NAVIGATOR SERIES

2000+ PROBLEMS

JEE Main & Advanced

Mechanics II

PRADEEP BENIWAL
IIT Kharagpur

arihant
SUCCESS AND NOTHING LESS

NAVIGATOR SERIES

ARIHANT PRAKASHAN (Series), MEERUT

Administrative & Production Offices

Regd. Office

'Ramchhaya' 4577/15, Agarwal Road, Darya Ganj, New Delhi -110002
Tele: 011- 47630600, 43518550

Head Office

Kalindi, TP Nagar, Meerut (UP) - 250002
Tel: 0121-7156203, 7156204

Sales & Support Offices

Agra, Ahmedabad, Bengaluru, Bareilly, Chennai, Delhi, Guwahati, Hyderabad, Jaipur, Jhansi, Kolkata, Lucknow, Nagpur & Pune.

PRICE :

PO No : TXT-XX-XXXXXXX-X-XX

Published by Arihant Publications (India) Ltd.

For further information about the books published by Arihant, log on to www.arihantbooks.com or e-mail at info@arihantbooks.com

Follow us on

PREFACE

Physics is a subject that requires a lot of practice to master it and the best way to practice Physics is to solve more & more problems right from the beginner's level to the most complex ones. That's why the search for a good Physics Problems book has always been the top notch task of each good student.

During the last 15 Years while teaching & mentoring thousands of students preparing for JEE Main, JEE Advanced, KVPY, Olympiads etc. I always felt the need of such a book that can offer quality problems of Physics for all the topics of different chapters. There are many problems books available in the market but unfortunately none of them serve the purpose perfectly.

To fulfil the need of a good Physics Problems book, I have prepared the book **JEE Navigator Mechanics-II**. All the problems given in this book are arranged conceptually and systematically in order to test the conceptual understanding & analytical ability of the students.

All the problems given in each chapter of this book have been developed with the utmost care and arranged in a way to enhance the problem-solving skills of the students & to boost their confidence to tackle complex JEE Problems.

The Points given below will help you to learn the basic structure of the book;

- Each chapter is divided into three major heads; **Level 1 'Starter Level', Level 2 'JEE Main Level' & Level 3 'JEE Advanced Level'.**
- **Level 1 'Starter Level'** consists of preliminary questions that test basic concepts. After completing this level student will have a solid understanding of fundamentals of the chapter necessary to solve the problems.
- **Level 2 'JEE Main Level'** has single choice correct questions and numerical value questions aimed especially for JEE Main.
- **Level 3 'JEE Advanced Level'** consists of various types of questions; MCQ with one or more than one correct answer, Comprehension Based Questions, Match the Columns and Numerical Value problems as per JEE Advanced Pattern.
- The problems given in JEE Advanced Level are made to be conceptually challenging resulting in practical and relevant practice for JEE Advanced.
- Detailed solutions to all the problems have been provided at the end of every chapter just to help the students in case they stuck somewhere while solving some questions.

At the end, I can say confidently that if you rigorously practice the problems given in this book then surely you will get an edge in Physics and will increase your chance of getting good JEE Score.

However, I have taken the utmost care while writing this book but if any error or whatsoever has skipped my attention then please bring it to my notice so that it can be rectified. I would also like to appeal all my fellow Physics Teachers to have a look at the book and share their valuable suggestions for its further improvement.

Pradeep Beniwal
B.Tech, IIT Kharagpur
problemsinphysics@yahoo.com

CONTENTS

CHAPTER~01

CENTRE OF MASS AND LINEAR MOMENTUM

LEVEL 01 Starter Level

1.1 Centre of Mass

1 Find distance of centre of mass of a system consisting of two particles of masses m_1 and m_2 separated by a distance L apart from m_1.

2 Four particles of masses 2 kg, 3 kg, 5 kg and 8 kg are placed at the four corners of a square of side 2 m. The square lies in XY-plane with 2 kg at origin and 3 kg on X-axis and 8 kg on Y-axis. Find the position of their centre of mass.

3 Three rods of the same mass are placed as shown in the figure. Calculate the coordinates of the centre of mass of the system.

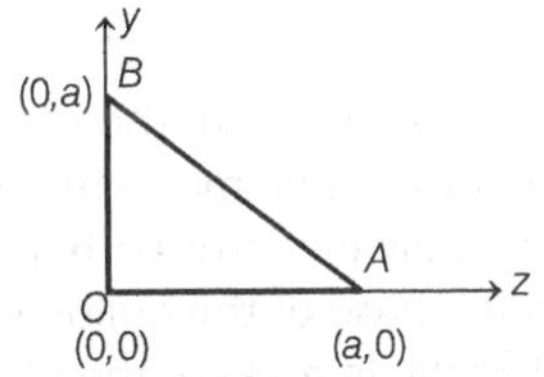

4 Centre of mass of a system of three particles of masses 1 kg, 2 kg and 3 kg is at the point (1 m, 2 m, 3 m) and centre of mass of another group of two particles of masses 2 kg and 3 kg is at point (−1 m, 3 m, −2 m). Where a 5 kg particle should be placed, so that centre of mass of the system of all these six particles shifts to centre of mass of the first system?

5 If linear density of a rod of length 3 m varies as $\lambda = 2 + x$, where x is the distance from the left end of the rod, then find the distance of the centre of mass of the rod from the left end.

6 Locate the centre of mass of a uniform

(a) semi-circular ring of radius R

(b) semi-circular disc of radius R

(c) solid hemisphere of radius R

(d) hemispherical shell of radius R

(e) hollow cone of height H

(f) solid cone of height H

7 Seven homogeneous bricks, each of length L, are arranged as shown in figure. Each brick is displaced with respect to the one in contact by $L/10$. Find the x-coordinate of the centre of mass relative to the origin O shown.

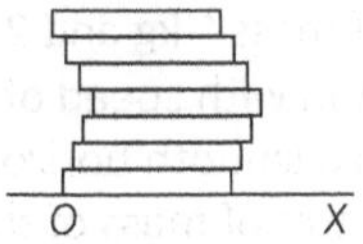

8 A man has constructed a toy as shown in figure. If density of the material of the sphere is 12 times of the cone, then find the distance of the centre of mass from O.

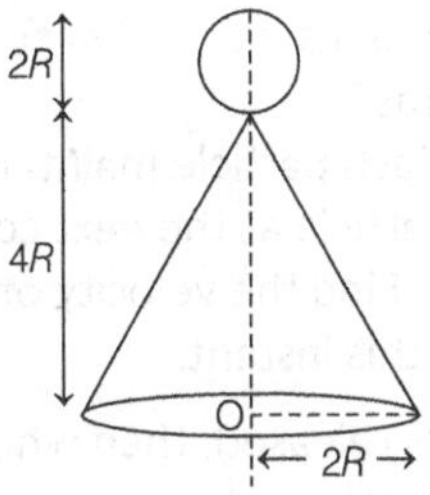

9 Find the position of the centre of mass of uniform lamina. (Take origin at E)

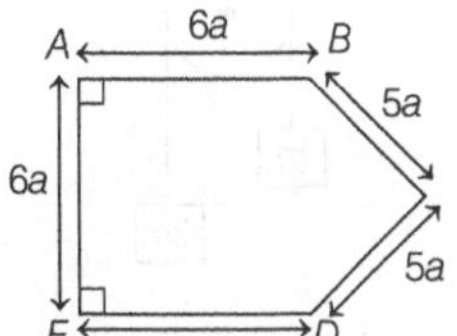

10 A spherical hollow is made in a lead sphere of radius R, such that its surface touches the outside surface of lead sphere and passes through the centre. What is the shift in the centre of mass of lead sphere due to the following?

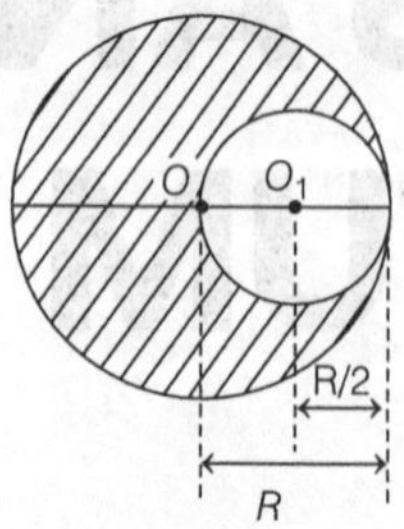

11 A semi-circular portion of radius r is cut from a uniform rectangular plate as shown in the figure. Find the distance of centre of mass C of remaining plate from O.

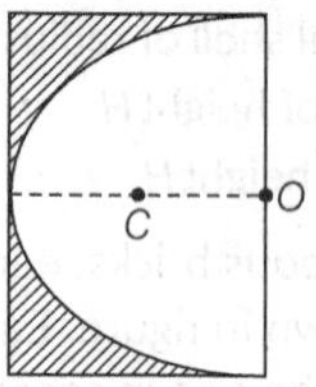

1.2 Motion of Centre of Mass

1 Two particles of mass 1 kg and 2 kg are moving in the opposite direction with speed of 8 m/s and 1m/s respectively, on a smooth horizontal surface. Find the speed of centre of mass of the system.

2 Three particles of masses 1 kg, 2 kg and 3 kg are situated at the corners of an equilateral triangle move at speed 6 ms^{-1}, 3 ms^{-1} and 2 ms^{-1}, respectively. Each particle maintains a direction towards the particle at the next corner symmetrically. Find the velocity of centre of mass of the system at this instant.

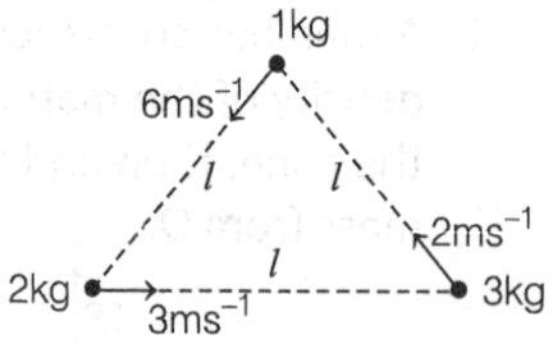

3 If the system is released, then what is the acceleration of the centre of mass of the system?

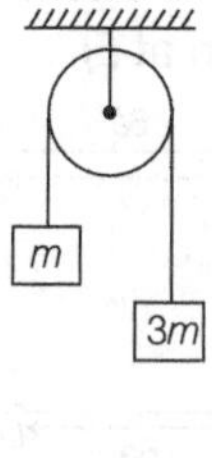

4 Two blocks each of mass m are kept on a smooth fixed wedge as shown in figure. Find the magnitude of acceleration of centre of mass of both the blocks.

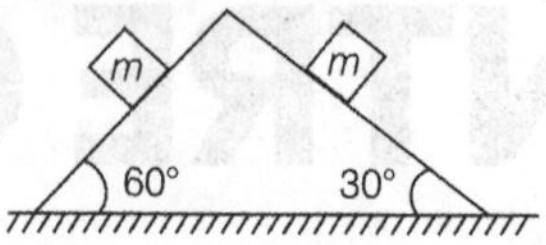

5 A ladder of mass 20 kg is hanging from ceiling as shown in figure. Three men A,B and C of masses 40 kg, 60 kg and 50 kg are climbing the ladder. Man A is climbing with upward retardation 2 m/s^2, B is climbing up with a constant speed of 0.5 m/s and C is climbing with upward acceleration of 1 m/s^2. Find the tension in the string supporting the ladder. ($g = 10\,m/s^2$)

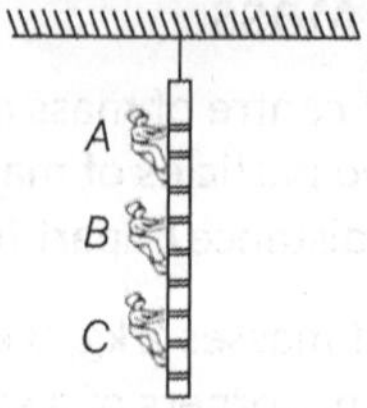

6 Two balls A and B of masses 100 g and 250 g respectively, are connected by a stretched spring of negligible mass and placed on a smooth table. When the balls are released simultaneously, the initial acceleration of B is 10 cm/s^2 westward. What is the magnitude and direction of initial acceleration of the ball A ?

7 An object A is dropped from the top of a 30 m high building and at the same moment another object B is projected vertically upwards with an initial speed of 15 m/s from the base of the building. Mass of the object A is 2 kg while mass of the object B is 4 kg. Find the maximum height above the ground level attained by the centre of mass of A and B system. ($g = 10\,m/s^2$)

1.3 Displacement of Centre of Mass

1 Two blocks of masses 10 kg and 30 kg are placed along a vertical line. The first block is raised through a height of 7 cm. By what distance should the second mass be moved to raise the centre of mass by 1 cm ?

2 A projectile is fired from a gun at an angle of 45° with the horizontal and with a speed of 20 m/s relative to ground. At the highest point in its flight, the projectile explodes into two fragments of equal mass.

One fragment, whose initial speed is zero falls vertically. How far from the gun does the other fragment land, assuming a horizontal ground? (Take, $g = 10 \text{ m/s}^2$)

3 A man of mass M stands at one end of a plank of length L which lies at rest on a frictionless surface. The man walks to the other end of the plank. If the mass of the plank is $3M$, find the distance that the plank moves relative to the ground.

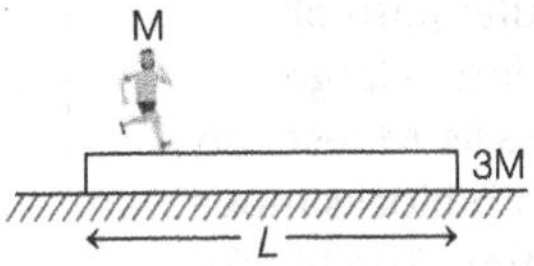

4 Ram (50 kg) and Shyam (60 kg) are sitting at the two extremes of a 4 m long boat (40 kg) standing still in water. To discuss a mechanics problem, they come to the middle of the boat. Neglecting friction with water, how far does the boat move in the water during the process?

5 A balloon of mass M with a light rope and man of mass m are at rest in mid air. If the man climbs up the rope and reaches the top of the rope, what is the distance by which man climbs? (The length of the rope $= L$)

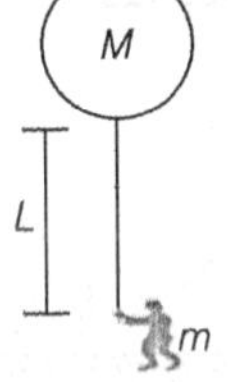

6 A block A (mass $= m$) is placed on the top of a wedge of height h (mass $= 5m$) as shown in figure. The system is released from rest. Find the distance moved by the wedge B till the block A reaches at lowest end of wedge. Assume all surfaces are frictionless.

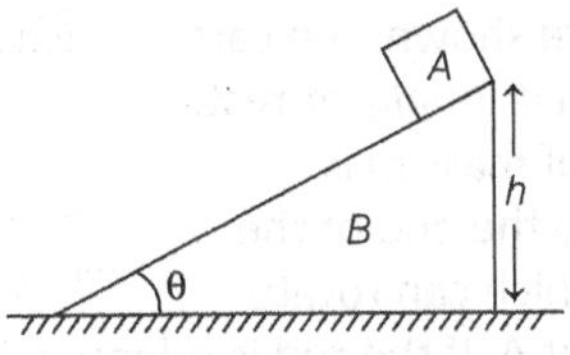

7 A block of mass M with a semicircular track of radius R rests on a horizontal frictionless surface. A uniform cylinder of radius r and mass m is released from rest from the top point A.

The cylinder slips on the semicircular frictionless track. Find the distance travelled by the block when the cylinder reaches the point B.

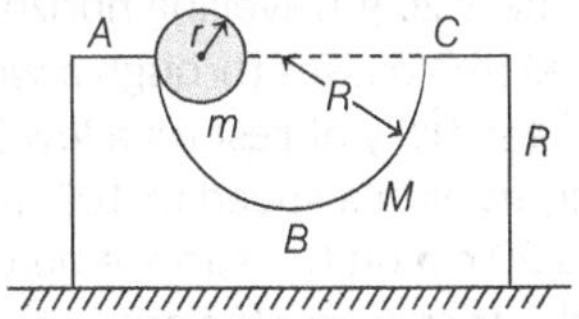

8 A uniform thin rod of mass M and length L is standing vertically along the Y-axis on a smooth horizontal surface, with its lower end at the origin (0, 0). A slight disturbance at $t=0$ causes the lower end to slip on the smooth surface along the positive X-axis, and the rod starts falling.

(a) What is the path followed by the centre of mass of the rod during its fall?

(b) Find the equation of the trajectory of a point on the rod located at a distance r from the lower end. What is the shape of the path of the point?

1.4 Conservation of Linear Momentum

1 A bomb of mass 16 kg at rest explodes into two pieces of masses 4 kg and 12 kg. The velocity of the 12 kg mass is 4 m/s. Find (a) the kinetic energy of other mass (b) the energy released in the explosion.

2 A particle of mass $4m$ which is at rest explodes into three fragments. Two of the fragments each of mass m are found to move with a speed v each in mutually perpendicular directions. Find

(a) the speed of third segment

(b) the energy released in the process of explosion

3 A shell is fired from a cannon with a speed of 100 m/s at an angle 30° with the vertical. At the highest point of its trajectory, the shell explodes into two fragments of masses in the ratio 1 : 2. The lighter fragment moves vertically upwards with an initial speed of 200 m/s. What is the speed of the heavier fragment at the time of explosion?

4 A bullet of mass m travelling horizontally with velocity v hits a pendulum bob of mass $2m$ at rest and gets embedded into it. The length of the pendulum is l. What is the minimum value of v such that the pendulum swings through an angle of 60° before coming to rest?

5 A bullet of mass 10 g and travelling at a speed of 500 m/s strikes a block of mass 2 kg which is suspended by string of length 5 m. The centre of gravity of the block is found to raise a vertical distance of 10 cm. What is the speed of the bullet after it emerges from the block? [$g = 9.8\ m/s^2$]

6 A bullet of mass 20 g travelling horizontally with a speed of 500 m/s passes through a wooden block of mass 10.0 kg initially at rest on a level surface. The bullet emerges with a speed of 100 m/s and the block slides 20 cm on the surface before coming to rest. Find the friction coefficient between the block and the surface.

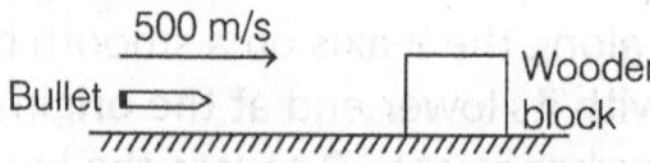

7 Blocks *A* and *B* have masses 40 kg and 60 kg, respectively. They are placed on a smooth surface and the spring connected between them is stretched by 1.5 m. If they are released from rest, determine the speeds of both blocks at the instant the spring becomes unstretched.

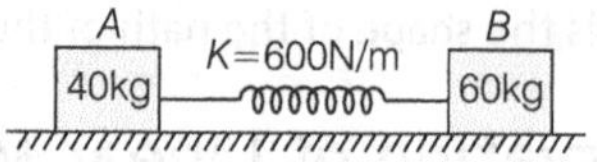

8 A small block of superdense material has a mass *M*/3, where *M* is the mass of earth. It is released from rest from a height *h* (<< radius of earth) from the surface of earth. What is the speed of the block at a height *h*/2?

9 A man of mass 100 kg is standing on a platform of mass 200 kg which is kept on a smooth ice surface. If the man starts moving on the platform with a speed 30 m/s relative to the platform, then with what velocity relative to the ice the platform will recoil?

10 A car with a gun mounted on it is kept on horizontal frictionless surface. Total mass of car, gun and shell is 50 kg. Mass of each shell is 1 kg. The shell is fired horizontally with relative velocity 100 m/s with respect to gun. What is the recoil speed of car after second shot?

11 Two persons *A* and *B* each of mass *m* are standing at the two ends of rail-road car of mass *M*. The person *A* jumps to the left with a horizontal speed *u* with respect to the car. The person *B* jumps to the right, again with the same horizontal speed *u* with respect to the car. Find the velocity of the car after both the persons have jumped off one after the other.

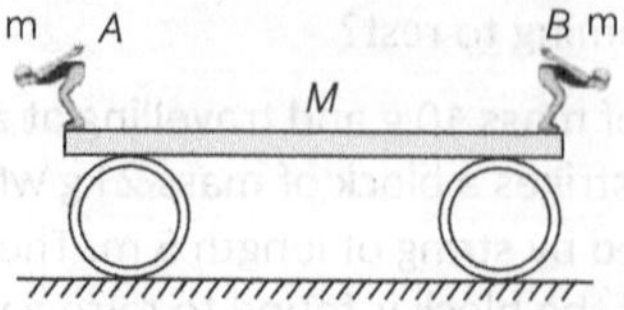

12 Two identical buggies move one after the other due to inertia (without friction) with the same velocity v_0. A man of mass *m* rides the rear buggy. At a certain moment the man jumps into the front buggy with a velocity *u* relative to his buggy. Knowing that the mass of each buggy is equal to *M*, find the velocities with which the buggies will move after that.

13 A small cube of mass *m* slides down a circular path of radius *R* cut into a large block of mass *M*. *M* rests on a table and both blocks move without friction. The blocks initially are at rest and *m* starts from the top of the path. Find the velocity *v* of the cube as it leaves the block. Initially the line joining *m* and the centre is horizontal.

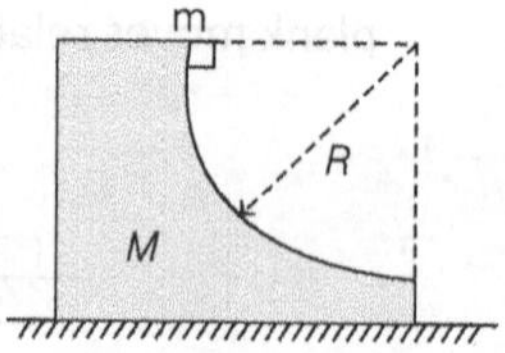

14 A small block of mass is thrown along the ground with speed $v_0 = \sqrt{2gh}$.

The larger block of mass 2*m* is initially at rest. Assume that all the surfaces are frictionless. Find

(a) the speed of the larger block when the smaller block reaches maximum height from ground

(b) the maximum height from the ground that the smaller mass ascends.

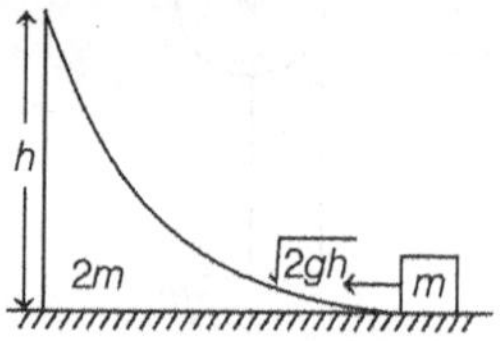

1.5 Centre of Mass Reference Frame

1 Find the linear momentum and kinetic energy of a system of two particles of masses m_1 and m_2 having velocities $\mathbf{v}_1$ and $\mathbf{v}_2$ relative to the centre of mass of the system.

2 In the figure shown, the cart of mass 6*m* is intially at rest. A particle of mass *m* is attached to the end of the light rod which can rotate freely about *A*. If the rod is released from rest in a horizontal position shown, determine the velocity v_{rel} of the particle with respect to the cart when the rod is vertical.

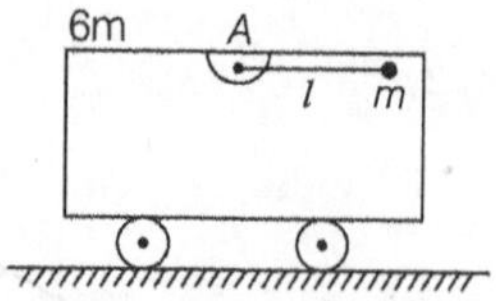

3 A block of mass m is pushed towards a movable wedge of mass $2m$ and height h with a velocity u. All surfaces are smooth. Find the minimum value of u for which the block will reach the top of the wedge.

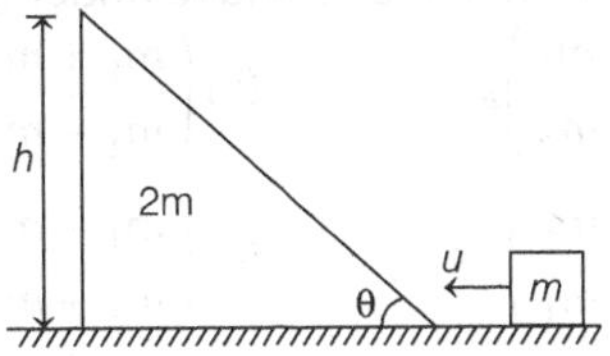

4 Each of the blocks shown in figure has mass 1 kg. The rear block moves with a speed of 2 m/s towards the front block kept at rest. The spring attached to the front block is light and has a spring constant 50 N/m. Find the maximum compression of the spring.

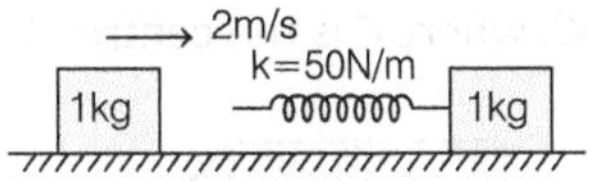

5 Two blocks of masses m and M connected by a spring are placed on frictionless horizontal ground. When the spring is relaxed, a constant force F is applied as shown. Find maximum extension of the spring during subsequent motion.

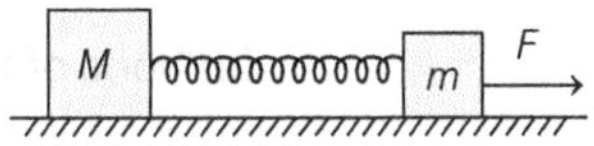

LEVEL 02 JEE Main Level

Single Choice Correct Questions

1 Masses of 1 g, 2 g, 3 g, ... 100 g are suspended from the 1cm, 2cm, 3cm...............100cm marks of a light metre scale. Find the position of their centre of mass.

(a) 67 cm (b) 70 cm (c) 75 cm (d) 80 cm

2 Seven particles, each of mass m are placed at the seven corners of a cube of side a but one corner is vacant, as shown in figure. The coordinates of the centre of mass of the system is

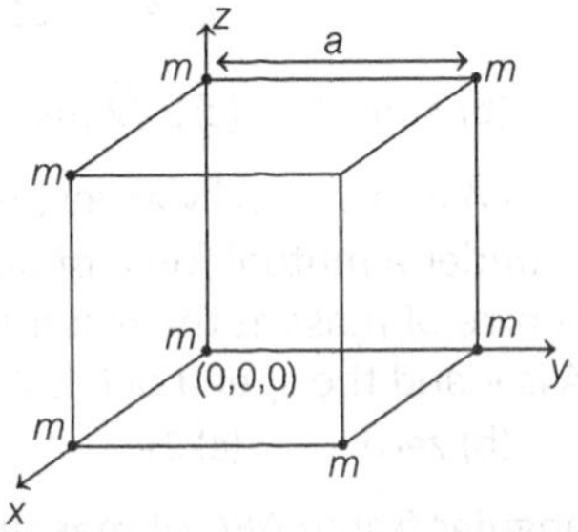

(a) $\left(\frac{2a}{7}, \frac{2a}{7}, \frac{2a}{7}\right)$ (b) $\left(\frac{3a}{7}, \frac{3a}{7}, \frac{3a}{7}\right)$

(c) $\left(\frac{a}{3}, \frac{a}{3}, \frac{a}{3}\right)$ (d) $\left(\frac{5a}{11}, \frac{5a}{11}, \frac{5a}{11}\right)$

3 Five uniform circular plates, each of diameter b and mass m are laid out in a pattern shown. Using the origin shown, find the y-coordinate of the centre of mass of the five-plate system.

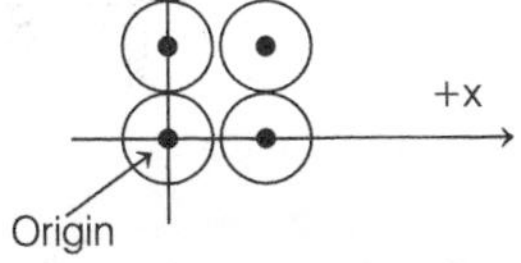

(a) $b/5$ (b) $b/3$ (c) $4b/5$ (d) $2b/5$

4 A thin uniform wire is bent to form the two equal sides AB and AC of triangle ABC, where $AB = AC = 5$ cm. The third side BC of length 6 cm is made from uniform wire of twice the density of the first. The distance of centre of mass from A is

(a) $\frac{34}{11}$ cm (b) $\frac{11}{34}$ cm (c) $\frac{34}{9}$ cm (d) $\frac{11}{45}$ cm

5 A wire is bent into the structure as shown in the figure, and placed on a table. It consists of two-half rings of radius R and two straight parts of length πR. The height of COM from the table is

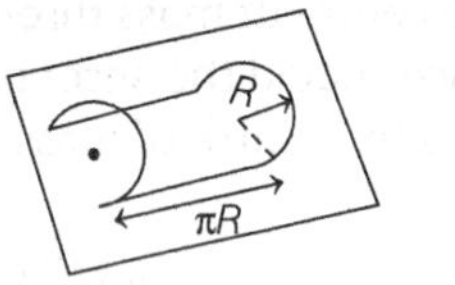

(a) $\frac{2R}{\pi}$ (b) $\frac{R}{\pi}$ (c) $\frac{R}{2}$ (d) zero

6 From the circular disc of radius $4R$ two small discs of radius R are cut off. The centre of mass of the new structure will be

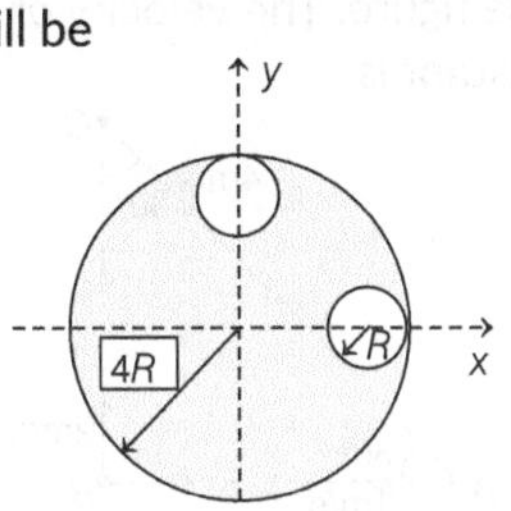

(a) $\frac{R}{5}\hat{\mathbf{i}} + \frac{R}{5}\hat{\mathbf{j}}$ (b) $-\frac{R}{5}\hat{\mathbf{i}} + \frac{R}{5}\hat{\mathbf{j}}$

(c) $\frac{-3R}{14}(\hat{\mathbf{i}} + \hat{\mathbf{j}})$ (d) None of these

7 An arrow sign is made by cutting and rejoining a quarter part of a square plate of side L as shown. The distance OC, where C is the centre of mass of the arrow, is

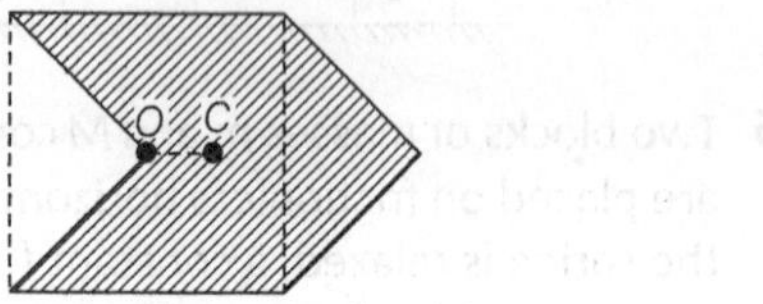

(a) $\frac{L}{3}$ (b) $\frac{L}{4}$

(c) $\frac{3L}{8}$ (d) None of these

8 A thin uniform sheet of metal of uniform thickness is cut into the shape bounded by the line $x = a$ and $y = \pm kx^2$, as shown. Find the coordinates of the centre of mass.

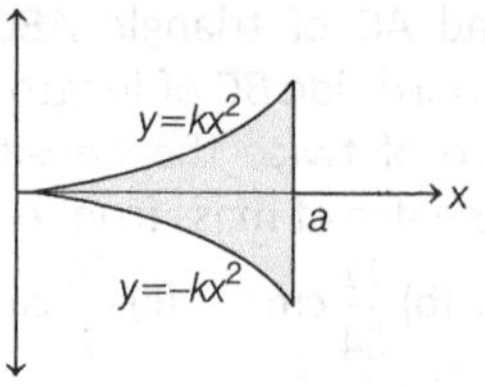

(a) $\frac{2}{3}a$ (b) $\frac{3}{4}a$ (c) $\frac{4}{5}a$ (d) $\frac{5}{6}a$

9 Consider a two particles system with particles having mass m_1 and m_2. If the first particle is pushed towards the centre of mass through a distance d, by what distance should the second particle be moved, so as to keep the centre of mass at the same position?

(a) d (b) $\frac{m_2}{m_1}d$

(c) $\frac{m_1}{m_1 + m_2}d$ (d) $\frac{m_1}{m_2}d$

10 Three particles of mass 2 kg each are moving as shown in the figure. The velocity of centre of mass at the given instant is

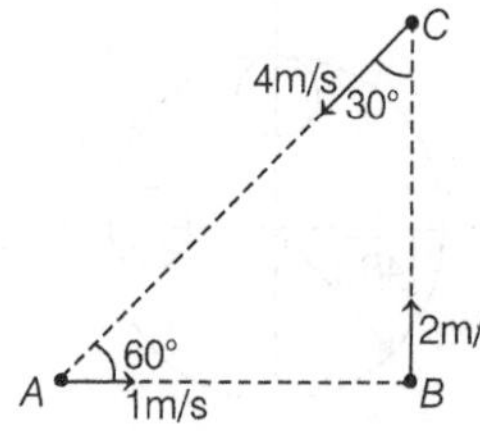

(a) $\frac{1}{3}[-\hat{\mathbf{i}} + 2(1 - \sqrt{3})\hat{\mathbf{j}}]$ (b) $\frac{1}{3}(-\hat{\mathbf{i}} + 2\sqrt{3}\hat{\mathbf{j}})$

(c) $\frac{1}{3}(-\hat{\mathbf{i}} + \sqrt{3}\hat{\mathbf{j}})$ (d) $\frac{1}{3}(-\hat{\mathbf{i}} - 2\sqrt{3}\hat{\mathbf{j}})$

11 Two blocks of mass m_1 and m_2 are connected by light inextensible string passing over smooth fixed pulley of negligible mass. The acceleration of the centre of the system when blocks move under gravity is

(a) $\left(\frac{m_2 - m_1}{m_1 + m_2}\right)g$ (b) $\left(\frac{m_1 + m_2}{m_1 - m_2}\right)g$

(c) $\left(\frac{m_2 + m_1}{m_2 - m_1}\right)^2 g$ (d) $\left(\frac{m_1 - m_2}{m_1 + m_2}\right)^2 g$

12 The masses are equal and are kept at height H. The wedges are fixed and frictionless. The magnitude of velocity of centre of mass of the system $(M + M)$ after 5 s is

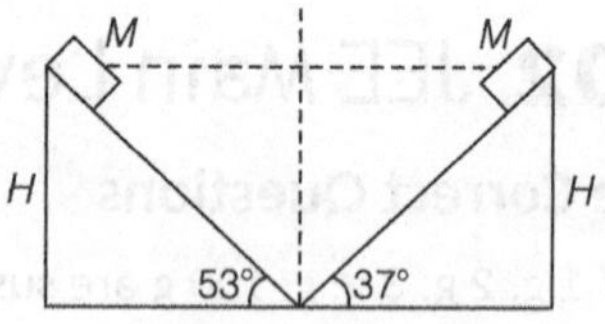

(a) 20 m/s (b) 25 m/s (c) 32 m/s (d) 16 m/s

13 The magnitude of acceleration of centre of mass of the system is $(g = 10\,\text{ms}^{-2})$

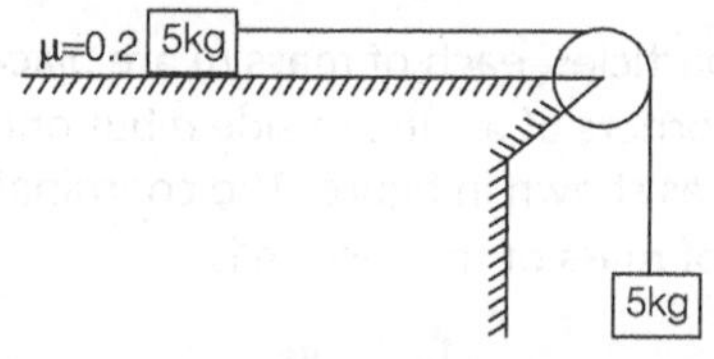

(a) 2 ms^{-2} (b) 4 ms^{-2} (c) $2\sqrt{2}\,\text{ms}^{-2}$ (d) $4\sqrt{2}\,\text{m/s}^{-2}$

14 Two particles A and B initially at rest move towards each other under a mutual force of attraction. The speed of centre of mass at the instant when the speed of A is v and the speed of B is $2v$ is

(a) v (b) zero (c) $2v$ (d) $3v/2$

15 A rigid triangular frame ABC of mass m is hanging from a rigid horizontal rod PQ. The frame is constrained to move along horizontal without friction. A bead of mass m is released from B that moves along BC. Magnitude of displacement of frame when bead reaches C is

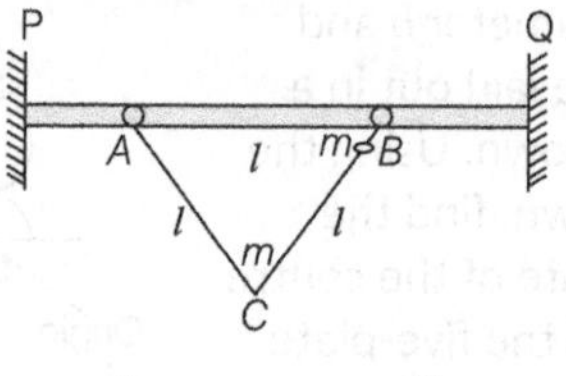

(a) $\frac{l}{2}$ (b) $\frac{l}{4}$ (c) $\frac{3l}{\sqrt{2}}$ (d) $\frac{\sqrt{3}l}{4}$

16 A dog of mass 10 kg is standing on a flat 10 m long boat so that it is 20 m from the shore. It walks 8 m on the boat towards the shore and then stops. The mass of the boat is 40 kg and friction between the boat and the water surface is negligible. How far is the dog from the shore now?

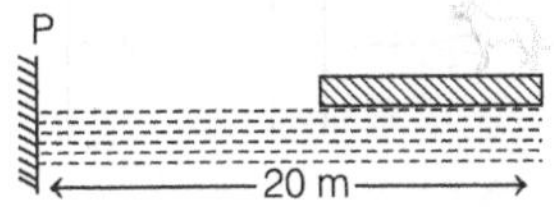

(a) 21.6 m (b) 18.4 m (c) 13.6 m (d) 12 m

17 A bomb of mass $3m$ is kept inside a closed box of mass $3m$ and length $4L$ at its centre. It explodes in two parts of masses m and $2m$. The two parts move in opposite direction and stick to the opposite side of the walls of box. Box is kept on a smooth horizontal surface. What is the distance moved by the box during this time interval?

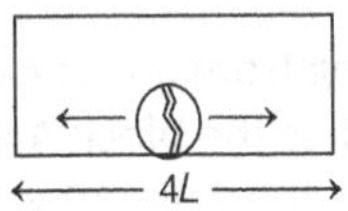

(a) 0 (b) $L/6$ (c) $L/12$ (d) $L/3$

18 Three man A, B and C of mass 40 kg, 50 kg and 60 kg are standing on a plank of mass 90 kg, which is kept on a smooth horizontal plane. If A and C exchange their positions, then mass B will shift

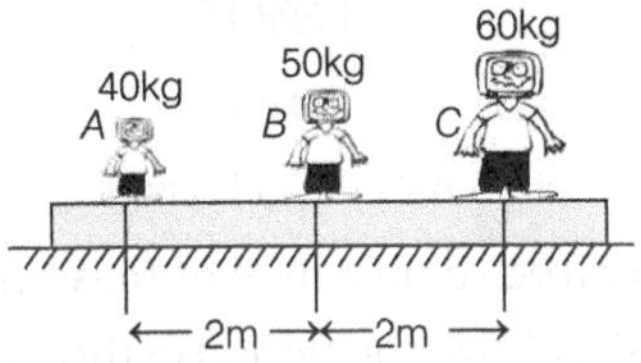

(a) (1/3) m towards left
(b) (1/3) m towards right
(c) will not move w.r.t. ground
(d) (5/3) m towards left

19 In a vertical plane inside a smooth hollow thin tube a block of same mass as that of tube is released as shown in figure. When it is slightly disturbed it moves towards right. By the time the block reaches the right end of the tube, the displacement of the tube will be (where R is mean radius of tube). Assume that the tube remains in vertical plane.

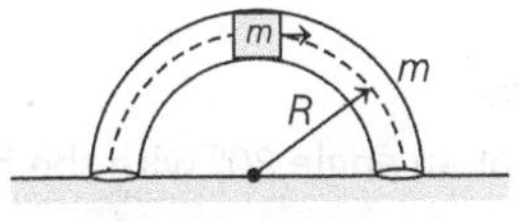

(a) $\frac{2R}{\pi}$ (b) $\frac{4R}{\pi}$ (c) $\frac{R}{2}$ (d) R

20 A projectile of mass $3m$ explodes at highest point of its path. It breaks into three equal parts. One part retraces its path, the second one comes to rest. The range of the projectile was 100 m if no explosion would have taken place. The distance of the third part from the point of projection when it finally lands on the ground is

(a) 100 m (b) 150 m (c) 250 m (d) 300 m

21 When a block is placed on a wedge as shown in the figure, the block starts sliding down and the wedge also start sliding on ground. All surfaces are rough. The centre of mass of (wedge + block) system will move

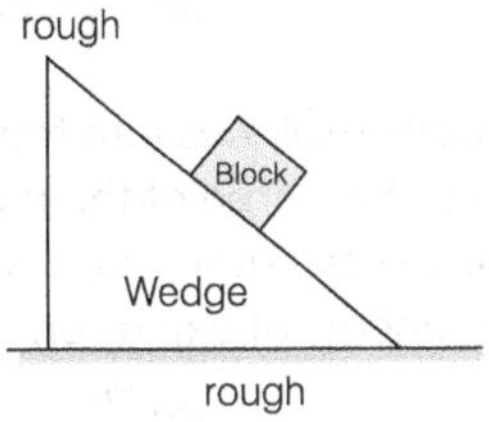

(a) leftward and downward
(b) rightward and downward
(c) leftward and upwards
(d) only downward

22 If a ball is thrown upwards from the surface of earth,
(a) the earth remains stationary while the ball moves upwards
(b) the ball remains stationary while the earth moves downwards
(c) the ball and earth both move towards each other
(d) the ball and earth both move away from each other

23 A train of mass M is moving on a circular track of radius R with constant speed v. The length of the train is half of the perimeter of the track. The linear momentum of the train will be

(a) 0 (b) $\frac{2Mv}{\pi}$ (c) MvR (d) Mv

24 A stationary body explodes into two fragments of masses m_1 and m_2. If momentum of one fragment is p, the energy of explosion is

(a) $\frac{p^2}{2(m_1+m_2)}$

(b) $\frac{p^2}{2\sqrt{m_1 m_2}}$

(c) $\frac{p^2(m_1+m_2)}{2m_1 m_2}$

(d) $\frac{p^2}{2(m_1-m_2)}$

25 A bomb of mass 12 kg at rest explodes into two fragments of masses in the ratio 1 : 3. The KE of the smaller fragment is 216 J. The momentum of heavier fragment is (in kg-m/s)

(a) 36 (b) 72
(c) 108 (d) Insufficient data

26 A spaceship of speed v_0 travelling along +Y-axis suddenly shots out one-fourth of its part with speed $2v_0$ along +X-axis. XY-axes are fixed with respect to ground. The speed of the remaining part is

(a) $\frac{2}{3}v_0$ (b) $\frac{\sqrt{20}}{3}v_0$
(c) $\frac{\sqrt{5}}{3}v_0$ (d) $\frac{\sqrt{13}}{3}v_0$

27 A stationary body explodes into four identical fragments such that three of them fly off mutually perpendicular to each other, each with same KE, E_0. The minimum energy of explosion will be

(a) $6E_0$ (b) $\frac{4E_0}{3}$
(c) $4E_0$ (d) $8E_0$

28 A machine gun fires a bullet of mass 40 g with a velocity 1200 m/s. The man holding it can exert a maximum force of 144 N on the gun. How many bullets can he fire per second at most?

(a) 1 (b) 2
(c) 3 (d) 4

29 A body of mass 5 kg moves along the X-axis with a velocity of 2 m/s. A second body of mass 10 kg moves along the Y-axis with a velocity of $\sqrt{3}$ m/s. They collide and stick together. The final velocity of combined mass after collision is

(a) $\frac{4}{3}$ m/ s (b) $\frac{5}{3}$ m/ s
(c) $\frac{6}{3}$ m/ s (d) $\frac{8}{3}$ m/ s

30 A bullet of mass m and velocity v passes through a pendulum of mass M and emerges with velocity v / 2. What is the minimum value of v such that the pendulum will swing through a complete cycle?

(a) $\frac{M}{m}\sqrt{2lg}$ (b) $\frac{2M}{m}\sqrt{2lg}$
(c) $\frac{M}{2m}\sqrt{5lg}$ (d) $\frac{2M}{m}\sqrt{5lg}$

31 A 20 g bullet pierces through a plate of mass $M_1 = 1$ kg and then comes to rest inside a second plate of mass $M_2 = 2.98$ kg as shown in figure. It is found that the two plates, initially at rest, now move with equal velocities. Find the percentage loss in the initial velocity of the bullet when it is between M_1 and M_2. Neglect any loss of material of the plates due to the action of bullet.

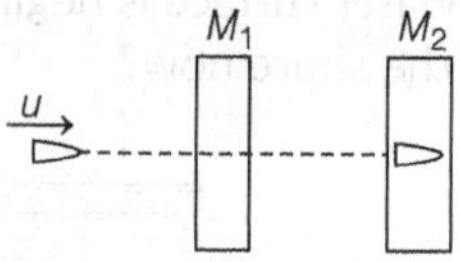

(a) 12.5 % (b) 25 % (c) 40 % (d) 50 %

32 A skater of mass m standing on ice throws a stone of mass M with a velocity v in a horizontal direction. The distance over which the skater will move back if coefficient of friction between skater and ice is μ will be

(a) $\frac{M^2v^2}{2m\mu g}$ (b) $\frac{Mv^2}{2m^2\mu g}$ (c) $\frac{M^2v^2}{2m^2\mu g}$ (d) $\frac{M^2v^2}{2m^2\mu^2 g}$

33 Block A is hanging from a vertical spring and is at rest. Block B strikes the block A with velocity v and sticks to it. Then, the value of v for which the spring just attains natural length is

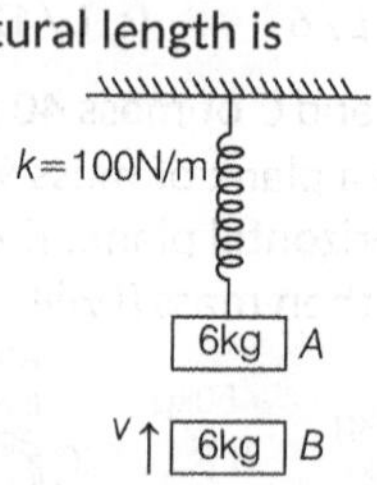

(a) 4 m/s (b) 5 m/s (c) 6 m/s (d) 8 m/s

34 In a gravity free room a man of mass m_1 is standing at a height h above the floor. He throws a ball of mass m_2 vertically downward with a speed u. Find the distance of man from the floor when the ball reaches the ground.

(a) $\left(1+\frac{m_2}{m_1}\right)h$ (b) $\left(1+\frac{m_1}{m_2}\right)h$
(c) $\left(1-\frac{m_2}{m_1}\right)h$ (d) $\left(1-\frac{m_1}{m_2}\right)h$

35 A gun fires a shell and recoils horizontally. If the shell travels along the barrel with muzzle speed v, the ratio of the speed with which the gun recoils if the barrel is

(i) horizontal
(ii) inclined at an angle 30° with the horizontal is

(a) 1 (b) $\frac{2}{\sqrt{3}}$ (d) $\frac{\sqrt{3}}{2}$ (d) $\frac{1}{2}$

36 A particle of mass m is projected at an angle of 60° with a velocity of 20 m/s relative to the ground from a plank of same mass m which is placed on smooth surface. Initially plank was at rest. The minimum length of the plank for which the ball will fall on the plank itself is ($g = 10$ m/s^2)

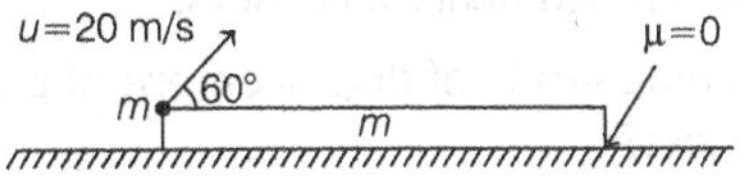

(a) $40\sqrt{3}$ m

(b) $20\sqrt{3}$ m

(c) $10\sqrt{3}$ m

(d) $60\sqrt{3}$ m

37 A block of mass $M = 2$ kg with a semicircular track of radius $R = 1.1$ m rests on a horizontal frictionless surface. A uniform cylinder of radius $r = 10$ cm and mass $m = 1.0$ kg is released from rest from the top point A. The cylinder slips on the semicircular frictionless track. The speed of the block when the cylinder reaches the bottom of the track at B is ($g = 10$ m/s^2)

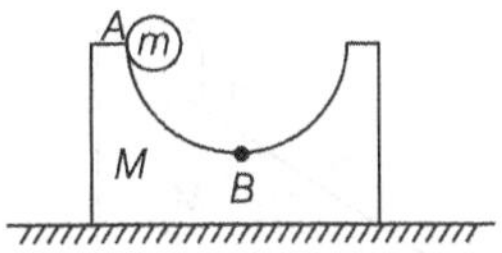

(a) $\sqrt{\frac{10}{3}}$ m/s (b) $\sqrt{\frac{4}{3}}$ m/s

(c) $\sqrt{\frac{5}{2}}$ m/s (d) $\sqrt{10}$ m/s

38 The system shown is released from rest. Mass of ball is m kg and that of wedge is M kg. When ball reaches at highest point on other side of the wedge, velocity of ball and wedge, is (initially wedge is kept at rest against a wall)

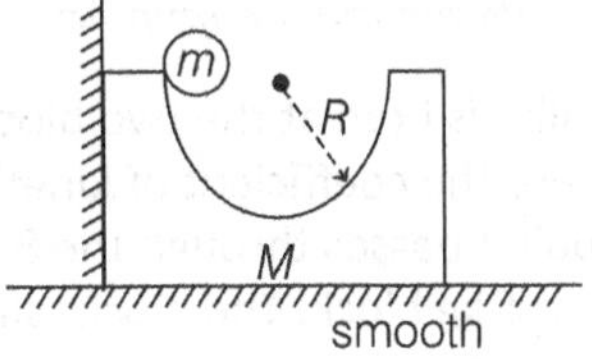

(a) $\frac{M\sqrt{2gR}}{m+M}$ (b) $\frac{m\sqrt{2gR}}{M}$

(c) $\frac{M}{m}\sqrt{2gR}$ (d) $\frac{m\sqrt{2gR}}{m+M}$

39 Block of mass $2m$ is kept on a smooth circular track of mass m which is kept on a smooth horizontal surface. The circular track is given a horizontal velocity $\sqrt{2gR}$ towards left. Find the maximum height reached by the block.

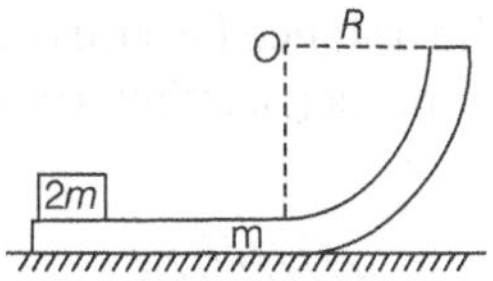

(a) $R/2$ (b) $R/3$ (c) $R/4$ (d) $R/6$

40 Two blocks of masses m_1 and m_2 connected by a light spring of stiffness k rest on a smooth horizontal plane, such that the block m_1 touches a vertical wall as shown in the figure. The block m_2 is shifted through a small distance x towards the wall and then released. The velocity of the centre of mass of the system after block m_1 breaks off the wall is

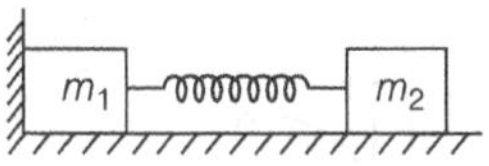

(a) $\frac{\sqrt{km_2}\,x}{m_1+m_2}$ (b) $\frac{\sqrt{km_1}\,x}{m_1+m_2}$

(c) $\frac{\sqrt{km_2}\,x}{m_1-m_2}$ (d) $\frac{\sqrt{km_1}\,x}{m_1-m_2}$

41 Two blocks of mass 3 kg and 6 kg respectively, are placed on a smooth horizontal surface. They are connected by a light spring of force constant $k = 200$N/m. Initially the spring is unstretched. The indicated velocities are imparted to the blocks. What will be the maximum extension of the spring?

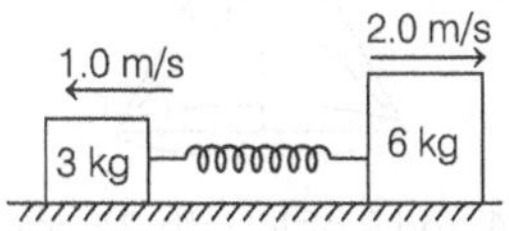

(a) 10 cm (b) 20 cm

(c) 30 cm (d) 40 cm

42 For shown situation find the maximum elongation in the spring. Neglect friction everywhere. Initially, the blocks are at rest and spring is unstretched.

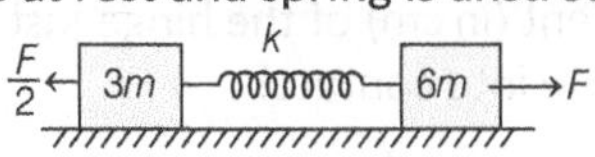

(a) $\frac{4F}{3k}$ (b) $\frac{3F}{4k}$

(c) $\frac{4F}{k}$ (d) $\frac{2F}{k}$

Numerical Value Questions

1 A circular plate of uniform thickness has a diameter of 56 cm. A circular portion of diameter 42 cm is removed from one edge of the plate as shown in figure. Find the distance (in cm) of the centre of mass of the remaining portion from the centre of the original plate.

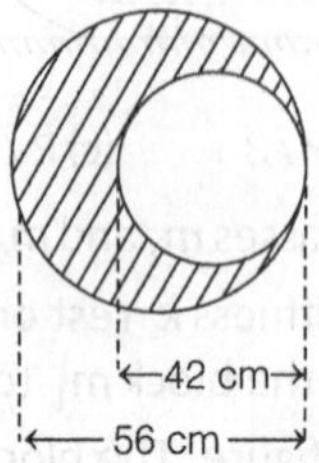

2 The centre of mass of an object which is formed by rotating a parabola $x = ky^2$ about X-axis having height of object as 6 m is given by (α m, β m). Find ($\alpha + \beta$).

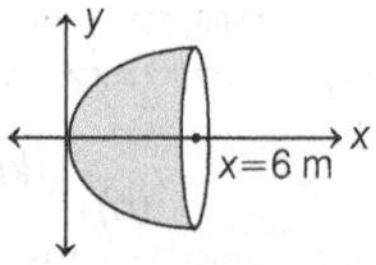

3 A uniform solid right circular cone of height 12 m has its base cut out in conical shape shown in figure such that the hollow is a right circular cone on the same base. Find what should be the height (in m) of the hollow so that the centre of mass of the remaining portion may coincide the vertex of the hollow part?

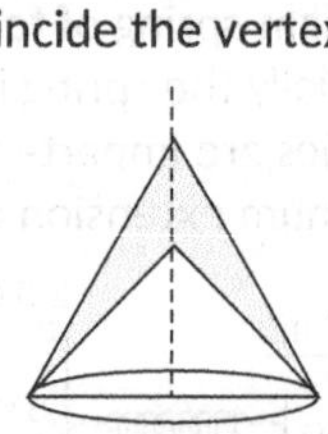

4 Two planks *A* and *B* of length 24 cm and 16 cm and mass 4 kg and 12 kg respectively, are connected by a frictionless, massless hinge as shown in the figure. Initially the system is at rest on a level, frictionless surface. The plank *A* falls clockwise and finally comes to rest on the top of the plank *B*. What is the displacement (in cm) of the hinge just after the two planks come into contact?

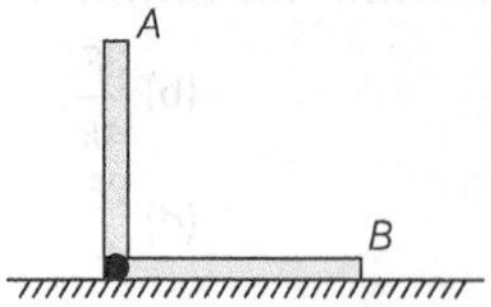

5 A square plank of mass $m_1 = 100$ kg and edge length $L = 20\sqrt{2}$ is placed on a smooth surface. Two person each of mass $m_2 = m_3 = 50$ kg are at corner of a plank as shown in figure. Two person begin to walk on the plank along two different paths as shown in figure and reach nearest corners.

What is magnitude of displacement of plank (in m) in the process?

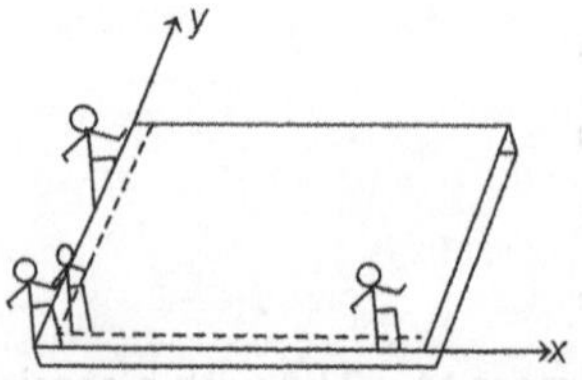

6 On the prism of mass $M = 2$ kg and length $l = 12$ m, another prism of mass $m = 1$ kg and length $l_1 = 3$ m is put as shown in the figure. The system is released from rest. Find the magnitude of horizontal displacement of *M* (in metres) when *m* reaches the bottom of *M*.

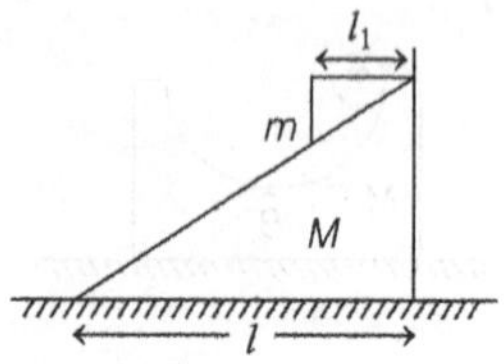

7 A 50 kg man is standing at one end of a 3 m long plank of mass 100 kg. The plank is sliding towards the right with uniform velocity of 2 m/s on the frictionless horizontal ground. The man walks to the other end of the plank in 5 s. Find distance (in m) travelled by the man relative to the ground in this 5 s interval.

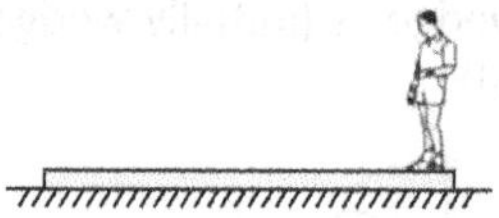

8 The 50 g bullet is fired at the two blocks resting on a surface where the coefficient of kinetic friction is 0.50. The bullet passes through the 8 kg block and lodges in the 6 kg block. The blocks slide the distances shown. Compute the initial velocity (in m/s) of the bullet.

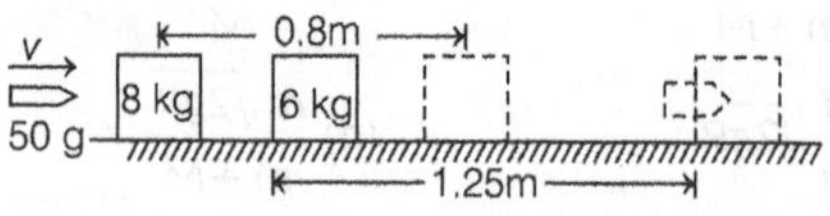

9 Two boats both having a mass of 150 kg including passengers in it are at rest. A sack of mass 50 kg makes first boat having total mass of 200 kg. It is thrown to the second boat with a velocity whose horizontal component is 6 m/s, relative to water. Calculate the distance (in m) between the boat 8.5 s after the throw if the sack spent 0.5 s in air. Neglect resistance of air and water.

10 A man of mass 56 kg having a bag of mass 2 kg slips from the roof of a tall building of height 50 m and starts falling vertically (figure). When at a height 32 m from the ground, he notices that the ground below him is pretty hard, but there is a pond at a horizontal distance 1 m from the line of fall. In order to save himself he throws the bag horizontally (with respect to himself) in the direction opposite to the pond so that the man lands in the water. Find the minimum horizontal velocity (in m/s) imparted to the bag. ($g = \pi^2$).

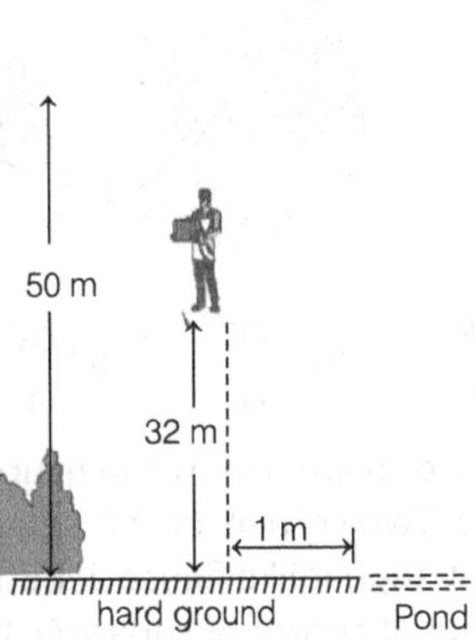

LEVEL 03 JEE Advanced Level

Single Choice Correct Questions

1 A uniform solid right circular cone of base radius R is joined to a uniform solid hemisphere of radius R and of the same density, as shown. The centre of mass of the composite solid lies at the centre of base of the cone. The height of the cone is

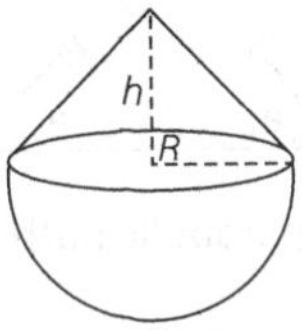

(a) $1.5R$ (b) $\sqrt{3}R$
(c) $3R$ (d) $2\sqrt{3}R$

2 A thin uniform semi-circular plate and a semi-circular ring of same mass and radius R are joined as shown. The centre of mass of the system w.r.t. shown coordinate system is

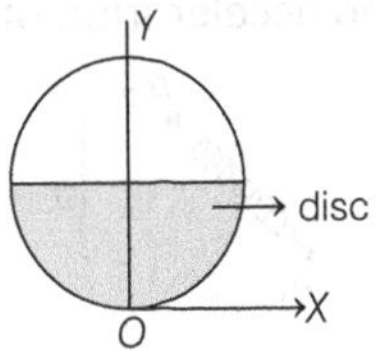

(a) $R\left(1+\frac{1}{3\pi}\right)$ (b) $R\left(1-\frac{1}{3\pi}\right)$
(c) $R\left(\pi+\frac{1}{3\pi}\right)$ (d) R

3 From a thin uniform, circular disc of radius $2R$ a semi-circular plate of radius R is removed as shown. The centre of mass of the remaining portion is

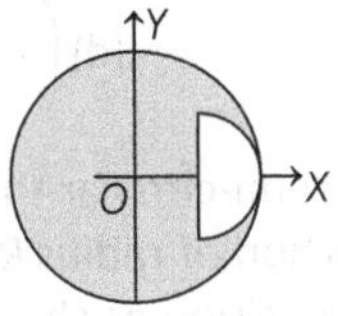

(a) $\frac{R(3\pi+4)}{21\pi}$
(b) $\frac{R(3\pi-4)}{21\pi}$
(c) $-\frac{R(3\pi+4)}{21\pi}$
(d) $-\frac{R(3\pi-4)}{21\pi}$

4 Eight solid uniform cubes of edge l are stacked together to form a single cube with center O. One cube is removed from this system. Distance of the centre of mass of remaining 7 cubes from O is

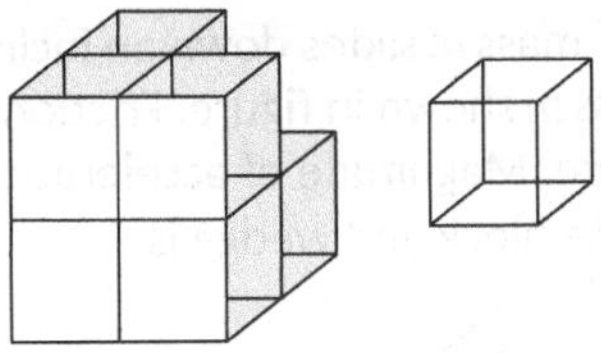

(a) $\frac{7\sqrt{3}l}{16}$ (b) $\frac{\sqrt{3}l}{16}$
(c) $\frac{\sqrt{3}l}{14}$ (d) zero

5 Find distance of centre of mass of section of a circular plate of uniform density as shown in the figure from O.

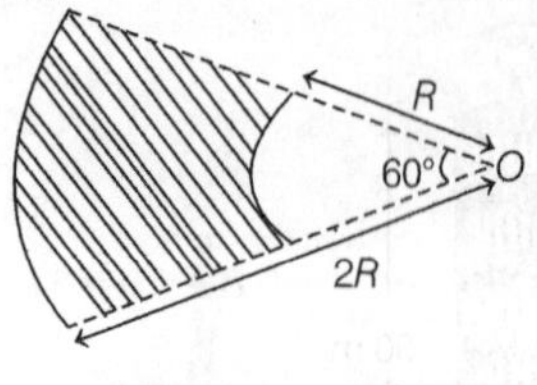

(a) $\frac{14R}{3\pi}$ (b) $\frac{14R}{5\pi}$ (c) $\frac{6R}{\pi}$ (d) $\frac{8R}{3\pi}$

6 A piece of paper (shown in figure 1) is in form of a square. Two corners of this square are folded to make it appear like figure 2. Both corners are put together at centre of square O. If O is taken to be (0, 0), the centre of mass of new system will be at

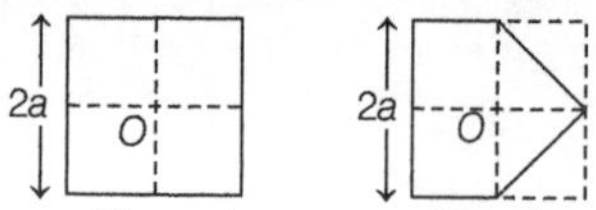

Figure 1 Figure 2

(a) $\left(-\frac{a}{8}, 0\right)$ (b) $\left(-\frac{a}{6}, 0\right)$

(c) $\left(\frac{a}{12}, 0\right)$ (d) $\left(-\frac{a}{12}, 0\right)$

7 From a uniform semi-circular thin disc of radius R, a semi-circular portion of radius $R/2$ is removed and placed in a new position as shown in figure. Taking O as origin and X and Y-axis as shown in figure, centre of mass of new setup is at

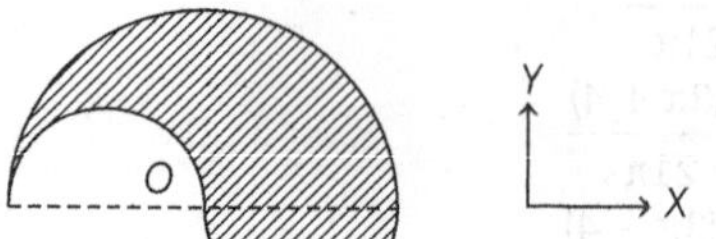

(a) $\frac{R}{4}, \frac{4R}{3\pi}$ (b) $-\frac{R}{4}, \frac{R}{3\pi}$

(c) $\frac{R}{4}, \frac{R}{\pi}$ (d) $\frac{R}{4}, \frac{R}{3\pi}$

8 A block of mass m slides down an inclined wedge of same mass m shown in figure. Friction is absent everywhere. Magnitude of acceleration of centre of mass of the block and wedge is

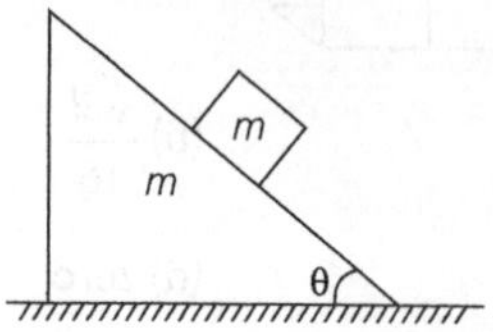

(a) 0 (b) $\frac{g\sin^2\theta}{1+\cos^2\theta}$

(c) $\frac{g\sin^2\theta}{1+\sin^2\theta}$ (d) $\frac{g\sin\theta}{1+\cos\theta}$

9 A rope thrown over a pulley has ladder of mass $(M-m)$ with a man of mass m on one of its ends and a counter balancing mass M on its other end. The man climbs with a velocity v_r relative to ladder. Ignoring the masses of the pulley and the rope as well as the friction on the pulley axis, the velocity of the centre of mass of this system is

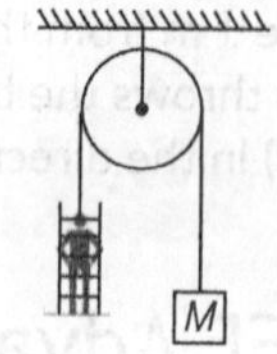

(a) $\frac{m}{M}v_r$ (b) $\frac{m}{2M}v_r$

(c) $\frac{M}{m}v_r$ (d) $\frac{2M}{m}v_r$

10 Two particles of equal mass m are projected from the ground with speed v_1 and v_2 at angle θ_1 and θ_2 as shown in figure. The centre of mass of the two particles

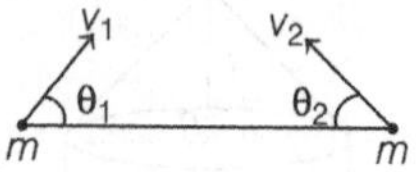

(a) will move in a parabolic path for any values of v_1, v_2, θ_1 and θ_2

(b) can move in a vertical line

(c) can move in a horizontal line

(d) will move in a straight line for any value of v_1, v_2, θ_1 and θ_2

11 Two particles are inter connected by an ideal spring (see figure). The spring is compressed and system is projected in air under gravity. If the acceleration of m_1 is $\mathbf{a}$ then find acceleration of m_2.

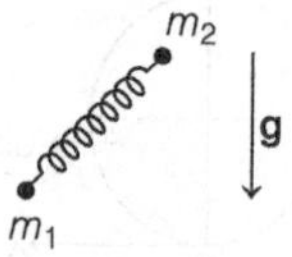

(a) $\mathbf{g}$

(b) $\mathbf{g}+\mathbf{a}$

(c) $\frac{m_1\mathbf{g}-m_1\mathbf{a}}{m_2}$

(d) $\frac{m_1\mathbf{g}+m_2\mathbf{g}-m_1\mathbf{a}}{m_2}$

12 A circular groove PQM of radius R is cut in an inclined plane as shown. A small ball of mass m is released from P. The magnitude of the displacement of wedge by the time ball reaches M is
$(\theta = 60°, R = 1\text{ m}, m = 2\text{ kg}, M = 3\text{ kg})$

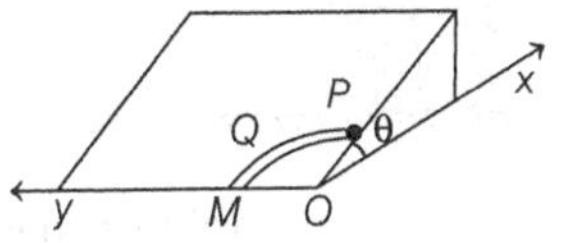

(a) $\sqrt{5}$ m (b) $\frac{1}{\sqrt{5}}$ m
(c) $\sqrt{\frac{17}{5}}$ m (d) None of these

13 A square plate $ABCD$ of mass 10 kg and side 1 m is placed on a frictionless surface. Two men having masses 85 kg and 35 kg are initially at the corners A and B, respectively. What is magnitude of displacement of plate when they move along the diagonals and reach to corners C and D, respectively?
(a) 1 m (b) $\sqrt{5}$ m (c) $\sqrt{12}$ m (d) 13 m

14 A ball of mass 1 kg is suspended by an inextensible string 1 m long attached to a point O of a smooth horizontal bar resting on a fixed smooth supports A and B. The ball is released from rest from the position when the string makes an angle of 30° with the vertical. The mass of the bar is 4 kg. The displacement of the bar when the string makes the maximum angle on the other side of the vertical is

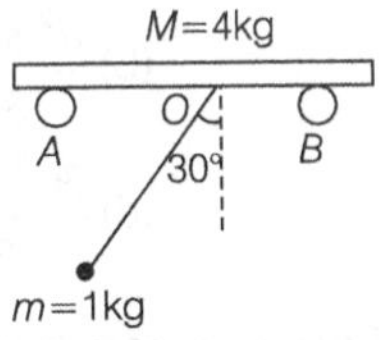

(a) 0 (b) 0.2 m (c) 0.25 m (d) 0.5 m

15 A system of two blocks A and B and a wedge C are released from rest as shown in figure. Masses of the blocks and the wedge are m, $2m$ and $2m$ respectively. The distance moved by the wedge C when block B slides down the plane a distance 10 cm is (neglect friction)

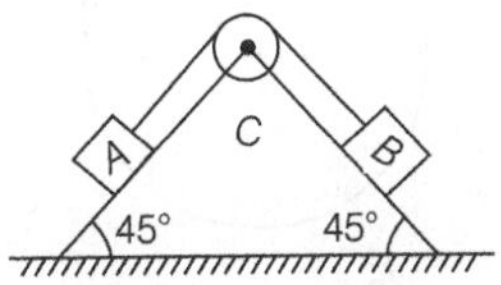

(a) $5\sqrt{2}$ cm (b) $3\sqrt{2}$ cm (c) 4 cm (d) $\frac{5}{\sqrt{2}}$ cm

16 Two men A and B are standing on a plank. B is at the middle of the plank and A is the left end of the plank. Surface of the plank is smooth. System is initially at rest and masses are as shown in figure. A and B start moving such that the position of B remains fixed with respect to ground then A meets B. Then the point where A meets B is located at

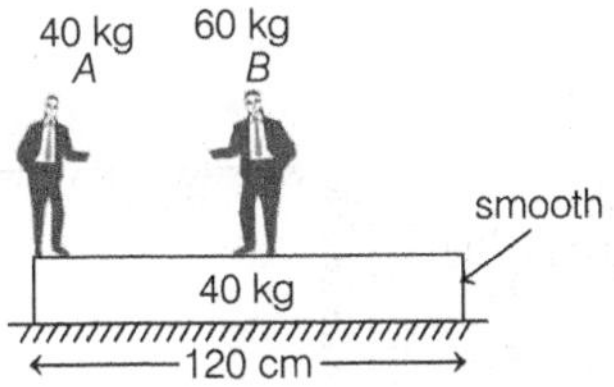

(a) the middle of the plank
(b) 30 cm from the left end of the plank
(c) the right end of the plank
(d) None of the above

17 In the figure shown block A of mass 1 kg and a plank B of mass 3 kg are placed on a frictionless surface where friction is also absent between A and B. Spring S_1 is compressed by amount x_0 and spring S_2 stretched by amount x_0 and held at rest. On releasing the block, the maximum distance the plank moves away from wall is

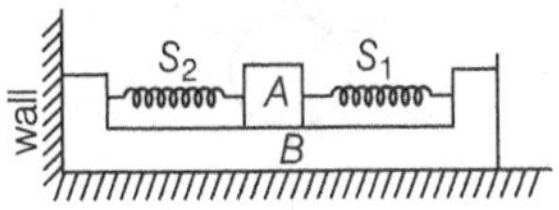

(a) $x_0/3$ (b) $x_0/2$ (c) $2x_0/3$ (d) x_0

18 Two blocks are connected by a spring and a thread as shown and are at rest. Initially spring is compressed by 20 cm. Now the thread is burnt and system is allowed to move. Total distance travelled by centre of mass is

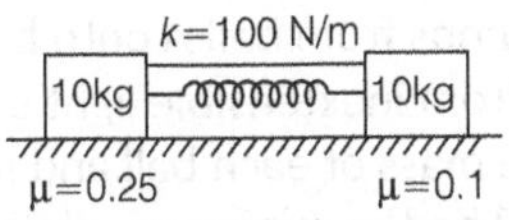

(a) 20 cm (b) 10 cm (c) zero (d) 5 cm

19 A buggy of mass 100 kg is free to move on a frictionless horizontal track. Two men, each of mass 50 kg, are standing on the buggy, which is initially stationary. The men jump off the buggy with velocity 10 m/s relative to the buggy. In one situation, the men jump one after the other. In another situation, the men jump simultaneously. What is the ratio of the recoil velocities of the buggy in two cases?
(a) 5 : 4 (b) 5 : 3 (c) 7 : 6 (d) 7 : 5

20 A man of mass m is standing on one end of a plank of mass $2m$ floating on a river. The other end just touches the bank of the river as shown in figure. With what minimum speed w.r.t. the plank, should the man jump to get out of the river? All surfaces are smooth and plank is always in level with the bank. Given that the length of the plank is 15 m.

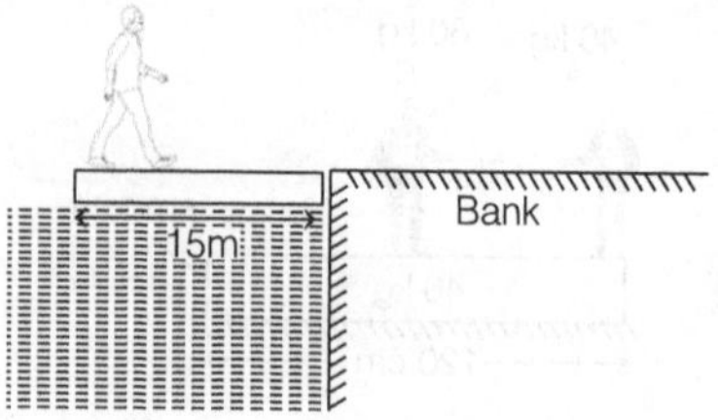

(a) 7 m/s (b) 7.5 m/s
(c) 9 m/s (d) 5 m/s

21 A rocket is projected straight up and explodes into three equally massive fragments just as it reaches the top of its flight. One of its fragment is observed to come straight down in time t_1. While other two land at a time t_2, after the burst. The height at which fragmentation occurs is

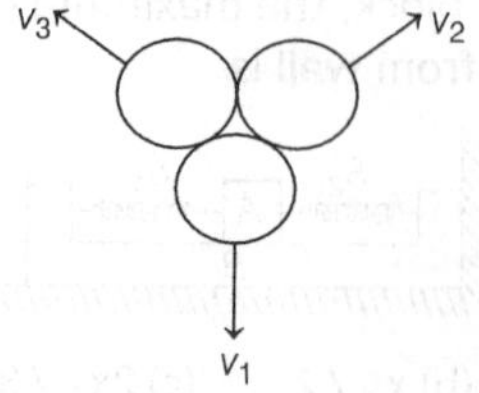

(a) $\frac{gt_1t_2}{2}\left(\frac{t_1+2t_2}{2t_1+2t_2}\right)$ (b) $\frac{gt_1t_2}{2}\left(\frac{2t_1+t_2}{t_1+2t_2}\right)$
(c) $\frac{gt_1t_2}{2}\left(\frac{t_1+t_2}{2t_1+t_2}\right)$ (d) $\frac{gt_1t_2}{2}\left(\frac{t_1+2t_2}{2t_1+t_2}\right)$

22 A monkey jumps from ball A onto ball B which are suspended from inextensible light string each of length L. The mass of each ball and monkey is same. What should be the minimum relative velocity of jump w.r.t. ball, if both the balls manage to complete the circle?

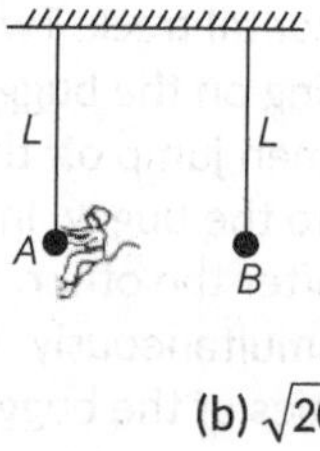

(a) $\sqrt{5gL}$ (b) $\sqrt{20gL}$
(c) $4\sqrt{5gL}$ (d) None of these

23 A gun fires a bullet as shown in figure. The barrel of the gun is inclined at an angle of 45° with horizontal. When the bullet leaves the barrel, it will be travelling at an angle to the horizontal of

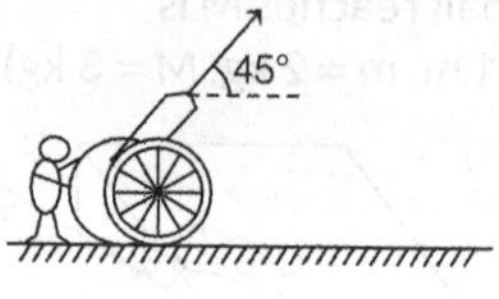

(a) 45° (b) less than 45°
(c) more than 45° (d) zero

24 A particle of mass $m = 0.1$ kg is released from rest from a point A of a wedge of mass $M = 2.4$ kg free to slide on a frictionless horizontal plane. The particle slides down the smooth face AB of the wedge. When the velocity of the wedge is 0.2 m/s the velocity of the particle relative to the wedge is

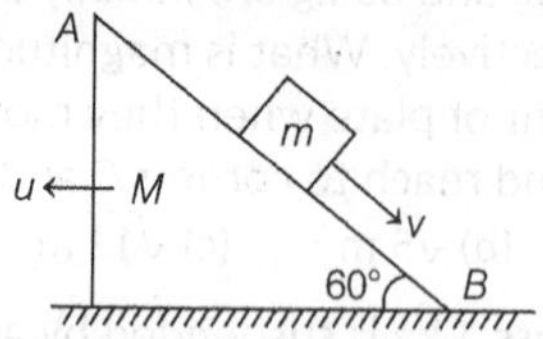

(a) 4.8 m/s (b) 5 m/s (c) 7.5 m/s (d) 10 m/s

25 A cannon of mass $5m$ (including a shell of mass m) is at rest on a smooth horizontal ground, fires the shell with its barrel at an angle θ with the horizontal at a velocity u relative to cannon. Find the horizontal distance of the point where shell strikes the ground from the initial position of the cannon

(a) $\frac{4u^2 \sin 2\theta}{5g}$ (b) $\frac{u^2 \sin 2\theta}{5g}$
(c) $\frac{3u^2 \sin 2\theta}{5g}$ (d) $\frac{8u^2 \sin 2\theta}{5g}$

26 Two particles of mass m, constrained to move along the circumference of a smooth circular loop of equal mass m, are initially located at opposite ends of a diameter and given equal velocities v_0 shown in the figure. The entire arrangement is located in gravity free space. Their velocity just before collision is

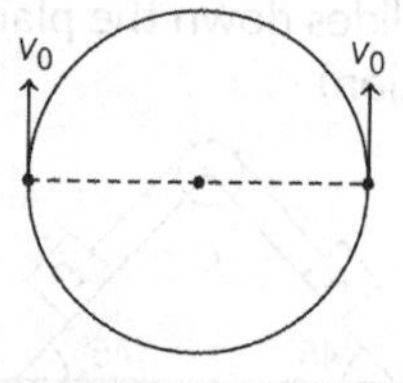

(a) $\frac{1}{\sqrt{3}}v_0$ (b) $\frac{\sqrt{3}}{2}v_0$ (c) $\frac{2}{\sqrt{3}}v_0$ (d) $\frac{\sqrt{7}}{3}v_0$

27 A man is standing on a cart of mass double the mass of the man. Initially cart is at rest on the smooth ground. Now, man jumps with relative velocity v horizontally towards right with respect to cart. The work done by man during the process of jumping is

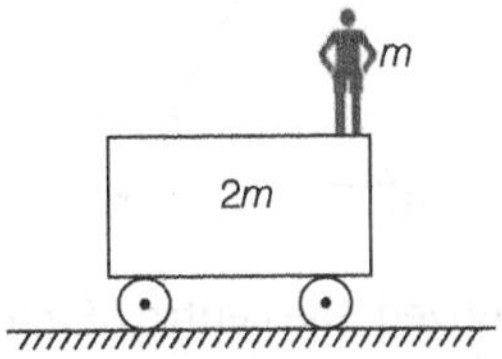

(a) $\frac{2mv^2}{9}$ (b) $\frac{mv^2}{9}$ (c) $\frac{mv^2}{3}$ (d) $\frac{4mv^2}{9}$

28 A block and wedge system is released from rest from the position as shown. After some time the block is moving with speed v on horizontal surface. What is work done by gravity on the block? (neglect friction)

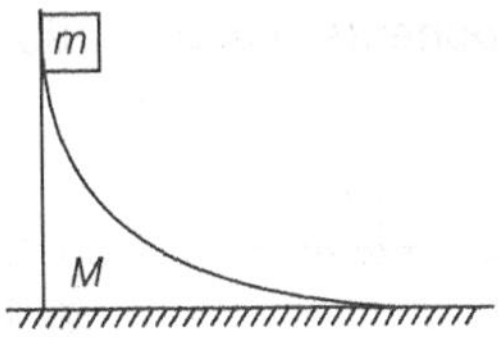

(a) $\frac{1}{2}\left(1+\frac{m}{M}\right)mv^2$ (b) $\frac{1}{2}mv^2$

(c) $\frac{1}{2}Mv^2$ (d) $\frac{1}{2}(m+M)v^2$

29 Figure shows an irregular wedge of mass m placed on a smooth horizontal surface. Part BC is rough. What minimum velocity should be imparted to a small block of same mass m so that it may reach point B?

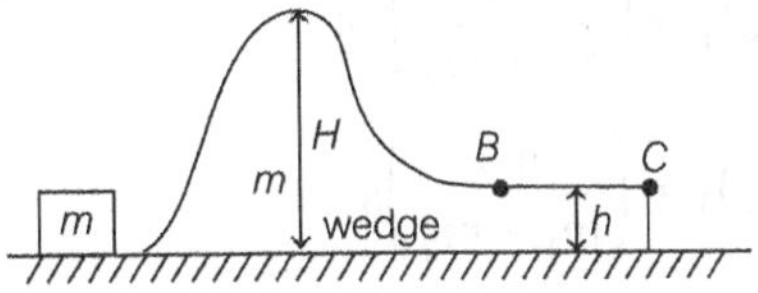

(a) $2\sqrt{gH}$ (b) $\sqrt{2gH}$ (c) $2\sqrt{g(H-h)}$ (d) $\sqrt{gH}$

30 A ball of mass m is released from A inside a smooth wedge of mass m as shown in the figure. What is the speed of the wedge when the ball reaches point B?

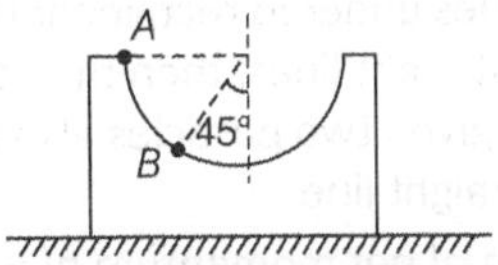

(a) $\left(\frac{gR}{3\sqrt{2}}\right)^{1/2}$ (b) $\sqrt{2gR}$ (c) $\left(\frac{5gR}{2\sqrt{3}}\right)^{1/2}$ (d) $\sqrt{\frac{3}{2}gR}$

31 A wedge of mass m, having a smooth semi-circular groove is resting against a vertical wall as shown in the diagram. A point mass m is released from top of groove. Neglecting friction everywhere, find maximum speed of wedge in subsequent motion

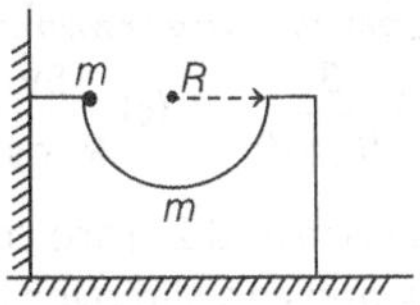

(a) $\sqrt{gR}$ (b) $2\sqrt{gR}$ (c) $\sqrt{2gR}$ (d) 0

32 A small bob of mass m is suspended by a massless string from a cart of the same mass m as shown in the figure. The friction between the cart and horizontal ground is negligible. The bob is given a velocity v_0 in horizontal direction as shown. The maximum height attained by the bob is [initially whole system (bob + string + cart) was at rest]

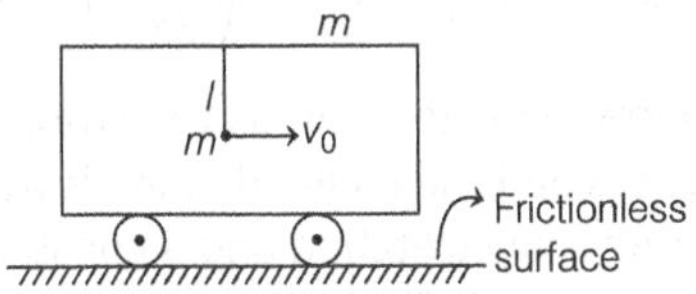

(a) $\frac{2v_0^2}{g}$ (b) $\frac{v_0^2}{g}$ (c) $\frac{v_0^2}{4g}$ (d) $\frac{v_0^2}{2g}$

33 A cart of mass M is at rest on smooth horizontal surface. A small sphere P of mass m is attached to ceiling of the cart by means of two strings PA and PB as shown. Initial tension in the string PA is T_1. Now the string PB is cut. Just after the cut tension in the string PA is T_2, then $\frac{T_2}{T_1}$ is

$\left[\text{Given that, } \theta = 37^0, \frac{m}{M} = \frac{5}{4}\right]$

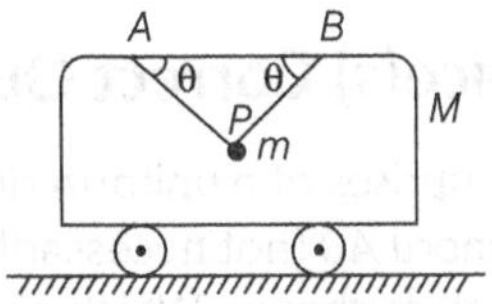

(a) $\frac{2}{5}$ (b) $\frac{9}{25}$ (c) $\frac{9}{20}$ (d) $\frac{3}{10}$

34 A hemisphere of mass $3m$ and radius R is free to slide with its base on a smooth horizontal table. A particle of mass m is placed on the top of the hemisphere. If particle is displaced with a negligible velocity, then find the angular velocity of the particle relative to the centre of the hemisphere at an angular displacement θ, when velocity of hemisphere is v.

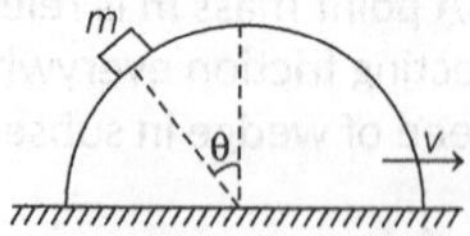

(a) $\frac{4v}{R\cos\theta}$ (b) $\frac{3v}{R\cos\theta}$ (c) $\frac{5v}{R\cos\theta}$ (d) $\frac{2v}{R\cos\theta}$

35 Two rings of mass m and $2m$ are connected with a massless spring and can slip over two frictionless parallel horizontal rails as shown in figure. Ring of mass m is given velocity v_0 in the direction shown. Maximum stretch in spring will be

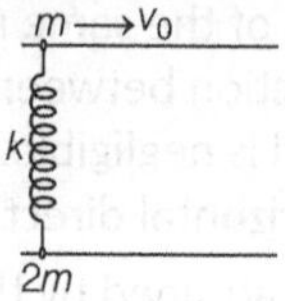

(a) $\sqrt{\frac{m}{k}}v_0$ (b) $\sqrt{\frac{3m}{k}}v_0$ (c) $\sqrt{\frac{2m}{3k}}v_0$ (d) $\sqrt{\frac{2m}{k}}v_0$

36 In the below arrangement, all the string and pulleys are massless and the inclined plane is frictionless. At $t = 0$, spring is unstretched and a constant force $F = mg$ starts to act. Find the maximum extension in the spring. (Assume incline to be sufficiently long).

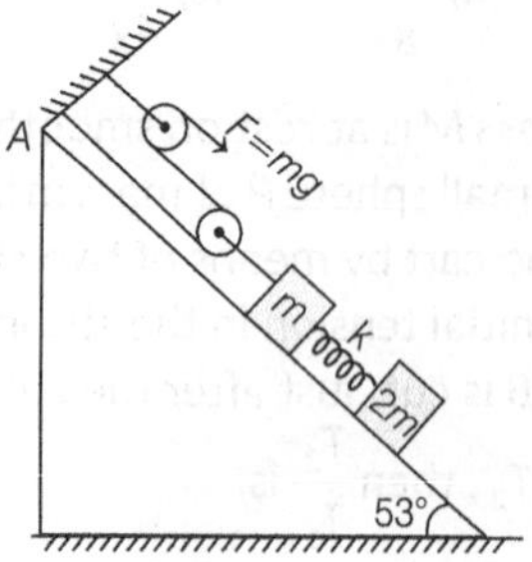

(a) $\frac{8mg}{k}$ (b) $\frac{4}{5}\frac{mg}{k}$ (c) $\frac{8}{15}\frac{mg}{k}$ (d) $\frac{8mg}{3k}$

Multiple Choice(s) Correct Questions

1 An object comprises of a uniform ring of radius R and its uniform chord AB (not necessarily made of the same material) as shown. Which of the following can not be the centre of mass of the object?

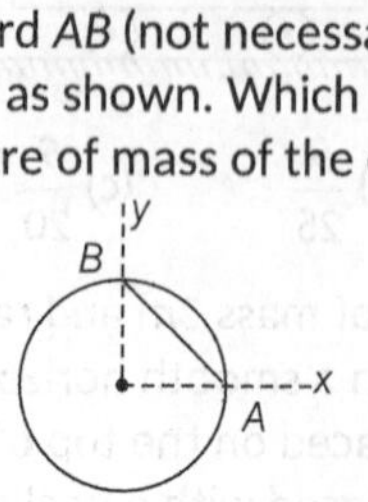

(a) $(R/3, R/3)$ (b) $(R/3, R/2)$
(c) $(R/4, R/4)$ (d) $(R/\sqrt{2}, R/\sqrt{2})$

2 A uniform wire frame ABC is in the shape of an equilateral triangle in XY-plane with centroid at the origin.

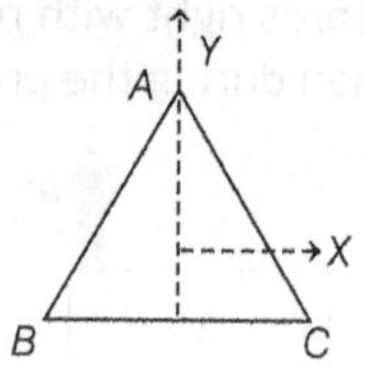

(a) If AB is removed, the centre of mass of the remaining figure is in fourth quadrant.
(b) If AC is removed, the centre of mass of the remaining figure is in first quadrant.
(c) If BC is removed, the centre of mass of the remaining figure is on the positive Y-axis.
(d) If AC is removed, the centre of mass of the remaining figure is in third quadrant.

3 X and Y components of acceleration of centre of mass are

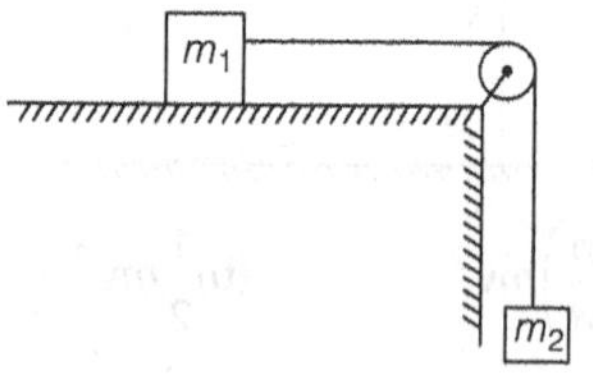

(a) $(a_{CM})_x = \frac{m_1 m_2 g}{m_1 + m_2}$

(b) $(a_{CM})_x = \frac{m_1 m_2 g}{(m_1 + m_2)^2}$

(c) $(a_{CM})_Y = \left(\frac{m_2}{m_1 + m_2}\right)^2 g$

(d) $(a_{CM})_Y = \left(\frac{m_2}{m_1 + m_2}\right) g$

4 Pick the correct statements.
(a) Non-zero work has to be done on a moving particle to change its momentum.
(b) To change momentum of a particle, a non-zero net force should act on it.
(c) Two particles undergo rectilinear motion along different straight lines, then the centre of mass of system of given two particles also always moves along a straight line.
(d) If direction of net momentum of a system of particles (having non-zero net momentum) is fixed, the centre of mass of given system moves along a straight line.

5 An object of mass 3*m*, initially at rest on a frictionless horizontal surface, explodes breaking into two fragments of mass *m* and 2*m*, respectively. Which of the following statements after the explosion are true?

(a) Velocity of centre of mass increases.

(b) Speed of smaller fragment will be twice that of larger fragment.

(c) Fragments have equal magnitude of momentum in ground frame but different magnitude of momentum in centre of mass frame.

(d) Kinetic energy of system increases.

6 Consider two skaters *A* and *B* initially at rest on ice (friction is negligible) with *A* holding a ball. *A* has greater mass than *B* and the ball has some significant mass. *A* throws the ball to *B*. *B* catches it and throws it back to *A* who catches it again. The magnitudes of the skaters' (excluding ball) final velocities, momentum and kinetic energies (denoted below as *v*, *p* and *K* respectively) are related as

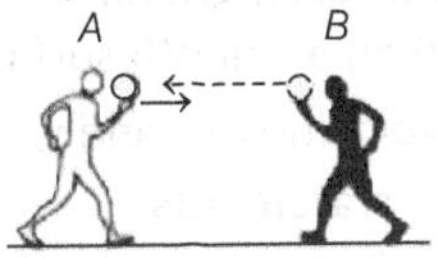

(a) $v_A = v_B$ (b) $v_A < v_B, p_A < p_B$

(c) $p_A = p_B, k_A < k_B$ (d) $p_A < p_B, k_A < k_B$

7 In the figure shown the system is at rest initially. Two persons A and B of masses 40 kg each move with speeds v_1 and v_2 respectively towards each other on a plank lying on a smooth horizontal surface as shown in figure. Plank travels a distance of 20 m towards right direction in 5 s (Here v_1 and v_2 are given with respect to the plank). Then, the possible condition(s) can be

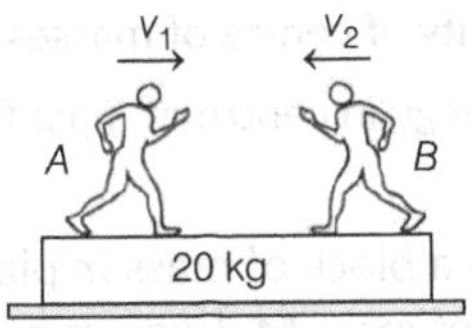

(a) $v_1 = 0$ m/s, $v_2 = 10$ m/s

(b) $v_1 = 5$ m/s, $v_2 = 15$ m/s

(c) $v_1 = 10$ m/s, $v_2 = 20$ m/s

(d) $v_1 = 2$ m/s, $v_2 = 12$ m/s

8 A rod of mass $(M - m)$ carries an insect of mass *m* at its bottom end and its top end is connected with a string which passes over a smooth pulley and the other end of the string is connected to a counter mass *M*. Initially the insect is at rest. Choose the correct option(s).

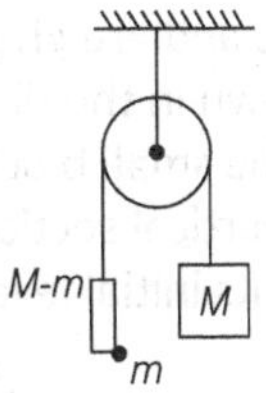

(a) As insect starts moving up relative to rod, the acceleration of centre of mass of the system (insect + rod + counter mass) becomes non-zero.

(b) As insect starts moving up relative to rod, tension in the string remains constant and is equal to *Mg*.

(c) As insect starts moving up relative to rod, the tension in the string becomes more than *Mg*.

(d) Acceleration of centre of mass of the system (insect + rod + counter mass) is zero when insect moves with constant velocity.

9 A man of mass *m* on an initially stationary boat gets off of the boat by leaping to the left in an exactly horizontal direction. Immediately after the leap, the boat of mass M, is observed to be moving to the right at speed *v*.

(a) Work done by man on boat is $\frac{1}{2}(m)v^2$.

(b) Increase in the mechanical energy of system of man and boat is $\frac{1}{2}\left(\frac{M^2}{m} + M\right)v^2$.

(c) Velocity of centre of mass of system is *v*.

(d) Increase in kinetic energy of man is $\frac{1}{2}\frac{M^2}{m}v^2$.

10 An insect of mass *m* is initially at rest at the one end of a stick of length *L* and mass *M*, which rests on a smooth horizontal floor. The coefficient of friction between the insect and stick is μ. The insect starts moving to reach the other end in shortest possible time.

(a) The centre of mass of the (stick + insect) system has speed $v = \left[\mu g\left(1 + \frac{m}{M}\right)\right]t$ at time *t*.

(b) Time taken by the insect to reach the other end is $t = \sqrt{\frac{2ML}{\mu(M + m)g}}$

(c) The magnitude of the linear momentum of the insect at time *t* is equal to μmgt.

(d) The maximum speed acquired by the stick is $v_{max} = \sqrt{\frac{2\mu L m^2 g}{(M + m)M}}$

11 A small block of mass m is placed on a smooth body of mass M, the combination is placed on a smooth horizontal surface and are given velocities u towards each other as shown in the diagram. The maximum height to which the small block of mass m rises after breaking off the vertical section of the body of mass M is H, relative to its initial level. Assume $M > m$.

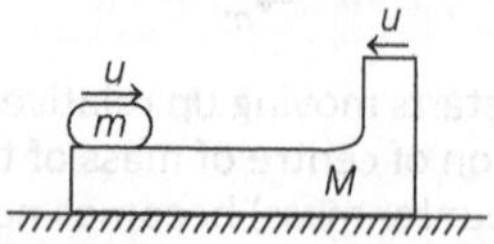

(a) $u < \sqrt{\dfrac{gH}{2}}$

(b) The work done in raising the two bodies through a height H equals 4 times the initial kinetic energy of the body of mass M.

(c) The final velocity of the small block at its highest point is $\left(\dfrac{M-m}{M+m}\right)u$.

(d) The kinetic energy of the system when the smaller block is at its highest point is $\dfrac{1}{4}(M-m)^2\dfrac{gH}{M}$.

12 A cart of mass M length L stands just at the end of a slope as shown in figure. A small block of mass m is released from rest at height h block slides on cart and comes to rest with respect to cart at the edge of cart. Friction exists between cart and block and all other surfaces are smooth. Coefficient of friction is μ.

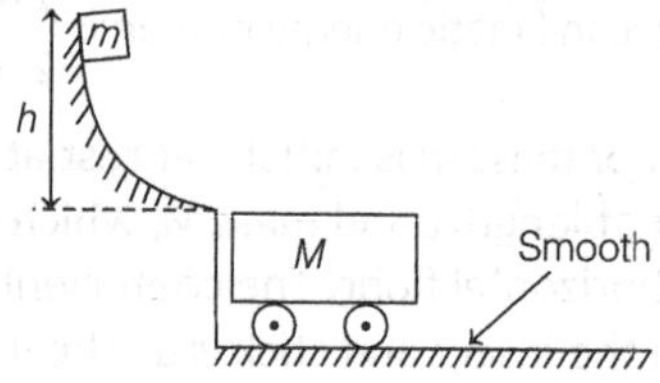

(a) Time for which block moves on cart is $\dfrac{\sqrt{2gh}\,M}{\mu g(m+M)}$.

(b) Net work done by kinetic friction is $-\mu mgL$.

(c) Final velocity of centre of mass of block and cart is $\dfrac{m\sqrt{2gh}}{m+M}$.

(d) Net impulse on cart is $\dfrac{mM\sqrt{2gh}}{m+M}$.

13 Two identical blocks each of mass $2M$ are joined by means of a light spring of spring constant k. A man of mass M is standing on one of the block as shown in the diagram. If man jumps horizontally with a velocity v relative to block and horizontal surface is smooth, then

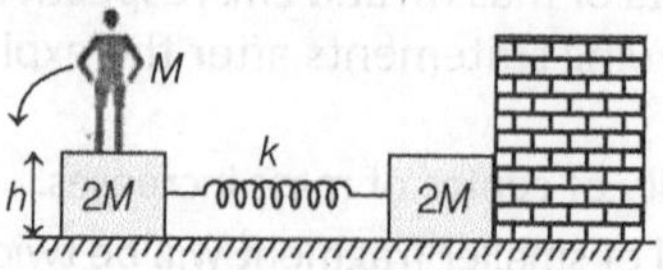

(a) the maximum compression in the spring is $\sqrt{\dfrac{2M}{k}}\left(\dfrac{v}{3}\right)$.

(b) man lands at horizontal distance $v\sqrt{\dfrac{2h}{g}}$ from initial position of the block.

(c) right block loses contact with wall when the elongation in spring is maximum.

(d) velocity of centre of mass of two blocks after $2M$ loses contact with wall is $\dfrac{v}{6}$.

14 Two blocks of mass m_1 and m_2 are connected by a spring in its natural length having spring constant k and are placed on a smooth surface. Block m_1 and m_2 are given velocities v_1 and v_2 as shown in figure. Choose correct statements

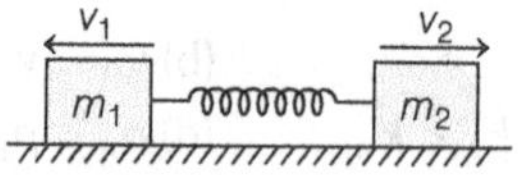

(a) Momentum of the system of m_1 and m_2 in the ground frame is conserved

(b) Momentum of the system of m_1 and m_2 in the frame attached to centre of masses of m_1 and m_2 is always zero.

(c) The term $\dfrac{1}{2}(m_1+m_2)v_c^2$ is always constant, where v_c is velocity of centre of masses of m_1 and m_2

(d) Kinetic energy in centre of mass frame remains constant.

15. Figure shows a block of mass m placed inside a smooth cart of mass M. Two springs of force constant of k and $4k$ are attached to wall of cart. The separation between springs in relaxed state is L. Initially at $t=0$, left spring is compressed by x_0 and block is released.

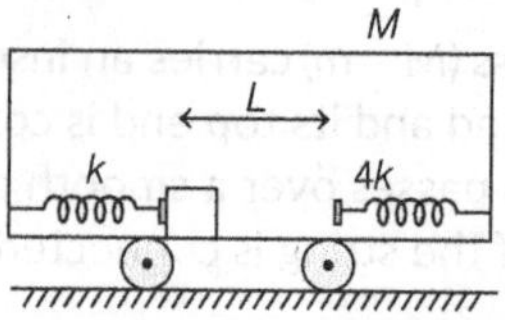

(a) Maximum compression of right spring is $\frac{x_0}{2}$.

(b) Time taken by block to travel distance L between springs is $\sqrt{\frac{mML^2}{k(m+M)x_0^2}}$.

(c) Distance travelled by cart from initial moment $t = 0$ to maximum compression of the right spring is $\frac{m(3x_0 + 2L)}{2(m+M)}$

(d) Centre of mass of cart remains at rest.

Comprehension Based Questions

Comprehension-1

A uniform bar length $12L$ and mass $48m$ is supported horizontally on two smooth tables as shown in the figure. A small fly of mass $8m$ is sitting on end A of the rod and a spider of mass $16m$ is sitting on the other end B. Both the insects start moving towards each other along the rod with fly moving at a speed $2v$ and the spider at a half of this speed. They meet at a point P on the rod and the spider eats the fly. After this the spider moves with a velocity $v/2$ relative to the rod towards the end A. The spider takes negligible time in eating the fly.

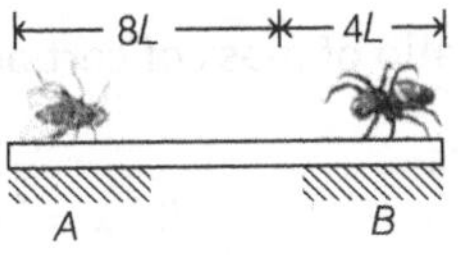

1 Displacement of the rod by the time when the insects meet is

(a) $L/2$ (b) L

(c) $3L/4$ (d) 0

2 The speed of the bar after the spider eats up the fly and moves towards A is

(a) $v/2$ (b) v

(c) $v/6$ (d) $2v$

3 By what distance the centre of mass of the rod shifts during this time?

(a) $8L/3$ (b) $4L/3$

(c) L (d) $L/3$

Comprehension - 2

Two friends A and B (each weighing 40 kg) are sitting on a frictionless platform some distance d apart. A rolls a ball of mass 4 kg on the platform towards B which B catches. Then B rolls the ball towards A and A catches it. The ball keeps on moving back and forth between A and B. The ball has a fixed speed of 5 m/s on the platform.

4 Find the speed of A after he catches the ball for the first time.

(a) $\frac{10}{21}$ m/s (b) $\frac{50}{11}$ m/s

(c) $\frac{10}{11}$ m/s (d) None of these

5 Find the speeds of A and B after the ball has made 5 round trips and is held by A

(a) $\frac{10}{11}$ m/s, $\frac{50}{11}$ m/s (b) $\frac{50}{11}$ m/s, $\frac{10}{11}$ m/s

(c) $\frac{50}{11}$ m/s, 5 m/s (d) None of these

6 How many times can A roll the ball?

(a) 6 (b) 5

(c) 7 (d) None of these

7 Where is the centre of mass of the system "$A + B +$ ball" at the end of the nth trip? (Give the distance from the initial position of A)

(a) $\frac{10}{11}d$ (b) $\frac{10}{21}d$

(c) $\frac{50}{11}d$ (d) None of these

Comprehension-3

A 1 kg block is given a velocity of 15 m/s towards right over a very long rough plank of mass 2 kg kept on a smooth horizontal plane as shown in figure. The coefficient of friction between the two blocks is equal to 0.4.

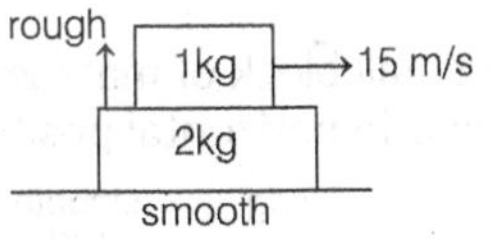

8 The correct graph showing linear momentum of 1 kg (i.e. p_1) and of 2 kg (i.e. p_2) *versus* time is

(a)
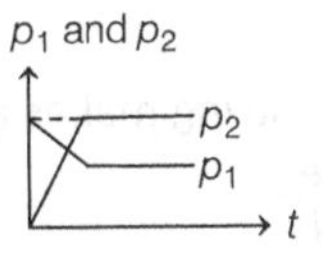

(b)
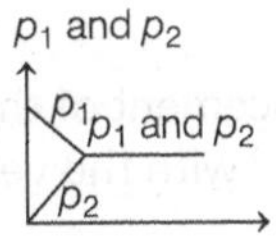

(c)
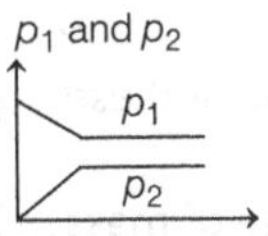

(d)
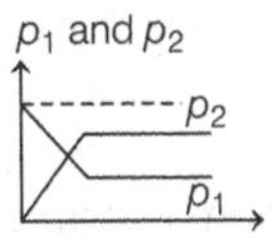

9 The magnitude of initial slope of p_1 *versus* t and p_2 *versus* t (in SI unit) will be

(a) 4 and 2 (b) 2 and 4

(c) 4 and 4 (d) 2 and 2

10 Momentum of both the blocks are equal at time $t =$ .... s

(a) 1.75 (b) 1.875 (c) 2.5 (d) 1.25

Comprehension 4

Block A is placed on wedge B at a height h above ground. Block and the two wedges are all of same mass m. Neglect friction everywhere.

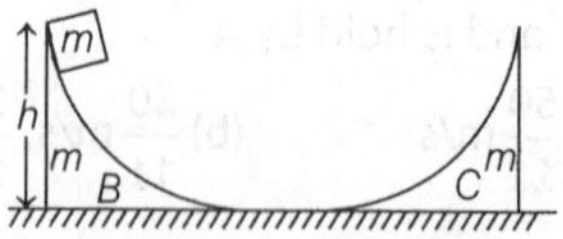

11. Find velocity of B when A has slid down from it.

(a) $\sqrt{gh}$ (b) $\sqrt{\frac{gh}{2}}$

(c) $\frac{\sqrt{gh}}{2}$ (d) None of these

12. Find maximum height upto which block A rises on wedge C.

(a) $h/2$ (b) $h/3$

(c) $h/4$ (d) None of these

13. Find velocity of A when it has slid down to ground from wedge C.

(a) 0 (b) $\sqrt{\frac{gh}{2}}$

(c) $\sqrt{\frac{gh}{4}}$ (d) None of these

Comprehension-5

In given figure, the small block of mass $2m$ is released from rest when the string is in horizontal position,

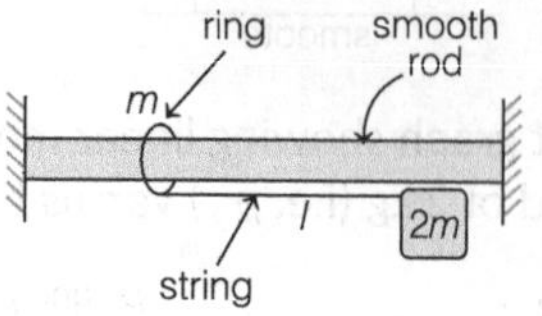

14. Displacement of the ring when string makes an angle $\theta = 37°$ with the vertical will be

(a) $\frac{4l}{15}$ (b) $\frac{l}{15}$

(c) $\frac{2l}{15}$ (d) None of these

15. Maximum possible velocity of ring of mass m is (assuming zero friction)

(a) $\sqrt{2gl}$ (b) $\sqrt{\frac{4gl}{3}}$

(c) $\sqrt{\frac{8gl}{3}}$ (d) None of these

16. Find the tension in the string when the block has maximum velocity.

(a) $12\,mg$ (b) $14\,mg$ (c) $8\,mg$ (d) $20\,mg$

Comprehension-6

A small object of mass $m = 1$ kg is released from rest at the top of an inclined plane that connects to a horizontal plane without an edge, it slides onto a cart of mass M that has a semi-cylindrical surface of radius $R = 0.36$ m fixed to the middle of it, as shown in the figure. The small object reaches the topmost point of the semi-cylinder and stops there. It continues to move vertically with free fall and hits the cart exactly at the edge. All friction can be neglected.

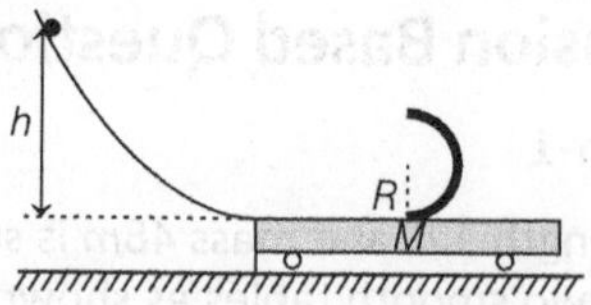

17. What is the minimum possible length of the cart?

(a) R (b) $2R$ (c) $3R$ (d) $4R$

18. At what height h was the small object released?

(a) $h = \frac{1}{2}\left(\frac{m}{M}\right)^2 R$ (b) $h = \frac{1}{2}\left(\frac{M}{m}\right)^2 R$

(c) $h = \frac{1}{2}\left(\frac{m}{M}\right) R$ (d) $h = \left(\frac{M}{m}\right)^2 R$

19. What is the ratio of mass of cart and mass of the particle?

(a) $k = \frac{1+\sqrt{17}}{2}$ (b) $k = \frac{1+\sqrt{14}}{2}$

(c) $k = \frac{1+\sqrt{16}}{2}$ (d) $k = \frac{1+\sqrt{18}}{2}$

Comprehension-7

A system consists of two small spheres of mass 1 kg and 2 kg interconnected by a weightless spring. At $t = 0$, the spheres are set in motion with initial velocities as shown in figure. Position vector of centre of mass at $t = 0$ is $20\hat{j}$. Initially spring is in its natural length. System moves in earth's gravitational field.

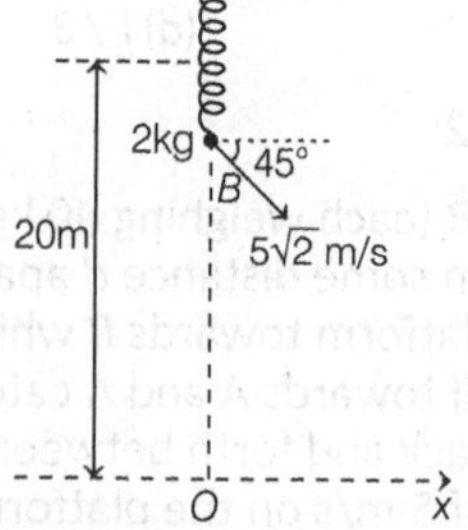

20. The momentum of the system at $t = 2$ s in kg m/s is ($g = 10\ \text{m/s}^2$)

(a) $(12\hat{i} - 32\hat{j})$ (b) $(16\hat{i} - 64\hat{j})$

(c) $(18\hat{i} - 64\hat{j})$ (d) $(12\hat{i} - 18\hat{j})$

21. The position vector of centre of mass of the system at $t = 1$ s is

(a) $4\hat{i} + \frac{24}{25}\hat{j}$ (b) $6\hat{i} + \frac{39}{2}\hat{j}$

(c) $4\hat{i} + \frac{29}{3}\hat{j}$ (d) $6\hat{i} + \frac{41}{3}\hat{j}$

Comprehension-8

Two blocks of equal mass m are connected by an unstretched spring and the system is kept at rest on a frictionless horizontal surface. A constant force F is applied on the first block pulling it away from the other as shown in figure.

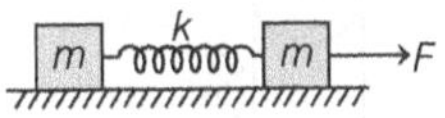

22. The displacement of the centre of mass at time t is

(a) $\frac{Ft^2}{2m}$ (b) $\frac{Ft^2}{3m}$

(c) $\frac{Ft^2}{4m}$ (d) $\frac{Ft^2}{m}$

23. If the extension of the spring is x_0 at time t, then the displacement of the first block at this instant is

(a) $\frac{1}{2}\left(\frac{Ft^2}{2m} + x_0\right)$ (b) $-\frac{1}{2}\left(\frac{Ft^2}{2m} + x_0\right)$

(c) $\frac{1}{2}\left(\frac{Ft^2}{2m} - x_0\right)$ (d) $\left(\frac{Ft^2}{2m} + x_0\right)$

24. If the extension of the spring is x_0 at time t, then the displacement of the second block at this instant is :

(a) $\left(\frac{Ft^2}{2m} - x_0\right)$ (b) $\frac{1}{2}\left(\frac{Ft^2}{2m} + x_0\right)$

(c) $\frac{1}{2}\left(\frac{2Ft^2}{m} - x_0\right)$ (d) $\frac{1}{2}\left(\frac{Ft^2}{2m} - x_0\right)$

Comprehension-9

A system consists of block A and B each of mass m connected by a light spring as shown with block B in contact with a wall. The block A compresses the spring by $3mg/k$ from natural length of spring and then released from rest. Neglect friction anywhere.

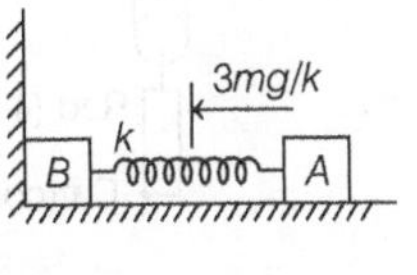

25. Acceleration of centre of mass of system comprising A and B just after A is released, is

(a) 0 (b) $\frac{3g}{2}$

(c) $3g$ (d) None of these

26. Velocity of centre of mass of system comprising A and B when block B just loses contact with the wall is

(a) $3g\sqrt{\frac{m}{K}}$ (b) $\frac{3g}{2}\sqrt{\frac{m}{k}}$

(c) $2g\sqrt{\frac{m}{k}}$ (d) None of these

27. Maximum extension in the spring after system loses contact with wall is

(a) $\frac{3mg}{\sqrt{2}k}$ (b) $\frac{\sqrt{3}mg}{2k}$

(c) $\frac{\sqrt{3}mg}{\sqrt{2}k}$ (d) None of these

Match the Columns Questions

1. In the figure shown, when the persons A and B exchange their positions, then match the Column I and Column II.

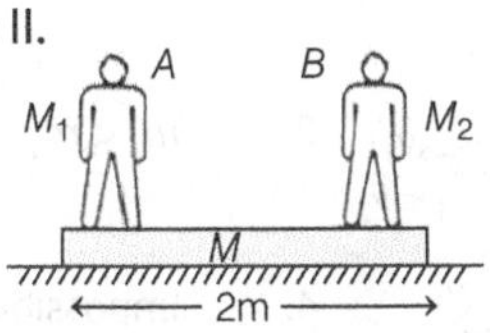

$M_1 = 50$ kg, $M_2 = 70$ kg, $M = 80$ kg

[There is no friction between the plank and ground]

Column I	Column II
A. The distance moved by the centre of mass of the system is	1. 0.2 m
B. The distance moved by the plank is	2. 1.8 m
C. The distance moved by A with respect to ground is	3. 0
D. The distance moved by B with respect to ground is	4. 2.2 m
	5. 1.2 m

2 Two men of mass 60 kg and 80 kg stand on a plank of mass 20 kg. Both of them can jump with a velocity of 1 m/s relative to the plank. In each event shown in Column I, find the velocity of plank after the event.

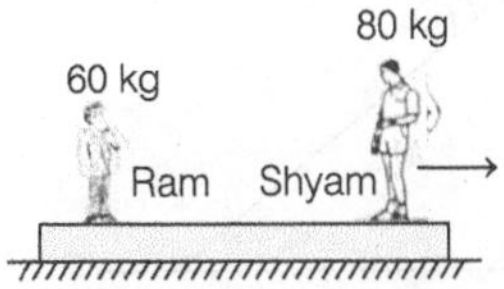

Smooth level ground

Column I	Column II
A. Ram alone jumps to the left	1. $-\frac{17}{40}$ m/s
B. Shyam alone jumps to the right	2. $-\frac{1}{2}$ m/s
C. Ram jumps to left and Shyam jumps to right simultaneously.	3. $\frac{3}{8}$ m/s
D. Ram jumps to left and after that Shyam jumps to right	4. $-\frac{1}{8}$ m/s

3 A body initially moving towards right explodes into two pieces 1 and 2. Direction of motion of the pieces is shown in Column I and possible mass ratio are shown in Column II.

Column I	Column II
A. 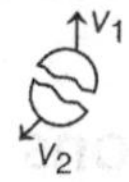	1. $m_1 > m_2$
B. 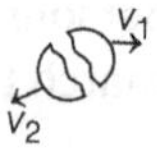	2. $m_1 = m_2$
C. 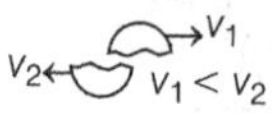	3. $m_1 < m_2$
D. 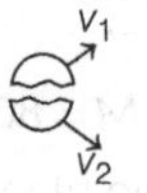	4. Impossible for any masses

4 In each situation of Column I, a system involving two bodies given. All the strings and pulleys are light and friction is absent every where. Initially each body of every system is at rest. Consider the system in all situation of Column I from rest till any collision occurs. Then match the statement in Column I with the corresponding results in Column II.

Column I	Column II
A. The block + wedge system is placed over smooth horizontal surface. After the system is released from rest, the centre of mass of system 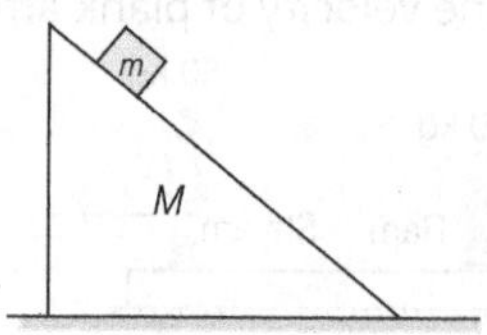	1 shifts towards right
B. The string connecting both the blocks of mass m is horizontal. Left block is placed over smooth horizontal table as shown. After the two block system is released from rest, the centre of mass of system 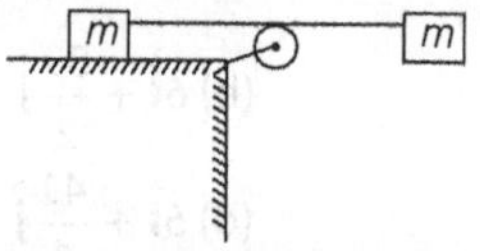	2 shifts towards left
C. The block and monkey have same mass. The monkey starts climbing up the rope. After the monkey starts climbing up, the centre of mass of monkey + block system 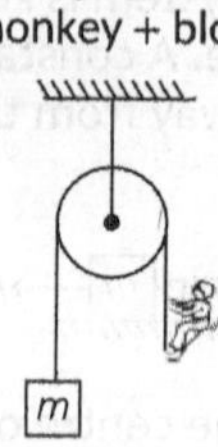	3. shifts downwards
D. Both blocks of mass m are initially at rest. The left block is given initial velocity u downwards, then the centre of mass of two blocks system afterwards 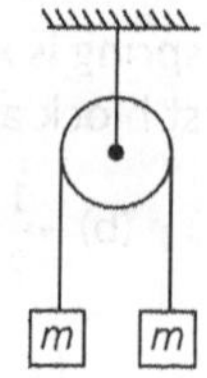	4. shifts upwards
	5. doesn't shift

5 A cat is intially hanging on a rod in static equillibrium as shown in figure. If the cat climbs up on the rod from its lower end towards its upper end with a monotonically increasing acceleration starting at $t = 0$ and crossing the midpoint of rod at $t = t_0$ and the average speed of cat in this time interval ($t = 0$ to $t = t_0$) is 2 m/s relative to the rod then in the time interval $t = 0$ to $t = t_0$, match the options (Use SI units)

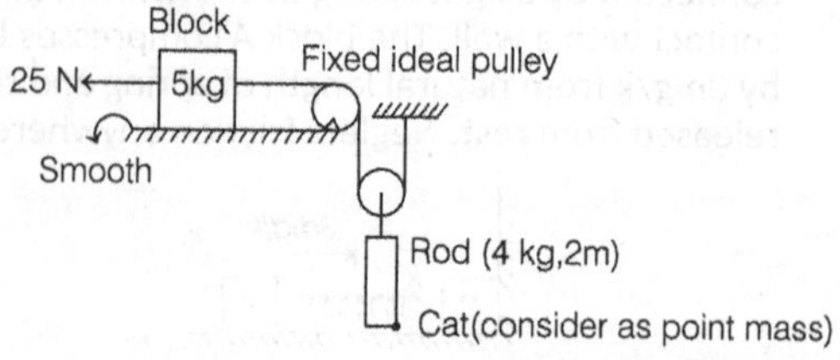

	Column I		Column II
A.	If the angle made by displacement of centre of mass of (block + cat) is ϕ with horizontal, then $\tan\phi$ is	1.	$\frac{2}{25}$
B.	The distance (in m) travelled by the block	2.	$\frac{2}{45}$
C.	Vertical displacement of the system (block + rod + cat) is	3.	$\frac{12}{5}$
D.	Horizontal displacement of the system (block + rod) is	4.	Zero
		5.	$\frac{1}{10}$

6 In the arrangement shown in figure, match the following columns.

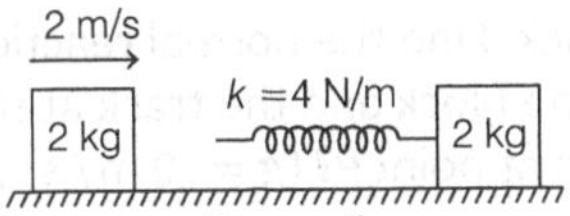

	Column I		Column II
A.	Velocity of centre of mass	1.	2 SI unit
B.	Velocity of combined mass when compression in the spring is maximum	2.	1 SI unit
C.	Maximum compression in the spring	3.	4 SI unit
D.	Maximum potential energy stored in the spring	4.	0.5 SI unit

Numerical Value Questions

1 A sector cut from a uniform disk of radius 12 cm and a uniform rod of the same mass bent into shape of an arc are arranged facing each other as shown in the figure. If centre of mass of the combination is at the origin, what is the radius (in cm) of the arc?

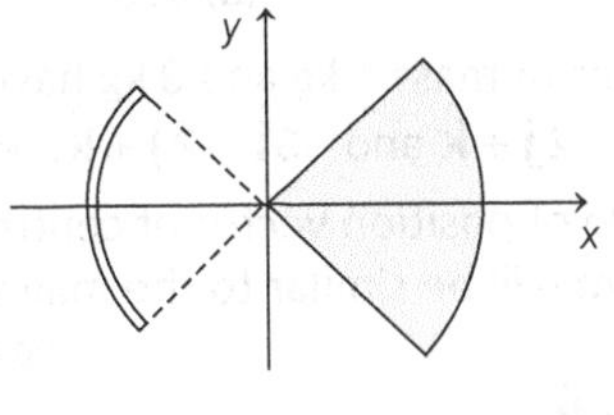

2 The figure shows a square metal plate of side l from which a square plate of side a has been cut as shown in the figure. If the ratio (a/l) so that the centre of mass of the remaining L-shaped plate coincides with the point A is $\frac{\sqrt{x}-y}{z}$, then find value of $x+y+z$.

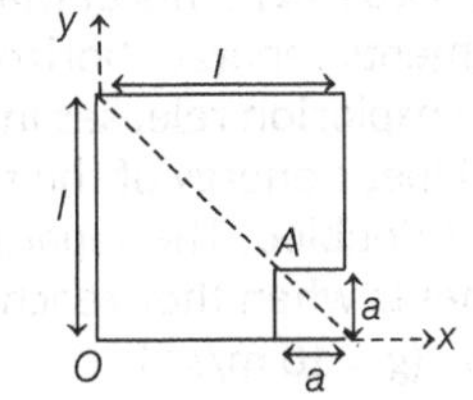

3 In the shown arrangement, all surfaces are smooth and system is released from rest. Mass of block A and B are equal ($m = 1$ kg), mass of block C is $M = 3$ kg. After releasing from rest block B strikes with the surfaces of block C after travelling height $h = 10$ cm. Find the displacement (in cm) of the block C, just before, the block B strikes to block C.

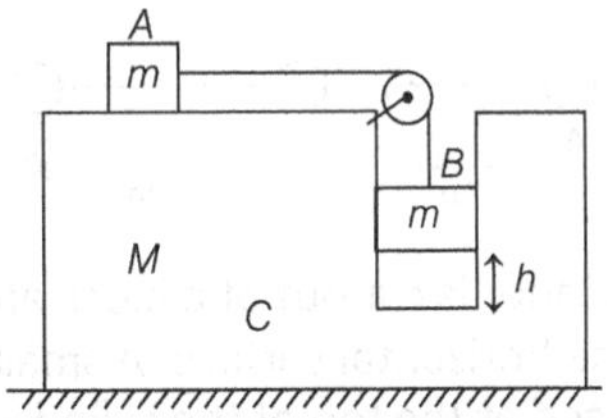

4 In a circus act, a 4 kg dog is trained to jump from B cart to A and then immediately back to the B cart. The carts each have a mass of 20 kg and they are initially at rest. In both cases the dog jumps at 6 m/s relative to the cart. If the cart moves along the same line with negligible friction with the final velocities of v_B and v_A respectively, find the value of $6v_B/5v_A$.

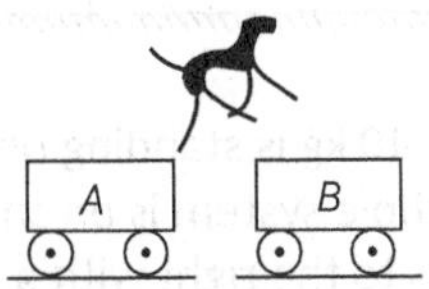

5 Three blocks A, B and C are kept as shown in the figure. The coefficient of the friction between A and B is 0.2, B and C is 0.1, C and ground is 0. The masses of A, B and C are 3 kg, 2 kg and 1 kg, respectively. A is given a horizontal velocity 10 m/s. A, B and C always remain in contact i.e., lies as shown in figure. The total work done by friction will be $-n$ J, then find n.

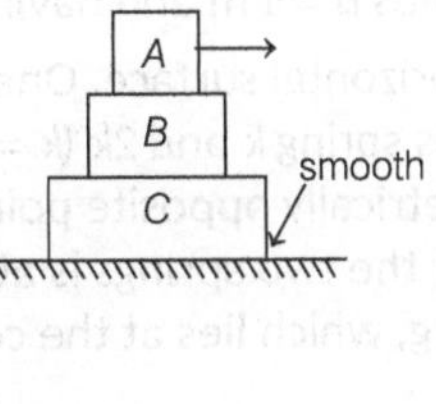

6 An object of mass 5 kg is projected with a velocity of 20 m/s at an angle of 60° to the horizontal. At the highest point of its path the projectile explodes and breaks up into two fragments of masses 1 kg and 4 kg. The fragments separate horizontally after the explosion. The explosion releases internal energy such that the kinetic energy of the system at the highest point is doubled. The separation between the two fragments when they reach the ground is $n\sqrt{3}$ m. Find n. $(g = 10\ m/s^2)$

7 Three identical balls A, B and C each of mass $m = 3$ kg are connected by strings AB and BC shown in the figure. The whole system is placed on a smooth horizontal surface. Now, the ball B is given an initial velocity $v_0 = \sqrt{3}$ m/s, perpendicular to the strings and along the horizontal surface. Find the tension (in N) in the string just before the balls A and C collide.

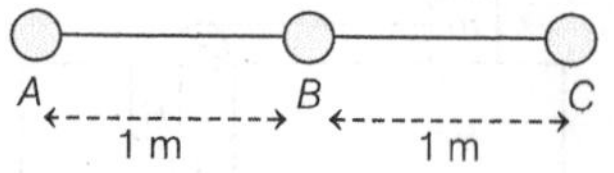

8 A semi-cylinder is cut out of a block and the block is kept on the horizontal surface. A small body of mass m is released at the top of the cylinder shaped hole. (Friction is negligible.) If the block is able to move on the horizontal surface without friction, then the force exerted on the block by the small body at the lowest point is $7mg/2$. Find the ratio of M/m.

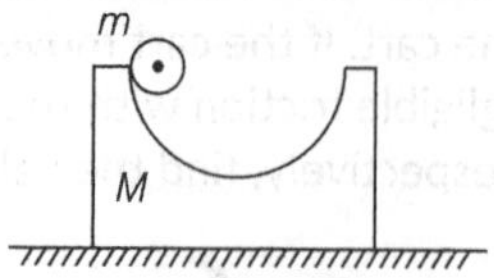

9 A boy of mass 10 kg is standing on a 4 kg block as shown. The whole system is on smooth level ground. The boy jumps to the right with a velocity of 7 m/s relative to the 4 kg block. Find the maximum velocity v of 1 kg block (in m/s) in the subsequent motion.

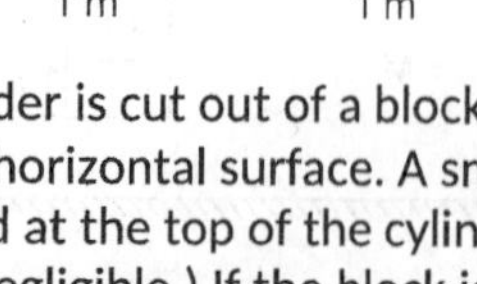

10 A ring of radius $a = 1$ m and having mass 4 kg lies on a smooth horizontal surface. One end of each of the two massless spring k and $2k$ $(k = 240$ N/m) are fixed to the diametrically opposite points of ring and the other end of the two springs is attached to a block of mass $m = 1$ kg, which lies at the centre of the ring and in this position springs are at their natural length. If the block is displaced by a distance $a/2$ along the length of springs such that spring of spring constant k is compressed $a/2$ and is released, then at the instant when each spring achieves its natural length. Find the velocity of the ring (in m/s).

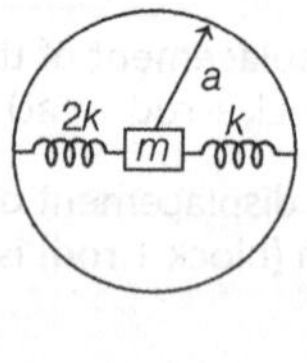

11 All the surfaces shown in the figure are smooth. The block of mass $m = \frac{21}{10}$ kg is projected with a speed $u = \sqrt{3gR}$, where $R = 20$ cm is the radius of the circular track. Find the normal reaction (in N) between the block and the track at the instant when the block is at point P? $(g = 10\ m/s^2)$

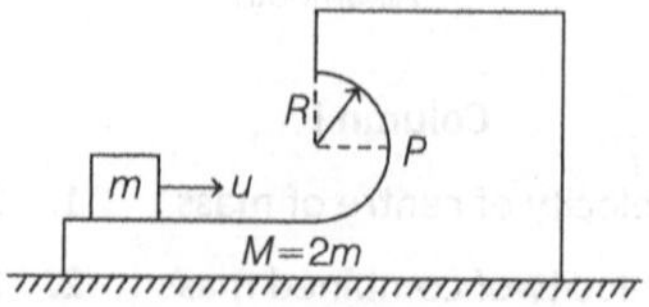

Previous Years Questions

JEE Main

1 A body of mass 1000 kg is moving horizontally with a velocity 6 m/s. If 200 kg extra mass is added, then the final velocity (in m/s) is **[2024, 27 Jan Shift-I]**

(a) 3 (b) 2
(c) 5 (d) 6

2 Two bodies of mass 4 g and 25 g are moving with equal kinetic energies. The ratio of magnitude of their linear momentum is **[2024, 27 Jan Shift-I]**

(a) 4 : 5 (b) 5 : 4
(c) 2 : 5 (d) 3 : 5

3 Two bodies of mass 1 kg and 3 kg have position vectors $\hat{\mathbf{i}} + 2\hat{\mathbf{j}} + \hat{\mathbf{k}}$ and $-3\hat{\mathbf{i}} - 2\hat{\mathbf{j}} + \hat{\mathbf{k}}$, respectively. The magnitude of position vector of centre of mass of this system will be similar to the magnitude of vector **[2022, 29 July Shift-I]**

(a) $\hat{\mathbf{i}} - 2\hat{\mathbf{j}} + \hat{\mathbf{k}}$
(b) $-3\hat{\mathbf{i}} - 2\hat{\mathbf{j}} + \hat{\mathbf{k}}$
(c) $-2\hat{\mathbf{i}} + 2\hat{\mathbf{k}}$
(d) $-2\hat{\mathbf{i}} - \hat{\mathbf{j}} + 2\hat{\mathbf{k}}$

4 The distance of centre of mass from end A of a one dimensional rod AB having mass density $\rho = \rho_0 \left(1 - \frac{x^2}{L^2}\right)$ kg/m and length L (in metre) is $\frac{3L}{\alpha}$ m. The value of α is .... (where, x is the distance from end A). **[2022, 28 July Shift-II]**

5 Three identical spheres each of mass M are placed at the corners of a right angled triangle with mutually perpendicular sides equal to 3 m each. Taking point of intersection of mutually perpendicular sides as origin, the magnitude of position vector of centre of mass of the system will be $\sqrt{x}$ m. The value of x is .... **[2022, 25 July Shift-II]**

6 Two masses A and B, each of mass M are fixed together by a massless spring. A force acts on the mass B as shown in figure. If the mass A starts moving away from mass B with acceleration a, then the acceleration of mass B wil be **[2021, 26 Feb Shift-II]**

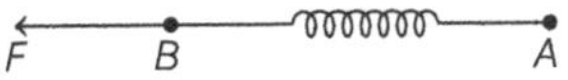

(a) $\frac{Ma - F}{M}$ (b) $\frac{MF}{F + Ma}$

(c) $\frac{F + Ma}{M}$ (d) $\frac{F - Ma}{M}$

7 A circular hole of radius $\left(\frac{a}{2}\right)$ is cut out of a circular disc of radius a as shown in figure. The centroid of the remaining circular portion with respect to point O will be **[2021, 24 Feb Shift-II]**

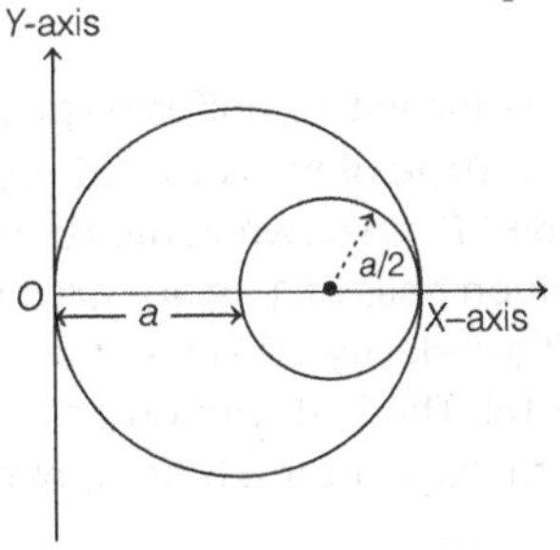

(a) $\frac{1}{6}a$ (b) $\frac{10}{11}a$

(c) $\frac{5}{6}a$ (d) $\frac{2}{3}a$

8 A large block of wood of mass $M = 5.99$ kg is hanging from two long massless cords. A bullet of mass $m = 10$ g is fired into the block and gets embedded in it. The system (block + bullet), then swing upwards, their centre of mass rising a vertical distance $h = 9.8$ cm before the (block + bullet) pendulum comes momentarily to rest at the end of its arc. The speed of the bullet just before collision is (Take $g = 9.8$ ms^{-2}) **[2021, 16 March Shift-II]**

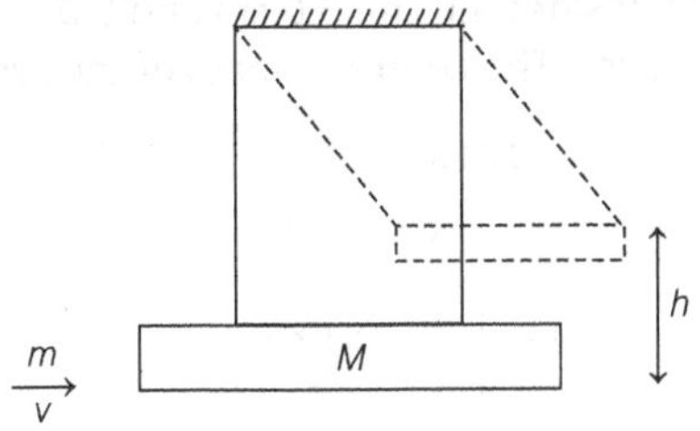

(a) 841.4 m/s (b) 811.4 m/s

(c) 831.4 m/s (d) 821.4 m/s

9 A ball of mass 10 kg moving with a velocity $10\sqrt{3}$ ms^{-1} along X-axis, hits another ball of mass 20 kg, which is at rest. After collision, the first ball comes to rest and the second one disintegrates into two equal pieces. One of the pieces starts moving along Y-axis at a speed of 10 m/s. The second piece starts moving at a speed of 20 m/s at an angle θ (degree) with respect to the X-axis.

The configuration of pieces after collision is shown in the figure. The value of θ to the nearest integer is .... **[2021, 16 March Shift-I]**

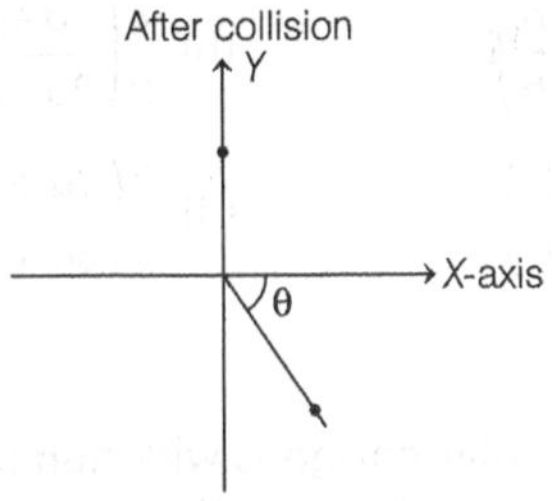

10 A square shaped hole of side $l = \frac{a}{2}$ is curved out at a distance $d = \frac{a}{2}$ from the centre O of a uniform circular disc of radius a. If the distance of the centre of mass of the remaining portion from O is $-a/X$, value of X (to the nearest integer) is .... **[2020, 02 Sep Shift-II]**

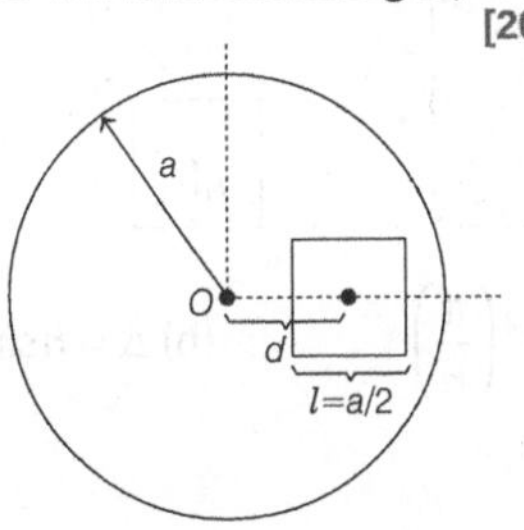

11 The centre of mass of a solid hemisphere of radius 8 cm is x cm from the centre of the flat surface. Then, value of x is .... **[2020, 06 Sep Shift-II]**

12 Three point particles of masses 1.0 kg, 1.5 kg and 2.5 kg are placed at three corners of a right angle triangle of sides 4.0 cm, 3.0 cm and 5.0 cm as shown in the figure. The centre of mass of the system is at a point **[2020, 7 Jan Shift-I]**

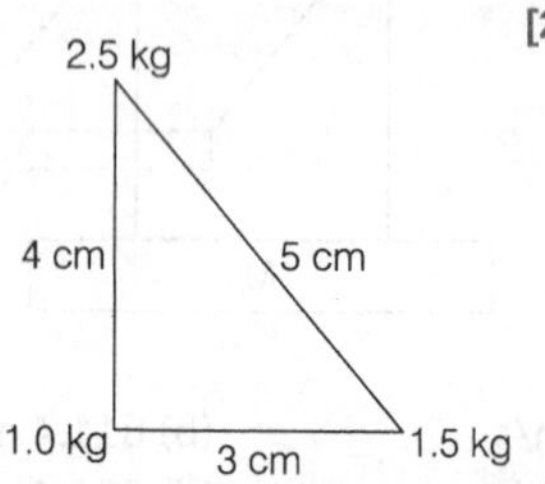

(a) 2.0 cm right and 0.9 cm above 1 kg mass
(b) 0.6 cm right and 2.0 cm above 1 kg mass
(c) 1.5 cm right and 1.2 cm above 1 kg mass
(d) 0.9 cm right and 2.0 cm above 1 kg mass

13 A rod of length L has non-uniform linear mass density given by

$$\rho(x) = a + b\left(\frac{x}{L}\right)^2,$$

where a and b are constants and $0 \le x \le L$. The value of x for the centre of mass of the rod is at **[2020, 9 Jan Shift-II]**

(a) $\frac{3}{4}\left(\frac{2a+b}{3a+b}\right)L$ (b) $\frac{4}{3}\left(\frac{a+b}{2a+3b}\right)L$

(c) $\frac{3}{2}\left(\frac{a+b}{2a+b}\right)L$ (d) $\frac{3}{2}\left(\frac{2a+b}{3a+b}\right)L$

JEE Advanced

1. Consider regular polygons with number of sides $n = 3, 4, 5$ ...... as shown in the figure. The centre of mass of all the polygons is at height h from the ground. They roll on a horizontal surface about the leading vertex without slipping and sliding as depicted. The maximum increase in height of the locus of the centre of mass for each polygon is Δ. Then, Δ depends on n and h as **(2017)**

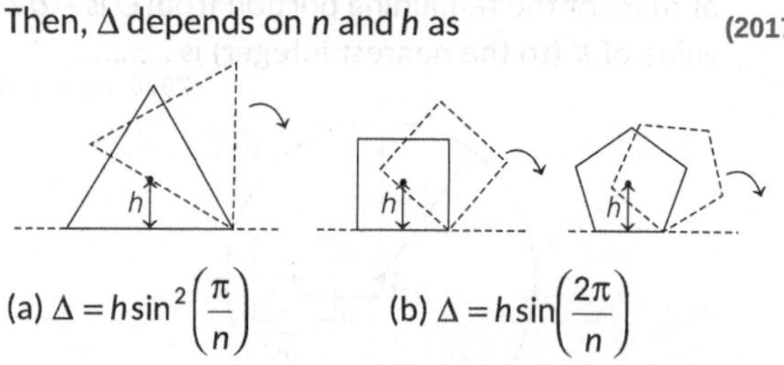

(a) $\Delta = h\sin^2\left(\frac{\pi}{n}\right)$ (b) $\Delta = h\sin\left(\frac{2\pi}{n}\right)$

(c) $\Delta = h\tan^2\left(\frac{\pi}{2n}\right)$ (d) $\Delta = h\left(\frac{1}{\cos\left(\frac{\pi}{n}\right)} - 1\right)$

2. A block of mass M has a circular cut with a frictionless surface as shown. The block rests on the horizontal frictionless surface of a fixed table. Initially the right edge of the block is at $x = 0$, in a coordinate system fixed to the table. A point mass m is released from rest at the topmost point of the path as shown and it slides down. When the mass loses contact with the block, its position is x and the velocity is v. At that instant, which of the following option is/are correct? **(2017)**

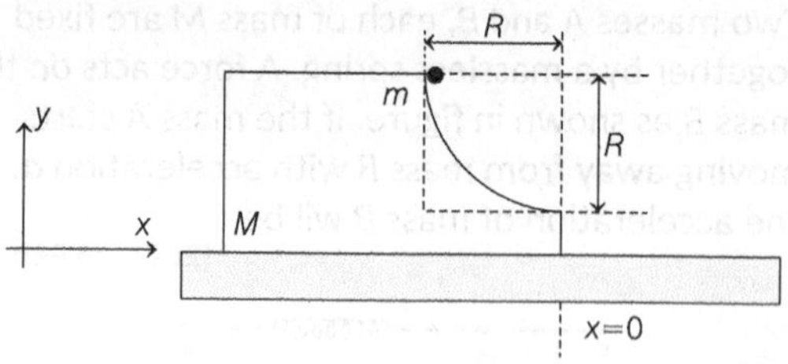

(a) The velocity of the point mass m is $v = \sqrt{\frac{2gR}{1 + \frac{m}{M}}}$

(b) The x component of displacement of the centre of mass of the block M is $-\frac{mR}{M+m}$

(c) The position of the point mass is $x = -\sqrt{2}\frac{mR}{M+m}$

(d) The velocity of the block M is $V = -\frac{m}{M}\sqrt{2gR}$

3. A car P is moving with a uniform speed of $5\sqrt{3}$ m/s towards a carriage of mass 9 kg at rest kept on the rails at a point B as shown in figure. The height AC is 120 m. Cannon balls of 1 kg are fired from the car with an initial velocity 100 m/s at an angle 30° with the horizontal. The first cannon ball hits the stationary carriage after a time t_0 and sticks to it.

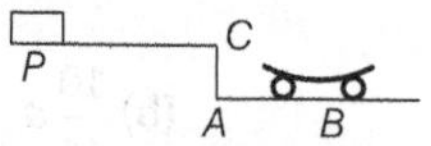

Determine t_0. At t_0, the second cannon ball is fired. Assume that the resistive force between the rails and the carriage is constant and ignore the vertical motion of the carriage throughout.

If the second ball also hits and sticks to the carriage, what will be the horizontal velocity of the carriage just after the second impact? **(2011)**

4. Look at the drawing given in the figure, which has been drawn with ink of uniform line-thickness. The mass of ink used to draw each of the two inner circles, and each of the two line segments is m. The mass of the ink used to draw the outer circle is $6m$. The coordinates of the centres of the different parts are : outer circle (0, 0), left inner circle $(-a, a)$, right inner circle (a, a), vertical line $(0, 0)$ and horizontal line $(0, -a)$. The y - coordinate of the centre of mass of the ink in this drawing is **(2009)**

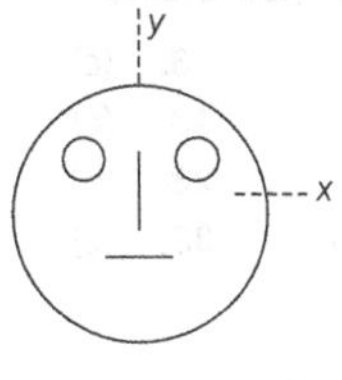

(a) $\frac{a}{10}$ (b) $\frac{a}{8}$ (c) $\frac{a}{12}$ (d) $\frac{a}{3}$

Answer Key

Level 1

1.1 Centre of Mass

1. $\frac{m_2L}{m_1+m_2}$ 2. $\left(\frac{8}{9},\frac{13}{9}\right)$ 3. $\left(\frac{a}{3},\frac{a}{3}\right)$ 4. (3 m, 1 m, 8 m) 5. $\frac{12}{7}$ m
6. (a) $\frac{2R}{\pi}$ (b) $\frac{4R}{3\pi}$ (c) $\frac{3R}{8}$ (d) $\frac{R}{2}$ (e) $\frac{H}{3}$ (f) $\frac{H}{4}$ 7. 22 L/35 8. 4R from O
9. $\left(\frac{49a}{12}, 3a\right)$ 10. $\frac{R}{14}$ 11. $\frac{2r}{3(4-\pi)}$

1.2 Motion of Centre of Mass

1. 2 m/s 2. 0 3. $g/4$ 4. $g/2$ 5. 1670 N 6. 25 cm/s^2 Eastward 7. 15 m

1.3 Displacement of Centre of Mass

1. 1 cm downward 2. 60 m 3. $L/4$ 4. 40/3 cm 5. $\frac{ML}{m+M}$ 6. $h\cot\theta/6$
7. $\frac{m(R-r)}{M+m}$ 8. (a) Straight line, (b) $\frac{x^2}{\left(\frac{L}{2}-r\right)^2}+\frac{y^2}{r^2}=1$, ellipse

1.4 Conservation of Linear Momentum

1. (a) 288 J (b) 384 J 2. (a) $v/\sqrt{2}$ (b) $(3/2)\,mv^2$ 3. 125 m/s
4. $3\sqrt{gl}$ 5. 220 m/s 6. 0.16 7. $v_1 = 4.5$ m/s, $v_2 = 3$ m/s
8. $\frac{\sqrt{3gh}}{2}$ 9. 10 m/s 10. $100\left(\frac{1}{49}+\frac{1}{50}\right)$ m/s 11. $\frac{m^2u}{(M+2m)(M+m)}$
12. $v_{rear} = v_0 - \frac{m}{M+m}u,\ v_{front} = v_0 + \frac{mMu}{(M+m)^2}$ 13. $v = \sqrt{\frac{2gR}{1+\frac{m}{M}}}$ 14. (a) $\sqrt{\frac{2gh}{9}}$ (b) $2h/3$

1.5 Centre of Mass Reference Frame

1. $P_{system,\,CM} = 0,\ K_{system,\,CM} = \frac{1}{2}\frac{m_1m_2}{m_1+m_2}|v_1 - v_2|^2 = \frac{1}{2}\mu v_{rel}^2$ 2. $\sqrt{\frac{7}{3}g\ell}$ 3. $\sqrt{3gh}$ 4. 20 cm 5. $x = \frac{2FM}{k(M+m)}$

Level 2

Single Choice Correct Questions

1. (a)	2. (b)	3. (c)	4. (a)	5. (b)	6. (c)	7. (b)	8. (b)	9. (d)	10. (a)
11. (d)	12. (b)	13. (c)	14. (b)	15. (b)	16. (c)	17. (d)	18. (b)	19. (c)	20. (c)
21. (b)	22. (d)	23. (b)	24. (c)	25. (a)	26. (b)	27. (a)	28. (c)	29. (a)	30. (d)
31. (b)	32. (c)	33. (c)	34. (a)	35. (b)	36. (a)	37. (a)	38. (d)	39. (b)	40. (a)
41. (c)	42. (a)								

Numerical Value Questions

1. 9	2. 4	3. 4	4. 3	5. 10	6. 3	7. 8
8. 871.5	9. 32	10. 22				

Level 3

Single Choice Correct Questions

1. (b)	2. (a)	3. (c)	4. (c)	5. (a)	6. (d)	7. (c)	8. (b)	9. (b)	10. (b)
11. (d)	12. (b)	13. (a)	14. (b)	15. (b)	16. (c)	17. (b)	18. (b)	19. (c)	20. (c)
21. (d)	22. (c)	23. (c)	24. (d)	25. (a)	26. (d)	27. (c)	28. (a)	29. (a)	30. (a)
31. (c)	32. (c)	33. (a)	34. (a)	35. (c)	36. (d)				

Multiple Choice(s) Correct Questions

1. (b, d)	2. (a, c, d)	3. (b, c)	4. (b, d)	5. (b, d)	6. (b, d)	7. (a, b, c, d)
8. (a, c, d)	9. (b, d)	10. (b, c, d)	11. (c, d)	12. (a, b, c, d)	13. (a, d)	14. (a, b, c)
15. (a, b, c)						

Comprehension Based Questions

1. (d)	2. (c)	3. (a)	4. (c)	5. (c)	6. (a)	7. (b)	8. (d)	9. (c)	10. (b)
11. (a)	12. (c)	13. (a)	14. (a)	15. (c)	16. (b)	17. (d)	18. (b)	19. (a)	20. (c)
21. (d)	22. (c)	23. (a)	24. (d)	25. (b)	26. (b)	27. (a)			

Match the Columns Questions

1. A→ 3; B→ 1; C→ 4; D→ 2
2. A→ 3; B→ 2; C→ 4; D→ 1
3. A→ 4; B→ 4; C→ 1; D→ 1,2,3
4. A→ 3; B→ 1,3; C→ 4; D→ 5
5. A→ 3; B→ 1; C→ 1; D→ 2
6. A→ 2; B→ 2; C→ 2; D→ 1

Numerical Value Questions

1. 8	2. 8	3. 2	4. 1	5. 75	6. 25	7. 1
8. 4	9. 8	10. 3	11. 0			

Previous Years Questions

JEE Main

1. (c)	2. (c)	3. (a)	4. (8)	5. (2)	6. (d)	7. (c)	8. (c)	9. (30)	10. (23)
11. (3)	12. (d)	13. (a)							

JEE Advanced

1. (d) 2. (a,b) 3. (12s, 15.75 m/s) 4. (a)

SOLUTIONS

Level 1

1.1 Centre of Mass

1. $x_{CM} = \dfrac{m_1x_1 + m_2x_2}{m_1 + m_2} = \dfrac{m_1(0) + m_2(L)}{m_1 + m_2} = \dfrac{m_2L}{m_1 + m_2}$

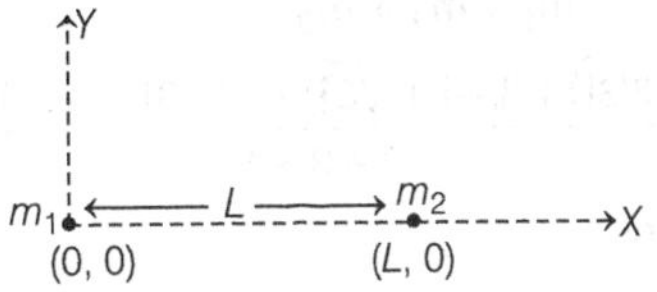

$y_{CM} = \dfrac{m_1y_1 + m_2y_2}{m_1 + m_2} = 0$

2. $x_{CM} = \dfrac{\Sigma m_ix_i}{\Sigma m_i} = \dfrac{2(0) + 3(2) + 5(2) + 8(0)}{2 + 3 + 5 + 8} = \dfrac{8}{9}$

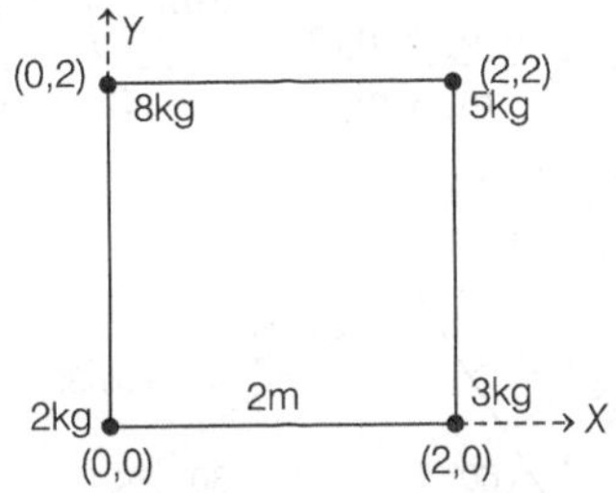

$y_{CM} = \dfrac{\Sigma m_iy_i}{\Sigma m_i} = \dfrac{2(0) + 3(0) + 5(2) + 8(2)}{2 + 3 + 5 + 8} = \dfrac{13}{9}$

3. Centre of mass of a uniform rod at its geometrical centre.

Coordinates of CM of rod $OA = \left(\dfrac{a}{2}, 0\right)$

rod $OB = \left(0, \dfrac{a}{2}\right)$, rod $AB = \left(\dfrac{a}{2}, \dfrac{a}{2}\right)$

$$x_{CM} = \frac{\Sigma m_ix_i}{\Sigma m_i} = \frac{m\left(\frac{a}{2}\right) + m(0) + m\left(\frac{a}{2}\right)}{m + m + m} = \frac{a}{3}$$

$$y_{CM} = \frac{\Sigma m_iy_i}{\Sigma m_i} = \frac{m(0) + m\left(\frac{a}{2}\right) + m\left(\frac{a}{2}\right)}{m + m + m} = \frac{a}{3}$$

4. According to the definition of centre of mass we can imagine one particle of mass $(1 + 2 + 3)$ kg at $(1, 2, 3)$, another particle of $(2 + 3)$ kg at $(-1, 3, -2)$.

Let the third particle of mass 5 kg put at (x, y, z).

$$x_{CM} = \frac{m_1x_1 + m_2x_2 + m_3x_3}{m_1 + m_2 + m_3}$$

$$\Rightarrow \quad 1 = \frac{6(1) + 5(-1) + 5x}{6 + 5 + 5} \Rightarrow x = 3$$

Similarly, $y = 1$ and $z = 8$

5. $x_{CM} = \dfrac{\int x dm}{\int dm} = \dfrac{\int_0^3 x(2 + x)\, dx}{\int_0^3 (2 + x)\, dx} = \dfrac{12}{7}$ m

6. (a) $\dfrac{2R}{\pi}$ above centre (b) $\dfrac{4R}{3\pi}$ above centre

(c) $\dfrac{3R}{8}$ above centre (d) $\dfrac{R}{2}$ above centre

(e) $\dfrac{H}{3}$ above base (f) $\dfrac{H}{4}$ above base

7. $x_{CM} = \dfrac{\Sigma m_ix_i}{\Sigma m_i}$

$$= \frac{m\left(\frac{L}{2}\right) + m\left(\frac{L}{2} + \frac{L}{10}\right) + m\left[\frac{L}{2} + 2\left(\frac{L}{10}\right)\right] + m\left[\frac{L}{2} + 3\left(\frac{L}{10}\right)\right] + m\left[\frac{L}{2} + 2\left(\frac{L}{10}\right)\right] + m\left(\frac{L}{2} + \frac{L}{10}\right) + m\left(\frac{L}{2}\right)}{7m}$$

$$= \frac{22L}{35}$$

8. Mass of cone $= \rho\left[\dfrac{1}{3}\pi(2R)^2(4R)\right] = \dfrac{16}{3}\rho\pi R^3$

Mass of sphere $= 12\rho\left(\dfrac{4}{3}\pi R^3\right) = 16\rho\pi R^3$

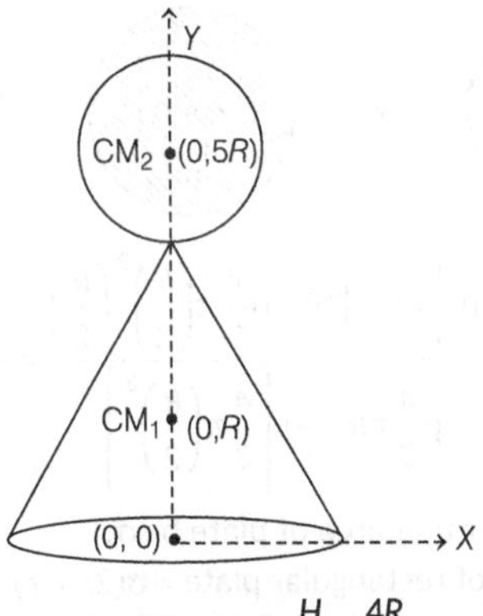

Centre of mass of solid cone is $\dfrac{H}{4} = \dfrac{4R}{4} = R$ above base.

$$y_{CM} = \frac{m_1y_1 + m_2y_2}{m_1 + m_2}$$

$$= \frac{\frac{16}{3}\rho\pi R^3(R) + 16\rho\pi R^3(5R)}{\frac{16}{3}\rho\pi R^3 + 16\rho\pi R^3} = 4R$$

9. Let mass per unit area of lamina $= \sigma$

For square lamina $ABDE$,

Mass $= \sigma(6a)^2 = 36\sigma a^2$

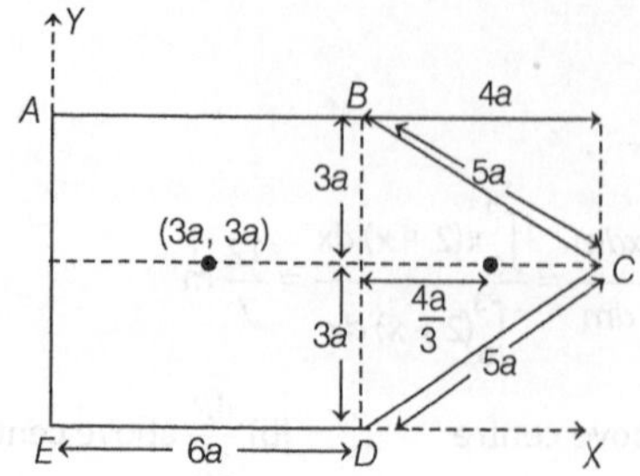

Coordinates of centre of mass = $(3a, 3a)$

For triangular lamina BCD,

$$\text{Mass} = \sigma \frac{1}{2}(6a)(4a) = 12\sigma a^2$$

Coordinates of centre of mass

$$= \left[\left(6a + \frac{4a}{3}\right), 3a\right] = \left(\frac{22a}{3}, 3a\right)$$

$$x_{CM} = \frac{m_1 x_1 + m_2 x_2}{m_1 + m_2}$$

$$= \frac{(36\sigma a^2)(3a) + (12\sigma a^2)\left(\frac{22a}{3}\right)}{36\sigma a^2 + 12\sigma a^2} = \frac{49a}{12}$$

$$y_{CM} = 3a$$

10. $x_{CM} = \dfrac{m_1 x_1 - m_2 x_2}{m_1 - m_2}$

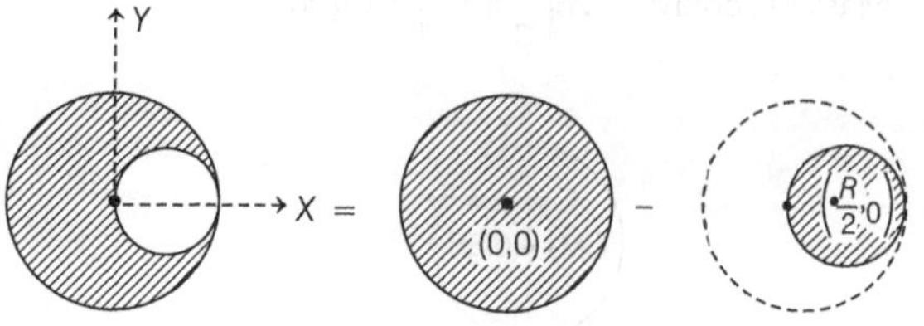

$$= \frac{\left(\rho \frac{4}{3}\pi R^3\right)(0) - \rho \frac{4}{3}\pi\left(\frac{R}{2}\right)^3\left(\frac{R}{2}\right)}{\rho \frac{4}{3}\pi R^3 - \rho\left[\frac{4}{3}\pi\left(\frac{R}{2}\right)^3\right]} = -\frac{R}{14}$$

11. Let mass per unit area of plate be σ.

m_1 = mass of rectangular plate $= \sigma(2r \times r) = 2\sigma r^2$,

m_2 = mass of semi-circular plate $= \sigma\left(\dfrac{\pi r^2}{2}\right)$

$$x_{CM} = \frac{m_1 x_1 - m_2 x_2}{m_1 - m_2}$$

$$= \frac{(2\sigma r^2)\left(\frac{r}{2}\right) - \sigma\left(\frac{\pi r^2}{2}\right)\left(\frac{4r}{3\pi}\right)}{2\sigma r^2 - \sigma\left(\frac{\pi r^2}{2}\right)}$$

$$= \frac{2r}{3(4 - \pi)}$$

1.2 Motion of Centre of Mass

1. $V_{CM} = \dfrac{m_1 v_1 + m_2 v_2}{m_1 + m_2} = \dfrac{1(8) + 2(-1)}{1 + 2} = 2 \text{ m/s}$

2. $\mathbf{v}_1 = 2\hat{\mathbf{i}}$

$$\mathbf{v}_2 = -2\cos 60° \hat{\mathbf{i}} + 2\sin 60° \hat{\mathbf{j}} = -\hat{\mathbf{i}} + \sqrt{3}\hat{\mathbf{j}}$$

$$\mathbf{v}_3 = -6\cos 60° \hat{\mathbf{i}} - 6\sin 60° \hat{\mathbf{j}} = -3\hat{\mathbf{i}} - 3\sqrt{3}\hat{\mathbf{j}}$$

$$\mathbf{v}_{CM} = \frac{m_1 \mathbf{v}_1 + m_2 \mathbf{v}_2 + m_3 \mathbf{v}_3}{m_1 + m_2 + m_3}$$

$$= \frac{2(3\hat{\mathbf{i}}) + 3(-\hat{\mathbf{i}} + \sqrt{3}\hat{\mathbf{j}}) + 1(-3\hat{\mathbf{i}} - 3\sqrt{3}\hat{\mathbf{j}})}{2 + 3 + 1}$$

$$= 0$$

3. $3mg - T = 3ma$ ... (i)

$T - mg = ma$ ... (ii)

Solving Eqs. (i) and (ii), we get $a = \dfrac{g}{2}$

$$a_{CM} = \frac{m_1 a_1 + m_2 a_2}{m_1 + m_2} = \frac{3m\left(\frac{g}{2}\right) + m\left(-\frac{g}{2}\right)}{3m + m} = \frac{g}{4}$$

4. $\mathbf{a}_{CM} = \dfrac{m_1 \mathbf{a}_1 + m_2 \mathbf{a}_2}{m_1 + m_2}$

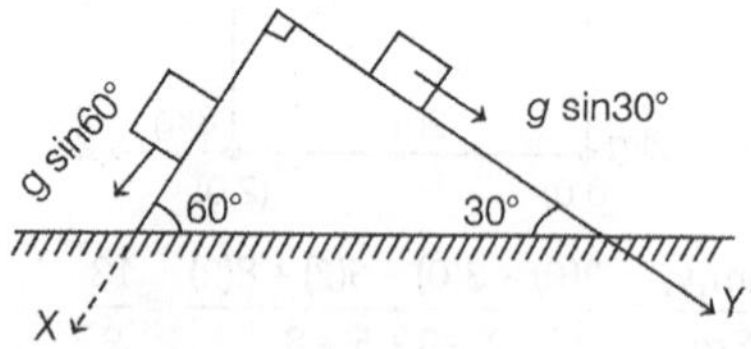

$$= \frac{m(g\sin 60°)\hat{\mathbf{i}} + m(g\sin 30°)\hat{\mathbf{j}}}{2m}$$

$$= \frac{\sqrt{3}g}{4}\hat{\mathbf{i}} + \frac{g}{4}\hat{\mathbf{j}}$$

$$a_{CM} = \sqrt{\left(\frac{\sqrt{3}g}{4}\right)^2 + \left(\frac{g}{4}\right)^2} = \frac{g}{2}$$

5. $\Sigma F_{ext} = Ma_{CM} = m_1 a_1 + m_2 a_2 + m_3 a_3 + m_4 a_4$

$\Rightarrow$ $T - 40g - 60g - 50g - 20g$

$= 40(-2) + 60(0) + 50(1) + 20(0)$

$\Rightarrow$ $T = 1670 \text{ N}$

6. $\Sigma F_{ext} = M\mathbf{a}_{CM} = m_1 \mathbf{a}_1 + m_2 \mathbf{a}_2$

$\Rightarrow$ $0 = 0.1\mathbf{a}_1 + (0.25)(-10 \text{ cm/s}^2 \hat{\mathbf{i}})$

$\Rightarrow$ $\mathbf{a}_1 = (25 \text{ cm/s}^2)\hat{\mathbf{i}} = 25 \text{ cm/s}^2$ eastward

7. $u_{CM} = \dfrac{m_1 u_1 + m_2 u_2}{m_1 + m_2} = \dfrac{2(0) + 4(15)}{2 + 4} = 10 \text{ m/s} \uparrow$

$$a_{CM} = \frac{m_1 a_1 + m_2 a_2}{m_1 + m_2} = \frac{2g + 4g}{2 + 4} = g \downarrow$$

$$H_{max} = \frac{u_{CM}^2}{2a_{CM}} = \frac{(10)^2}{2(10)} = 5 \text{ m}$$

Initial height of CM from ground

$$= \frac{m_1y_1 + m_2y_2}{m_1 + m_2} = \frac{2(30) + 4(0)}{2+4} = 10 \text{ m}$$

Maximum height attained by CM from the ground $= 10 + 5 = 15$ m

1.3 Displacement of Centre of Mass

1. $\Delta y_{CM} = \dfrac{m_1 \Delta y_1 + m_2 \Delta y_2}{m_1 + m_2}$

$\Rightarrow \quad 1 = \dfrac{10(7) + 30(\Delta y_2)}{10 + 30}$

$\Rightarrow \quad \Delta y_2 = -1$ cm $= 1$ cm, down

2. Explosion is due to internal forces. Since external forces are unchanged, centre of mass of the two fragments will continue to follow the original parabolic trajectory of the projectile.

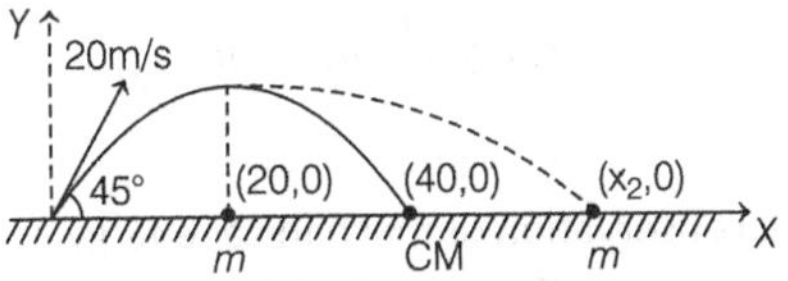

$$R = \frac{u^2 \sin 2\theta}{g} = \frac{(20)^2 \sin 90°}{10} = 40 \text{ m}$$

$$x_{CM} = \frac{m_1x_1 + m_2x_2}{m_1 + m_2}$$

$\Rightarrow \quad 40 = \dfrac{m(20) + m(x_2)}{2m}$

$\Rightarrow \quad x_2 = 60$ m

3. Let displacement of plank $= s_p$

Displacement of man w.r.t. plank $= s_{mp} = L$

$\Rightarrow \quad s_m - s_p = L \Rightarrow s_m = L + s_p$

Since, external forces on (man + plank) system are zero in horizontal direction and initial velocity of CM of (man + plank) system is zero,

$\Rightarrow \quad (s_{CM})_x = 0 \Rightarrow \dfrac{m_1s_p + m_2s_m}{m_1 + m_2} = 0$

$\Rightarrow \quad \dfrac{3Ms_p + M(L + s_p)}{4M} = 0$

$\Rightarrow \quad s_p = -\dfrac{L}{4} = \dfrac{L}{4}$, left

4. Let displacement of boat $= s_b$

Displacement of Ram w.r.t. boat $= s_{Ab} = +2$

$\Rightarrow \quad s_A = 2 + s_b$

Displacement of Shyam w.r.t. boat $= s_{Bb} = -2$

$\Rightarrow \quad s_B = -2 + s_b$

$(s_{CM})_x = 0$

$\Rightarrow \quad \dfrac{40s_b + 50(2 + s_b) + 60(-2 + s_b)}{40 + 50 + 60} = 0$

$\Rightarrow \quad s_b = \dfrac{2}{15} \text{ m} = \dfrac{40}{3} \text{ cm}$

5. Let displacmenet of balloon $= S_b$

Displacement of man w.r.t. balloon $= s_{mb} = L$

$\Rightarrow \quad s_m = L + s_b$

$(s_{CM})_x = 0 \Rightarrow \dfrac{Ms_b + m(L + s_b)}{M + m} = 0$

$\Rightarrow \quad s_b = -\dfrac{mL}{M + m}$

$s_m = L + s_b = L + \left(\dfrac{-mL}{M + m}\right) = \dfrac{ML}{M + m}$

6. Let displacement of wedge $= s_w$

Displacement of block w.r.t. wedge in horizontal

$= s_{bw} = -h\cot\theta$

$\Rightarrow \quad s_b = -h\cot\theta + s_w$

$(s_{CM})_x = 0 \Rightarrow \dfrac{m(-h\cot\theta + s_w) + 5ms_w}{m + 5m} = 0$

$\Rightarrow \quad s_w = \dfrac{h\cot\theta}{6}$

7. Let displacement of block $= s_b$

Displacement of cylinder w.r.t. block in horizontal

$= s_{cb} = R - r$

$\Rightarrow \quad s_c = (R - r) + s_b$

$(s_{CM})_x = 0$

$\Rightarrow \quad \dfrac{Ms_b + m[(R - r) + s_b]}{M + m} = 0$

$\Rightarrow \quad s_b = -\dfrac{m(R - r)}{M + m}$

8. (a) There is no force on the rod in horizontal. So acceleration of centre of mass in horizontal direction will be zero. Centre of mass will go vertically down along a straight line.

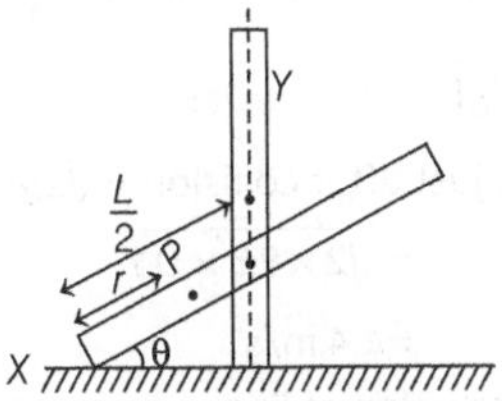

(b) Let coordinates of point P be (x, y).

$$x = \left(\frac{L}{2} - r\right)\cos\theta \text{ and } y = r\sin\theta$$

$$\sin^2\theta + \cos^2\theta = 1$$

$$\Rightarrow \quad \frac{x^2}{\left(\frac{L}{2} - r\right)^2} + \frac{y^2}{r^2} = 1$$

which is an equation of ellipse.

1.4 Conservation of Linear Momentum

1. (a) Applying conservation of linear momentum,

$$16(0) = 4v_1 + 12(4)$$

$$\Rightarrow \quad v_1 = -12 \text{ m/s}$$

Kinetic energy of 4 kg mass $= \frac{1}{2}(4)(12)^2 = 288$ J

(b) Energy released $= K_1 + K_2 = \frac{1}{2}(4)(12)^2 + \frac{1}{2}(12)(4)^2$

$$= 384 \text{ J}$$

2. (a) Applying conservation of linear momentum,

$$4m(0) = m(v\hat{\mathbf{i}}) + m(v\hat{\mathbf{j}}) + 2m\mathbf{v}$$

$$\Rightarrow \quad \mathbf{v} = -\frac{v}{2}\hat{\mathbf{i}} - \frac{v}{2}\hat{\mathbf{j}}$$

Speed of third fragment $= \sqrt{\left(\frac{v}{2}\right)^2 + \left(\frac{v}{2}\right)^2} = \frac{v}{\sqrt{2}}$

(b) Energy released

$$= \frac{1}{2}mv^2 + \frac{1}{2}mv^2 + \frac{1}{2}(2m)\left(\frac{v}{\sqrt{2}}\right)^2 = \frac{3}{2}mv^2$$

3. Applying conservation of linear momentum at the highest point,

$$m(100\cos 60\hat{\mathbf{i}}) = \frac{m}{3}(200\hat{\mathbf{j}}) + \left(\frac{2m}{3}\right)\mathbf{v}$$

$$\mathbf{v} = 75\hat{\mathbf{i}} - 100\hat{\mathbf{j}}$$

Speed of heavier fragment $= \sqrt{(75)^2 + (100)^2} = 125$ m/s

4. Applying conservation of linear momentum

$$mv + 2m(0) = 3mv'$$

$$\Rightarrow \quad v' = \frac{v}{3}$$

Applying work-energy theorem after collision,

$$W_{mg} + W_T = \Delta K$$

$$\Rightarrow \quad -3mgl(1 - \cos 60°) + 0 = 0 - \frac{1}{2}(3m)\left(\frac{v}{3}\right)^2$$

$$\Rightarrow \quad v = 3\sqrt{gl}$$

5. Speed of block just after collision $= \sqrt{2gh}$

$$= \sqrt{2 \times 9.8 \times 0.1}$$

$$= 1.4 \text{ m/s}$$

Applying conservation of linear momentum,

$$\left(\frac{10}{1000}\right)(500) + 2 \times 0 = \left(\frac{10}{1000}\right)v + 2 \times 1.4$$

$$\Rightarrow \quad v = 220 \text{ m/s}$$

6. Using conservation of linear momentum,

$$\left(\frac{20}{1000}\right)(500) + 10(0) = \left(\frac{20}{1000}\right)(100) + 10v$$

$$\Rightarrow \quad v = 0.8 \text{ m/s}$$

For block, $v^2 = u^2 + 2as$

$$\Rightarrow \quad 0^2 = (0.8)^2 + 2[-\mu(10)](0.2)$$

$$\Rightarrow \quad \mu = 0.16$$

7. Let their velocities be v_1 and v_2 when spring becomes unstrectched.

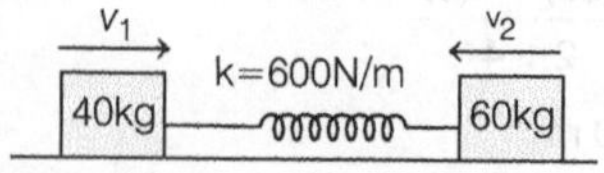

Applying conservation of linear momentum,

$$40(0) + 60(0) = 40v_1 + 60(-v_2)$$

$$\Rightarrow \quad v_1 = \frac{3v_2}{2} \quad \text{... (i)}$$

Applying conservation of mechanical energy,

$$K_1 + U_1 = K_2 + U_2$$

$$\Rightarrow (0+0) + \frac{1}{2} \times 600 \times (1.5)^2 = \left(\frac{1}{2} \times 40v_1^2 + \frac{1}{2} \times 60v_2^2\right) + 0$$

$$\Rightarrow \quad 2v_1^2 + 3v_2^2 = 67.5 \quad \text{... (ii)}$$

Solving Eqs. (i) and (ii), we get

$$v_1 = 4.5 \text{ m/s and } v_2 = 3 \text{ m/s}$$

8. Let velocities of block and earth be v_1 and v_2 respectively.

Applying conservation of linear momentum,

$$0 + 0 = \frac{M}{3}v_1 + M(-v_2)$$

$$\Rightarrow \quad v_1 = 3v_2 \quad \text{... (i)}$$

Applying conservation of mechanical energy,

$$K_1 + U_1 = K_2 + U_2$$

$$\Rightarrow \quad (0+0) + \frac{M}{3}gh = \left[\frac{1}{2}\left(\frac{M}{3}\right)v_1^2 + \frac{1}{2}Mv_2^2\right] + \frac{M}{3}g\left(\frac{h}{2}\right)$$

$$\Rightarrow \quad v_1^2 + 3v_2^2 = gh \quad \text{... (ii)}$$

Solving Eqs. (i) and (ii), we get

$$v_1 = \sqrt{\frac{3gh}{4}}$$

9. Let velocity of platform $= v_p$

Velocity of man w.r.t. platform $= v_{mp} = 30$

$$\Rightarrow \quad v_m - v_p = 30$$

$$\Rightarrow \quad v_m = (30 + v_p)$$

Applying linear momentum conservation for (man + platform) system in horizontal,

$$0 + 0 = 100(30 + v_p) + 200v_p$$

$$\Rightarrow \quad v_p = -10 \text{ m/s}$$

10. Let velocity of car after the first shot $= v_c$

Applying conservation of linear momentum for the first shot,

$$0 + 0 = 49v_c + 1(100 + v_c)$$

$$\Rightarrow \quad v_c = -\frac{100}{50} \text{ m/s}$$

Let velocity of car after the second shot $= v_c'$

Applying conservation of linear momentum for the second shot,

$$49\left(\frac{-100}{50}\right) = 48v_c' + 1(100 + v_c')$$

$$\Rightarrow \quad v_c' = -100\left(\frac{1}{50} + \frac{1}{49}\right) \text{ m/s}$$

11. Applying conservation of linear momentum when *A* jumps

$$0 + 0 = (M + m)v_c + m(-u + v_c)$$

$$\Rightarrow \quad v_c = \frac{mu}{M + 2m}$$

Applying conservation of linear momentum when *B* jumps

$$(M + m)\left(\frac{mu}{M + 2m}\right) = Mv_c' + m(u + v_c')$$

$$\Rightarrow \quad v_c' = -\frac{m^2u}{(M + 2m)(M + m)}$$

12. Applying conservation of linear momentum when man leaves the rear buggy,

$$(M + m)v_0 = Mv_{rear} + m(u + v_{rear})$$

$$\Rightarrow \quad v_{rear} = v_0 - \frac{mu}{M + m}$$

Applying conservation of linear momentum when man jumps into the front buggy

$$m\left[u + \left(v_0 - \frac{mu}{M + m}\right)\right] + Mv_0 = (M + m)v_{front}$$

$$\Rightarrow \quad v_{front} = v_0 + \frac{mMu}{(M + m)^2}$$

13. Applying conservation of linear momentum in horizontal,

$$0 + 0 = mv_1 + m(-v_2)$$

$$\Rightarrow \quad v_2 = \frac{mv_1}{M}$$

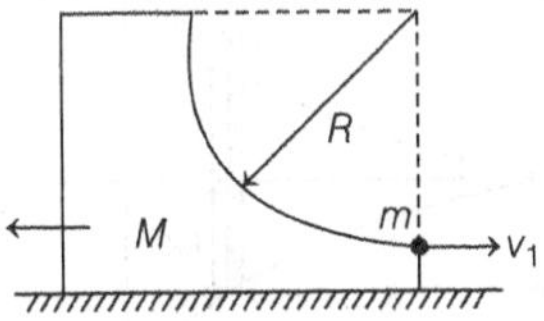

Applying work-energy theorem,

$$W_{gravity} + W_{internal\ normal} + W_{normal\ from\ ground} = \Delta K$$

$$\Rightarrow \quad mgR + 0 + 0 = \left(\frac{1}{2}Mv_1^2 + \frac{1}{2}Mv_2^2\right) - (0 + 0)$$

$$\Rightarrow \quad 2mgR = mv_1^2 + M\left(\frac{mv_1}{M}\right)^2 \Rightarrow v_1 = \sqrt{\frac{2gR}{1 + \frac{m}{M}}}$$

14. (a)

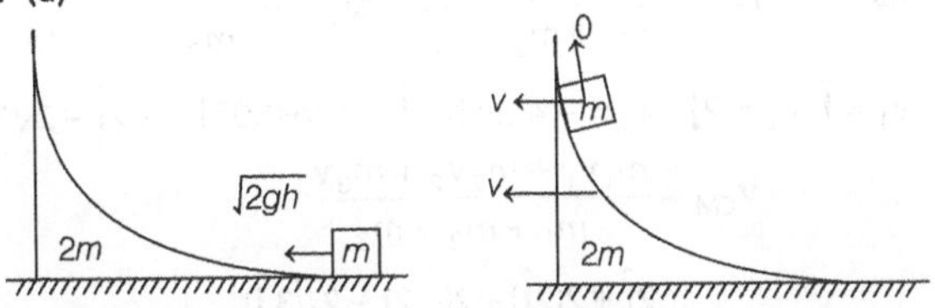

When the smaller block reaches maximum height from ground, its velocity w.r.t. the larger block is zero.

Using conservation of linear momentum,

$$2m(0) + m(\sqrt{2gh}) = 2mv + mv$$

$$\Rightarrow \quad v = \frac{\sqrt{2gh}}{3}$$

(b) Using energy conservation,

$$K_1 + U_1 = K_2 + U_2$$

$$\Rightarrow \left[\frac{1}{2}m(\sqrt{2gh})^2 + 0\right] + 0 = \frac{1}{2}(3m)\left(\frac{\sqrt{2gh}}{3}\right)^2 + mgh_{max}$$

$$\Rightarrow \quad h_{max} = \frac{2h}{3}$$

1.5 Centre of Mass Reference Frame

1. $\mathbf{v}_{CM} = \dfrac{m_1\mathbf{v}_1 + m_2\mathbf{v}_2}{m_1 + m_2}$

$$\mathbf{v}_{1,\,CM} = \mathbf{v}_1 - \mathbf{v}_{CM} = \frac{m_2(\mathbf{v}_1 - \mathbf{v}_2)}{m_1 + m_2}$$

$$\mathbf{v}_{2,\,CM} = \mathbf{v}_2 - \mathbf{v}_{CM} = \frac{m_1(\mathbf{v}_2 - \mathbf{v}_1)}{m_1 + m_2}$$

$$\mathbf{P}_{system,\,CM} = m_1\mathbf{v}_{1,\,CM} + m_2\mathbf{v}_{2,\,CM} = 0$$

$$\mathbf{K}_{system,\,CM} = \frac{1}{2}m_1\left(\frac{m_2|\mathbf{v}_1 - \mathbf{v}_2|}{m_1 + m_2}\right)^2 + \frac{1}{2}m_2\left(\frac{m_1|\mathbf{v}_2 - \mathbf{v}_1|}{m_1 + m_2}\right)^2$$

$$= \frac{1}{2}\left(\frac{m_1m_2}{m_1 + m_2}\right)|\mathbf{v}_1 - \mathbf{v}_2|^2 = \frac{1}{2}\mu v_{rel}^2$$

2. In CM reference frame, using work-energy theorem,

$$W_{gravity} + W_T = \Delta K$$

$$\Rightarrow \quad mgl + 0 = \frac{1}{2}\cdot\frac{(6m)(m)}{6m + m}v_{rel}^2 - 0$$

$$\Rightarrow \quad v_{rel} = \sqrt{\frac{7gl}{3}}$$

3. Using energy conservation in CM reference frame,

$$K_1 + U_1 = K_2 + U_2$$

$$\Rightarrow \frac{1}{2}\left[\frac{(2m)(m)}{2m + m}\right](u - 0)^2 + 0 = 0 + mgh$$

$$\Rightarrow \quad u = \sqrt{3gh}$$

4. In CM reference frame,

$$\frac{1}{2}\mu v_{rel}^2 = \frac{1}{2}kx^2$$

$$\Rightarrow \quad \frac{1}{2}\left[\frac{1(1)}{1 + 1}\right](2 - 0)^2 = \frac{1}{2} \times 50x^2$$

$$\Rightarrow \quad x = 20 \text{ cm}$$

5. $F_{ext} = Ma_{CM} \Rightarrow F = (M + m)a_{CM}$

$$\Rightarrow \quad a_{CM} = \frac{F}{M + m}$$

In CM reference frame, each block experiences pseudo force.

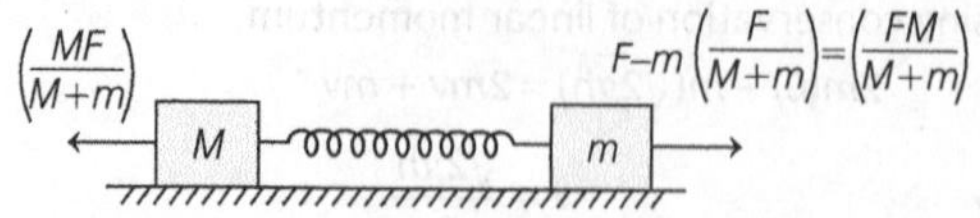

Let $\frac{FM}{M+m}=F_1$

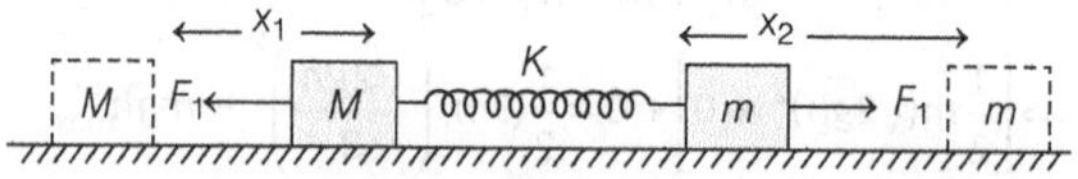

Using work-energy theorem,

$$W_{ext}+W_{spring}=\Delta K$$

$$\Rightarrow \quad F_1x_1+F_1x_2+\frac{1}{2}K[0-(x_1+x_2)^2]=(0+0)-(0+0)$$

$$\Rightarrow \quad x_1+x_2=\frac{2F_1}{K}=\frac{2FM}{(M+m)K}$$

Level 2

Single Choice Correct Questions

1. $x_{CM}=\frac{m_1x_1+m_2x_2+m_3x_3+...+m_{100}x_{100}}{m_1+m_2+m_3+....+m_{100}}$

$$=\frac{(1)(1)+(2)(2)+(3)(3)+....+(100)(100)}{1+2+3+....+100}$$

$$=\frac{n(n+1)(2n+1)/6}{\frac{n(n+1)}{2}}=\frac{2n+1}{3}$$

$$=\frac{2(100)+1}{3}=67\text{ cm}$$

2. $x_{CM}=\frac{m_1x_1+m_2x_2+m_3x_3+m_4x_4+m_5x_5+m_6x_6+m_7x_7}{m_1+m_2+m_3+m_4+m_5+m_6+m_7}$

$$=\frac{ma+ma+ma+m(0)+m(0)+m(0)+m(0)}{7m}=\frac{3a}{7}$$

Similarly, $y_{CM}=\frac{3a}{7}$ and $z_{CM}=\frac{3a}{7}$

3. $y_{CM}=\frac{m_1y_1+m_2y_2+m_3y_3+m_4y_4+m_5y_5}{m_1+m_2+m_3+m_4+m_5}$

$$=\frac{m(0)+m(0)+m(b)+m(b)+m(2b)}{5m}=\frac{4b}{5}$$

4.

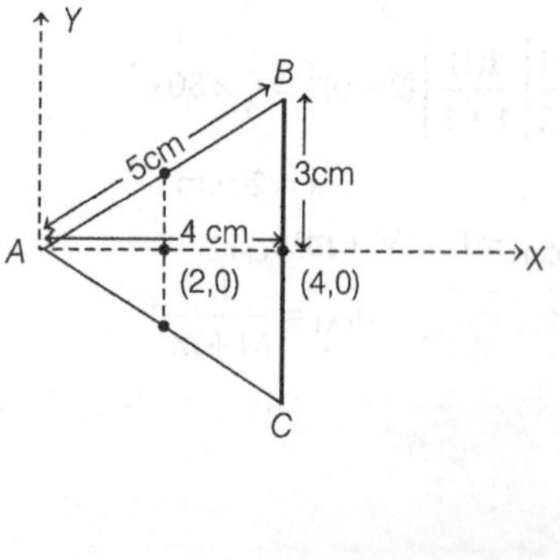

$$x_{CM}=\frac{m_1x_1+m_2x_2+m_3x_3}{m_1+m_2+m_3}$$

$$=\frac{\lambda(5)(2)+\lambda(5)(2)+(2\lambda)(6)(4)}{\lambda(5)+\lambda(5)+2\lambda(6)}=\frac{34}{11}\text{ cm}$$

5. $y_{CM}=\frac{m_1y_1+m_2y_2+m_3y_3+m_4y_4}{m_1+m_2+m_3+m_4}$

$$=\frac{m(0)+m(0)+m\left(\frac{2R}{\pi}\right)+m\left(\frac{2R}{\pi}\right)}{4m}$$

$$=\frac{R}{\pi}$$

6. $\mathbf{r}_{CM}=\frac{m_1\mathbf{r}_1-m_2\mathbf{r}_2-m_3\mathbf{r}_3}{m_1-m_2-m_3}$

$$=\frac{[\sigma\pi(4R)^2](0\hat{i}+0\hat{j})-(\sigma\pi R^2)(3R\hat{i})-(\sigma\pi R^2)(3R\hat{j})}{\sigma\pi(4R)^2-\sigma\pi R^2-\sigma\pi R^2}$$

$$=\frac{-3R}{14}(\hat{i}+\hat{j})$$

7. $x_{CM}=\frac{m_1x_1+m_2x_2-m_3x_3}{m_1+m_2-m_3}$

$$=\frac{(\sigma L^2)(0)+\left(\frac{\sigma L^2}{4}\right)\left[\frac{L}{2}+\frac{1}{3}\left(\frac{L}{2}\right)\right]-\left(\frac{\sigma L^2}{4}\right)\left[-\frac{2}{3}\left(\frac{L}{2}\right)\right]}{\sigma L^2+\frac{\sigma L^2}{4}-\frac{\sigma L^2}{4}}$$

$$=\frac{L}{4}$$

8. $dm=\sigma[(2kx^2)dx)]$

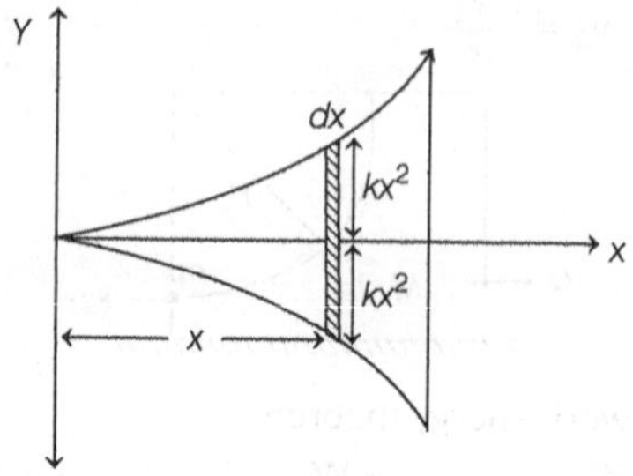

$$x_{CM}=\frac{\int dm\, x}{\int dm}=\frac{2\sigma K\int_0^a x^3dx}{2\sigma K\int_0^a x^2dx}=\frac{3a}{4}$$

9. $\Delta r_{CM}=\frac{m_1\Delta r_1+m_2\Delta r_2}{m_1+m_2}$

$$\Rightarrow \quad 0=\frac{m_1(d)+m_2(\Delta r_2)}{m_1+m_2}\Rightarrow \Delta r_2=-\frac{m_1d}{m_2}$$

10. $\mathbf{v}_1=\hat{i},\ \mathbf{v}_2=2\hat{j},\ \mathbf{v}_3=-4\sin30°\hat{i}-4\cos30°\hat{j}=-2\hat{i}-2\sqrt{3}\hat{j}$

$$\mathbf{v}_{CM}=\frac{m_1\mathbf{v}_1+m_2\mathbf{v}_2+m_3\mathbf{v}_3}{m_1+m_2+m_3}$$

$$=\frac{2\hat{i}+2(2\hat{j})+2(-2\hat{i}-2\sqrt{3}\hat{j})}{2+2+2}$$

$$= \frac{1}{3}[-\hat{i} + 2(1-\sqrt{3})\hat{j}]$$

11. $m_1 g - T = m_1 a$ ... (i)

$T - m_2 g = m_2 a$ ... (ii)

Solving Eqs. (i) and (ii), we get

$$a = \frac{(m_1 - m_2)}{m_1 + m_2}$$

$$a_{CM} = \frac{m_1 a_1 + m_2 a_2}{m_1 + m_2} = \frac{m_1 a + m_2(-a)}{m_1 + m_2}$$

$$= \left(\frac{m_1 - m_2}{m_1 + m_2}\right)^2 g$$

12. $\mathbf{a}_1 = g \sin 53° \hat{\mathbf{i}}, \mathbf{a}_2 = g \sin 37° \hat{\mathbf{j}}$

$$\mathbf{a}_{CM} = \frac{m_1 \mathbf{a}_1 + m_2 \mathbf{a}_2}{m_1 + m_2} = \frac{Mg \sin 53° \hat{\mathbf{i}} + Mg \sin 37° \hat{\mathbf{j}}}{2M}$$

$$= 4\hat{\mathbf{i}} + 3\hat{\mathbf{j}}$$

$$\mathbf{v}_{CM} = \mathbf{u}_{CM} + \mathbf{a}_{CM} t = 0 + (4\hat{\mathbf{i}} + 3\hat{\mathbf{j}})(5)$$

$$= 20\hat{\mathbf{i}} + 15\hat{\mathbf{j}}$$

$$v_{CM} = \sqrt{(20)^2 + (15)^2} = 25 \text{ m/s}$$

13. $50 - T = 5a$ ... (i)

$T - 0.2(50) = 5a$ ... (ii)

Solving Eqs. (i) and (ii), we get

$$a = 4 \text{ m/s}^2$$

$$\mathbf{a}_{CM} = \frac{m_1 \mathbf{a}_1 + m_2 \mathbf{a}_2}{m_1 + m_2} = \frac{5(4\hat{\mathbf{i}}) + 5(4\hat{\mathbf{j}})}{10}$$

$$= 2\hat{\mathbf{i}} + 2\hat{\mathbf{j}}$$

$$\mathbf{a}_{CM} = \sqrt{(2)^2 + (2)^2} = 2\sqrt{2} \text{ m/s}^2$$

14. $\mathbf{F}_{ext} = M\mathbf{a}_{CM}$

Since, external forces on the system are zero, acceleration of centre of mass will be zero. So, velocity of centre of mass will be constant. Initially centre of mass is at rest. So, velocity of centre of mass will be zero at any time.

15. Displacement of bead w.r.t. frame in horizontal $= -\frac{l}{2}$

$$\Rightarrow \quad s_{bf} = -\frac{l}{2}$$

$$\Rightarrow \quad s_b - s_f = \frac{-l}{2} \Rightarrow s_b = -\frac{l}{2} + s_f$$

$$(s_{CM})_x = \frac{m_1 s_1 + m_2 s_2}{m_1 + m_2}$$

$$\Rightarrow \quad 0 = \frac{m s_f + m\left(-\frac{l}{2} + s_f\right)}{2m}$$

$$\Rightarrow \quad s_f = \frac{l}{4}$$

16. Displacement of dog w.r.t. boat $= -8$

$$\Rightarrow \quad s_{db} = -8$$

$$\Rightarrow \quad s_d - s_b = -8 \Rightarrow s_d = -8 + s_b$$

$$(s_{CM})_x = \frac{m_1 s_1 + m_2 s_2}{m_1 + m_2}$$

$$\Rightarrow \quad 0 = \frac{40\, s_b + 10(-8 + s_b)}{50}$$

$$\Rightarrow \quad s_b = 1.6 \text{ m}$$

$$s_d = -8 + 1.6 = -6.4 \text{ m}$$

Distance of dog from the shore $= 20 - 6.4 = 13.6$ m

17. $s_{AC} = 2L \Rightarrow s_A = 2L + s_C$

$s_{BC} = -2L \Rightarrow s_B = -2L + s_C$

$$s_{CM} = \frac{m_A s_A + m_B s_B + m_C s_C}{m_A + m_B + m_C} = 0$$

$$\Rightarrow \quad \frac{m(2L + s_C) + 2m(-2L + s_C) + 3m s_C}{6m} = 0$$

$$\Rightarrow \quad s_C = \frac{L}{3}$$

18. $s_{AP} = +4 \Rightarrow s_A = 4 + s_P$

$s_{CP} = -4 \Rightarrow s_C = -4 + s_P$

$$s_{CM} = \frac{m_1 s_1 + m_2 s_2 + m_3 s_3 + m_4 s_4}{m_1 + m_2 + m_3 + m_4}$$

$$\Rightarrow 0 = \frac{40(4 + s_p) + 60(-4 + s_p) + 50 s_p + 90 s_p}{40 + 60 + 50 + 90}$$

$$\Rightarrow s_p = \frac{1}{3} \text{ m towards right}$$

19. Displacement of block w.r.t. tube in horizontal $= +R$

$$\Rightarrow \quad s_{BT} = R \Rightarrow s_B = R + s_T$$

$$s_{CM} = \frac{m_1 s_1 + m_2 s_2}{m_1 + m_2}$$

$$\Rightarrow \quad 0 = \frac{m s_T + m(R + s_T)}{2m}$$

$$\Rightarrow \quad s_T = \frac{-R}{2}$$

20.

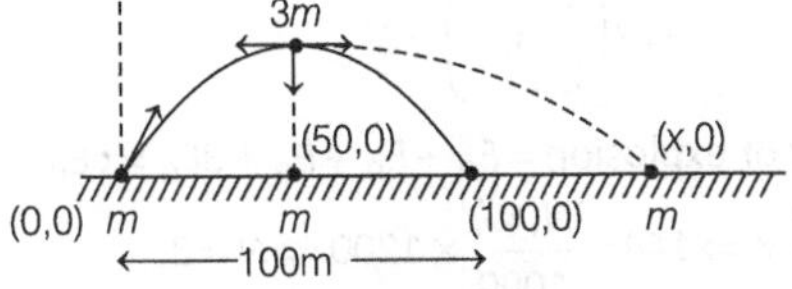

$$x_{CM} = \frac{m_1 x_1 + m_2 x_2 + m_3 x_3}{m_1 + m_2 + m_3}$$

$$\Rightarrow \quad 100 = \frac{m(0) + m(50) + mx}{3m} \Rightarrow x = 250 \text{ m}$$

21. Friction on wedge will be acting towards right. Due to friction, centre of mass of (wedge + block) system will move rightward and due to gravity centre of mass will move downward.

22. External forces on the (Earth + ball) system is zero. So to keep centre of mass stationary both will move away from each other.

23. $dm = \frac{M}{\pi R} R d\theta = \frac{M}{\pi} d\theta$

$d\mathbf{p} = d\,mv \sin\theta \hat{\mathbf{i}} + dmv \cos\theta \hat{\mathbf{j}}$

$\Rightarrow \int d\mathbf{p} = \frac{Mv}{\pi} \int_0^{\pi} \sin\theta d\theta \hat{\mathbf{i}} + \frac{Mv}{\pi} \int_0^{\pi} \cos\theta\, d\theta\, \hat{\mathbf{j}}$

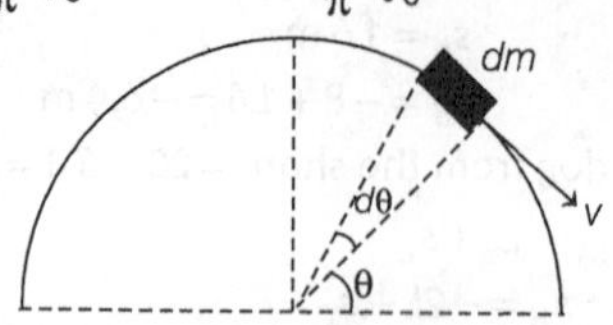

$\Rightarrow \quad \mathbf{p} = \frac{2Mv}{\pi} \hat{\mathbf{i}} \Rightarrow p = \frac{2Mv}{\pi}$

24. From linear momentum conservation, linear momentum of other fragment will be $-p$.

$$K = \frac{p^2}{2m_1} + \frac{|-p|^2}{2m_2} = \frac{p^2(m_1 + m_2)}{2m_1 m_2}$$

25. $K_{smaller} = \frac{p^2}{2m} \Rightarrow 216 = \frac{p^2}{2(3)}$

$\Rightarrow \quad p = 36$ kg-m/s

26. From linear momentum conservation,

$$mv_0\hat{\mathbf{j}} = \left(\frac{m}{4}\right)(2v_0\hat{\mathbf{i}}) + \left(\frac{3m}{4}\right)\mathbf{v}$$

$$\Rightarrow \quad \mathbf{v} = -\frac{2v_0}{3}\hat{\mathbf{i}} + \frac{4v_0}{3}\hat{\mathbf{j}}$$

$$\text{Speed} = \sqrt{\left(\frac{2v_0}{3}\right)^2 + \left(\frac{4v_0}{3}\right)^2} = \frac{\sqrt{20}}{3} v_0$$

27. From linear momentum conservation.

$$4m(0) = mv\hat{\mathbf{i}} + mv\hat{\mathbf{j}} + mv\hat{\mathbf{k}} + m\mathbf{v}$$

$$\mathbf{v} = -v(\hat{\mathbf{i}} + \hat{\mathbf{j}} + \hat{\mathbf{k}})$$

Kinetic energy of the fourth fragment $= \frac{1}{2} m(\sqrt{3}\, v)^2$

$$= 3\left(\frac{1}{2} mv^2\right) = 3E_0$$

Energy of explosion $= E_0 + E_0 + E_0 + 3E_0 = 6E_0$

28. $F = \frac{dm}{dt} v \Rightarrow 144 = \frac{N(40)}{1000} \times 1200 \Rightarrow N = 3$

29. Applying linear momentum conservation,

$$5(2\hat{\mathbf{i}}) + 10(\sqrt{3}\hat{\mathbf{j}}) = (5 + 10)\mathbf{v}$$

$$\Rightarrow \quad \mathbf{v} = \frac{2}{3}\hat{\mathbf{i}} + \frac{2}{\sqrt{3}}\hat{\mathbf{j}}$$

$$\text{Speed} = \sqrt{\left(\frac{2}{3}\right)^2 + \left(\frac{2}{\sqrt{3}}\right)^2} = \frac{4}{3} \text{ m/s}$$

30. Applying linear momentum conservation,

$$mv + M(0) = m\frac{v}{2} + M(\sqrt{5gl})$$

$$\Rightarrow \quad v = \frac{2M}{m}\sqrt{5gl}$$

31. Applying linear momentum conservation,

$$\left(\frac{20}{1000}\right)v = 1(v_2) + \left(\frac{20}{1000}\right)v_1 \quad \text{... (i)}$$

$$\left(\frac{20}{1000}\right)v_1 = \left(2.98 + \frac{20}{1000}\right)v_2 \quad \text{... (ii)}$$

Solving Eqs. (i) and (ii), we get

$$v_1 = \frac{3v}{4}$$

$$\% \text{ loss in velocity} = \frac{v - (3v/4)}{v} \times 100 = 25\%$$

32. Applying linear momentum conservation,

$$0 + 0 = Mv + mv_{recoil}$$

$$\Rightarrow \quad v_{recoil} = -\frac{Mv}{m}$$

$$v^2 = u^2 + 2as \Rightarrow 0^2 = \left(\frac{Mv}{m}\right)^2 + 2(-\mu g)s$$

$$\Rightarrow \quad s = \frac{M^2v^2}{2m^2\mu g}$$

33. Applying linear momentum conservation,

$$6v + 6(0) = (6 + 6)v_1$$

$$\Rightarrow \quad v_1 = \frac{v}{2}$$

Applying work-energy theorem,

$W_{mg} + W_{spring} = \Delta K$

$$\Rightarrow \quad -12 \times 10 \times \left(\frac{60}{100}\right) + \frac{1}{2} \times 100\left[\left(\frac{60}{100}\right)^2 - 0^2\right]$$

$$= 0 - \frac{1}{2} \times 12 \times \left(\frac{v}{2}\right)^2$$

$\Rightarrow \quad v = 6$ m/s

34. Time taken by the ball to hit the floor $= \frac{h}{u}$

Applying conservation of linear momentum,

$$0 + 0 = m_2 u + m_1 v_{man}$$

$$\Rightarrow \quad v_{man} = -\frac{m_2 u}{m_1}$$

Distance of man from the floor

$$= h + \left(\frac{m_2 u}{m_1}\right)\left(\frac{h}{u}\right) = \left(1 + \frac{m_2}{m_1}\right)h$$

35. When the barrel is horizontal,

$$v_{SG} = v \Rightarrow v_s = v + v_G$$

Applying conservation of linear momentum,

$0 + 0 = m(v + v_G) + Mv_G$

$\Rightarrow v_G = -\frac{mv}{M + m}$

When the barrel is inclined at an angle of 30° with the horizontal,

Applying linear momentum conservation in horizontal,

$$0+0=m(v\cos 30^\circ + v_G') + Mv_G'$$

$$\Rightarrow v_G' = -\frac{mv\cos 30^\circ}{M+m}$$

So, $\frac{v_G}{v_G'} = \frac{2}{\sqrt{3}}$

36. $T = \frac{2u\sin\theta}{g} = \frac{2\times 20\times \sin 60^\circ}{10} = 2\sqrt{3}$ s

Applying linear momentum conservation in horizontal,

$0+0=m(20\cos 60^\circ)+mv_{plank}$

$v_{plank} = -10$ m/s

Velocity of particle w.r.t. plank in horizontal

$$= 10-(-10) = 20 \text{ m/s}$$

In horizontal,

$$s_{particle,\ plank} = u_{particle,\ plank}t + \frac{1}{2}a_{particle,\ plank}t^2$$

$$\Rightarrow \quad L = 20(2\sqrt{3}) + 0 = 40\sqrt{3} \text{ m}$$

37. Applying linear momentum conservation in horizontal

$$0+0 = 1v_1 + 2(-v_2)$$

$$\Rightarrow \quad v_1 = 2v_2$$

Applying work-energy theorem,

$$W_{gravity} + W_{internal\ normal} + W_{normal\ from\ ground} = \Delta K$$

$$\Rightarrow \quad 1\times 10\,(1.1-0.1)+0+0$$

$$= \left(\frac{1}{2}\times 1v_1^2 + \frac{1}{2}\times 2v_2^2\right) - (0+0)$$

$$\Rightarrow \quad 10 = \frac{1}{2}(2v_2)^2 + v_2^2$$

$$\Rightarrow \quad v_2 = \sqrt{\frac{10}{3}} \text{ m/s}$$

38. Wedge will remain stationary till the ball reaches the bottom most position of circular track

Applying work-energy theorem for the ball,

$$W_{gravity} + W_N = \Delta K$$

$$\Rightarrow \quad mgR + 0 = \frac{1}{2}mv^2 - 0 \Rightarrow v = \sqrt{2gR}$$

When the ball reaches at the highest position on the other side of the wedge, velocity of the ball w.r.t. the wedge is zero.

Applying linear momentum conservation in horizontal

$m(\sqrt{2gR}) + M(0) = (M+m)v'$

$$\Rightarrow \quad v' = \frac{m\sqrt{2gR}}{M+m}$$

39. Using work-energy theorem in CM reference frame,

$$W_{mg} + W_N = \Delta K$$

$$\Rightarrow \quad -2mgh + 0 = \frac{1}{2}\left(\frac{2m}{3}\right)(0)^2 - \frac{1}{2}\left(\frac{2m}{3}\right)(\sqrt{2gR})^2$$

$$\Rightarrow \quad h = \frac{R}{3}$$

40. m_1 will break off the wall when the spring acquires natural length,

Applying work-energy theorem,

$$W_{spring} + W_{mg} + W_N = \Delta K$$

$$\Rightarrow \quad \frac{1}{2}K(x^2-0^2)+0+0 = \frac{1}{2}m_2v^2 - 0$$

$$\Rightarrow \quad v = \left(\sqrt{\frac{K}{m_2}}\right)x$$

$$v_{CM} = \frac{m_1v_1+m_2v_2}{m_1+m_2}$$

$$= \frac{m_1(0)+m_2\left(\sqrt{\frac{K}{m_2}}\right)x}{m_1+m_2} = \frac{(\sqrt{Km_2})x}{m_1+m_2}$$

41. Using energy conservation in CM reference frame,

$$K_1 + U_1 = K_2 + U_2$$

$$\Rightarrow \quad \frac{1}{2}\left[\frac{3(6)}{3+6}\right][2-(-1)]^2 + 0 = \frac{1}{2}\left[\frac{3(6)}{3+6}\right](0)^2 + \frac{1}{2}\times 200\,x^2$$

$$\Rightarrow \quad x = 30 \text{ cm}$$

42. $F_{ext} = m\,a_{CM} \Rightarrow F - \frac{F}{2} = (6m+3m)\,a_{CM}$

$$\Rightarrow \quad a_{CM} = \frac{F}{18m}$$

In CM reference frame, each block experiences pseudo force.

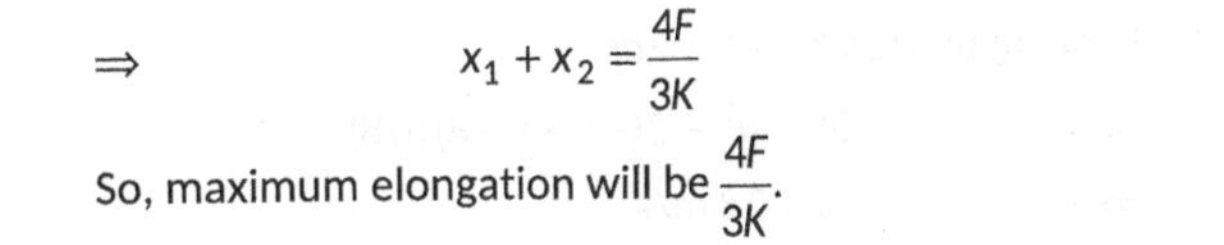

Using work-energy theorem in CM reference frame,

$$W_{ext} + W_{spring} = \Delta K$$

$$\Rightarrow \quad \left(\frac{2F}{3}\right)x_1 + \left(\frac{2F}{3}\right)x_2 + \frac{1}{2}K[0^2-(x_1+x_2)^2] = 0-0$$

$$\Rightarrow \quad x_1 + x_2 = \frac{4F}{3K}$$

So, maximum elongation will be $\frac{4F}{3K}$.

Numerical Value Questions

1. $x_{CM} = \frac{m_1x_1 - m_2x_2}{m_1-m_2} = \frac{\sigma\pi(28)^2(0) - \sigma\pi(21)^2(7)}{\sigma\pi(28)^2 - \sigma\pi(21)^2} = -9$ cm

2. $x_{CM} = \frac{\int x\,dm}{\int dm} = \frac{\int x\rho\pi y^2 dx}{\int \rho\pi y^2 dx} = \frac{\int_0^6 x\rho\pi\left(\frac{x}{k}\right)dx}{\int_0^6 \rho\pi\left(\frac{x}{k}\right)dx} = 4$m

$y_{CM} = 0$

So, $\quad \alpha + \beta = 4 + 0 = 4$

3. $y_{CM} = \frac{m_1y_1 - m_2y_2}{m_1-m_2}$

$$\Rightarrow \quad h = \frac{\rho\frac{1}{3}\pi R^2(12)\left(\frac{12}{4}\right) - \rho\frac{1}{3}\pi R^2 h\left(\frac{h}{4}\right)}{\rho\frac{1}{3}\pi R^2(12) - \rho\frac{1}{3}\pi R^2 h}$$

$$\Rightarrow \quad h^2 - 16h + 48 = 0$$

$$\Rightarrow \quad h = 4 \text{ cm}$$

4. In horizontal direction, centre of mass doesn't move.

$$(x_{CM})_i = (x_{CM})_f$$

$$\Rightarrow \quad \frac{4(0) + 12(8)}{16} = x_0 + \frac{4(12) + 12(8)}{16}$$

$$\Rightarrow \quad x_0 = -3 \text{ cm}$$

5. $s_{CM} = \dfrac{m_1 s_1 + m_2 s_2 + m_3 s_3}{m_1 + m_2 + m_3}$

$$\Rightarrow \quad 0 = \frac{100\,\mathbf{s}_p + 50(20\sqrt{2}\hat{\mathbf{i}} + \mathbf{s}_p) + 50(20\sqrt{2}\hat{\mathbf{j}} + \mathbf{s}_p)}{100 + 50 + 50}$$

$$\Rightarrow \quad \mathbf{s}_p = -5\sqrt{2}\hat{\mathbf{i}} - 5\sqrt{2}\hat{\mathbf{j}}$$

Magnitude of displacement of plank

$$= \sqrt{(5\sqrt{2})^2 + (5\sqrt{2})^2}$$

$$= 10 \text{ m}$$

6. $(s_{CM})_x = \dfrac{m_1 s_1 + m_2 s_2}{m_1 + m_2}$

$$\Rightarrow \quad 0 = \frac{2s_m + 1(S_m - 9)}{2 + 1} \Rightarrow s_m = 3\text{m}$$

7. $(s_{CM})_x = \dfrac{m_1 s_1 + m_2 s_2}{m_1 + m_2}$

$$\Rightarrow \quad 0 = \frac{50(-3 + s_p) + 100\,s_p}{50 + 100}$$

$$\Rightarrow \quad s_p = 1 \text{ m}$$

$$s_m = -3 + 1 = -2\text{m}$$

Distance travelled by plank in 5 s $= 2 \times 5 = 10$ m

Distance travelled by man w.r.t. ground $= 10 - 2 = 8$ m

8. For 8 kg block, $v^2 = u^2 + 2as$

$$\Rightarrow \quad 0^2 = u^2 + 2(-0.5 \times 9.8)(0.8)$$

$$\Rightarrow \quad u = 2.8 \text{ m/s}$$

For 6 kg block, $v^2 = u^2 + 2as$

$$\Rightarrow \quad 0^2 = u^2 + 2(-0.5 \times 9.8)(1.25)$$

$$\Rightarrow \quad u = 3.5 \text{ m/s}$$

Applying conservation of linear momentum,

$0.05\,v = 8 \times 2.8 + 6.05 \times 3.5$

$\Rightarrow v = 871.5$ m/s

9. Applying linear momentum conservation for throwing of sack,

$$0 + 0 = 150\,v_{boat} + 50(6)$$

$$v_{boat} = -2 \text{ m/s}$$

Applying linear momentum conservation for landing of sack in the second boat,

$$50 \times 6 + 150 \times 0 = 200\,v'_{boat}$$

$$v'_{boat} = 1.5 \text{ m/s}$$

$$T = \frac{2u_y}{g} \Rightarrow 0.5 = \frac{2u_y}{10} \Rightarrow u_y = 2.5 \text{ m/s}$$

$$R = \frac{2u_x u_y}{g} = \frac{2(6)(2.5)}{10} = 3 \text{ m}$$

Initial separation between boats $= 3$m

Distance travelled by first boat while the sack is in the air $= 2 \times 0.5 = 1$ m

Distance $= u_{rel}t = [2 - (-1.5)](8) = 28$ m

Total distance $= 3 + 1 + 28 = 32$ m

10. $T = \sqrt{\dfrac{2H}{g}} - \sqrt{\dfrac{2h}{g}} = \dfrac{1}{\sqrt{g}}(\sqrt{2 \times 50} - \sqrt{2 \times 18}) = \dfrac{4}{\sqrt{g}}$

$$s_x = u_x t \Rightarrow 1 = u_x\left(\frac{4}{\sqrt{g}}\right) \Rightarrow u_x = \frac{\sqrt{g}}{4}$$

Applying conservation of linear momentum in horizontal,

$$\Rightarrow \quad 0 + 0 = -2\,v_{bag} + 56\left(\frac{\sqrt{g}}{4}\right)$$

$$\Rightarrow \quad v_{bag} = 7\sqrt{g} = 7 \times \frac{22}{7} = 22 \text{ m/s}$$

Level 3

Single Choice Correct Questions

1. $y_{CM} = \dfrac{m_1 y_1 + m_2 y_2}{m_1 + m_2}$

$$\Rightarrow \quad 0 = \frac{\left(\rho\frac{1}{3}\pi R^2 H\right)\left(\frac{H}{4}\right) + \left(\rho\frac{2}{3}\pi R^3\right)\left(\frac{-3R}{8}\right)}{\rho\left(\frac{1}{3}\pi R^2 H\right) + \rho\left(\frac{2}{3}\pi R^3\right)}$$

$$\Rightarrow \quad H = \sqrt{3}R$$

2. $y_{CM} = \dfrac{m_1 y_1 + m_2 y_2}{m_1 + m_2} = \dfrac{m\left(R - \frac{4R}{3\pi}\right) + m\left(R + \frac{2R}{\pi}\right)}{2m}$

$$= R\left(1 + \frac{1}{3\pi}\right)$$

3. $x_{CM} = \dfrac{m_1 x_1 - m_2 x_2}{m_1 - m_2}$

$$= \frac{\sigma\pi(2R)^2(0) - \sigma\left(\frac{\pi R^2}{2}\right)\left(R + \frac{4R}{3\pi}\right)}{\sigma\pi(2R)^2 - \sigma\left(\frac{\pi R^2}{2}\right)}$$

$$= -\frac{R}{21\pi}(3\pi + 4)$$

4. $x_{CM} = \dfrac{m_1x_1 - m_2x_2}{m_1 - m_2} = \dfrac{(8m)(0) - m\left(\dfrac{l}{2}\right)}{8m - m} = -\dfrac{l}{14}$

Similarly, $y_{CM} = z_{CM} = -\dfrac{l}{14}$

Distance of CM from O $= \sqrt{\left(\dfrac{l}{14}\right)^2 + \left(\dfrac{l}{14}\right)^2 + \left(\dfrac{l}{14}\right)^2}$

$= \dfrac{\sqrt{3}l}{14}$

5. For a sector,

$$r_{CM} = \frac{4R}{3\theta}\sin\left(\frac{\theta}{2}\right) = \frac{4R}{3\left(\frac{\pi}{3}\right)}\sin\left(\frac{\pi/3}{2}\right) = \frac{2R}{\pi}$$

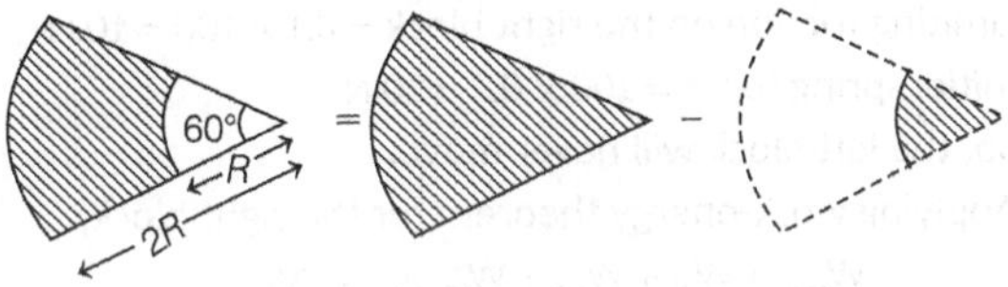

$$x_{CM} = \frac{m_1x_1 - m_2x_2}{m_1 - m_2}$$

$$= \frac{\left[\sigma(2R)^2\left(\frac{\pi}{3}\right)\right]\left[\frac{2(2R)}{\pi}\right] - \sigma R^2\left(\frac{\pi}{3}\right)\left(\frac{2R}{\pi}\right)}{\sigma(2R)^2\frac{\pi}{3} - \sigma R^2\left(\frac{\pi}{3}\right)}$$

$$= \frac{14R}{3\pi}$$

6. $x_{CM} = \dfrac{m_1x_1 + m_2x_2 + m_3x_3 - m_4x_4 - m_5x_5}{m_1 + m_2 + m_3 - m_4 - m_5}$

$$= \frac{m(0) + \frac{m}{8}\left(\frac{a}{3}\right) + \frac{m}{8}\left(\frac{a}{3}\right) - \frac{m}{8}\left(\frac{2a}{3}\right) - \frac{m}{8}\left(\frac{2a}{3}\right)}{m + \frac{m}{8} + \frac{m}{8} - \frac{m}{8} - \frac{m}{8}}$$

$$= -\frac{a}{12}$$

7. $x_{CM} = \dfrac{m_1x_1 + m_2x_2 - m_3x_3}{m_1 + m_2 - m_3}$

$$= \frac{M(0) + \frac{M}{4}\left(\frac{R}{2}\right) - \frac{M}{4}\left(-\frac{R}{2}\right)}{M + \frac{M}{4} - \frac{M}{4}} = \frac{R}{4}$$

$$y_{CM} = \frac{m_1y_1 + m_2y_2 - m_3y_3}{m_1 + m_2 - m_3}$$

$$= \frac{M\left(\frac{4R}{3\pi}\right) + \frac{M}{4}\left[-\frac{4\left(\frac{R}{2}\right)}{3\pi}\right] - \frac{M}{4}\left[\frac{4\left(\frac{R}{2}\right)}{3\pi}\right]}{M + \frac{M}{4} - \frac{M}{4}} = \frac{R}{\pi}$$

8.

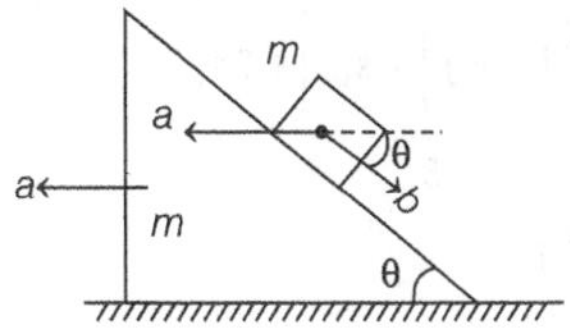

$(\Sigma F_{ext})_x = 0 \Rightarrow -ma + m(b\cos\theta - a) = 0$

$\Rightarrow \quad b\cos\theta = 2a$

For the block along the inclined plane,

$$mg\sin\theta = m(b - a\cos\theta)$$

$$\Rightarrow \quad mg\sin\theta = m\left[\left(b - \frac{b\cos\theta}{2}\right)\cos\theta\right]$$

$$\Rightarrow \quad b = \frac{2g\sin\theta}{2 - \cos^2\theta} = \frac{2g\sin\theta}{1 + \sin^2\theta}$$

$$(a_{CM})_x = 0,\ (a_{CM})_y = \frac{m_1a_{1y} + ma_{2y}}{m_1 + m_2}$$

$$= \frac{m(0) + m(b\sin\theta)}{2m}$$

$$= \frac{b\sin\theta}{2} = \frac{g\sin^2\theta}{1 + \sin^2\theta}$$

9. $v_{CM} = \dfrac{m_1v_1 + m_2v_2 + m_3v_3}{m_1 + m_2 + m_3}$

$$= \frac{m(v_r + v_{ladder}) + (M - m)v_{ladder} + M(-v_{ladder})}{m + (M - m) + M}$$

$$= \frac{mv_r}{2M}$$

10. $(u_{CM})_x = \dfrac{m(v_1\cos\theta_1) - (-v_2\cos\theta_2)m}{2m}$

$$= \frac{v_1\cos\theta_1 + v_2\cos\theta_2}{2}$$

$$(u_{CM})_y = \frac{m(v_1\sin\theta_1) - m(v_2\sin\theta_2)}{2m} = \frac{v_1\sin\theta_1 - v_2\sin\theta_2}{2}$$

$$(a_{CM})_y = \frac{mg + mg}{2m} = g$$

If $(u_{CM})_x = 0 \Rightarrow \mathbf{u}_{CM} \parallel \mathbf{a}_{CM}$, path will be a vertical line other wise path will be parabolic.

11. $\mathbf{F}_{ext} = M\,\mathbf{a}_{CM}$

$\Rightarrow m_1\mathbf{g} + m_2\mathbf{g} = m_1\mathbf{a} + m_2\mathbf{a}_2$

$$\Rightarrow \quad \mathbf{a}_2 = \frac{m_1\mathbf{g} + m_2\mathbf{g} - m_1\mathbf{a}}{m_2}$$

12. $\mathbf{s}_{bw} = \mathbf{r}_m - \mathbf{r}_p = -R\hat{j} - (R\cos 60°\,\hat{i} + R\sin 60°\,\hat{j})$

$$= -\frac{R}{2}\hat{i} - R\hat{j} - \frac{\sqrt{3}R}{2}\hat{k}$$

$$\mathbf{s}_b = \mathbf{s}_{bw} + \mathbf{s}_w = \left(-\frac{R}{2}\hat{i} - R\hat{j} - \frac{\sqrt{3}R}{2}\hat{k}\right) + \mathbf{s}_w$$

$$(\mathbf{s}_{CM})_{xy} = \frac{m_1\mathbf{s}_1 + m_2\mathbf{s}_2}{m_1 + m_2}$$

$$\Rightarrow 0=\frac{2\left[\left(\frac{-R}{2}\hat{i}-R\hat{j}\right)+\mathbf{s}_w\right]+3\mathbf{s}_w}{5}$$

$$\mathbf{s}_w=\frac{R}{5}\hat{i}+\frac{2R}{5}\hat{j}$$

Displacement of wedge

$$=\sqrt{\left(\frac{R}{5}\right)^2+\left(\frac{2R}{5}\right)^2}=\frac{R}{\sqrt{5}}=\frac{1}{5}\text{ m}$$

13.

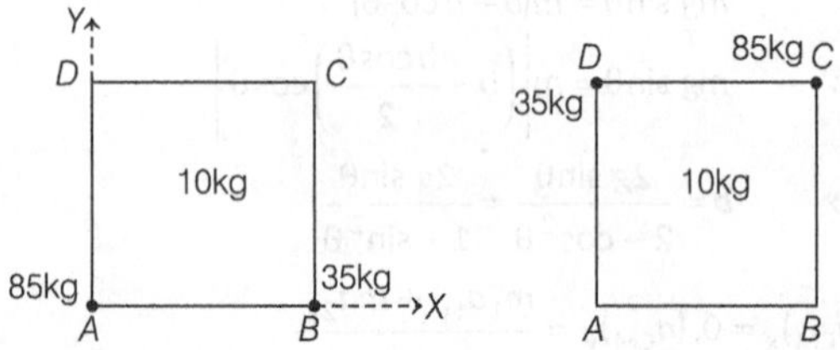

$$\mathbf{s}_{AP}=1(\hat{i}+\hat{j})\Rightarrow \mathbf{s}_A=(\hat{i}+\hat{j})+\mathbf{s}_p$$

$$\mathbf{s}_{BP}=1(-\hat{i}+\hat{j})\Rightarrow \mathbf{s}_B=(-\hat{i}+\hat{j})+\mathbf{s}_p$$

$$\mathbf{s}_{CM}=0$$

$$\Rightarrow \frac{10\,\mathbf{s}_p+85[(\hat{i}+\hat{j})+\mathbf{s}_p]+35[(-\hat{i}+\hat{j})+\mathbf{s}_p]}{10+85+35}=0$$

$$\Rightarrow \quad \mathbf{s}_p=-\frac{5}{13}\hat{i}-\frac{12}{13}\hat{j}$$

Magnitude of displacement of plate

$$=\sqrt{\left(\frac{5}{13}\right)^2+\left(\frac{12}{13}\right)^2}=1\text{ m}$$

14. Displacement of ball w.r.t. bar in horizontal $=2(1\sin 30°)$

$$\Rightarrow \quad s_{\text{ball, bar}}=1$$

$$\Rightarrow \quad s_{\text{ball}}=1+s_{\text{bar}}$$

$$(s_{CM})_x=0\Rightarrow\frac{4s_{\text{bar}}+1(1+s_{\text{bar}})}{5}=0$$

$$\Rightarrow \quad s_{\text{bar}}=-0.2\text{ m}$$

15. Displacement of A w.r.t. wedge in horizontal $=10\cos 45°$

$$\Rightarrow \quad s_{AC}=5\sqrt{2}$$

$$\Rightarrow \quad s_A=5\sqrt{2}+s_C$$

Displacement of B w.r.t. wedge in horizontal $=10\cos 45°$

$$\Rightarrow \quad s_{BC}=5\sqrt{2}$$

$$\Rightarrow \quad s_B=5\sqrt{2}+s_C$$

$$(s_{CM})_x=0$$

$$\Rightarrow \frac{m(5\sqrt{2}+s_c)+2m(5\sqrt{2}+s_c)+2ms_c}{5m}=1$$

$$\Rightarrow \quad s_c=-3\sqrt{2}\text{ cm}$$

16. Let $s_{AP}=x\Rightarrow s_A=x+s_P$

$$s_{BP}=(x-60)$$

$$\Rightarrow \quad s_B=(x-60)+s_P=0$$

$$s_{CM}=0\Rightarrow\frac{40(x+s_P)+60(0)+40s_P}{140}=0$$

$$\Rightarrow \quad 2s_P+x=0\Rightarrow s_P=-\frac{x}{2}$$

$$s_B=(x-60)-\frac{x}{2}=0$$

$$\Rightarrow \quad x=120\text{ cm}$$

So, A will meet B at the right end of the plank.

17. When B is at maximum distance from the wall, A will be at the other extreme position

$$s_{AB}=-2x_0\Rightarrow s_A=-2x_0+s_B$$

$$(s_{CM})_x=\frac{1(-2x_0+s_B)+3s_B}{4}=0$$

$$\Rightarrow \quad s_B=\frac{x_0}{2}$$

18. Limiting friction on the left block $=0.25\times 100=25$ N

Limiting friction on the right block $=0.1\times 100=10$ N

Initial spring force $=100\times 0.2=20$ N

So, the left block will never move.

Applying work-energy theorem for the right block,

$$W_{mg}+W_N+W_{sp}+W_{\text{friction}}=\Delta K$$

$$\Rightarrow \quad 0+0+\frac{1}{2}(100)[(0.2)^2-(0.2-x)^2]-10(x)=0-0$$

$$\Rightarrow \quad x=0.2\text{ m}=20\text{ cm}$$

So, the right block will come to permanently rest when the spring acquires natural length.

$$s_{CM}=\frac{m_1x_1+m_2x_2}{m_1+m_2}=\frac{10(0)+10(20)}{20}=10\text{ cm}$$

19. When first man jumps,

$$0+0=150v_1+50(10+v_1)$$

$$\Rightarrow \quad v_1=-2.5\text{ m/s}$$

When 2nd man jumps

$$150(-2.5)=100v_2+50(10+v_2)$$

$$\Rightarrow \quad v_2=-\frac{35}{6}\text{ m/s}$$

When both men jump simultaneously,

$$0+0+0=100v_2'+50(10+v_2')+50(10+v_2')$$

$$\Rightarrow \quad v_2'=-5\text{ m/s}$$

$$\frac{v_2}{v_2'}=\frac{35/6}{5}=\frac{7}{6}$$

20. When the man walks to the other end of the plank

$$s_{CM}=0=\frac{2ms_P+m(15+S_P)}{3m}$$

$$\Rightarrow \quad S_P=-5\text{ m}$$

So, now man has to jump 5 m.

$$R_{\max}=\frac{u^2}{g}=5\Rightarrow u=5\sqrt{2}\text{ m/s}$$

$$u_x=5\sqrt{2}\cos 45°=5\text{ m/s}$$

$$u_y=5\sqrt{2}\sin 45°=5\text{ m/s}$$

From linear momentum conservation in horizontal,

$$0+0=2mv_{\text{plank}}+m(5)$$

$$v_{plank} = -2.5 \text{ m/s}$$
$$(v_{man,\ plank})_x = 5 - (-2.5) = 7.5 \text{ m/s}$$
$$v_{man,\ plank} = \sqrt{(7.5)^2 + (5)^2} = 9 \text{ m/s}$$

21. Since second and third fragment take equal time to reach ground, $\Rightarrow v_{2y} = v_{3y}$

From linear momentum conservation in horizontal,
$$v_{2x} = v_{3x}$$
So, we get $v_2 = v_3$

From linear momentum conservation in vertical,
$$0 = mv_{2y} + mv_{3y} - mv_1$$
$$\Rightarrow \quad v_1 = 2v_{2y} = 2v_{3y}$$
$$\Rightarrow \quad v_{2y} = v_{3y} = \frac{v_1}{2}$$
$$s_y = u_y t + \frac{1}{2}a_y t^2$$
$$+h = v_1 t_1 + \frac{1}{2}gt_1^2 \quad \text{...(i)}$$
$$-h = \left(\frac{v_1}{2}\right)t_2 - \frac{1}{2}gt_2^2 \quad \text{...(ii)}$$
Solving Eqs. (i) and (ii), we get
$$h = \frac{gt_1t_2}{2}\left(\frac{t_1 + 2t_2}{2t_1 + t_2}\right)$$

22. Applying linear momentum conservation when monkey jumps on to ball B,
$$mu_{monkey} + m(0) = (m + m)\sqrt{5gL}$$
$$u_{monkey} = 2\sqrt{5gL}$$
Applying linear momentum conservation when monkey jumps from ball A,
$$0 + 0 = -mv_A + m(2\sqrt{5gL})$$
$$v_A = 2\sqrt{5gL}$$
$$v_{monkey,\ ball\ A} = 2\sqrt{5gL} - (-2\sqrt{5gL}) = 4\sqrt{5gL}$$

23. Lets take velocity of bullet w.r.t. barrel to be v and recoil velocity of gun to be u.
$$\mathbf{v}_{bullet} = \mathbf{v}_{bullet,\ gun} + \mathbf{v}_{gun}$$
$$= (v\cos 45°\,\hat{\mathbf{i}} + v\sin 45°\,\hat{\mathbf{j}}) - u\hat{\mathbf{i}}$$
$$= (v\cos 45° - u)\hat{\mathbf{i}} + v\sin 45°\,\hat{\mathbf{j}}$$
$$\tan\phi = \frac{v\sin 45°}{v\cos 45° - u}$$
So, $\phi > 45°$

24. Using linear momentum conservation for (wedge + block) system in horizontal

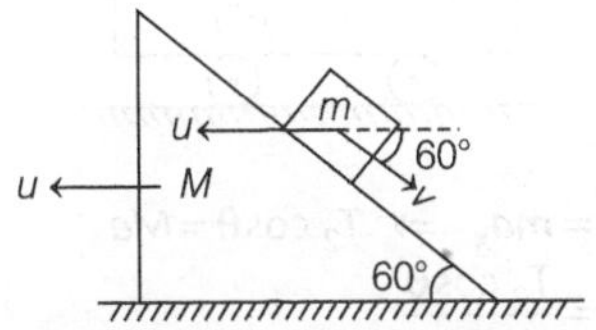

$$0 + 0 = -Mu + m(v\cos 60° - u)$$
$$\Rightarrow \quad 0 = -2.4(0.2) + 0.1\left(\frac{v}{2} - 0.2\right)$$
$$\Rightarrow \quad v = 10 \text{ m/s}$$

25. Using linear momentum conservation in horizontal,
$$0 + 0 = m(u\cos\theta + v_{cannon}) + 4m\,v_{cannon}$$
$$\Rightarrow \quad v_{cannon} = -\frac{u\cos\theta}{5}$$
In horizontal,
$$(v_{shell})_x = v_{shell,\ cannon} + v_{cannon}$$
$$= u\cos\theta - \frac{u\cos\theta}{5} = \frac{4u\cos\theta}{5}$$
$$T = \frac{2u_y}{g} = \frac{2u\sin\theta}{g}$$
$$R = (v_{shell})_x T = \left(\frac{4u\cos\theta}{5}\right)\left(\frac{2u\sin\theta}{g}\right)$$
$$= \frac{4u^2\sin 2\theta}{5g}$$

26.

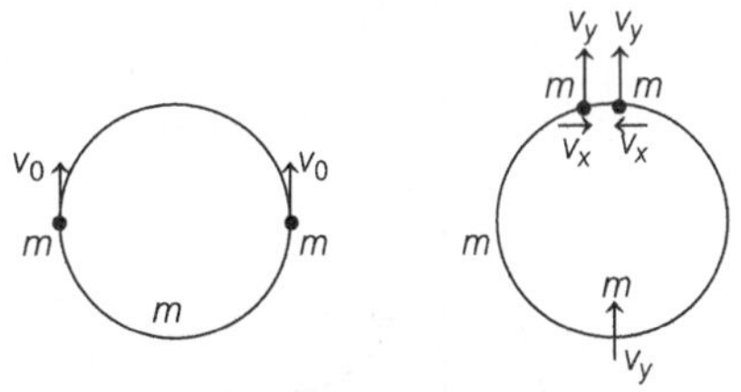

Applying linear momentum conservation,
$$mv_0 + mv_0 + m(0) = mv_y + mv_y + mv_y$$
$$v_y = \frac{2v_0}{3}$$
Applying energy conservation,
$$\frac{1}{2}mv_0^2 + \frac{1}{2}mv_0^2 + 0 = \frac{1}{2}mv_y^2 + \frac{1}{2}m\left(\sqrt{v_x^2 + v_y^2}\right)^2 + \frac{1}{2}m\left(\sqrt{v_x^2 + v_y^2}\right)^2$$
$$\Rightarrow \quad v_x = \frac{v_0}{\sqrt{3}}$$
Velocity of particle just before collision
$$= \sqrt{\left(\frac{v_0}{\sqrt{3}}\right)^2 + \left(\frac{2v_0}{3}\right)^2} = \frac{\sqrt{7}v_0}{3}$$

27. $v_{mc} = v \Rightarrow v_m - v_c = v \Rightarrow v_m = v + v_c$

Applying linear momentum conservation,
$$0 + 0 = 2mv_c + m(v + v_c)$$
$$\Rightarrow \quad v_c = -\frac{v}{3}$$
$$v_m = v_{mc} + v_c = v - \frac{v}{3} = \frac{2v}{3}$$
Using work-energy theorem,

$$W_{man} = \Delta K_{system} = \left[\frac{1}{2}(2m)\left(\frac{v}{3}\right)^2 + \frac{1}{2}m\left(\frac{2v}{3}\right)^2\right] - (0+0)$$

$$= \frac{mv^2}{3}$$

28. Using linear momentum conservation for (wedge + block) system in horizontal,

$$0 + 0 = mv + Mv_{wedge}$$

$$\Rightarrow \quad v_{wedge} = -\frac{mv}{M}$$

Using work-energy theorem,

$$W_{gravity} + W_{internal\ normal} + W_{normal\ by\ ground} = \Delta K$$

$$\Rightarrow \quad W_{gravity} + 0 + 0 = \left[\frac{1}{2}mv^2 + \frac{1}{2}M\left(\frac{mv}{M}\right)^2\right] - (0+0)$$

$$\Rightarrow \quad W_{gravity} = \frac{1}{2}mv^2\left[1 + \frac{m}{M}\right]$$

29.

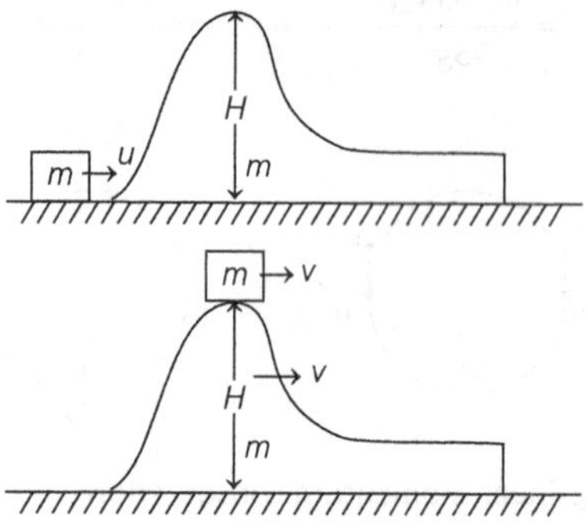

Using linear momentum conservation in horizontal,

$$mu + m(0) = mv + mv$$

$$v = \frac{u}{2}$$

Using energy conservation,

$$K_1 + U_1 = K_2 + U_2$$

$$\Rightarrow \quad \left(\frac{1}{2}mu^2 + 0\right) + 0 = \frac{1}{2}(m+m)\left(\frac{u}{2}\right)^2 + mgH$$

$$\Rightarrow \quad u = 2\sqrt{gH}$$

30. Using linear momentum conservation in horizontal,

$$0 + 0 = m(v\cos 45° - u) + m(-u)$$

$$\Rightarrow \quad v = 2\sqrt{2}u$$

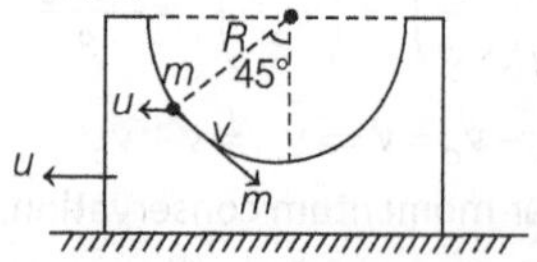

Using energy conservation

$$K_1 + U_1 = K_2 + U_2$$

$$(0+0) + mgR\cos 45°$$

$$= \left[\frac{1}{2}mu^2 + \frac{1}{2}m\left(\sqrt{v^2 + u^2 + 2uv\cos 135°}\right)^2\right] + 0$$

$$\Rightarrow \quad u = \sqrt{\frac{gR}{3\sqrt{2}}}$$

31. Wedge will not break off the wall till the point mass reaches the bottom most position of the groove.

Using work-energy theorem for the point mass,

$$W_{mg} + W_N = \Delta K$$

$$\Rightarrow \quad mgR + 0 = \frac{1}{2}mv^2 - 0 \Rightarrow v = \sqrt{2gR}$$

Now, the point mass will slide on the right half of groove and the wedge will keep speeding due to horizontal component of normal till the point mass returns to the bottom most position of the groove.

Using linear momentum conservation in horizontal,

$$m(\sqrt{2gR}) + m(0) = mv - mu$$

$$\Rightarrow \quad v - u = \sqrt{2gR} \qquad \text{... (i)}$$

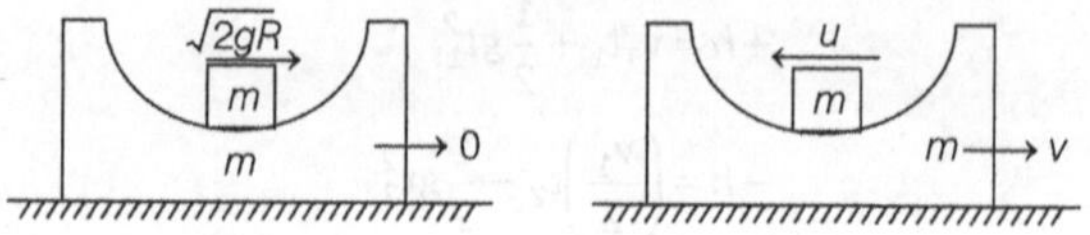

Using energy conservation,

$$K_1 + U_1 = K_2 + U_2$$

$$\Rightarrow \quad \left[\frac{1}{2}m(\sqrt{2gR})^2 + 0\right] + 0 = \left(\frac{1}{2}mv^2 + \frac{1}{2}mu^2\right) + 0$$

$$\Rightarrow \quad v^2 + u^2 = 2gR \qquad \text{... (ii)}$$

Solving Eqs. (i) and (ii), we get

$$v = \sqrt{2gR} \text{ and } u = 0$$

32. $(v_{rel})_i = v_0; (v_{rel})_f = 0$

Reduced mass $= \dfrac{m(m)}{m+m} = \dfrac{m}{2}$

Using work-energy theorem in CM reference frame,

$$W_{mg} + W_T + W_N = \Delta K$$

$$\Rightarrow \quad -mgh + 0 + 0 = \frac{1}{2}\left(\frac{m}{2}\right)(0)^2 - \frac{1}{2}\left(\frac{m}{2}\right)(v_0 - 0)^2$$

$$\Rightarrow \quad h = \frac{v_0^2}{4g}$$

33. Initially, $2T_1 \sin\theta = mg$

$$\Rightarrow \quad T_1 = \frac{mg}{2\sin\theta} = \frac{5mg}{6}$$

Just after cutting the string PB,

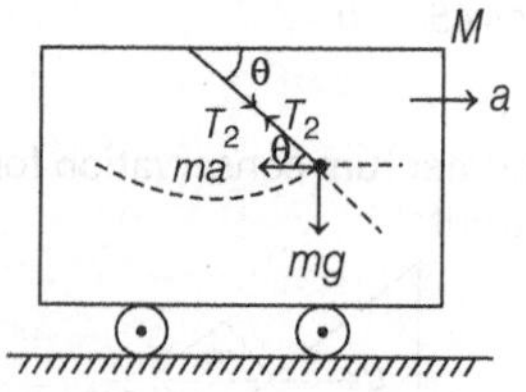

For the cart,

$$\Sigma F_x = ma_x \Rightarrow T_2\cos\theta = Ma$$

$$\Rightarrow \quad a = \frac{T_2\cos\theta}{M}$$

The motion of the sphere w.r.t. the cart is circular motion.

$$T_2 + ma\cos\theta - mg\sin\theta = \frac{m(0)^2}{l}$$

$$\Rightarrow \quad T_2 + m\left(\frac{T_2\cos\theta}{M}\right)\cos\theta - mg\sin\theta = 0$$

$$\Rightarrow \quad T_2 = \frac{mg}{3}$$

So, $\frac{T_2}{T_1} = \frac{2}{5}$

34.

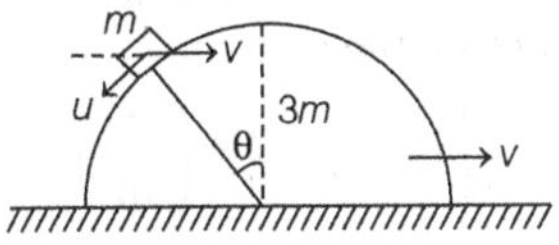

Using linear momentum conservation in horizontal,

$$0 + 0 = 3mv + m(v - u\cos\theta)$$

$$\Rightarrow \quad u = \frac{4v}{\cos\theta}$$

$$\omega = \frac{u}{R} = \frac{4v}{R\cos\theta}$$

35. Using energy conservation in CM reference frame,

$$K_1 + U_1 = K_2 + U_2$$

$$\Rightarrow \quad \frac{1}{2}\left(\frac{2m}{3}\right)(v_0 - 0)^2 + 0 = \frac{1}{2}\left(\frac{2m}{3}\right)(0)^2 + \frac{1}{2}kx^2$$

$$\Rightarrow \quad x = \sqrt{\frac{2m}{3K}}\, v_0$$

36. $F_{ext} = ma_{CM}$

$$\Rightarrow \quad 3mg\sin 53° - 2mg = 3m\,a_{CM}$$

$$\Rightarrow \quad a_{CM} = \frac{2g}{15}$$

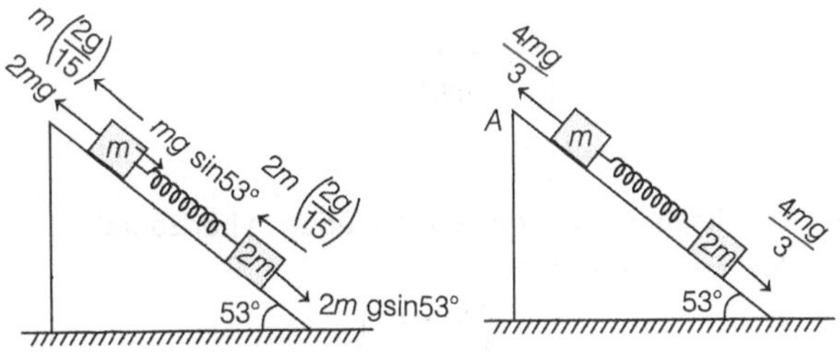

In CM reference frame, each block experiences pseudo force.

Using work-energy theorem in CM reference frame

$$W_{spring} + W_{ext} = \Delta K$$

$$\Rightarrow \quad \frac{1}{2}K[0^2 - (x_1 + x_2)^2] + \frac{4mg}{3}x_1 + \frac{4mg}{3}x_2 = 0 - 0$$

$$\Rightarrow \quad x_1 + x_2 = \frac{8mg}{3K}$$

$$\Rightarrow \quad x_{max} = \frac{8mg}{3K}$$

Multiple Choice(s) Correct Questions

1. Centre of mass of ring will be at its geometrical centre and centre of mass of uniform chord AB will be at its mid point, so centre of mass of the object will lie on the line CD.

   Equation of line CD,

   $y = x$, where $\left(x < \frac{R}{2}, y < \frac{R}{2}\right)$

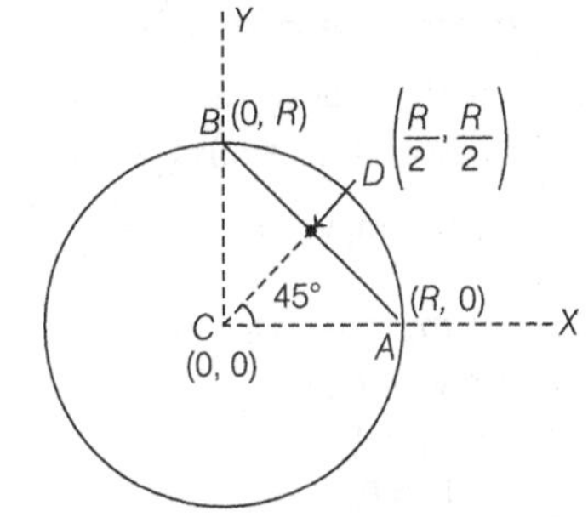

2. If AB is removed, centre of mass will shift right and down, so centre of mass will be in the fourth quadrant. If AC is removed, centre of mass will shift left and down, so centre of mass will be in the third quadrant.

   If BC is removed, CM will shift up. So, CM will be on the positive Y-axis.

3. $m_2g - T = m_2a$ ... (i)

   $T = m_1a$ ... (ii)

   Solving Eqs. (i) and (ii), we get

$$a = \frac{m_2g}{m_1 + m_2}$$

$$\mathbf{a}_{CM} = \frac{m_1\mathbf{a}_1 + m_2\mathbf{a}_2}{m_1 + m_2} = \frac{m_1\left(\frac{m_2g}{m_1+m_2}\right)\hat{i} + m_2\left(\frac{m_2g}{m_1+m_2}\right)g\hat{j}}{m_1 + m_2}$$

So, $$(a_{CM})_x = \frac{m_1m_2g}{(m_1 + m_2)^2}$$

and $$(a_{CM})_y = \left(\frac{m_2}{m_1 + m_2}\right)^2 g$$

4. (A) To just change direction of momentum, no work has to be done. e.g. uniform circular motion.

   (B) $\mathbf{F} = \frac{d\mathbf{P}}{dt}$

   (C) If particles have acceleration, then CM need not move along a straight line.

   (D) $\mathbf{P} = m\mathbf{v}_{CM}$, If $\mathbf{P}$ has fixed direction, then $\mathbf{v}_{CM}$ will also have fixed direction, so CM moves along a straight line.

5. (A) Velocity of CM will remain unchanged as explosion is due to internal forces.

   (B) From linear momentum conservation,

$$3m(0) = m\mathbf{v}_1 + 2m\mathbf{v}_2$$

$$\Rightarrow \quad \mathbf{v}_1 = -2\mathbf{v}_2$$

$$\Rightarrow \quad |\mathbf{v}_1| = 2|\mathbf{v}_2|$$

   (C) In centre of mass frame, total momentum is zero. So fragments have equal magnitude of momentum.

(D) Kinetic energy of system increases due to internal forces.

6. Let after the process of catching is over, final velocities are as shown.

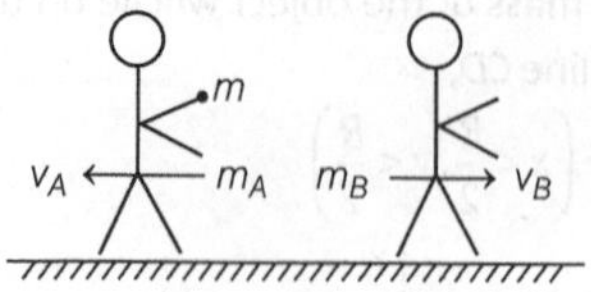

From linear momentum conservation for the entire system.

$$0 = -(m_A + m)v_A + m_B v_B$$

$$\Rightarrow \quad (m_A + m)v_A = m_B v_B \Rightarrow \frac{v_B}{v_A} = \frac{m_A + m}{m_B}$$

Since, $\quad m_A > m_B;\ v_B > v_A$

$$m_A v_A + m v_A = m_B v_B$$

$$\Rightarrow \quad P_A + m v_A = P_B$$

$$\Rightarrow \quad P_B > P_A$$

$$K = \frac{P^2}{2m}$$

Since, $\quad P_B > P_A$ and $m_B < m_A$

$$\Rightarrow \quad K_B > K_A$$

7. Let velocity of plank $= v_P$

$$v_{AP} = v_1 \Rightarrow v_A = v_1 + v_P$$

$$v_{BP} = -v_2 \Rightarrow v_B = -v_2 + v_P$$

From linear momentum conservation in horizontal,

$$0 = 20v_P + 40(v_1 + v_P) + 40(-v_2 + v_P)$$

$$\Rightarrow \quad 100v_P = 40(v_2 - v_1)$$

$$\Rightarrow \quad 100\left(\frac{20}{5}\right) = 40(v_2 - v_1) \Rightarrow v_2 - v_1 = 10$$

8. When the insect starts moving up relative to rod, the friction force between the insect and rod increases. This increased friction increases the tension in the string ($T' > Mg$). So, the system experiences a net force in upward direction. Hence, centre of mass of the system will accelerate in upward direction.

If the insect moves up with constant velocity, friction force on the insect equals weight of the insect, so net force on the (insect + rod + counter mass) system is zero and its acceleration will be zero.

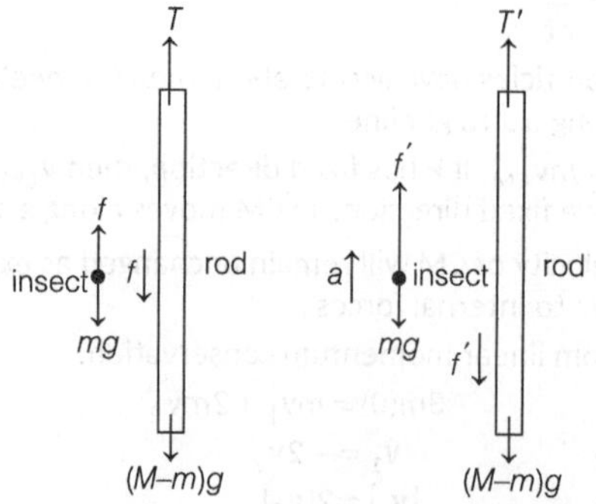

9. From linear momentum conservation in horizontal,

$$0 + 0 = Mv - mv_{man}$$

$$\Rightarrow \quad v_{man} = \frac{Mv}{m}$$

$$W_{man} = \Delta K_{system} = \frac{1}{2}Mv^2 + \frac{1}{2}m\left(\frac{Mv}{m}\right)^2$$

$$= \frac{1}{2}\left(\frac{M^2}{m} + M\right)v^2$$

$$\Delta E_{system} = \Delta K_{system} = \frac{1}{2}\left(\frac{M^2}{m} + M\right)v^2$$

Velocity of CM is zero as CM is initially at rest and there is no external force on the system.

$$\Delta K_{man} = \frac{1}{2}mv_{man}^2 = \frac{1}{2}m\left(\frac{Mv}{m}\right)^2 = \frac{1}{2}\frac{M^2}{m}v^2$$

10. Maximum friction force on insect $= \mu mg$

Maximum possible acceleration of insect $= \dfrac{\mu mg}{m} = \mu g$

Acceleration of stick $= -\dfrac{\mu mg}{M}$

$$a_{rel} = a_{insect} - a_{stick} = \mu g\left(1 + \frac{m}{M}\right)$$

$$s_{rel} = u_{rel}t + \frac{1}{2}a_{rel}t^2$$

$$\Rightarrow \quad L = 0 + \frac{1}{2}\mu g\left(1 + \frac{m}{M}\right)t^2$$

$$\Rightarrow \quad t = \sqrt{\frac{2ML}{\mu(M + m)g}}$$

Velocity of centre of mass is zero at any time

$$v_{stick} = u + at$$

$$\Rightarrow \quad v_{stick} = 0 + \left(\frac{\mu mg}{M}\right)\left[\sqrt{\frac{2ML}{\mu(M + m)g}}\right]$$

$$= \sqrt{\frac{2u L m^2 g}{(M + m)M}}$$

$$P_{insect} = \int F dt = (\mu mg)t$$

11. From linear momentum conservation in horizontal,

$$Mu - mu = (M + m)v$$

$$\Rightarrow \quad v = \left(\frac{M - m}{M + m}\right)u$$

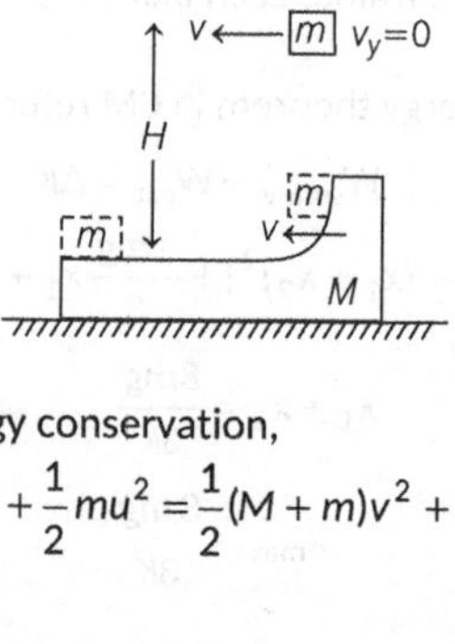

Applying energy conservation,

$$\frac{1}{2}Mu^2 + \frac{1}{2}mu^2 = \frac{1}{2}(M + m)v^2 + mgH$$

$$\Rightarrow \quad u = \sqrt{\frac{gH}{2}\left(1+\frac{m}{M}\right)} \Rightarrow u > \sqrt{\frac{gH}{2}}$$

Kinetic energy of the system when smaller block is at its highest point $= \frac{1}{2}(M+m)v^2$

$$= \frac{1}{2}(M+m)\left(\frac{M-m}{M+m}\right)u^2$$

$$= \frac{1}{2}(M+m)\left(\frac{M-m}{M+m}\right)\left[\frac{gH}{2}\left(\frac{M+m}{M}\right)\right]$$

$$= \frac{1}{4}(M-m)^2\frac{gH}{M}$$

12.

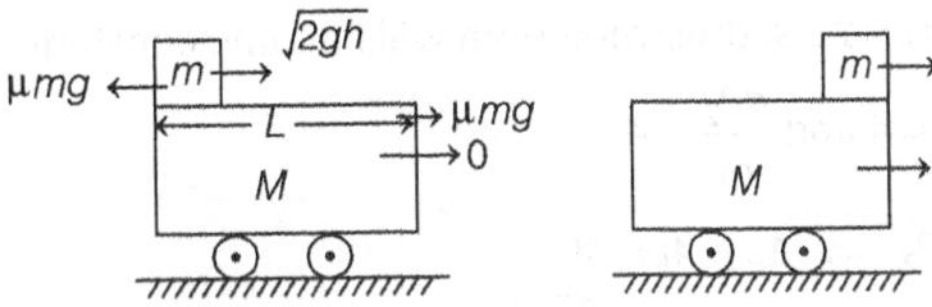

From linear momentum conservation in horizontal,

$$m\sqrt{2gh} + M(0) = (M+m)v$$

$$\Rightarrow \quad v = \frac{m\sqrt{2gh}}{M+m}$$

For block, $v = u + at$

$$\Rightarrow \quad \frac{m\sqrt{2gh}}{M+m} = \sqrt{2gh} + (-\mu g)t$$

$$\Rightarrow \quad t = \frac{M\sqrt{2gh}}{\mu g(M+m)}$$

Lets take displacement of cart to be x.

$$W_{friction} = -\mu mg\,(L+x) + \mu mg\,x = -\mu mgL$$

Net impulse on cart $= Mv_{cart} - 0 = M\left(\frac{m\sqrt{2gh}}{M+m}\right)$

13. $v_{man,\,block} = -v \Rightarrow v_{man} = -v + v_{block}$

Applying conservation of linear momentum,

$$0 + 0 = M(-v + v_{block}) + 2Mv_{block}$$

$$\Rightarrow \quad v_{block} = \frac{v}{3}$$

Right block will be at rest as long as spring is compressed. Right block will lose contact when the left block is moving left and spring acquires natural length.

Applying energy conservation,

$$\frac{1}{2}(2M)\left(\frac{v}{3}\right)^2 = \frac{1}{2}Kx_{max}^2$$

$$\Rightarrow \quad x_{max} = \sqrt{\frac{2M}{K}}\left(\frac{v}{3}\right)$$

$$v_{CM} = \frac{m_1v_1 + m_2v_2}{m_1+m_2} = \frac{2M\left(\frac{v}{3}\right)+0}{4M} = \frac{v}{6}$$

14. External force on the system is zero. So, linear momentum will be conserved in the ground frame.

Momentum of a system in the frame attached to CM is always zero.

Since, v_C is constant, $\frac{1}{2}(m_1+m_2)v_C^2$ is always constant.

Kinetic energy in centre of mass frame is not constant due to work done by spring force on the system.

15. Let velocities of block and cart be v_1 and v_2 when block loses contact with the left spring.

Applying linear momentum conservation,

$$0 + 0 = mv_1 + M(-v_2) \Rightarrow v_2 = \frac{mv_1}{M}$$

Applying energy conservation,

$$K_1 + U_1 = K_2 + U_2$$

$$\Rightarrow \quad (0+0) + \frac{1}{2}Kx_0^2 = \left(\frac{1}{2}mv_1^2 + \frac{1}{2}Mv_2^2\right) + 0$$

$$\Rightarrow \quad v_1 = \sqrt{\frac{KMx_0^2}{(M+m)m}}$$

and $$v_2 = \frac{m}{M}\sqrt{\frac{KMx_0^2}{(M+m)m}}$$

Time taken to travel distance $L = \frac{L}{v_{rel}} = \frac{L}{v_1+v_2}$

$$= \sqrt{\frac{mML^2}{K(M+m)x_0^2}}$$

Applying energy conservation in CM reference frame to find maximum compression in the right spring.

$$K_1 + U_1 = K_2 + U_2$$

$$\Rightarrow \quad \frac{1}{2}\mu v_{real}^2 + 0 = 0 + \frac{1}{2}(4K)x_{max}^2$$

$$\Rightarrow \quad \frac{1}{2}\frac{Mm}{M+m}(v_1+v_2)^2 = \frac{1}{2}(4K)x_{max}^2$$

$$\Rightarrow \quad x_{max} = \frac{x_0}{2}$$

$$s_{block,\,cart} = x_0 + L + \frac{x_0}{2} = \frac{3x_0}{2} + L$$

$$\Rightarrow \quad s_{block} = \left(\frac{3x_0}{2} + L\right) + s_{cart}$$

$$s_{CM} = \frac{m_1s_1 + m_2s_2}{m_1+m_2}$$

$$0 = \frac{m\left[\left(\frac{3x_0}{2}+L\right) + s_{cart}\right] + Ms_{cart}}{M+m}$$

$$\Rightarrow \quad s_{cart} = \frac{m(3x_0+2L)}{2(M+m)}$$

Comprehension Based Questions

1. Applying linear momentum conservation for the system,

$$+0+0=(8m)(2v)+(16m)(-v)+(48m)v_{bar}$$

$$\Rightarrow \quad v_{bar}=0$$

So, displacement of bar when the insects meet is zero.

2. $v_{spider,\ bar}=-\frac{v}{2}\Rightarrow v_{spider}=-\frac{v}{2}+v_{bar}$

Applying conservation of linear momentum,

$$0+0=24m\left(-\frac{v}{2}+v_{bar}\right)+48m\ v_{bar}$$

$$v_{bar}=\frac{v}{6}$$

3. $s_{CM}=0$

$$\Rightarrow \quad \frac{24m(-8L+s_{bar})+48m\ s_{bar}}{72m}=0$$

$$\Rightarrow \quad s_{bar}=\frac{8L}{3}$$

4. Applying conservation of linear momentum when A rolls the ball for the first time,

$0+0=40v_A+4(5)\Rightarrow v_A=-0.5$ m/s

Applying conservation of linear momentum when A catches the ball for the first time

$$40(-0.5)+4(-5)=(40+4)v_A'$$

$$v_A'=-\frac{40}{44}=-\frac{10}{11}\text{ m/s}$$

5. In one round trip momentum imparted to $B=20-(-20)$

$$=40\text{ kgm/s}$$

In 5 round trips, momentum imparted to B

$$=40\times 5=200\text{ kg-m/s}$$

Now, $200=40v_B\Rightarrow v_B=5$ m/s

Similarly for A,

$$200=(40+4)v_A\Rightarrow v_A=\frac{50}{11}\text{ m/s}$$

6. After n round trips, $v_A=\frac{40n}{44}=\frac{10n}{11}$

For A to be able to catch the ball,

$$\frac{10n}{11}<5\Rightarrow n<5.5$$

So, A can roll the ball 6 times but he can't catch the fall sixth time as his speed will be greater than speed of ball.

7. CM of the system will not move. So

$$x_{CM}=\frac{m_1x_1+m_2x_2+m_3x_3}{m_1+m_2+m_3}$$

$$=\frac{40(0)+4(0)+40d}{40+4+40}=\frac{10d}{21}$$

8. $f_k=\mu mg=0.4\times 1\times 10=4$ N

For 1 kg, $\Sigma F=ma\Rightarrow -4=1a_1$

$$\Rightarrow \quad a_1=-4\text{ m/s}^2$$

For 2 kg, $\Sigma F=ma\Rightarrow 4=2a_2$

$$\Rightarrow \quad a_2=2\text{ m/s}^2$$

$$v=u+at\Rightarrow v_1=15-4t$$

and $$v_2=2t$$

$$P_1=m_1v_1=15-4t$$

$$P_2=m_2v_2=4t$$

From linear momentum conservation,

$$1\times 15+2\times 0=(2+1)v$$

$$v=5\text{ m/s}$$

When their velocity becomes 5 m/s, kinetic friction will stop acting.

$$v_1=v_2=5\text{ m/s}$$

$$\Rightarrow \quad 2t=5\Rightarrow t=2.5\text{ s}$$

After $t=2.5$ s, their momenta will become constant.

9. $\left|\frac{dP_1}{dt}\right|=4$ and $\frac{dP_2}{dt}=4$

10. $P_1=P_2\Rightarrow 15-4t=4t$

$$t=\frac{15}{8}=1.875\text{ s}$$

11.

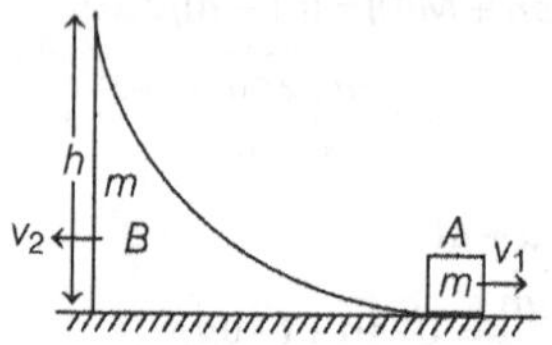

Applying linear momentum conservation for $(A+B)$ system in horizontal,

$$0+0=-mv_2+mv_1\Rightarrow v_1=v_2 \quad \text{... (i)}$$

Applying energy conservation for $(A+B)$ system

$$K_1+U_1=K_2+U_2$$

$$\Rightarrow \quad (0+0)+mgh=\left(\frac{1}{2}mv_1^2+\frac{1}{2}mv_2^2\right)+0$$

$$\Rightarrow \quad v_1^2+v_2^2=2gh \quad \text{... (ii)}$$

Solving Eqs. (i) and (ii), we get

$$v_1=v_2=\sqrt{gh}$$

12. When A reaches maximum height on wedge C, velocity of A w.r.t. C will be zero.

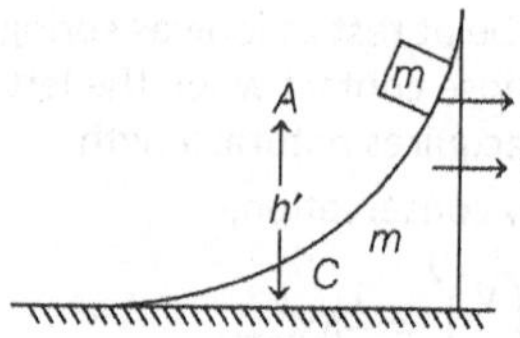

Applying linear momentum conservation for $(A+C)$ system in horizontal

$$m\sqrt{gh}+0=(m+m)v_3$$

$$\Rightarrow \quad v_3=\frac{1}{2}\sqrt{gh}$$

Applying energy conservation for $(A+C)$ system

$$K_1+U_1=K_2+U_2$$

$$\frac{1}{2}m(\sqrt{gh})^2 + 0 = \frac{1}{2}(2m)\left(\frac{\sqrt{gh}}{2}\right)^2 + mgh'$$

$$\Rightarrow \quad h' = \frac{h}{4}$$

13.

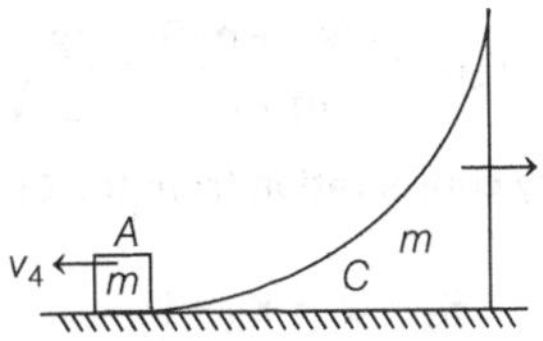

Applying linear momentum conservation for $(A + C)$ system in horizontal

$$m\sqrt{gh} + 0 = -mv_4 + mv_5$$

$$\Rightarrow \quad v_5 - v_4 = \sqrt{gh} \qquad \text{... (i)}$$

Applying energy conservation for $(A + C)$ system

$$K_1 + U_1 = K_2 + U_2$$

$$\left[\frac{1}{2}m(\sqrt{gh})^2 + 0\right] + 0 = \left(\frac{1}{2}mv_4^2 + \frac{1}{2}mv_5^2\right) + 0$$

$$v_4^2 + v_5^2 = gh \qquad \text{... (ii)}$$

Solving Eqs. (i) and (ii), we get

$$v_4 = 0 \text{ and } v_5 = \sqrt{gh}$$

14. $(s_{\text{block, ring}})_x = -l(1 - \sin 37°) = -\frac{2l}{5}$

$$(s_{\text{block}})_x = -\frac{2l}{5} + s_{\text{ring}}$$

$$(s_{CM})_x = \frac{m_1 s_1 + m_2 s_2}{m_1 + m_2}$$

$$\Rightarrow \quad 0 = \frac{ms_{\text{ring}} + 2m\left(-\frac{2l}{5} + s_{\text{ring}}\right)}{3m}$$

$$\Rightarrow \quad s_{\text{ring}} = \frac{4l}{15}$$

15. Velocity of ring will be maximum when string becomes vertical.

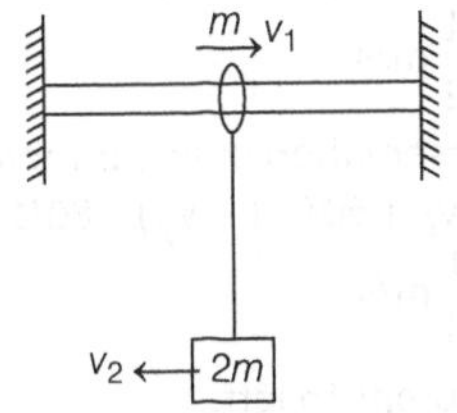

Applying linear momentum conservation for the system in horizontal.

$$0 + 0 = mv_1 + 2m(-v_2)$$

$$\Rightarrow \quad v_1 = 2v_2 \qquad \text{... (i)}$$

Applying energy conservation

$$K_1 + U_1 = K_2 + U_2$$

$$(0 + 0) + 2mgl = \left[\frac{1}{2}mv_1^2 + \frac{1}{2}(2m)v_2^2\right] + 0$$

$$v_1^2 + 2v_2^2 = 4gl \qquad \text{... (ii)}$$

Solving Eqs. (i) and (ii), we get

$$v_1 = \sqrt{\frac{8gl}{3}}$$

16. Block is going in circular motion w.r.t. the ring.

$$T - 2mg = \frac{(2m)v_{\text{rel}}^2}{l}$$

$$\Rightarrow \quad T - 2mg = \frac{(2m)(v_1 + v_2)^2}{l}$$

$$\Rightarrow \quad T - 2mg = 12mg$$

$$\Rightarrow \quad T = 14mg$$

17.

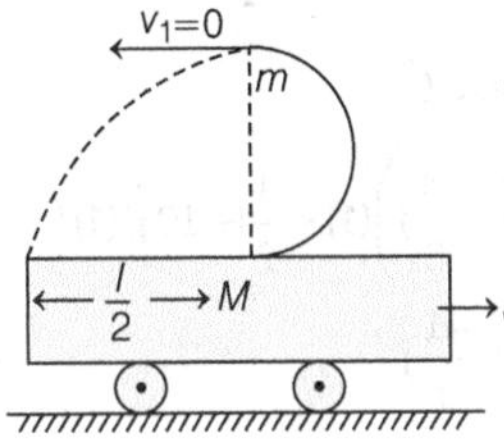

$$s_y = u_y t + \frac{1}{2}a_y t^2 \Rightarrow 2R = \frac{1}{2}gT^2$$

$$\Rightarrow \quad T = \sqrt{\frac{4R}{g}}$$

At the highest point

$$mg + N_A = \frac{mv_{\text{rel}}^2}{R}$$

$$\Rightarrow \quad v_{\text{rel}} = \sqrt{gR}$$

$\because$ $[N_A = 0$ for v_{rel} to be minimum$]$

In horizontal,

$$s_{\text{rel}} = U_{\text{rel}}t + \frac{1}{2}a_{\text{rel}}t^2$$

$$\Rightarrow \quad \frac{l}{2} = (\sqrt{gR})\sqrt{\frac{4R}{g}}$$

$$\Rightarrow \quad l = 4R$$

18. $v_{\text{rel}} = v_2 - v_1 \Rightarrow \sqrt{gR} = v_2 - 0$

$$\Rightarrow \quad v_2 = \sqrt{gR}$$

Applying linear momentum conservation,

$$m\sqrt{2gh} = Mv_2$$

$$\Rightarrow \quad m\sqrt{2gh} = M\sqrt{gR}$$

$$\Rightarrow \quad h = \frac{1}{2}\left(\frac{M}{m}\right)^2 R$$

19. Applying energy conservation,

$$mgh = mg(2R) + \frac{1}{2}Mv_2^2$$

$$\Rightarrow \quad mg\frac{1}{2}\left(\frac{M}{m}\right)^2 R = mg(2R) + \frac{1}{2}M(\sqrt{gR})^2$$

$$\Rightarrow \quad \left(\frac{M}{m}\right)^2 = 4 + \left(\frac{M}{m}\right) \Rightarrow \left(\frac{M}{m}\right)^2 - \left(\frac{M}{m}\right) - 4 = 0$$

$$\Rightarrow \quad \frac{M}{m} = \frac{1+\sqrt{17}}{2}$$

20. $\mathbf{P}_1 = (10)\cos 37°\,\hat{\mathbf{i}} + 1(10)\sin 37°\,\hat{\mathbf{j}} + 2(5\sqrt{2})\cos 45°\,\hat{\mathbf{i}} + 2(5\sqrt{2})\sin 45°(-\hat{\mathbf{j}})$

$$= 18\hat{\mathbf{i}} - 4\hat{\mathbf{j}}$$

$$\Delta \mathbf{P} = \mathbf{F}_{\text{ext}}\Delta t$$

$$\Rightarrow \mathbf{P}_2 - (18\hat{\mathbf{i}} - 4\hat{\mathbf{j}}) = -(1g + 2g)(2)\hat{\mathbf{j}}$$

$$\Rightarrow \quad \mathbf{P}_2 = 18\hat{\mathbf{i}} - 64\hat{\mathbf{j}}$$

21. $\mathbf{S}_{\text{CM}} = \mathbf{u}_{\text{rel}}t + \frac{1}{2}\mathbf{a}_{\text{CM}}t^2$

$$\Rightarrow \mathbf{r} - 20\hat{\mathbf{j}} = \left(6\hat{\mathbf{i}} - \frac{4}{3}\hat{\mathbf{j}}\right)(1) + \frac{1}{2}(-10\hat{\mathbf{j}})(1)^2$$

$$\Rightarrow \quad \mathbf{r} = 6\hat{\mathbf{i}} + \frac{41}{3}\hat{\mathbf{j}}$$

22. $F_{\text{ext}} = Ma_{\text{CM}} \Rightarrow F = (2m)\,a_{\text{CM}}$

$$\Rightarrow \quad a_{\text{CM}} = \frac{F}{2m}$$

$$s_{\text{CM}} = u_{\text{CM}}t + \frac{1}{2}a_{\text{CM}}t^2 = 0 + \frac{1}{2}\left(\frac{F}{2m}\right)t^2 = \frac{Ft^2}{4m}$$

23. and **24.** Suppose the displacement of first block and second block be x_1 and x_2 respectively.

$$x_1 - x_2 = x_0 \quad \text{...(i)}$$

$$S_{\text{CM}} = \frac{mx_1 + mx_2}{2} = \frac{Ft^2}{4m}$$

$$\Rightarrow \quad x_1 + x_2 = \frac{Ft^2}{2m} \quad \text{... (ii)}$$

Solving Eqs. (i) and (ii), we get

$$x_1 = \frac{1}{2}\left(\frac{Ft^2}{2m} + x_0\right),\ x_2 = \frac{1}{2}\left(\frac{Ft^2}{2m} - x_0\right)$$

25.

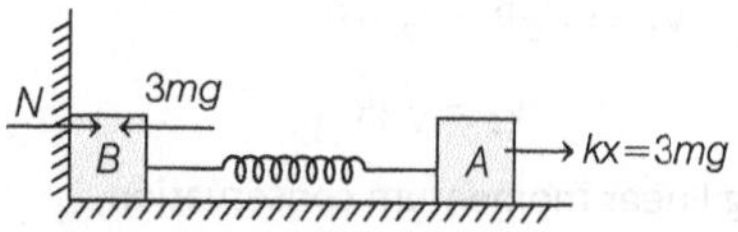

B will remain at rest as long as the spring is compressed.

So, $\quad a_B = 0,\ a_A = \frac{3mg}{m} = 3g$

$$a_{\text{CM}} = \frac{m(3g) + m(0)}{2m} = \frac{3g}{2}$$

26. Block B will lose contact when spring acquires natural length.

Applying energy conservation,

$$\frac{1}{2}K\left(\frac{3mg}{K}\right)^2 = \frac{1}{2}mv_A^2$$

$$v_A = 3g\sqrt{\frac{m}{K}}$$

$$v_{\text{CM}} = \frac{mv_A + m(0)}{m+m} = \frac{3g}{2}\sqrt{\frac{m}{K}}$$

27. Applying energy conservation from the CM reference frame,

$$K_1 + U_1 = K_2 + U_2$$

$$\Rightarrow \quad \frac{1}{2}\left[\frac{m(m)}{m+m}\right]\left(3g\sqrt{\frac{m}{K}} - 0\right)^2 = 0 + \frac{1}{2}Kx_{\max}^2$$

$$\Rightarrow \quad x_{\max} = \frac{3mg}{\sqrt{2K}}$$

Match the Columns Questions

1. $s_{AP} = +2 \Rightarrow s_A - s_P = 2$

$$\Rightarrow \quad s_A = 2 + s_P$$

$$s_{BP} = -2$$

$$\Rightarrow \quad s_B - s_P = -2$$

$$\Rightarrow \quad s_B = -2 + s_P$$

$$s_{\text{CM}} = \frac{m_1s_1 + m_2s_2 + m_3s_3}{m_1 + m_2 + m_3}$$

$$\Rightarrow \quad 0 = \frac{50(2+s_p) + 70(-2+s_p) + 80s_p}{50 + 80 + 70}$$

$$\Rightarrow \quad s_p = 0.2 \text{ m}$$

$$s_A = 2 + 0.2 = 2.2 \text{ m}$$

$$s_B = -2 + 0.2 = -1.8 \text{ m}$$

2. (A) $v_{RP} = -1 \Rightarrow v_R = -1 + v_P$

Applying conservation of linear momentum,

$$0 = 60(-1 + v_P) + 100\,v_P \Rightarrow v_p = \frac{3}{8}\text{ m/s}$$

(B) $v_{sp} = 1 \Rightarrow v_s = 1 + v_p$

Applying conservation of linear momentum,

$$0 = 80(1 + v_p) + 80\,v_p$$

$$\Rightarrow \quad v_P = -\frac{1}{2}\text{ m/s}$$

(C) Applying conservation of linear momentum,

$$0 = 20v_P + 60(-1 + v_p) + 80(1 + v_p)$$

$$\Rightarrow \quad v_P = -\frac{1}{8}\text{ m/s}$$

(D) When Ram jumps to left,

$$0 = 60(-1 + v_p) + 100\,v_p$$

$$\Rightarrow \quad v_p = \frac{3}{8}\text{ m/s}$$

Now, when Shyam jumps to right,

$$100\left(\frac{3}{8}\right) = 80(1 + v_p') + 20v_p'$$

$$\Rightarrow \quad v_p' = \frac{-17}{40}\text{ m/s}$$

3. (A) In this case, there is net momentum towards left which is not possible.

(B) In this case, there is net momentum in vertical which is not possible.

(C) $m_1v_1 - m_2v_2 = (m_1 + m_2)v$

$\Rightarrow \quad m_1v_1 > m_2v_2$

$\Rightarrow \quad m_1 > m_2 \quad [\because v_1 < v_2]$

(D) $m_1v_1 \cos\alpha + m_2v_2 \cos\beta = (m_1 + m_2)v$

$m_1v_1 \sin\alpha = m_2v_2 \sin\beta$

So, all three possibilities are there i.e.

$m_1 > m_2,\ m_1 = m_2$ and $m_1 < m_2$

4. (A) Centre of mass is initially at rest and net external force is in downward direction. So, the centre of mass will shift downwards.

(B) Due to gravity, centre of mass will shift downwards. The pulley exerts a force on string which has a horizontal component towards right, so the centre of mass will also shift towards right.

(C) Both block and monkey move up. So CM will shift upwards.

(D) The system is in equilibrium. So centre of mass will not shift.

5.

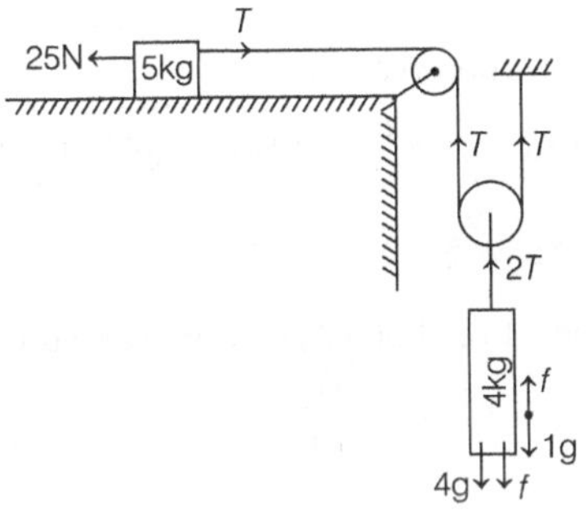

$$t_0 = \frac{1}{2}\,s$$

Since the system is in equilibrium, mass of cat will be 1 kg

For cat, $f - 1g = a_1$ ... (i)

For rod, $4g + f - 2T = 4a_2$ ... (ii)

For block; $T - 25 = 5(2a_2)$ ... (iii)

Solving Eqs. (i), (ii) and (iii)

$$a_1 = 24a_2$$

So, average velocity will have same relation.

$$v_1 = 24v_2$$

Relative velocity of cat w.r.t. rod

$$v_1 + v_2 = 2 \text{ m/s}$$

$$\Rightarrow \quad v_1 = \frac{48}{25} \text{ m/s and } v_2 = \frac{2}{25} \text{ m/s}$$

(A) $\tan\phi = \dfrac{M_{cat}\,y_{cat}}{M_{block}x_{block}} = \dfrac{1 \times \left(\frac{48}{25}t_0\right)}{5 \times \left(\frac{4}{25}t_0\right)} = \dfrac{12}{5}$

(B) $x_{block} = \left(\frac{4}{25}\right)t_0 = \left(\frac{4}{25}\right)\left(\frac{1}{2}\right) = \frac{2}{25}$ m

(C) $y_{CM} = \dfrac{1 \times \frac{48}{25}\left(\frac{1}{2}\right) - 4\left(\frac{2}{25}\right)\left(\frac{1}{2}\right) + 5(0)}{10} = \dfrac{2}{25}$ m

(D) Horizontal displacement of (block + rod)

$$= \frac{5 \times \frac{4}{25} \times \frac{1}{2} + 4 \times 0}{9} = \frac{2}{45} \text{ m}$$

6. (A) $v_{CM} = \dfrac{2(2) + 2(0)}{2 + 2} = 1$ m/s

(B) v_{CM} is constant.

(C) Applying energy conservation in CM reference frame,

$$\frac{1}{2}\left[\frac{2(2)}{2+2}\right](2-0)^2 = \frac{1}{2}(4)x_{max}^2$$

$$x_{max} = 1 \text{ m}$$

(D) $U_{max} = \dfrac{1}{2}Kx_{max}^2 = \dfrac{1}{2}(4)(1)^2 = 2$ J

Numerical Value Questions

1. For a sector, $x_{CM} = \dfrac{4R\sin\left(\frac{\theta}{2}\right)}{3\theta}$

For an arc, $x_{CM} = \dfrac{2R\sin\left(\frac{\theta}{2}\right)}{\theta}$

$$x_{CM} = \frac{m_1x_1 + m_2x_2}{m_1 + m_2}$$

$$\Rightarrow \quad 0 = \frac{m\left[\dfrac{4R_1\sin\left(\frac{\theta}{2}\right)}{3\theta}\right] + m\left[\dfrac{-2R_2\sin\left(\frac{\theta}{2}\right)}{\theta}\right]}{m + m}$$

$$\Rightarrow \quad R_2 = \frac{2R_1}{3} = 8 \text{ cm}$$

2. $y_{CM} = \dfrac{m_1y_1 - m_2y_2}{m_1 - m_2}$

$$\Rightarrow \quad a = \frac{(\sigma l^2)\left(\frac{l}{2}\right) - (\sigma a^2)\left(\frac{a}{2}\right)}{\sigma l^2 - \sigma a^2}$$

$$\Rightarrow \quad l^3 - a^3 = 2a(l^2 - a^2)$$

$$\Rightarrow \quad (l-a)(l^2 + a^2 + al) = 2a(l+a)(l-a)$$

$$\Rightarrow \quad l^2 - al - a^2 = 0$$

$$\Rightarrow \quad \left(\frac{a}{l}\right)^2 + \left(\frac{a}{l}\right) - 1 = 0$$

$$\Rightarrow \quad \frac{a}{l} = \frac{\sqrt{5} - 1}{2}$$

3. $s_{AC} = +10 \Rightarrow s_A - s_C = 10$

$\Rightarrow \quad s_A = (10 + s_C)$

$(s_B)_x = (s_C)_x$

$$(s_{CM})_x = \frac{m_1 s_1 + m_2 s_2 + m_3 s_3}{m_1 + m_2 + m_3}$$

$$\Rightarrow \quad 0 = \frac{1(10 + s_C) + 1 s_C + 3 s_C}{5}$$

$\Rightarrow \quad s_C = -2$ cm

4. When dog jumps from B to A.

$20 v_1 = 4 v_2$ ... (i)

$v_1 + v_2 = 6$ ...(ii)

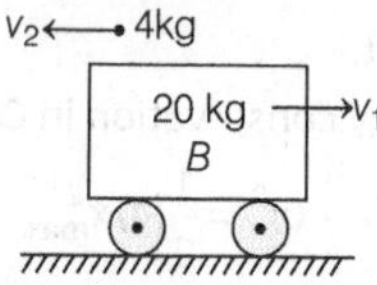

So, we get $v_1 = 1$ m/s and $v_2 = 5$ m/s

When dog lands on A,

$4 \times 5 = (20 + 4) v_3$

$$v_3 = \frac{5}{6} \text{ m/s}$$

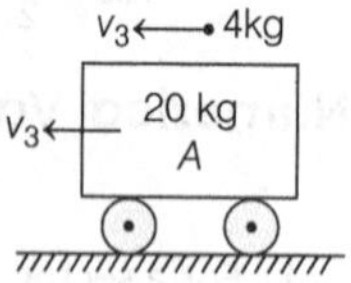

When dog jumps from A to B,

$v_A + v_4 = 6$

$24 v_3 = 20 v_A - 4 v_4$

So, we get

$$v_A = \frac{11}{6} \text{ m/s}, \ v_4 = \frac{25}{6} \text{ m/s}$$

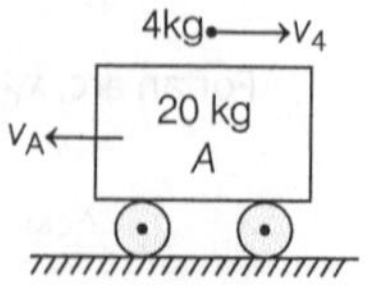

When dog lands on B,

$$20 \times 1 + 4\left(\frac{25}{6}\right) = 24 v_B$$

$$v_B = \frac{55}{36} \text{ m/s}$$

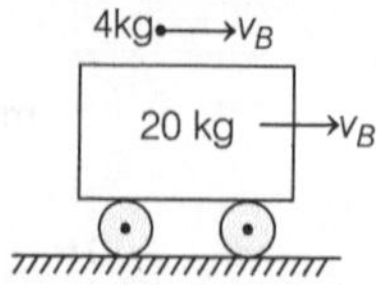

Now, $\frac{6 v_B}{5 v_A} = 1$

5. From linear momentum conservation for $(A + B + C)$ system in horizontal,

$3(10) = (3 + 2 + 1)v$

$\Rightarrow \quad v = 5$ m/s

$W_{friction} = -$ Loss in KE of $(A + B + C)$ system

$$= -\left[\frac{1}{2} \times 3 \times (10)^2 - \frac{1}{2}(3 + 2 + 1)(5)^2\right]$$

$= -(150 - 75) = -75$ J

6. Let velocities of fragments be v_1 and v_2 after explosion. Applying linear momentum conservation at the highest point

$5(20 \cos 60°) = 1 v_1 + 4 v_2$

$\Rightarrow \quad v_1 + 4 v_2 = 50$ ... (i)

$K_2 = 2K_1$

$$\Rightarrow \frac{1}{2} \times 1 \times v_1^2 + \frac{1}{2} \times 4 \times v_2^2 = 2\left[\frac{1}{2} \times 5 \times (10)^2\right]$$

$\Rightarrow \quad v_1^2 + 4 v_2^2 = 1000$ ... (ii)

On solving Eqs. (i) and (ii), we get

$v_1 = 30$ m/s and $v_2 = 5$ m/s

$$t = \text{Time taken to reach maximum height} = \frac{u \sin\theta}{g}$$

$$= \frac{20 \sin 60°}{10} = \sqrt{3} \text{ s}$$

Separation between the two fragment on ground

$= (v_1 - v_2)t$

$= (30 - 5)\sqrt{3} = 25\sqrt{3}$ m

7.

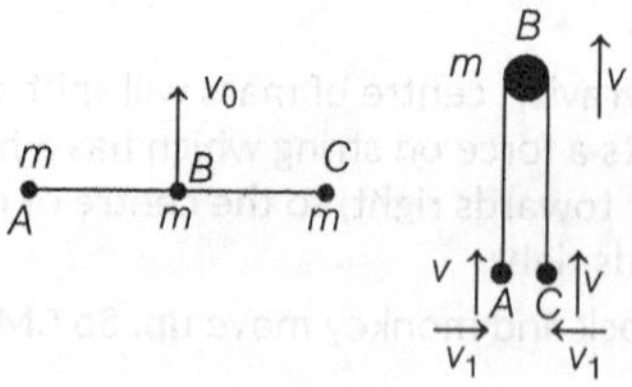

From momentum conservation,

$$m v_0 = mv + mv + mv \Rightarrow v = \frac{v_0}{3}$$

From energy conservation

$$\frac{1}{2} m v_0^2 = \frac{1}{2} m v^2 + \frac{1}{2} m\left(\sqrt{v^2 + v_1^2}\right)^2 + \frac{1}{2} m\left(\sqrt{v^2 + v_1^2}\right)^2$$

$$\Rightarrow \quad v_1 = \frac{v_0}{\sqrt{3}}$$

With respect to B, A and C go in circular motion.

$$a_B = \frac{2T}{m}$$

FBD of A,

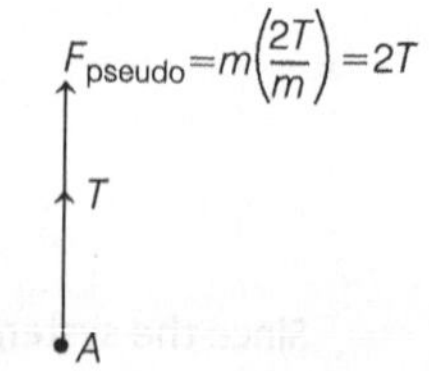

$$2T + T = \frac{m v_1^2}{l} \Rightarrow 3T = \frac{m v_0^2}{3l}$$

$$\Rightarrow \quad T = \frac{m v_0^2}{9l} = 1 \text{ N}$$

8. Using energy conservation in CM reference frame,

$K_1 + U_1 = K_2 + U_2$

$$0 + mgR = \frac{1}{2}\left(\frac{Mm}{M + m}\right) v_{rel}^2 + 0$$

$$\Rightarrow \quad v_{rel} = \sqrt{\frac{2(M + m) gR}{M}}$$

For the body, $N - mg = \frac{m v_{rel}^2}{R}$

$$\Rightarrow \quad \frac{7mg}{2} - mg = \frac{m}{R}\left[\frac{2(M + m)gR}{M}\right]$$

$$\Rightarrow \quad \frac{M}{m} = 4$$

9. $v_{boy, 4\,kg} = 7 \Rightarrow v_{boy} = 7 + v_{4\,kg}$

Using linear momentum conservation,

$$0 + 0 = 4v_{4\,kg} + 10(7 + v_{4\,kg})$$

$$v_{4\,kg} = -5 \text{ m/s}$$

Velocity of 1 kg will be maximum when spring again acquires natural length,

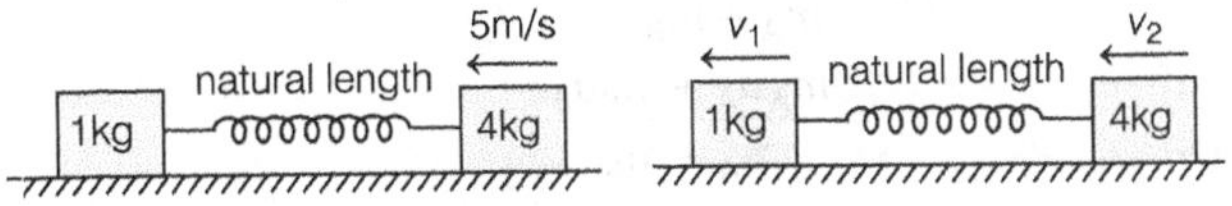

$$4 \times 5 + 1 \times 0 = 1v_1 + 4v_2$$

$$v_1 + 4v_2 = 20 \quad \text{... (i)}$$

$$\frac{1}{2} \times 4 \times 5^2 = \frac{1}{2} \times 1 \times v_1^2 + \frac{1}{2} \times 4 \times v_2^2$$

$$v_1^2 + 4v_2^2 = 100 \quad \text{... (ii)}$$

Solving Eqs. (i) and (ii), we get

$$v_1 = 8 \text{ m/s}$$

and $\quad v_2 = 3$ m/s

10.

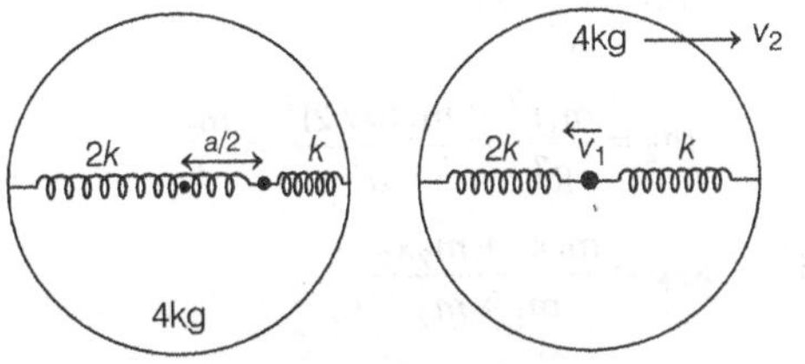

Using linear momentum conservation,

$$0 + 0 = 4v_2 + 1(-v_1)$$

$$\Rightarrow \quad v_1 = 4v_2 \quad \text{... (i)}$$

Using energy conservation

$$K_1 + U_1 = K_2 + U_2$$

$$\Rightarrow (0+0) + \left[\frac{1}{2}K\left(\frac{a}{2}\right)^2 + \frac{1}{2} \times 2K\left(\frac{a}{2}\right)^2\right]$$

$$= \left(\frac{1}{2} \times 1 \times v_1^2 + \frac{1}{2} \times 4 \times v_2^2\right) + (0+0)$$

$$\Rightarrow v_1^2 + 4v_2^2 = \frac{3Ka^2}{4}$$

$$\Rightarrow \quad v_1^2 + 4v_2^2 = 180 \quad \text{... (ii)}$$

Solving Eqs. (i) and (ii), we get

$$v_2 = 3 \text{ m/s}$$

11.

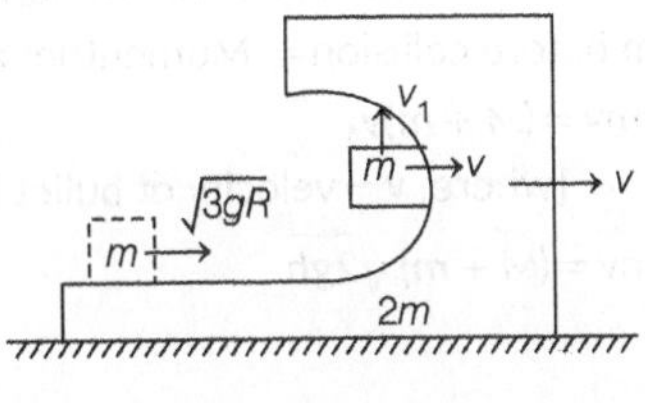

Applying linear momentum conservation in horizontal

$$m\sqrt{3gR} + 0 = (2m + m)v$$

$$\Rightarrow \quad v = \frac{\sqrt{3gR}}{3}$$

For the bigger block, $\Sigma F_x = ma_x$

$$N = 2ma$$

$$\Rightarrow \quad a = \frac{N}{2m}$$

Block is in circular motion w.r.t. the bigger block.

FBD of m,

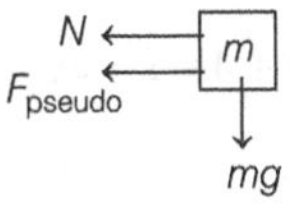

$$F_{pseudo} = m\left(\frac{N}{2m}\right) = \frac{N}{2}$$

$$N + \frac{N}{2} = \frac{mv_1^2}{R}$$

$$\Rightarrow \quad N = \frac{2mv_1^2}{3R}$$

Using energy conservation

$$\frac{1}{2}m(\sqrt{3gR})^2 = \frac{1}{2}(2m)v^2 + \frac{1}{2}m\left(\sqrt{v^2 + v_1^2}\right)^2 + mgR$$

$$\Rightarrow \quad v_1 = 0$$

So, $\quad N = 0$

Previous Years Questions

JEE Main

1. Linear momentum is conserved,

$$p_i = p_f$$

$$m_1 v_1 = m_2 v_2$$

$$1000 \times 6 = 1200 \times v_2$$

$$v_2 = 5 \text{ m/s}$$

2. $KE = \frac{1}{2}mv^2 = \frac{m^2v^2}{2m} = \frac{p^2}{2m}$

Given,

$$KE_1 = KE_2$$

So, $\quad \frac{p_1^2}{2m_1} = \frac{p_2^2}{2m_2}$

$$\Rightarrow \quad \frac{p_1}{p_2} = \sqrt{\frac{m_1}{m_2}}$$

$$\frac{p_1}{p_2} = \sqrt{\frac{4}{25}} = \frac{2}{5}$$

$$\Rightarrow \quad \frac{p_1}{p_2} = \frac{2}{5}$$

3. $$\mathbf{r}_{CM} = \frac{m_1\mathbf{r}_1 + m_2\mathbf{r}_2}{m_1 + m_2}$$

$$\Rightarrow \quad \mathbf{r}_{CM} = \frac{1(\hat{\mathbf{i}}+2\hat{\mathbf{j}}+\hat{\mathbf{k}})+3(-3\hat{\mathbf{i}}-2\hat{\mathbf{j}}+\hat{\mathbf{k}})}{4}$$

$$\Rightarrow \quad \mathbf{r}_{CM} = \frac{-8\hat{\mathbf{i}}-4\hat{\mathbf{j}}+4\hat{\mathbf{k}}}{4} = -2\hat{\mathbf{i}}-\hat{\mathbf{j}}+\hat{\mathbf{k}}$$

$$\therefore \quad |\mathbf{r}_{CM}| = \sqrt{(-2)^2+(-1)^2+(1)^2} = \sqrt{6}$$

Now, on checking option (a) we find the magnitude

$$= \sqrt{1^2+(-2)^2+(1)^2}$$

$$= \sqrt{1+4+1} = \sqrt{6}$$

4. Given, mass density,

$$\rho = \rho_0\left(1-\frac{x^2}{L^2}\right)\text{kg/m}$$

Mass of element, $dm = \rho dx = \rho_0\left(1-\frac{x^2}{L^2}\right)dx$

The distance of centre of mass is

$$x_{CM} = \frac{\int_0^L x\,dm}{\int_0^L dm} = \frac{\int_0^L \rho_0\left(1-\frac{x^2}{L^2}\right)x\,dx}{\int_0^L \rho_0\left(1-\frac{x^2}{L^2}\right)dx}$$

$$= \frac{L^2/4}{2L/3} = \frac{3L}{8} = \frac{3L}{\alpha} \quad \text{(Given)}$$

$$\therefore \quad \alpha = 8$$

5. The given situation is shown below.

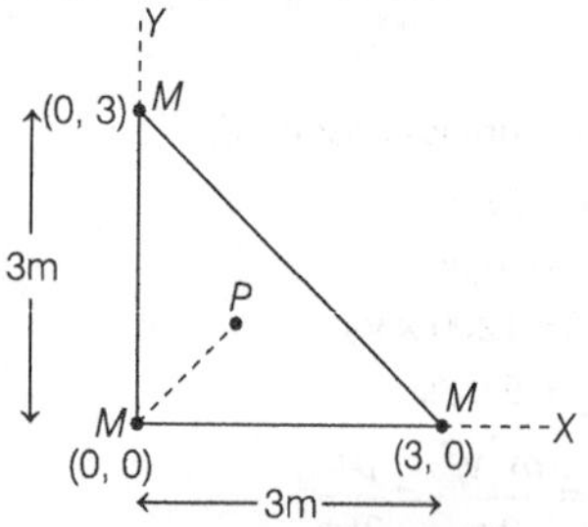

If $(\mathbf{X}_{CM}, \mathbf{Y}_{CM})$ be the positions of centre of mass, then

$$\mathbf{X}_{CM} = \frac{\mathbf{x}_1 m_1 + \mathbf{x}_2 m_2 + \mathbf{x}_3 m_3}{m_1+m_2+m_3}$$

$$= \frac{0\times m + 3\hat{\mathbf{i}}\times m + 0\times m}{m+m+m} = \hat{\mathbf{i}}$$

Similarly, $\mathbf{Y}_{CM} = \frac{\mathbf{y}_1 m_1 + \mathbf{y}_2 m_2 + \mathbf{y}_3 m_3}{m_1+m_2+m_3}$

$$= \frac{0\times m + 3\hat{\mathbf{j}}\times m + 0\times m}{3} = \hat{\mathbf{j}}$$

$\therefore$ Position vector of centre of mass,

$$\mathbf{OP} = \mathbf{X}_{CM} + \mathbf{Y}_{CM}$$

$$\mathbf{OP} = \hat{\mathbf{i}} + \hat{\mathbf{j}}$$

$\therefore$ Magnitude of position of centre of mass,

$$|\mathbf{OP}| = \sqrt{1^2+1^2} = \sqrt{2} = \sqrt{x} \quad \text{(given)}$$

$$\therefore \quad x = 2$$

6. Let a_{CM} be the acceleration of centre of mass of system and F be the applied force on spring.

$$\therefore \quad a_{CM} = \frac{F}{m_A + m_B}$$

$$= \frac{m_A a_A + m_B a_B}{m_A + m_B}$$

$$\Rightarrow \quad a_{CM} = \frac{F}{2M} = \frac{Ma_A + Ma_B}{2M} \quad (\because m_A = m_B = M)$$

$$\Rightarrow \quad a_B = \frac{F - Ma_A}{M} = \frac{F - Ma}{M}$$

7. Given, radius of hole, $r = a/2$

and radius of disc, $R = a$

Let x_{CM} be the centre of mass of system,

m_1, x_1 be the mass and centre of mass of disc

m_2, x_2 be the mass and centre of mass of circular hole.

$$\therefore \quad m_2 = \frac{m_1}{\pi R^2}\pi r^2$$

$$\Rightarrow \quad m_2 = \frac{m_1 r^2}{R^2} = \frac{m_1(a/2)^2}{a^2} = \frac{m_1}{4}$$

and $$x_{CM} = \frac{m_1x_1 + m_2x_2}{m_1+m_2}$$

$$\therefore \quad x_{CM} = \frac{m_1 a - (m_1/4)(3a/2)}{m_1 - (m_1/4)}$$

$$\Rightarrow \quad x_{CM} = \frac{5a}{6}$$

8. Given,

Mass of large block of wood, $M = 5.99$ kg

Mass of bullet, $m = 10$ g

Height at which their centre of mass rise, $h = 9.8$ cm

From the law of conservation of energy,

Energy of the system when bullet gets embedded = Energy of the system till it momentarily comes to rest.

$$\Rightarrow \quad \frac{1}{2}(M+m)v_1^2 = (M+m)gh$$

where, v_1 = velocity of bullet + block system

$$\Rightarrow \quad v_1 = \sqrt{2gh} \quad \text{... (i)}$$

According to law of conservation of momentum,

Momentum before collision = Momentum after collision.

$$\Rightarrow \quad mv = (M+m)v_1$$

[where, v = velocity of bullet before collision]

$$\Rightarrow \quad mv = (M+m)\sqrt{2gh} \quad \text{[using Eq. (i)]}$$

$$\Rightarrow \quad v = \left(\frac{M+m}{m}\right)\sqrt{2gh}$$

$$\Rightarrow \quad v = \frac{(5.99+0.01)}{10\times10^{-3}} \times \sqrt{2\times9.8\times9.8\times10^{-2}}$$

$$\Rightarrow \quad v = 831.55\ \text{ms}^{-1}$$

9. We can represent the given situation in figure as

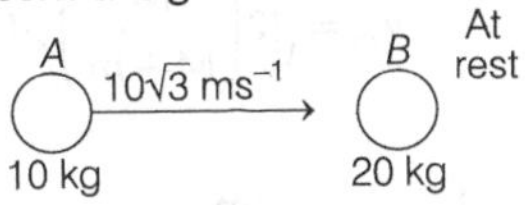

Before collision

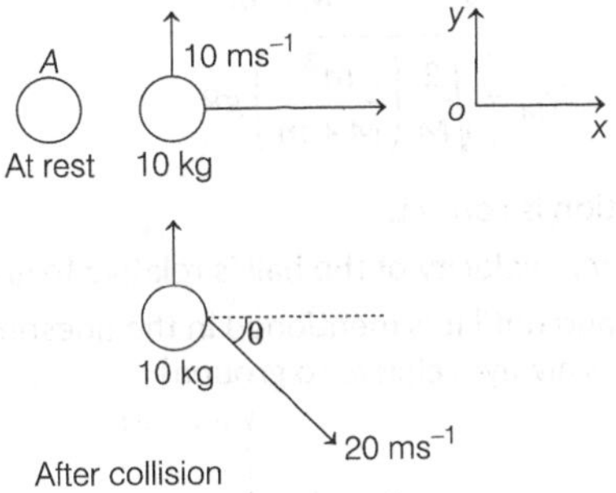

After collision

It means linear momentum is conserved along X-axis.

According to the law of conservation of linear momentum,

$$p_i = p_f$$

$$m_A u_A + m_B u_B = m_A v_A + (m_B v_B \cos\theta)$$

$$= m_A v_A + m_{B_1} v_{B_1} \cos 90° + m_{B_2} v_{B_2} \cos\theta$$

$$\Rightarrow 10\times10\sqrt{3} + 20\times0 = 10\times0 + 10\times10\times0 + 10\times20\cos\theta$$

$$\Rightarrow \quad 10\times10\sqrt{3} = 200\cos\theta$$

where, $\cos\theta$ being the horizontal component i.e., along X-axis

$$\Rightarrow \quad \cos\theta = \frac{\sqrt{3}}{2}$$

$$\Rightarrow \quad \theta = 30° \qquad [\because \cos 30° = \sqrt{3}/2]$$

10. Centre of mass of remaining portion is given by

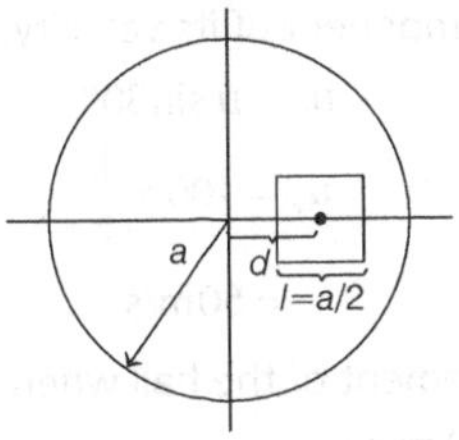

$$X_{CM} = \frac{m_1 x_1 - m_2 x_2}{m_1 - m_2}$$

Here note that, removed mass (m_2) is treated as a negative mass.

Let x = mass per unit area of uniform disc.

Then, m_1 = mass of complete disc $= x \cdot \pi a^2$

m_2 = mass of square portion $= x \cdot \dfrac{a^2}{4}$

Also,

x_1 = x-coordinate of centre of mass of $m_1 = 0$

x_2 = x - coordinate of centre of mass of $m_2 = d$

$$\Rightarrow \quad X_{CM} = \frac{x\pi a^2 \times 0 - x\dfrac{a^2}{4} \times d}{x\pi a^2 - x\dfrac{a^2}{4}} = \frac{-a}{2(4\pi - 1)} \qquad \text{...(i)}$$

$$\left[\text{Since}, d = \frac{a}{2}\right]$$

$$\text{Given,} \quad X_{CM} = -\frac{a}{X} \qquad \text{...(ii)}$$

Comparing the Eqs. (i) and (ii), we get

$$\therefore \quad X = 2(4\pi - 1) = 23.12 \quad \text{or } X \approx 23$$

11. The distance of centre of mass of a solid hemisphere from the centre of the flate surface is given by

$$d = \frac{3R}{8}$$

Here, $R = 8$ cm

$$\therefore \quad d = \frac{3\times8}{8} = 3 \text{ cm}$$

Given, $d = x$ cm

$\therefore$ $x = 3$

12. We choose origin as shown in the figure.

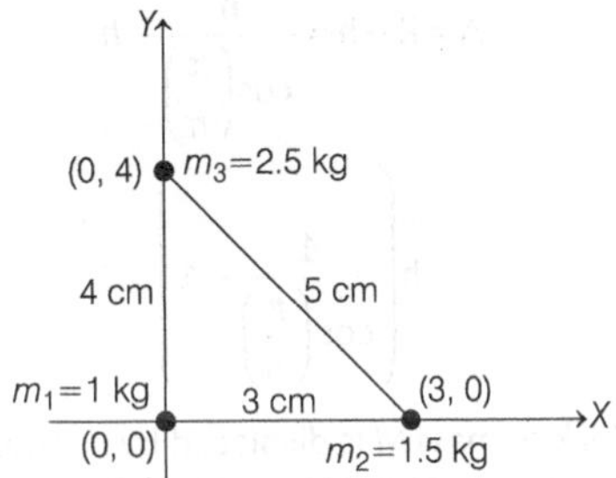

Using $x_{CM} = \dfrac{m_1 x_1 + m_2 x_2 + m_3 x_3}{m_1 + m_2 + m_3}$, we have

$$x_{CM} = \frac{1\times0 + 1.5\times3 + 2.5\times0}{1 + 1.5 + 2.5} = 0.9 \text{ cm}$$

Similarly,

$$y_{CM} = \frac{1\times0 + 1.5\times0 + 2.5\times4}{1 + 1.5 + 2.5} = 2.0 \text{ cm}$$

So, centre of mass (CM) is 0.9 cm right and 2.0 cm above 1 kg mass.

13. For a continuous mass distribution,

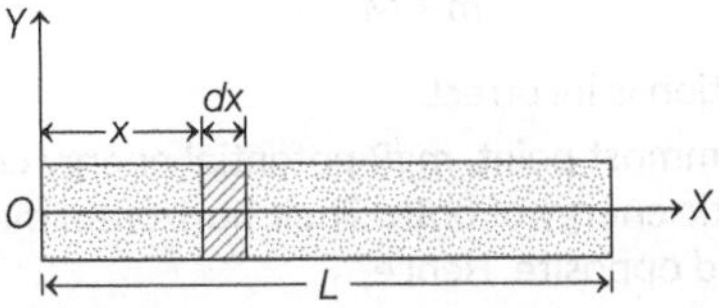

$$x_{CM} = \frac{\int x\,dm}{\int dm}$$

Here, mass of an elemental length dx of rod,

$$dm = \rho dx = \left(a + b\left(\frac{x}{L}\right)^2\right)dx$$

So, $$x_{CM} = \frac{\int_0^L x\left(a + \frac{bx^2}{L^2}\right)dx}{\int_0^L \left(a + \frac{bx^2}{L^2}\right)dx}$$

So, $x_{CM} = \frac{3}{4}\left(\frac{2a+b}{3a+b}\right)L$

JEE Advanced

1.

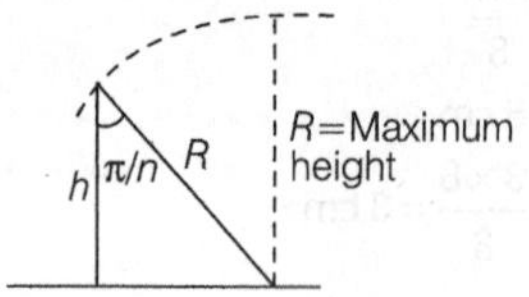

$$\cos\left(\frac{\pi}{n}\right) = \frac{h}{R}$$

$$\Delta = R - h = \frac{h}{\cos\left(\frac{\pi}{n}\right)} - h$$

$$= h\left(\frac{1}{\cos\left(\frac{\pi}{n}\right)} - 1\right)$$

2. Let the block of mass M is displaced by d. Then net displacement of mass m in horizontal direction will be $(d + R)$. In horizontal direction displacement of centre of mas will be zero. Hence,

$$\frac{dM + (d+R)m}{M+m} = 0$$

$$\Rightarrow \quad d = -\frac{mR}{M+m}$$

∴ (b) option is correct.

Position of the point mass at this instant is,

$$x = x_i + \text{displacement of } m$$
$$= -R + (d + R)$$
$$= d = -\frac{mR}{m+M}$$

∴ (c) option is incorrect.

At bottommost point, mgR potential energy converts into the kinetic energy of both. Their horizontal momenta are equal and opposite. Hence,

$$P_m = P_M \qquad \text{(magnitude wise)}$$

$$\therefore \quad \sqrt{2K_m m} = \sqrt{2K_M M}$$

or $$\frac{K_m}{K_M} = \frac{M}{m}$$

$$\therefore \quad K_m = \frac{1}{2}mv_m^2 = \frac{M}{M+m}(mgR)$$

or $$v_m = \sqrt{2\left(\frac{M}{M+m}\right)gR}$$

Similarly,

$$K_M = \frac{1}{2}Mv_M^2 = \frac{m}{M+m}(mgR)$$

$$\therefore \quad v_M = \sqrt{\frac{2}{M}\left(\frac{m^2}{M+m}\right)gR}$$

∴ (a) option is correct.

3. (a) 100 m/s velocity of the ball is relative to ground. [Unless and until it is mentioned in the question, the velocity is always relative to ground]

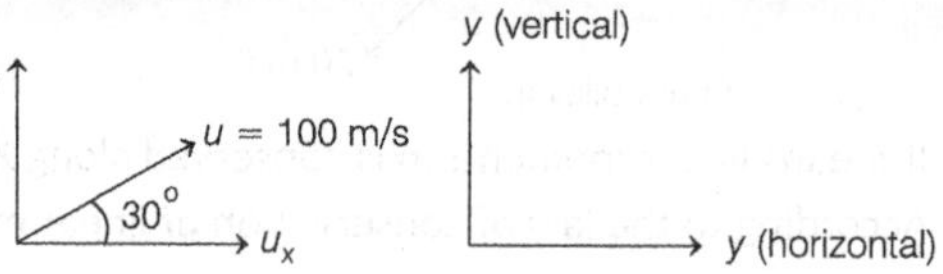

$a_x = 0$ and
$a_y = -g = -10$ m/s²

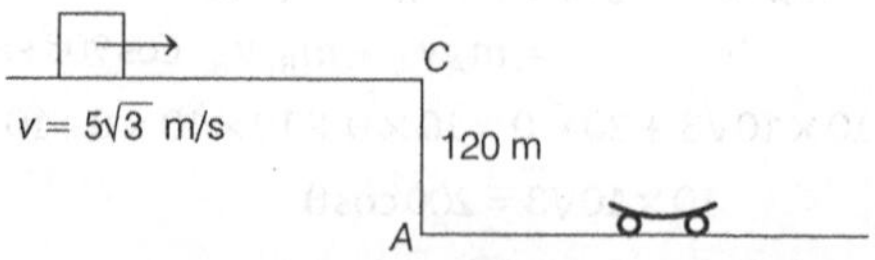

Horizontal component of velocity of cannon ball,

$$u_x = u\cos 30°$$

or $$u_x = (100) \times \frac{\sqrt{3}}{2}$$
$$= 50\sqrt{3}\text{ m/ s}$$

and vertical component of its velocity,

$$u_y = u\sin 30°$$
$$u_y = 100 \times \frac{1}{2}$$
$$= 50\text{ m/s}$$

Vertical displacement of the ball when it strikes the carriage is – 120 m or

$$s_y = u_y t + \frac{1}{2}a_y t^2$$

$$\Rightarrow \quad -120 = (50t) + \left(\frac{1}{2}\right)(-10)t^2$$

$$\Rightarrow \quad t^2 - 10t - 24 = 0$$

$$\Rightarrow \quad t = 12\text{s} \quad \text{or} \quad -2\text{s}$$

Ignoring the negative time, we have

$$t_0 = 12\text{s}$$

(b) When it strikes the carriage, its horizontal component of velocity is still $50\sqrt{3}$ m/s. It strikes to the carriage. Let v_2 be the velocity of (carriage + ball) system after collision. Then, applying conservation of linear momentum in horizontal direction

(mass of ball) (horizontal component of its velocity before collision) = (mass of ball + carriage) (v_2)

$$\therefore \quad (1\text{kg})(50\sqrt{3}\text{ m/ s}) = (10\text{kg})(v_2)$$

$$\therefore \quad v_2 = 5\sqrt{3}\text{ m/s}$$

The second ball is fired when the first ball strikes the carriage i.e. after 12 s. In these 12 s, the car will move forward a distance of $12v_1$ or $60\sqrt{3}$ m.

The second ball also takes 12 s to travel a vertical displacement of - 120 m. This ball will strike the carriage only when the carriage also covers the same distance of $60\sqrt{3}$ m in these 12 s. This is possible only when resistive forces are zero because velocity of car

(v_1) = velocity of carriage after first collision.

$$(v_2) = 5\sqrt{3}\text{ m/s.}$$

Hence, at the time of second collision

Horizontal component of velocity of ball $=50\sqrt{3}$ m/s and horizontal velocity of carriage + first ball $=5\sqrt{3}$ m/s. Let v be the desired velocity of carriage after second collision. Then, conservation of linear momentum in horizontal direction gives

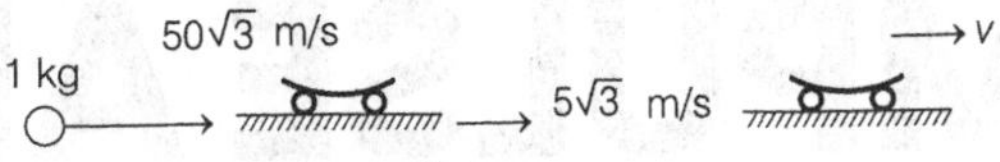

Before collision

$$11v = (1)(50\sqrt{3}) + (10)(5\sqrt{3}) = 100\sqrt{3}$$

$$\therefore \quad v = \frac{100\sqrt{3}}{11}\text{ m/s}$$

or $\quad v = 15.75$ m/s

In this particular problem, values are so adjusted that even if we take the velocity of ball with respect to car, we get the same results of both the parts, although the method will be wrong.

4. $$y_{CM} = \frac{m_1y_1 + m_2y_2 + m_3y_3 + m_4y_4 + m_5y_5}{m_1 + m_2 + m_3 + m_4 + m_5}$$

$$= \frac{(6m)(0) + (m)(a) + m(a) + m(0) + m(-a)}{6m + m + m + m + m} = \frac{a}{10}$$

CHAPTER~02

IMPULSE AND COLISIONS

LEVEL 01 Starter Level

2.1 Impulse

1 A bullet is fired from a gun. The force on the bullet is given by $F = 600 - (2 \times 10^5)t$. Here, F is in newton and t in second. The force on the bullet becomes zero as soon as it leaves the barrel. What is the impulse imparted to the bullet?

2 The figure shows the force-time graph of a 2 kg particle. At $t = 0$, particle is at rest. Find the

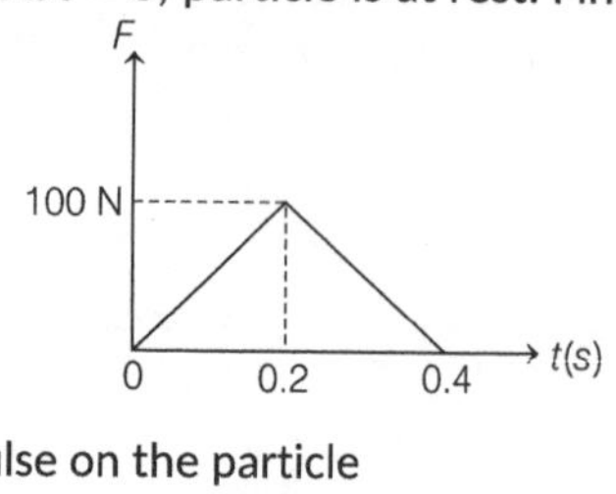

(a) impulse on the particle
(b) final velocity of the particle

3 A steel ball with a mass of $m = 100$ g falls from a height of $h_1 = 80$ cm onto a steel plate and rebounds to a height of $h_2 = 45$ cm. Find the impulse of the force received by the plate during the impact.

4 A ball of mass 100 g moving with a speed of 4 m/s strikes a horizontal surface at an angle of 30° from the surface. The ball is reflected back with same speed and same angle of reflection find (a) the impulse imparted to the ball (b) change in magnitude of momentum of the ball.

5 A ball of mass m is suspended from a point A by an inextensible string of length L. Ball is drawn to a side and held at same level as A but at a distance $\sqrt{3}L/2$ from A as shown. Now the ball is released. Find

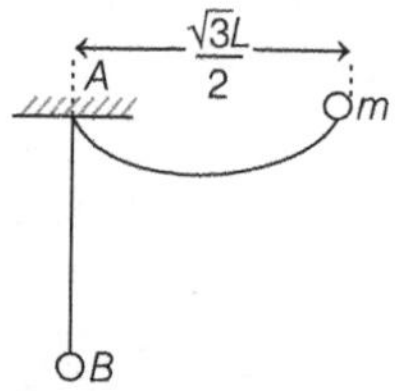

(a) speed of ball just after the jerk in the string
(b) impulse applied by string.

6 Two particles A and B of equal mass m each are attached by a string of length $2l$ and initially placed over a smooth horizontal table in the position shown in figure. Particle B is projected across the table with speed u perpendicular to AB as shown in figure. Find the velocities of each particle after the string becomes taut and the magnitude of the impulsive tension.

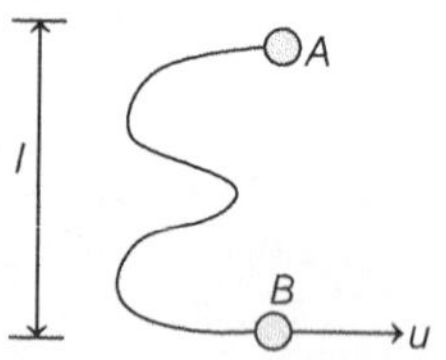

7 Two masses $3m$ and m are tied with a string which passes over a smooth pulley. If the mass m is raised vertically through a distance h and is then dropped, then

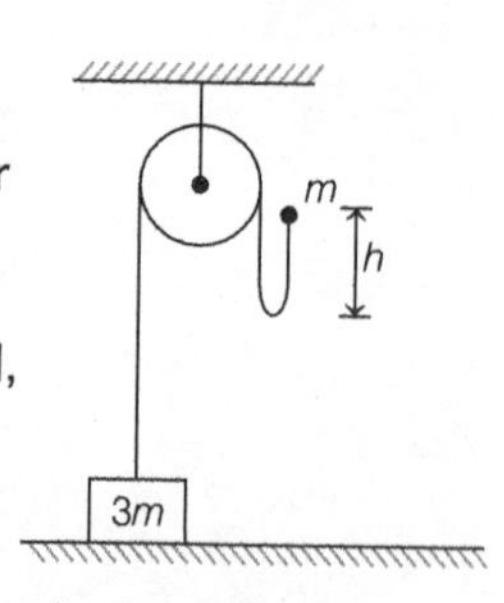

(a) what is the speed with which $3m$ begins to rise?
(b) what is the impulse of tension in the string?

8 A bob of mass M is suspended by an inextensible string. A particle of mass m, moving with velocity v_0 strikes the bob as shown in the figure. The particle comes to rest just after collision. Then calculate

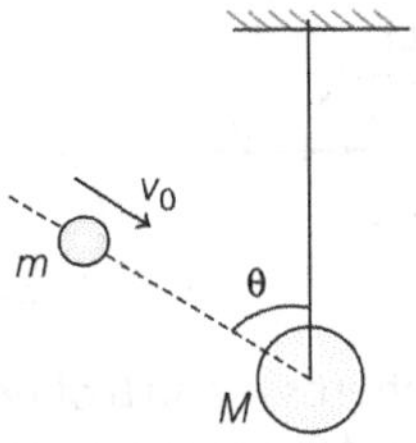

(a) the velocity of the bob just after collision.
(b) impulse of tension in the string.

9 Two identical block A and B, connected by a massless string are placed on a frictionless horizontal plane. A bullet having same mass, moving with speed u strikes block B from behind as shown. If the bullet gets embedded into the block B then find

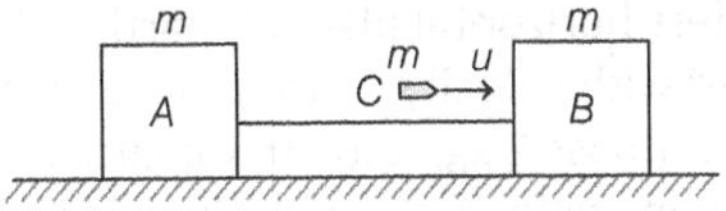

(a) the velocity of A, B and C after collision.
(b) impulse on A due to tension in the string
(c) impulse of normal force between B and C.

10 A ball of mass m is dropped from height h on a stationary wedge of mass $2m$ as shown in figure. If after the collision, the ball rebounds horizontally then find

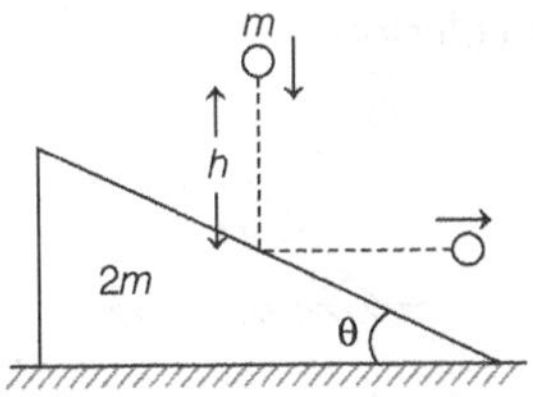

(a) velocity of the ball and the wedge just after collision
(b) impulse of normal force between the ball and the wedge
(c) impulse of normal force exerted by the ground on the wedge.

2.2 Head-on Collisions

1 A ball of mass 2 kg moving with speed 5 m/s collides directly with another of mass 3 kg moving in the same direction with speed 4 m/s. The coefficient of restitution is 2/3. Find the velocities after collision

2 A block of mass 5 kg moves from left to right with a velocity of 2 m/s and collides with another block of mass 3 kg moving along the same line in the opposite direction with velocity 4 m/s. If coefficient of restitution is 0.6, determine velocities of both the blocks after their collision.

3 A 3 kg block A moving with 4 m/s on a smooth table collide inelastically and head on with an 8kg block B moving with speed 1.5 m/s towards A.
(Given $e = 1/2$)
(a) What is final velocities of both the blocks?
(b) Find out the impulse of reformation and deformation.
(c) Find out the maximum potential energy of deformation.
(d) Find out loss in kinetic energy of system.

4 A block of mass 2.0 kg moving at 2.0 m/s collides head on with another block of equal mass kept at rest.
(a) Find the maximum possible loss in kinetic energy due to the collision.
(b) If the actual loss in kinetic energy is half of this maximum, find the coefficient of restitution.

5 A particle moving with kinetic energy K makes a head on elastic collision with an identical particle at rest.

Find the maximum elastic potential energy of the system during collision.

6 Three balls A, B and C are placed on a smooth horizontal surface. Given that $m_A = m_C = 4m_B$. Ball B collides with ball C with an initial velocity v as shown in figure. Find the total number of collisions between the balls. All collisions are elastic.

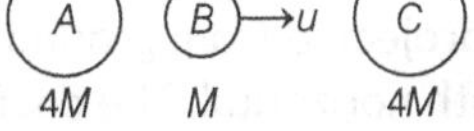

7 Two pendulum bobs of masses m_1 and $m_2 (= 2m_1)$ collide elastically at the lowest point in their motion, when the centres are at the same level, as in figure. If both are released from height H above the lowest point, to what heights do they rise for the first time?

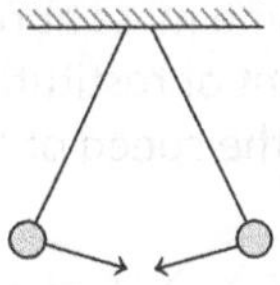

8 The 4 kg sphere released from rest when $\theta = 60°$ strikes a block mass of 5 kg placed on a rough horizontal plane and comes to rest after collision. The 5 kg block comes to rest after moving a distance

of 0.8m. Find μ of ground and block and coefficient of restitution e.

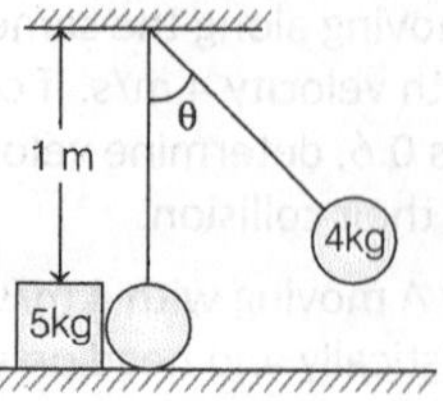

9 A ball is released from rest from a height h from ground. The coefficient of restitution between the ball and the ground is e. Find

(a) the velocity of the ball just after nth collision.

(b) the total distance covered before the ball stops.

(c) the total time after which the ball stops.

10 A particle of mass m moves with velocity $v_0 = 20$ m/s towards a heavy wall that is moving with velocity $v = 6$ m/s. If the coefficient of restitution between the ball and the wall is 0.5 then what is the speed of the particle just after the collision?

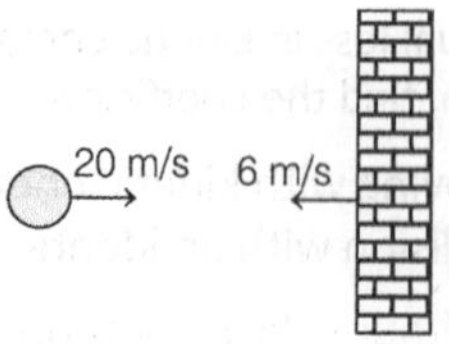

2.3 Oblique Collisions

1 A ball of mass m hits a floor with a speed v_0 making an angle of incidence α with the normal. The coefficient of restitution is e. Find the speed of the reflected ball and the angle of reflection of the ball.

2 A particle is projected from ground with speed u at an angle θ with horizontal. The coefficient of restitution of collision between the particle and the ground is e. How far from the starting point the particle makes it third collision with the ground?

3 A ball of mass 1 kg moving with speed of 10 m/s on a smooth horizontal plane collides obliquely with another ball of same mass at rest as shown in the figure. If coefficient of restitution for the collision is 0.5, what will be the speed of the striking ball after the collision?

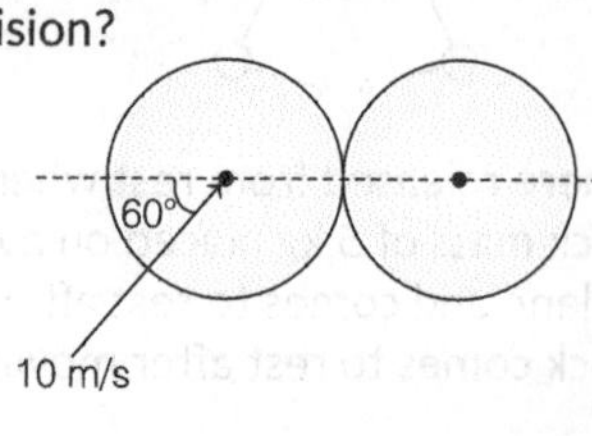

4 A disk sliding with velocity u on a smooth horizontal plane strikes another identical disk kept at rest as shown in the figure. If the impact between the disks is perfectly elastic impact, find velocities of the disks after the impact.

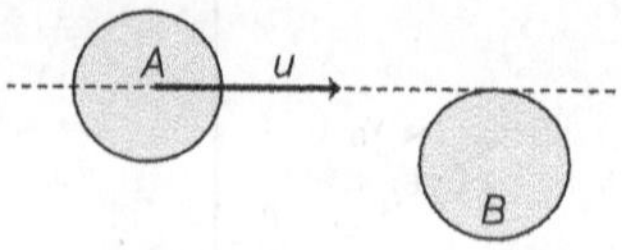

5 Two smooth spheres A and B of equal radius, lie on a horizontal table. A is of mass m and B is of mass $3m$, the spheres are projected towards each other with velocity vectors $5\hat{i} + 2\hat{j}$ and $2\hat{i} - \hat{j}$ respectively and when they collides the line joining their centres is parallel to the vector $\hat{i}$. If the coefficient of restitution between A and B is 1/3, find their velocities after impact.

6 Two point particles A and B are placed in line on a frictionless horizontal plane. If particle A (mass 1 kg) is moved with velocity 10 m/s towards stationary particle B (mass 2 kg) and after collision the two move at an angle of 45° with the initial direction of motion, then find coefficient of restitution.

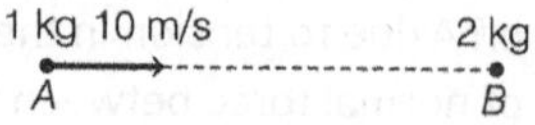

7 In the figure shown, a ball of mass m collides perpendicularly on a smooth stationary wedge of mass $M = 2m$. If the coefficient of restitution of collision is e (< 1) then determine the velocity of the wedge after collision.

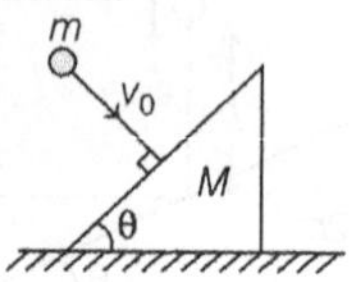

8 A 1 kg ball moving horizontally with velocity 10.0 m/s strikes inclined surface of a 3 kg smooth wedge as shown in the figure. The wedge is placed at rest on a frictionless horizontal ground. If the coefficient of restitution is 0.4, calculate the velocity of the wedge after the impact.

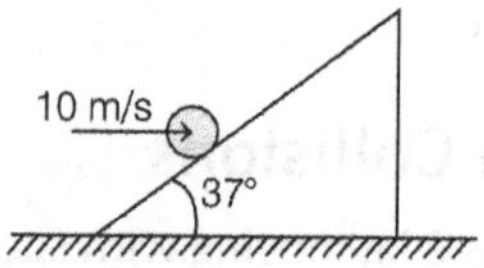

9 A hemisphere S and a particle P are of same mass m. P is dropped from a height h. S is kept on a smooth horizontal surface.

The friction between P and S is also absent. P collides elastically with S at the point shown in the figure. After collision the velocity of the particle becomes horizontal.

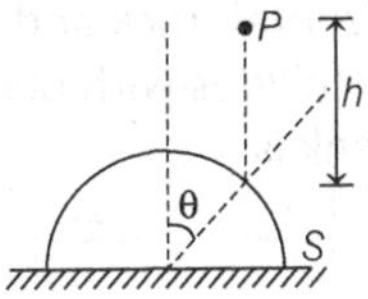

Find

(a) $\tan\theta$

(b) speed of the hemisphere after collision.

(c) impulse of ground on the hemisphere

2.4 Variable Mass System

1 A hopper drops gravel at a rate of 75 kg/s onto a conveyor belt moving at a constant speed of 2.20m/s,

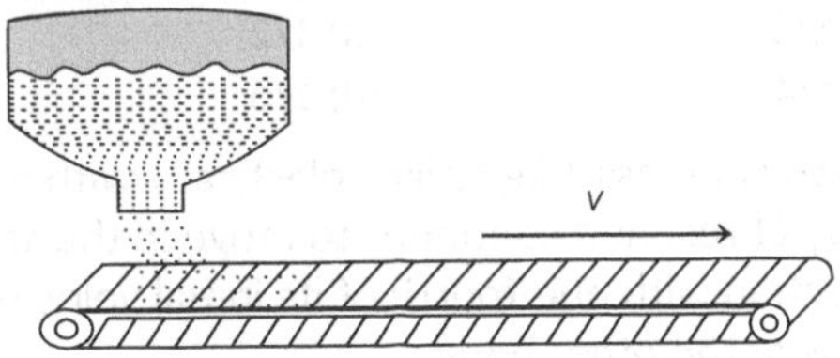

(a) Determine the force needed to keep the conveyor belt moving.

(b) What power output must the motor have that drives the conveyor belt?

(c) What is the rate of increase of kinetic energy of the conveyor belt?

2 A flat car of mass m_0 starts moving to the right due to a constant horizontal force F. Sand spills on the flat car from a stationary hopper. The rate of loading is constant and equal to μ kg/s. Find the time dependence of the velocity and the acceleration of the flat car in the process of loading. The friction is negligibly small.

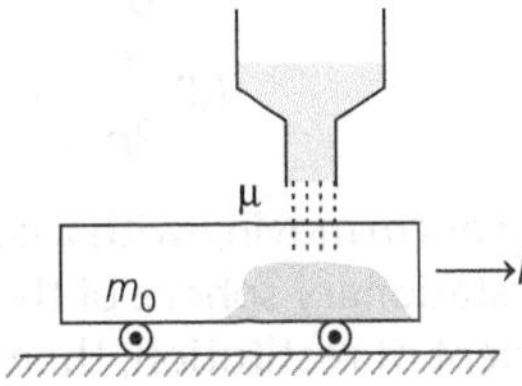

3 A cart loaded with sand moves along a horizontal floor due to a constant force F coinciding in direction with the cart's velocity vector. In the process sand spills through a hole in the bottom with a constant rate μ kg/s.

Find the acceleration and velocity of the cart at the moment t, if at the initial moment $t = 0$ the cart with loaded sand had the mass m_0 and its velocity was equal to zero. Friction is to be neglected.

4 A rocket has a mass of 21000 kg of which 15000 kg is fuel. The rocket engine can exhaust fuel at the rate of 190 kg/s with an exhaust velocity of 2800 m/s relative to the rocket. The rocket is fired vertically upward. Assume that acceleration due to gravity is constant at $g = 10\ \text{ms}^{-2}$ and there is no air resistance.

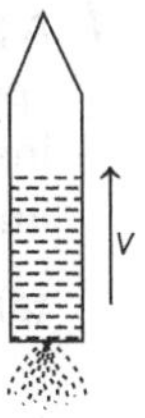

Calculate

(a) the thrust of the rocket.

(b) the net force on the rocket at blast-off

(c) the rocket's velocity as a function of time

(d) final velocity at the burn out

5 A pile of loose link chain of mass per unit length λ lies on a rough surface with coefficient of kinetic friction μ_k. One end of the chain is being pulled horizontal along the surface by a constant force F. Determine the acceleration of chain in terms of x and $dx/dt = v$.

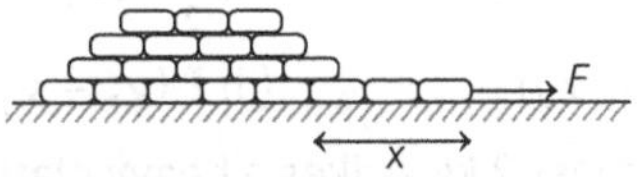

6 A chain of length L and mass M lies in a pile on the floor. If its end A is raised vertically at a constant speed v_0, express in terms of the length y of chain which is off the floor at any given instant.

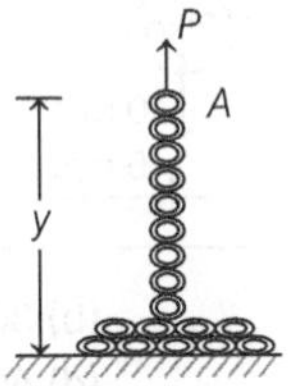

(a) The magnitude of the force P applied to end A.

(b) Energy lost during the lifting of the chain.

7 A uniform chain of mass m and length l hangs on a thread and touches the surface of a table by its lower end. Find the force exerted by the table on the chain when x length of chain has fallen on the table. The fallen part does not form heap.

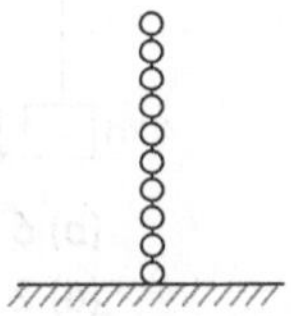

LEVEL 02 JEE Main Level

Single Choice Correct Questions

1 A particle of mass m is made to move with uniform speed v_0 along the perimeter of a regular hexagon, inscribed in a circle of radius R. The magnitude of impulse applied at each corner of the hexagon is

(a) $2mv_0 \sin\frac{\pi}{6}$ (b) $mv_0 \sin\frac{\pi}{6}$

(c) $mv_0 \sin\frac{\pi}{3}$ (d) $2mv_0 \sin\frac{\pi}{3}$

2 Two balls of same mass are dropped from the same height h, on to the floor. The first ball bounces to a height $h/4$ after the collision and the second ball to a height $h/16$. The impulse applied by the first and second ball on the floor are I_1 and I_2 respectively. Then

(a) $5I_1 = 6I_2$ (b) $6I_1 = 5I_2$

(c) $I_1 = 2I_2$ (d) $2I_1 = I_2$

3 An impulse $\mathbf{I}$ changes the velocity of a particle from $\mathbf{v}_1$ to $\mathbf{v}_2$. Kinetic energy gained by the particle is

(a) $\frac{1}{2}\mathbf{I}\cdot(\mathbf{v}_1 + \mathbf{v}_2)$ (b) $\frac{1}{2}\mathbf{I}\cdot(\mathbf{v}_1 - \mathbf{v}_2)$

(c) $\mathbf{I}\cdot(\mathbf{v}_1 - \mathbf{v}_2)$ (d) $\mathbf{I}\cdot(\mathbf{v}_1 + \mathbf{v}_2)$

4 A ball of mass 2 kg strikes a heavy platform, elastically, moving upwards with a velocity of 5m/s. The speed of the ball just before the collision is 10m/s downwards. Then the impulse imparted by the platform on the ball is.

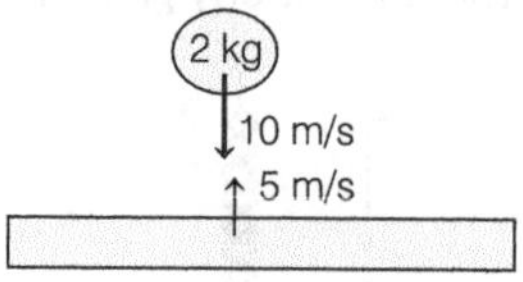

(a) 20 N-s (b) 30 N-s

(c) 40 N-s (d) 60 N-s

5 Two blocks of same mass (4 kg) are placed according to diagram. Initial velocities of bodies are 4 m/s and 2 m/s and the string is taut. Find the impulse on 4 kg when the string again becomes taut.

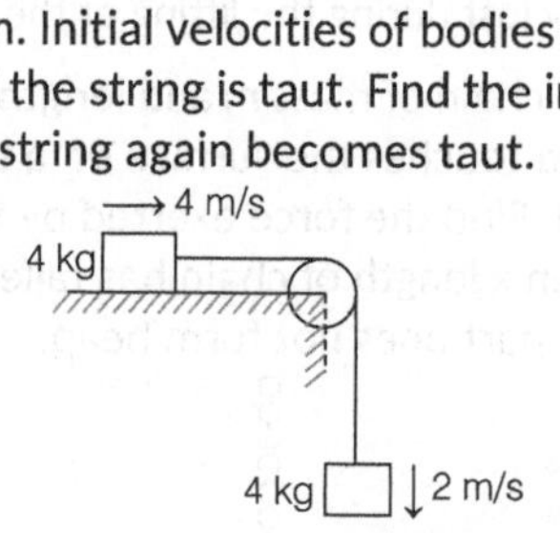

(a) 24 N-s (b) 6 N-s

(c) 4 N-s (d) 2 N-s

6 A plank of mass m moving with a velocity v along a frictionless horizontal track and a body of mass $m/2$ moving with 2v collides with plank elastically. Final speed of the plank is

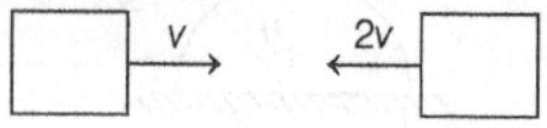

(a) 5v / 3 (b) v

(c) 2v / 3 (D) None of these

7 Ball 1 collides with an another identical ball 2 at rest as shown in figure. For what value of coefficient of restitution e, the velocity of second ball becomes two times that of 1 after collision?

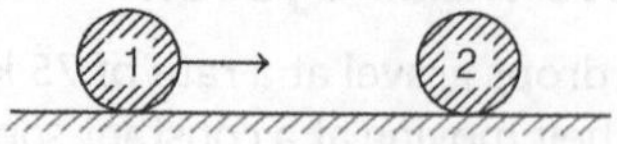

(a) 1/3 (b) 1/2

(c) 1/4 (d) 1/6

8 A body of mass 1 kg strikes elastically with another body at rest and continues to move in the same direction with one-fourth of its initial velocity. The mass of the other body is

(a) 0.6 kg (b) 2.4 kg

(c) 3 kg (d) 4 kg

9 A solid iron ball A of radius r collides head on with another stationary solid iron ball B of radius $2r$. The ratio of their speeds just after the collision ($e = 0.5$) is

(a) 3 (b) 4

(c) 2 (d) 1

10 In a one dimensional collision between two identical particles A and B, B is stationary and A has momentum p before impact. During impact, B gives impulse J to A. The coefficient of restitution is

(a) $\frac{2J}{p} - 1$ (b) $\frac{J}{p} + 1$

(c) $\frac{J}{p} - 1$ (d) $\frac{J}{2p} - 1$

11 A sphere of mass m moving with a constant velocity hits another stationary sphere of the same mass. If e is the coefficient of restitution, then ratio of speed of the first sphere to the speed of the second sphere after collision will be

(a) $\left(\frac{1-e}{1+e}\right)$ (b) $\left(\frac{1+e}{1-e}\right)$

(c) $\left(\frac{e+1}{e-1}\right)$ (d) $\left(\frac{e-1}{e+1}\right)$

12 The friction coefficient between the horizontal surface and each of the block shown in the figure is 0.2. The collision between the blocks is perfectly elastic. The separation between them when they come to rest is

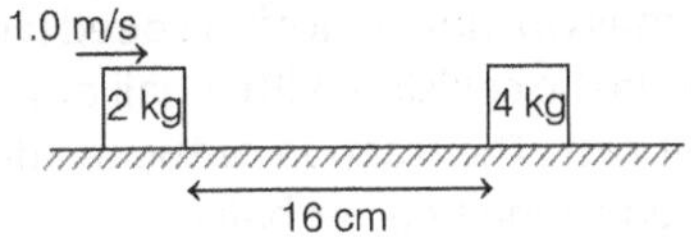

(a) 5 cm (b) 8 cm (c) 10 cm (d) 12 cm

13 Three blocks are initially placed as shown in the figure. Block *A* has mass *m* and initial velocity *v* to the right. Block *B* with mass *m* and block *C* with mass 4*m* are both initially at rest. Neglect friction. All collisions are elastic. The final velocity of block *A* is

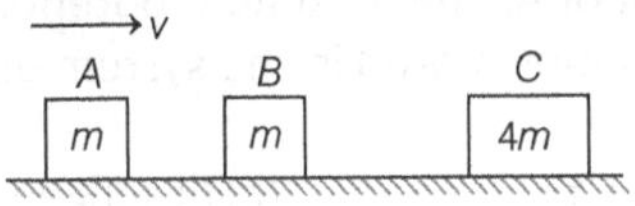

(a) 0.6 *v* to the left
(b) 1.4 *v* to the left
(c) *v* to the left
(d) 0.4 *v* to the right

14 As shown above, a ball of mass *m*, suspended on the end of a wire, is released from height *h* and collides elastically, when it is at its lowest point, with a block of mass 2*m* at rest on a frictionless surface. After the collision, the ball rises to a final height equal to

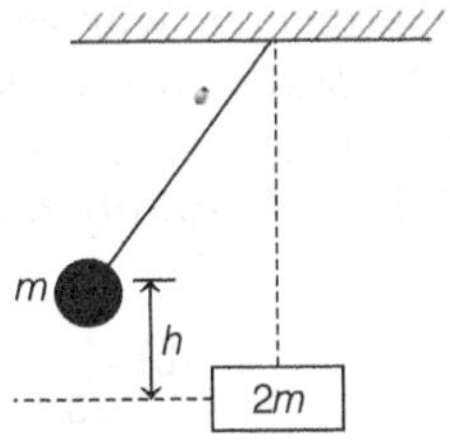

(a) $h/9$ (b) $h/8$
(c) $h/3$ (d) $h/2$

15 Two masses *m* and 2*m* are placed in fixed horizontal circular smooth hollow tube of radius *r* as shown. The mass *m* is moving with speed *u* and the mass 2*m* is stationary. After their first collision, the time elapsed for next collision is (coefficient of restitution $e = 1/2$)

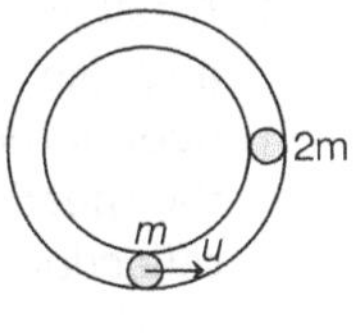

(a) $\frac{2\pi r}{u}$ (b) $\frac{4\pi r}{u}$
(c) $\frac{3\pi r}{u}$ (d) $\frac{12\pi r}{u}$

16 A ball of mass 0.2 kg rests on a vertical post of height 5*m*. A bullet of mass 0.01 kg, traveling with a velocity *v* in a horizontal direction, hits the centre of the ball. After the collision, the ball and bullet travel independently. The ball hits the ground at a distance of 20 m and the bullet at a distance of 100 m from the foot of the post. The initial velocity *v* of the bullet is

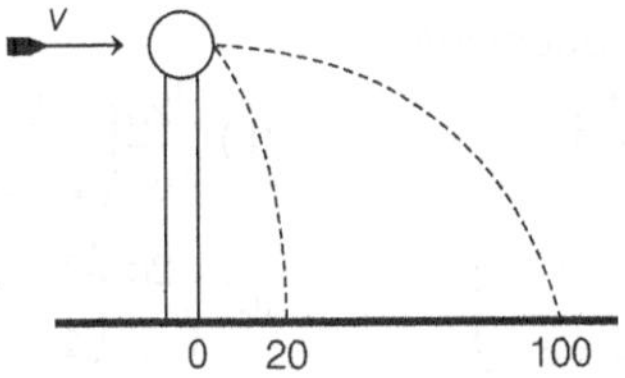

(a) 250 m/s (b) $250\sqrt{2}$ m/s
(c) 400 m/s (d) 500 m/s

17 Two identical balls of equal masses *A* and *B* are lying on a smooth surface as shown in figure. Ball *A* hits the ball *B* (which is at rest) with a velocity $v = 16$ m/s. What should be the minimum value of coefficient of restitution between *A* and *B* so that *B* just reaches the highest point of inclined plane? ($g = 10$ m/s^2)

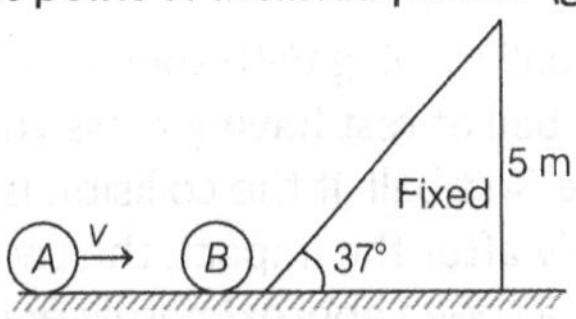

(a) 2/3 (b) 1/4 (c) 1/2 (d) 1/3

18 A bead of mass *m* and diameter *d* is sliding back and forth with velocity *v* on a wire held between two rigid walls of length *L*. Assume that the collisions with the wall are perfectly elastic and there is no friction. The average force that the bouncing bead exerts on the one of the walls is

(a) $\frac{mv^2}{L-d}$ (b) $\frac{mv^2}{L+d}$ (c) $\frac{2mv^2}{L-d}$ (d) $\frac{2mv^2}{L+d}$

19 A small ball on a frictionless horizontal surface moves towards right with a velocity *v*. It collides with the wall and returns back and continues to and fro motion. If the average speed for first to and fro motion of the ball is $2v/3$, then the coefficient of restitution of impact is

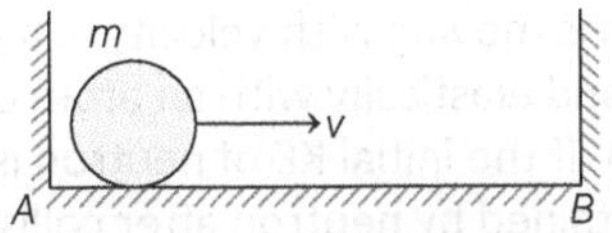

(a) 0.5 (b) 0.8
(c) 0.25 (d) 0.75

20 After falling from a height h and striking the ground twice, a ball rise up to the height (e = coefficient of restitution)

(a) he (b) he^2

(c) he^3 (d) he^4

21 A ball is dropped from a height h above a horizontal concrete surface. The coefficient of restitution for the collision involved is e. The time after which the ball stops bouncing is

(a) $\sqrt{\frac{2h}{g}}\left(\frac{1}{e}\right)$ (b) $\sqrt{\frac{2h}{g}}\left(\frac{1}{1-e}\right)$

(c) $\sqrt{\frac{2h}{g}}\left(\frac{1}{1-e^2}\right)$ (d) $\sqrt{\frac{2h}{g}}\left(\frac{1+e}{1-e}\right)$

22 A ball falls vertically on to a floor, with momentum p, and then bounces repeatedly, the coefficient of restitution is e. The total momentum imparted by the ball to the floor is

(a) $p(1+e)$ (b) $\frac{p}{1-e}$

(c) $\frac{p(1+e)}{(1-e)}$ (d) $p\left(1-\frac{1}{e}\right)$

23 A massive ball moving with speed v collides head-on with a tiny ball at rest having mass very less than the mass of the first ball. If the collision is elastic, then immediately after the impact, the second ball will move with a speed approximately equal to

(a) v (b) $2v$

(c) $v/2$ (d) ∞

24 A sphere moving with velocity v strikes a wall moving towards the sphere with a velocity u. If the mass of the wall is infinitely large the work done by the wall during elastic collision will be

(a) $mu(v+u)$ (b) $2m\,u(v+u)$

(c) $2\,mv(v+u)$ (d) $2\,m(v+u)$

25 Two identical balls each of mass 2 kg are moving towards each other with the same speed of 5 m/s. They collide with each other, stick together and come to rest what is the work done by the internal forces?

(a) 25 J (b) – 25 J

(c) 50 J (d) – 50 J

26 A neutron is moving with velocity u. It collides head-on and elastically with an atom of mass number A. If the initial KE of neutron is E. Kinetic energy retained by neutron after collision

(a) $\left(\frac{A}{A+1}\right)^2 E$ (b) $\left(\frac{A}{A-1}\right)^2 E$

(c) $\left(\frac{A-1}{A+1}\right)^2 E$ (d) $\left(\frac{A^2-1}{A^2+1}\right)E$

27 A ball of mass m moving with a speed u undergoes a head-on elastic collision with a ball of mass nm initially at rest. The fraction of the incident energy transferred to the heavier ball is

(a) $\frac{n}{1+n}$ (b) $\frac{n}{(1+n)^2}$

(c) $\frac{2n}{(1+n)^2}$ (d) $\frac{4n}{(1+n)^2}$

28 A ball A moving with kinetic energy E, makes a head on elastic collision with a stationary ball with mass n times that of A. The maximum potential energy due to deformation stored in the system during the collision is

(a) $nE/(n+1)$ (b) $(n+1)E/n$

(c) $(n-1)E/n$ (d) E/n

29 During the head-on collision of two masses 1kg and 2 kg the maximum energy of deformation is 100/3 J. If before collision the masses are moving in the same direction, then their velocity of approach before the collision is

(a) 10 m/s (b) 5 m/s

(c) 20 m/s (d) $10\sqrt{2}$ m/s

30 A smooth small spherical ball of mass m, moving with velocity u collides head on with another small spherical ball of mass $3m$, which was initially at rest. Two-third of the initial kinetic energy of the system is lost. The coefficient of restitution between the spheres is

(a) $\frac{1}{3}$ (b) $\frac{1}{\sqrt{3}}$

(c) $\frac{1}{2}$ (d) zero

31 A ball of mass m hits the floor with a speed v making an angle of incidence $\theta = 45°$ with the normal to the floor. If the coefficient of restitution $e = 1/\sqrt{2}$, then the speed of the reflected ball and the angle of reflection are

(a) $\frac{\sqrt{3}}{2}v, \tan^{-1}\sqrt{2}$ (b) $\frac{\sqrt{3}}{4}v, \tan^{-1}\sqrt{3}$

(c) $\frac{2\sqrt{3}}{5}v, \tan^{-1}\sqrt{3}$ (d) $\frac{\sqrt{3}}{5}v, \tan^{-1}\sqrt{2}$

32 A particle travelling horizontally strikes a smooth fixed spherical surface as shown. If coefficient of restitution is $e = 1/3$, what should be angle θ, so that it rebounds vertically?

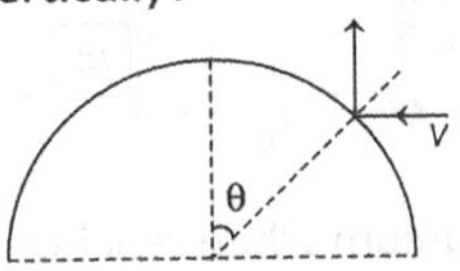

(a) 30° (b) 37°
(c) 45° (d) 60°

33 A glass ball collides with a smooth horizontal surface in XZ-plane with a velocity $\mathbf{v} = a\hat{\mathbf{i}} - b\hat{\mathbf{j}}$. If the coefficient of restitution of collision is e, then the velocity of the ball just after the impact will be

(a) $a\hat{\mathbf{i}} + b\hat{\mathbf{j}}$
(b) $a\hat{\mathbf{i}} + eb\hat{\mathbf{j}}$
(c) $a\hat{\mathbf{i}} - b\hat{\mathbf{j}}$
(d) $a\hat{\mathbf{i}} - eb\hat{\mathbf{j}}$

34 A sphere is moving with a velocity $4\hat{\mathbf{i}} + 3\hat{\mathbf{j}} - 5\hat{\mathbf{k}}$ when it hits a smooth wall and rebounds with velocity $2\hat{\mathbf{i}} + 2\hat{\mathbf{j}} + 3\hat{\mathbf{k}}$. The coefficient of restitution between the sphere and the wall is

(a) 6/17 (b) 2/3
(c) 9/16 (d) 4/13

35 A spherical ball of mass 1 kg moving with a uniform speed of 1 m/s collides symmetrically with two identical spherical balls of mass 1 kg each at rest touching each other. If the two balls move with 0.5m/s in two directions at the same angle of 60° with the direction of the first ball, the loss of kinetic energy on account of the collision is

(a) 0.125 J (b) 0.5 J
(c) 1.0 J (d) 0.75 J

36 There are three identical balls on a horizontal surface. Two of them are at rest touching each other and third one comes and strikes these two balls symmetrically and stops after collision. The coefficient of restitution for any one of the two impacts that took place is

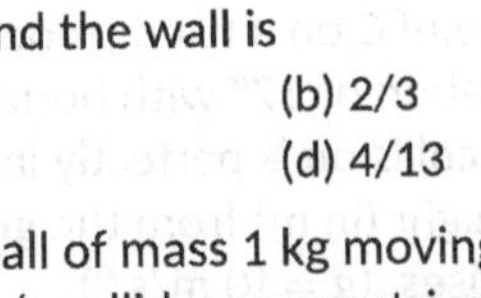

(a) 2/3 (b) 4/9
(c) 9/16 (d) 1/3

37 A disk A of radius r moving on perfectly smooth surface at a speed v undergoes an elastic collision with an identical stationary disk B. Find the velocity of the disk B after collision if the impact parameter is r / 2 as shown in the figure

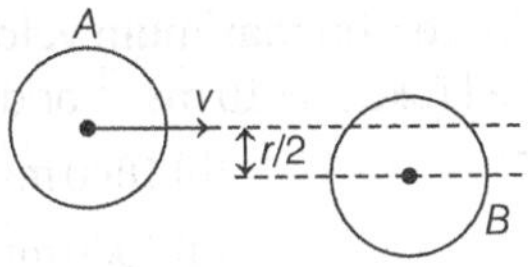

(a) $\frac{v\sqrt{15}}{4}$ (b) $\frac{v}{4}$
(c) $\frac{v}{2}$ (d) $\frac{\sqrt{3}v}{2}$

38 A ball of mass M strikes another ball of mass m at rest. If they separate in mutually perpendicular directions, then the coefficient of restitution (e) is

(a) $\frac{M}{m}$ (b) $\frac{m}{M}$
(c) $\frac{m}{2M}$ (d) zero

39 A ball is released from position A and travels 5 m before striking the smooth fixed inclined plane as shown. If the coefficient of restitution in the impact is $e = 0.5$, the time taken by the ball to strike the plane again is

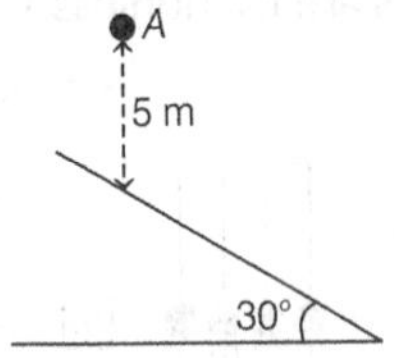

(a) 1 s (b) 2 s
(c) 2.5 s (d) 3 s

40 A 5000 kg rocket is set of vertical firing. The relative speed of burnt gas is 800 ms^{-1}. To give an initial upwards acceleration of 20 ms^{-2}, the amount of gas ejected per second to supply the needed thrust will be

(a) 127.5 kg s^{-1} (b) 187.5 kg s^{-1}
(c) 185.5 kg s^{-1} (d) 137.5 kg s^{-1}

41 A balloon having mass m is filled with gas and is held in hands of a boy. Then suddenly it gets released and gas starts coming out of it with a constant rate. The velocity of the ejected gas is 2 m/s with respect to the balloon. Find out the velocity of the balloon when the mass of gas is reduced to half.

(a) ln2 (b) 2ln4
(c) 2ln2 (d) None of these

42 A rocket, with an initial mass of 1000 kg, is launched vertically upwards from rest under gravity. The rocket burns fuel at the rate of 10 kg s^{-1}. The burnt matter is ejected vertically downwards with a speed of 2000 ms^{-1} relative to the rocket. If burning stops after one minute, the maximum velocity of the rocket will be [Take $g = 10$ ms^{-2} and $\ln(2.5) = 0.92$]

(a) 1240 ms^{-1} (b) 1840 ms^{-1}
(c) 2440 ms^{-1} (d) 2000 ms^{-1}

Numerical Value Questions

1 A block of mass 4 kg is moving with a velocity of 7 m/s on a surface. It collides with another block of mass 3 kg elastically. The surface is smooth for 4 kg block but rough for 3 kg block ($\mu = 0.4$). Find the time (in s) after which next collision will occur.

2 In the given arrangement four identical balls of mass 1kg are hanging from light string such that they are very close to each other. Suddenly, first ball gets impulse of 16 N-s to the right as shown in figure. Block of mass is 1kg just able to complete one circular turn for radius *r*. If value of $r = \left(\frac{3}{2}\right)^n \times \frac{1}{5g}$ m, find the value of *n* (Coefficient of restitution $e = 0.5$ and all surfaces are frictionless.)

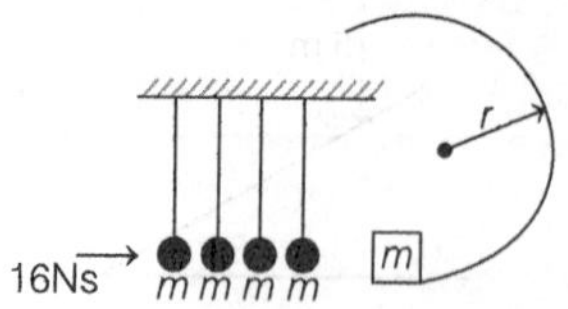

3 A sphere *A* of mass 2 kg moving with velocity v_0 collides with bob of mass 1kg as shown in the figure. Value of tension at which string of pendulum breaks is 40 N. If length of pendulum is 30 cm, then find the maximum value of v_0 (in m/s) so that string does not break. Coefficient of restitution is 1/2.

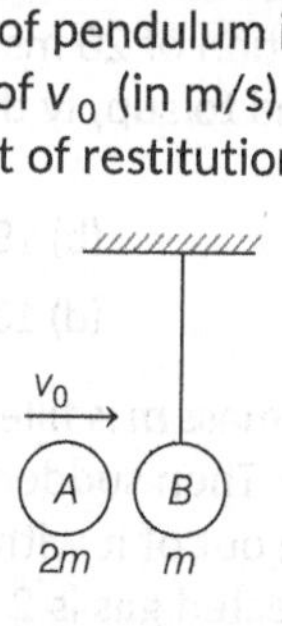

4 Consider a hypothetical field in which force acting on a particle varies with its horizontal distance from wall *AB* is $F = \alpha x$ and always towards wall. Coefficient of restitution for collision between particle and wall is $e = 1/2$. Find the maximum force (in N) acting on the particle after 3rd collision. (Use $\alpha x_0 = 16$ N)

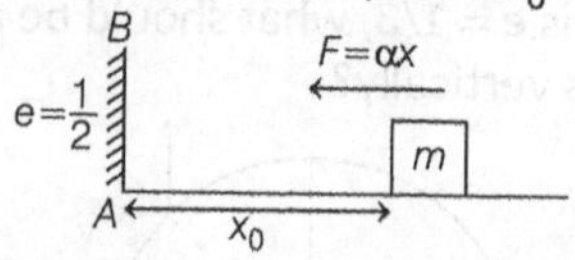

5 A simple pendulum when reaches its maximum angular displacement of 60° from the vertical is hit by a bullet moving horizontally with velocity 200 m/s. The bullet comes out of the bob horizontally with velocity 100 m/s. Find velocity of the bob immediately after the bullet comes out. Neglect loss of mass of the bob due to piercing by the bullet. Mass of the bob is 10 times of that of the bullet.

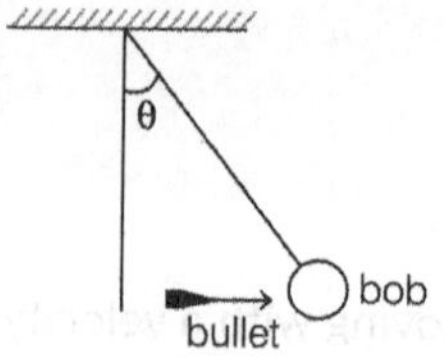

6 A particle is projected from point *O* on the ground with velocity $u = 5\sqrt{5}$ m/s at angle $\alpha = \tan^{-1}(0.5)$. It strikes at a point *C* on a fixed smooth plane *AB* having inclination of 37° with horizontal as shown in figure. If the collision is perfectly inelastic, calculate maximum height (in m) from the ground to which the particle rises. ($g = 10$ m/s^2)

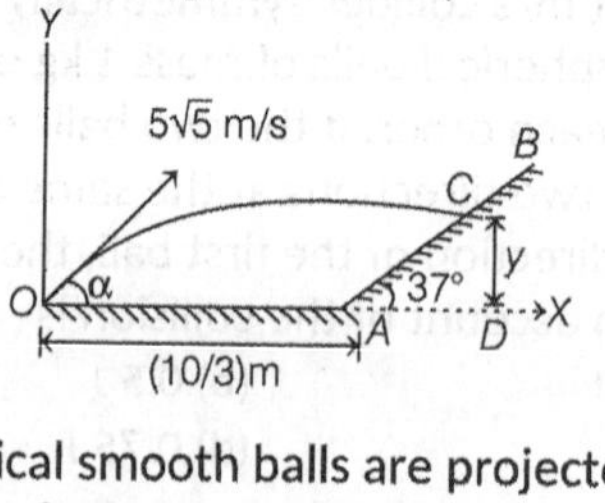

7 Two identical smooth balls are projected from points O and A on the horizontal ground with same speed of projection. The angle of projection in each case in 30° (see figure). The distance between O and A is 100 m. The balls collide in mid air and return to their respective points of projection. If the coefficient of restitution is 0.7, find the speed of projection *u* of either ball (in m/s) .Fill the value of $\frac{u\sqrt{7}}{25}$

(Take $\sqrt{3} = 1.7$)

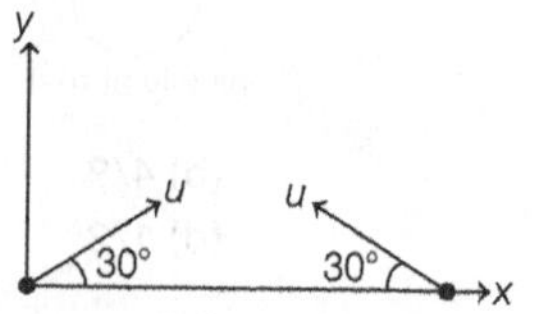

8 A particle is thrown on to a rough floor at an angle of $\alpha = 45°$. If it rebounds at the same angle $\beta = 45°$, determine the coefficient of kinetic friction between the floor and the particle. The coefficient of restitution is $e = 0.6$.

9 A massive disc of radius R is moved with a constant velocity u on a frictionless table. Another small disc collides with it elastically with a speed of $v_0 = 12$ m/s, the velocities of the discs are parallel. The distance d shown in the figure is equal to $R/2$, friction between the discs is negligible. For which u (in m/s) will the small disc move perpendicularly to its original motion after the collision?

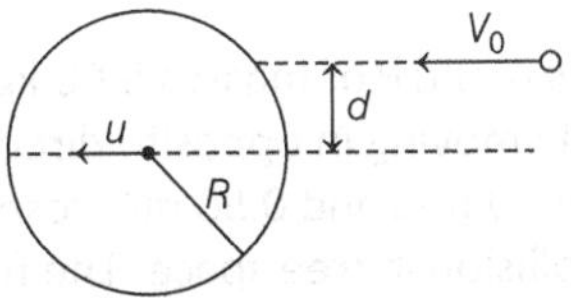

10 A ball moving translationally collides elastically with another, stationary ball of the same mass. At the moment of impact the angle between the straight line passing through the centres of the balls and the direction of the initial motion of the striking ball is equal to $\alpha = 45°$. Assuming the balls to the smooth, find the fraction η of the kinetic energy of the striking ball that turned into potential energy at the moment of the maximum deformation.

LEVEL 03 JEE Advanced Level

Single Choice Correct Questions

1 Three blocks are placed on smooth horizontal surface and lie on same horizontal straight line. Block 1 and block 3 have mass m each and block 2 has mass $M(M > m)$. Block 2 and block 3 are initially stationary, while block 1 is initially moving towards block 2 with speed v as shown. Assume that all collisions are head-on and perfectly elastic. What value of M/m ensures that block 1 and block 3 have the same final speed ?

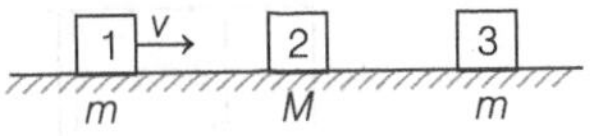

(a) $5 + \sqrt{2}$
(b) $5 - \sqrt{2}$
(c) $2 + \sqrt{5}$
(d) $3 + \sqrt{5}$

2 Two identical balls are released from positions as shown. They collide elastically on horizontal surface. Ratio of heights attained by A and B after collision is (All surfaces are smooth, neglect energy loss at M and N)

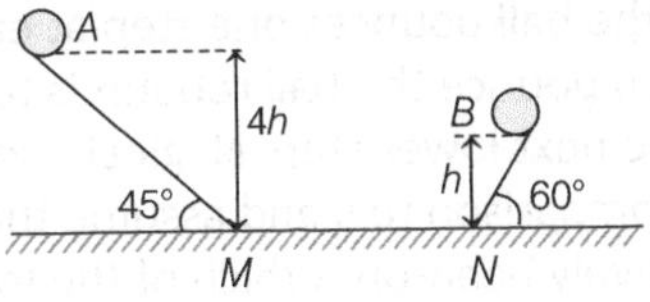

(a) 1 : 4 (b) 2 : 1
(c) 4 : 13 (d) 2 :5

3 A uniform sphere of mass m moving along a smooth horizontal surface strikes another uniform sphere of mass $2m$ (initially at rest) head-on. If loss in KE of first sphere is maximum, then value of coefficient of restitution is

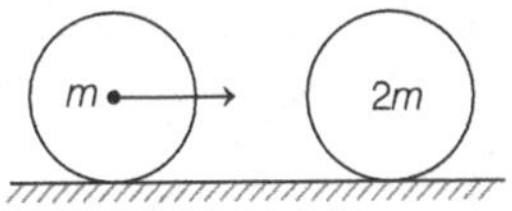

(a) 0.2 (b) 0.5
(c) 0.7 (d) 1

4 Block A of mass m is moving with a speed v_0 on a frictionless horizontal surface as shown in figure. It collides with a massive block B of mass $M = \alpha m$ $(\alpha > 1)$ initially at rest. All collisions are elastic. Condition on α for which the two blocks will undergo only one collision is

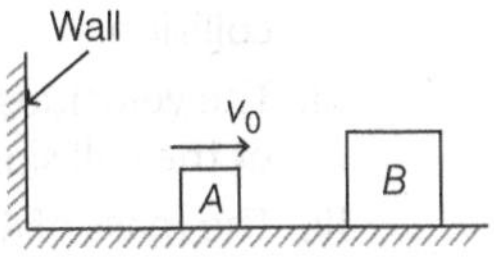

(a) $\alpha < 3$ (b) $\alpha < 4$
(c) $\alpha < 5$ (d) $\alpha < 6$

5 In figure, there are two pendulums with bobs having identical mass. The pendulum A is released from rest in the position shown. If the maximum angle θ_B formed by cord BD with the vertical in the subsequent motion of sphere B is to be equal to the angle θ_A, what is the required value of the ratio l_B/l_A of the lengths of the two cords in terms of coefficient of restitution e between the two spheres.

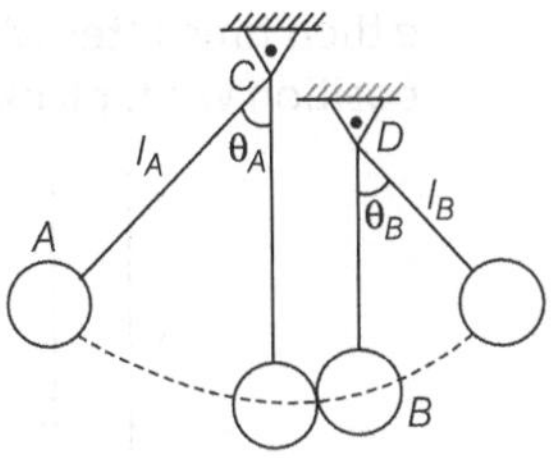

(a) $\frac{(1-e^2)}{4}$ (b) $\frac{(1+e)^2}{4}$ (c) $\frac{(1-e^2)}{3}$ (d) $\frac{2(1-e)^2}{3}$

6 Two bodies A and B of masses 5.00 kg and 10.0 kg respectively moving in opposite directions with velocities 4.00 m/s and 0.50 m/s respectively make head-on collision in free space. The force of their mutual interaction varies according to the given graph. The coefficient of restitution is

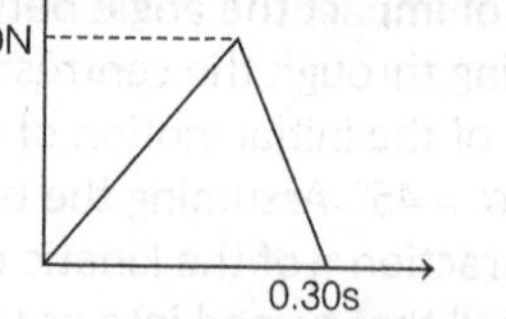

(a) 0.25
(b) 0.33
(c) 0.50
(d) 0.75

7 The diagram shows the velocity-time graph for two masses R and S that collided elastically. Which of the following statements is true?

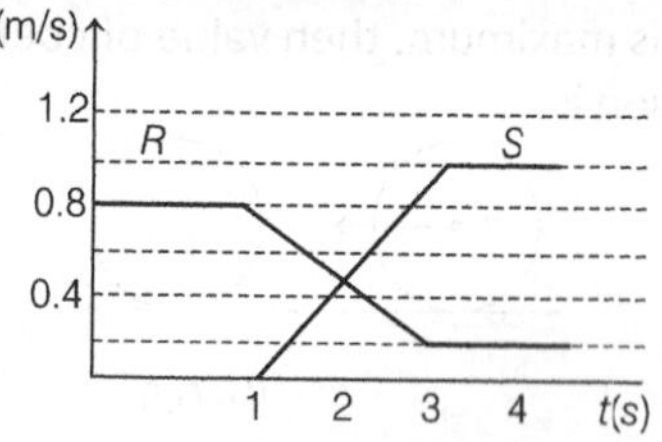

I. R and S moved in the same direction after the collision.
II. The velocities of R and S were equal at the mid time of the collision.
III. The mass of R was greater than mass of S.

(a) I only
(b) II only
(c) I and II only
(d) I, II and III

8 A smooth plank having two vertical walls are kept on a smooth surface. A small block of mass m is projected towards one of the vertical wall with a velocity v. If all collision has coefficient of restitution e then time after which block comes to same position w.r.t. plank is

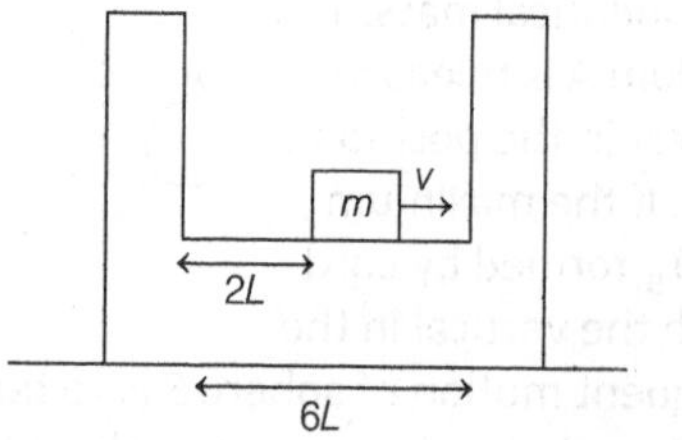

(a) $\frac{4L}{v} + \frac{6L}{ev} + \frac{2L}{e^2v}$
(b) $\frac{4L}{ev} + \frac{6L}{e^2v} + \frac{2L}{e^3v}$
(c) $\frac{10L}{ev} + \frac{2L}{e^2v}$
(d) Data not sufficient

9 A bullet of mass m is shot with a velocity u at an angle $\theta = 60°$ with the horizontal which strikes the box of mass $2m$ resting at the edge of a smooth surface OB as shown in figure. Bullet strikes the box horizontally after that bullet passes through the box and moves with velocity $u/4$ along horizontal direction. If bullet rebounds elastically with wall AB, then find the final position where bullet again strikes mass $2m$.

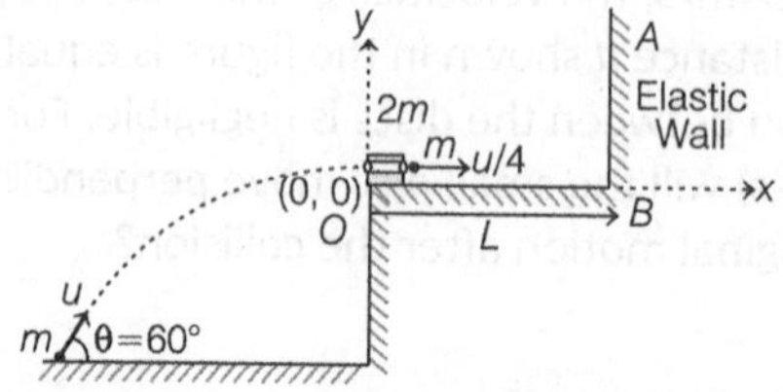

(a) $\frac{L}{2}, 0$
(b) $\frac{L}{3}, 0$
(c) $\frac{2L}{3}, 0$
(d) $\frac{L}{4}, 0$

10 A shell of mass 1 kg is projected with velocity 20 m/s at an angle 60° with horizontal. It collides inelastically with a ball of mass 1 kg which is suspended through a thread of length 2 m. The other end of the thread is attached to the ceiling of the trolley of mass 18 kg as shown in figure. Initially, the trolley is stationary and it is free to move along horizontal rails without any friction. What is the maximum deflection of the thread with vertical? (Take $g = 10 \text{ m/s}^2$)

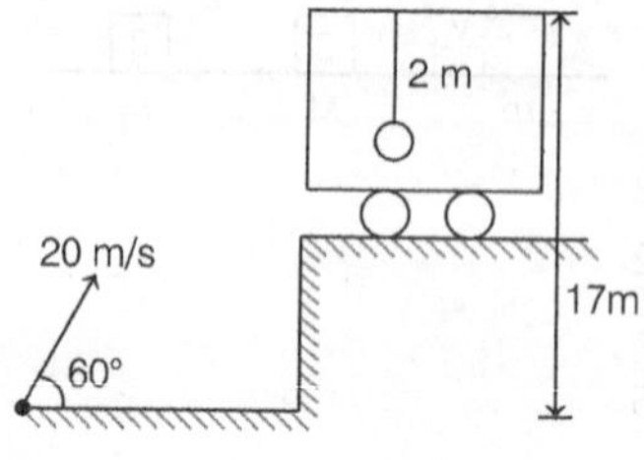

(a) $\cos^{-1}(3/8)$
(b) $\cos^{-1}(5/12)$
(c) $\cos^{-1}(7/16)$
(d) $\cos^{-1}(1/2)$

11 A ball is bouncing down a set of stairs. The coefficient of restitution is e. The height of each step is d and the ball bounces one step at each bounce. After each bounce the ball rebounds to a height h above the next lower step. Neglect width of each step in comparison to h and assume the impacts to be effectively head-on. Which of the following relation is correct ?

(a) $\frac{h}{d} = 1 - e^2$
(b) $\frac{h}{d} = 1 - e$
(c) $\frac{h}{d} = \frac{1}{1 - e^2}$
(d) $\frac{h}{d} = \frac{1}{1 - e}$

12 A particle collides elastically with two moving walls one by one as shown on a horizontal plane. Find the final speed of the particle after two collisions

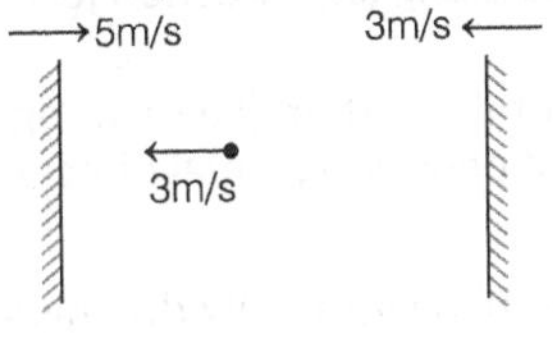

(a) 11 m/s (b) 19 m/s (c) 21 m/s (d) 5 m/s

13 From what minimum height h must the system be released when spring is unstretched so that after perfectly inelastic collision ($e = 0$) with ground, B may be lifted off the ground (Spring constant $= k$).

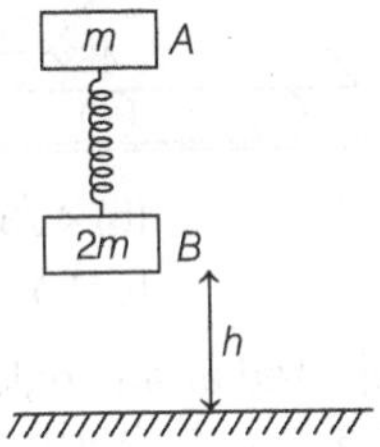

(a) $mg/(4k)$
(b) $4mg/k$
(c) $mg/(2k)$
(d) None of these

14 A uniform horizontal rod of length l falls vertically from height h on two identical blocks placed symmetrically below the rod as shown in figure. The coefficients of restitution are e_1 and e_2. The maximum height through which the centre of mass of the rod will rise after bouncing off the blocks is

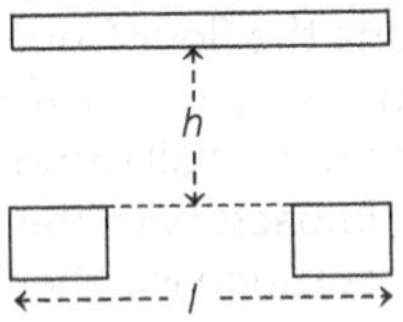

(a) $\dfrac{h}{(e_1 + e_2)}$
(b) $\dfrac{(e_1 + e_2)^2 h}{4}$
(c) $\dfrac{(e_1 + e_2)^2 h}{2}$
(d) $\dfrac{4h}{(e_1^2 + e_2^2)}$

15 A ball thrown from position A against a smooth vertical semi-circular wall rebounds and hits position B at the other end of the diameter through A. If the coefficient of restitution is 1/3, then the value of θ is

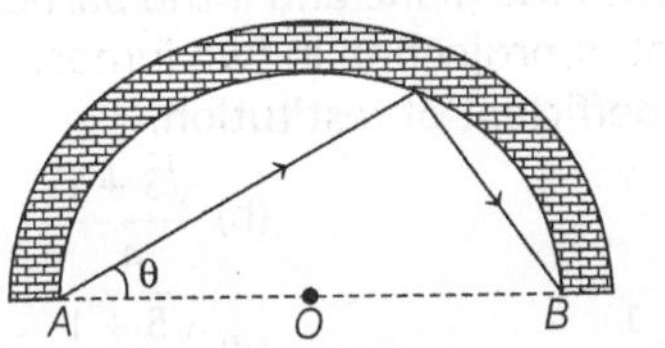

(a) 30° (b) 37° (c) 45° (d) 53°

16 AB is a L-shaped obstacle fixed on a horizontal smooth table. A ball strikes it at A, gets deflected and restrikes it at B. If the velocity vector before collision is $\mathbf{v}$ and coefficient of restitution of each collision is e, then the velocity of ball after its second collision at B is

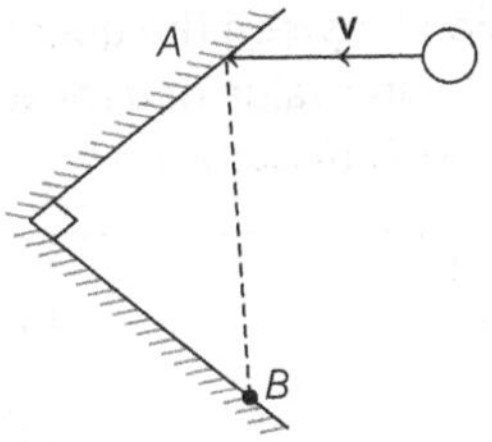

(a) $e^2\mathbf{v}$
(b) $-e^2\mathbf{v}$
(c) $-e\mathbf{v}$
(d) Data insufficient

17 The body having mass m_1 moving with a speed of v, collides elastically with a motionless body and after impact jumps aside from it at an angle 90° to the initial direction of motion with speed of $v/2$. find the mass of motionless body.

(a) $m_1/6$
(b) $5m_1/3$
(c) $4m_1/3$
(d) $3m_1/5$

18 A moving 2 kg ball with a speed of 2 ms^{-1} hits obliquely a stationary identical ball inelastically as shown. If the first ball moves away at an angle $\alpha = 30°$ to the original path, find the total KE lost after the collision

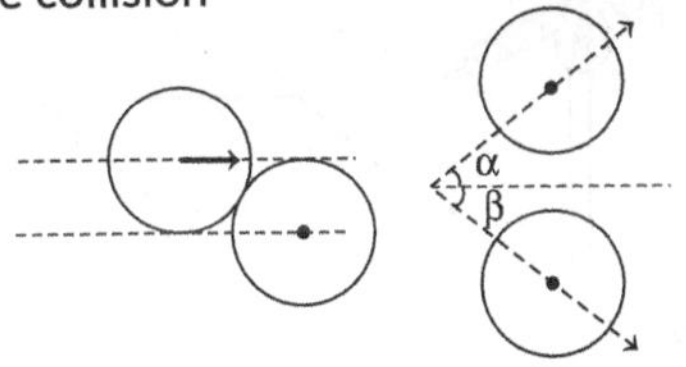

(a) (4/3) J (b) (5/4) J (c) (6/5) J (d) (7/6) J

19 A ball of mass 3 kg and radius 3 cm moving with velocity of 10 m/s collides obliquely with another ball of mass 2 kg and radius 2 cm, kept at rest. The impact parameter is 3 cm. It is found that after collision, the 3 kg ball has a velocity component of 2 m/s along the common normal. Find the coefficient of restitution.

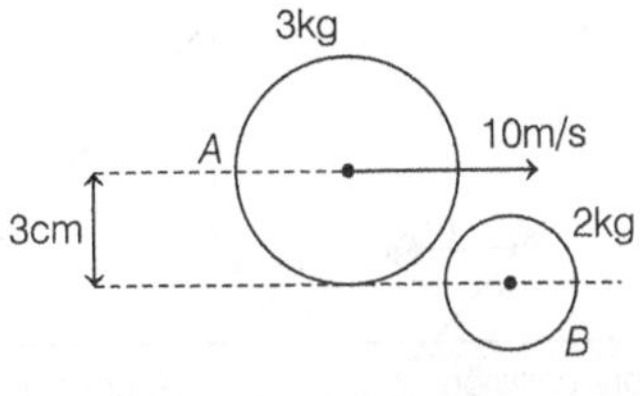

(a) 1/2
(b) 8/9
(c) 7/8
(d) 2/3

20 The queen is put at the center of a perfectly smooth carom board (square with side l). The striker strikes the queen with a speed v_0 as shown in the figure. Radius of the queen is $\sqrt{10}$ cm and that of the striker is $2\sqrt{10}$ cm. Coefficient of restitution for the collision between the queen and the striker is 1/2 and that for the collision between the queen and the walls of the board is 1. Find value of d for which the queen gets in the hole A. (Assume $l >>>$ radius of queen)

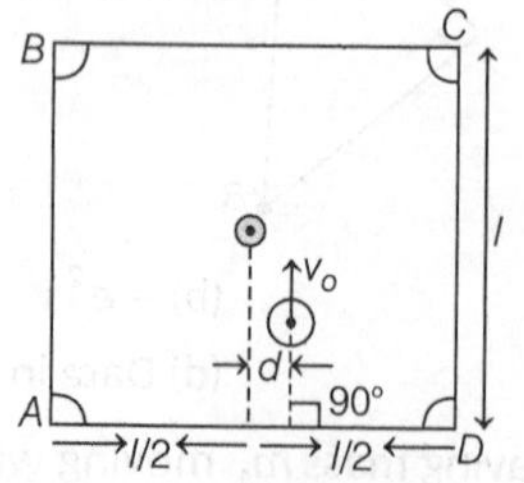

(a) 1 cm (b) 2 cm
(c) 3 cm (d) 4 cm

21 A gun which fires small balls of mass 20 g is firing 20 balls per second on the smooth horizontal table surface *ABCD*. If the collision is perfectly elastic and balls are striking at the centre of table with a speed 5 m/s at an angle of 60° with the vertical just before collision, then force exerted by one of the leg on ground is (assume total weight of the table is 0.2 kg and $g = 10\ m/s^2$)

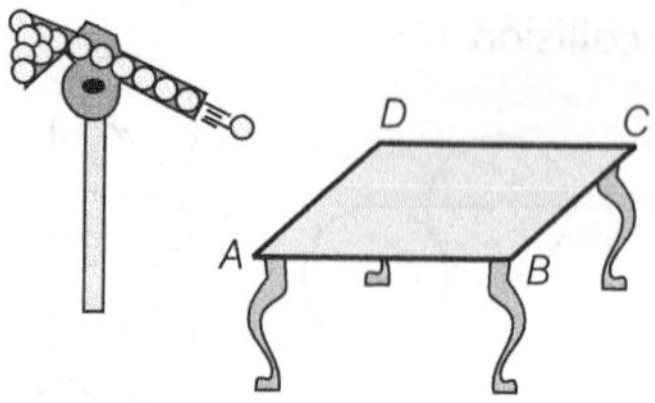

(a) 0.5 N (b) 1 N
(c) 0.25 N (d) 0.75 N

22 Consider a situation in which a ball collides horizontally with a wedge as shown in figure. All surface are smooth. It is observed that after collision ball starts moving on the incline as shown in figure. Which of the following statement(s) is/are not correct for this situation?

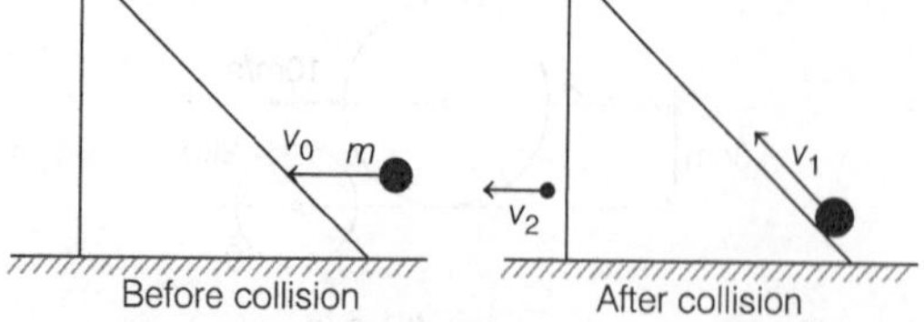

(a) Collision between ball and wedge is perfectly inelastic ($e = 0$).
(b) Momentum of the ball can be conserved only along incline just before and after collision.
(c) Momentum of system (ball + wedge) can be conserved along any direction just before and after collision.
(d) Momentum of system (ball + wedge) can be conserved only initial direction of motion of the ball.

23 A small ball falling vertically downward with constant velocity 4m/s strikes elastically a massive inclined cart moving with velocity 4m/s horizontally as shown. The velocity of the rebound of the ball is

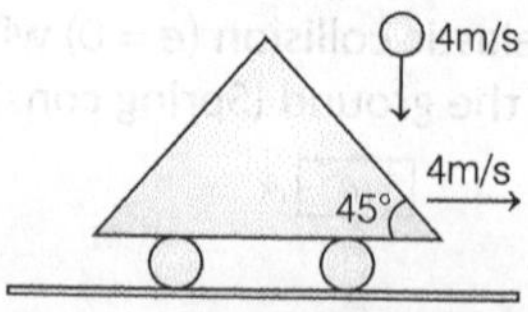

(a) $4\sqrt{2}$ m/s (b) $4\sqrt{3}$ m/s
(c) 4 m/s (d*) $4\sqrt{5}$ m/s

24 A particle is projected at an angle θ to the horizontal from a point on a smooth horizontal floor. It is found that ratio of the first maximum height attained to maximum height reached by it after 3rd collision with the floor is $\frac{10^{12}}{2^{36}}$. Find coefficient of restitution between particle and floor.
(a) 0.72 (b) 0.64
(c) 0.56 (d) None of these

25 A cylindrical hall has a horizontal smooth floor. A ball is projected along the floor from a point on the wall in a direction making an angle θ with the radius through the point, the ball returns back to the initial point after two impacts with the wall. If the coefficient of restitution is e then $\tan^2\theta$ will be

(a) $\frac{1+e+e^2}{e^3}$ (b) $\frac{1+e}{e^2}$

(c) $\frac{e^2}{1+e}$ (d) $\frac{e^3}{1+e+e^2}$

26 A particle is projected from the foot of an inclined plane at an angle α in the vertical plane through the line of greatest slope and hits the plane at right angles. If β be the angle the direction of projection makes with the plane and if the particle returns to the point of projection in two jumps, find the value of the coefficient of restitution.

(a) $\frac{\sqrt{3}-1}{2}$ (b) $\frac{\sqrt{3}+1}{4}$

(c) $\frac{\sqrt{5}-1}{2}$ (d) $\frac{\sqrt{5}+1}{4}$

27 A wedge of mass M rests on a horizontal surface. The inclination of the wedge is α. A ball of mass m moving horizontally with speed u hits the inclined face of the wedge inelastically and after hitting slides up the inclined face of the wedge. The velocity of the wedge just after the collision is (Neglect any friction)

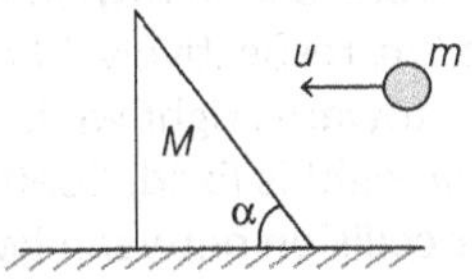

(a) $\frac{mu\sin\alpha}{M+m\sin\alpha}$ (b) $\frac{mu\cos\alpha}{M+m\cos\alpha}$

(c) $\frac{mu\sin^2\alpha}{M+m\sin^2\alpha}$ (d) $\frac{mu\cos^2\alpha}{M+m\cos^2\alpha}$

28 A ball A is falling vertically downwards with velocity v_1. It strikes elastically with a wedge moving horizontally with velocity v_2 as shown in figure. What must be the ratio v_1/v_2, so that the ball bounces back in vertically upward direction relative to the wedge?

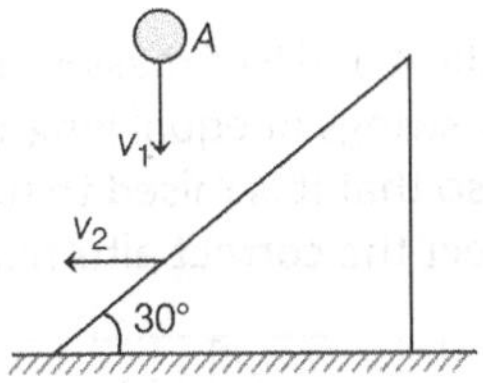

(a) $\sqrt{3}$ (b) $\frac{1}{\sqrt{3}}$

(c) 2 (d) $\frac{1}{2}$

29 A ball of mass m is attached to the lower end of a vertical string whose upper end is fixed. An identical ball B moving with a velocity $v_0 = 6$ m/s at an angle $\theta = 45°$ from vertical collides elastically with the ball A as shown. The velocity of the ball B just after collision is

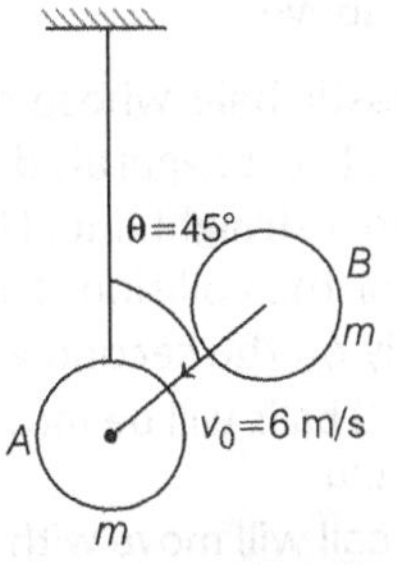

(a) 5 m/s (b) 4 m/s
(c) 3 m/s (d) 2 m/s

30 A bob of mass $10m$ is suspended through an inextensible string of length l. When the bob is at rest at the equilibrium position, two particles of mass m each moving with velocity u making an angle 60° with the string strike and get simultaneously attached to the bob. What is the value of impulsive tension in the string during the impact ?

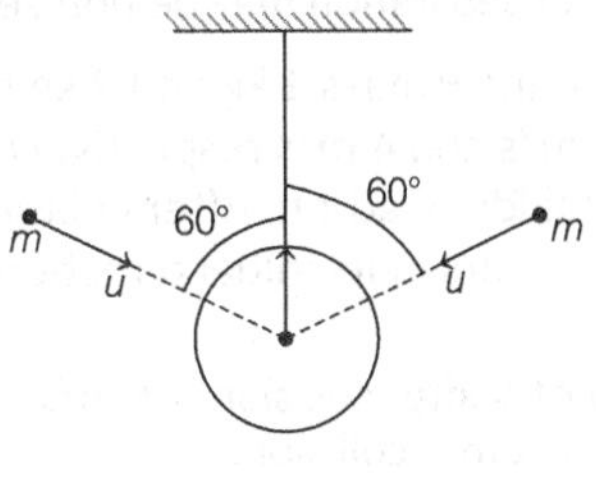

(a) zero
(b) $2mu$
(c) mu
(d) $12mu$

31 Two blocks A and B of mass $2m$ and m respectively are connected to a massless spring of spring constant k. A and B are moving on the horizontal frictionless surface with velocity v to right. If A collides with C of mass m elastically and head-on, then the maximum compressions of the spring will be

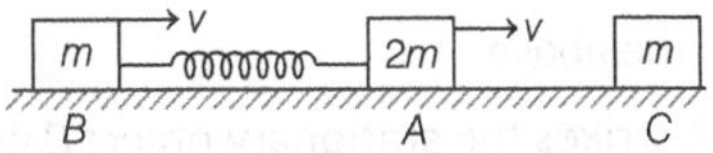

(a) $v\sqrt{\frac{3m}{2k}}$ (b) $v\sqrt{\frac{27m}{8k}}$

(c) $v\sqrt{\frac{9m}{8k}}$ (d) $v\sqrt{\frac{8m}{27k}}$

32 A mass m_1 is connected by a weightless cable passing over a frictionless pulley to a container of water, whose mass is m_0 at $t = 0$. If the container ejects water in downward direction at a constant rate b kg/s, with a velocity v_0 relative to the container, then acceleration of m_1 as a function of time is

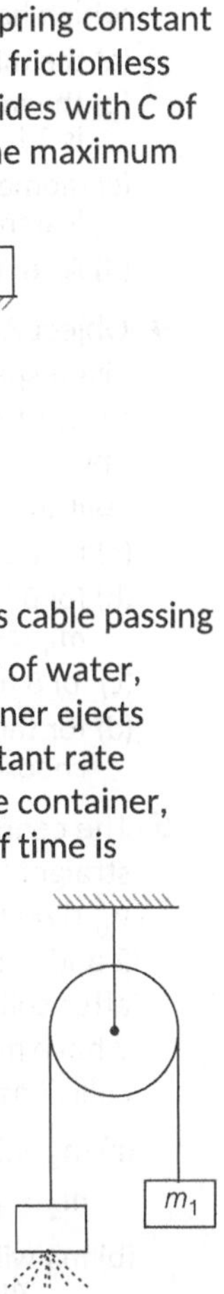

(a) $\frac{(m_1 - m_0)g}{m_1 + (m_0 - bt)}$

(b) $\frac{m_1 - (m_0 - bt)g}{m_1 + (m_0 - bt)}$

(c) $\frac{m_1 g - (m_0 - bt)g + v_0 b}{m_1 + (m_0 - bt)}$

(d) $\frac{m_1 g - (m_0 - bt)g + v_0 b}{m_1 - (m_0 - bt)}$

Multiple Choice(s) Correct Questions

1 In an inelastic collision,
(a) the final velocities of both the particles must be same
(b) kinetic energy of the system is not conserved
(c) linear momentum of the system is not conserved
(d) velocity of separation may be non-zero

2 Two balls A and B mass 1 kg and 2 kg moving with speeds 21 m/s and 4 m/s respectively in opposite direction collide head-on. After collision A moves with speed 1 m/s in its initial direction. Which is /are correct?
(a) Velocity of B after collision is 6 m/s opposite to its direction before collision.
(b) $e = 0.2$
(c) Loss of kinetic energy due to collision is 200 J.
(d) Impulse of force between 2 balls is 400 N-s.

3 A particle moving with kinetic energy = 3 J makes an elastic head-on collision with a stationary particle which has twice its mass. During the impact
(a) the minimum kinetic energy of the system is 1 J.
(b) the maximum elastic potential energy of the system is 2 J.
(c) momentum and total energy are conserved at every instant.
(d) All of the above

4 Object A strikes the stationary object B with a certain given speed u head-on in an elastic collision. The mass of A is fixed, you may only choose the mass of B appropriately for following cases. Then after the collision
(a) for B to have the greatest speed, choose $m_B = m_A$
(b) for B to have the greatest momentum, choose $m_B << m_A$
(c) for B to have the greatest speed, choose $m_B << m_A$
(d) for the maximum fraction of kinetic energy transfer, choose $m_B = m_A$

5 The centres of three spheres 1, 2 and 3 lie on a single straight line. Sphere 1 is moving with an initial speed v_0 directed along this line towards sphere 2. Spheres 2 and 3 are initially at rest. Acquiring some speed after collision, sphere 2 hits sphere 3. Spheres 1 and 3 have masses m_1 and m_3 respectively, and all the collisions are perfectly elastic and head on. Then
(a) m_3 will acquire maximum speed, when $m_2 = \sqrt{m_1 m_3}$
(b) m_3 will acquire maximum speed equal to $\dfrac{4m_1 v_0}{(\sqrt{m_1} + \sqrt{m_3})^2}$
(c) m_3 will acquire maximum speed, when $m_2 = \dfrac{m_1 + m_3}{2}$
(d) m_3 will acquire maximum speed equal to $\dfrac{m_1 m_3}{2}$

6 The two balls A and B as shown in figure are of masses m and $2m$, respectively. The ball A moves with velocity u towards right while B is at rest. The wall at extreme right is fixed. Coefficient of restitution for collision between two balls is 1/2 and between either ball and wall is 1. Then speeds of A and B after all possible collisions are

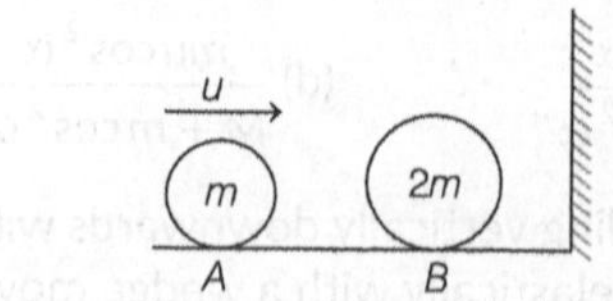

(a) $v_A = \dfrac{u}{2}$
(b) $v_A = \dfrac{u}{4}$
(c) $v_B = \dfrac{u}{8}$
(d) $v_B = \dfrac{u}{4}$

7 Two small balls A and B of mass M and 3M hang from the ceiling by strings of equal length. The ball A is drawn aside so that it is raised to height H and then released. Select the correct alternatives.

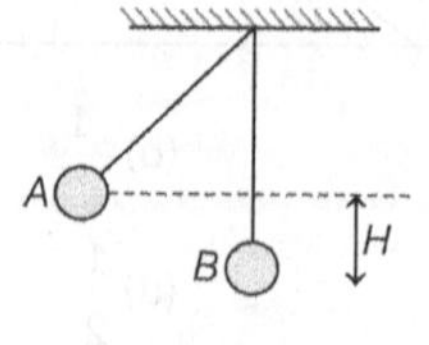

(a) If collision is perfectly elastic, the ball B will rise to height $H/4$.
(b) If collision is perfectly inelastic combined mass will rise to height $H/16$.
(c) If collision is perfectly elastic, the ball A will rise to a height $H/4$.
(d) None of the above

8 A series of n elastic balls whose masses are m, em, e^2m ... etc. are at rest separated by intervals with their centres on a straight line. Here, e is coefficient of restitution for the collision. The first is made to impinge directly on the second with velocity u. Then
(a) the first $(n-1)$ balls will be moving with the same velocity $(1-e)u$
(b) the last one ball will move with velocity u
(c) the kinetic energy of the system is $\dfrac{1}{2}mu^2(1 - e + e^n)$
(d) None of the above

9 A ball moving with a velocity v hits a massive wall moving towards the ball with a velocity u. An elastic impact lasts for a time Δt.

(a) The average elastic force acting on the ball is $\frac{m(u+v)}{\Delta t}$.

(b) The average elastic force acting on the ball is $\frac{2m(u+v)}{\Delta t}$.

(c) The kinetic energy of the ball increases by $2mu(u+v)$.

(d) The kinetic energy of the ball remains the same after the collision.

10 A massive vertical wall is approaching a man at a speed u. When it is at a distance of 10 m, the man throws a ball with speed 10 m/s at an angle 37° which after completely elastic rebound reaches back directly into his hands. ($g = 10$ m/s^2)

(a) Velocity u of the wall is (13/3) m/s.

(b) Velocity u of the wall is (1/3) m/s.

(c) Time of flight of the ball is 1.2 s

(d) time taken by the ball to collide with the wall is (30/37) s.

11 In the figure, the block B of mass m starts from rest at the top of a wedge W of mass M. All surfaces are without friction. W can slide on the ground. B slides down onto the ground, moves along ground with a speed v has an elastic collision with the wall, and climbs back onto W.

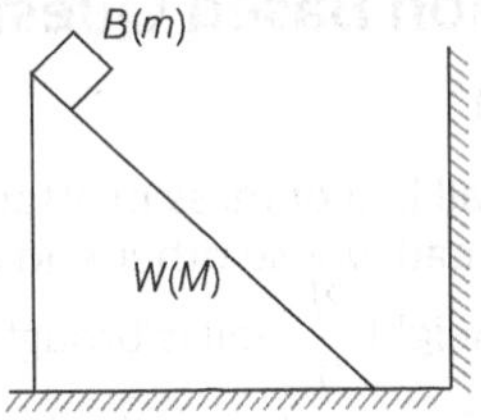

(a) B will reach the top of W again.

(b) From the beginning, till the collision with the wall, the centre of mass of '$B + W$' is stationary in horizontal direction.

(c) After the collision the centre of mass of $B + W$ moves with the velocity $\frac{2mv}{m+M}$.

(d) When B reaches its highest position on W, the speed of W is $\frac{2mv}{m+M}$.

12 Two particles of mass m_1 and m_2 are moving with velocity $\mathbf{v}_1$ and $\mathbf{v}_2$, respectively. Mark the correct statements about a perfectly inelastic collision between m_1 and m_2.

(a) Impulse by m_1 to m_2 is $\frac{m_1 m_2}{m_1 + m_2}(\mathbf{v}_1 - \mathbf{v}_2)$

(b) Momentum transfered by m_2 to m_1 is $\frac{m_1 m_2}{m_1 + m_2}(\mathbf{v}_2 - \mathbf{v}_1)$

(c) Impulse by m_1 on m_2 in CM frame is $\frac{m_1 m_2}{m_1 + m_2}(\mathbf{v}_1 - \mathbf{v}_2)$

(d) In CM frame both the particles come to rest after perfectly inelastic collision.

13 A block of mass m is given a horizontal velocity v_0 from one end of a sledge of mass M and length l. If the block stops after 1st collision with sledge and all surfaces are frictionless then (Assume coefficient of restitution does not change i.e. e remains constant) $m = 2$ kg, $M = 4$ kg, $v_0 = 16$ m/s, $l = 8$ m)

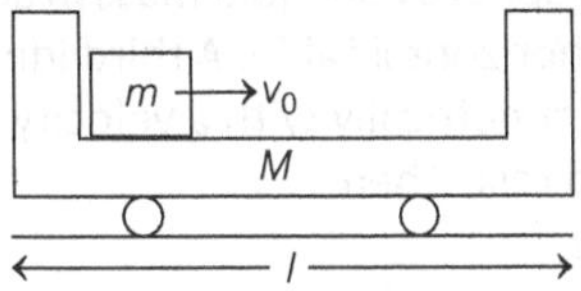

(a) Speed of the sledge and block after 2nd collision are 4 m/s and 8 m/s respectively.

(b) Speed of the sledge and block after 2nd collision are 6 m/s and 4 m/s respectively.

(c) Distance travelled by CM of the (block + sledge) system just before 4th collision is 40 m.

(d) Distance travelled by CM of the (block + sledge) system just before 4th collision is (32/3) m.

14 Two identical blocks A and B each of mass 2 kg are hanging stationary by a light inextensible flexible string, passing over a light and frictionless pulley, as shown in figure. At $t = 0$, a shell C of mass 1kg moving vertically upwards with velocity 9 m/s collides with block B and gets stuck to it.

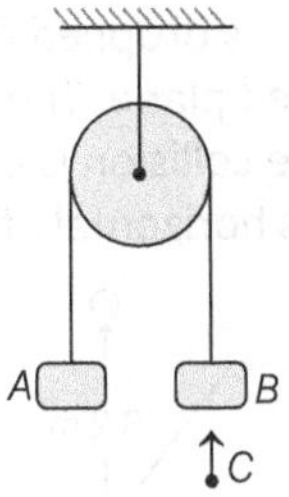

(a) String gets taut again at $t = 0.3$ s.

(b) Time at which block B starts moving downwards is 0.9 s.

(c) Maximum height reached by B is 0.81 m.

(d) Loss of energy due to jerk in the string is 5.4 J.

15 A ball A collides elastically with an another identical ball B with velocity 10 m/s at an angle of 30° from the line joining their centres C_1 and C_2. Select the correct alternative(s).

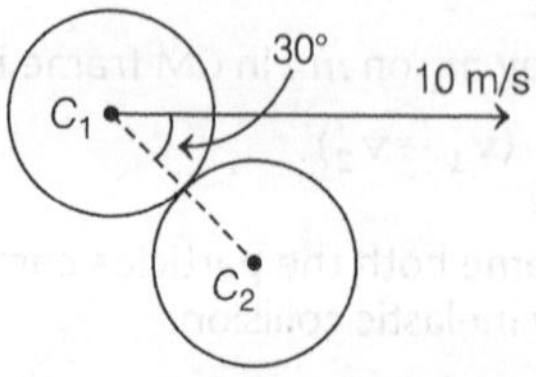

(a) Velocity of ball A after collision is 5 m/s.
(b) Velocity of ball B after collision is $5\sqrt{3}$ m/s.
(c) Both the balls move at right angles after collision.
(d) Kinetic energy will not be conserved here, because collision is not head-on.

16 Two equal spheres of equal mass m are in contact on a smooth horizontal table. A third identical sphere collides symmetrically with a velocity u on them and reduced to rest. Then
(a) $e = 2/3$
(b) $e = 1/3$
(c) loss of kinetic energy is $\frac{1}{2}mu^2$
(d) loss of kinetic energy is $\frac{1}{6}mu^2$

17. A projectile is fired on a horizontal ground. Coefficient of restitution between projectile and ground is e. Let a, b and c be the ratio of time of flight, maximum height and horizontal range in first two collisions with the ground. Then
(a) $a = \frac{1}{e}$ (b) $b = \frac{1}{e^2}$
(c) $c = \frac{1}{e^2}$ (d) All of these

18 A ball of mass 1kg is dropped from a height of 3.2 m on smooth inclined plane. The coefficient of restitution for the collision is $e = 1/2$. The ball's velocity becomes horizontal after the collision.

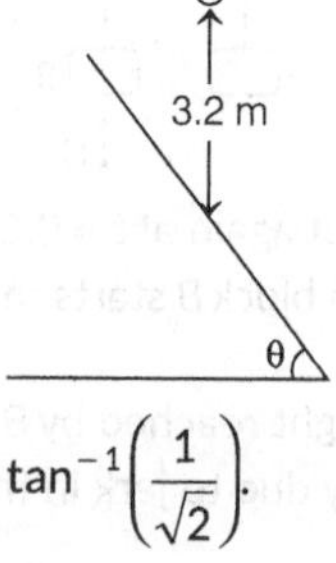

(a) The angle $\theta = \tan^{-1}\left(\frac{1}{\sqrt{2}}\right)$
(b) The speed of the ball after the collision $= 4\sqrt{2}$ m/s.
(c) The total loss in kinetic energy during the collision is 8 J.
(d) The ball hits the inclined plane again while travelling vertically downward.

19 On a smooth horizontal surface, a ball of mass 1kg is placed, tied to a nail O on the same horizontal surface with a string of length 50 cm. Another ball of same mass travelling on the horizontal surface with a speed of 10 m/s, its velocity making an angle of 45° with string as shown, collides with the first ball. The balls stick to each other after collision

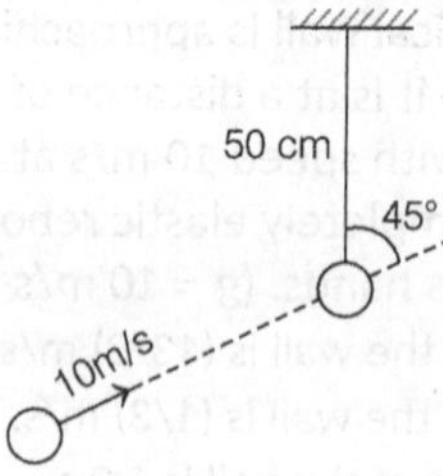

(a) momentum will not be conserved during collision.
(b) tension in the string just after collision is zero.
(c) time for which the string remains slack after collision is 0.141 s.
(d) velocity of the balls just after the string is taut again is $\frac{5}{\sqrt{2}}$ m/s.

Comprehension Based Questions

Comprehension-1

Figure shows a small ball of mass m attached to one end of an inextensible thread whose other end is connected to a fixed point O at a height $\frac{2l}{3}$. Ball is brought to horizontal level and released from rest. Length of the thread is l. Horizontal surface is smooth.

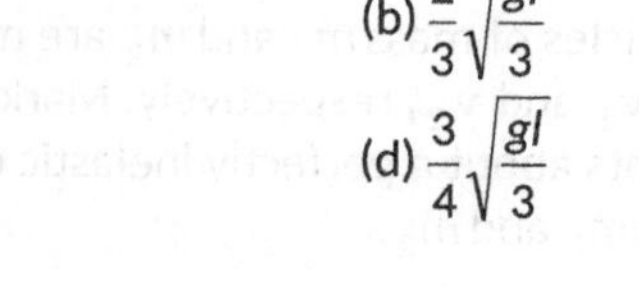

1 Velocity of the ball just after it strikes the surface (collision is perfectly inelastic) will be
(a) $2\sqrt{\frac{gl}{3}}$ (b) $\frac{2}{3}\sqrt{\frac{gl}{3}}$
(c) $\frac{4}{3}\sqrt{\frac{gl}{3}}$ (d) $\frac{3}{4}\sqrt{\frac{gl}{3}}$

2 Magnitude of the impulse on the ball due to the tension, as it loses contact with the surface is

(a) $\frac{2\sqrt{3}}{5\sqrt{5}}m\sqrt{gl}$ (b) $\frac{4\sqrt{5}}{9\sqrt{3}}m\sqrt{gl}$

(c) $\frac{2\sqrt{6}}{5}m\sqrt{gl}$ (d) $\frac{4\sqrt{5}}{9}m\sqrt{gl}$

3 The maximum height attained by the ball after striking the floor is (floor is smooth)

(a) $\frac{32l}{243}$ (b) $\frac{23}{43}l$ (c) $\frac{43}{264}l$ (d) $\frac{8}{27}l$

Comprehension-2

A narrow U-shaped tube of mass $2m$ is placed at rest on a smooth fixed horizontal surface. The curved surface of tube as shown is semicircular in shape. Two identical smooth spherical balls (of small size) each of mass m and of diameter slightly less than the inner diameter of tube enter into the tube simultaneously with a velocity u as shown. (Assume no loss of energy anywhere and all collisions to be elastic).

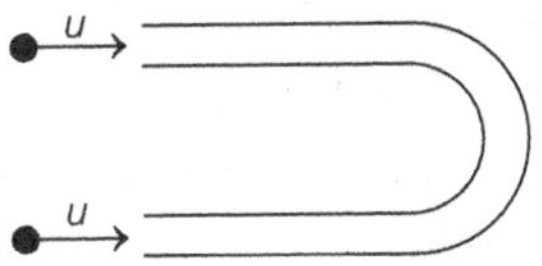

4 Speed of each spherical ball, just before their collision is

(a) $\frac{u}{\sqrt{3}}$ (b) $\frac{2u}{3\sqrt{3}}$ (c) $\frac{u}{2}$ (d) $\frac{\sqrt{3}u}{2}$

5 The angle between velocity vectors of both balls just before collision, as observed in the ground frame is

(a) $2\tan^{-1}\sqrt{2}$ (b) $2\tan^{-1}\frac{1}{\sqrt{2}}$

(c) $\tan^{-1}\sqrt{2}$ (d) π

6 Speed of the spheres when they come out of the tube is

(a) u (b) $u/2$

(c) $\frac{\sqrt{3}u}{2}$ (d) 0

Comprehension-3

A block of mass 1 kg is moving towards a movable wedge of mass 2 kg as shown in figure. All surfaces are smooth. When the block leaves the wedge from top, its velocity is making an angle $\theta = 30°$ with horizontal.

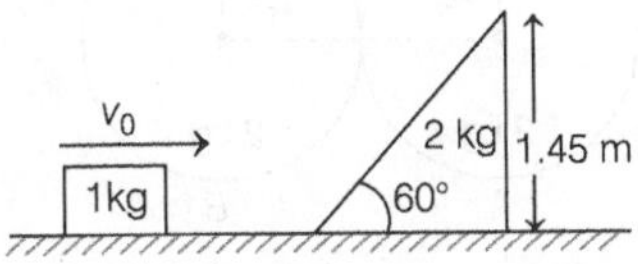

7 The value of v_0 (in m/s) is

(a) 4 (b) 7

(c) 10 (d) 9

8 To what maximum height will the block rise

(a) 1.9 m (b) 2.7 m

(c) 1.6 m (d) 1.45 m

9 In the whole process let J be the magnitude of net impulse given to the block by the wedge, J_H its horizontal component and J_V its vertical component. Then

(a) $J = \frac{8}{\sqrt{3}}$ N-s (b) $J_H = 4$ N-s

(c) $J_V = \frac{4}{\sqrt{3}}$ N-s (d) All of these

Comprehension-4

A smooth ball A moving with velocity u collides with another smooth identical ball at rest. After collision both the balls move with same speed with angle between their velocities 60°. No external force acts on the system of balls.

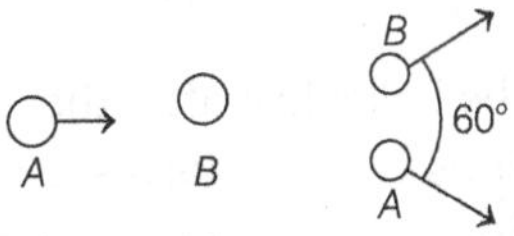

10 The speed of each ball after the collision is

(a) $\frac{u}{2}$ (b) $\frac{u}{3}$ (c) $\frac{u}{\sqrt{3}}$ (d) $\frac{2u}{\sqrt{3}}$

11 If the kinetic energy lost is fully converted to heat then heat produced is

(a) $\frac{1}{3}mu^2$ (b) $\frac{2}{3}mu^2$ (c) 0 (d) $\frac{1}{6}mu^2$

12 The value of coefficient of restitution is

(a) 1 (b) $\frac{1}{3}$ (c) $\frac{1}{\sqrt{3}}$ (d) 0

Comprehension-5

A ball of mass $m = 1$ kg is colliding with a wedge of mass $M = 0.9$ kg with a velocity of 15 m/s as shown in the figure. After striking the wedge, the ball rebounds in some arbitrary direction and due to the impulse the wedge recoils in backward direction with a speed of 10 m/s. Assume all the surfaces to be smooth take $\theta = 37°$ and $g = 10\ m/s^2$.

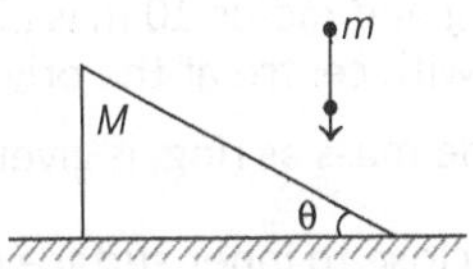

13 Velocity of ball after collision would
(a) $\sqrt{90}$ m / s (b) 10 m / s
(c) 5 m / s (d) 14.3 m/s

14 The coefficient of restitution between ball and wedge is
(a) 0.5 (b) 0.75 (c) 0.68 (d) 0.4

15 Magnitude of impulse between wedge and ball would be
(a) 18 N-s (b) 110 N-s (c) 8 N-s (d) 15 N-s

Comprehension-6

Two smooth balls A and B, each of mass m and radius R, have their centres as shown in figure. Ball A, moving along positive X-axis, collides with ball B. Just before the collision, speed of ball A is 4 m/s and ball B is stationary. The collision between the balls is elastic.

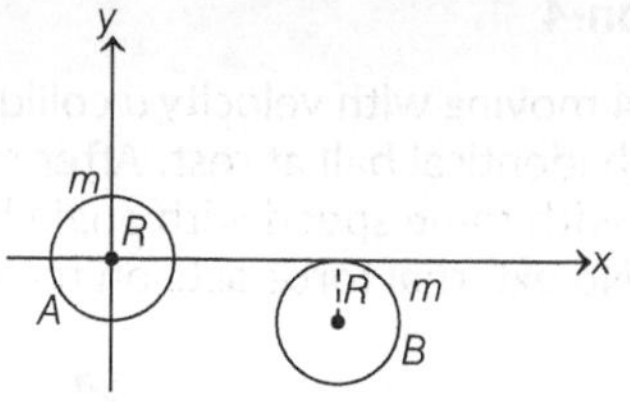

16 Velocity of the ball A just after the collision is
(a) $(\hat{i}+\sqrt{3}\,\hat{j})$ m/s (b) $(\hat{i}-\sqrt{3}\,\hat{j})$ m/s
(c) $(2\hat{i}+\sqrt{3}\,\hat{j})$ m/s (d) $(2\hat{i}+2\,\hat{j})$ m/s

17 Velocity of the ball B after the collision is
(a) $(3\hat{i}-\sqrt{3}\,\hat{j})$ m/s (b) $(2\sqrt{3}-2\sqrt{3}\,\hat{j})$ m/s
(c) $(2\hat{i}-2\sqrt{3}\,\hat{j})$ m/s (d) $(\sqrt{3}\,\hat{i}-\sqrt{3}\,\hat{j})$ m/s

18 Impulse(in kg-m/s) of the force exerted by A on B during the collision is equal to
(a) $(\sqrt{3}m\hat{i}+3m\hat{j})$ (b) $\left(\frac{\sqrt{3}}{2}m\hat{i}-3m\hat{j}\right)$
(c) $(3m\hat{i}-\sqrt{3}m\hat{j})$ (d) $(2\sqrt{3}m\hat{i}-3m\hat{j})$

19 Coefficient of restitution during the collision is changed to 1/2, keeping all other parameters un changed. What is the velocity of the ball B after the collision?
(a) $\frac{1}{2}(3\sqrt{3}\,\hat{i}+9\,\hat{j})$ m/s (b) $\frac{1}{4}(9\,\hat{i}-3\sqrt{3}\,\hat{j})$ m/s
(c) $(6\,\hat{i}+3\sqrt{3}\,\hat{j})$ m/s (d) $(6\,\hat{i}-3\sqrt{3}\,\hat{j})$ m/s

Comprehension-7

A ring of mass 200 g and radius 10 m is placed on a smooth horizontal surface with centre at the origin. A small particle, of the same mass as ring, is given velocity $\frac{5}{\sqrt{2}}$ m/s from point A (very close to inner surface of the ring) towards point B (at $t=0$). Initially, particle was not in contact with ring. Assume all collisions between the ring and the particle as perfectly elastic.

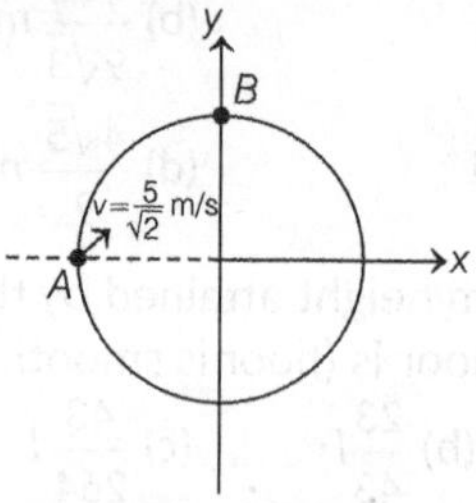

20 Particle will collide with point A for the first time after a time interval of
(a) 8 s (b) 16 s
(c) 12 s (d) 24 s

21 Coordinate of centre of mass of ring when particle reach back to point A for the first time
(a) (10, 10) (b) (0, 0)
(c) (20, 20) (d) (– 20, – 20)

22 Which of the following conclusion can be drawn
(i) between $t=8$ to 12 s particle is at rest.
(ii) between $t=12$ to 16 s particle is moving along + y-direction.
(iii) between $t=4$ to 8 s particle is moving along + x-direction.
(iv) between $t=8$ to 12 s ring is moving at 45° with + x-direction.

Correct alternatives are
(a) (i), (ii), (iii) (b) (ii), (iii), (iv)
(c) (i), (iv) (d) (i), (ii), (iii), (iv)

Comprehension-8

Two identical balls A and B each of mass 2 kg and radius R are suspended vertically from inextensible strings as shown. Third ball C of mass 1 kg and radius $r=(\sqrt{2}-1)R$ falls and hits both the balls A and B symmetrically with 10 m/s. Speed of both the balls A and B just after the collision is 3 m/s.

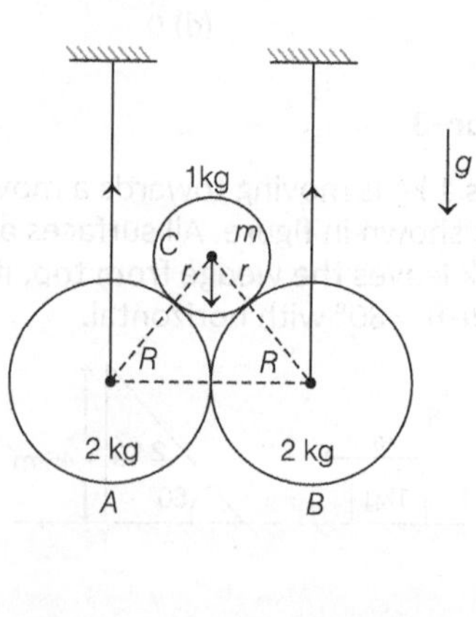

23 Speed of balls C just after collision is

(a) 2 m/s (b) $2\sqrt{2}$ m/s

(c) 5 m/s (d) $(\sqrt{2}-1)$ m/s

24 Impulse provided by each string during collision is

(a) $6\sqrt{2}$ N-s (b) 12 N-s

(c) $3\sqrt{2}$ N-s (d) 6 N-s

25 The value of coefficient of restitution is

(a) $\frac{1}{4}$ (b) $\frac{1}{\sqrt{2}}$

(c) $(\sqrt{2}-1)$ (d) $\frac{1}{2}$

Comprehension-9

Three spheres, each of mass m, can slide freely on a frictionless, horizontal surface. Spheres A and B are attached to an inextensible inelastic cord of length l and are at rest in the position shown when sphere B is struck directly by sphere C which is moving to the right with a velocity v_0. Knowing that the cord is taut when sphere B is struck by sphere C and assume perfectly elastic impact between spheres B and C.

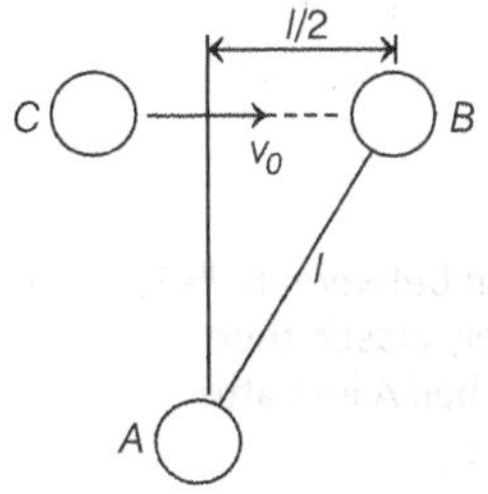

26 The velocity of sphere C immediately after impact is

(a) $\frac{v_0}{15}$ (b) $\frac{2v_0}{15}$

(c) $\frac{3v_0}{15}$ (d) $\frac{4v_0}{15}$

27 The velocity of sphere B immediately after impact is

(a) $\frac{4\sqrt{3}\,v_0}{15}$

(b) $\frac{8\sqrt{3}\,v_0}{15}$

(c) $\frac{4\sqrt{13}\,v_0}{15}$

(d) $\frac{4\sqrt{17}\,v_0}{15}$

28 Impulse of tension in the string is

(a) $\frac{mv_0}{15}$ (b) $\frac{2mv_0}{15}$

(c) $\frac{3mv_0}{15}$ (d) $\frac{4mv_0}{15}$

Match The Columns Questions

1 Match the following

	Column I		Column II
A.	Elastic collision	1.	Kinetic energy is conserved
B.	Inelastic collision	2.	Momentum conserved
C.	Perfectly inelastic collision	3.	Kinetic energy is not conserved
D.	Collision between two cars moving at high speeds.	4.	Total energy is conserved
		5.	Mechanical energy is not conserved

2 A smooth disk (mass M_1) moving on smooth floor undergoes elastic collision with another smooth disk (mass M_2) at rest. Quantities in Column II refer to possible values after collision.

($v \to$ speed, $p \to$ momentum, $K \to$ kinetic energy)

	Column I		Column II
A.	$M_1 >> M_2$, collision is head on	1.	$\lvert \mathbf{v}_{2_f} \rvert > \lvert \mathbf{v}_{1_f} \rvert$
B.	$M_1 << M_2$, collision is head on	2.	$\lvert \mathbf{p}_{2_f} \rvert > \lvert \mathbf{p}_{1_f} \rvert$
C.	$M_1 = M_2$, collision is head-on	3.	$K_{2_f} > K_{1_f}$
D.	$M_1 = M_2$, collision is head-on	4.	$K_{2_f} < K_{1_f}$

3. A heavy ball of mass $2m$ moving with a velocity u_0 collides elastically head-on with a cradle of three identical balls each of mass m as shown in figure.

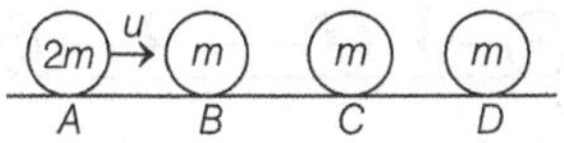

	Column I		Column II
A.	Total impulse of all collisions on A	1.	$4mu/9$
B.	Total impulse of all collisions on B	2.	$4mu/27$
C.	Total impulse of all collision on C	3.	$4mu/3$
D.	Total impulse of all collisions on D	4.	$52mu/27$

4 Block A moving on frictionless horizontal plane collides head-on with block B initially at rest. The collision is not ($0 < e < 1$) perfectly elastic.

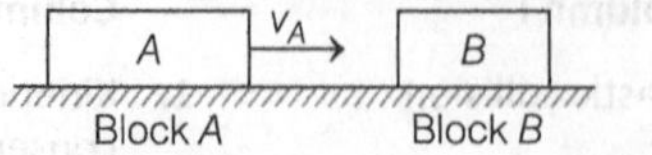

	Column I		Column II
A.	Forces exerted by the blocks	1.	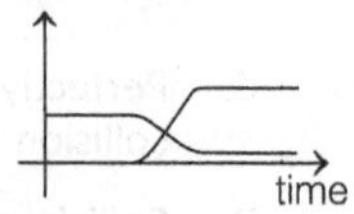
B.	The position of mass centres of the two block system	2.	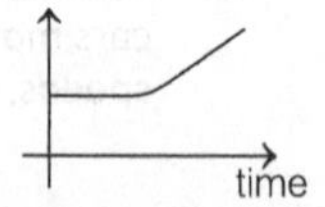
C.	Velocity of blocks	3.	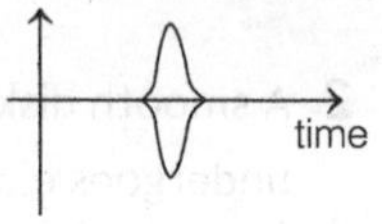
D.	Position of block B	4.	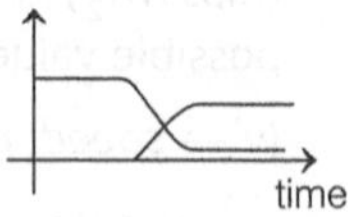
		5.	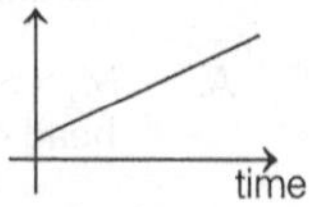

5 Two spheres A and B moving on a smooth horizontal surface with same velocity v. A third sphere C is moving in opposite direction on same surface with same speed. All the spheres are of equal mass. The collisions are elastic. v_{CM} represents the centre of mass velocity of the three sphere system. In Column I are mentioned values of some physical quantities after all possible collisions having occurred and in Column II are mentioned different physical setups.

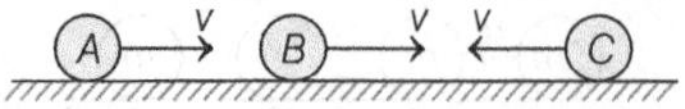

	Column I		Column II
A.	v_{CM} during all the collisions $= v/3$	1.	If A and B were connected by an ideal spring which is initially at natural length.
B.	Only one collision takes place in	2.	If A and B were connected to each other by a massless rigid rod
C.	Mechanical energy is not conserved	3.	If A and B are connected by just taut ideal string.
D.	A and B can be approximated as a diatomic molecule having activated or frozen vibrational degree of freedom.	4.	If A and B were not connected to each other.
		5.	If A and B were initially moving in contact with each other.

6 A smooth ball A of mass m is attached to one end of a light inextensible string, and is suspended from fixed point O. Another identical ball B, is dropped from a height h, so that the string just touches the surface of the sphere.

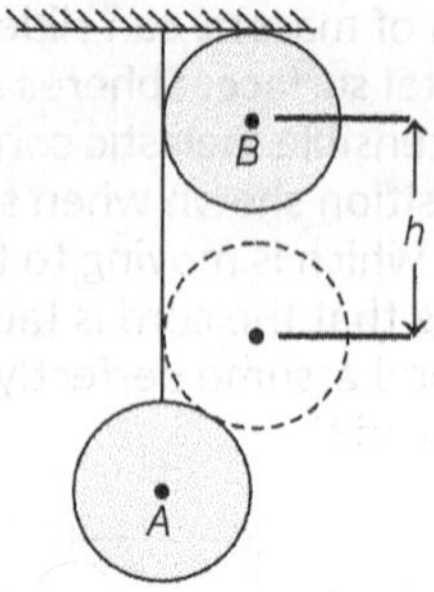

	Column I		Column II
A.	If collision between balls is completely elastic then speed of ball A just after collision is	1.	$\frac{3m}{5}\sqrt{2gh}$
B.	If collision between balls is completely elastic then impulsive tension provided by string is	2.	$\frac{\sqrt{6gh}}{5}$
C.	If collision between balls is completely inelastic then speed of ball A just after collision is	3.	$\frac{6m}{5}\sqrt{2gh}$
D.	If collision between balls is completely inelastic then impulsive tension provided by string is	4.	$\frac{2\sqrt{6gh}}{5}$

7 A block of A of mass $M_A = 1$ kg is kept on a smooth horizontal surface and attached by a light thread to another block B of mass $M_A = 2$ kg. Block B is resting on ground, and thread and pulley are massless and frictionless. A bullet of mass $m = 0.25$ kg moving horizontally with velocity of $u = 200$ m/s penetrates through block A and comes out with a velocity of 100 m/s.

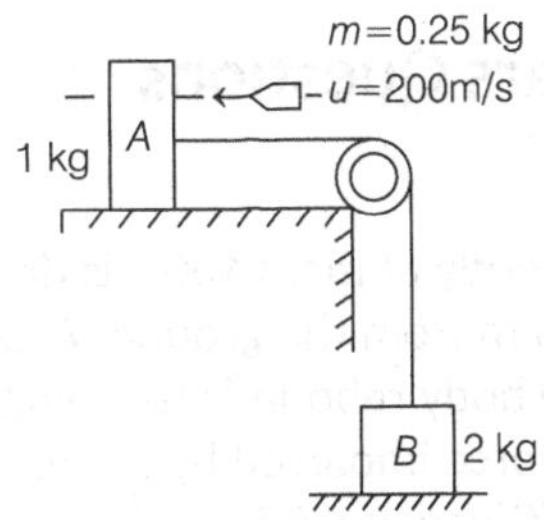

Column I		Column II (Values in SI unit)
A. Velocity of the 2 kg block just after the bullet comes out	1.	50/3
B. Maximum displacement of 1 kg block in left direction	2.	25
C. Impulse by the string on block *B*	3.	25/3
D. Impulse by the particle on block *A*	4.	5.2

Numerical Value Questions

1 3 blocks shown are identical. *A* and *C* are moving together at 12 m/s. *B* is at rest, when *A* hits *B* as shown. Collision is perfectly inelastic. The friction coefficient between *A* and *C* is same as that between *B* and *C* and is equal to 0.2. Finally *C* is on top of *B* and all are moving together with same speed. What is the length of each block (in m) ? Ground is smooth.

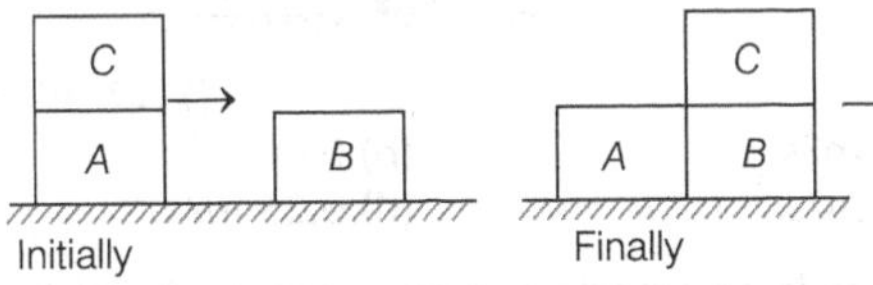

2 A small ball of mass *m* is placed on a super ball of mass *M* and the two balls are dropped from height *H* (*H* is very large compared to radius of balls). How high (in m) does small ball rise after collision? All collisions are head-on elastic and $m << M$. ($H = 1$ m and $g = 10$ m/s^2)

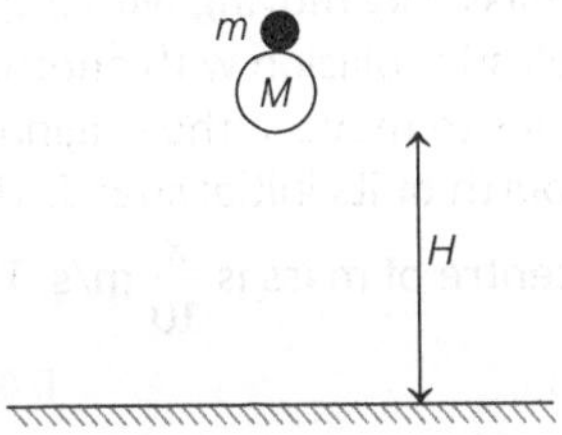

3 A small block *A* is released from the top of a fixed incline at height of $h = 512$ m. All surfaces are frictionless. The block collides with the ground inelastically but does not stick to it. After collision with the spring, it returns back and collides with the incline inelastically but again does not stick to it. Find the maximum height (in m) from the ground attained by block *A* when it climbs up the incline.

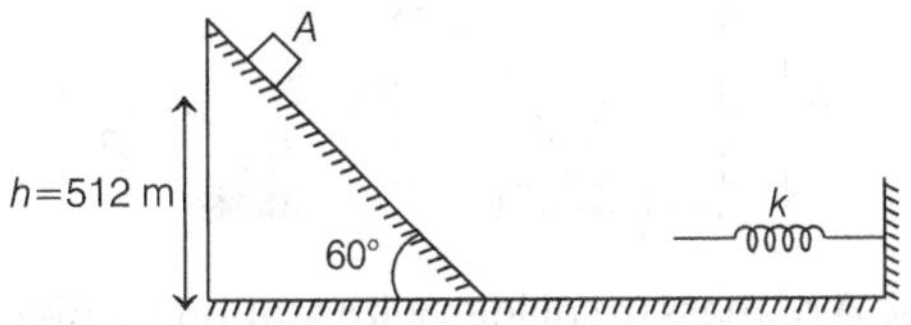

4 Consider a horizontal surface moving vertically upward with velocity 2 m/s. A small ball of mass 2 kg is moving with velocity $2\hat{i} - 2\hat{j}$ (m/s). If coefficient of restitution is 1/2 and friction coefficient is 1/3, find horizontal component of velocity of ball after collision.

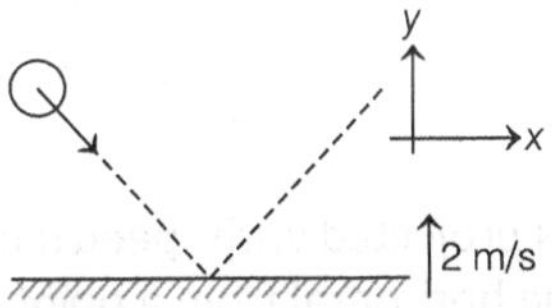

5 A small steel ball *A* is suspended by an inextensible thread of length $l = 1.5$ m from *O*. Another identical ball is thrown vertically downwards such that its surface remains just in contact with thread during downward motion and collides elastically with the suspended ball. If the suspended ball just completes vertical circle after collision, calculate the velocity (in m/s) of the falling ball just before collision. ($g = 10$ ms^{-2})

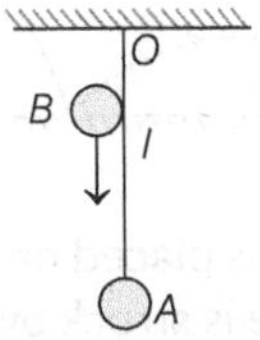

6 Two equal discs initially at rest are in contact on a table. A third disc of same mass but of double radius strikes them symmetrically and itself comes to rest after impact. The coefficient of restitution is *n*/32. Find *n*.

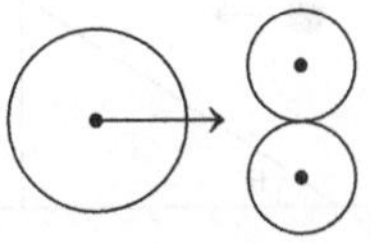

7 A 70 g ball B dropped from a height h_0 = 9 m reaches a height h_2 = 0.25 m after bouncing twice from identical 210 g plates. Plate A rests directly on hard ground, while plate C rests on a foam-rubber mat. Determine the height h_1 (in m) of the ball's first bounce.

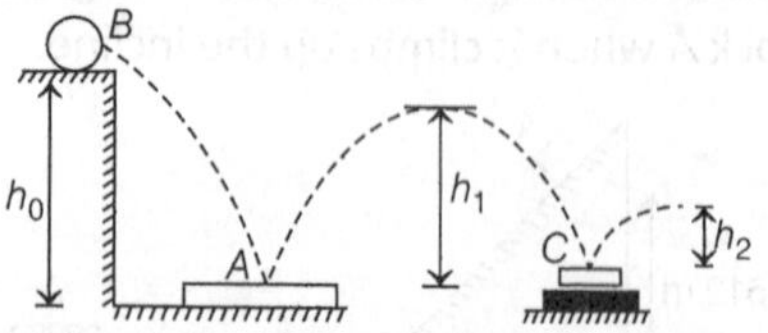

8 Disc A of mass m collides with stationary disk B of mass $2m$ as shown in figure. Find the value of coefficient of restitution for which the two disks move in perpendicular direction after collision.

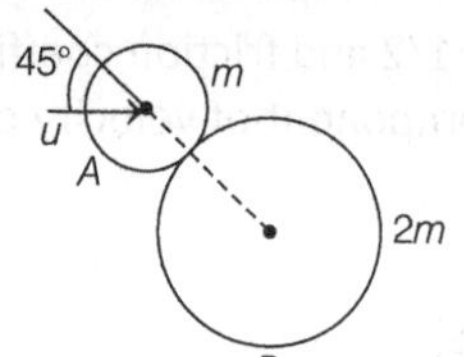

9 A particle is projected with speed u making an angle 30° with the horizontal from a point A on the ground. The vertical wall is smooth. The particle hits the wall at highest point of its trajectory, after which it rebounds from the smooth ground and reaches point A as shown in the diagram. If coefficient of restitution e is same for all the collision then find the value of $4e$.

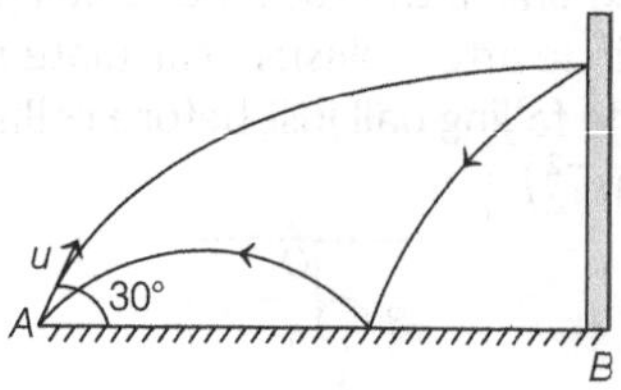

10 An inclined plane is placed on a horizontal smooth surface. The plane is struck by an elastic ball whose velocity is horizontal just before the impact. The ball bounces off the inclined plane and then lands on it again at the point of first impact. Find the ratio of the masses of the ball and the inclined plane. ($\theta = 30°$)

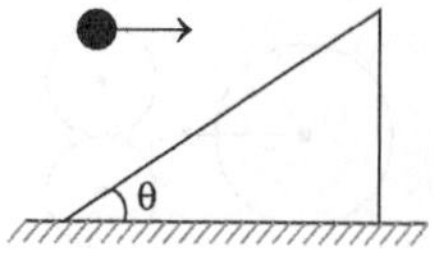

Previous Years Questions

JEE Main

1 A spherical body of mass 100 g is dropped from a height of 10 m from the ground. After hitting the ground, the body rebounds to a height of 5 m. The impulse of force imparted by the ground to the body is given by (Given, $g = 9.8 \text{ m/s}^2$) **[2024, 30 Jan Shift-I]**

(a) 43.2 kg ms^{-1} (b) 4.32 kg ms^{-1}
(c) 23.9 kg ms^{-1} (d) 2.39 kg ms^{-1}

2 A bullet of mass 0.1 kg moving horizontally with speed 400 ms^{-1} hits a wooden block of mass 3.9 kg kept on a horizontal rough surface. The bullet gets embedded into the block and moves 20 m before coming to rest. The coefficient of friction between the block and the surface is (Given, $g = 10 \text{ m/s}^2$) **[2023, 8 April Shift-II]**

(a) 0.50 (b) 0.90
(c) 0.25 (d) 0.65

3 As per the given figure, a small ball P slides down the quadrant of a circle and hits the other ball Q of equal mass which is initially at rest. Neglecting the effect of friction and assume the collision to be elastic, the velocity of ball Q after collision will be ($g = 10 \text{ m/s}^2$)

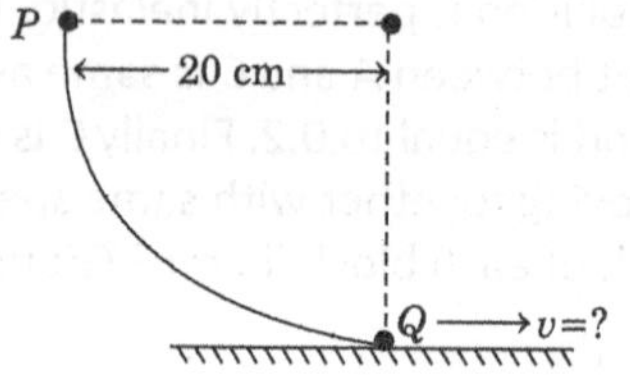

[2023, 30 Jan Shift-I]

(a) 4 m/s (b) 0
(c) 2 m/s (d) 0.25 m/s

4 A body is dropped on ground from a height h_1 and afer hitting the ground, it rebounds to a height h_2. If the ratio of velocities of the body just before and after hitting ground is 4, then percentage loss in kinetic energy of the body is $\frac{x}{4}$. The value of x is ……… **[2023, 6 April Shift-II]**

5 A body of mass 2 kg moving with a speed of 4 m/s makes an elastic collision with another body at rest and continues to move in the original direction but with one-fourth of its initial speed. The speed of the two body centre of mass is $\frac{x}{10}$ m/s. Then, the value of x is ……… . **[2021, 25 July Shift-1]**

6 A bullet of 10 g, moving with velocity v, collides head-on with the stationary bob of a pendulum and recoils with velocity 100 m/s. The length of the pendulum is 0.5 m and mass of the bob is 1 kg. The minimum value of v .... m/s, so that the pendulum describes a circle. (Assume, the string to be inextensible and $g = 10\ \text{m/s}^2$) **[2021, 27 Aug Shift-II]**

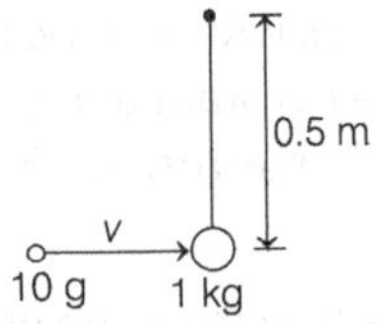

7 Three objects A, B and C are kept in a straight line on a frictionless horizontal surface. The masses of A, B and C are m, $2m$ and $2m$, respectively. A moves towards B with a speed of 9 m/s and makes an elastic collision with it. There after B makes a completely inelastic collision with C. All motions occur along same straight line. The final speed of C is **[2021, 27 July Shift-I]**

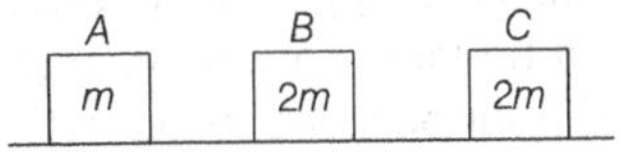

(a) 6 m/s (b) 9 m/s (c) 4 m/s (d) 3 m/s

8 A ball of mass 4 kg, moving with a velocity of $10\ \text{ms}^{-1}$, collides with a spring of length 8 m and force constant $100\ \text{Nm}^{-1}$. The length of the compressed spring is x m. The value of x to the nearest integer, is .... **[2021, 18 March Shift-II]**

9 An object of mass m_1 collides with another object of mass m_2, which is at rest. After the collision, the objects move with equal speeds in opposite direction. The ratio of the masses $m_2 : m_1$ is **[2021, 18 March Shift-II]**

(a) 3 : 1 (b) 2 : 1 (c) 1 : 2 (d) 1 : 1

10 Two identical blocks A and B each of mass m resting on the smooth horizontal floor are connected by a light spring of natural length L and spring constant k. A third block C of mass m moving with a speed v along the line joining A and B collides with A. The maximum compression in the spring is **[2021, 17 March Shift-II]**

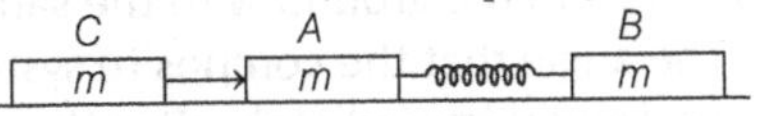

(a) $v\sqrt{\dfrac{m}{2k}}$ (b) $\sqrt{\dfrac{mv}{2k}}$

(c) $\sqrt{\dfrac{mv}{k}}$ (d) $\sqrt{\dfrac{m}{2k}}$

11 A boy is rolling a 0.5 kg ball on the frictionless floor with the speed of $20\ \text{ms}^{-1}$. The ball gets deflected by an obstacle on the way. After deflection it moves with 5% of its initial kinetic energy. What is the speed of the ball now ? **[2021, 17 March Shift-I]**

(a) $19.0\ \text{ms}^{-1}$ (b) $4.47\ \text{ms}^{-1}$

(c) $14.41\ \text{ms}^{-1}$ (d) $1.00\ \text{ms}^{-1}$

12 Given below are two statements : one is labelled as Assertion A and the other is labelled as Reason R.

Assertion (A) Body P having mass M moving with speed u has head-on collision elastically with another body Q having mass m initially at rest. If $m << M$, body Q will have a maximum speed equal to $2u$ after collision.

Reason (R) During elastic collision, the momentum and kinetic energy are both conserved. In the light of the above statements, choose the most appropriate answer from the options given below. **[2021, 26 Feb Shift-I]**

(a) A is not correct but R is correct.
(b) Both A and R are correct but R is not the correct explanation of A.
(c) Both A and R are correct and R is the correct explanation of A.
(d) A is correct but R is not correct.

13 A ball with a speed of 9 m/s collides with another identical ball at rest. After the collision, the direction of each ball makes an angle of 30° with the original direction. The ratio of velocities of the balls after collision is $x : y$, where x is .... **[2021, 24 Feb Shift-I]**

14 A particle of mass m with an initial velocity $u\hat{\mathbf{i}}$ collides perfectly elastically with a mass $3m$ at rest. It moves with a velocity $v\hat{\mathbf{j}}$ after collision, then v is given by **[2020, 2 Sep Shift-I]**

(a) $v = \sqrt{\dfrac{2}{3}}u$ (b) $v = \dfrac{1}{\sqrt{6}}u$ (c) $v = \dfrac{u}{\sqrt{2}}$ (d) $v = \dfrac{u}{\sqrt{3}}$

15 A particle of mass m is moving along the X-axis with initial velocity $u\hat{\mathbf{i}}$. It collides elastically with a particle of mass $10\ m$ at rest and then moves with half its initial kinetic energy (see figure). If $\sin\theta_1 = \sqrt{n}\sin\theta_2$, then value of n is .... **[2020, 2 Sep Shift-II]**

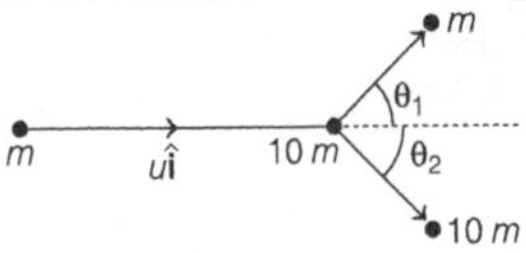

16 A block of mass 1.9 kg is at rest at the edge of a table of height 1 m. A bullet of mass 0.1 kg collides with the block and sticks to it. If the velocity of the bullet is 20 m/s in the horizontal direction just before the collision, then the kinetic energy just before the combined system strikes the floor, is

(Take, $g = 10\ m/s^2$ and assume there is no rotational motion and loss of energy after the collision is negligible) [2020, 3 Sep Shift-II]

(a) 20 J (b) 19 J (c) 21 J (d) 23 J

17 Blocks of masses m, $2m$, $4m$ and $8m$ are arranged in a line on a frictionless floor. Another block of mass m, moving with speed v along the same line (see figure) collides with mass m in perfectly inelastic manner. All the subsequent collisions are also perfectly inelasti(c) By the time, the last block of mass $8m$ starts moving, the total energy loss is p% of the original energy. Value of p is close to [2020, 4 Sep Shift-I]

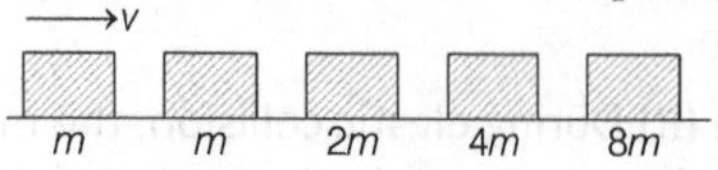

(a) 77 (b) 87 (c) 94 (d) 37

18 A body A, of mass $m = 0.1$ kg has an initial velocity of $3\hat{\mathbf{i}}\ ms^{-1}$. It collides elastically with another body, B of the same mass which has an initial velocity of $5\hat{\mathbf{j}}$ ms $^{-1}$. After collision, A moves with a velocity $\mathbf{v} = 4(\hat{\mathbf{i}} + \hat{\mathbf{j}})$. The energy of B after collision is written as $\frac{x}{10}$ J. The value of x is .... [2020, 8 Jan Shift-I]

JEE Advanced

1. A slide with a frictionless curved surface, which becomes horizontal at its lower end, is fixed on the terrace of a building of height $3h$ from the ground, as shown in the figure. A spherical ball of mass m is released on the slide from rest at a height h from the top of the terrace. The ball leaves the slide with a velocity $\mathbf{u}_0 = \mathbf{u}_0\hat{\mathbf{x}}$ and falls on the ground at a distance d from the building making an angle θ with the horizontal. It bounces off with a velocity $\mathbf{v}$ and reaches a maximum height h_1. The acceleration due to gravity is g and the coefficient of restitution of the ground is $\frac{1}{\sqrt{3}}$. Which of the following statement (s) is/are correct? (2023)

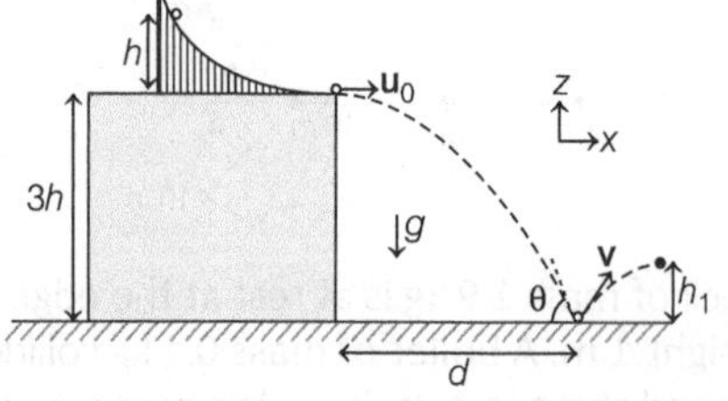

(a) $\mathbf{u}_0 = \sqrt{2gh}\hat{\mathbf{x}}$ (b) $\mathbf{v} = \sqrt{2gh}(\hat{\mathbf{x}} - \hat{\mathbf{z}})$

(c) $\theta = 60°$ (d) $\frac{d}{h_1} = 2\sqrt{3}$

2. A solid horizontal surface is covered with a thin layer of oil. A rectangular block of mass $m = 0.4$ kg is at rest on this surface. An impulse of 1.0 N-s is applied to the block at time $t = 0$, so that it starts moving along the X-axis with a velocity $v(t) = v_0 e^{-t/\tau}$, where v_0 is a constant and $\tau = 4$ s. The displacement of the block, in metres, at $t = \tau$ is.............. (Take, $e^{-1} = 0.37$). (2018)

3. A ball is projected from the ground at an angle of 45° with the horizontal surface. It reaches a maximum height of 120 m and returns to the ground. Upon hitting the ground for the first time, it loses half of its kinetic energy. Immediately after the bounce, the velocity of the ball makes an angle of 30° with the horizontal surface. The maximum height it reaches after the bounce, in metres, is .... (2018)

4. A tennis ball is dropped on a horizontal smooth surface. It bounces back to its original position after hitting the surface. The force on the ball during the collision is proportional to the length of compression of the ball. Which one of the following sketches describes the variation of its kinetic energy K with time t most appropriately? The figures are only illustrative and not to the scale. (2014)

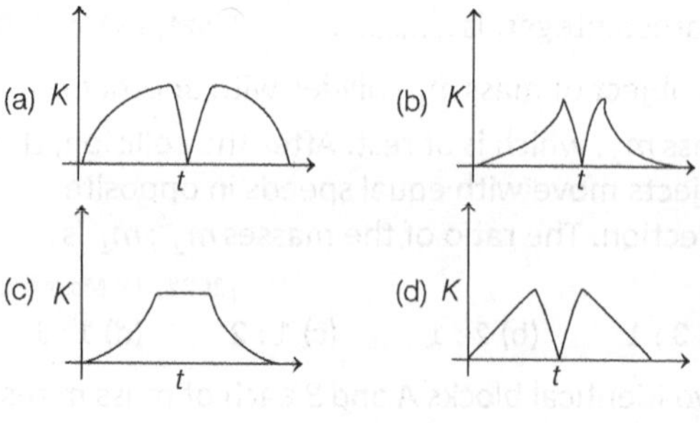

5. A particle of mass m is projected from the ground with an initial speed u_0 at an angle α with the horizontal. At the highest point of its trajectory, it makes a completely inelastic collision with another identical particle, which was thrown vertically upward from the ground with the same initial speed u_0. The angle that the composite system makes with the horizontal immediately after the collision is (2013)

(a) $\frac{\pi}{4}$ (b) $\frac{\pi}{4} + \alpha$ (c) $\frac{\pi}{4} - \alpha$ (d) $\frac{\pi}{2}$

6. A ball of mass 0.2 kg rests on a vertical post of height 5 m. A bullet of mass 0.01 kg, travelling with a velocity v m/s in a horizontal direction, hits the centre of the ball. After the collision, the ball and bullet travel independently. The ball hits the ground at a distance of 20 m and the bullet at a distance of 100 m from the foot of the post. The initial velocity v of the bullet is **(2011)**

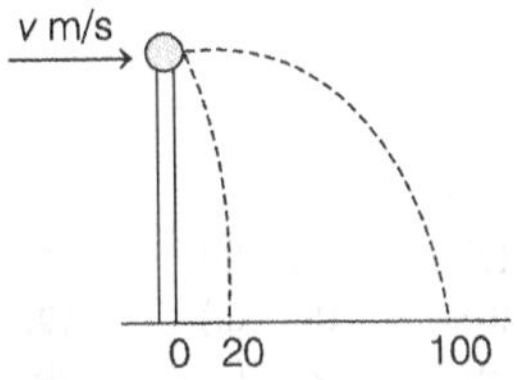

(a) 250 m/s
(b) $250\sqrt{2}$ m/s
(c) 400 m/s
(d) 500 m/s

7. A point mass of 1 kg collides elastically with a stationary point mass of 5 kg. After their collision, the 1 kg mass reverses its direction and moves with a speed of 2 ms^{-1}. Which of the following statement(s) is/are correct for the system of these two masses? **(2010)**

(a) Total momentum of the system is 3 kg-ms^{-1}
(b) Momentum of 5 kg mass after collision is 4 kg -ms^{-1}
(c) Kinetic energy of the centre of mass is 0.75 J
(d) Total kinetic energy of the system is 4 J

8. Two small particles of equal masses start moving in opposite directions from a point A in a horizontal circular orbit. Their tangential velocities are v and 2v respectively, as shown in the figure. Between collisions, the particles move with constant speeds. After making how many elastic collisions, other than that at A, these two particles will again reach the point A? **(2009)**

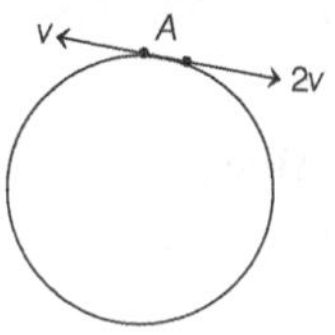

(a) 4 (b) 3 (c) 2 (d) 1

Answer Key

Level 1

2.1 Impulse

1. 0.9 N-s
2. (a) 20 N-s (b) 10 m/s
3. 0.7 N-s
4. (a) 0.4 N-s (b) zero
5. (a) $\frac{\sqrt{3gL}}{2}$ (b) $\frac{m\sqrt{gL}}{2}$
6. $v_A = \frac{\sqrt{3}}{4}u$, $v_B = \frac{\sqrt{7}}{4}u$, $J = \frac{\sqrt{3}}{4}mu$
7. (a) $\sqrt{\frac{gh}{2}}$ (b) $3m\frac{\sqrt{gh}}{2}$
8. (a) $mv_0 \sin\theta / M$ (b) $mv_0 \cos\theta$
9. (a) $u/3$ (b) $mu/3$ (c) $2mu/3$
10. (a) $\sqrt{2gh}\tan\theta$, $\sqrt{\frac{gh}{2}}\tan\theta$ (b) $m\sqrt{2gh}\sec\theta$ (c) $m\sqrt{2gh}$

2.2 Head-on Collisions

1. $v_1 = 4$ m/s and $v_2 = 4.67$ m/s
2. $v_A = -1.6$ m/s and $v_B = 2.0$ m/s
3. (a) -2 m/s, $\frac{3}{4}$ m/s (b) 6 N-s, 12 N-s, (c) 33 J (d) $\frac{99}{4}$ J
4. (a) 2 J, (b) $1/\sqrt{2}$
5. $K/2$
6. 2
7. $\frac{25}{9}H, \frac{H}{9}$
8. $e = 0.8, \mu = 0.4$
9. (a) $e^n\sqrt{2gh}$ (b) $\left(\frac{1+e^2}{1-e^2}\right)h$ (c) $\sqrt{\frac{2h}{g}}\left(\frac{1+e}{1-e}\right)$
10. 19 m/s

2.3 Oblique Collisions

1. $v_0\sqrt{\sin^2\alpha + e^2\cos^2\alpha}$, $\tan^{-1}\left(\frac{\tan\alpha}{e}\right)$
2. $\frac{(1+e+e^2)u^2\sin 2\theta}{g}$
3. 8.75 m/s
4. $v_A = u/2$, $v_B = \frac{\sqrt{3}u}{2}$
5. $\mathbf{v}_A = 2\hat{i} + 2\hat{j}$, $\mathbf{v}_B = 3\hat{i} - \hat{j}$
6. $\frac{1}{2}$
7. $\frac{(1+e)v_0\sin\theta}{2+\sin^2\theta}$
8. $v_{Wedge} = 1.5$ m/s
9. (a) $\frac{1}{\sqrt{2}}$ (b) $\sqrt{gh}$ (c) $m\sqrt{2gh}$

2.4 Variable Mass System

1. (a) 165 N (b) 363 W (c) 181.5 W 2. $v = \frac{Ft}{m_0 + \mu t}$, $a = \frac{Fm_0}{(m_0 + \mu t)^2}$ 3. $v = \frac{F}{\mu} \ln\left(\frac{m_0}{m_0 - \mu t}\right)$; $a = \frac{F}{m_0 - \mu t}$

4. (a) 5.32×10^5 N (b) 3.22×10^5N (c) $v_0 - gt + v_{rel} \ln\frac{M_0}{M}$ (d) 2718 m/s

5. $\frac{F}{\lambda x} - \mu_k g - \frac{v^2}{x}$ 6. (a) $\frac{M}{L}(gy + v_0^2)$ (b) $\frac{Myv_0^2}{2L}$ 7. $3mg\frac{x}{l}$

Level 2

Single Choice Correct Questions

1. (a)	2. (a)	3. (a)	4. (d)	5. (c)	6. (b)	7. (a)	8. (a)	9. (c)	10. (a)
11. (a)	12. (a)	13. (a)	14. (a)	15. (b)	16. (d)	17. (b)	18. (a)	19. (a)	20. (d)
21. (d)	22. (c)	23. (b)	24. (b)	25. (d)	26. (c)	27. (d)	28. (a)	29. (a)	30. (a)
31. (a)	32. (d)	33. (b)	34. (a)	35. (a)	36. (a)	37. (a)	38. (a)	39. (a)	40. (b)
41. (c)	42. (a)								

Numerical Value Questions

1. (8)	2. (8)	3. (3)	4. (2)	5. (5)	6. (4.45)	7. (4)	8. (0.25)	9. (4)	10. (0.25)

Level 3

Single Choice Correct Questions

1. (c)	2. (c)	3. (b)	4. (a)	5. (b)	6. (c)	7. (d)	8. (a)	9. (c)	10. (c)
11. (c)	12. (b)	13. (b)	14. (b)	15. (a)	16. (c)	17. (b)	18. (a)	19. (c)	20. (c)
21. (b)	22. (c)	23. (d)	24. (b)	25. (d)	26. (c)	27. (c)	28. (b)	29. (d)	30. (c)
31. (d)	32. (c)								

Multiple Choice (s) Correct Questions

1. (b, d)	2. (a,b,c)	3. (a,b,c,d)	4. (b,c,d)	5. (a,b)	6. (a,d)	7. (a,b,c)	8. (a,b,c)	9. (b,c)	10. (a,c,d)
11. (b,c,d)	12. (a,b,c,d)	13. (a,c)	14. (a,b,c,d)	15. (a,b,c)	16. (a,d)	17. (a,b)	18. (a,b)	19. (b,c,d)	

Comprehension Based Questions

1. (c)	2. (b)	3. (a)	4. (d)	5. (a)	6. (d)	7. (b)	8. (c)	9. (d)	10. (c)
11. (d)	12. (b)	13. (a)	14. (b)	15. (d)	16. (a)	17. (a)	18. (c)	19. (b)	20. (b)
21. (c)	22. (d)	23. (a)	24. (d)	25. (d)	26. (a)	27. (c)	28. (d)		

Match the Columns Questions

1. A→ 2,3,4; B→ 2,3,4,5; C→ 2,3,4,5; D→ 2,3,4,5 2. A→ 1,4; B→ 2,4; C→ 1,2,3; D→ 1, 2,3,4

3. A→ 4; B→ 2; C→ 1; D→ 3, 4. A→ 3; B→ 5; C→ 4; D→ 2 5. A→ 1,2,3,4,5; B→ 1,2; C→ 3; D→ 1,2

6. A→ 4; B→ 3; C→ 2; D→ 1 7. A→ 3; B→ 4; C→ 1; D→ 2

Numerical Value Questions

1. 6 2. 9 3. 32 4. 0 5. 12.5 6. 18 7. 4 8. 0.5 9. 2 10. 2

Previous Year Questions

JEE Main

1. (d)	2. (c)	3. (c)	4. (375)	5. (25)	6. (400)	7. (d)	8. (6)	9. (a)	10. (a)
11. (b)	12. (c)	13. (1)	14. (c)	15. (10)	16. (c)	17. (c)	18. (1)		

JEE Advanced

1. (a,c,d)	2. (6.30 m)	3. (30)	4. (b)	5. (a)	6. (d)	7. (a,c)	8. (c)

SOLUTIONS

Level 1

2.1 Impulse

1. $F = 600 - (2 \times 10^5)t = 0$

$\Rightarrow \quad t = 3 \times 10^{-3}$ s

$$\text{Impulse} = \int F dt = \int_0^{3 \times 10^{-3}} [(600 - (2 \times 10^5)t)]\, dt$$

$$= [600t - 10^5 t^2]_0^{3 \times 10^{-3}}$$

$$= 0.9 \text{ N-s}$$

2. (a) Impulse $= \int F dt =$ Area under F-t graph

$$= \frac{1}{2} \times 0.4 \times 100 = 20 \text{ N-s}$$

(b) Impulse = Change in linear momentum

$\Rightarrow \quad 20 = 2v - 2(0) \quad \Rightarrow v = 10$ m/s

3. $u = \sqrt{2gh_1} = \sqrt{2 \times 10 \times 0.8} = 4$ m/s

$v = \sqrt{2gh_2} = \sqrt{2 \times 10 \times 0.45} = 3$ m/s

Impulse $= \Delta p = m[v - (-u)] = 0.1[(4 - (-3))] = 0.7$ N-s

4. (a) $\mathbf{p}_1 = mu \cos 30° \,\hat{\mathbf{i}} - mu \sin 30° \,\hat{\mathbf{j}}$

$\mathbf{p}_2 = mu \cos 30 \hat{\mathbf{i}} + mu \sin 30 \hat{\mathbf{j}}$

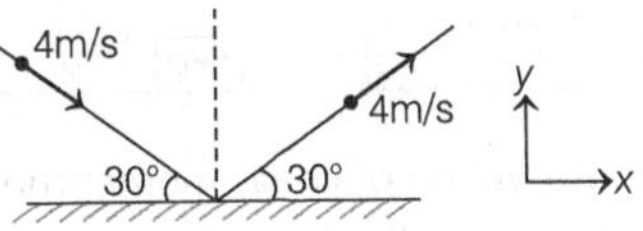

Impulse $= \Delta \mathbf{p} = 2mu \sin 30° \,\hat{\mathbf{j}}$

$$|\text{Impulse}| = 2 \times 0.1 \times 4 \times \frac{1}{2} = 0.4 \text{ N-s}$$

(b) Magnitude of momentum is constant. So, change in magnitude of momentum is zero.

5. (a)

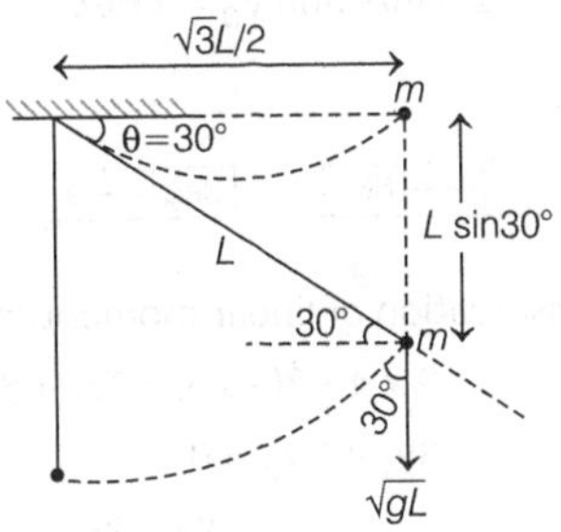

$$\cos\theta = \frac{\sqrt{3}\, L/2}{L}$$

$\Rightarrow \quad \theta = 30°$

Speed of fall just before jerk in the string

$$= \sqrt{2gh} = \sqrt{2g(L \sin 30°)} = \sqrt{gL}$$

Due to jerk, component of velocity of ball along the string will become zero. So, velocity of ball just after jerk will be

$$\sqrt{gL} \cos 30° = \sqrt{\frac{3gL}{2}}$$

(b) Impulse due to string $= \int T dt$

$$= 0 - (-m\sqrt{gL} \sin 30°) = \frac{m\sqrt{gL}}{2}$$

6.

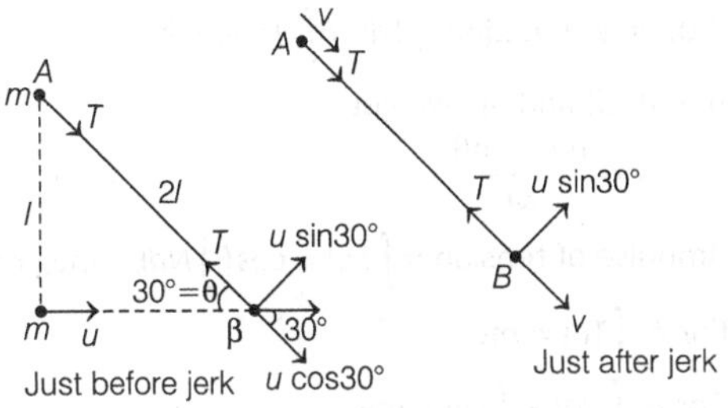

$$\sin\theta = \frac{l}{2l} = \frac{1}{2} \Rightarrow \theta = 30°$$

Component of velocity of B perpendicular to string will remain unchanged.

For B, $-\int T dt = mv - mu \cos 30°$ ... (i)

For A, $\int T dt = mv - 0$ ... (ii)

Adding Eqs. (i) and (ii), we get

$$v = \frac{\sqrt{3}u}{4}$$

So, $v_A = \dfrac{\sqrt{3}u}{4}$, $v_B = \sqrt{\left(\dfrac{\sqrt{3}u}{4}\right)^2 + \left(\dfrac{u}{2}\right)^2} = \dfrac{\sqrt{7}u}{4}$

Impulse of tension $= \int T dt = mv = \dfrac{\sqrt{3}mu}{4}$

7. (a)

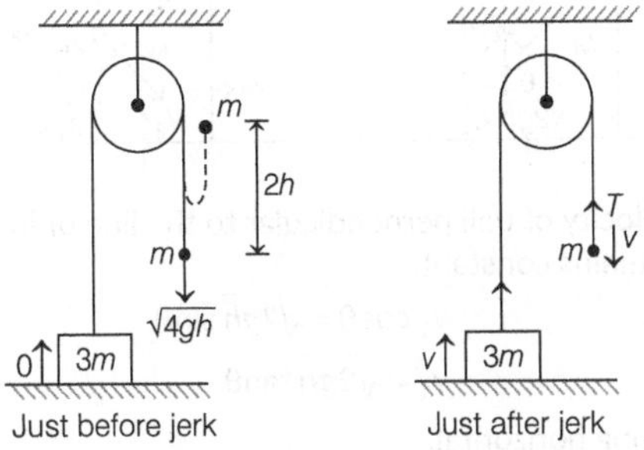

For mass $3m$, $\int T dt = 3mv - 0$ ... (i)

For mass m, $-\int T dt = mv - m\sqrt{4gh}$ ... (ii)

From Eqs. (i) and (ii), we get

$$v = \frac{\sqrt{gh}}{2}$$

(b) Impulse of tension $= \int T dt = 3mv = \dfrac{3m\sqrt{gh}}{2}$

8.

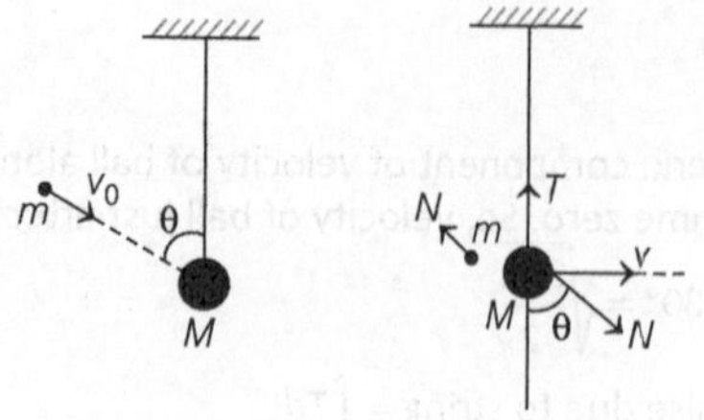

For particle, $-\int N dt = 0 - mv_0$ ...(i)

For bob in x-direction, $\int N \sin\theta dt = Mv - 0$ ...(ii)

For bob in y-direction, $\int T dt = \int N \cos\theta\, dt$

From Eqs. (i) and (ii), we get

$$v = \frac{mv_0 \sin\theta}{M}$$

(b) Impulse of tension $= \int T dt = \cos\theta \int N dt = mv_0 \cos\theta$

9. (a) For A, $\int T dt = mv$ ...(i)

For B, $\int N dt - \int T dt = mv$ ...(ii)

For C, $-\int N dt = mv - mu$ ... (iii)

Adding Eqs. (i), (ii) and (iii), we get

$$v = \frac{u}{3}$$

(b) $\int T dt = mv = \frac{mu}{3}$

(c) $-\int N dt = mv - mu$

$$\Rightarrow \quad -\int N dt = \frac{mu}{3} - mu = -\frac{2mu}{3}$$

$$\Rightarrow \quad \int N dt = \frac{2mu}{3}$$

10.

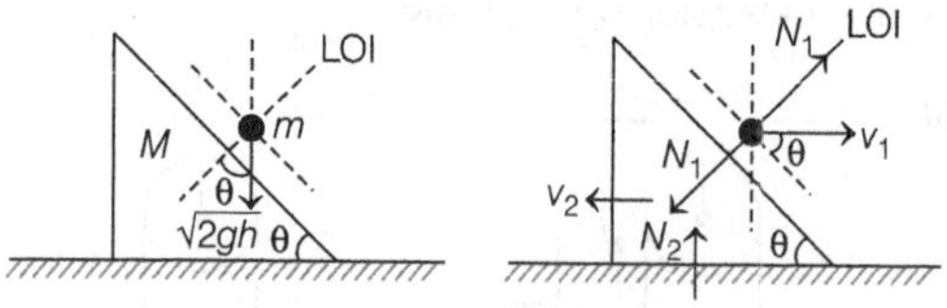

(a) Velocity of ball perpendicular to the line of impact remains constant.

$$\Rightarrow \quad v_1 \cos\theta = \sqrt{2gh} \sin\theta$$

$$\Rightarrow \quad v_1 = \sqrt{2gh} \tan\theta$$

Along horizontal,

For ball, $\int N_1 \sin\theta dt = mv_1 - 0$ ...(i)

For wedge, $\int N_1 \sin\theta dt = 2mv_2 - 0$ ...(ii)

Solving Eqs. (i) and (ii), we get

$$mv_1 = 2mv_2$$

$$\Rightarrow \quad v_2 = \frac{v_1}{2} = \sqrt{\frac{gh}{2}} \tan\theta$$

(b) $\int N_1 \sin\theta dt = mv_1$

$$\Rightarrow \quad (\sin\theta) \int N_1 dt = m\sqrt{2gh} \tan\theta$$

$$\Rightarrow \quad \int N_1 dt = m\sqrt{2gh} \sec\theta$$

(c) For wedge, along vertical,

$$\int N_2 dt - \int N_1 \cos\theta dt = 0$$

$$\Rightarrow \quad \int N_2 dt = (\cos\theta) \int N_1 dt = (\cos\theta) m\sqrt{2gh} \sec\theta = m\sqrt{2gh}$$

2.2 Head-on Collisions

1.

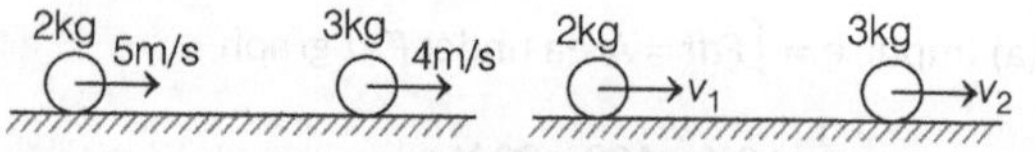

Applying conservation of linear momentum,

$$2 \times 5 + 3 \times 4 = 2v_1 + 3v_2$$

$$2v_1 + 3v_2 = 22 \quad \text{...(i)}$$

$$e = \frac{2}{3} = \frac{v_2 - v_1}{5 - 4}$$

$$\Rightarrow \quad v_2 - v_1 = 2/3 \quad \text{... (ii)}$$

Solving Eqs. (i) and (ii), we get

$$v_1 = 4 \text{ m/s and } v_2 = 4.67 \text{ m/s}$$

2.

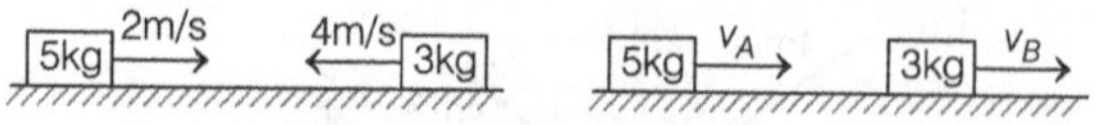

Applying conservation of linear momentum,

$$5 \times 2 + 3 \times (-4) = 5v_A + 3v_B$$

$$\Rightarrow \quad 5v_A + 3v_B = -2 \quad \text{... (i)}$$

$$e = 0.6 = \frac{v_B - v_A}{2 - (-4)}$$

$$\Rightarrow \quad v_B - v_A = 3.6 \quad \text{... (ii)}$$

Solving Eqs. (i) and (ii), we get

$$v_A = -1.6 \text{ m/s and } v_B = 2 \text{ m/s}$$

3. (a)

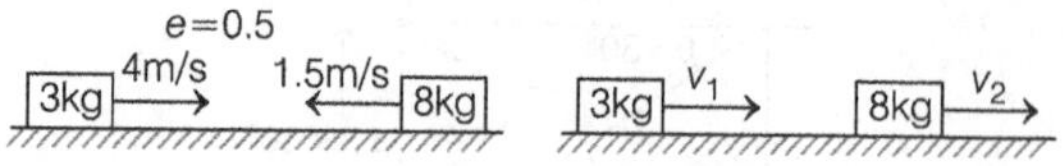

Applying conservation of linear momentum,

$$3 \times 4 + 8(-1.5) = 3v_1 + 8v_2$$

$$\Rightarrow \quad 3v_1 + 8v_2 = 0 \quad \text{... (i)}$$

$$e = 0.5 = \frac{v_2 - v_1}{4 - (-1.5)}$$

$$\Rightarrow \quad v_2 - v_1 = 2.75 \quad \text{... (ii)}$$

Solving Eqs. (i) and (ii), we get

$$v_1 = -2 \text{ m/s and } v_2 = \frac{3}{4} \text{ m/s}$$

(b) During max deformation,

$$3\times4+8(-1.5)=(3+8)v$$

$$\Rightarrow \quad v=0$$

Impulse of reformation $=8(v_2-v)=6$ N-s

Impulse of deformation $=3(u_1-v)=12$ N-s.

(c) $U_{max}=K_1-K=\left[\frac{1}{2}\times3\times4^2+\frac{1}{2}\times8\times(1.5)^2\right]-\frac{1}{2}(3+8)(0)^2$

$$=33\text{ J}$$

(d) Loss in KE $=K_1-K_2$

$$=\left[\frac{1}{2}\times3\times4^2+\frac{1}{2}\times8\times(1.5)^2\right]-\left[\frac{1}{2}\times3\times2^2+\frac{1}{2}\times8\times\left(\frac{3}{4}\right)^2\right]$$

$$=\frac{99}{4}\text{ J}$$

4. (a) Maximum loss in kinetic energy takes place in perfectly inelastic collision.

Using conservation of linear momentum,

$$2\times2+2\times0=(2+2)v$$

$$\Rightarrow \quad v=1\text{ m/s}$$

$$(\text{Loss in KE})_{max}=K_1-K_2=\left(\frac{1}{2}\times2\times2^2+0\right)-\left(\frac{1}{2}\times4\times1^2\right)=2\text{ J}$$

(b) Loss in KE $=\frac{1}{2}\times2=1$ J

$$\Rightarrow \quad K_1-K_2=1$$

$$\Rightarrow \quad \left(\frac{1}{2}\times2\times2^2+0\right)-\left(\frac{1}{2}\times2v_1^2+\frac{1}{2}\times2v_2^2\right)=1$$

$$\Rightarrow \quad v_1^2+v_2^2=3 \quad \text{... (i)}$$

Using linear momentum conservation,

$$2\times2+2\times0=2v_1+2v_2$$

$$v_1+v_2=2 \quad \text{... (ii)}$$

$$e=\frac{v_2-v_1}{2-0}$$

$$\Rightarrow \quad v_2-v_1=2e \quad \text{... (iii)}$$

Solving Eqs. (ii) and (iii), we get

$$v_2=e+1 \text{ and } v_1=1-e$$

Now from Eq. (i),

$$(1-e)^2+(1+e)^2=3$$

$$\Rightarrow \quad e=\frac{1}{\sqrt{2}}$$

5. Maximum elastic potential energy is stored at the point of maximum deformation.

Using momentum conservation,

$$mu+0=(m+m)v$$

$$\Rightarrow \quad v=\frac{u}{2}$$

$$U_{max}=\text{Loss in KE}$$

$$=\left(\frac{1}{2}mu^2+0\right)-\frac{1}{2}\times2m\left(\frac{u}{2}\right)^2$$

$$=\frac{1}{4}mu^2=\frac{1}{2}\left(\frac{1}{2}mu^2\right)=\frac{K}{2}$$

6. When B collides C,

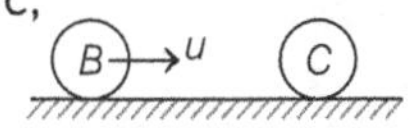

$$Mu+0=Mv_B+4Mv_C$$

$$\Rightarrow \quad v_B+4v_C=u \quad \text{... (i)}$$

$$e=1-\frac{v_C-v_B}{u-0}$$

$$\Rightarrow \quad v_C-v_B=u \quad \text{... (ii)}$$

Solving Eqs. (i) and (ii), we get

$$v_B=-\frac{3u}{5} \text{ and } v_C=\frac{2u}{5}$$

Now, B collides with A

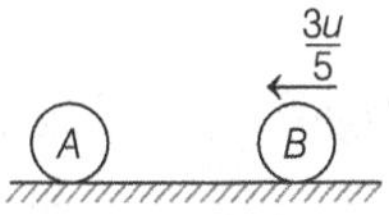

$$v_A=-\frac{2}{5}\left(\frac{3u}{5}\right)=-\frac{6u}{25}$$

and $$v_B=-\frac{3}{5}\left(\frac{-3u}{5}\right)=\frac{9u}{25}$$

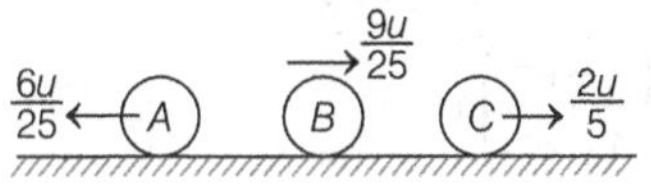

Now, ball C is faster than ball B. So, no more collisions will take place. So, total number of collision is 2.

7.

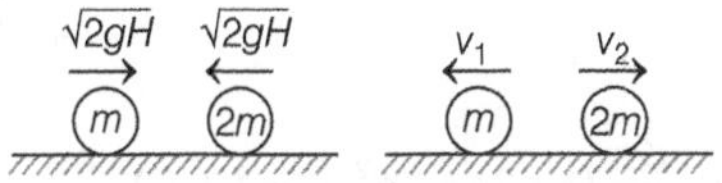

$$m(\sqrt{2gH})+2m(-\sqrt{2gH})=-mv_1+2mv_2$$

$$\Rightarrow \quad v_1-2v_2=\sqrt{2gH} \quad \text{... (i)}$$

$$e=1=\frac{v_1+v_2}{2\sqrt{2gH}}$$

$$\Rightarrow \quad v_1+v_2=2\sqrt{2gH} \quad \text{... (ii)}$$

Solving Eqs. (i) and (ii), we get

$$v_1=\frac{5}{3}\sqrt{2gH} \text{ and } v_2=\frac{\sqrt{2gH}}{3}$$

Maximum height reached by $1=\frac{v_1^2}{2g}=\frac{25H}{9}$

Maximum height reached by $2=\frac{v_2^2}{2g}=\frac{H}{9}$

8. Speed of 4 kg just before collision $= \sqrt{2gl(1-\cos\theta)}$

$$= \sqrt{2\times 10\times 1(1-\cos 60^\circ)}$$

$$= \sqrt{10}\text{ m/s}$$

Applying conservation of linear momentum,

$$4\sqrt{10} + 5(0) = 4(0) + 5v$$

$$v = \frac{4\sqrt{10}}{5}\text{ m/s}$$

For block, $v^2 = u^2 + 2as$

$$\Rightarrow \quad 0^2 = \left(\frac{4\sqrt{10}}{5}\right)^2 + 2[(-\mu(10))](0.8)$$

$$\Rightarrow \quad \mu = 0.4$$

$$e = \frac{\frac{4\sqrt{10}}{5} - 0}{\sqrt{10} - 0} = 0.8$$

9. (a) Velocity of ball just before first collision $= \sqrt{2gh}$

Velocity of ball just after first collision $= e\sqrt{2gh}$

So, velocity of ball just after nth collision $= e^n\sqrt{2gh}$

(b) Total distance

$$= h + \frac{(e\sqrt{2gh})^2}{2g}\times 2 + \frac{(e^2\sqrt{2gh})^2}{2g}\times 2 + \ldots$$

$$= h + 2e^2h + 2e^4h + \ldots$$

$$= h + 2e^2h(1 + e^2 + e^4 + \ldots)$$

$$= h + 2e^2h\left(\frac{1}{1-e^2}\right)$$

$$= \left(\frac{1+e^2}{1-e^2}\right)h$$

(c) Total time $= \sqrt{\frac{2h}{g}} + \frac{2(e\sqrt{2gh})}{g} + \frac{2(e^2\sqrt{2gh})}{g} + \frac{2(e^3\sqrt{2gh})}{g} + \ldots$

$$= \sqrt{\frac{2h}{g}}(1 + 2e + 2e^2 + 2e^3 + \ldots)$$

$$= \sqrt{\frac{2h}{g}}[(1 + 2e(1 + e + e^2 + \ldots)]$$

$$= \sqrt{\frac{2h}{g}}\left[1 + 2e\left(\frac{1}{1-e}\right)\right]$$

$$= \sqrt{\frac{2h}{g}}\left(\frac{1+e}{1-e}\right)$$

10.

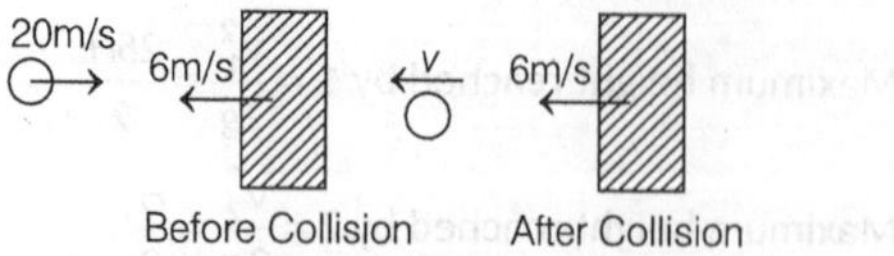

$$e = 0.5 = \frac{v-6}{20-(-6)}$$

$$\Rightarrow \quad v = 19\text{ m/s}$$

2.3 Oblique Collisions

1. Component of velocity perpendicular to line of impact will remain constant.

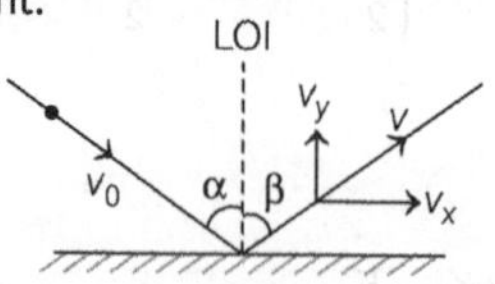

So, $\quad v_x = v_0\sin\alpha$

$$e = \frac{v_y}{v_0\cos\alpha}$$

$$\Rightarrow \quad v_y = ev_0\cos\alpha$$

$$\tan\beta = \frac{v_x}{v_y} = \frac{v_0\sin\alpha}{ev_0\cos\alpha}$$

$$\Rightarrow \quad \tan\beta = \frac{\tan\alpha}{e}$$

$$\Rightarrow \quad \beta = \tan^{-1}\left(\frac{\tan\alpha}{e}\right)$$

Speed of the reflected ball $= \sqrt{v_x^2 + v_y^2}$

$$= \sqrt{(v_0\sin\alpha)^2 + (ev_0\cos\alpha)^2}$$

$$= v_0\sqrt{\sin^2\alpha + e^2\cos^2\alpha}$$

2. $T = \frac{2u\sin\theta}{g} + \frac{2eu\sin\theta}{g} + \frac{2e^2u\sin\theta}{g}$

$$= \frac{2u\sin\theta}{g}(1 + e + e^2)$$

$$s_x = u_xt + \frac{1}{2}a_xt^2$$

$$\Rightarrow \quad R = (u\cos\theta)T = \frac{u^2\sin 2\theta}{g}(1 + e + e^2)$$

3.

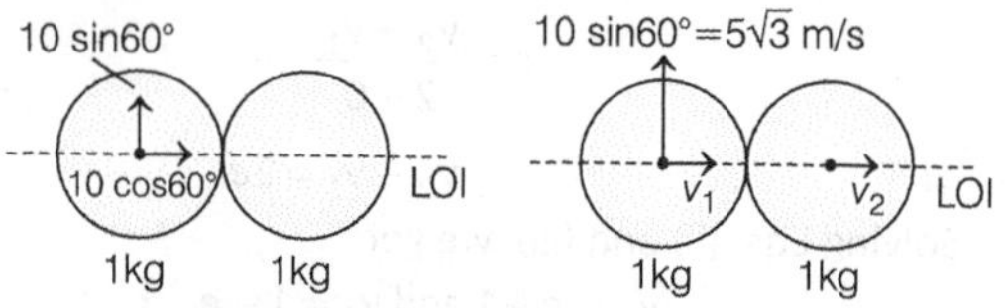

Using momentum conservation along LOI,

$$1(10\cos 60^\circ) + 1(0) = 1v_1 + 1v_2$$

$$v_1 + v_2 = 5 \quad \ldots\text{(i)}$$

$$e = 0.5 = \frac{v_2 - v_1}{10\cos 60^\circ}$$

$$\Rightarrow \quad v_2 - v_1 = 2.5 \quad \ldots\text{(ii)}$$

Solving Eqs. (i) and (ii), we get

$$v_1 = 1.25\text{ m/s and } v_2 = 3.75\text{ m/s}$$

Speed of striking ball $= \sqrt{(1.25)^2 + (5\sqrt{3})^2} = 8.75\text{ m/s}$

4. $$\sin\theta = \frac{r}{2r} = \frac{1}{2}$$

$$\Rightarrow \quad \theta = 30^\circ$$

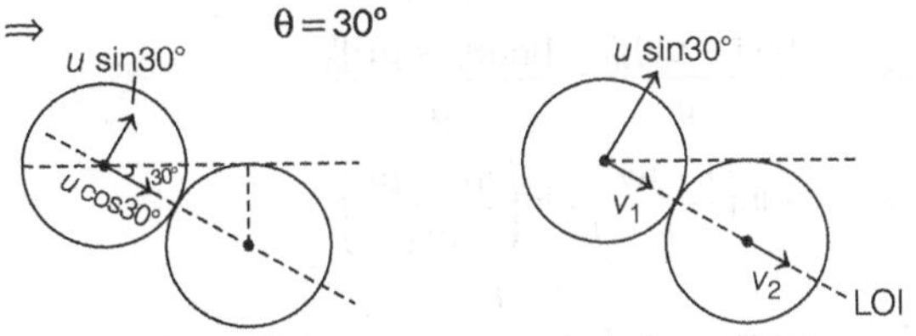

Just before collision   Just after collision

Using linear momentum conservation along the line of impact,

$$mu\cos 30^\circ + 0 = mv_1 + mv_2$$

$$\Rightarrow \quad v_1 + v_1 = \frac{\sqrt{3}u}{2} \quad \text{...(i)}$$

$$e = 1 = \frac{v_2 - v_1}{u\cos 30^\circ}$$

$$\Rightarrow \quad v_2 - v_1 = \frac{\sqrt{3}u}{2} \quad \text{...(ii)}$$

Solving Eqs. (i) and (ii), we get

$$v_1 = 0 \text{ and } v_2 = \frac{\sqrt{3}u}{2}$$

So, $$v_A = u\sin 30^\circ = \frac{u}{2}$$

and $$v_B = \frac{\sqrt{3}u}{2}$$

5. Component of velocity of each ball perpendicular to the line of impact will remain unchanged.

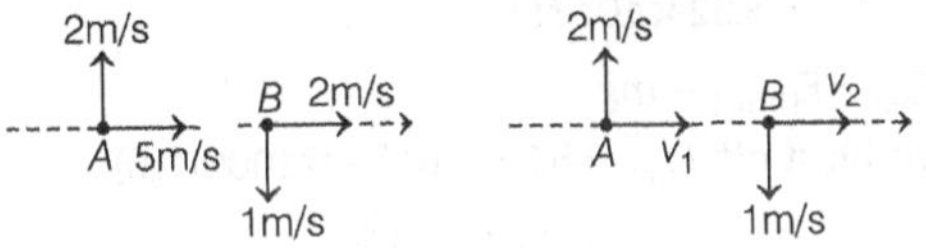

Before collision   After collision

Using momentum conservation along the line of impact

$$m(5) + 3m(2) = mv_1 + 3mv_2$$

$$v_1 + 3v_2 = 11 \quad \text{... (i)}$$

$$e = \frac{1}{3} = \frac{v_2 - v_1}{5 - 2}$$

$$\Rightarrow \quad v_2 - v_1 = 1 \quad \text{... (ii)}$$

Solving Eqs. (i) and (ii), we get

$$v_1 = 2 \text{ m/s}, \; v_2 = 3 \text{ m/s}$$

So, $$\mathbf{v}_A = 2\hat{\mathbf{i}} + 2\hat{\mathbf{j}}$$

and $$\mathbf{v}_B = 3\hat{\mathbf{i}} - \hat{\mathbf{j}}$$

6.

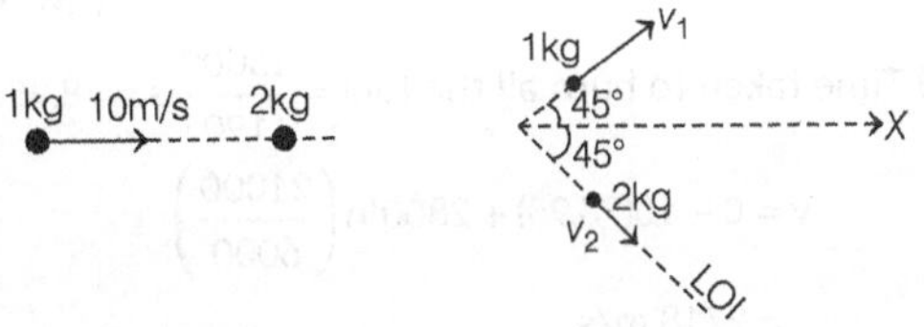

Using linear momentum conservation,

In X-direction,

$$1 \times 10 + 2 \times 0 = 1v_1 \cos 45^\circ + 2v_2 \cos 45^\circ$$

$$\Rightarrow \quad v_1 + 2v_2 = 10\sqrt{2} \quad \text{... (i)}$$

In Y-direction, $0 + 0 = 1v_1 \sin 45^\circ - 2v_2 \sin 45^\circ$

$$\Rightarrow \quad v_1 = 2v_2 \quad \text{... (ii)}$$

Solving Eqs. (i) and (ii), we get

$$v_1 = \frac{10}{\sqrt{2}} \text{ m/s and } v_2 = \frac{5}{\sqrt{2}} \text{ m/s}$$

Line of impact will be along the line of motion of 2 kg after collision.

$$= \frac{v_2 - v_1 \cos 90^\circ}{10\cos 45^\circ - 0} = \frac{5/\sqrt{2}}{10/\sqrt{2}} = \frac{1}{2}$$

7. Using linear momentum consevation for (wedge + ball) system is horizontal,

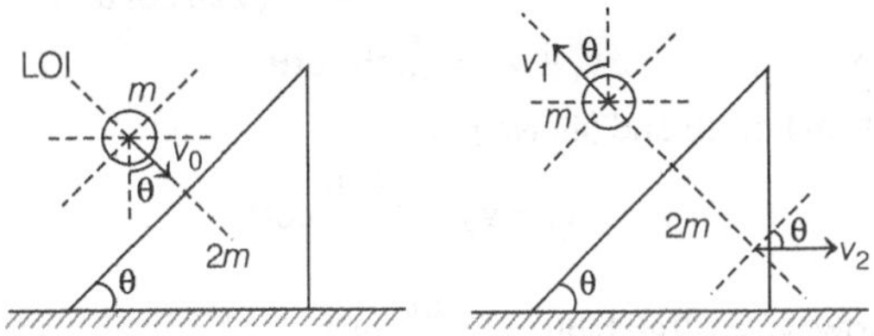

Before collision   After collision

$$mv_0 \sin\theta = -mv_1 \sin\theta + 2mv_2$$

$$\Rightarrow \quad 2v_2 - v_1 \sin\theta = v_0 \sin\theta \quad \text{...(i)}$$

$$e = \frac{v_{sep}}{v_{app}} = \frac{v_1 + v_2 \sin\theta}{v_0}$$

$$\Rightarrow \quad v_1 + v_2 \sin\theta = ev_0 \quad \text{...(ii)}$$

Solving Eqs. (i) and (ii), we get

$$v_2 = \frac{(e+1)v_0 \sin\theta}{2 + \sin^2\theta}$$

8. Component of velocity of ball perpendicular to the line of impact remains unchanged.

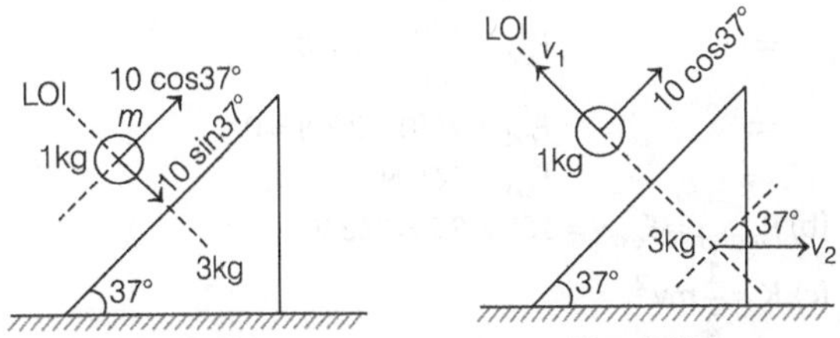

Before Collision   After Collision

Using conservation of momentum for (wedge + ball) system in horizontal

$$1(10) + 3(0) = 3v_2 + 1((10\cos 37^\circ)\cos 37^\circ - v_1 \sin 37^\circ)$$

$$\Rightarrow \quad 5v_2 - v_1 = 6 \quad \text{...(i)}$$

$$e = \frac{v_2 \sin 37^\circ - (-v_1)}{10\sin 37^\circ} = 0.4$$

$$\Rightarrow \quad 5v_1 + 3v_2 = 12 \quad \text{...(ii)}$$

Solving Eqs. (i) and (ii), we get

$$v_2 = 1.5 \text{ m/s}$$

9. (a) Component of velocity of particle perpendicular to the line of impact remains unchanged.

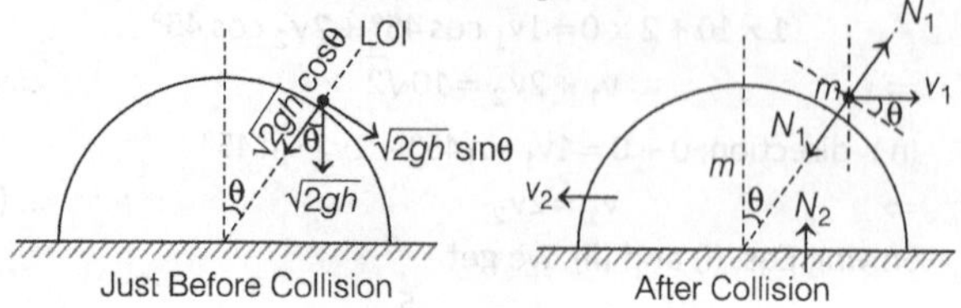

Just Before Collision After Collision

$\Rightarrow \qquad v_1 \cos\theta = \sqrt{2gh}\sin\theta$

$\Rightarrow \qquad v_1 = \sqrt{2gh}\tan\theta$ ...(i)

Using linear momentum conservation in horizontal for (hemisphere + particle) system

$$0 + 0 = -mv_2 + mv_1$$

$\Rightarrow \qquad v_1 = v_2$ ...(ii)

Coefficient of restitution $= e = 1 = \dfrac{v_1 \sin\theta + v_2 \sin\theta}{\sqrt{2gh}\cos\theta}$

$\Rightarrow \qquad v_1 + v_2 = \sqrt{2gh}\cot\theta$ ...(iii)

From Eqs. (i) and (ii), we get

$$v_1 = v_2 = \frac{\sqrt{2gh}}{2}\cot\theta$$

Now, $v_1 = \sqrt{2gh}\tan\theta = \dfrac{\sqrt{2gh}}{2}\cot\theta$

$\Rightarrow \qquad \tan^2\theta = \dfrac{1}{2} \Rightarrow \tan\theta = \dfrac{1}{\sqrt{2}}$

(b) $\qquad v_2 = \dfrac{\sqrt{2gh}}{2}\cot\theta = \dfrac{\sqrt{2gh}}{2}(\sqrt{2}) = \sqrt{gh}$

(c) For (hemisphere + particle) system in vertical

$$\int N_2 dt = m[(0 - (-\sqrt{2gh}))] + m(0 - 0) = m\sqrt{2gh}$$

2.4 Variable Mass System

1. (a) $\Sigma F = ma$

$\Rightarrow \qquad F_{ext} + F_{thrust} = 0$

$\Rightarrow \qquad F_{ext} + \dfrac{dm}{dt} v_{rel} = 0$

$\Rightarrow \qquad F_{ext} + 75(0 - 2.20) = 0$

$\Rightarrow \qquad F_{ext} = 165 \text{ N}$

(b) $P_{motor} = F_{ext} v = 165 \times 2.2 = 363 \text{ W}$

(c) $K = \dfrac{1}{2} mv^2$

$\Rightarrow \qquad \dfrac{dK}{dt} = \dfrac{1}{2}\dfrac{dm}{dt} v^2 = 181.5 \text{ W}$

2. Let velocity of car at any time be v.

$$F_{Thrust} = \frac{dm}{dt} v_{rel} = \mu(0 - v) = -\mu v$$

For car, $\Sigma F = ma$

$\Rightarrow \qquad F_{ext} + F_{Thrust} = ma$

$\Rightarrow \qquad F - \mu v = (m_0 + \mu t)\dfrac{dv}{dt}$

$\Rightarrow \qquad \displaystyle\int_0^v \frac{dv}{F - \mu v} = \int_0^t \frac{dt}{m_0 + \mu t}$

$\Rightarrow \qquad \dfrac{[\ln(F - \mu v)]_0^v}{-\mu} = \dfrac{[\ln(m_0 + \mu t)]_0^t}{\mu}$

$\Rightarrow \qquad -\ln\left(\dfrac{F - \mu v}{F}\right) = \ln\left(\dfrac{m_0 + \mu t}{m_0}\right)$

$\Rightarrow \qquad v = \dfrac{Ft}{m_0 + \mu t}$

$$a = \frac{F - \mu v}{m_0 + \mu t} = \frac{F - \dfrac{\mu F t}{m_0 + ut}}{m_0 + ut} = \frac{Fm_0}{(m_0 + \mu t)^2}$$

3. Let velocity of cart at any time be v. Velocity of sand spilling out of cart will also be v.

$$F_{Thrust} = \frac{dm}{dt} v_{rel} = \mu(v - v) = 0$$

$$\Sigma F = ma \Rightarrow F_{ext} + F_{Thrust} = m\frac{dv}{dt}$$

$\Rightarrow \qquad F + 0 = (m_0 - \mu t)\dfrac{dv}{dt}$

$\Rightarrow \qquad a = \dfrac{dv}{dt} = \dfrac{F}{m_0 - \mu t}$

$$\int_0^v dv = F\int_0^t \frac{dt}{m_0 - \mu t} \Rightarrow v = \frac{F}{\mu}\ln\left(\frac{m_0}{m_0 - \mu t}\right)$$

4. (a) $F_{Thrust} = \dfrac{dm}{dt} v_{rel} = 190 \times 2800$

$$= 5.32 \times 10^5 \text{ N}$$

(b) $F_{net} = F_{Thrust} - mg$

At blast off, $F_{net} = 5.32 \times 10^5 - (21000)(10)$

$$= 3.22 \times 10^5 \text{N}$$

(c) $\Sigma F = m\dfrac{dv}{dt}$

$\Rightarrow \qquad F_{ext} + F_{Thrust} = m\dfrac{dv}{dt}$

$\Rightarrow \qquad -mg + \left(-\dfrac{dm}{dt}\right)v_{rel} = \dfrac{m\,dv}{dt}$

$\Rightarrow \qquad -\displaystyle\int_0^t g\,dt - \int_{M_0}^{M} \frac{dm}{m} v_{rel} = \int_{V_0}^{V} dv$

$\Rightarrow \qquad -gt + \left[\ln\left(\dfrac{M_0}{M}\right)\right] v_{rel} = v - v_0$

$\Rightarrow \qquad v = v_0 - gt + v_{rel}\ln\left(\dfrac{M_0}{M}\right)$

(d) Time taken to burn all the fuel $= \dfrac{15000}{190}\text{ s} = 78.95 \text{ s}$

$$v = 0 - 10(78.95) + 2800\ln\left(\frac{21000}{6000}\right)$$

$$= 2718 \text{ m/s}$$

5. $m = \lambda x \Rightarrow \frac{dm}{dt} = \lambda \frac{dx}{dt} = \lambda v$

$$F_{ext} + F_{Thrust} = m\frac{dv}{dt}$$

$$\Rightarrow \quad F - \mu_k(\lambda x g) - (\lambda v)v = (\lambda x)\frac{dv}{dt}$$

$$\Rightarrow \quad \frac{dv}{dt} = \frac{F}{\lambda x} - \mu_k g - \frac{v^2}{x}$$

6. (a) $F_{Thrust} = \frac{dm}{dt} v_{rel} = \frac{d\left(\frac{M}{L}y\right)}{dt}(0 - v_0) = -\frac{M}{L}v_0^2$

$$F_{ext} + F_{Thrust} = m\frac{dv}{dt}$$

$$\Rightarrow \quad P - \frac{M}{L}yg - \frac{M}{L}v_0^2 = 0$$

$$\Rightarrow \quad P = \frac{M}{L}(gy + v_0^2)$$

(b) Energy lost during the lifting = Work done by applied force – Increase in mechanical energy of chain

$$= \int_0^y P dy - \left(\left(\frac{m}{L}y\right)g\left(\frac{y}{2}\right) + \frac{1}{2}\left(\frac{M}{L}y\right)v_0^2\right)$$

$$= \frac{Myv_0^2}{2L}$$

7.

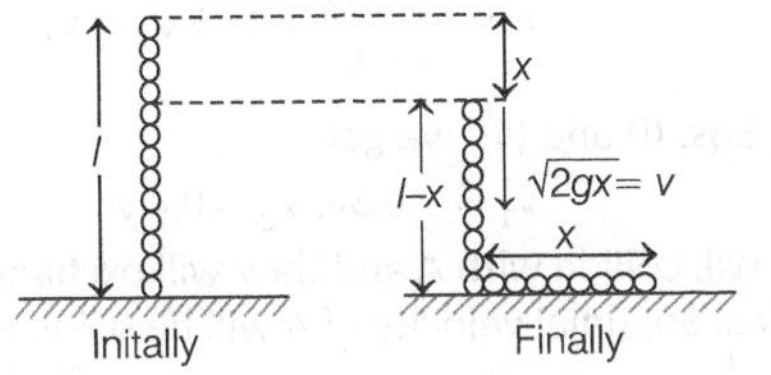

$$F_{Thrust} = \frac{dm}{dt} v_{rel} = \frac{d\left(\frac{m}{l}x\right)}{dt}(v - 0)$$

$$= \frac{m}{l}\frac{dx}{dt}v = \frac{m}{l}v^2 = \frac{2mgx}{l}$$

$$N = F_{Thrust} + \left(\frac{m}{l}x\right)g$$

$$= \frac{2mgx}{l} + \frac{mgx}{l} = \frac{3mgx}{l}$$

Level 2

Single Choice Correct Questions

1. (a) $|\Delta \mathbf{p}| = |\mathbf{p}_2 - \mathbf{p}_1|$

$$= \sqrt{(mv_0)^2 + (mv_0)^2 - 2(mv_0)(mv_0)\cos\left(\frac{\pi}{3}\right)}$$

$$= 2mv_0 \sin\left(\frac{\pi}{6}\right)$$

$$J = |\Delta \mathbf{p}| = 2mv_0 \sin\left(\frac{\pi}{6}\right)$$

2. (a) $I_1 = m\left[\sqrt{2gh} - \left\{-\sqrt{2g\left(\frac{h}{4}\right)}\right\}\right] = \frac{3m}{2}\sqrt{2gh}$

$$I_2 = m\left[\sqrt{2gh} - \left\{-\sqrt{2g\left(\frac{h}{16}\right)}\right\}\right] = \frac{5}{4}m\sqrt{2gh}$$

$$m\sqrt{2gh} = \frac{2I_1}{3} = \frac{4}{5}I_2$$

$$\Rightarrow \quad 5I_1 = 6I_2$$

3. (a) $\Delta K = \frac{1}{2}m(v_2^2 - v_1^2) = \frac{1}{2}m(\mathbf{v}_2 - \mathbf{v}_1)\cdot(\mathbf{v}_2 + \mathbf{v}_1)$

$$= \frac{1}{2}\mathbf{I}\cdot(\mathbf{v}_2 + \mathbf{v}_1)$$

4. (d)

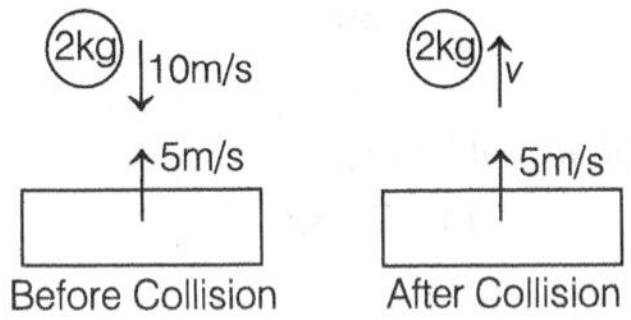

$$e = 1 = \frac{v - 5}{10 - (-5)}$$

$$\Rightarrow \quad v = 20 \text{ m/s}$$

$$I = m(v_2 - v_1) = 2[20 - (-10)]$$

$$= 60 \text{ N-s}$$

5. (c) Let time be t when string again gets taut

$$s_1 = s_2 \Rightarrow 4t = 2t + \frac{1}{2}(10)t^2 \Rightarrow t = 0.4 \text{ s}$$

At $t = 0.4$ s, velocity of lower block

$$v = u + at = 2 + (10)(0.4) = 6 \text{ m/s}$$

Using linear momentum conservation,

$$4(4) + 4(6) = (4 + 4)v$$

$$v = 5 \text{ m/s}$$

$$I = \int T dt = 4(5 - 4) = 4 \text{ N-s}$$

6. (b) Using conservation of linear momentum,

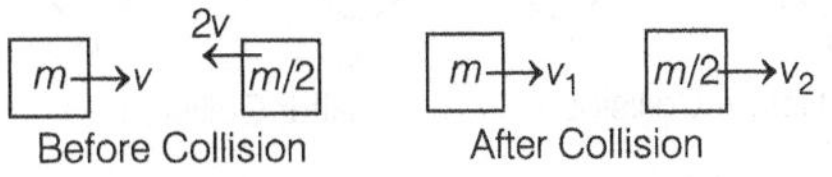

$$mv + \frac{m}{2}(-2v) = mv_1 + \frac{m}{2}v_2$$

$$\Rightarrow \quad 2v_1 + v_2 = 0 \quad \text{... (i)}$$

$$e = \frac{v_2 - v_1}{v - (-2v)} = 1$$

$$\Rightarrow \quad v_2 - v_1 = 3v \quad \text{... (ii)}$$

Solving Eqs. (i) and (ii), we get

$$v_1 = -v \text{ and } v_2 = 2v$$

7. (a) $mu + m(0) = mv + m(2v)$

$\Rightarrow \quad v = \frac{u}{3}$

$$e = \frac{v_2 - v_1}{u_1 - u_2} = \frac{2v - v}{u - 0} = \frac{v}{u} = \frac{1}{3}$$

8. (a)

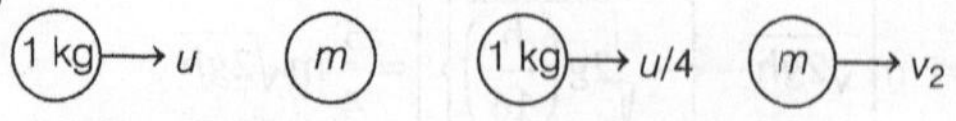

Before Collision After Collision

$$1(u) + m(0) = 1\left(\frac{u}{4}\right) + mv_2$$

$\Rightarrow \quad mv_2 = \frac{3u}{4}$ ...(i)

$$e = \frac{v_2 - v_1}{u_1 - u_2} = \frac{v_2 - \frac{u}{4}}{u} = 1$$

$\Rightarrow \quad v_2 = \frac{5u}{4}$ ...(ii)

From Eqs. (i) and (iii), we get

$$m = 0.6 \text{ kg}$$

9. (c) $m \propto r^3 \Rightarrow m_B = 8m_A$

$$m_A u + 0 = m_A v_1 + m_B v_2$$

$\Rightarrow \quad u = v_1 + 8v_2$ ...(i)

$$e = \frac{v_2 - v_1}{u - 0} = 0.5$$

$\Rightarrow \quad v_2 - v_1 = \frac{u}{2}$ ...(ii)

Solving Eqs. (i) and (ii), we get

$$v_1 = \frac{-u}{3} \text{ and } v_2 = \frac{u}{6}$$

$$\frac{|v_1|}{|v_2|} = \frac{u/3}{u/6} = 2$$

10. (a) $e = \frac{v_2 - v_1}{u_1 - u_2} = \frac{\frac{J}{m} - \frac{p - J}{m}}{\frac{p}{m} - 0} = \frac{2J}{p} - 1$

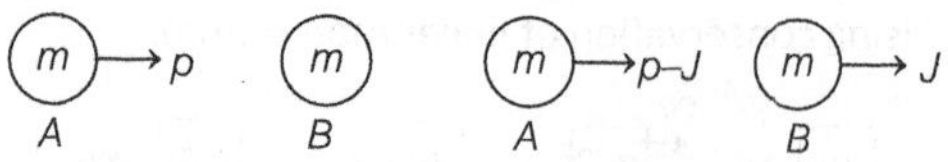

Before Collision After Collision

11. (a) $mu + m(0) = mv_1 + mv_2$

$\Rightarrow \quad v_1 + v_2 = u$ ...(i)

$e = \frac{v_2 - v_1}{u - 0} \Rightarrow v_2 - v_1 = eu$ ...(ii)

Solving Eqs. (i) and (ii), we get

$$v_1 = \frac{(1-e)u}{2}, v_2 = \frac{(e+1)u}{2}$$

$$\frac{v_1}{v_2} = \left(\frac{1-e}{1+e}\right)$$

12. (a) Speed of 2 kg just before collision,

$$v^2 = u^2 + 2as$$

$\Rightarrow \quad v^2 = (1)^2 + 2(-0.2 \times 10)(0.16)$

$\Rightarrow \quad v = 0.6 \text{ m/s}$

Using linear momentum conservation,

$$2(0.6) + 4(0) = 2v_1 + 4v_2$$

$v_1 + 2v_2 = 0.6$ ... (i)

$$e = \frac{v_2 - v_1}{0.6 - 0} = 1$$

$\Rightarrow \quad v_2 - v_1 = 0.6$ ...(ii)

Solving Eqs. (i) and (ii), we get

$$v_1 = -0.2 \text{ m/s and } v_2 = 0.4 \text{ m/s}$$

Separation between them when they come to rest,

$$= \frac{v_1^2}{2\mu g} + \frac{v_2^2}{2\mu g} = 0.05 \text{ m} = 5 \text{ cm}$$

13. (a) When A collides with B, they will exchange their velocities.

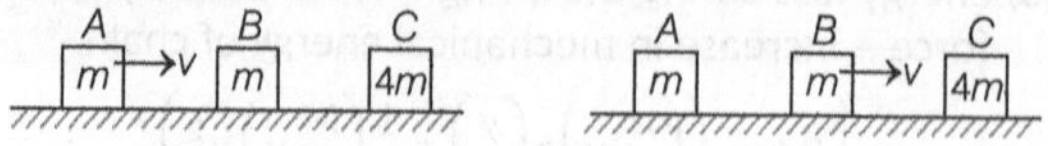

For collision between B and C

$$mv + 4m(0) = mv_1 + 4mv_2$$

$\Rightarrow \quad v_1 + 4v_2 = v$ ...(i)

$e = \frac{v_2 - v_1}{v - 0} = 1 \Rightarrow v_2 - v_1 = v$ ... (ii)

Solving Eqs. (i) and (ii), we get

$$v_1 = -0.6v, v_2 = 0.4v$$

Now, B will collide with A and they will exchange their velocities. So, finial velocity of A will be 0.6 v, left.

14. (a) Velocity of ball just before collision = $\sqrt{2gh}$

$$m(\sqrt{2gh}) + 2m(0) = mv_1 + 2mv_2$$

$\Rightarrow \quad v_1 + 2v_2 = \sqrt{2gh}$ ...(i)

$$e = 1 = \frac{v_2 - v_1}{\sqrt{2gh} - 0}$$

$\Rightarrow \quad v_2 - v_1 = \sqrt{2gh}$ ... (ii)

Solving Eqs. (i) and (ii), we get

$$v_1 = -\frac{\sqrt{2gh}}{3}, v_2 = \frac{2\sqrt{2gh}}{3}$$

Maximum height reached by ball after collision,

$$h_{max} = \frac{v_1^2}{2g} = \frac{h}{9}$$

15. (b) $v_{app} = u$

$$e = \frac{v_{sep}}{v_{app}} \Rightarrow \frac{1}{2} = \frac{v_{sep}}{u}$$

$\Rightarrow \quad v_{sep} = \frac{u}{2}$

$$T = \frac{2\pi r}{v_{sep}} = \frac{2\pi r}{u/2} = \frac{4\pi r}{u}$$

16. (d) $R = u\sqrt{\dfrac{2h}{g}} \Rightarrow 20 = v_1\sqrt{\dfrac{2(5)}{10}} \Rightarrow v_1 = 20 \text{ m/s}$

and $100 = v_1\sqrt{\dfrac{2(5)}{10}} \Rightarrow v_2 = 100 \text{ m/s}$

Using linear momentum conservation,

$$0.01v + 0.2 \times 0 = 0.01 \times 100 + 0.2 \times 20$$

$$\Rightarrow \quad v = 500 \text{ m/s}$$

17. (b) Velocity of ball B just after collision $= \sqrt{2gh}$

$$= \sqrt{2 \times 10 \times 5}$$

$$= 10 \text{ m/s}$$

Using linear momentum conservation,

$$m(16) + m(0) = mv_1 + m(10)$$

$$\Rightarrow \quad v_1 = 6 \text{ m/s}$$

$$e = \frac{v_2 - v_1}{u_1 - u_2} = \frac{10 - 6}{16 - 0} = \frac{1}{4}$$

18. (a) $F_{avg} = \dfrac{\Delta P}{\Delta t} = \dfrac{mv - (-mv)}{\left[\dfrac{2(L-d)}{v}\right]} = \dfrac{mv^2}{L-d}$

19. (a) $v_{avg} = \dfrac{\text{Total distance}}{\text{Total time}} \Rightarrow \dfrac{2v}{3} = \dfrac{2L}{\dfrac{L}{v} + \dfrac{L}{ev}}$

$$\Rightarrow \quad e = 0.5$$

20. (d) Speed of ball just after first collision $= e\sqrt{2gh}$

Speed of ball just after second collision $= e(e\sqrt{2gh})$

$$= e^2\sqrt{2gh}$$

$$H_{max} = \frac{u^2}{2g} = \frac{(e^2\sqrt{2gh})^2}{2g} = e^4h$$

21. (d) $T = \sqrt{\dfrac{2h}{g}} + \dfrac{2(e\sqrt{2gh})}{g} + \dfrac{2(e^2\sqrt{2gh})}{g} + \dfrac{2(e^3\sqrt{2gh})}{g} + \ldots$

$$= \sqrt{\frac{2h}{g}}(1 + 2e + 2e^2 + 2e^3 + \ldots)$$

$$= \sqrt{\frac{2h}{g}}[1 + 2e(1 + e + e^2 + \ldots)]$$

$$= \sqrt{\frac{2h}{g}}\left(1 + 2e\left[\frac{1}{1-e}\right]\right)$$

$$= \sqrt{\frac{2h}{g}}\left(\frac{1+e}{1-e}\right)$$

22. (c) Momentum imparted to floor in first collision $= ep - (-p)$

$$= (e+1)p$$

Momentum imparted to floor in second collision

$$= e^2p - (-ep) = e(e+1)p$$

Total momentum imparted to floor

$$= (e+1)p + e(e+1)p + e^2(e+1)p + \ldots$$

$$= (e+1)p(1 + e + e^2 + \ldots)$$

$$= \left(\frac{1+e}{1-e}\right)p$$

23. (b)

Before collision   After collision

Since $M >> m$, velocity of first ball will remain unchanged.

$$e = \frac{v_2 - v}{v - 0} = 1$$

$$\Rightarrow \quad v_2 = 2v$$

24. (b)

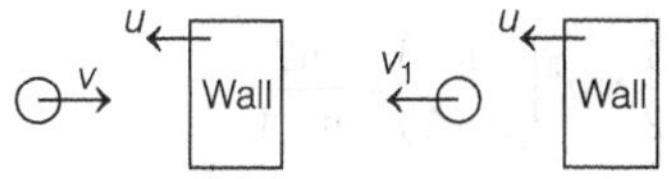

Before Collision   After Collision

$$e = \frac{v_1 - u}{v - (-4)} = 1$$

$$\Rightarrow \quad v_1 = v + 2u$$

$$W = \Delta K = \frac{1}{2}m(v_1^2 - v^2) = \frac{1}{2}m((v + 2u)^2 - v^2)$$

$$= 2mu(v + u)$$

25. (d) $W_{\text{internal forces}} = \Delta K_{\text{system}}$

$$= 0 - \left(\frac{1}{2} \times 2 \times 5^2 + \frac{1}{2} \times 2 \times 5^2\right) = -50 \text{ J}$$

26. (c)

Before Collision   After Collision

$$mu + 0 = mv_1 + Amv_2$$

$$\Rightarrow \quad v_1 + v_2 = u \quad \ldots\text{(i)}$$

$$e = \frac{v_2 - v_1}{u - 0} = 1$$

$$\Rightarrow \quad v_2 - v_1 = u \quad \ldots\text{(ii)}$$

Solving Eqs. (i) and (ii), we get

$$v_1 = -\left(\frac{A-1}{A+1}\right)u$$

Kinetic energy retained by neutron $= \dfrac{1}{2}mu^2\left(\dfrac{A-1}{A+1}\right)^2$

$$= \left(\frac{A-1}{A+1}\right)^2 E$$

27. (d) $mu + 0 = mv_1 + nmv_2$

$$\Rightarrow \quad v_1 + nv_2 = u \quad \ldots\text{(i)}$$

$$e = \frac{v_2 - v_1}{u - 0} = 1$$

$$\Rightarrow \quad v_2 - v_1 = u \quad \ldots\text{(ii)}$$

Solving Eqs. (i) and (ii), we get

$$v_2 = \frac{2u}{(n+1)}$$

$$K_2 = \frac{1}{2}(nm)v_2^2$$

Fraction of incident energy transferred to the heavier ball

$$=\frac{\frac{1}{2}(nm)\left(\frac{2u}{n+1}\right)^2}{\frac{1}{2}mu^2}=\frac{4n}{(1+n)^2}$$

28. (a) $mu+0=(m+nm)v$

$\Rightarrow \quad v=\frac{u}{n+1}$

$$U_{max}=K_1-K=\left(\frac{1}{2}mu^2+0\right)-\frac{1}{2}(m+nm)\left(\frac{u}{n+1}\right)^2$$

$$=\frac{1}{2}mu^2\left(\frac{n}{n+1}\right)=\frac{nE}{n+1}$$

29. (a) Energy loss $=\frac{1}{2}\mu v_{rel}^2$

$\Rightarrow \quad \frac{100}{3}=\frac{1}{2}\left[\frac{(2)(1)}{2+1}\right]v_{rel}^2$

$\Rightarrow \quad v_{rel}=10$ m/s

30. (a) Loss in KE $=\frac{1}{2}\left(\frac{m_1m_2}{m_1+m_2}\right)(1-e^2)(u_1-u_2)^2$

$\Rightarrow \quad \frac{2}{3}\times\frac{1}{2}mu^2=\frac{1}{2}\left[\frac{m(3m)}{m+3m}\right](1-e^2)(u-0)^2$

$\Rightarrow \quad e=\frac{1}{3}$

31. (a) $\tan\phi=\frac{\tan\theta}{e}=\frac{\tan 45^\circ}{\left(\frac{1}{\sqrt{2}}\right)}$

$\Rightarrow \quad \phi=\tan^{-1}(\sqrt{2})$

$$v'=\sqrt{(ev\cos\theta)^2+(v\sin\theta)^2}=\frac{\sqrt{3}}{2}v$$

32. (d) $\tan\phi=\frac{\tan\theta}{e}$

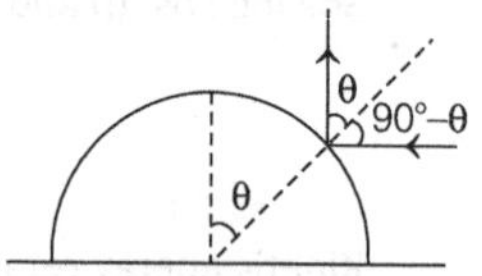

$\Rightarrow \quad \tan\theta=\frac{\tan(90^\circ-\theta)}{(1/3)}$

$\Rightarrow \quad \tan^2\theta=3$

$\Rightarrow \quad \tan\theta=\sqrt{3}$

$\Rightarrow \quad \theta=60^\circ$

33. (b) Component of velocity of ball parallel to surface will remain unchanged and component of velocity of ball normal to surface will become e times in magnitude and direction will get reversed.

So, velocity after collision $=a\hat{i}-(-eb)\hat{j}=a\hat{i}+eb\hat{j}$

34. (a) $\mathbf{n}=(2\hat{i}+2\hat{j}+3\hat{k})-(4\hat{i}+3\hat{j}-5\hat{k})=-2\hat{i}-\hat{j}+8\hat{k}$

$$e=\frac{v_{sep}}{v_{app}}=\frac{|\mathbf{v}\cdot\mathbf{n}|}{|\mathbf{u}\cdot\mathbf{n}|}$$

$$=\frac{-4-2+24}{|-8-3-40|}$$

$$=\frac{18}{51}=\frac{6}{17}$$

35. (a)

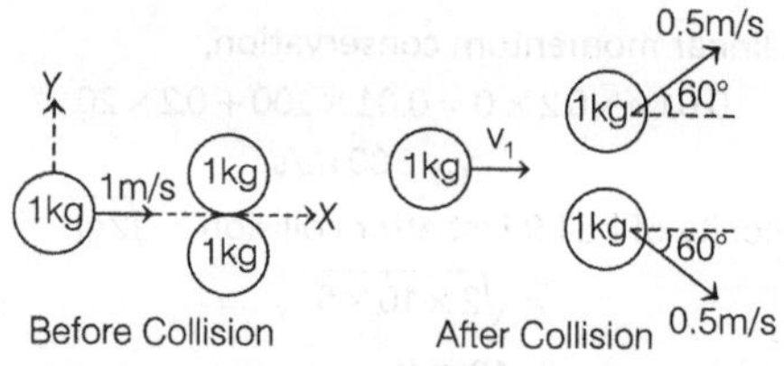

Using linear momentum conservation along X-axis

$$1(1)+0+0=1v_1+1(0.5\cos 60^\circ)+1(0.5\cos 60^\circ)$$

$$v_1=0.5 \text{ m/s}$$

Loss of K.E. $=K_1-K_2$

$$=\frac{1}{2}\times1\times1^2-\left[\frac{1}{2}\times1\times(0.5)^2\times3\right]$$

$$=0.125 \text{ J}$$

36. (a) Applying linear momentum conservation,

$$mu+0+0=0+mv\cos 30^\circ+mv\cos 30^\circ$$

$\Rightarrow \quad v=\frac{u}{\sqrt{3}}$

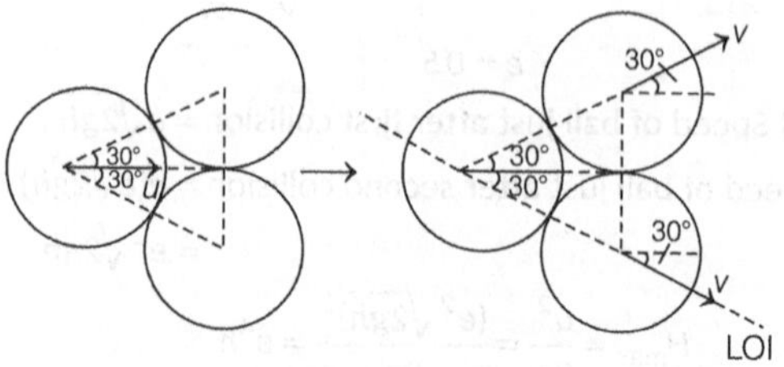

$$e=\frac{v_{sep}}{v_{app}}=\frac{v-0}{u\cos 30^\circ}=\frac{u/\sqrt{3}}{\left(\frac{\sqrt{3}u}{2}\right)}=\frac{2}{3}$$

37. (a)

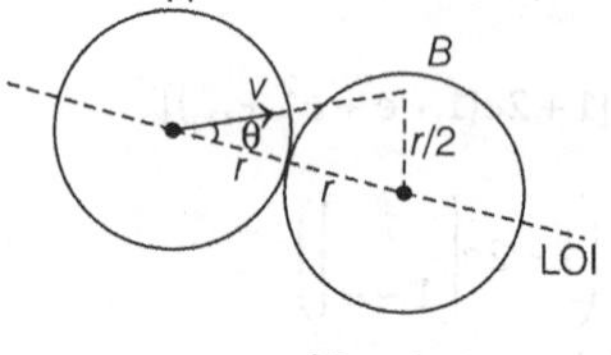

$$\sin\theta=\frac{r/2}{2r}=\frac{1}{4}$$

Velocity of A along the line of impact before collision

$$=v\cos\theta=v\sqrt{1-\left(\frac{1}{4}\right)^2}=\frac{\sqrt{15}v}{4}$$

Along the LOI, velocities of two balls will get exchanged. So, velocity of ball B after collision $=\frac{\sqrt{15}}{4}v$

38. (a) Using linear momentum conservation along the line of impact,

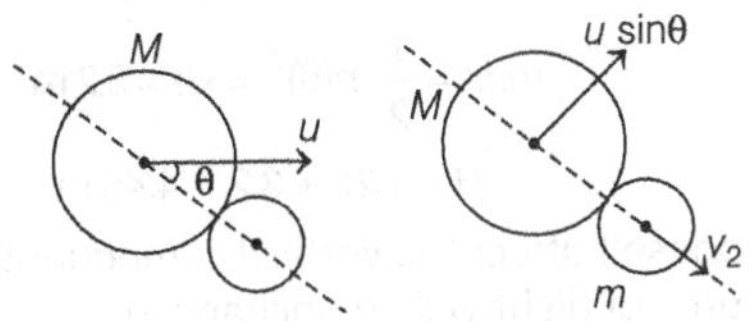

Before Collision After Collision

$$M(u\cos\theta) + 0 = 0 + mv_2$$

$$\Rightarrow \quad v_2 = \frac{Mu\cos\theta}{m}$$

$$e = \frac{v_{sep}}{v_{app}} = \frac{v_2}{u\cos\theta} = \frac{M}{m}$$

39. (a) Velocity of ball just before hitting the inclined plane

$$= \sqrt{2gh} = 10\text{ m / s}$$

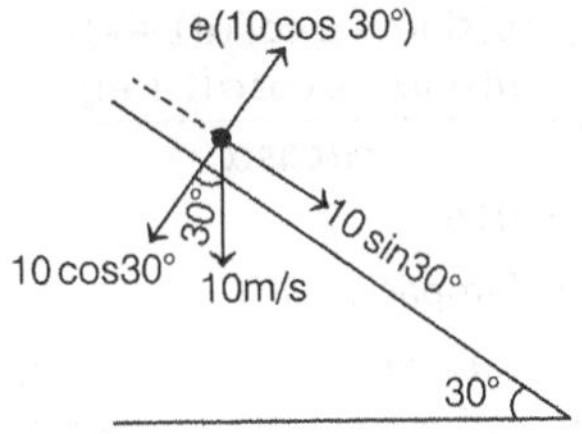

$$T = \frac{2u_y}{g\cos 30^\circ} = \frac{2[0.5(10\cos 30^\circ)]}{10\cos 30^\circ} = 1\text{ s}$$

40. (b) $F_{ext} + F_{Thrust} = ma$

$$\Rightarrow \quad -mg + \frac{dm}{dt}v_{rel} = ma$$

$$\Rightarrow \quad -5000\times 10 + \frac{dm}{dt}(800) = 5000\times 20$$

$$\Rightarrow \quad \frac{dm}{dt} = 187.5\text{ kgs}^{-1}$$

41. (c) $F_{Thrust} = m\dfrac{dv}{dt}$

$$\Rightarrow \quad -\frac{dm}{dt}v_{rel} = m\frac{dv}{dt}$$

$$\Rightarrow \quad \int_0^v dv = -\int_{m_0}^{m_0/2}\frac{dm}{m}v_{rel}$$

$$\Rightarrow \quad v = 2\ln 2$$

42. (a) $M = M_0 - \mu t = 1000 - 10(60) = 400$

$$v = v_0 - gt + v_r\ln\left(\frac{M_0}{M}\right)$$

$$= 0 - 10\times 60 + 2000\ln\left(\frac{1000}{400}\right)$$

$$= 1240\text{ m/s}$$

Numerical Value Questions

1. Using linear momentum conservation,

$$4\times 7 + 3\times 0 = 4v_1 + 3v_2$$

$$\Rightarrow \quad 4v_1 + 3v_2 = 28 \qquad \text{...(i)}$$

$$e = \frac{v_2 - v_1}{7 - 0} = 1$$

$$\Rightarrow \quad v_2 - v_1 = 7 \qquad \text{...(ii)}$$

Solving Eqs. (i) and (ii), we get

$$v_1 = 1\text{ m/s}, v_2 = 8\text{ m/s}$$

Distance travelled by 3 kg block before coming to rest,

$$v^2 = u^2 + 2as$$

$$\Rightarrow \quad 0^2 = (8)^2 + 2(-0.4\times 10)s \Rightarrow s = 8\text{ m}$$

Time taken by 4 kg block to reach 3 kg block,

$$s = ut + \frac{1}{2}at^2$$

$$8 = 1t \Rightarrow t = 8\text{ s}$$

2. Let speed of first ball be u.

$$16 = 1(u) \Rightarrow u = 16\text{ m/s}$$

For first collision between first ball and second ball,

$$mu + m(0) = mv_1 + mv_2$$

$$\Rightarrow \quad v_1 + v_2 = u \qquad \text{... (i)}$$

$$e = 0.5 = \frac{v_2 - v_1}{u - 0}$$

$$\Rightarrow \quad v_2 - v_1 = \frac{u}{2} \qquad \text{... (ii)}$$

Solving Eqs. (i) and (ii), we get

$$v_2 = \frac{3u}{4}$$

Similarly, $v_5 = \left(\dfrac{3}{4}\right)^4 u$

For block to just complete vertical circle

$$\left(\frac{3}{4}\right)^4 u = \sqrt{5gr}$$

$$\Rightarrow \quad \left(\left(\frac{3}{4}\right)^4(16)\right)^2 = 5gr \Rightarrow r = \left(\frac{3}{2}\right)^8\frac{1}{5g}$$

So, $\quad n = 8$

3. For ball B, $T - mg = \dfrac{mv_2^2}{l}$

$$\Rightarrow \quad 40 - 10 = \frac{1v_2^2}{0.3} \Rightarrow v_2 = 3\text{ m/s}$$

Using momentum conservation,

$$2v_0 + 0 = 2v_1 + 1(3)$$

$$2v_0 = 2v_1 + 3 \qquad \text{... (i)}$$

$$e = \frac{1}{2} = \frac{3 - v_1}{v_0 - 0}$$

$$\Rightarrow \quad 6 - 2v_1 = v_0 \qquad \text{...(ii)}$$

Solving Eqs. (i) and (ii), we get

$$v_0 = 3\text{ m/s}$$

4. $W = \int F dx = \Delta K$

$$\Rightarrow \quad -\int_0^0 \alpha x\, dx = K_0 - 0 \Rightarrow K_0 = \frac{\alpha x_0^2}{2}$$

Kinetic energy just after 3rd collision $= \left(\frac{1}{2}\right)^6 K_0 = \frac{K_0}{64}$

$$\frac{1}{64}\left(\frac{1}{2}\alpha x_0^2\right) = \frac{1}{2}\alpha x^2 \Rightarrow x = \frac{x_0}{8}$$

$$F = \alpha x = \frac{\alpha x_0}{8} = \frac{16}{8} = 2\,\text{N}$$

5. $m(200) + 0 = m(100) + 10mv$

$$v = 10\ \text{m/s}$$

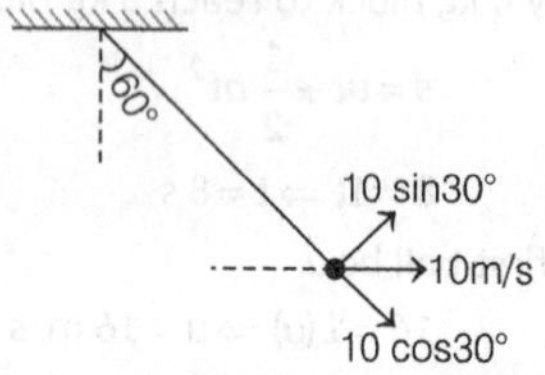

Due to jerk in the string, component of velocity of bob along the string will become zero. So, velocity of bob after jerk will be $10\sin 30° = 5$ m/s.

6. Let coordinates of point C be (x, y)

$$\tan 37° = \frac{y}{x - \frac{10}{3}} \Rightarrow y = \frac{3x}{4} - \frac{5}{2}$$

Equation of trajectory,

$$y = x\tan\alpha - \frac{gx^2}{2(u\cos\alpha)^2}$$

$$\Rightarrow \quad \frac{3x}{4} - \frac{5}{2} = x\left(\frac{1}{2}\right) - \frac{10x^2}{2\left[5\sqrt{5}\left(\frac{2}{\sqrt{5}}\right)\right]^2}$$

$$\Rightarrow \quad x^2 + 5x - 50 = 0 \Rightarrow x = 5\,\text{m}$$

$$y = \frac{3(5)}{4} - \frac{5}{2} = 1.25\,\text{m}$$

$$v_y^2 = u_y^2 + 2a_y s_y$$

$$\Rightarrow \quad v_y^2 = \left[5\sqrt{5}\left(\frac{1}{\sqrt{5}}\right)\right]^2 + 2(-10)(1.25)$$

$$\Rightarrow \quad v_y = 0$$

So, the particle strikes the inclined plane at point C horizontal with velocity $u\cos\alpha = 10$ m/s

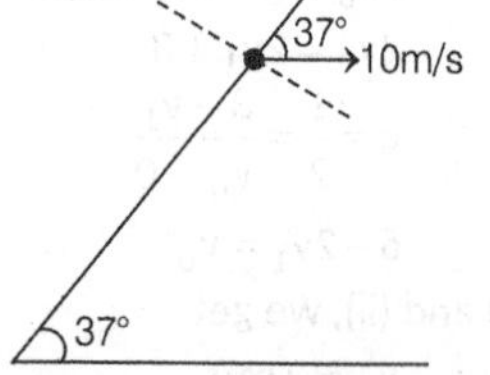

Velocity of particle just after collision $= 10\cos 37°$, along the inclined plane. Component of velocity normal to the inclined plane will become zero as $e = 0$.

Let h be further height raised by the particle.

$$mgh = \frac{1}{2}m(8)^2 \Rightarrow h = 3.2\,\text{m}$$

$$H = 1.25 + 3.2 = 4.45\,\text{m}$$

7. Collision doesn't affect the vertical component of velocity. So, total time of flight will be unchanged.

$$T = t_1 + t_2$$

$$\Rightarrow \quad \frac{2u\sin 30°}{g} = \frac{50}{u\cos 30°} + \frac{50}{eu\cos 30°}$$

$$\Rightarrow \quad u = \frac{100}{\sqrt{7}}\ \text{m/s}$$

8. $\int N dt = m[(eu\cos\alpha - (-u\cos\alpha)] = mu\cos\alpha(1+e)$

Impulse due to friction $= -\int \mu N\, dt$

$$\Rightarrow \quad mv_x - mu\sin\alpha = -\mu[mu\cos\alpha(1+e)]$$

$$\Rightarrow \quad v_x = u[\sin\alpha - \mu\cos\alpha(1+e)]$$

$$\tan\beta = \frac{u[\sin\alpha - u\cos\alpha(1+e)]}{eu\cos\alpha}$$

$$\Rightarrow \quad \mu = 0.25$$

9. Along the line of impact,

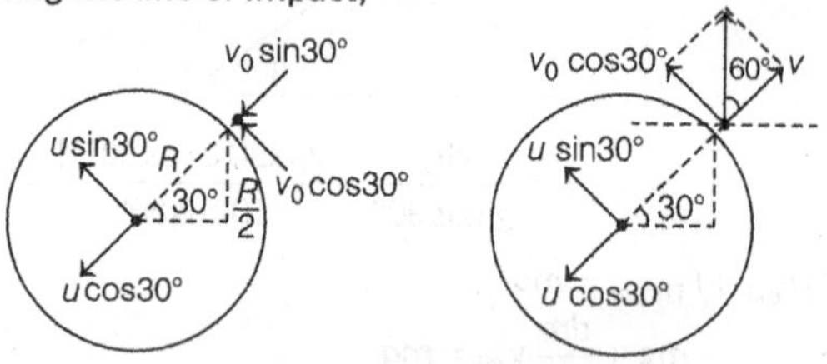

$$e = \frac{u\cos 30° - (-v)}{v_0\cos 30° - u\cos 30°} = 1$$

$$\Rightarrow \quad v = v_0\cos 30° - 2u\cos 30°$$

$$\tan 60° = \frac{v_0\sin 30°}{v_0\cos 30° - 2u\cos 30°}$$

$$\Rightarrow \quad u = \frac{v_0}{3} = 4\ \text{m/s}$$

10. Using momentum conservation along the line of impact

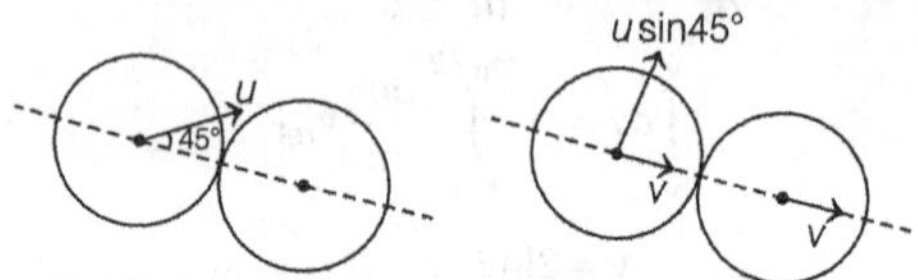

Just Before Collision — During Maximum deformation

$$mu\cos 45° + 0 = mv + mv$$

$$\Rightarrow \quad v = \frac{u\cos 45°}{2}$$

KE of striking ball that turned into potential energy.

$$= \frac{1}{2}m(u\cos 45°)^2 - \left[\frac{1}{2}m\left(\frac{u\cos 45°}{2}\right)^2 \times 2\right] = \frac{1}{8}mu^2$$

$$\eta = \frac{U}{K_1} = \frac{\frac{1}{8}mu^2}{\frac{1}{2}mu^2} = 0.25$$

Level 3

Single Choice correct Questions

1. (c)

$$mv + 0 = mv_1 + Mv_2$$

and $\dfrac{v_2 - v_1}{v - 0} = 1$

Solving, we get

$$v_1 = -\left(\frac{M-m}{M+m}\right)v \text{ and } v_2 = \left(\frac{2m}{M+m}\right)v$$

$$v_3 = \left(\frac{2M}{M+m}\right)v_2 = \frac{4Mmv}{(M+m)^2}$$

Now, $|v_1| = v_3$

$\Rightarrow$ $\left(\dfrac{M-m}{M+m}\right)v = \dfrac{4Mmv}{(M+m)^2}$

$\Rightarrow$ $M^2 - m^2 = 4Mm$

$\Rightarrow$ $\dfrac{M}{m} = 2 + \sqrt{5}$

2. (c)

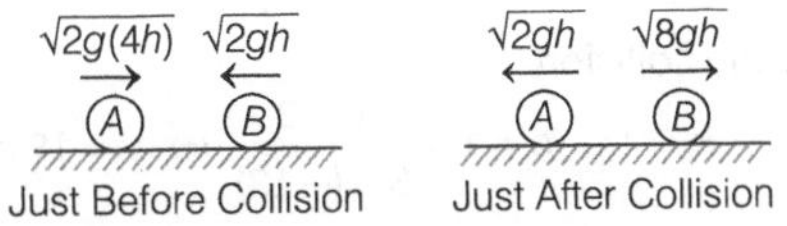

h_A = maximum height reached by $A = \dfrac{(\sqrt{2gh})^2}{2g} = h$

Velocity of B when it leaves the inclined surface,

$$W_{mg} + W_N = \Delta K$$

$\Rightarrow$ $-mgh + 0 = \dfrac{1}{2}mv^2 - \dfrac{1}{2}m(\sqrt{8gh})^2$

$\Rightarrow$ $v = \sqrt{6gh}$

$$h_1 = \frac{u^2 \sin^2\theta}{2g} = \frac{(\sqrt{6gh})^2 \sin^2 60°}{2g} = \frac{9h}{4}$$

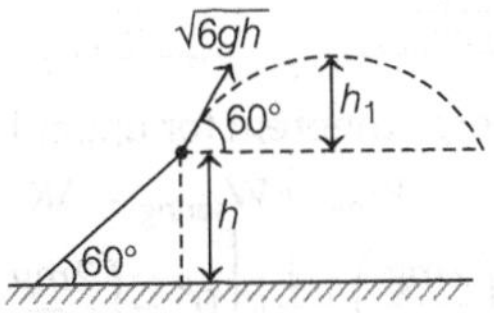

h_B = maximum height reached by $B = h + \dfrac{9h}{4} = \dfrac{13h}{4}$

$$\frac{h_A}{h_B} = \frac{h}{\left(\frac{13h}{4}\right)} = \frac{4}{13}$$

3. (b)

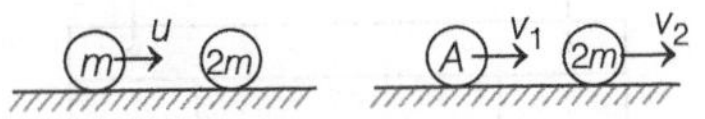

$$mu + 0 = mv_1 + 2mv_2$$

$\Rightarrow$ $v_1 + 2v_2 = u$ ... (i)

$$e = \frac{v_2 - v_1}{u - 0}$$

$\Rightarrow$ $v_2 - v_1 = eu$ ... (ii)

Solving, we get $v_1 = \dfrac{u}{3}(1 - 2e)$

For maximum loss of KE of first sphere,

$$v_1 = \frac{u}{3}(1 - 2e) = 0 \Rightarrow e = 0.5$$

4. (a) $mv_0 + 0 = mv_1 + (\alpha m)v_2$

$\Rightarrow$ $v_1 + \alpha v_2 = v_0 \Rightarrow 1 = e = \dfrac{v_2 - v_1}{v_0 - 0}$

$\Rightarrow$ $v_2 - v_1 = v_0$

Solving, we get $v_2 = \dfrac{2v_0}{1+\alpha}$ and $v_1 = -\left(\dfrac{\alpha - 1}{\alpha + 1}\right)v_0$

Now, block A will collide with the wall and rebound with the same speed.

For blocks not to collide again,

$$v_2 > |v_1| \Rightarrow \frac{2v_0}{1+\alpha} > \left(\frac{\alpha-1}{\alpha+1}\right)v_0$$

$\Rightarrow$ $\alpha < 3$

5. (b) u_A = Velocity of A just before collision $= \sqrt{2gl_A(1 - \cos\theta_A)}$

v_B = Velocity of B just after collision $= \sqrt{2gl_B(1 - \cos\theta_B)}$

Using linear momentum conservation,

$$mu_A = mv_A + mv_B \Rightarrow v_A + v_B = u_A \quad \text{... (i)}$$

$$e = \frac{v_B - v_A}{u_B - 0} \Rightarrow v_B - v_A = eu_A \quad \text{... (ii)}$$

Solving, we get

$$v_B = \left(\frac{e+1}{2}\right)u_A$$

$\Rightarrow$ $\sqrt{2gl_B(1 - \cos\theta)} = \left(\dfrac{e+1}{2}\right)\sqrt{2gl_A(1 - \cos\theta)}$

$\Rightarrow$ $\dfrac{l_B}{l_A} = \dfrac{(1+e)^2}{4}$

6. (c) At maximum deformation,

$$5(4) + 10(-0.5) = (5 + 10)v$$

$\Rightarrow$ $v = 1$ m/s

$|\Delta p_A|$ = Impulse of deformation $= 5(4 - 1) = 15$ N-s

Let deformation time be t.

So, Area under F-t graph = 15

$\Rightarrow$ $\dfrac{1}{2} \times t \times 150 = 15$

$\Rightarrow$ $t = 0.2$ s

So, reformation time $= 0.3 - 0.2 = 0.1$ s

Impulse of reformation $= \dfrac{1}{2} \times 0.1 \times 150 = 7.5$ N-s

$$e = \frac{\text{Impulse of reformation}}{\text{Impulse of deformation}} = \frac{7.5}{15} = \frac{1}{2}$$

7. (d) R and S have positive velocities after the collision, hence they are moving in the same direction.

At the midpoint of the collision, both the velocity-time curves intersect. Hence they have the same velocities at the mid-point of the collision.

After the collision, R has lesser velocity, hence it has a higher mass in order to keep the momentum conserved.

8. (a) Time taken to strike the front wall $= \dfrac{4L}{v}$

Velocity of approach of the block and plank after collision at front wall $= ev$

Further time taken to strike the rear wall $= \dfrac{6L}{ev}$

Velocity of separation after collision at rear wall

$$= e(ev) = e^2 v$$

So, total time $= \dfrac{4L}{v} + \dfrac{6L}{ev} + \dfrac{2L}{e^2 v}$

9. (c) Using linear momentum conservation,

$$m(u\cos 60°) = 2mv_{\text{block}} + m\left(\frac{u}{4}\right)$$

$$\Rightarrow \qquad v_{\text{block}} = \frac{u}{8}$$

Time taken by the bullet to hit the wall $= \dfrac{L}{(u/4)} = \dfrac{4L}{u}$

Distance travelled by the block by the time bullet hits the wall $= \left(\dfrac{u}{8}\right)\left(\dfrac{4L}{u}\right) = \dfrac{L}{2}$

The bullet will rebound from the wall with the same speed.

Further time taken for bullet to strike the block

$$= \frac{L-(L/2)}{\frac{u}{4}+\frac{u}{8}} = \frac{4L}{3u}$$

Position of block $= \dfrac{L}{2} + \dfrac{u}{8}\left(\dfrac{4L}{3u}\right) = \dfrac{2L}{3}$

10. (c) $v_y^2 = u_y^2 + 2a_y s_y$

$$\Rightarrow \qquad v_y^2 = (20\sin 60°)^2 + 2(-10)(15)$$

$$\Rightarrow \qquad v_y = 0$$

So, the shell's velocity is horizontal when it hits the ball.

Using linear momentum conservation,

$$1(20\cos 60°) + 0 = (1+1)v$$

$$\Rightarrow \qquad v = 5\text{ m/s}$$

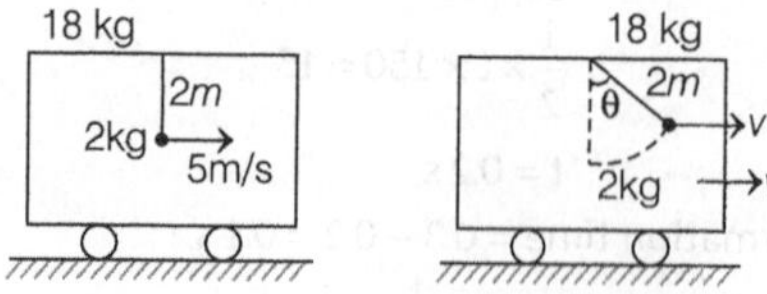

Using linear momentum conservation

$$2\times 5 + 18\times 0 = (2+18)v_1$$

$$\Rightarrow \qquad v_1 = 0.5\text{ m/s}$$

Using work-energy theorem.

$$W_{mg} + W_T = \Delta K_{\text{system}}$$

$$\Rightarrow \qquad -2\times 10\times 2(1-\cos\theta) + 0$$

$$= \frac{1}{2}\times 20\times (0.5)^2 - \frac{1}{2}\times 2\times 5^2$$

$$\Rightarrow \qquad \theta = \cos^{-1}\left(\frac{7}{16}\right)$$

11. (c) Speed just before hitting a step $= \sqrt{2gh}$

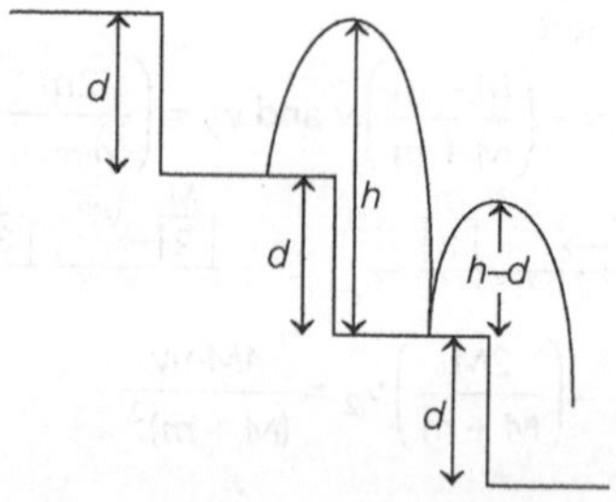

Speed just after hitting a step $= \sqrt{2g(h-d)}$

$$e = \frac{\sqrt{2g(h-d)}}{\sqrt{2gh}} \Rightarrow \frac{h}{d} = \frac{1}{1-e^2}$$

12. (b) For first collision,

$$e = 1 = \frac{v-5}{5-(-3)} \Rightarrow v = 13\text{ m/s}$$

For Second collision

$$e = 1 = \frac{v-3}{3-(-13)} \Rightarrow v = 19\text{ m/s}$$

13. (b) Speed of lower block will become zero immediately after hitting the ground. To lift the lower block, elongation in the spring should be $\dfrac{2mg}{k}$.

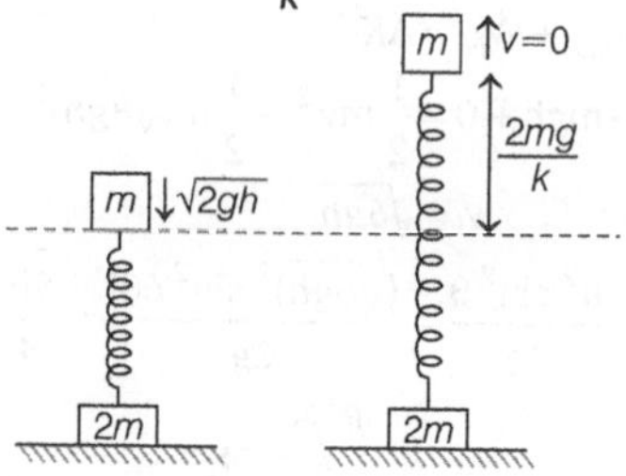

Using work-energy theorem for upper block,

$$W_{mg} + W_{\text{spring}} = \Delta K$$

$$\Rightarrow \qquad -mg\left(\frac{2mg}{k}\right) + \frac{1}{2}k\left[0^2 - \left(\frac{2mg}{k}\right)^2\right]$$

$$= 0 - \frac{1}{2}m(\sqrt{2gh})^2 \Rightarrow h = \frac{4mg}{k}$$

14. (b)

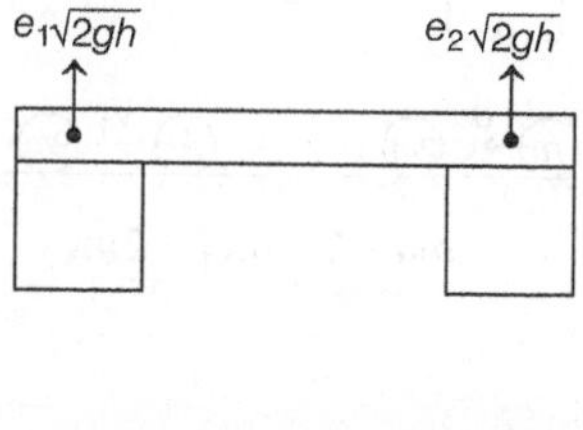

$$v_{CM} = \frac{e_1\sqrt{2gh} + e_2\sqrt{2gh}}{2} = \left(\frac{e_1+e_2}{2}\right)\sqrt{2gh}$$

$$h_{max} = \frac{v_{CM}^2}{2g} = \frac{(e_1+e_2)^2 h}{4}$$

15. (a) $\tan\beta = \dfrac{\tan\alpha}{e}$

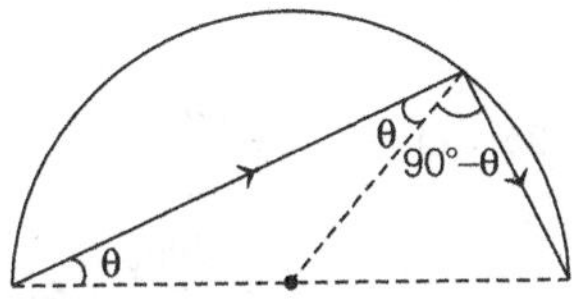

$\Rightarrow \quad \tan(90° - \theta) = \dfrac{\tan\theta}{(1/3)}$

$\Rightarrow \quad \tan^2\theta = \dfrac{1}{3}$

$\Rightarrow \quad \tan\theta = \dfrac{1}{\sqrt{3}}$

$\Rightarrow \quad \theta = 30°$

16. (c) Both components of velocity become e times in magnitude and direction gets reversed. So, new velocity $= -e\mathbf{v}$

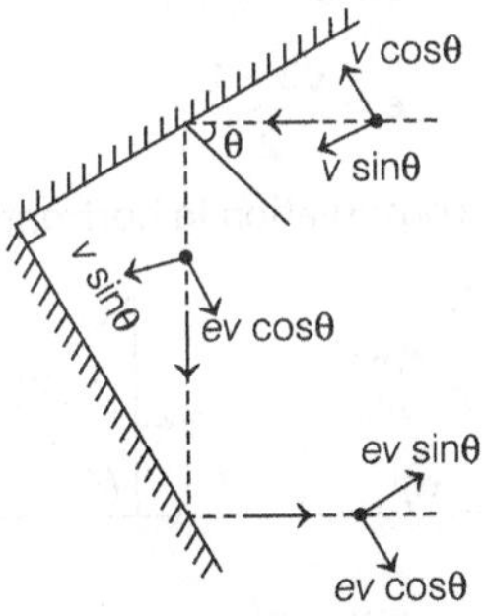

17. (b) Applying linear momentum conservation in X-direction.

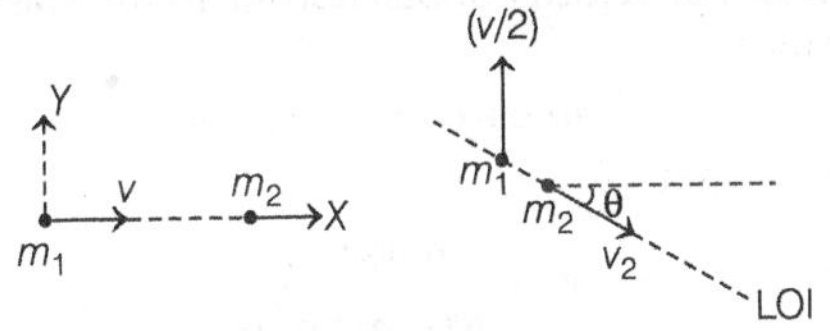

$$m_1 v + 0 = 0 + m_2 v_2 \cos\theta \quad \text{...(i)}$$

Applying linear momentum conservation in Y-direction

$$0 + 0 = m_1\left(\frac{v}{2}\right) - m_2 v_2 \sin\theta \quad \text{...(ii)}$$

Solving, we get $\tan\theta = \dfrac{1}{2}$

$$e = \frac{v_2 + \left(\frac{v}{2}\right)\sin\theta}{v\cos\theta} = 1$$

$$\Rightarrow \quad v_2 + \left(\frac{v}{2}\right)\sin\theta = v\cos\theta$$

$$\Rightarrow \quad \frac{m_1 v}{m_2\cos\theta} + \left(\frac{v}{2}\right)\sin\theta = v\cos\theta$$

$$\Rightarrow \quad \frac{m_1}{m_2} = \left(\cos^2\theta - \frac{\sin\theta\cos\theta}{2}\right) = \frac{3}{5}$$

$$\Rightarrow \quad m_2 = \frac{5m_1}{3}$$

18. (a)

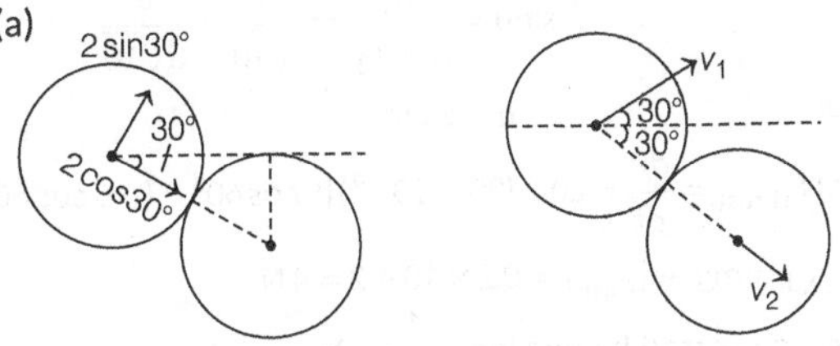

$$v_1 \sin 60° = 2\sin 30°$$

$$\Rightarrow \quad v_1 = \frac{2}{\sqrt{3}} \text{ m/s}$$

Momentum conservation along the line of impact,

$$2(2\cos 30°) + 0 = 2(v_1\cos 60°) + 2v_2$$

$$\Rightarrow \quad v_2 = \frac{2}{\sqrt{3}} \text{ m/s}$$

$$KE_{Lost} = \frac{1}{2}\times 2\times 2^2 - \left[\frac{1}{2}\times 2\times\left(\frac{2}{\sqrt{3}}\right)^2 + \frac{1}{2}\times 2\times\left(\frac{2}{\sqrt{3}}\right)^2\right]$$

$$= \frac{4}{3} \text{ J}$$

19. (c)

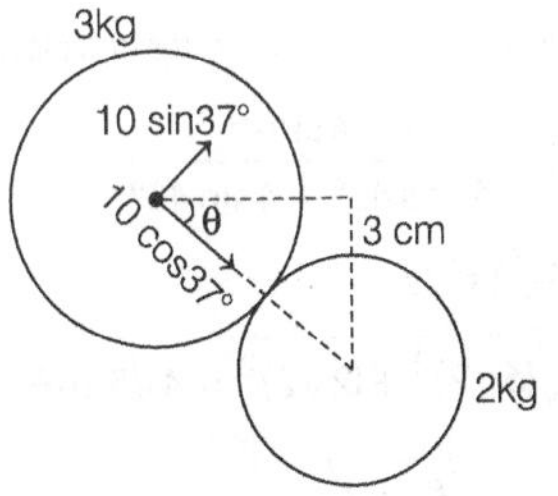

$$\sin\theta = \frac{3}{3+2} \Rightarrow \theta = 37°$$

Momentum conservation along the common normal.

$$3(10\cos 37°) + 2(0) = 3(2) + 2v_2$$

$$v_2 = 9 \text{ m/s}$$

$$e = \frac{9-2}{10\cos 37° - 0} = \frac{7}{8}$$

20. (c)

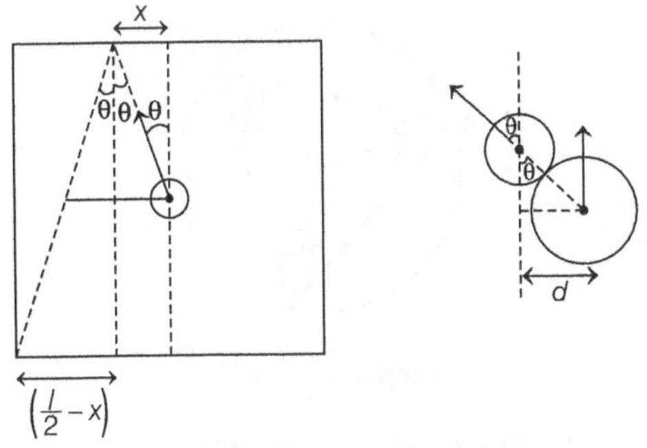

$$\tan\theta = \frac{x}{l/2} = \frac{\frac{l}{2} - x}{l} \Rightarrow x = l/6$$

$$\Rightarrow \quad \tan\theta = \frac{1}{3}$$

$$\sin\theta = \frac{d}{r_1 + r_2} \Rightarrow \frac{1}{\sqrt{10}} = \frac{d}{3\sqrt{10}}$$

$\Rightarrow \qquad d = 3\text{ cm}$

21. (b) $F_{Thrust} = \frac{dP}{dt} = 20 \times (20 \times 10^{-3})[5\cos 60° - (-5\cos 60°)]$

$F_{Total} = mg + F_{Thrust} = 0.2 \times 10 + 2 = 4\text{ N}$

Force exerted by one leg $= \frac{4}{4} = 1\text{ N}$

22. (c) Wedge will exert normal force on the ball normal to the incline. So, momentum of ball can be conserved only along incline just before and after collision.
Normal force on wedge from ground is impulsive. So, momentum of (wedge + ball) system can be conserved only along horizontal.

23. (d)

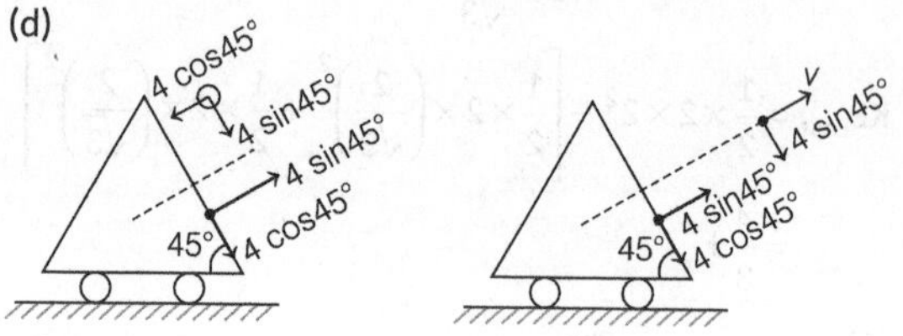

Before collision   After collision

$$e = 1 = \frac{v - 4\sin 45°}{4\cos 45° + 4\sin 45°}$$

$\Rightarrow \qquad v = 6\sqrt{2}\text{ m/s}$

$$v_{ball} = \sqrt{(6\sqrt{2})^2 + (2\sqrt{2})^2} = 4\sqrt{5}\text{ m/s}$$

24. (b) $H_1 = \frac{u_y^2}{2g}; H_4 = \frac{(e^3 u_y)^2}{2g}$

$$\frac{H_1}{H_4} = \frac{1}{e^6} = \frac{10^{12}}{2^{36}}$$

$\Rightarrow \qquad e = \frac{2^6}{10^2} = 0.64$

25. (d) $\tan\alpha = \frac{\tan\theta}{e}$

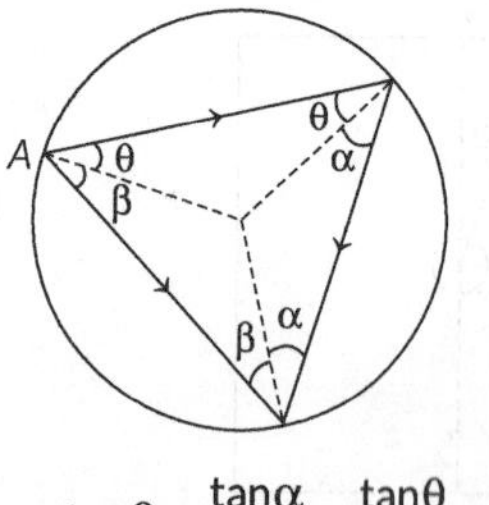

$$\tan\beta = \frac{\tan\alpha}{e} = \frac{\tan\theta}{e^2}$$

$$(\theta + \beta) + (\theta + \alpha) + (\alpha + \beta) = 180°$$

$\Rightarrow \qquad \alpha + \beta = 90° - \theta$

$\Rightarrow \qquad \tan(\alpha + \beta) = \tan(90° - \theta)$

$\Rightarrow \qquad \frac{\tan\alpha + \tan\beta}{1 - \tan\alpha\tan\beta} = \frac{1}{\tan\theta}$

$\Rightarrow \qquad \frac{\frac{\tan\theta}{e} + \frac{\tan\theta}{e^2}}{1 - \left(\frac{\tan\theta}{e}\right)\left(\frac{\tan\theta}{e^2}\right)} = \frac{1}{\tan\theta}$

$\Rightarrow \qquad \tan^2\theta = \frac{e^3}{1 + e + e^2}$

26. (c) $T = \frac{2u_y}{g}$

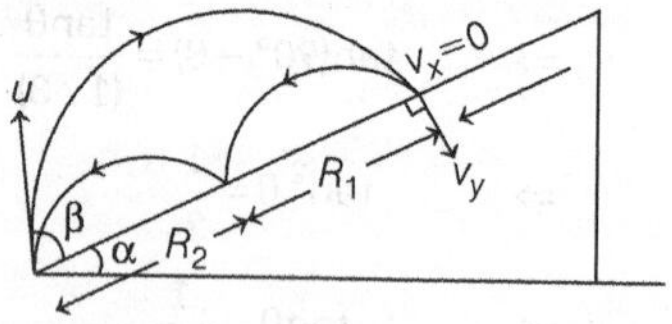

$T_1 = \frac{2eu_y}{g} = eT$

$T_2 = \frac{2e^2u_y}{g} = e^2T$

$R = R_1 + R_2$

$\Rightarrow \qquad \frac{1}{2}(g\sin\alpha)T^2 = \frac{1}{2}(g\sin\alpha)(eT + e^2T)^2$

$\Rightarrow \qquad e^2 + e - 1 = 0$

$\Rightarrow \qquad e = \frac{\sqrt{5} - 1}{2}$

27. (c) Momentum conservation in horizontal.

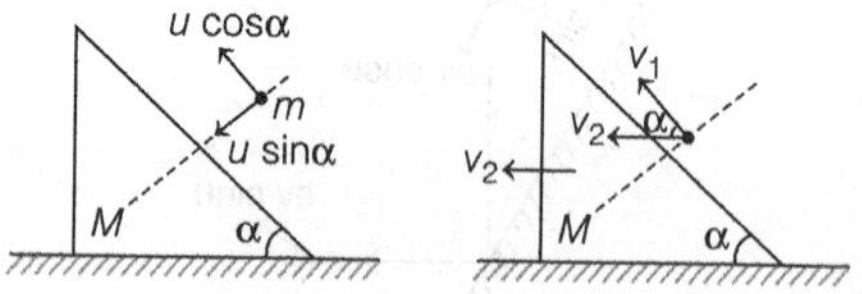

$$mu = m(v_2 + v_1\cos\alpha) + Mv_2 \qquad \text{... (i)}$$

Component of velocity of ball normal to the line of impact is constant.

$\Rightarrow \qquad u\cos\alpha = v_1 + v_2\cos\alpha \qquad \text{... (ii)}$

Solving, we get

$$v_2 = \frac{mu\sin^2\alpha}{M + m\sin^2\alpha}$$

28. (b)

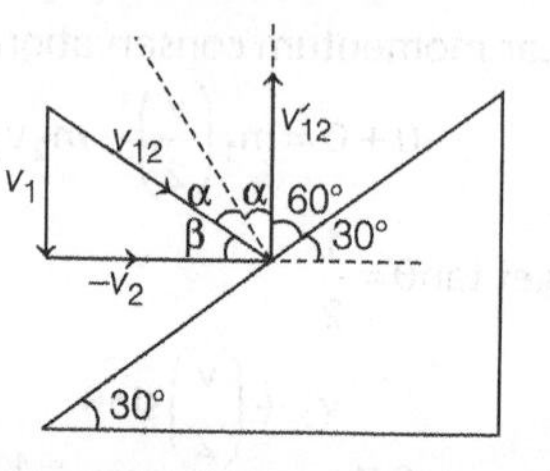

$\mathbf{v}_{12}$ = Velocity of ball w.r.t. wedge before collision.

$\mathbf{v}'_{12}$ = Velocity of ball w.r.t. wedge after collision.

In elastic collision $\mathbf{v}_{12}$ and $\mathbf{v}'_{12}$ will make equal angles with the normal.

$\alpha = 30°$ and $\alpha + \beta = 60°$

$\Rightarrow \qquad \beta = 30°$

$$\tan\beta = \frac{v_1}{v_2} = \frac{1}{\sqrt{3}}$$

29. (d) Using linear momentum conservation in horizontal,

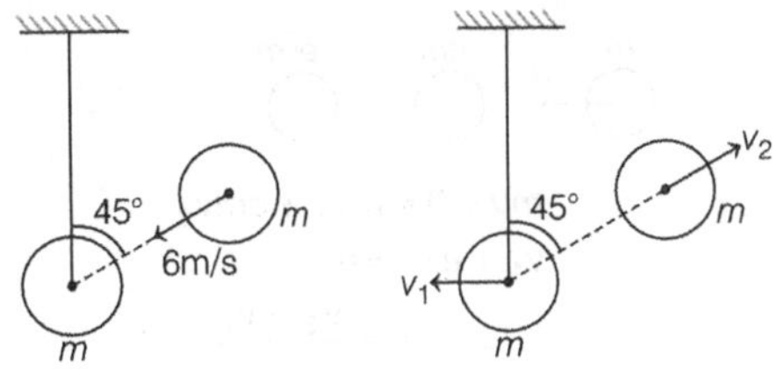

$$m(6\cos 45°) = mv_1 + m(-v_2\cos 45°)$$

$$\Rightarrow \quad v_1 - \frac{v_2}{\sqrt{2}} = 3\sqrt{2} \quad \text{... (i)}$$

$$e = 1 = \frac{v_2 + v_1\cos 45°}{6}$$

$$\Rightarrow \quad v_2 + \frac{v_1}{\sqrt{2}} = 6 \quad \text{... (ii)}$$

Solving Eqs. (i) and (ii), we get

$$v_2 = 2\text{ m/s}$$

30. (c) $\int T dt = 0 - [-(mu\cos 60° + mu\cos 60°)] = mu$

31. (d) For collision between A and C,

$$2mv + 0 = 2mv_A + mv_C \quad \text{... (i)}$$

$$e = \frac{v_C - v_A}{v} = 1 \quad \text{... (ii)}$$

Solving, we get $v_A = \frac{v}{3}$

Applying energy conservation in CM reference frame,

$$\frac{1}{2}\mu v_{rel}^2 = \frac{1}{2}kx_{max}^2$$

$$\Rightarrow \quad \frac{1}{2}\left[\frac{m(2m)}{m+2m}\right]\left(v - \frac{v}{3}\right)^2 = \frac{1}{2}kx_{max}^2$$

$$\Rightarrow \quad x_{max} = v\sqrt{\frac{8m}{27k}}$$

32. (c) $F_{Thrust} = \frac{dm}{dt}v_{rel} = bv_0$

$$\Rightarrow \quad F_{ext} + F_{Thrust} = Ma$$

$$\Rightarrow \quad m_1 g - (m_0 - bt)g + bv_0 = [m_1 + (m_0 - bt)]a$$

$$\Rightarrow \quad a = \frac{m_1 g - (m_0 - bt)g + bv_0}{m_1 + (m_0 - bt)}$$

Multiple Choice(s) Correct Questions

1. Linear momentum is conserved but kinetic energy is not conserved in an elastic collision.

   In perfectly inelastic collision, velocity of separation is zero.

2. (a,b,c) Using linear momentum conservation,

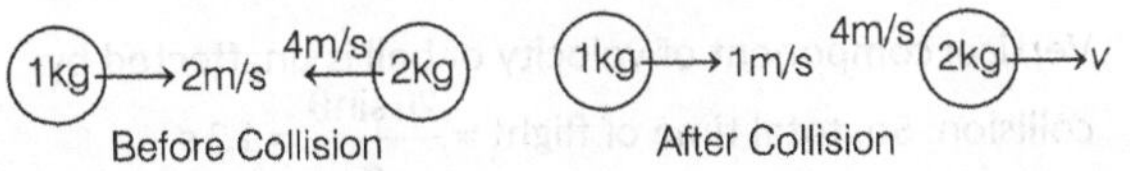

Before Collision After Collision

$$1 \times 21 + 2(-4) = 1(1) + 2v$$

$$\Rightarrow \quad v = 6\text{ m/s}$$

$$e = \frac{6-1}{21-(-4)} = 0.2$$

$$K_{Loss} = \left[\frac{1}{2}\times 1\times(21)^2 + \frac{1}{2}\times 2\times 4^2\right] - \left(\frac{1}{2}\times 1\times 1^2 + \frac{1}{2}\times 2\times 6^2\right)$$

$$= 200\text{ J}$$

$$J = 1(21-1) = 20\text{ N-s}$$

3. (a,b,c,d) At maximum deformation,

$$mu + 0 = (m+2m)v$$

$$\Rightarrow \quad v = \frac{u}{3}$$

$$K_1 = \frac{1}{2}mu^2 = 3\text{ J}$$

$$K_{min} = \frac{1}{2}(3m)\left(\frac{u}{3}\right)^2 = \frac{1}{6}mu^2 = 1\text{ J}$$

$$U_{max} = K_1 - K_{min} = 3 - 1 = 2\text{ J}$$

4. (b,c,d) $m_A u = m_A v_A + m_B v_B$ ... (i)

   and $e = \frac{v_B - v_A}{u} = 1 \Rightarrow v_B - v_A = u$ ...(ii)

   Solving Eqs. (i) and (ii), we get

$$v_1 = \left(\frac{m_A - m_B}{m_A + m_B}\right)u \text{ and } v_B = \frac{2m_A u}{m_A + m_B}$$

   For $m_A >> m_B$, $v_B = 2u$

   $m_A = m_B$, $v_A = 0$, $v_B = u$

   $m_A << m_B$, $v_B = 0$

5. (a,b) For collision between (1) and (2)

$$m_1 v_0 = m_1 v_1 + m_2 v_2 \quad \text{... (i)}$$

$$e = \frac{v_2 - v_1}{v_0} = 1$$

$$\Rightarrow \quad v_2 - v_1 = v_0 \quad \text{...(ii)}$$

Solving, we get

$$v_2 = \frac{2m_1 v_0}{m_1 + m_2}$$

Similarly for collision between (2) and (3), we get

$$v_3 = \frac{2m_2}{m_2 + m_3}\left(\frac{2m_1 v_0}{m_1 + m_2}\right)$$

$$= \frac{4m_1 v_0}{m_2 + (m_1 + m_3) + \frac{m_1 m_3}{m_2}}$$

To maximize v_3, $y = m_2 + (m_1 + m_3) + \frac{m_1 m_3}{m_2}$ is to be minimized.

$$\frac{dy}{dm_2} = 1 + 0 - \frac{m_1 m_3}{m_2^2} = 0$$

$$\Rightarrow \quad m_2 = \sqrt{m_1 m_3}$$

$$(v_3)_{max} = \frac{4m_1 v_0}{\sqrt{m_1 m_3} + m_1 + m_3 + \dfrac{m_1 m_3}{\sqrt{m_1 m_3}}}$$

$$= \frac{4m_1 v_0}{(\sqrt{m_1} + \sqrt{m_3})^2}$$

6. (a,d) For collision between A and B,

$$mu + 0 = mv_1 + 2mv_2 \quad \text{... (i)}$$

$$e = \frac{1}{2} = \frac{v_2 - v_1}{u} \quad \text{... (ii)}$$

Solving, we get, $v_1 = 0$ and $v_2 = \dfrac{u}{2}$

Now, ball B will collide with the wall and rebound with the same speed.

Now, B will collide with A

$$m \times 0 + 2m\left(\frac{u}{2}\right) = mv_A + 2mv_B$$

$$e = \frac{1}{2} = \frac{v_A - v_B}{(u/2)} \quad \text{... (iv)}$$

Solving, we get $v_A = \dfrac{u}{2}$ and $v_B = \dfrac{u}{4}$

7. (a,b,c) If $e = 1$,

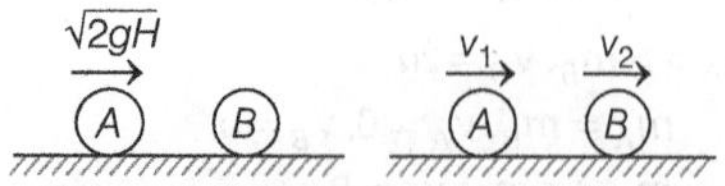

Before Collision After Collision

$$M(\sqrt{2gH}) + 0 = Mv_1 + 3Mv_2$$

$$\Rightarrow \quad v_1 + 3v_2 = \sqrt{2gH} \quad \text{... (i)}$$

$$e = 1 = \frac{v_2 - v_1}{\sqrt{2gH}}$$

$$\Rightarrow \quad v_2 - v_1 = \sqrt{2gH} \quad \text{... (ii)}$$

Solving Eqs. (i) and (ii), we get

$$v_1 = -\frac{\sqrt{2gH}}{2}$$

and

$$v_2 = \frac{\sqrt{2gH}}{2}$$

$$(H_A)_{max} = \frac{v_1^2}{2g} = \frac{H}{4}$$

$$(H_B)_{max} = \frac{v_2^2}{2g} = \frac{H}{4}$$

For perfectly inelastic collision,

$$M(\sqrt{2gH}) + 0 = (M + 3M)v$$

$$v = \frac{1}{4}\sqrt{2gH}$$

$$H_{max} = \frac{v^2}{2g} = \frac{H}{16}$$

8. (a,b,c) For the first collision,

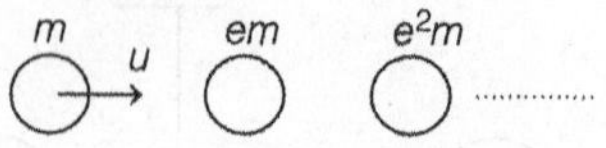

$$mu + 0 = mv_1 + emv_2$$

$$\Rightarrow \quad v_1 + ev_2 = u \quad \text{... (i)}$$

$$e = \frac{v_2 - v_1}{u}$$

$$\Rightarrow \quad v_2 - v_1 = eu \quad \text{...(ii)}$$

Solving, we get $v_1 = (1 - e)u$ and $v_2 = u$

So, finally first $(n - 1)$ balls will be moving with the same velocity $(1 - e)u$ and the last ball will move with velocity u.

$$K = \frac{1}{2}(m + em + e^2 m + \ldots + e^{n-2} m)$$

$$[(1 - e)u]^2 + \frac{1}{2}(e^{n-1} m)u^2$$

$$= \frac{1}{2} mu^2 (1 - e + e^n)$$

9. (b,c)

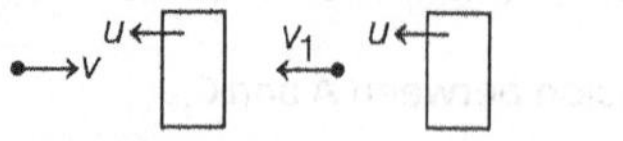

Before Collision After Collision

$$e = 1 = \frac{v_1 - u}{v + u}$$

$$\Rightarrow \quad v_1 = v + 2u$$

$$F_{avg} = \frac{\Delta P}{\Delta t} = \frac{m(v + 2u) - (-mv)}{\Delta t}$$

$$= \frac{2m(v + u)}{\Delta t}$$

$$\Delta K = \frac{1}{2} m(v + 2u)^2 - \frac{1}{2} mv^2$$

$$= 2mu(v + u)$$

10. (a,c,d) t_1 = Time taken to hit the wall $= \dfrac{10}{u + 8}$

Distance covered by the wall by

time $t_1 = u\left(\dfrac{10}{8 + u}\right)$

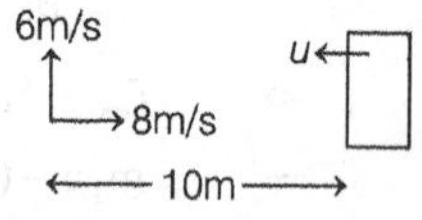

For collision, $e = \dfrac{v_{sep}}{v_{app}} = 1$

$$\Rightarrow \quad \frac{v - u}{8 + u} = 1 \Rightarrow v = 8 + 2u$$

Distance covered by the ball in return journey

$$= 10 - u\left(\frac{10}{8 + u}\right) = \frac{80}{8 + u}$$

Return time $= t_2 = \dfrac{(80/8 + u)}{8 + 2u}$

Vertical component of velocity of ball is unaffected by collision. So, total time of flight $= \dfrac{2u \sin\theta}{g} = 1.2$ s

$$t_1 + t_2 = T$$

$$\Rightarrow \quad \frac{10}{8+u} + \frac{80}{(8+u)(8+2u)} = 1.2$$

$$\Rightarrow \quad u = \frac{13}{3} \text{ m/s}$$

$$t_1 = \frac{10}{8+u} = \frac{30}{37} \text{ s}$$

11. (b,c,d) Since, no external force in horizontal on (wedge + block) system, applying momentum conservation in horizontal.

$$0 + 0 = -MV_1 + mv$$

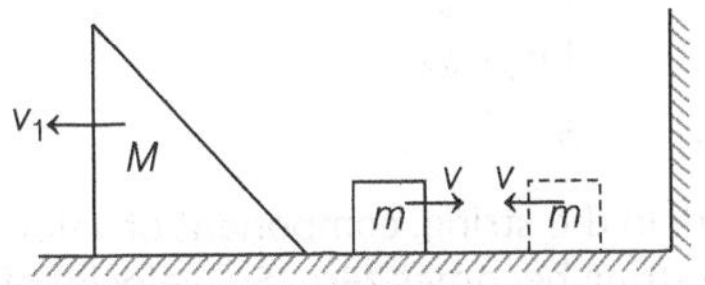

$$\Rightarrow \quad V_1 = \frac{mv}{M}$$

After elastic collision with the wall, velocity of block will get reversed.

After collision, $v_{CM} = \dfrac{Mv_1 + mv}{M+m} = \dfrac{2mv}{M+m}$

When, B reaches highest position on W,

$Mv_1 + mv = (M+m)v_2$

$$\Rightarrow \quad v_2 = \frac{2mv}{M+m}$$

12. (a,b,c,d) For perfectly inelastic collision,

$$m_1\mathbf{v}_1 + m_2\mathbf{v}_2 = (m_1+m_2)\mathbf{v}$$

$$\Rightarrow \quad \mathbf{v} = \frac{m_1\mathbf{v}_1 + m_2\mathbf{v}_2}{m_1+m_2}$$

Impulse by m_1 to $m_2 = m_2(\mathbf{v} - \mathbf{v}_2)$

$$= \frac{m_1 m_2}{m_1+m_2}(\mathbf{v}_1 - \mathbf{v}_2)$$

Momentum transferred by m_2 to $m_1 = m_1(\mathbf{v} - \mathbf{v}_1)$

$$= \frac{m_1 m_2}{m_1+m_2}(\mathbf{v}_2 - \mathbf{v}_1)$$

In CM frame, $(\mathbf{p}_{2,\,CM})_i = m_2(\mathbf{v}_2 - \mathbf{v}_{CM})$

$$= \frac{m_1 m_2}{m_1+m_2}(\mathbf{v}_2 - \mathbf{v}_1)$$

$$(\mathbf{p}_{2,\,CM})_f = 0$$

Impulse by m_1 on m_2 in CM frame $= (\mathbf{p}_{2,\,CM})_f - (\mathbf{p}_{2,\,CM})_i$

$$= \frac{m_1 m_2}{m_1+m_2}(\mathbf{v}_1 - \mathbf{v}_2)$$

13. (a,b,c,d) For first collision,

$$2(16) + 4(0) = 2(0) + 4v$$

$$\Rightarrow \quad v = 8 \text{ m/s}$$

$$e = \frac{v_{sep}}{v_{app}} = \frac{8-0}{16-0} = 0.5$$

For second collision,

$$2(0) + 4(8) = 2v_1 + 4v_2$$

$$\Rightarrow \quad v_1 + 2v_2 = 16 \qquad \text{...(i)}$$

$$e = \frac{v_1 - v_2}{8-0} = 0.5$$

$$\Rightarrow \quad v_1 - v_2 = 4 \qquad \text{...(ii)}$$

Solving, we get $v_1 = 8$ m/s, $v_2 = 4$ m/s

$$t = \frac{8}{16} + \frac{8}{16e} + \frac{8}{16e^2} + \frac{8}{16e^3} = 7.5 \text{ s}$$

$$v_{CM} = \frac{2\times 16 + 4\times 0}{2+4} = \frac{16}{3} \text{ m/s}$$

$$s_{CM} = v_{CM}T = \frac{16}{3}\times 7.5 = 40 \text{ m}$$

14. (a,b,c,d) When C strikes B, the combined body starts to rise vertically upward.

$$1\times 9 = (2+1)v_0 \Rightarrow v_0 = 3 \text{ m/s}$$

Now, string gets slack and both the bodies move under gravity. Let string gets taut at $t = t_1$

$$s_A = s_B \Rightarrow \frac{1}{2}gt_1^2 = 3t_1 - \frac{1}{2}gt_1^2$$

$$\Rightarrow \quad t_1 = 0.3 \text{ s}$$

At $t = t_1$, $v_{(B+C)} = 3 - 10(0.3) = 0$ and $V_A = 10(0.3) = 3$ m/s

Due to different velocities, there will be a jerk in the string and there after both bodies will have same velocity.

$$2\times 3 + 3\times 0 = (2+3)v$$

$$\Rightarrow \quad v = 1.2 \text{ m/s}$$

Now, the combined mass starts going up with velocity 1.2 m/s but its acceleration is downward.

$$a = \frac{(3-2)10}{3+2} = 2 \text{ m/s}^2$$

For combined body, $v = u + at$

$$0 = 1.2 + (-2)t_2 \Rightarrow t_2 = 0.6 \text{ s}$$

After this instant, combined body starts moving down. Height ascended by combined body in time t_1

$$= 3t_1 - \frac{1}{2}gt_1^2 = 0.45 \text{ m}$$

Height ascended by combined body in time t_2

$$= 1.2t_2 + \frac{1}{2}(-2)t_2^2 = 0.36 \text{ m}$$

Maximum height ascended by combined body

$$= 0.45 + 0.36 = 0.81 \text{ m}$$

Loss of energy due to jerk in the string.

$$= \left[\frac{1}{2}\times 2\times (3)^2 + 0\right] - \frac{1}{2}\times 5\times (1.2)^2 = 5.4 \text{ J}$$

15. (a,b,c)

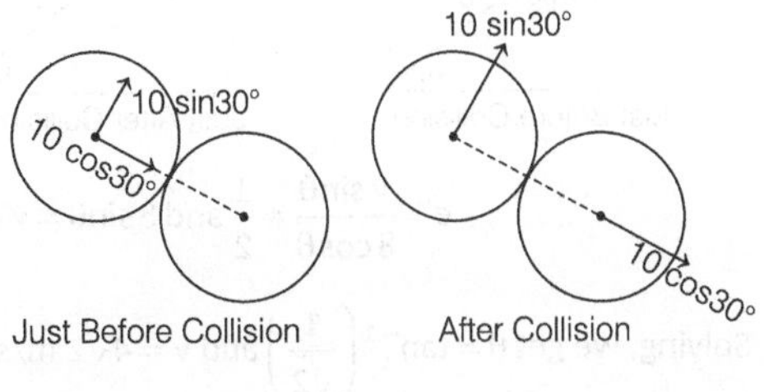

Component of velocity of ball A perpendicular to the line of impact remains unchanged and their velocities along the line of impact will be exchanged.

So, velocity of ball A after collision $= 10\sin 30° = 5$ m/s

Velocity of ball A after collision $= 10\cos 30° = 5\sqrt{3}$ m/s

Both the balls move at right angle after collision.

16. (a,d) Using linear momentum conservation along X-axis,

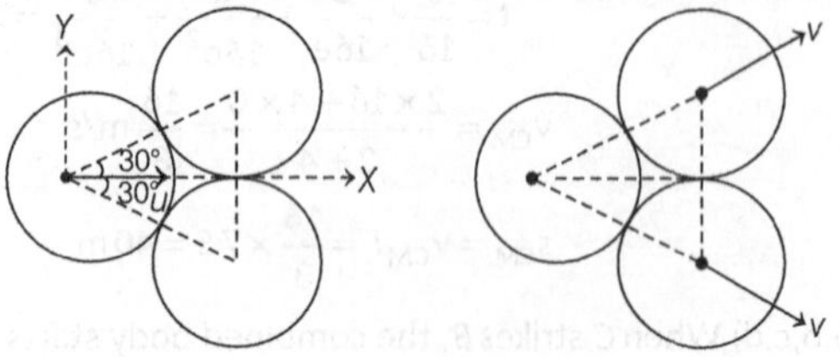

$$mu = 0 + mv\cos 30° + mv\cos 30°$$

$$\Rightarrow \quad v = \frac{u}{\sqrt{3}}$$

$$e = \frac{v_{sep}}{v_{app}} = \frac{v - 0}{u\cos 30° - 0} = \frac{2}{3}$$

$$\text{Loss of KE} = \frac{1}{2}mu^2 - \left[\frac{1}{2}m\left(\frac{u}{\sqrt{3}}\right)^2 \times 2\right] = \frac{1}{6}mu^2$$

17. (a,b) $u_y' = eu_y$ and $u_y'' = e^2u_y$

$$T = \frac{2u_y}{g}$$

$$\Rightarrow \quad a = \frac{T_1}{T_2} = \frac{1}{e}$$

$$H = \frac{u_y^2}{2g}$$

$$\Rightarrow \quad b = \frac{H_1}{H_2} = \frac{1}{e^2}$$

$$R = \frac{2u_xu_y}{g}$$

$$\Rightarrow \quad c = \frac{R_1}{R_2} = \frac{1}{e}$$

18. (a,b) Speed just before collision

$$= \sqrt{2gh} = \sqrt{2 \times 10 \times 3.2} = 8 \text{ m/s}$$

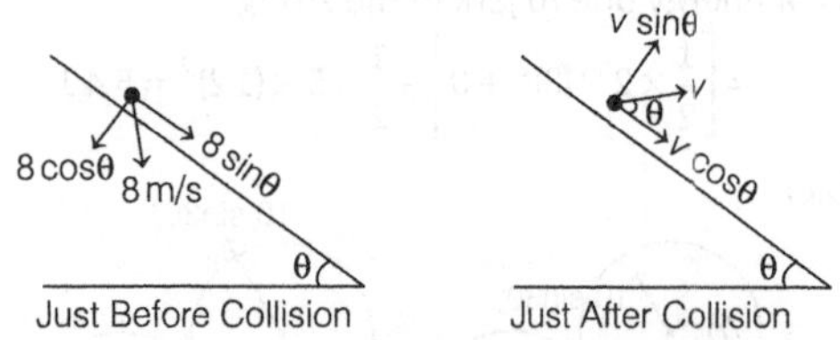

$$e = \frac{v\sin\theta}{8\cos\theta} = \frac{1}{2} \text{ and } 8\sin\theta = v\cos\theta$$

Solving, we get $\theta = \tan^{-1}\left(\frac{1}{\sqrt{2}}\right)$ and $v = 4\sqrt{2}$ m/s

$$\text{Loss in KE} = \frac{1}{2} \times 1 \times 8^2 - \frac{1}{2} \times 1 \times (4\sqrt{2})^2 = 16 \text{ J}$$

19. (b,c,d) For collision, conserving linear momentum,

$$m(10) + m(0) = 2mv$$

$$\Rightarrow \quad v = 5 \text{ m/s}$$

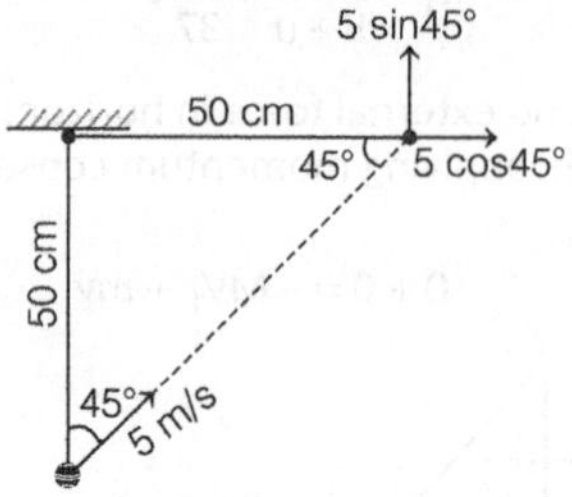

Due to jerk in the string, component of velocity of ball along the string becomes zero. So, velocity of ball after the jerk will be $5\sin 45° = \frac{5}{\sqrt{2}}$ m/s.

$$\text{Time for which the string remains slack} = \frac{50\sqrt{2} \text{ cm}}{5 \text{ m/s}} = 0.141 \text{ s}$$

Comprehension Based Questions

1. (c) Velocity of ball just before hitting the ground,

$$u = \sqrt{2g\left(\frac{2l}{3}\right)} = \sqrt{\frac{4gl}{3}}$$

Since $e = 0$, component of velocity of ball perpendicular to ground will become zero after hitting the ground and ball will slide along the ground with velocity $u\sin\theta$.

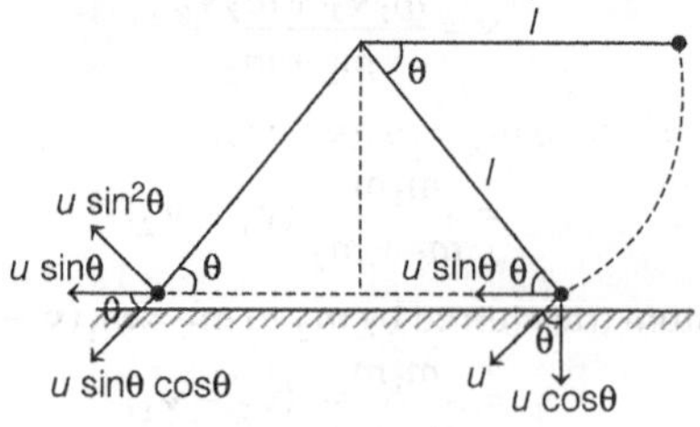

$$u\sin\theta = \sqrt{\frac{4gl}{3}}\left(\frac{2l/3}{l}\right) = \frac{4}{3}\sqrt{\frac{gl}{3}}$$

2. (b) $\int T\,dt = 0 - (-mu\sin\theta\cos\theta) = mu\sin\theta\cos\theta$

$$= \sqrt{\frac{4gl}{3}}\left(\frac{2l/3}{l}\right)\left(\frac{\sqrt{5}}{3}\right)$$

$$= \frac{4\sqrt{5}}{9\sqrt{3}}m\sqrt{gl}$$

3. (a) After the jerk in the string, velocity of ball will be $u\sin^2\theta$.

$$H_{max} = \frac{(u\sin^2\theta)^2}{2g} = \frac{32l}{243}$$

4. (d) Using linear momentum conservation in horizontal.

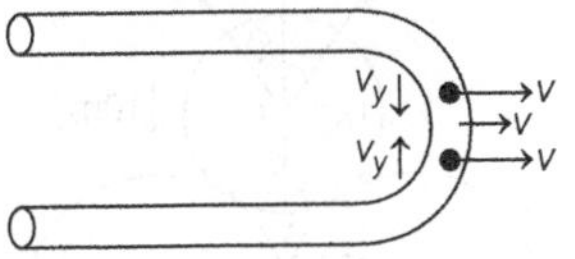

$$mu + mu + 2m(0) = 4mv$$

$$\Rightarrow \qquad v = \frac{u}{2}$$

Using energy conservation,

$$\frac{1}{2}mu^2 + \frac{1}{2}mu^2 + 0 = \frac{1}{2}(2m)v^2 + \frac{1}{2}mv_B^2 + \frac{1}{2}mv_B^2$$

$$\Rightarrow \qquad v_B = \frac{\sqrt{3}u}{2}$$

5. (a) $\sqrt{v^2 + v_y^2} = \frac{\sqrt{3}u}{2}$

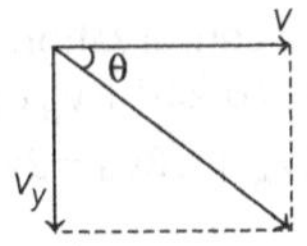

$$\Rightarrow \qquad v_y = \frac{u}{\sqrt{2}}$$

$$\tan\theta = \frac{v_y}{v} = \frac{u/\sqrt{2}}{u/2} = \sqrt{2}$$

Angle between velocity vectors of both balls $= 2\theta$

$$= 2\tan^{-1}(\sqrt{2})$$

6. (d) $mu + mu + 0 = 2mv_T + mv_1 + mv_2$

$$\Rightarrow \qquad 2u = 2v_T + v_1 + v_2$$

From symmetry and energy conservation,

$$v_T = u$$

and $\qquad v_1 = v_2 = 0$

7. (b) Since, velocity of block is equally inclined with $\mathbf{v}$ and $\mathbf{v}_r$

$\Rightarrow v = v_r$ and $v_B = 2v\cos 30° = \sqrt{3}v$

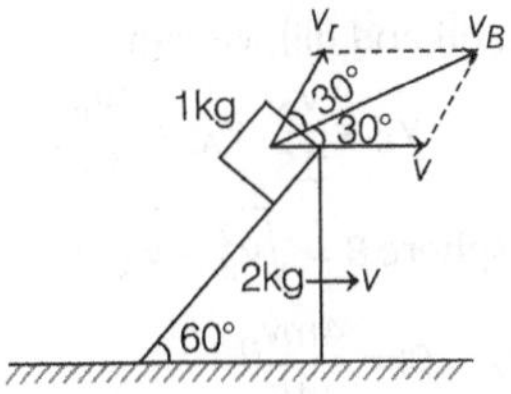

Using linear momentum conservation in horizontal.

$$1(v_0) + 2(0) = 2v + 1(v + v_r\cos 60°)$$

$$\Rightarrow \qquad v_0 = \frac{7v}{2}$$

Using energy conservation,

$$\frac{1}{2}\times 1\times v_0^2 = \frac{1}{2}\times 2\times v^2 + \frac{1}{2}\times 1\times(\sqrt{3}v)^2 + 1\times 10\times 1.45$$

$$\Rightarrow \qquad v_0 = 7\text{ m/s}$$

8. (c) $H = \frac{v_B^2\sin^2 30°}{2g} = 0.15\text{ m}$

Maximum height from ground $= 1.45 + 0.15 = 1.6$ m

9. (d) $J_H = m(v_0 - v_B\cos 30°) = 4$ N-s

$$\tan 30° = \frac{J_V}{J_H}$$

$$\Rightarrow \qquad \frac{1}{\sqrt{3}} = \frac{J_V}{4}$$

$$\Rightarrow \qquad J_V = \frac{4}{\sqrt{3}}$$

$$J = \sqrt{J_H^2 + J_V^2} = \frac{8}{\sqrt{3}}\text{ N-s}$$

10. (c) Using linear momentum conservation,

$$mu + 0 = mv\cos 30° + mv\cos 30°$$

$$v = \frac{u}{\sqrt{3}}$$

11. (d) Heat produced $= K_1 - K_2$

$$= \left(\frac{1}{2}mu^2 + 0\right) - \left(\frac{1}{2}mv^2 + \frac{1}{2}mv^2\right)$$

$$= \frac{1}{6}mu^2$$

12. **(b)** Line of impact will be along the line of motion of *B* after collision.

$$e = \frac{v_{sep}}{v_{app}} = \frac{v - v\cos 60°}{u\cos 30°} = \frac{1}{3}$$

13. (a) Using linear momentum conservation in horizontal,

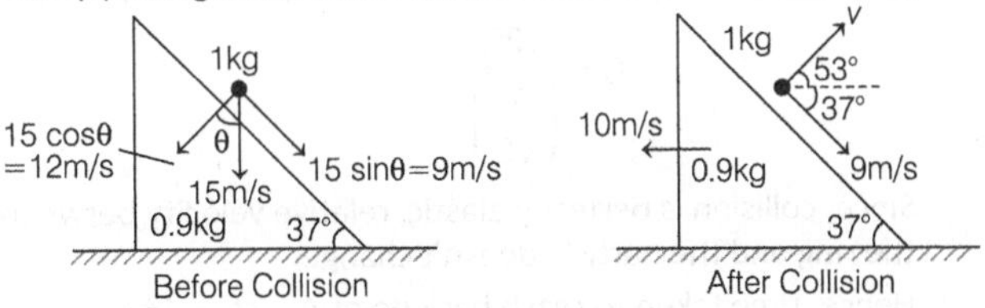

$$0 + 0 = 0.9(-10) + 1(9\cos 37° + v\cos 53°)$$

$$\Rightarrow \qquad v = 3\text{ m/s}$$

So, velocity of ball $= \sqrt{9^2 + 3^2} = \sqrt{90}$ m/s

14. (b) $e = \frac{v_{sep}}{v_{app}} = \frac{v + 10\sin 37°}{15\cos 37°} = 0.75$

15. (d) Impulse on the ball $= 1[(3 - (-12)] = 15$ N-s

16. (a)

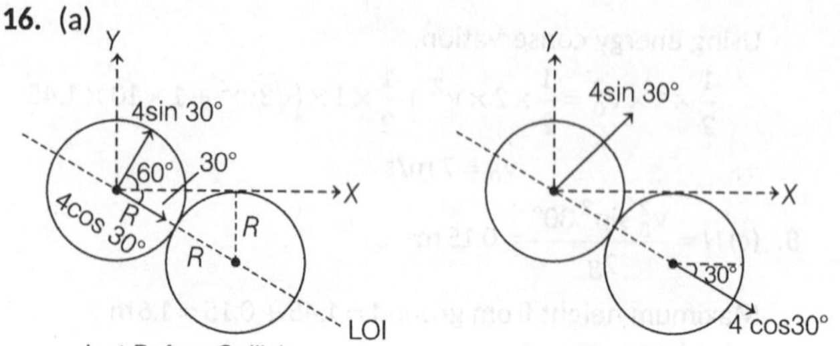

Just Before Collision Just After Collision

Since collision is head-on elastic collision of identical bodies, they will exchange their velocities along the line of impact.

So, $\mathbf{v}_A = 4\sin 30° \cos 60° \hat{\mathbf{i}} + 4\sin 30° \sin 60° \hat{\mathbf{j}}$

$= (\hat{\mathbf{i}} + \sqrt{3}\hat{\mathbf{j}})$ m/s

17. (a) $\mathbf{v}_B = 4\cos 30° \cos 30° \hat{\mathbf{i}} - 4\cos 30° \sin 30° \hat{\mathbf{j}}$

$= (3\hat{\mathbf{i}} - \sqrt{3}\hat{\mathbf{j}})$m/s

18. (c) $I = m(v_B - 0) = m(3\hat{\mathbf{i}} - \sqrt{3}\hat{\mathbf{j}})$

19. (b) $e = \dfrac{1}{2} = \dfrac{v_2 - v_1}{4\cos 30°}$

$\Rightarrow \quad v_2 - v_1 = \sqrt{3}$ ... (i)

$m(4\cos 30°) + 0 = mv_1 + mv_2$

$\Rightarrow \quad v_1 + v_2 = 2\sqrt{3}$ ... (ii)

Solving, we get, $v_2 = \dfrac{3\sqrt{3}}{2}$ m/s

So, $\mathbf{v}_B = \dfrac{3\sqrt{3}}{2} \cos 30 \hat{\mathbf{i}} - \dfrac{3\sqrt{3}}{2} \sin 30° \hat{\mathbf{j}}$

$= \left(\dfrac{9}{4}\hat{\mathbf{i}} - \dfrac{3\sqrt{3}}{4}\hat{\mathbf{j}}\right)$ m/s

20. (b) Time taken by particle to move from point A to point B is

$t_1 = \dfrac{\sqrt{2}R}{\left(\dfrac{5}{\sqrt{2}}\right)} = 4$ s

Since, collision is perfectly elastic, relative velocity between the ring and the particle doesn't change.

Hence, time taken to reach back point $A = 4t_1 = 16$ s

21. (c) For particle,

x-component of velocity $= \dfrac{5}{2}$ m/s

y-component of velocity $= \dfrac{5}{2}$ m/s

For 8 s ring moves along x-direction and for 8 s it moves along y-direction. So, its centre of mass co-ordinates

$= \left(\dfrac{5}{2} \times 8, \dfrac{5}{2} \times 8\right) = (20, 20)$

22. (d) Since collisions are elastic, along normal direction velocities will be exchanged. Hence, all these conclusions are correct.

23. (a) Lets take ball C rebounds with velocity v.

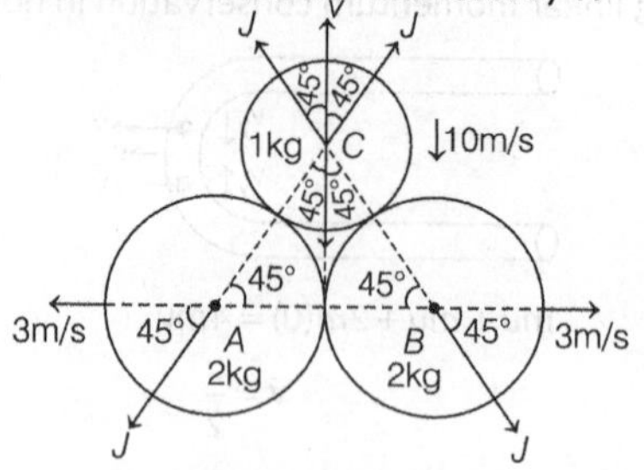

For A or B, $J\cos 45° = 2(3) - 0$ ... (i)

For C, $2J\cos 45° = 1[v - (-10)]$ ... (ii)

Solving, we get, $v = 2$ m/s

24. (d) $\int T dt = J \sin 45° = 6$ N-s

25. (d) $e = \dfrac{v_{sep}}{v_{app}} = \dfrac{3\cos 45° + v\cos 45°}{10\cos 45°} = \dfrac{1}{2}$

26. (a) Using momentum conservation along X-axis,

$mv_0 = -mv_C + m(v_A \cos 60° + v_B \cos 30°) + mv_A \cos 60°$

$\Rightarrow \quad 2v_A + \sqrt{3}v_B = 2v_0 + 2v_C$ ... (i)

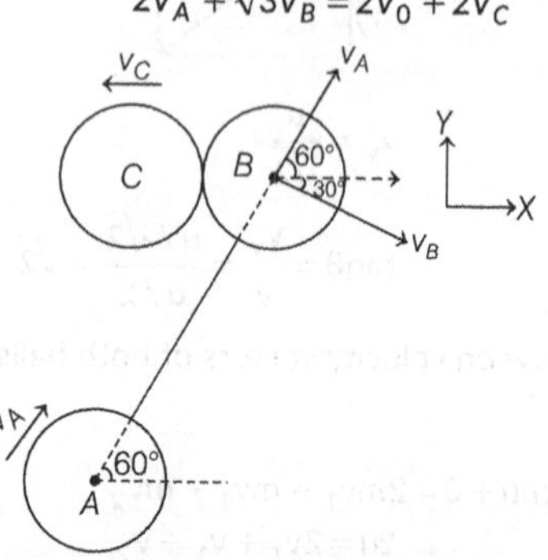

Using momentum conservation along Y-axis.

$0 = m(v_A \sin 60° - v_B \sin 30°) + m(v_A \sin 60°)$

$\Rightarrow \quad v_B = 2\sqrt{3}\, v_A$ ... (ii)

and $\quad e = 1 = \dfrac{v_A \cos 60° + v_B \cos 30° - (-v_C)}{v_0}$

$v_A + \sqrt{3}\, v_B + 2v_C = 2v_0$ ...(iii)

Solving Eqs. (i), (ii) and (iii), we get

$v_C = \dfrac{v_0}{15}, v_A = \dfrac{4v_0}{15}, v_B = \dfrac{8\sqrt{3}v_0}{15}$

27. (c) Velocity of sphere $B = \sqrt{v_B^2 + v_A^2}$

28. (d) $\int T dt = m(v_A - 0) = \dfrac{4mv_0}{15}$

Match The Columns Questions

1. (A) In elastic collision, momentum and total energy are conserved. Initial and final kinetic energy are same but kinetic energy is not conserved during collision.

(B) Momentum is conserved but kinetic energy and mechanical energy are not conserved as some energy is lost in the form of heat and sound.

(C) Same as inelastic collision

(D) Same as inelastic collision

2. $M_1u = M_1v_1 + M_2v_2$ ...(i)

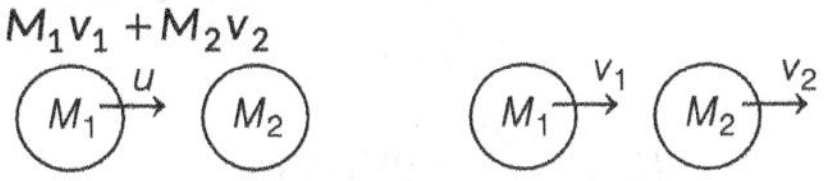

$$e = 1 = \frac{v_2 - v_1}{u} \quad \text{... (ii)}$$

Solving we get,

$$v_1 = \left(\frac{M_1 - M_2}{M_1 + M_2}\right)u \text{ and } v_2 = \frac{2M_1u}{M_1 + M_2}$$

(A) $M_1 >> M_2$

$v_1 = u$ and $v_2 = 2u$

$p_1 = M_1u$ and $p_2 = M_2(2u)$

$K_1 = \frac{1}{2}M_1u^2$ and $K_2 = \frac{1}{2}M_2(2u)^2$

$\Rightarrow$ $(v_2)_f > (v_1)_f$ and $(K_1)_f > (K_2)_f$ and $(p_1)_f > (p_2)_f$

(B) $M_1 << M_2$

$v_1 = -u$ and $v_2 = 0$

$p_1 = -M_1u$ and $p_2 = 2M_1u$

$K_1 = \frac{1}{2}M_1u^2$ and $K_2 = \frac{(2M_1u)^2}{2M_2} = \frac{2M_1^2u^2}{M_2}$

So, $|\mathbf{v}_{1f}| > |\mathbf{v}_{2f}|, |\mathbf{p}_{2f}| > |\mathbf{p}_{1f}|$ and $K_{1f} > K_{2f}$

(C) $M_1 = M_2$

$v_1 = 0$ and $v_2 = u$

$p_1 = 0$ and $p_2 = M_2u$

$K_1 = 0$ and $K_2 = \frac{1}{2}M_2u^2$

So, $|\mathbf{v}_{2f}| > |\mathbf{v}_{1f}|, |\mathbf{p}_{2f}| > |\mathbf{p}_{1f}|$ and $K_{2f} > K_{1f}$

(D) $M_1 = M_2$ and collision is oblique so components of velocities along the line of impact will be exchanged and component of velocity perpendicular to the line of impact will remain unchanged.

3.

Initially	(2m) $\to u$	(m)	(m)	(m)
Ist collision	(2m) $\to \frac{u}{3}$	(m) $\to \frac{4u}{3}$	(m)	(m)
2nd collision	(2m) $\to \frac{u}{3}$	(m)	(m) $\to \frac{4u}{3}$	(m)
3rd collision	(2m) $\to \frac{u}{3}$	(m)	(m)	(m) $\to \frac{4u}{3}$
4th collision	(2m) $\to \frac{u}{9}$	(m) $\to \frac{4u}{9}$	(m)	(m) $\to \frac{4u}{3}$
5th collision	(2m) $\to \frac{u}{9}$	(m)	(m) $\to \frac{4u}{9}$	(m) $\to \frac{4u}{3}$
6th collision	(2m) $\to \frac{u}{27}$	(m) $\to \frac{4u}{27}$	(m) $\to \frac{4u}{9}$	(m) $\to \frac{4u}{3}$

Total impulse on $A = 2m\left(u - \frac{u}{27}\right) = \frac{52}{27}mu$

Total impulse on $B = m\left(\frac{4u}{27} - 0\right) = \frac{4}{27}mu$

Total impulse on $C = m\left(\frac{4u}{9} - 0\right) = \frac{4}{9}mu$

Total impulse on $D = m\left(\frac{4u}{3} - 0\right) = \frac{4}{3}mu$

4. (A) During collision, forces are action-reaction pair. So they are same in magnitude.

(B) $s_{CM} = v_{CM}t$ and $v_{CM} = \text{constant} \Rightarrow s_{CM} \propto t$

(C) $e = \frac{v_{sep}}{v_{app}} < 1 \Rightarrow v_{sep} < v_{app}$

So, correct graph will be s not P.

(D) Initially B is at rest and then moves with constant velocity.

5. (A) $v_{CM} = \text{constant} = \frac{v}{3}$ as $F_{ext} = 0$ in all cases.

(B) If A and B are connected by an ideal spring on massless rigid rod then only one collision will take place as C will move away from them.

(C) Due to jerk in the string, mechanical energy is not conserved.

(D) A and B will oscillate, if connected by a spring. A and B don't oscillate if connected with a rigid rod.

6. (A)

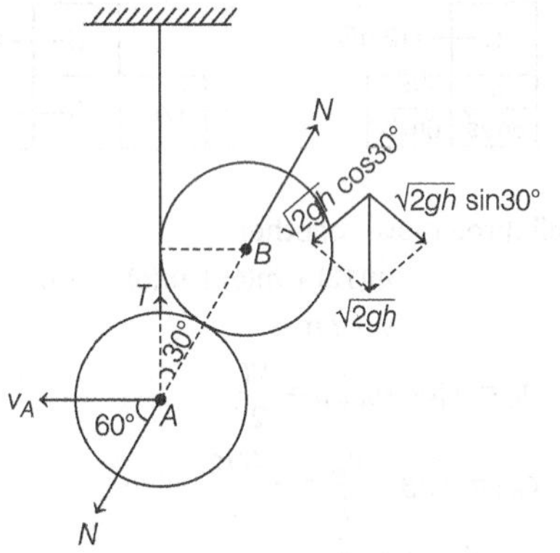

Lets take ball B is rebounded along the line of impact with velocity v.

For B, $\int N dt = m[v - (-\sqrt{2gh}\cos 30°)]$ ... (i)

For A, $\int N dt \cos 60° = mv_A$ ... (ii)

$$e = 1 - \frac{v + v_A \cos 60°}{\sqrt{2gh}\cos 30°} \quad \text{... (iii)}$$

Solving, we get $v_A = \frac{2\sqrt{6gh}}{5}$

(B) $\int T dt = \int N \sin 60° dt = \frac{6m\sqrt{2gh}}{5}$

(C) $e = 0 = \dfrac{v + v_A \cos 60^\circ}{\sqrt{2gh}\cos 30^\circ}$

$\Rightarrow \qquad v = -\dfrac{v_A}{2}$ ... (iv)

Solving Eqs. (i), (ii) and (iv), we get $v_A = \dfrac{\sqrt{6gh}}{5}$

(D) $\int T dt = \int N \sin 60^\circ \, dt = \dfrac{3m}{5}\sqrt{2gh}$

7. For bullet, $\int F dt = m(v_f - v_i) = 0.25[-100 - (-200)] = 25$ N-S

This is also impulse by particle on A.

For block A, $\int (F - T)\, dt = M_A(v - 0)$ ... (i)

For block B, $\int T dt = M_B(v - 0)$ ... (ii)

Adding Eqs. (i) and (ii),

$$\int F dt = (M_A + M_B)v$$

$\Rightarrow \qquad 25 = 3v \Rightarrow v = \dfrac{25}{3}$ m/s

So, $\qquad \int T dt = M_B v = 2 \times \dfrac{25}{3} = \dfrac{50}{3}$ N-s

Applying conservation of energy,

$$M_B gh = \frac{1}{2}(M_A + M_B)v^2 \Rightarrow h = 5.21 \text{ m}$$

Numerical Value Questions

1. When A and B collide,

$$m(12) + 0 = 2mv \Rightarrow v = 6 \text{ m/s}$$

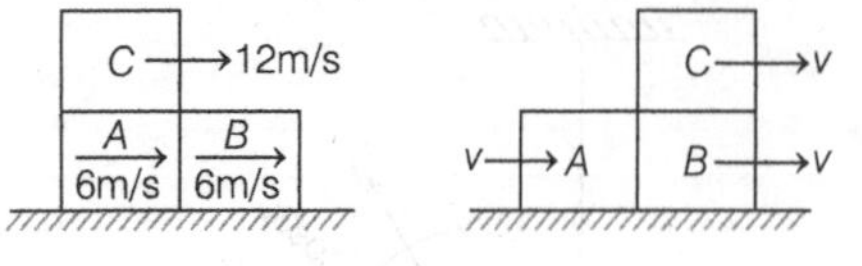

When all three move together,

$$m(12) + m(6) + m(6) = 3mv$$

$\Rightarrow \qquad v = 8$ m/s

$$a_C = -\mu g, \; a_{A+B} = \frac{\mu g}{2}$$

$$a_{rel} = -\mu g - \frac{\mu g}{2} = -\frac{3\mu g}{2}$$

For C, $v_{rel}^2 = u_{rel}^2 + 2a_{rel}s_{rel}$

$\Rightarrow \qquad 0 = 6^2 + 2\left[\dfrac{-3(0.2)(10)}{2}\right]l$

$\Rightarrow \qquad l = 6$ m

2. The bigger ball will hit the ground with speed $\sqrt{2gH}$ and rebound with the same speed.

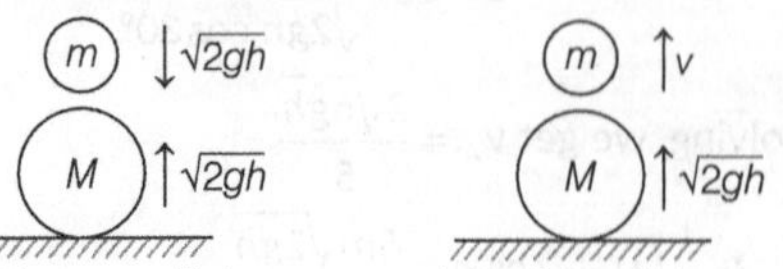

Just before collision between the balls

Just after collision

$$e = 1 = \frac{v - \sqrt{2gH}}{\sqrt{2gH} - (-\sqrt{2gH})}$$

$\Rightarrow \qquad v = 3\sqrt{2gH}$

$$H_{max} = \frac{v^2}{2g} = 9H = 9 \text{ m}$$

3. Speed just before reaching ground $= \sqrt{2gh}$

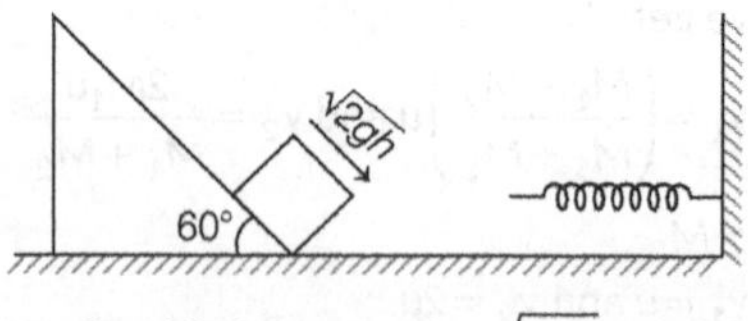

Speed just after hitting ground $= \sqrt{2gh}\cos 60^\circ$ as component of velocity of block perpendicular to ground will become zero. ($\because e = 0$)

Now, the block rebounds from the spring with the same speed.

Speed of the block just after hitting the incline

$$= (\sqrt{2gh}\cos 60^\circ)\cos 60^\circ = \frac{1}{4}\sqrt{2gh}$$

$$h_{max} = \frac{v^2}{2g} = \frac{(\sqrt{2gh}/4)^2}{2g} = \frac{h}{16} = \frac{512}{16} = 32 \text{ m}$$

4. Let velocity of ball after collision $= v_x\hat{i} + v_y\hat{j}$

$$e = \frac{v_y - 2}{2 + 2} = \frac{1}{2} \Rightarrow v_y = 4 \text{ m/s}$$

$$\int N dt = 2[4 - (-2)] = 12 \text{ N-s}$$

$$\int \mu N dt = \frac{1}{3}(12) = 4 \text{ N-s}$$

$$-\int \mu N dt = m(v_x - 2)$$

$\Rightarrow \qquad -4 = 2(v_x - 2) \Rightarrow v_x = 0$

5. For ball B,

$\int N dt = m[v_1 - (-u\cos 30^\circ)]$ ... (i)

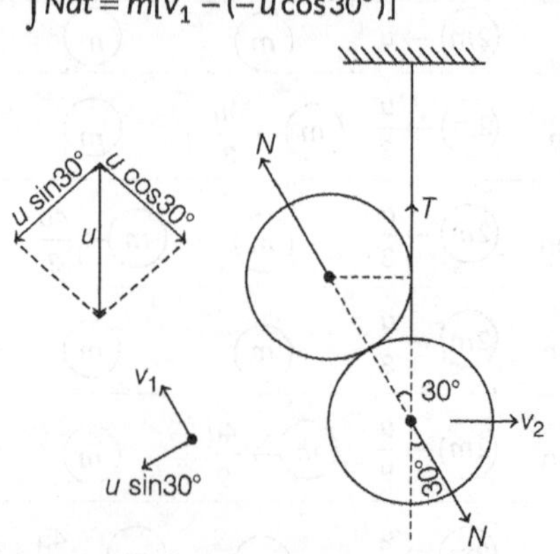

For ball A, $\int N dt \sin 30^\circ = mv_2$ ... (ii)

$e = \dfrac{v_1 + v_2 \sin 30^\circ}{u\cos 30^\circ} = 1$ ... (iii)

Solving, we get

$$v_2 = \frac{2\sqrt{3}u}{5}$$

For ball A to complete vertical circle,

$$v_2 = \sqrt{5gl}$$

$$\Rightarrow \quad \frac{2\sqrt{3}u}{5} = \sqrt{5 \times 10 \times 1.5}$$

$$\Rightarrow \quad u = 12.5 \text{ m/s}$$

6. $\sin\theta = \frac{R}{3R} = \frac{1}{3}$ and $\cos\theta = \frac{2\sqrt{2}}{3}$

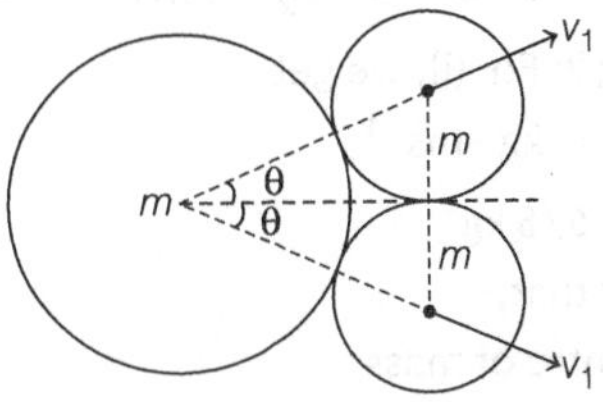

Using linear momentum conservation in horizontal,

$$mu + 0 + 0 = 0 + mv_1 \cos\theta + mv_1 \cos\theta$$

$$\Rightarrow \quad v_1 \cos\theta = \frac{u}{2}$$

Along the line of impact, $e = \frac{v_{sep}}{v_{app}} = \frac{v_1 - 0}{u\cos\theta} = \frac{1}{2\cos^2\theta} = \frac{9}{16}$

7. Speed just before hitting plate $A = \sqrt{2gh_0}$

Speed with which it rebounds from plate $A = e\sqrt{2gh_0}$

For plate $(B + C)$, using momentum conservation,

$$m(e\sqrt{2gh_0}) + 0 = (m + 3m)v$$

$$\Rightarrow \quad v = \frac{e}{4}\sqrt{2gh_0}$$

$$h_2 = \frac{v^2}{2g} \Rightarrow 0.25 = \frac{e^2(9)}{16}$$

$$\Rightarrow \quad e = \frac{2}{3}$$

$$h_1 = \frac{(e\sqrt{2gh_0})^2}{2g}$$

$$\Rightarrow \quad e^2 h_0 = 4\text{m}$$

8. For discs to go in perpendicular directions, component of velocity of ball A along the line of impact should become zero.

$$mu\cos 45° + 2m(0) = 0 + 2mv_2$$

$$\Rightarrow \quad v_2 = \frac{u\cos 45°}{2}$$

$$e = \frac{v_2 - v_1}{u\cos 45° - 0} = \frac{\frac{u\cos 45°}{2} - 0}{u\cos 45° - 0} = 0.5$$

9. $(u\cos\theta)t_{AB} = (eu\cos\theta)t_{BC} + (eu\cos\theta)t_{CA}$

$$\Rightarrow \quad (u\cos\theta)\left(\frac{u\sin\theta}{g}\right) = (eu\cos\theta)\left(\frac{u\sin\theta}{2}\right) + (eu\cos\theta)\left(\frac{2eu\cos\theta}{g}\right)$$

$$\Rightarrow \quad 1 = e + 2e^2$$

$$\Rightarrow \quad e = 0.5$$

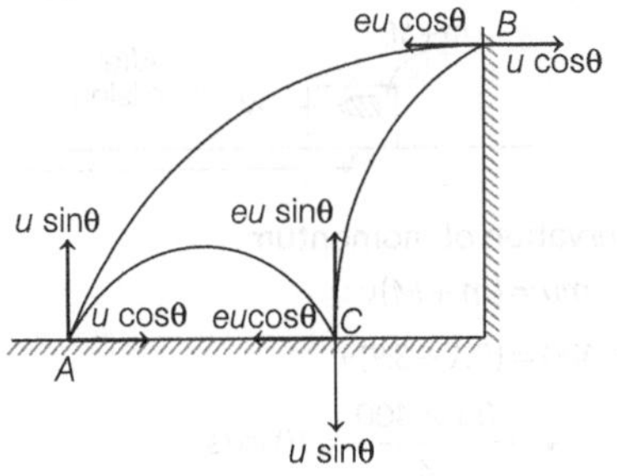

10. Using linear momentum conservation in horizontal.

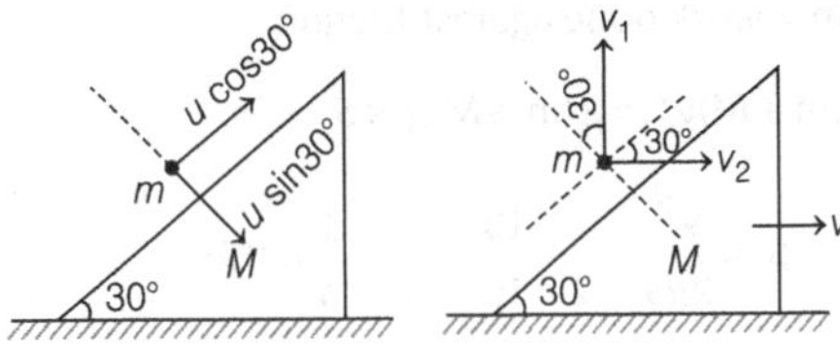

$$mu = (M + m)v_2 \qquad \text{... (i)}$$

$$v_2 \cos 30° + v_1 \sin 30° = u\cos 30° \qquad \text{... (ii)}$$

$$e = \frac{v_1 \cos 30°}{u\sin 30°} = 1 \qquad \text{... (iii)}$$

Solving, we get $\frac{M}{m} = 2$

Previous Years Questions

JEE Main

1. Given,

Mass of body $(m) = 100$ g $= 0.1$ kg

Height from where it dropped,

$$h_1 = 10 \text{ m}$$

Rebound height, $h_2 = 5$ m

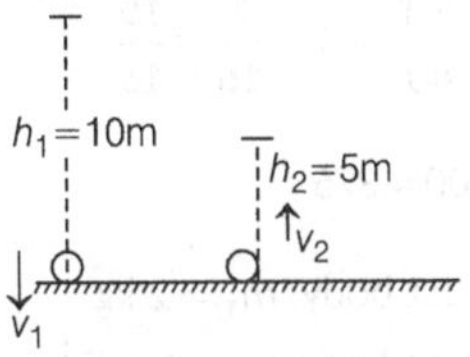

Impulse is given by

$J = \Delta p$

$J = mv_2 - (-mv_1)$

$= m(v_2 + v_1)$

$= m(\sqrt{2gh_1} + \sqrt{2gh_2})$

$= 0.1\,(\sqrt{2 \times 9.8 \times 10} + \sqrt{2 \times 9.8 \times 5})$

$= 2.39$ kg-m/s

2. Before collision

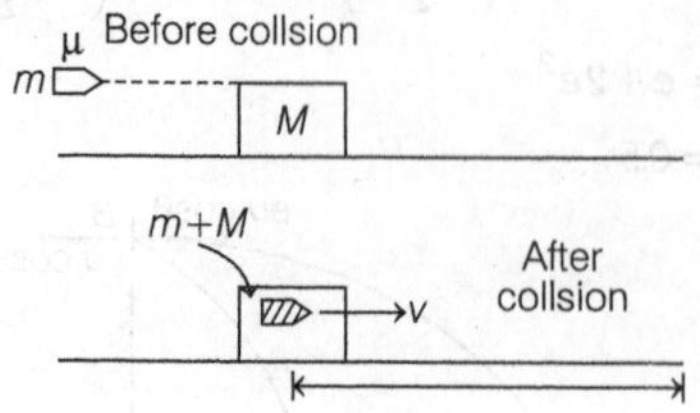

By conservation of momentum,

$$mu = (m+M)v$$

$\Rightarrow 0.1 \times 400 = (0.1 + 3.9)v$

$$\Rightarrow \quad v = \frac{0.1 \times 400}{4} = 10 \text{ m/s}$$

K.E of block and bullet system = work done against friction

$$\Rightarrow \frac{1}{2}(m+M)v^2 = \mu(m+M)g \times S$$

$$\Rightarrow \quad \mu = \frac{v^2}{2gS} = \frac{10^2}{2 \times 10 \times 20} = \frac{1}{4} = 0.25$$

3. Velocity of a ball P when it strikes ball Q is given by,

$$v = \sqrt{2gh}$$
$$= \sqrt{2 \times 10 \times 0.2}$$
$$= 2 \text{ ms}^{-1}$$

As balls are identical, they exchange velocities in an elastic collision. So, velocity of Q = 2 m/s.

4. Let u and v be speeds, just before and after body strikes the ground.

Given, $\frac{u}{v} = \frac{4}{1}$

$$\text{loss in KE} \Rightarrow \Delta K = \frac{\frac{1}{2}mu^2 - \frac{1}{2}mv^2}{\frac{1}{2}mu^2}$$

$$\Delta \text{KE} = 1 - \left(\frac{v}{4}\right)^2 = 1 - \frac{1}{16} = \frac{15}{16}$$

$$\% \text{ loss} = \frac{15}{16} \times 100 = 375$$

5. Given, mass of 1st body, $m_1 = 2$ kg

Initial speed of 1st body, $u_1 = 4 \text{ ms}^{-1}$

Initial speed of 2nd body, $u_2 = 0 \text{ ms}^{-1}$

Let v_1 be the speed of 1st body after collision. So, as per question,

$$v_1 = \frac{u_1}{4} = \frac{4}{4} = 1 \text{ ms}^{-1}$$

and v_2 be the speed of 2nd body after collision.

By using law of conservation of momentum,

Initial momentum of system (p_i)

= Final momentum of system (p_f)

$$\Rightarrow \quad m_1u_1 + m_2u_2 = m_1v_1 + m_2v_2$$
$$\Rightarrow \quad 2 \times 4 + m_2 \times 0 = 2 \times 1 + m_2v_2$$
$$\Rightarrow \quad m_2v_2 = 8 - 2 = 6 \text{ kg - ms}^{-1} \quad \text{...(i)}$$

Since it is an elastic collision.

$$\text{Coefficient of restitution } (e) = \frac{v_2 - v_1}{u_1 - u_2} = 1$$

$$\Rightarrow \quad v_2 - 1 = 4 - 0 \Rightarrow v_2 = 5 \text{ ms}^{-1}$$

Substituting in Eq. (i), we get

$$m_2 \times 5 = 6 \text{kg - ms}^{-1}$$
$$\Rightarrow \quad m_2 = 6/5 \text{ kg}$$

As we know that,

Speed of centre of mass,

$$v_{CM} = \frac{m_1v_1 + m_2v_2}{m_1 + m_2} = \frac{2 \times 1 + \frac{6}{5} \times 5}{2 + \frac{6}{5}}$$

$$= \frac{5}{2} = 2.5 \text{ ms}^{-1} = \frac{25}{10} \text{ms}^{-1}$$

$$\therefore \quad x = 25$$

6. Given, mass of bullet (m_b) = 10 g

$= 10 \times 10^{-3}$ kg

Initial speed of bullet is v.

Length of pendulum, $l = 0.5$ m

Mass of bob, $m = 1$ kg

Initial speed of bob, $u = 0$

Final speed of bullet, $v_b = 100 \text{ ms}^{-1}$

Final speed of bob for making complete circle at bottom,
$v' = \sqrt{5gl}$

Acceleration due to gravity, $g = 10 \text{ ms}^{-2}$

By using law of conservation of momentum

$$m_bu_b + mu = -m_bv_b + mv'$$

$$\Rightarrow \frac{10}{1000}v + 0 = \frac{-10}{1000} \times 100 + 1\sqrt{5gl}$$

$$\Rightarrow \quad \frac{v}{100} = -1 + \sqrt{5 \times 10 \times \frac{5}{10}}$$

$$\Rightarrow \quad \frac{v}{100} = -1 + 5$$

$$\Rightarrow \quad v = 4 \times 100 = 400 \text{ ms}^{-1}$$

7. If v'_A and v'_B be the velocity of body A and B after first collision, then by conservation of linear momentum

$$mv_A = mv'_A + 2m\,v'_B$$
$$v_A = v'_A + 2v'_B \quad \text{...(i)}$$

$$\text{Again, } e = \frac{v'_A - v'_B}{0 - v_A}$$

$$1 = \frac{v'_A - v'_B}{-v_A} \quad \text{[For elastic collision, } e = 1\text{]}$$

$\Rightarrow \quad -v_A = v'_A - v'_B$ ...(ii)

Adding Eqs. (i) and (ii), we have

$$0 = 2v'_A + v'_B$$

$\Rightarrow \quad v'_B = -2v'_A$ ...(iii)

From Eqs. (ii) and (iii), we get

$$-v_A = v'_A - (-2v'_A)$$

$\Rightarrow \quad -v_A = v'_A + 2v'_A = 3v'_A$

$\Rightarrow \quad v'_A = -\frac{v_A}{3} = -\frac{9}{3} = -3\text{m/s}$

$\therefore$ From Eq. (iii), $v'_B = -2(-3) = 6$ m/s

Again, after 2nd collision,

$$2mv'_B = (2m + 2m)v_c = 4mv_c$$

$\Rightarrow \quad v_c = \frac{v'_B}{2} = \frac{6}{2} = 3$ m/s

8. Given, mass of the ball, $m = 4$ kg

Velocity of the ball, $v = 10$ m/s

Force constant, $k = 100$ N/m

The length of the spring, $x = 8$ m

Let x is the compressed length of the spring.

Using the work-energy theorem,

"It states that kinetic energy of the ball is converted into the stored energy of spring".

$$\frac{mv^2}{2} = \frac{kx^2}{2}$$

$\Rightarrow \quad \frac{4(10)^2}{2} = \frac{(100)\,x^2}{2}$

$\Rightarrow \quad x = 2\text{m}$

The final length (compressed) of the spring

$= 8 - 2 = 6$ m

Hence, the value of x to the nearest integer is 6.

9. The mass m_1 is moving with speed u_1 initially and mass m_2 is at rest. After the collision, the mass m_1 and m_2 move with speed v in opposite directions.

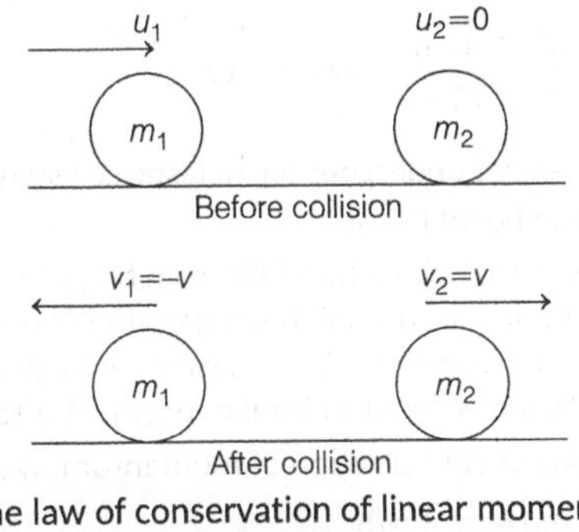

Using the law of conservation of linear momentum,

$$m_1u_1 + m_2u_2 = m_1v_1 + m_2v_2$$

$\Rightarrow \quad m_1u_1 + m_2(0) = m_1(-v) + m_2v$

$\Rightarrow \quad m_1u_1 = (-m_1 + m_2)v$ ...(i)

Since, the collision is elastic because they move with same speed after the collision. Hence, coefficient of restitution, $e = 1$

$\therefore \quad e = \frac{v_2 - v_1}{u_1 - u_2} \Rightarrow 1 = \frac{v - (-v)}{u_1 - 0}$

$u_1 = 2v$ ...(ii)

Putting the above value in Eq. (i), we get

$$m_1(2v) = (-m_1 + m_2)v$$

$\Rightarrow \quad 3m_1 = m_2 \Rightarrow \frac{m_2}{m_1} = \frac{3}{1}$

$\Rightarrow \quad m_2 : m_1 = 3 : 1$

10. Let v is the speed of the third block C.

The velocity of centre of mass of A and B is

$$v_{CM} = \frac{v}{2}$$

The spring is compressed maximum by x distance.

Using the law of conservation of energy.

$$\frac{1}{2}mv^2 = \frac{1}{2}m\left(\frac{v}{2}\right)^2 + \frac{1}{2}m\left(\frac{v}{2}\right)^2 + \frac{1}{2}kx^2$$

$\Rightarrow \quad \frac{1}{4}mv^2 = \frac{1}{2}kx^2$

$\Rightarrow \quad x = \sqrt{\frac{mv^2}{2k}}$

$\Rightarrow \quad x = v\sqrt{\frac{m}{2k}}$

11. Given, mass of rolling ball, $m = 0.5$ kg

Speed of ball, $u = 20\text{ ms}^{-1}$

Before deflection,

Initial kinetic energy, $KE_i = \frac{1}{2}mu^2$

$$= \frac{1}{2} \times 0.5 \times (20)^2 = 100\text{J}$$

It is given in the question that after deflection the ball moves with 5% of its initial kinetic energy

$$KE_f = 5\% \text{ of } KE_i \Rightarrow KE_f = \frac{5}{100} \times 100 = 5\text{ J}$$

If the final speed of the ball is $v\text{ ms}^{-1}$, then

$$KE_f = \frac{1}{2}mv^2$$

$\Rightarrow \quad 5 = \frac{1}{2} \times 0.5 \times v^2$

$\Rightarrow \quad v = \sqrt{20} = 4.47\text{ ms}^{-1}$

$\Rightarrow \quad v = 4.47\text{ ms}^{-1}$

12. Let v_1 and v_2 are the speed of P and Q after collision.

By using law of conservation of mementum,

$$m_1u_1 + m_2u_2 = m_1v_1 + m_2v_2$$

$\Rightarrow \quad Mu + m \cdot 0 = Mv_1 + mv_2$

$$\Rightarrow \frac{M(u - v_1)}{m} = v_2 \quad \text{...(i)}$$

and by using law of conservation of energy,

$$\frac{1}{2}m_1u_1^2 + \frac{1}{2}m_2u_2^2 = \frac{1}{2}m_1v_1^2 + \frac{1}{2}m_2v_2^2$$

$$\Rightarrow \quad Mu^2 + 0 = Mv_1^2 + mv_2^2$$

$$\Rightarrow \quad M(u^2 - v_1^2) = mv_2^2$$

$$\Rightarrow M(u - v_1)(u + v_1)/m = v_2^2 \quad \text{...(ii)}$$

Substituting the value of $M\frac{(u - v_1)}{m}$ from Eq. (i) in Eq. (ii), we get

$$v_2(u + v_1) = v_2^2 \Rightarrow u + v_1 = v_2$$

$\because \quad M >> m$

$\therefore \quad v_1 = u$ and $v_2 = 2u$

Hence, option (c) is the correct.

13. The situation is shown below

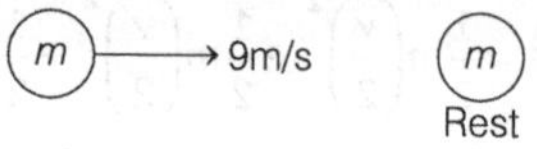

Before collision

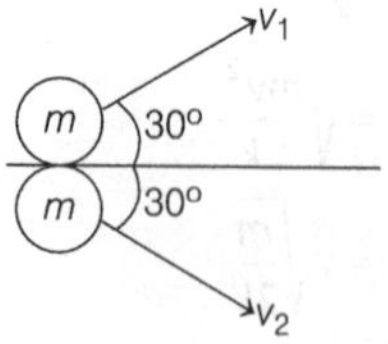

After collision

Using conservation of linear momentum in y-direction,

$$p_i = p_f$$

As, $p_i = 0$

and $\quad p_f = mv_1 \sin 30° - mv_2 \sin 30°$

$$\Rightarrow \quad 0 = m \times \frac{1}{2}v_1 - m \times \frac{1}{2}v_2$$

$\Rightarrow \quad v_1 = v_2$ or $v_1 : v_2 = 1:1$

Since, $v_1 : v_2 = x : y$ (gi ven)

$\therefore \quad x = 1$

14. As collision is elastic as shown below, both momentum and KE are conserve(d)

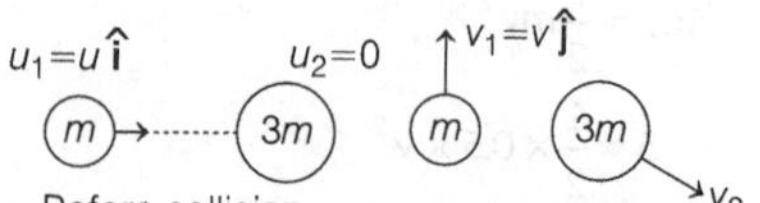

Before collision After collision

Momentum conservation gives,

$$mu\hat{i} = mv\hat{j} + 3mv_2$$

$$\Rightarrow \quad v_2 = \frac{1}{3}(u\hat{i} - v\hat{j})$$

$$\Rightarrow \quad |v_2| = \sqrt{\frac{u^2 + v^2}{9}}$$

or $\quad v_2^2 = (u^2 + v^2)/9 \quad$ ...(i)

Kinetic energy conservation gives,

$$\Rightarrow \quad \frac{1}{2}mu^2 = \frac{1}{2}mv^2 + \frac{1}{2}3mv_2^2$$

$$\Rightarrow \quad u^2 = v^2 + 3v_2^2 \quad \text{...(ii)}$$

Substituting value of v_2 from Eq (i) into Eq (ii), we get

$$u^2 = v^2 + 3\left(\frac{u^2 + v^2}{9}\right)$$

$$\Rightarrow \quad \frac{2}{3}u^2 = \frac{4}{3}v^2 \Rightarrow v = \frac{u}{\sqrt{2}}$$

Hence, correct option is (c).

15. Given, impact is shown below,

For particle 1, final KE is equals to half of its initial value,

$$\Rightarrow \quad K_f = \frac{1}{2}K_i$$

$$\Rightarrow \quad \frac{1}{2}m_1v_1^2 = \left(\frac{1}{2}m_1u^2\right) \times \frac{1}{2}$$

$\Rightarrow$ Final velocity of m_1 will be, $v_1 = \frac{u}{\sqrt{2}}$

Momentum in y-direction is conserved,

i.e. $\quad 10mv_2 \sin\theta_2 = mv_1 \sin\theta_1$

Here, $v_1 = \frac{u}{\sqrt{2}}$ and $\sin\theta_1 = \sqrt{n}\sin\theta_2$

So, we have

$$10mv_2 \cdot \sin\theta_2 = \frac{mu}{\sqrt{2}} \cdot \sqrt{n}\sin\theta_2$$

$$\Rightarrow \quad v_2 = \frac{u\sqrt{n}}{10\sqrt{2}} \quad \text{...(i)}$$

Also collision is elastic, so KE is conserve(d)

$$\Rightarrow \quad \frac{1}{2}mu^2 = \frac{1}{2}mv_1^2 + \frac{1}{2}(10m)v_2^2$$

Substituting values of v_1 and v_2, we have

$$u^2 = \left(\frac{u}{\sqrt{2}}\right)^2 + 10\left(\frac{u^2n}{100 \times 2}\right)$$

$$\Rightarrow \quad \frac{u^2}{2} = \frac{u^2n}{10 \times 2} \Rightarrow n = 10$$

16. When the bullet undergoes an inelastic collision with block, a part of KE of bullet is lost.

When bullet + block system falls from height h, then its total energy (kinetic + potential) becomes kinetic energy, so kinetic energy of bullet + block system at bottom just before collision is equal to total energy just after collision.

Now, by law of conservation of momentum, we have

$$mu = (m + M)v$$

$$\Rightarrow \quad v = \frac{mu}{m + M} = \frac{0.1 \times 20}{(0.1 + 1.9)} = 1\,\text{ms}^{-1}$$

Total energy of bullet and block just after collision

$$= KE + PE = \frac{1}{2}(m+M)v^2 + (m+M)gh$$

$$= \frac{1}{2}\times 2\times 1^2 + 2\times 10\times 1$$

$$= 1 + 20 = 21\text{ J}$$

Hence, correct option is (c).

17. Since, all the collisions are perfectly inelastic, so after the final collision, all blocks will be moving together. Let their final velocity be v'.

By law of conservation of linear momentum,

$$(p_{sys})_i = (p_{sys})_f$$

$$\Rightarrow mv + m(0) + 2m(0) + 4m(0) + 8m(0) = (m + m + 2m + 4m + 8m)v'$$

$$\Rightarrow mv = 16mv'$$

$$\Rightarrow v' = \frac{v}{16} \quad \text{...(i)}$$

Now, initial kinetic energy of system,

$$(K_{sys})_i = \frac{1}{2}mv^2 + 0 + 0 + 0 + 0 = \frac{1}{2}mv^2$$

And final kinetic energy of system,

$$(K_{sys})_f = \frac{1}{2}(m + m + 2m + 4m + 8m)(v')^2$$

$$= \frac{1}{2}\times 16m \times \left(\frac{v}{16}\right)^2 = \frac{1}{32}mv^2$$

Loss in kinetic energy,

$$(\Delta K_{sys})_{loss} = (K_{sys})_i - (K_{sys})_f = \frac{1}{2}mv^2 - \frac{1}{32}mv^2 = \frac{15}{32}mv^2$$

% loss in kinetic energy,

$$\%(\Delta K_{sys})_{loss} = \frac{(\Delta K_{sys})_{loss}}{(K_{sys})_i}\times 100\%$$

$$= \frac{\frac{15}{32}mv^2}{\frac{1}{2}mv^2}\times 100\% = \frac{15}{16}\times 100\% = 93.75\%$$

Given that $\%(\Delta K_{sys})_{loss} = p\%$

so, $p = 93.75 \simeq 94$

Hence, correct option is (c).

18. Given situation in as shown in the figure.

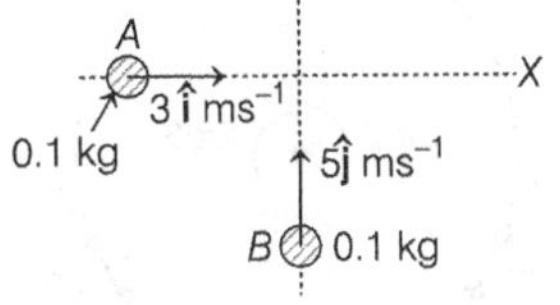

Total initial momentum,

$$p_i = m_A v_A + m_B v_B$$

$$= 0.1\times 3\hat{i} + 0.1\times 5\hat{j} = 0.3\,\hat{i} + 0.5\,\hat{j}\ (\text{kg-ms}^{-1})$$

Final velocity of A, $v_A = 4(\hat{i}+\hat{j})$

Let final velocity of B is v_B.

Then, final momentum after collision,

$$p_f = m_A v_A + m_B v_B$$

$$= 0.1\times 4(\hat{i}+\hat{j}) + 0.1\times v_B$$

Now, by conservation of momentum, we have

$$p_i = p_f$$

$$\Rightarrow 0.3\hat{i} + 0.5\hat{j} = 0.4\hat{i} + 0.4\hat{j} + 0.1v_B$$

$$\Rightarrow v_B = -\hat{i} + \hat{j}$$

Kinetic energy of B after collision will be

$$K = \frac{1}{2}mv^2 = \frac{1}{2}\times 0.1\times |(-\hat{i}+\hat{j})|^2$$

$$= \frac{1}{2}\times 0.1\times 2 = 0.1\text{ J}$$

It is given, energy of B after collision is $\frac{x}{10}$.

So, $\frac{x}{10} = 0.1$ or $x = 1$

JEE Advanced

1. From energy conservation :

$$\frac{1}{2}mu_0 = mgh$$

$$\Rightarrow u_0 = \sqrt{2gh}$$

Option (a) is correct

$$\mathbf{v}_0 = \sqrt{2gh}\,\hat{\mathbf{i}} - \sqrt{2gh(3h)}\,\hat{\mathbf{k}}$$

$$= \sqrt{2gh}\,(\hat{\mathbf{i}} - \sqrt{3}\,\hat{\mathbf{k}})$$

$$\tan\theta = \frac{v_z}{v_x} = \frac{\sqrt{2g(3h)}}{\sqrt{2gh}} = \sqrt{3}$$

$$\Rightarrow \theta = 60^\circ$$

Option (c) is correct

$$\sqrt{\frac{h_1}{3h}} = e = \frac{1}{\sqrt{3}}$$

$$\Rightarrow h_1 = h \quad \text{...(i)}$$

$$d = u_0\sqrt{\frac{2(3h)}{g}} = \sqrt{2gh}\sqrt{\frac{2\times 3h}{g}}$$

$$d = 2h\sqrt{3}$$

$$\Rightarrow \frac{d}{h} = \frac{d}{h_1} = 2\sqrt{3} \quad \text{[from Eq. (i)]}$$

Option (d) is correct.

2. Linear impulse, $J = mv_0$

$$v_0 = \frac{J}{m} = 2.5\text{ m/s}$$

$$\therefore \quad v = v_0 e^{-t/\tau} \Rightarrow \frac{dx}{dt} = v_0 e^{-t/\tau}$$

$$\int_0^x dx = v_0 \int_0^\tau e^{-t/\tau} dt$$

$$x = v_0 \left[\frac{e^{-t/\tau}}{-\frac{1}{\tau}} \right]_0^\tau$$

$$x = 2.5(-4)(e^{-1} - e^0) = 2.5(-4)(0.37 - 1)$$

$$x = 6.30 \text{ m}$$

3. $\because \; H = \dfrac{u^2 \sin^2 45^\circ}{2g} = 120 \text{ m} \Rightarrow \dfrac{u^2}{4g} = 120 \text{ m}$

If speed is v after the first collision, then speed should remain $1/\sqrt{2}$ times, as kinetic energy has reduced to half.

$$\Rightarrow \quad v = \frac{u}{\sqrt{2}}$$

$$\therefore \quad h_{max} = \frac{v^2 \sin^2 30^\circ}{2g} = \frac{(u/\sqrt{2})^2 \sin^2 30^\circ}{2g}$$

$$= \left(\frac{u^2/4g}{4} \right) = \frac{120}{4} = 30$$

4.

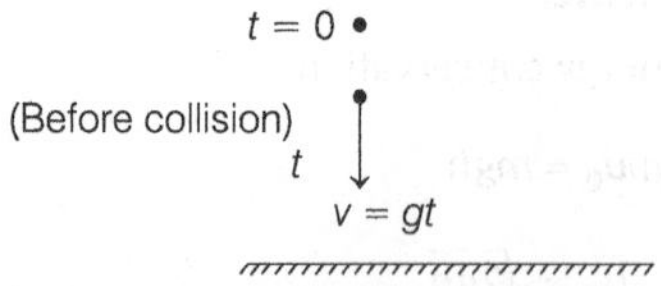

$$K = \frac{1}{2} m g^2 t^2$$

$K \propto t^2$ Therefore, K-t graph is parabola.

During collision, retarding force is just like the spring force ($F \propto x$), therefore kinetic energy first decreases to elastic potential energy and then increases.

5. From momentum conservation equation, we have

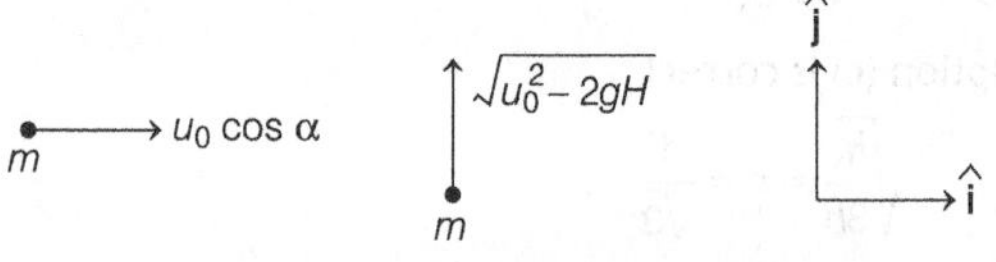

$$\mathbf{p}_i = \mathbf{p}_f$$

$$\therefore \quad m(u_0 \cos\alpha)\hat{\mathbf{i}} + m(\sqrt{u_0^2 - 2gH})\hat{\mathbf{j}} = (2m)\mathbf{v} \qquad \text{...(i)}$$

$$H = \frac{u_0^2 \sin^2 \alpha}{2g} \qquad \text{...(ii)}$$

From Eqs. (i) and (ii)

$$\mathbf{v} = \frac{u_0 \cos\alpha}{2} \hat{\mathbf{i}} + \frac{u_0 \cos\alpha}{2} \hat{\mathbf{j}}$$

Since both components of $\mathbf{v}$ are equal. Therefore, it is making 45° with horizontal.

6. $R = u\sqrt{\dfrac{2h}{g}}$

$$\Rightarrow \quad 20 = v_1 \sqrt{\frac{2 \times 5}{10}}$$

$$\text{and} \quad 100 = v_2 \sqrt{\frac{2 \times 5}{10}}$$

$$\Rightarrow \quad v_1 = 20 \text{ m/s}$$

$$\Rightarrow \quad v_2 = 100 \text{ m/s.}$$

Applying momentum conservation just before and just after the collision

$$(0.01)(v) = (0.2)(20) + (0.01)(100) \; v = 500 \text{ m/s}$$

7.

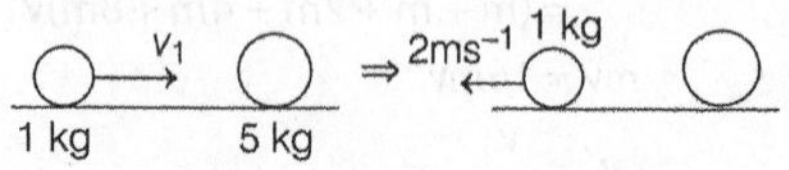

$$v_1' = \left(\frac{m_1 - m_2}{m_1 + m_2} \right) v_1 + \left(\frac{2m_2}{m_1 + m_2} \right) v_2$$

$$-2 = \left(\frac{1-5}{1+5} \right) v_1 + 0 \qquad (\text{as } v_2 = 0)$$

$$\therefore \quad v_1 = 3 \text{ ms}^{-1}$$

$$v_2' = \left(\frac{m_2 - m_1}{m_1 + m_2} \right) v_2 + \left(\frac{2m_1}{m_1 + m_2} \right) v_1$$

$$P_{CM} = P_i = (1)(3) = 3 \text{ kg -m/s}$$

$$P_5' = (5)(1) = 5 \text{ kg -m/s}$$

$$K_{CM} = \frac{p_{CM}^2}{2M_{CM}} = \frac{9}{2 \times 6} = 0.75 \text{ J}$$

$$K_{total} = \frac{1}{2} \times 1 \times (3)^2 = 4.5 \text{ J}$$

8. At first collision one particle having speed $2v$ will rotate $240^\circ \left(\text{or } \dfrac{4\pi}{3} \right)$ while other particle having speed v will rotate $120^\circ \left(\text{or } \dfrac{2\pi}{3} \right)$. At first collision, they will exchange their velocities. Now, as shown in figure, after two collisions they will again reach at point A.

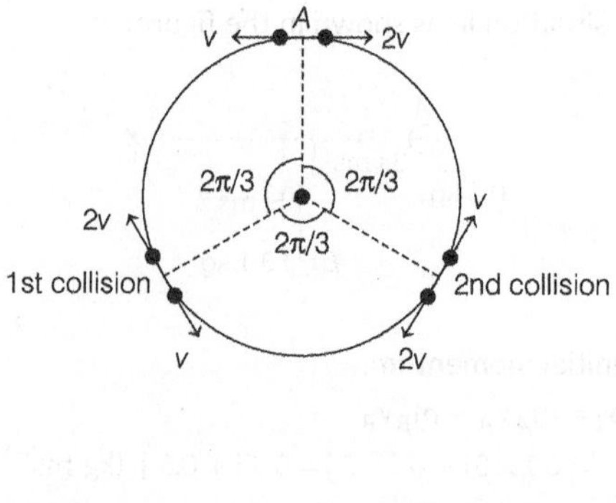

CHAPTER~03

ROTATIONAL MOTION

LEVEL 01 Starter Level

3.1 Moment of Inertia

1. Two point masses m_1 and m_2 are joined by a weightless rod of length r. Prove that the moment of inertia of the system about an axis passing through the centre of mass and perpendicular to the rod is $I = \mu r^2$, where $\mu = \dfrac{m_1 m_2}{m_1 + m_2}$ and is called reduced mass of system.

2. Four particles each of mass m are kept at the four corners of a square frame of edge a. Find the moment of inertia of the system about

(i) an axis perpendicular to the plane of the square and passing through the centre of the square.

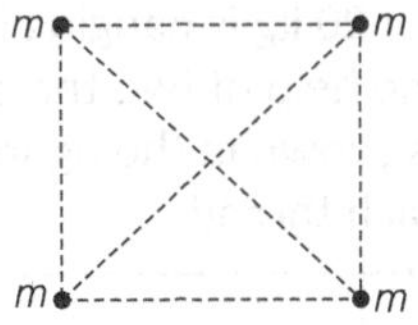

(ii) perpendicular to the plane of the square and passing through one of particles.

(iii) one of the sides of the square

(iv) one of the diagonals of the square

3. Find out the moment of inertia of figures shown each having mass M, radius R and having uniform mass distribution about an axis passing through the centre and perpendicular to the plane.

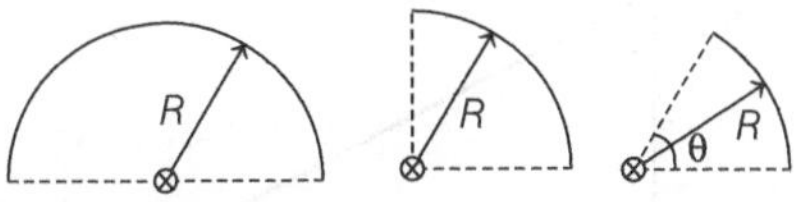

(a) (b) (c)

4. The surface mass density (mass/area) of a circular disc of radius R depends on the distance from the centre x given as, $\sigma(x) = \alpha + \beta x$, where α and β are positive constant. Find its moment of inertia about the line perpendicular to the plane of the disc through its centre.

5. Find out the moment of inertia of a ring having uniform mass distribution of mass M and radius R about an axis which is tangent to the ring

(i) in the plane of the ring

(i) (ii)

(ii) perpendicular to the plane of the ring.

6. Calculate the moment of inertia of a uniform rod of mass M and length L about axes 1, 2, 3 and 4.

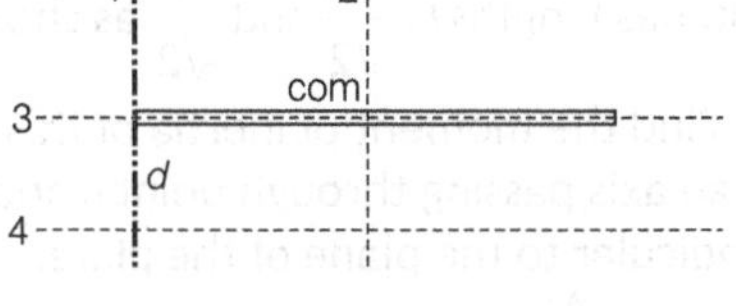

7. Find the moment of inertia of the two uniform joint rods having mass m each about point P as shown in figure.

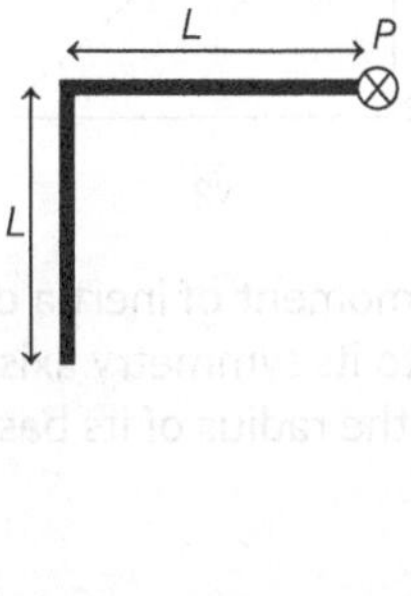

8. Three identical uniform rods, each of length L, are joined to form a rigid equilateral triangle. Find its radius of gyration about an axis parallel to its one side and passing through the opposite vertex.

9. In the figure shown, find moment of inertia of a plate having mass M, length l and width b about axes 1, 2, 3 and 4. Assume that mass is uniformly distributed.

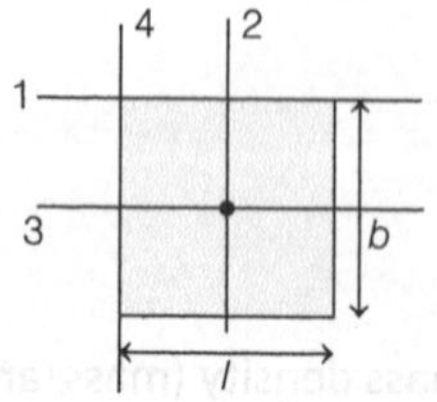

10. Find moment of inertia of a uniform square plate of mass M and edge L about an axis

(i) passing through one corner and perpendicular to the plane of the plate

(ii) along one of the diagonals of the plate

11. Find out the moment of inertia of a semi-circular disc about an axis passing through its centre of mass and perpendicular to the plane.

12. Four spheres each mass M and radius R are arranged as shown in the figure.

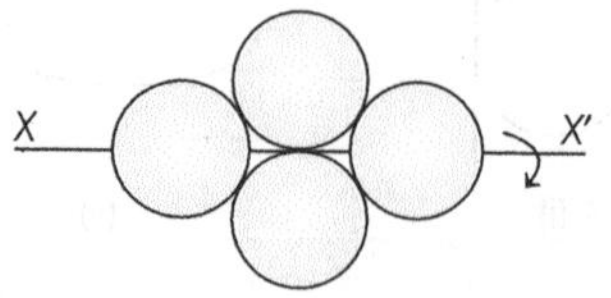

Find the moment of inertia of the system about axis XX'.

13. A uniform triangular plate of mass M whose vertices are ABC has lengths l, $\frac{l}{\sqrt{2}}$ and $\frac{l}{\sqrt{2}}$ as shown in figure. Find the moment of inertia of this plate about an axis passing through point B and perpendicular to the plane of the plate.

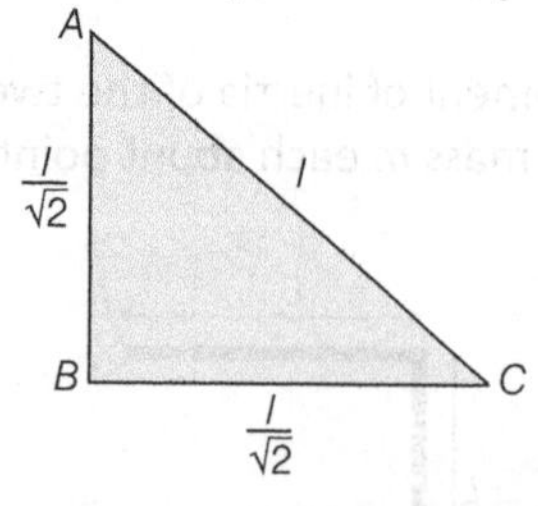

14. Calculate the moment of inertia of a uniform solid cone relative to its symmetry axis, if the mass of the cone is m and the radius of its base is R.

15. From a circular disc of radius R and mass $9M$, a small disc of radius $R/3$ is removed from the disc. Find the moment of inertia of the remaining disc about an axis perpendicular to the plane of the disc and passing through O.

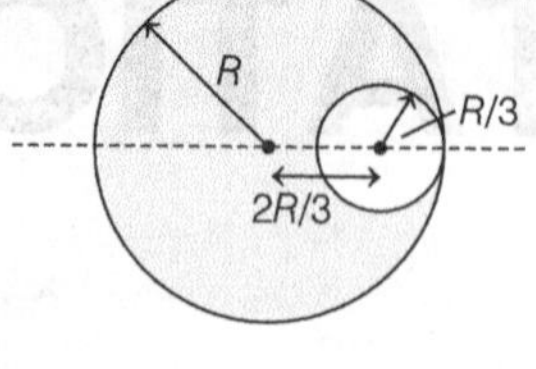

3.2 Torque

1. A simple pendulum of length l is pulled aside to make an angle θ with the vertical. Find the magnitude of the torque of the weight w of the bob about the point of suspension. When is the torque zero?

2. A particle of mass m is projected with a speed u at an angle θ with horizontal. Find the torque of the weight of the particle about the point of projection when the particle is at the highest point.

3. In an experiment with a beam balance, an unknown mass m is balanced by two known masses of 16 kg and 4 kg as shown in figure. Find the value of the unknown mass m.

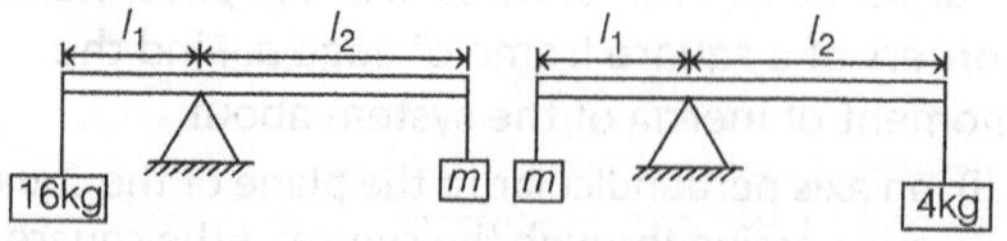

4. A uniform rod of 20 kg is hanging in horizontal position with the help of two threads. It also supports a 40 kg mass as shown in the figure. Find the tension developed in each thread.

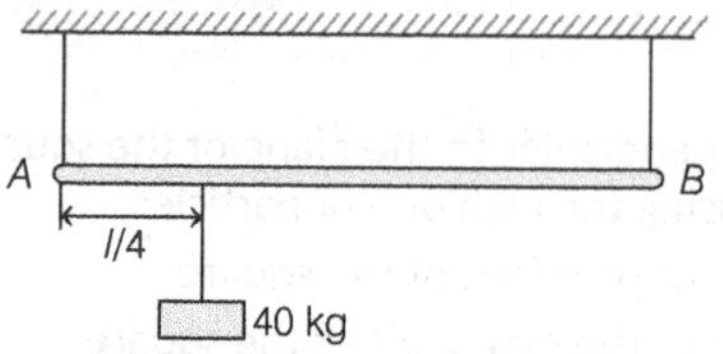

5. Assuming frictionless contacts, determine the magnitude of external horizontal force P applied at the lower end for equilibrium of the rod. The rod is uniform and its mass is m.

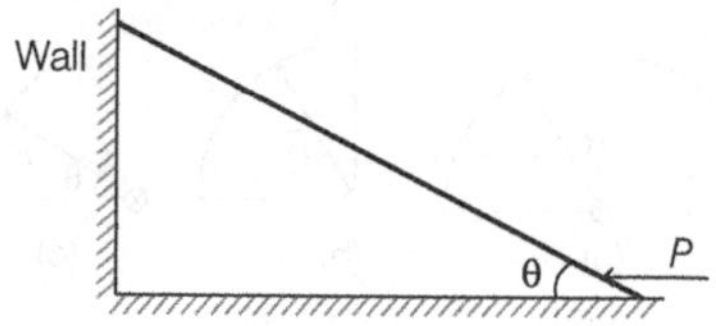

6. A uniform rod of length L rests against a smooth wall as shown in figure. Find the friction coefficient between the ground and the lower end, if the minimum angle that the rod can make with the horizontal is θ.

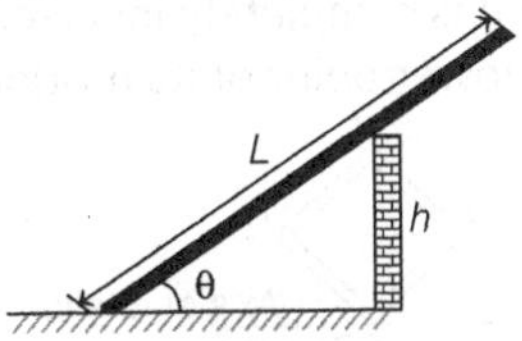

7. In the system as shown in figure, AB is a uniform rod of mass 10 kg and BC is a light string which is connected between wall and rod, in vertical plane. There is block of mass 15kg connected at B with a light string. [Take, $g = 10\ m/s^2$] If whole of the system is in equilibrium, then find

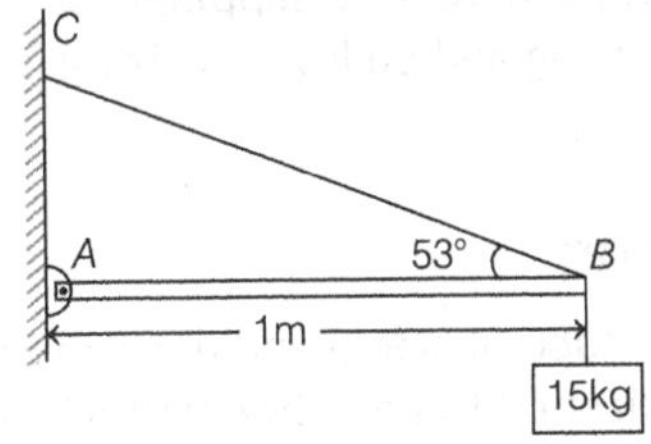

(i) tension in the string BC

(ii) hinge force exerted on beam at point A.

8. A cylinder of length 20 cm and radius 10 cm is rotating about its central axis at an angular speed of 100 rad/s. The moment of inertia of the cylinder about its axis of rotation is 0.8 kgm^2. Find the tangential force that will stop the cylinder at a uniform rate in 10 s.

9. A bar of length L and mass m has a frictionless pivot through its mid-point. There is an additional point mass $2m$ on the right end of the bar and an additional point mass m on the left end of the bar.

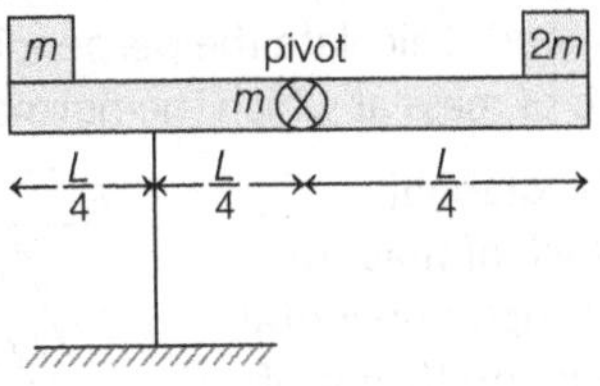

The bar is held in horizontal position by a vertical cord attached at $L/4$ from the left end as shown in the figure. The additional masses m and $2m$ are fixed to the rod. The rod is initially horizontal.

(a) Find the tension in the cord.

(b) Find the force that the pivot exerts on the bar.

(c) If the cord is cut, what is the angular acceleration of the bar immediately after the cord is cut?

10. A uniform rod of mass m and length L can rotate in vertical plane about a smooth horizontal axis hinged at point H. Find

(i) angular acceleration of the rod just after it is released from initial horizontal position from rest.

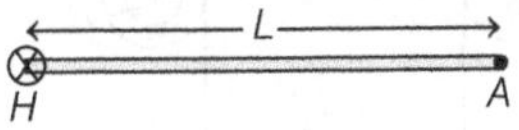

(ii) the acceleration (tangential and radial) of point A at this moment.

(iii) net hinge force acting at this moment.

11. The uniform rod AB of mass m is released from rest when $\beta = 60°$. Assuming that the friction force between end A and the surface is large enough to prevent sliding, determine (for the instant just after release)

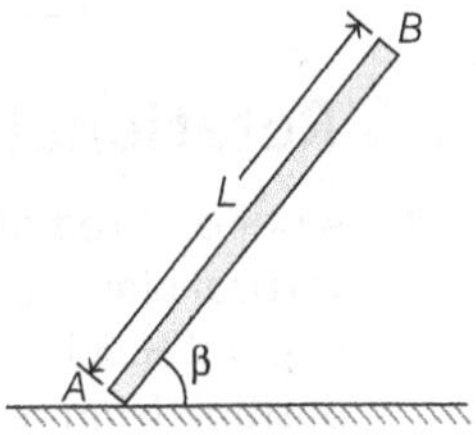

(a) the angular acceleration of the rod

(b) the normal reaction and the friction force at A.

12. A uniform square plate of mass m is supported as shown. If the cable suddenly breaks, determine just after that moment;

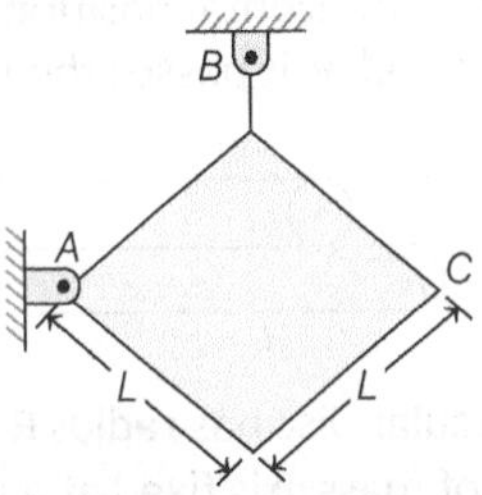

(a) the angular acceleration of the plate.

(b) the acceleration of corner C.

(c) the reaction at A.

13. A block of mass m is suspended with the help of a light cord wrapped over a cylindrical pulley of mass $2m$ and radius R as shown in the figure.

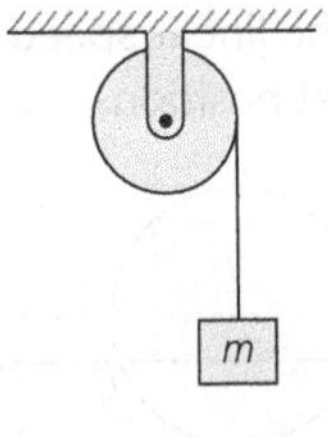

The system is released from rest. Find the angular acceleration of the pulley and the acceleration of the block.

14. In the arrangements shown, pulleys are rough enough so that slipping can't take place. The mass of blocks, moment of inertia of pulley and radius are indicated. Find acceleration of blocks.

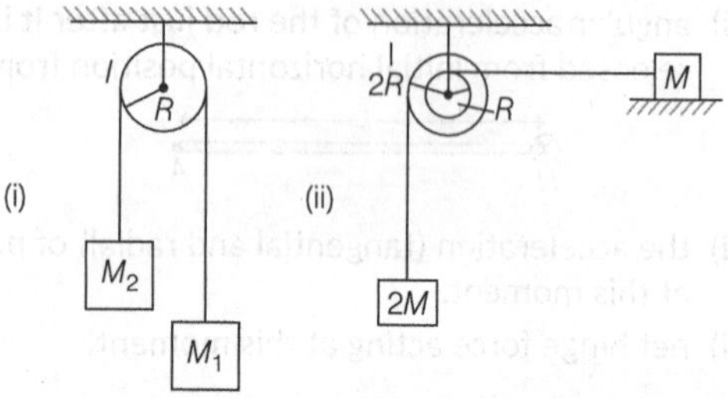

3.3 Rotational Kinetic Energy

1. A uniform rod of mass m and length l can rotate in vertical plane about a smooth horizontal axis hinged at point H. It is released from initial horizontal position from rest. When it becomes vertical, find

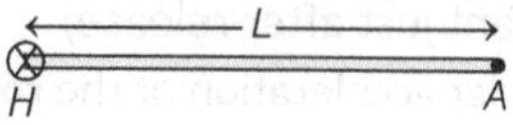

(i) the angular speed

(ii) the reaction at hinge

2. A uniform rod is hinged as shown in the figure and is released from a horizontal position. Find the angular velocity of the rod as it passes the vertical position.

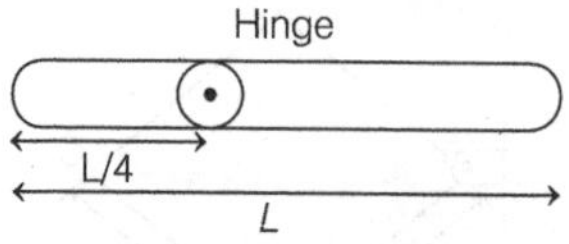

3. A uniform circular disc has radius R and mass m. A particle also of mass m is fixed at a point A on the edge of the disc as shown in the figure. The disc can rotate freely about a fixed horizontal chord PQ that is at a distance $R/4$ from the centre C of the disc. The line AC is perpendicular to PQ. Initially, the disc is held vertical with the point A at its highest position. It is then allowed to fall, so that it starts rotating about PQ. Find the linear speed of the particle as it reaches its lowest position.

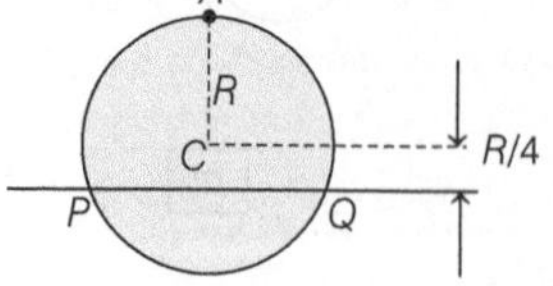

4. A square frame, made of 4 equal rods of length L, mass m each is hinged at corner A, so that it can rotate about a horizontal axis parallel to line DB as shown. It is slightly disturbed and it starts falling about hinge axis. Calculate angular speed of the frame when it is completely inverted and point C reaches the lower point of its motion.

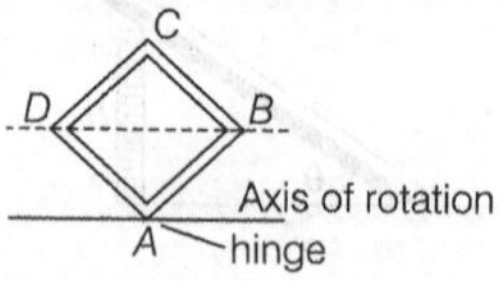

5. The moment of inertia of the pulley system as shown in figure is 3 kgm^2. Its radius is 1m. The system is released from rest. Find the linear velocity of the block, when it has descended through 40 cm. (Assume that there is no slipping between string and pulley and string is light) [Take, $g = 10$ m/s^2]

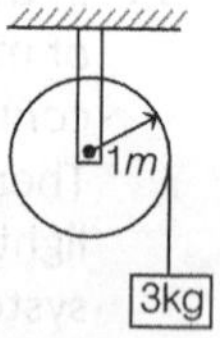

3.4 Toppling

1. A uniform cube of side a and mass m rests on a rough horizontal table. A horizontal force F is applied normal to one of the faces at a point that is directly above the centre of the face, at a height $3a/4$ above the base. (Assume that the cube does not slide).

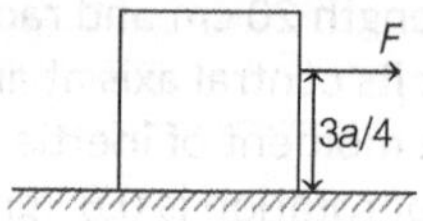

(i) If $F = \dfrac{mg}{3}$, then find the distance of line of action of normal force acting on the cube from its centre.

(ii) Find the minimum value of F for which the cube begins to tilt about the edge.

2. A solid cubical block of mass m and side a slides down a rough inclined plane of inclination θ with a constant speed. Calculate the perpendicular distance x from centre of mass at which the normal force is acting.

3. A regular hexagonal uniform block of mass m rests on a rough horizontal surface with coefficient of friction μ as shown in figure. A constant horizontal force is applied on the block as shown. If the coefficient of friction is sufficient to prevent slipping before toppling, then the minimum force required to topple the block about its corner A.

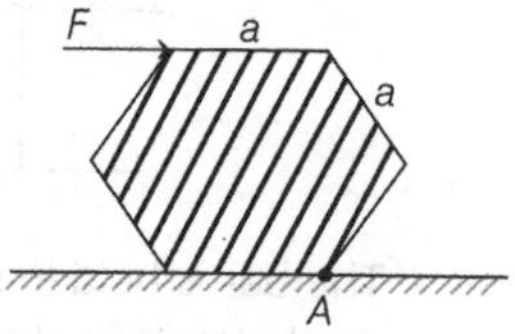

4. A box of dimensions l and b is kept on a truck moving with an acceleration a. If box does not slide, find the minimum acceleration of the truck for which it topples.

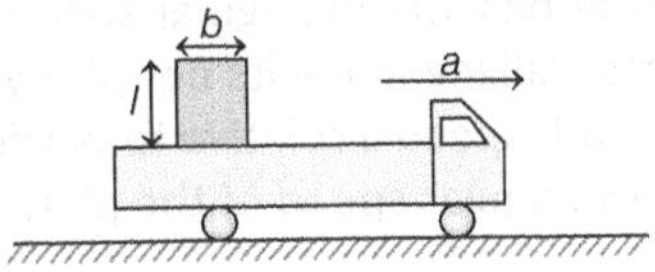

3.5 Angular Momentum

1. A particle having mass 2 kg is moving along straight line $3x + 4y = 5$ with speed 8 m/s. Find angular momentum of the particle about origin. x and y are in meters.

2. A particle of mass m is projected on horizontal ground with an initial velocity of u making an angle θ with horizontal. Find out the angular momentum of particle about the point of projection when it is at highest point of path.

3. A uniform circular ring of mass 400 g and radius 10 cm is rotated about one of its diameter at an angular speed of 20 rad/s. Find the kinetic energy of the ring and its angular momentum about the axis of rotation.

4. If the radius of the earth is reduced to half of its present day value without change in its mass, what will be the length of the day?

5. A uniform ring is rotating about vertical axis with angular velocity ω initially. A point insect (S) having the same mass as that of the ring starts walking from the lowest point P_1 and finally reaches the point P_2 (as shown in figure). What is the final angular velocity of the ring?

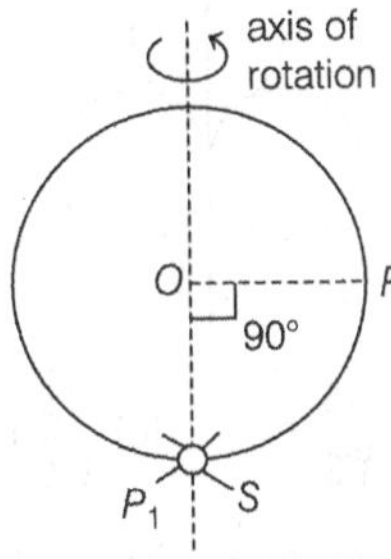

6. The moment of inertia of a uniform disc about an axis passing through its centre and perpendicular to its plane is 1 kg-m^2. It is rotating with an angular velocity 100 rad/s. Another identical disc is gently placed on it, so that their centres coincide.

   Now, these two discs together continue to rotate about the same axis. Find the loss in kinetic energy.

7. Two beads (each of mass m) can move freely on a frictionless rod of mass $2m$ and length L. The system is rotated with an angular velocity ω_0 when the beads are at a distance $L/4$ from the centre of the rod. What is the angular velocity of the system when the beads reach the respective ends of the rod?

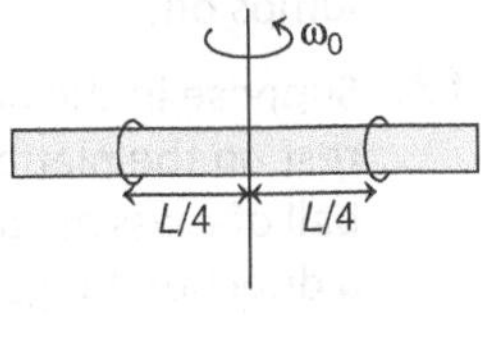

8. A uniform rod of mass m and length L can rotate freely on a smooth horizontal plane about a vertical axis hinged at point H. A point mass having same mass m coming with an initial speed u perpendicular to the rod, strikes the rod and sticks to it at a distance of $3L/4$ from hinge point. Find out the angular velocity of the rod just after collision.

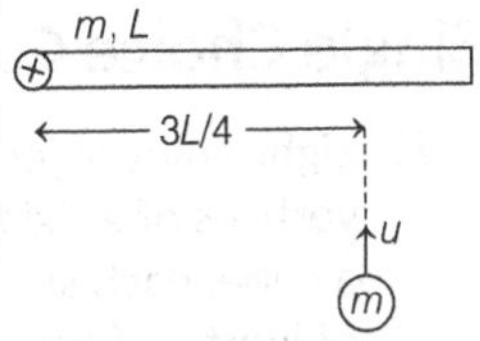

9. A block of mass m is attached to a pulley disc of equal mass m, radius r by means of a slack string as shown. The pulley is hinged about its centre on a horizontal table and the block is projected with an initial velocity of 5 m/s. Find the velocity when the string becomes taut.

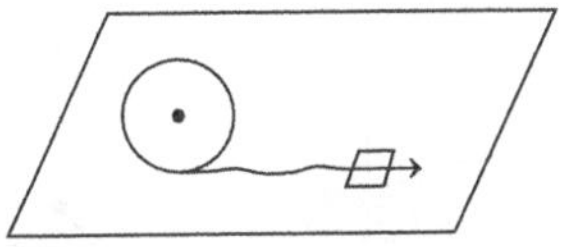

10. A particle of mass m is attached to the end of a string and moves with speed v along a circle of radius r_0 on a frictionless table. The string passes through a frictionless hole in the table. Find the work done by external agent, if the string is slowly pulled so that the radius of circular orbit changes from r_0 to $r_0/2$.

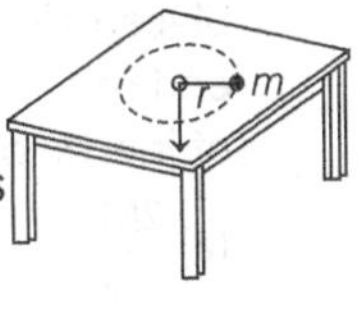

11. A 2 kg sphere moving horizontally to the right with an initial velocity of 5 m/s strikes the lower end of an 8 kg rigid rod AB. The rod is suspended from a hinge at A and is initially at rest. Knowing that the coefficient of restitution between the rod and sphere is 0.8, determine the angular velocity of the rod and the velocity of the sphere immediately after the impact.

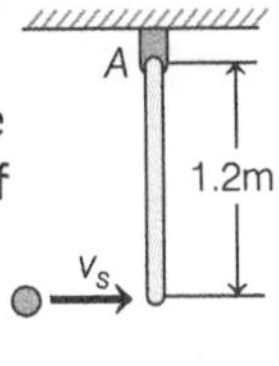

12. A child of mass m is standing, on the periphery of a circular platform of radius R, which can rotate about its central axis. The moment of inertia of the platform is I. Child jumps off from the platform with

a velocity u tangentially relative to the platform. Find the angular speed of the platform after the child jumps off.

13. Suppose in the previous problem, the child stays at rest on the platform and one of his friend throws a ball of mass m_1 towards him with a velocity of v from a direction tangential to the platform and the child on the platform catches the ball. Find the angular velocity of the platform after he catches the ball.

14. In previous problem, if initially the platform with the child is rotating with an angular speed ω_0 and the child starts walking along its periphery in opposite direction with speed u relative to platform, what will be the new angular speed of the platform?

LEVEL 02 JEE Main Level

Single Choice Correct Questions

1. Eight point objects, each of mass M, are at the vertices of a rigid, massless framework in the form of a cube; each side is of length a. What is the moment of inertia of this arrangement about an axis passing through one edge of the cube?

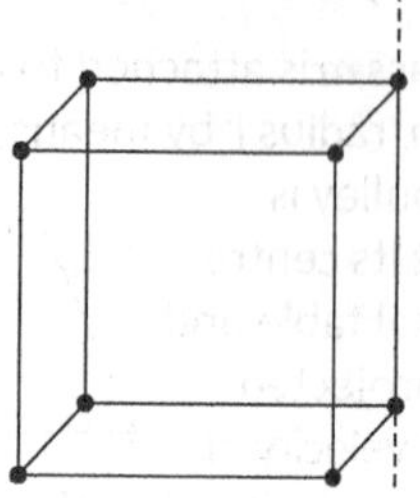

(a) $4Ma^2$ (b) $6Ma^2$
(c) $8Ma^2$ (d) $10Ma^2$

2. Three thin rods each of length L and mass M are placed along X, Y and Z-axes in such a way that one end of each of the rods is at the origin. The moment of inertia of this system about Z-axis is:

(a) $\frac{2ML^2}{3}$ (b) $\frac{4ML^2}{3}$ (c) $\frac{5ML^2}{3}$ (d) $\frac{ML^2}{3}$

3. AB and CD are two identical rods each of length l and mass m joined to form a cross is fixed inside a ring of mass m and radius $l/2$. Moment of inertia of the system about a bisector of the angle between the rods (XY) is

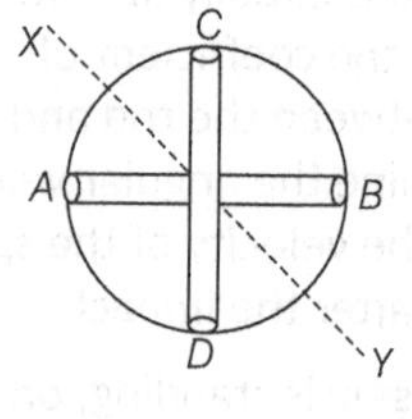

(a) $\frac{7ml^2}{6}$ (b) $\frac{13ml^2}{12}$
(c) $\frac{ml^2}{12}$ (d) $\frac{5ml^2}{24}$

4. A thin wire of length L and uniform linear mass density ρ is bent into a circular loop with centre at O as shown in the figure. The moment of inertia of the loop about the axis XX' is

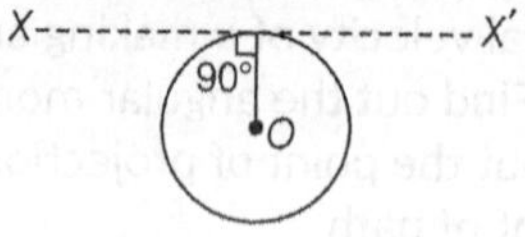

(a) $\frac{3\rho L^3}{16\pi^2}$ (b) $\frac{\rho L^3}{16\pi^2}$ (c) $\frac{5\rho L^3}{16\pi^2}$ (d) $\frac{3\rho L^3}{8\pi^2}$

5. If the moment of inertia of a disc about an axis tangentially and parallel to its surface be I, then the moment of inertia about the axis tangential but perpendicular to the surface will be

(a) $\frac{6}{5}I$ (b) $\frac{3}{4}I$ (c) $\frac{3}{2}I$ (d) $\frac{5}{4}I$

6. Three rings each of mass m and radius r are placed in a plane touching each other as shown. The radius of gyration of the system about the axis as shown in the figure is

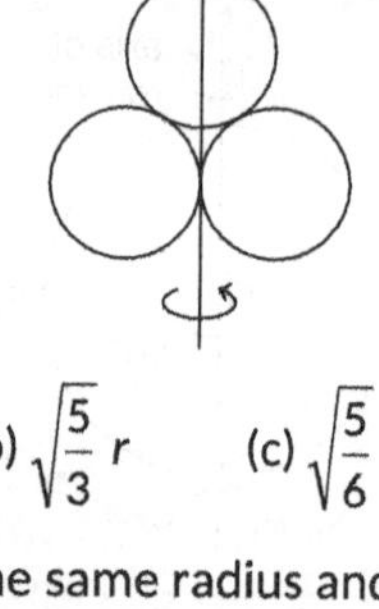

(a) $\sqrt{\frac{7}{6}}r$ (b) $\sqrt{\frac{5}{3}}r$ (c) $\sqrt{\frac{5}{6}}r$ (d) $\sqrt{\frac{7}{2}}r$

7. Two rings of the same radius and mass are placed, such that their centres are at a common point and their planes are perpendicular to each other. The moment of inertia of the system about an axis passing through the centre and perpendicular to the plane of one of the rings is (mass of the ring $= m$, radius $= r$)

(a) $\frac{1}{2}mr^2$ (b) mr^2 (c) $\frac{3}{2}mr^2$ (d) $2mr^2$

8. A circular disc of radius R and thickness $R/6$ has moment of inertia I about an axis passing through its centre and perpendicular to its plane. It is melted and recasted into a solid sphere. The moment of inertia of the sphere about its diameter as axis of rotation is

(a) I (b) $\frac{2I}{8}$

(c) $\frac{I}{5}$ (d) $\frac{I}{10}$

9. A rigid body can be hinged about any point on the X-axis. When it is hinged such that the hinge is at x, the moment of inertia is given by $I = x^2 - 2x + 99$. The X-coordinate of centre of mass is

(a) $x = 2$ (b) $x = 0$

(c) $x = 1$ (d) $x = 3$

10. A uniform disc of radius R lies in the XY-plane with its center at origin. Its moment of inertia about Z-axis is equal to its moment of inertia about line $y = x + c$. The value of c can be

(a) $-\frac{R}{2}$ (b) $\frac{R}{\sqrt{2}}$

(c) $\frac{R}{4}$ (d) None

11. The moment of inertia of semi-circular plate of radius R and mass M about axis AA' in its plane passing through its centre is

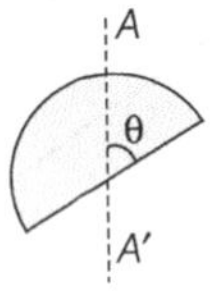

(a) $\frac{MR^2}{2}$ (b) $\frac{MR^2}{4}\cos^2\theta$

(c) $\frac{MR^2}{4}\sin^2\theta$ (d) $\frac{MR^2}{4}$

12. Moment of inertia of a thin uniform semi-circular wire having mass M, radius R and centre C about an axis passing through point O and perpendicular to its plane is

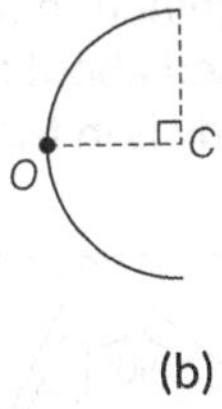

(a) $2MR^2$ (b) $2MR^2\left(1-\frac{1}{\pi}\right)$

(c) $MR^2\left(1-\frac{2}{\pi}\right)$ (d) $2MR^2\left(1-\frac{2}{\pi}\right)$

13. In the given triangular sheet, $PQ = QR = l$ and $\angle PQR = 90°$. If M is the mass of the sheet, then its moment of inertia about PR is

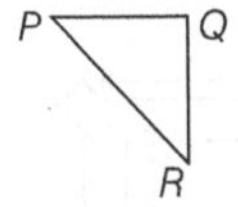

(a) $\frac{Ml^2}{24}$ (b) $\frac{Ml^2}{12}$ (c) $\frac{Ml^2}{6}$ (d) $\frac{Ml^2}{3}$

14. The figure shows a uniform rod lying along the X-axis. The locus of all the points lying on the rectangular coordinate axis, about which the moment of inertia of the rod is same as that about O is

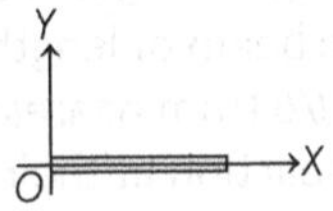

(a) an ellipse (b) a circle

(c) a parabola (d) a straight line

15. Let I be the moment of inertia of a uniform square plate about an axis AB that passes through its centre and is parallel to two of its sides. CD is a line in the plane of the plate the passes through the centre of the plate and makes an angle θ with AB. The moment of inertia of the plate about the axis CD is then equal to

(a) I (b) $I\sin^2\theta$ (c) $I\cos^2\theta$ (d) $I\cos^2\left(\frac{\theta}{2}\right)$

16. The moment of inertia of a hollow cubical box of mass M and side a about an axis passing through the centres of two opposite faces is equal to

(a) $\frac{5Ma^2}{3}$ (b) $\frac{5Ma^2}{6}$ (c) $\frac{5Ma^2}{12}$ (d) $\frac{5Ma^2}{18}$

17. The moment of inertia of a cylinder about its own axis is equal to its moment of inertia about an axis passing through its centre and perpendicular to its length. The ratio of length to radius is

(a) $2:1$ (b) $\sqrt{2}:1$

(c) $\sqrt{3}:1$ (d) $3:1$

18. A uniform solid sphere of radius R has a cavity of radius $R/2$ as shown. Mass of this system is M. Find moment of inertia of this sphere about an axis passing through centre of sphere.

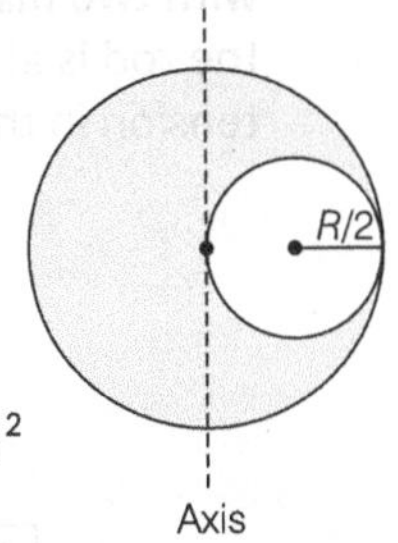

(a) $\frac{57}{140}MR^2$ (b) $\frac{16}{35}MR^2$

(c) $\frac{MR^2}{28}$ (d) $\frac{1}{20}MR^2$

19. Find force F required to keep the system in equilibrium. The dimensions of the system are $d = 0.3$ m and $a = 0.2$ m. Assume the rods to be massless.

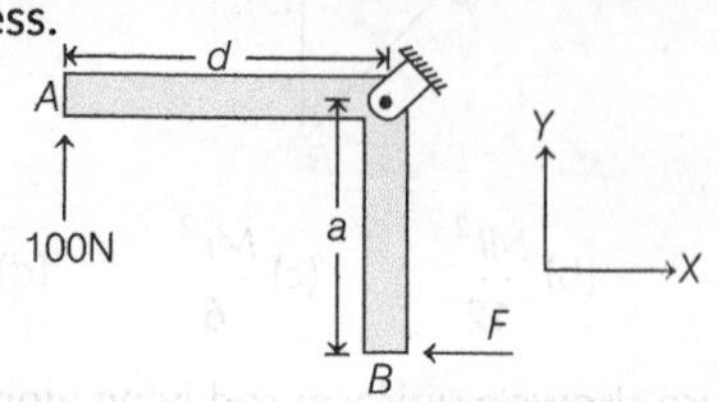

(a) $150(\hat{i})$ (b) $150(-\hat{k})$
(c) $150(-\hat{i})$ (d) It cannot be in equilibrium

20. Two persons of equal height are carrying a long uniform wooden beam of length l. They are at distance $l/4$ and $l/6$ from nearest end of the rod. The ratio of normal reaction at their heads is

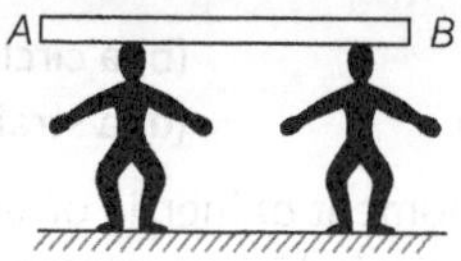

(a) 2 : 3 (b) 1 : 3 (c) 4 : 3 (d) 1 : 2

21. Figure shows a pair of pin jointed gripper tongs holding an object weighing 2000 N. The coefficient of friction μ at the gripping surface is 0.1. X-X' is the line of action of the input force and Y-Y' is the line of application of normal gripping force. If the pin-joint is assumed as frictionless, the magnitude of force F required to hold the weight is

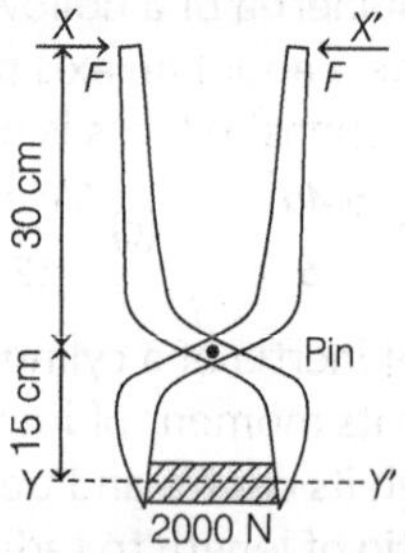

(a) 1000 N (b) 2000 N (c) 2500 N (d) 5000 N

22. A uniform rod of mass $3m$ and length L is suspended with two massless strings as shown in the figure. If the rod is at rest in a horizontal position the ratio of tension in the two strings T_1/T_2 is

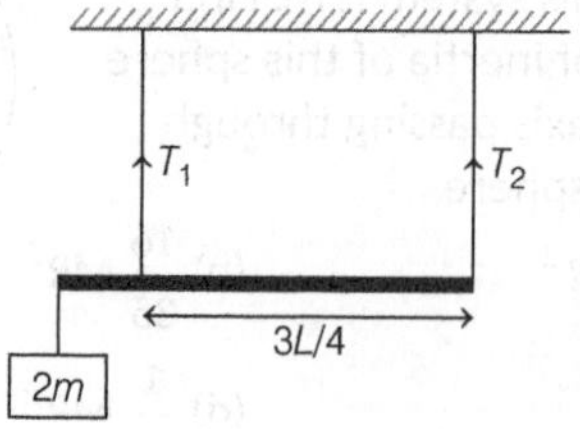

(a) 1 : 14 (b) 14 : 1 (c) 14 : 3 (d) 3 : 14

23. A ladder 5 m long rests on a rough horizontal plane and against a smooth vertical wall. The ladder is about to slip on the rough plane when its lower end is at a distance 4 m from the wall. The coefficient of friction is

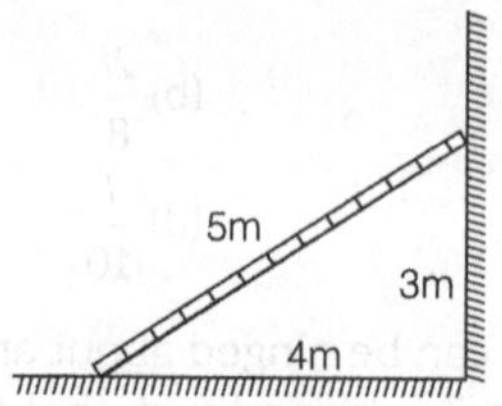

(a) $\frac{2}{3}$ (b) $\frac{1}{2}$ (c) $\frac{3}{5}$ (d) $\frac{4}{5}$

24. A smooth rod of length l is kept inside a trolley at an angle θ as shown in the figure. What should be the acceleration a of the trolley, so that the rod remains in equilibrium with respect to it?

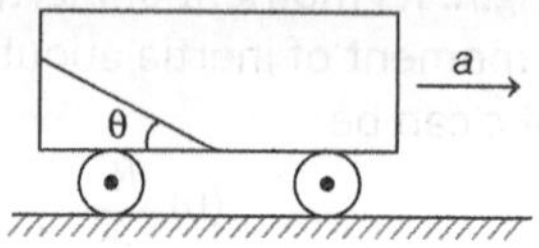

(a) $g \tan\theta$ (b) $g \cos\theta$ (c) $g \sin\theta$ (d) $g \cot\theta$

25. A thin hoop of weight 500 N and radius 1 m rests on a rough inclined plane as shown in the figure. The minimum coefficient of friction needed for this configuration is

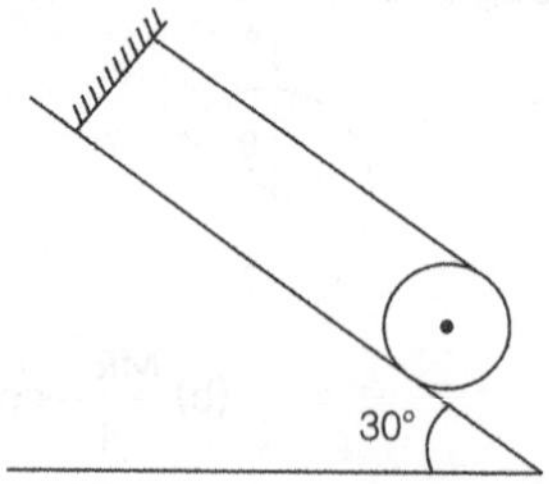

(a) $\frac{1}{3\sqrt{3}}$ (b) $\frac{1}{\sqrt{3}}$
(c) $\frac{1}{2}$ (d) $\frac{1}{2\sqrt{3}}$

26. Two uniform rods of equal length but different masses are rigidly joined to form an L-shaped body, which is then pivoted about O as shown. If in equilibrium the body is in the shown configuration, ratio M/m will be

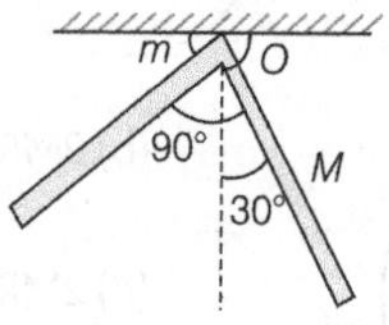

(a) 2 (b) 3 (c) $\sqrt{2}$ (d) $\sqrt{3}$

27. Two equal rods each of length $2l$ and weight w are freely joined at one end. The system is placed in a vertical position with the other ends of the two rods on a smooth horizontal plane and the middle points of the rods are joined by a string of length L which is kept taut in equilibrium position. The tension of the string is

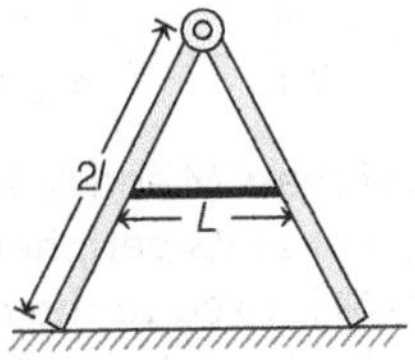

(a) $\frac{wL}{2l}$ (b) $\frac{wl}{\sqrt{4l^2 - L^2}}$

(c) $\frac{2wl}{\sqrt{4l^2 - L^2}}$ (d) $\frac{wL}{\sqrt{4l^2 - L^2}}$

28. In figure the uniform gate weighs 300 N and is 3 m wide and 2 m high. It is supported by a hinge at the bottom left corner and a horizontal cable at the top left corner, as shown , the tension in the cable and the force that the hinge exerts on the gate (magnitude and direction)

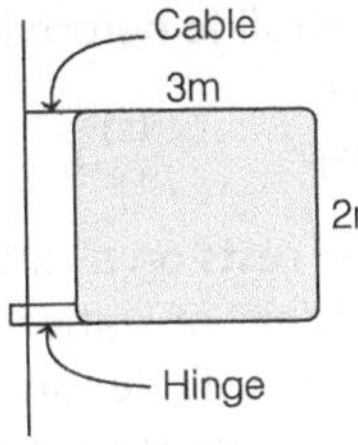

(a) $T = 225$ N , $F_X = 225$ N, $F_Y = 300$ N
(b) $T = 300$ N , $F_X = 225$ N, $F_Y = 300$ N
(c) $T = 225$ N , $F_X = 300$ N, $F_Y = 250$ N
(d) $T = 300$ N , $F_X = 300$ N, $F_Y = 250$ N

29. A light rod of length 1 m pivoted at its centre and two masses of 5 kg and 2 kg are hung from the ends as shown in figure. Assuming that it was horizontal in the beginning, the initial angular acceleration of the rod is [$g = 10$ m/s^2]

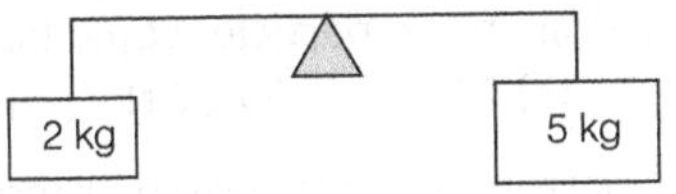

(a) 8.2 rad/s^2 (b) 8.6 rad/s^2
(c) 7.2 rad/s^2 (d) 6.2 rad/s^2

30. In the arrangement shown in figure, two equal masses hung from light cords wrapped around a uniform solid cylinder of mass M and radius R. The cylinder is free to rotate about a horizontal axis. If the system is released from rest, then, the linear acceleration of each mass is

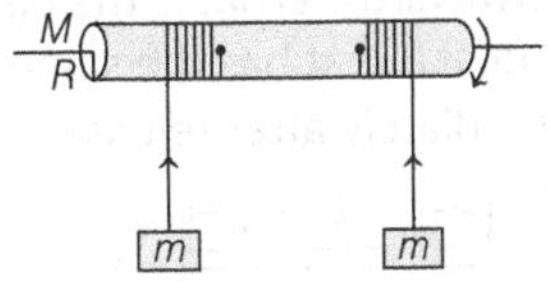

(a) $\frac{2mg}{M + 4m}$ (b) $\frac{mg}{M + m}$

(c) $\frac{4mg}{M + 4m}$ (d) $\frac{2mg}{M + 4m}$

31. The moment of inertia of the pulley system shown in figure is 4 kgm^2. The radii of bigger and smaller pulleys are 2 m and 1 m, respectively. The angular acceleration of the pulley system is

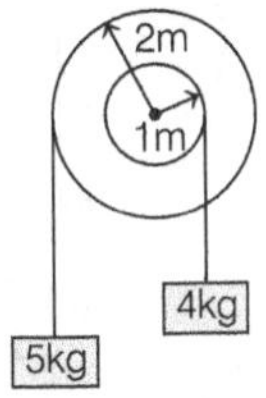

(a) 2.1 rad/s^2 (b) 4.2 rad/s^2
(c) 1.2 rad/s^2 (d) 0.6 rad/s^2

32. A wheel 4 m in diameter rotates about a fixed frictionless horizontal axis, about which its moment of inertia is 10 kg m^2. A constant tension of 40 N is maintained on a rope wrapped around the rim of the wheel. If the wheel starts from rest at $t = 0$ s, find the length of rope unwounded till $t = 3$ s.

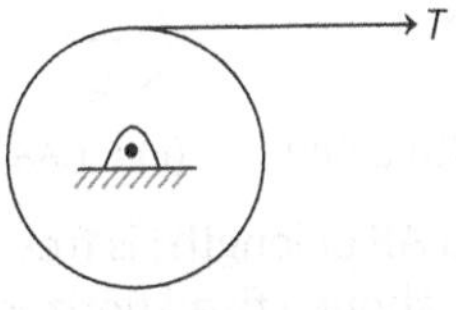

(a) 36.0 m (b) 72.0 m (c) 18.0 m (d) 720 m

33. A rod is hinged at its centre and rotated by applying a constant torque starting from rest. The power developed by the external torque as a function of time is

(a)
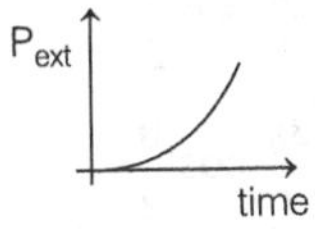

(b)
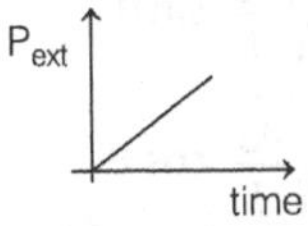

(c)
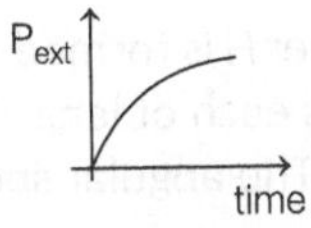

(d)
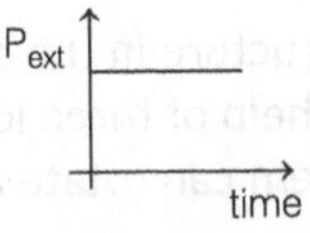

34. A uniform bar AB of mass m and a ball of the same mass are released from rest from the same horizontal position. The bar is hinged at end A. There is gravity downwards. What is the distance of the point from point B that has the same acceleration as the ball, immediately after release?

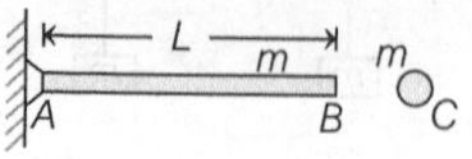

(a) $\frac{2L}{3}$ (b) $\frac{L}{3}$ (c) $\frac{L}{2}$ (d) $\frac{3L}{4}$

35. A uniform cylinder free to turn around a fixed axis has a string wrapped around it as shown to the right. The string is pulled with a force F equal to the cylinders weight. What is the acceleration of the string?

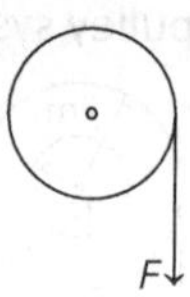

(a) $2g$ (b) g (c) $\frac{g}{2}$ (d) $\frac{g}{4}$

36. The figure shows a 15 kg solid cylinder mounted on a fixed axle, with a radius 25 cm rotating at an angular speed of 500 rotations per minute. If a 100 N braking force is applied normal to the curved surface of the cylinder bringing it to rest in 15 s, what is the coefficient of kinetic friction between the brake shoe and the cylinder (approx.)?

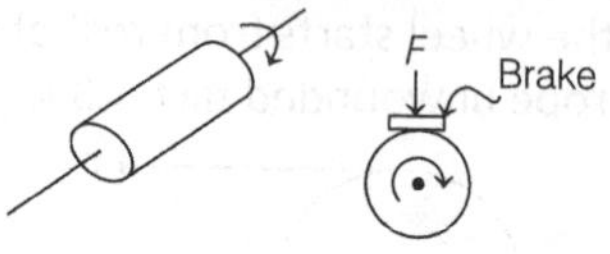

(a) 0.027 (b) 0.042 (c) 0.066 (d) 0.140

37. A uniform rod AB of length l is free to rotate in the vertical plane about a fixed horizontal axis passing through the end A. It starts rotating from rest from the vertical position as shown in figure. Its angular velocity after turning through an angle θ is

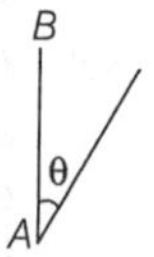

(a) $\sqrt{\frac{3g}{l}}\sin\theta$ (b) $\sqrt{\frac{6g}{l}}\sin\frac{\theta}{2}$

(c) $\sqrt{\frac{3g}{l}}\cos\theta$ (d) $\sqrt{\frac{3g}{l}}\cos\frac{\theta}{2}$

38. A structure in the shape of letter H is formed with the help of three identical rods each of length l. The system can rotate along axis I. The angular speed of the system when plane of H becomes vertical from its original position of rest along the horizontal, is

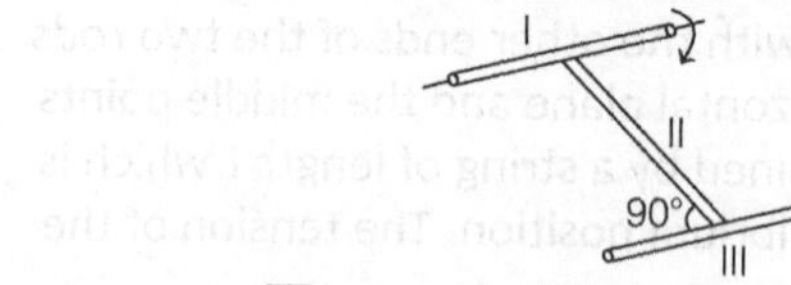

(a) $\frac{3}{2}\sqrt{\frac{g}{l}}$ (b) $\frac{2}{3}\sqrt{\frac{g}{l}}$ (c) $\frac{1}{3}\sqrt{\frac{g}{l}}$ (d) $\frac{3}{4}\sqrt{\frac{g}{l}}$

39. A uniform disc of mass M and radius R is supported vertically by a pivot at its periphery as shown. A particle of mass M is fixed to the rim and raised to the highest point above the centre. The system is then released from rest and it can rotate about its pivot freely. The angular speed of the system when the attached object is directly beneath the pivot is

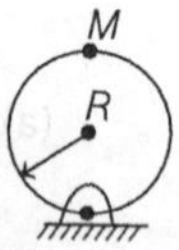

(a) $\sqrt{\frac{24g}{11R}}$ (b) $\sqrt{\frac{8g}{11R}}$ (c) $\sqrt{\frac{8g}{3R}}$ (d) $\sqrt{\frac{3g}{8R}}$

40. A cone of radius r and height h rests on a rough horizontal surface, the coefficient of friction between the cone and the surface being μ. A gradually increasing horizontal force F is applied to the vertex of the cone. The largest value of μ for which the cone will slide before it topples is

(a) $\frac{r}{2h}$ (b) $\frac{2r}{5h}$ (c) $\frac{r}{h}$ (d) $\sqrt{\frac{r}{h}}$

41. A uniform cylinder rests on a cart as shown. The coefficient of static friction between the cylinder and the cart is 0.5. If the cylinder is 4 cm in diameter and 10 cm in height, which of the following is the minimum acceleration of the cart needed to cause the cylinder to tip over?

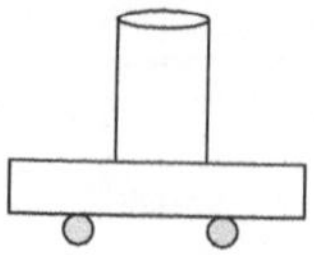

(a) 2 m/s^2
(b) 4 m/s^2
(c) 5 m/s^2
(d) The cylinder would slide before it begins to tip over.

42. The angular momentum of a particle about origin is varying as $L = 4t + 8$ (SI units) when it moves along a straight line $y = x - 4$ (x, y in meters). The magnitude of force acting on the particle would be

(a) 1 N (b) 2 N (c) $\sqrt{2}$ N (d) $\sqrt{3}$ N

43. A particle performs uniform circular motion with an angular momentum L. If the frequency of the particle's motion is tripled and its kinetic energy is halved, the angular momentum becomes

(a) $\frac{2L}{3}$ (b) $\frac{3L}{2}$ (c) $\frac{L}{6}$ (d) $6L$

44. A uniform disk turns at 2.4 rev/s around a frictionless axis. A non-rotating rod, of the same mass as the disk and length equal to the disk's diameter is dropped onto the freely spinning disk figure. They then both turn around the axis with their centres superposed. What is the angular frequency of the combination?

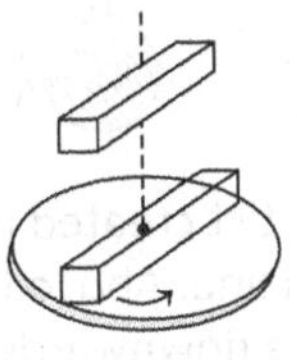

(a) 1.2 rev/s (b) 2.0 rev/s
(c) 1.44 rev/s (d) 0.96 rev/s

45. A cubical block of side *a* moving with velocity v on a horizontal smooth plane as shown. It hits a ridge at point O. The angular speed of the block after it hits O is

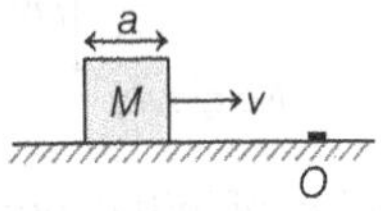

(a) $\frac{3v}{4a}$ (b) $\frac{3v}{2a}$ (c) $\frac{\sqrt{3}}{\sqrt{2}}a$ (d) zero

46. A smooth uniform rod of length *L* and mass *M* has two identical beads of negligible size, each of mass *m*, which can slide freely along the rod. Initially, the two beads are at the centre of the rod and the system is rotating with angular velocity ω_0 about an axis perpendicular to rod and passing through the midpoint of rod. There are no external forces. When the beads reach the ends of the rod, then angular velocity of the system is

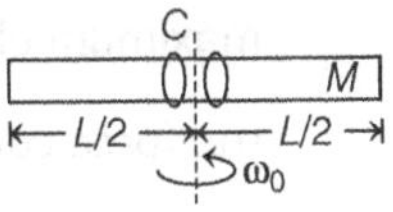

(a) $\frac{M}{M+3m}\omega_0$ (b) $\frac{M}{M+6m}\omega_0$
(c) $\frac{M+6m}{M}\omega_0$ (d) ω_0

47. A uniform rectangular plate of mass *m* which is free to rotate about the smooth vertical hinge passing through the centre and perpendicular to the plate, is lying on a smooth horizontal surface. A particle of mass *m* moving with speed *u* collides with the plate and sticks to it as shown in figure. The angular velocity of the plate after collision will be

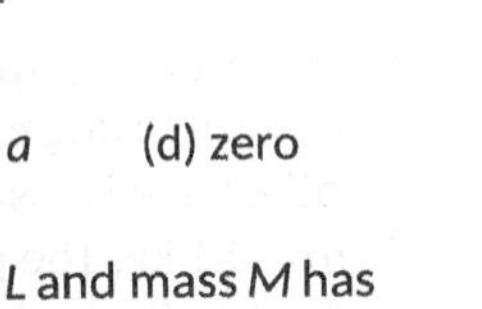

(a) $\frac{12u}{5a}$ (b) $\frac{12u}{19a}$ (c) $\frac{3u}{2a}$ (d) $\frac{3u}{5a}$

48. A circular platform is mounted on a vertical frictionless axle. Its radius is $r = 2$m and its moment of inertia $I = 220$ kgm^2. It is initially at rest. A 70 kg man stands on the edge of the platform and begins to walk along the edge at speed $v_0 = 10$ ms^{-1} relative to the platform. The angular velocity of the platform is

(a) 1.5 rad/s (b) 1.8 rad/s
(c) 2.0 rad/s (d) 2.8 rad/s

49. A uniform rod of mass *M* is hinged at its upper end. A particle of mass *m* moving horizontally strikes the rod at its mid-point elastically. If the particle comes to rest after collision, then the value of *M/m* is

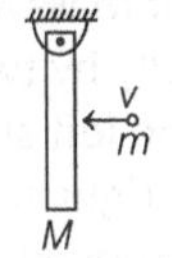

(a) $\frac{3}{4}$ (b) $\frac{4}{3}$ (c) $\frac{2}{3}$ (d) None

50. A child is standing on the edge of a merry-go-round that has the shape of a disk, as shown in the figure above. The mass of the child is 40 kg. The merry-go-round has a mass of 200 kg and a radius of 2.5 m, and it is rotating with an angular velocity of $\omega = 2.0$ rad/s. The child then walks slowly toward the center of the merry-go-round. What will be the final angular velocity of the merry-go-round when the child reaches the centre? (The size of the child can be neglected)

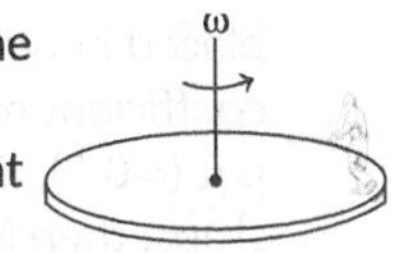

(a) 2.0 rad/s (b) 2.2 rad/s
(c) 2.4 rad/s (d) 2.8 rad/s

Numerical Value Questions

1. A square frame is made of four identical uniform rods of length 3 m and mass 0.5 kg each. What is the moment of inertia about axis which is parallel to the diagonal and is passing through a vertex in kg m^2?

2. A uniform iron ribbon of mass 3*m* and length 3*d* is bent at *B* as shown and placed on a horizontal table in vertical plane. A fly of mass *m* is sitting at point *A*. What is the angle α at which the ribbon is just about to topple ? Find 32 cos α and fill in OMR sheet.

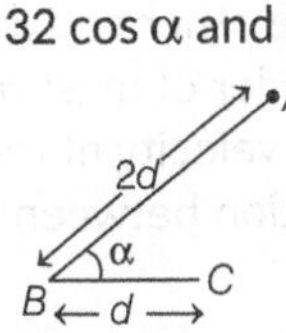

3. A drinking straw of mass $2m$ is placed on a smooth table orthogonally to the edge, such that half of it extends beyond the table. A fly of mass m lands on the A end of the straw and walks along the straw until it reaches the B end. It does not tip even when another fly gently lands on the top of the first one. If the largest mass that the second fly can have is nm then find n.

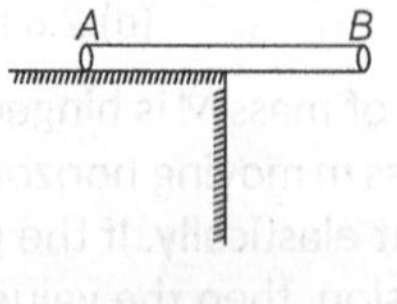

4. A uniform thin rod of mass M and length L is supported horizontally by two supports, one at each end. At time $t=0$, the left support is removed. Normal force on the right support immediately after the left support is removed is Mg/x. Fill x in OMR sheet.

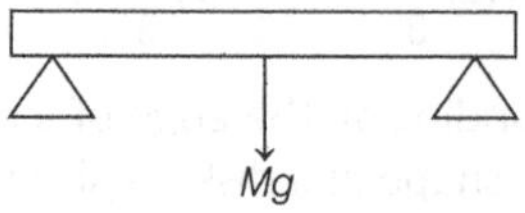

5. A uniform cylinder of radius R $(=3\text{ m})$ is spun about its axis at an angular velocity ω_0 $(=40\sqrt{\pi}\text{ rad/s})$ and placed between two perpendicular walls. The coefficient of friction between the walls and cylinder is μ $(=0.2)$. If this cylinder makes N turns before it stops, then find the value of N.

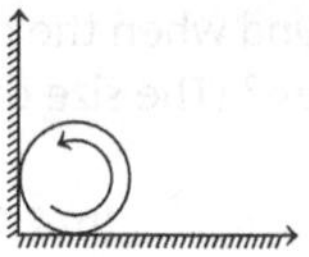

6. A semicircular disc of radius R and mass M is pulled by a horizontal force F, so that it moves with uniform velocity. The coefficient of friction between disc and ground is $\mu=\frac{4}{3\pi}$. Find the value of θ in degree.

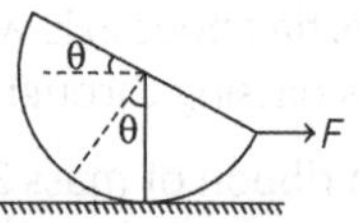

7. Figure shows a uniform rigid rod of L shape whose mass is m and is lying in a vertical plane. It is hinged at one end and the other end is rubbing with a rotating solid cylinder of mass m and radius $R=1\text{ m}$. The initial angular velocity of the cylinder is 30 rad/s. co-efficient of friction between the rod and the cylinder is $\mu=0.5$. After how much time (in s) will the cylinder stop rotating?
(Take, $g=10\text{ m/s}^2$)

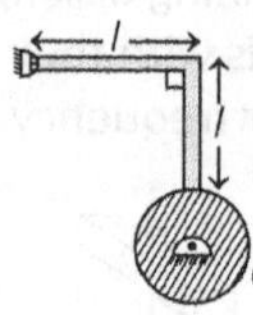

8. Some how a scientist created no gravity region below the broken line. Above the broken line gravity is unchanged i.e. g downwards. If a hinged uniform rod is released from horizontal position, then its angular speed when it becomes vertical is $\sqrt{\frac{\eta g}{4L}}$. Find η.

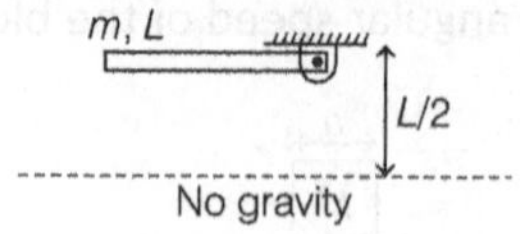

9. One side of a spring of initial, unstretched length $l_0=1\text{ m}$, lying on a frictionless table, is fixed, the other one is fastened to a small puck of mass $m=0.1\text{ kg}$. The puck is given velocity in a direction perpendicular to the spring, at an initial speed $v_0=11\text{ m/s}$. In the course of the motion, the maximum elongation of the spring is $l=\frac{l_0}{10}$. What is the force constant of the spring (in SI units)?

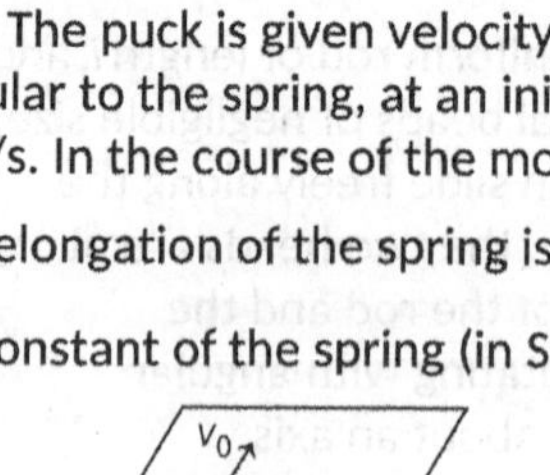

10. The pulley shown in figure has a radius of 10 cm and moment of inertia 0.1 kg-m^2. The string going over it attached at one end to a vertical spring of spring constant 100 N/m fixed from below, and supports a 11kg mass at the other end. The system is released from rest with the spring at its natural length. Find the speed (in m/s) of the block when it has descended through 10 cm. (Take, $g=10\text{ m/s}^2$ and assume that the there is no slipping between string and pulley).

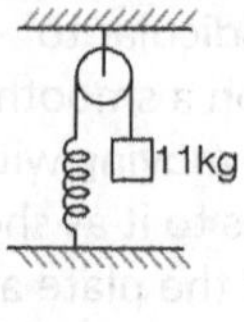

LEVEL 03 JEE Advanced Level

Single Choice Correct Questions

1. A slender rod of mass M and length L is hinged about an end to swing freely in a vertical plane. However, its density is non-uniform and varies linearly from hinged end to the free end, doubling its value. The moment of inertia of the rod, about the rotation axis passing through the hinge point is

(a) $\frac{2ML^2}{9}$ (b) $\frac{3ML^2}{16}$ (c) $\frac{7ML^2}{18}$ (d) None

2. What must be the relation between length and radius of a cylinder of given mass and density, so that its moment of inertia about an axis through its centre of mass and perpendicular to its length may be minimum?

(a) $\frac{3}{2}$ (b) $\frac{2}{3}$ (c) $\sqrt{\frac{3}{2}}$ (d) $\sqrt{\frac{2}{3}}$

3. Two identical rings each of mass m with their planes mutually perpendicular, radius R are welded at their point of contact O. If the system is free to rotate about an axis passing through the point P perpendicular to the plane of the paper, the moment of inertia of the system about this axis is equal to

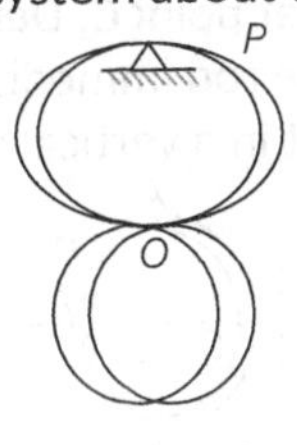

(a) 6.5 mR^2 (b) 12 mR^2
(c) 6 mR^2 (d) 11.5 mR^2

4. Figure shows an isosceles triangular plate of mass M and base length l. The apex lies at the origin and the angle at the apex is 90°. The base is parallel to X-axis. The moment of inertia of the plate about the X-axis is

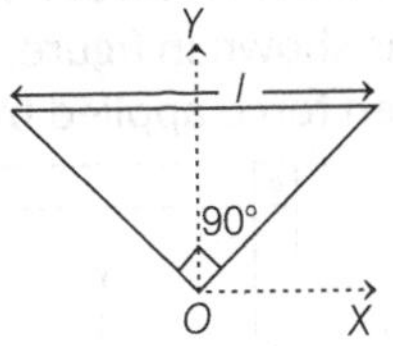

(a) $\frac{Ml^2}{6}$ (b) $\frac{Ml^2}{8}$
(c) $\frac{Ml^2}{12}$ (d) $\frac{Ml^2}{4}$

5. The radius of gyration of a solid hemisphere of mass M and radius R about an axis parallel to the diameter at a distance $\frac{3R}{4}$ from this plane is given by

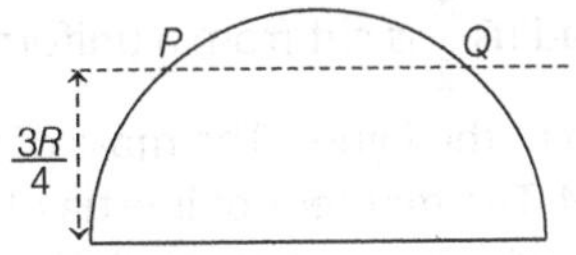

(a) $\frac{3R}{\sqrt{10}}$ (b) $\frac{5R}{4}$ (c) $\frac{5R}{8}$ (d) $\sqrt{\frac{2}{5}}R$

6. A uniform rod of mass $2M$ is bent into four adjacent semi-circles each of radius r, all lying in the same plane. The moment of inertia of the bent rod about an axis through one end A and perpendicular to plane of rod is

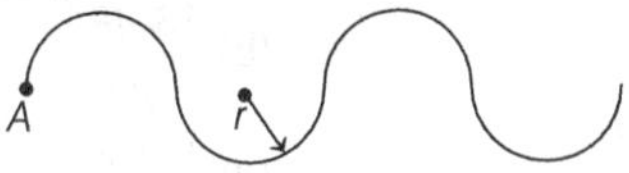

(a) 22 Mr^2 (b) 88 Mr^2
(c) 44 Mr^2 (d) 66 Mr^2

7. The moment of inertia of a cube of mass m and side a about the diagonal of one of its face is

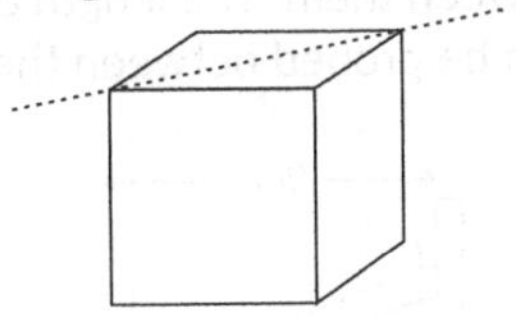

(a) $\frac{ma^2}{12}$ (b) $\frac{ma^2}{6}$
(c) $\frac{5ma^2}{12}$ (d) $\frac{2ma^2}{3}$

8. A square plate of mass M and edge L is shown in figure. The moment of inertia of the plate about the axis in the plane of plate passing through one of its vertex making an angle 15° from horizontal is

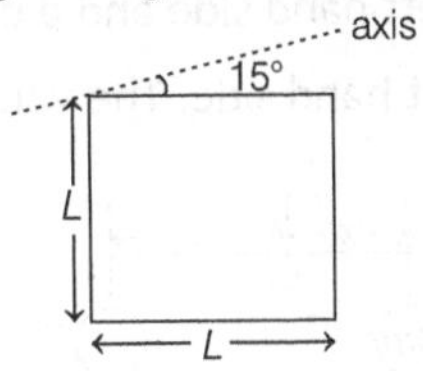

(a) $\frac{ML^2}{12}$ (b) $\frac{11ML^2}{24}$
(c) $\frac{7ML^2}{12}$ (d) None of these

9. A cubical frame is made of 12 rods each of mass M and length L. The moment of inertia of cube about its face diagonal is

(a) $\frac{19}{3}ML^2$ (b) $\frac{23}{3}ML^2$ (c) $\frac{31}{3}ML^2$ (d) $\frac{37}{3}ML^2$

10. A disc of radius $\frac{R}{2}$ is cut from a uniform disc of radius R as shown in the figure. The mass of the disc (with cavity) is M. The moment of inertia of this disc about an axis XX' which passes through the centre O of the disc and is in the plane of the disc will be

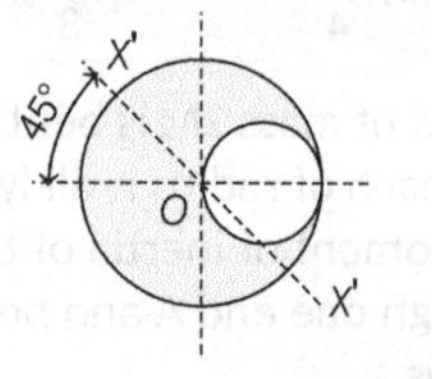

(a) $\frac{7MR^2}{12}$ (b) $\frac{13MR^2}{24}$

(c) $\frac{13MR^2}{48}$ (d) $\frac{11MR^2}{36}$

11. Two vertical walls are separated by a distance of 2 m. Wall A is smooth while wall B is rough with a coefficient of friction $\mu = 0.5$ A uniform rod is probed between them. The length of the longest rod that can be probed between the walls is equal to

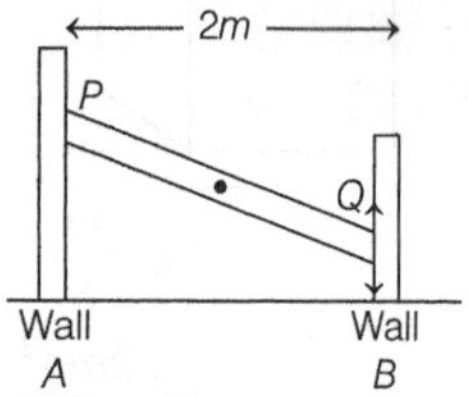

(a) 2 m (b) $2\sqrt{2}$ m

(c) $\sqrt{5}$ m (d) $\frac{\sqrt{17}}{2}$ m

12. A rigid massless beam is balanced by a particle of mass 4 m in left hand side and a pulley particle system in right hand side. The value of $\frac{x}{y}$ is

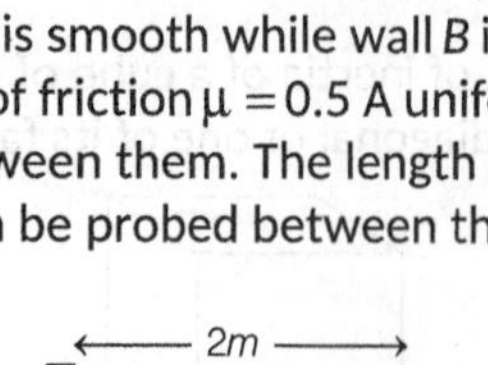

(a) $\frac{7}{6}$ (b) $\frac{5}{6}$ (c) 1 : 1 (d) $\frac{11}{12}$

13. A solid hemisphere of weight P rests with its curved surface in contact with a rough inclined plane. A weight Q is placed at some point on the rim of the hemisphere to keep its plane surface horizontal, then its minimum coefficient of friction is

(a) $\frac{Q}{\sqrt{P(P+2Q)}}$ (b) $\frac{Q}{\sqrt{P(Q+2P)}}$

(c) $\frac{P+Q}{\sqrt{P(P+2Q)}}$ (d) $\frac{P-Q}{\sqrt{P(P+2Q)}}$

14. A uniform bar of mass M and length L is hinged to a shaft which is rotating with constant angular velocity ω. Find angle made by bar with vertical in equilibrium position.

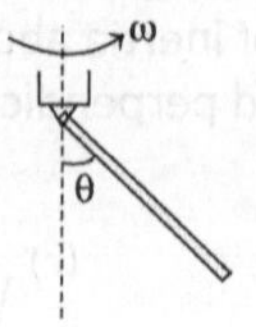

(a) $\cos^{-1}\left(\frac{g}{\omega^2 L}\right)$ (b) $\cos^{-1}\left(\frac{3g}{2\omega^2 L}\right)$

(c) $\sin^{-1}\left(\frac{g}{\omega^2 L}\right)$ (d) $\sin^{-1}\left(\frac{3g}{2\omega^2 L}\right)$

15. A uniform rod AB is bent in the shape of an arc of circle and hinged at point C. Determine the angular acceleration of the rod immediately after it is released from rest in a vertical plane.

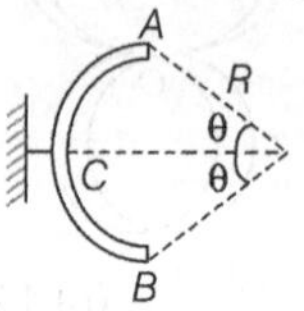

(a) $\frac{g}{R}\sin\theta$ (b) $\frac{2g}{R}\sin 2\theta$

(c) $\frac{g}{2R}$ (d) $\left(\frac{g}{2R}\right)\left(\frac{5\sin\theta}{\theta}\right)$

16. Two identical rods each of mass m and length l are hinged at one end at P. A force F is applied at one end of vertical rod as shown in figure, system is in equilibrium. Then force applied by the hinge is

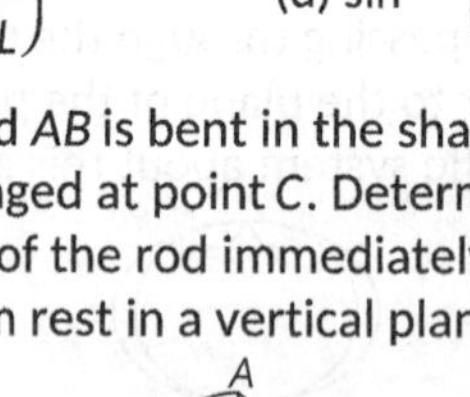

(a) $\frac{1}{2}mg\hat{i}$ (b) $-mg\hat{i} + mg\hat{j}$

(c) $-\frac{mg}{2}\hat{i} + 2mg\hat{j}$ (d) $-mg\hat{i} + 2mg\hat{j}$

17. A non-uniform rod OA of linear mass density $\lambda = \lambda_0 x$ (λ_0 = constant.) is suspended from ceiling with hinge joint O and light string as shown in figure. Find the angular acceleration of rod just after the string is cut.

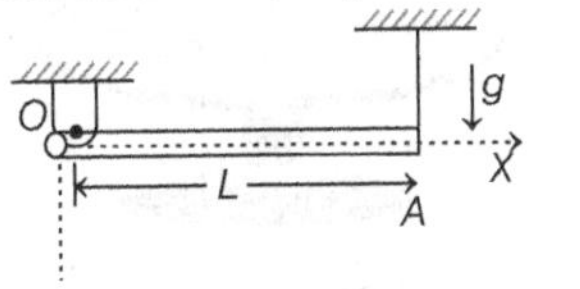

(a) $\frac{2g}{L}$ (b) $\frac{g}{L}$

(c) $\frac{4g}{3L}$ (d) none of these

18. The minimum value of θ, if the rod does not slip is

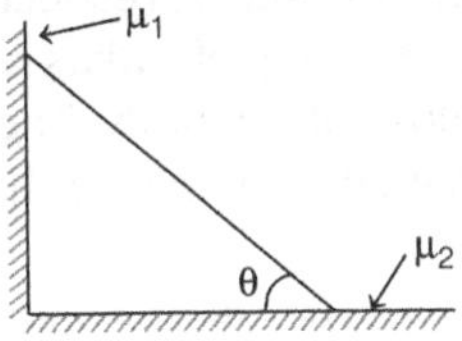

(a) 45° (b) $\tan^{-1}\left[\frac{1-\mu_1\mu_2}{2\mu_2}\right]$

(c) $\tan^{-1}\left(\frac{\mu_1}{\mu_2}\right)$ (d) $\tan^{-1}\left[\frac{1-\mu_1\mu_2}{2\mu_1}\right]$

19. Figure shows a uniform rod of $M = 5$ kg and length 8 m supported horizontally by a string of length 10 m and breaking tension 52 N. A ball of mass 1 kg starts rolling at $t = 0$ from end A with constant speed of 50 cm/s towards end B. Find the time when the string breaks. ($g = 10$ m/s^2)

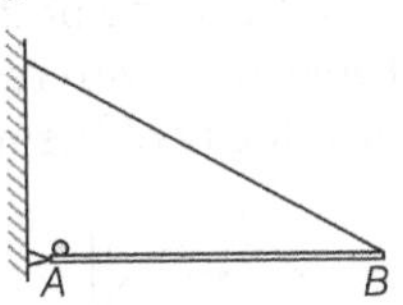

(a) 7.92 s (b) 8.92 s
(c) 9.92 s (d) 10.92 s

20. Figure shows a vertical force F that is applied tangentially to a uniform cylinder of weight w. The coefficient of static friction between the cylinder and all surfaces is 0.5. The maximum force that can be applied without causing the cylinder to rotate is

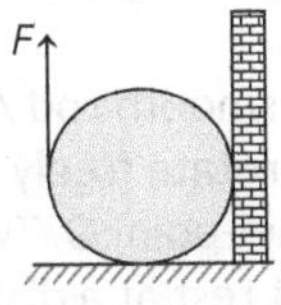

(a) $\frac{w}{2}$ (b) $\frac{w}{4}$ (c) $\frac{3w}{4}$ (d) $\frac{3w}{8}$

21. A disc of mass 54 kg and radius of gyration 0.75 m is rotating ($600/\pi$) rev/min as shown in figure. What force F must be applied to braking mechanism to stop the disc in 25 s? Coefficient of friction between the disc and rod is 0.3. (Neglect mass of the rod)

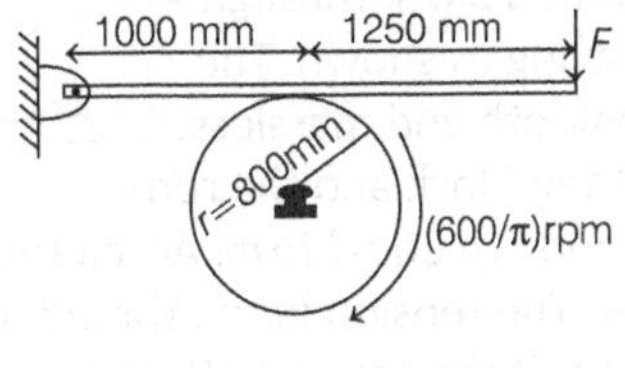

(a) 30 N (b) 45 N (c) 60 N (d) 75 N

22. A uniform block A of mass 25 kg and length 6 m is hinged at C and is supported by a small block B as shown in the Figure . A constant force F of magnitude 157.5 N is applied to block B horizontally . What is the speed of B after it moves 1.5 m ? The mass of block B is 2.5 kg and the coefficient of friction for all contact surfaces is 0.3. [Use, ln (3/2) ≅ 0.4 and $g = 10$ ms^{-2}]

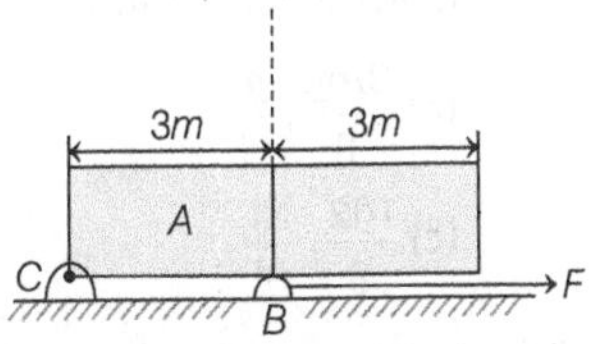

(a) 2 m/s (b) 6 m/s (c) 8 m/s (d) 10 m/s

23. A sphere is placed rotating with its centre initially at rest in a corner as shown in figure (a) and (b). Coefficient of friction between all surfaces and the sphere is 1/3 . The ratio of the frictional force $\frac{f_a}{f_b}$ by ground in situations (a) & (b) is

(a) (b)

(a) 1 (b) $\frac{9}{10}$

(c) $\frac{10}{9}$ (d) None of these

24. A uniform rod of mass m and length l can rotate in vertical plane about a smooth horizontal axis hinged at point H. It is released from rest making an angle of 37° with horizontal. The force exerted by the hinge just after the rod is released is

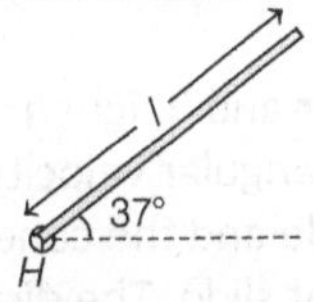

(a) $\frac{9mg}{25}$ (b) $\frac{13mg}{25}$ (c) $\frac{mg\sqrt{10}}{5}$ (d) $\frac{mg\sqrt{10}}{25}$

25. Uniform rod AB is hinged at the end A in a horizontal position as shown in the figure (the hinge is frictionless, that is, it does not exert any friction force on the rod). The other end of the rod is connected to a block through a massless string as shown. The pulley is smooth and massless. Masses of the block and the rod are same and are equal to m. Acceleration due to gravity is g. The tension in the thread, and angular acceleration of the rod just after release of block from this position

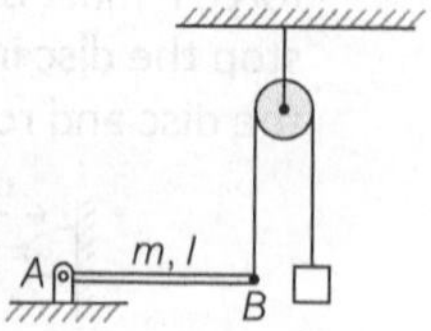

(a) $\frac{3mg}{8}, \frac{g}{8l}$ (b) $\frac{5mg}{8}, \frac{3g}{8l}$

(c) $\frac{mg}{8}, \frac{5g}{8l}$ (d) $\frac{7mg}{8}, \frac{7g}{8l}$

26. In the system shown in figure blocks A and B have masses $m_1 = 2$ kg and $m_2 = \frac{26}{7}$ kg, respectively.

Pulley having moment of inertia, $I = 0.11$ kg-m^2 can rotate without friction about a fixed axis. Inner and outer radii of pulley are $a = 10$ cm and $b = 15$ cm respectively. B is hanging with the thread wrapped around the pulley, while A lies on a rough inclined plane. Coefficient of friction being $\mu = \frac{\sqrt{3}}{10}$.

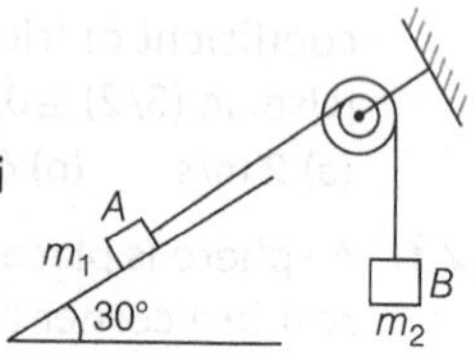

Acceleration of 2 kg block is
($g = 10$ ms^{-2})

(a) 2 ms^{-2} (b) 3 ms^{-2}

(c) 4 ms^{-2} (d) 5 ms^{-2}

27. A uniform hemi-solid sphere is placed with flat surface on rough inclined plane as shown in figure. If friction is large for no sliding, then the minimum angle θ at which toppling occur is

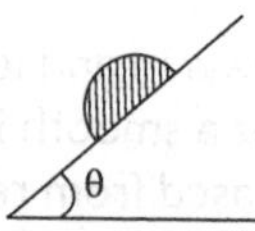

(a) $\tan^{-1}\left(\frac{1}{2}\right)$ (b) 45° (c) $\tan^{-1}\left(\frac{8}{3}\right)$ (d) $\tan^{-1}\left(\frac{4}{3}\right)$

28. A cone of radius r and height h is kept on a turntable rotating with an angular velocity. The friction between the table and the cone is sufficient so that the cone does not slide. The distance between the axis of the cone and the axis of turntable is R ($R >> r$). The maximum value of ω for which the cone does not topple is

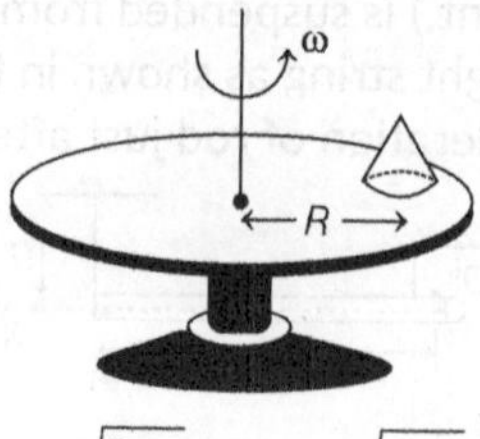

(a) $\sqrt{\frac{gr}{Rh}}$ (b) $\sqrt{\frac{2gr}{Rh}}$ (c) $\sqrt{\frac{3gr}{Rh}}$ (d) $\sqrt{\frac{4gr}{Rh}}$

29. A solid uniform cylindrical rod of radius r has a conical nose is placed on smooth horizontal surface as shown in figure. The length of the cylindrical and conical nose are $4r$ and $3r$, respectively. Mass of the conical part is M. A ring of radius $r/2$ is to be tightly fitted on the nose of the body. The maximum permissible mass of the ring, so that the body does not topple is

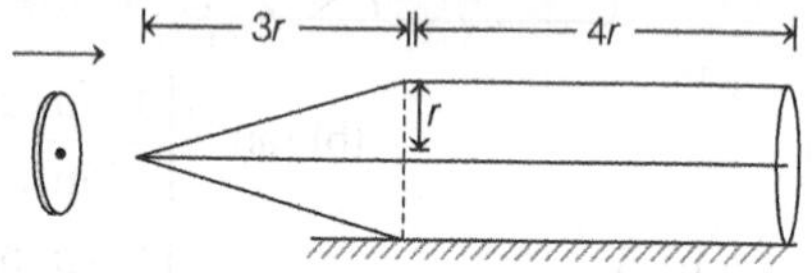

(a) $\frac{21M}{5}$ (b) $\frac{29M}{6}$

(c) $\frac{11M}{3}$ (d) $\frac{16M}{3}$

30. A child with mass m is standing at the edge of a merry-go-round having moment of inertia I, radius R and initial angular velocity ω as shown in the figure. The child jumps off the edge of the merry-go-round with tangential velocity v with respect to the ground. The new angular velocity of the merry-go-round is

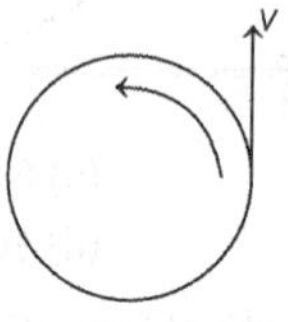

(a) $\sqrt{\frac{I\omega^2 - mv^2}{I}}$ (b) $\sqrt{\frac{(I + mR^2)\omega^2 - mv^2}{I}}$

(c) $\frac{I\omega - mvR}{I}$ (d) $\frac{(I + mR^2)\omega - mvR}{I}$

31. A rigid horizontal smooth rod AB of mass 0.75 kg and length 40 cm can rotate freely about a fixed vertical axis through its mid-point O. Two rings each of mass 1 kg are initially at rest at a distance of 10 cm from O on either side of the rod. The rod is set in rotation with an angular velocity of 30 rad/s. The velocity of each ring along the length of the rod, then they reach the ends of the rod is

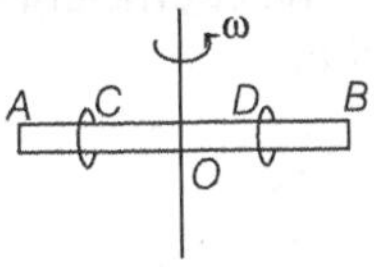

(a) 3 m/s (b) 2 m/s
(c) 1 m/s (d) 0.5 m/s

32. A uniform disc of mass m_0 rotates freely about a fixed horizontal axis passing through its centre. A thin cotton pad is fixed to its rim, which can absorb water. The mass of water dripping onto the pad per unit time is μ. After what time will the angular velocity of the disc get reduced to half its initial value ?

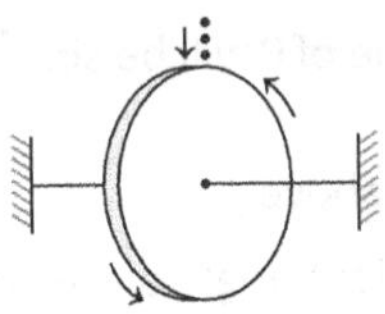

(a) $\frac{2m_0}{\mu}$ (b) $\frac{3m_0}{\mu}$ (c) $\frac{m_0}{\mu}$ (d) $\frac{m_0}{2\mu}$

33. A thin uniform straight rod of mass 2 kg and length 1 m is free to rotate about its upper end when at rest. It receives an impulsive blow of 10 Ns at its lowest point, normal to its length as shown in figure. The kinetic energy of rod just after impact is

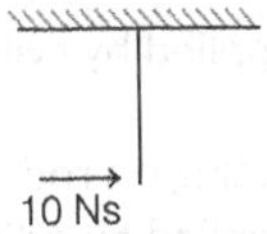

(a) 75 J (b) 100 J
(c) 200 J (d) None of these

34. A cube with sides of length $2a$ and mass M is moving with an initial speed v_0 along a frictionless table. When the cube reaches the end of the table it is caught abruptly by a short lip and begins to rotate. The minimum speed v_0 such that the cube falls off the table is

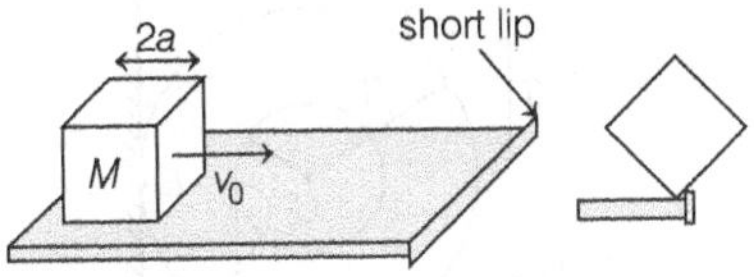

(a) $\sqrt{\frac{16ag(\sqrt{2}-1)}{3}}$ (b) $\sqrt{16ag(\sqrt{2}-1)}$

(c) $\sqrt{ag(\sqrt{2}-1)}$ (d) $\sqrt{\frac{ag}{3}(\sqrt{2}-1)}$

Multiple Choice(s) Correct Questions

1. Three particles, each of mass m are placed at the points (x_1, y_1, z_1), (x_2, y_2, z_2) and (x_3, y_3, z_3) on the inner surface of a paraboloid of revolution obtained by rotating the parabola, $x^2 = 4ay$ about the Y-axis. Neglect the mass of the paraboloid. (Y-axis is along the vertical)

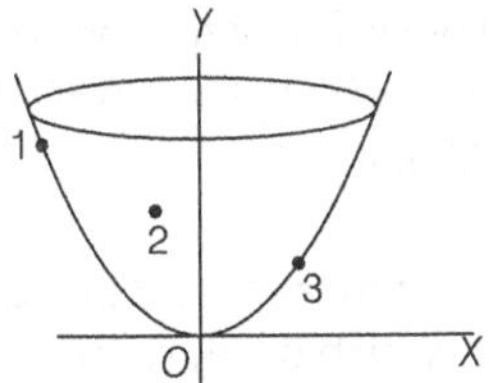

(a) The moment of inertia of the system about the axis of the paraboloid is $I = 4ma(y_1 + y_2 + y_3)$.
(b) If potential energy at O is taken to be zero, the potential energy of the system is $mg(y_1 + y_2 + y_3)$.
(c) If the particle at (x_1, y_1, z_1) slides down the smooth surface, its speed at O is $\sqrt{2gy_1}$
(d) If the paraboloid spins about OY with an angular speed ω, the kinetic energy of the system will be $2ma(y_1 + y_2 + y_3)\omega^2$.

2. A rigid body is in pure rotation.
(a) You can find two points in the body in a plane perpendicular to the axis of rotation having same velocity.
(b) You can find two points in the body in a plane perpendicular to the axis of rotation having same acceleration.
(c) Speed of all the particles lying on the curved surface of a cylinder whose axis coincides with the axis of rotation is same.
(d) Angular speed of the body is same as seen from any point in the body.

3. In the figure shown, the rod is uniform and has a mass m, length L. The horizontal thread is connected to the rod at a point at a distance $\frac{L}{3}$ along the rod from lower end and angle between rod and wall is 60°.

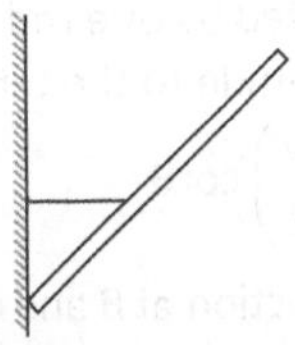

(a) In equilibrium, tension in the thread is $\frac{3mg}{2}$.

(b) In equilibrium, tension in the thread is $\frac{3\sqrt{3}mg}{2}$.

(c) The minimum value of friction coefficient between the lower end of rod and the vertical wall for the rod be in equilibrium is $\frac{2}{3\sqrt{3}}$.

(d) The minimum value of friction coefficient between the lower end of rod and the vertical wall for the rod be in equilibrium is $\frac{2}{3}$.

4. A uniform rod of mass M and length L is hinged at point A about which it can rotate freely. The rod is kept horizontal by means of a vertical string as shown. A small block is placed at other end B of the rod. Now string is cut, then

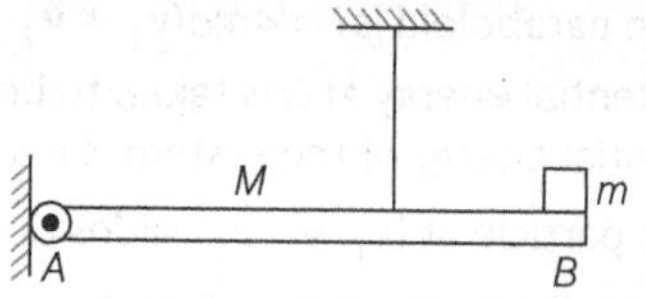

(a) Just after cut relative acceleration between block m and end B of the rod is $\frac{g}{2}$.

(b) Just after cut relative acceleration between block m and end B of the rod is zero.

(c) Tension in the rod at its mid-point when the rod becomes vertical is $\frac{13Mg}{8}$.

(d) Tension in the rod at its mid-point when the rod becomes vertical is $\frac{9Mg}{8}$.

5. Two uniform equal ladders AB and AC, each of weight w lean against each other and a string is tied between E and F. They stand on a smooth horizontal surface. Then

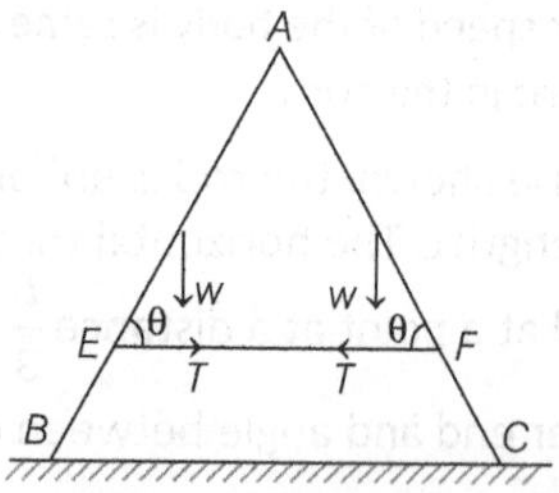

(a) the force exerted by one rod on the other at A is equal in magnitude to the tension T in the string

(b) tension $T = \left(\frac{w}{2}\right)\cot\theta$

(c) the normal reaction at B and C are equal

(d) the normal reaction at B or C is greater than w

6. A semi-circular disc rests in a vertical plane with its curved edge on rough horizontal and equally rough vertical surface. The coefficient of friction is μ for both surfaces, then

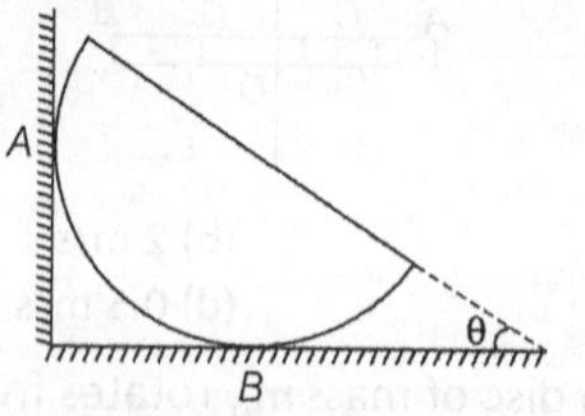

(a) friction acts upwards at A and towards left at B

(b) for greatest value of θ (for no slipping) normal contact force at A is $\frac{\mu w}{1+\mu^2}$, where w = weight of disc

(c) greatest value of θ will be $\sin^{-1}\left[\frac{3\pi}{4}\left(\frac{\mu+\mu^2}{1+\mu^2}\right)\right]$

(d) None of the above

7. A rod bent at right angle along its centre line, is placed on a rough horizontal fixed cylinder of radius R as shown in figure. Mass of rod is $2m$ and rod is in equilibrium.

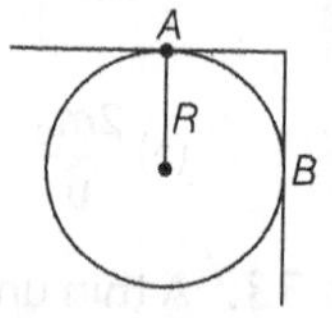

Assume that friction force on rod at A and B are equal in magnitude.

(a) Normal force applied by cylinder on rod at A is $\frac{3mg}{2}$.

(b) Normal force applied by cylinder on rod at B must be zero.

(c) Friction force acting on rod at B is upward.

(d) Normal force applied by cylinder on rod at A is mg.

8. A massless spool of inner radius r, outer radius R is placed against vertical wall and tilted split floor as shown. A light inextensible thread is tightly wound around the spool through which a mass m is hanging. There exists no friction at point A, while the coefficient of friction between spool and point B is μ. The angle between two surfaces is θ.

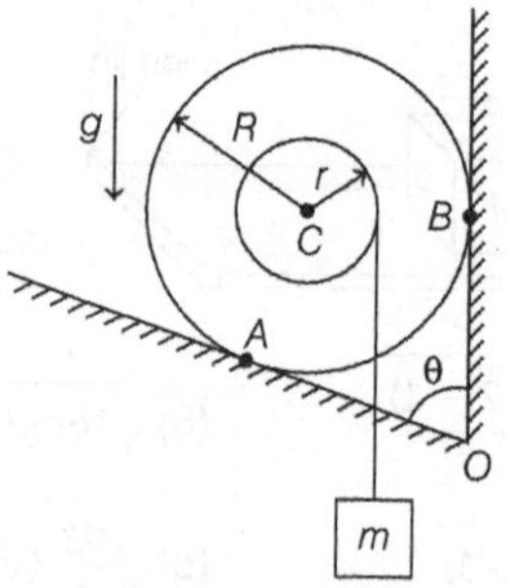

(a) the magnitude of force on the spool at B in order to maintain equilibrium is $mg\sqrt{\left(\frac{r}{R}\right)^2+\left(1-\frac{r}{R}\right)^2\frac{1}{\tan^2\theta}}$

(b) the magnitude of force on the spool at B in order to maintain equilibrium is $mg\left(1-\frac{r}{R}\right)\frac{1}{\tan\theta}$

(c) the minimum value of μ for the system to remain in equilibrium is $\frac{\cot\theta}{\left(\frac{R}{r}\right)-1}$

(d) the minimum value of μ for the system to remain in equilibrium is $\frac{\tan\theta}{\left(\frac{R}{r}\right)-1}$

9. A block with a square base ($a \times a$) and height h, is placed on an inclined plane. The coefficient of friction is μ. The angle of inclination θ of the plane is gradually increased. The block will

(a) topple before sliding if $\mu > \frac{a}{h}$

(b) topple before sliding if $\mu < \frac{a}{h}$

(c) slide before toppling if $\mu > \frac{a}{h}$

(d) slide before toppling if $\mu < \frac{a}{h}$

10. A uniform rod of mass $M = 2$kg and length L is suspended by two smooth hinges 1 and 2 as shown in the figure. A force $F = 4$ N is applied downward at a distance $\frac{L}{4}$ from the hinge 2. Due to the application of force F, the hinge 2 breaks. At this instant, applied force F is also removed. The rod starts to rotate downward about hinge 1. ($g = 10$ m/s^2). Choose the correct statement(s).

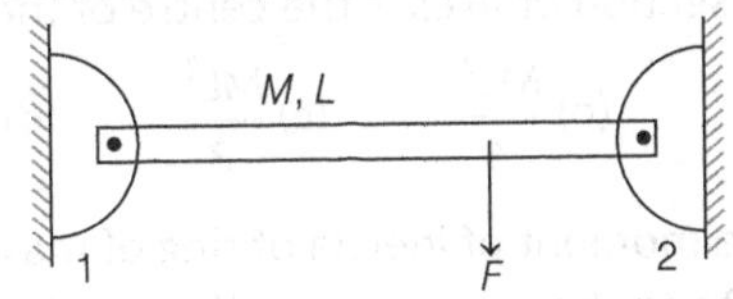

(a) The reaction at hinge 1, before hinge 2 breaks, is 11 N.

(b) The reaction at hinge 1, before hinge 2 breaks, is 24 N.

(c) The reaction at hinge 1, just after breaking of hinge 2 is 5 N.

(d) The reaction at hinge 1, just after breaking of hinge 2 is 8 N.

11. A uniform rod AB of length l and mass M hangs from point A at which it is freely hinged in a car moving with velocity v_0. The rod can rotate in vertical plane about the axis at A. If the car suddenly stops,

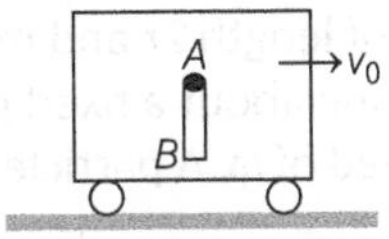

(a) the angular speed ω with which the rod starts rotating is $\frac{3v_0}{2l}$

(b) the minimum value of v_0, so that the rod completes the rotation is $\sqrt{\frac{8}{3}gl}$

(c) loss of energy during the process is $\frac{1}{8}Mv_0^2$

(d) there is no loss of energy

12. In the figure, the block on the smooth table is set into motion in a circular orbit of radius r around the centre hole. The hanging mass is identical to the mass on the table and remains in equilibrium (Neglect friction). The string connecting the two blocks is massless and inextensible. Select the correct answer.

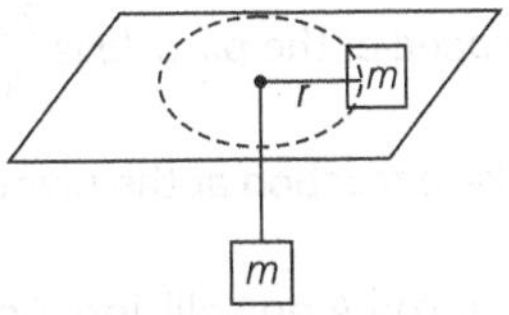

(a) The angular speed ω of the block in its circular motion is $\sqrt{\frac{g}{r}}$

(b) Kinetic energy as function of r is given by $\frac{mgr}{2}$

(c) Angular momentum about the hole is conserved even if hanging block is pulled down.

(d) The block on table is in equilibrium.

13. A particle of mass m is suspended from point O and undergoes circular motion in horizontal plane as conical pendulum as shown in figure.

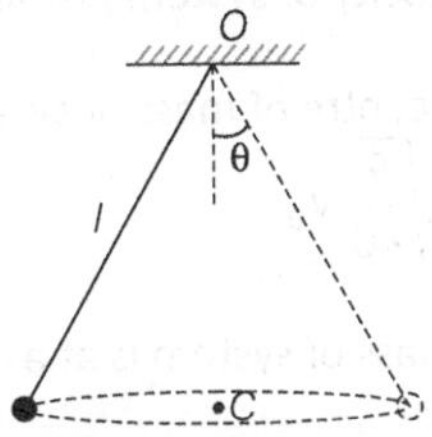

(a) Angular momentum of particle about point of suspension does not remain constant.

(b) Angular momentum of particle about centre of circle remains constant.

(c) Average force during half rotation is $\frac{2mg \tan\theta}{\pi}$

(d) Average torque about axis OC during half rotation is zero.

14. A uniform rod of length $2r$ and mass m is rotating in a horizontal plane about a fixed pivot through centre at a steady speed of ω. A particle of mass m moving with speed $\frac{\omega r}{4}$ strikes an end of the rod perpendicularly. The rod and the particle are moving towards each other and the coefficient of restitution is 1/2.

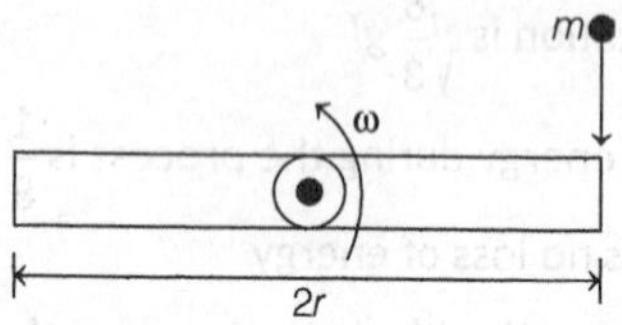

(a) The new angular speed of the rod is $\frac{13\omega}{32}$ in clockwise direction as seen from the above.

(b) The new angular speed of the rod is $\frac{13\omega}{32}$ in anti-clockwise direction as seen from the above.

(c) The new speed of the particle is $\frac{7\omega r}{32}$.

(d) The impulsive reaction at the pivot is $\frac{15m\omega r}{32}$.

15. Rod B sticks to rod A on collision. Collision takes place on horizontal plane. Rod A is hinged at O. Friction is absent everywhere.

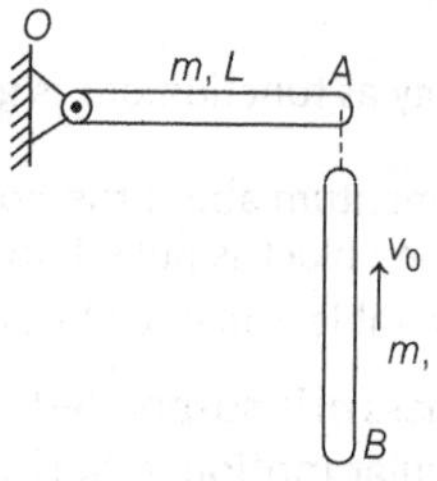

(a) Angular velocity of system just after collision is $\frac{2v_0}{5L}$

(b) Velocity of centre of mass of system just after collision is $\sqrt{\frac{9}{40}}\, v_0$

(c) Centre of mass of system is at a distance of $\frac{\sqrt{10}\, L}{4}$ from O

(d) Kinetic energy of system just after collision is $\frac{9}{40} mv^2$.

Comprehension Based Questions

Comprehension-1

In the treatment of moments of inertia, introductory textbooks often present two theorems, generally called the parallel axis theorem and the perpendicular axis theorem. There is another theorem of this same genre, which is not usually included, but which is interesting and useful. It is $I_x + I_y + I_z = 2\,\Sigma m_i r_i^2$. Here, I_x, I_y and I_z are the moments of inertia about three mutually perpendicular intersecting axes, m_i is the mass of the ith particle and r_i is its distance from the intersection. The proof is simple : taking the three axes as coordinate axes, we have

$$I_x + I_y + I_z$$
$$= \Sigma m_i (y_i^2 + z_i^2) + \Sigma m_i (z_i^2 + x_i^2) + \Sigma m_i (x_i^2 + y_i^2)$$
$$= 2\Sigma m_i (x_i^2 + y_i^2 + z_i^2) = 2\Sigma m_i r_i^2$$

One important application is the calculation of the moment of inertia I_d of a uniform thin-walled spherical shell, of mass M and radius R, about a diameter. Taking the center as the origin of coordinates, we have $I_x = I_y = I_z = I_d$, and $r_i = R$. The theorem gives $3I_d = 2\Sigma m_i R^2 = 2(\Sigma m_i)R^2 = 2MR^2$

Therefore, $I_d = \frac{2MR^2}{3}$.

1. Which of following can be derived from above theorem?

(a) Parallel axis theorem
(b) Perpendicular axis theorem
(c) Both
(d) None of these

2. Consider a solid cube of mass m and side L. What will be the value of $\Sigma m_i r_i^2$ for this body, when the point of intersection of axes is the centre of the cube?

(a) $\frac{ML^2}{2}$ (b) $\frac{ML^2}{4}$ (c) $\frac{ML^2}{3}$ (d) $\frac{ML^2}{6}$

3. Find the moment of inertia of ring of mass m and radius R about an axis passing through its centre and making an angle of 45° with its plane

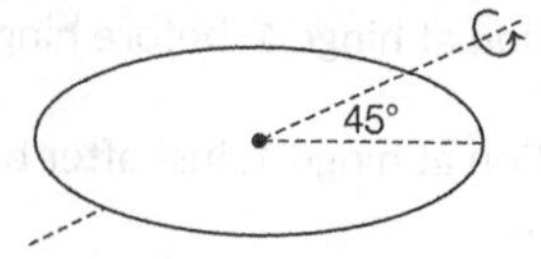

(a) $\frac{MR^2}{4}$ (b) $\frac{MR^2}{2}$ (c) $\frac{3}{4}MR^2$ (d) MR^2

Comprehension-2

A horizontal uniform rod of mass m has its left end hinged to the fixed inclined plane, while its right end rests on the top of a uniform cylinder of mass m which in turn is at rest on the fixed inclined plane as shown. The coefficient of friction between the cylinder and rod, and between the cylinder and inclined plane, is sufficient to keep the cylinder at rest

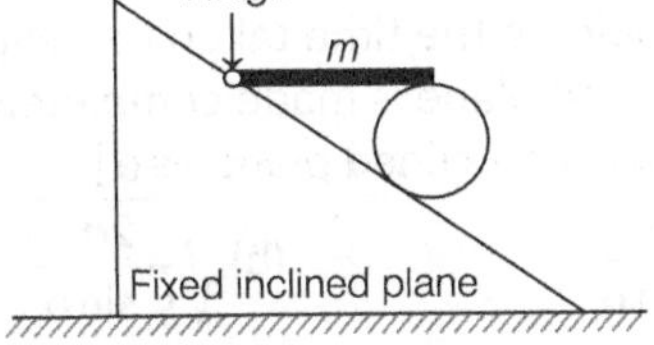

4. The magnitude of normal reaction exerted by the rod on the cylinder is

(a) $\frac{mg}{4}$ (b) $\frac{mg}{3}$ (c) $\frac{mg}{2}$ (d) $\frac{2mg}{3}$

5. The ratio of magnitude of frictional force on the cylinder due to the rod and the magnitude of frictional force on the cylinder due to the inclined plane is

(a) 1 : 1 (b) $2:\sqrt{3}$ (c) 2 : 1 (d) $\sqrt{2}:1$

6. The magnitude of normal reaction exerted by the inclined plane on the cylinder is

(a) mg (b) $\frac{3mg}{2}$ (c) $2mg$ (d) $\frac{5mg}{4}$

Comprehension-3

There is a man of mass 100 kg sitting on a motorbike of mass 150 kg. The distance of the axles of the wheels (wheelbase) is 1.5 m. The common mass center of the man and the motorbike is at a 1 m height above the ground level, and at a 0.6 m distance from the vertical line going through the rear axle.

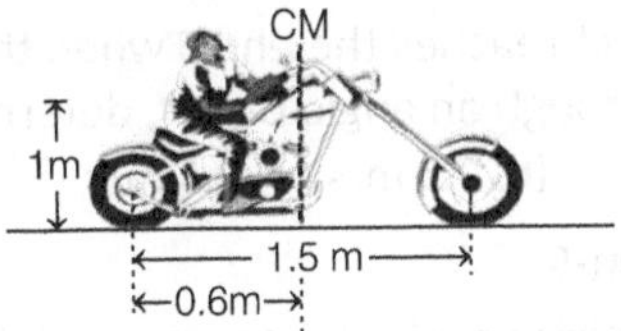

7. What normal force is exerted on the rear wheel by the ground, when the motorbike starts off with an acceleration of $a = 2\ \text{m/s}^2$?

(a) 1000 N (b) 1250 N

(c) $\frac{2000}{3}$ N (d) $\frac{5500}{3}$ N

8. What acceleration is needed to lift the front wheel ?

(a) 10 m/s^2 (b) 5 m/s^2

(c) 6 m/s^2 (d) None of these

9. What minimum friction coefficient can ensure the above acceleration?

(a) 1 (b) 0.6 (c) 0.5 (d) 0.8

Comprehension-4

A thin uniform rod of mass m and length L is hinged at one end and is free to rotate in the vertical plane. A small ball of mass m is fixed to the other end of the rod. A constant horizontal force $F = \frac{mg}{2}$ is also acting on the rod at the free end when the rod is released from horizontal position as shown in figure.

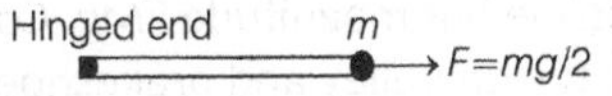

10. Find acceleration of the ball at the instant of releasing the rod

(a) $\frac{3g}{2}$ (b) $\frac{9g}{8}$

(c) $\frac{3g}{4}$ (d) None of these

11. Find the vertical component of reaction force exerted by the hinge when the rod has just been released.

(a) $\frac{mg}{2}$ (b) $\frac{5mg}{8}$ (c) $\frac{5mg}{16}$ (d) $\frac{3mg}{4}$

12. What is the speed of ball when the rod becomes vertical?

(a) $\sqrt{\frac{3gl}{2}}$ (b) $\sqrt{2gl}$

(c) $\sqrt{\frac{3gl}{4}}$ (d) None of these

Comprehension-5

A square frame, made of 4 equal rods of length l, mass m each is hinged at corner A, so that it can rotate about a horizontal axis parallel to line DB as shown. It is slightly disturbed and it starts falling about hinge axis. Calculate following parameters when the frame is completely inverted and point C reaches the lower point of its motion.

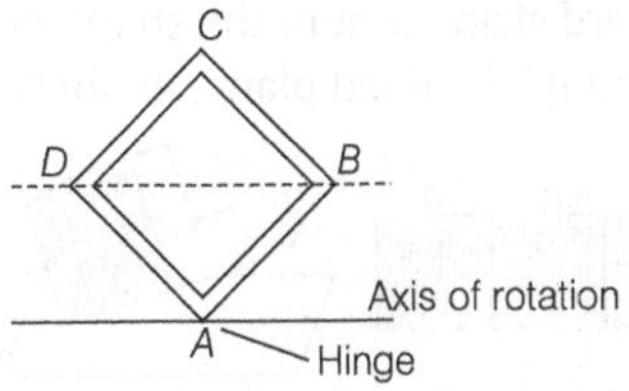

13. Angular velocity of frame

(a) $\sqrt{3\sqrt{2}\frac{g}{l}}$ (b) $\sqrt{\frac{3g}{l}}$ (c) $\sqrt{\frac{3}{\sqrt{2}}\frac{g}{l}}$ (d) $\sqrt{\frac{6g}{l}}$

14. Velocity of point B

(a) $\sqrt{\frac{3}{\sqrt{2}}gl}$ (b) $\sqrt{3\sqrt{2}\,gl}$ (c) $\sqrt{3\frac{g}{l}}$ (d) $\sqrt{6\frac{g}{l}}$

15. Hinge reaction

(a) 4 mg (b) 8 mg (c) 12 mg (d) 16 mg

Comprehension-6

A block of mass M slides on a smooth incline as shown in figure. The compound pulley has moment of inertia $I = 2MR^2$. A brakeshoe can be pressed against pulley to stop it. The normal force applied on the brakeshoe has magnitude $2Mg$. Coefficient of friction between pulley and brakeshoe is $\mu = 0.5$. Initially, block is rest and pulley rotates on a frictionless pivot.

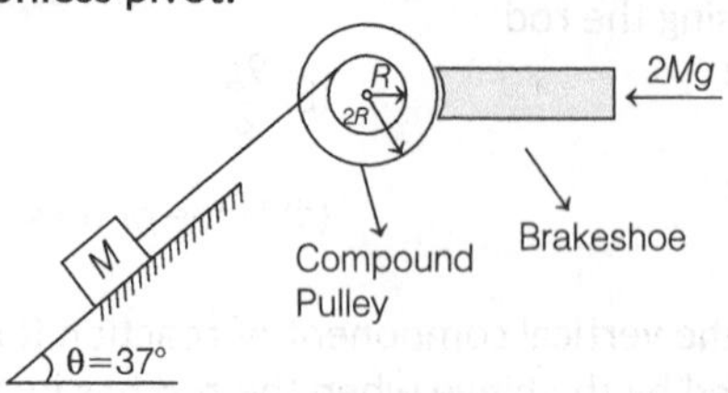

16. Initially at $t = 0$, brakeshoe is not in contact with the pulley. What is acceleration of block along the incline?

(a) 4 m/s^2 (b) 3 m/s^2
(c) 2 m/s^2 (d) 1 m/s^2

17. At $t = 7$ s brakeshoe is applied on the compound pulley. What is magnitude of acceleration of block thereafter?

(a) $\frac{13}{15}g$ (b) $\frac{g}{5}$
(c) $\frac{11}{15}g$ (d) $\frac{7}{15}g$

18. Determine time taken by block and pulley system to come to stop after the brake is applied.

(a) 7 s (b) 10 s (c) 3 s (d) 5 s

Comprehension-7

A cardboard strip, bent in the shape of the letter C, is put on a rough inclined plane, as shown in the figure.

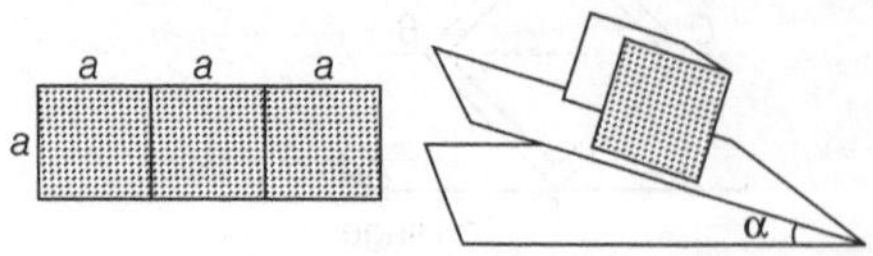

19. At what angle of inclination to the horizontal plane will it topple? (assume that it does not slide).

(a) $\tan^{-1}\left(\frac{2}{3}\right)$ (b) $\tan^{-1}\left(\frac{3}{2}\right)$

(c) 45° (d) $\tan^{-1}\left(\frac{1}{3}\right)$

20. What should be the minimum coefficient of friction, so that it does not slide before toppling.

(a) 0.66 (b) 0.75 (c) 1.0 (d) 0.33

21. What should be the time taken to travel a distance a, if the inclined plane is made completely smooth? [Take, angle of inclined plane as α]

(a) $\sqrt{\frac{a}{g\sin\alpha}}$ (b) $\sqrt{\frac{2a}{g\sin\alpha}}$

(c) $\sqrt{\frac{2a}{3g\sin\alpha}}$ (d) None of these

Comprehension-8

A homogeneous rod AB of length $L = 1.8$ m and mass M is pivoted at the centre O in such a way that it can rotate freely in the vertical plane (figure). The rod is initially in the horizontal position. An insect S of the same mass M falls vertically with speed v on the point C, mid-way between the points O and B. Immediately after falling, the insect moves towards the end B such that the rod rotates with a constant angular velocity ω.

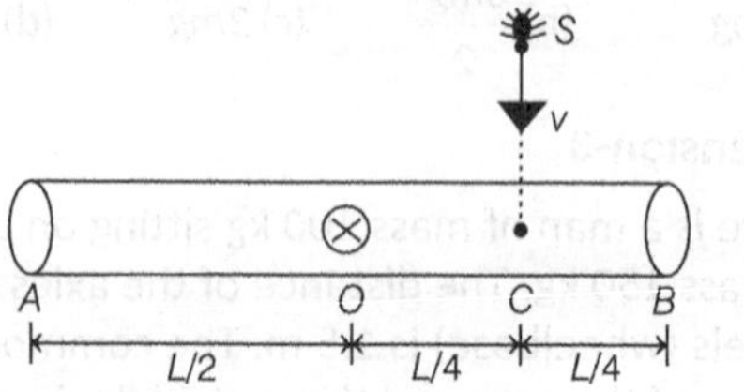

22. Determine the angular velocity ω in terms of v and L.

(a) $\frac{2v}{3L}$ (b) $\frac{12v}{7L}$ (c) $\frac{24v}{7L}$ (d) $\frac{9v}{8L}$

23. If the insect reaches the end B when the rod has turned through an angle of 90°, determine v.

(a) 2 m/s (b) 3.5 m/s (c) 5 m/s (d) 6 m/s

Comprehension-9

Three particles each of mass m can slide on fixed frictionless circular tracks in the same horizontal plane as shown in fig. Particle A moves with velocity v_0 and hits particle B. The coefficient of restitution being $e = \frac{1}{2}$. Assuming that B and C are initially at rest, lie along the radial line before impact, the spring initially is unstretched, and it has a spring constant k.

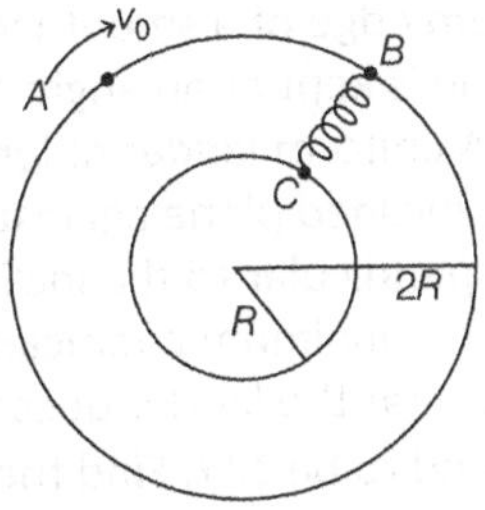

24. The velocity of B immediately after impact is

(a) v_0 (b) $\frac{3v_0}{4}$ (c) $\frac{v_0}{2}$ (d) $\frac{v_0}{4}$

25. The maximum velocity of C is

(a) $\frac{3v_0}{10}$ (b) $\frac{3v_0}{8}$ (c) $\frac{3v_0}{5}$ (d) $\frac{3v_0}{4}$

26. The maximum stretch in the spring is

(a) $v_0\sqrt{\frac{m}{5k}}$ (b) $\frac{v_0}{2}\sqrt{\frac{m}{5k}}$ (c) $\frac{3v_0}{4}\sqrt{\frac{m}{5k}}$ (d) $\frac{v_0}{4}\sqrt{\frac{m}{5k}}$

Match The Columns Questions

1. Square frame is made of four uniform rods. Mass of each rod is M and length L.

Column-I (Axis of rotation)	Column-II (Moment of inertia about axis of rotation)
A. 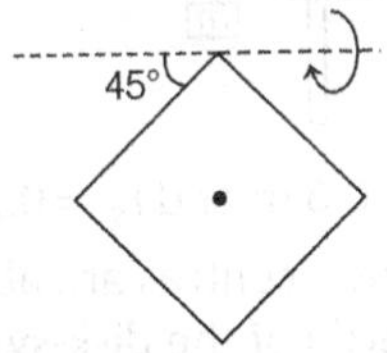	P. $\frac{2}{3}ML^2$
B. 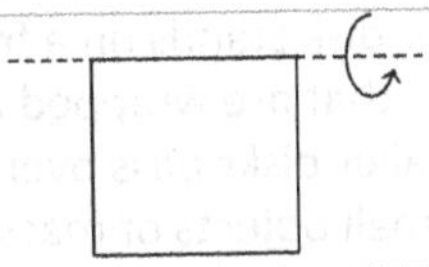	Q. $\frac{5}{3}ML^2$
C. 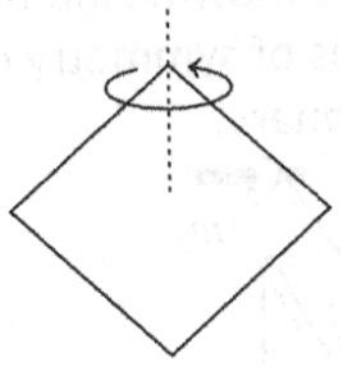	R. $\frac{7}{3}ML^2$
D. 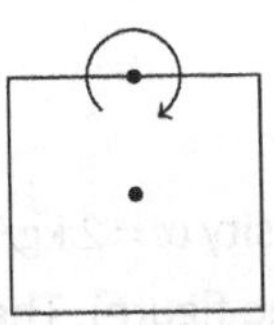	S. $\frac{8}{3}ML^2$

2.

Column-I	Column-II
A. 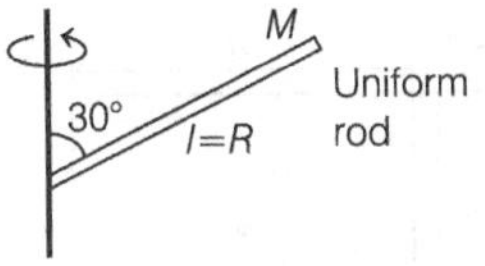	P. $\frac{8MR^2}{11}$
B. 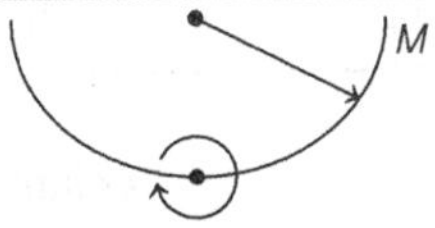 $[\pi = 22/7]$ Uniform Semi-circular ring. Axis is perpendicular to plane of ring	Q. $\frac{MR^2}{12}$
C. 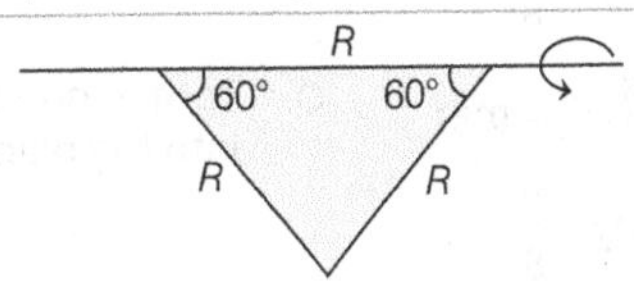 Uniform triangular plate of mass M	R. $\frac{13MR^2}{8}$
D. 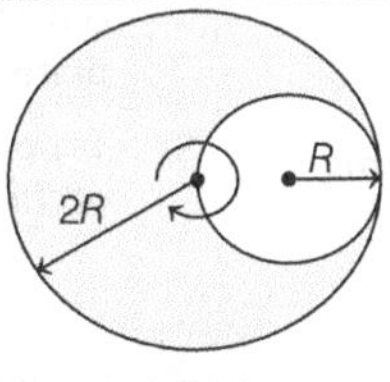 Uniform disk of initial mass M from which circular portion of radius R is then removed. MI of remaining mass about axis which is perpendicular to plane of plate.	S. $\frac{MR^2}{8}$

3. A projectile is launched at angle θ to horizontal from L and it hits the target T on level ground.

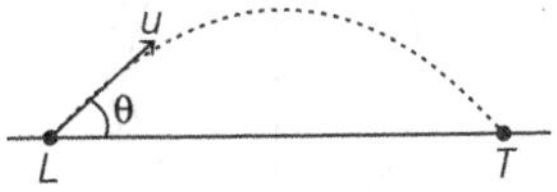

Column-I	Column-II
A. Magnitude of radial acceleration	P. Increases
B. Magnitude of tangential acceleration	Q. Decreases
C. Power delivered by gravity	R. First increases, then decreases
D. Torque of gravity about T	S. First decreases, then increases

4. Consider a square plate of mass m kept on a rough horizontal ground with friction coefficient $\mu = 1$. Two anti-parallel forces F_1 and F_2 are applied at height h_1 and h_2 respectively as shown in figure. Column I gives various values of forces and height of point of application of that force while column II gives various effects.

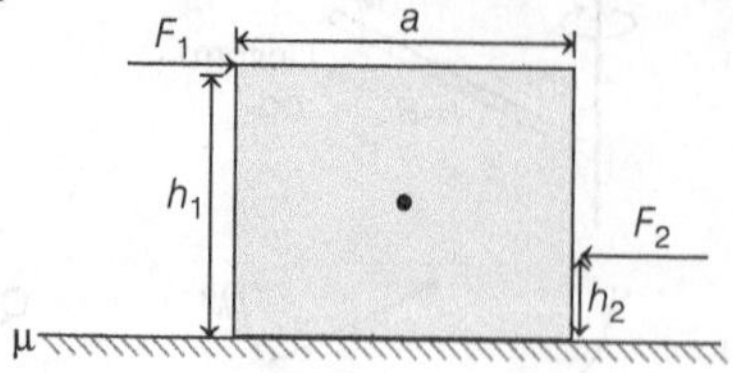

	Column-I		Column-II
A.	$F_1 = F_2 = \frac{mg}{2}$; $h_1 = a$; $h_2 = \frac{a}{8}$	P.	Normal reaction shifts towards right.
B.	$F_1 = \frac{mg}{2}$; $F_2 = mg$; $h_1 = a$; $h_2 = \frac{a}{8}$	Q.	Torque due to friction is into the plane of plate.
C.	$F_1 = mg$; $F_2 = 0$; $h_1 = a$	R.	Torque due to friction is out of the plane of plate.
D.	$F_1 = \frac{mg}{2}$; $F_2 = mg$; $h_1 = h_2 = \frac{a}{2}$	S.	Toppling of plate occurs.
		T.	Friction force is zero.

5. A solid sphere is rotating about an axis as shown in the figure. An insect follows the dotted path on the circumference of sphere as shown. Match the following

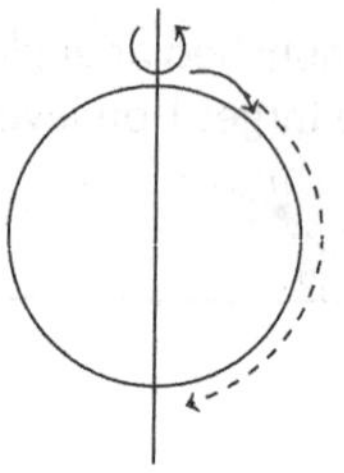

	Column-I		Column-II
A.	Moment of inertia	P.	will remain constant
B.	Angular velocity	Q.	will first increase, then decrease
C.	Angular momentum	R.	will first decrease, then increase
D.	Rotational kinetic energy	S.	will continuously decrease
		T.	will continuously increase

Numerical Value Questions

1. At the bottom edge of a smooth vertical wall, an inclined plane is kept at an angle of 45° from the horizontal. A uniform ladder of length l and mass M rests on the inclined plane against the wall, such that it is perpendicular to the inclined, as shown in the figure. The minimum coefficient of friction necessary so that the ladder does not slip on the incline is found to be $1/\alpha$. Find the value of α.

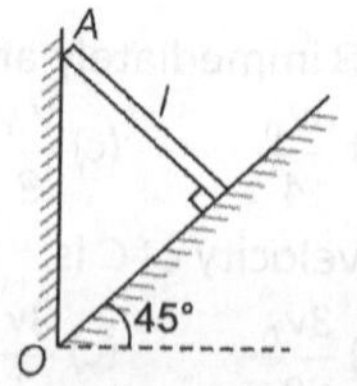

2. A cylinder of height h, diameter $h/2$ and mass M and with a homogeneous mass distribution is placed on a horizontal table. One end of a string running over a pulley is fastened to the top of the cylinder, a body of mass m is hung from the other end and the system is released. Friction is negligible everywhere. At what minimum ratio $\frac{m}{M}$ will the cylinder tilt?

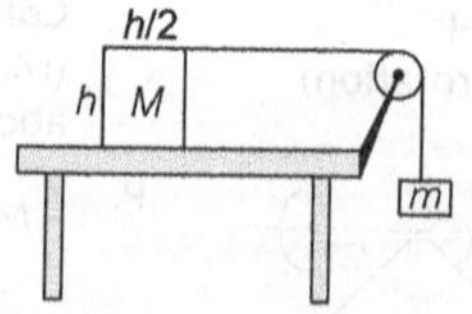

3. Two disks with radii $r_1 = 0.3$ m and $r_2 = 0.2$ m are fixed together, so that their centres are above each other. The rotational inertia of the disk-system is 0.25 kg-m^2. The larger disk stands on a frictionless table. Massless chords that are wrapped around the larger and the smaller disks pass over pulleys and are attached to small objects of masses $m_1 = 5$ kg and m_2, respectively as shown. Find the value of m_2 (in kg) at which the axis of symmetry of the disk-system remains stationary.

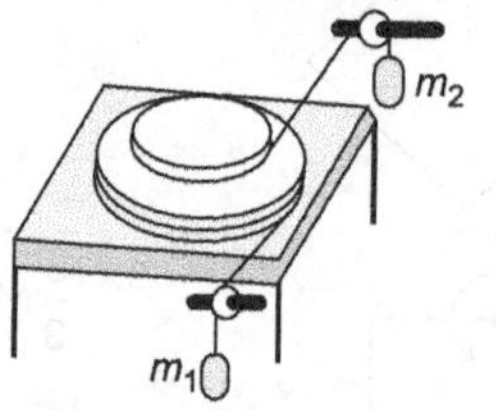

4. A thin rod of linear mass density $\alpha = 2$ kg/m rests on a disc of radius $R = 1$ m (see figure). The thin rod makes an angle $\theta = 60°$ with the horizontal and is

tangent to the disc at its upper end. Friction exists at all points of contact, and assume that it is large enough to keep the system at rest. Find the friction force (in N) between the ground and the disc.

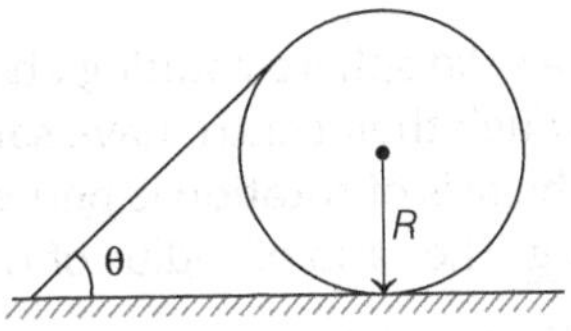

5. A thin rod of mass m and length $2l$ is placed horizontal and perpendicular to a horizontal rough nail, as shown in figure and set free.The point of contact of the rod with the nail is $\frac{l}{3}$ distance away from the centre of rod. If the rod starts slipping when it forms an angle 37° with the horizontal, then find the coefficient of friction of rod with nail.

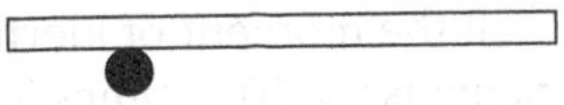

6. A rod is released from vertical position shown in the diagram. The value of sin θ, at which net hinge reaction is in vertical direction (neglect any friction), is x. Then find the value of $3x$.

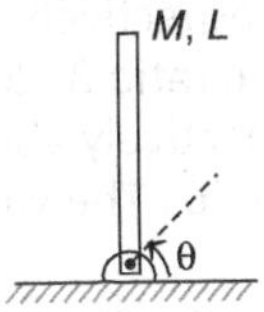

7. Consider an L-shaped rod of uniform mass density, hinged at point O is held at rest initially. The mass of the rod is $m = 1$ kg. The earth's gravitational field is assumed to be uniform and directed downwards. Assume no friction at hinges. The rod is now released. Find the maximum magnitude of angular speed of the rod (in rad/s). (Take $L = 1$ m, $\sqrt{10} = 19/6$)

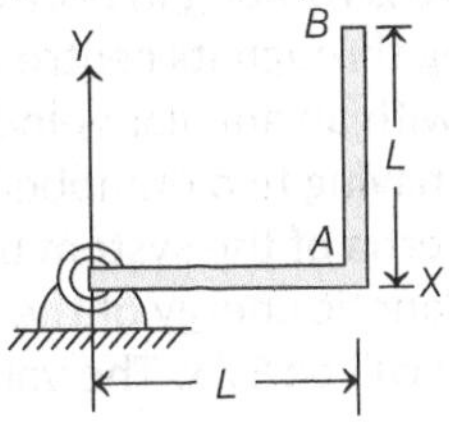

8. A rod of length R and mass M is free to rotate about a horizontal axis passing through hinge P as in figure. First it is taken aside such that it becomes horizontal and then released. At the lowest point the rod hits the block B of mass m and stops. Find the ratio of masses $\frac{M}{m}$ such that the block B completes the circle. Neglect any friction. If your answer is N fill value of N_2.

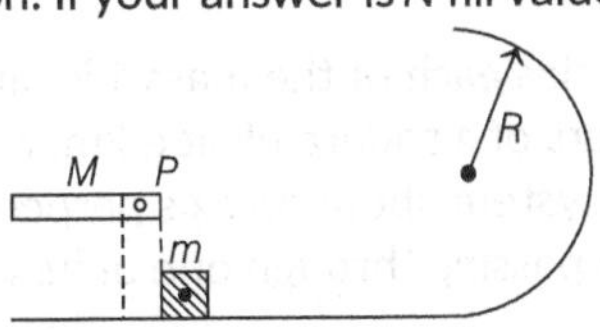

9. A uniform rod of length 0.72 m is pivoted at one end and is hanging as shown. It receives a horizontal impulse at a distance x below the pivot as shown. If impulse applied by the pivot is zero, then find the value of x (in cm).

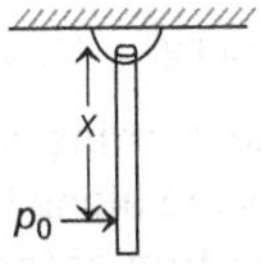

10. A solid uniform cylinder of mass $m = 6$ kg and radius $r = 0.1$ m is kept in balance on a slope of inclination $\alpha = 37°$ with the help of a thread fastened to its jacket. The cylinder does not slip on the slope. The minimum required coefficient of friction to keep the cylinder in balance when the thread is held vertically is given as μ. Find the value of 4μ.

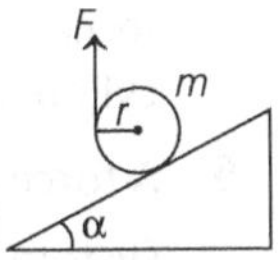

11. A boy is standing on a platform which is free to rotate about its vertical axis. The boy holds an open umberella in his hand. The axis of the umbrella coincides with that of the platform. The moment of inertia of the platform plus the boy system is 6.0×10^{-3} kg-m^2 and that of the umbrella is 4.0×10^{-3} kg-m^2. The boy starts spinning the umbrella about the axis at an angular speed of 3.0 rev/s with respect to himself. If the angular velocity imparted to the platform is $z/5$ rev/s, find the value of z.

12. Two uniform rods A and B of length 0.6 m each and of masses 0.01 kg and 0.02 kg respectively, are rigidly joined end to end. The combination is pivoted at the lighter end, P as shown in figure such that it can freely rotate about point P in a vertical plane. A small object of mass 0.05 kg, moving horizontally, hits the lower end of the combination and sticks to it. What should be the velocity (in m/s) of the object, so that the system could just be raised to the horizontal position?

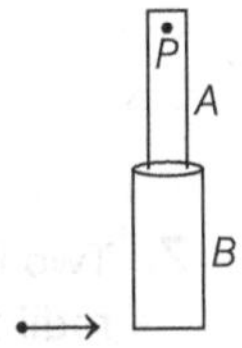

Previous Years Questions

JEE Main

1. Four particles each of the mass 1 kg are placed at four corners of a square of side 2m. Moment of inertia of system about an axis perpendicular to its plane and passing through one of its vertex is .... kg m^2. **[2024, 27 Jan Shift-I]**

2. A heavy iron bar of weight 12 kg is having its one end on the ground and the other on the shoulder of a man. The rod makes an angle 60° with the horizontal, the weight experienced by the man is **[2024, 27 Jan Shift-II]**

   (a) 6 kg (b) $6\sqrt{3}$ kg (c) 3 kg (d) 12 kg

3. A body of mass 5 kg moving with a uniform speed $3\sqrt{2}\ \text{ms}^{-1}$ in X-Y-plane along the line $y = x - 4$. The angular momentum of the particle about the origin will be .... kg m^2s^{-1} **[2024, 29 Jan Shift-II]**

4. A light rope is wound around a hollow cylinder of mass 5 kg and radius 70 cm. The rope is pulled with a force of 52.5 N. The angular acceleration of the cylinder will be .... rad s^{-2}. **[2023, 13 April Shift-II]**

5. A force of $-P\hat{k}$ acts on the origin of the coordinate system. The torque about the point (2, – 3) is $P(a\hat{i} + b\hat{j})$, The ratio of $\frac{a}{b}$ is $\frac{x}{2}$. The value of x is **[2023, 10 April Shift-II]**

6. A particle of mass 100 g is projected at time $t = 0$ with a speed $20\ \text{ms}^{-1}$ at an angle 45° to the horizontal as given in the figure. The magnitude of the angular momentum of the particle about the starting point at time $t = 2$ s is found to be $\sqrt{K}$ kg-m^2/s. The value of K is .... (Take, $g = 10\ \text{ms}^{-2}$) **[2023, 29 Jan Shift-II]**

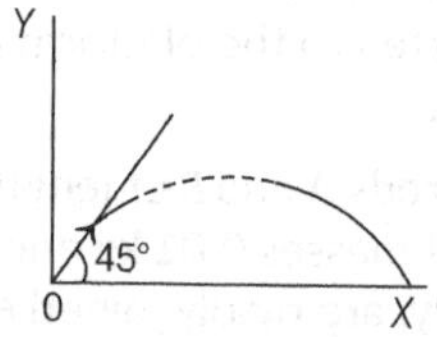

7. Two identical solid spheres each of mass 2 kg and radii 10 cm are fixed at the ends of a light rod. The separation between the centres of the spheres is 40 cm. The moment of inertia of the system about an axis perpendicular to the rod passing through its middle point is .... $\times 10^{-3}$ kg-m^2 **[2023, 6 April Shift-I]**

8. The moment of inertia of a semicircular ring about an axis, passing through the centre and perpendicular to the plane of ring, is $\frac{1}{x}MR^2$ where R is the radius and M is the mass of the semicircular ring. The value of x will be .... **[2023, 8 April Shift-I]**

9. A ring and a solid sphere rotating about an axis passing through their centre have same radii of gyration. The axis of rotation is perpendicular to plane of ring. The ratio of radius of ring to that of sphere is $\sqrt{\frac{2}{x}}$. The value of x is .... **[2023, 6 April Shift-II]**

10. A solid sphere and a solid cylinder of same mass and radius are rolling on a horizontal surface without slipping. The radio of their radius of gyrations respectively ($k_{sph} : k_{cyl}$) is $2 : \sqrt{x}$. The value of x is .... **[2023, 15 April Shift-I]**

11. A solid sphere of mass 500 g and radius 5 cm is rotated about one of its diameter with angular speed of 10 rad s^{-1}. If the moment of inertia of the sphere about its tangent is $x \times 10^{-2}$ times its angular momentum about the diameter. Then the value of x will be .... **[2023, 11 April Shift-I]**

12. Two discs of same mass and different radii are made of different materials such that their thicknesses are 1 cm and 0.5 cm respectively. The densities of materials are in the ratio 3 : 5. The moment of inertia of these discs respectively about their diameters will be in the ratio of $x/6$. The value of x is .... **[2023, 31 Jan Shift-II]**

13. Moment of inertia of a disc of mass M and radius R about any of its diameter is $\frac{MR^2}{4}$. The moment of inertia of this disc about an axis normal to the disc and passing through a point on its edge will be, $\frac{x}{2}MR^2$. The value of x is .... **[2023, 1 Feb Shift-II]**

14. A circular plate is rotating in horizontal plane, about an axis passing through its centre and perpendicular to the plate, with an angular velocity ω. A person sits at the centre having two dumbbells in his hands, the moment of inertia of the system become triple. If E be the initial kinetic energy of the system, then final kinetic energy will be E/x. The value of x is **[2023, 11 April Shift-II]**

15. The torque of a force $5\hat{\mathbf{i}} + 3\hat{\mathbf{j}} - 7\hat{\mathbf{k}}$ about the origin is τ. If the force acts on a particle whose position vector is $2\hat{\mathbf{i}} + 2\hat{\mathbf{j}} + \hat{\mathbf{k}}$, then the value of τ will be **[2022, 29 July Shift-II]**

    (a) $11\hat{\mathbf{i}} + 19\hat{\mathbf{j}} - 4\hat{\mathbf{k}}$ (b) $-11\hat{\mathbf{i}} + 9\hat{\mathbf{j}} - 16\hat{\mathbf{k}}$
    (c) $-17\hat{\mathbf{i}} + 19\hat{\mathbf{j}} - 4\hat{\mathbf{k}}$ (d) $17\hat{\mathbf{i}} + 9\hat{\mathbf{j}} + 16\hat{\mathbf{k}}$

16. The position vector of 1 kg object is $\mathbf{r} = (3\hat{\mathbf{i}} - \hat{\mathbf{j}})$ m and its velocity, $\mathbf{v} = (3\hat{\mathbf{j}} + \hat{\mathbf{k}})$ ms^{-1}. The magnitude of its angular momentum is $\sqrt{x}$ N-m, where x is ______ . [2022, 28 June Shift-I]

17. A metre scale is balanced on a knife edge at its centre. When two coins, each of mass 10 g are put one on the top of the other at the 10.0 cm mark the scale is found to be balanced at 40.0 cm mark.

The mass of the metre scale is found to be $x \times 10^{-2}$ kg. The value of x is .... [2022, 24 June Shift-I]

18. The radius of gyration of a cylindrical rod about an axis of rotation perpendicular to its length and passing through the center will be .... m.

(Given, the length of the rod is $10\sqrt{3}$ m) [2022, 26 July Shift-II]

19. A disc with a flat small bottom beaker placed on it at a distance R from its centre is revolving about an axis passing through the centre and perpendicular to its plane with an angular velocity ω. The coefficient of static friction between the bottom of the beaker and the surface of the disc is μ. The beaker will revolve with the disc, if [2022, 25 June Shift-II]

(a) $R \le \frac{\mu g}{2\omega^2}$ (b) $R \le \frac{\mu g}{\omega^2}$

(c) $R \ge \frac{\mu g}{2\omega^2}$ (d) $R \ge \frac{\mu g}{\omega^2}$

20. A fly wheel is accelerated uniformly from rest and rotates through 5 rad in the first second. The angle rotated by the fly wheel in the next second, will be [2022, 24 June Shift-II]

(a) 7.5 rad (b) 15 rad (c) 20 rad (d) 30 rad

21. Angular momentum of a single particle moving with constant speed along circular path [2021, 31 Aug Shift-I]

(a) changes in magnitude but remains same in the direction
(b) remains same in magnitude and direction
(c) remains same in magnitude but changes in the direction
(d) is zero

22. A solid disc of radius 20 cm and mass 10 kg is rotating with an angular velocity of 600 rpm, about an axis normal to its circular plane and passing through its centre of mass. The retarding torque required to bring the disc at rest in 10 s is $\pi \times 10^{-1}$ N-m. [2021, 25 July Shift-I]

23. A particle of mass m is moving in time t on a trajectory given by

$$\mathbf{r} = 10\alpha t^2 \hat{\mathbf{i}} + 5\beta(t-5)\hat{\mathbf{j}}$$

where, α and β are dimensional constants. The angular momentum of the particle becomes the same as it was for $t = 0$ at time t is ...... s. [2021, 25 July Shift-I]

24. A thin circular ring of mass M and radius r is rotating about its axis with an angular speed ω. Two particles having mass m each are now attached at diametrically opposite points. The angular speed of the ring will become [2021, 18 March Shift-I]

(a) $\omega \frac{M}{M+m}$ (b) $\omega \frac{M+2m}{M}$

(c) $\omega \frac{M}{M+2m}$ (d) $\omega \frac{M-2m}{M+2m}$

25. A mass M hangs on a massless rod of length l which rotates at a constant angular frequency. The mass M moves with steady speed in a circular path of constant radius. Assume that the system is in steady circular motion with constant angular velocity ω. The angular momentum of M about point A is L_A which lies in the positive z-direction and the angular momentum of M about B is L_B. The correct statement for this system is [2021, 17 March Shift-I]

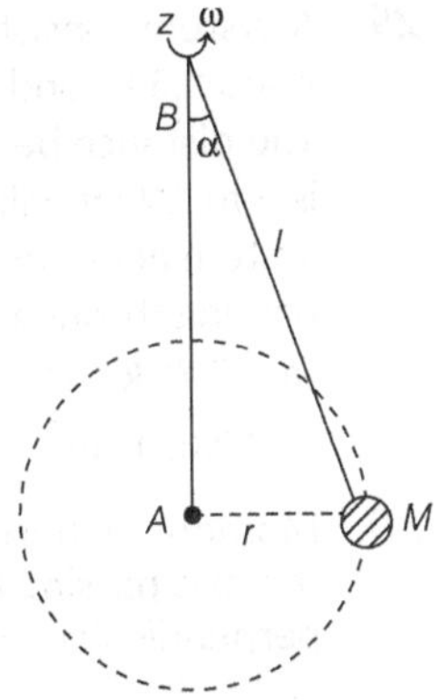

(a) L_A and L_B are both constant in magnitude and direction
(b) L_B is constant in direction with varying magnitude
(c) L_B is constant, both in magnitude and direction
(d) L_A is constant, both in magnitude and direction

26. A triangular plate is shown below. A force $\mathbf{F} = 4\hat{\mathbf{i}} - 3\hat{\mathbf{j}}$ is applied at point P. The torque at point P with respect to point O and Q are [2021, 17 March Shift-I]

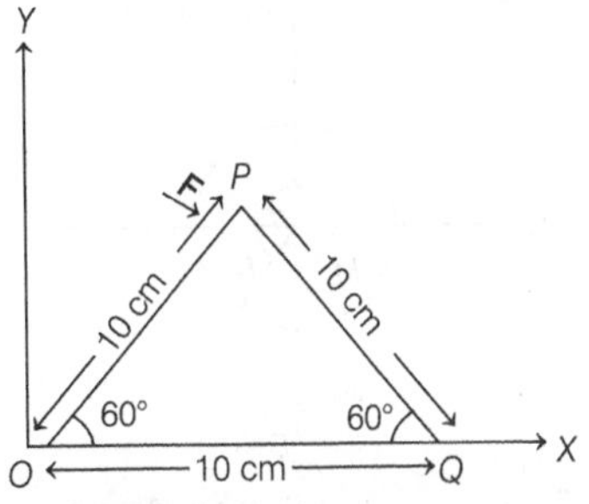

(a) $-15 - 20\sqrt{3}, 15 - 20\sqrt{3}$
(b) $15 + 20\sqrt{3}, 15 - 20\sqrt{3}$

(c) $15 - 20\sqrt{3}, 15 + 20\sqrt{3}$
(d) $-15 + 20\sqrt{3}, 15 + 20\sqrt{3}$

27. A force $F = 4\hat{i} + 3\hat{j} + 4\hat{k}$ is applied on an intersection point of $x = 2$ plane and X-axis. The magnitude of torque of this force about a point (2, 3, 4) is .... (Round off to the nearest integer) **[2021, 16 March Shift-II]**

28. A 2 kg steel rod of length 0.6 m is clamped on a table vertically at its lower end and is free to rotate in vertical plane. The upper end is pushed so that the rod falls under gravity. Ignoring the friction due to clamping at its lower end, the speed of the free end of rod when it passes through its lowest position is .... ms^{-1}. (Take, $g = 10\ ms^{-2}$) **[2021, 31 Aug Shift-I]**

29. A system consists of two identical spheres each of mass 1.5 kg and radius 50 cm at the end of light rod. The distance between the centres of the two spheres is 5 m. What will be the moment of inertia of the system about an axis perpendicular to the rod passing through its mid-point ? **[2021, 31 Aug Shift-II]**

(a) $18.75\ kgm^2$ (b) $1.905 \times 10^5\ kgm^2$
(c) $19.05\ kgm^2$ (d) $1.875 \times 10^5\ kgm^2$

30. Moment of inertia of a square plate of side l about the axis passing through one of the corner and perpendicular to the plane of square plate is given by **[2021, 27 Aug Shift-I]**

(a) $\frac{Ml^2}{6}$ (b) Ml^2 (c) $\frac{Ml^2}{12}$ (d) $\frac{2}{3}Ml^2$

31. The figure shows two solid discs with radius R and r, respectively. If mass per unit area is same for both, what is the ratio of MI of bigger disc around axis AB (which is perpendicular to the plane of the disc and passing through its centre) of MI of smaller disc around one of its diameters lying on its plane? **[2021, 27 July Shift-I]**

Given, M is the mass of the larger disc. (MI stands for moment of inertia)

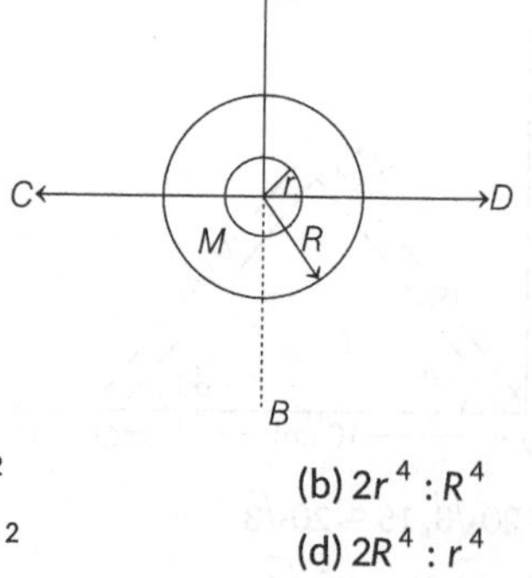

(a) $R^2 : r^2$ (b) $2r^4 : R^4$
(c) $2R^2 : r^2$ (d) $2R^4 : r^4$

32. **Assertion (A)** Moment of inertia of a circular disc of mass M and radius R about X, Y-axes (passing through its plane) and Z-axis which is perpendicular to its plane were found to be I_x, I_y and I_z, respectively. The respective radii of gyration about all the three axes will be the same.

Reason (R) A rigid body making rotational motion has fixed mass and shape.

In the light of the above statements, choose the most appropriate answer from the options given below. **[2021, 25 July Shift-I]**

(a) Both A and R are correct and R is the correct explanation of A.
(b) Both A and R are correct but R is not the correct explanation of A.
(c) A is correct but R is not correct.
(d) A is not correct but R is correct.

33. Consider a uniform wire of mass M and length L. It is bent into a semicircle. Its moment of inertia about a line perpendicular to the plane of the wire passing through the centre is **[2021, 18 March Shift-II]**

(a) $\frac{1}{4}\frac{ML^2}{\pi^2}$ (b) $\frac{2}{5}\frac{ML^2}{\pi^2}$
(c) $\frac{ML^2}{\pi^2}$ (d) $\frac{1}{2}\frac{ML^2}{\pi^2}$

34. Four equal masses, m each are placed at the corners of a square of length (l) as shown in the figure. The moment of inertia of the system about an axis passing through A and parallel to DB would be **[2021, 16 March Shift-I]**

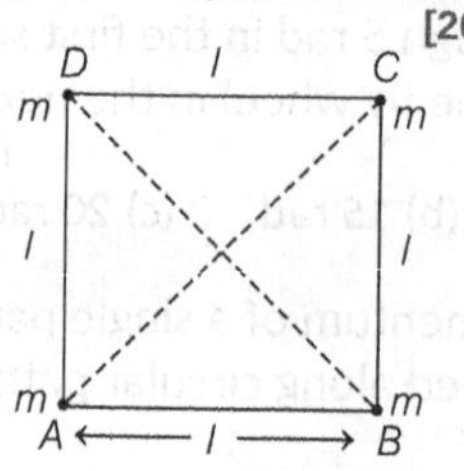

(a) $1ml^2$ (b) $2ml^2$
(c) $3ml^2$ (d) $\sqrt{3}ml^2$

35. Four identical solid spheres each of mass m and radius a are placed with their centres on the four corners of a square of side b. The moment of inertia of the system about one side of square, where the axis of rotation is parallel to the plane of the square is **[2021, 26 Feb Shift-I]**

(a) $\frac{4}{5}ma^2 + 2mb^2$ (b) $\frac{8}{5}ma^2 + mb^2$
(c) $\frac{8}{5}ma^2 + 2mb^2$ (d) $\frac{4}{5}ma^2$

36. A uniform thin bar of mass 6 kg and length 2.4 m is bent to make an equilateral hexagon. The moment of inertia about an axis passing through the centre of mass and perpendicular to the plane of hexagon is .... $\times 10^{-1}$ kg-m^2. **[2021, 24 Feb Shift-II]**

37. Moment of inertia (MI) of four bodies, having same mass and radius, are reported as
I_1 = MI of thin circular ring about its diameter,
I_2 = MI of circular disk about an axis perpendicular to the disk and going through the centre,
I_3 = MI of solid cylinder about its axis
and I_4 = MI of solid sphere about its diameter. Then, **[2021, 24 Feb Shift-I]**

(a) $I_1 + I_2 = I_3 + \frac{5}{2} I_4$
(b) $I_1 + I_3 < I_2 + I_4$
(c) $I_1 = I_2 = I_3 < I_4$
(d) $I_1 = I_2 = I_3 > I_4$

38. Two discs have moments of inertia I_1 and I_2 about their respective axes perpendicular to the plane and passing through the centre. They are rotating with angular speeds, ω_1 and ω_2 respectively and are brought into contact face to face with their axes of rotation co-axial. The loss in kinetic energy of the system in the process is given by **[2021, 27 Aug Shift-II]**

(a) $\frac{I_1 I_2}{(I_1 + I_2)}(\omega_1 - \omega_2)^2$ (b) $\frac{(I_1 - I_2)^2 \omega_1 \omega_2}{2(I_1 + I_2)}$

(c) $\frac{I_1 I_2}{2(I_1 + I_2)}(\omega_1 - \omega_2)^2$ (d) $\frac{(\omega_1 - \omega_2)^2}{2(I_1 + I_2)}$

39. In the given figure, two wheels P and Q are connected by a belt B. The radius of P is three times as that of Q. In case of same rotational kinetic energy, the ratio of rotational inertias $\left(\frac{I_1}{I_2}\right)$ will be $x : 1$. The value of x will be .... **[2021, 27 July Shift-II]**

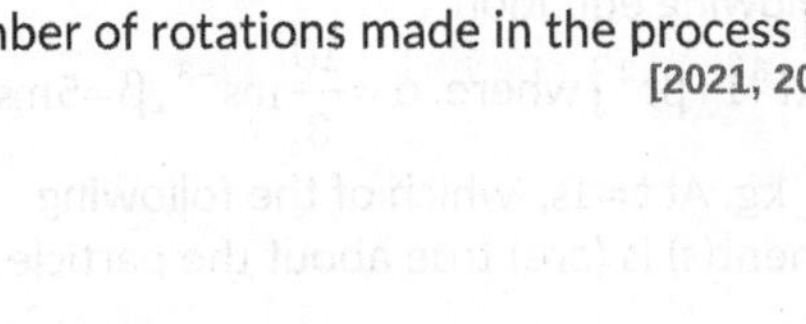

40. A body rotating with an angular speed of 600 rpm is uniformly accelerated to 1800 rpm in 10 s. The number of rotations made in the process is .... **[2021, 20 July Shift-II]**

41. A cord is wound round the circumference of wheel of radius r. The axis of the wheel is horizontal and the moment of inertia about it is I. A weight mg is attached to the cord at the end. The weight falls from rest. After falling through a distance h, the square of angular velocity of wheel will be **[2021, 26 Feb Shift-II]**

(a) $\frac{2mgh}{I + 2mr^2}$ (b) $\frac{2mgh}{I + mr^2}$

(c) $2gh$ (d) $\frac{2gh}{I + mr^2}$

42. A person of 80 kg mass is standing on the rim of a circular platform of mass 200 kg rotating about its axis at 5 rpm. The person now starts moving towards the centre of the platform. What will be the rotational speed (in rpm) of the platform when the person reaches its centre? **[2020, 03 Sep Shift-I]**

43. A thin rod of mass 0.9 kg and length 1 m is suspended at rest from one end, so that it can freely oscillate in the vertical plane.
A particle of mass 0.1 kg moving in a straight line with velocity 80 m/s hits the rod at its bottom-most point and sticks to it (see figure). The angular speed (in rad/s) of the rod immediately after the collision will be .... **[2020, 05 Sep Shift-II]**

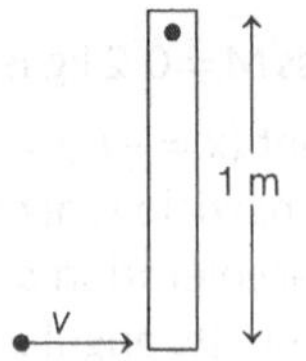

44. Four point masses, each of mass m are fixed at the corners of a square of side l. The square is rotating with angular frequency ω, about an axis passing through one of the corners of the square and parallel to its diagonal, as shown in the figure. The angular momentum of the square about this axis is **[2020, 06 Sep Shift-I]**

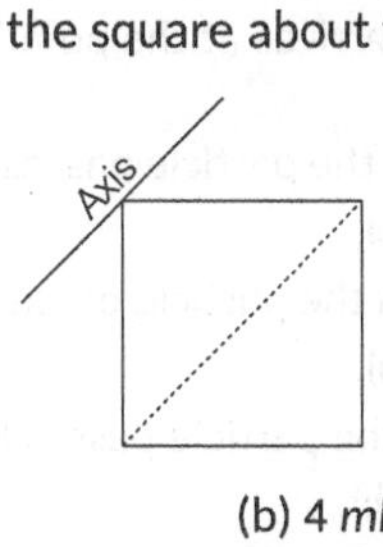

(a) $ml^2\omega$ (b) $4\,ml^2\omega$
(c) $3\,ml^2\omega$ (d) $2\,ml^2\omega$

JEE Advanced

1. A bar of mass $M = 1.00$ kg and length $L = 0.20$ m is lying on a horizontal frictionless surface. One end of the bar is pivoted at a point about which it is free to rotate. A small mass $m = 0.10$ kg is moving on the same horizontal surface with $5.00\ \text{ms}^{-1}$ speed on a path perpendicular to the bar. It hits the bar at a distance $L/2$ from the pivoted end and returns back on the same path with speed v. After this elastic collision, the bar rotates with an angular velocity ω. Which of the following statement is correct? **(2023)**

(a) $\omega = 6.98\ \text{rad s}^{-1}$ and $v = 4.30\ \text{ms}^{-1}$
(b) $\omega = 3.75\ \text{rad s}^{-1}$ and $v = 4.30\ \text{ms}^{-1}$
(c) $\omega = 3.75\ \text{rad s}^{-1}$ and $v = 10.0\ \text{ms}^{-1}$
(d) $\omega = 6.80\ \text{rad s}^{-1}$ and $v = 4.10\ \text{ms}^{-1}$

2. A cord is wound round the circumference of wheel of radius r. The axis of the wheel is horizontal and the moment of inertia about it is I. A weight mg is attached to the cord at the end. The weight falls from rest. After falling through a distance h, the square of angular velocity of wheel will be **(2021)**

(a) $\dfrac{2mgh}{I + 2mr^2}$ (b) $\dfrac{2mgh}{I + mr^2}$
(c) $2gh$ (d) $\dfrac{2gh}{I + mr^2}$

3. A particle of mass $M = 0.2$ kg is initially at rest in the xy-plane at a point $(x = -l, y = -h)$, where $l = 10$ m and $h = 1$ m. The particle is accelerated at time $t = 0$ with a constant acceleration $a = 10\ \text{m/s}^2$ along the positive x-direction. Its angular momentum and torque with respect to the origin, in SI units, are represented by $\mathbf{L}$ and τ, respectively. $\hat{\mathbf{i}}, \hat{\mathbf{j}}$ and $\hat{\mathbf{k}}$ are unit vectors along the positive x, y and z-directions, respectively. If $\hat{\mathbf{k}} = \hat{\mathbf{i}} \times \hat{\mathbf{j}}$, then, which of the following statement(s) is(are) correct? **(2021)**

(a) The particle arrives at the point $(x = l, y = -h)$ at time $t = 2$ s.
(b) $\tau = 2\hat{\mathbf{k}}$ when the particle passes through the point $(x = l, y = -h)$.
(c) $\mathbf{L} = 4\hat{\mathbf{k}}$ when the particle passes through the point $(x = l, y = -h)$.
(d) $\tau = \hat{\mathbf{k}}$ when the particle passes through the point $(x = 0, y = -h)$.

4. A rod of mass m and length L, pivoted at one of its ends, is hanging vertically. A bullet of the same mass moving at speed v strikes the rod horizontally at a distance x from its pivoted end and gets embedded in it. The combined system now rotates with angular speed ω about the pivot. The maximum angular speed ω_M is achieved for $x = x_M$. Then **(2020)**

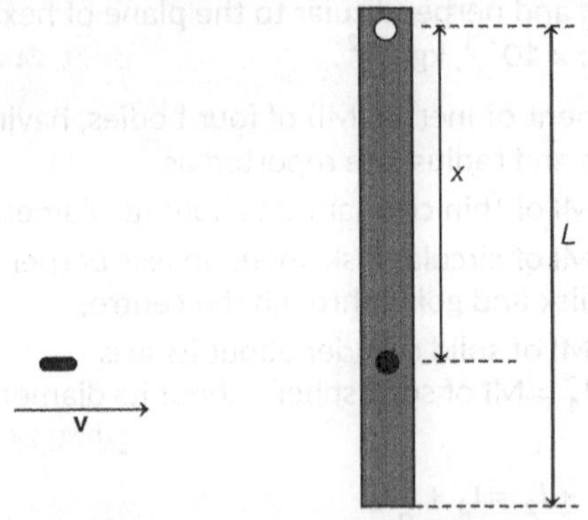

(a) $\omega = \dfrac{3vx}{L^2 + 3x^2}$ (b) $\omega = \dfrac{12vx}{L^2 + 12x^2}$
(c) $x_M = \dfrac{L}{\sqrt{3}}$ (d) $\omega_M = \dfrac{v}{2L}\sqrt{3}$

5. In the column-I below, four different paths of a particle are given as functions of time. In these functions, α and β are positive constants of appropriate dimensions and $\alpha \neq \beta$. In each case, the force acting on the particle is either zero or conservative. In column-II, five physical quantities of the particle are mentioned: $\mathbf{p}$ is the linear momentum, $\mathbf{L}$ is the angular momentum about the origin, K is the kinetic energy, U is the potential energy and E is the total energy. Match each path in Column-I with those quantities in Column-II, which are conserved for that path. **(2018)**

	Column I		Column II
A.	$\mathbf{r}(t) = \alpha t\,\hat{\mathbf{i}} + \beta t\,\hat{\mathbf{j}}$	p.	$\mathbf{p}$
B.	$\mathbf{r}(t) = \alpha \cos \omega t\,\hat{\mathbf{i}} + \beta \sin \omega t\,\hat{\mathbf{j}}$	q.	$\mathbf{L}$
C.	$\mathbf{r}(t) = \alpha(\cos \omega t\,\hat{\mathbf{i}} + \sin \omega t\,\hat{\mathbf{j}})$	r.	K
D.	$\mathbf{r}(t) = a t\,\hat{\mathbf{i}} + \dfrac{\beta}{2} t^2\,\hat{\mathbf{j}}$	s.	U
		t.	E

(a) A $\to$ p, q, r, s, t; B $\to$ q, t; C $\to$ q, r, s, t; D $\to$ t
(b) A $\to$ p, q, r, s, t; B $\to$ r, t; C $\to$ q, r, s, t; D $\to$ q, t
(c) A $\to$ q, r, s; B $\to$ t; C $\to$ p, q, s; D $\to$ q, t
(d) A $\to$ p, q, r, t; B $\to$ q, t; C $\to$ q, r, s, t; D $\to$ q, t

6. The position vector $\mathbf{r}$ of particle of mass m is given by the following equation
$\mathbf{r}(t) = \alpha t^3\hat{\mathbf{i}} + \beta t^2\hat{\mathbf{j}}$ where, $\alpha = \dfrac{10}{3}\text{ms}^{-3}$, $\beta = 5\text{ms}^{-2}$ and $m = 0.1$ kg. At $t = 1$s, which of the following statement(s) is (are) true about the particle? **(2016)**

(a) The velocity $\mathbf{v}$ is given by $\mathbf{v}=(10\hat{\mathbf{i}}+10\hat{\mathbf{j}})\,\text{ms}^{-1}$
(b) The angular momentum $\mathbf{L}$ with respect to the origin is given by $\mathbf{L}=(-5/3)\hat{\mathbf{k}}$ Nms
(c) The force $\mathbf{F}$ is given by $\mathbf{F}=(\hat{\mathbf{i}}+2\hat{\mathbf{j}})$N
(d) The torque τ with respect to the origin is given by $\tau=-\frac{20}{3}\hat{\mathbf{k}}$ Nm

7. A ring of mass M and radius R is rotating with angular speed ω about a fixed vertical axis passing through its centre O with two point masses each of mass $\frac{M}{8}$ at rest at O. These masses can move radially outwards along two massless rods fixed on the ring as shown in the figure.
At some instant, the angular speed of the system is $\frac{8}{9}\omega$ and one of the masses is at a distance of $\frac{3}{5}R$ from O. At this instant, the distance of the other mass from O is **(2015)**

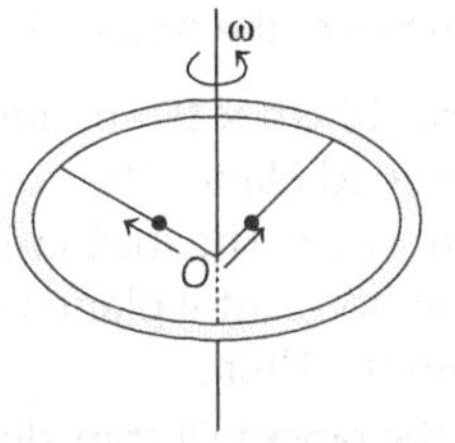

(a) $\frac{2}{3}R$ (b) $\frac{1}{3}R$ (c) $\frac{3}{5}R$ (d) $\frac{4}{5}R$

8. A horizontal circular platform of radius 0.5 m and mass 0.45 kg is free to rotate about its axis. Two massless spring toy-guns, each carrying a steel ball of mass 0.05 kg are attached to the platform at a distance 0.25 m from the centre on its either sides along its diameter (see figure). Each gun simultaneously fires the balls horizontally and perpendicular to the diameter in opposite directions. After leaving the platform, the balls have horizontal speed of 9 ms^{-1} with respect to the ground. The rotational speed of the platform in rad s^{-1} after the balls leave the platform is **(2014)**

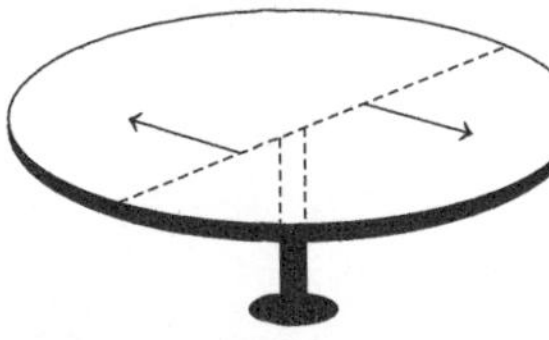

9. A uniform circular disc of mass 50 kg and radius 0.4 m is rotating with an angular velocity of 10 rad/s about its own axis, which is vertical. Two uniform circular rings, each of mass 6.25 kg and radius 0.2 m, are gently placed symmetrically on the disc in such a manner that they are touching each other along the axis of the disc and are horizontal. Assume that the friction is large enough such that the rings are at rest relative to the disc and the system rotates about the original axis. The new angular velocity (in rad s^{-1}) of the system is **(2013)**

10. Consider a disc rotating in the horizontal plane with a constant angular speed ω about its centre O.

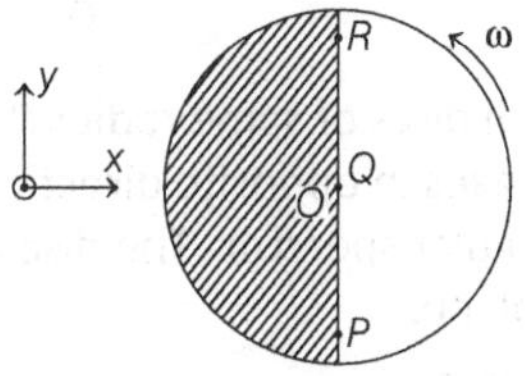

The disc has a shaded region on one side of the diameter and an unshaded region on the other side as shown in the figure. When the disc is in the orientation as shown, two pebbles P and Q are simultaneously projected at an angle towards R. The velocity of projection is in the y-z plane and is same for both pebbles with respect to the disc.
Assume that (i) they land back on the disc before the disc has completed 1/8 rotation, (ii) their range is less than half the disc radius, and (iii) ω remains constant throughout. Then **(2012)**
(a) P lands in the shaded region and Q in the unshaded region
(b) P lands in the unshaded region and Q in the shaded region
(c) both P and Q land in the unshaded region
(d) both P and Q land in the shaded region

11. A thin uniform rod, pivoted at O, is rotating in the horizontal plane with constant angular speed ω, as shown in the figure. At time $t = 0$, a small insect starts from O and moves with constant speed v with respect to the rod towards the other end. It reaches the end of the rod at $t = T$ and stops. The angular speed of the system remains ω throughout.
The magnitude of the torque $|\tau|$ on the system about O, as a function of time is best represented by which plot? **(2012)**

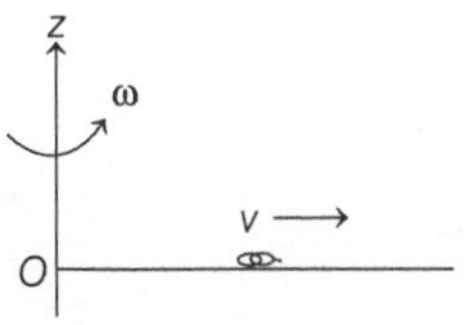

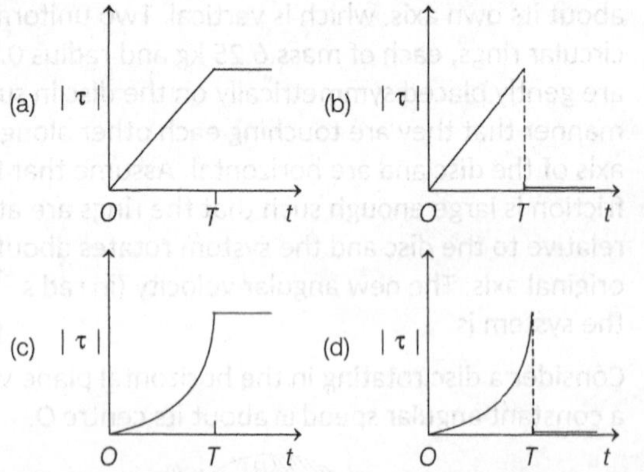

12. Two identical discs of same radius R are rotating about their axes in opposite directions with the same constant angular speed ω. The discs are in the same horizontal plane.

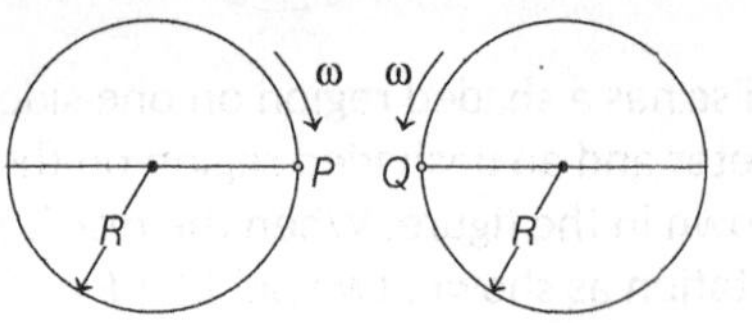

At time $t = 0$, the points P and Q are facing each other as shown in the figure. The relative speed between the two points P and Q is v_r. In one time period (T) of rotation of the discs, v_r as a function of time is best represented by **(2012)**

Note Language of the question is wrong. Magnitude of relative velocity should be asked.

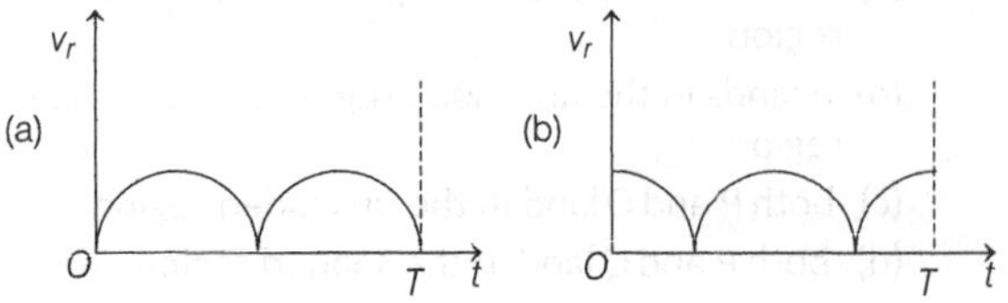

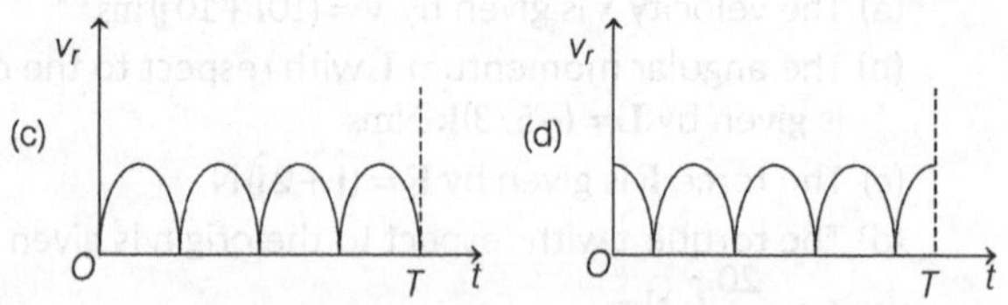

13. Four solid spheres each of diameter $\sqrt{5}$ cm and mass 0.5 kg are placed with their centres at the corners of a square of side 4 cm. The moment of inertia of the system about the diagonal of the square is $N \times 10^{-4}$ kg-m^2, then N is **(2011)**

14. If the resultant of all the external forces acting on a system of particles is zero, then from an inertial frame, one can surely say that **(2009)**

(a) linear momentum of the system does not change in time

(b) kinetic energy of the system does not change in time

(c) angular momentum of the system does not change in time

(d) potential energy of the system does not change in time

15. A block of base 10 cm × 10 cm and height 15 cm is kept on an inclined plane. The coefficient of friction between them is $\sqrt{3}$. The inclination θ of this inclined plane from the horizontal plane is gradually increased from 0°. Then, **(2009)**

(a) at $\theta = 30°$, the block will start sliding down the plane

(b) the block will remain at rest on the plane up to certain θ and then it will topple

(c) at $\theta = 60°$, the block will start sliding down the plane and continue to do so at higher angles

(d) at $\theta = 60°$, the block will start sliding down the plane and on further increasing θ, it will topple at certain θ

Answer Key

Level 1

3.1 Moment of Inertia

2. (i) $2ma^2$ (ii) $4ma^2$ (iii) $2ma^2$ (iv) ma^2

3. (a) MR^2 (b) MR^2 (c) MR^2

4. $2\pi\left(\frac{\alpha R^4}{4}+\frac{\beta R^5}{5}\right)$

5. (i) $\frac{3MR^2}{2}$ (ii) $2MR^2$

6. $I_1=\frac{ML^2}{3}, I_2=\frac{ML^2}{12}, I_3=0, I_4=Md^2$

7. $\frac{5ML^2}{3}$

8. $\frac{L}{2}\sqrt{\frac{5}{3}}$

9. $I_1=\frac{Mb^2}{3}; I_2=\frac{Ml^2}{12}; I_3=\frac{Mb^2}{12}, I_4=\frac{Ml^2}{3}$

10. (i) $\frac{2ML^2}{3}$ (ii) $\frac{ML^2}{12}$

11. $\left[\frac{MR^2}{2}-M\left(\frac{4R}{3\pi}\right)^2\right]$

12. $\frac{18}{5}mR^2$

13. $\frac{Ml^2}{6}$

14. $I=\frac{3}{10}mR^2$

15. $4MR^2$

3.2 Torque

1. $wl\sin\theta$, when the bob is at the lowest point

2. $mu^2\sin\theta\cos\theta$ perpendicular to the plane of motion

3. 8 kg

4. 400 N (left string) and 200 N (right string)

5. $P=\left(\frac{mg}{2}\right)\cot\theta$

6. $\frac{L\cos\theta\sin^2\theta}{2h-L\cos^2\theta\sin\theta}$

7. (i) 250 N (ii) $50\sqrt{10}$ N

8. 80 N

9. (a) $T=2mg$ (b) $N=6mg$ (c) $\frac{3g}{5L}$

10. (i) $\frac{3g}{2L}$ (ii) $a_{\text{radial}}=0, a_{\text{tangential}}=\frac{3g}{2}$ (iii) $\frac{mg}{4}$

11. (a) $\frac{3g}{4L}$ (cw) (b) $N=\frac{13mg}{16}, f=\left(\frac{3\sqrt{3}}{16}\right)mg$

12. (a) $\frac{3g}{2\sqrt{2}L}$ (cw) (b) $\frac{3}{2}g$ (c) $\frac{mg}{4}$

13. $\frac{g}{2R}, \frac{g}{2}$

14. (i) $a=\frac{(M_1-M_2)g}{M_1+M_2+\frac{1}{R^2}}$ (ii) $a_{2M}=\frac{8MgR^2}{I+9MR^2}, a_M=\frac{4MgR^2}{I+9MR^2}$

3.3 Rotational Kinetic Energy

1. (i) $\omega=\sqrt{\frac{3g}{l}}$ (ii) $\frac{5mg}{2}$

2. $\sqrt{\frac{24g}{7L}}$

3. $\sqrt{5gR}$

4. $\sqrt{3\sqrt{2}\frac{g}{L}}$

5. 2 m/s

3.4 Toppling

1. (i) $\frac{a}{4}$ (ii) $\frac{2mg}{3}$

2. $x=\frac{a\tan\theta}{2}$

3. $\frac{mg}{2\sqrt{3}}$

4. $\frac{gb}{l}$

3.5 Angular Momentum

1. 16 kg m^2/s

2. $\frac{mu^3\sin^2\theta\cos\theta}{2g}$

3. $K=0.4$ J, $L=0.04$ kg-m^2/s

4. 6 h

5. $\frac{\omega}{3}$

6. 2500 J

7. $\frac{7\omega_0}{16}$

8. $\frac{36u}{43L}$

9. $\frac{10}{3}$ m/s

10. $\left(\frac{3}{2}\right)mv^2$

11. $\omega=\frac{45}{14}$ rad/s, $v_s=\frac{1}{7}$ m/s

12. $\frac{muR}{mR^2+I}$

13. $\frac{m_1vR}{I+(m+m_1)R^2}$

14. $\frac{(I+mR^2)\omega_0+muR}{I+mR^2}$

Level 2

Single Choice Correct Questions

1. (c)	2. (a)	3. (c)	4. (d)	5. (a)	6. (a)	7. (c)	8. (c)	9. (c)	10. (b)
11. (d)	12. (d)	13. (b)	14. (b)	15. (a)	16. (d)	17. (c)	18. (a)	19. (c)	20. (c)
21. (d)	22. (b)	23. (a)	24. (d)	25. (d)	26. (d)	27. (d)	28. (a)	29. (b)	30. (c)
31. (a)	32. (b)	33. (b)	34. (b)	35. (a)	36. (c)	37. (b)	38. (a)	39. (a)	40. (c)
41. (b)	42. (c)	43. (c)	44. (c)	45. (a)	46. (b)	47. (d)	48. (d)	49. (a)	50. (d)

Numerical Value Questions

1. 12	2. 28	3. 3	4. 4	5. 260	6. 30	7. 4
8. 9	9. 210	10. 1				

Level 3

Single Choice Correct Questions

1. (c)	2. (c)	3. (d)	4. (b)	5. (d)	6. (c)	7. (c)	8. (b)	9. (b)	10. (c)
11. (d)	12. (d)	13. (a)	14. (b)	15. (c)	16. (c)	17. (c)	18. (b)	19. (c)	20. (d)
21. (b)	22. (b)	23. (b)	24. (c)	25. (b)	26. (a)	27. (c)	28. (d)	29. (b)	30. (d)
31. (a)	32. (d)	33. (a)	34. (a)						

Multiple Choice(s) Correct Questions

1. (a,b,c,d)	2. (c,d)	3. (b,c)	4. (a,c)	5. (a,c)	6. (a,b,c)	7. (a,c)	8. (a,d)	9. (a,d)	10. (a,c)
11. (a,b,c)	12. (a,b,c)	13. (a,b,c,d)	14. (a,c,d)	15. (b,c)					

Comprehension Based Questions

1. (b)	2. (b)	3. (c)	4. (c)	5. (a)	6. (b)	7. (d)	8. (c)	9. (b)	10. (b)
11. (c)	12. (a)	13. (a)	14. (a)	15. (d)	16. (c)	17. (d)	18. (c)	19. (a)	20. (a)
21. (b)	22. (b)	23. (b)	24. (b)	25. (c)	26. (c)				

Match the Columns Questions

1. A→ S; B →Q; C →P; D →R
2. A→ Q; B→ P; C→ S; D→ R
3. A→ R; B→ S; C→ P; D→ Q
4. A→ P,T; B→ P,R; C→ P,Q,S; D→ R
5. A→ Q; B→ R; C→ P; D→ R

Numerical Value Questions

1. (3)	2. (1)	3. (2.5)	4. (5)	5. (1.5)	6. (2)	7. (5)	8. (15)	9. (48)	10. (3)
11. (6)	12. (6)								

Previous Year Questions

JEE Main

1. (16)	2. (c)	3. (60)	4. (15)	5. (3)	6. (800)	7. (176)	8. (2)	9. (5)	10. (5)
11. (350)	12. (5)	13. (3)	14. (3)	15. (c)	16. (91)	17. (6)	18. (5)	19. (b)	20. (b)
21. (b)	22. (4)	23. (10)	24. (c)	25. (d)	26. (b)	27. (20)	28. (6)	29. (c)	30. (d)
31. (d)	32. (d)	33. (c)	34. (c)	35. (c)	36. (8)	37. (d)	38. (c)	39. (9)	40. (32)
41. (b)	42. (9)	43. (20)	44. (c)						

JEE Advanced

1. (4.30)	2. (b)	3. (a,b,c)	4. (a,c,d)	5. (a)	6. (ab,d)	7. (d)	8. (4)	9. (8)	10. (*)
11. (b)	12. (a)	13. (9)	14. (a)	15. (b)					

SOLUTIONS

Level 1

3.1 Moment of Inertia

1.

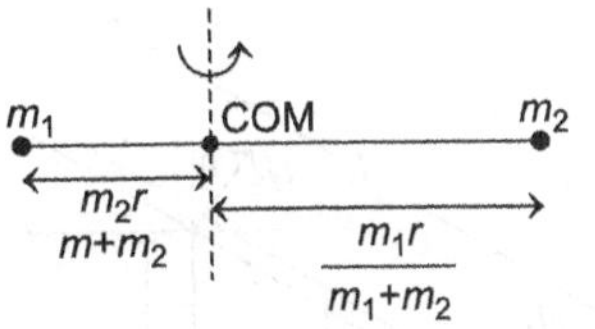

$$I = m_1\left(\frac{m_2 r}{m_1+m_2}\right)^2 + m_2\left(\frac{m_1 r}{m_1+m_2}\right)^2 = \left(\frac{m_1 m_2}{m_1+m_2}\right) r^2$$

$$= \mu r^2$$

2. (i) $I_1 = m\left(\frac{a}{\sqrt{2}}\right)^2 + m\left(\frac{a}{\sqrt{2}}\right)^2 + m\left(\frac{a}{\sqrt{2}}\right)^2 + m\left(\frac{a}{\sqrt{2}}\right)^2 = 2ma^2$

(ii) $I_2 = 0 + ma^2 + ma^2 + m(\sqrt{2}a)^2 = 4ma^2$

(iii) $I_3 = 0 + 0 + ma^2 + ma^2 = 2ma^2$

(iv) $I_4 = 0 + 0 + m\left(\frac{a}{\sqrt{2}}\right)^2 + m\left(\frac{a}{\sqrt{2}}\right)^2 = ma^2$

3. (a) $I = \int dmR^2 = (\int dm)R^2 = MR^2$

(b) $I = \int dmR^2 = MR^2$ (c) $I = \int dmR^2 = MR^2$

4. $dm = \sigma 2\pi x\, dx = (\alpha + \beta x)2\pi x\, dx$

$$I = \int dmx^2 = 2\pi\int_0^R (\alpha x^3 + \beta x^4)dx = 2\pi\left(\frac{\alpha R^4}{4} + \frac{\beta R^5}{5}\right)$$

5. (i) $I = I_{CM} + md^2 = \frac{MR^2}{2} + MR^2 = \frac{3}{2}MR^2$

(ii) $I = I_{CM} + md^2 = MR^2 + MR^2 = 2MR^2$

6. $I_1 = \frac{ML^2}{3}; I_2 = \frac{ML^2}{12}; I_3 = 0; I_4 = Md^2$

7. $I = I_1 + I_2 = \frac{ML^2}{3} + \left[\frac{ML^2}{12} + M\left(\frac{\sqrt{5}L}{2}\right)^2\right] = \frac{5}{3}ML^2$

8. $I = I_1 + I_2 + I_3$

$$= \frac{ML^2}{3}\sin^2 60° + \frac{ML^2}{3}\sin^2 60° + M\left(\frac{\sqrt{3}L}{2}\right)^2 = \frac{5}{4}ML^2$$

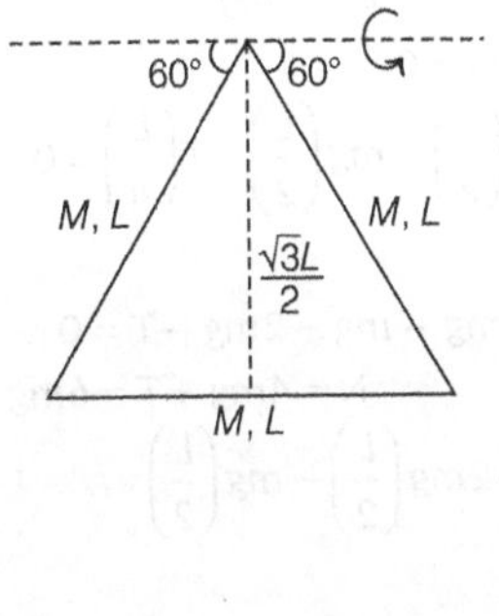

$$I = (3M)K^2 = \frac{5}{4}ML^2 \Rightarrow K = \frac{L}{2}\sqrt{\frac{5}{3}}$$

9. $I_1 = \frac{Mb^2}{3}; I_2 = \frac{Ml^2}{12}; I_3 = \frac{Mb^2}{12}$ and $I_4 = \frac{Ml^2}{3}$

10. (i) $I = I_x + I_y = \frac{ML^2}{3} + \frac{ML^2}{3} = \frac{2}{3}ML^2$

(ii) $I = I_1 + I_2 \Rightarrow \frac{ML^2}{6} = 2I_1 \Rightarrow I_1 = \frac{ML^2}{12}$

11.

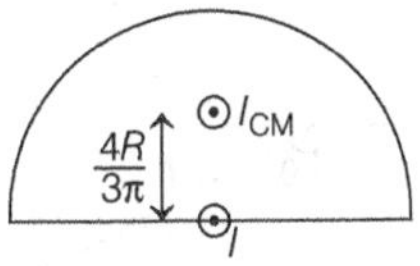

$$I = I_{CM} + md^2$$

$$\Rightarrow \frac{MR^2}{2} = I_{CM} + M\left(\frac{4R}{3\pi}\right)^2$$

$$\Rightarrow I_{CM} = \frac{MR^2}{2} - M\left(\frac{4R}{3\pi}\right)^2$$

12. $I = I_1 + I_2 + I_3 + I_4$

$$= \frac{2}{5}MR^2 + \frac{2}{5}MR^2 + \left(\frac{2}{5}MR^2 + MR^2\right) + \left(\frac{2}{5}MR^2 + MR^2\right)$$

$$= \frac{18MR^2}{5}$$

13. $I = \frac{Ml^2}{6}$

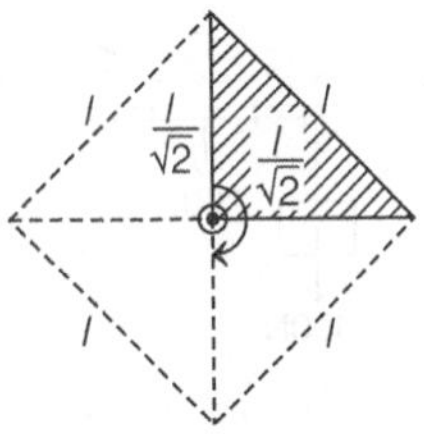

14. Lets take an elemental disc at a distance x from apex and of thickness dx.

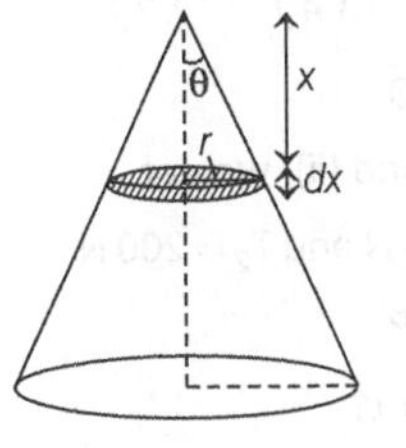

$$dm = \frac{M}{\frac{1}{3}\pi R^2 H}\left(\pi\left(\frac{Rx}{H}\right)^2 dx\right) = \frac{3M}{H^3}x^2 dx$$

$$\tan\theta = \frac{r}{x} = \frac{R}{H} \Rightarrow r = \frac{Rx}{H}$$

$$dI = \frac{dmr^2}{2} \Rightarrow \int dI = \int_0^H \frac{3M}{H^3}\frac{x^2dx}{2}\left(\frac{Rx}{H}\right)^2$$

$$\Rightarrow \quad I = \frac{3}{10}MR^2$$

15. $I = I_1 - I_2 = \dfrac{(9M)R^2}{2} - \left(\dfrac{M\left(\dfrac{R}{3}\right)^2}{2} + M\left(\dfrac{2R}{3}\right)^2\right) = 4MR^2$

3.2 Torque

1. $\tau = r_\perp F = wl \sin\theta$

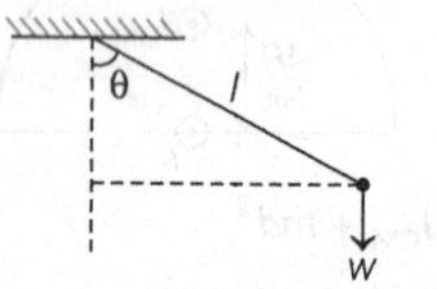

Torque will be zero when the bob is at the lowest point.

2. $\tau = r_\perp F = \left(\dfrac{R}{2}\right)mg = \left(\dfrac{u^2 \sin 2\theta}{2g}\right)mg = mu^2 \sin\theta \cos\theta$

3. $(16g)l_1 = (mg)l_2 \Rightarrow \dfrac{l_1}{l_2} = \dfrac{m}{16}$ ...(i)

$(mg)l_1 = (4g)l_2 \Rightarrow \dfrac{l_1}{l_2} = \dfrac{4}{m}$ ...(ii)

From Eqs. (i) and (ii), we get $\dfrac{m}{16} = \dfrac{4}{m} \Rightarrow m^2 = 64 \Rightarrow m = 8$ kg

4. $\Sigma F_y = 0 \Rightarrow T_1 + T_2 = 600$ ...(i)

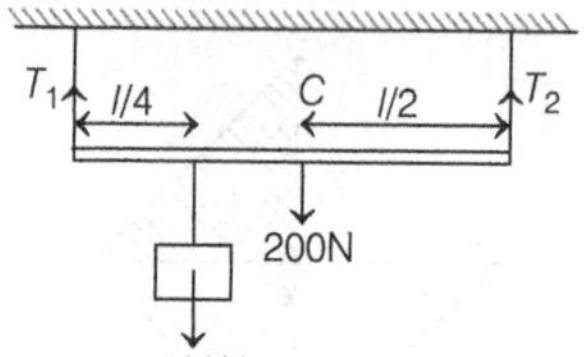

About C, $\Sigma\tau = 0$

$$\Rightarrow \quad T_1\left(\frac{l}{2}\right) - (400)\left(\frac{l}{4}\right) - T_2\left(\frac{l}{2}\right) = 0$$

$\Rightarrow \quad T_1 - T_2 = 200$ ...(ii)

Solving Eqs. (i) and (ii), we get

$T_1 = 400$ N and $T_2 = 200$ N

5. $\Sigma F_x = 0 \Rightarrow N_2 = P$

$\Sigma F_y = 0 \Rightarrow N_1 = mg$

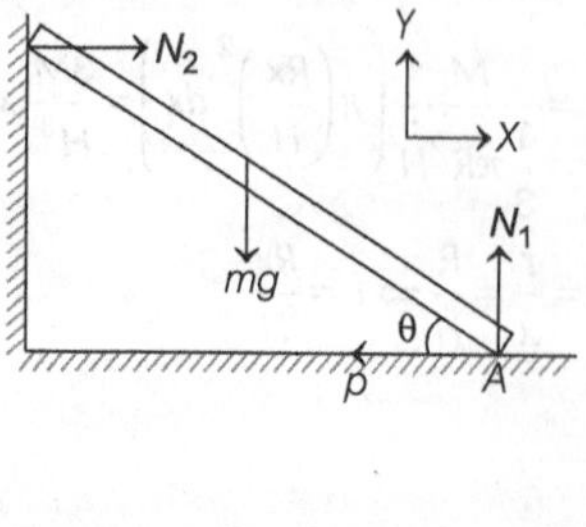

About point A, $\Sigma\tau = 0$

$$\Rightarrow N_2(L\sin\theta) - mg\left(\frac{L}{2}\cos\theta\right) = 0 \Rightarrow N_2 = \frac{mg\cot\theta}{2}$$

So, $P = \dfrac{mg\cot\theta}{2}$

6.

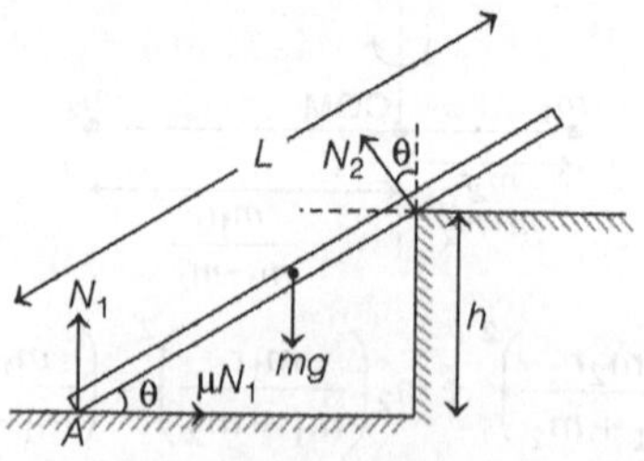

$\Sigma F_x = 0 \Rightarrow \mu N_1 = N_2 \sin\theta$ ...(i)

$\Sigma F_y = 0 \Rightarrow N_1 + N_2 \cos\theta = mg$ ...(ii)

About point A, $\Sigma\tau = 0 \Rightarrow mg\left(\dfrac{L}{2}\cos\theta\right) - N_2\left(\dfrac{h}{\sin\theta}\right) = 0$ ...(iii)

Solving we get, $\mu = \dfrac{L\cos\theta\sin^2\theta}{2h - L\cos^2\theta\sin\theta}$

7. (i)

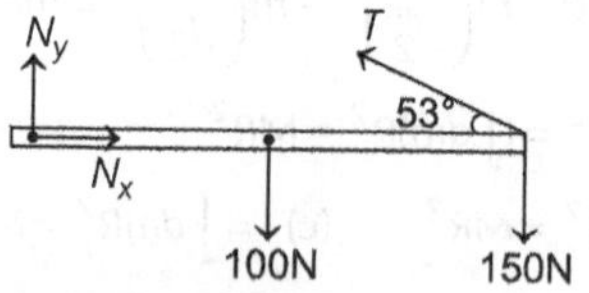

$\Sigma F_x = 0 \Rightarrow N_x = T\cos 53°$ ...(i)

$\Sigma F_y = 0 \Rightarrow N_y + T\sin 53° = 250$ ...(ii)

About hinge, $\Sigma\tau = 0 \Rightarrow 100(0.5) + 150(1) - (T\sin 53°)(1) = 0$

$\Rightarrow \quad T = 250$ N

(ii) $N_x = 250\cos 53° = 150$ N

$N_y = 250 - 250\sin 53° = 50$ N

Hinge force $= \sqrt{N_x^2 + N_y^2} = 50\sqrt{10}$ N

8. $\omega = \omega_0 + \alpha t \Rightarrow 0 = 100 + \alpha(10) \Rightarrow \alpha = -10$ rad/s

$\tau = I\alpha = 0.8 \times 10 = 8$ N-m

$\tau = r_\perp F \Rightarrow 8 = (0.1)F \Rightarrow F = 80$ N

9. (a)

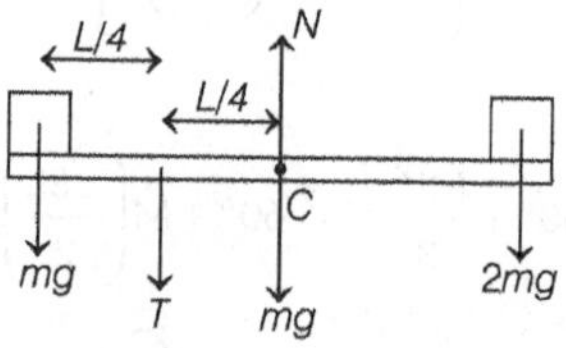

About C, $\Sigma\tau = 0$

$$\Rightarrow \quad 2mg\left(\frac{L}{2}\right) - mg\left(\frac{L}{2}\right) - T\left(\frac{L}{4}\right) = 0 \Rightarrow T = 2mg$$

(b) $\Sigma F_y = 0$

$\Rightarrow \quad N - mg - mg - 2mg - T = 0$

$\Rightarrow \quad N = 4mg + T = 6mg$

(c) $\Sigma\tau = I\alpha \Rightarrow 2mg\left(\dfrac{L}{2}\right) - mg\left(\dfrac{L}{2}\right)$

$$= \left(\frac{mL^2}{12} + m\left(\frac{L}{2}\right)^2 + 2m\left(\frac{L}{2}\right)^2\right)\alpha \Rightarrow \alpha = \frac{3g}{5L}$$

10. (i) About hinge, $\Sigma\tau = I\alpha$

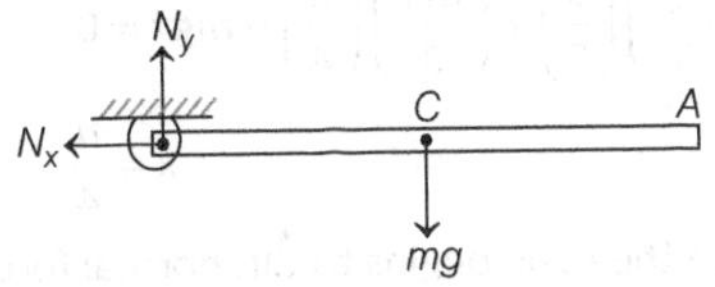

$$\Rightarrow mg\left(\frac{L}{2}\right) = \left(\frac{mL^2}{3}\right)\alpha \Rightarrow \alpha = \frac{3g}{2L}$$

(ii) For point A, $a_{radial} = \omega^2 L = 0$

$$a_{tangential} = L\alpha = \frac{3g}{2}$$

(iii) $(\Sigma F_{ext})_x = m(a_{CM})_x \Rightarrow N_x = m\left(\omega^2 \frac{L}{2}\right) = 0 \quad [\because \omega = 0]$

$(\Sigma F_{ext})_y = m(a_{CM})_y \Rightarrow mg - N_y = m\left(\frac{L}{2}\alpha\right)$

$$\Rightarrow \quad N_y = \frac{mg}{4}$$

So, net hinge force $= \sqrt{N_x^2 + N_y^2} = \frac{mg}{4}$

11. (a) Since end A is not sliding, the rod is in pure rotational motion about A.

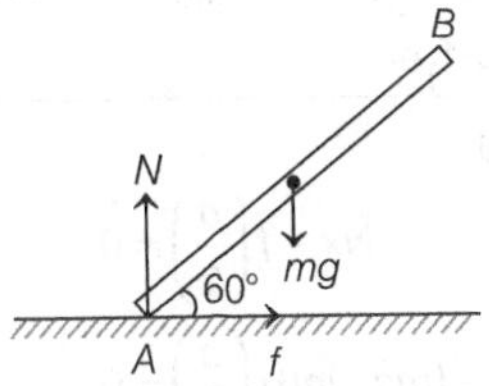

About A, $\Sigma\tau = I\alpha$

$$\Rightarrow mg\left(\frac{L}{2}\cos 60°\right) = \left(\frac{mL^2}{3}\right)\alpha \Rightarrow \alpha = \frac{3g}{4L}$$

(b) $(\Sigma F_{ext})_x = m(a_{CM})_x$

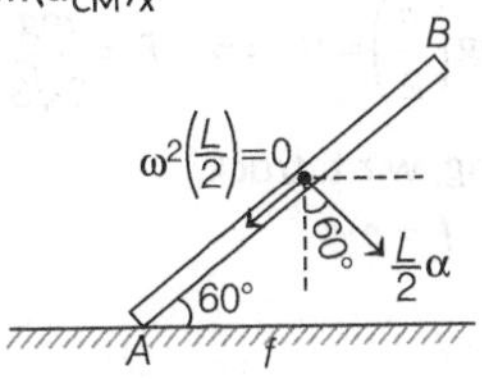

$$\Rightarrow \quad f = m\left(\frac{L}{2}\alpha \sin 60°\right) = \frac{3\sqrt{3}\, mg}{16}$$

$(\Sigma F_{ext})_y = m(a_{CM})_y$

$$\Rightarrow mg - N = m\left(\frac{L}{2}\alpha \cos 60°\right) \Rightarrow N = \frac{13mg}{16}$$

12. (a) $\Sigma\tau = I\alpha \Rightarrow mg\left(\frac{L}{\sqrt{2}}\right) = \left(\frac{2mL^2}{3}\right)\alpha \Rightarrow \alpha = \frac{3g}{2\sqrt{2}L}$

(b) $a_c = r\alpha = (\sqrt{2}L)\left(\frac{3g}{2\sqrt{2}L}\right) = \frac{3g}{2}$

(c) $(\Sigma F_{ext})_y = m(a_{CM})_y$

$$\Rightarrow mg - N_y = m\left(\frac{L}{\sqrt{2}}\alpha\right) \Rightarrow N_y = \frac{mg}{4}$$

13. For block, $\Sigma F = ma \Rightarrow mg - T = ma$ ...(i)

For pulley,

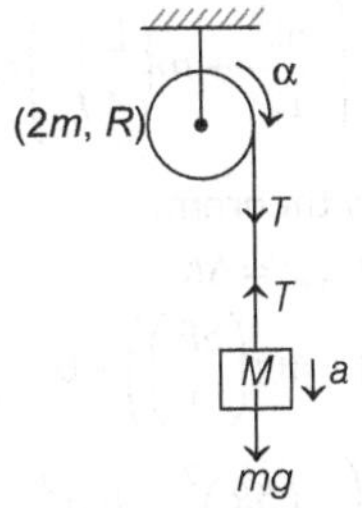

$$\Sigma\tau = I\alpha \Rightarrow TR = \left(\frac{2mR^2}{2}\right)\alpha \quad \text{...(ii)}$$

Constraint, $a = R\alpha$ ...(iii)

Solving Eqs. (i), (ii) and (iii), we get

$$\alpha = \frac{g}{2R} \text{ and } a = \frac{g}{2}$$

14. (i) $M_1 g - T_1 = M_1 a$ ...(i)

$T_2 - M_2 g = M_2 a$ ...(ii)

$T_1 R - T_2 R = I\alpha$ ...(iii)

$a = R\alpha$ ...(iv)

Solving we get, $a = \dfrac{(M_1 - M_2)g}{M_1 + M_2 + \dfrac{I}{R^2}}$

(ii) $2Mg - T_1 = 2Ma_1$ ...(i)

$T_2 = Ma_2$ ...(ii)

$T_1(2R) - T_2(R) = I\alpha$ ...(iii)

$a_1 = 2R\alpha$ ...(iv)

$a_2 = R\alpha$ ...(v)

Solving we get,

$$a_1 = \frac{8MgR^2}{I + 9MR^2} \text{ and } a_2 = \frac{4MgR^2}{I + 9MR^2}$$

3.3 Rotational Kinetic Energy

1. (i) Applying work-energy theorem,

$W_{mg} + W_{hinge} = \Delta K$

$$\Rightarrow mg\left(\frac{L}{2}\right) + 0 = \frac{1}{2}\left(\frac{mL^2}{3}\right)\omega^2 - 0 \Rightarrow \omega = \sqrt{\frac{3g}{L}}$$

(ii) $(\Sigma F_{ext})_y = M(a_{CM})_y$

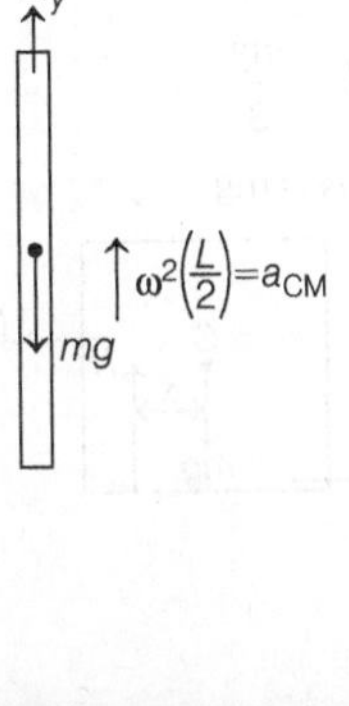

$$\Rightarrow N_y - mg = m\left(\omega^2\left(\frac{L}{2}\right)\right) \Rightarrow N_y = \frac{5mg}{2}$$

2. Using work-energy theorem,

$$W_{mg} + W_{hinge} = \Delta K$$

$$\Rightarrow mg\left(\frac{L}{4}\right) + 0 = \frac{1}{2}\left(\frac{mL^2}{12} + m\left(\frac{L}{4}\right)^2\right)\omega^2 \Rightarrow \omega = \sqrt{\frac{24g}{7L}}$$

3. Using work-energy theorem,

$$W_{mg} + W_{hinge} = \Delta K$$

$$\Rightarrow \left(+mg\left(\frac{R}{2}\right) + mg\left(\frac{5R}{2}\right)\right) + 0$$

$$= \frac{1}{2}\left(m\left(\frac{5R}{4}\right)^2 + \frac{mR^2}{4} + m\left(\frac{R}{4}\right)^2\right)\omega^2$$

$$\Rightarrow \omega = \sqrt{\frac{16g}{5R}}$$

Linear speed of particle $= \omega\left(\frac{5R}{4}\right) = \sqrt{5gR}$

4. $I_{AB} = I_{AD} = \frac{ML^2}{3}\sin^2 45°$

$$I_{BC} = I_{CD} = \frac{ML^2}{12}\sin^2 45° + M\left(\frac{3\sqrt{2}L}{4}\right)^2$$

$$I = I_{AB} + I_{BC} + I_{CD} + I_{AD} = \frac{8}{3}ML^2$$

$$W_{mg} + W_{hinge} = \Delta K$$

$$\Rightarrow + 4Mg(\sqrt{2}\,L) + 0 = \frac{1}{2}\left(\frac{8}{3}ML^2\right)\omega^2$$

$$\Rightarrow \omega = \sqrt{\frac{3\sqrt{2}g}{L}}$$

5. Using work-energy theorem for (block + pulley) system,

$$W_{mg} + W_T = \Delta K_{system}$$

$$\Rightarrow 3 \times 10 \times 0.4 + 0 = \left(\frac{1}{2} \times 3 \times v^2 + \frac{1}{2} \times 3\omega^2\right) - (0 + 0)$$

$$\Rightarrow 12 = \frac{3}{2}(v^2) + \frac{3}{2}\left(\frac{v}{1}\right)^2 \qquad \left[\because \omega = \frac{v}{R}\right]$$

$$\Rightarrow v = 2 \text{ m/s}$$

3.4 Toppling

1. (i) $\Sigma F_x = 0 \Rightarrow f = \frac{mg}{3}$

$\Sigma F_y = 0 \Rightarrow N = mg$

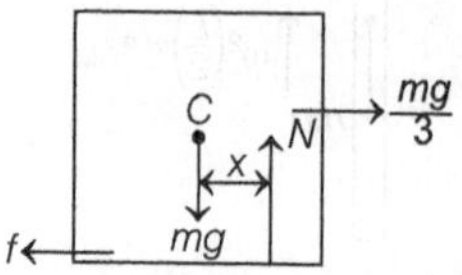

About C, $\Sigma\tau = 0$

$$\Rightarrow f\left(\frac{a}{2}\right) + \left(\frac{mg}{3}\right)\left(\frac{a}{4}\right) - Nx = 0$$

$$\Rightarrow \left(\frac{mg}{3}\right)\left(\frac{a}{2}\right) + \left(\frac{mg}{3}\right)\left(\frac{a}{4}\right) - mgx = 0$$

$$\Rightarrow x = \frac{a}{4}$$

(ii) When the cube begins to tilt, normal force passes through the rightmost end of the cube.

About A, $\Sigma\tau = 0$

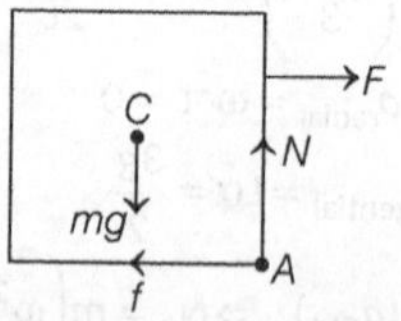

$$F\left(\frac{3a}{4}\right) - mg\left(\frac{a}{2}\right) = 0 \Rightarrow F = \frac{2mg}{3}$$

2. Since the cube is sliding down with constant speed, $mg\sin\theta = f$

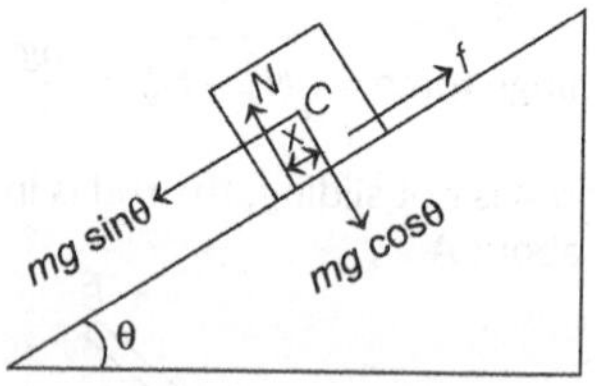

About C, $\Sigma\tau = 0$

$$\Rightarrow Nx - f\left(\frac{a}{2}\right) = 0$$

$$\Rightarrow (mg\cos\theta)x - (mg\sin\theta)\left(\frac{a}{2}\right) = 0$$

$$\Rightarrow x = \frac{a}{2}\tan\theta$$

3. About A, $\Sigma\tau = 0$

$$\Rightarrow F(\sqrt{3}a) - mg\left(\frac{a}{2}\right) = 0 \Rightarrow F = \frac{mg}{2\sqrt{3}}$$

4. Box is not sliding, w.r.t. truck,

$$\Rightarrow f = ma$$

For toppling,

About A,

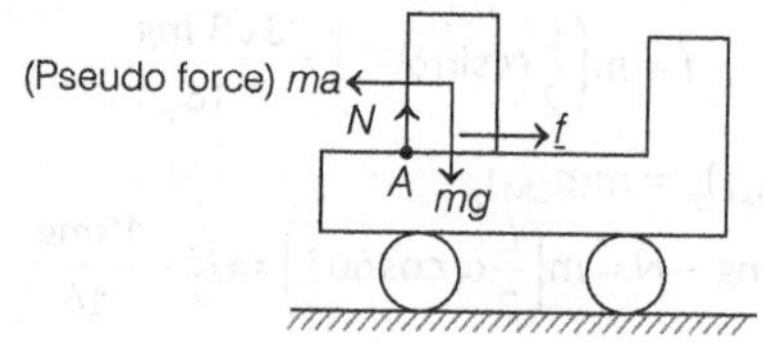

$$\Sigma\tau = 0 \Rightarrow ma\left(\frac{l}{2}\right) - mg\left(\frac{b}{2}\right) = 0$$

$$\Rightarrow a = \frac{gb}{l}$$

3.5 Angular Momentum

1. $L = r_{\perp}p = \dfrac{|3(0)+4(0)-5|}{\sqrt{3^2+4^2}}(2\times 8) = 16\ \text{kg m}^2/\text{s}$

2. $L = r_{\perp}p = \left(\dfrac{u^2\sin^2\theta}{2g}\right)(mu\cos\theta) = \dfrac{mu^3\sin^2\theta\cos\theta}{2g}$

3. $I = \left(\dfrac{mR^2}{2}\right) = \dfrac{0.4\times(0.1)^2}{2} = 2\times 10^{-3}\text{kg m}^2$

$K = \dfrac{1}{2}I\omega^2 = \dfrac{1}{2}\times 2\times 10^{-3}\times(20)^2 = 0.4\ \text{J}$

$L = I\omega = 2\times 10^{-3}\times 20 = 0.04\ \text{kg m}^2/\text{s}$

4. Conserving angular momentum,

$I_1\omega_1 = I_2\omega_2$

$\Rightarrow \left(\dfrac{2}{5}MR^2\right)\left(\dfrac{2\pi}{(24\,\text{h})}\right) = \dfrac{2}{5}M\left(\dfrac{R}{2}\right)^2\left(\dfrac{2\pi}{T}\right)$

$\Rightarrow T = 6\ \text{h}$

5. $I_1\omega_1 = I_2\omega_2$

$\Rightarrow \left(\dfrac{mR^2}{2}+0\right)\omega = \left(\dfrac{mR^2}{2}+mR^2\right)\omega' \Rightarrow \omega' = \dfrac{\omega}{3}$

6. $I_1\omega_1 = I_2\omega_2 \Rightarrow 1\times 100 = (1+1)\omega \Rightarrow \omega = 50\ \text{rad/s}$

$K_{\text{loss}} = K_1 - K_2 = \left(\dfrac{1}{2}\times 1\times(100)^2+0\right) - \left(\dfrac{1}{2}\times 2\times(50)^2\right)$

$= 2500\ \text{J}$

7. $I_1\omega_1 = I_2\omega_2$

$\Rightarrow \left(2m\dfrac{L^2}{12}+m\left(\dfrac{L}{4}\right)^2+m\left(\dfrac{L}{4}\right)^2\right)\omega_0$

$= \left(2m\left(\dfrac{L^2}{12}\right)+m\left(\dfrac{L}{2}\right)^2+m\left(\dfrac{L}{2}\right)^2\right)\omega$

$\Rightarrow \quad \omega = \dfrac{7\omega_0}{16}$

8. $mu\left(\dfrac{3L}{4}\right)+0 = \left(\dfrac{mL^2}{3}+m\left(\dfrac{3L}{4}\right)^2\right)\omega \Rightarrow \omega = \dfrac{36u}{43L}$

9. Conserving angular momentum about the hinge,

$m(5)r + 0 = mvr + \left(\dfrac{mr^2}{2}\right)\omega$

$\Rightarrow \quad 5 = v + \dfrac{\omega r}{2}$

$\Rightarrow \quad 5 = v + \dfrac{v}{2} \qquad \because (v = \omega r)$

$\Rightarrow \quad v = \dfrac{10}{3}\ \text{m/s}$

10. $mv_1r_1 = mv_2r_2 \Rightarrow mvr_0 = mv'\left(\dfrac{r_0}{2}\right) \Rightarrow v' = 2v$

$W_{\text{ext}} = \Delta K = \dfrac{1}{2}m(2v)^2 - \dfrac{1}{2}mv^2 = \dfrac{3}{2}mv^2$

11. Conserving angular momentum for (rod + sphere) system about the hinge

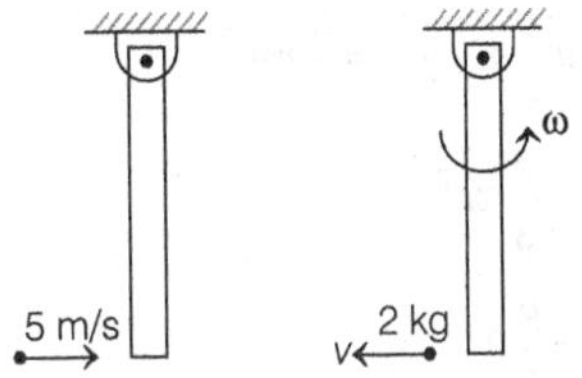

Before Collision After Collision

$2\times 5\times 1.2 + 0 = -2v(1.2) + \dfrac{8(1.2)^2}{3}\omega$

$\Rightarrow \quad 12 + 2.4v = 3.84\omega \qquad \text{...(i)}$

$e = 0.8 = \dfrac{v+\omega(1.2)}{5-0} \Rightarrow v + 1.2\omega = 4 \qquad \text{...(ii)}$

Solving Eqs. (i) and (ii), we get

$v = \dfrac{1}{7}\ \text{m/s and } \omega = \dfrac{45}{14}\ \text{rad/s}$

12. $v_{\text{child, platform}} = u \Rightarrow v_{\text{child}} = u + v_{\text{platform}} = u + \omega R$

Conserving angular momentum for (child + platform) system,

$0 + 0 = I\omega + m(u+\omega R)R \Rightarrow \omega = -\dfrac{muR}{I+mR^2}$

13. $m_1vR + 0 = (I + mR^2 + m_1R^2)\omega \Rightarrow \omega = \dfrac{m_1vR}{I+(m+m_1)R^2}$

14. $(I+mR^2)\omega_0 = I\omega + m(-u+\omega R)R$

$\Rightarrow \quad \omega = \dfrac{(I+mR^2)\omega_0 + muR}{I+mR^2}$

Level 2

Single Choice Correct Questions

1. $I = 0 + 0 + Ma^2\times 4 + M(\sqrt{2}a)^2\times 2 = 8Ma^2$

2. $I = I_1 + I_2 + I_3 = \dfrac{ML^2}{3} + \dfrac{ML^2}{3} + 0 = \dfrac{2ML^2}{3}$

3. $I = I_1 + I_2 = \dfrac{ml^2}{12}\sin^2 45^\circ + \dfrac{ml^2}{12}\sin^2 45^\circ = \dfrac{ml^2}{12}$

4. $I = I_{CM} + md^2 = \dfrac{MR^2}{2} + MR^2 = \dfrac{3}{2}MR^2$

$= \dfrac{3}{2}(\rho L)\left(\dfrac{L}{2\pi}\right)^2 = \dfrac{3\rho L^3}{8\pi^2}$

5. $\dfrac{5}{4}MR^2 = I \Rightarrow MR^2 = \dfrac{4I}{5}$

$I' = \dfrac{3}{2}MR^2 = \dfrac{3}{2}\left(\dfrac{4I}{5}\right) = \dfrac{6I}{5}$

6. $I = I_1 + I_2 + I_3 = \dfrac{mr^2}{2} + \left(\dfrac{mr^2}{2}+mr^2\right) + \left(\dfrac{mr^2}{2}+mr^2\right)$

$= \dfrac{7}{2}mr^2$

$$I=\frac{7}{2}mr^2=(3m)k^2 \Rightarrow k=\sqrt{\frac{7}{6}}\,r$$

7. $I=I_1+I_2=mr^2+\frac{mr^2}{2}=\frac{3}{2}mr^2$

8. $v=\pi R^2\left(\frac{R}{6}\right)=\frac{4}{3}\pi r^3$

$$\Rightarrow \quad r=\frac{R}{2}$$

$$I=\frac{MR^2}{2}, I'=\frac{2}{5}Mr^2=\frac{2}{5}\left(\frac{2I}{R^2}\right)\left(\frac{R}{2}\right)^2=\frac{I}{5}$$

9. I is minimum about the axis passing through the centre of mass.

$$\frac{dI}{dx}=2x-2=0 \Rightarrow x=1$$

10. $I_1=I_2 \Rightarrow \frac{MR^2}{2}=\frac{MR^2}{4}+M\left(\frac{C}{\sqrt{2}}\right)^2$

$$\Rightarrow \quad C=\frac{R}{\sqrt{2}}$$

11. Sector 1 can be shifted in place of sector 2 as they have similar mass distribution about axis AA'. So, $I=\frac{MR^2}{4}$.

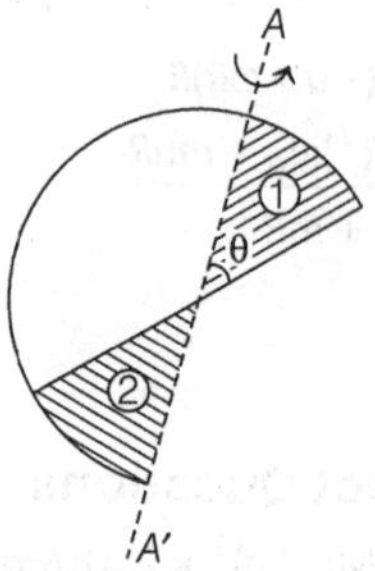

12. $I_C=MR^2=I_{CM}+M\left(\frac{2R}{\pi}\right)^2$

$$\Rightarrow \quad I_{CM}=MR^2-M\left(\frac{2R}{\pi}\right)^2$$

$$I_0=I_{CM}+M\left(R-\frac{2R}{\pi}\right)^2$$

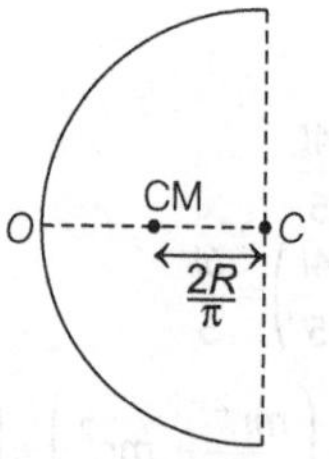

$$\Rightarrow \quad I_0=\left(MR^2-M\left(\frac{2R}{\pi}\right)^2\right)+M\left(R-\frac{2R}{\pi}\right)^2$$

$$=2MR^2\left(1-\frac{2}{\pi}\right)$$

13. For square sheet, moment of inertia about diagonal

$$=\frac{(2M)l^2}{12}$$

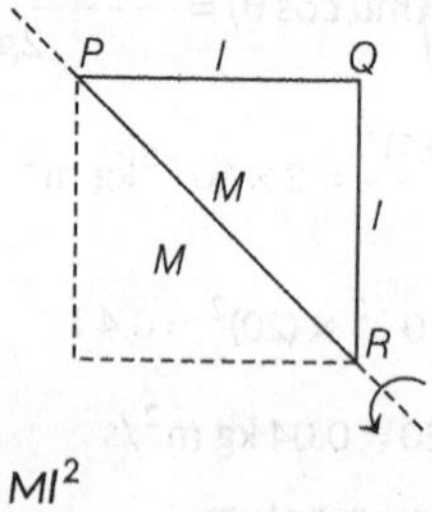

$$\text{So, } I=\frac{1}{2}\left(\frac{(2M)l^2}{12}\right)=\frac{Ml^2}{12}$$

14. $I_1=I_2$

$$\Rightarrow \quad \frac{ML^2}{3}=\frac{ML^2}{12}+M\left(\sqrt{\left(x-\frac{L}{2}\right)^2+y^2}\right)^2$$

$$\Rightarrow \quad \left(x-\frac{L}{2}\right)^2+y^2=\frac{L^2}{4}$$

So, locus will be circle.

15. $I_{AB}=I_{EF}=I$

$I_{CD}=I_{GH}=I'$

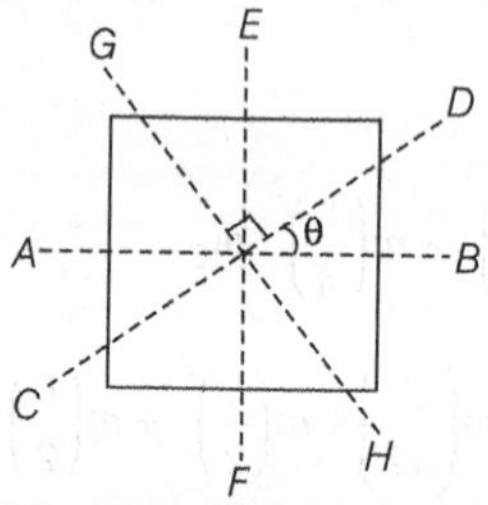

Using perpendicular axis theorem,

$$I_z=I_{AB}+I_{EF}=I_{CD}+I_{GH}$$

$$\Rightarrow \quad I+I=I'+I' \Rightarrow I'=I$$

16. $I=\left(\left(\frac{M}{6}\right)\frac{a^2}{6}\right)\times 2+\left(\left(\frac{M}{6}\right)\left(\frac{a^2}{12}\right)+\left(\frac{M}{6}\right)\left(\frac{a}{2}\right)^2\right)\times 4=\frac{5Ma^2}{18}$

17. $I_1=I_2 \Rightarrow \frac{MR^2}{2}=\frac{MR^2}{4}+\frac{ML^2}{12} \Rightarrow \frac{L}{R}=\sqrt{3}$

18. $\rho=\frac{M}{\frac{4}{3}\pi R^3-\frac{4}{3}\pi\left(\frac{R}{2}\right)^3}=\left(\frac{M}{\frac{4}{3}\pi R^3}\right)\left(\frac{8}{7}\right)$

$$M_1=\rho\frac{4}{3}\pi R^3=\frac{8M}{7} \text{ and } M_2=\rho\frac{4}{3}\pi\left(\frac{R}{2}\right)^3=\frac{M}{7}$$

$$I=I_1-I_2$$

$$= \frac{2}{5}\left(\frac{8M}{7}\right)R^2 - \left(\frac{2}{5}\left(\frac{M}{7}\right)\left(\frac{R}{2}\right)^2 + \left(\frac{M}{7}\right)\left(\frac{R}{2}\right)^2\right) = \frac{57}{140}MR^2$$

19. $\Sigma\tau = 0 \Rightarrow 100(0.3) + F(0.2) = 0$

$\Rightarrow \quad F = -150$ N

So, $\quad \mathbf{F} = -150\hat{\mathbf{i}}$

20. About C,

$$\Sigma\tau = 0 \Rightarrow N_1\left(\frac{l}{4}\right) - N_2\left(\frac{l}{3}\right) = 0$$

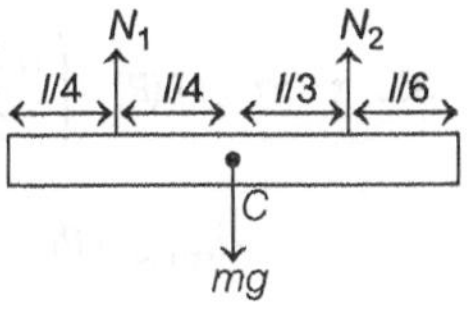

$$\Rightarrow \quad \frac{N_1}{N_2} = \frac{4}{3}$$

21. For the object,

$$\Sigma F_y = 0 \Rightarrow 2\mu N_1 = 2000$$

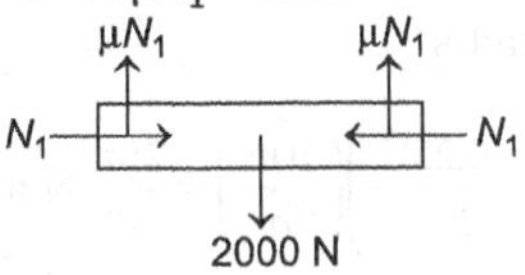

$\Rightarrow 2(0.1)N_1 = 2000 \Rightarrow N_1 = 10000$ N

For a tong, $\Sigma\tau = 0$

$\Rightarrow \quad N_1(15 \text{ cm}) - F(30 \text{ cm}) = 0$

$\Rightarrow \quad F = \frac{N_1}{2} = 5000$ N

22. $\Sigma F_y = 0 \Rightarrow T_1 + T_2 = 5\,mg$ ...(i)

About C, $\Sigma\tau = 0$

$$\Rightarrow \quad T_1\left(\frac{L}{4}\right) - T_2\left(\frac{L}{2}\right) - 2mg\left(\frac{L}{2}\right) = 0$$

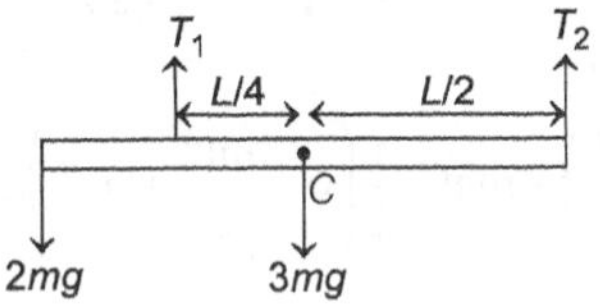

$\Rightarrow \quad T_1 - 2T_2 = 4mg$ ...(ii)

Solving, we get $T_1 = \frac{14mg}{3}$, $T_2 = \frac{mg}{3}$

So, $\frac{T_1}{T_2} = 14:1$

23. $\Sigma F_x = 0 \Rightarrow N_2 = \mu N_1$ ...(i)

$\Sigma F_y = 0 \Rightarrow N_1 = mg$ ...(ii)

About the lower end, $\Sigma\tau = 0$

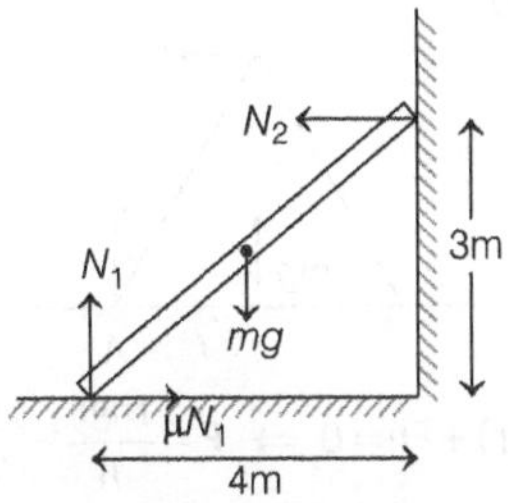

$\Rightarrow \quad mg(2) - N_2(3) = 0 \Rightarrow N_2 = \frac{2mg}{3}$ ...(iii)

Solving, we get $\mu = \frac{2}{3}$

24. $\Sigma F_x = 0 \Rightarrow N_2 = ma$ ...(i)

$\Sigma F_y = 0 \Rightarrow N_1 = mg$ ...(ii)

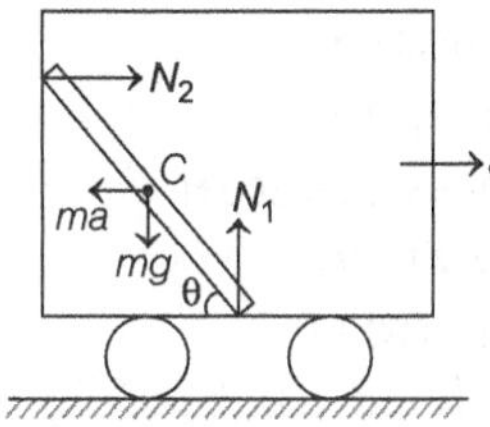

About C, $\Sigma\tau = 0$

$\Rightarrow \quad N_1\left(\frac{l}{2}\cos\theta\right) - N_2\left(\frac{l}{2}\sin\theta\right) = 0$ ...(iii)

$\Rightarrow \quad N_1 = N_2 \tan\theta$

Solving we get, $a = g\cot\theta$

25. $\Sigma F_x = 0 \Rightarrow T + f = mg\sin 30°$ ...(i)

$\Sigma F_y = 0 \Rightarrow N = mg\cos 30°$ ...(ii)

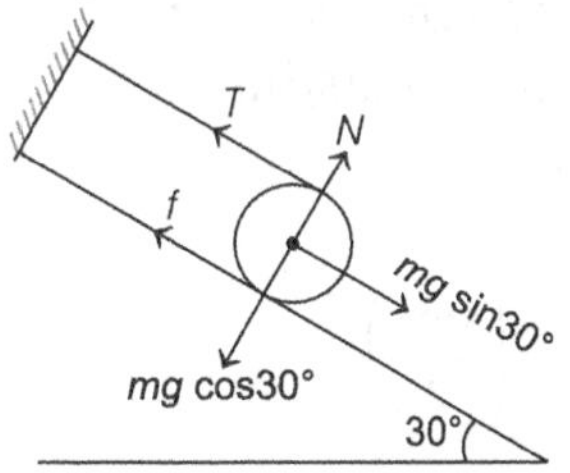

About the point of contact,

$\Sigma\tau = 0 \Rightarrow -T(2R) + (mg\sin 30°)R = 0 \Rightarrow T = \frac{mg}{4}$ ...(iii)

Solving we get, $T = \frac{mg}{4}$ and $f = \frac{mg}{4}$

Now, $f \le f_L \Rightarrow \frac{mg}{4} \le \mu(mg\cos 30°) \Rightarrow \mu_{min} = \frac{1}{2\sqrt{3}}$

26. $\Sigma\tau = 0$

$\Rightarrow \quad Mg\left(\frac{L}{2}\sin 30°\right) - mg\left(\frac{L}{2}\sin 60°\right) = 0$

$\Rightarrow \quad \frac{M}{m} = \sqrt{3}$

27. For the system, $\Sigma F_y = 0$

$\Rightarrow \quad 2N_1 - 2w = 0$

$\Rightarrow \quad N_1 = w$

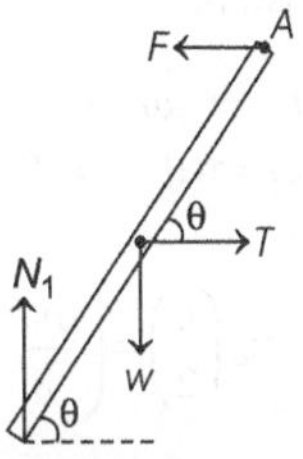

FBD of left rod

About point A,

$\Sigma\tau = 0 \Rightarrow N_1(2l\cos\theta) - w(l\cos\theta) - T(l\sin\theta) = 0$

$\Rightarrow \quad T = w\cot\theta = \dfrac{wL}{\sqrt{4l^2 - L^2}}$

28. For equilibrium of plate,

$\Sigma F_x = 0 \Rightarrow T = F_x$

$\Sigma F_y = 0 \Rightarrow F_y = 300\text{ N}$

About the hinge, $\Sigma\tau = 0$

$\Rightarrow \quad 300(1.5) - T(2) = 0$

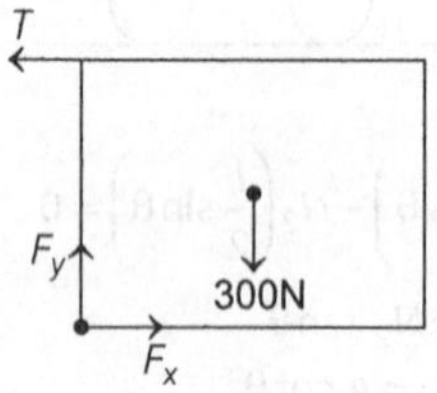

$\Rightarrow \quad T = 225\text{ N}$

So, $F_x = 225$ N, $T = 225$ N and $F_y = 300$ N

29. $\tau = I\alpha \Rightarrow 50\times0.5 - 20\times0.5$

$= (5\times(0.5)^2 + 2\times(0.5)^2)\alpha$

$\Rightarrow \alpha = 8.6\text{ rad/s}^2$

30. $mg - T = ma$ ...(i)

$(2T)R = \left(\dfrac{MR^2}{2}\right)\alpha$ ...(ii)

$a = R\alpha$ ...(iii)

Solving we get $a = \dfrac{4mg}{M+4m}$

31. $50 - T_1 = 5a_1$ ...(i)

$T_2 - 40 = 4a_2$ ...(ii)

$T_1(2) - T_2(1) = 4\alpha$ ...(iii)

$a_1 = 2\alpha$ ...(iv)

$a_2 = (1)\alpha$ ...(v)

Solving, we get $\alpha = \dfrac{15}{7}\text{ rad/s}^2 = 2.1\text{ rad/s}^2$

32. $\tau = I\alpha \Rightarrow 40(2) = 10\alpha \Rightarrow \alpha = 8\text{ rad/s}^2$

$a = R\alpha = 2(8) = 16\text{ m/s}^2$

$s = ut + \dfrac{1}{2}at^2 = \dfrac{1}{2}(16)(3)^2 = 72\text{ m}$

33. $\tau = I\alpha \Rightarrow \alpha = \dfrac{\tau}{I} = \text{constant}$ $(\because \tau = \text{constant})$

$\omega = \omega_0 + \alpha t \Rightarrow \omega = \alpha t$

$P = \tau\cdot\omega = \tau\omega = \tau\alpha t \Rightarrow P \propto t$

34. $a_{\text{ball}} = g$

For bar, $\tau = I\alpha \Rightarrow mg\left(\dfrac{L}{2}\right) = \left(\dfrac{mL^2}{3}\right)\alpha$

$\Rightarrow \quad \alpha = \dfrac{3g}{2L}$

a = Acceleration of any point on the bar $= r\alpha = r\left(\dfrac{3g}{2L}\right)$

$a = g \Rightarrow r\left(\dfrac{3g}{2L}\right) = g \Rightarrow r = \dfrac{2L}{3}$

Distance of the point from $B = L - \dfrac{2L}{3} = \dfrac{L}{3}$

35. $\tau = I\alpha \Rightarrow F(R) = \left(\dfrac{mR^2}{2}\right)\alpha \Rightarrow \alpha = \dfrac{2F}{mR}$

$a_{\text{string}} = R\alpha = R\left(\dfrac{2(mg)}{mR}\right) = 2g$

36. $\omega = \omega_0 + \alpha t \Rightarrow 0 = \dfrac{500\times2\pi}{60} + \alpha(15)$

$\Rightarrow \alpha = -\dfrac{10\pi}{9}\text{ rad/s}^2$

$\tau = I\alpha = \left(\dfrac{15(0.25)^2}{2}\right)\left(\dfrac{10\pi}{a}\right) = \dfrac{25\pi}{48}$ N-m

$\tau = \mu N = \mu(100)$

$\Rightarrow \tau = fR \Rightarrow \dfrac{25\pi}{48} = \mu(100)(0.25)$

$\Rightarrow \mu = 0.066$

37. $W_{mg} + W_{\text{hinge}} = \Delta K$

$\Rightarrow \quad mg\dfrac{l}{2}(1-\cos\theta) + 0 = \dfrac{1}{2}\left(\dfrac{ml^2}{3}\right)\omega^2 - 0$

$\Rightarrow \quad \omega = \sqrt{\dfrac{6g}{l}}\sin\left(\dfrac{\theta}{2}\right)$

38. $W_{\text{gravity}} = \Delta K$

$\Rightarrow 0 + mg\left(\dfrac{l}{2}\right) + mgl = \dfrac{1}{2}\left(0 + \dfrac{ml^2}{3} + ml^2\right)\omega^2$

$\Rightarrow \omega = \dfrac{3}{2}\sqrt{\dfrac{g}{l}}$

39. $W_{\text{hinge}} + W_{\text{gravity}} = \Delta K$

$\Rightarrow 0 + [(Mg(4R) + Mg(2R)] = \dfrac{1}{2}\left[\dfrac{3}{2}MR^2 + M(2R)^2\right]\omega^2$

$\Rightarrow \quad \omega = \sqrt{\dfrac{24g}{11R}}$

40. For cone to just topple,

About A, $\Sigma\tau = 0$

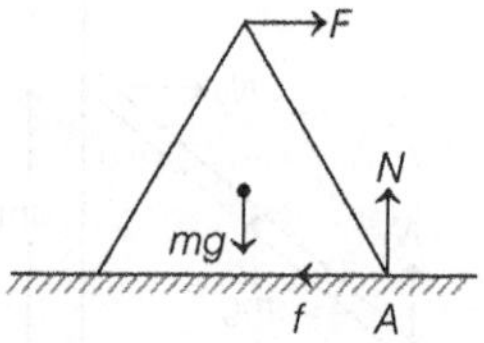

$\Rightarrow \quad -mg(r) + Fh = 0 \Rightarrow F = \dfrac{mgr}{h}$

$\Sigma F_x = 0 \Rightarrow F = f$

$\Sigma F_y = 0 \Rightarrow N = mg$

For cone to slide before it topples, $F > f_L$

$$\Rightarrow \quad \frac{mgr}{h} > \mu(mg) \Rightarrow \mu < \frac{r}{h}$$

$$\Rightarrow \quad \mu_{\max} = \frac{r}{h}$$

41. For cylinder to just tip over,
About A, $\Sigma\tau = 0$

$$\Rightarrow \quad ma\left(\frac{h}{2}\right) - mgr = 0$$

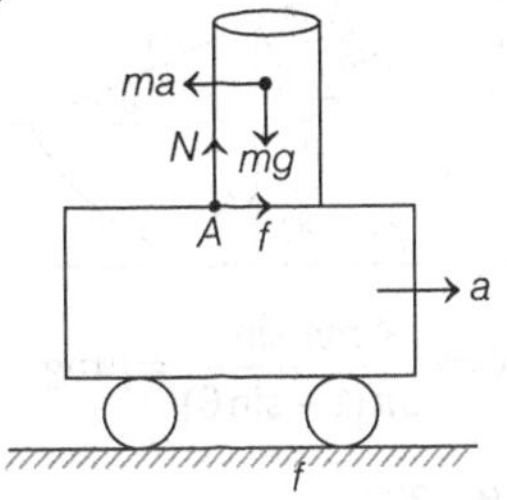

$$\Rightarrow \quad a = \frac{2gr}{h} = 4\text{ m/s}^2$$

42. $\tau = \frac{dL}{dt} = 4$ N-m

$$\tau = r_\perp F \Rightarrow 4 = \left(\frac{4}{\sqrt{2}}\right)F \Rightarrow F = \sqrt{2}\text{ N}$$

43. $K = \frac{1}{2}I\omega^2 \Rightarrow \frac{K}{2} = \frac{1}{2}I'(3\omega)^2 \Rightarrow I' = \frac{I}{18}$

$$L = I\omega \Rightarrow L' = \left(\frac{I}{18}\right)(3\omega) = \frac{L}{6}$$

44. $\left(\frac{mR^2}{2}\right)(2.4) + 0 = \left(\frac{mR^2}{2} + \frac{m(2R)^2}{12}\right)\omega \Rightarrow \omega = 1.44$ rev/s

45. Conserving angular momentum about O,

$$Mv\left(\frac{a}{2}\right) = \left(\frac{2Ma^2}{3}\right)\omega \Rightarrow \omega = \frac{3v}{4a}$$

46. $\left(\frac{ML^2}{12} + 0 + 0\right)\omega_0 = \left(\frac{ML^2}{12} + m\left(\frac{L}{2}\right)^2 + m\left(\frac{L}{2}\right)^2\right)\omega$

$$\Rightarrow \quad \omega = \left(\frac{M}{M + 6m}\right)\omega_0$$

47. $mua = \left(\frac{m}{12}((2a)^2 + a^2) + m\left(\frac{\sqrt{5}a}{2}\right)^2\right)\omega \quad \Rightarrow \quad \omega = \frac{3u}{5a}$

48. $L_1 = L_2 \Rightarrow 0 + 0 = 2200\omega + 70(10 + \omega(2))2$

$$\Rightarrow \quad \omega = -2.8\text{ rad/s}$$

49. Conserving angular momentum about the hinge,

$$mv\left(\frac{L}{2}\right) + 0 = \frac{ML^2}{3}\omega + 0 \quad \text{...(i)}$$

$$e = \frac{\left(\frac{\omega L}{2}\right) - 0}{v - 0} = 1 \quad \text{...(ii)}$$

Solving, we get $\frac{M}{m} = \frac{3}{4}$

50. Conserving angular momentum for the system,

$$\left(\frac{(200)(2.5)^2}{2} + 40(2.5)^2\right)(2) = \left(\frac{200(2.5)^2}{2} + 0\right)\omega$$

$$\Rightarrow \quad \omega = 2.8\text{ rad/s}$$

Numerical Value Questions

1. $I_{AB} = I_{AC} = \frac{ML^2}{3}\sin^2 45° = \frac{ML^2}{6}$

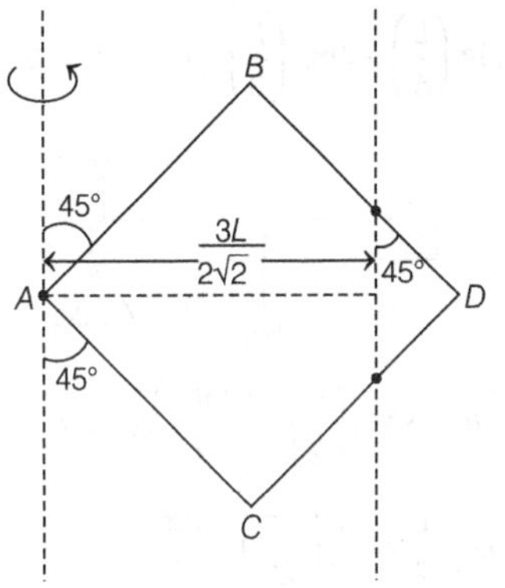

$$I_{BD} = I_{CD} = \frac{ML^2}{12}\sin^2 45° + M\left(\frac{3L}{2\sqrt{2}}\right)^2 = \frac{7}{6}ML^2$$

$$I = 2\left(\frac{ML^2}{6}\right) + 2\left(\frac{7}{6}ML^2\right)$$

$$= \frac{8}{3}ML^2 = \frac{8}{3} \times \frac{1}{2} \times (3)^2$$

$$= 12\text{ kg-m}^2$$

2.

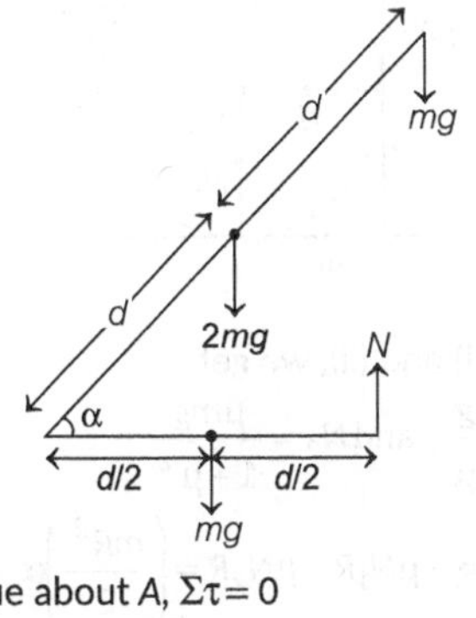

Taking torque about A, $\Sigma\tau = 0$

$$\Rightarrow \quad mg(2d\cos\alpha - d) = mg\frac{d}{2} + 2mg(d - d\cos\alpha)$$

$$\Rightarrow \quad \cos\alpha = \frac{7}{8}$$

So, value of $32\cos\alpha = 32 \times \frac{7}{8} = 28$

3. $S_{\text{fly, straw}} = L \Rightarrow S_{\text{fly}} = L + S_{\text{straw}}$

$$S_{CM} = \frac{2m\,S_{\text{straw}} + m\,(L + S_{\text{straw}})}{3m} = 0 \Rightarrow S_{\text{straw}} = -\frac{L}{3}$$

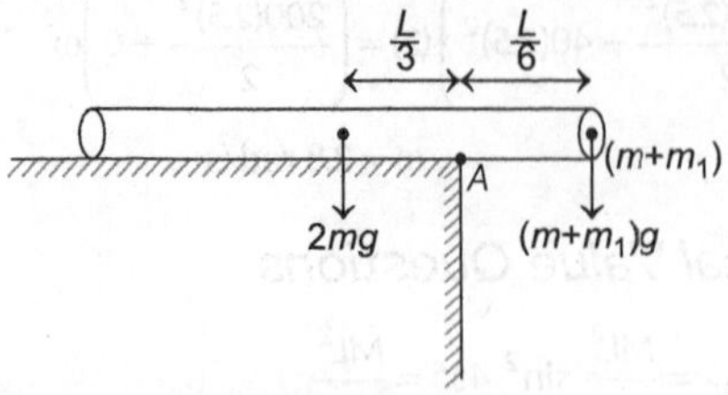

About the edge of the table, $\Sigma\tau = 0$

$$\Rightarrow (m + m_1)g\left(\frac{L}{6}\right) - 2mg\left(\frac{L}{3}\right) = 0 \Rightarrow m_1 = 3m$$

4.

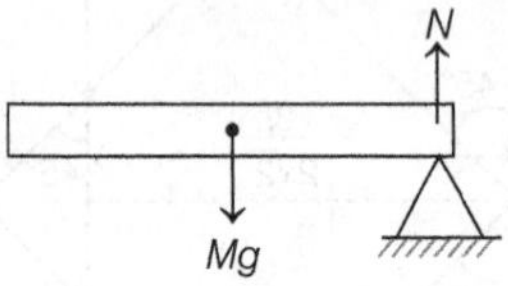

$$\tau = I\alpha \Rightarrow Mg\left(\frac{L}{2}\right) = \left(\frac{ML^2}{3}\right)\alpha \Rightarrow \alpha = \frac{3g}{2L}$$

$$a_{CM} = \frac{L}{2}\alpha = \frac{L}{2}\left(\frac{3g}{2L}\right) = \frac{3g}{4}$$

$$(\Sigma F_{\text{ext}})_y = M(a_{CM})_y \Rightarrow Mg - N = M\left(\frac{3g}{4}\right)$$

$$\Rightarrow \quad N = \frac{Mg}{4}$$

5. $\Sigma F_x = 0 \Rightarrow \mu N_1 = N_2$ ...(i)

$\Sigma F_y = 0 \Rightarrow N_1 + \mu N_2 = mg$ ...(ii)

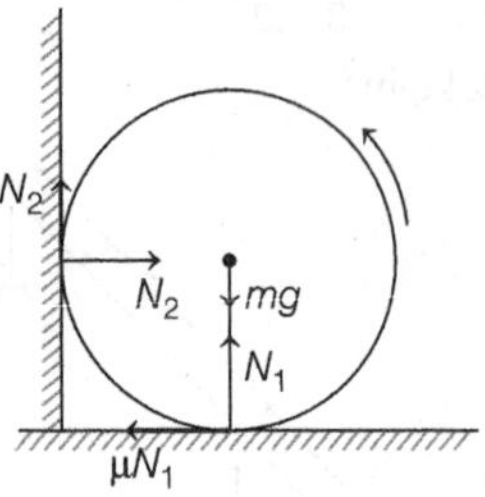

Solving Eqs. (i) and (ii), we get

$$N_1 = \frac{mg}{1 + \mu^2} \text{ and } N_2 = \frac{\mu mg}{1 + \mu^2}$$

$$\tau = I\alpha \Rightarrow -\mu N_1 R - \mu N_2 R = \left(\frac{mR^2}{2}\right)\alpha$$

$$\Rightarrow \quad \alpha = -\frac{20\mu(\mu + 1)}{3(1 + \mu^2)} = -\frac{20}{13}\ \text{rad/s}^2$$

$$\omega^2 = \omega_0^2 + 2\alpha\theta$$

$$\Rightarrow \quad 0^2 = (40\sqrt{\pi})^2 + 2\left(-\frac{20}{13}\right)\theta \Rightarrow \theta = 520\pi$$

Number of revolutions $= \dfrac{\theta}{2\pi} = 260$

6. $\Sigma F_x = 0 \Rightarrow F = f$

$\Sigma F_y = 0 \Rightarrow N = mg$

About the point of contact,

$$\Sigma\tau = 0 \;\Rightarrow\; FR(1 - \sin\theta) - mg\frac{4R}{3\pi}\sin\theta = 0$$

$$\Rightarrow \quad F = \frac{4mg\sin\theta}{3\pi(1 - \sin\theta)}$$

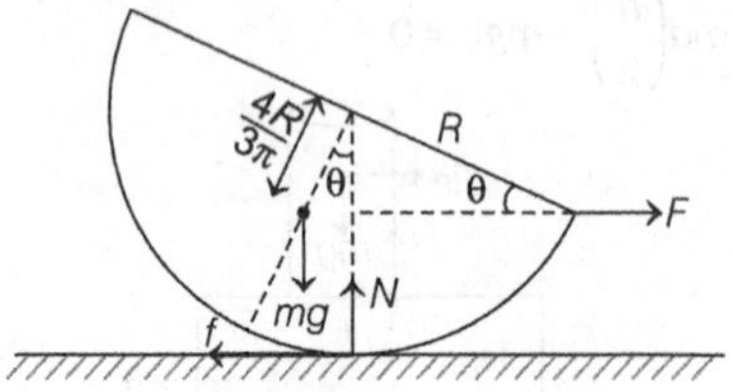

$$f \le f_L \Rightarrow F = \mu N \Rightarrow \frac{4\,mg\sin\theta}{3\pi(1 - \sin\theta)} = \mu mg$$

$$\Rightarrow \sin\theta = \frac{1}{2} \Rightarrow \theta = 30°$$

7. About the hinge, $\Sigma\tau = 0$

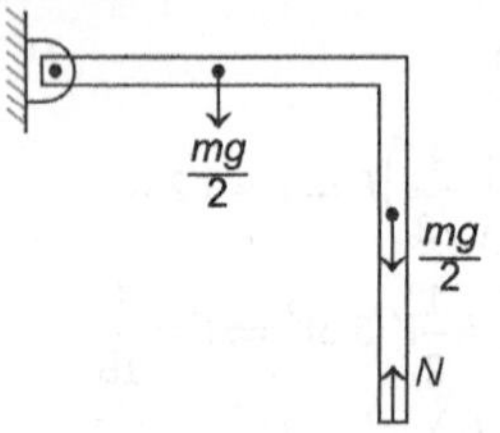

$$\Rightarrow \frac{mg}{2}\left(\frac{L}{2}\right) + \frac{mg}{2}L - N(L) = 0 \Rightarrow N = \frac{3mg}{4}$$

$$f = \mu N = 0.5\left(\frac{3mg}{4}\right) = \frac{3mg}{8}$$

For cylinder, $\tau = I\alpha \Rightarrow -\left(\dfrac{3mg}{8}\right) = \left(\dfrac{mR^2}{2}\right)\alpha$

$$\Rightarrow \quad \alpha = -\frac{3g}{4R} = -7.5\ \text{m/s}^2$$

$$\omega = \omega_0 + \alpha t \Rightarrow 0 = 30 - 7.5t \Rightarrow t = 4\ \text{s}$$

8. $U_1 = mg\left(\dfrac{L}{2}\right),\ U_2 = \left(\dfrac{m}{2}\right)g\left(\dfrac{L}{4}\right)$

Applying mechanical energy conservation,

$$K_1 + U_1 = K_2 + U_2$$

$$\Rightarrow 0 + mg\left(\frac{L}{2}\right) = \frac{1}{2}\left(\frac{mL^2}{3}\right)\omega^2 + \frac{mgL}{8} \Rightarrow \omega = \sqrt{\frac{9g}{4L}}$$

9. Using angular momentum conservation,

$$mv_0 l_0 = mv\left(l_0 + \frac{l_0}{10}\right) \Rightarrow v = 10\ \text{m/s}$$

Using mechanical energy conservation, $K_1 + U_1 = K_2 + U_2$

$$\Rightarrow \quad \frac{1}{2}(0.1)(11)^2 + 0 = \frac{1}{2}(0.1)(10)^2 + \frac{1}{2}k(0.1)^2$$

$$\Rightarrow \quad k = 210\ \text{N/m}$$

10. $W_{gravity} + W_{spring} = \Delta K_{system}$

$$\Rightarrow 11 \times 10 \times 0.1 + \frac{1}{2} \times 100 \times (0^2 - (0.1)^2)$$

$$= \left(\frac{1}{2} \times 11 \times v^2 \times \frac{1}{2} \times 0.1\omega^2\right) - (0+0)$$

$$\Rightarrow \quad 21 = 11v^2 + 0.1\left(\frac{v}{0.1}\right)^2 \qquad \{\because v = \omega R\}$$

$$\Rightarrow \quad v = 1 \text{ m/s}$$

Level 3

Single Choice Correct Questions

1. $\lambda = \lambda_0\left(\frac{x}{L} + 1\right)$

$$I = \int dm x^2 = \int_0^L \left(\lambda_0\left(\frac{x}{L}+1\right)dx\right)x^2 = \frac{7\lambda_0 L^3}{12}$$

$$M = \int dm = \int_0^L \lambda_0\left(\frac{x}{L}+1\right)dx = \frac{3\lambda_0 L}{2}$$

$$\text{So, } I = \frac{7}{12}\left(\frac{2M}{3L}\right)L^3 = \frac{7ML^3}{18}$$

2. $I = \frac{MR^2}{4} + \frac{ML^2}{12}$

and $\quad V = \pi R^2 L = \text{constant}$

$$I = \frac{M}{4}\left(\frac{V}{\pi L}\right) + \frac{ML^2}{12}$$

$$\frac{dI}{dL} = \frac{MV}{4\pi}\left(-\frac{1}{L^2}\right) + \frac{2ML}{12} = 0$$

$$\Rightarrow \quad \frac{3V}{2\pi} = L^3 \Rightarrow \frac{3}{2\pi}(\pi R^2 L) = L^3 \Rightarrow \frac{L}{R} = \sqrt{\frac{3}{2}}$$

3. $I = I_1 + I_2 = (mR^2 + mR^2) + \left(\frac{mR^2}{2} + m(3R)^2\right) = 11.5\, mR^2$

4. $dm = \dfrac{M}{\frac{1}{2}\left(\frac{l}{\sqrt{2}}\right)\left(\frac{l}{\sqrt{2}}\right)} \times 2x\,dx = \dfrac{8Mx\,dx}{l^2}$

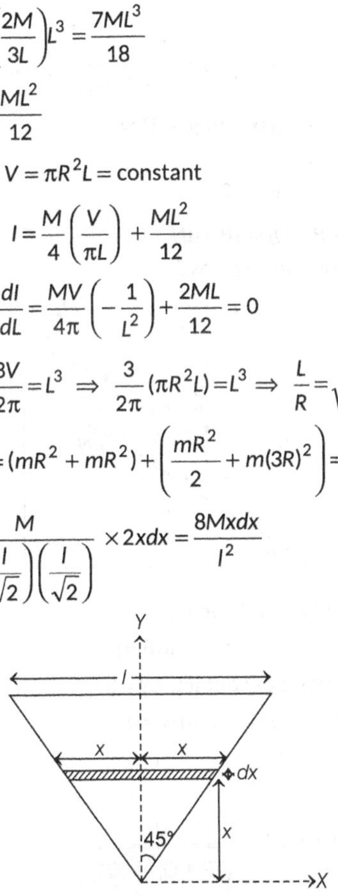

$$I = \int dm x^2 = \frac{8M}{l^2}\int_0^{l/2} x^3 dx = \frac{Ml^2}{8}$$

5. $I = \frac{2}{5}mR^2$

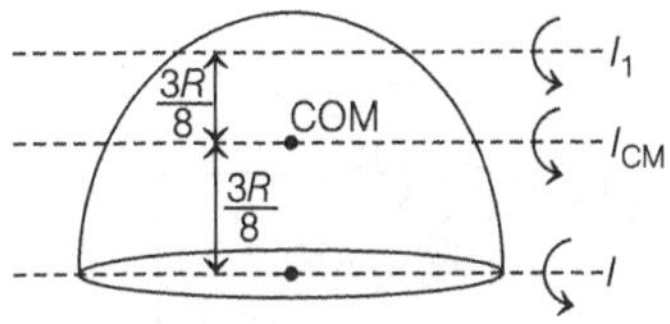

$$I = I_{CM} + \left(\frac{3R}{8}\right)^2 \qquad \text{...(i)}$$

$$I_1 = I_{CM} + \left(\frac{3R}{8}\right)^2 \qquad \text{...(ii)}$$

From Eqs. (i) and (ii), we get

$$I_1 = I = \frac{2}{5}mR^2$$

$$\Rightarrow \quad mK^2 = \frac{2}{5}mR^2$$

$$\Rightarrow \quad K = \sqrt{\frac{2}{5}}R$$

6. $I_1 = I_{CM} + \left(\frac{M}{2}\right)y^2$

$$= \left(\left(\frac{M}{2}\right)r^2 - \left(\frac{M}{2}\right)x^2\right) + \left(\frac{M}{2}\right)y^2$$

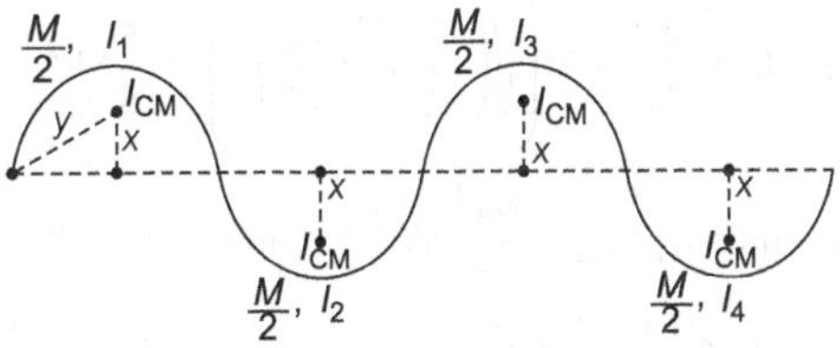

$$= \frac{M}{2}(r^2 + (y^2 - x^2)) = Mr^2$$

$$\text{Similarly, } I_2 = \frac{M}{2}(r^2 + (3r)^2) = 5Mr^2$$

$$I_3 = \frac{M}{2}(r^2 + (5r)^2) = 13Mr^2$$

$$I_4 = \frac{M}{2}(r^2 + (7r)^2) = 25Mr^2$$

$$I = I_1 + I_2 + I_3 + I_4 = 44Mr^2$$

7. $I = \int_0^a \left(\frac{M}{a}dx\right)\left(\frac{a^2}{12} + x^2\right) = \frac{5Ma^2}{12}$

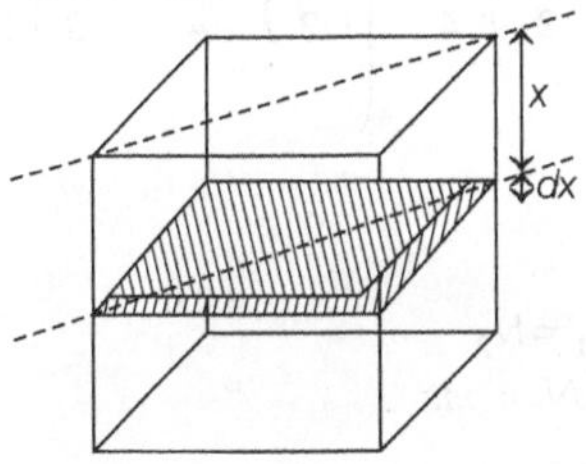

8. $I = I_{CM} + Md^2 = \dfrac{ML^2}{12} + M\left(\dfrac{L}{\sqrt{2}}\cos 30°\right)^2 = \dfrac{11ML^2}{24}$

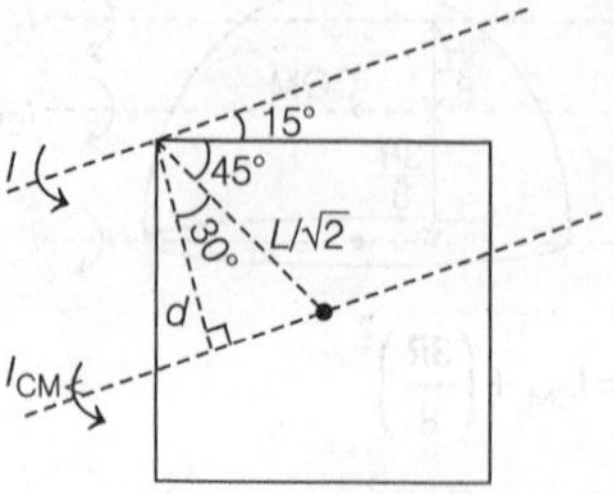

9. $I_1 = I_2 = I_3 = I_4 = \dfrac{ML^2}{3}\sin^2 45° = \dfrac{ML^2}{6}$

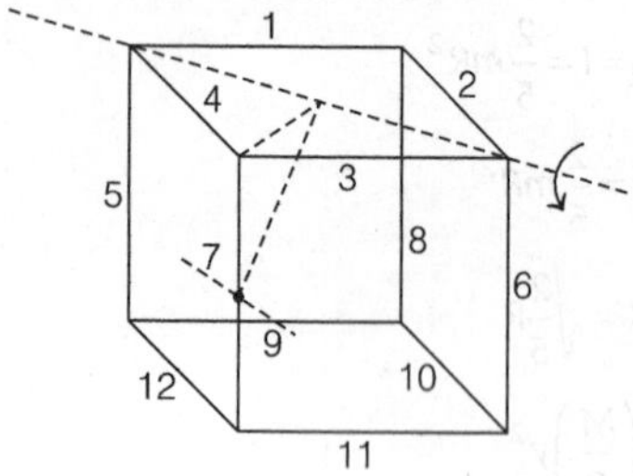

$$I_5 = I_6 = \frac{ML^2}{3}$$

$$I_7 = I_8 = \frac{ML^2}{12} + M\left(\sqrt{\left(\frac{L}{\sqrt{2}}\right)^2 + \left(\frac{L}{2}\right)^2}\right)^2 = \frac{5}{6}ML^2$$

$$I_9 = I_{10} = I_{11} = I_{12} = \frac{ML^2}{3}\sin^2 45° + ML^2 = \frac{7}{6}ML^2$$

$$I = 4\left(\frac{ML^2}{6}\right) + 2\left(\frac{ML^2}{3}\right) + 2\left(\frac{5}{6}ML^2\right) + 4\left(\frac{7}{6}ML^2\right) = \frac{23}{3}ML^2$$

10. $\sigma = \dfrac{M}{\pi R^2 - \pi\left(\dfrac{R}{2}\right)^2} = \dfrac{4M}{3\pi R^2}$

$$M_1 = \sigma\pi R^2 = \frac{4M}{3}$$

and $M_2 = \sigma\left(\dfrac{\pi R^2}{4}\right) = \dfrac{M}{3}$

$$I = I_1 - I_2 = \left(\frac{4M}{3}\right)\frac{R^2}{4} - \left(\left(\frac{M}{3}\right)\frac{\left(\frac{R}{2}\right)^2}{4} + \frac{M}{3}\left(\frac{R}{2}\sin 45°\right)^2\right)$$

$$= \frac{13MR^2}{48}$$

11. $\Sigma F_x = 0 \Rightarrow N_1 = N_2$

$\Sigma F_y = 0 \Rightarrow \mu N_2 = mg$

$\Sigma\tau = 0 \Rightarrow N_1(L\sin\theta) - mg\left(\dfrac{L}{2}\cos\theta\right) = 0$

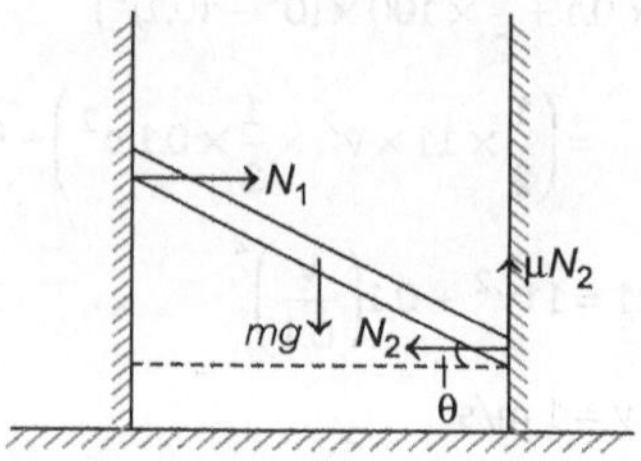

$\Rightarrow \quad N_1 = \dfrac{mg\cot\theta}{2}$

$\mu N_2 = mg$

$\Rightarrow \quad \mu N_1 = mg \qquad \because \{N_1 = N_2\}$

$\Rightarrow \quad \mu\left(\dfrac{mg\cot\theta}{2}\right) = mg$

$\Rightarrow \quad \cot\theta = 4$

$\Rightarrow \quad \dfrac{2}{\sqrt{L^2 - 4}} = 4$

$\Rightarrow \quad L = \dfrac{\sqrt{17}}{2}$ m

12. T = Tension in the string $= \dfrac{2m_1m_2g}{m_1 + m_2} = \dfrac{4}{3}mg$

$\Sigma\tau = 0 \Rightarrow (4mg)x = (mg + 2T)y$

$\Rightarrow \quad \dfrac{x}{y} = \dfrac{11}{12}$

13. $\Sigma F_x = 0 \Rightarrow (P + Q)\sin\theta = \mu N$ ...(i)

$\Sigma F_y = 0 \Rightarrow N = (P + Q)\cos\theta$ ...(ii)

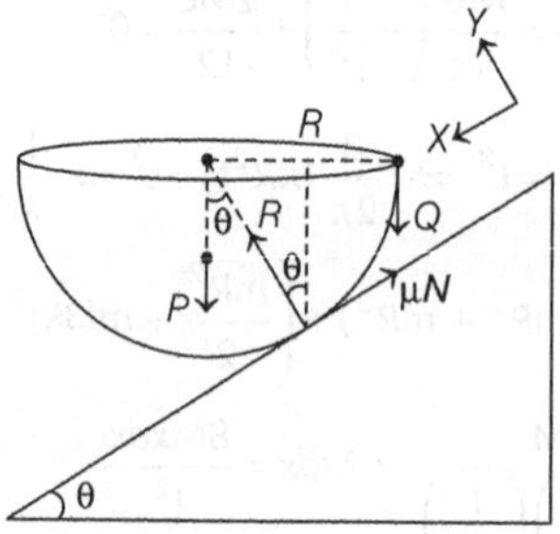

From Eqs. (i) and (ii), we get

$$\tan\theta = \mu$$

About the point of contact, $\Sigma\tau = 0$

$\Rightarrow P(R\sin\theta) - Q(R(1 - \sin\theta)) = 0$

$\Rightarrow \quad \sin\theta = \dfrac{Q}{P + Q}$

$$\mu = \tan\theta = \frac{Q}{\sqrt{(P+Q)^2 - Q^2}}$$

$$= \frac{Q}{\sqrt{P(P + 2Q)}}$$

14. $\tau_{\text{centrifugal}} = \int_0^L \left(\frac{M}{L}dx\right)\omega^2 x \sin\theta (x\cos\theta)$

$= \frac{M\omega^2 L^2 \sin\theta\cos\theta}{3}$

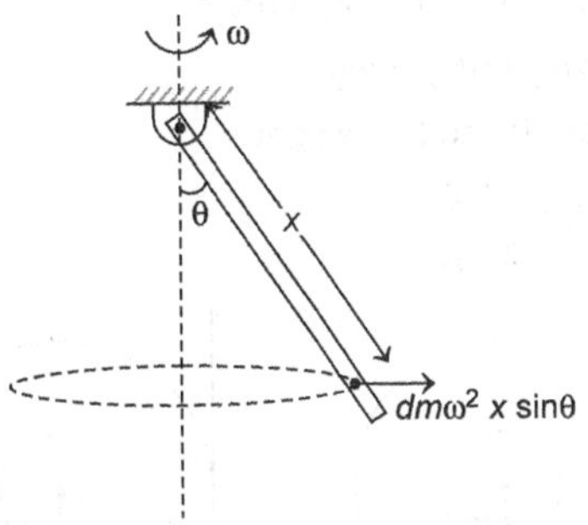

About hinge, $\Sigma\tau = 0 \Rightarrow \tau_{\text{gravity}} = \tau_{\text{centrifugal}}$

$\Rightarrow Mg\left(\frac{L}{2}\sin\theta\right) = \frac{M\omega^2 L^2 \sin\theta\cos\theta}{3} \Rightarrow \theta = \cos^{-1}\left(\frac{3g}{2\omega^2 L}\right)$

15. For an arc, $r_{CM} = \frac{R\sin\theta}{\theta}$

$I_{\text{hinge}} = I_{CM} + M\left(R\left(1-\frac{\sin\theta}{\theta}\right)\right)^2$

$= \left(MR^2 - M\left(\frac{R\sin\theta}{\theta}\right)^2\right) + M\left(R\left(1-\frac{\sin\theta}{\theta}\right)\right)^2$

$= 2MR^2\left(1-\frac{\sin\theta}{\theta}\right)$

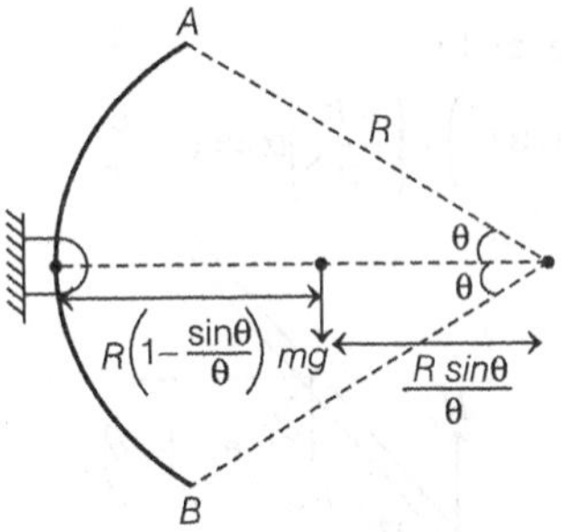

$\tau = I\alpha$

$\Rightarrow mgR\left(1-\frac{\sin\theta}{\theta}\right) = \left(2MR^2\left(1-\frac{\sin\theta}{\theta}\right)\right)\alpha \Rightarrow \alpha = \frac{g}{2R}$

16. $\Sigma F_x = 0 \Rightarrow N_x = F$

$\Sigma F_y = 0 \Rightarrow N_y = 2mg$

About hinge, $\Sigma\tau = 0$

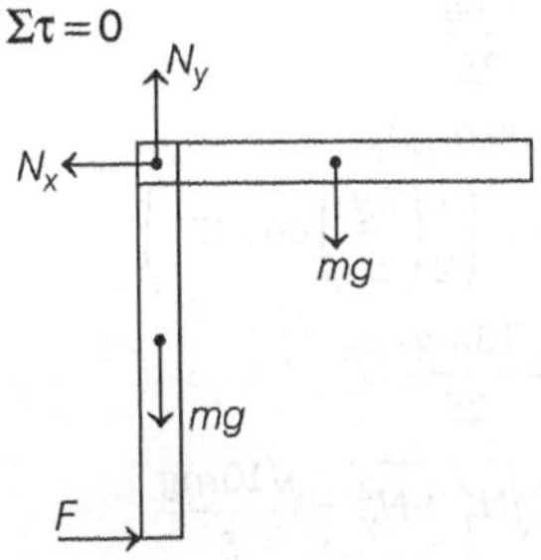

$\Rightarrow F(L) - mg\left(\frac{L}{2}\right) = 0 \Rightarrow F = \frac{mg}{2}$

Hinge force $= -N_x\hat{\mathbf{i}} + N_y\hat{\mathbf{j}} = -\frac{mg}{2}\hat{\mathbf{i}} + 2mg\hat{\mathbf{j}}$

17. $x_{CM} = \frac{\int dm x}{\int dm} = \frac{\int_0^L (\lambda_0 x dx)x}{\int_0^L \lambda_0 x dx} = \frac{2L}{3}$

$I = \int dm x^2 = \int_0^L (\lambda_0 x dx)x^2 = \frac{\lambda_0 L^4}{4}$

$\tau = I\alpha \Rightarrow (Mg)\left(\frac{2L}{3}\right) = \left(\frac{\lambda_0 L^4}{4}\right)\alpha$

$\Rightarrow \left(\frac{\lambda_0 L^2}{2}g\right)\left(\frac{2L}{3}\right) = \left(\frac{\lambda_0 L^4}{4}\right)\alpha \Rightarrow \alpha = \frac{4g}{3L}$

18. $\Sigma F_x = 0 \Rightarrow N_1 = \mu_2 N_2$ ...(i)

$\Sigma F_y = 0 \Rightarrow \mu_1 N_1 + mg = N_2$ ...(ii)

About A, $\Sigma\tau = 0$

$\Rightarrow N_1(L\sin\theta) + \mu_1 N_1(L\cos\theta) - mg\left(\frac{L}{2}\cos\theta\right) = 0$

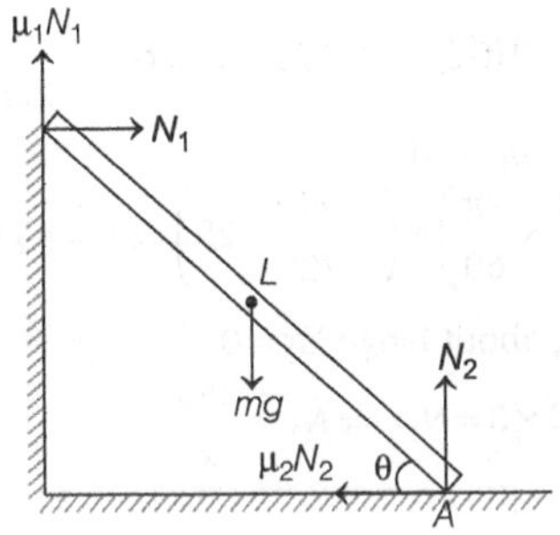

$\Rightarrow N_1\tan\theta + \mu_1 N_1 = \frac{mg}{2}$ ...(iii)

Solving Eqs. (i), (ii) and (iii), we get

$\theta = \tan^{-1}\left(\frac{1-\mu_1\mu_2}{2\mu_2}\right)$

19. About hinge, $\Sigma\tau = 0$

$\Rightarrow 10x + 50(4) - (52\sin 37°)(8) = 0$

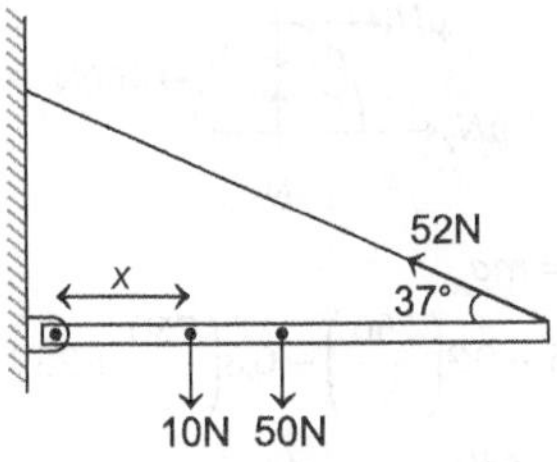

$\Rightarrow x = \frac{124}{25}$ m

$t = \frac{x}{v} = \frac{124}{25\times 0.5} = 9.92$ s

20. $\Sigma F_x = 0 \Rightarrow N_2 = \mu N_1$ ...(i)

$\Sigma F_y = 0 \Rightarrow F + N_1 + \mu N_2 = w$ ...(ii)

About A, $\Sigma\tau = 0$

$\Rightarrow \quad FR - N_2R - \mu N_2 R = 0$

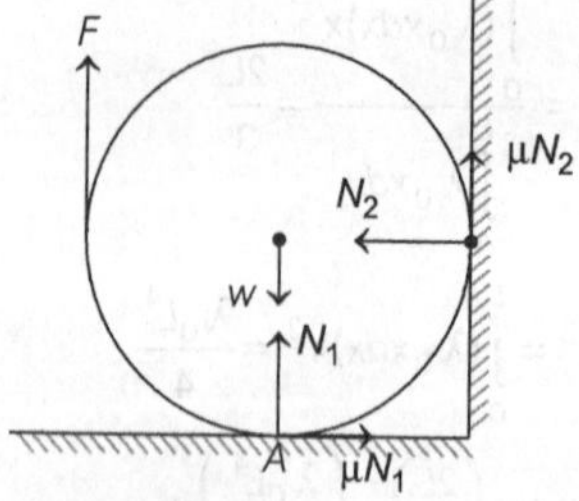

$\Rightarrow \quad F = N_2 + \mu N_2$ ...(iii)

Solving Eqs. (i), (ii) and (iii), we get

$$F = \frac{\mu(\mu+1)w}{2\mu^2 + \mu + 1} = \frac{3w}{8}$$

21. For the rod about the hinge, $\Sigma\tau = 0$

$\Rightarrow \quad N(1000) - F(2250) = 0$

$\Rightarrow \quad N = 2.25F$

$f = \mu N = 0.3(2.25F)$

For disc, $\Sigma\tau = I\alpha$

$$\Rightarrow -0.3(2.25F)(0.8) = 54(0.75)^2\alpha \Rightarrow \alpha = -\frac{4F}{225}$$

$\omega = \omega_0 + \alpha t$

$$\Rightarrow 0 = \left(\frac{600}{\pi} \times \frac{2\pi}{60}\right) + \left(-\frac{4F}{225} \times 25\right) \Rightarrow F = 45\text{ N}$$

22. For block A, about hinge $\Sigma\tau = 0$

$$\Rightarrow \quad 250 \times 3 = N_1 x \Rightarrow N_1 = \frac{750}{x}$$

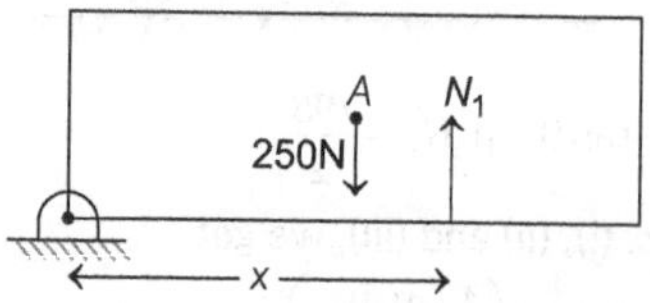

For block B,

$$\Sigma F_y = 0 \Rightarrow N_2 = N_1 + (2.5)(10) = \frac{750}{x} + 25$$

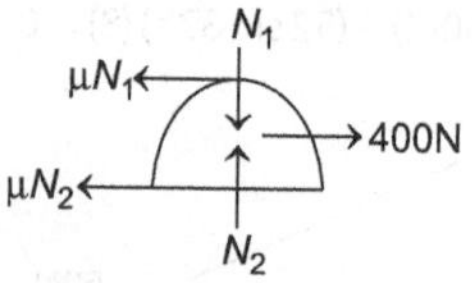

$\Sigma F_x = ma_x$

$$\Rightarrow \quad 157.5 - 0.3\left(\frac{750}{x}\right) - 0.3\left(\frac{750}{x} + 25\right) = 2.5a$$

$$\Rightarrow \quad 150 - \frac{450}{x} = 2.5\,v\frac{dv}{dx}$$

$$\Rightarrow \quad \int v\,dv = \int_3^{4.5}\left(60 - \frac{180}{x}\right)dx$$

$$\Rightarrow \quad \frac{v^2}{2} = 60(1.5) - 180\ln\left(\frac{3}{2}\right)$$

$\Rightarrow \quad v = 6\text{ m/s}$

23. In figure (a), $\Sigma F_x = 0 \Rightarrow N_2 = \mu N_1$ ...(i)

$\Sigma F_y = 0 \Rightarrow N_1 + \mu N_2 = mg$ ...(ii)

Solving Eqs. (i) and (ii), we get

$$N_1 = \frac{mg}{1+\mu^2}$$

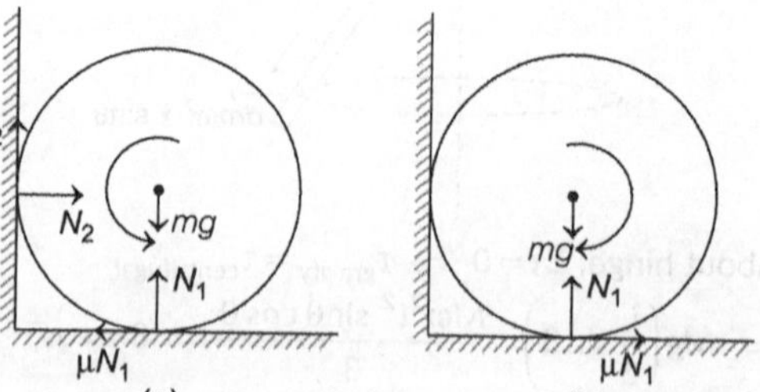

(a) (b)

So, $f_a = \mu N_1 = \dfrac{\mu mg}{1+\mu^2} = \dfrac{3mg}{10}$

In figure (b), due to friction on ground, the sphere will move towards right and hence it will lose contact with the wall.

$$f_b = \mu N_1 = \mu(mg) = \frac{mg}{3}$$

So, $\dfrac{f_a}{f_b} = \dfrac{9}{10}$

24. About hinge, $\tau = I\alpha$

$$\Rightarrow mg\left(\frac{l}{2}\cos 37°\right) = \left(\frac{ml^2}{3}\right)\alpha \Rightarrow \alpha = \frac{6g}{5l}$$

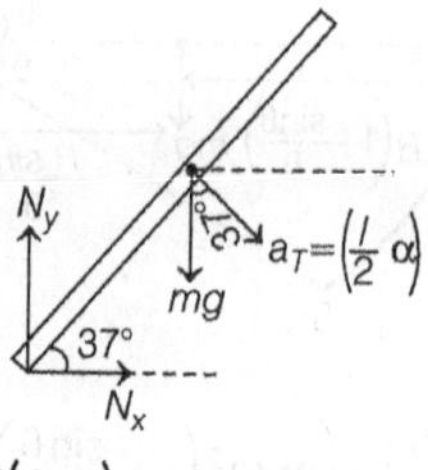

$(\Sigma F_{\text{ext}})_x = m(a_{\text{CM}})_x$

$$\Rightarrow \quad N_x = m\left(\frac{l}{2}\left(\frac{6g}{5l}\right)\sin 37°\right)$$

$$N_x = \frac{9mg}{25}$$

$(\Sigma F_{\text{ext}})_y = m(a_{\text{CM}})_y$

$$\Rightarrow \quad mg - N_y = m\left(\frac{l}{2}\left(\frac{6g}{5l}\right)\cos 37°\right)$$

$$\Rightarrow \quad N_y = \frac{13mg}{25}$$

$$\text{Hinge force} = \sqrt{N_x^2 + N_y^2} = \frac{\sqrt{10}mg}{5}$$

25. $mg - T = ma$ ...(i)

$$Tl - mg\left(\frac{l}{2}\right) = \left(\frac{ml^2}{3}\right)\alpha$$ ...(ii)

$$a = l\alpha$$ ...(iii)

Solving Eqs. (i), (ii) and (iii), we get

$$\alpha = \frac{3g}{8l} \text{ and } T = \frac{5mg}{8}$$

26. $m_2 g - T_2 = m_2 a_2$ ...(i)

$T_1 - \mu m_1 g \cos 30° - m_1 g \sin 30° = m_1 a_1$ ...(ii)

$T_2 b - T_1 a = I\alpha$ ...(iii)

$a_1 = a\alpha$ ...(iv)

$a_2 = b\alpha$ ...(v)

Solving equations, we get $a_1 = 2 \text{ m/s}^2$

27. About A, $\Sigma\tau = 0 \Rightarrow mg \sin\theta\left(\frac{3R}{8}\right) - mg\cos\theta(R) = 0$

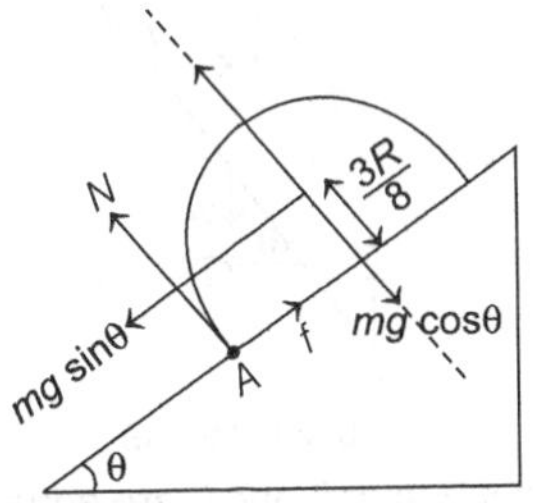

$$\Rightarrow \theta = \tan^{-1}\left(\frac{8}{3}\right)$$

28. About A, $\Sigma\tau = 0 \Rightarrow m\omega^2 R\left(\frac{h}{4}\right) - mgr = 0$

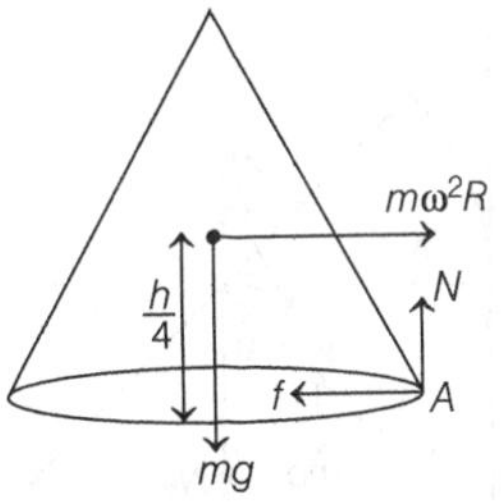

$$\Rightarrow \quad \omega = \sqrt{\frac{4gr}{Rh}}$$

29. $M = \rho\left(\frac{1}{3}\pi r^2 (3r)\right) \Rightarrow \rho = \frac{M}{\pi r^3}$

Mass of cylindrical part $= \rho\pi r^2(4r) = 4M$

About A, $\Sigma\tau = 0$

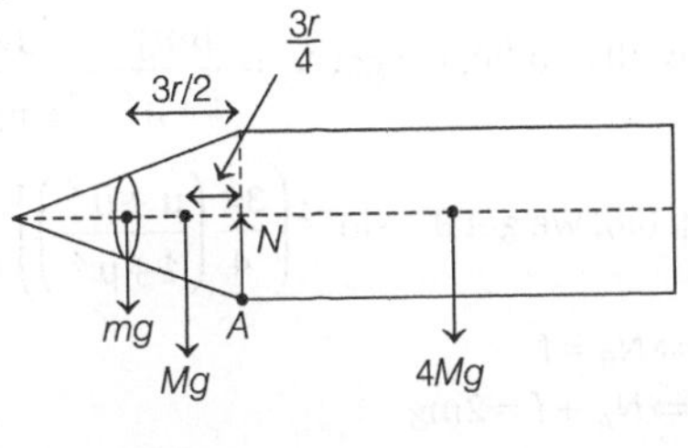

$$\Rightarrow 4Mg(2r) - Mg\left(\frac{3r}{4}\right) - mg\left(\frac{3r}{2}\right) = 0 \Rightarrow m = \frac{29M}{6}$$

30. $(I + mR^2)\omega = mvR + I\omega'$

$$\Rightarrow \quad \omega' = \frac{(I + mR^2)\omega - mvR}{I}$$

31. Conserving angular momentum,

$$\left(\frac{(0.75)(0.4)^2}{12} + 1(0.1)^2 + 1(0.1)^2\right)30$$

$$= \left(\frac{(0.75)(0.4)^2}{12} + 1(0.2)^2 + 1(0.2)^2\right)\omega$$

$$\Rightarrow \quad \omega = 10 \text{ rad/s}$$

Using energy conservation,

$$\frac{1}{2}(0.01 + 0.01 + 0.01)(30)^2 = \frac{1}{2}(0.01 + 0.04 + 0.04)(10)^2 + \frac{1}{2}\times 1\times v^2 + \frac{1}{2}\times 1\times v^2$$

$$\Rightarrow \quad v = 3 \text{ m/s}$$

32. $I_1\omega_1 = I_2\omega_2$

$$\Rightarrow \left(\frac{m_0 R^2}{2}\right)\omega_0 = \left(\frac{m_0 R^2}{2} + (\mu t)R^2\right)\left(\frac{\omega_0}{2}\right) \Rightarrow t = \frac{m_0}{2\mu}$$

33. $JL = I\omega \Rightarrow 10 \times 1 = \frac{(2)(1)^2}{3}\omega \Rightarrow \omega = 15 \text{ rad/s}$

$$K = \frac{1}{2}I\omega^2 = \frac{1}{2}\times\frac{2}{3}\times(15)^2 = 75 \text{ J}$$

34. Applying angular momentum conservation,

$$Mv_0 a = \left(\frac{2}{3}M(2a)^2\right)\omega \Rightarrow \omega = \frac{3v_0}{8a}$$

Applying energy conservation,

$$K_1 + U_1 = K_2 + U_2$$

$$\Rightarrow \quad \frac{1}{2}\left(\frac{2}{3}M(2a)^2\right)\left(\frac{3v_0}{8a}\right)^2 + Mga = 0 + Mg(\sqrt{2}a)$$

$$\Rightarrow \quad v_0 = \sqrt{\frac{16ag(\sqrt{2}-1)}{3}}$$

Multiple Choice(s) Correct Questions

1. (A) For any point on the surface of paraboloid, $x^2 + z^2 = 4ay$

$$I = \sum_{i=1}^{3} m_i(x_i^2 + z_i^2) = 4ma(y_1 + y_2 + y_3)$$

(B) $U = \sum_{i=1}^{3} m_i g h_i = mg(y_1 + y_2 + y_3)$

(C) $K_1 + U_1 = K_2 + U_2$

$$\Rightarrow 0 + mgy_1 = \frac{1}{2}mv^2 + 0$$

$$\Rightarrow v = \sqrt{2gy_1}$$

(D) $K = \frac{1}{2} I\omega^2 = \frac{1}{2}(4ma(y_1 + y_2 + y_3))\omega^2$

$= 2ma(y_1 + y_2 + y_3)\omega^2$

2. (A) Particles having same speed on a circle have different directions. Particles having same direction on different circles have different speeds. So, no two particles in a plane perpendicular to the axis of rotation have same velocity.

(B) No two particles in a plane perpendicular to the axis of rotation have same acceleration.

(C) Speed $= \omega r =$ constant

(D) $\omega = \frac{v_\perp}{r} =$ constant

3. $\Sigma F_x = 0 \Rightarrow N = T$

$\Sigma F_y = 0 \Rightarrow f = mg$

About A, $\Sigma\tau = 0$

$\Rightarrow mg\left(\frac{L}{2}\sin 60°\right) - T\left(\frac{L}{3}\cos 60°\right) = 0$

$\Rightarrow T = \frac{3\sqrt{3}mg}{2}$

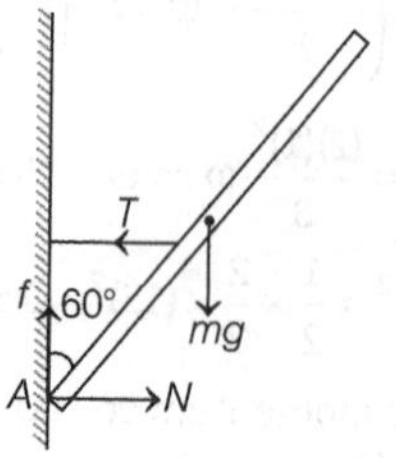

$f \le f_L$

$\Rightarrow mg \le \mu\left(\frac{3\sqrt{3}mg}{2}\right) \Rightarrow \mu \ge \frac{2}{3\sqrt{3}}$

4. For rod, $\Sigma\tau = I\alpha$

$\Rightarrow Mg\left(\frac{L}{2}\right) = \left(\frac{ML^2}{3}\right)\alpha \Rightarrow \alpha = \frac{3g}{2L}$

$a_B = L\alpha = \frac{3g}{2}$

$a_{\text{block}} = g$, So, $a_{\text{rel}} = \frac{3g}{2} - g = \frac{g}{2}$

For rod, when it becomes vertical,

$W_{\text{gravity}} + W_{\text{hinge}} = \Delta K$

$\Rightarrow Mg\left(\frac{L}{2}\right) + 0 = \frac{1}{2}\left(\frac{ML^2}{3}\right)\omega^2 - 0$

$\Rightarrow \omega = \sqrt{\frac{3g}{L}}$

$\Sigma\tau = I\alpha$

$\Rightarrow 0 = \left(\frac{ML^2}{3}\right)\alpha \Rightarrow \alpha = 0$

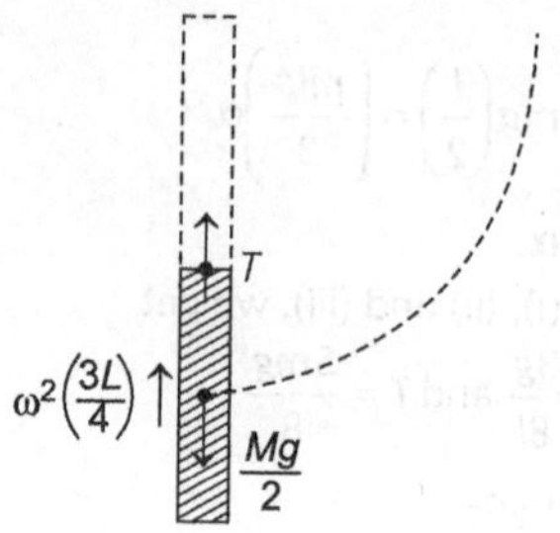

For lower half of rod,

$(\Sigma F_{\text{ext}})_y = m(a_{\text{CM}})_y$

$T - \frac{Mg}{2} = \frac{M}{2}\omega^2\left(\frac{3L}{4}\right) \Rightarrow T = \frac{13Mg}{8}$

5. (A) $\Sigma F_x = 0 \Rightarrow F = T$

(B) $\tan\theta = \frac{w}{T} \Rightarrow T = w\cot\theta$

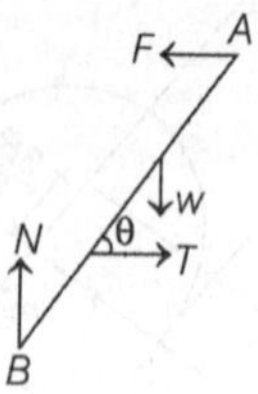

FBD of ladder AB

(C) Normal reaction at B and C are equal.

(D) $\Sigma F_y = 0 \Rightarrow N = w$

6. $\Sigma F_x = 0 \Rightarrow N_1 = \mu N_2$ ...(i)

$\Sigma F_y = 0 \Rightarrow \mu N_1 + N_2 = mg$ ...(ii)

About B, $\Sigma\tau = 0$

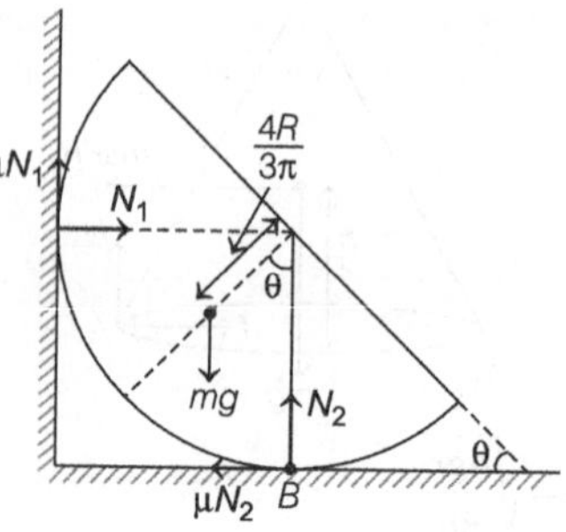

$mg\left(\frac{4R}{3R}\sin\theta\right) - N_1 R - (\mu N_1)R = 0$

$\Rightarrow N_1 = \left(\frac{mg\sin\theta}{1+\mu}\right)\frac{4}{3\pi}$ ...(iii)

From Eqs. (i) and (ii), we get $N_1 = \frac{\mu mg}{1+\mu^2} = \frac{\mu w}{1+\mu^2}$

From Eq. (iii), we get $\theta = \sin^{-1}\left(\frac{3\pi}{4}\left(\frac{\mu+\mu^2}{1+\mu^2}\right)\right)$

7. $\Sigma F_x = 0 \Rightarrow N_B = f$ ...(i)

$\Sigma F_y = 0 \Rightarrow N_A + f = 2mg$ ...(ii)

About C, $\Sigma\tau = 0$

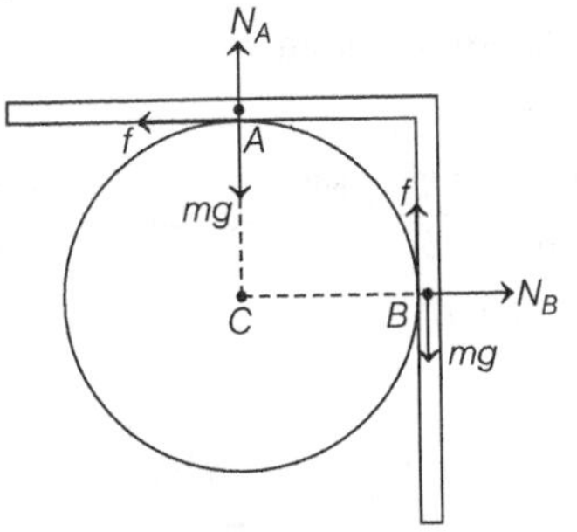

$$\Rightarrow \qquad mgR - fR - fR = 0 \Rightarrow f = \frac{mg}{2} \qquad \text{...(iii)}$$

Solving, we get $N_A = \dfrac{3mg}{2}$; $N_B = \dfrac{mg}{2}$

8. $\Sigma F_x = 0 \Rightarrow N_1 \cos\theta = N_2$ ...(i)

$\Sigma F_y = 0 \Rightarrow N_1 \sin\theta + f = mg$ ...(ii)

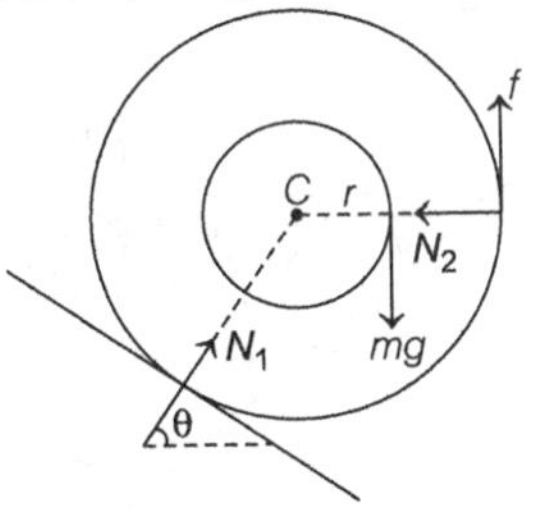

About C, $\Sigma\tau = 0$

$$mgr - fR = 0 \qquad \text{...(iii)}$$

Solving Eqs. (i), (ii) and (iii), we get

$$N_2 = \frac{mg}{\tan\theta}\left(1 - \frac{r}{R}\right)$$

Net force at B, $F_B = \sqrt{N_2^2 + f^2}$

For minimum value of μ, $f \le f_L$

$$\Rightarrow \qquad \frac{mgr}{R} \le \frac{\mu mg}{\tan\theta}\left(1 - \frac{r}{R}\right) \Rightarrow \mu \ge \frac{\tan\theta}{\left(\frac{R}{r}\right) - 1}$$

9. For block to topple, $\tau > 0$

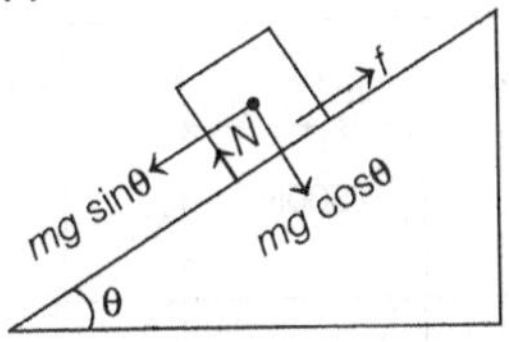

$$(mg \sin\theta)\left(\frac{h}{2}\right) - (mg \cos\theta)\frac{a}{2} > 0$$

$$\Rightarrow \qquad \tan\theta > \frac{a}{h}$$

For block to slide, $mg \sin\theta > f_L$

$\Rightarrow \qquad mg \sin\theta > \mu\, mg \cos\theta$

$\Rightarrow \qquad \tan\theta > \mu$

For block to topple before sliding,

$$\mu > \tan\theta > \frac{a}{h} \Rightarrow \mu > \frac{a}{h}$$

For block to slide before toppling,

$$\mu < \tan\theta < \frac{a}{h} \Rightarrow \mu < \frac{a}{h}$$

10. $\Sigma F_y = 0 \Rightarrow N_1 + N_2 = 24\text{ N}$

About hinge 2, $\Sigma\tau = 0$

$$\Rightarrow \qquad N_1(L) - 20\left(\frac{L}{4}\right) - 4\left(\frac{L}{4}\right) = 0 \Rightarrow N_1 = 11\text{ N}$$

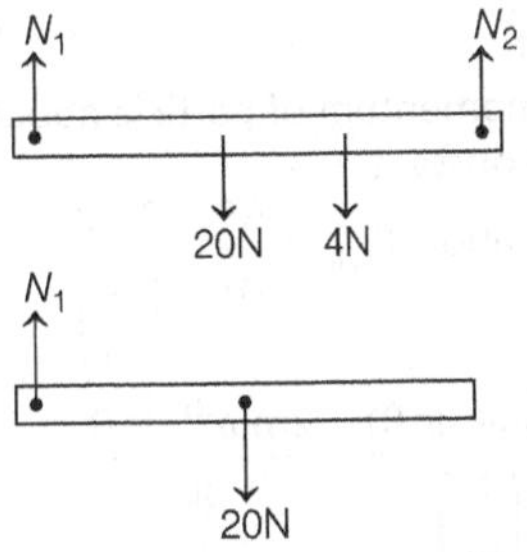

Now when hinge 2 breaks and force F is removed,

$$\Sigma\tau = I\alpha \Rightarrow 20\left(\frac{L}{2}\right) = \frac{2(L^2)}{3}\alpha \Rightarrow \alpha = \frac{15}{L}$$

$$(a_{CM})_y = r\alpha = \left(\frac{L}{2}\right)\left(\frac{15}{L}\right) = 7.5\text{ m/s}^2$$

$$(\Sigma F_{ext})_y = m(a_{CM})_y \Rightarrow 20 - N_1 = 2(7.5)$$

$$\Rightarrow \qquad N_1 = 5\text{ N}$$

11. (A) Using angular momentum conservation for rod about the hinge,

$$Mv_0\left(\frac{l}{2}\right) = \left(\frac{Ml^2}{3}\right)\omega \Rightarrow \omega = \frac{3v_0}{2l}$$

(B) For rod to complete the rotation,

$$K_1 + U_1 = K_2 + U_2$$

$$\Rightarrow \frac{1}{2}\left(\frac{Ml^2}{3}\right)\left(\frac{3v_0}{2l}\right)^2 - Mg\frac{l}{2} = 0 + Mg\frac{l}{2}$$

$$\Rightarrow v_0 = \sqrt{\frac{8gl}{3}}$$

(C) Loss of energy $= \dfrac{1}{2}Mv_0^2 - \dfrac{1}{2}\left(\dfrac{Ml^2}{3}\right)\left(\dfrac{3v_0}{2l}\right)^2$

$$= \frac{1}{8}Mv_0^2$$

12. For equilibrium of hanging block, $T = mg$

For the block on table, $T = m\omega^2 r$

$$\Rightarrow \qquad mg = m\omega^2 r \Rightarrow \omega = \sqrt{\frac{g}{r}}$$

$$K = \frac{1}{2}mv^2 = \frac{1}{2}m(\omega r)^2 = \frac{mgr}{2}$$

Torque of tension about the hole is zero. So, angular momentum will be conserved.

13. (A) Angular momentum of particle about the point of suspension is constant in magnitude but its direction is continuously changing.

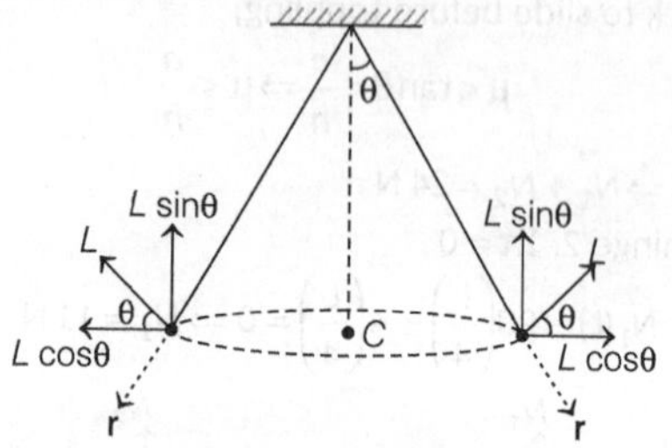

(B) Angular momentum of particle about centre of circle remains constant.

(C) In half rotation, $F_{\text{avg}} = \dfrac{\Delta P}{\Delta t} = \dfrac{2mv}{\left(\dfrac{\pi}{\omega}\right)}$

$$= \frac{2m\omega(l\sin\theta)}{\left(\dfrac{\pi}{\omega}\right)} = \frac{2m\omega^2 l\sin\theta}{\pi}$$

$$= \frac{2m}{\pi}\left(\frac{g}{l\cos\theta}\right) l\sin\theta = \frac{2mg\tan\theta}{\pi}$$

(D) About OC, L is constant

So, $\tau_{\text{avg.}} = \dfrac{\Delta L}{\Delta t} = 0$

14. $\dfrac{m(2r)^2\omega}{12} - m\left(\dfrac{\omega r}{4}\right) r = \dfrac{m(2r)^2}{12}\omega' + mvr$

$\Rightarrow \quad \dfrac{\omega r}{4} = \omega' r + 3v$ ...(i)

$e = \dfrac{1}{2} = \dfrac{v - \omega' r}{\dfrac{\omega r}{4} + \omega r} \Rightarrow 8v - 8\omega' r = 5\omega r$ ...(ii)

Solving Eqs. (i) and (ii), we get $\omega' = -\dfrac{13\omega}{32} = \dfrac{13\omega}{32}$, clockwise

and $v = \dfrac{7\omega r}{32}$

For system, $\int N\,dt = \Delta p_{\text{system}} = 0 + m\left(v - \left(-\dfrac{\omega r}{4}\right)\right) = \dfrac{15\,m\omega r}{32}$

$$= \Delta p_{\text{rod}} + \Delta p_{\text{particle}}$$

15.

(A) $mv_0 L = \left(\left(\dfrac{mL^2}{3}\right) + \left(\dfrac{mL^2}{12} + m\left(\dfrac{\sqrt{5}L}{2}\right)^2\right)\right)\omega$

$\Rightarrow \omega = \dfrac{3v_0}{5L}$

(B) $V_{CM} = \omega r = \left(\dfrac{3v_0}{5L}\right)\sqrt{\left(\dfrac{3L}{4}\right)^2 + \left(\dfrac{L}{4}\right)^2} = \sqrt{\dfrac{9}{40}}\,v_0$

(C) $r_{CM} = \sqrt{\left(\dfrac{3L}{4}\right)^2 + \left(\dfrac{L}{4}\right)^2} = \dfrac{\sqrt{10}L}{4}$

(D) $K = \dfrac{1}{2}I\omega^2 = \dfrac{1}{2}\left(\dfrac{5}{3}mL^2\right)\left(\dfrac{3v_0}{5L}\right)^2 = \dfrac{3}{10}mv_0^2$

Comprehension Based Questions

1. Perpendicular axis theorem

2. $2\Sigma m_i r_i^2 = I_x + I_y + I_z$

$$= \frac{ML^2}{6} + \frac{ML^2}{6} + \frac{ML^2}{6} \Rightarrow \Sigma m_i r_i^2 = \frac{ML^2}{4}$$

3. $I_x + I_y + I_z = 2\Sigma m_i r_i^2$

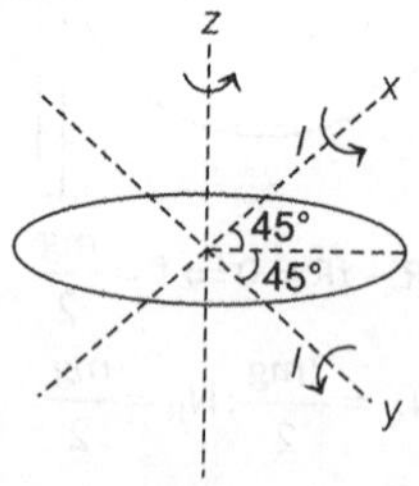

$\Rightarrow \quad I + I + \dfrac{MR^2}{2} = 2MR^2 \Rightarrow I = \dfrac{3}{4}MR^2$

4. For rod, $\Sigma\tau = 0$

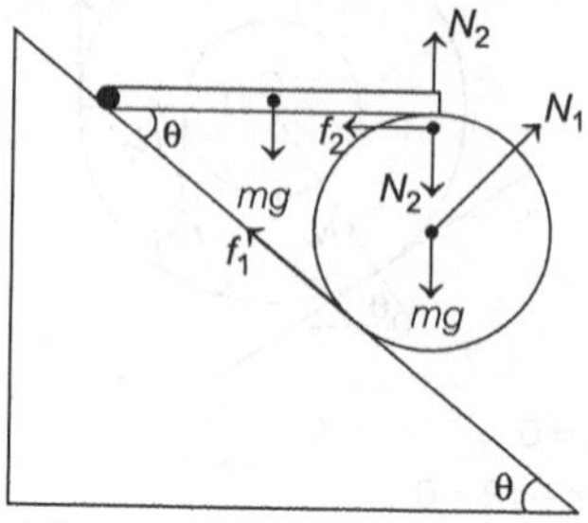

$\Rightarrow \quad mg\left(\dfrac{l}{2}\right) - N_2 l = 0 \Rightarrow N_2 = \dfrac{mg}{2}$

5. For cylinder, $\Sigma\tau = 0$ about its centre

$\Rightarrow \quad f_1 R - f_2 R = 0 \Rightarrow f_1 = f_2 \Rightarrow \dfrac{f_1}{f_2} = 1:1$

6. About hinge, for cylinder $\Sigma\tau = 0$

$\Rightarrow \quad mgL + N_2 L - N_1 L = 0 \Rightarrow N_1 = \dfrac{3mg}{2}$

7. $\Sigma F_y = 0 \Rightarrow N_1 + N_2 = 2500$ ...(i)

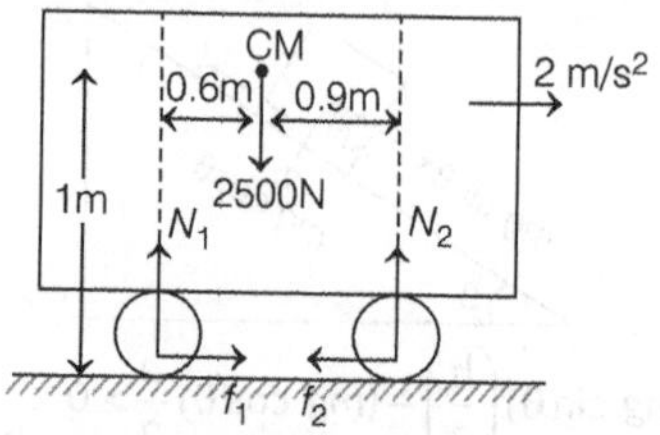

$\Sigma F_x = m(a_{CM})_x \Rightarrow f_1 - f_2 = 250 \times 2 = 500$ ...(ii)

About centre of mass, $\Sigma\tau = 0$

$\Rightarrow \quad N_1(0.6) + f_2(1) - f_1(1) - N_2(0.9) = 0$ ...(iii)

Solving Eqs. (i), (ii) and (iii), we get

$N_1 = \dfrac{5500}{3}$ N

8. To lift the front wheel, $N_2 = 0 \Rightarrow f_2 = 0$

$$\Sigma F_y = 0 \Rightarrow N_1 + N_2 = 2500$$
$$\Rightarrow \quad N_1 = 2500\,\text{N}$$
$$\Sigma F_x = ma_x \Rightarrow f_1 = 250a$$

About CM, $\Sigma\tau = 0$

$$\Rightarrow \quad N_1(0.6) - f_1(1) = 0$$

Solving we get, $a = 6\ \text{m/s}^2$

9. $f_1 = 250 \times 6 = 1500$ N

$$f_1 \le f_L \Rightarrow 1500 \le \mu(2500)$$
$$\Rightarrow \quad \mu \ge 0.6$$

10. $\Sigma\tau = I\alpha$

$$\Rightarrow \quad mg\left(\frac{L}{2}\right) + mgL = \left(\frac{mL^2}{3} + mL^2\right)\alpha$$
$$\Rightarrow \quad \alpha = \frac{9g}{8L}$$
$$a_{\text{ball}} = r\alpha = L\left(\frac{9g}{8L}\right) = \frac{9g}{8}$$

11. $(\Sigma F_{\text{ext}})_y = (ma_{CM})_y$

$$\Rightarrow \quad 2mg - N_y = 2m\left(\frac{3L}{4}\alpha\right) \Rightarrow N_y = \frac{5mg}{16}$$

12. Applying work-energy theorem,

$$W_{\text{gravity}} + W_F + W_{\text{hinge}} = \Delta K_{\text{system}}$$
$$\Rightarrow \left(+mg\frac{L}{2} + mgL\right) + \left(\frac{mg}{2}L\cos 180°\right)$$
$$= \frac{1}{2}\left(\frac{mL^2}{3} + mL^2\right)\omega^2 - 0$$
$$\Rightarrow \quad \omega = \sqrt{\frac{3g}{2l}}$$
$$v_{\text{ball}} = \omega l = \sqrt{\frac{3gl}{2}}$$

13. $$I = \left(\frac{ml^2}{3}\sin^2 45°\right) \times 2 + \left(\frac{ml^2}{12}\sin^2 45° + m\left(\frac{3l}{2\sqrt{2}}\right)^2\right) \times 2$$
$$= \frac{8}{3}ml^2$$

Using energy conservation,

$$K_1 + U_1 = K_2 + U_2$$
$$\Rightarrow \quad 0 + 4mg\left(\frac{l}{\sqrt{2}}\right) = \frac{1}{2}\left(\frac{8}{3}ml^2\right)\omega^2 - 4mg\left(\frac{l}{\sqrt{2}}\right)$$
$$\Rightarrow \quad \omega = \sqrt{\frac{3\sqrt{2}g}{l}}$$

14. $$v_B = \omega\left(\frac{l}{\sqrt{2}}\right) = \sqrt{\frac{3gl}{\sqrt{2}}}$$

15. $$N_y - 4mg = 4m\omega^2\left(\frac{l}{\sqrt{2}}\right)$$
$$\Rightarrow \quad N_y = 16\,mg$$

16. $mg\sin 37° - T = ma$ ...(i)

$$TR = (2MR^2)\alpha \quad \text{...(ii)}$$
$$a = R\alpha \quad \text{...(iii)}$$

Solving Eqs. (i), (ii) and (iii) we get

$$a = 2\ \text{m/s}^2$$

17. $f = \mu N = 0.5(2Mg) = Mg$ ...(i)

$$Mg\sin 37° - T = Ma \quad \text{...(ii)}$$
$$TR - f(2R) = (2MR^2)\alpha \quad \text{...(iii)}$$
$$a = R\alpha \quad \text{...(iv)}$$

Solving equations, we get

$$a = -\frac{7g}{15}$$

18. At $t = 7$, $v = u + at \Rightarrow v = 0 + 2(7) = 14$ m/s

After applying brake, $v = u + at$

$$\Rightarrow \quad 0 = 14 - \left(\frac{7g}{15}\right)t$$
$$\Rightarrow \quad t = 3\ \text{s}$$

19. Taking torque about the edge, $\Sigma\tau = 0$

$$\Rightarrow (3mg\sin\alpha)\frac{a}{2} - (3mg\cos\alpha)\left(\frac{2}{3}\left(\frac{a}{2}\right)\right) = 0$$
$$\Rightarrow \quad \alpha = \tan^{-1}\left(\frac{2}{3}\right)$$

20. $\mu = \tan\alpha = \dfrac{2}{3} = 0.66$

21. $s = ut + \dfrac{1}{2}at^2 \Rightarrow a = \dfrac{1}{2}(g\sin\alpha)t^2$

$$\Rightarrow \quad t = \sqrt{\frac{2a}{g\sin\alpha}}$$

22. Conserving angular momentum of the system about the point O,

$$Mv\left(\frac{L}{4}\right) = \left(\frac{ML^2}{12} + M\left(\frac{L}{4}\right)^2\right)\omega$$
$$\Rightarrow \quad \omega = \frac{12v}{7L}$$

23.

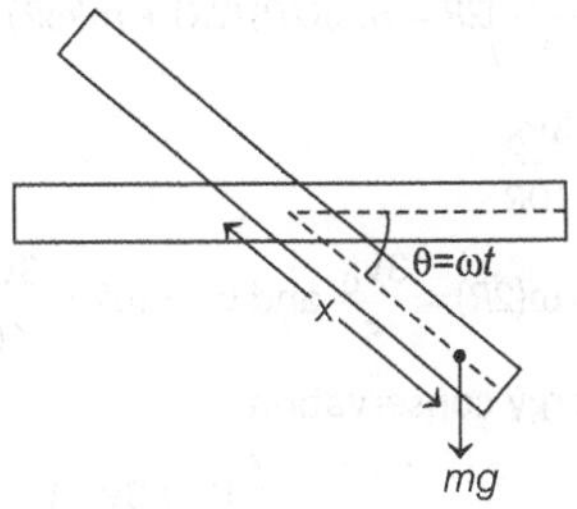

$$L = \left(\frac{ML^2}{12} + Mx^2\right)\omega$$
$$\tau = \frac{dL}{dt} = \omega\left(M2x\frac{dx}{dt}\right) \text{ and } \tau_{\text{gravity}} = Mgx\cos\omega t$$

$$\Rightarrow \quad 2M\omega x\frac{dx}{dt} = Mgx\cos\omega t$$

$$\Rightarrow \quad \int_{L/4}^{L/2} dx = \frac{g}{2\omega}\int_0^{\pi/2\omega}\cos\omega t\, dt$$

$$\Rightarrow \quad \omega = \sqrt{\frac{2g}{L}} = \frac{12v}{7L}$$

$$\Rightarrow \quad v = \frac{7}{12}\sqrt{2gL} = 3.5 \text{ m/s}$$

24. $mv_0 + 0 = mv_1 + mv_2$ ...(i)

$$e = \frac{1}{2} = \frac{v_2 - v_1}{v_0 - 0} \qquad \text{...(ii)}$$

Solving Eqs. (i) and (ii), we get

$$v_2 = \frac{3v_0}{4}$$

25. After collision B will start moving with speed $\frac{3v_0}{4}$ and C will also start moving when spring applies force on it. Subsequently speed of B decreases and that of C increases continuously. After some time, when the spring is again in unstreched position, speed of C becomes maximum.

Applying mechanical energy conservation,

$$\frac{1}{2}m\left(\frac{3v_0}{4}\right)^2 = \frac{1}{2}mv_B^2 + \frac{1}{2}mv_C^2 \qquad \text{...(i)}$$

Applying conservation of angular momentum about centre about centre of the track,

$$m\left(\frac{3v_0}{4}\right)2R = mv_B(2R) + mv_C(R) \qquad \text{...(ii)}$$

Solving Eqs. (i) and (ii), we get

$$v_C = \frac{3v_0}{5}$$

26. Stretch in the spring will be maximum when angular velocities of B and C will be same about the centre of the track.

Conserving angular momentum,

$$m\left(\frac{3v_0}{4}\right)2R = m\omega(2R)(2R) + m(\omega R)(R)$$

$$\Rightarrow \quad \omega = \frac{3v_0}{10R}$$

$$v_B = \omega(2R) = \frac{3v_0}{5} \text{ and } v_C = \omega R = \frac{3v_0}{10}$$

Applying energy conservation,

$$\left(\frac{1}{2}m\left(\frac{3v_0}{4}\right)^2 + 0\right) + 0 = \left(\frac{1}{2}m\left(\frac{3v_0}{5}\right)^2 + \frac{1}{2}m\left(\frac{3v_0}{10}\right)^2\right) + \frac{1}{2}kx_{max}^2$$

$$\Rightarrow \quad x_{max} = \frac{3v_0}{4}\sqrt{\frac{m}{5k}}$$

Match the Columns Questions

1. (A) $I = \left(\frac{ML^2}{3}\sin^2 45°\right)\times 2 + \left(\frac{ML^2}{12}\sin^2 45° + M\left(\frac{3L}{2\sqrt{2}}\right)^2\right)\times 2$

$$= \frac{8}{3}ML^2$$

(B) $I = 0 + \frac{ML^2}{3} + \frac{ML^2}{3} + ML^2 = \frac{5}{3}ML^2$

(C) $I = \left(\frac{ML^2}{3}\sin^2 45°\right)\times 4 = \frac{2}{3}ML^2$

(D) $I = \frac{ML^2}{12} + \left(\frac{ML^2}{12} + M\left(\frac{L}{2}\sqrt{2}\right)^2\right)\times 2 + \left(\frac{ML^2}{12} + ML^2\right)$

$$= \frac{7}{3}ML^2$$

2. (A) $I = \frac{MR^2}{3}\sin^2 30° = \frac{MR^2}{12}$

(B) $MR^2 = I_{CM} + M\left(\frac{2R}{\pi}\right)^2$ ...(i)

$$I = I_{CM} + M\left(R - \frac{2R}{\pi}\right)^2 \qquad \text{...(ii)}$$

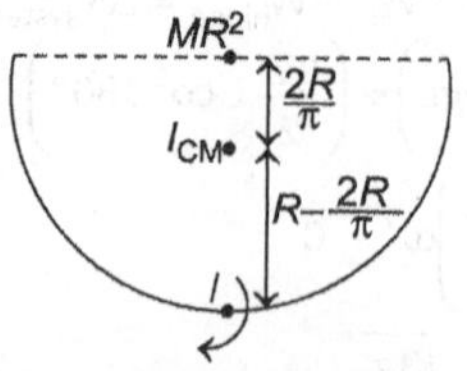

Solving Eqs. (i) and (ii), we get

$$I = MR^2 + M\left(R - \frac{2R}{\pi}\right)^2 - M\left(\frac{2R}{\pi}\right)^2$$

$$= MR^2\left[1 + 1 - \frac{4}{\pi}\right] = \frac{8MR^2}{11}$$

(C) $dm = \frac{M}{\left(\frac{\sqrt{3}R^2}{4}\right)}(\sqrt{3}x\,dx) = \frac{4Mx\,dx}{R^2}$

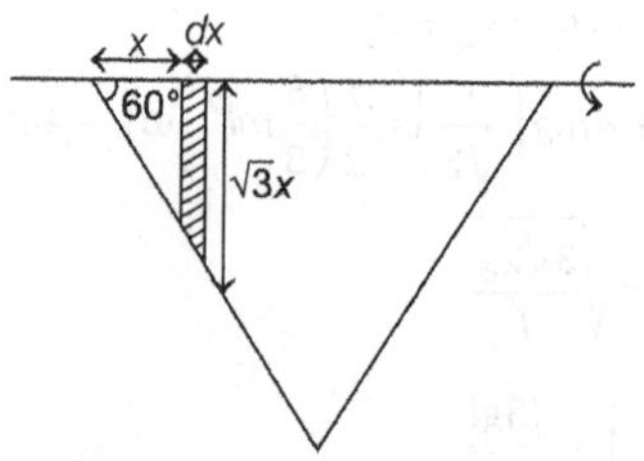

$$I = 2\int_0^{R/2}\left(\frac{4Mx\,dx}{R^2}\right)\frac{(\sqrt{3}x)^2}{3} \Rightarrow I = \frac{MR^2}{8}$$

(D) $I = I_1 - I_2 = \frac{M(2R)^2}{2} - \left(\left(\frac{M}{4}\right)\frac{R^2}{2} + \left(\frac{M}{4}\right)R^2\right) = \frac{13MR^2}{8}$

3.

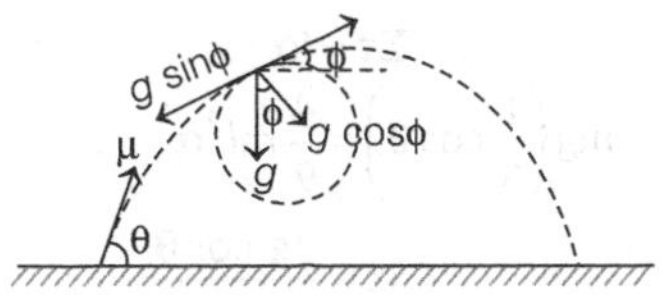

ϕ first decreases till highest point and thereafter ϕ increases.

(A) | Radial acceleration | $= g\cos\phi$. So, it first increases and then decreases.

(B) | Tangential acceleration | $= g\sin\phi$. So, it first decreases and then increases.

(C) $P = \mathbf{F}\cdot\mathbf{v} = (-mg\hat{\mathbf{j}})\cdot((u\cos\theta\hat{\mathbf{i}} + (u\sin\theta - gt)\hat{\mathbf{j}})$

$= -mg(u\sin\theta - gt)$

During ascent power is negative. At the highest point, power is zero and during descent power is positive. So, power increases with time.

(D) $\tau_{mg} = mg(R - (u\cos\theta)t)$

As time increases, torque due to gravity about T decreases.

4. (A) $\Sigma F = 0 \Rightarrow f = 0$

$$\Sigma\tau = F_1h_1 - F_2h_2 = \left(\frac{mg}{2}\right)a - \left(\frac{mg}{2}\right)\frac{a}{8}$$

$$= \frac{7mga}{16}, \text{ clockwise}$$

Due to clockwise torque of applied forces, normal reaction shifts towards right.

Minimum torque required to topple the plate about the right most edge $= mg\left(\frac{a}{2}\right)$.

Since $\Sigma\tau < mg\left(\frac{a}{2}\right)$, plate will not topple.

(B) $\Sigma F_{\text{applied}} = \frac{mg}{2} - mg = \frac{mg}{2}$ towards left

$f_L = \mu mg = 1\,(mg) = mg$

So, the plate won't slide and friction will be $\left(\frac{mg}{2}\right)$ (static) towards right. Torque due to friction is out of the plane of plate.

$\Sigma\tau = \left(\frac{mg}{2}\right)(a) - (mg)\left(\frac{a}{8}\right) = \frac{3mga}{8}$, clockwise. Hence, normal reaction shifts towards right.

Since $\Sigma\tau = \frac{3mga}{8} < mg\left(\frac{a}{2}\right)$, plate won't topple.

(C) $\Sigma F = mg - 0 = mg$ towards right. So, friction will be mg (limiting) towards left and plate will not slide.

Torque due to friction will be into the plane of plate. $\Sigma\tau = mga$, clockwise. So, the normal reaction shifts towards right.

Since $\Sigma\tau = mga > mg\left(\frac{a}{2}\right)$, toppling of plate occurs.

(D) $\Sigma F = \frac{mg}{2} - mg = \frac{mg}{2}$, left. Since net force is less than limiting friction, block won't slide and friction will be $\frac{mg}{2}$ (static) towards right. So, torque due to friction is out of the plane of plate.

About the centre of the plate, torque of applied forces and gravity is zero. Due to counter clockwise torque of friction, normal reaction shifts towards left.

About the centre, $\tau_{\text{friction}} = \left(\frac{mg}{2}\right)\left(\frac{a}{2}\right)$ and maximum torque of normal reaction $= mg\left(\frac{a}{2}\right)$.

Since, $\tau_{\text{friction}} < (\tau_N)_{\max}$, toppling doesn't take place.

5. (A) Distance of the insect from the axis first increases and then decreases. So, momentum of inertia will first increase and then decrease.

(B) $I\omega = \text{constant} \Rightarrow \omega \propto \frac{1}{I}$

(C) $L = I\omega = \text{constant}$

(D) $K = \frac{L^2}{2I} \Rightarrow K \propto \frac{1}{I}$

Numerical Value Questions

1. $\Sigma F_y = 0 \Rightarrow N_2\cos 45° + \mu N_2\sin 45° = Mg$

$$\Rightarrow \quad N_2 = \frac{\sqrt{2}mg}{\mu + 1} \qquad \text{...(i)}$$

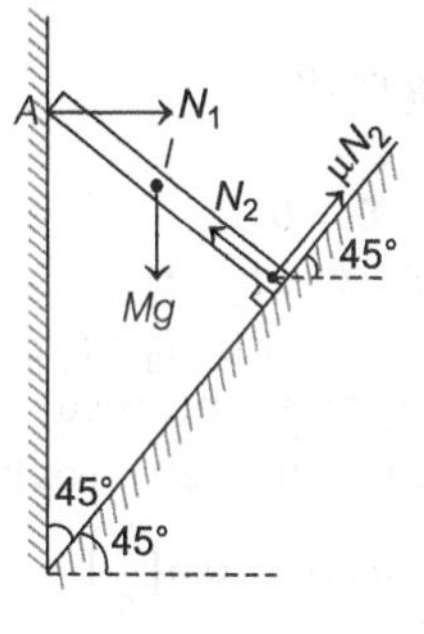

About A, $\Sigma\tau = 0$

$$\Rightarrow \quad Mg\left(\frac{l}{2}\sin 45°\right) - \mu N_2 l = 0$$

$$\Rightarrow \quad N_2 = \frac{Mg}{2\sqrt{2}\mu} \qquad \text{...(ii)}$$

From Eqs. (i) and (ii), we get

$$\mu = \frac{1}{3}$$

2. $mg - T = ma$ ...(i)

$T = ma$ ...(ii)

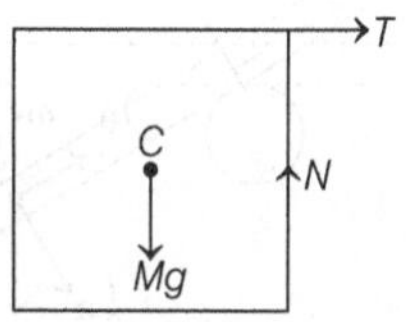

From Eqs. (i) and (ii), we get

$$T=\frac{Mmg}{M+m}$$

For just toppling about C, $\Sigma\tau=0$

$$\Rightarrow \quad T\left(\frac{h}{2}\right)-N\left(\frac{h}{4}\right)=0$$

$$\Rightarrow \quad 2T=N \;\Rightarrow\; 2\frac{Mmg}{M+m}=Mg \;\Rightarrow\; \frac{m}{M}=1$$

3. For m_1, $\Sigma F = ma \Rightarrow 50-T_1=5a_1$ ...(i)

For m_2, $\Sigma F = ma \Rightarrow T_2 - m_2(10)=m_2a_2$ ...(ii)

For disk system; $\Sigma F_{ext}=ma_{CM} \Rightarrow T_1-T_2=0$ ...(iii)

$\Sigma\tau = I\alpha \Rightarrow T_1(0.3)-T_2(0.2)=0.25\alpha$ ...(iv)

Constraints, $a_1=(0.3)\alpha$ ...(v)

$a_2=(0.2)\alpha$ ...(vi)

Solving we get, $m_2=2.5$ kg

4.

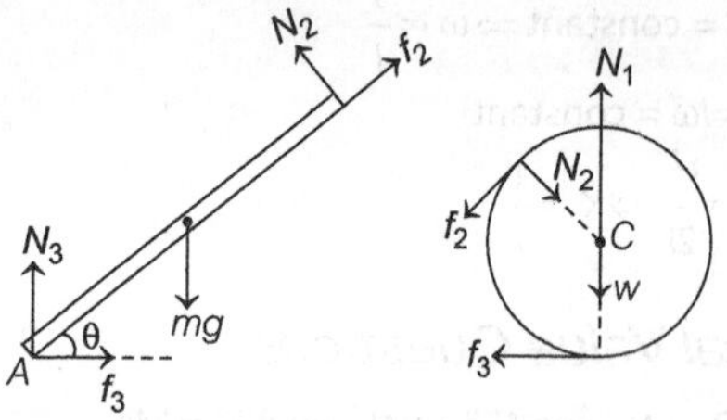

For rod, about A, $\Sigma\tau=0$

$$\Rightarrow \quad mg\left(\frac{L}{2}\cos\theta\right)-N_2(L)=0$$

$$\Rightarrow \quad N_2=\frac{mg\cos\theta}{2}$$

For disc, about C, $\Sigma\tau=0$

$$\Rightarrow \quad f_2R-f_3R=0 \Rightarrow f_3=f_2$$

$$\Sigma F_x=0 \Rightarrow N_2\sin\theta = f_3+f_2\cos\theta$$

$$\Rightarrow \quad f_3=\frac{N_2\sin\theta}{1+\cos\theta}=\frac{mg\cos\theta\sin\theta}{2(1+\cos\theta)}$$

$$=\frac{1}{2}mg\cos\theta\tan\left(\frac{\theta}{2}\right)$$

Mass of rod $= m = \lambda L = \lambda R\cot\left(\frac{\theta}{2}\right)$

So, $f_3=\dfrac{\lambda gR\cos\theta}{2}=5$ N

5. $I=\dfrac{m(2l)^2}{12}+m\left(\dfrac{l}{3}\right)^2=\dfrac{4}{9}ml^2$

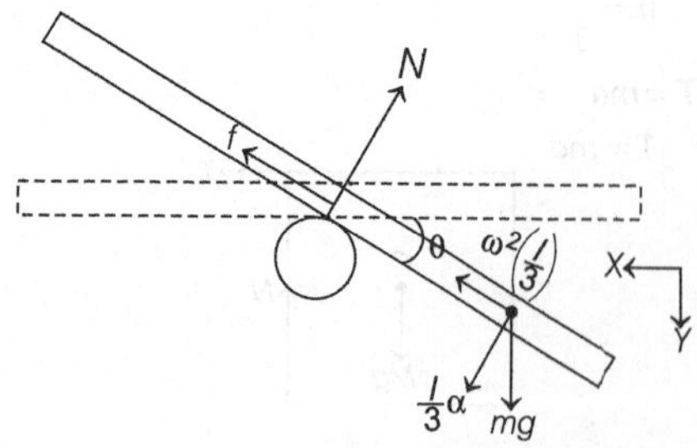

$$\Sigma\tau=I\alpha$$

$$\Rightarrow \quad mg\left(\frac{l}{3}\cos\theta\right)=\frac{4}{9}ml^2\alpha$$

$$\Rightarrow \quad \alpha=\frac{3g\cos\theta}{4l}$$

Applying work-energy theorem,

$$W_{mg}+W_N+W_f=\Delta K$$

$$mg\frac{l}{3}\sin\theta+0+0=\frac{1}{2}\left(\frac{4}{9}ml^2\right)\omega^2-0$$

$$\Rightarrow \quad \omega=\sqrt{\frac{3g\sin\theta}{2l}}$$

In x-direction, $\Sigma F = ma_{CM}$

$$\Rightarrow \quad f-mg\sin\theta=m\omega^2\left(\frac{l}{3}\right)$$

$$\Rightarrow \quad f=\frac{3mg\sin\theta}{2}$$

In y-direction, $\Sigma F=ma_{CM}$

$$\Rightarrow \quad mg\cos\theta-N=m\left(\frac{l}{3}\alpha\right)$$

$$\Rightarrow \quad N=\frac{3mg\cos\theta}{4}$$

$$f\le f_L$$

$$\Rightarrow \quad \frac{3mg\sin\theta}{2}=\mu\left(\frac{3mg\cos\theta}{4}\right)$$

$$\Rightarrow \quad \mu=2\tan\theta=1.5$$

6. $\Sigma\tau=I\alpha$

$$\Rightarrow \quad mg\frac{L}{2}\cos\theta=\frac{mL^2}{3}\alpha$$

$$\Rightarrow \quad \alpha=\frac{3g\cos\theta}{2L}$$

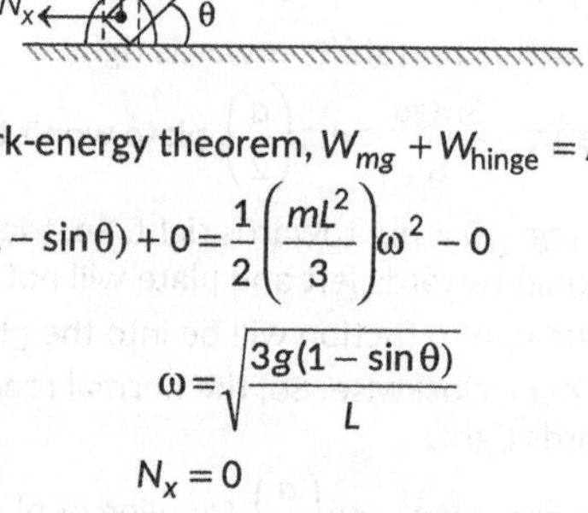

Using work-energy theorem, $W_{mg}+W_{hinge}=\Delta K$

$$\Rightarrow mg\frac{L}{2}(1-\sin\theta)+0=\frac{1}{2}\left(\frac{mL^2}{3}\right)\omega^2-0$$

$$\Rightarrow \quad \omega=\sqrt{\frac{3g(1-\sin\theta)}{L}}$$

$$N_x=0$$

$$\Rightarrow \quad (a_{CM})_x=0$$

$$\Rightarrow \quad \frac{L}{2}\alpha \sin\theta = \omega^2 \frac{L}{2}\cos\theta$$

$$\Rightarrow \quad \sin\theta = \frac{2}{3}$$

7. $I = \left(\frac{m}{2}\right)\frac{L^2}{3} + \left(\frac{m}{2}\left(\frac{L^2}{12}\right) + \left(\frac{m}{2}\right)\left(\frac{\sqrt{5}L}{2}\right)^2\right) = \frac{5}{6}mL^2$

$$PC = \sqrt{\left(\frac{3L}{4}\right)^2 + \left(\frac{L}{4}\right)^2} = \frac{\sqrt{10}L}{4}$$

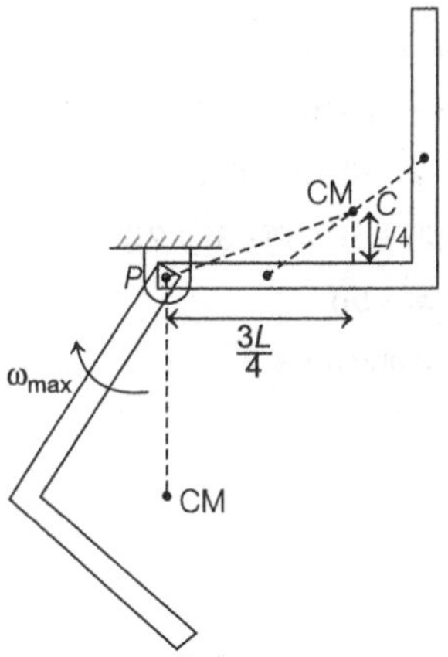

Using work-energy theorem,

$$W_{mg} + W_{hinge} = \Delta K$$

$$\Rightarrow \quad mg\left(\frac{\sqrt{10}L}{4} + \frac{L}{4}\right) + 0 = \frac{1}{2}\left(\frac{5}{6}mL^2\right)\omega_{max}^2$$

$$\Rightarrow \quad \omega_{max} = \sqrt{\frac{3g}{5L}(\sqrt{10}+1)} = 5 \text{ rad/s}$$

8. Applying work-energy for rod,

$$W_{mg} = \Delta K$$

$$\Rightarrow +Mg\left(\frac{R}{2}\right) = \frac{1}{2}\left(\frac{MR^2}{3}\right)\omega^2 \Rightarrow \omega = \sqrt{\frac{3g}{R}}$$

Speed of block just after collision $= \sqrt{5gR}$

Applying angular momentum conservation for the system just before and and just after collision,

$$\left(\frac{MR^2}{3}\right)\sqrt{\frac{3g}{R}} + 0 = 0 + m(\sqrt{5gR})R$$

$$\Rightarrow \quad \frac{M}{m} = \sqrt{15}$$

9. $I_{pivot} + I_{ext} = \Delta p$

$\Rightarrow \quad 0 + p_0 = mv_{CM} - 0$

$$\Rightarrow \quad v_{CM} = \frac{p_0}{m} \quad \text{...(i)}$$

Angular impulse $= \Delta L$

$$\Rightarrow \quad p_0 x = \left(\frac{mL^2}{3}\right)\omega \quad \text{...(ii)}$$

and $\quad v_{CM} = \frac{\omega L}{2} \quad$ ...(iii)

Solving Eqs. (i), (ii) and (iii), we get

$$\Rightarrow \quad x = \frac{2L}{3} = 48 \text{ cm}$$

10.

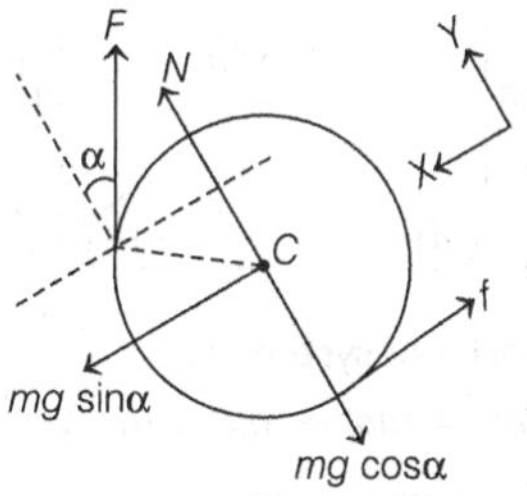

About C, $\Sigma\tau = 0$

$\Rightarrow \quad FR - fR = 0$

$\Rightarrow \quad F = f \quad$ ...(i)

$\Sigma F_x = 0$

$\Rightarrow \quad mg\sin\alpha = F\sin\alpha + f \quad$ ...(ii)

$\Sigma F_y = 0$

$\Rightarrow \quad N = mg\cos\alpha - F\cos\alpha \quad$ ...(iii)

Solving Eqs. (i), (ii) and (iii), we get

$$f = \frac{mg\sin\alpha}{1+\sin\alpha}$$

and $\quad N = \dfrac{mg\cos\alpha}{1+\sin\alpha}$

$f \le f_L$

$\Rightarrow \quad f \le \mu N$

$\Rightarrow \quad \mu = \tan\alpha = \frac{3}{4}$

11. $\omega_{umbrella,\ boy} = 3$ rev/s

$\Rightarrow \omega_{umbrella} = 3 + \omega_{boy}$

Applying angular momentum conservation,

$$0 + 0 = 6\times10^{-3}\,\omega_{platform} + 4\times10^{-3}(3+\omega_{platform})$$

$\Rightarrow \omega_{platform} = 1.2$ rev/s

12. $I = I_A + I_B = \dfrac{(0.01)(0.6)^2}{3} + \left(\dfrac{(0.02)(0.6)^2}{12} + (0.02)(0.9)^2\right)$

$= 0.018$ kg-m^2

Using energy conservation for the system,

$$K_1 + U_1 = K_2 + U_2$$

$$\Rightarrow \frac{1}{2}(0.018 + (0.05)(1.2)^2)\omega^2 + (-(0.01)10(0.3) - (0.01)$$
$$(10)(0.9) - (0.05)(10)(1.2) = 0 + 0$$

$\Rightarrow \quad \omega = 4$ rad/s

Using angular momentum conservation for collision,

$0.05u(1.2) + 0 = (0.018 + (0.05)(1.2)^2)(4)$

$\Rightarrow \quad u = 6$ m/s

Previous Years Questions

JEE Main

1.

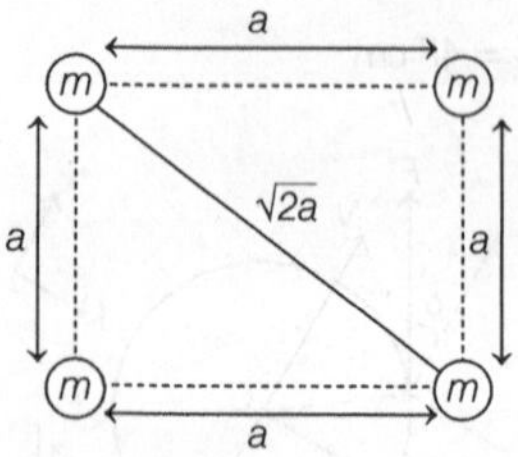

Moment of inertia of system is,

$$I = \Sigma mr^2 = ma^2 + ma^2 + m(\sqrt{2}a)^2$$
$$= ma^2 + ma^2 + 2ma^2$$
$$= 4ma^2$$
$$I = 4 \times 1 \times (2)^2$$
$$= 4 \times 1 \times 4 = 16\ \text{kg/m}^2$$

2.

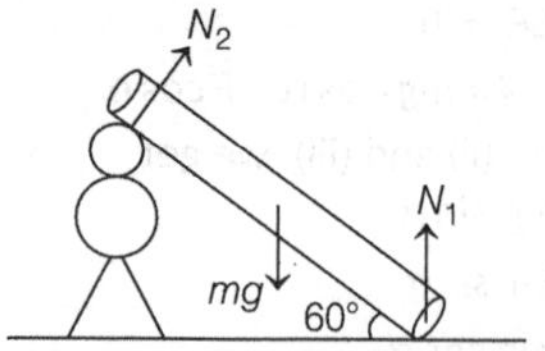

Taking torque about N_1,

$$mg\frac{l}{2}\cos 60° = N_2 l$$
$$12 \times 10 \times \frac{l}{2} \times \frac{1}{2} = N_2 \times l$$
$$N_2 = \frac{120}{4} = 30\,\text{N}$$
$$N_2 = 30\ \text{N}$$
$$\therefore \quad \text{Mass} = \frac{N_2}{g} = \frac{30}{10} = 3\ \text{kg}$$

3. Given, $m = 5$ kg

$$v = 3\sqrt{2}\ \text{ms}^{-1}$$
$$y = x + 4$$
$$x - y + 4 = 0$$

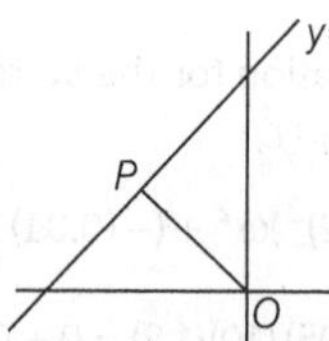

Perpendicular difference on the line from origin,

$$OP = \frac{4}{\sqrt{1^2 + 1^2}} = 2\sqrt{2}$$

$\therefore$ Angular momentum

$$L = mv \times OP = 5 \times 3\sqrt{2} \times 2\sqrt{2} = 60\ \text{kg m}^2\text{s}^{-1}$$

4.

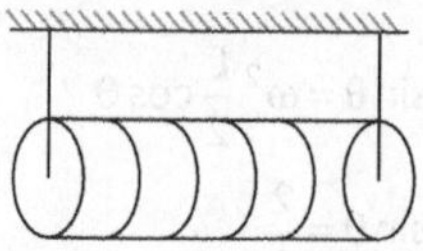

We know that

$$\tau = I\alpha$$
$$\Rightarrow \quad FR = mR^2\alpha$$
$$\Rightarrow \quad \alpha = \frac{F}{mR} = \frac{52.5}{5 \times 0.7}$$
$$\Rightarrow \quad \alpha = 15\ \text{rad/s}^2$$

5. We know that, $\tau = \mathbf{r} \times \mathbf{F}$

Where, $\mathbf{r} = 2\hat{i} - 3\hat{j}$ and $\mathbf{F} = -P\hat{k}$

$$\Rightarrow \quad \tau = (+2\hat{i} - 3\hat{j}) \times (-P)\hat{k}$$
$$= P(2\hat{j} + 3\hat{i}) = P(+3\hat{i} + 2\hat{j})$$
$$= P(a\hat{i} + b\hat{j}) \qquad \text{(Given)}$$

So, $\quad a = +3$ and $b = +2$

Thus, $\quad \dfrac{a}{b} = \dfrac{3}{2} = \dfrac{x}{2}$

$\therefore \quad x = 3$

6.

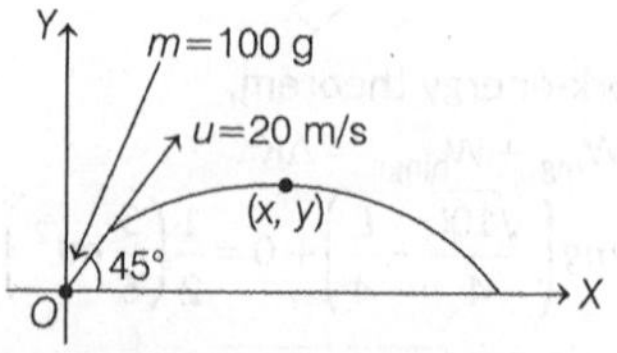

At time $t = 2$ s; let particle is at point (x, y)

Then, $x = v_x t = x\cos\theta t$

$$= 20 \times \cos 45° \times 2 = \frac{40}{\sqrt{2}} = 20\sqrt{2}\ \text{m}$$

and $\quad y = u\sin\theta \cdot t - \dfrac{1}{2}gt^2$

$$= 20 \times \frac{1}{\sqrt{2}} \times 2 - \frac{1}{2} \times 10 \times 2^2$$
$$= 20\sqrt{2} - 20 = 20(\sqrt{2} - 1)\,\text{m}$$

So, position vector of particle,

$$\mathbf{r} = x\hat{i} + y\hat{j} = 20\sqrt{2}\hat{i} + 20(\sqrt{2} - 1)\hat{j}$$

Also, velocity of particle at $t = 2$ s is

$$\mathbf{v} = \mathbf{u} + \mathbf{a}t$$
$$\Rightarrow \quad \mathbf{v} = (u\cos\theta\hat{i} + u\sin\theta\hat{j}) - (g\hat{j}t)$$
$$= \frac{20}{\sqrt{2}}\hat{i} + \frac{20}{\sqrt{2}}\hat{j} - 20\hat{j}$$
$$= 10\sqrt{2}\hat{i} + 10\sqrt{2}\hat{j} - 20\hat{j}$$
$$= 10\sqrt{2}\hat{i} + 10(\sqrt{2} - 2)\hat{j}$$

So, Angular momentum at $t = 2$s is given by,

$$\mathbf{L} = m(\mathbf{r} \times \mathbf{v})$$

$$= 0.1 \begin{vmatrix} \hat{i} & \hat{j} & \hat{k} \\ 20\sqrt{2} & 20(\sqrt{2}-1) & 0 \\ 10\sqrt{2} & 10(\sqrt{2}-2) & 0 \end{vmatrix}$$

$$= 0 \cdot 1(-200\sqrt{2})\,\hat{k} = -20\sqrt{2}\,\hat{k}$$

So, magnitude of angular momentum is

$$|\mathbf{L}| = |-20\sqrt{2}\,\hat{k}| = 20\sqrt{2} = \sqrt{800}$$

$$= \sqrt{K} \quad \text{(Given)}$$

$\therefore \quad K = 800$

7. Using parallel axis theorem

$$I_{sys} = \left(\frac{2}{5}mr^2 + md^2\right) \times 2$$

Here, $r = 10$ cm $= 0.1$ m

$$d = \frac{40}{2}\text{ cm} = 0.2 \text{ m}$$

$$I_{sys} = \left(\frac{2}{5} \times 2 \times 0.01 + 2 \times 0.04\right) \times 2$$

$$= (0.008 + 0.08) \times 2 = 0.088 \times 2$$

$$= 176 \times 10^{-3} \text{ kg-m}^2$$

8. Moment of inertia of a semicirular ring about an axis through centre and perpendicular to plane of ring is;

$$I = \frac{1}{2}MR^2$$

And given $I = \frac{1}{x}MR^2$

$\therefore \quad x = 2$

9. Given radius of gyration is same for ring and solid sphere

$$K_R = K_{SS}$$

$$\Rightarrow \quad R_R = \sqrt{\frac{2}{5}}R_{SS}$$

$$\Rightarrow \quad \frac{R_R}{R_{SS}} = \sqrt{\frac{2}{5}} = \sqrt{\frac{2}{x}}$$

$$x = 5$$

10. For solid sphere,

$$K_{sph}^2 = \frac{2}{5}R^2 \quad \Rightarrow K_{sph} = \sqrt{\frac{2}{5}}R$$

For solid cylinder,

$$K_{cyl}^2 = \frac{R^2}{2} \quad \Rightarrow K_{cyl} = \frac{R}{\sqrt{2}}$$

$$\therefore \quad K_{sph} : K_{cyl} = \sqrt{\frac{2}{5}}R : \frac{R}{\sqrt{2}} = \sqrt{\frac{2}{5}} : \frac{1}{\sqrt{2}}$$

$$= \sqrt{\frac{2}{5}} \cdot \sqrt{10} : \frac{\sqrt{10}}{\sqrt{2}} = 2 : \sqrt{5} = 2 : \sqrt{x} \quad \text{(given)}$$

$\therefore \quad x = 5$

11. Moment of inertia of sphere about its diameter

$$I_1 = \frac{2}{5}mR^2$$

Moment of inertia of the sphere about its tangent,

$$I_2 = \frac{2}{5}MR^2 + MR^2 = \frac{7}{5}MR^2$$

Angular momentum about diameter,

$$L = I_1\omega = \frac{2}{5}MR^2\omega$$

$$\therefore \quad \frac{I_2}{L} = \frac{7}{2\omega} = \frac{7}{2 \times 10} = \frac{7}{20}$$

$$= \frac{7}{2} \times 100 \times 10^{-2}$$

$$= 350 \times 10^{-2} = x \times 10^{-2} \quad \text{(given)}$$

$\therefore \quad x = 350$

12. Given that, both discs have same mass.

$$M_1 = M_2$$

$$\rho_1 V_1 = \rho_2 V_2$$

$$\rho_1 \pi R_1^2 t_1 = \rho_2 \pi R_2^2 t_2$$

$$\text{or} \quad \frac{R_1^2}{R_2^2} = \left(\frac{\rho_2}{\rho_1}\right)\left(\frac{t_2}{t_1}\right) \quad \text{...(i)}$$

Moment of inertia of a disc about diameter is given as

$$I = \frac{MR^2}{4}$$

$$\text{or} \quad \frac{I_1}{I_2} = \frac{M_1}{M_2} \cdot \frac{R_1^2}{R_2^2}$$

$$\frac{I_1}{I_2} = \frac{M_1}{M_2} \cdot \frac{\rho_2}{\rho_1} \cdot \frac{t_2}{t_1} \quad \text{[from Eq. (i)]}$$

Given that,

$$\frac{M_1}{M_2} = 1, \frac{\rho_2}{\rho_1} = \frac{3}{5}, \frac{t_2}{t_1} = \frac{1}{0.5}$$

$$\frac{I_1}{I_2} = (1)\left(\frac{5}{3}\right)\left(\frac{0.5}{1}\right) = \frac{5}{6} = \frac{x}{6} \quad \text{(given)}$$

$\therefore \quad x = 5$

13. For disc,

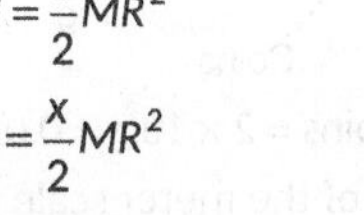

By using parallel axis theorem,

$$I = I_{CM} + Md^2$$

$$= \frac{MR^2}{2} + MR^2$$

$$\Rightarrow \quad I = \frac{3}{2}MR^2$$

Given, $\quad I = \frac{x}{2}MR^2$

On comparing, we get, $x = 3$

14. We know that,

Rotational kinetic energy

$$E=\frac{1}{2}I\omega^2=\frac{(I\omega)^2}{2I}=\frac{L^2}{2I} \quad (\because L=I\omega)$$

$$\therefore \quad E\propto\frac{1}{I}$$

$$\Rightarrow \quad \frac{E_f}{E_i}=\frac{I_i}{I_f}=\frac{I}{3I}=\frac{1}{3}$$

$$\Rightarrow \quad E_f=\frac{E_i}{3}=\frac{E}{3}=\frac{E}{x} \quad \text{(given)}$$

$$\therefore \quad x=3$$

15. Given, force applied on the body,

$$\mathbf{F}=5\hat{\mathbf{i}}+3\hat{\mathbf{j}}-7\hat{\mathbf{k}}$$

Position vector, $r=2\hat{\mathbf{i}}+2\hat{\mathbf{j}}+\hat{\mathbf{k}}$

$\therefore$ Torque applied on the body,

$$\tau=\mathbf{r}\times\mathbf{F}=(2\hat{\mathbf{i}}+2\hat{\mathbf{j}}+\hat{\mathbf{k}})\times(5\hat{\mathbf{i}}+3\hat{\mathbf{j}}-7\hat{\mathbf{k}})$$

$$=\begin{vmatrix}\hat{\mathbf{i}} & \hat{\mathbf{j}} & \hat{\mathbf{k}}\\ 2 & 2 & 1\\ 5 & 3 & -7\end{vmatrix}$$

$$=\hat{\mathbf{i}}(-14-3)-\hat{\mathbf{j}}(-14-5)+\hat{\mathbf{k}}(6-10)$$

$$=-17\hat{\mathbf{i}}+19\hat{\mathbf{j}}-4\hat{\mathbf{k}}$$

16. Angular momentum of a body,

$$\mathbf{L}=\mathbf{r}\times\mathbf{p}=(\mathbf{r}\times m\mathbf{v})$$

Here, $\mathbf{r}=(3\hat{\mathbf{i}}-\hat{\mathbf{j}})$ m

$$\mathbf{v}=(3\hat{\mathbf{j}}+\hat{\mathbf{k}})\text{ m/s}$$

and $\quad m=1$ kg

So, $\quad \mathbf{L}=\begin{vmatrix}\hat{\mathbf{i}} & \hat{\mathbf{j}} & \hat{\mathbf{k}}\\ 3 & -1 & 0\\ 0 & 3 & 1\end{vmatrix}$

Or $\quad \mathbf{L}=-\hat{\mathbf{i}}-3\hat{\mathbf{j}}+9\hat{\mathbf{k}}$

Magnitude of angular momentum will be

$$|\mathbf{L}|=\sqrt{1^2+3^2+9^2}=\sqrt{91}\text{ N-m}$$

17. The given situation is shown below

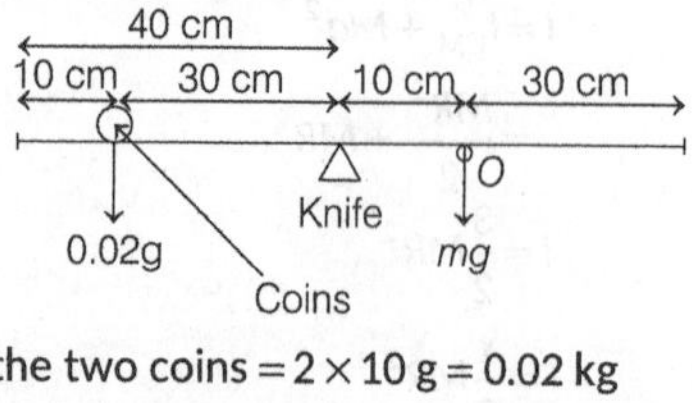

Mass of the two coins $=2\times10$ g $=0.02$ kg

Let m be the mass of the meter scale which is balanced at point O.

By the principle of moments about knife edge.

$$(0.02\,g)\times(30\times10^{-2})=mg\times10\times10^{-2}$$

$$\Rightarrow \quad m=6\times10^{-2}\text{ kg}$$

$$x=6$$

18. Given, length of cylindrical rod,

$$l=10\sqrt{3}\text{ m}$$

Moment of inertia of rod about an axis passing through the centre and perpendicular to the length of rod,

$$I=Ml^2/12 \quad \text{...(i)}$$

If K be the radius of gyration, then

$$I=MK^2 \quad \text{...(ii)}$$

From Eqs. (i), and (ii), we get

$$MK^2=Ml^2/12$$

$$\Rightarrow \quad K=\frac{l}{\sqrt{12}}=\frac{l}{2\sqrt{3}}=\frac{10\sqrt{3}}{2\sqrt{3}}=5\text{ m}$$

19. According to given situation, the beaker will revolve with the disc if centrifugal force $\leq$ friction force

i.e. $\quad m\omega^2R\leq\mu mg$

$$R\leq\frac{\mu g}{\omega^2}$$

20. When, $t=1$ s, then $\theta=5$ rad

$$\omega_0=0\text{ rad/s},$$

Let α be the angular acceleration of the wheel, then by using the equation of rotational motion,

$$\theta=\omega_0t+\frac{1}{2}\alpha t^2$$

$$\Rightarrow \quad 5=0\times1+\frac{1}{2}\alpha\times1^2$$

$$\Rightarrow \quad 5=\frac{\alpha}{2}$$

$$\Rightarrow \quad \alpha=10\text{ rad/s}^2$$

If θ' be angle rotated by wheel in $t'=2$s, then

$$\theta'=\omega_0t'+\frac{1}{2}\alpha(t')^2=0\times2+\frac{1}{2}\times10\times(2)^2$$

$$\theta'=20\text{ rad}$$

$\therefore$ Angle rotated by wheel is $\Delta\theta=\theta'-\theta=20-5=15$ rad

21. As we know that,

Angular momentum, $L=r\times p=mvr\sin\theta$

where, $m=$ mass, $v=$ velocity, $r=$ radius,

$\theta=$ angle between v and $r=90°$ (for circular motion) Since, m, v, r are constant.

$\therefore L$ will always remain same in magnitude and direction.

22. Angular velocity, $\omega=600$ rpm

$$\omega=600\times\frac{2\pi}{60}=20\pi\text{ rads}^{-1}$$

$$\alpha = \frac{\omega}{t} = \frac{20\pi}{10} = 2\pi \text{rads}^{-2}$$

$$\tau = I\alpha \Rightarrow \tau = \frac{1}{2}MR^2\alpha = \frac{1}{2} \times 10 \times \left(\frac{20}{100}\right)^2 \times 2\pi$$

$$= 0.4\pi \; = 4\pi \times 10^{-1} \text{ N-m}$$

23. Velocity $(\mathbf{v}) = \frac{d\mathbf{r}}{dt}$

$$\Rightarrow \quad \mathbf{v} = \frac{d}{dt}[10\alpha t^2\hat{i} + 5\beta(t-5)\hat{j}] = 20\alpha t\hat{i} + 5\beta\hat{j}$$

Now $\mathbf{v}(t=0) = 5\beta\hat{j}$

and $\quad r(t=0) = 5\beta(0-5)\hat{j} = -25\beta\hat{j}$

$$\mathbf{L}(t=0) = m(\mathbf{r} \times \mathbf{v}) = 0$$

[$\because$ $\sin\theta$ (angle between v and r) is 0].

Now, $\mathbf{r}(t) \times \mathbf{v}(t) = \mathbf{v}(t) \times \mathbf{r}(t) = 0$

$$\Rightarrow \quad \mathbf{v} \times \mathbf{r} = \begin{vmatrix} \hat{i} & \hat{j} & \hat{k} \\ 20\alpha t & 5\beta & 0 \\ 10\alpha t^2 & 5\beta(t-5) & 0 \end{vmatrix}$$

$$\Rightarrow \quad \hat{k}[100\alpha\beta t(t-5) - 50\alpha\beta t^2] = 0$$

$$\Rightarrow \quad 2t - 10 = t \;\Rightarrow\; t = 10 \text{ s}$$

24. Using the law of conservation of angular momentum

$$I\omega = I'\omega'$$

$$\Rightarrow \quad Mr^2\omega = (Mr^2 + 2mr^2)\omega'$$

$$\Rightarrow \quad \omega' = \frac{M}{M+2m}\omega$$

25. It is given that the system is assumed to be in steady circular motion with constant angular velocity ω.

We know that $\mathbf{L} = m(\mathbf{r} \times \mathbf{v})$

Since, L_A is the angular momentum of M about point A which lies in positive z-direction. Therefore, with respect to point A, we will get the direction of **L** along positive Z-axis and of constant magnitude of mvr.

Since, L_B is the angular momentum of M about point B, so with respect to point B, we will get the constant magnitude of **L** but its direction will be continuously changing. Hence, option (d) is correct.

26. Given, $\mathbf{F} = 4\hat{i} - 3\hat{j}$

$\therefore$ Position vector of P w.r.t. O, $\mathbf{r}_O = 5\hat{i} + 5\sqrt{3}\hat{j}$

and position vector of P w.r.t. Q,

$$\mathbf{r}_Q = -5\hat{i} + 5\sqrt{3}\hat{j}$$

Torque at point P w.r.t. O,

$$\tau_O = \mathbf{r}_O \times \mathbf{F} = (5\hat{i} + 5\sqrt{3}\hat{j}) \times (4\hat{i} - 3\hat{j})$$

$$= (-15 - 20\sqrt{3})\hat{k} = (15 + 20\sqrt{3})(-\hat{k})$$

Torque at point P w.r.t. Q,

$$\tau_Q = \mathbf{r}_Q \times \mathbf{F} = (4\hat{i} - 3\hat{j}) \times (-5\hat{i} + 5\sqrt{3}\hat{j})$$

$$= (-15 + 20\sqrt{3})\hat{k}$$

$$= (15 - 20\sqrt{3})(-\hat{k})$$

27. $\mathbf{r} = (2\hat{i}) - (2\hat{i} + 3\hat{j} + 4\hat{k}) = -3\hat{j} - 4\hat{k}$

$$\Rightarrow \quad \tau = \mathbf{r} \times \mathbf{F} = \begin{vmatrix} \hat{i} & \hat{j} & \hat{k} \\ 0 & -3 & -4 \\ 4 & 3 & 4 \end{vmatrix}$$

$$\Rightarrow \quad \tau = -16\hat{j} + 12\hat{k}$$

$$\Rightarrow \quad |\tau| = 20$$

28. By using the energy conservation,

$$mgl = \frac{1}{2}I\omega^2$$

$$mgl = \frac{1}{2} \times \frac{ml^2}{3} \times \omega^2$$

$$\Rightarrow \quad \omega = \sqrt{\frac{6g}{l}}$$

$$v = \omega r = \omega l = \sqrt{6gl}$$

$$\Rightarrow \quad v = \sqrt{6 \times 10 \times 0.6} = 6 \text{ m/s}$$

29. Given, mass of each sphere, $M = 1.5$ kg

Radius of each sphere, $R = 50$ cm

$= 50 \times 10^{-2}$ m

Distance between centre of spheres,

$l = 5$ m

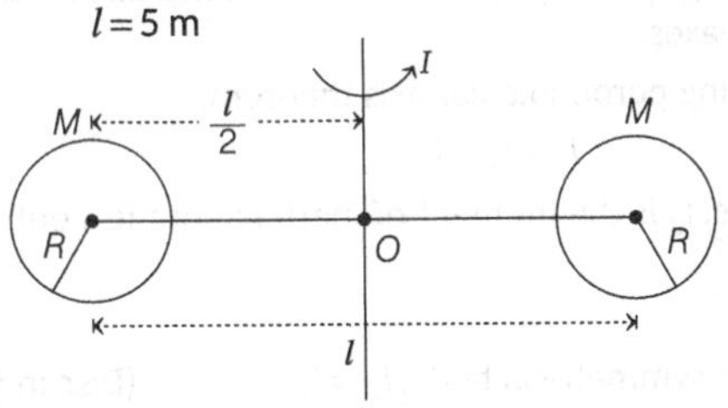

By using parallel axis theorem, moment of inertia of system is

$$I = 2\left[\frac{2}{5}MR^2 + \frac{Ml^2}{4}\right] \Rightarrow I = 2M\left[\frac{2}{5}R^2 + \frac{l^2}{4}\right]$$

Substituting the values, we get

$$I = 2 \times 1.5\left[\frac{2}{5} \times (50 \times 10^{-2})^2 + \frac{(5)^2}{4}\right] = 19.05 \text{ kg-m}^2$$

30.

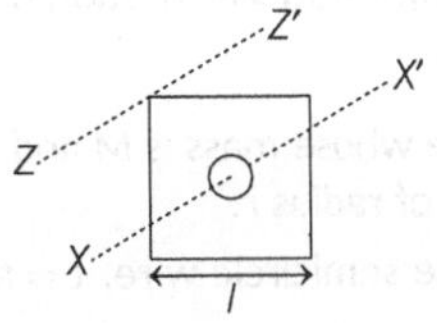

By parallel axis theorem, moment of inertia of square plate about axis $Z - Z'$ will be

$$I_{zz'} = I_{xx'} + M\left(\frac{l}{\sqrt{2}}\right)^2$$

$$I_{zz'} = \frac{Ml^2}{6} + \frac{Ml^2}{2} = Ml^2\left[\frac{1}{6} + \frac{1}{2}\right]$$

$$\Rightarrow \quad I_{zz'} = \frac{2Ml^2}{3}$$

31. As per question, mass per unit area of both disc is same.

Let mass per unit area be σ.

$\therefore$ Mass of smaller disc, $M' = \pi r^2 \sigma$

Mass of larger disc, $M = \pi R^2 \sigma$

$\therefore$ Moment of inertia of smaller disc around one of its diameter lying on its plane, $I' = \frac{1}{4} M' r^2$

$$\Rightarrow \quad I' = \frac{\pi \sigma r^4}{4}$$

and moment of inertia of bigger disc around axis AB (perpendicular to the plane) of disc and passing through its centre,

$$I = \frac{1}{2} MR^2 = \frac{\pi \sigma R^4}{2}$$

$$\therefore \quad \frac{I}{I'} = \frac{\frac{\pi \sigma R^4}{2}}{\frac{\pi \sigma r^4}{4}} = \frac{2R^4}{r^4} \Rightarrow \frac{I}{I'} = \frac{2R^4}{r^4}$$

32. Given, I_X, I_Y and I_Z be the moment of inertia of disc about X, Y and Z-axes.

By using perpendicular axis theorem,

$$I_Z = I_X + I_Y$$

where, I_Z is the moment of inertia about its centre of mass $= \frac{MR^2}{2}$

and in symmetrical body, $I_X = I_Y$ (Disc in given case)

$$\therefore \quad I_Z = 2I_X$$

$$\Rightarrow \quad I_X = I_Y = \frac{I_Z}{2} = \frac{MR^2}{4}$$

Now, $I_X = I_Y \neq I_Z$

As, radius of gyration, $k = \sqrt{I/M}$

$$\Rightarrow \quad k \propto I$$

So, radii of gyration about all axis will nor be the same.

$\therefore$ Assertion is not correct but Reason is correct because in a rigid body making rotational motion has fixed mass M and radius R ($I_X = I_Y$).

33. The uniform wire whose mass is M and length is L and bent into a semicircle of radius r.

The length of the semicircle wire, $L = \pi r$

$$\Rightarrow \quad r = \frac{L}{\pi}$$

The moment of inertia,

$$I = Mr^2$$

$$\Rightarrow \quad I = M\left(\frac{L}{\pi}\right)^2 \Rightarrow I = \frac{ML^2}{\pi^2}$$

34. The given situation can be represented as follows

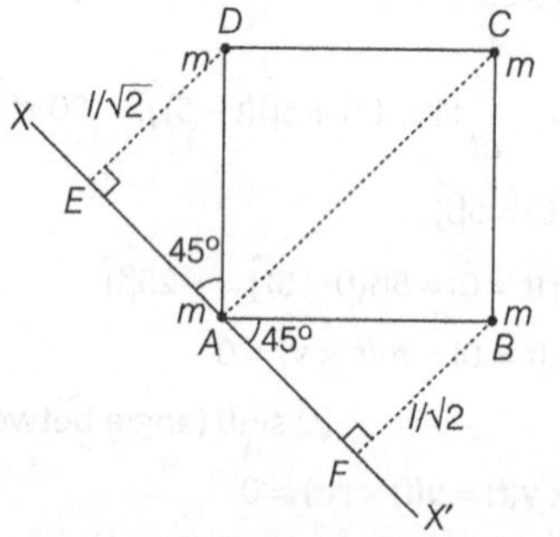

In the above figure, XX' be the axis which passes through A and is parallel to DB.

$\therefore$ Moment of inertia of the system

$$= \text{Mass} \times (\text{Perpendicular distance from axis})^2$$

$$I = m(AC)^2 + m(ED)^2 + m(FB)^2$$

$$= m(0)^2 + m(l\sqrt{2})^2 + m\left(\frac{l}{\sqrt{2}}\right)^2 + m\left(\frac{l}{\sqrt{2}}\right)^2$$

$$= 3ml^2$$

35. Given, mass of solid sphere $= m$

Radius of solid sphere $= a$

Side of square $= b$

Let I_{net} be the net moment of inertia of system.

Moment of inertia of sphere, $I_s = \frac{2}{5} ma^2$

Axis of rotation is BC.

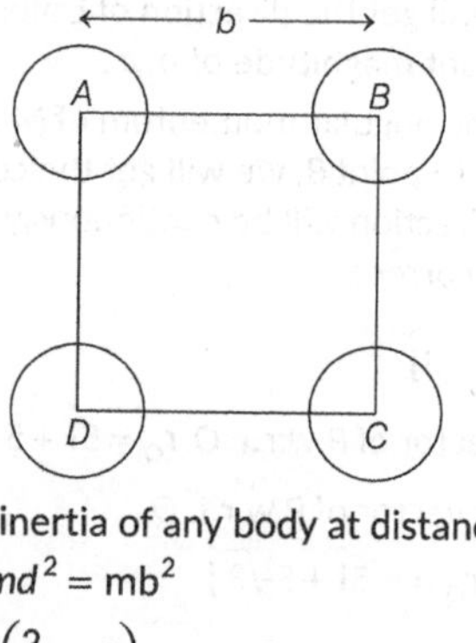

$\therefore$ Moment of inertia of any body at distance,

$$d = md^2 = mb^2 \qquad (\because d = b)$$

$$\therefore \quad I_{net} = 4\left(\frac{2}{5} ma^2\right) + 2(mb^2)$$

$$\Rightarrow \quad I_{net} = \frac{8}{5} ma^2 + 2mb^2$$

36.

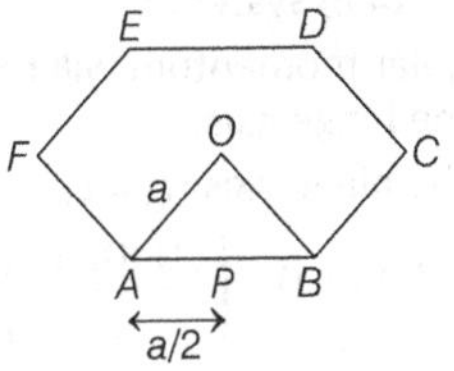

Side of hexagon, $a = \frac{2.4}{6} = 0.4$ m

Mass of each side, $m' = 6/6 = 1$ kg

and $OP = \sqrt{a^2 - a^2/4} = a\sqrt{3}/2$

Now, by using parallel axes theorem,

$$I_{OP} = \frac{m'a^2}{12} + m'\left(\frac{\sqrt{3}a}{2}\right)^2 = \frac{5a^2}{6}$$

$$\Rightarrow \quad I_{OP} = \frac{5}{6} \times 0.4 \times 0.4$$

and I_{net} (net moment of inertia at O)

$$= 6 \times \frac{5}{6} \times 0.4 \times 0.4$$

$$= 8 \times 10^{-1} \text{ kg-m}^2$$

37. Let M and R be the mass and radius of four bodies. Then, as per question, their moment of inertia are

$$I_1 = \frac{MR^2}{2}, I_2 = \frac{MR^2}{2}, I_3 = \frac{MR^2}{2},$$

$$I_4 = \frac{2}{5}MR^2$$

Clearly, $I_1 = I_2 = I_3 > I_4$

38. By using law of conservation of angular momentum,

$$I_1\omega_1 + I_2\omega_2 = (I_1 + I_2)\omega$$

$$\Rightarrow \quad \omega = \frac{I_1\omega_1 + I_2\omega_2}{I_1 + I_2}$$

$\therefore$ Change in kinetic energy ΔKE

$$= \frac{1}{2}I_1\omega_1^2 + \frac{1}{2}I_2\omega_2^2 - \frac{1}{2}(I_1 + I_2)\omega^2$$

$$= \frac{1}{2}I_1\omega_1^2 + \frac{1}{2}I_2\omega_2^2 - \frac{1}{2}(I_1 + I_2)\left(\frac{I_1\omega_1 + I_2\omega_2}{I_1 + I_2}\right)^2$$

$$= \frac{1}{2}I_1 I_2 \frac{(\omega_1 - \omega_2)^2}{I_1 + I_2}$$

39. From the given situation,

$$KE_P = KE_Q$$

$$\Rightarrow \quad \frac{1}{2}I_1(\omega_1)^2 = \frac{1}{2}I_2(\omega_2)^2$$

$$\Rightarrow \quad \frac{1}{2}I_1\left(\frac{v}{3R}\right)^2 = \frac{1}{2}I_2\left(\frac{v}{R^2}\right)$$

[$\because$ Radius of P is 3 times to that of Q]

$$\Rightarrow \quad I_1 \times \frac{v^2}{9R^2} = I_2 \times \frac{v^2}{R^2}$$

$$\Rightarrow \quad \frac{I_1}{9} = I_2 \Rightarrow \frac{I_1}{I_2} = \frac{9}{1} \quad \text{...(i)}$$

$\because$ According to question, the ratio of rotational inertias $\frac{I_1}{I_2} = \frac{x}{1}$. So, on comparing it with Eq. (i), we can write $x = 9$.

40. $\because$ We know that

$$\omega_F = \omega_0 + \alpha t$$

$$\Rightarrow \quad 30 = 10 + \alpha \times 10$$

$$\Rightarrow \quad \frac{30 - 10}{10} = \alpha$$

$$\Rightarrow \quad \alpha = \frac{20}{10} = 2 \text{ rps}^2$$

Angular displacement is calculated by the rotational equation of motion as

$$\theta = \omega_0 t + \frac{1}{2}\alpha t^2$$

where, θ is the angular displacement.

$$\Rightarrow \quad \theta = 10 \times 10 + \frac{1}{2} \times 2 \times (10)^2$$

$$\Rightarrow \quad \theta = 100 + 100$$

$$\Rightarrow \quad \theta = 200 \text{ rad}$$

Number of rotations

$$= \frac{\theta}{2\pi} = \frac{200}{2\pi} = 31.8 \approx 32$$

41. Moment of inertia of wheel, $I = mR^2$

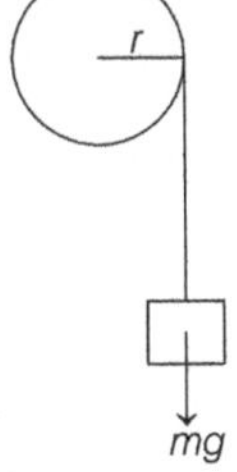

Let v be the velocity and $v = r\omega$

$$\Rightarrow \quad \omega = v/r$$

By using law of conservation of energy,

$$1/2(I + mr^2)\omega^2 = mgh$$

$$\Rightarrow \quad \omega^2 = \frac{2mgh}{I + mr^2}$$

42.

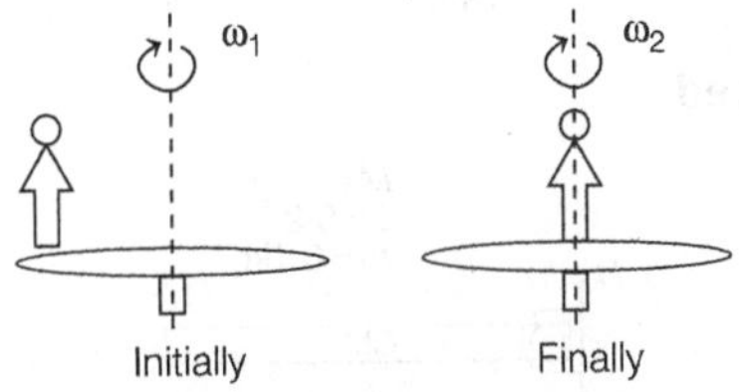

According to conservation of angular momentum,

$$I_1\omega_1 = I_2\omega_2$$

$$\Rightarrow \quad \left(80R^2 + \frac{200R^2}{2}\right)\omega_1 = \left(\frac{200R^2}{2}\right)\omega_2$$

$$\Rightarrow \quad \frac{360R^2}{2} \times 5 = \frac{200R^2}{2} \times \omega_2$$

$$\omega_2 = 9 \text{ rpm}$$

43. The given situation is shown in the following fig.,

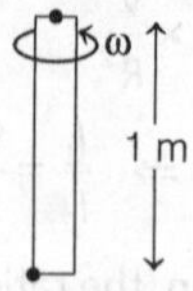

Applying law of conservation of angular momentum about pivotal point,

$$L_i = L_f \Rightarrow mvl = I\omega$$

$$\Rightarrow \quad mvl = \left(\frac{1}{3}ML^2 + ml^2\right)\omega \qquad \text{...(i)}$$

Given, $m = 0.1$ kg, $v = 80\ \text{ms}^{-1}$, $M = 0.9$ kg, $l = 1$ m

Substituting these values in eq. (i), we get

$$0.1 \times 80 \times 1 = \left(\frac{0.9 \times 1^2}{3} + 0.1 \times 1^2\right)\omega$$

$$8 = \left(\frac{3}{10} + \frac{1}{10}\right)\omega \Rightarrow 8 = \frac{4}{10}\omega \Rightarrow \omega = 20 \text{ rad/s}$$

44. The angular momentum of the square about the given axis will be the sum of angular momentum due to each point masses.

i.e. $\quad L = L_1 + L_2 + L_3 + L_4 = I_1\omega_1 + I_2\omega_2 + I_3\omega_3 + I_4\omega_4$

Here, angular frequency will be same.

i.e., $\quad \omega_1 = \omega_2 = \omega_3 = \omega_4 = \omega$ (say)

$\therefore \quad L = (I_1 + I_2 + I_3 + I_4)\omega$

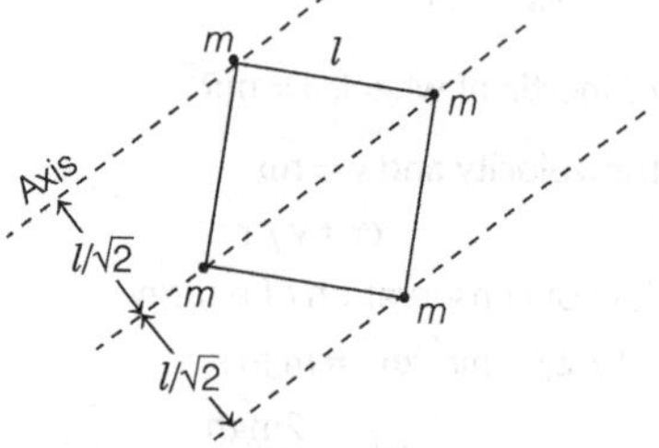

$$L = \left\{m(0)^2 + 2 \times m\left(\frac{l}{\sqrt{2}}\right)^2 + m(\sqrt{2}l)^2\right\}\omega = 3ml^2\omega$$

JEE Advanced

1.

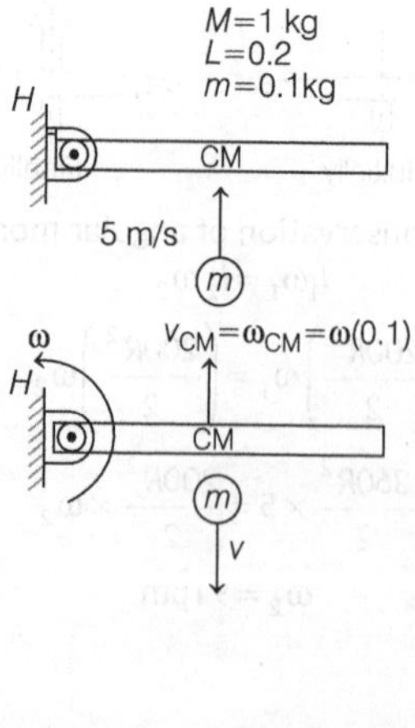

For the (rod + ball) system :

(i) The angular momentum will remain conserved only about the hinge axis.

About the hinge axis : $L_i = L_f$

$$0 + (0.1)(5)(0.1) = \left(\frac{(1)(0.2)^2}{3}\right)\omega - (0.1)(v)(0.1)$$

$$\Rightarrow \frac{4\omega}{3} - v = 5 \qquad \text{...(i)}$$

(ii) $e = \dfrac{v_2 - v_1}{v_1 - v_2} = \dfrac{\omega(0.1) + v}{5}$ where, $e = 1$

$$\frac{\omega}{10} + v = 5 \qquad \text{...(ii)}$$

Solving Eqs. (i) and (ii) we get,

$$\omega = \frac{300}{43} = 6.98 \text{ rad/s}$$

and $\quad v = 4.30$ m/s

2. Moment of inertia of wheel, $I = mR^2$

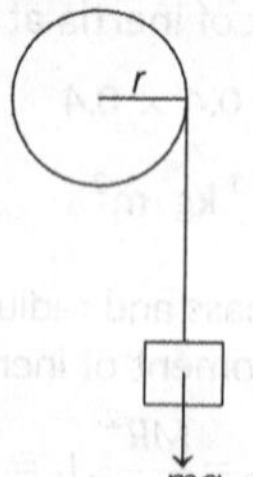

Let v be the velocity and $v = r\omega \Rightarrow \omega = v/r$

By using law of conservation of energy,

$$1/2(I + mr^2)\omega^2 = mgh$$

$$\Rightarrow \quad \omega^2 = \frac{2mgh}{I + mr^2}$$

3.

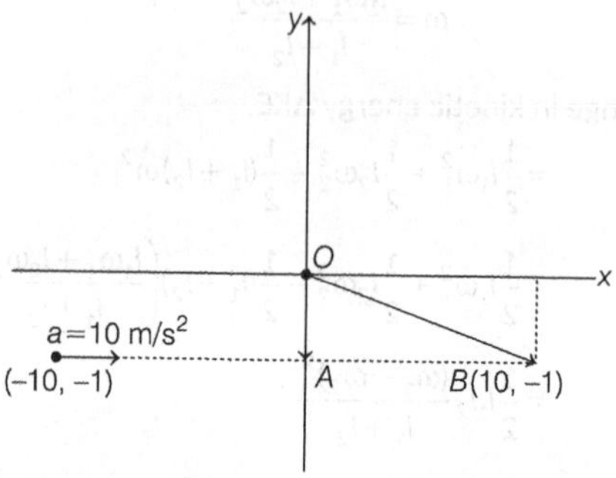

$$\mathbf{r}_A = -\hat{\mathbf{j}}$$

$$s = \frac{1}{2}at^2$$

$$20 = \frac{1}{2} \times 10 \times t^2$$

$$t = 2 \text{ s}$$

$$\tau_0 = \mathbf{r} \times \mathbf{F};\ \mathbf{r}_B = 10\hat{\mathbf{i}} - \hat{\mathbf{j}}$$

$$\mathbf{F} = m\mathbf{a} = 0.2 \times 10\hat{\mathbf{i}} = 2\hat{\mathbf{i}}$$

$\tau_0 = (10\hat{\mathbf{i}} - \hat{\mathbf{j}}) \times (2\hat{\mathbf{i}})$

$\tau_0 = 2\hat{\mathbf{k}}$

$\mathbf{L}_0 = \mathbf{r}_B \times \mathbf{p} = \mathbf{r}_B \times m\mathbf{v}$

$\mathbf{v} = \mathbf{a}t = 10\hat{\mathbf{i}} \times 2 = 20\hat{\mathbf{i}}$

$\mathbf{L}_0 = (0.2)[(10\hat{\mathbf{i}} - \hat{\mathbf{j}}) \times 20\hat{\mathbf{i}}] = 4\hat{\mathbf{k}}$

At point $A(0, -1)$

$\tau_0 = \mathbf{r}_A \times \mathbf{F} = (-\hat{\mathbf{j}}) \times 2\hat{\mathbf{i}} = 2\hat{\mathbf{k}}$

4. According to conservation of angular momentum about suspension point,

$$mvx = \left(\frac{mL^2}{3} + mx^2\right)\omega$$

$$vx = \left(\frac{L^2}{3} + x^2\right)\omega \quad \Rightarrow \quad \omega = \frac{3vx}{L^2 + 3x^2}$$

For maximum,

$$\frac{d\omega}{dx} = 0 \quad \Rightarrow \quad x = \frac{L}{\sqrt{3}}$$

$$\omega = \frac{\sqrt{3}\,v}{2L}$$

5. When force $\mathbf{F} = 0 \Rightarrow$ potential energy $U =$ constant

$\mathbf{F} \neq 0 \Rightarrow$ force is conservative $\Rightarrow$ Total energy $E =$ constant

Column I

(A) $\mathbf{r}(t) = \alpha t\hat{\mathbf{i}} + \beta t\hat{\mathbf{j}}$

$\frac{d\mathbf{r}}{dt} = \mathbf{v} = \alpha\hat{\mathbf{i}} + \beta\hat{\mathbf{j}} =$ constant $\Rightarrow \mathbf{p} =$ constant

$|\mathbf{v}| = \sqrt{\alpha^2 + \beta^2} =$ constant $\Rightarrow K =$ constant

$\frac{d\mathbf{v}}{dt} = \mathbf{a} = 0 \Rightarrow \mathbf{F} = 0 \Rightarrow U =$ constant

$E = U + K =$ constant

$\mathbf{L} = m(\mathbf{r} \times \mathbf{v}) = 0$

$\mathbf{L} =$ constant

A $\rightarrow$ p, q, r, s, t

(B) $\mathbf{r}(t) = \alpha\cos\omega t\hat{\mathbf{i}} + \beta\sin\omega t\hat{\mathbf{j}}$

$\frac{d\mathbf{r}}{dt} = \mathbf{v} = \alpha\omega\sin\omega t(-\hat{\mathbf{i}}) + \beta\omega\cos\omega t\hat{\mathbf{j}} \neq$ constant

$\Rightarrow \mathbf{p} \neq$ constant

$|\mathbf{v}| = \omega\sqrt{(\alpha\sin\omega t)^2 + (\beta\cos\omega t)^2} \neq$ constant

$\Rightarrow \quad K \neq$ constant

$\mathbf{a} = \frac{d\mathbf{v}}{dt} = -\omega^2\mathbf{r} \neq 0 \quad \Rightarrow \mathbf{F} \neq 0$

So, it is conservative

$\Rightarrow \quad E =$ constant $= K + U$

But $K \neq$ constant $\Rightarrow U \neq$ constant

$\mathbf{L} = m(\mathbf{r} \times \mathbf{v}) = m\omega\alpha\beta\,(\hat{\mathbf{k}}) =$ constant

B $\rightarrow$ q, t

(C) $\mathbf{r}(t) = \alpha\,(\cos\omega t\hat{\mathbf{i}} + \sin\omega t\hat{\mathbf{j}})$

$\frac{d\mathbf{r}}{dt} = \mathbf{v} = \alpha\omega\,[\sin\omega t(-\hat{\mathbf{i}}) + \cos\omega t\,\hat{\mathbf{j}}] \neq$ constant

$\Rightarrow \mathbf{p} \neq$ constant

$|\mathbf{v}| = \alpha\omega =$ constant $\Rightarrow K =$ constant

$\mathbf{a} = \frac{d\mathbf{v}}{dt} = -\omega^2\mathbf{r} \neq 0 \Rightarrow E =$ constant,

$U =$ constant

$\mathbf{L} = m(\mathbf{r} \times \mathbf{v}) = m\omega\alpha^2\,\hat{\mathbf{k}} =$ constant

C $\rightarrow$ q, r, s, t

(D) $\mathbf{r}(t) = \alpha t\hat{\mathbf{i}} + \frac{\beta}{2}t^2\hat{\mathbf{j}}$

$\frac{d\mathbf{r}}{dt} = \mathbf{v} = \alpha\hat{\mathbf{i}} + \beta t\,\hat{\mathbf{j}} \neq$ constant $\Rightarrow \mathbf{p} \neq$ constant

$|\mathbf{v}| = \sqrt{\alpha^2 + (\beta t)^2} \neq$ constant $\quad \Rightarrow \quad K \neq$ constant

$\mathbf{a} = \frac{d\mathbf{v}}{dt} = \beta\,\hat{\mathbf{j}} \neq 0 \Rightarrow E =$ constant $= K + U$

But $K \neq$ constant

$\therefore \quad U \neq$ constant

$\mathbf{L} = m\,(\mathbf{r} \times \mathbf{v}) = \frac{1}{2}\alpha\beta t^2\,\hat{\mathbf{k}} \neq$ constant

D $\rightarrow$ t

6. $\mathbf{r} = \alpha t^3\hat{\mathbf{i}} + \beta t^2\hat{\mathbf{j}}$

$\mathbf{v} = \frac{d\mathbf{r}}{dt} = 3\alpha t^2\hat{\mathbf{i}} + 2\beta t\hat{\mathbf{j}}$ and $\mathbf{a} = \frac{d\mathbf{v}}{dt} = 6\alpha t\hat{\mathbf{i}} + 2\beta\hat{\mathbf{j}}$

At $t = 1$ s,

(a) $\mathbf{v} = 3 \times \frac{10}{3} \times 1\hat{\mathbf{i}} + 2 \times 5 \times 1\hat{\mathbf{j}} = (10\hat{\mathbf{i}} + 10\hat{\mathbf{j}})$ m/s

(b) $\mathbf{L} = \mathbf{r} \times \mathbf{p} = \left(\frac{10}{3} \times 1\hat{\mathbf{i}} + 5 \times 1\hat{\mathbf{j}}\right) \times 0.1(10\hat{\mathbf{i}} + 10\hat{\mathbf{j}})$

$= \left(-\frac{5}{3}\hat{\mathbf{k}}\right)$ N-ms

(c) $\mathbf{F} = m\mathbf{a} = 0.1 \times \left(6 \times \frac{10}{3} \times 1\hat{\mathbf{i}} + 2 \times 5\hat{\mathbf{j}}\right) = (2\hat{\mathbf{i}} + \hat{\mathbf{j}})$N

(d) $\tau = r \times \mathbf{F} = \left(\frac{10}{3}\hat{\mathbf{i}} + 5\hat{\mathbf{j}}\right) \times (2\hat{\mathbf{i}} + \hat{\mathbf{j}})$

$= +\frac{10}{3}\hat{\mathbf{k}} + 10(-\hat{\mathbf{k}}) = \left(\frac{-20}{3}\hat{\mathbf{k}}\right)$N-m

7. Let the other mass at this instant is at a distance of x from the centre O. Applying law of conservation of angular momentum, we have

$$I_1\omega_1 = I_2\omega_2$$

$$\therefore \quad (MR^2)(\omega) = \left[MR^2 + \frac{M}{8}\left(\frac{3}{5}R\right)^2 + \frac{M}{8}x^2\right]\left(\frac{8}{9}\omega\right)$$

Solving this equation, we get $x = \frac{4}{5}R$.

NOTE If we take identical situations with both point masses, then answer will be (c). But in that case, angular momentum is not conserved.

8. Applying conservation of angular momentum

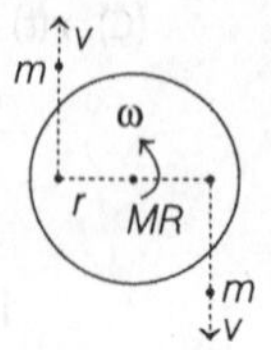

$$L_i = L_f$$

$$\Rightarrow \quad 2mvr - \frac{MR^2}{2}\omega = 0$$

$$\Rightarrow \quad \omega = \frac{4mvr}{MR^2}$$

Substituting the values, we get

$$\omega = \frac{(4)(5\times10^{-2})(9)\left(\frac{1}{4}\right)}{45\times10^{-2}\times\frac{1}{4}}$$

$$\Rightarrow \quad \omega = 4 \text{ rad/s}$$

9. $I_1\omega_1 = I_2\omega_2$

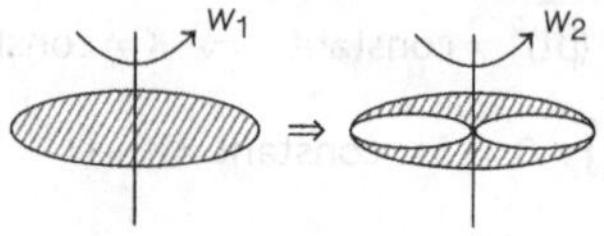

$$\omega_2 = \left(\frac{I_1}{I_2}\right)\omega_1$$

$$= \left[\frac{\frac{1}{2}MR^2}{\frac{1}{2}MR^2 + 4(mr^2)}\right]\omega_1$$

$$= \left[\frac{50(0.4)^2}{50(0.4)^2 + 8\times(6.25)\times(0.2)^2}\right](10)$$

$$= 8 \text{ rad/s}$$

10. Language of question is not very clear. For example, disc is rotating. Its different points have different velocities. Relative velocity of pebble with respect to which point, it is not clear. Further, actual initial positions of P and Q are also not given.

11. $|\mathbf{L}|$ or $L = I\omega$ (about axis of rod)

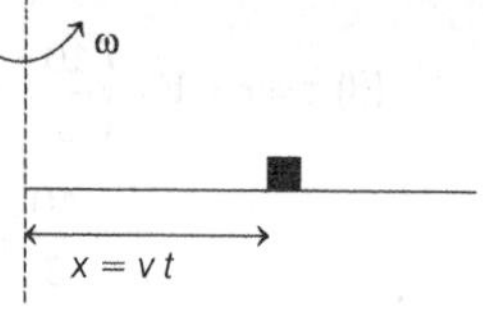

$$I = I_{rod} + mx^2 = I_{rod} + mv^2t^2$$

Here, m = mass of insect

$$\therefore \quad L = (I_{rod} + mv^2t^2)\,\omega$$

Now $|\tau| = \frac{dL}{dt} = (2mv^2t\omega)$ or $|\tau| \propto t$

i.e. the graph is straight line passing through origin.

After time T, L = constant

$$\therefore \quad |\tau| \text{ or } \frac{dL}{dt} = 0$$

12. Language of question is wrong because relative speed is not the correct word. Relative speed between two is always zero.

The correct word is magnitude of relative velocity.

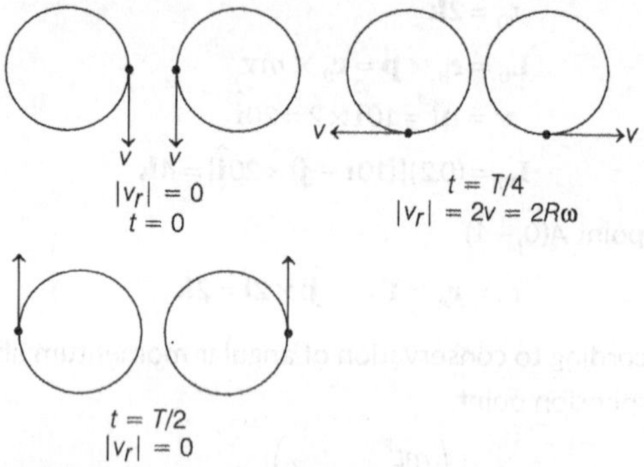

Corresponding to above values, the correct graph is (a).

13. $r = \frac{d}{2} = \frac{\sqrt{5}}{2}$ cm $= \frac{\sqrt{5}}{2}\times10^{-2}$ m

$$\Rightarrow \quad m = 0.5 \text{ kg}$$

$$a = 4 \text{ cm} = 4\times10^{-2} \text{ m}$$

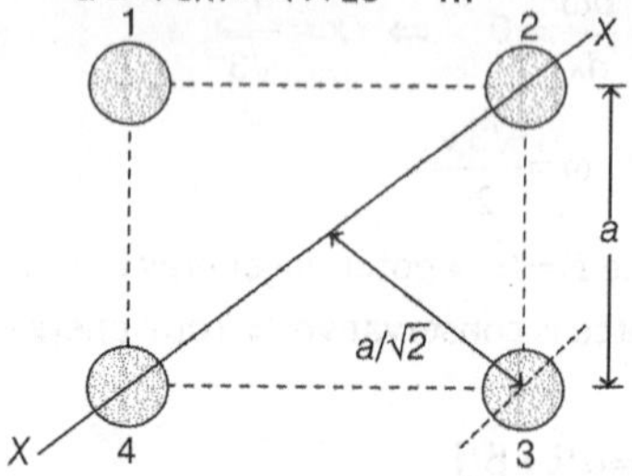

$$I_{XX} = I_1 + I_2 + I_3 + I_4$$

$$= \left[\frac{2}{5}mr^2 + m\left(\frac{a}{\sqrt{2}}\right)^2\right] + \frac{2}{5}mr^2 + \left[\frac{2}{5}mr^2 + m\left(\frac{a}{\sqrt{2}}\right)^2\right] + \frac{2}{5}mr^2$$

Substituting the values, we get

$$I_{XX} = 9\times10^{-4} \text{ kg-m}^2 \quad \Rightarrow \quad N = 9$$

14. On a system of particles if,

$$\Sigma \mathbf{F}_{\text{ext.}} = 0$$

then, $\quad \mathbf{p}_{\text{system}} = \text{constant}$

No other conclusions can be drawn.

15. Condition of sliding is :

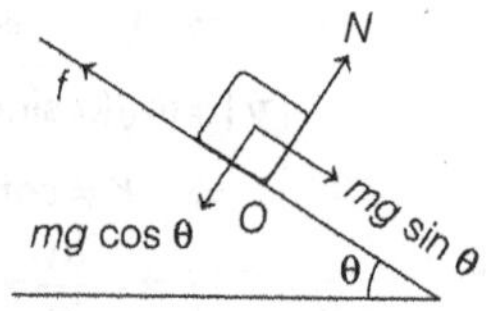

$mg \sin\theta > \mu mg \cos\theta$

or $\tan\theta > \mu$ or $\tan\theta > \sqrt{3}$ ...(i)

Condition of toppling is :

Torque of $mg \sin\theta$ about O > torque of $mg\cos\theta$

$$\therefore \quad (mg\sin\theta)\left(\frac{15}{2}\right) > (mg\cos\theta)\left(\frac{10}{2}\right)$$

or $\quad \tan\theta > \frac{2}{3}$ ...(ii)

With increase in value of θ, condition of toppling is satisfied first.

CHAPTER~04

COMBINED TRANSLATIONAL AND ROTATIONAL MOTION

LEVEL 01 Starter Level

4.1 Kinematics of Combined Motion

1 A wheel of radius *r* rolls (rolling without slipping) on a level road as shown in figure. Find out velocity of points *A*, *B* and *C*.

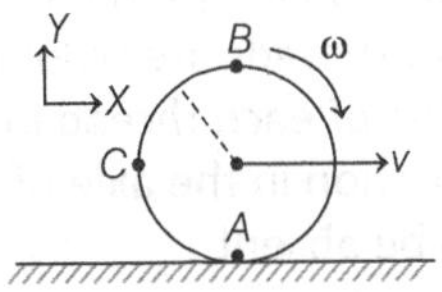

2 The centre of mass of a uniform rod of length 10 m is moving with a translational velocity of 50 m/s on a frictionless horizontal surface as shown in the figure and the rod rotates about its centre of mass with an angular velocity of 5 rad/s. Find out velocities of points *A* and *B*.

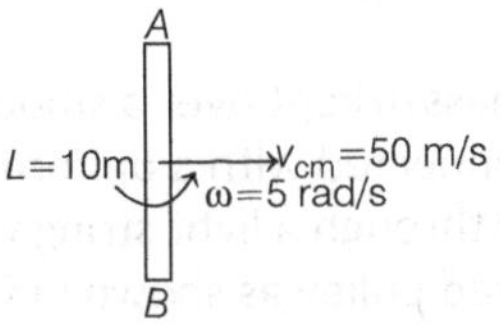

3 A plank is moving with a velocity of 4 m/s. A disc of radius 2 m rolls without slipping on it with an angular velocity of 3 rad/s as shown in figure. What is the velocity of centre of the disc?

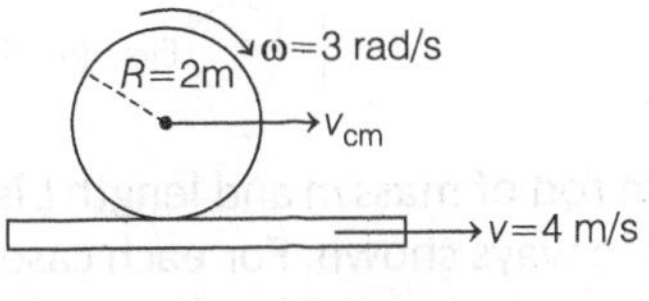

4 The disc of the radius *r* is confined to roll without slipping at *A* and *B*. If the plates have the velocities shown, what is the angular velocity of the disc?

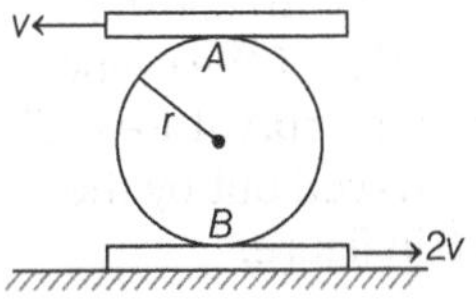

5 A bobbin with thread wound around it lies on a horizontal floor and can roll along it without sliding. If the block starts to descend with constant velocity *v* as shown in the figure, what is the velocity of centre of bobbin? (The inner radius of the bobbin is *r* and external one *R*)

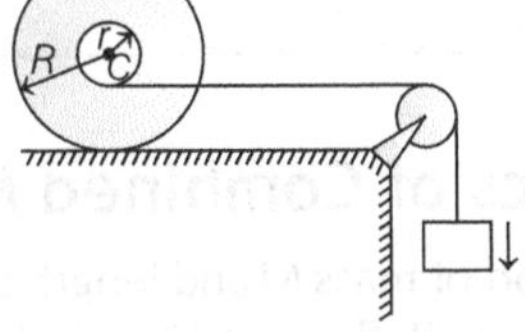

6 Cylinders *B* and *C* weigh 2 kg each and have radius of 2 m. Body A weighing 10 kg rides on the cylinders. If there is no slipping anywhere, find the kinetic energy of the system when the body A is moving at a speed $v = 10$ m/s.

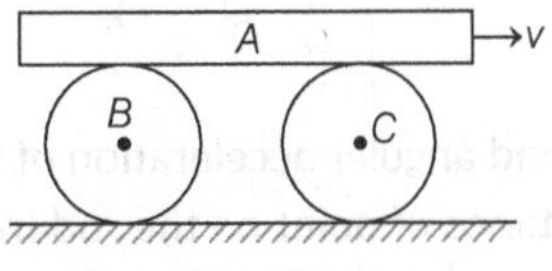

7 A body of round section of radius 10 cm starts rolling on a horizontal stationary surface with uniform angular acceleration 2 rad/s^2.

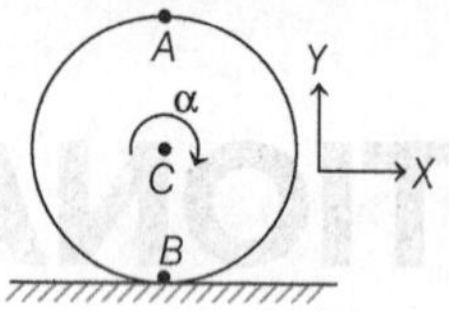

(a) Find initial acceleration of the center C and top point A.

(b) Find expression for acceleration of the top point A as function of time.

8 Two identical disks, each of radius r, are connected by a cord as shown in the figure. The disk I rotates with constant angular acceleration α in anti-clockwise direction. Find acceleration of the center of disk II and its angular acceleration.

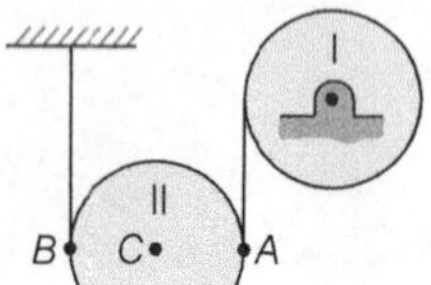

9 A cylinder rolls without slipping over a horizontal plane with constant velocity. The radius of the cylinder is equal to r. Find the curvature radii of trajectories traced out by the points A and B in figure.

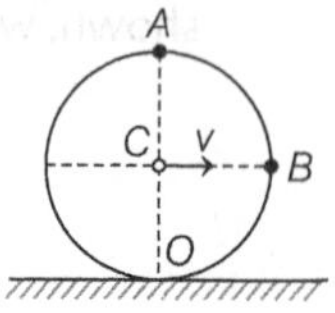

10 A wheel of radius r rolls without slipping along the X-axis with constant speed v_0 as shown in the figure. Find the total distance covered by the point between two successive moments at which it touches the surface.

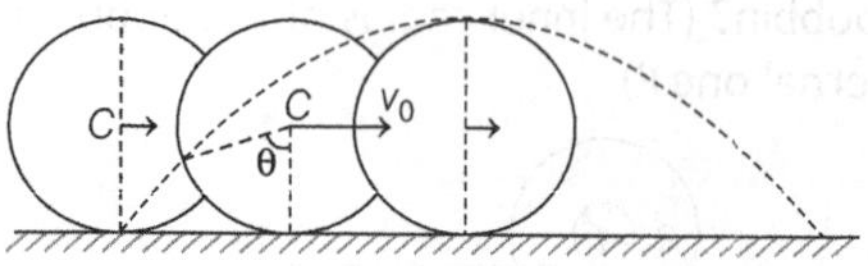

4.2 Dynamics of Combined Motion

1 A uniform rod of mass M and length L is kept on a horizontal smooth floor and is acted upon by the forces as shown in figure. Find

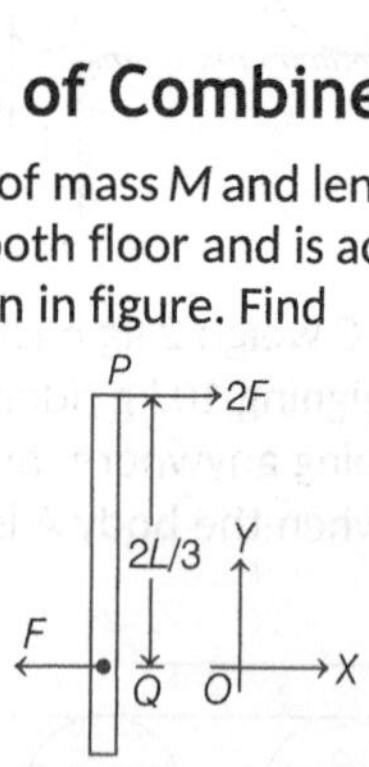

(a) linear and angular acceleration of the rod

(b) the distance of point on the rod from the centre whose acceleration is zero

2 A uniform solid sphere of radius R is placed on a smooth horizontal surface. It is pulled by a constant force acting along the tangent from the highest point. Calculate the distance travelled by the centre of mass of the solid sphere during the time it makes one full revolution.

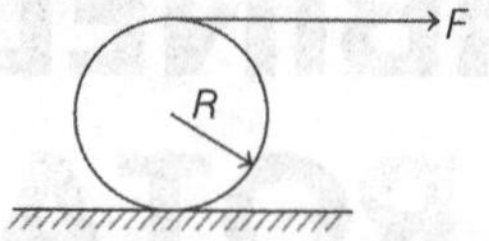

3 A uniform cylinder of mass m and radius R (figure) starts descending at a moment $t = 0$ due to gravity. Neglecting the mass of the thread, find the tension of each thread and the angular acceleration of the cylinder.

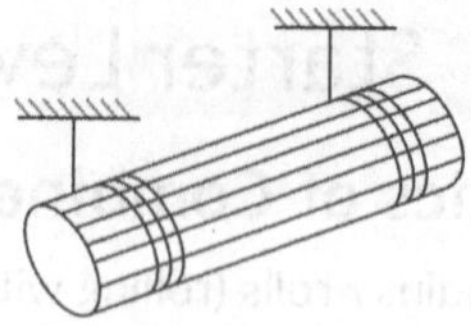

4 The arrangement shown in figure consists of two identical uniform solid cylinders, each of mass m, on which two light threads are wound symmetrically. Find the tension of each thread in the process of motion. The friction in the axle of the upper cylinder is assumed to be absent.

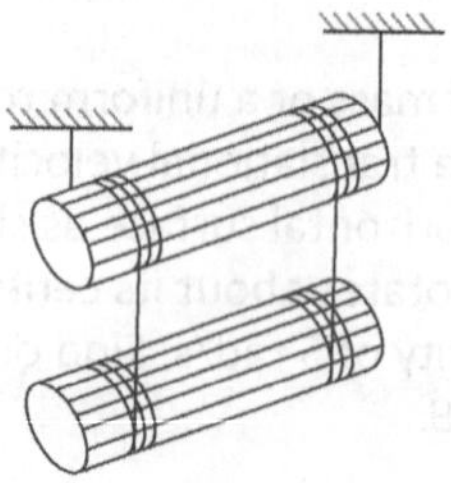

5 A block of mass m kept over a smooth horizontal surface is connected with a uniform disc of mass m and radius R through a light string which passes over a smooth fixed pulley as shown in figure. Calculate acceleration of the block.

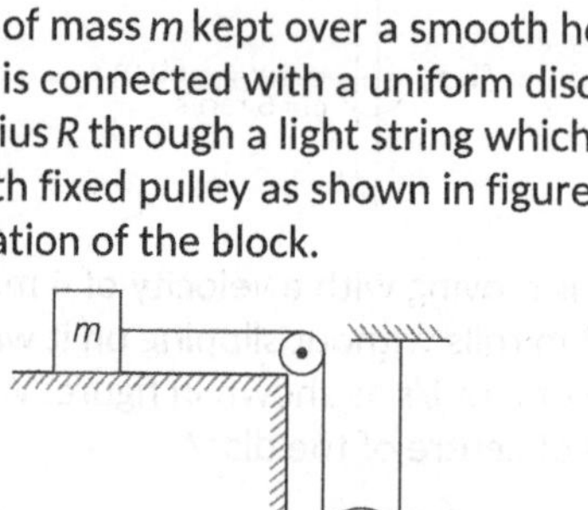

6 A uniform rod of mass m and length L is suspended in each of the ways shown. For each case immediately after the connection at B has been released, determine the acceleration of centre of mass and angular acceleration of the rod

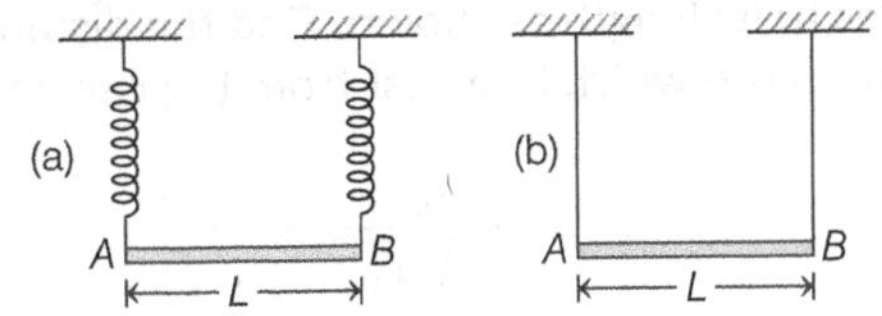

4.3 Dynamics of Rolling on a Plane Surface

1 A hollow cylinder of mass M and radius R kept on a rough horizontal plane is given linear velocity v_0 as shown in figure. Calculate the linear velocity after the hollow cylinder starts pure rolling.

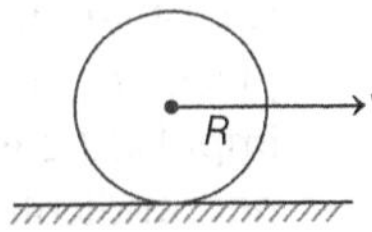

2 A cylinder is given angular velocity ω_0 and kept on a horizontal rough surface. The initial velocity is zero. Find out distance travelled by the cylinder before it performs pure rolling and work done by friction force.

3 A hollow sphere is set into motion on a rough horizontal surface with a speed v_0 in the forward direction and an rotational speed $\frac{v_0}{R}$ in the anti-clockwise direction as shown in figure. Find the translational speed of the sphere (a) when it stops rotating and (b) when slipping finally ceases and pure rolling starts.

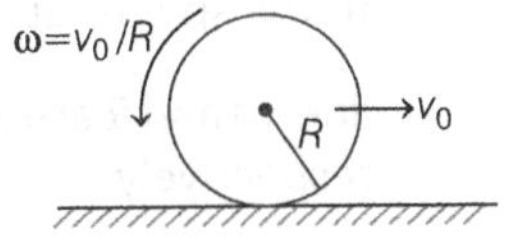

4 A constant force F acts tangentially at the highest point of a uniform disc of mass m kept on a rough horizontal surface as shown in figure. If the disc rolls without slipping, calculate (i) the acceleration of the centre (ii) friction acting on the disc.

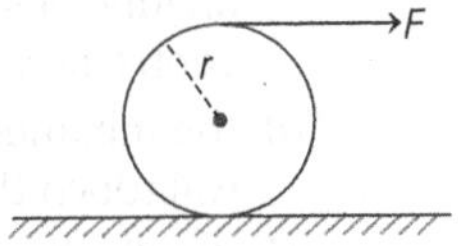

5 In the figure, a sphere of mass M and radius R is being pulled by a horizontal force $F = Mg$ at its centre. Find the minimum coefficient of friction needed to prevent slipping.

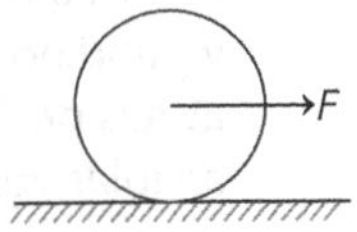

6 The free end of the string wound on the surface of a solid cylinder of mass M and radius R is pulled up by a force F as shown. If there is sufficient friction between cylinder and floor, so that the cylinder is able to roll without slipping, find the maximum angular acceleration that the cylinder can have.

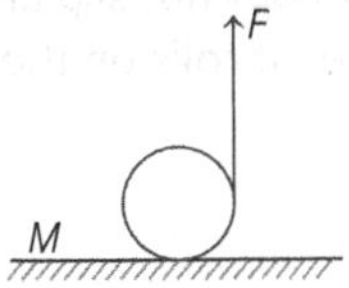

7 A block of mass m is attached at one end of a thin light cord, which passes over an ideal pulley. At the other end, it is wrapped around a cylinder of mass m, which can roll without slipping over a horizontal plane.

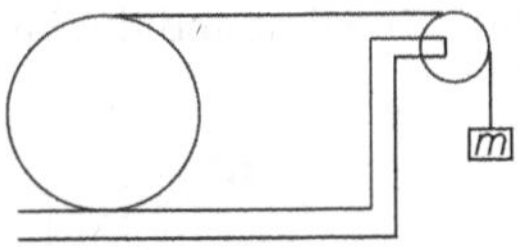

(a) What is the acceleration of the block?
(b) What is the friction force on the cylinder?

8 A plank of mass $2m$ with a uniform sphere of mass m placed on it rests on a smooth horizontal plane. A constant horizontal force F is applied to the plank. With what accelerations will the plank and the centre of the sphere move provided there is no sliding between the plank and the sphere?

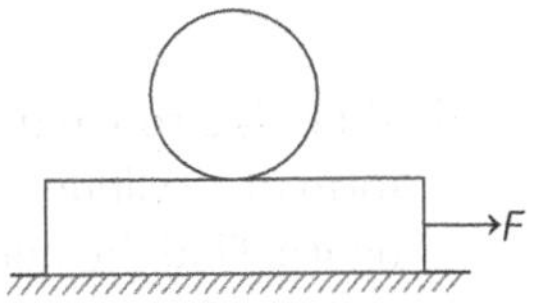

9 A man pushes a cylinder of mass m with the help of a plank of mass m as shown. There is no slipping at any contact. The horizontal component of the force applied by the man is F. Find

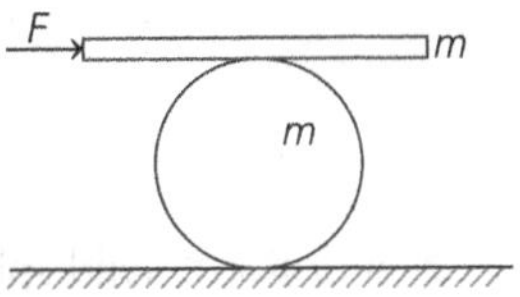

(i) the acceleration of the plank and the centre of mass of the cylinder and
(ii) the magnitude and directions of frictional forces at contact points.

4.4 Rolling on an Inclined Surface

1 A sphere of mass m rolls without slipping on an inclined plane of inclination θ. Find the linear acceleration of the sphere and force of friction on it.

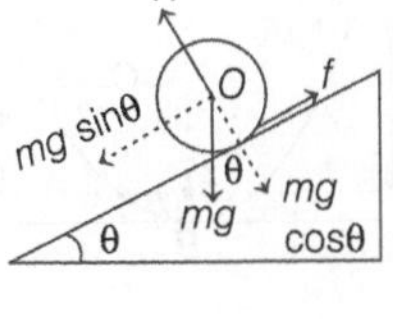

2 A small solid cylinder is released from a point at a height h on a rough as track shown in figure. Assuming that it does not slip anywhere, calculate its linear speed when it rolls on the horizontal part of the track.

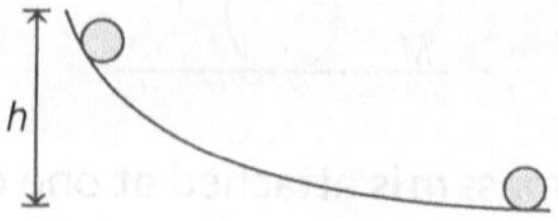

3 A uniform ring, a cylinder and a sphere are allowed to roll down without slipping simultaneously from the top of an inclined plane of inclination θ and of height h. Who is the first and the last to reach the bottom?

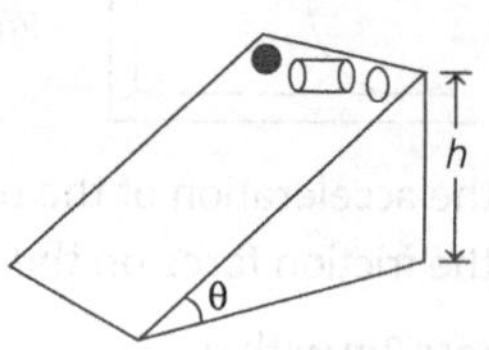

4 There is a rough track, a portion of which is in the form of a cylinder of radius R as shown in the figure. Find the minimum linear speed of a uniform sphere of radius r with which it should be set rolling without sliding on the horizontal part, so that it can complete round the circle without sliding on the cylindrical part.

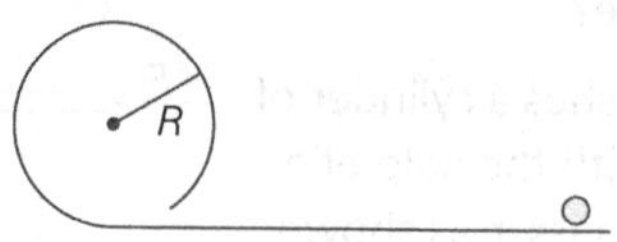

5 A uniform solid sphere is released from the top of an inclined plane of inclination θ.

(a) Find the minimum coefficient of friction between the sphere and the plane to prevent sliding.

(b) Find the kinetic energy of the sphere as it moves down a distance l on the incline, if the friction coefficient is half the value calculated in part (a).

6 A uniform cylinder rolls from rest down the side of a parabolic trough from height h. The cylinder does not slip from A to B but the surface of the trough is smooth from B to C. How far will the cylinder ascend towards C?

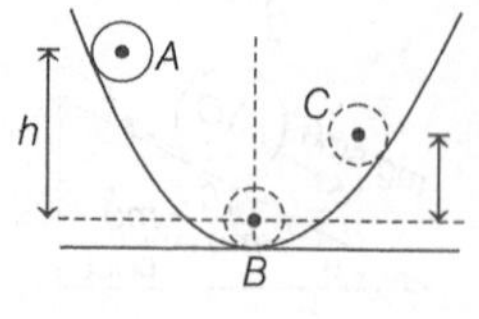

4.5 Angular Impulse

1 A uniform rod of length L is given an impulse at right angles to its length as shown. Find the distance of point on rod which is at rest from the centre of the rod.

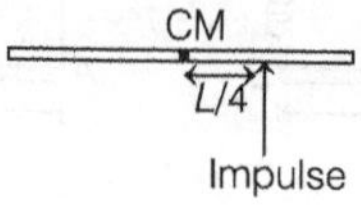

2 Two particles of masses m and $2m$ are attached at the ends A and B of a light rigid rod of length l. The system (m + rod + $2m$) is placed on a smooth horizontal surface. An impulse J is given at the end A of the rod perpendicular to its length as shown in figure.

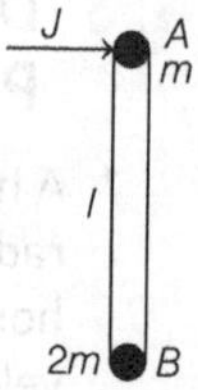

Find the

(i) velocity of centre of mass of the system.

(ii) angular velocity of the rod.

(iii) velocities of end A and end B of the rod.

3 A uniform solid sphere is placed on a smooth horizontal surface. An impulse I is given horizontally to the sphere at a height $h = \frac{4R}{5}$ above the centre line. m and R are mass and radius of sphere, respectively.

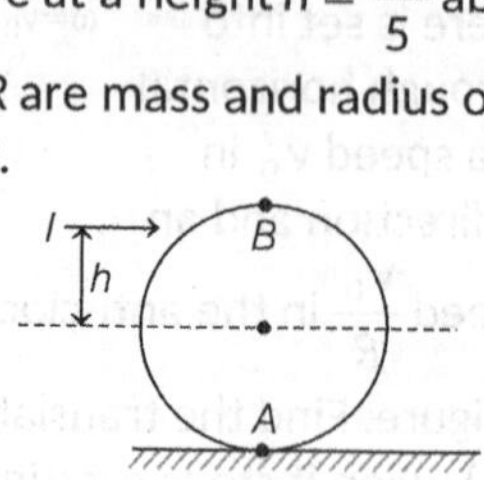

Find

(a) angular velocity of sphere and linear velocity of centre of mass of the sphere.

(b) the minimum time after which the highest point B will touch the ground.

(c) the displacement of the centre of mass during this interval.

4 A rod of length L forming an angle β with the vertical strikes a frictionless floor at A with a vertical velocity v_1 and no angular velocity. Assuming that the impact at A is perfectly elastic, derive an expression for the angular velocity of the rod immediately after the impact.

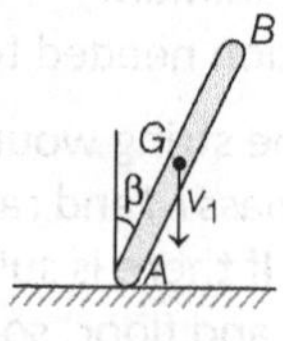

5 An elastic spherical ball of mass M and radius a moving with velocity v strikes a rigid surface at an angle θ to the normal. Assuming it skids while in contact with the surface, the tangential frictional force being a constant fraction μ of the normal reaction force, show that

(a) the ball is reflected at an angle θ to the normal, where $(\tan\theta - \tan\phi) = 2\mu$

(b) the angular velocity of the rebounding ball changes by an amount $\dfrac{5\mu v}{a}\cos\theta$

You may assume that the component of velocity perpendicular to the surface is reversed in direction without change of magnitude.

4.6 Anglular Momentum in Combined Motion

1 A disc of mass M and radius R is rolling with angular speed ω on a horizontal plane as shown. Find the magnitude of angular momentum of the disc about the origin O.

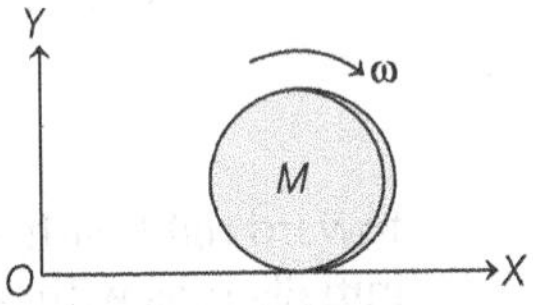

2 A rod AB of mass M and length L is lying on a horizontal frictionless surface. A particle of mass m travelling along the surface hits the end A of the rod with a velocity v_0 in a direction perpendicular to AB.

The collision is elastic. After the collision, the particle comes to rest.

(i) Find the ratio m/M.

(ii) A point P on the rod is at rest immediately after collision. Find the distance AP.

(iii) Find the linear speed of the point P after a time $\dfrac{\pi L}{3V_0}$ after the collision.

3 A uniform bar of length $6a$ and mass $8m$ lies on a smooth horizontal table. Two point masses m and $2\,m$ moving in the same horizontal plane with speeds $2v$ and v respectively, strike the bar as shown and stick to the bar after collision.

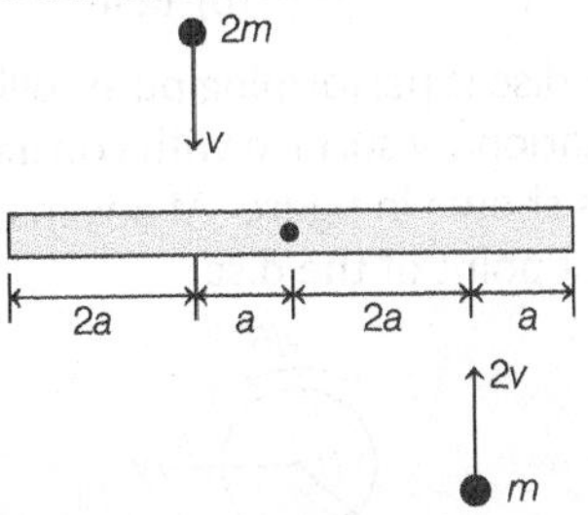

Find out

(i) Velocity of the centre of mass of the system.

(ii) Angular velocity of the rod about centre of mass of the system.

(iii) Total kinetic energy of the system, just after the collision.

4 Two small particles A and B of masses M and $2M$ respectively, are joined rigidly to the ends of a light rod of length l as shown in the figure. The system translates on a smooth horizontal surface with a velocity u in a direction perpendicular to the rod. A particle P of mass M kept at rest on the surface sticks to the particle A as the particle P collides with it.

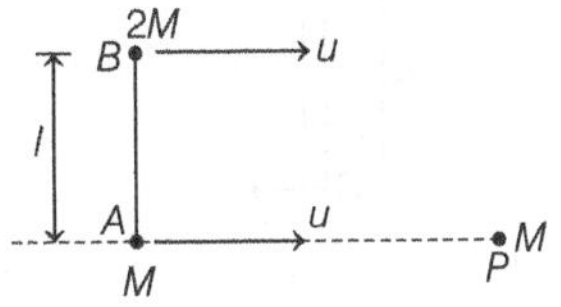

Calculate

(a) the linear speeds of the particles A and B after the collision,

(b) the velocity of the centre of mass C of the system $A + B + P$ and

(c) the angular speed of the system about C after the collision.

5 A uniform disc of mass M, radius R is moving towards right with velocity v_0 and having angular velocity ω_0 about the axis perpendicular to plane of disc passing through centre of disc. Suddenly, top point of the disc gets hinged about a fixed smooth axis. What is the angular velocity of disk about new rotation axis?

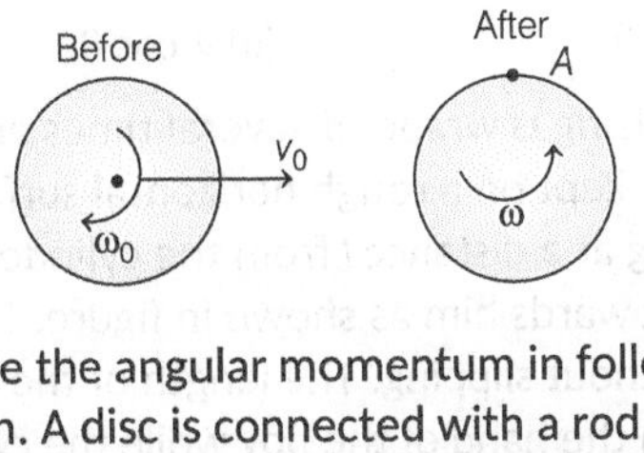

6 Calculate the angular momentum in following situation. A disc is connected with a rod of mass m and length l. The disc is free to rotate about its own axis. If whole system is rotating with $\omega_1\hat{j}$ and disc also rotate about its own axis with $\omega_2\hat{i}$, then calculate $\mathbf{L}$ about origin.

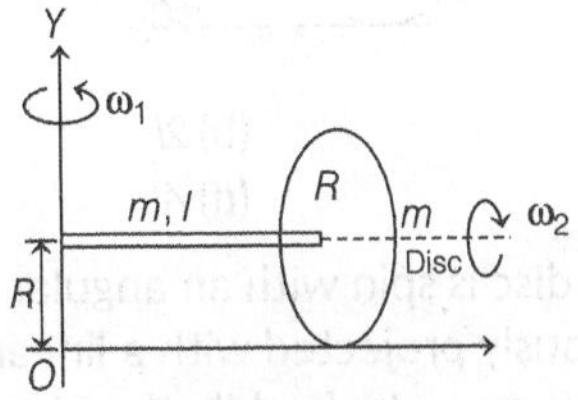

4.7 Instantaneous Axis of Rotation

1 A 100 cm rod is moving on a horizontal surface. At an instant, when it is parallel to the X-axis its ends A and B have velocities 30 cm/s and 20 cm/s as shown in the figure.

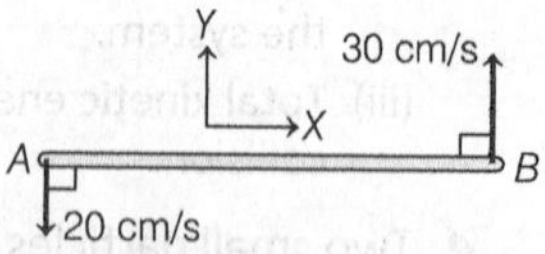

(a) Find its angular velocity and velocity of its centre.
(b) Locate its instantaneous axis of rotation.

2 A uniform rod AB of length L and mass m is moving as shown in figure.

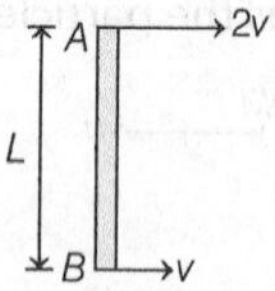

Find
(a) location of instantaneous axis of rotation
(b) angular velocity and velocity of its centre
(c) kinetic energy of the rod

3 **A uniform bar of length l and mass m stands vertically touching a vertical wall (Y-axis). When slightly displaced, its lower end begins to slide along the floor (X-axis). Obtain an expression for the angular velocity (ω) of the bar as a function of θ. Neglect friction everywhere.**

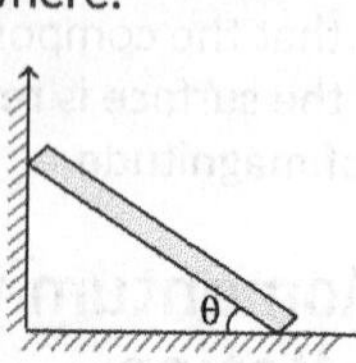

LEVEL 02 JEE Main Level

Single Choice Correct Questions

1 A hoop rolls on a horizontal ground without slipping with linear speed v. Speed of a particle P on the circumference of the hoop at angle θ is

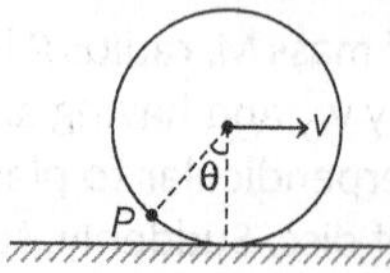

(a) $2v \sin\left(\frac{\theta}{2}\right)$ (b) $2v \cos\left(\frac{\theta}{2}\right)$
(c) $v \sin\theta$ (d) $v \cos\theta$

2 A thin string is wrapped several times around a cylinder kept on a rough horizontal surface. A boy standing at a distance l from the cylinder draws the string towards him as shown in figure. The cylinder rolls without slipping. The length of the string passed through the hand of the boy while the cylinder reaches his hand is

(a) l (b) $2l$
(c) $3l$ (d) $4l$

3 A uniform disc is spin with an angular velocity ω and simultaneously projected with a linear velocity v towards left on a plank while the plank moves toward right with a constant velocity $2v$. If the disc initially rolls without slipping on the plank, then angular velocity ω is

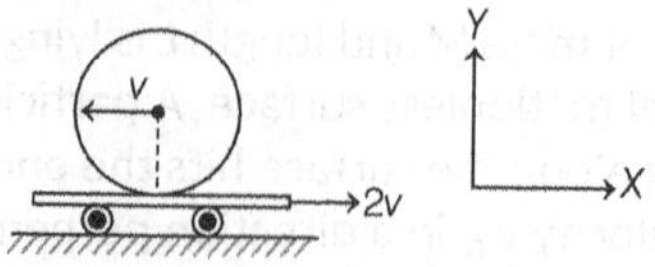

(a) $\frac{2v}{R}\hat{k}$ (b) $\frac{2v}{R}(-\hat{k})$ (c) $\frac{3v}{R}\hat{k}$ (d) $\frac{3v}{R}(-\hat{k})$

4 A plank P is placed on a solid cylinder S, which rolls on a horizontal surface. The two are of equal mass. There is no slipping at any of the surfaces in contact. The ratio of the kinetic energy of P to the kinetic energy of S is

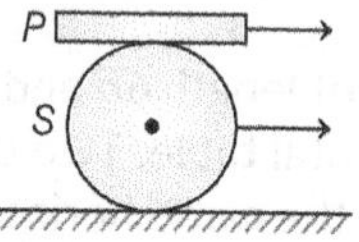

(a) 1 : 1 (b) 2 : 1
(c) 8 : 3 (d) 1 : 4

5 A uniform disc is performing pure rolling on a smooth stationary surface with constant angular velocity as shown in figure. At any instant, for the lower most point of the disc

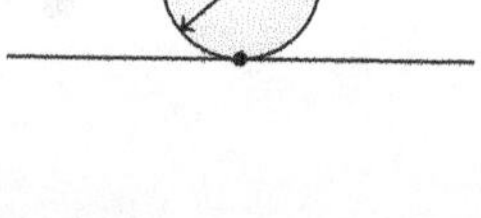

(a) velocity is v, acceleration is zero
(b) velocity is zero, acceleration is zero
(c) velocity is v, acceleration is $\frac{v^2}{R}$.
(d) velocity is zero, acceleration is $\frac{v^2}{R}$

6 A disc rolls without slipping on a horizontal surface. A point on the disc at a distance $R/2$ from the centre moves in a curved path. The radius of curvature at the highest point of the path is

(a) $4R$ (b) $\frac{R}{2}$ (c) $\frac{3R}{2}$ (d) $4.5R$

7 A disc of radius R is rolling purely on a flat horizontal surface, with a constant angular velocity. The angle between the velocity and acceleration vectors of point P is

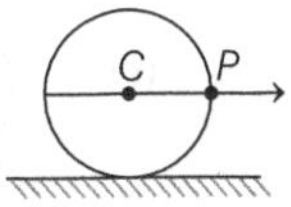

(a) zero (b) 45°
(c) 135° (d) $\tan^{-1}\left(\frac{1}{2}\right)$

8 A disc of radius R rolls on a horizontal ground with linear acceleration a and angular acceleration α as shown in figure. The magnitude of acceleration of point P shown in figure at an instant when its angular velocity of ω, will be

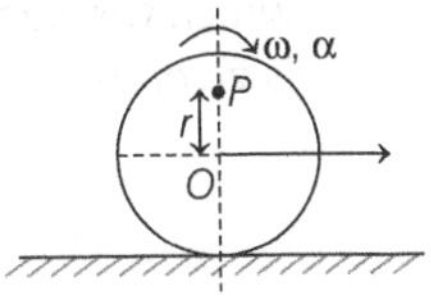

(a) $\sqrt{(a+r\alpha)^2+(r\omega^2)^2}$ (b) $\frac{ar}{R}$
(c) $\sqrt{r^2\alpha^2+r^2\omega^4}$ (d) $r\alpha$

9 A uniform ring of radius R is given a back spin of angular velocity $\frac{v_0}{2R}$ and thrown on a horizontal rough surface with velocity of centre to be v_0. The velocity of the centre of the ring when it starts pure rolling will be

(a) $\frac{v_0}{2}$ (b) $\frac{v_0}{4}$ (c) $\frac{3v_0}{4}$ (d) 0

10 A uniform disc of radius $R=0.2$ m kept over a rough horizontal surface is given velocity v_0 and angular velocity ω_0. After some time its kinetic energy becomes zero. If $v_0=10$ m/s, find ω_0

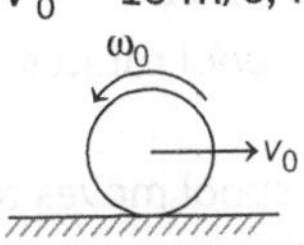

(a) 50 rad/s (b) 100 rad/s
(c) 150 rad/s (d) 200 rad/s

11 A uniform sphere of mass m is given some angular velocity about a horizontal axis through its centre and gently placed on a plank of mass $3m$. The coefficient of friction between the two is μ. The plank rests on a smooth horizontal surface. The initial acceleration of the centre of sphere relative to the plank will be

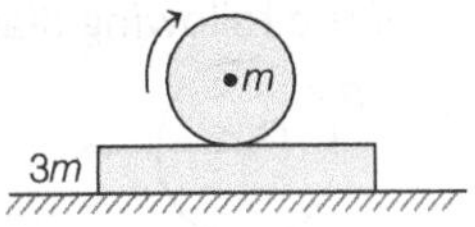

(a) zero (b) $\left(\frac{4}{3}\right)\mu g$ (c) $\left(\frac{7}{5}\right)\mu g$ (d) $2\mu g$

12 A hollow sphere of mass 2 kg is kept on a rough horizontal surface. A force of $10\sqrt{3}$ N is applied as shown in the figure. Find the minimum value of μ, so that the sphere starts pure rolling. (Take, $g=10$ m/s^2)

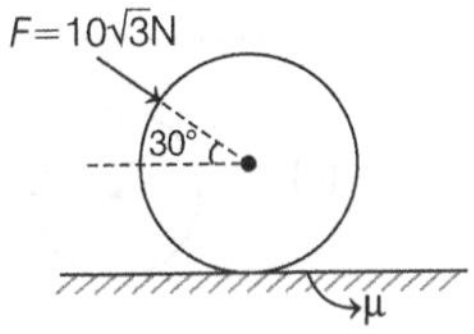

(a) 0.3
(b) 0.2
(c) 0.1
(d) For no value of μ it will start pure rolling.

13 The rope shown in figure is wound around a cylinder of mass 4 kg and radius 0.1 m. If the cylinder rolls without slipping, then the linear acceleration of its centre of mass is

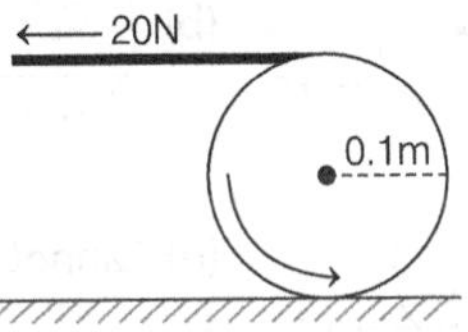

(a) 6.7 m/s^2 (b) 10.0 m/s^2
(c) 9.0 m/s^2 (d) None of these

14 How much is the magnitude of the frictional force acting at the point of contact for a cylinder which is rolling (without slipping) under the action of an external force F as shown in the diagram below? (Assume F to be constant and applied constantly at the same point on the cylinder as shown)

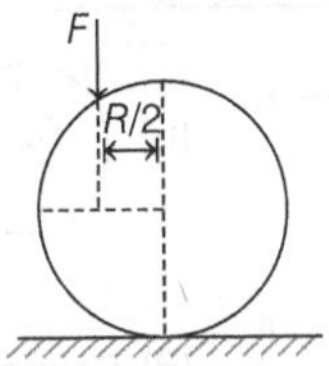

(a) $\frac{F}{3}$ (b) $\frac{2F}{3}$ (c) $\frac{F}{2}$ (d) $\frac{3F}{2}$

(Direction Q. Nos. 15-18) In the following problems, indicate the correct direction of friction force acting on the cylinder, which is pulled on a rough surface by a constant force F.

15 A cylinder of mass M and radius R is pulled horizontally by a force F. The friction force can be given by which of the following diagrams

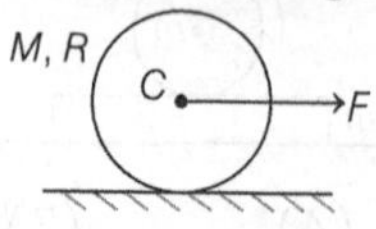

(a) 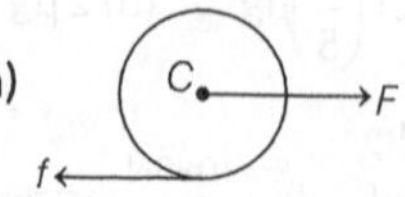

(b) 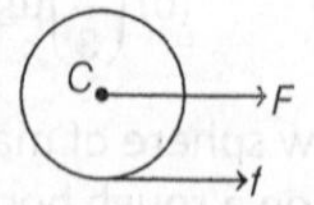

(c) 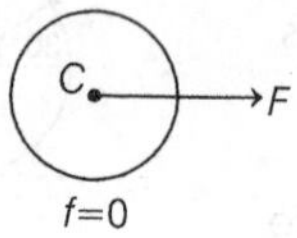

(d) Cannot be interpreted

16 A cylinder is pulled horizontally by a force F acting at a point below the centre of mass of the cylinder, as shown in figure. The friction force can be given by which of the following diagrams

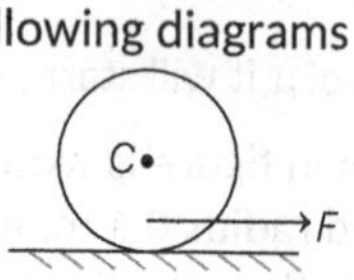

(a) 

(b) 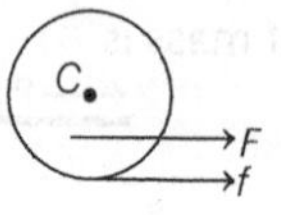

(c) 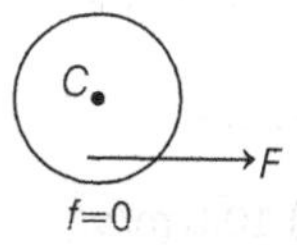

(d) Cannot be interpreted

17 A cylinder is pulled horizontally by a force F acting at a point above the centre of mass of the cylinder, as shown in figure. The friction force can be given by which of the following diagrams

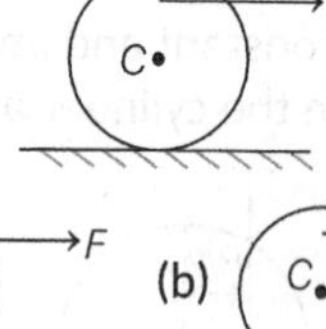

(a) 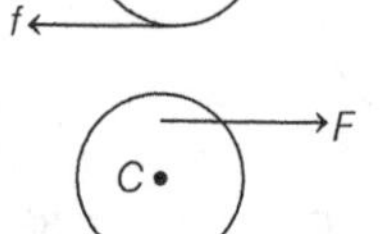

(b) 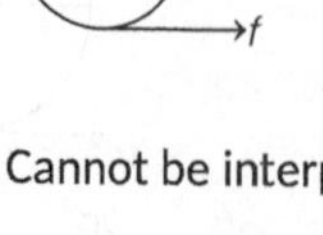

(c) 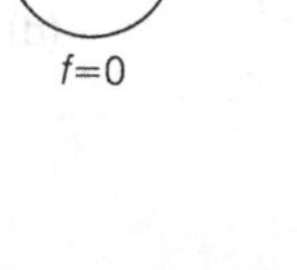

(d) Cannot be interpreted

18 A cylinder is placed on a rough plank which in turn is placed on a smooth surface. The plank is pulled with a constant force F. The friction force can be given by which of the following diagrams

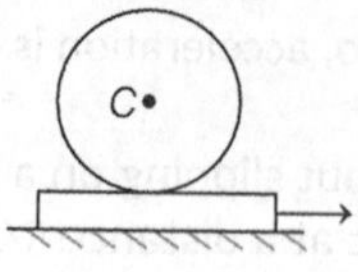

(a) 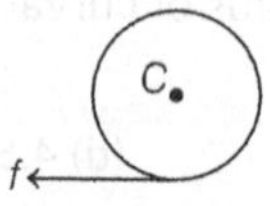

(b) 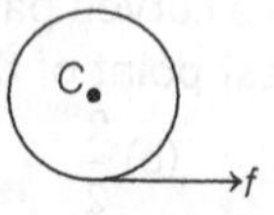

(c) 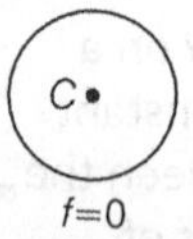

(d) Cannot be interpreted

19 The spool shown in figure is placed on rough horizontal surface and has inner radius r and outer radius R. The angle θ between the applied force and the horizontal can be varied. The critical angle (θ) for which the spool does not roll and remains stationary is given by

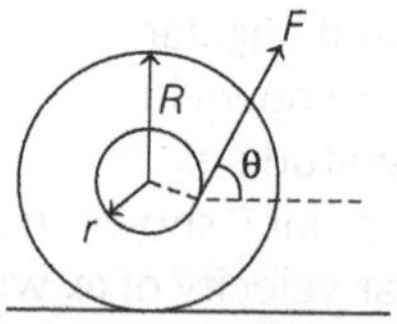

(a) $\cos^{-1}\sqrt{\dfrac{r}{R}}$

(b) $\cos^{-1}\left(\dfrac{2r}{R}\right)$

(c) $\cos^{-1}\left(\dfrac{r}{R}\right)$

(d) $\sin^{-1}\left(\dfrac{r}{R}\right)$

20 Inner and outer radii of a spool are r and R, respectively. A thread is wound over its inner surface and placed over a rough horizontal surface. Thread is pulled by a force F as shown in figure, then in case of pure rolling

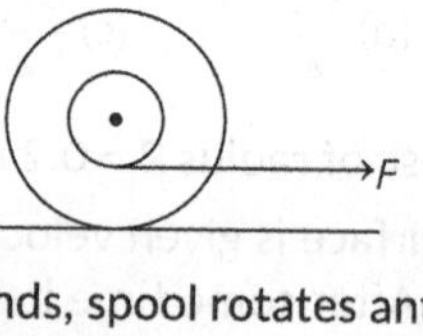

(a) thread unwinds, spool rotates anti-clockwise and friction act leftwards

(b) thread winds, spool rotates clockwise and friction acts leftwards

(c) thread winds, spool moves to the right and friction act rightwards

(d) thread winds, spool moves to the right and friction does not come into existence.

21 A spool of mass M and radius $2R$ lies on an inclined plane as shown in figure. A light thread is wound around the connecting tube of the spool and its free end carries a weight of mass m. The value of m, so that system is in equilibrium is

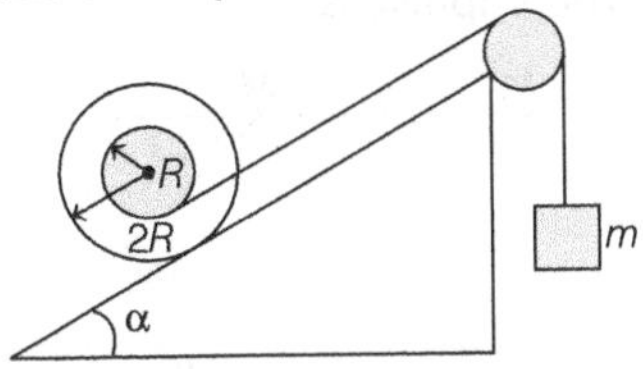

(a) $2M \sin \alpha$ (b) $M \sin \alpha$
(c) $2M \tan \alpha$ (d) $M \tan \alpha$

22 A spool of mass m and radius R has wrapped with a string and other end of string is connected with a mass m as shown in figure. If moment of inertia of spool is $\frac{5}{3}mR^2$ and friction is sufficient to prevent slipping, then find acceleration of block.

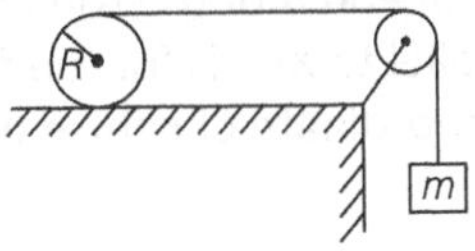

(a) 2 m/s^2 (b) 4 m/s^2 (c) 5 m/s^2 (d) 6 m/s^2

23 A disc having a thread tightly wound on it, is being pulled upwards by the thread such that the disc starts moving upwards with an acceleration g. Find acceleration of the free end of the thread.

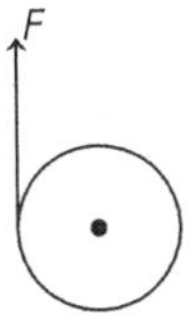

(a) $2g$ (b) $3g$
(c) $4g$ (d) $5g$

24 A solid sphere and a solid cylinder having the same mass and radius roll down the same incline. The ratio of their acceleration is

(a) 14 : 15 (b) 1 : 2
(c) 15 : 14 (d) 2 : 1

25 Two solid cylinders P and Q of same mass and same radius start rolling down a fixed inclined plane from the same height at the same time. Cylinder P has most of its mass concentrated near its surface, while Q has most of its mass concentrated near the axis. Which statement(s) is(are) correct?

(a) Both cylinders P and Q reach the ground at the same time.
(b) Cylinder P has larger linear acceleration than cylinder Q.
(c) Both cylinder reach the ground with same translational kinetic energy.
(d) Cylinder Q reaches the ground with larger angular speed.

26 The body shown, with mass M and radius R, starts from rest and rolls without slipping down an inclined plane of height H. At the bottom of the plane its translational speed is $\left(\frac{8gH}{7}\right)^{\frac{1}{2}}$. Which of the following is the moment of inertia of the body?

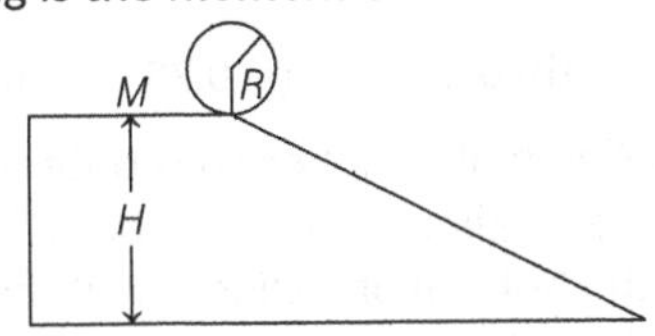

(a) $\frac{MR^2}{2}$ (b) $\frac{3MR^2}{4}$
(c) $\frac{7MR^2}{8}$ (d) MR^2

27 A ball rolls down an inclined plane as shown in figure. The ball is first released from rest from P and then later from Q. Which of the following statement is/ are correct?

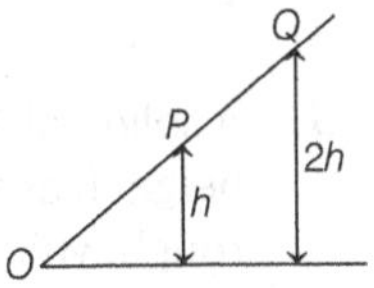

(i) The ball takes twice as much time to roll from Q to O as it does to roll from P to O.
(ii) The acceleration of the ball at Q is twice as large as the acceleration at P.
(iii) The ball has twice as much KE at O when rolling from Q as it does when rolling from P.

(a) (i), (ii) only (b) (ii), (iii) only
(c) (i) only (d) (iii) only

28. A small sphere A of mass m and radius r rolls without slipping inside a large fixed hemispherical bowl of radius R as shown in figure. If the sphere starts from rest at the top point of the hemisphere, find the normal force exerted by the small sphere on the hemisphere when it is at the bottom B of the hemisphere.

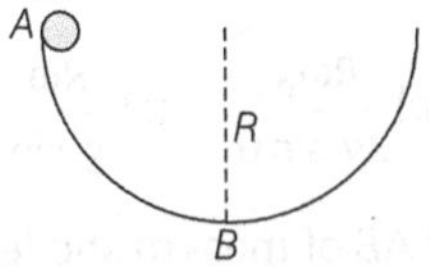

(a) $\frac{10mg}{7}$ (b) $\frac{17mg}{7}$
(c) $\frac{5mg}{7}$ (d) $\frac{7mg}{5}$

29 Three identical slender rods each of mass M are welded at their ends to form an equilateral triangle, and the corners are then welded to a light metal hoop of radius R. If the rigid assembly of rods and hoop is allowed to roll down the incline of inclination

θ, the minimum value of the coefficient of static friction is

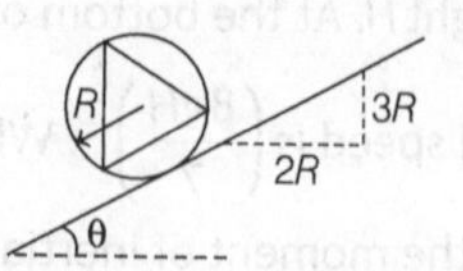

(a) 0.25 (b) 0.5 (c) 0.75 (d) 0.9

30 A thick walled hollow sphere has outer radius R. It rolls down an inclined plane without slipping and its speed at the bottom of incline is v. If the inclined plane is frictionless and the sphere slides down without rolling, its speed at the bottom is $\frac{5v}{4}$. What is the radius of gyration of the sphere?

(a) $\frac{R}{\sqrt{2}}$ (b) $\frac{R}{2}$ (c) $\frac{3R}{4}$ (d) $\frac{\sqrt{3}R}{4}$

31 A solid ball rolls down a parabolic path ABC from a height h as shown in figure. Portion AB of the path is rough while BC is smooth. How high will the ball climb in BC?

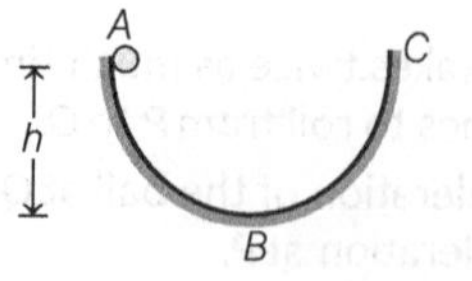

(a) $\frac{2}{3}h$ (b) $\frac{5}{7}h$ (c) $\frac{3}{5}h$ (d) $\frac{2}{7}h$

32 A cylinder of radius R is spinned with angular velocity ω_0 and then placed on an incline having coefficient of friction $\mu = \tan\theta$ (θ is the angle of incline). The cylinder continues to spin without falling for time

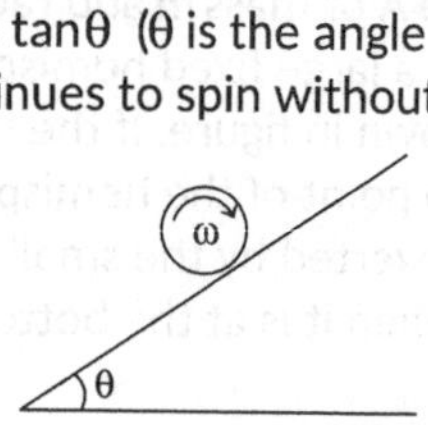

(a) $\frac{R\omega_0}{3g\sin\theta}$ (b) $\frac{R\omega_0}{2g\sin\theta}$ (c) $\frac{R\omega_0}{g\sin\theta}$ (d) $\frac{2R\omega_0}{g\sin\theta}$

33 A uniform rod AB of mass m and length l is at rest on a smooth horizontal surface. An impulse J is applied to the end B, perpendicular to the rod in the horizontal direction. Speed of particle P at a distance $\frac{l}{6}$ from the centre towards A of the rod after time $t = \frac{\pi m l}{12J}$ is

(a) $2\frac{J}{m}$ (b) $\frac{J}{\sqrt{2}m}$ (c) $\frac{J}{m}$ (d) $\sqrt{2}\frac{J}{m}$

34 Two equal masses each of mass M are joined by a massless rod of length L. Now, an impulse Mv is given to the mass M making an angle of 30° with the length of the rod. The angular velocity of the rod just after imparting the impulse is

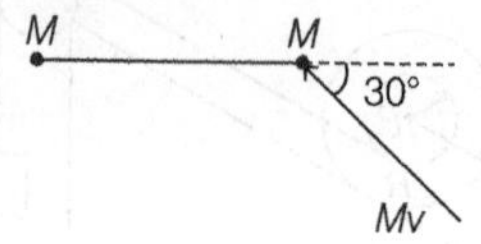

(a) $\frac{v}{L}$ (b) $\frac{2v}{L}$

(c) $\frac{v}{2L}$ (d) None of these

35 A uniform rod of mass m, length l is placed over a smooth horizontal surface along Y-axis and is at rest as shown in figure. An impulsive force F is applied for a small time Δt along x-direction at point A. The X-coordinate of end A of the rod when the rod becomes parallel to X-axis for the first time is (initially the coordinate of centre of mass of the rod is (0, 0))

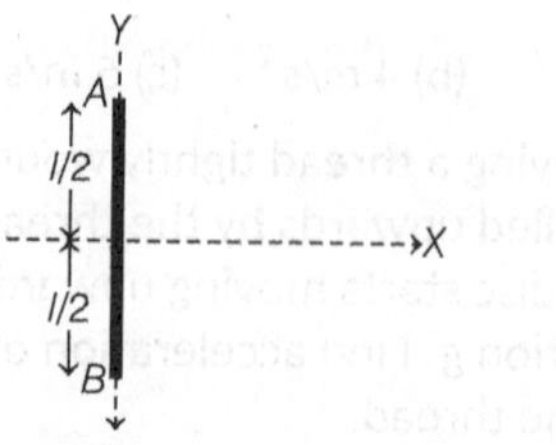

(a) $\frac{\pi l}{12}$ (b) $\frac{l}{2}\left(1+\frac{\pi}{12}\right)$

(c) $\frac{l}{2}\left(1-\frac{\pi}{6}\right)$ (d) $\frac{l}{2}\left(1+\frac{\pi}{6}\right)$

36 A solid sphere is placed on a horizontal plane. A horizontal impulse I is applied at a distance h above the central line as shown in the figure. Soon after giving the impulse the sphere starts rolling. The ratio $\frac{h}{R}$ would be

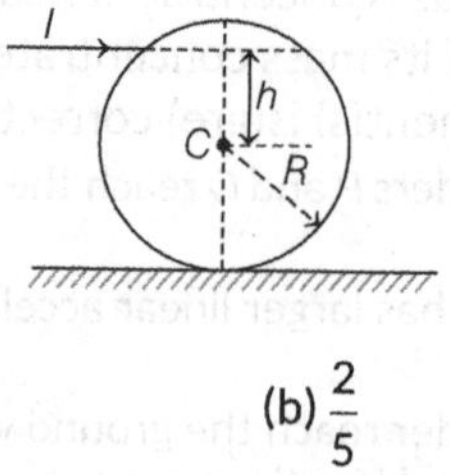

(a) $\frac{1}{2}$ (b) $\frac{2}{5}$

(c) $\frac{1}{4}$ (d) $\frac{1}{5}$

37 A disc of mass m and radius R moves in the XY-plane as shown in the figure. The angular momentum of the disc about the origin O at the instant shown is

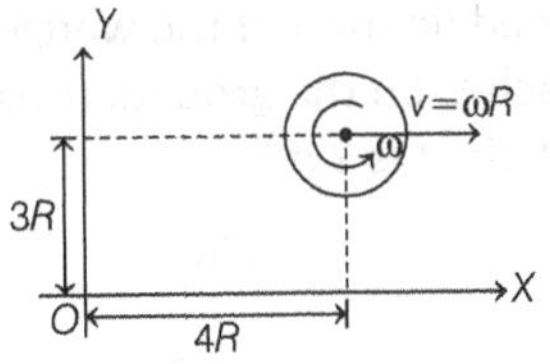

(a) $-\frac{5}{2}mR^2\omega\hat{k}$ (b) $\frac{7}{2}mR^2\omega\hat{k}$

(c) $-\frac{9}{2}mR^2\omega\hat{k}$ (d) $\frac{5}{2}mR^2\omega\hat{k}$

38 A circular wooden loop of mass m and radius R rests flat on a horizontal frictionless surface. A bullet, also of mass m, and moving with a velocity v, strikes the loop and gets embedded in it. The thickness of the loop is much smaller than R. The angular velocity with which the system rotates just after the bullet strikes the loop is

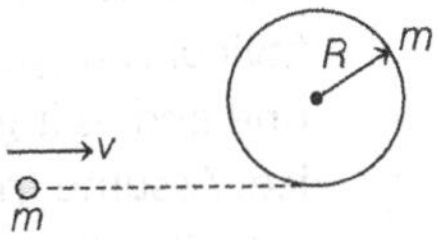

(a) $\frac{v}{4R}$ (b) $\frac{v}{3R}$ (c) $\frac{2v}{3R}$ (d) $\frac{3v}{4R}$

39 A thin rod of mass M and length L is struck at one end by a ball of clay of mass m, moving with speed v as shown in figure. The ball sticks to the rod. After the collision, the angular momentum of the clay-rod system about A, the mid-point of the rod, is

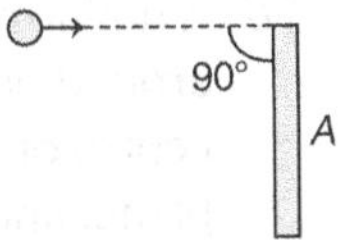

(a) $\left(m+\frac{M}{3}\right)\left(\frac{vL}{2}\right)$ (b) $\left(m+\frac{M}{12}\right)\left(\frac{vL}{2}\right)$

(c) $\frac{mvL}{2}$ (d) mvL

40 The end A of a ladder AP of length 5m, kept inclined to a vertical wall is slipping over a horizontal surface, when A is at a distance of 3m from the wall. If velocity of centre of mass at this moment is 1.25 m/s then velocity of the lowest point A of the ladder at this instant is

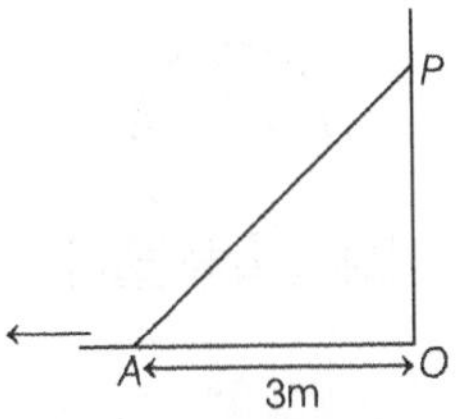

(a) 1.25 m/s (b) 0 m/s

(c) 1 m/s (d) 2 m/s

41 A rod of mass M and length l is at rest on plane horizontal smooth surface. A particle of same mass M strike one end with velocity u perpendicular to rod, elastically. Now, just after collision what is the kinetic energy of upper half part of rod?

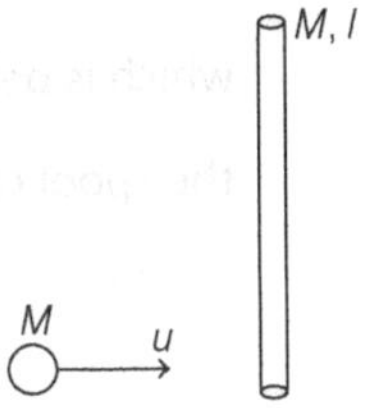

(a) $\frac{Mu^2}{25}$ (b) $\frac{Mu^2}{16}$

(c) $\frac{Mu^2}{9}$ (d) $\frac{Mu^2}{4}$

Numerical Value Questions

1 We apply a force of 10 N on a cord wrapped around a cylinder of mass 20 kg. The cylinder rolls without slipping on the floor. Find its kinetic energy (in J) after 6 s.

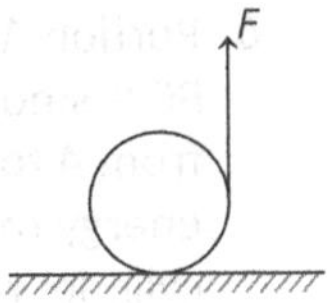

2 A uniform solid sphere of mass 1 kg and radius R is resting on a rough horizontal surface. After applying an impulse of magnitude $\frac{1}{\sqrt{3}}$ kg-m/s on sphere as shown in figure it starts pure rolling. If friction coefficient is $\frac{x\sqrt{3}}{7}$, then find x.

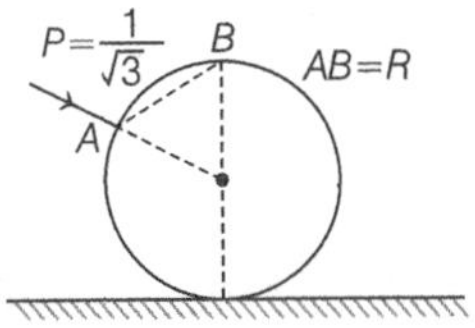

3 A uniform solid sphere rolls down on a vertical rigid surface without slipping. The vertical surface moves with an acceleration $a=\frac{g}{2}$ in horizontal direction as shown. The minimum coefficient of friction between the sphere and vertical surface so as to prevent slipping is μ. Write 14μ as answer.

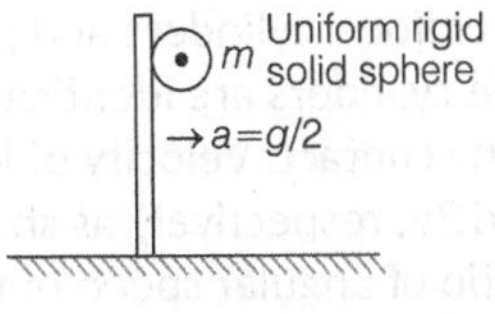

4 A spool of inner radius R and outer radius $3R$ has a moment of inertia $=MR^2$ about an axis passing through its geometric centre, where M is the mass of the spool. A thread wound on the inner surface of the spool is pulled horizontally with a constant force $=Mg$. If the acceleration of the point on the thread which is being pulled is $\frac{ng}{5}$, then find n. Assume that the spool rolls purely on the floor.

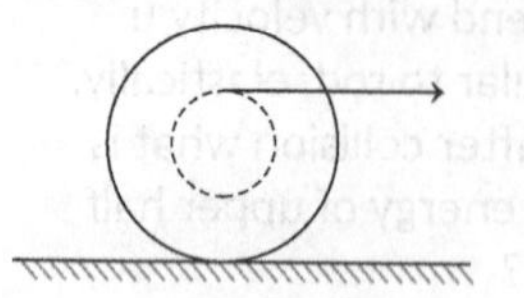

5 A solid cylinder is released from rest from the top of an inclined plane of inclination 60°, where friction coefficient varies with distance x as $\mu = \frac{13-3x}{\sqrt{3}}$. Find the distance (in m) travelled by the cylinder on incline before it starts slipping.

6 Portion AB of the wedge shown in figure is rough and BC is smooth. A solid sphere rolls without slipping from A to B. Find the ratio of translational kinetic energy to rotational kinetic energy, when the cylinder reaches point C.

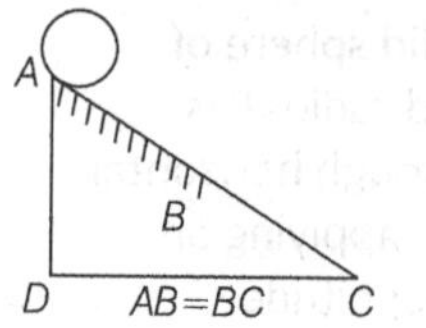

7 A solid cylinder C and a hollow pipe P of same diameter are in contact when they are released from rest as shown in the figure on a long incline plane. Cylinder C and pipe P roll without slipping. Determine the clear gap (in m) between them after 4 s.

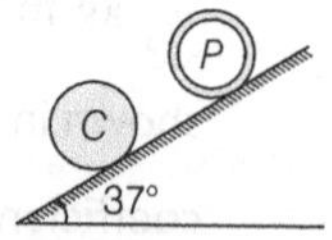

8 A wedge of mass m is placed on a smooth horizontal surface. A solid cylinder having same mass m starts rolling without slipping down the wedge as shown. Find the speed (in m/s) of the wedge when the cylinder reaches on the ground. (Angle of wedge is 60° and its height is 2 m)

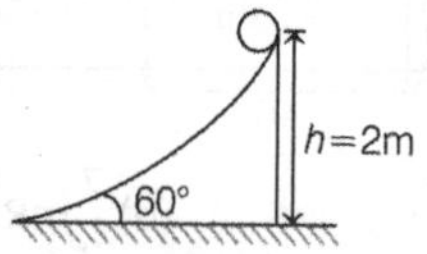

9 A 200 kg beam 2.0 m in length slides broadside down the ice with a speed of 16 m/s (figure). A 50 kg small favicol can (guaranteed sticking !!!) at rest sticks at one end as it goes past, both go spinning down the ice. Assume frictionless motion. What is the angular velocity of combined mass in rad/s?

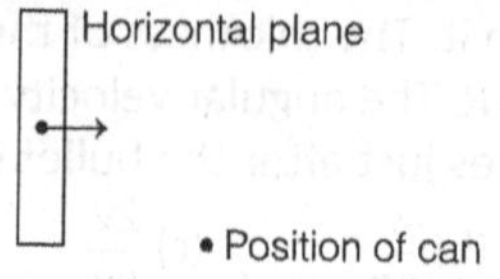

10 A uniform stick of mass 18 kg and length 3 m spins around on a frictionless horizontal plane, with its centre of mass stationary. A mass M is placed on the plane, and the stick collides elastically with it, as shown (with the contact point being the end of the stick). What should M (in kg) be so that after the collision the stick has translational motion, but no rotational motion?

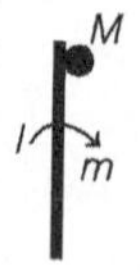

LEVEL 03 JEE Advanced Level

Single Choice Correct Questions

1 A system of uniform cylinders and plates is shown in figure. All the cylinders are identical and there is no slipping at any contact. Velocity of lower and upper plate is v and $2v$, respectively as shown in figure. Then, the ratio of angular speed of the upper cylinders to lower cylinders is

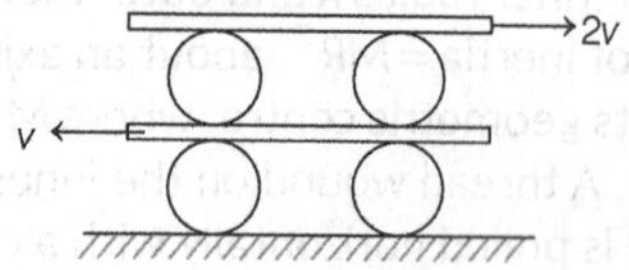

(a) 3 (b) 1/3
(c) 1 (d) None of these

2 A ring of mass m and radius R has three particles attached to the ring as shown in the figure. The centre of the ring has a speed v_0. The kinetic energy of the system is (slipping is absent)

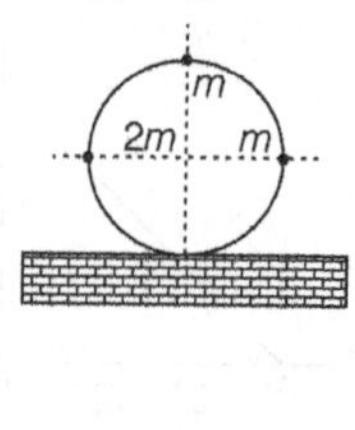

(a) $6\ mv_0^2$
(b) $12\ mv_0^2$
(c) $4\ mv_0^2$
(d) $8\ mv_0^2$

3 On a train moving with acceleration $10\ m/s^2$ a ball starts rolling on floor of train along the width of the train with angular acceleration $2\ rad/s^2$, radius of ball is 1 m. Find the acceleration of the top point of ball at the time $t = 3$ s as seen from ground.

(a) $10\ m/s^2$ (b) $\sqrt{1412}\ m/s^2$
(c) $100\ m/s^2$ (d) $\sqrt{1396}\ m/s^2$

4 A solid sphere of mass M and radius R is lying on a rough horizontal plane. A constant force $F = 4\ Mg$ acts vertically at point P, such that OP makes 60° with horizontal. The minimum value of coefficient of friction, so that sphere does pure rolling is

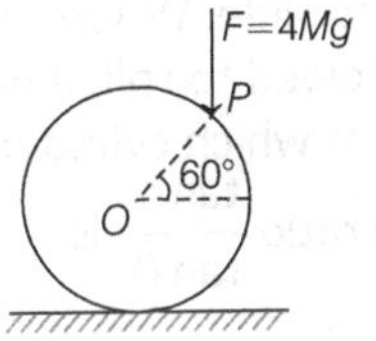

(a) $\frac{3}{7}$ (b) $\frac{4}{7}$
(c) $\frac{2}{7}$ (d) $\frac{2}{5}$

5 A ring of radius R is rolling purely on the outer surface of a pipe of radius $4R$. At some instant, the centre of the ring has a constant speed $= v$. Then, the acceleration of the point on the ring which is in contact with the surface of the pipe is

(a) $\frac{4v^2}{5R}$ (b) $\frac{3v^2}{5R}$
(c) $\frac{v^2}{4R}$ (d) zero

6 A cylinder is sandwiched between two planks. Two constant horizontal forces F and $2F$ are applied on the planks as shown. Masses of planks and cylinder are indicated in the figure. Radius of the cylinder is as shown. Determine the acceleration of the centre of mass of cylinder, if there is no slipping at the top and bottom of cylinder. ($F = 1300$ N, $M = 10$ kg)

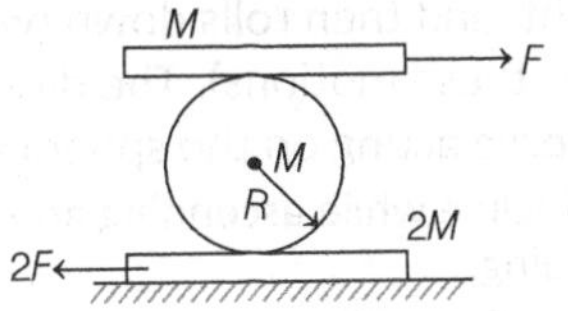

(a) $2\ ms^{-2}$ (b) $3\ ms^{-2}$
(c) $5\ ms^{-2}$ (d) $10\ ms^{-2}$

7 A small block of mass m is rigidly attached at P to a ring of mass $3m$ and radius r. The system is released from rest at $\theta = 90°$ and rolls without sliding. The angular acceleration of ring just after release is

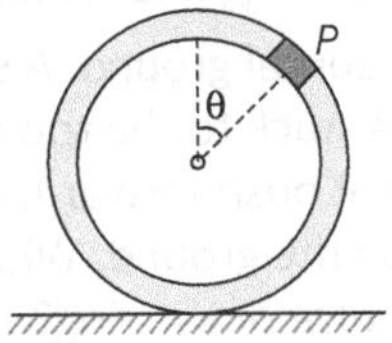

(a) $\frac{g}{4r}$ (b) $\frac{g}{8r}$
(c) $\frac{g}{3r}$ (d) $\frac{g}{2r}$

8 A hollow smooth uniform sphere A of mass m rolls without sliding on a smooth horizontal surface. It collides head on elastically with another stationary smooth solid sphere B of the same mass m and same radius. The ratio of kinetic energy of B to that of A just after the collision is

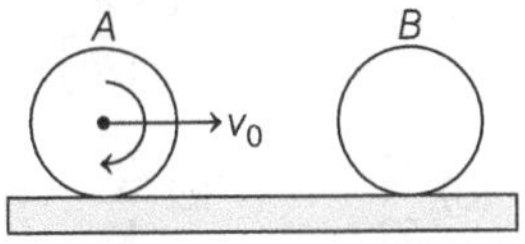

(a) 1 : 1 (b) 2 : 3
(c) 3 : 2 (d) None

9 A uniform rod of mass m and length l is sliding between smooth vertical wall and smooth horizontal floor as shown in figure. At this moment, kinetic energy of rod is

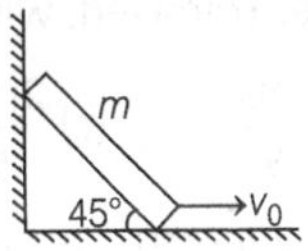

(a) mv_0^2 (b) $\frac{1}{3}mv_0^2$
(c) $\frac{1}{2}mv_0^2$ (d) $\frac{1}{4}mv_0^2$

10 A cylinder of mass m is kept on the edge of a plank of mass $2m$ and length 12 m, which in turn is kept on smooth ground. Coefficient of friction between the plank and the cylinder is 0.1. The cylinder is given an impulse which imparts it a velocity 7 m/s but no angular velocity. The time after which the cylinder falls off the plank is

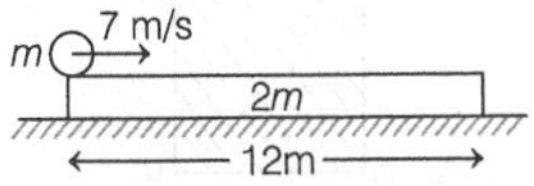

(a) 2 s (b) 2.25 s
(c) 2.5 s (d) 2.75 s

11 A ring of mass $m = 1$ kg and radius $R = 1.25$ m is kept on a rough horizontal ground. A small body of same mass $m = 1$ kg is stuck to the top of the ring. When it was given a slight push forward, the ring started rolling purely on the ground. What is the maximum speed of the centre of the ring?

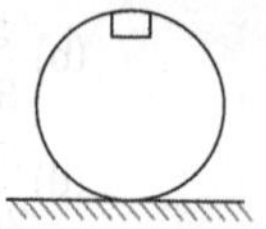

(a) 1 m/s (b) 5 m/s
(c) 2 m/s (d) 10 m/s

12 Angular acceleration of the cylinder C shown in figure is (all strings and pulley are ideal)

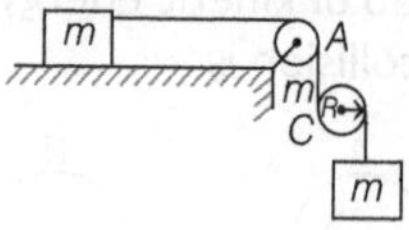

(a) $\frac{2g}{3R}$ (b) $\frac{2g}{5R}$ (c) $\frac{2g}{R}$ (d) $\frac{g}{2R}$

13 A uniform slender rod of mass m and length L is released from rest, with its lower end touching a frictionless horizontal floor as shown. At the initial moment, the rod is inclined at an angle $= 30°$ with the vertical. Then, the value of normal reaction from the floor just after released, will be

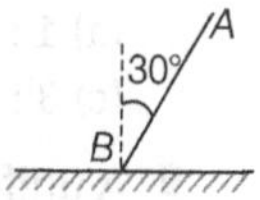

(a) $\frac{4mg}{7}$ (b) $\frac{5mg}{9}$ (c) $\frac{2mg}{5}$ (d) none

14 In the above problem, the initial acceleration of the lower end of the rod will be

(a) $\frac{g\sqrt{3}}{4}$ (b) $\frac{g\sqrt{3}}{5}$ (c) $\frac{3g\sqrt{3}}{7}$ (d) None

15 A thin uniform square plate $ABCD$ of side a and mass m is suspended in vertical plane as shown in the figure. AE and BF are two massless inextensible strings. The line AB is horizontal. The tension in the string AE just after BF is cut is

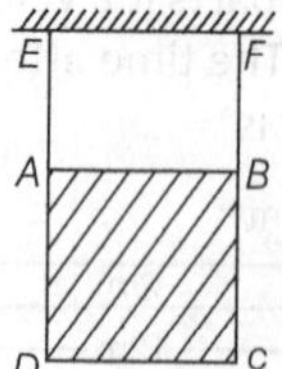

(a) $\frac{2mg}{5}$ (b) $\frac{3mg}{5}$ (c) $\frac{3mg}{7}$ (d) $\frac{4mg}{7}$

16 A uniform ball of radius r rolls without slipping down from the top of a fixed sphere of radius R. Find the angular velocity of the ball at the moment it breaks-off the sphere. The initial velocity of the ball is negligible.

(a) $\sqrt{\frac{10g(R+r)}{17r^2}}$ (b) $\sqrt{\frac{17g(R+r)}{10r^2}}$

(c) $\sqrt{\frac{7g(R+r)}{27r^2}}$ (d) $\sqrt{\frac{5g(R+r)}{27r^2}}$

17 A solid cylinder is placed in ends on position on an inclined plane. It is found that at an angle θ the cylinder starts to slide. When the cylinder turns on its sides and allowed to roll, it is found that the steepest angle at which cylinder performs pure rolling is θ. The ratio $\frac{\tan\phi}{\tan\theta}$, is

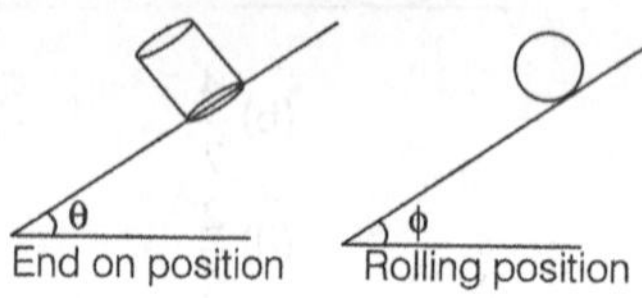

(a) $\frac{1}{3}$ (b) 1 (c) 3 (d) $\frac{1}{2}$

18 The wedge shown in the figure has a mass M and incline angle 37°. The floor is frictionless. The mass of the solid sphere is also M. Friction between the incline surface of the wedge and the sphere is sufficient to prevent any sliding, so that the sphere rolls purely down the inclined surface of the wedge. Find the acceleration of the wedge.

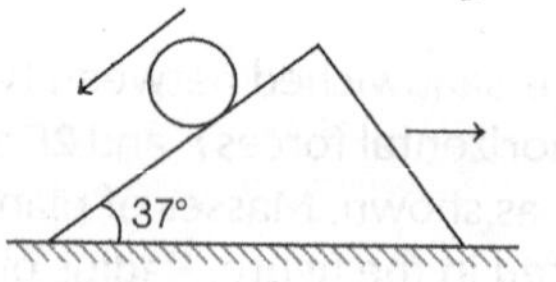

(a) $\frac{2g}{5}$ (b) $\frac{2g}{7}$ (c) $\frac{2g}{9}$ (d) $\frac{2g}{11}$

19 A spherical shell rolls up an inclined plane, reaches some height, and then rolls down (without slipping throughout these motions). The direction of the frictional force acting on the spherical shell are

(a) up the incline while ascending and down the incline descending.
(b) up the incline while ascending as well as descending.
(c) down the incline while ascending and up the incline while descending.
(d) down the incline while ascending as well as descending.

20 A length $L = 15$ m of flexible tape is tightly wound. It is then allowed to unwind as it rolls down a fixed incline that makes an angle $\theta = 30°$ with the horizontal, the upper end of the tape being fixed. Find the time taken by the tape to unwind completely. Neglect radius at any time w.r.t. the length of the rope.

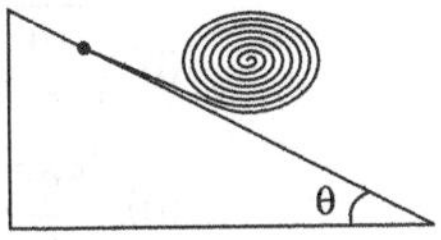

(a) 2 s (b) 3 s (c) 5 s (d) 6 s

21 A ring and sphere having same mass m and radius r each are connected by a massless rod which maintains constant distance between their centres, and rotation is friction free about the hinges at centre. There is sufficient friction on incline to maintain rolling. The force which acts through the rod during motion is

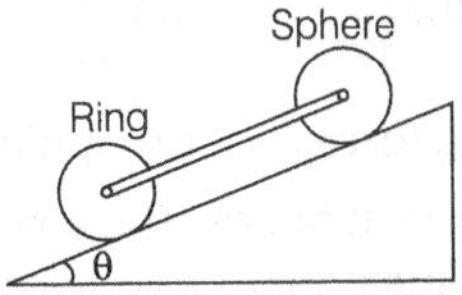

(a) $\frac{2}{17} mg \sin\theta$ (b) $\frac{3}{17} mg \sin\theta$

(c) $\frac{5}{17} mg \sin\theta$ (d) $\frac{7}{17} mg \sin\theta$

22 A disc is set rolling on an inclined plane of angle 30° at its base as shown. It is in continuous rolling on plane upto height $h = 1$ m, then leaves the plane. If initially it had kinetic energy of 4 J, find the ratio of kinetic energy due to translation and rotation at maximum height of its trajectory (mass of disc is 0.1 kg)

(a) $\frac{1}{2}$ (b) $\frac{3}{2}$ (c) $\frac{3}{4}$ (d) 2

23 A cylinder having radius 0.4 m, initially rotating (at $t = 0$) with $\omega_0 =$ 54 rad/s is placed on a rough inclined plane with $\theta = 37°$ having friction coefficient $\mu = 0.5$. The time taken by the cylinder to start pure rolling is

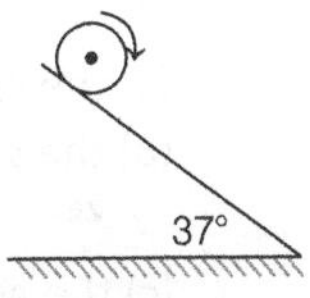

(a) 5.4 s (b) 1.4 s (c) 1.2 s (d) 1.8 s

24 A uniform disc of mass $m = 12$ kg slides down along smooth, frictionless hill, which ends in a horizontal plane without break. The disc is released from rest at a height of $h = 1.25$ m (it has no initial speed and it does not rotate), and lands on the top of a cart of mass $M = 6$ kg, which can move on a frictionless surface. The coefficient of kinetic friction between the cart and the disc is $\mu = 0.4$. Find minimum length of the cart so that the disc begins to roll without slipping before losing contact with the cart.

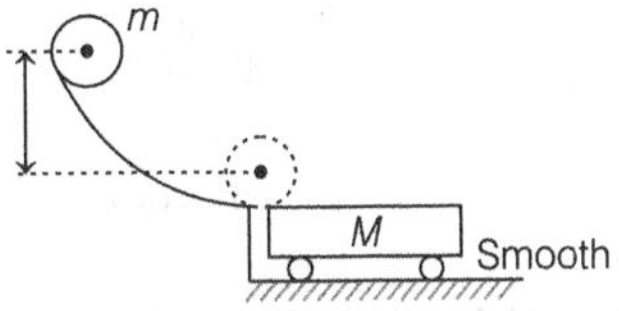

(a) $\frac{7}{8}$ m (b) $\frac{7}{4}$ m (c) $\frac{21}{4}$ m (d) $\frac{3}{8}$ m

25 In the figure shown a ring A is rolling without sliding with a velocity v on the horizontal surface of the body B (of same mass as A). All surfaces are smooth. B has no initial velocity. What will be the maximum height (from initial position) reached by A on B?

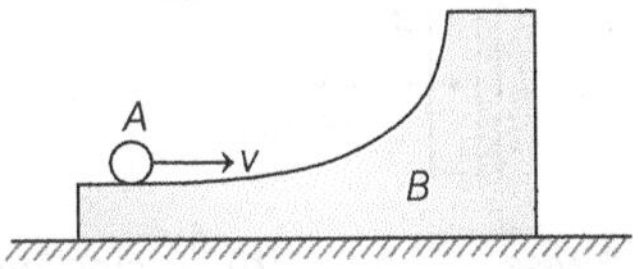

(a) $\frac{3v^2}{4g}$ (b) $\frac{v^2}{4g}$

(c) $\frac{v^2}{2g}$ (d) $\frac{v^2}{3g}$

26 A uniform solid square plate $ABCD$ of mass m and side a is moving in XY horizontal smooth plane. The velocity of centre of mass is $v_0(2\hat{i} + 4\hat{j})$ m/s. The end A of square plate is suddenly fixed by a pin, find the new velocity of centre of mass of square

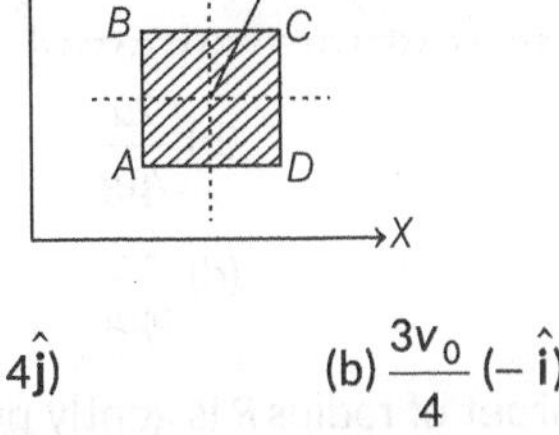

(a) $v_0(2\hat{i} + 4\hat{j})$ (b) $\frac{3v_0}{4}(-\hat{i}) + \frac{3v_0}{4}\hat{j}$

(c) $\frac{3v_0}{4}\hat{i} - \frac{3v_0}{2}\hat{j}$ (d) $3v_0\hat{i} - 3v_0\hat{j}$

27 A disc of mass M and radius R is rolling purely with centre's velocity v_0 on a flat horizontal floor when it hits a step in the floor of height $\frac{R}{4}$. The corner of the step is sufficiently rough to prevent any slipping of the disc against itself. What is the velocity of the centre of the disc just after impact?

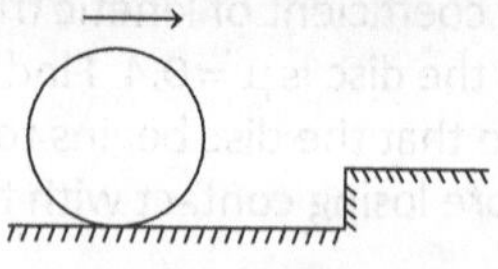

(a) $\frac{4v_0}{5}$ (b) $\frac{4v_0}{7}$

(c) $\frac{5v_0}{6}$ (d) None

28 A bar of mass M and length L is in pure translatory motion with its centre of mass velocity v. It collides with and sticks to a second identical bar which is initially at rest. (Assume that it becomes one composite bar of length $2L$). The angular velocity of the composite bar will be

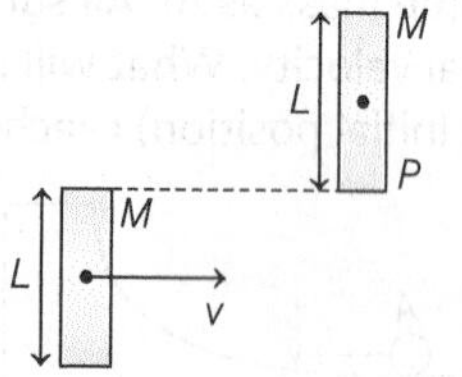

(a) $\frac{3v}{4L}$ clockwise (b) $\frac{4v}{3L}$ clockwise

(c) $\frac{3v}{4L}$ counter clockwise (d) $\frac{v}{L}$ counter clockwise

29 A solid sphere is rolling purely on a rough horizontal surface (coefficient of kinetic friction $= \mu$) with speed of centre $= u$. It collides inelastically with a smooth vertical wall at a certain moment, the coefficient of restitution being 1/2. The sphere will begin pure rolling after a time

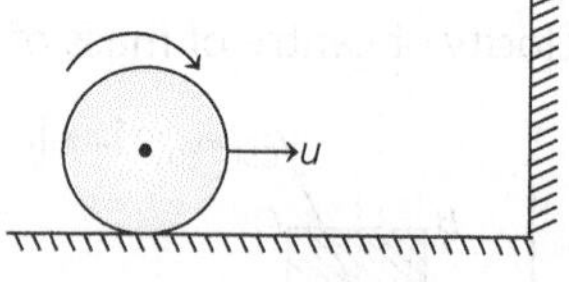

(a) $\frac{3u}{7\mu g}$ (b) $\frac{2u}{7\mu g}$

(c) $\frac{3u}{5\mu g}$ (d) $\frac{2u}{5\mu g}$

30 A reeled carpet of radius R is gently pushed. If it rolls without sliding and unreels, the speed of the centre of mass of the rolling portion when its radius is halved is (Neglect the vertical motion of the centre of mass)

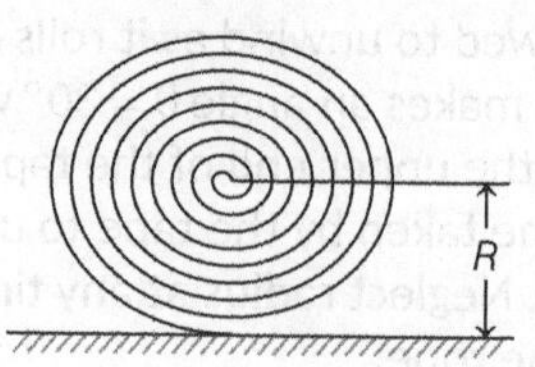

(a) $\sqrt{\frac{7}{3}gR}$ (b) $\sqrt{\frac{14}{3}gR}$

(c) $\sqrt{\frac{8gR}{3}}$ (d) $\sqrt{\frac{5gR}{3}}$

31 A bullet of mass m moving with velocity u just grazes the top of a solid cylinder of mass m and radius R resting on a rough horizontal surface as shown in figure. Assuming that the cylinder rolls without slipping, then the final velocity of bullet is

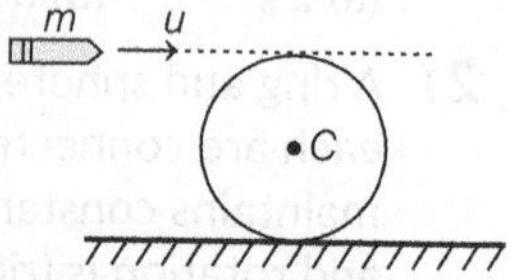

(a) $\frac{8u}{11}$ (b) $\frac{7u}{17}$ (c) $\frac{5u}{12}$ (d) $\frac{9u}{13}$

32 A time varying force $F = 2t$ is applied on a spool rolling as shown in figure. The angular momentum of the spool at time t about bottom-most point is

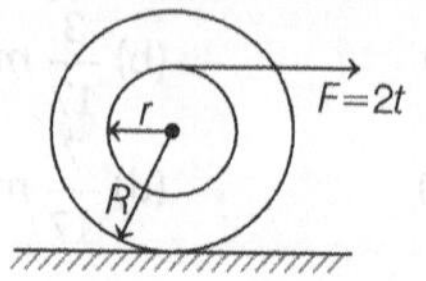

(a) $\frac{r^2t^2}{R}$ (b) $\frac{(R+r)^2t^2}{r}$

(c) $(R+r)t^2$ (d) insufficient data

Multiple Choice(s) Correct Questions

1 In the figure shown, the plank is being pulled to the right with a constant speed v. If the cylinder does not slip, then

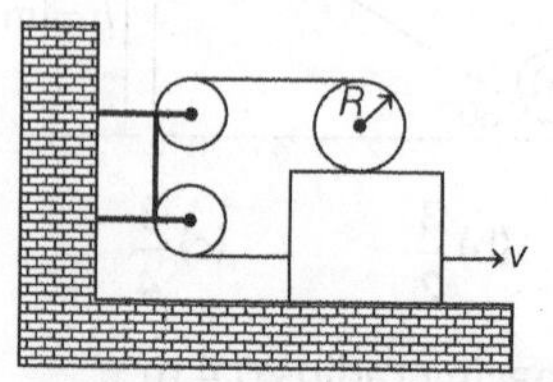

(a) the speed of the centre of mass of the cylinder is $2v$

(b) the speed of the centre of mass of the cylinder is zero

(c) the angular velocity of the cylinder is $\frac{v}{R}$

(d) the angular velocity of the cylinder is zero

2 A wheel is rolling without slipping on a horizontal plane with velocity v and acceleration a as shown in figure. Acceleration at

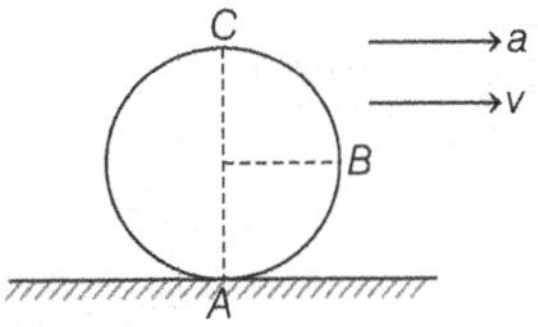

(a) A is vertically upwards
(b) B may be vertically downwards
(c) C cannot be horizontal.
(d) a point on the rim may be horizontally leftward.

3 On a uniform solid sphere lying on a horizontal surface a force F is applied at a height of $\frac{R}{2}$ from the centre of mass. There is no slipping anywhere.

(a) The acceleration of the centre of mass of the sphere is $\frac{15F}{14M}$.
(b) The acceleration of a point at the top of the sphere is $\frac{15F}{14M}$.
(c) Frictional force acting on the sphere is $\frac{F}{14}$ in the forward direction.
(d) Frictional force acting on the sphere is $\frac{F}{14}$ in the backward direction.

4 A spool is pulled horizontally on rough surface by two equal and opposite forces as shown in the figure. Select correct statement(s).

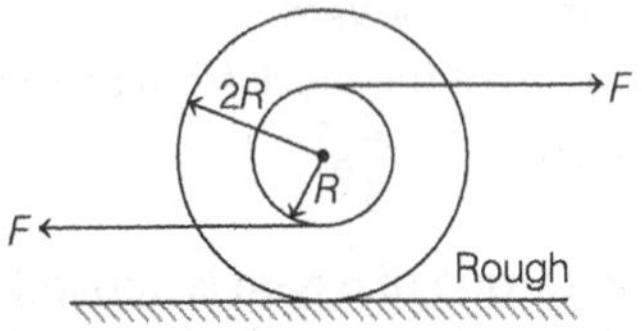

(a) Frictional force acts rightward.
(b) Frictional force acts leftward.
(c) The centre of mass remains stationary.
(d) The centre of mass moves towards right.

5 A disc of circumference s is at rest at a point A on a horizontal surface when a constant horizontal force begins to act on its centre. Between A and B, there is sufficient friction to prevent slipping and the surface is smooth to the right of B. $AB = s$. The disc moves from A to B in time T. To the right of B,

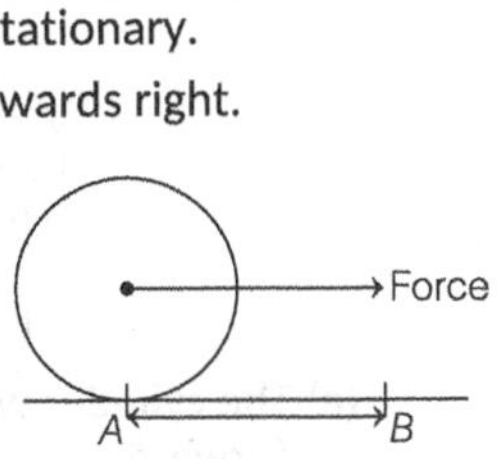

(a) the angular acceleration of the disc will disappear, linear acceleration will remain unchanged
(b) linear acceleration of the disc will increase
(c) the disc will make one rotation in time $\frac{T}{2}$
(d) the disc will cover a distance greater than s in further time T.

6 A hollow cylinder, a spherical shell, a solid cylinder and a solid sphere are allowed to roll on an inclined rough surface of coefficient of friction μ and inclination θ. The correct statements are

(a) if hollow cylinder can roll on inclined plane, all other objects will also roll.
(b) if all the objects are rolling and have same mass, the KE of all the objects will be same at the bottom of inclined plane.
(c) work done by the frictional force will be zero, if objects are rolling.
(d) frictional force will be equal for all the objects, if having same mass.

7 A ring rolls without slipping on a horizontal surface. At any instant, its position is as shown in the figure. Choose the CORRECT statement(s).

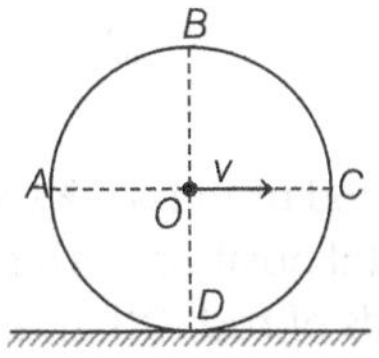

(a) Section ABC has greater kinetic energy than section ADC.
(b) Section BC has greater kinetic energy than section CD.
(c) Section BC has the same kinetic energy as section DA.
(d) The sections AB, BC, CD and DA have the same kinetic energy.

8 A solid sphere of mass m is released on the plank of mass M which lies on an inclined plane of inclination θ as shown in figure. There is sufficient friction force between sphere and plank.

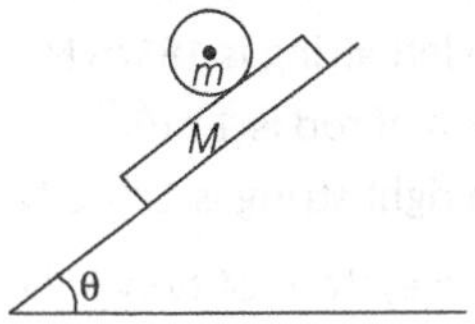

(a) The minimum value of μ so that the plank remains at rest is $\frac{7M + 2m}{7(M + m)} \tan\theta$.

(b) If the plank is at rest, frictional force between sphere and plank is $\frac{2}{7}$ $mg \sin\theta$.

(c) If there is no friction between the plank and inclined plane, then acceleration of plank is less than $g \sin\theta$.

(d) If there is no friction between plank and inclined plane, then friction force on this sphere is zero.

9 A disc is given an angular speed ω_0 and released from a certain height (as shown in figure). Motion of disc is observed after collision with the rough surface. Velocity of centre of mass of ball and direction of ω is shown in figure after the collision. Mark possible path(s), disc cannot follow after the collision.

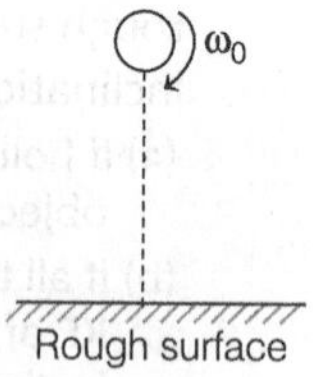

(a) 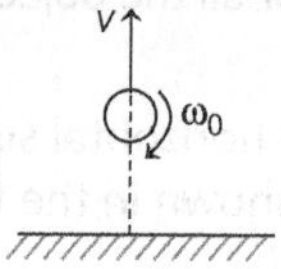

(b) 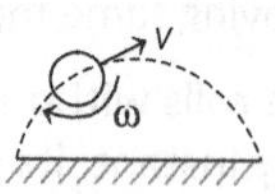

(c) 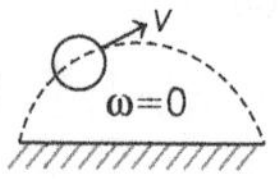

(d) 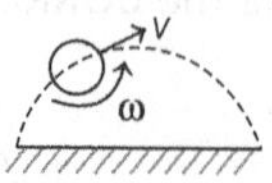

10 A thin uniform rod of mass 5 kg and length 1m is held in horizontal position with the help of strings attached to ends of rod. Other ends of strings are held by some external agent. Now, end *A* is pulled down with speed $v_A = 3t$ and end *B* is pulled down with speed $v_B = t$, where *t* is time in s. Choose the correct choice (s) at time $t = 0$

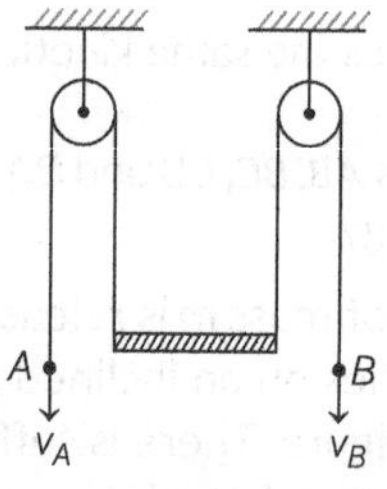

(a) Angular acceleration of rod is 2 rad/s^2

(b) Tension in left string is 185/6 N

(c) Acceleration of rod is 1 m/s^2

(d) Tension in right string is 170/3 N

11 Figure shows a system of two pulleys. Block of mass *m* is suspended from the pulley *P* which is fixed by a frictionless bearing. As the mass *m* desends string *AB* winds on the pulley *P*. The block starts from rest with a constant acceleration of 4.75 m/s^2. String in the section *AB* is parallel to the incline. Choose the correct option(s) after 4 s of the motion. (Assume no slipping every where)

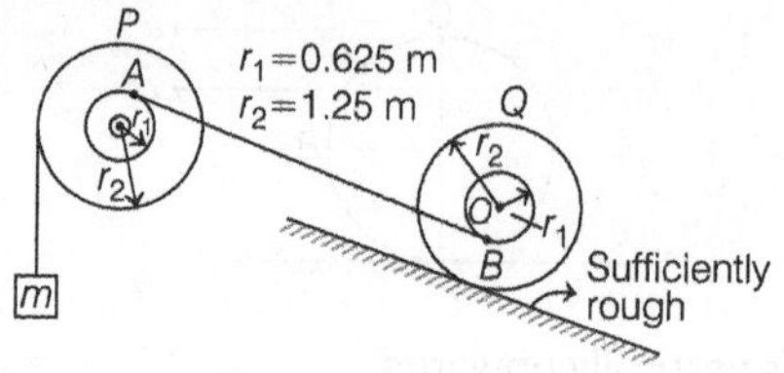

(a) Velocity of *B* is 9.5 m/s

(b) Velocity of centre O is 19 m/s

(c) Acceleration of centre O is 4.75 m/s^2

(d) Work done by friction by the incline on pulley Q is negative.

12 A disc of mass *M*, radius *R* has massless string wrapped over it, the other end of the string connects a block of mass *M* as shown. Initially, the system was at rest. If released, no slipping takes place at any contact surface. Immediately after system is released, mark the correct options.

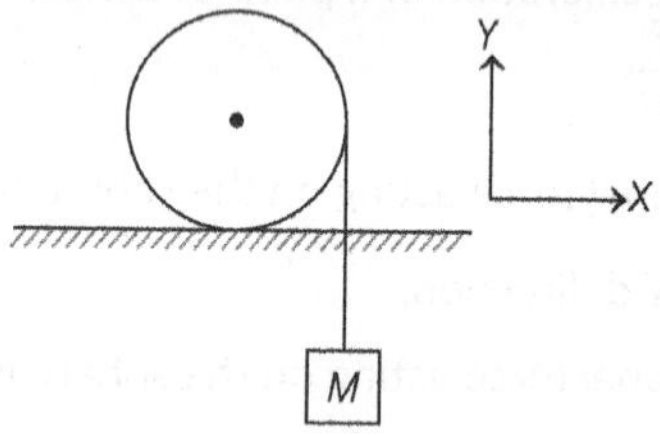

(a) Tension in the string is $\frac{3Mg}{5}$

(B) Acceleration of the block is $+\frac{2}{5}g\hat{i} - \frac{2}{5}g\hat{j}$

(c) The disc moves forward

(d) Acceleration of the block from centre of mass frame of the system is $-\frac{2}{5}g\hat{j}$

13 A clockwise torque of 6 N-m is applied to the circular solid cylinder as shown in the figure. There is no friction between the cylinder and the block. Mark the CORRECT statement (s)

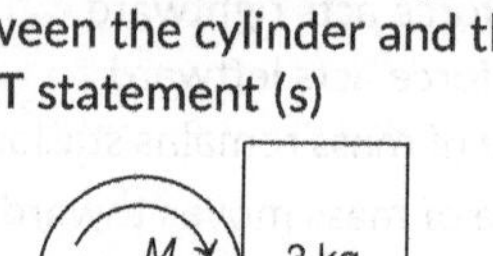

(a) The cylinder will slip but the system does not move forward.

(b) The system cannot move forward for any torque applied to the cylinder.

(c) The acceleration of the system will be 1m/s^2 forward.

(d) The angular acceleration of the cylinder is 10 rad/s^2.

14 A disc of mass $m = 1$ kg and radius $r = 1$ m is hanging from the roof with a light rod of length $L = 2$ m as shown in the figure. Disc can rotate freely about hinge point C and rod can also rotate freely about hinge point O. At the given instant angular velocity $\omega_1 = 2$ rad/s and $\omega_2 = 4$ rad/s, then

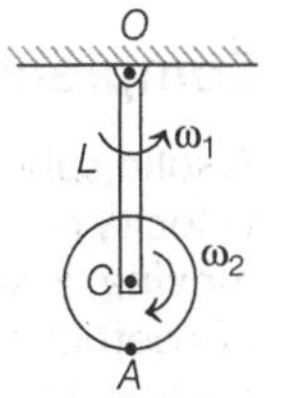

(a) total energy of the disc is 12 J.
(b) the magnitude of total angular momentum of the disc about hinge point O is 6 kg- m^2/s.
(c) the magnitude of the angular momentum of the disc about a point A on the disc is 6 kg-m^2/s.
(d) the magnitude of the angular momentum of the disc about point C is 2 kg-m^2/s.

15 A uniform rod of length l and mass $2m$ rests on a smooth horizontal table. A point mass m moving horizontally at right angle to the rod with velocity v collides with one end of the rod and sticks to it, then

(a) angular velocity of the system after collision is $\frac{v}{l}$.
(b) angular velocity of the system after collision is $\frac{v}{2l}$.
(c) the loss in kinetic energy of the system as a whole as a result of the collision is $\frac{mv^2}{6}$.
(d) the loss in kinetic energy of the system as a whole as a result of the collision is $\frac{7mv^2}{24}$.

16 A smooth rod AC of length l and mass m is kept on a horizontal smooth plane. It is free to rotate and move. A particle of same mass m moving on the plane with velocity v strikes rod at point B making angle 37° with the rod. The collision is elastic. After collision,

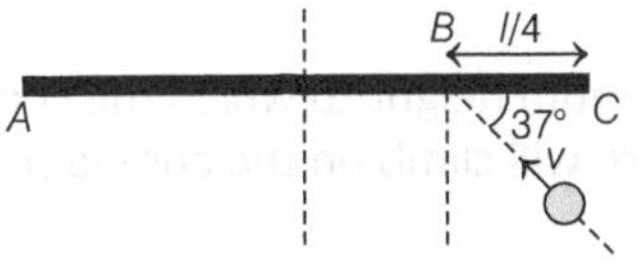

(a) the angular velocity of the rod will be $\frac{72}{55}\frac{v}{l}$
(b) impulse of the impact force is $\frac{24mv}{55}$
(c) the centre of the rod will travel a distance $\frac{\pi l}{3}$ in the time in which it makes half rotation
(d) None of the above

17. Two particles A and B, of mass m each, are joined by a rigid massless rod of length l. A particle P of mass m, moving with a speed u normal to AB, strikes A and sticks to it. The centre of mass of the $A + B + P$ system is C.

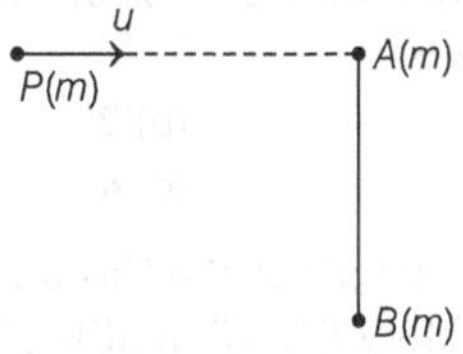

(a) The velocity of C before impact is $\frac{u}{3}$
(b) The velocity of C after impact is $\frac{u}{3}$
(c) The velocity of $A + P$ immediately after impact is $\frac{u}{2}$.
(d) The velocity of B immediately after impact is zero.

18. A wheel (to be considered as a ring) of mass m and radius R rolls without sliding on a horizontal surface with constant velocity v. It encounters a step of height $\frac{R}{2}$ at which it ascends without sliding.

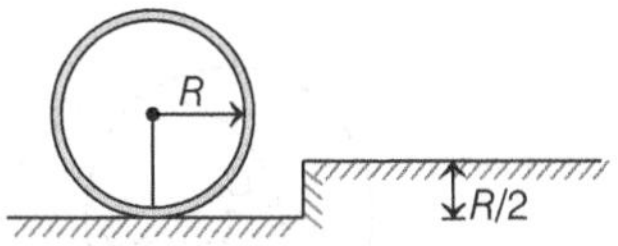

(a) The angular velocity of the ring just after it comes in contact with the step is $\frac{3v}{4R}$
(b) The normal reaction due to the step on the wheel just after the impact is $\frac{mg}{2} - \frac{9mv^2}{16R}$
(c) The normal reaction due to the step on the wheel increases as the wheel ascends
(d) The friction will be absent during the ascent.

Comprehension Based Questions

Comprehension-1

Figure shows a uniform smooth solid cylinder A of radius 4m rolling without slipping on the 8 kg plank which in turn, is supported by a fixed smooth surface. Block B is known to accelerate down with 6 m/s^2 and block C moves down with acceleration 2 m/s^2.

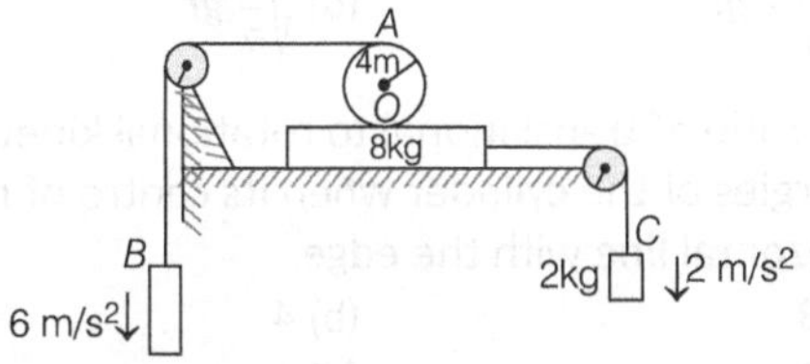

1 What is the angular acceleration of the cylinder ?
(a) 0.8 rad/s^2 (b) 1.2 rad/s^2
(c) 2 rad/s^2 (d) 1 rad/s^2

2 What is the ratio of the mass of the cylinder to the mass of block *B*?
(a) 1 (b) 2
(c) 3 (d) 4

3 If unwrapped length of the thread between the cylinder and block *B* is 20 m at the beginning, when the system was released from rest, what would it be 2 s later?
(a) 28 m (b) 30 m
(c) 22 m (d) 32.5 m

Comprehension-2

A rectangular rigid fixed block has a long horizontal edge. A solid homogeneous cylinder of radius *r* is placed horizontally at rest with its length parallel to the edge such that the axis of the cylinder and the edge of the block are in the same vertical plane. There is sufficient friction present at the edge, so that a very small displacement causes the cylinder to roll-off the edge without slipping. Determine

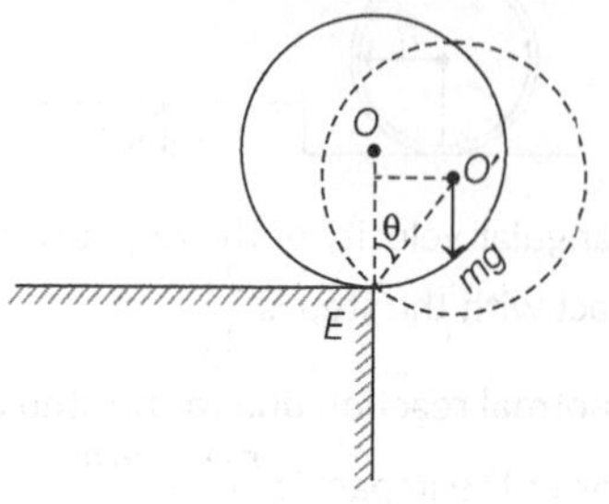

4 The angle θ_c through which the cylinder rotates before it leaves contact with the edge.
(a) $\cos^{-1}\frac{2}{7}$ (b) $\cos^{-1}\frac{3}{7}$
(c) $\cos^{-1}\frac{4}{7}$ (d) $\cos^{-1}\frac{6}{7}$

5 The speed of the centre of mass of the cylinder before leaving contact with the edge.
(a) $\sqrt{\frac{20}{21}gr}$ (b) $\sqrt{\frac{16}{21}gr}$
(c) $\sqrt{\frac{4}{7}gr}$ (d) $\sqrt{\frac{3}{7}gr}$

6 The ratio of translational to rotational kinetic energies of the cylinder when its centre of mass is in horizontal line with the edge.
(a) 3 (b) 4
(c) 5 (d) 6

Comprehension-3

A solid sphere has linear velocity $v_0 = 4$ m/s and angular velocity $\omega_0 = 9$ rad/s as shown. Ground on which it is moving, is smooth. It collides elastically with a rough wall of coefficient of friction μ. Radius of the sphere is 1 m and mass is 2 kg.

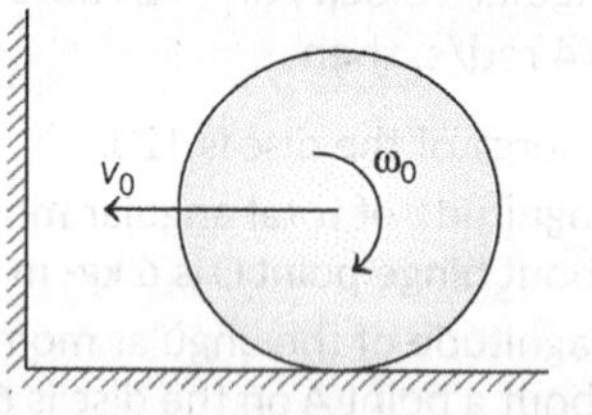

7. If the sphere after colliding with the wall rolls without slipping in opposite direction, then coefficient of friction μ is
(a) $\frac{1}{2}$ (b) $\frac{2}{3}$
(c) $\frac{1}{3}$ (d) $\frac{1}{4}$

8 What is net linear impulse imparted by the wall on the sphere during impact ?
(a) $\sqrt{32}$ N-s (b) $4\sqrt{17}$ N-s
(c) $4\sqrt{5}$ N-s (d) $15\sqrt{2}$ N-s

Comprehension-4

A wedge of mass 4*m* is placed at rest on a smooth horizontal surface. A uniform solid sphere of mass *m* and radius *r* is placed at rest on the flat portion of the wedge at the point *Q* as shown in the figure. A sharp horizontal impulse *P* is given to the sphere at a point below $h = 0.4r$ from the centre of the sphere. The radius of curvature of the curved portion of the wedge is *R*. All surfaces are smooth.

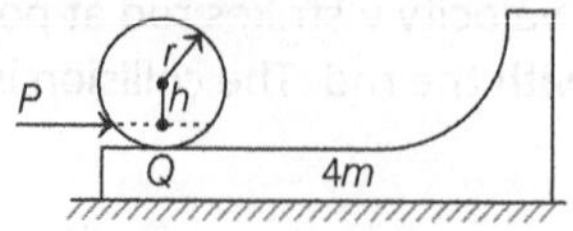

9 The maximum height to which the centre of mass of the sphere will climb on the curved portion of the wedge is
(a) $\frac{2P^2}{5m^2g}$ (b) $\frac{P^2}{5m^2g}$
(c) $\frac{P^2}{2m^2g}$ (d) None of these

10 Kinetic energy of the system when sphere is at the highest point is
(a) $\frac{P^2}{10m}$ (b) $\frac{P^2}{5m}$ (c) $\frac{3P^2}{10m}$ (d) $\frac{3P^2}{5m}$

11 Speed of the wedge when sphere reaches the flat portion again

(a) $\frac{2P}{5m}$ (b) $\frac{3P}{5m}$ (c) $\frac{8P}{5m}$ (d) $\frac{P}{5m}$

Comprehension-5

The system described in figure is composed of a wheel of mass M and radius R, a massless rope which is wrapped at one end around the wheel and is connected at the other end to a block of mass m. The block is placed on a slanted plane with a lift angle θ, and the rope is passed over a massless pulley connected to the higher end of the incline. Initially, the system is held at rest.

As the system is released the block remains at rest, while the wheel unwraps the rope while rolling down. The wheel is made up of five identical rods of length R which are connected at the centre of the wheel and distributed evenly over its massless circumference.

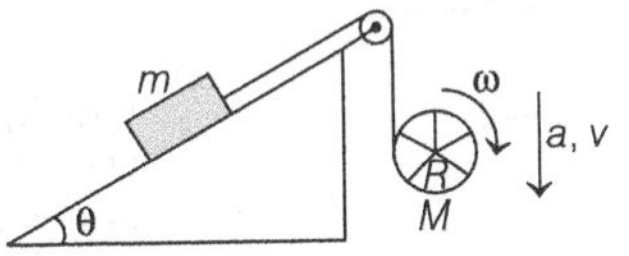

12 The angular acceleration of the wheel is

(a) $\frac{3g}{4R}$ (b) $\frac{4g}{3R}$

(c) $\frac{2g}{3R}$ (d) $\frac{3g}{2R}$

13 The mass of the block is

(a) $\frac{M}{\sin\theta}$ (b) $\frac{M}{2\sin\theta}$ (c) $\frac{M}{3\sin\theta}$ (d) $\frac{M}{4\sin\theta}$

14 The initial acceleration of the centre of mass of wheel is

(a) zero (b) $\frac{3g}{4}$

(c) $\frac{4g}{3}$ (d) None of these

Comprehension-6

A thin rod of length L is falling freely in horizontal position from a height H above the surface of the table, in such a way that the end of the rod just hits the edge of the table. This collision is instantaneous and totally elastic.

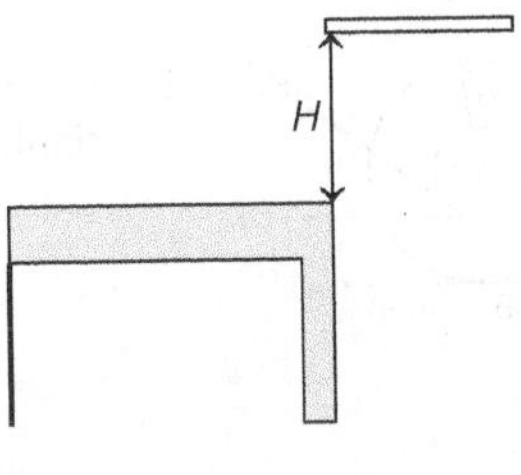

15 At what time after the collision does the rod perform a whole revolution?

(a) $\frac{2\pi}{3\sqrt{2gH}}L$ (b) $\frac{3\pi}{2\sqrt{2gH}}L$

(c) $\frac{3\pi}{2\sqrt{gH}}L$ (d) $\frac{\pi}{2\sqrt{gH}}L$

16 In the above question, where is its centre of mass of the rod at that moment from the level of table?

(a) $\frac{\pi}{2}L\left(1+\frac{\pi}{3}\frac{L}{H}\right)$ (b) $\frac{\pi}{2}L\left(1+\frac{3\pi}{2}\frac{L}{H}\right)$

(c) $\pi L\left(2+\frac{\pi}{3}\frac{L}{H}\right)$ (d) $\frac{\pi}{3}L\left(1+\frac{\pi}{3}\frac{L}{H}\right)$

Comprehension-7

A ring of masss m and radius r is projected with velocity v_0 while spinning with angular velocity $\frac{v_0}{4r}$ at the bottom of an inclined plane of angle of inclination $\theta = 60°$ as shown in figure. The ring begins to roll without slipping after colliding with the inclined plane. Before collision, sense of rotation is depicted in the figure.

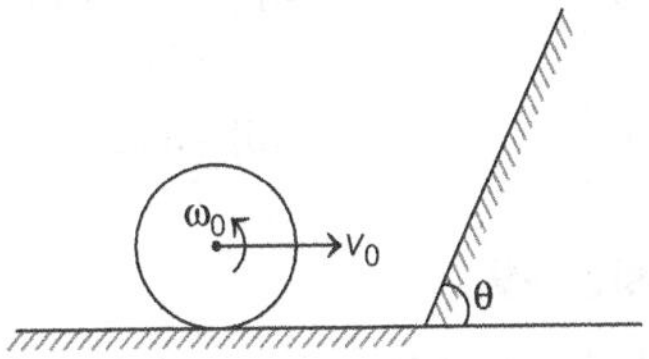

17 Velocity of centre of mass of the ring just after the collision is

(a) v_0 (b) $\frac{v_0}{2}$ (c) $\frac{v_0}{4}$ (d) $\frac{v_0}{8}$

18 Loss of kinetic energy of ring during collision is

(a) $\frac{9}{32}mv_0^2$ (b) $\frac{33}{64}mv_0^2$ (c) $\frac{1}{2}mv_0^2$ (d) zero

19 If the ring after collision rolling up the incline, then maximum height attained by it is

(a) $\frac{v_0^2}{2g}$ (b) $\frac{v_0^2}{128g}$ (c) $\frac{v_0^2}{64g}$ (d) $\frac{v_0^2}{32g}$

Comprehension-8

A uniform slender rod of mass $2m$ and length L is lying on a frictionless horizontal surface. Two insects, of mass m each, moving horizontally with velocities v and $2v$ hit the rod simultaneously and symmetrically and stick to it. The initial velocities of the insects are perpendicular to the rod, as shown.

The distance of each insect's hit-point from the centre of the rod is $L/6$. Just after hitting the rod, each insect starts walking along the rod, away from its centre, with constant speed $=v$ relative to the rod. As the rod rotates and moves, the insects finally reach the ends.

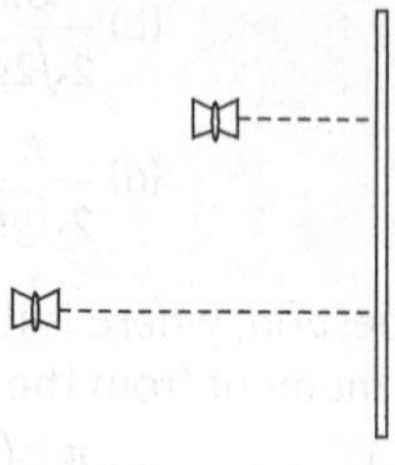

20 The angular velocity of the rod immediately after the insects stick to the rod is

(a) $\frac{3v}{4L}$ (b) $\frac{3v}{2L}$ (c) $\frac{v}{2L}$ (d) $\frac{3v}{8L}$

21 The angular velocity of the rod when insects reach the ends of the rod is

(a) $\frac{v}{4L}$ (b) $\frac{v}{2L}$ (c) $\frac{v}{3L}$ (d) $\frac{v}{8L}$

22 The angle rotated by the rod till the insects reach the ends is

(a) $\frac{\pi}{6\sqrt{3}}$ rad (b) $\frac{\pi}{12\sqrt{3}}$ rad

(c) $\frac{\pi}{2\sqrt{3}}$ rad (d) $\frac{\pi}{3}$ rad

Comprehension-9

A spherical ball of mass M moving with initial velocity v collides elastically with another ball of mass M, which is fixed at one end of L-shaped rigid massless frame as shown in figure (a). The L-shaped frame contains another mass M connected at the other end.

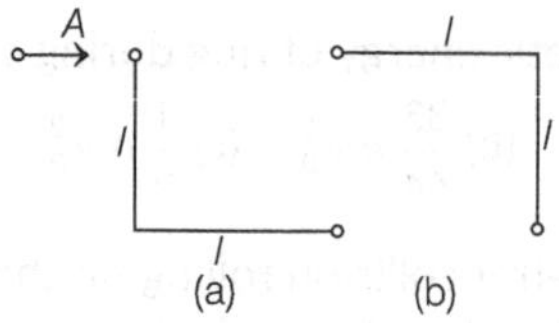

23 The speed of the striking mass after collision is

(a) $\frac{v}{2}$ backwards (b) 0

(c) $\frac{v}{3}$ in same direction (d) $\frac{v}{7}$ backwards

24 How soon will the frame come to the orientation shown in figure (b) after collision?

(a) $\frac{\pi l}{4v}$ (b) $\frac{7\pi l}{2v}$

(c) $\frac{2\pi l}{v}$ (d) $\frac{7\pi l}{4v}$

Match The Columns Questions

1 Four different situations of a moving disc are shown in Column I and predictions about its final motion and forces acting on it are given in Column II.

Column I	Column II
A. 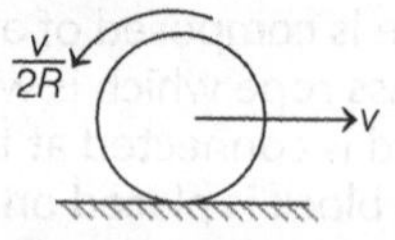	P. Finally, disc will roll along the initial direction of velocity v.
B. 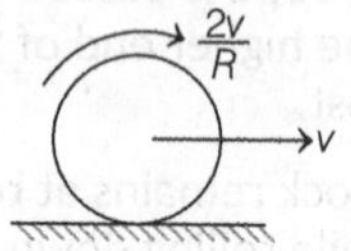	Q. Finally, disc will roll in direction opposite to the initial direction of velocity v.
C. 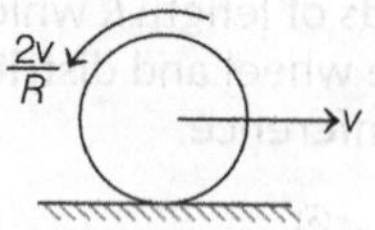	R. Finally, disc stops
D. 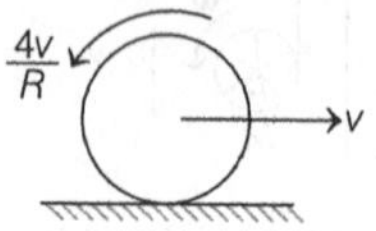	S. Initially, friction force acts in the direction opposite to that of initial velocity.
	T. None of these

2 A yo-yo is resting on a perfectly rough horizontal table. Forces F_1, F_2, F_3 and F_4 are applied separately as shown.

Column I	Column II
A. 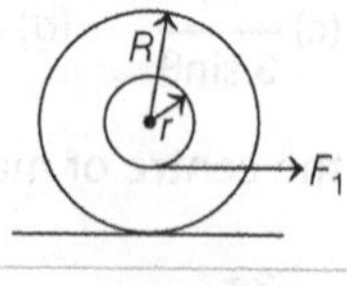	P. Centre of mass accelerates towards left.
B. 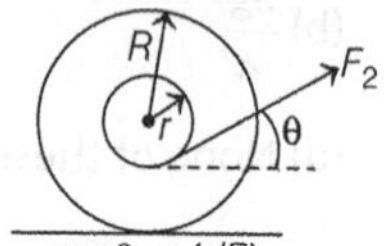 $\cos\theta < (r/R)$	Q. Centre of mass accelerates towards right.
C. 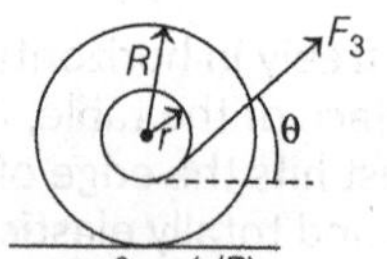 $\cos\theta < (r/R)$	R. Friction acts towards left.
D. 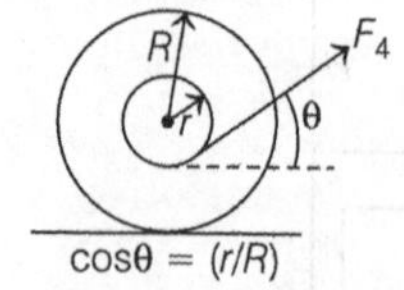 $\cos\theta = (r/R)$	S. Friction acts towards right.

3 Body X may be a solid or hollow cylinder, solid or hollow sphere (each of mass m and radius R). It is placed on a horizontal smooth platform P, in a carriage moving with acceleration a horizontal leftwards. If platform P is gently removed, body X rolls down along the rough vertical wall of the carriage.

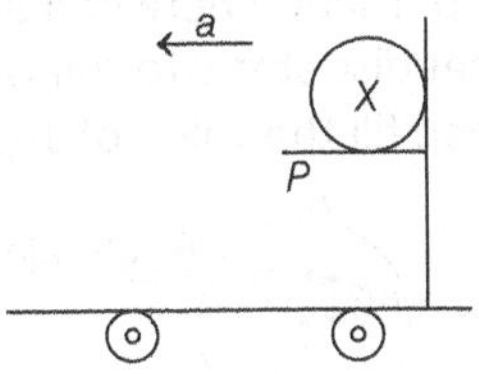

	Column I		Column II
A.	X is hollow cylinder.	P.	Downward acceleration (w.r.t. to carriage) = $5g/7$
B.	X is solid cylinder.	Q.	Downward acceleration (w.r.t to carriage) = $g/2$
C.	X is hollow sphere.	R.	Static friction = $mg/3$
D.	X is solid sphere.	S.	Static friction = $2mg/5$

4 A hollow sphere, ring, disc, solid sphere and solid cylinder are released from rest on an inclined plane of inclination 37°. ($\tan 37° = 3/4$ and $g = 10\ m/s^2$). The co-efficient of friction between body and surface is μ. Mass of each body is 1 kg and radius 1 m. Then, match the column.

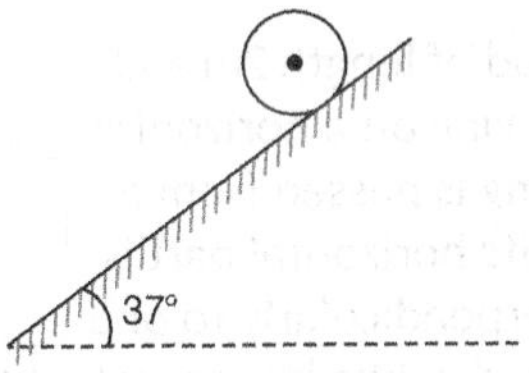

	Column I		Column II
A.	If $\mu = 0.2$, then acceleration is maximum for	P.	ring
B.	If $\mu = 0.3$, then there is no work done by friction	Q.	disc
C.	If $\mu = 0.2$, then pure rolling does not take place for	R.	hollow sphere
D.	If $\mu = 0.5$, then maximum friction force is acting on	S.	solid sphere
		T.	solid cylinder

5 Match the following

	Column I		Column II
A.	A ring of mass m is projected on rough horizontal plane with velocity v_0. The magnitude of work done by frictional force to start rolling. 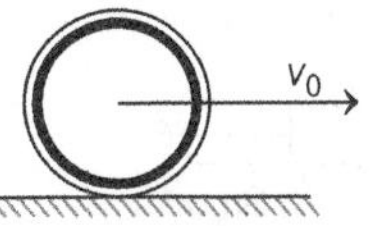	P.	$\frac{1}{3}mv_0^2$
B.	Kinetic energy of pivoted rod of mass m, velocity of centre of mass is v_0. 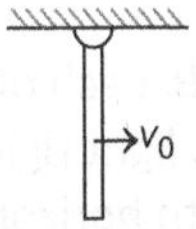	Q.	$\frac{1}{8}mv_0^2$
C.	Kinetic energy of translation of a smooth rod of mass m, where velocity of one end is v_0. 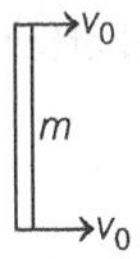	R.	$\frac{1}{4}mv_0^2$
D.	Kinetic energy of a rod of mass m, as shown in figure. 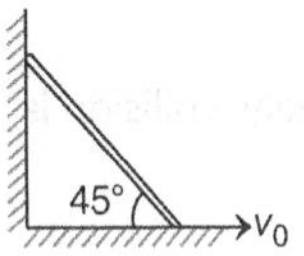	S.	$\frac{2}{3}mv_0^2$
		T.	$\frac{1}{9}mv_0^2$

6 In Column I, certain situations are depicted. In all cases, there is a cylinder on a rough plank. Assume friction is sufficient for pure rolling. Match with appropriate descriptions in column II. The mass of cylinder is equal to that of plank.

	Column I		Column II
A.	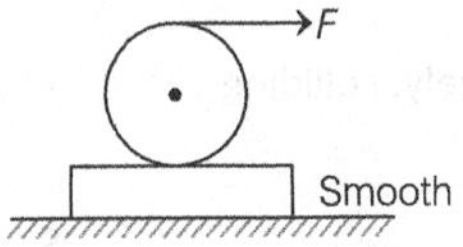	P.	Plank accelerates to the left.
B.	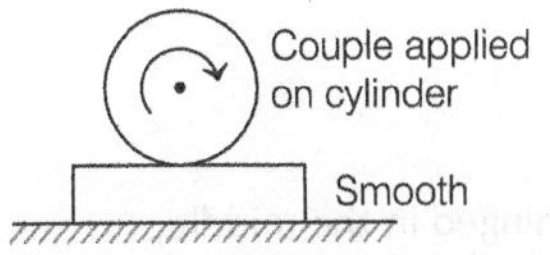	Q.	Friction on cylinder is towards right.

Column I	Column II
C. 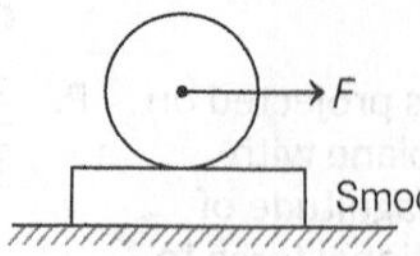	R. Friction on cylinder is in direction opposite to its acceleration.
D. 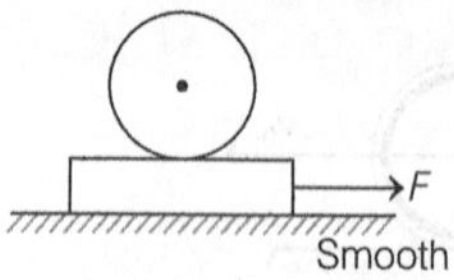	S. The acceleration of cylinder is greater in magnitude than that of the plank.
	T. Acceleration of cylinder is towards right.

7 Two small balls A and B, each of mass m, are joined rigidly to the ends of a light rigid rod of length l. The system lies on a smooth horizontal table. A particle of same mass moving with speed u perpendicularly to rod on the table strikes particle B, as shown, consider the following four situations and find the angular velocity ω of rod after collision.

Column I	Column II
A. 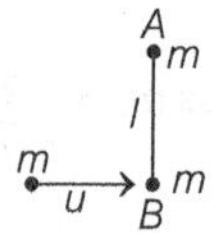 Rod AB lies freely, collision is elastic.	P. $\omega = \dfrac{u}{l}$
B. 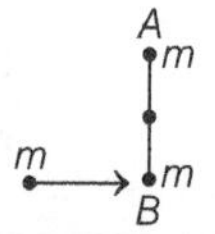 Rod AB is hinged in the middle, collision is elastic.	Q. $\omega = \dfrac{u}{2l}$
C. 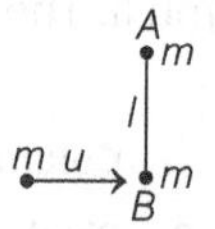 Rod AB lies freely, colliding particle sticks.	R. $\omega = \dfrac{4u}{3l}$
D. 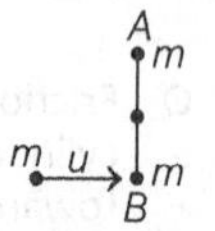 Rod AB is hinged in the middle, colliding particle sticks.	S. $\omega = \dfrac{2u}{3l}$

Numerical Value Questions

1 A disc of mass M and radius R is placed on a rough horizontal surface. A light rod of length $2R$ is fixed to the disc at point A as shown in the figure and force $\dfrac{3Mg}{2}$ is applied at the other end. The minimum value of coefficient of friction between disc and horizontal surface, so that disc starts to roll without slipping is given by μ, then fill the value of 10μ in OMR sheet.

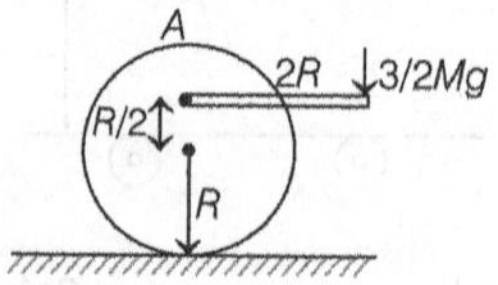

2 A box of mass 1 kg is mounted with two cylinders each of mass 1 kg, moment of inertia 0.5 kg m^2 and radius 1 m as shown in figure. Cylinders are mounted on their central axis of rotation and this system is placed on a rough horizontal surface. The rear cylinder is connected to battery operated motor which provides a torque of 100 N-m to this cylinder via a belt as shown. If sufficient friction is present between cylinder and horizontal surface for pure rolling, then what is the acceleration (in m/s^2) of the vehicle? (Neglect mass of motor, belt and other accessories of vehicle).

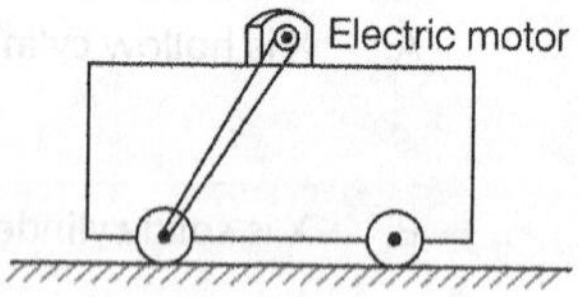

3 There is a rod of length 2m and mass 10 kg lying on a horizontal table. A string is passed from a pulley, and its horizontal part is attached perpendicularly to one end of the rod, while its vertical part is attached to a weight of mass 5 kg. Mass of pulley and friction are negligible. Initially, system is released from rest. What is angular acceleration (in rad/s^2) of rod at the initial moment ?

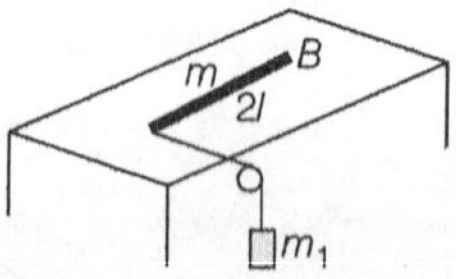

4 A uniform solid cylinder A of mass m_1 can freely rotate about a horizontal axis fixed to a mount of mass m_2. A constant horizontal force F is applied to the end K of a light thread tightly wound on the cylinder. The friction between the mount and the supporting horizontal plane is assumed to be absent. Take, $m_1 = m_2 = 5$ kg and $F = 10$ N. What is the acceleration (in m/s^2) of the point K?

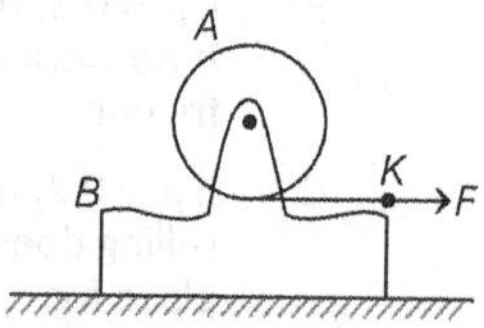

5 Inside a uniformly accelerating thin-walled spherical shell of radius $R = 1$ m, which is rolling on horizontal surface, there is a small body slipping around. Angle of friction between body and inner surface of sphere (i.e., angle between total reaction and normal) is 23°. The acceleration $a = 7.5\ \text{m/s}^2$ of the centre of sphere ensures that the small body stays at a fixed distance h from the surface. Find the value of h in cm.

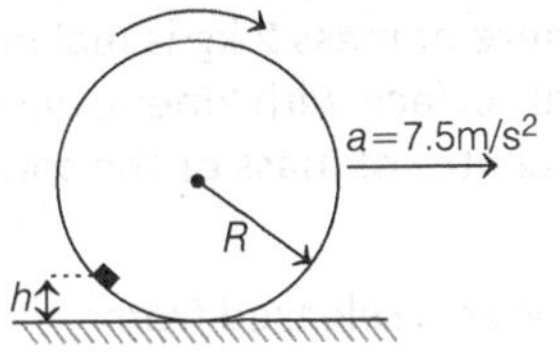

6 A uniform disc of mass 15 kg and radius 4 m, initially stands vertically on a horizontal plank of same mass and sufficient length L, so that the disc always remains over the plank, as shown. The plank rests on smooth horizontal floor and friction between disc and plank is sufficiently high such that disc rolls on plank without slipping. The plank is pulled to right and disc is pulled to left with constant horizontal force of magnitude 42 N each. The magnitude of work done by friction on the plank in time in which disc rotates by one revolution on plank is given by n J. Fill $(n + 300)$ in OMR sheet. (Take, $\pi = 22/7$)

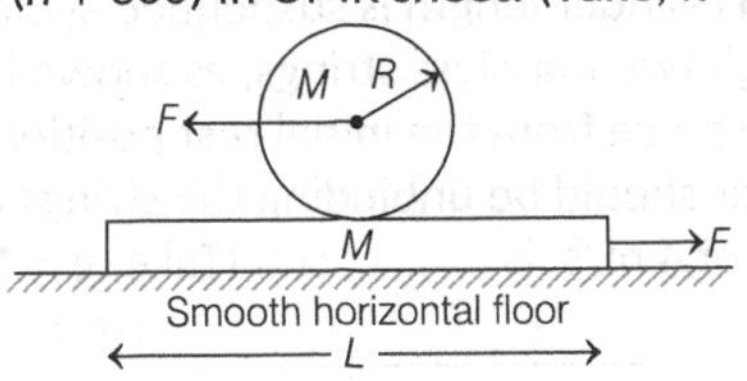

7 A solid sphere of mass m and radius R is rolling without slipping over a horizontal surface, with a velocity v_0. Subsequently, sphere climbs onto a curved surface of a wedge of mass M, which is initially at rest. Given that $M = 2m/3$ and there is no friction between the wedge and horizontal plane. But sufficient friction is present between the sphere and the curved surface of the wedge allowing pure rolling of the solid sphere. Find minimum value of v_0 (in m/s) for which the sphere can reach the top of the wedge. Take, $g = 10\ \text{m/s}^2$ and $h = 9$ m.

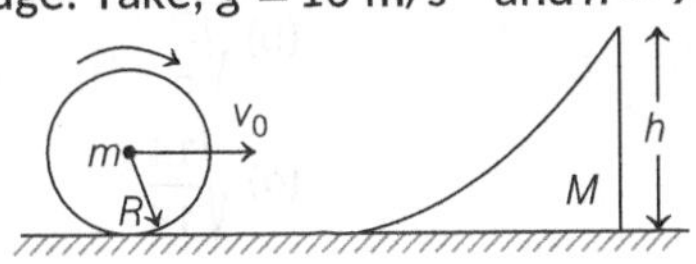

8 A uniform ring of mass m and radius R is performing uniform pure rolling motion on a horizontal surface. The velocity of the centre of the ring is v_0. If the kinetic energy of the semi-circular arc AOB is $mv_0^2\left(\frac{1}{\alpha} - \frac{\beta}{\pi}\right)$, then find the value of $\alpha + \beta$.

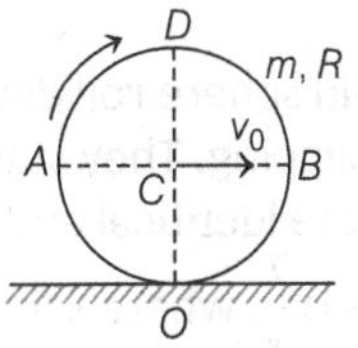

9 A small putty C of mass 1 kg moving with speed 8 m/s strikes to ball A of a dumb-bell and sticks to it as shown in figure. The dumb-bell consists of balls A (1 kg) and B (2 kg) joined by a rigid rod of mass 12 kg. The dumb-bell balls is to be treated as particles. How much thermal energy (in J) is produced ?

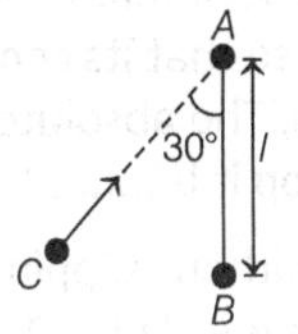

10 A long thin rod of length $l = 90$ cm and mass 600 g, is rotating clockwise on a frictionless horizontal table about its centre of mass, which is stationary. A small ball of mass 300 g is placed on the table at distance x from the centre of mass of the rod. The rod collides elastically with the ball. After the collision, the rod is translating to the left without rotating and the ball moves to the right. What is the distance x (in cm)?

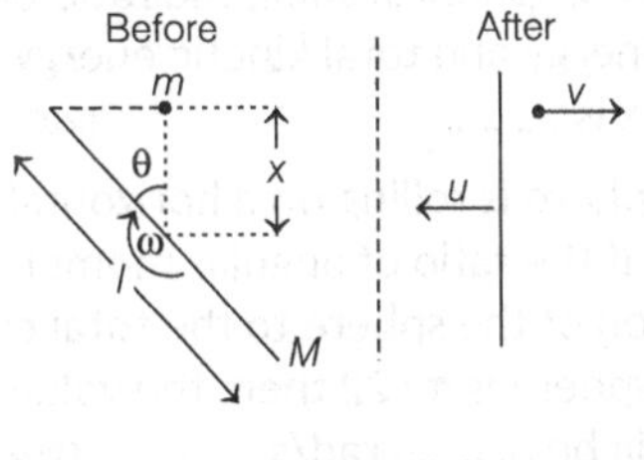

11 A uniform rod AB of mass M and length $\sqrt{2}R$ is moving in a vertical plane inside a hollow sphere of radius R. The sphere is rolling on a fixed horizontal surface without slipping with velocity of its centre $2v$. When the end B is at the lowest position, its speed is found to be v as shown in the figure. If the kinetic energy of the rod at this instant is $\frac{4}{K}Mv^2$.

Find K.

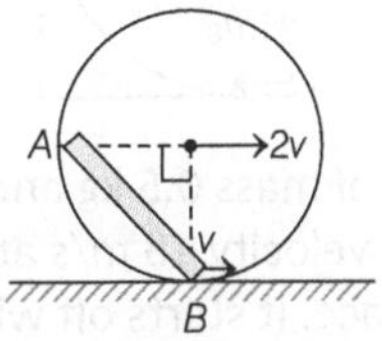

Previous Years Questions

JEE Main

1 A ring and a solid sphere roll down the same inclined plane without slipping. They start from rest. The radii of both bodies are identical and the ratio of their kinetic energies is $\frac{7}{x}$, where x is **[2024, 27 Jan Shift-II]**

2 A cylinder is rolling down on an inclined plane of inclination 60°. It's acceleration during rolling down will be $\frac{x}{\sqrt{3}}\ m/s^2$, where $x =$ ...... (use $g = 10\ m/s^2$). **[2024, 29 Jan Shift-I]**

3 A solid circular disc of mass 50 kg rolls along a horizontal floor, so that its center of mass has a speed of 0.4 m/s. The absolute value of work done on the disc to stop it is .... J. **[2024, 31 Jan Shift-I]**

4 A disc is rolling without slipping on a surface. The radius of the disc is R. At $t = 0$, the topmost point on the disc is A as shown in figure. When the disc completes half of its rotation, the displacement of point A from its initial position is **[2023, 13 April Shift-I]**

(a) $2R\sqrt{(1 + 4\pi^2)}$

(b) $R\sqrt{\pi^2 + 4}$

(c) $2R$

(d) $R\sqrt{\pi^2 + 1}$

5 For a rolling spherical shell, the ratio of rotational kinetic energy and total kinetic energy is $x/5$. The value of x is .... **[2023, 12 April Shift-I]**

6 A solid sphere is rolling on a horizontal plane without slipping. If the ratio of angular momentum about axis of rotation of the sphere to the total energy of moving sphere is $\pi : 22$ then, the value of its angular speed will be .... rad/s **[2023, 13 April Shift-I]**

7 A hollow spherical ball of uniform density rolls up a curved surface with an initial velocity 3 m/s (as shown in figure). Maximum height with respect to the initial position covered by it will be .... cm (take, $g = 10\ m/s^2$) **[2023, 8 April Shift-II]**

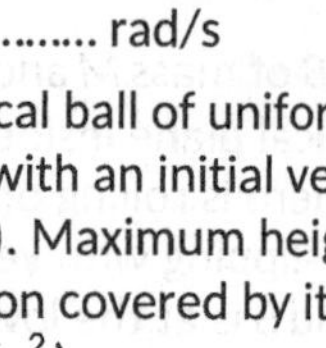

8 A uniform disc of mass 0.5 kg and radius r is projected with velocity 18 m/s at $t = 0$ s on a rough horizontal surface. It starts off with a purely sliding motion at $t = 0$ s. After 2 s it acquires a purely rolling motion (see figure). The total kinetic energy of the disc after 2 s will be .... J (given, coefficient of friction is 0.3 and $g = 10\ m/s^2$). **[2023, 30 Jan Shift-II]**

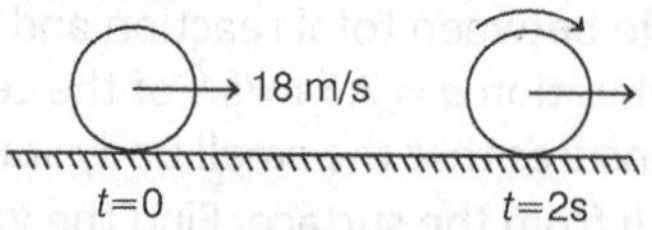

9 A solid sphere of mass 2 kg is making pure rolling on a horizontal surface with kinetic energy 2240 J. The velocity of centre of mass of the sphere will be .... ms^{-1}. **[2023, 29 Jan Shift-I]**

10 A solid cylinder is released from rest from the top of an inclined plane of inclination 30° and length 60 cm. If the cylinder rolls without slipping, its speed upon reaching the bottom of the inclined plane is .... ms^{-1}. (Given, $g = 10\ ms^{-2}$) **[2023, 1Feb Shift-I]**

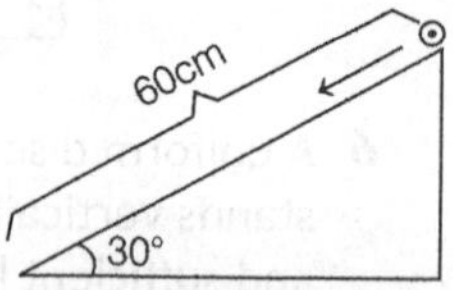

11 A solid sphere of mass 1 kg rolls without slipping on a plane surface. Its kinetic energy is 7×10^{-3} J. The speed of the centre of mass of the sphere is .... $cm\ s^{-1}$. **[2023, 31 Jan Shift-I]**

12 A solid cylinder length is suspended symmetrically through two massless strings, as shown in the figure. The distance from the initial rest position, the cylinder should be unbinding the strings to achieve a speed of 4 m/s, is .... cm. (Take, $g = 10\ m/s^2$). **[2022, 27 July Shift-II]**

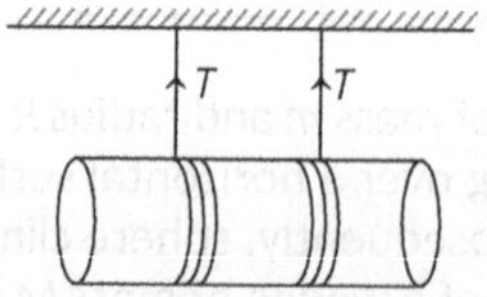

13 A solid cylinder and a solid sphere, having same mass M and radius R, roll down the same inclined plane from top without slipping. They start from rest. The ratio of velocity of the solid cylinder to that of the solid sphere, with which they reach the ground, will be **[2022, 25 July Shift-I]**

(a) $\sqrt{\frac{5}{3}}$ (b) $\sqrt{\frac{4}{5}}$

(c) $\sqrt{\frac{3}{5}}$ (d) $\sqrt{\frac{14}{15}}$

14 The centre of a wheel rolling on a plane surface moves with a speed v_0. A particle on the rim of the wheel at the same level as the centre will be moving at a speed $\sqrt{x}\, v_0$. Then, the value of x is .... **[2021, 22 July Shift-II]**

15 Consider a situation in which a ring, a solid cylinder and a solid sphere roll down on the same inclined plane without slipping. Assume that they start rolling from rest and having identical diameter.

The correct statement for this situation.
[2021, 22 July Shift-II]

(a) The sphere has the greatest and the ring has the least velocity of the centre of mass at the bottom of the inclined plane.
(b) The ring has the greatest and the cylinder has the least velocity of the centre of mass at the bottom of the inclined plane.
(c) All of them will have same velocity.
(d) The cylinder has the greatest and the sphere has the least velocity of the centre of mass at the bottom of the inclined plane.

16 A body rolls down an inclined plane without slipping. The kinetic energy of rotation is 50% of its translational kinetic energy. The body is
[2021, 20 July Shift-II]

(a) solid sphere
(b) solid cylinder
(c) hollow cylinder
(d) ring

JEE Advanced

1 An annular disk of mass M, inner radius a and outer radius b is placed on a horizontal surface with coefficient of friction μ, as shown in the figure.

At some time, an impulse $J_0\,\hat{\mathbf{x}}$ is applied at a height h above the centre of the disk. If $h = h_m$, then the disk rolls without slipping along the X-axis. Which of the following statement(s) is(are) correct? **(2023)**

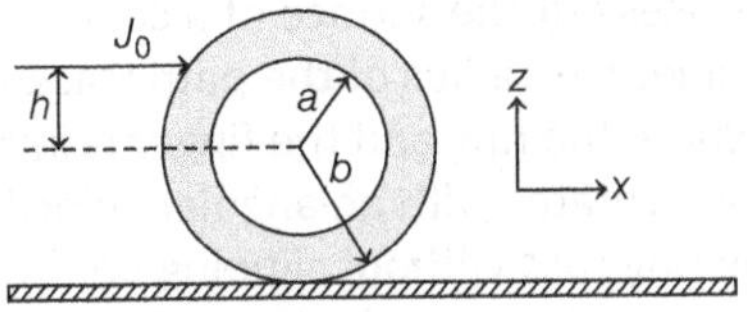

(a) For $\mu \neq 0$ and $a \to 0$, $h_m = b/2$.
(b) For $\mu \neq 0$ and $a \to b$, $h_m = b$.
(c) For $h = h_m$ the initial angular velocity does not depend on the inner radius a.
(d) For $\mu = 0$ and $h = 0$, the wheel always slides without rolling.

2 A thin circular coin of mass 5 g and radius 4/3 cm is initially in a horizontal XY-plane. The coin is tossed vertically up (+z direction) by applying an impulse of $\sqrt{\frac{\pi}{2}} \times 10^{-2}$ N-s at a distance 2/3 cm from its centre.The coin spins about its diameter and moves along the +z direction. By the time the coin reaches back to its initial position, it completes n rotations. The value of n is .... [Given : The acceleration due to gravity $g = 10\ \text{ms}^{-2}$] **(2023)**

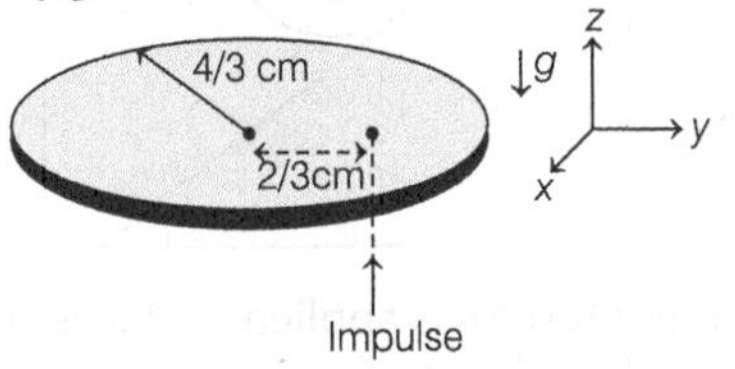

3 A flat surface of a thin uniform disk A of radius R is glued to a horizontal table. Another thin uniform disk B of mass M and with the same radius R rolls without slipping on the circumference of A, as shown in the figure. A flat surface of B also lies on the plane of the table. The centre of mass of B has fixed angular speed ω about the vertical axis passing through the centre of A. The angular momentum of B is $nM\omega R^2$ with respect to the centre of A. Which of the following is the value of n? **(2022)**

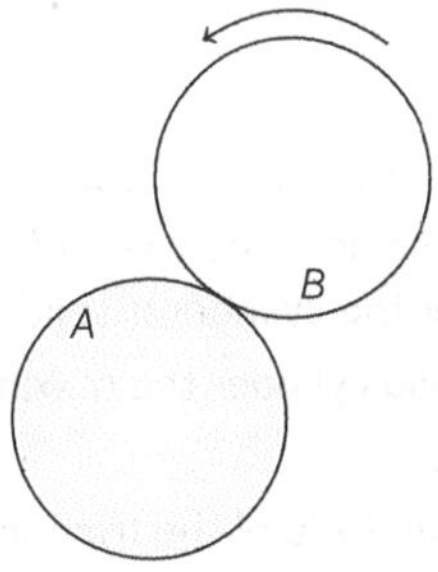

(a) 2 (b) 5 (c) 7/2 (d) 9/2

4 At time $t = 0$, a disk of radius 1 m starts to roll without slipping on a horizontal plane with an angular acceleration of $\alpha = \frac{2}{3}$ rad s^{-2}. A small stone is stuck to the disk. At $t = 0$, it is at the contact point of the disk and the plane. Later, at time $t = \sqrt{\pi}$ s, the stone detaches itself and flies off tangentially from the disk. The maximum height (in m) reached by the stone measured from the plane is $\frac{1}{2} + \frac{x}{10}$. The value of x is .... [Take, $g = 10\ \text{ms}^{-2}$] **(2022)**

5 A solid sphere of mass 1 kg and radius 1 m rolls without slipping on a fixed inclined plane with an angle of inclination $\theta = 30°$ from the horizontal. Two forces of magnitude 1 N each, parallel to the incline, act on the sphere, both at distance $r = 0.5$ m from the centre of the sphere, as shown in the figure.

The acceleration of the sphere down the plane is .... ms^{-2}. (Take, $g = 10\ ms^{-2}$) **(2022)**

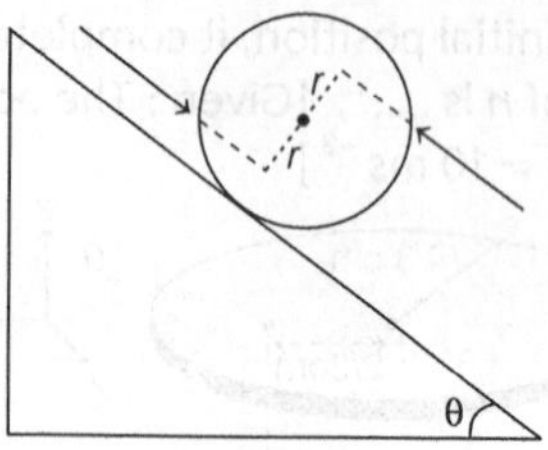

6 A horizontal force F is applied at the centre of mass of a cylindrical object of mass m and radius R, perpendicular to its axis as shown in the figure. The coefficient of friction between the object and the ground is μ. The centre of mass of the object has an acceleration a. The acceleration due to gravity is g. Given that, the object rolls without slipping, which of the following statement(s) is(are) correct? **(2021)**

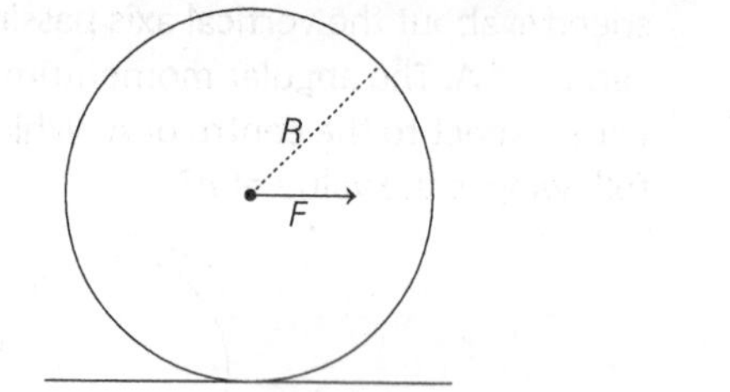

(a) For the same F, the value of a does not depend on whether the cylinder is solid or hollow.

(b) For a solid cylinder,the maximum possible value of a is $2\mu g$.

(c) The magnitude of the frictional force on the object due to the ground is always μmg.

(d) For a thin-walled hollow cylinder, $a = \frac{F}{2m}$.

7 A thin rod of mass M and length a is free to rotate in horizontal plane about a fixed vertical axis passing through point O. A thin circular disc of mass M and of radius $a/4$ is pivoted on this rod with its centre at a distance $a/4$ from the free end, so that it can rotate freely about its vertical axis, as shown in the figure. Assume that, both the rod and the disc have uniform density and they remain horizontal during the motion. An outside stationary observer finds the rod rotating with an angular velocity Ω and the disc rotating about its vertical axis with angular velocity 4Ω. The total angular momentum of the system about the point O is $\left(\frac{Ma^2\Omega}{48}\right) n$.

The value of n is ____. **(2021)**

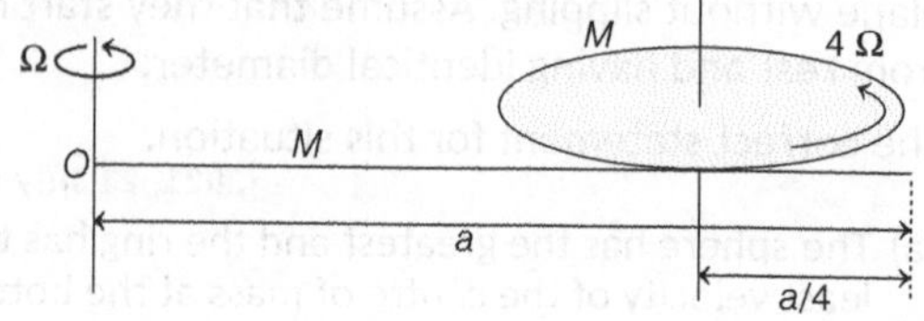

8 A rigid uniform bar AB of length L is slipping from its vertical position on a frictionless floor (as shown in the figure). At some instant of time, the angle made by the bar with the vertical is θ. Which of the following statements about its motion is/are correct? **(2017)**

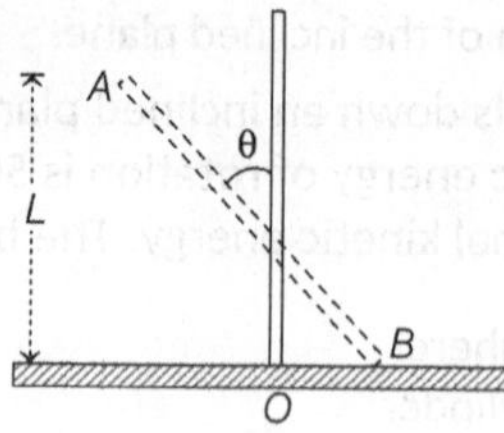

(a) Instantaneous torque about the point in contact with the floor is proportional to $\sin\theta$.

(b) The trajectory of the point A is parabola.

(c) The mid-point of the bar will fall vertically downward.

(d) When the bar makes an angle θ with the vertical, the displacement of its mid-point from the initial position is proportional to $(1 - \cos\theta)$.

Direction (Q. Nos. 8 and 9) One twirls a circular ring (of mass M and radius R) near the tip of one's finger as shown in Figure 1. In the process the finger never loses contact with the inner rim of the ring. The finger traces out the surface of a cone, shown by the dotted line. The radius of the path traced out by the point where the ring and the finger is in contact is r. The finger rotates with an angular velocity ω_0. The rotating ring rolls without slipping on the outside of a smaller circle described by the point where the ring and the finger is in contact (Figure 2). The coefficient of friction between the ring and the finger is μ and the acceleration due to gravity is g.

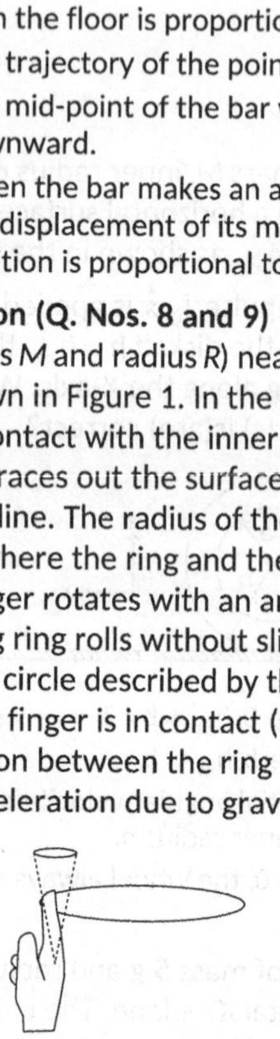
Figure 1

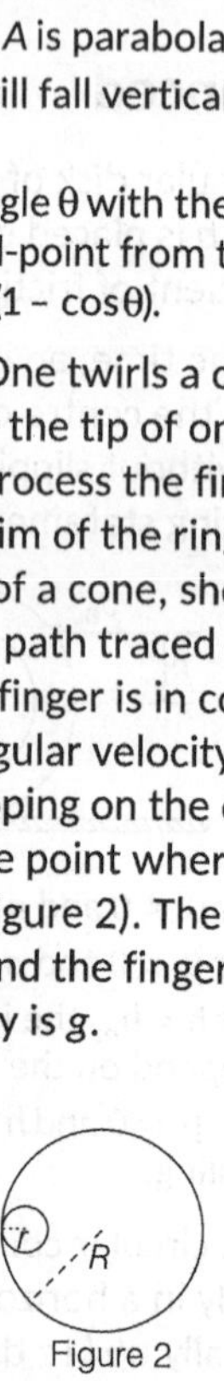

Figure 2

8 The total kinetic energy of the ring is **(2017)**

(a) $M\omega_0^2(R-r)^2$ (b) $\frac{1}{2}M\omega_0^2(R-r)^2$

(c) $M\omega_0^2R^2$ (d) $\frac{3}{2}M\omega_0^2(R-r)^2$

10 The minimum value of ω_0 below which the ring will drop down is **(2017)**

(a) $\sqrt{\frac{g}{2\mu(R-r)}}$ (b) $\sqrt{\frac{3g}{2\mu(R-r)}}$

(c) $\sqrt{\frac{g}{\mu(R-r)}}$ (d) $\sqrt{\frac{2g}{\mu(R-r)}}$

11 A wheel of radius R and mass M is placed at the bottom of a fixed step of height R as shown in the figure. A constant force is continuously applied on the surface of the wheel so that it just climbs the step without slipping. Consider the torque τ about an axis normal to the plane of the paper passing through the point Q. Which of the following options is/are correct? **(2017)**

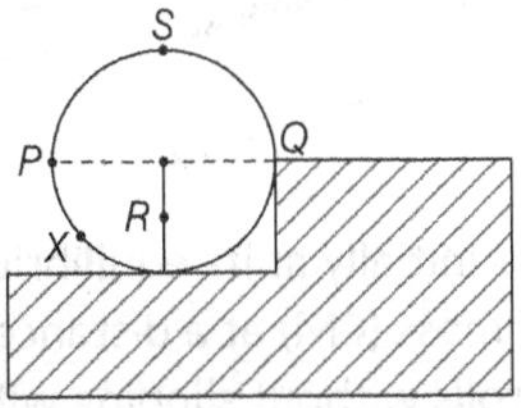

(a) If the force is applied normal to the circumference at point P, then τ is zero

(b) If the force is applied tangentially at point S, then $\tau \neq 0$ but the wheel never climbs the step

(c) If the force is applied at point P tangentially, then τ decreases continuously as the wheel climbs

(d) If the force is applied normal to the circumference at point X, then τ is constant

12 Two thin circular discs of mass m and $4m$, having radii of a and $2a$, respectively, are rigidly fixed by a massless, rigid rod of length $l = \sqrt{24}\,a$ through their centers. This assembly is laid on a firm and flat surface and set rolling without slipping on the surface so that the angular speed about the axis of the rod is ω. The angular momentum of the entire assembly about the point 'O' is $\mathbf{L}$ (see the figure). Which of the following statement(s) is (are) true? **(2016)**

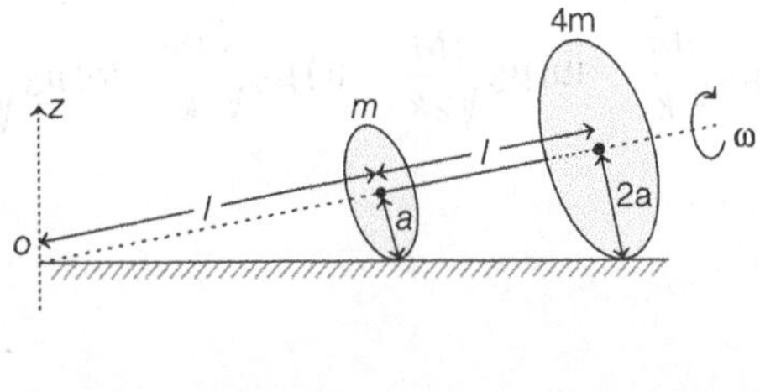

(a) The magnitude of the z-component of $\mathbf{L}$ is $55\,ma^2\omega$

(b) The magnitude of angular momentum of centre of mass of the assembly about the point O is $81\,ma^2\omega$

(c) The centre of mass of the assembly rotates about the Z-axis with an angular speed of $\frac{\omega}{5}$

(d) The magnitude of angular momentum of the assembly about its centre of mass is $17\,ma^2\frac{\omega}{2}$

13 Two identical uniform discs roll without slipping on two different surfaces AB and CD (see figure) starting at A and C with linear speeds v_1 and v_2, respectively, and always remain in contact with the surfaces. If they reach B and D with the same linear speed and $v_1 = 3$ m/s, then v_2 in m/s is ($g = 10\ \text{m/s}^2$) **(2015)**

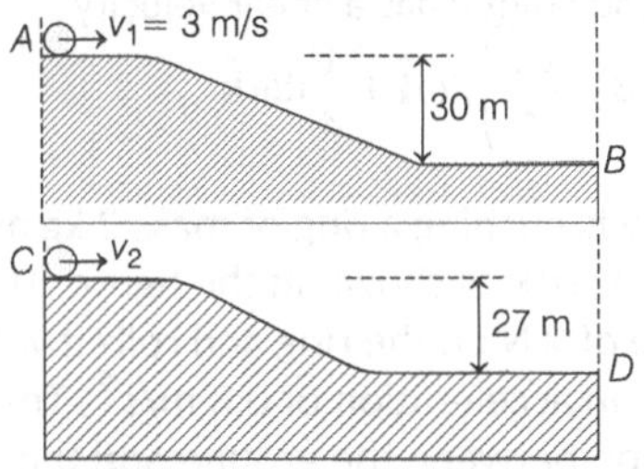

14 Two solid cylinders P and Q of same mass and same radius start rolling down a fixed inclined plane from the same height at the same time. Cylinder P has most of its mass concentrated near its surface, while Q has most of its mass concentrated near the axis. Which statement(s) is(are) correct? **(2012)**

(a) Both cylinders P and Q reach the ground at the same time

(b) Cylinder P has larger linear acceleration than cylinder Q

(c) Both cylinders reach the ground with same translational kinetic energy

(d) Cylinder Q reaches the ground with larger angular speed

15 The figure shows a system consisting of (i) a ring of outer radius $3R$ rolling clockwise without slipping on a horizontal surface with angular speed ω and (ii) an inner disc of radius $2R$ rotating anti-clockwise with angular speed $\omega/2$.

The ring and disc are separated by frictionless ball bearings. The system is in the x-z plane. The point P on the inner disc is at a distance R from the origin, where OP makes an angle of 30° with the horizontal. Then with respect to the horizontal surface, **(2012)**

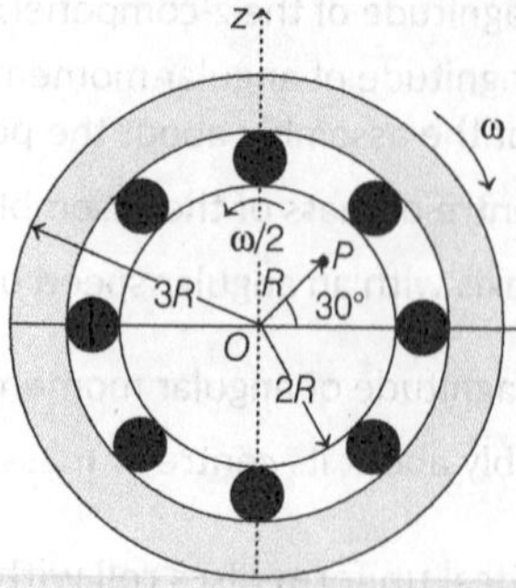

(a) the point O has a linear velocity $3R\omega\hat{\mathbf{i}}$

(b) the point P has a linear velocity $\frac{11}{4}R\omega\hat{\mathbf{i}}+\frac{\sqrt{3}}{4}R\omega\hat{\mathbf{k}}$

(c) the point P has a linear velocity $\frac{13}{4}R\omega\hat{\mathbf{i}}-\frac{\sqrt{3}}{4}R\omega\hat{\mathbf{k}}$

(d) the point P has a linear velocity $\left(3-\frac{\sqrt{3}}{4}\right)R\omega\hat{\mathbf{i}}+\frac{1}{4}R\omega\hat{\mathbf{k}}$

16 A boy is pushing a ring of mass 2 kg and radius 0.5 m with a stick as shown in the figure. The stick applies a force of 2 N on the ring and rolls it without slipping with an acceleration of 0.3 m/s^2. The coefficient of friction between the ground and the ring is large enough that rolling always occurs and the coefficient of friction between the stick and the ring is $(P/10)$. The value of P is .... **(2011)**

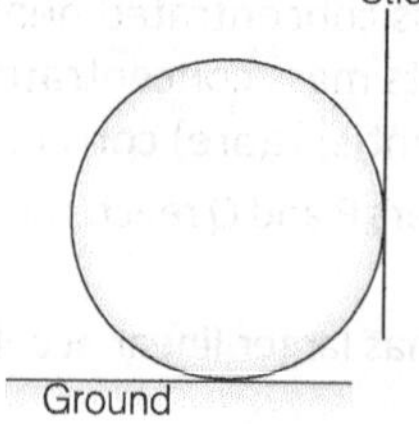

17 A thin ring of mass 2 kg and radius 0.5 m is rolling without slipping on a horizontal plane with velocity 1 m/s. A small ball of mass 0.1 kg, moving with velocity 20 m/s in the opposite direction, hits the ring at a height of 0.75 m and goes vertically up with velocity 10 m/s. Immediately after the collision, **(2011)**

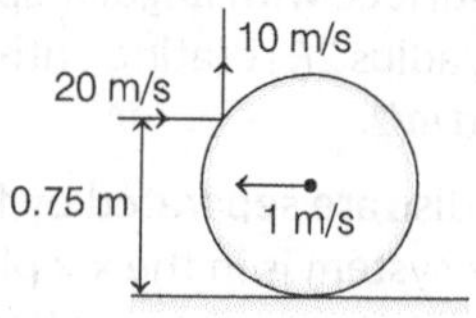

(a) the ring has pure rotation about its stationary CM

(b) the ring comes to a complete stop

(c) friction between the ring and the ground is to the left

(d) there is no friction between the ring and the ground

Direction (Q. Nos. 16-18) A uniform thin cylindrical disk of mass M and radius R is attached to two identical massless springs of spring constant k which are fixed to the wall as shown in the figure. The springs are attached to the axle of the disk diammetrically on either side at a distance d from its centre. The axle is massless and both the springs and the axle are in a horizontal plane. The unstretched length of each spring is L.

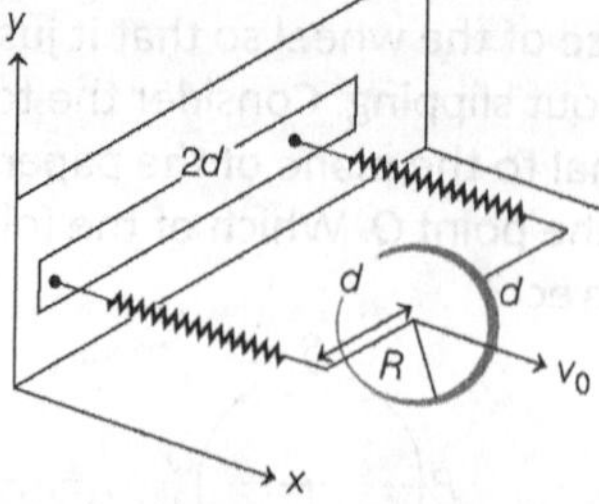

The disk is initially at its equilibrium position with its centre of mass (CM) at a distance L from the wall. The disk rolls without slipping with velocity $\mathbf{v}_0 = v_0\hat{\mathbf{i}}$. The coefficient of friction is μ.

18 The net external force acting on the disk when its centre of mass is at displacement x with respect to its equilibrium position is **(2008)**

(a) $-kx$ (b) $-2kx$ (c) $-\frac{2kx}{3}$ (d) $-\frac{4kx}{3}$

19 The centre of mass of the disk undergoes simple harmonic motion with angular frequency ω equal to **(2008)**

(a) $\sqrt{\frac{k}{M}}$ (b) $\sqrt{\frac{2k}{M}}$

(c) $\sqrt{\frac{2k}{3M}}$ (d) $\sqrt{\frac{4k}{3M}}$

20 The maximum value of v_0 for which the disk will roll without slipping is **(2008)**

(a) $\mu g\sqrt{\frac{M}{k}}$ (b) $\mu g\sqrt{\frac{M}{2k}}$ (c) $\mu g\sqrt{\frac{3M}{k}}$ (d) $\mu g\sqrt{\frac{5M}{2k}}$

Answer Key

Level 1

4.1 Kinematics of Combined Motion

1. $\mathbf{v}_A = 0$; $\mathbf{v}_B = 2v\hat{\mathbf{i}}$; $\mathbf{v}_C = v\hat{\mathbf{i}} + v\hat{\mathbf{j}}$
2. $v_A = 25$ m/s, $v_B = 75$ m/s
3. $v_{CM} = 10$ m/s
4. $\frac{3v}{2r}$, counter clockwise
5. $\frac{vR}{R-r}$
6. 575 J
7. (a) $\mathbf{a}_c = 20\hat{\mathbf{i}}$ cm/s^2; $\mathbf{a}_A = 40\hat{\mathbf{i}}$ cm/s^2 (b) $\mathbf{a}_A = 40\hat{\mathbf{i}} - 40t^2\hat{\mathbf{j}}$ cm/s^2
8. $a_{CM} = \frac{r\alpha}{2}, \alpha' = \frac{\alpha}{2}$
9. $R_A = 4r, R_B = 2\sqrt{2}r$
10. $8r$

4.2 Dynamics of Combined Motion

1. (a) $\frac{F}{m}, \frac{14F}{mL}$ (b) $\frac{L}{14}$ below centre
2. $\frac{4\pi R}{5}$
3. $T = \frac{mg}{6}, \alpha = \frac{2g}{3R}$
4. $T = \frac{mg}{10}$
5. $\frac{8g}{11}$
6. (a) $a_{CM} = \frac{g}{2}, \alpha = \frac{3g}{L}$ (b) $a_{CM} = \frac{3g}{4}, \alpha = \frac{3g}{2L}$

4.3 Dynamics of Rolling on a Plane Surface

1. $\frac{v_0}{2}$
2. $s = \left(\frac{\omega_0^2 R^2}{18\mu g}\right)$; $W_f = \frac{-m\omega_0^2 R^2}{6}$
3. (a) $\frac{v_0}{3}$ (b) $\frac{v_0}{5}$
4. $a_{CM} = \frac{4F}{3m}, f = \frac{F}{3}$
5. $\frac{2}{7}$
6. $\alpha_{max} = \frac{2g}{3R}$
7. (a) $\frac{8g}{11}$ (b) $\frac{mg}{11}$
8. $a_{CM} = \frac{F}{8m}, a_{plank} = \frac{7F}{16m}$
9. (i) $a_{CM} = \frac{4F}{11m}, a_{plank} = \frac{8F}{11m}$ (ii) $f_1 = \frac{3F}{11}, f_2 = \frac{F}{11}$

4.4 Rolling on an Inclined Surface

1. $a = \frac{5}{7}g\sin\theta, f = \frac{2}{7}mg\sin\theta$
2. $\sqrt{\frac{4gh}{3}}$
3. Sphere reaches first and ring last
4. $\sqrt{\frac{27g(R-r)}{7}}$
5. (a) $\frac{2}{7}\tan\theta$ (b) $\frac{11}{12}mgl\sin\theta$
6. $\frac{2h}{3}$

4.5 Angular Impulse

1. $\frac{L}{3}$ to the left of centre
2. (i) $\frac{J}{3m}$ (ii) $\frac{J}{ml}$ (iii) $v_A = \frac{J}{m}, v_B = 0$
3. (a) $\frac{I}{m}, \frac{2I}{mR}$ (b) $\frac{\pi mR}{2I}$ (c) $\frac{\pi R}{2}$
4. $\frac{v_1}{L}\left(\frac{12\sin\beta}{3\sin^2\beta + 1}\right)(c\omega)$

4.6 Anglular Momentum in Combined Motion

1. $\frac{3}{2}MR^2\omega$
2. (i) $\frac{1}{4}$ (ii) $\frac{2}{3}L$ (iii) $\frac{v_0}{2\sqrt{2}}$
3. (i) Zero (ii) $\frac{v}{5a}$ (iii) $\frac{3}{5}mv^2$
4. (a) $u, \frac{u}{2}$ (b) $\frac{3u}{4}$ (c) $\frac{u}{2l}$
5. $\frac{2v_0 - 3\omega_0 R}{3R}$
6. $\left(\frac{4}{3}ml^2\omega_1 + \frac{1}{4}mR^2\omega_1\right)\hat{\mathbf{j}} + \left(\frac{1}{2}mR^2\omega_2 - \frac{3}{2}m\omega_1 lR\right)\hat{\mathbf{i}}$

4.7 Instantaneous Axis of Rotation

1. (a) $\omega = 0.5$ rad/s; $\mathbf{v}_c = 5.0\hat{\mathbf{j}}$ cm/s (b) 40 cm from A
2. (a) Distance L below B along the rod (b) $\frac{v}{L}, \frac{3v}{2}$ (c) $\frac{7}{6}mv^2$
3. $\sqrt{\frac{3g(1-\sin\theta)}{l}}$

Level 2

Single Choice Correct Questions

1. (a)	2. (b)	3. (c)	4. (c)	5. (d)	6. (d)	7. (c)	8. (a)	9. (b)	10. (b)
11. (b)	12. (b)	13. (a)	14. (b)	15. (a)	16. (a)	17. (d)	18. (b)	19. (c)	20. (b)
21. (a)	22. (d)	23. (d)	24. (c)	25. (d)	26. (b)	27. (d)	28. (b)	29. (b)	30. (c)
31. (b)	32. (b)	33. (d)	34. (c)	35. (d)	36. (b)	37. (a)	38. (b)	39. (c)	40. (d)
41. (a)									

Numerical Value Questions

1. (60)	2. (2)	3. (8)	4. (8)	5. (4)	6. (6)	7. (8)	8. (4)	9. (6)	10. (9)

Level 3

Single Choice Correct Questions

1. (a)	2. (a)	3. (b)	4. (c)	5. (a)	6. (c)	7. (b)	8. (c)	9. (b)	10. (b)
11. (b)	12. (b)	13. (a)	14. (c)	15. (a)	16. (a)	17. (c)	18. (c)	19. (b)	20. (b)
21. (b)	22. (b)	23. (c)	24. (a)	25. (b)	26. (b)	27. (c)	28. (c)	29. (a)	30. (b)
31. (a)	32. (c)								

Multiple Choice(s) Correct Questions

1. (b, c)	2. (a, b, c)	3. (a, c)	4. (a, d)	5. (b, c, d)	6. (a, b, c)	7. (a, b)	8. (a, b, d)
9. (a, c, d)	10. (a, b)	11. (a, b, c)	12. (a, c)	13. (c, d)	14. (a, b, c, d)	15. (a, c)	16. (a, b, c)
17. (a, b, c, d)	18. (a, b, c)						

Comprehension Based Questions

1. (d)	2. (b)	3. (a)	4. (c)	5. (c)	6. (d)	7. (d)	8. (b)	9. (a)	10. (c)
11. (a)	12. (a)	13. (d)	14. (b)	15. (a)	16. (d)	17. (d)	18. (b)	19. (c)	20. (a)
21. (a)	22. (a)	23. (d)	24. (d)						

Match the Columns Questions

1. A→ PS; B→ P; C→ RS; D→ QS
2. A→ QR; B→ PR; C→ QR; D→ R
3. A→ Q; B→ R; C→ S; D→ P
4. A→ PQRST; B→ QRST; C→ PQRST; D→ P
5. A→ R; B→ S; C→ Q; D→ P
6. A→ PQST; B→ PQT; C→ RST; D→ QT
7. A→ P; B→ R; C→ Q; D→ S

Numerical Value Questions

1. (8)	2. (25)	3. (5)	4. (5)	5. (50)	6. (36)	7. (15)	8. (3)	9. (29)	10. (45)
11. (3)									

Previous Years Questions

JEE Main

1. (10)	2. (10)	3. (6)	4. (b)	5. (2)	6. (4)	7. (45)	8. (54)	9. (40)	10. (4)
11. (10)	12. (120)	13. (d)	14. (4)	15. (a)	16. (b)				

JEE Advanced

1. (a,b,c,d)	2. (30)	3. (b)	4. (0.52)	5. (2.86≈3)	6. (b,d)	7. (49)	8. (a,c,d)	9. ()	10. (c)
11. (b,c)	12. (c,d)	13. (7)	14. (d)	15. (a,b)	16. (3.6 ≈ 4)	17. (a,c)	18. (d)	19. (d)	20. (c)

SOLUTIONS

Level 1

4.1 Kinematics of Combined Motion

1. $\mathbf{v}_A = v\hat{\mathbf{i}} - \omega r\hat{\mathbf{i}} = 0 \Rightarrow \omega = \dfrac{v}{r}$

$\mathbf{v}_B = v\hat{\mathbf{i}} + \omega r\hat{\mathbf{i}} = 2v\hat{\mathbf{i}}$

$\mathbf{v}_C = v\hat{\mathbf{i}} + \omega r\hat{\mathbf{j}} = v\hat{\mathbf{i}} + v\hat{\mathbf{j}}$

2. $v_A = v_{CM} - \omega r = 50 - 5(5) = 25$ m/s

$v_B = v_{CM} + \omega r = 50 + 5(5) = 75$ m/s

3. $v_{CM} - \omega R = v \Rightarrow v_{CM} - 3(2) = 4 \Rightarrow v_{CM} = 10$ m/s

4. $v_A = v_{CM} + \omega r = -v$ ...(i)

$v_B = v_{CM} - \omega r = 2v$ ...(ii)

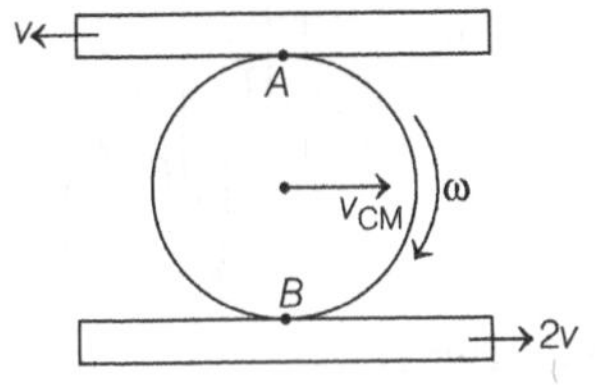

Solving we get,

$$v_{CM} = \frac{v}{2} \text{ and } \omega = -\frac{3v}{2r} = \frac{3v}{2r}, \text{ counter clockwise}$$

5. $v_A = v_{CM} - \omega r = v$ ...(i)

$v_B = v_{CM} - \omega R = 0$ ...(ii)

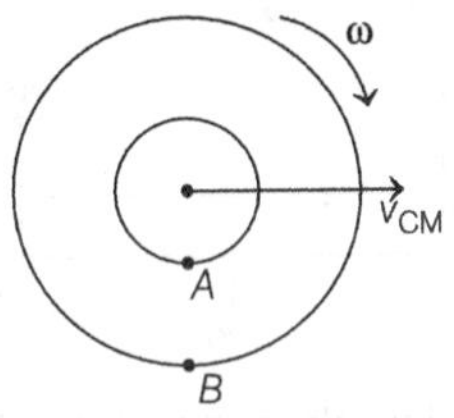

From Eqs. (i) and (ii), we get

$$v_{CM} = \frac{vR}{R - r}$$

6. $v_{CM} - \omega r = 0$ ...(i)

$v_{CM} + \omega r = v$ ...(ii)

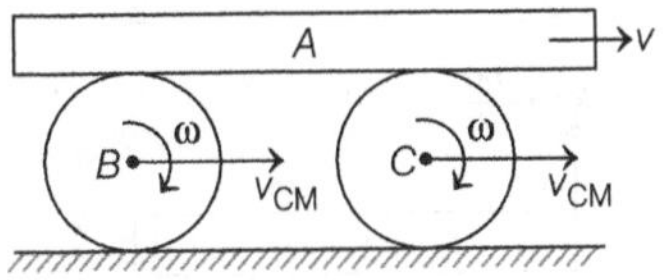

Solving, we get $v_{CM} = \dfrac{v}{2}$ and $\omega = \dfrac{v}{2r}$

$K = K_A + K_B + K_C$

$$= \frac{1}{2} \times 10 \times (10)^2 + \left(\frac{1}{2} \times 2 \times 5^2 + \frac{1}{2}\left(\frac{(2)(2)^2}{2}\right)(2.5)^2\right) \times 2$$

$= 575$ J

7. (a) Tangential acceleration of $P = \mathbf{a}_c - R\alpha\hat{\mathbf{i}} = 0$

$\Rightarrow \mathbf{a}_c = 20\hat{\mathbf{i}}$ cm/s^2

Centripetal acceleration of $A = \omega^2 R = 0$

Tangential acceleration of $A = a_c + R\alpha = 40$ cm/s^2

So, $\mathbf{a}_A = 40\hat{\mathbf{i}}$

(b) $\omega = \alpha t$,

$$\mathbf{a}_A = (a_c + R\alpha)\hat{\mathbf{i}} - \omega^2 R\hat{\mathbf{j}} = 40\hat{\mathbf{i}} - 40t^2\hat{\mathbf{j}}$$

8. $a_C = r\alpha$ ...(i)

$a_{CM} + r\alpha' = a_A$ ...(ii)

$a_{CM} - r\alpha' = a_B = 0$ ...(iii)

$a_A = a_C$ ...(iv)

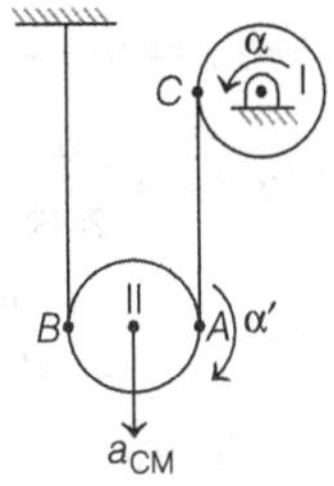

Solving we get,

$$a_{CM} = \frac{r\alpha}{2} \text{ and } \alpha' = \frac{\alpha}{2}$$

9. $a_A = \dfrac{v^2}{r} = \dfrac{(2v)^2}{R_A} \Rightarrow R_A = 4r$

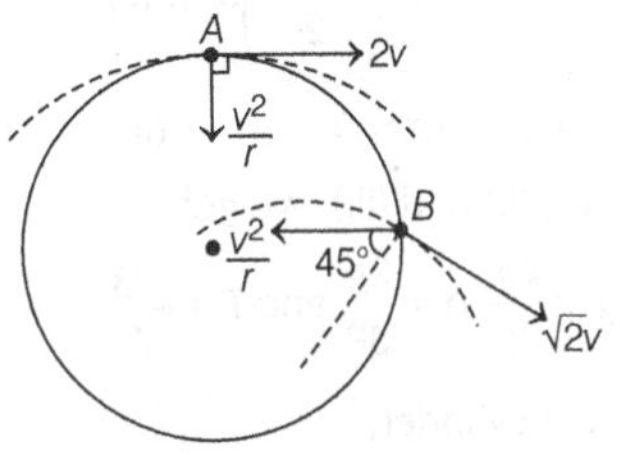

$$a_B = \frac{v^2}{r}\cos 45° = \frac{(\sqrt{2}v)^2}{R_B}$$

$\Rightarrow \quad R_B = 2\sqrt{2}r$

10. $v_p = \sqrt{v_0^2 + v_0^2 + 2v_0^2 \cos(180 - \theta)} = 2v_0 \sin\left(\dfrac{\theta}{2}\right)$

Distance $= \int (\text{Speed})dt$

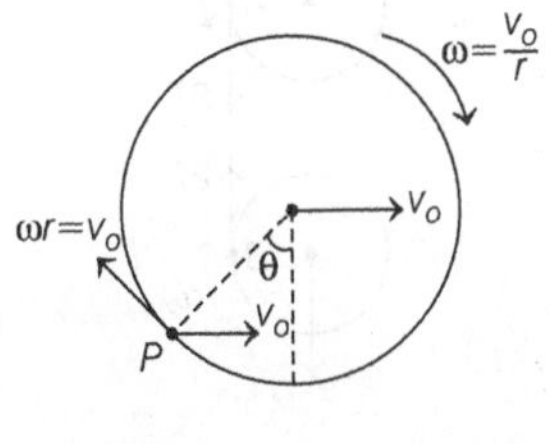

$$= \int_0^{\frac{2\pi}{\omega}} 2v_0 \sin\left(\frac{\omega t}{2}\right) dt = 8r$$

4.2 Dynamics of Combined Motion

1. (a) $\Sigma F_{ext} = Ma_{CM} \Rightarrow 2F - F = Ma_{CM}$

$$\Rightarrow \quad a_{CM} = \frac{F}{M}$$

$$\Sigma\tau = I\alpha \Rightarrow 2F\left(\frac{L}{2}\right) + F\left(\frac{L}{6}\right) = \left(\frac{ML^2}{12}\right)\alpha$$

$$\Rightarrow \quad \alpha = \frac{14F}{ML}$$

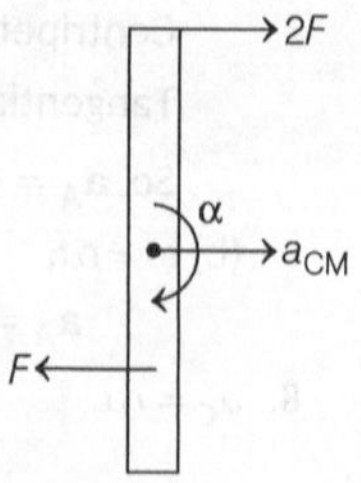

(b) $a_p = a_{CM} - r\alpha = 0 \Rightarrow r = \dfrac{L}{14}$

2. $\Sigma F_{ext} = Ma_{CM} \Rightarrow F = Ma_{CM} \Rightarrow a_{CM} = \dfrac{F}{M}$

$$\Sigma\tau = I\alpha \Rightarrow FR = \frac{2}{5}MR^2\alpha \Rightarrow \alpha = \frac{5F}{2MR}$$

$$\theta = \omega_0 t + \frac{1}{2}\alpha t^2 \Rightarrow 2\pi = 0 + \frac{1}{2}\left(\frac{5F}{2MR}\right)T^2$$

$$\Rightarrow \quad T = \sqrt{\frac{8\pi MR}{5F}}$$

$$s_{CM} = ut + \frac{1}{2}at^2 = 0 + \frac{1}{2}\left(\frac{F}{M}\right)\left(\frac{8\pi MR}{5F}\right) = \frac{4\pi R}{5}$$

3. $\Sigma F_{ext} = ma_{CM} \Rightarrow mg - 2T = ma_{CM}$ ...(i)

$\Sigma\tau = I\alpha \Rightarrow TR + TR = \left(\dfrac{mR^2}{2}\right)\alpha$ ...(ii)

$a_p = 0 \Rightarrow a_{CM} - R\alpha = 0$ ...(iii)

Solving Eqs. (i), (ii) and (iii), we get

$$a_{CM} = \frac{2g}{3}, \alpha = \frac{2g}{3R} \text{ and } T = \frac{mg}{6}$$

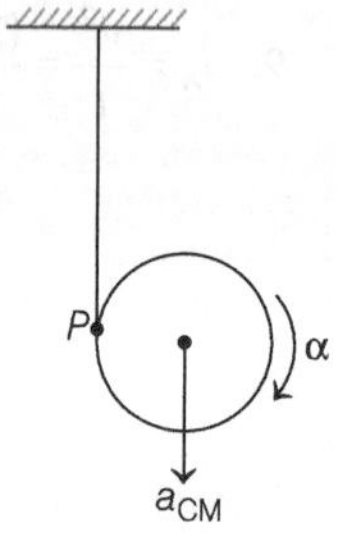

4. For upper fixed cylinder,

$$\Sigma\tau = I\alpha \Rightarrow TR + TR = \left(\frac{mR^2}{2}\right)\alpha_1 \quad \text{...(i)}$$

For lower cylinder,

$$\Sigma F_{ext} = ma_{CM} \Rightarrow mg - 2T = ma_{CM} \quad \text{...(ii)}$$

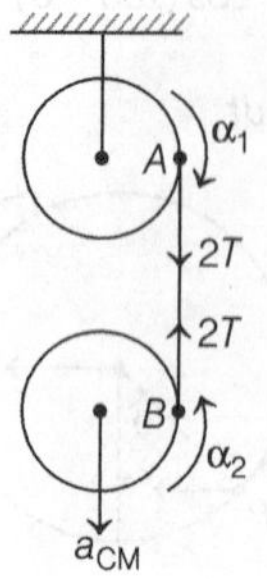

$$\Sigma\tau = I\alpha \Rightarrow 2TR = \left(\frac{mR^2}{2}\right)\alpha_2 \quad \text{...(iii)}$$

Constraint, $a_A = a_B \Rightarrow R\alpha_1 = a_{CM} - R\alpha_2$ ...(iv)

Solving Eqs. (i), (ii), (iii) and (iv), we get

$$T = \frac{mg}{10}$$

5. For block, $\Sigma F_x = ma_x \Rightarrow T_1 = ma$ ...(i)

For disc, $\Sigma F_{ext} = ma_{CM} \Rightarrow mg - T_1 - T_2 = ma_{CM}$ ...(ii)

$$\Sigma\tau = I\alpha \Rightarrow T_2R - T_1R = \left(\frac{mR^2}{2}\right)\alpha \quad \text{...(iii)}$$

Constraints, $a_A = a_{CM} + R\alpha = a$ ...(iv)

$a_B = a_{CM} - R\alpha = 0$ ...(v)

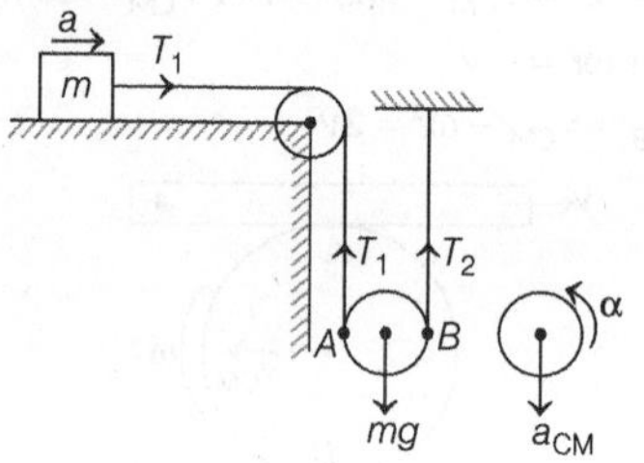

Solving equations we get,

$$a = \frac{4g}{11}$$

6. (a) Initially, the rod is in equilibrium. So,

$$\Sigma F_y = 0 \Rightarrow kx + kx - mg = 0$$

$$\Rightarrow \quad kx = \frac{mg}{2}$$

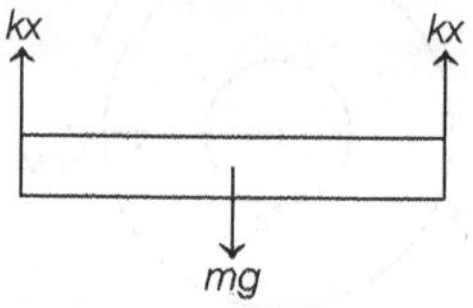

Spring force doesn't change instantly. So, just after the right spring is removed, spring force in the left spring will be $Kx = \dfrac{mg}{2}$.

$$\Sigma F_{ext} = ma_{CM}$$

$$\Rightarrow \quad mg - \frac{mg}{2} = ma_{CM} \Rightarrow a_{CM} = \frac{g}{2}$$

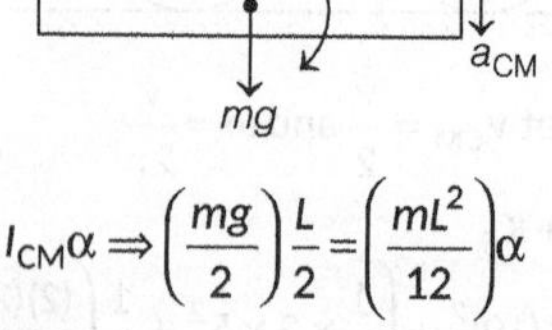

$$\Sigma\tau = I_{CM}\alpha \Rightarrow \left(\frac{mg}{2}\right)\frac{L}{2} = \left(\frac{mL^2}{12}\right)\alpha$$

$$\Rightarrow \quad \alpha = \frac{3g}{L}$$

(b) $\Sigma F_{ext} = ma_{CM} \Rightarrow mg - T = ma_{CM}$ ...(i)

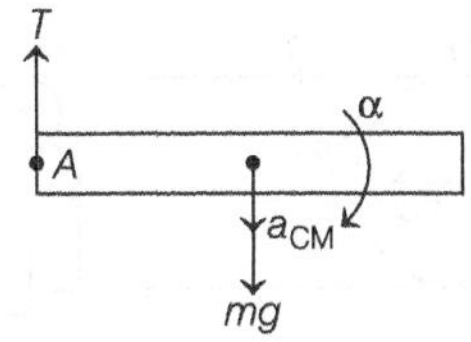

$$\Sigma\tau = I\alpha \Rightarrow T\left(\frac{L}{2}\right) = \left(\frac{mL^2}{12}\right)\alpha \quad ...(ii)$$

$$a_A = a_{CM} - \left(\frac{L}{2}\right)\alpha = 0 \quad ...(iii)$$

Solving Eqs. (i), (ii) and (iii), we get

$$a_{CM} = \frac{3g}{4}, \alpha = \frac{3g}{2L}$$

4.3 Dynamics of Rolling on a Plane Surface

1. $\Sigma F_{ext} = ma_{CM} \Rightarrow -\mu mg = ma_{CM}$

$\Rightarrow$ $a_{CM} = -\mu g$

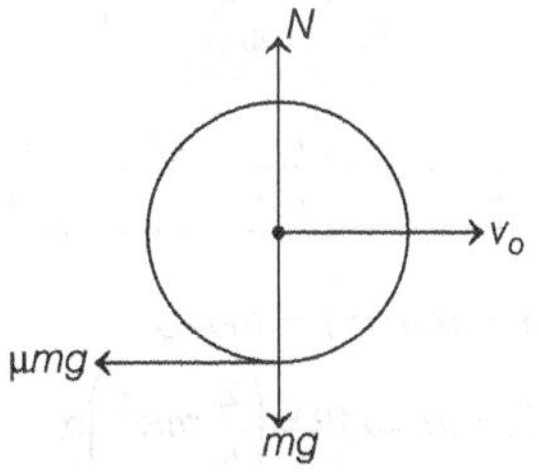

$$\Sigma\tau = I\alpha \Rightarrow \mu mgR = (mR^2)\alpha$$

$\Rightarrow$ $\alpha = \frac{\mu g}{R}$

$$v = u + at \Rightarrow v_{CM} = v_0 - \mu gt$$

$$\omega = \omega_0 + \alpha t \Rightarrow \omega = \left(\frac{\mu g}{R}\right)t$$

For pure rolling, $v_{CM} = \omega R$

$\Rightarrow$ $v_0 - \mu gt = \left(\left(\frac{\mu g}{R}\right)t\right)R$

$\Rightarrow$ $t = \frac{v_0}{2\mu g}$

$$v_{CM} = v_0 - \mu g\left(\frac{v_0}{2\mu g}\right) = \frac{v_0}{2}$$

2. $\Sigma F_{ext} = ma_{CM} \Rightarrow \mu mg = ma_{CM} \Rightarrow a_{CM} = \mu g$

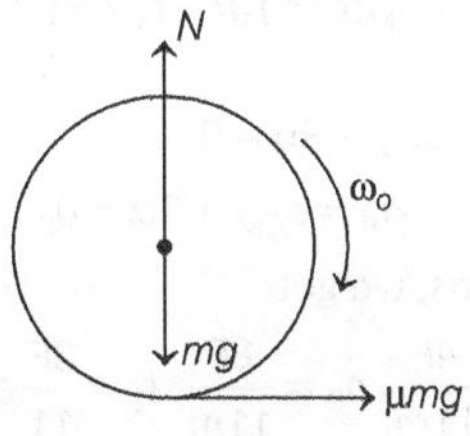

$$\Sigma\tau = I\alpha \Rightarrow -\mu mgR = \left(\frac{mR^2}{2}\right)\alpha \Rightarrow \alpha = \frac{2\mu g}{R}$$

$$v = u + at \Rightarrow v_{CM} = (\mu g)t$$

$$\omega = \omega_0 + \alpha t \Rightarrow \omega = \omega_0 - \left(\frac{2\mu g}{R}\right)t$$

For pure rolling, $v_{CM} = \omega R$

$\Rightarrow$ $(\mu g)t = \left(\omega_0 - \left(\frac{2\mu g}{R}\right)t\right)R$

$\Rightarrow$ $t = \frac{\omega_0 R}{3\mu g}$

$$s = ut + \frac{1}{2}at^2 \Rightarrow s_{CM} = \frac{1}{2}(\mu g)\left(\frac{\omega_0 R}{3\mu g}\right)^2 = \frac{\omega_0^2 R^2}{18\mu g}$$

Applying work-energy theorem,

$W_{mg} + W_N + W_F = \Delta K$

$$\Rightarrow 0 + 0 + W_f = \left(\frac{1}{2}m\left(\frac{\omega_0 R}{3}\right)^2 + \frac{1}{2}\left(\frac{mR^2}{2}\right)\left(\frac{\omega_0}{3}\right)^2\right) - \left(\frac{1}{2}\left(\frac{mR^2}{2}\right)\omega_0^2\right)$$

$\Rightarrow$ $W_f = -\frac{m\omega_0^2 R^2}{6}$

3. (a) $\Sigma F_{ext} = ma_{CM} \Rightarrow -\mu mg = ma_{CM} \Rightarrow a_{CM} = -\mu g$

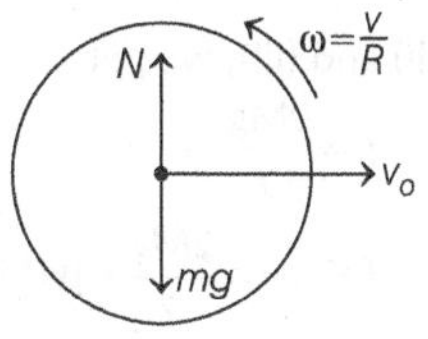

$$\Sigma\tau = I\alpha \Rightarrow \mu mgR = \frac{2}{3}mR^2\alpha \Rightarrow \alpha = \frac{3\mu g}{2R}$$

$$v = u + at \Rightarrow v_{CM} = v_0 - \mu gt$$

$$\omega = \omega_0 + \alpha t \Rightarrow \omega = -\frac{v}{R} + \left(\frac{3\mu g}{2R}\right)t$$

When it stops rotating, $\omega = -\frac{v_0}{R} + \left(\frac{3\mu g}{2R}\right)t = 0$

$\Rightarrow$ $t = \frac{2v_0}{3\mu g}$

$$v_{CM} = v_0 - \mu g\left(\frac{2v_0}{3\mu g}\right) = \frac{v_0}{3}$$

When pure rolling starts, $v_{CM} = \omega R$

$\Rightarrow$ $v_0 - \mu gt = \left(-\frac{v_0}{R} + \left(\frac{3\mu g}{2R}\right)t\right)R$

$\Rightarrow$ $t = \frac{4v_0}{5\mu g}$

$$v_{CM} = v_0 - \mu g\left(\frac{4v_0}{5\mu g}\right) = \frac{v_0}{5}$$

4. $\Sigma F_{ext} = ma_{CM} \Rightarrow F + f = ma_{CM}$ ...(i)

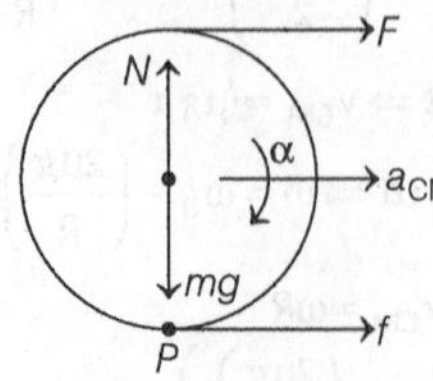

$$\Sigma\tau = I_{CM}\alpha \Rightarrow FR - fR = \left(\frac{mR^2}{2}\right)\alpha \quad \text{...(ii)}$$

$$a_p = 0 \Rightarrow a_{CM} - R\alpha = 0 \quad \text{...(iii)}$$

Solving Eqs. (i), (ii) and (iii), we get

$$a_{CM} = \frac{4F}{3m}, f = \frac{F}{3}$$

5. $\Sigma F_{ext} = Ma_{CM} \Rightarrow Mg - f = Ma_{CM}$ ...(i)

$$\Sigma\tau = I_{CM}\alpha \Rightarrow fR = \left(\frac{2}{5}MR^2\right)\alpha \quad \text{...(ii)}$$

$$a_p = 0 \Rightarrow a_{CM} - R\alpha = 0 \quad \text{...(iii)}$$

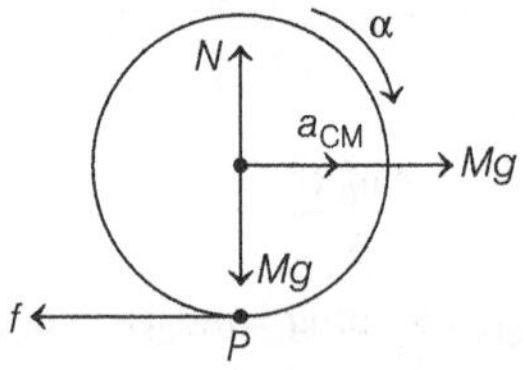

Solving Eqs. (i), (ii) and (iii), we get

$$f = \frac{2Mg}{7}$$

$$f \le f_L \Rightarrow \frac{2Mg}{7} \le \mu(Mg) \Rightarrow \mu_{min} = \frac{2}{7}$$

6. $\Sigma F_x = ma_x \Rightarrow f = ma_{CM}$ ...(i)

$\Sigma F_y = 0 \Rightarrow N + F = mg$ ...(ii)

$$\Sigma\tau = I_{CM}\alpha \Rightarrow FR - fR = \left(\frac{mR^2}{2}\right)\alpha \quad \text{...(iii)}$$

$$a_p = 0 \Rightarrow a_{CM} - R\alpha = 0 \quad \text{...(iv)}$$

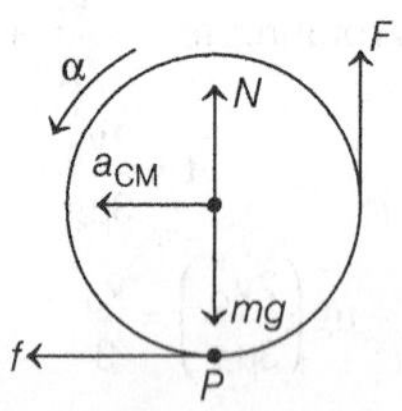

Solving equations, we get

$$\alpha = \frac{2F}{3mR}$$

$$N_{min} = mg - F_{max} = 0$$

$$\Rightarrow \quad F_{max} = mg$$

So, $\alpha_{max} = \frac{2(mg)}{3mR} = \frac{2g}{3R}$

7. For block, $\Sigma F_y = ma_y \Rightarrow mg - T = ma$ ...(i)

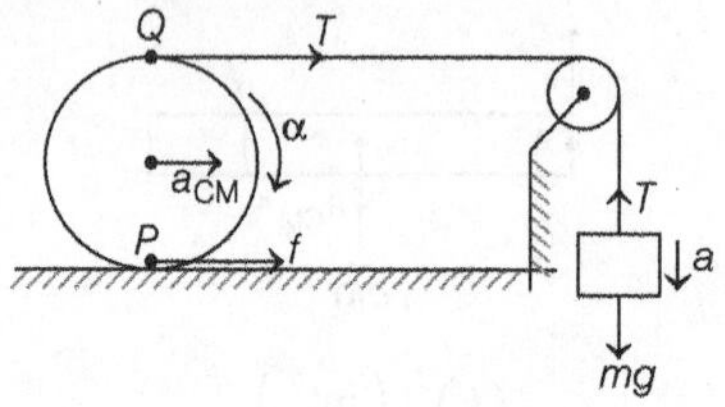

For cylinder, $\Sigma F_x = ma_x \Rightarrow T + f = ma_{CM}$ ...(ii)

$$\Sigma\tau = I_{CM}\alpha \Rightarrow TR - fR = \left(\frac{mR^2}{2}\right)\alpha \quad \text{...(iii)}$$

Constraints, $a_P = 0 \Rightarrow a_{CM} - R\alpha = 0$ ...(iv)

$a_Q = a \Rightarrow a_{CM} + R\alpha = a$ ...(v)

Solving the equations, we get

$$a = \frac{8g}{11} \text{ and } f = \frac{mg}{11}$$

8. For plank, $\Sigma F = ma \Rightarrow F - f = 2ma$ ...(i)

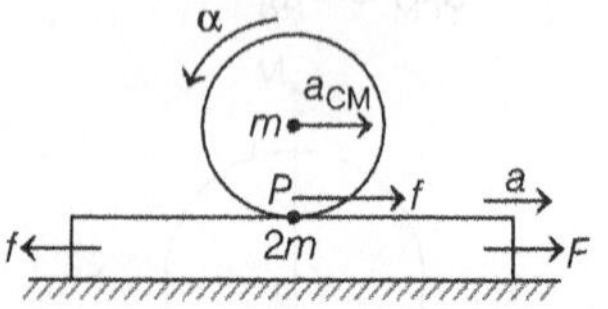

For sphere, $\Sigma F = ma \Rightarrow f = ma_{CM}$ ...(ii)

$$\Sigma\tau = I\alpha \Rightarrow fR = \left(\frac{2}{5}mR^2\right)\alpha \quad \text{...(iii)}$$

Constrains, $a_P = a_{CM} + R\alpha = a$ ...(iv)

Solving equations, we get

$$a = \frac{7F}{16m} \text{ and } a_{CM} = \frac{F}{8m}$$

9. For plank, $\Sigma F = ma \Rightarrow F - f_1 = ma_P$ ...(i)

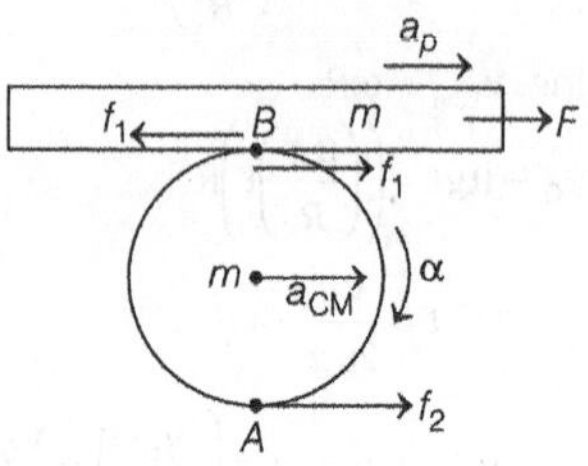

For cylinder, $\Sigma F = ma \Rightarrow f_1 + f_2 = ma_{CM}$ ...(ii)

$$\Sigma\tau = I_{CM}\alpha \Rightarrow f_1R - f_2R = \left(\frac{mR^2}{2}\right)\alpha \quad \text{...(iii)}$$

Constraint, $a_A = a_{CM} - R\alpha = 0$ ...(iv)

$a_B = a_{CM} + R\alpha = a_P$ ...(v)

Solving equations, we get

$$a_{CM} = \frac{4F}{11m}, a_P = \frac{8F}{11m}, f_1 = \frac{3F}{11} \text{ and } f_2 = \frac{F}{11}$$

4.4 Rolling on an Inclined Surface

1. $\Sigma F = ma \Rightarrow mg\sin\theta - f = ma_{CM}$ ...(i)

$$\Sigma\tau = I\alpha \Rightarrow fR = \left(\frac{2}{3}mR^2\right)\alpha$$ ...(ii)

$$a_P = 0 \Rightarrow a_{CM} - R\alpha = 0$$ ...(iii)

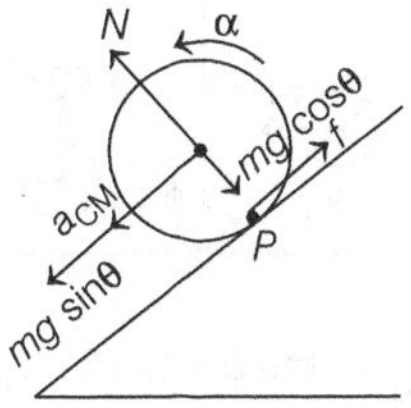

Solving we get, $a_{CM} = \dfrac{5g\sin\theta}{7}$ and $f = \dfrac{2mg\sin\theta}{7}$

2. $W_{mg} + W_N + W_f = \Delta K$

$$\Rightarrow +mgh + 0 + 0 = \left(\frac{1}{2}mv^2 + \frac{1}{2}\left(\frac{mR^2}{2}\right)\left(\frac{v}{r}\right)^2\right) - (0+0)$$

$$\Rightarrow \quad v = \sqrt{\frac{4gh}{3}}$$

3 $a_{CM} = \dfrac{mg\sin\theta}{m + \dfrac{I_{CM}}{R^2}}$

$$s = ut + \frac{1}{2}at^2 \Rightarrow \frac{h}{\sin\theta} = 0 + \frac{1}{2}\left(\frac{mg\sin\theta}{m + \frac{I_{CM}}{R^2}}\right)T^2$$

$$\Rightarrow \quad T = \sqrt{\frac{2h(I_{CM} + mR^2)}{mR^2 g\sin^2\theta}}$$

$$T_{ring} = \sqrt{\frac{4h}{g\sin^2\theta}},\ T_{cylinder} = \sqrt{\frac{3h}{g\sin^2\theta}}$$

$$T_{sphere} = \sqrt{\frac{14h}{5g\sin^2\theta}}$$

Solid sphere takes the least time and the ring takes the maximum time.

4. At the highest point, $N + mg = \dfrac{mv^2}{R-r}$

$$\Rightarrow \quad 0 + mg = \frac{mv_{min}^2}{R-r}$$

$$\Rightarrow \quad v_{min} = \sqrt{g(R-r)}$$

Applying energy conservation between the bottom most and topmost point,

$$K_1 + U_1 = K_2 + U_2$$

$$\Rightarrow \quad \frac{7}{10}mu^2 + 0 = \frac{7}{10}mv_{min}^2 + mg2(R-r)$$

$$\Rightarrow \quad u = \sqrt{\frac{27g(R-r)}{7}}$$

5. (a) $mg\sin\theta - f = ma_{CM}$ ...(i)

$$fR = \frac{2}{5}mR^2\alpha$$ ...(ii)

$$a_{CM} = R\alpha$$ ...(iii)

Solving we get, $f = \dfrac{2mg\sin\theta}{7}$

$$f \le f_L \Rightarrow \frac{2\,mg\sin\theta}{7} \le \mu mg\cos\theta$$

$$\Rightarrow \quad \mu_{min} = \frac{2\tan\theta}{7}$$

(b) $\mu = \dfrac{1}{2}\mu_{min} = \dfrac{\tan\theta}{7}$

$$\Sigma F = ma_{CM} \Rightarrow mg\sin\theta - \mu\, mg\cos\theta = ma_{CM}$$

$$\Rightarrow \quad a_{CM} = \frac{6g\sin\theta}{7}$$

$$\Sigma\tau = I\alpha \Rightarrow (\mu\, mg\cos\theta)R = \frac{2}{5}mR^2\alpha$$

$$\Rightarrow \quad \alpha = \frac{5g\sin\theta}{14R}$$

$$s = ut + \frac{1}{2}at^2 \Rightarrow l = \frac{1}{2}\left(\frac{6g\sin\theta}{7}\right)T^2$$

$$T = \sqrt{\frac{7l}{3g\sin\theta}}$$

$$K = \frac{1}{2}mv_{CM}^2 + \frac{1}{2}I_{CM}\omega^2 = \frac{1}{2}m(2al) + \frac{1}{2}\left(\frac{2}{5}mR^2\right)(\alpha T)^2$$

$$= \frac{11}{12}mgl\sin\theta$$

6. From A to B,

$$W_{mg} + W_N + W_f = \Delta K$$

$$\Rightarrow \quad +mgh + 0 + 0 = \frac{3}{4}mv_{CM}^2 - 0$$

$$\Rightarrow \quad v_{CM} = \sqrt{\frac{4gh}{3}}$$

From B to C,

$$W_{mg} + W_N + W_f = \Delta K$$

$$\Rightarrow -mgh' + 0 + 0 = \left(0 + \frac{1}{2}I_{CM}\omega^2\right) - \left(\frac{1}{2}mv_{CM}^2 + \frac{1}{2}I_{CM}\omega^2\right)$$

$$\Rightarrow h' = \frac{2h}{3}$$

4.5 Angular Impulse

1. Linear impulse $= \Delta P \Rightarrow J = mv_{CM} - 0$

$$\Rightarrow \quad v_{CM} = \frac{J}{m}$$

Angular impulse $= \Delta L \Rightarrow J\left(\dfrac{L}{4}\right) = \left(\dfrac{mL^2}{12}\right)\omega - 0$

$$\Rightarrow \quad \omega = \frac{3J}{mL}$$

$$v_P = v_{CM} - \omega x = \frac{J}{m} - \left(\frac{3J}{mL}\right)x = 0 \Rightarrow x = \frac{L}{3}$$

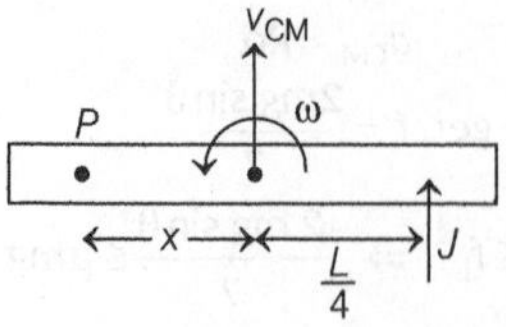

2. (i) Linear impulse $= \Delta P \Rightarrow J = 3mv_{CM} \Rightarrow v_{CM} = \frac{J}{3m}$

(ii) Angular impulse $= \Delta L$

$$\Rightarrow \quad J\left(\frac{2l}{3}\right) = \left(m\left(\frac{2l}{3}\right)^2 + 2m\left(\frac{l}{3}\right)^2\right)\omega$$

$$\Rightarrow \quad \omega = \frac{J}{ml}$$

(iii) $v_A = v_{CM} + \omega\left(\frac{2l}{3}\right) = \frac{J}{m}$

$$v_B = v_{CM} - \omega\left(\frac{l}{3}\right) = 0$$

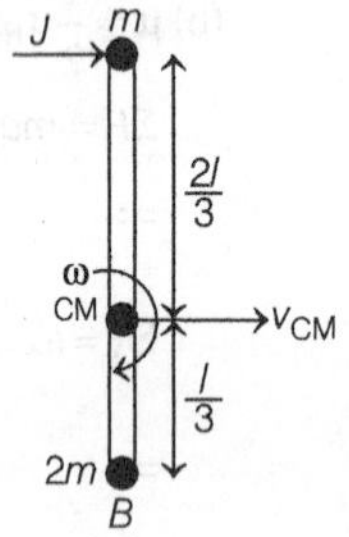

3. (a) Linear impulse $= \Delta P \Rightarrow I = mv_{CM} - 0$

$$\Rightarrow \quad v_{CM} = \frac{I}{m}$$

Angular impulse $= \Delta L \Rightarrow I\left(\frac{4R}{5}\right) = \left(\frac{2}{5}mR^2\right)\omega - 0$

$$\Rightarrow \quad \omega = \frac{2I}{mR}$$

(b) $\theta = \omega_0 t + \frac{1}{2}\alpha t^2 \Rightarrow \pi = \left(\frac{2I}{mR}\right)t \Rightarrow t = \frac{mR\pi}{2I}$

(c) $s = ut + \frac{1}{2}at^2 \Rightarrow s_{CM} = \left(\frac{I}{m}\right)\left(\frac{mR\pi}{2I}\right) = \frac{\pi R}{2}$

4. Linear impulse $= \Delta P \Rightarrow \int N dt = mv_{CM} - (-mv_1)$

$$\Rightarrow \quad \int N dt = m(v_{CM} + v_1) \qquad \text{...(i)}$$

Angular impulse $= \Delta L \Rightarrow \left(\int N \sin\beta \, dt\right)\frac{L}{2} = \left(\frac{mL^2}{12}\right)\omega \qquad \text{...(ii)}$

$$e = \frac{v_{CM} + \frac{\omega L}{2}\sin\beta}{v_1} = 1 \qquad \text{...(iii)}$$

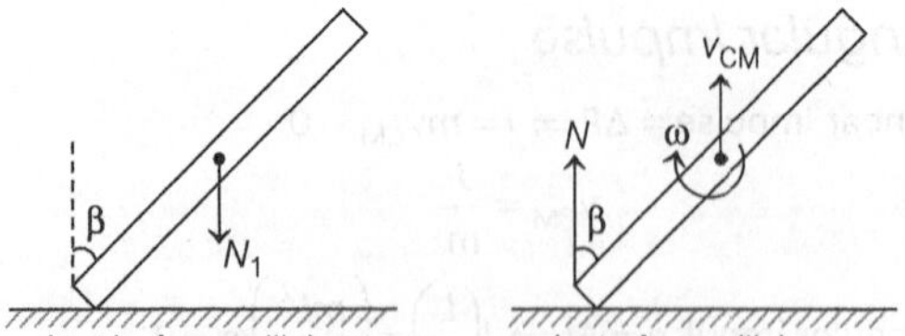

Just before collision Just after collision

Solving Eqs. (i), (ii) and (iii), we get

$$\omega = \frac{v_1}{L}\left(\frac{12\sin\beta}{3\sin^2\beta + 1}\right)$$

5. (a) $\int N dt = mv\cos\theta - (-mv\cos\theta) = 2mv\cos\theta$

$$-\int \mu N dt = mv_x - mv\sin\theta$$

$$\Rightarrow -\mu(2mv\cos\theta) = mv_x - mv\sin\theta$$

$$\Rightarrow \quad v_x = v\sin\theta - 2\mu v\cos\theta$$

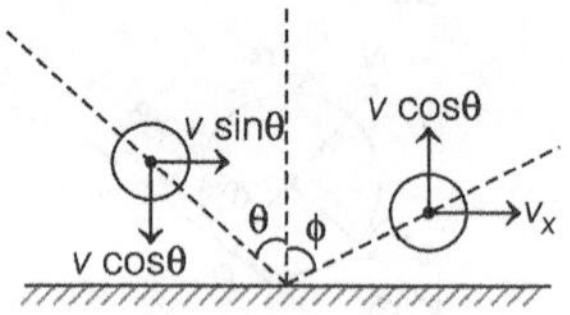

$$\tan\phi = \frac{v_x}{v\cos\theta} \Rightarrow \tan\phi = \tan\theta - 2\mu$$

$$\Rightarrow \tan\theta - \tan\phi = 2\mu$$

(b) Angular impulse due to friction $= \left(\int \mu N dt\right)R$

$$\left(\mu \int N dt\right)a = \left(\frac{2}{5}ma^2\right)\Delta\omega$$

$$\Rightarrow \quad \Delta\omega = \frac{5\mu v\cos\theta}{a}$$

4.6 Angular Momentum in Combined Motion

1. $\mathbf{L} = \mathbf{L}_{CM} + m(\mathbf{r}_{CM} \times \mathbf{v}_{CM})$

$$\Rightarrow L = \left(\frac{MR^2}{2}\right)\omega + MvR = \frac{MR^2\omega}{2} + M(\omega R)R = \frac{3}{2}MR^2\omega$$

2. Applying linear momentum for the system,

$$mv_0 + 0 = 0 + Mv_{CM} \qquad \text{...(i)}$$

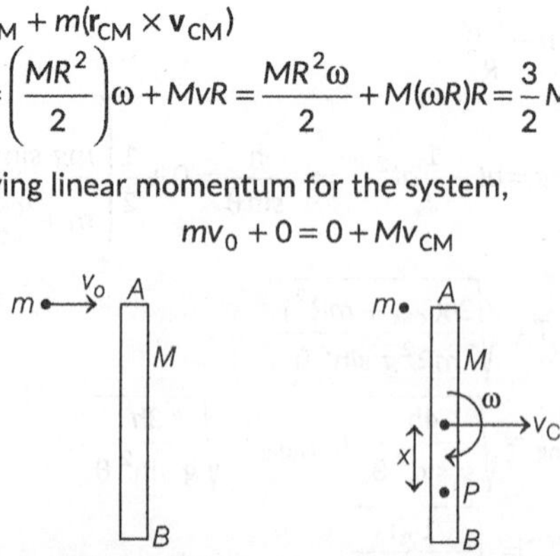

Before collision Just after collision

Applying angular momentum conservation for the system about the centre of the rod,

$$mv_0\left(\frac{L}{2}\right) + 0 = 0 + \left(\frac{ML^2}{12}\right)\omega \qquad \text{...(ii)}$$

$$e = \frac{\left(v_{CM} + \frac{\omega L}{2}\right) - 0}{v_0 - 0} = 1 \qquad \text{...(iii)}$$

Solving Eqs. (i), (ii) and (iii), we get

$$\frac{m}{M} = \frac{1}{4}, \; v_{CM} = \frac{v_0}{4}, \; \omega = \frac{3v_0}{2L}$$

(ii) $v_P = v_{CM} - \omega x = 0 \Rightarrow \frac{v_0}{4} - \left(\frac{3v_0}{2L}\right)x = 0$ and $x = \frac{L}{6}$

$$AP = \frac{L}{2} + \frac{L}{6} = \frac{2L}{3}$$

(iii) $\theta = \omega t = \left(\frac{3v_0}{2L}\right)\left(\frac{\pi L}{3v_0}\right) = \frac{\pi}{2}$

$$\mathbf{v}_P = \frac{v_0}{4}\hat{\mathbf{i}} + \left(\frac{\omega L}{6}\right)\hat{\mathbf{j}}$$

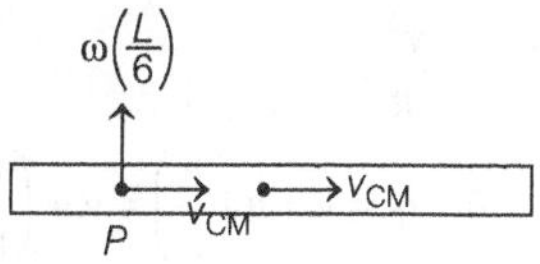

$$v_P = \sqrt{\left(\frac{v_0}{4}\right)^2 + \left(\frac{v_0}{4}\right)^2} = \frac{v_0}{2\sqrt{2}}$$

3. (i) $v_{CM} = \frac{8m(0) + (2m)v + m(-2v)}{12m} = 0$

Since, $F_{ext} = 0$, $v_{CM} = \text{constant} = 0$

(ii) Applying angular momentum conservation about the centre of mass of system,

$$0 + (2m)va + m(2v)(2a) = \left(\frac{8m(6a)^2}{12} + 2ma^2 + m(2a)^2\right)\omega$$

$$\Rightarrow \quad \omega = \frac{v}{5a}$$

(iii) $K = \frac{1}{2}I\omega^2 = \frac{1}{2}\left(\frac{8m(6a)^2}{12} + 2ma^2 + m(2a)^2\right)\left(\frac{v}{5a}\right)^2$

$$= \frac{3}{5}mv^2$$

4. Using linear momentum conservation for $(A + B + P)$ system,

$$2Mu + Mu + 0 = 4Mv_{CM}$$

$$\Rightarrow \quad v_{CM} = \frac{3u}{4}$$

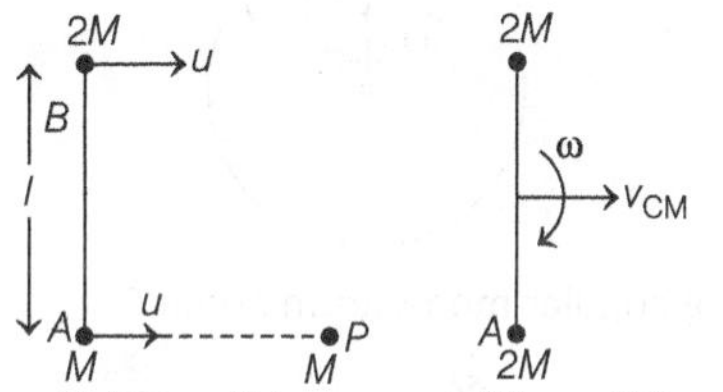

Before collision After collision

Using angular momentum conservation for $(A + B + P)$ system about its centre of mass,

$$(2M)u\frac{l}{2} - Mu\left(\frac{l}{2}\right) = \left[2M\left(\frac{l}{2}\right)^2 + 2M\left(\frac{l}{2}\right)^2\right]\omega$$

$$\Rightarrow \quad \omega = \frac{u}{2l}$$

$$v_B = v_{CM} - \omega\left(\frac{l}{2}\right) = \frac{u}{2}$$

$$v_A = v_{CM} + \omega\left(\frac{l}{2}\right) = u$$

5. Conserving angular momentum about A,

$$-\left(\frac{MR^2}{2}\right)\omega_0 + Mv_0R = \left(\frac{MR^2}{2} + MR^2\right)\omega$$

$$\Rightarrow \quad \omega = \frac{2v_0 - 3\omega_0 R}{3R}$$

6. $\mathbf{L} = \mathbf{L}_{CM} + \mathbf{r} \times m\mathbf{v}_{CM}$

For rod, $\mathbf{L}_1 = \left(\frac{ml^2}{12}\right)\omega_1\hat{\mathbf{j}} + \left(\frac{l}{2}\hat{\mathbf{i}} + R\hat{\mathbf{j}}\right) \times m\left(-\omega_1\left(\frac{l}{2}\right)\hat{\mathbf{k}}\right)$

$$= \frac{ml^2\omega_1}{12}\hat{\mathbf{j}} + \frac{ml^2\omega_1}{4}\hat{\mathbf{j}} - \frac{m\omega_1 lR}{2}\hat{\mathbf{i}}$$

$$= \left(\frac{ml^2}{3}\omega_1\right)\hat{\mathbf{j}} - \left(\frac{m\omega_1 lR}{2}\right)\hat{\mathbf{i}}$$

For disc $\mathbf{L}_2 = \left(+\frac{mR^2}{2}\omega_2\hat{\mathbf{i}}\right) + \left(\frac{mR^2}{4}\omega_1\hat{\mathbf{j}}\right)$

$$+ (l\hat{\mathbf{i}} + R\hat{\mathbf{j}}) \times m(-\omega_1 l\hat{\mathbf{k}})$$

$$= \left(+\frac{mR^2}{2}\omega_2\right)\hat{\mathbf{i}} + \left(\frac{mR^2}{4}\omega_1\right)\hat{\mathbf{j}} + (ml^2\omega_1)\hat{\mathbf{j}} - (mRl\omega_1)\hat{\mathbf{i}}$$

So, $\mathbf{L} = \mathbf{L}_1 + \mathbf{L}_2$

$$= \left(\frac{4}{3}ml^2\omega_1 + \frac{mR^2}{4}\omega_1\right)\hat{\mathbf{j}} + \left(\frac{mR^2}{2}\omega_2 - \frac{3}{2}m\omega_1 lR\right)\hat{\mathbf{i}}$$

4.7 Instantaneous Axis of Rotation

1. (a) $v_B = v_{CM} + \omega(50) = 30$ ...(i)

$v_A = v_{CM} - \omega(50) = -20$ ...(ii)

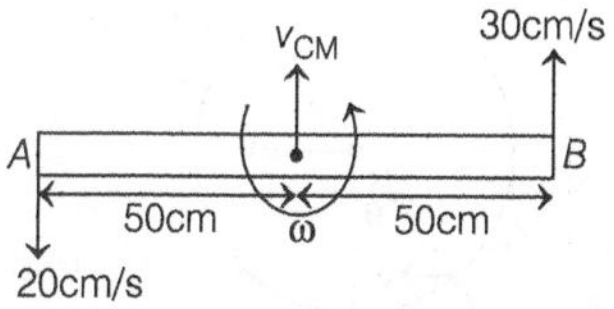

Solving (i) and (ii), we get

$$v_{CM} = 5 \text{ cm/s and } \omega = 0.5 \text{ rad/s}$$

(b) $v_A = \omega x = 20$ ...(i)

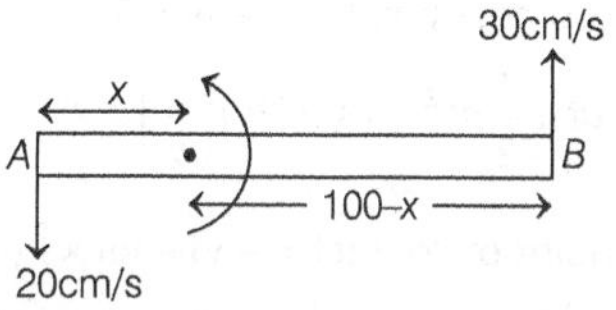

$v_B = \omega(100 - x) = 30$ ...(ii)

Solving Eqs. (i) and (ii), we get $x = 40$ cm

2. (a) $v_A = \omega(L + x) = 2v$ ...(i)

$v_B = \omega x = v$ ...(ii)

Solving, we get

$$x = L$$

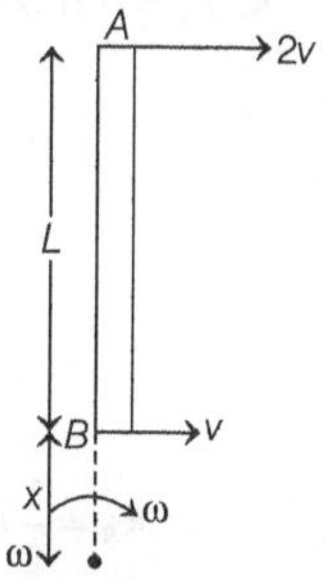

(b) $\omega L = v \Rightarrow \omega = \frac{v}{L}$

$$v_{CM} = \omega\left(\frac{3L}{2}\right) = \frac{3v}{2}$$

(c) $K = \frac{1}{2}mv_{CM}^2 + \frac{1}{2}I_{CM}\omega^2$

$$= \frac{1}{2}m\left(\frac{3v}{2}\right)^2 + \frac{1}{2}\left(\frac{mL^2}{12}\right)\left(\frac{v}{L}\right)^2 = \frac{7}{6}mv^2$$

3. Applying work-energy theorem,

$$W_{mg} + W_{N_1} + W_{N_2} = \Delta K$$

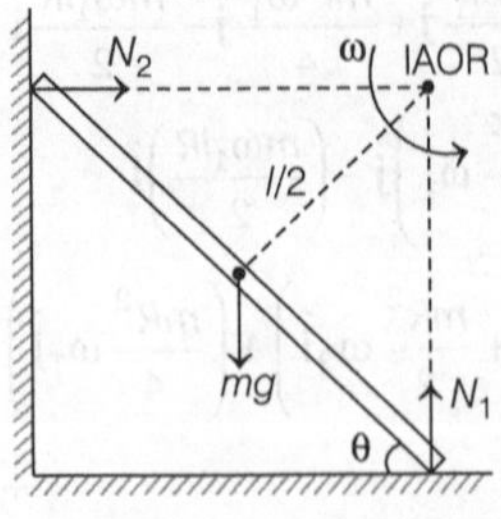

$$\Rightarrow + mg\frac{l}{2}(1-\sin\theta) + 0 + 0 = \frac{1}{2}\left(\frac{ml^2}{12} + m\left(\frac{l}{2}\right)^2\right)\omega^2$$

$$\omega = \sqrt{\frac{3g(1-\sin\theta)}{l}}$$

Level 2

Single Choice Correct Questions

1. $v_P = \sqrt{v^2 + v^2 + 2v(v)\cos(180° - \theta)} = 2v\sin\left(\frac{\theta}{2}\right)$

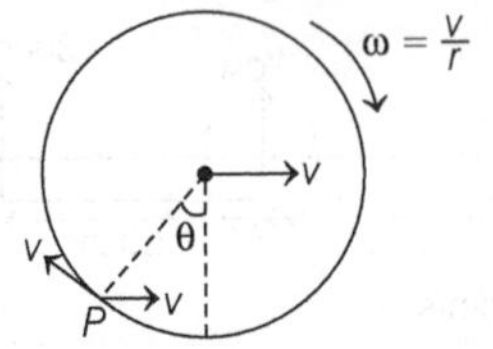

2. $s_{CM} = u_{CM}t + \frac{1}{2}a_{CM}t^2 \Rightarrow l = vt \Rightarrow t = \frac{l}{v}$

Velocity of topmost point $= v + \omega r = 2v$

$$s = ut + \frac{1}{2}at^2 \Rightarrow s = (2v)\left(\frac{l}{v}\right) = 2l$$

3. Velocity of point of contact $= -v\hat{i} + (\omega \times R(-\hat{j})) = 2v\hat{i}$

$$\Rightarrow \quad \omega \times \hat{j} = -\left(\frac{3v}{R}\right)\hat{i} \Rightarrow \omega = \left(\frac{3v}{R}\right)\hat{k}$$

4. $K_P = \frac{1}{2}m(2v)^2 = 2mv^2$

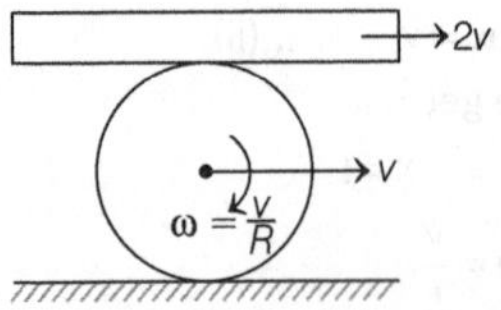

$$K_S = \frac{1}{2}mv^2 + \frac{1}{2}\left(\frac{mR^2}{2}\right)\left(\frac{v}{R}\right)^2 = \frac{3}{4}mv^2$$

$K_P : K_S = 8 : 3$

5. For the lowermost point, velocity is zero and acceleration is $\frac{v^2}{R}$.

6. $v_P = v + \omega\left(\frac{R}{2}\right) = v + \left(\frac{v}{R}\right)\left(\frac{R}{2}\right) = \frac{3v}{2}$

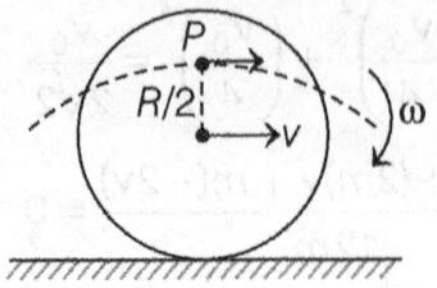

$$\text{Centripetal acceleration of } P = \omega^2\left(\frac{R}{2}\right) = \frac{\left(\frac{3v}{2}\right)^2}{r}$$

$$\Rightarrow \quad r = 4.5R$$

7. $\mathbf{v_P} = v\hat{i} - v\hat{j}$

$$\mathbf{a_P} = -\frac{v^2}{R}\hat{i}$$

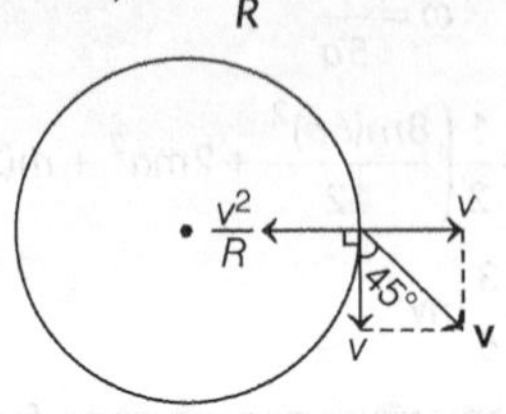

Angle between velocity and acceleration at $P = 135°$

8. $a_P = \sqrt{(a + r\alpha)^2 + (\omega^2 r)^2}$

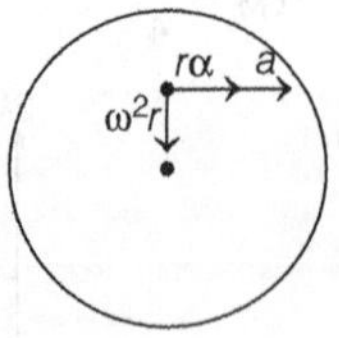

9. Conserving angular momentum about P,

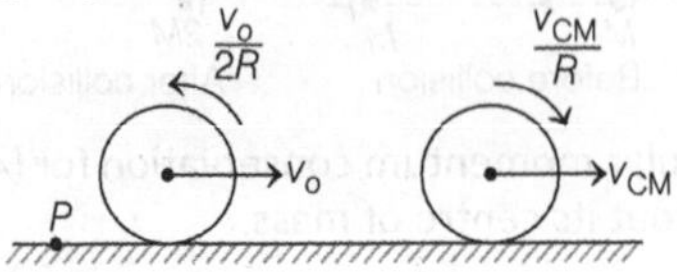

$$-(mR^2)\left(\frac{v_0}{2R}\right) + mv_0R = (mR^2)\left(\frac{v_{CM}}{R}\right) + mv_{CM}R$$

$$\Rightarrow \quad v_{CM} = \frac{v_0}{4}$$

10. Conserving angular momentum about P,

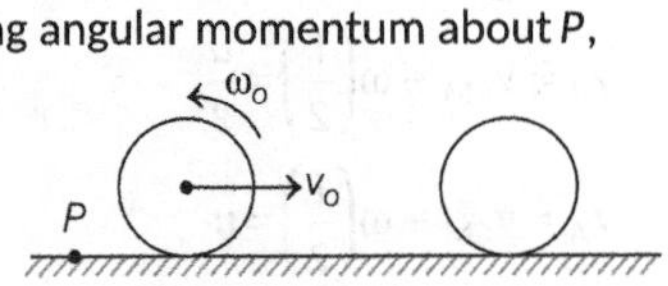

$$-\left(\frac{mR^2}{2}\right)\omega_0 + mv_0R = 0 + 0$$

$$\Rightarrow \quad \omega_0 = \frac{2v_0}{R} = 100 \text{ rad/s}$$

11. $a_1 = \dfrac{\mu mg}{m} = \mu g$

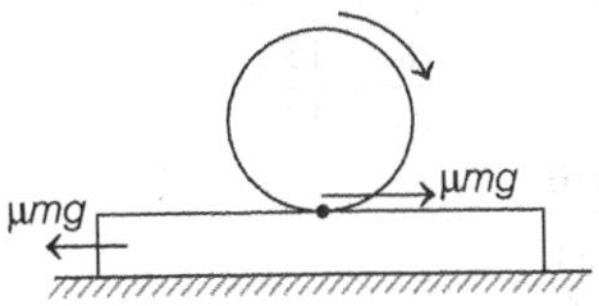

$$a_2 = -\frac{\mu mg}{3m} = -\frac{\mu g}{3}$$

$$a_{12} = a_1 - a_2 = \mu g - \left(-\frac{\mu g}{3}\right) = \frac{4\mu g}{3}$$

12. $\Sigma F_x = ma_x \Rightarrow 10\sqrt{3}\cos 30° - f = 2a_{CM}$ ...(i)

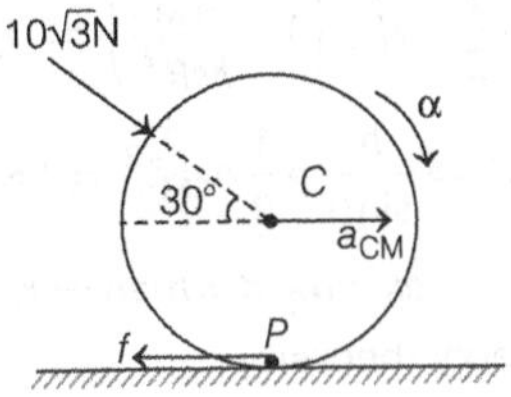

About C, $\Sigma\tau = I\alpha$

$\Rightarrow$ $fR = \dfrac{2}{3}((2)R^2)\alpha$ ...(ii)

$a_P = a_{CM} - R\alpha = 0$ ...(iii)

Solving equation, we get $f = 6$ N

$\Sigma F_y = 0 \Rightarrow N = mg + (10\sqrt{3})\sin 30° = (20 + 5\sqrt{3})$ N

$f \le f_L \Rightarrow 6 \le (20 + 5\sqrt{3})\mu$, $\mu_{min} = \dfrac{6}{20 + 5\sqrt{3}} = 0.2$

13. $\Sigma F_x = ma_x \Rightarrow 20 + f = 4a_{CM}$ ...(i)

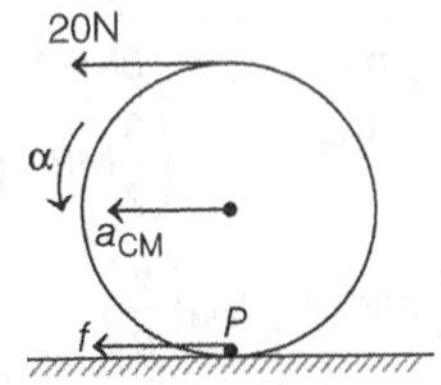

$\Sigma\tau = I\alpha \Rightarrow 20R - fR = 0.02\alpha$ ...(ii)

$a_P = 0 \Rightarrow a_{CM} - R\alpha = 0$ ...(iii)

Solving Eqs. (i), (ii) and (iii), we get

$a_{CM} = 6.7 \text{ m/s}^2$

14. $\Sigma F_x = ma_x \Rightarrow f = ma_{CM}$ ...(i)

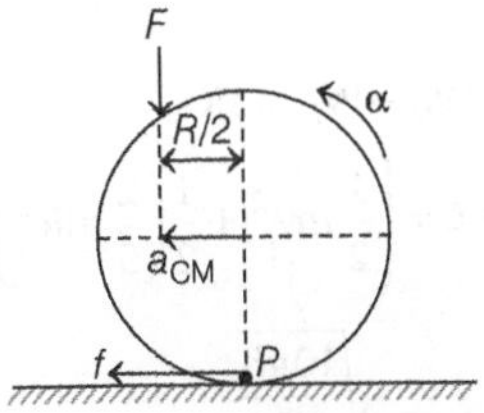

$\Sigma\tau = I_{CM}\alpha \Rightarrow -fR + F\left(\dfrac{R}{2}\right) = \left(\dfrac{mR^2}{2}\right)\alpha$ ...(ii)

$a_P = 0 \Rightarrow a_{CM} - R\alpha = 0$ ...(iii)

Solving Eqs. (i), (ii) and (iii), we get

$$f = \frac{2F}{3}$$

15. In absence of friction, acceleration of centre of mass is towards right and angular acceleration is zero. So, the point of contact has the tendency to move towards right and friction will act towards left.

16. In absence of friction, a_{CM} is towards right and angular acceleration about the centre will be anti-clockwise. So, point of contact has the tendency to move towards right and friction will act towards left.

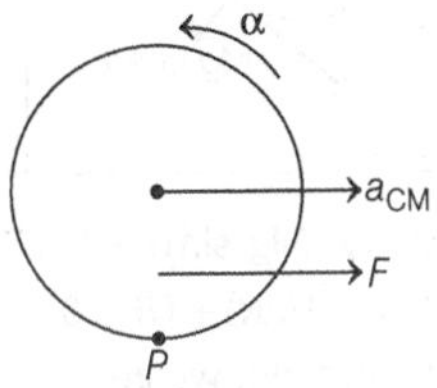

$$a_P = a_{CM} + R\alpha$$

17. In absence of friction, a_{CM} will be towards right and α will be clockwise.

So, $a_P = a_{CM} - R\alpha$

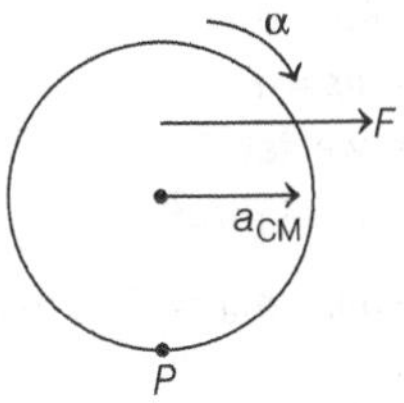

Since, we don't know whether $a_{CM} > R\alpha$ or $a_{CM} < R\alpha$ or $a_{CM} = R\alpha$, we can't find direction of friction.

18. Friction on the plank will be towards left, so friction on the cylinder will be towards right.

19. $\Sigma F_x = 0 \Rightarrow F\cos\theta = f$ ...(i)

$\Sigma\tau = 0 \Rightarrow fR - Fr = 0$ ...(ii)

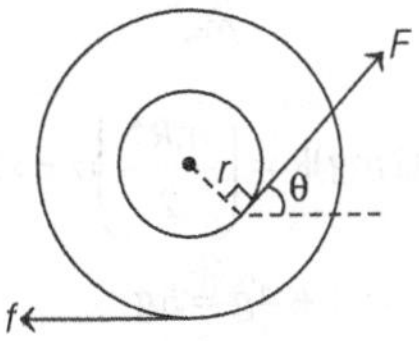

From Eqs. (i) and (ii), we get

$$\theta = \cos^{-1}\left(\frac{r}{R}\right)$$

20. In absence of friction, a_{CM} is towards right and α is anti-clockwise, so tendency of bottom most point is to go towards right. Hence, friction will act leftwards. Now for pure rolling, a_{CM} is towards right and α will be clockwise. So, thread winds and spool rotates clockwise.

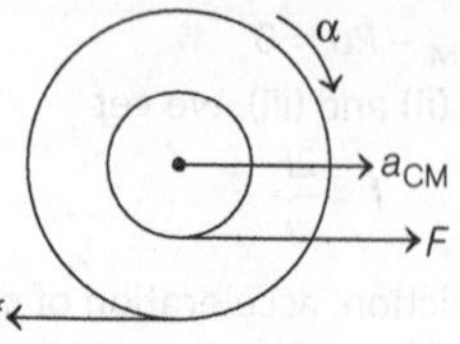

21. For block, $\Sigma F_y = 0 \Rightarrow T - mg = 0$ ...(i)

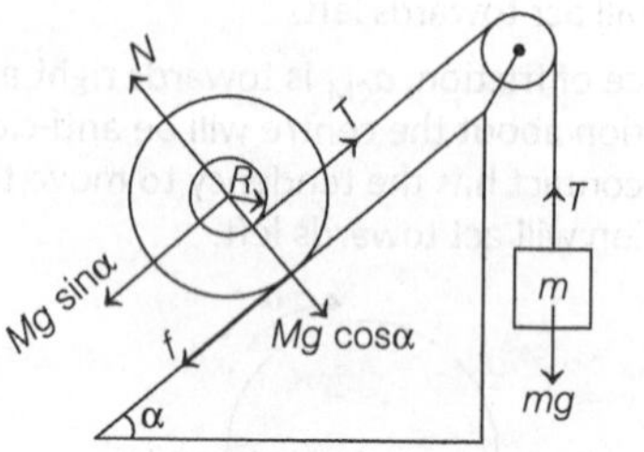

For spool, $\Sigma F = 0 \;\Rightarrow\; Mg\sin\alpha + f = T$ ...(ii)

$\Sigma\tau = 0 \;\Rightarrow\; f(2R) + TR = 0$ ...(iii)

Solving Eqs. (i), (ii) and (iii), we get $m = 2M\sin\alpha$

22. For block, $mg - T = ma$ ...(i)

For spool, $T + f = ma_{CM}$ ...(ii)

$$TR - fR = \frac{5}{3}mR^2\alpha \quad ...(iii)$$

Constraint, $a_{CM} - R\alpha = 0$ ...(iv)

$a_{CM} + R\alpha = a$ ...(v)

Solving equations, we get

$$a = 6\ \text{m/s}^2$$

23. $\Sigma F = ma_{CM} \Rightarrow F - mg = mg \Rightarrow F = 2mg$

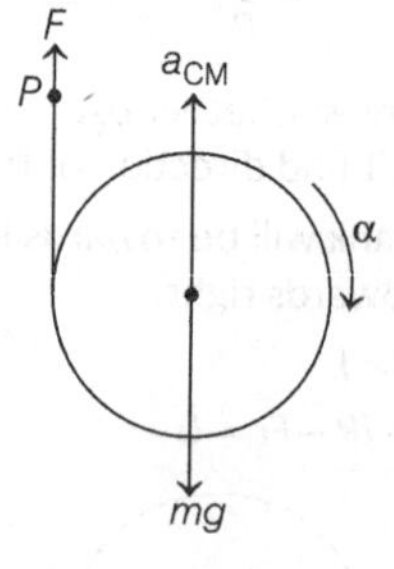

$$\Sigma\tau = I_{CM}\alpha \Rightarrow (2mg)R = \left(\frac{mR^2}{2}\right)\alpha \Rightarrow R\alpha = 4g$$

$$a_P = a_{CM} + R\alpha = g + 4g = 5g$$

24. $a_{CM} = \dfrac{mg\sin\theta}{m + \dfrac{I_{CM}}{R^2}}$

For solid sphere, $I_{CM} = \dfrac{2}{5}mR^2$

For solid cylinder, $I_{CM} = \dfrac{mR^2}{2}$

So, $a_1 = \dfrac{5g\sin\theta}{7}$ and $a_2 = \dfrac{2g\sin\theta}{3}$

$$\frac{a_1}{a_2} = \frac{15}{14}$$

25. $a_{CM} = \dfrac{mg\sin\theta}{m + \dfrac{I_{CM}}{R^2}}$

$$I_P > I_Q \Rightarrow a_P < a_Q$$

So, cylinder Q reaches ground with larger speed and larger angular speed and takes lesser time than P.

26. $MgH = \dfrac{1}{2}Mv_{CM}^2 + \dfrac{1}{2}I_{CM}\left(\dfrac{v_{CM}}{R}\right)^2$

$$\Rightarrow \quad MgH = \frac{1}{2}mv_{CM}^2\left(1 + \frac{I_{CM}}{MR^2}\right) \Rightarrow I_{CM} = \frac{3}{4}MR^2$$

27. $S_{CM} = ut + \dfrac{1}{2}at^2 \Rightarrow \dfrac{h}{\sin\theta} = \dfrac{1}{2}a_{CM}t^2 \Rightarrow t \propto \sqrt{h}$

$$a_P = a_Q, K = mgh \Rightarrow K \propto h$$

28. Using work-energy theorem,

$$W_{mg} + W_N + W_f = \Delta K$$

$$\Rightarrow \quad +mg(R - r) + 0 + 0 = \frac{7}{10}mv_{CM}^2 - 0$$

$$\Rightarrow \quad v_{CM} = \sqrt{\frac{10g(R - r)}{7}}$$

At point B, $N - mg = \dfrac{mv_{CM}^2}{R - r} \Rightarrow N = \dfrac{17mg}{7}$

29. $I_{CM} = \left(\dfrac{M(2R\sin 60°)^2}{12} + M(R\cos 60°)^2\right) \times 3 = \dfrac{3}{2}MR^2$

$$\mu_{min} = \frac{\tan\theta}{1 + \dfrac{mR^2}{I_{CM}}} = \frac{\dfrac{3}{2}}{1 + \dfrac{3MR^2}{\left(\dfrac{3}{2}MR^2\right)}} = \frac{1}{2}$$

30. $mgh = \dfrac{1}{2}mv^2 + \dfrac{1}{2}I_{CM}\left(\dfrac{v}{R}\right)^2$ ...(i)

$mgh = \dfrac{1}{2}m\left(\dfrac{5v}{4}\right)^2$ ...(ii)

Solving we get, $I_{CM} = \dfrac{9}{16}mR^2$

Now, $I_{CM} = mK^2 = \dfrac{9}{16}mR^2 \Rightarrow K = \dfrac{3R}{4}$

31. From A to B,

$$W_{mg} + W_N + W_f = \Delta K$$

$$\Rightarrow +mgh + 0 + 0 = \left(\frac{1}{2}mv^2 + \frac{1}{2}\left(\frac{2}{5}mR^2\right)\left(\frac{v}{R}\right)^2\right) - (0 + 0)$$

$$\Rightarrow \quad v = \sqrt{\frac{10gh}{7}}$$

From B to C,

$$W_{mg} + W_N = \Delta K$$

$$\Rightarrow -mgh' + 0 = \left(0 + \frac{1}{2}(I_{CM})\omega^2\right) - \left(\frac{1}{2}mv^2 + \frac{1}{2}(I_{CM})\omega^2\right)$$

$$\Rightarrow \quad h' = \frac{5h}{7}$$

32. $f = \mu\, mg\cos\theta = mg\sin\theta$

$$\Sigma F = ma_{CM} \Rightarrow mg\sin\theta - mg\sin\theta = ma_{CM}$$

$$\Rightarrow \quad a_{CM} = 0$$

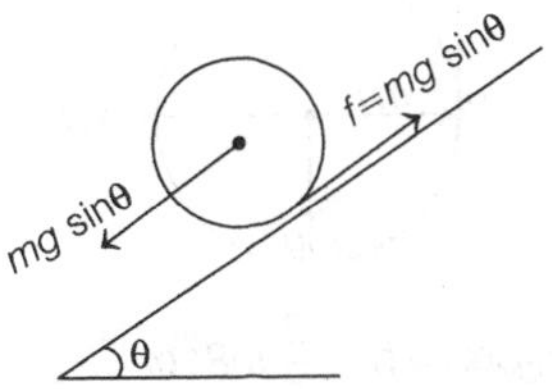

So, centre of mass of cylinder is stationary,

$$\Sigma\tau = I_{CM}\alpha \Rightarrow -(mg\sin\theta)R = \left(\frac{mR^2}{2}\right)\alpha$$

$$\Rightarrow \quad \alpha = -\frac{2g\sin\theta}{R}$$

$$\omega = \omega_0 + \alpha t \Rightarrow 0 = \omega_0 - \left(\frac{2g\sin\theta}{R}\right)t$$

$$t = \frac{\omega_0 R}{2g\sin\theta}$$

33. Linear impulse $= \Delta P \Rightarrow J = mv_{CM} \Rightarrow v_{CM} = \dfrac{J}{m}$

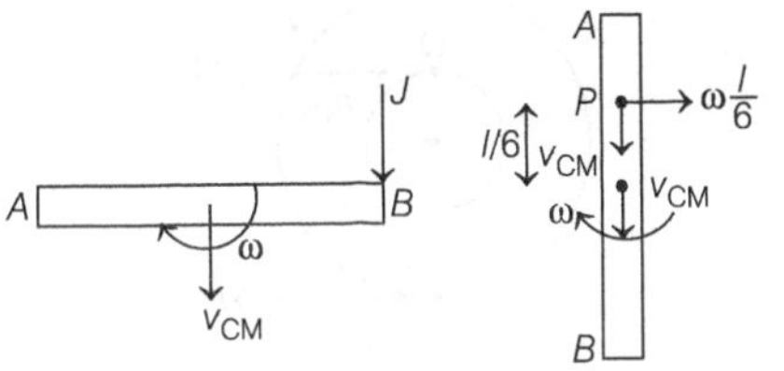

$$\text{Angular impulse} = \Delta L \Rightarrow J\frac{l}{2} = \left(\frac{ml^2}{12}\right)\omega \Rightarrow \omega = \frac{6J}{ml}$$

$$\theta = \omega t = \left(\frac{6J}{ml}\right)\left(\frac{\pi ml}{12J}\right) = \frac{\pi}{2}$$

$$v_P = \sqrt{v_{cm}^2 + \left(\frac{\omega l}{6}\right)^2} = \sqrt{2}\frac{J}{m}$$

34. Angular impulse $= \Delta L$

$$\Rightarrow (Mv\sin 30^\circ)\frac{L}{2} = \left(M\left(\frac{L}{2}\right)^2 + M\left(\frac{L}{2}\right)^2\right)\omega \Rightarrow \omega = \frac{v}{2L}$$

35. Linear impulse $= \Delta P \Rightarrow F\Delta t = mv_{CM} \Rightarrow v_{CM} = \dfrac{F\Delta t}{m}$

$$\text{Angular impulse} = \Delta L \Rightarrow (F\Delta t)\left(\frac{l}{2}\right) = \left(\frac{ml^2}{12}\right)\omega \Rightarrow \omega = \frac{6F\Delta t}{ml}$$

$$\theta = \omega t = \frac{\pi}{2} \Rightarrow t = \frac{\pi ml}{12F\Delta t}$$

$$s_{CM} = v_{CM}t = \frac{\pi l}{12}$$

$$X\text{-coordinate of end } A = \frac{l}{2} + \frac{\pi l}{12} = \frac{l}{2}\left(1 + \frac{\pi}{6}\right)$$

36. $I = \Delta P \Rightarrow I = mv_{CM} \Rightarrow v_{CM} = \dfrac{I}{m}$

$$I \times h = \Delta L \Rightarrow I \times h = \left(\frac{2}{5}mR^2\right)\omega \Rightarrow \omega = \frac{5Ih}{2mR^2}$$

For pure rolling, $v_{CM} = \omega R$

$$\Rightarrow \quad \frac{h}{R} = \frac{2}{5}$$

37. $\mathbf{L} = \mathbf{L}_{CM} + m(\mathbf{r}_{CM} \times \mathbf{v}_{CM})$

$$\mathbf{L} = \left(\frac{mR^2}{2}\right)\omega\hat{\mathbf{k}} + m((4R\hat{\mathbf{i}} + 3R\hat{\mathbf{j}}) \times (\omega r)\hat{\mathbf{i}}) = -\frac{5}{2}mR^2\omega\hat{\mathbf{k}}$$

38. Conserving angular momentum of system about the centre of mass of the system,

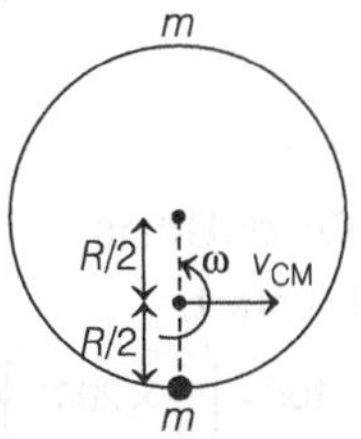

$$mv\left(\frac{R}{2}\right) + 0 = \left(\left(mR^2 + m\left(\frac{R}{2}\right)^2\right) + m\left(\frac{R}{2}\right)^2\right)\omega$$

$$\Rightarrow \quad \omega = \frac{v}{3R}$$

39. $L_i = mv\left(\dfrac{L}{2}\right)$, since external torque on the system is zero, angular momentum of system is conserved about A. So, $L_f = mv\left(\dfrac{L}{2}\right)$

40. $v_{CM} = \omega(2.5) \Rightarrow 1.25 = \omega(2.5)$

$$\omega = 0.5 \text{ rad/s}$$

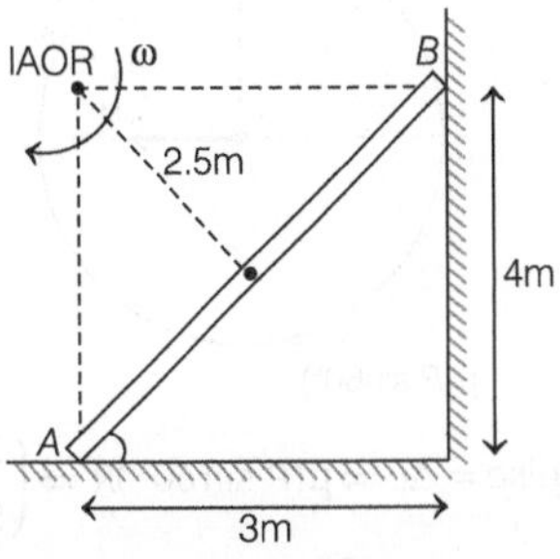

$$\Rightarrow \quad v_A = \omega(4) = 0.5 \times 4 = 2 \text{ m/s}$$

41. $Mu + 0 = Mv + Mv_{CM}$ ...(i)

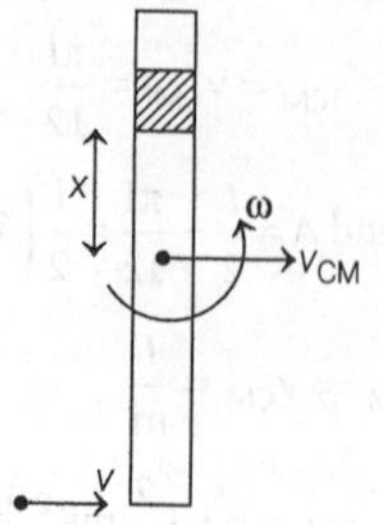

$$Mu\frac{L}{2} = Mv\frac{L}{2} + \frac{ML^2}{12}\omega \quad \text{...(ii)}$$

$$e = \frac{\left(v_{CM} + \frac{\omega L}{2}\right) - v}{u} = 1 \quad \text{...(iii)}$$

Solving, we get $v_{CM} = \frac{2u}{5}$ and $\omega = \frac{12u}{5L}$

$$K = \int_0^{L/2} \frac{1}{2}\left(\frac{M}{L}dx\right)(v_{CM} - \omega x)^2 = \frac{M}{2L}\left[\frac{(v_{CM} - \omega x)^3}{-3\omega}\right]_0^{L/2}$$

$$= \frac{Mu^2}{25}$$

Numerical Value Questions

1. About the point of contact,

$$\Sigma\tau = I\alpha \Rightarrow 10R = \left(\frac{3}{2} \times 20R^2\right)\alpha$$

$$\Rightarrow \quad \alpha = \frac{1}{3R}$$

$$\omega = \omega_0 + \alpha t = 0 + \left(\frac{1}{3R}\right)(6) = \frac{2}{R}$$

$$K = \frac{1}{2}I_P\omega^2 = \frac{1}{2}\left(\frac{3}{2} \times 20R^2\right)\left(\frac{2}{R}\right)^2 = 60 \text{ J}$$

2. Linear impulse $= \Delta P \Rightarrow P\cos 60° - \mu(P\sin 60°) = mv_{CM}$

$$\Rightarrow \quad v_{CM} = \frac{1}{2\sqrt{3}} - \frac{\mu}{2}$$

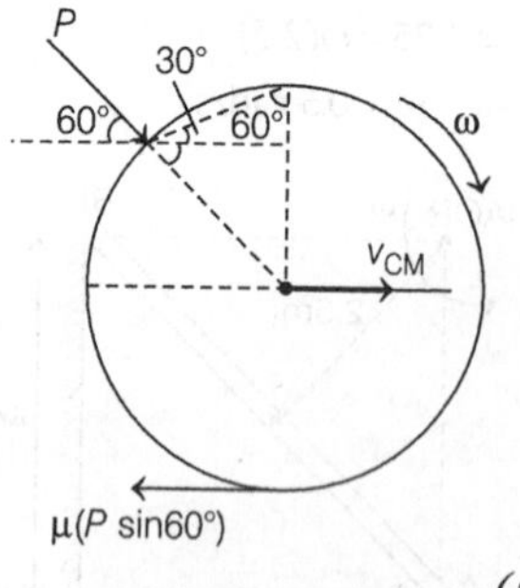

Angular impulse $= \Delta L \Rightarrow \mu(P\sin 60°)R \Rightarrow \left(\frac{2}{5}mR^2\right)\omega$

$$\Rightarrow \quad \omega = \frac{5\mu}{4R}$$

For pure rolling, $v_{CM} = \omega R$

$$\Rightarrow \quad \frac{1}{2\sqrt{3}} - \frac{\mu}{2} = \frac{5\mu}{4}$$

$$\Rightarrow \quad \mu = \frac{2\sqrt{3}}{7}$$

3. $\Sigma F_x = 0 \Rightarrow N = ma$

$$\Sigma F_y = ma_{CM} \Rightarrow mg - f = ma_{CM}$$

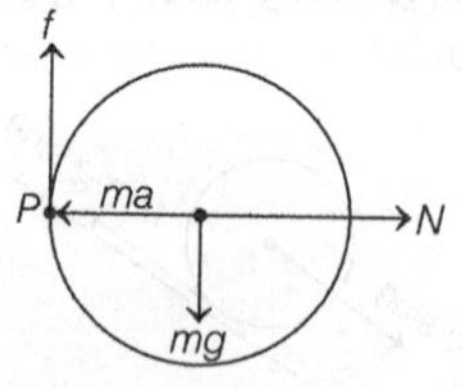

$$\Sigma\tau = I_{CM}\alpha \Rightarrow fR = \frac{2}{5}mR^2\alpha$$

$$(a_P)_{tangential} = 0 \Rightarrow a_{CM} - R\alpha = 0$$

Solving equations, we get $f = \frac{2mg}{7}$

$$f \le f_L \Rightarrow \frac{2mg}{7} \le \mu\left(\frac{mg}{2}\right)$$

$$\Rightarrow \quad \mu_{min} = \frac{4}{7}$$

4. $\Sigma F = ma_{CM} \Rightarrow Mg + f = Ma_{CM}$ ...(i)

$\Sigma\tau = I_{CM}\alpha \Rightarrow MgR - f(3R) = (MR^2)\alpha$ ...(ii)

$(a_P)_{tangential} = 0 \Rightarrow a_{CM} - 3R\alpha = 0$ ...(iii)

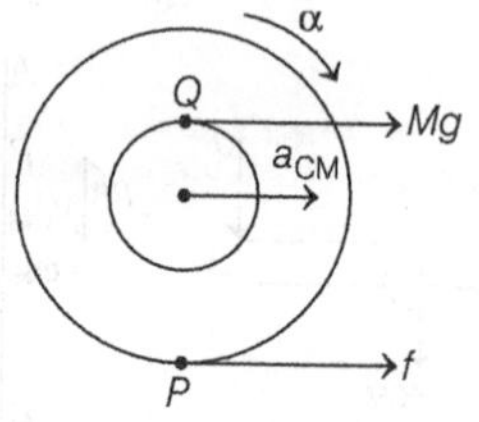

Solving we get, $a_{CM} = \frac{6g}{5}$ and $\alpha = \frac{2g}{5R}$

$$a_Q = a_{CM} + R\alpha = \frac{6g}{5} + \frac{2g}{5} = \frac{8g}{5}$$

5. $\mu_{min} = \dfrac{\tan\theta}{1 + \dfrac{mR^2}{I_{CM}}} = \dfrac{\tan\theta}{3}$

So, $\mu = \dfrac{13 - 3x}{\sqrt{3}} = \dfrac{\tan 60°}{3} \Rightarrow x = 4$

6. From A to B,

$$W_{mg} + W_N + W_f = \Delta K$$

$$\Rightarrow \quad + mgh + 0 + 0 = \frac{1}{2}mv_{CM}^2 + \frac{1}{2}\left(\frac{2}{5}mR^2\right)\left(\frac{v_{CM}}{R}\right)^2$$

$$\Rightarrow \quad v_{CM} = \sqrt{\frac{10gh}{7}}$$

So at point B, $K_T = \frac{1}{2} mv_{CM}^2 = \frac{5mgh}{7}$

and $K_R = \frac{1}{2} I_{CM}\omega^2 = \frac{2mgh}{7}$

From B to C, work done by gravity will increase only transactional kinetic energy, so at point C,

$$K_T = \frac{5mgh}{7} + mgh = \frac{12mgh}{7}$$

$$K_R = \frac{2mgh}{7}$$

So, $\frac{K_T}{K_R} = 6$

7. $a = \dfrac{mg \sin\theta}{m + \dfrac{I_{CM}}{R^2}}$

$$a_P = \frac{g \sin\theta}{2} \text{ and } a_C = \frac{2g \sin\theta}{3}$$

$$a_{rel} = a_C - a_P = \frac{g \sin\theta}{6} = 1 \text{ m/s}^2$$

$$s = ut + \frac{1}{2} at^2 = 0 + \frac{1}{2}(1)(4)^2 = 8 \text{ m}$$

8. Applying linear momentum conservation,

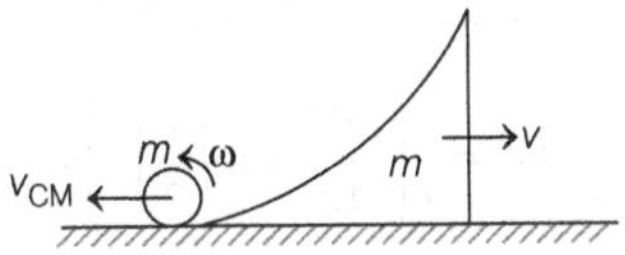

$$0 + 0 = -mv_{CM} + mv \quad \text{...(i)}$$

Applying energy conservation,

$$mgh = \frac{1}{2} mv^2 + \frac{3}{4} mv_{CM}^2 \quad \text{...(ii)}$$

Solving Eqs. (i) and (ii), we get

$$v = \sqrt{\frac{4gh}{5}} = 4 \text{ m/s}$$

9. Conserving linear momentum of system,

$$200 \times 16 = 200v + 50(v - \omega(1)) \quad \text{...(i)}$$

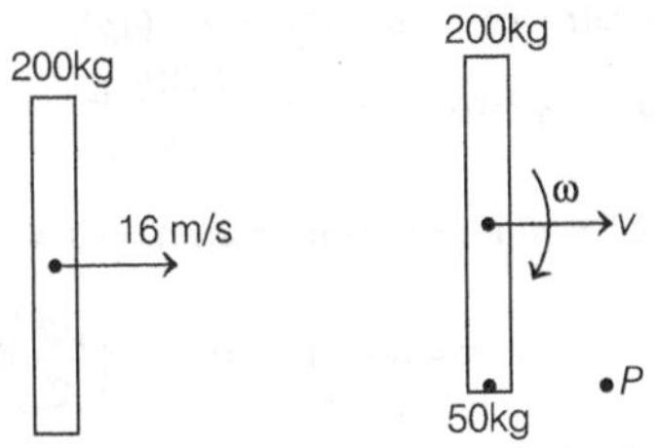

Conserving angular momentum of system about point P on ground,

$$200 \times 16 \times 1 = \left(\left(\frac{(200)(2)^2}{12}\right)\omega + 200v(1)\right) + 0 \quad \text{...(ii)}$$

Solving Eqs. (i) and (ii), we get

$$\omega = 6 \text{ rad/s}$$

10. Conserving linear momentum of the system,

$$0 + 0 = 18(-v_1) + Mv_2 \quad \text{...(i)}$$

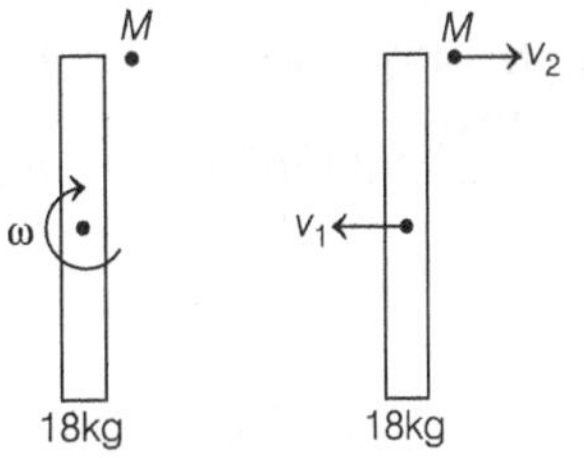

Conserving angular momentum of the system about the centre of the rod,

$$\left(\frac{18(3)^2}{12}\right)\omega + 0 = 0 + Mv_2(1.5) \quad \text{...(ii)}$$

$$e = \frac{v_1 + v_2}{\omega(1.5)} = 1 \quad \text{...(iii)}$$

Solving Eqs. (i), (ii) and (iii), we get

$$M = 9 \text{ kg}$$

Level 3

Single Choice Correct Questions

1. $\omega_1 = \frac{v}{2R}$; $\omega_2 = \frac{2v - (-v)}{2R} = \frac{3v}{2R}$

$$\frac{\omega_2}{\omega_1} = 3$$

2. $K = \left(\frac{1}{2} mv_0^2 + \frac{1}{2}(mR^2)\left(\frac{v_0}{R}\right)^2\right) + \frac{1}{2} m(2v_0)^2 + \frac{1}{2} m(\sqrt{2}v_0)^2 + \frac{1}{2}(2m)(\sqrt{2}v_0)^2$

$$= 6mv_0^2$$

3. $\omega = \alpha t = 2(3) = 6$ rad/s

$$a_c = \omega^2 R = 36 \text{ m/s}^2$$

$$a_T = 2R\alpha = 4 \text{ m/s}^2$$

$$a_{net} = \sqrt{(10)^2 + (36)^2 + (4)^2}$$

$$= \sqrt{1412} \text{ m/s}^2$$

4. $\Sigma F_x = ma_x \Rightarrow f = Ma_{CM}$ ...(i)

$\Sigma\tau = I_{CM}\alpha \Rightarrow (4Mg)R \cos 60° - fR = \left(\frac{2}{5} mR^2\right)\alpha$ ...(ii)

$$a_{CM} - R\alpha = 0 \quad \text{...(iii)}$$

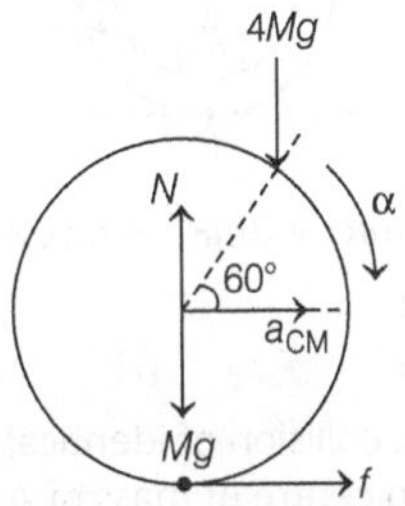

Solving Eqs. (i), (ii) and (iii), we get

$$f = \frac{10Mg}{7}$$

$$\Sigma F_y = 0 \Rightarrow N - 4Mg - Mg = 0 \Rightarrow N = 5Mg$$

$$f \le f_L \Rightarrow \frac{10Mg}{7} \le \mu\,(5Mg) \Rightarrow \mu_{min} = \frac{2}{7}$$

5. $\mathbf{a}_C = \frac{v^2}{5R}\downarrow$

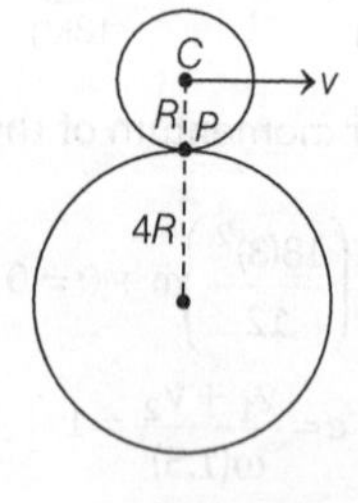

$$\mathbf{a}_P = \mathbf{a}_{PC} + \mathbf{a}_C = \frac{v^2}{R}\uparrow + \frac{v^2}{5R}\downarrow = \frac{4v^2}{5R}\uparrow$$

6. For upper plank, $F - f_1 = Ma_1$ ...(i)

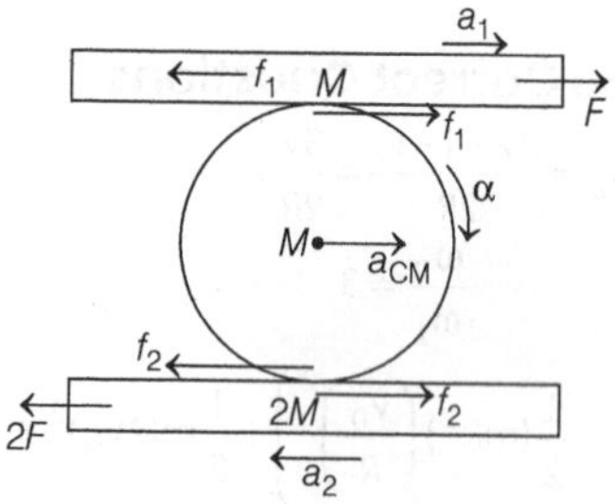

For lower plank, $2F - f_2 = 2Ma_2$ ...(ii)

For cylinder, $f_1 + f_2 = Ma_{CM}$ ...(iii)

$$f_1R - f_2R = \left(\frac{MR^2}{2}\right)\alpha \qquad \text{...(iv)}$$

$$a_{CM} + R\alpha = a_1 \qquad \text{...(v)}$$

$$a_{CM} - R\alpha = -a_2 \qquad \text{...(vi)}$$

Solving equations, we get $a_{CM} = 5\ \text{m/s}^2$

7. About the point of contact,

$$\Sigma\tau = I\alpha$$

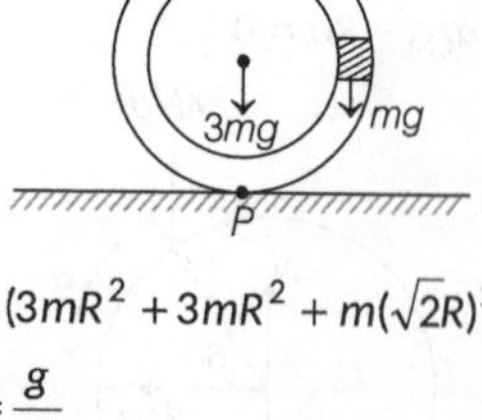

$$\Rightarrow \quad mgr = (3mR^2 + 3mR^2 + m(\sqrt{2}R)^2)\alpha$$

$$\Rightarrow \quad \alpha = \frac{g}{8r}$$

8. In head on elastic collision of identical masses, velocities get exchanged, so centre of mass of A comes to rest and centre of mass of B starts moving with velocity v_0. Angular speed of A will remain unchanged in collision.

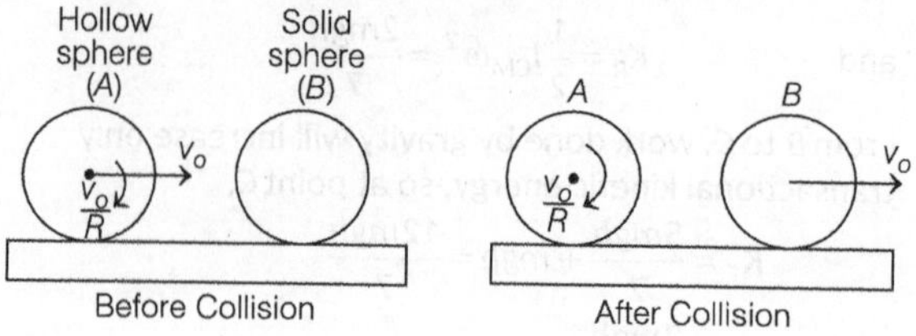

So, $K_B = \frac{1}{2}mv_0^2$ and $K_A = \frac{1}{2}\left(\frac{2}{3}mR^2\right)\left(\frac{v_0}{R}\right)^2$

$$\Rightarrow \quad \frac{K_B}{K_A} = \frac{3}{2}$$

9. $v_A = \omega(l\sin 45°) = v_0$

$$\Rightarrow \quad \omega = \frac{\sqrt{2}v_0}{l}$$

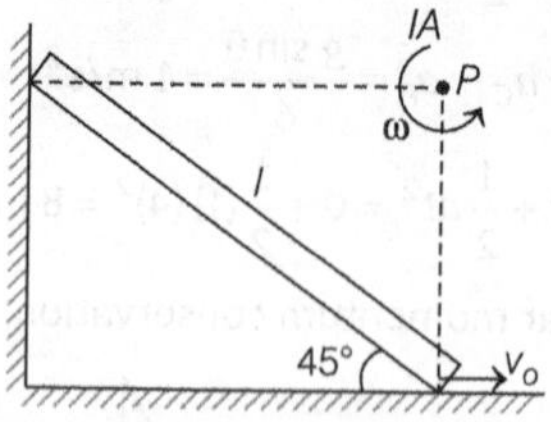

$$K = \frac{1}{2}I_P\omega^2 = \frac{1}{2}\left(\frac{ml^2}{12} + m\left(\frac{l}{2}\right)^2\right)\omega^2 = \frac{1}{3}mv_0^2$$

10. For cylinder, $\Sigma F = ma_{CM} \Rightarrow -\mu mg = ma_{CM}$

$$\Rightarrow \quad a_{CM} = -\mu g$$

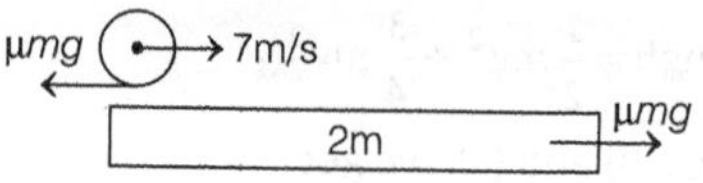

$$\Sigma\tau = I_{CM}\alpha \Rightarrow \mu mgR = \left(\frac{mR^2}{2}\right)\alpha$$

$$\Rightarrow \quad \alpha = \frac{2\mu g}{R}$$

$$v = u + at \Rightarrow v_{CM} = 7 - (\mu g)t$$

$$\omega = \omega_0 + \alpha t \Rightarrow \omega = \left(\frac{2\mu g}{R}\right)t$$

For plank, $\Sigma F = ma \Rightarrow \mu mg = 2ma \Rightarrow a = \frac{\mu g}{2}$

$$v = u + at \Rightarrow v = \left(\frac{\mu g}{2}\right)t$$

For pure rolling to begin, $v = v_{CM} - \omega R$

$$\Rightarrow \quad \left(\frac{\mu g}{2}\right)t = (7 - \mu g t) - (2\mu g)t$$

$$\Rightarrow \quad t = 2\ \text{s}$$

$$s_{rel} = u_{rel}t + \frac{1}{2}a_{rel}t^2 = 7(2) + \frac{1}{2}\left(-\mu g - \frac{\mu g}{2}\right)(2)^2$$

$$= 11\ \text{m}$$

So, by the time pure rolling begins, the cylinder has travelled 11 m on the plank. Now, velocities become constant as friction vanishes.

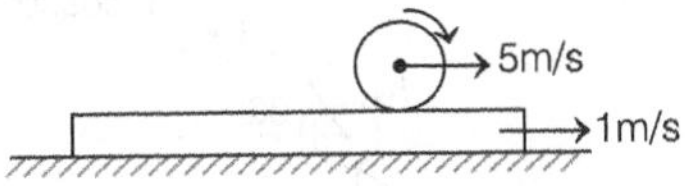

Further time taken to cover remaining 1 m

$$=\frac{1}{(5-1)}=0.25\text{ s}$$

Total time $= 2 + 0.25 = 2.25$ s

11. Speed of the ring will be maximum when the small body will be at its lowest position.

$$W_{mg} = \Delta K$$

$$\Rightarrow +1\times10\times2.5=\left(\frac{1}{2}\times1\times v_{CM}^2+\frac{1}{2}\times1\times(1.25)^2\left(\frac{v_{CM}}{1.25}\right)^2\right)+0$$

$$\Rightarrow \quad v_{CM} = 5\text{ m/s}$$

12. $mg - T_1 = ma_1$ ...(i)

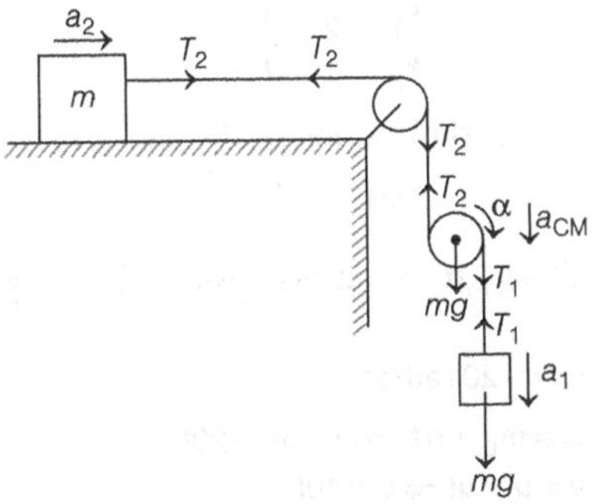

$$mg + T_1 - T_2 = ma_{CM} \quad \text{...(ii)}$$

$$T_1R + T_2R = \left(\frac{mR^2}{2}\right)\alpha \quad \text{...(iii)}$$

$$T_2 = ma_2 \quad \text{...(iv)}$$

$$a_1 = a_{CM} + R\alpha \quad \text{...(v)}$$

$$a_2 = a_{CM} - R\alpha \quad \text{...(vi)}$$

Solving equation, we get $\alpha = \frac{2g}{5R}$

13. About P, $\Sigma\tau = I_P\alpha$

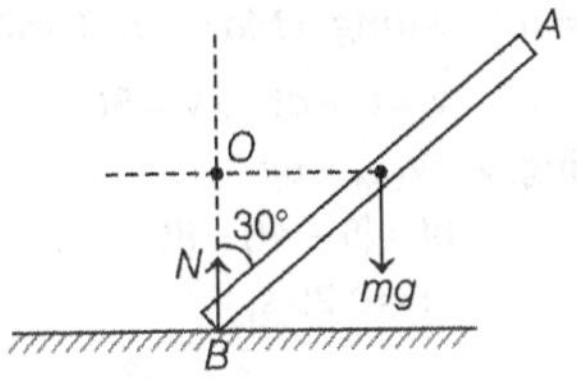

$$\Rightarrow \quad mg\left(\frac{l}{2}\sin 30°\right)=\left(\frac{ml^2}{12}+m\left(\frac{l}{2}\sin 30°\right)^2\right)\alpha$$

$$\Rightarrow \quad \alpha = \frac{12g}{7l}$$

$$a_C = \left(\frac{l}{2}\sin 30°\right)\alpha = \frac{3g}{7}$$

$$\Sigma F = ma_{CM}$$

$$\Rightarrow \quad mg - N = m\left(\frac{3g}{7}\right)$$

$$\Rightarrow \quad N = \frac{4mg}{7}$$

14. $a_B = \left(\frac{l}{2}\cos 30°\right)\alpha = \frac{3\sqrt{3}g}{7}$

15. $\Sigma F = ma \Rightarrow mg - T = ma_{CM}$ ...(i)

$$\Sigma\tau = I_{CM}\alpha \quad \Rightarrow T\left(\frac{l}{2}\right)=\left(\frac{ml^2}{6}\right)\alpha \quad \text{...(ii)}$$

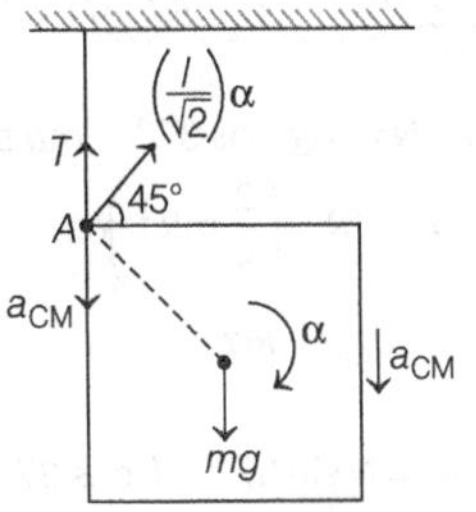

Initial acceleration of point A along the string will be zero.

$$\Rightarrow \quad a_{CM} - \left(\frac{l}{\sqrt{2}}\right)\alpha\sin 45° = 0 \quad \text{...(iii)}$$

Solving Eqs. (i), (ii) and (iii), we get

$$T = \frac{2mg}{5}$$

16. Using energy conservation,

$$mg(R+r) + 0 = mg(R+r)\cos\theta + \frac{7}{10}mv_{CM}^2$$

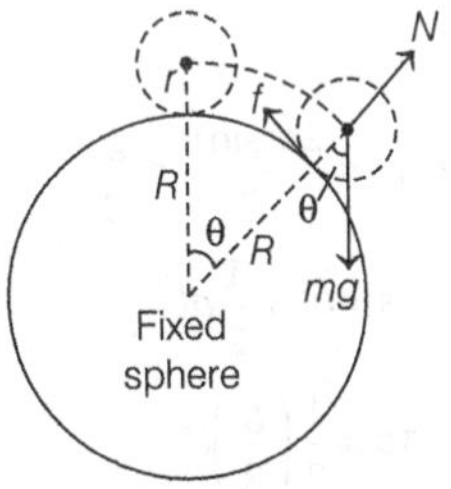

$$\Rightarrow \quad mg(R+r)(1-\cos\theta) = \frac{7}{10}mv_{CM}^2 \quad \text{...(i)}$$

$$mg\cos\theta - N = \frac{mv_{CM}^2}{R+r} \quad \text{...(ii)}$$

$$N = 0 \quad \text{...(iii)}$$

Solving equations, we get

$$v_{CM} = \sqrt{\frac{10g(R+r)}{17}}$$

So, $\omega = \frac{v_{CM}}{r} = \sqrt{\frac{10g(R+r)}{17r^2}}$

17. $\tan\theta = \mu$ and $\mu = \dfrac{\tan\phi}{1+\dfrac{mR^2}{I_{cm}}} = \dfrac{\tan\phi}{3}$

So, $\dfrac{\tan\phi}{\tan\theta} = 3$

18. For sphere,

$$\Sigma F_x = ma_x \Rightarrow mg\sin 37° + ma\cos 37° - f = ma_{CM} \quad \text{...(i)}$$

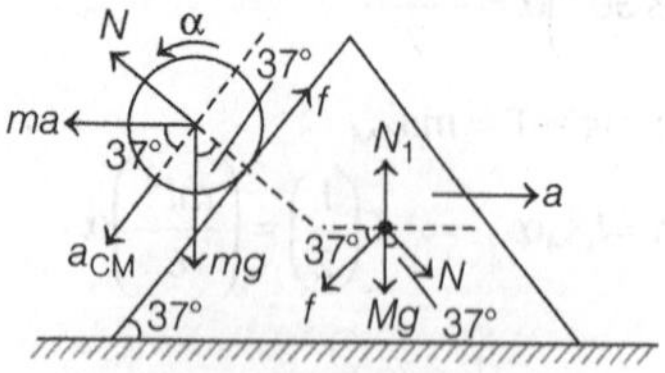

$$\Sigma F_y = 0 \Rightarrow N = mg\cos 37° - ma\sin 37° \quad \text{...(ii)}$$

$$\Sigma\tau = I_{CM}\alpha \Rightarrow fR = \left(\frac{2}{5}mR^2\right)\alpha \quad \text{...(iii)}$$

$$a_{CM} = R\alpha \quad \text{...(iv)}$$

For wedge,

$$\Sigma F = ma \Rightarrow N\sin 37° - f\cos 37° = ma \quad \text{...(v)}$$

Solving Eqs. (i), (ii), (iii), (iv) and (v), we get

$$a = \frac{2g}{9}$$

19. During upward journey velocity decreases and friction acts upwards to reduce angular velocity. Similarly, during downward journey, velocity increases and to increase angular velocity friction acts upwards.

20. $mg\sin\theta - f = ma_{CM}$ ...(i)

$$fR = \left(\frac{mR^2}{2}\right)\alpha \quad \text{...(ii)}$$

$$a_{CM} = R\alpha \quad \text{...(iii)}$$

Solving, we get $a_{CM} = \dfrac{2g\sin\theta}{3} = \dfrac{g}{3}$

$$s = ut + \frac{1}{2}at^2$$

$$\Rightarrow \quad 15 = \frac{1}{2}\left(\frac{g}{3}\right)t^2$$

$$\Rightarrow \quad t = 3\text{ s}$$

21. For ring, $mg\sin\theta + F - f_1 = ma_{CM}$ ...(i)

$$f_1R = (mR^2)\alpha \quad \text{...(ii)}$$

For sphere, $mg\sin\theta - F - f_2 = ma_{CM}$ ...(iii)

$$f_2R = \left(\frac{2}{5}mR^2\right)\alpha \quad \text{...(iv)}$$

For both, $a_{CM} = R\alpha$ ...(v)

Solving equations, we get

$$F = \frac{3mg\sin\theta}{17}$$

22. Using energy conservation,

$$K + U = K_1 + U_1 \Rightarrow 4 + 0 = K_1 + 0.1\times 10\times 1$$

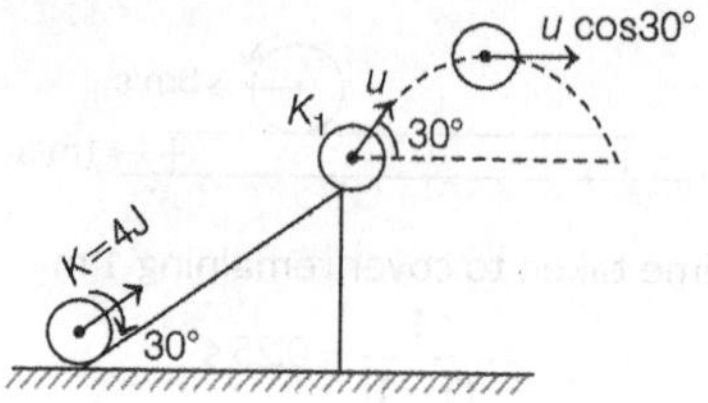

$$\Rightarrow \quad K_1 = 3\text{ J}$$

$$\frac{K_T}{K_R} = \frac{\frac{1}{2}mv_{CM}^2}{\frac{1}{2}\left(\frac{mR^2}{2}\right)\left(\frac{v_{CM}}{R}\right)^2} = 2$$

$$\Rightarrow \quad K_T = 2\text{ J and } K_R = 1\text{ J}$$

K_T at the highest point $= 2\cos^2 30° = \dfrac{3}{2}$ J

So, $\dfrac{K_T}{K_R} = \dfrac{\frac{3}{2}}{1} = \dfrac{3}{2}$

23. $\Sigma F = ma \Rightarrow mg\sin\theta + \mu\, mg\cos\theta = ma_{CM}$

$$\Rightarrow \quad a_{CM} = 10\text{ m/s}^2$$

$$\Sigma\tau = I_{CM}\alpha \Rightarrow -(\mu\, mg\cos\theta)R = \left(\frac{mR^2}{2}\right)\alpha$$

$$\Rightarrow \quad \alpha = -20\text{ rad/s}^2$$

$$\omega = \omega_0 + \alpha t \Rightarrow \omega = 54 - 20t$$

$$v = u + at \Rightarrow v = 10t$$

For pure rolling, $v = \omega R \Rightarrow 10t = (54 - 20t)(0.4)$

$$\Rightarrow \quad t = 1.2\text{ s}$$

24. Speed of disc at the bottom $= \sqrt{2gh} = 5$ m/s

For disc, $\Sigma F = ma \Rightarrow -\mu mg = ma \Rightarrow a_{CM} = -4\text{ m/s}^2$

$$\Sigma\tau = I_{CM}\alpha \Rightarrow \mu mgR = \left(\frac{mR^2}{2}\right)\alpha \Rightarrow \alpha = \frac{8}{R}$$

$$v = u + at \Rightarrow v_{CM} = 5 - 4t$$

$$\omega = \omega_0 + \alpha t \Rightarrow \omega = \left(\frac{8}{R}\right)t$$

For cart, $\Sigma F = ma \Rightarrow \mu mg = Ma \Rightarrow a = 8\text{ m/s}^2$

$$v = u + at \Rightarrow v = 8t$$

For pure rolling, $v = v_{CM} - \omega r$

$$\Rightarrow \quad 8t = (5 - 4t) - 8t$$

$$\Rightarrow \quad t = 0.25\text{ s}$$

$$s_{rel} = u_{rel}t + \frac{1}{2}a_{rel}t^2$$

$$\Rightarrow \quad l = 5(0.25) + \frac{1}{2}(-12)(0.25)^2$$

$$= \frac{7}{8}\text{ m}$$

25. Rotational kinetic energy of ring will not change as there is no friction.
Using linear momentum conservation,

$$mv + 0 = mv' + mv' \Rightarrow v' = \frac{v}{2}$$

Using energy conservation,

$$\left(\frac{1}{2}mv^2 + \frac{1}{2}I_{CM}\omega^2\right) + 0 = \left(0 + \frac{1}{2}I_{CM}\omega^2\right) + \frac{1}{2}(2m)\left(\frac{v}{2}\right)^2 + mgh$$

$$\Rightarrow \quad h = \frac{v^2}{4g}$$

26. Applying angular momentum conservation about A,

$$m\left(\left(\frac{a}{2}\hat{\mathbf{i}} + \frac{a}{2}\hat{\mathbf{j}}\right) \times (2\hat{\mathbf{i}} + 4\hat{\mathbf{j}})v_0\right) = \left(\frac{2ma^2}{3}\right)\omega$$

$$\Rightarrow \quad \omega = \frac{3v_0}{2a}\hat{\mathbf{k}}$$

$$\mathbf{v}_{CM} = \omega \times \mathbf{r}_{CM} = \left(\frac{3v_0}{2a}\right)\hat{\mathbf{k}} \times \left(\frac{a}{2}\hat{\mathbf{i}} + \frac{a}{2}\hat{\mathbf{j}}\right)$$

$$= \frac{3v_0}{4}(-\hat{\mathbf{i}} + \hat{\mathbf{j}})$$

27. Conserving angular momentum about the corner of step,

$$\left(\frac{MR^2}{2}\right)\left(\frac{v_0}{R}\right) + Mv_0\left(\frac{3R}{4}\right) = \left(\frac{MR^2}{2} + MR^2\right)\omega$$

$$\Rightarrow \quad \omega = \frac{5v_0}{6}$$

So, $$v_{CM} = \omega R = \frac{5v_0}{6}$$

28. Conserving angular momentum about point P on ground,

$$Mv\left(\frac{L}{2}\right) = \left(\frac{(2M)(2L)^2}{12}\right)\omega$$

$$\Rightarrow \quad \omega = \frac{3v}{4L}, \text{ counter-clockwise}$$

29. $\Sigma F = ma \Rightarrow -\mu mg = ma_{CM} \Rightarrow a_{CM} = -\mu g$

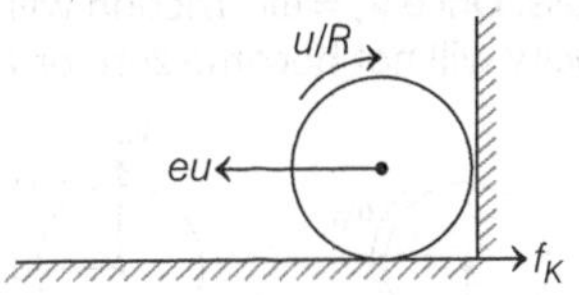

$$\Sigma\tau = I\alpha \;\Rightarrow\; (\mu mg)R = \left(\frac{2}{5}mR^2\right)\alpha \;\Rightarrow\; \alpha = \frac{5\mu g}{2R}$$

$$v = u + at \;\Rightarrow\; v_{CM} = eu - \mu gt$$

$$\omega = \omega_0 + \alpha t \;\Rightarrow\; \omega = -\frac{u}{R} + \left(\frac{5\mu g}{2R}\right)t$$

For pure rolling, $v_{CM} = \omega R$

$$\Rightarrow \quad \frac{u}{2} - \mu gt = -u + \left(\frac{5\mu g}{2}\right)t$$

$$\Rightarrow \quad t = \frac{3u}{7\mu g}$$

30. Using energy conservation,

$$mgR + 0 = \left(\frac{m}{4}\right)g\frac{R}{2} + \frac{3}{4}\left(\frac{m}{4}\right)v_{CM}^2$$

$$\Rightarrow \quad v_{CM} = \sqrt{\frac{14gR}{3}}$$

31. Impulse of friction on the cylinder about point A will be zero.

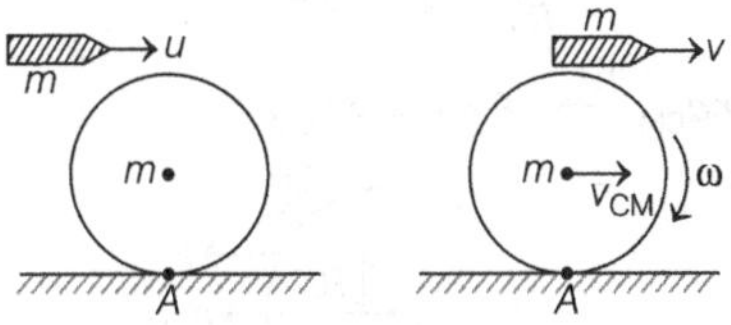

So conserving angular momentum of system about point A on the ground,

$$mu(2R) = \left(\frac{3}{2}mR^2\right)\omega + mv(2R) \qquad \text{...(i)}$$

When the bullet leaves, there is no relative motion between cylinder and bullet. So, $v = 2\omega R$ ...(ii)

Solving Eqs. (i) and (ii), we get

$$v = \frac{8u}{11}$$

32. About the bottommost point,

$$\tau = \frac{dL}{dt} \Rightarrow (2t)(R + r) = \frac{dL}{dt}$$

$$\Rightarrow \quad L = \int_0^t 2(R + r)\,t\,dt$$

$$\Rightarrow \quad L = (R + r)t^2$$

Multiple Choice(s) Correct Questions

1. $v_A = v_{CM} + \omega R = v$ ...(i)

$v_B = v_{CM} - \omega R = -v$ ...(ii)

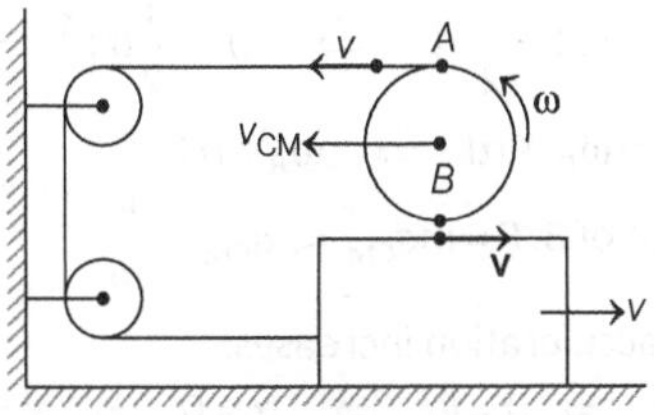

Solving Eqs. (i) and (ii), we get

$$v_{CM} = 0 \text{ and } \omega = \frac{v}{R}$$

2. (A) Tangential acceleration of A is zero. Centripetal acceleration is vertically up.

(B) If $a = \dfrac{v^2}{R}$, then net acceleration will be vertically downward.

(C) Acceleration of C will be resultant of $a+R\alpha$ and $\frac{v^2}{R}$

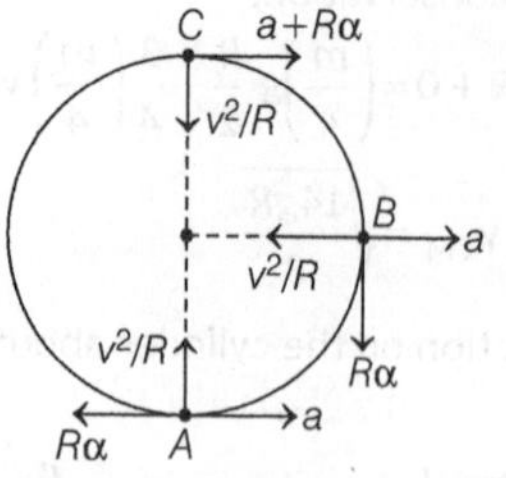

3. $\Sigma F_{ext} = ma_{CM} \Rightarrow F + f = Ma_{CM}$ ...(i)

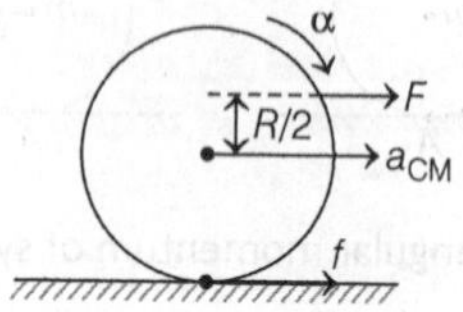

$$\Sigma\tau = I_{CM}\alpha \Rightarrow F\left(\frac{R}{2}\right) - fR = \left(\frac{2}{5}MR^2\right)\alpha \quad \text{...(ii)}$$

$$a_{CM} = R\alpha \quad \text{...(iii)}$$

Solving Eqs. (i), (ii) and (iii), we get

$$a_{CM} = \frac{15F}{14M} \text{ and } f = \frac{F}{14} \text{ (forward)}$$

4. In absence of friction, $a_{CM} = 0$ and α will be clockwise. So, the bottommost point has tendency to move leftward. So, to oppose this, friction will act rightward. So, centre of mass moves towards right due to friction.

5. From A to B,

$$F - f = ma_{CM} \quad \text{...(i)}$$

$$fR = \left(\frac{mR^2}{2}\right)\alpha \quad \text{...(ii)}$$

$$a_{CM} = R\alpha \quad \text{...(iii)}$$

Solving we get, $a_{CM} = \frac{2F}{3m}$ and $\alpha = \frac{2F}{3mR}$

$$\theta = \omega_0 t + \frac{1}{2}\alpha t^2 \Rightarrow 2\pi = \frac{1}{2}\alpha T^2 \Rightarrow T = \sqrt{\frac{4\pi}{\alpha}}$$

$$\omega = \omega_0 + \alpha t \Rightarrow \omega_B = \alpha T$$

To the right of B, $F = ma_{CM} \Rightarrow a_{CM} = \frac{F}{m}$

So, linear acceleration increases.

$$\Sigma\tau = I\alpha \Rightarrow 0 = I\alpha \Rightarrow \alpha = 0 \Rightarrow \omega = \text{constant}$$

$$\theta = \omega_0 t + \frac{1}{2}\alpha t^2 \Rightarrow 2\pi = (2\alpha T)t \Rightarrow t = \frac{2\pi}{\alpha T} = \frac{T}{2}$$

Due to initial speed at B and greater linear acceleration, disc will cover a distance greater than s in further time T.

$$s = ut + \frac{1}{2}at^2; \ s' > s$$

6. (A) $\mu = \dfrac{\tan\theta}{1 + \dfrac{mR^2}{I_{CM}}}$ hollow cylinder requires maximum friction as it has maximum moment of inertia, so if hollow cylinder can roll, then all other objects will also roll.

(B) $K = mgh$ for all objects

(C) Work done by friction is zero in rolling as no relative motion is there at the point of contact.

7. About the instantaneous axis of rotation (bottommost point), $v = \omega r$, so upper half ring has greater kinetic energy than lower half ring.

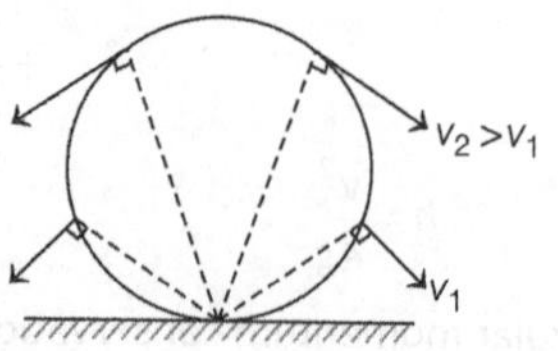

8.

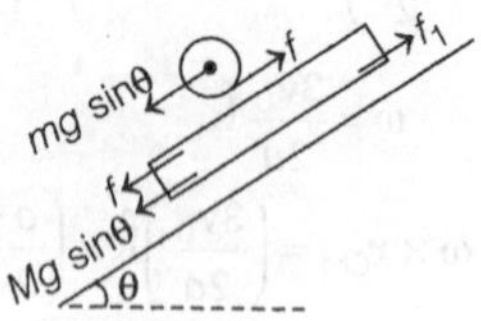

For sphere, $mg\sin\theta - f = ma_{CM}$ ...(i)

$$fR = \frac{2}{5}mR^2\alpha \quad \text{...(ii)}$$

$$a_{CM} = R\alpha \quad \text{...(iii)}$$

Solving we get, $f = \frac{2mg\sin\theta}{7}$

If plank is at rest, then $f = \frac{2mg\sin\theta}{7}$

and $f + Mg\sin\theta = \mu_{min}(M+m)g\cos\theta$

$$\Rightarrow \mu_{min} = \frac{7M + 2m}{7(M+m)}\tan\theta$$

If there is no friction between the plank and inclined plane, then acceleration of both sphere and plank will be $g\sin\theta$ and friction force on sphere will be zero.

9. Since, normal is impulsive, friction will also be impulsive and it will reduce ω and give some horizontal velocity to centre of mass. Once $v_x = \omega r$, friction will stop acting. So, angular velocity will not become zero or get reversed.

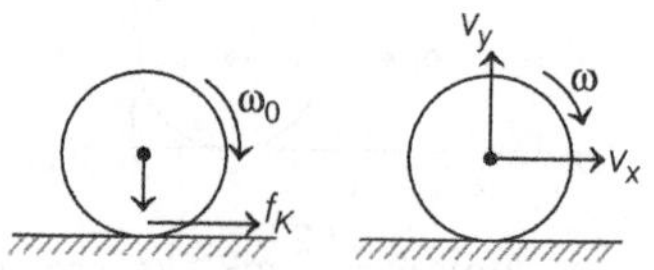

10. $a_A = \frac{dv_A}{dt} = 3$ and $a_B = \frac{dv_B}{dt} = 1$

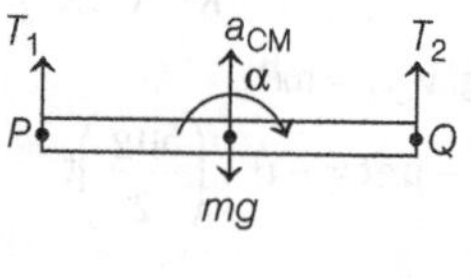

$$a_P = a_{CM} + (0.5)\alpha = 3 \quad ...(i)$$
$$a_Q = a_{CM} - (0.5)\alpha = 1 \quad ...(ii)$$

Solving we get, $a_{CM} = 2\text{ m/s}^2$ and $\alpha = 2\text{ rad/s}^2$

$$\Sigma F_{ext} = ma_{CM} \Rightarrow T_1 + T_2 - mg = ma_{CM} \quad ...(iii)$$
$$\Sigma\tau = I_{CM}\alpha \Rightarrow T_1(0.5) - T_2(0.5) = \left(\frac{ml^2}{12}\right)\alpha \quad ...(iv)$$

Solving Eqs. (iii) and (iv), we get

$$T_1 = \frac{185}{6}\text{ N and } T_2 = \frac{175}{6}\text{ N}$$

11. $4.75 = r_2\alpha_1$

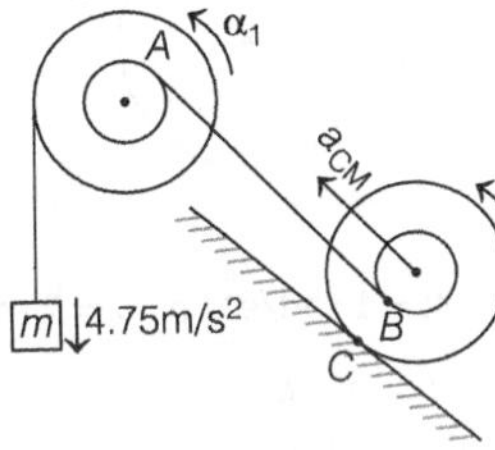

$$a_A = r_1\alpha_1$$
$$a_B = a_{CM} - r_1\alpha_2 = a_A$$
$$a_{CM} - r_2\alpha_2 = 0$$

Solving we get,

$$a_{CM} = \frac{r_1(4.75)}{r_2 - r_1} = 4.75\text{ m/s}^2$$
$$v = u + at \Rightarrow v_{CM} = (4.75)4 = 19\text{ m/s}$$
$$\Rightarrow \quad v_B = a_B t = \left(\frac{4.75}{2}\right) \times 4 = 9.5\text{ m/s}$$

Work done by friction on pulley Q is zero.

12. For block,

$$Mg - T = Ma \quad ...(i)$$

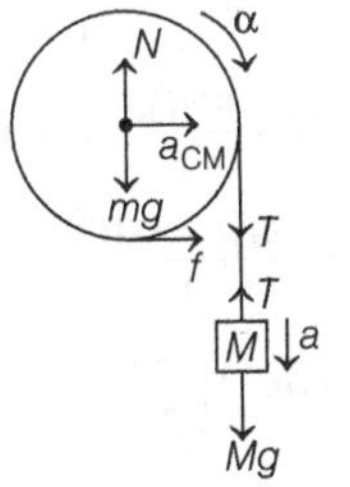

For disc,

$$f = Ma_{CM} \quad ...(ii)$$
$$TR - fR = \left(\frac{MR^2}{2}\right)\alpha \quad ...(iii)$$
$$a_{CM} = R\alpha \quad ...(iv)$$

and $\quad R\alpha = a \quad ...(v)$

Solving we get $a = a_{CM} = \frac{2g}{5}, T = \frac{3Mg}{5}$

13. For system, $\Sigma F = ma \Rightarrow 24 - 15 = 9a$

$$\Rightarrow \quad a = 1\text{ m/s}^2$$

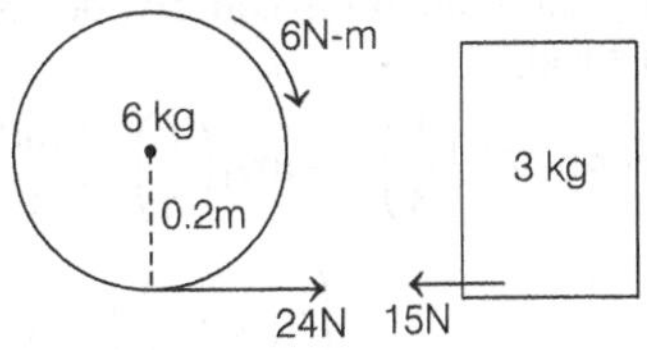

For cylinder, $\Sigma\tau = I_{CM}\alpha \Rightarrow 6 - 24(0.2) = I_{CM}\alpha$

$$\Rightarrow \quad \alpha = 10\text{ rad/s}^2$$

14. (A) For disc, $I_{CM} = \frac{mR^2}{2} = 0.5\text{ kg-m}^2$

$$v_{CM} = \omega_1 L = 4\text{ m/s}$$
$$K_{disc} = \frac{1}{2}I_{CM}\omega_2^2 + \frac{1}{2}Mv_{CM}^2 = 12\text{ J}$$

(B) $\mathbf{L}_0 = \mathbf{L}_{CM} + m(\mathbf{r} \times \mathbf{v}_{CM}) = -0.5 \times 4 + 1(4)(2)$
$= 6\text{ kg m}^2/\text{s}$

(C) $\mathbf{v}_A = \mathbf{v}_C + \mathbf{v}_{AC} = \omega_1 L - \omega_2 R = 0$
$\mathbf{L}_A = \mathbf{L}_{CM} + m(\mathbf{r} \times (\mathbf{v}_{CM} - \mathbf{v}_A)) = 6\text{ kg m}^2/\text{s}$

(D) $\mathbf{L}_C = I_{CM}\omega = 2\text{ kg m}^2/\text{s}$

15. Conserving angular momentum about the centre of mass of the system,

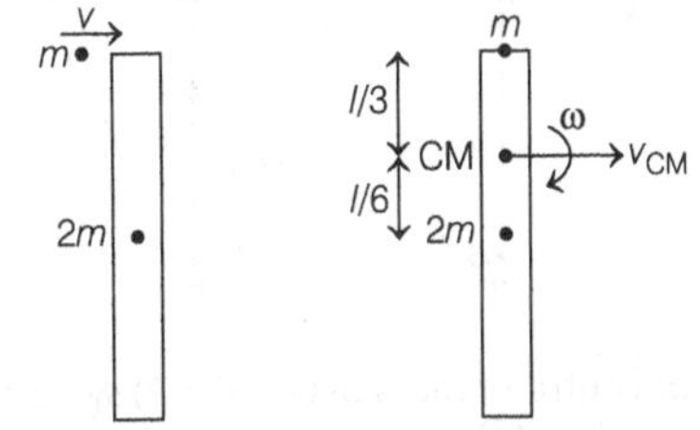

just before collision just after collision

$$mv\left(\frac{l}{3}\right) + 0 = \left(\frac{2ml^2}{12} + 2m\left(\frac{l}{6}\right)^2 + m\left(\frac{l}{3}\right)^2\right)\omega$$
$$\Rightarrow \quad \omega = \frac{v}{l}$$

Final kinetic energy $= \frac{1}{2}I_{CM}\omega^2 + \frac{1}{2}Mv_{CM}^2$

$$= \frac{1}{2}\left(\frac{ml^2}{3}\right)\left(\frac{v}{l}\right)^2 + \frac{1}{2}(3m)\left(\frac{v}{3}\right)^2$$
$$= \frac{1}{3}mv^2$$

Loss in KE $= \frac{1}{2}mv^2 - \frac{1}{3}mv^2 = \frac{mv^2}{6}$

16. Applying linear momentum conservation,

$$mv\sin 37° = mv_{CM} + m(-v_1) \quad ...(i)$$

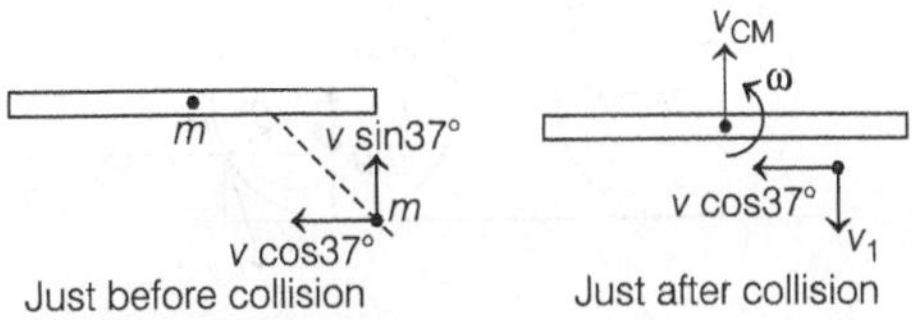

Just before collision Just after collision

Applying angular momentum conservation about the centre of the rod,

$$(mv\sin 37°)\left(\frac{l}{4}\right) = -mv_1\left(\frac{l}{4}\right) + \left(\frac{ml^2}{12}\right)\omega \quad \text{...(ii)}$$

$$e = \frac{\left(v_{CM} + \frac{\omega l}{4}\right) + v_1}{v\sin 37°} = 1 \quad \text{...(iii)}$$

Solving Eqs. (i), (ii) and (iii), we get

$$\omega = \frac{72v}{55l},\ v_1 = -\frac{9v}{55} \text{ and } v_{CM} = \frac{24v}{55}$$

Impulse of the impact force $= \int N dt = \Delta P_{rod}$

$$= mv_{CM} = \frac{24mv}{55}$$

$$\theta = \omega t + \frac{1}{2}\alpha t^2 \Rightarrow \pi = \frac{72v}{55l}t \Rightarrow t = \frac{55\pi l}{72v'}$$

$$s = ut + \frac{1}{2}at^2 \Rightarrow s_{CM} = \left(\frac{24v}{55}\right)\left(\frac{55\pi l}{72v}\right) = \frac{\pi l}{3}$$

17. $v_C = \dfrac{mu + 0 + 0}{m + m + m} = \dfrac{u}{3}$

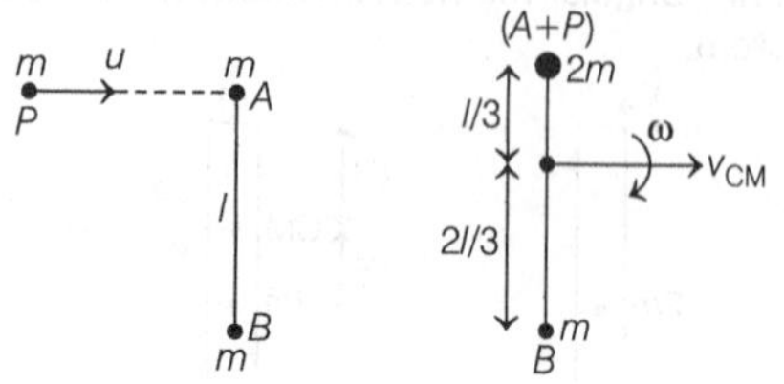

Velocity of centre of mass of $(A + B + P)$ system will not change during collision.

Conserving angular momentum about C.

$$mu\left(\frac{l}{3}\right) = \left(2m\left(\frac{l}{3}\right)^2 + m\left(\frac{2l}{3}\right)^2\right)\omega$$

$$\Rightarrow \quad \omega = \frac{u}{2l}$$

$$v_{(A+P)} = v_{CM} + \frac{\omega l}{3} = \frac{u}{3} + \left(\frac{u}{2l}\right)\left(\frac{l}{3}\right) = \frac{u}{2}$$

$$v_B = v_{CM} - \omega\left(\frac{2l}{3}\right) = \frac{u}{3} - \left(\frac{u}{2l}\right)\left(\frac{2l}{3}\right) = 0$$

18. Conserving angular momentum about P,

$$(mR^2)\left(\frac{v}{R}\right) + mv\left(\frac{R}{2}\right) = (2mR^2)\omega$$

$$\Rightarrow \quad \omega = \frac{3v}{4R}$$

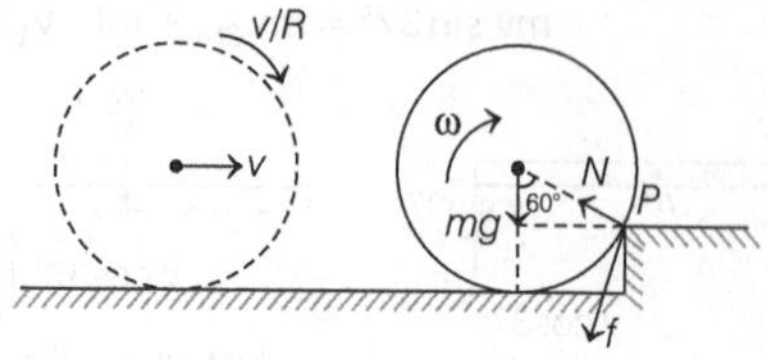

$$mg\cos 60° - N = \frac{mv_{CM}^2}{R} \text{ where } v_{CM} = \omega R = \frac{3v}{4}$$

$$\Rightarrow \quad N = \frac{mg}{2} - \frac{9mv^2}{16R}$$

As the wheel ascends $mg\cos\theta$ increases and v decreases. So, N will increase. Friction is static during ascent.

Comprehension Based Questions

1. $a_{CM} + R\alpha = 6$ ...(i)

$a_{CM} - R\alpha = -2$ ...(ii)

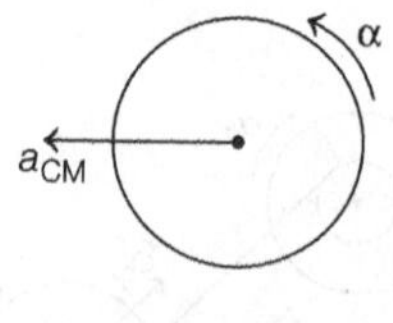

Solving, we get

$$\alpha = 1 \text{ rad/s}^2,\ a_{CM} = 2 \text{ m/s}^2$$

2. For block B; $m_B g - T = m_B(6)$ ...(iii)

For cylinder; $T = m_{cylinder}(2)$ ...(iv)

Solving Eqs. (iii) and (iv), we get

$$m_{cylinder} : m_B = 2:1$$

3. The acceleration of the topmost point of the cylinder with respect to its centre of mass is

$$a_{AO} = R\alpha = 4(1) = 4 \text{ m/s}^2$$

Length of the thread $= 20 + \frac{1}{2}(4)(2)^2 = 28$ m

4. Using work-energy theorem,

$$W_{mg} + W_N + W_f = \Delta K$$

$$\Rightarrow \quad +mgr(1 - \cos\theta) + 0 + 0 = \frac{1}{2}\left(\frac{3}{2}mr^2\right)\omega^2 - 0$$

$$\Rightarrow \quad \omega = \sqrt{\frac{4g(1-\cos\theta)}{3r}}$$

$$mg\cos\theta - N = \frac{mv_{CM}^2}{r}, \text{ where } v_{CM} = \omega r$$

$$\Rightarrow mg\cos\theta - 0 = \frac{4mg(1-\cos\theta)}{3} \quad [N = 0 \text{ for losing contact}]$$

$$\Rightarrow \quad \theta = \cos^{-1}\left(\frac{4}{7}\right)$$

5. $v_{CM} = \omega r = \sqrt{\dfrac{4gr}{7}}$

6. Just after leaving contact,

$$K_T = \frac{1}{2}mv_{CM}^2 = \frac{2mgr}{7}$$

$$K_R = \frac{1}{2}I_{CM}\omega^2 = \frac{mgr}{7}$$

When centre of mass is in horizontal line,

$$K_T = \frac{2mgr}{7} + mg\left(\frac{4r}{7}\right) = \frac{6mgr}{7}$$

$$K_R = \frac{mgr}{7}$$

So, $\frac{K_T}{K_R} = 6$

7. $v_{CM} = ev_0 = 4$ m/s

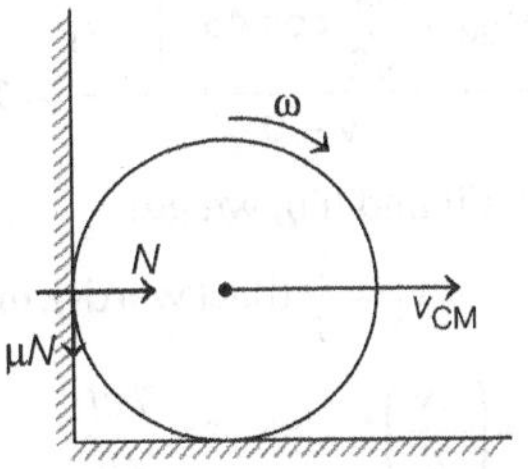

$$\int N dt = 2(4 - (-4)) = 16 \text{ N-s}$$

$$I_{CM} = \frac{2}{5} mR^2 = 0.8 \text{ kg-m}^2$$

Angular impulse due to friction $= -(\mu \int N dt)R = -16\mu$

$$\omega = \frac{v_{CM}}{R} = 4 \text{ rad/s}$$

Angular impulse = Change in angular momentum

$$-16\mu = 0.8(4 - 9)$$

$$\Rightarrow \quad \mu = \frac{1}{4}$$

8.
$$J_N = \int N dt = 16 \text{ N-s}$$

$$J_f = \mu \int N dt = 4 \text{ N-s}$$

$$J = \sqrt{J_N^2 + J_f^2} = 4\sqrt{17} \text{ N-s}$$

9. Using linear momentum conservation,

$$p = (4m + m)v \Rightarrow v = \frac{p}{5m}$$

Using energy conservation,

$$\frac{p^2}{2m} = \frac{p^2}{2(5m)} + mgh$$

$$\Rightarrow \quad h = \frac{2p^2}{5m^2 g}$$

10. Angular impulse $= \Delta L$

$$\Rightarrow \quad p(0.4r) = \left(\frac{2}{5} mr^2\right)\omega$$

$$\Rightarrow \quad \omega = \frac{p}{mr}$$

$$K_R = \frac{1}{2} I_{CM}\omega^2 = \frac{1}{2}\left(\frac{2}{5} mr^2\right)\left(\frac{p}{mr}\right)^2 = \frac{p^2}{5m}$$

$$K_T = \frac{1}{2}(5m)\left(\frac{p}{5m}\right)^2 = \frac{p^2}{10m}$$

$$K = K_R + K_T = \frac{3p^2}{10m}$$

11. Using linear momentum conservation

$$p = -mv_1 + 4mv_2 \quad \text{...(i)}$$

Using energy conservation,

$$\frac{p^2}{2m} = \frac{1}{2} mv_1^2 + \frac{1}{2}(4m)v_2^2 \quad \text{...(ii)}$$

Solving Eqs. (i) and (ii), we get

$$v_2 = \frac{2p}{5m}$$

12. For block; $T - mg \sin\theta = 0$

$$\Rightarrow \quad T = mg \sin\theta$$

For wheel,

$$Mg - T = ma \quad \text{...(i)}$$

$$TR = \left(\frac{MR^2}{3}\right)\alpha \quad \text{...(ii)}$$

$$a = R\alpha \quad \text{...(iii)}$$

Solving, we get $\alpha = \frac{3g}{4R}$ and $T = \frac{mg}{4}$

13. $T = \frac{Mg}{4} = mg \sin\theta \Rightarrow m = \frac{M}{4 \sin\theta}$

14. $a = \frac{3g}{4}$

15. $\int N dt = m(v_{CM} - (-\sqrt{2gH}))$ ...(i)

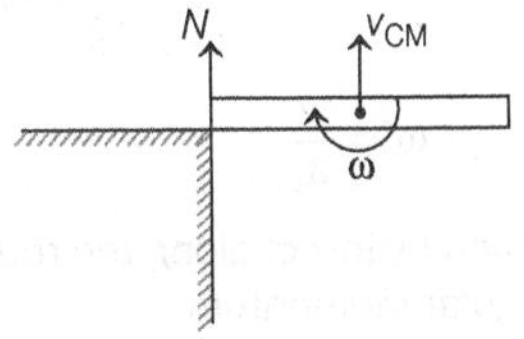

$$\left(\int N dt\right)\frac{L}{2} = \left(\frac{mL^2}{12}\right)\omega \quad \text{...(ii)}$$

$$e = \frac{v_{CM} + \frac{\omega L}{2}}{\sqrt{2gH}} = 1 \quad \text{...(iii)}$$

Solving, we get $\omega = \frac{3\sqrt{2gH}}{L}$ and $v_{CM} = -\frac{\sqrt{2gH}}{2}$

$$T = \frac{2\pi}{\omega} = \frac{2\pi L}{3\sqrt{2gH}}$$

16. $s = ut + \frac{1}{2}at^2 = \left(\frac{\sqrt{2gH}}{2}\right)T + \frac{1}{2}gT^2 = \frac{\pi L}{3}\left(1 + \frac{\pi L}{3H}\right)$

17. Applying angular momentum conservation about P,

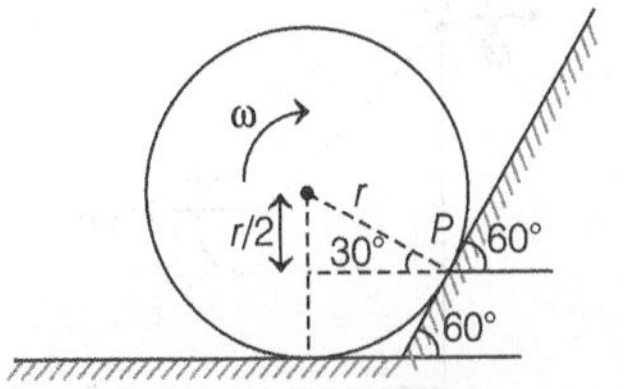

$$-(mr^2)\left(\frac{v_0}{4}\right)+mv_0\left(\frac{r}{2}\right)=(2mr^2)\omega$$

$$\Rightarrow \quad \omega=\frac{v_0}{8r}$$

18. $K_1=\frac{1}{2}mv_0^2+\frac{1}{2}(mr^2)\left(\frac{v_0}{4}\right)^2=\frac{17}{32}mv_0^2$

$$K_2=\frac{1}{2}(2mr^2)\left(\frac{v_0}{8r}\right)^2=\frac{1}{64}mv_0^2$$

$$\text{Loss in KE}=K_1-K_2=\frac{33}{64}mv_0^2$$

19. $K_2=\frac{1}{64}mv_0^2=mgh \Rightarrow h=\frac{v_0^2}{64g}$

20. Conserving angular momentum about the centre of mass of the system,

$$m(2v)\frac{L}{6}-mv\frac{L}{6}=\left(2m\left(\frac{L^2}{12}\right)+m\left(\frac{L}{6}\right)^2+m\left(\frac{L}{6}\right)^2\right)\omega$$

$$\Rightarrow \quad \omega=\frac{3v}{4L}$$

21. $\left(2m\left(\frac{L^2}{12}\right)+m\left(\frac{L}{6}\right)^2+m\left(\frac{L}{6}\right)^2\right)\left(\frac{3v}{4L}\right)$

$$=\left(2m\frac{L^2}{12}+m\left(\frac{L}{2}\right)^2+m\left(\frac{L}{2}\right)^2\right)\omega'$$

$$\omega'=\frac{v}{4L}$$

22. Distance travelled by insect along the rod in time $t=vt$

Conserving angular momentum

$$m(2v)\left(\frac{L}{6}\right)-mv\left(\frac{L}{6}\right)=\left(2m\frac{L^2}{12}+m(vt)^2+m(vt)^2\right)\omega$$

$$\Rightarrow \quad \omega=\frac{L}{12v}\frac{1}{\left(t^2+\left(\frac{L}{2\sqrt{3}}\right)^2\right)}$$

$$\int d\theta=\frac{L}{12v}\int_0^{L/2v}\frac{dt}{\left(t^2+\left(\frac{L}{2\sqrt{3}}\right)^2\right)}$$

$$\Rightarrow \quad \theta=\frac{\pi}{6\sqrt{3}}\text{ rad}$$

23. Conserving linear momentum of system

$$Mv=-Mv_1+2Mv_{CM} \quad \text{...(i)}$$

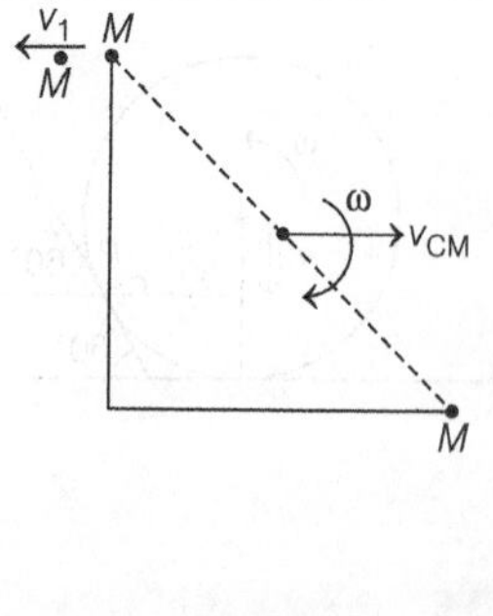

Conserving angular momentum about the centre of mass of the frame

$$Mv\left(\frac{l}{2}\right)=-Mv_1\left(\frac{l}{2}\right)+\left(M\left(\frac{l}{\sqrt{2}}\right)^2+M\left(\frac{l}{\sqrt{2}}\right)^2\right)\omega \quad \text{...(ii)}$$

$$e=\frac{\left(v_{CM}+\frac{\omega l}{\sqrt{2}}\cos 45°\right)+v_1}{v-0}=1 \quad \text{...(iii)}$$

Solving Eqs. (i), (ii) and (iii), we get

$$v_1=\frac{v}{7}\text{ (backwards)}, \omega=\frac{4v}{7l}$$

24. $\theta=\omega t \Rightarrow \pi=\left(\frac{4v}{7l}\right)t \Rightarrow t=\frac{7\pi l}{4v}$

Match the Columns Questions

1. Let L_i = Angular momentum about the bottommost point

v_P = Initial velocity of bottommost point

(A) $L_i=mvR+\left(\frac{1}{2}mR^2\right)\left(-\frac{v}{2R}\right)=\frac{3mvR}{4}$, clockwise

$v_P=v+\left(\frac{v}{2R}\right)R \Rightarrow \frac{3v}{2}$, towards right. So, finally the disc will roll along the initial direction of velocity (v). Friction will act towards left as the bottommost point has velocity towards right.

(B) $L_i=mvR+\left(\frac{mR^2}{2}\right)\left(\frac{2v}{R}\right)=2mvR$, clockwise

$v_P=v-\left(\frac{2v}{R}\right)R=-v=v$ towards left

(C) $L_i=mvR+\left(\frac{mR^2}{2}\right)\left(-\frac{2v}{R}\right)=0$

So, the disc will finally stop.

$v_P=v+\left(\frac{2v}{R}\right)R=3v$, towards right

(D) $L_i=mvR+\left(\frac{mR^2}{2}\right)\left(-\frac{4v}{R}\right)=-mvR$

$=mvR$, anti-clockwise

So, finally the disc will roll towards left,

$v_P=v+\left(\frac{4v}{R}\right)R=5v$, towards right.

2. $F\cos\theta-f=ma_{CM}$ ...(i)

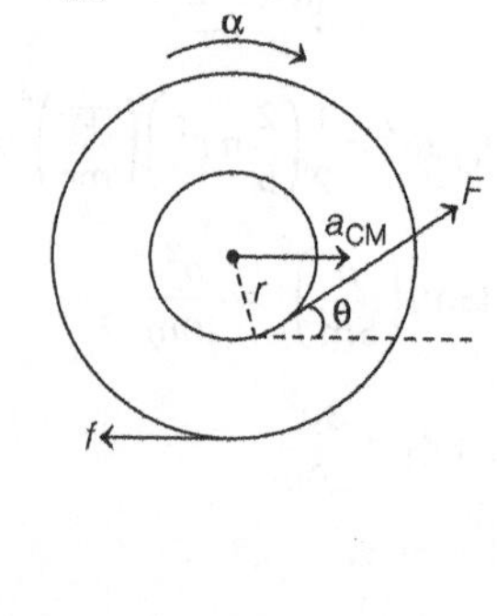

$$fR - Fr = I_{CM}\alpha \quad ...(ii)$$
$$a_{CM} = R\alpha \quad ...(iii)$$

Solving Eqs. (i), (ii) and (iii), we get

$$a_{CM} = \frac{F\left(\cos\theta - \frac{r}{R}\right)}{m + \frac{I_{CM}}{R^2}} \text{ and } f = \frac{F(I_{CM}\cos\theta + mRr)}{I_{CM} + mR^2}$$

(A) $\theta = 0°$; So $a_{CM} > 0$ and f will act towards left.

(B) $\cos\theta < \frac{r}{R}$; $a_{CM} < 0$ and f will act towards left

(C) $\cos\theta > \frac{r}{R}$; $a_{CM} > 0$ and f will act towards left

(D) $\cos\theta = \frac{r}{R}$; $a_{CM} = 0$ and f will act towards left

3. $mg - f = ma_{CM}$ ...(i)

$fR = I_{CM}\alpha$ ...(ii)

$a_{CM} = R\alpha$ ...(iii)

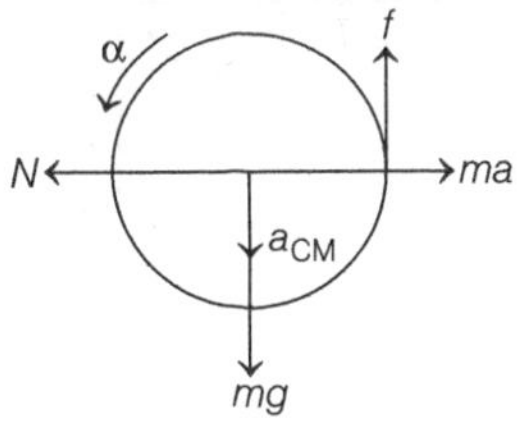

Solving, we get

$$a_{CM} = \frac{mg}{m + \frac{I_{CM}}{R^2}} \text{ and } f = \frac{mg}{1 + \frac{mR^2}{I_{CM}}}$$

(P) $I_{CM} = mR^2$; $a_{CM} = \frac{g}{2}$; $f = \frac{mg}{2}$

(Q) $I_{CM} = \frac{mR^2}{2}$; $a_{CM} = \frac{2g}{3}$; $f = \frac{mg}{3}$

(R) $I_{CM} = \frac{2}{3}mR^2$; $a_{CM} = \frac{3g}{5}$; $f = \frac{2mg}{5}$

(S) $I_{CM} = \frac{2}{5}mR^2$; $a_{CM} = \frac{5g}{7}$; $f = \frac{2mg}{7}$

4. $\mu_{min} = \frac{\tan\theta}{1 + \frac{mR^2}{I_{CM}}}$

μ_{min} for ring $= \frac{\tan\theta}{2} = \frac{3}{8} = 0.375$

μ_{min} for solid sphere $= \frac{2\tan\theta}{7} = \frac{3}{14} = 0.214$

μ_{min} for disc $= \frac{\tan\theta}{3} = 0.25$

(A) $\mu = 0.2$, no object can do pure rolling. So, $a = g\sin\theta - \mu g\cos\theta$ for all of them.

(B) $\mu = 0.3$, only ring can't do pure rolling. For all other objects friction will be static.

(C) $\mu = 0.2$, no object can do pure rolling.

(D) $\mu = 0.5$, all objects doing pure rolling. Maximum friction is required for ring as it has maximum I_{CM}.

5. (A) Conserving angular momentum about the point of contact

$$mv_0R = (2mR^2)\omega \Rightarrow \omega = \frac{v_0}{2R}$$

$$K_1 = \frac{1}{2}mv_0^2 \text{ and } K_2 = \frac{1}{2}(2mR^2)\left(\frac{v_0}{2R}\right)^2 = \frac{mv_0^2}{4}$$

$$W_f = \Delta K = K_2 - K_1 = -\frac{mv_0^2}{4}$$

(B) $\omega = \frac{v_0}{\left(\frac{l}{2}\right)} = \frac{2v_0}{l} \Rightarrow K = \frac{1}{2}\left(\frac{ml^2}{3}\right)\left(\frac{2v_0}{l}\right)^2 = \frac{2}{3}mv_0^2$

(C) $v_{CM} = \frac{v_0}{2}$; $K = \frac{1}{2}m\left(\frac{v_0}{2}\right)^2 = \frac{mv_0^2}{8}$

(D) $\omega = \frac{v_0}{l\sin 45°}$ $K = \frac{1}{2}I_P\omega^2 = \frac{1}{2}\left(\frac{ml^2}{12} + m\left(\frac{l}{2}\right)^2\right)\omega^2 = \frac{mv_0^2}{3}$

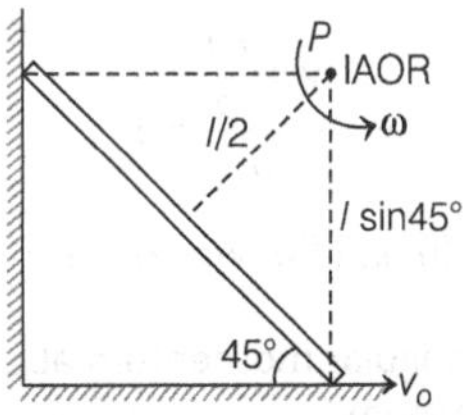

6. (A) In absence of friction, $a_{CM} = \frac{F}{m}$ and $\alpha = \frac{2F}{mR}$ clockwise

Acceleration of bottommost point $= a_{CM} - R\alpha = \frac{F}{m}$, left

So, friction on cylinder will be towards right and on the plank left.

$$a_p = a_{CM} - R\alpha$$

So, $a_{CM} > a_p$

(B) Due to external torque, tendency of the bottommost point of cylinder is to move towards left. So, friction on cylinder will be towards right and on the plank left.

(C) In absence of friction, $a_{CM} = \frac{F}{m}$ and $\alpha = 0$

So, tendency of bottommost point of cylinder is to move towards right. So, friction on cylinder will be towards left and on the plank right.

$$a_p = a_{CM} - R\alpha \Rightarrow a_{CM} > a_p$$

(D) To oppose motion of plank, clyinder will exert friction on the plank towards left. So, friction on the cylinder will be towards right.

$$a_{CM} + R\alpha = a_p$$

7. (A) $mu + 0 = -mv + 2mv_{CM}$ ...(i)

$$mu\left(\frac{l}{2}\right) = -mv\left(\frac{l}{2}\right) + \left(m\left(\frac{l}{2}\right)^2 + m\left(\frac{l}{2}\right)^2\right)\omega \quad ...(ii)$$

$$e = \frac{v_{CM} + \frac{\omega l}{2} + v}{u} = 1 \quad \text{...(iii)}$$

Solving Eqs. (i), (ii) and (iii), we get $\omega = \frac{u}{l}$

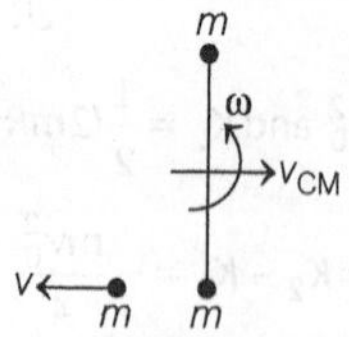

(B) $$mu\left(\frac{l}{2}\right) = -mv\left(\frac{l}{2}\right) + \left\{m\left(\frac{l}{2}\right)^2 + m\left(\frac{l}{2}\right)^2\right\}\omega \quad \text{...(i)}$$

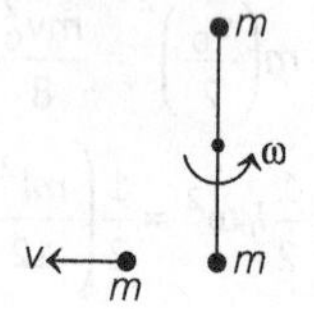

$$e = \frac{v + \frac{\omega l}{2}}{u} = 1 \quad \text{...(ii)}$$

Solving Eqs. (i) and (ii), we get, $\omega = \frac{4u}{3l}$

(C) Conserving angular momentum about the CM of system,

$$mu\left(\frac{l}{3}\right) = \left\{2m\left(\frac{l}{3}\right)^2 + m\left(\frac{2l}{3}\right)^2\right\}\omega$$

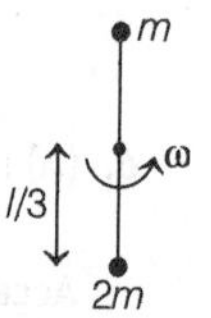

$$\omega = \frac{u}{2l}$$

(D) Conserving angular momentum about the hinge.

$$mu\left(\frac{l}{2}\right) = \left\{2m\left(\frac{l}{2}\right)^2 + m\left(\frac{l}{2}\right)^2\right\}\omega \Rightarrow \omega = \frac{2u}{3l}$$

Numercial Value Questions

1. $\Sigma F = ma \Rightarrow f = Ma_{CM}$ ...(i)

$$\Sigma\tau = I_{CM}\alpha \Rightarrow \left(\frac{3}{2}Mg\right)2R - fR = \left(\frac{MR^2}{2}\right)\alpha \quad \text{...(ii)}$$

$$a_{CM} = R\alpha \quad \text{...(iii)}$$

Solving, we get $f = 2Mg$

$$f \le f_L \Rightarrow 2Mg \le \mu\left(\frac{5}{2}Mg\right) \Rightarrow \mu_{min} = 0.8$$

2. For rear wheel; $\Sigma\tau = I_{CM}\alpha \Rightarrow 100 - f_1R = (0.5)\alpha$ ...(i)

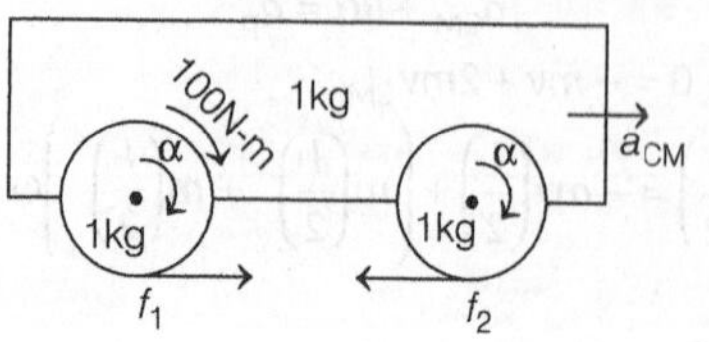

For front wheel; $\Sigma\tau = I_{CM}\alpha \Rightarrow f_2R = (0.5)\alpha$ ...(ii)

For system, $\Sigma F_{ext} = Ma_{CM} \Rightarrow f_1 - f_2 = 3a_{CM}$ ...(iii)

$a_{CM} = R\alpha$ ...(iv)

Solving Eqs. (i), (ii), (iii) and (iv), we get $a_{CM} = 25 \text{ m/s}^2$

3. $m_1g - T = m_1a$ ...(i)

$T = ma_{CM}$ ...(ii)

$$Tl = \left(\frac{m(2l)^2}{12}\right)\alpha \quad \text{...(iii)}$$

$a_{CM} + l\alpha = a$ ...(iv)

Solving Eqs. (i), (ii), (iii) and (iv) we get $\alpha = 5 \text{ rad/s}^2$

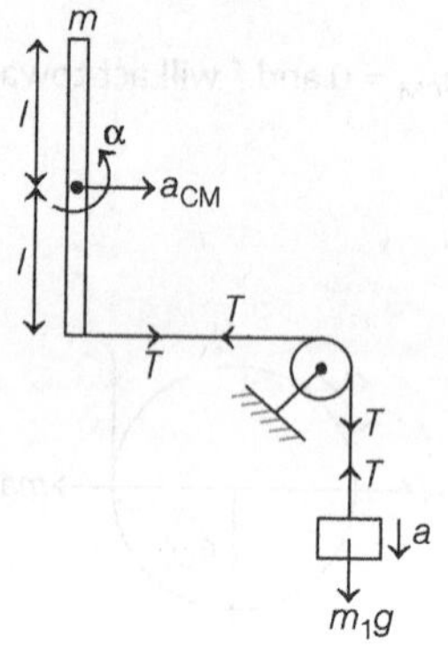

4. $\Sigma F = ma_{CM} \Rightarrow 10 = (5+5)a_{CM} \Rightarrow a_{CM} = 1 \text{ m/s}^2$

$$\Sigma\tau = I_{CM}\alpha \Rightarrow 10R = \left(\frac{5R^2}{2}\right)\alpha \Rightarrow R\alpha = 4 \text{ m/s}^2$$

$a_k = a_{CM} + R\alpha = 1 + 4 = 5 \text{ m/s}^2$

5. Let R be the resultant of normal force and friction.

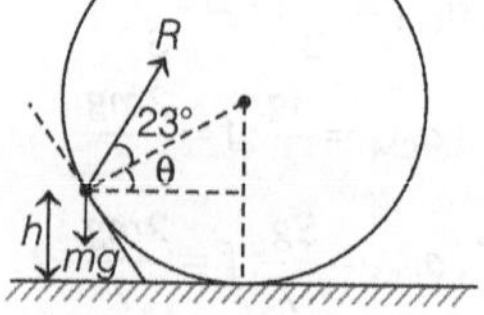

$R\cos(\theta + 23°) = ma$ ...(i)

$R\sin(\theta + 23°) = mg$ ...(ii)

Dividing Eq. (ii) by Eq. (i),

$$\tan(\theta + 23°) = \frac{4}{3} \Rightarrow \theta = 30°$$

$$\sin\theta = \frac{R-h}{R} = \frac{1}{2} \Rightarrow h = \frac{R}{2} = 50 \text{ cm}$$

6. For plank, $F - f = 15a_P$ ...(i)

For disc, $f - F = 15a_{CM}$ ...(ii)

$$fR = \left(\frac{15R^2}{2}\right)\alpha \quad \text{...(iii)}$$

Constraint: $a_{CM} + R\alpha = a_P$ ...(iv)

Solving, we get, $f=\frac{F}{2};\ \alpha=\frac{F}{15R};\ a_P=\frac{F}{30}$

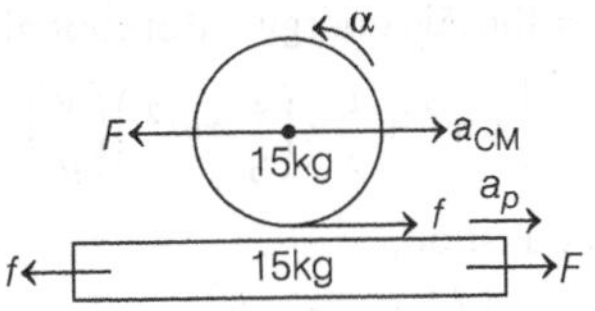

$$\theta=\omega_0 t+\frac{1}{2}\alpha t^2 \Rightarrow 2\pi=\frac{1}{2}\left(\frac{F}{15R}\right)t^2 \Rightarrow t=\sqrt{\frac{60\pi R}{F}}$$

$$s=ut+\frac{1}{2}at^2 \Rightarrow s_P=\frac{1}{2}\left(\frac{F}{30}\right)\left(\frac{60\pi R}{F}\right)=\pi R$$

Work done by friction on plank $=-f(\pi R)$

$$=-\frac{F}{2}\pi R=-264\text{ J}$$

7. Using linear momentum conservation for the system,

$$mv_0+0=(M+m)v \Rightarrow v=\frac{mv_0}{M+m}$$

Using energy conservation for system

$$K_1+U_1=K_2+U_2$$

$$\Rightarrow \frac{7}{10}mv_0^2+0=\frac{1}{2}(M+m)\left(\frac{mv_0}{M+m}\right)^2+mgh$$

$$\Rightarrow \quad v_0=\sqrt{\frac{5gh}{2}}=15\text{ m/s}$$

8. $v_P=\sqrt{v_0^2+v_0^2+2(v_0)(v_0)\cos(180°-\theta)}=2v_0\sin\left(\frac{\theta}{2}\right)$

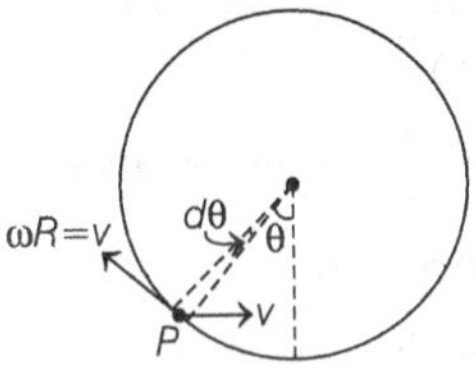

$$K=\int_{-\frac{\pi}{2}}^{+\frac{\pi}{2}}\frac{1}{2}\left(\frac{m}{2\pi}d\theta\right)\left(2v_0\sin\left(\frac{\theta}{2}\right)\right)^2$$

$$=mv_0^2\left(\frac{1}{2}-\frac{1}{\pi}\right)$$

So, $\qquad \alpha+\beta=2+1=3$

9. Using linear momentum conservation for the system,

$$1(8)=(2+2+12)v_{CM} \Rightarrow v_{CM}=0.5\text{ m/s}$$

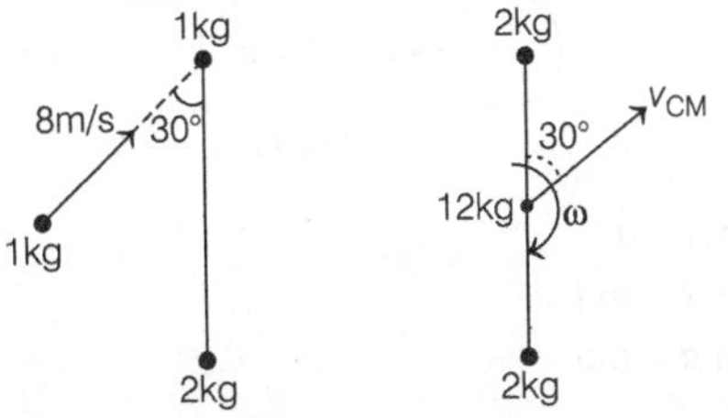

Using angular momentum conservation about the CM,

$$(1(8)\sin 30°)\frac{L}{2}=\left(\frac{(12)L^2}{12}+2\left(\frac{L}{2}\right)^2+2\left(\frac{L}{2}\right)^2\right)\omega$$

$$\Rightarrow \quad \omega=\frac{1}{L}$$

Heat produced

$$=\frac{1}{2}\times1\times8^2-\left(\frac{1}{2}\times16\times(0.5)^2+\frac{1}{2}(2L^2)\left(\frac{1}{L}\right)^2\right)=29\text{ J}$$

10. Applying linear momentum conservation for system

$$0+0=0.6(-u)+(0.3)v$$

$$\Rightarrow \quad v=2u \qquad \text{...(i)}$$

Applying angular momentum conservation about the centre of mass of rod,

$$\left(\frac{(0.6)(0.9)^2}{12}\right)\omega=(0.3)vx \Rightarrow \frac{27}{200}\omega=vx \qquad \text{...(ii)}$$

$$e=\frac{v+u}{\omega x}=1 \Rightarrow v+u=\omega x \qquad \text{...(iii)}$$

Solving Eqs. (i), (ii) and (iii), we get

$$x=45\text{ cm}$$

11. Let vertical velocity of A be v_1.

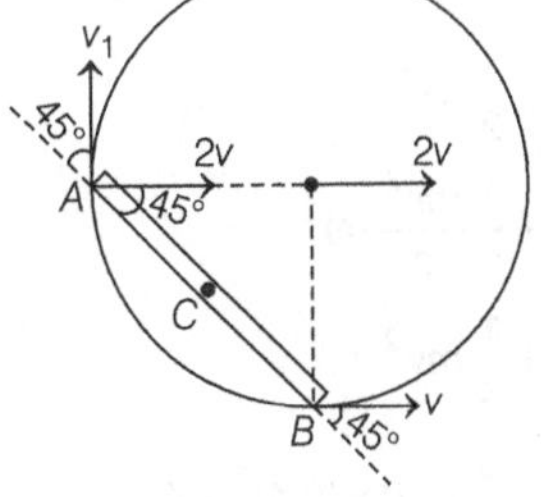

Velocities of A and B will be same along the rod.

$$2v\cos45°-v_1\cos45°=v\cos45°$$

$$\Rightarrow \quad v_1=v$$

$$v_{CM}=\frac{3v}{2}\hat{i}+\frac{v}{2}\hat{j}\text{ and }\omega=\frac{\sqrt{2}v}{\sqrt{2}R}=\frac{v}{R}$$

$$K=\frac{1}{2}mv_{CM}^2+\frac{1}{2}I_{CM}\omega^2=\frac{4}{3}Mv^2$$

Previous Years Questions

JEE Main

1. $$\frac{E_{K_{\text{ring}}}}{E_{K_{\text{sphere}}}}=\frac{\frac{1}{2}mv^2\left(1+\frac{K_R^2}{R^2}\right)}{\frac{1}{2}mv^2\left(1+\frac{K_S^2}{R^2}\right)}=\frac{1+\frac{K_R^2}{R^2}}{1+\frac{K_S^2}{R^2}}=\frac{1+\frac{R^2}{R^2}}{1+\frac{\frac{2}{5}R^2}{R^2}}$$

$$=\frac{1+1}{\frac{7}{5}}=\frac{10}{7}$$

$$\therefore \quad \frac{E_{K_{\text{sphere}}}}{E_{K_{\text{ring}}}} = \frac{7}{10} = \frac{7}{x} \quad \text{(given)}$$

$$x = 10$$

2.

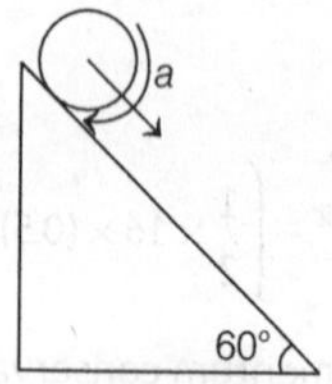

For rolling motion, $a = \dfrac{g\sin\theta}{1 + \dfrac{I_{cm}}{MR^2}}$

$$a = \frac{g\sin\theta}{1 + \frac{1}{2}} = \frac{2 \times 10 \times \sin 60°}{3}$$

$$= \frac{2 \times 10 \times \sqrt{3}}{3 \times 2} = \frac{10}{\sqrt{3}}$$

Therefore, $x = 10$

3. To stop a rolling disc,

Work done = Total energy of the disc

$\therefore$ Work done = KE of COM + Rotational KE of body about its COM

$$= \frac{1}{2}mv^2 + \frac{1}{2}I\omega^2$$

$$= \frac{1}{2}mv^2 + \frac{1}{2}\frac{mr^2}{2}\cdot\omega^2$$

$$= \frac{1}{2}mv^2 + \frac{1}{4}mv^2 \qquad \left[\because \omega = \frac{v}{r}\right]$$

$$= \frac{3}{4}mv^2 = \frac{3}{4} \times 50 \times (0.4)^2 = 6 \text{ J}$$

4. The given situation is show below.

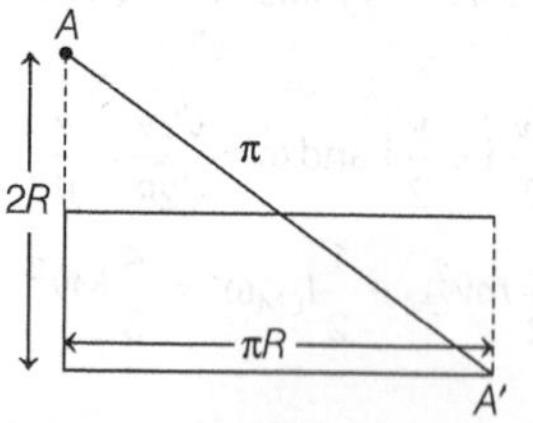

A is the initial top most position of disc.

A' is the final position of disc after completing half rotation.

$\therefore$ Required displacement,

$$AA' = \sqrt{(\pi R)^2 + (2R)^2} = R\sqrt{\pi^2 + 4}$$

5.

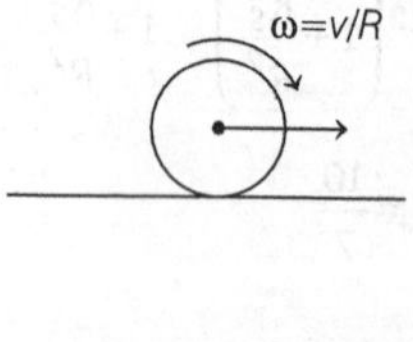

$$\text{Rotational energy} = \frac{1}{2}I\omega^2 = \frac{1}{2}\left(\frac{2}{3}mR^2\right)\left(\frac{v}{R}\right)^2$$

Total energy = Kinetic energy + Rotational energy

$$= \frac{1}{2}mv^2 + \frac{1}{2} \times \left(\frac{2}{3}mR^2\right)\left(\frac{v}{R}\right)^2$$

According to question,

$$\frac{K_{\text{rot}}}{K_{\text{Total}}} = \frac{\frac{1}{2}\left(\frac{2}{3}\right)mR^2 \times \frac{v^2}{R^2}}{\frac{1}{2}mv^2 + \frac{1}{2} \times \frac{2}{3}mR^2 \times \frac{v^2}{R^2}} = \frac{2}{5} = \frac{x}{5} \quad \text{(given)}$$

Thus, $x = 2$

6. For solid sphere Angular momentum,

$$L = I\omega = \frac{2}{5}MR^2 \times \frac{v}{R}$$

$$L = \frac{2MRv}{5} \qquad \text{...(i)}$$

Total energy of sphere,

$$E = \frac{1}{2}I\omega^2 + \frac{1}{2}mv^2$$

$$= \frac{1}{2}\left(\frac{2}{5}MR^2\right)\frac{v^2}{R^2} + \frac{1}{2}mv_0^2$$

$$\Rightarrow \quad E = \frac{7}{10}Mv^2 \qquad \text{...(ii)}$$

From Eqs. (i) and (ii), we get

$$\frac{L}{E} = \frac{\frac{2MRv}{5}}{\frac{7Mv^2}{10}} \Rightarrow \frac{\pi}{22} = \frac{4R}{7v}$$

$$\Rightarrow \quad \frac{V}{R} = \frac{4}{7} \times \frac{22}{\pi} \Rightarrow \omega = 4 \text{ rad/s}$$

7. By energy conservation;

$$\frac{1}{2}mv^2 = mgh$$

$$\Rightarrow \quad h = \frac{v^2}{2g} = \frac{3^2}{2 \times 10} \text{ m}$$

$$= \frac{3^2 \times 100}{2 \times 10} \text{ cm} = 45 \text{ cm}$$

8. Given, $m = 0.5$ kg,

$$u = 18 \text{ m/s}, \mu = 0.3$$

For disc, $I = \dfrac{1}{2}mR^2$

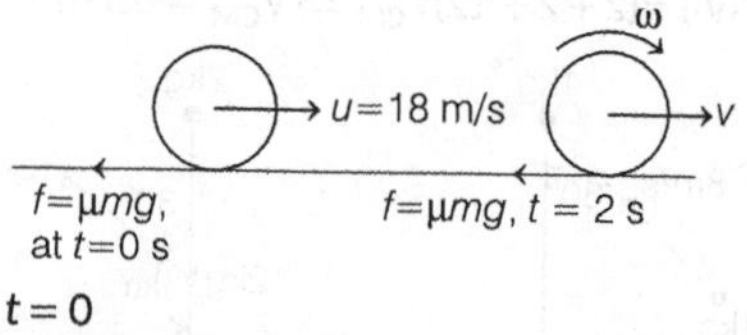

At time, $t = 0$ (Pure sliding)

$$f = ma$$

$$\Rightarrow \quad \mu mg = ma$$

$\therefore \quad a = \mu g = 0.3 \times 10 = 3$ m/s

At time, $t = 2$ s (Pure rolling)

$$v = u - at$$
$$= 18 - 3 \times 2 = 12 \text{ m/s}$$

$\therefore \quad v = 12$ m/s

Also, $\quad v = \omega r$

$$\Rightarrow \quad \omega = \frac{v}{r} = \frac{12}{r}$$

$$\therefore \ (\text{KE})_{\text{Total}} = \frac{1}{2}mv^2 + \frac{1}{2}I\omega^2$$

$$= \frac{1}{2} \times 0.5 \times 12^2 + \frac{1}{2} \times \frac{0.5 \times r^2}{2} \times \frac{12^2}{r^2}$$

$$= 54 \text{ J}$$

9. For a rolling sphere, KE

$$= \text{KE}_{\text{rotational}} + \text{KE}_{\text{translational}}$$

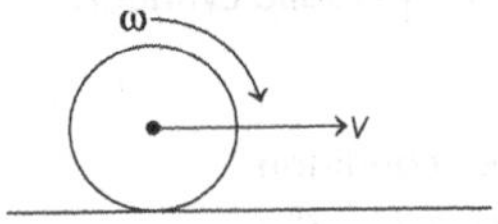

$$\text{KE} = \frac{1}{2}I\omega^2 + \frac{1}{2}mv^2 = \frac{1}{2} \times \frac{2}{5}mr^2\omega^2 + \frac{1}{2}mv^2$$

$$= \left(\frac{1}{5} + \frac{1}{2}\right)mv^2$$

$$\therefore \quad \left[I = \frac{2}{5}mr^2 \text{ and } v = r\omega\right] = \frac{7}{10}mv^2 \qquad (\therefore m = 2 \text{ kg})$$

$$= \frac{14}{10}v^2$$

Given, KE = 2240 J

So, $\frac{14}{10}v^2 = 2240$

$$\Rightarrow \quad v^2 = 1600 \quad \Rightarrow v = 40 \text{ m/s}$$

10. Given that, $\theta = 30°$, $l = 60$ cm

For solid cylinder, $\frac{K^2}{R^2} = \frac{1}{2}$

Speed of a body in pure rolling motion is given as

$$v = \sqrt{\frac{2gs\sin\theta}{1 + \frac{K^2}{R^2}}} = \sqrt{\frac{2 \times 10 \times 0.6 \times \sin 30°}{1 + \frac{1}{2}}}$$

$$v = 4 \text{ m/s}$$

11. Given that, mass, $m = 1$ kg

Total kinetic energy, $K_T = 7 \times 10^{-3}$ J

In pure rolling motion,

$$K_T = \frac{1}{2}mv_{\text{CM}}^2\left(1 + \frac{K^2}{R^2}\right)$$

For solid sphere, $\frac{K^2}{R^2} = \frac{2}{5}$

$$\therefore \quad K_T = \frac{1}{2}mv_{\text{CM}}^2\left(1 + \frac{2}{5}\right)$$

$$\Rightarrow \quad K_T = \frac{7}{10}mv_{\text{CM}}^2 \text{ or } v_{\text{CM}}^2 = \frac{10K_T}{7m}$$

$$\text{or} \quad v_{\text{CM}} = \sqrt{\frac{10K_T}{7m}} = \sqrt{\frac{10 \times 7 \times 10^{-3}}{7 \times 1}}$$

$$v_{\text{CM}} = 10^{-1} \text{ m/s} \Rightarrow v_{\text{CM}} = 10 \text{ cm/s}$$

12. By energy conservation as number of non-conservative forces are acting:

Let it unbinds and falls h height to attain speed of 4 m/s

$$\therefore \quad mgh = \frac{1}{2}mv^2 + \frac{1}{2}I\omega^2$$

($\because$ Decrease in gravitational potential energy = increase in translational kinetic energy + increase in rotational kinetic energy)

$$\Rightarrow \quad mgh = \frac{1}{2}mv^2 + \frac{1}{2}\frac{mR^2}{2}\omega^2$$

$$\Rightarrow \quad gh = \frac{1}{2}v^2 + \frac{1}{4}R^2\omega^2$$

$$\Rightarrow \quad 10h = \frac{4^2}{2} + \frac{1}{4}(v^2) \qquad (\because v = R\omega)$$

$$\Rightarrow \quad 10h = \frac{16}{2} + \frac{4^2}{4} \Rightarrow 10h = \frac{16}{2} + \frac{16}{4}$$

$$\Rightarrow \quad 10h = 12 \Rightarrow h = \frac{12}{10} \text{ m} = 1.2 \text{ m}$$

$$= 1.2 \times 100 \text{ cm} = 120 \text{ cm}$$

13. When a body rolls down an inclined plane,

Potential energy at top of incline = Kinetic energy of rotation + Kinetic energy of translation of CM

$$\Rightarrow \quad Mgh = \frac{1}{2}I\omega^2 + \frac{1}{2}Mv^2$$

$$\Rightarrow Mgh = \frac{1}{2}MK^2\left(\frac{v^2}{r^2}\right) + \frac{1}{2}Mv^2 \qquad \left[\because \omega = \frac{v}{r}\right]$$

$$\Rightarrow \quad Mgh = \frac{1}{2}Mv^2\left(1 + \frac{K^2}{R^2}\right) \qquad \text{...(i)}$$

Here, I = moment of inertia = MK^2, K = radius of gyration.

For solid cylinder, $\frac{K^2}{R^2} = \frac{1}{2}$

For solid sphere, $\frac{K^2}{R^2} = \frac{2}{5}$

Now, if we take ratio of Eq. (i) for solid cylinder and solid sphere

(for both mgh term will be same), we have

$$\frac{(mgh)_{\text{cyl}}}{(mgh)_{\text{sphere}}} = \frac{\frac{1}{2}Mv_{\text{cyl}}^2\left(1 + \frac{K^2}{R}\right)_{\text{cyl}}}{\frac{1}{2}Mv_{\text{sphere}}^2\left(1 + \frac{K^2}{R^2}\right)_{\text{sphere}}}$$

(For both bodies, mass and height are same)

$$\Rightarrow \quad 1 = \frac{v_{cyl}^2}{v_{sphere}^2} \cdot \frac{\left(1+\frac{1}{2}\right)}{\left(1+\frac{2}{5}\right)}$$

$$\Rightarrow \quad \frac{v_{cyl}^2}{v_{sphere}^2} = \frac{1+\frac{2}{5}}{1+\frac{1}{2}} = \frac{7}{5} \times \frac{2}{3}$$

$$\Rightarrow \quad \frac{v_{cyl}}{v_{sphere}} = \sqrt{\frac{14}{15}}$$

14. Given, speed of centre of mass of wheel be v_0

Speed of particle at rim be $v_0\sqrt{x}$.

$\therefore$ Velocity of particle placed at rim of wheel will be

$$v_0\sqrt{x} = v_0 + R\omega = v_0 + R \cdot \frac{v_0}{R}$$

$$\Rightarrow \quad v_0\sqrt{x} = 2v_0 \quad \Rightarrow \quad \sqrt{x} = 2 \quad \Rightarrow x = 4$$

15. Given, three shapes be ring, solid cylinder and solid sphere.

As we know that,

Moment of inertia of ring, solid cylinder and solid sphere about its centre of mass be

$$I_{ring} = MR^2 \quad \text{...(i)}$$

$$I_{solid\ cylinder} = \frac{MR^2}{2} \quad \text{...(ii)}$$

$$I_{solid\ sphere} = \frac{2}{5}MR^2 \quad \text{...(iii)}$$

and speed of body to roll on inclined plane is

$$v = \sqrt{\frac{2gh}{1+\frac{k^2}{R^2}}} \quad \text{...(iv)}$$

where, k is the of gyration.

Now from Eqs. (i), (ii) and (iii), we get

$$k_{ring} = R$$

$$k_{solid\ cylinder} = \frac{R}{\sqrt{2}} \quad \text{and} \quad k_{solid\ sphere} = R\sqrt{\frac{2}{5}}$$

Substituting these values sequently in Eq. (iv), we get

$$v_{ring} = \sqrt{\frac{2gh}{1+\frac{R^2}{R^2}}} = \sqrt{gh}$$

$$v_{solid\ cylinder} = \sqrt{\frac{2gh}{1+\frac{R^2/2}{R^2}}} = \sqrt{\frac{4gh}{3}} = \sqrt{1.33gh}$$

$$v_{solid\ sphere} = \sqrt{\frac{2gh}{1+\frac{\frac{2}{5}R^2}{R^2}}} = \sqrt{\frac{10}{7}gh} = \sqrt{1.43gh}$$

$v_{solid\ sphere} > v_{solid\ cylinder} > v_{ring}$.

Hence, the sphere has the greatest and the ring has the least velocity of the centre of mass at the bottom of the inclined plane.

16. It is given that $K_{rotational} = 50\%$ of $K_{translational}$

$$\Rightarrow \quad \frac{1}{2}I\omega^2 = \frac{1}{2}\left(\frac{1}{2}mv^2\right) \quad \text{...(i)}$$

where, I is moment of inertia, ω is angular speed, m is mass and v is linear speed.

$\because$ This case is of pure rolling, therefore

$$v = \omega R \quad \text{...(iii)}$$

From Eqs. (i) and (ii), we get

$$\frac{1}{2}I\omega^2 = \frac{1}{4}mR^2\omega^2 \Rightarrow I = \frac{1}{2}mR^2$$

As this the value of moment of inertia is for solid cylinder. Therefore, the body is solid cylinder.

JEE Advanced

1. Accordig to given condition

Impulse, $J = \Delta p = M(v - 0)$

$$\Rightarrow \quad J = Mv \quad \text{...(i)}$$

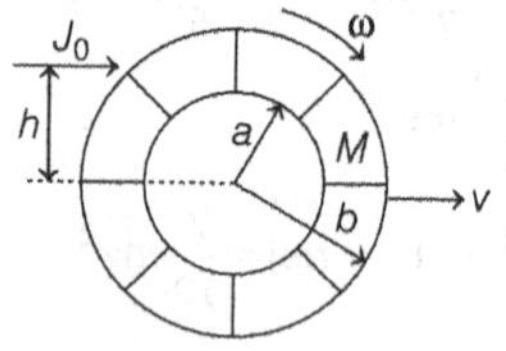

As, $J_0 \times h = I\omega$

$$\Rightarrow \quad J_0h = \frac{M}{2}(a^2+b^2)\omega$$

If $h = h_M$, then $\omega = \frac{v}{b}$

$$\therefore \quad J_0 \times h_M = \left(\frac{M}{2}\right)(a^2+b^2)\frac{v}{b} \quad \text{...(ii)}$$

From Eqs. (i) and (ii), we get

$$h_M = \frac{a^2+b^2}{2b}$$

If $a \to 0 \Rightarrow h_M = \frac{b}{2}$

if $a \to b$ then $h_M = \frac{b}{2}$

if $a \to b$ then $h_M = b$

Thus, if $h = h_M$, then from Eq. (i), we see that ω is independent of a

If $\mu = 0, h = 0$ i.e. the wheel always slides without rolling.

2. $$\omega = \frac{J \times \frac{R}{2}}{\frac{MR^2}{4}} = \frac{J}{MR} \times 2 = \frac{\sqrt{\frac{\pi}{2}} \times 2}{\frac{5}{1000} \times \frac{4}{3} \times \frac{1}{100}}$$

$2 \times 75\sqrt{2\pi}$ rad/s

$\Rightarrow$ Number of rotations $= \dfrac{\omega \cdot \Delta t}{2\pi}$

$$= \frac{2 \times 75\sqrt{2\pi} \times \dfrac{\sqrt{2\pi}}{5}}{2\pi} = 30$$

$\Rightarrow$ $n = 30$

3. $v = \omega(2R)$

$v = \omega_0 R$ (For no slipping)

$\therefore$ $\omega_0 = 2\omega$

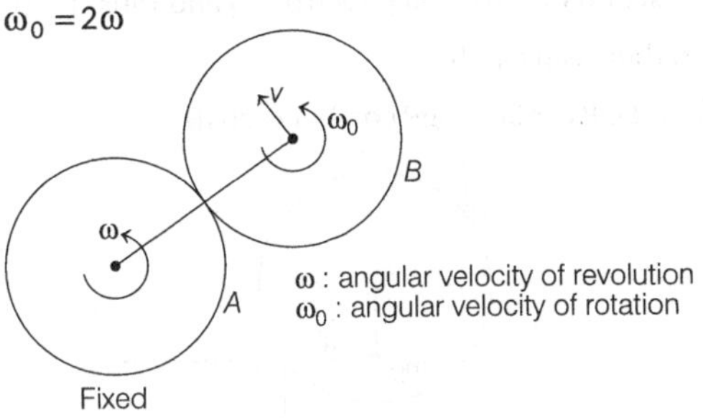

$$\mathbf{L} = m\,\mathbf{r} \times \mathbf{v}_c + I_c\omega_0 = M2Rv + \frac{1}{2}MR^2\omega_0$$

$$= 4MR^2\omega + \frac{1}{2}MR^2(2\omega) = 5MR^2\omega$$

$\therefore$ $n = 5$

4.

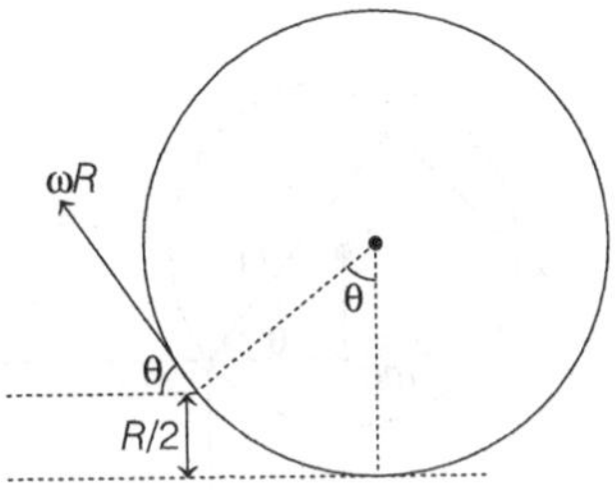

At $t = 0$, $\omega = 0$

At $t = \sqrt{\pi}$, $\omega = \alpha t = \dfrac{2}{3}\sqrt{\pi}$ $\therefore$ $v = \omega R = \dfrac{2}{3}\sqrt{\pi}R$

$\Rightarrow$ $v = \dfrac{2}{3}\sqrt{\pi}$ $[\because R = 1\text{ m}]$

$\Rightarrow$ $\theta = \dfrac{1}{2}\alpha t^2$ $\Rightarrow$ $\theta = \dfrac{1}{2} \times \dfrac{2}{3} \times \pi = \dfrac{\pi}{3}$ $\Rightarrow \theta = 60°$

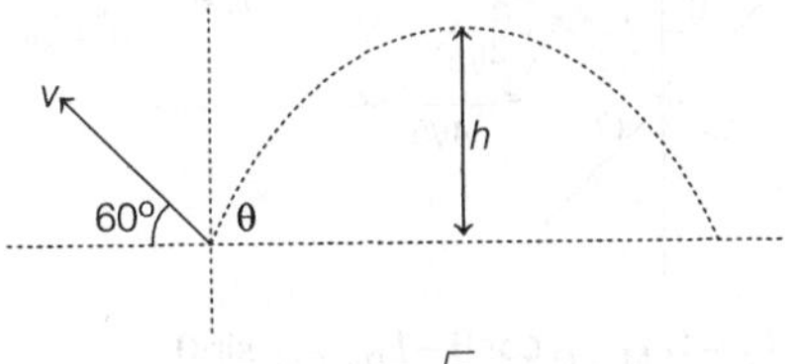

$\because$ $v_y = v\sin 60° = \dfrac{\sqrt{3}}{2}v$

$\therefore$ $h = \dfrac{u_y^2}{2g} = \dfrac{\frac{3}{4}v^2}{2g}$ $[\because v_y = u_y]$

$\Rightarrow$ $h = \dfrac{\frac{3}{4} \times \frac{4}{9}\pi}{2g}$ $\Rightarrow$ $h = \dfrac{3\pi}{9 \times 2g} = \dfrac{\pi}{6g}$

Maximum height from plane, $H = \dfrac{R}{2} + h$

$$H = \frac{1}{2} + \frac{\pi}{6 \times 10} \Rightarrow x = \frac{\pi}{6};\ x = 0.52$$

5.

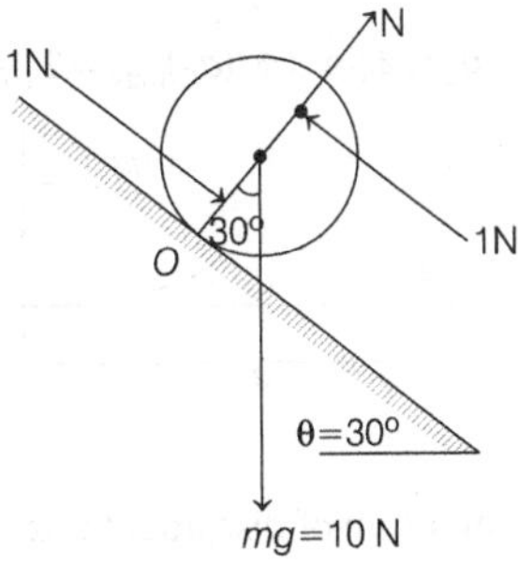

Taking torque about contact point O,

$\tau = 10 \times R \times \sin 30° + 1 \times 0.5 - 1 \times 1.5$ (clockwise)

$= 10 \times 1 \times \dfrac{1}{2} + 0.5 - 1.5$

$= 4$ N-m (clockwise)

Now, $\tau = I\alpha = \dfrac{7}{5}mR^2\alpha = \dfrac{7}{5} \times (1)(1)^2\alpha = \dfrac{7}{5}\alpha$

$\therefore$ $4 = \dfrac{7}{5}\alpha \Rightarrow \alpha = \dfrac{20}{7}$ rad/s^2

So, $a_{CM} = \alpha R = \dfrac{20}{7}$ m/s^2 $\Rightarrow a_{CM} = 2.86$ m/s^2

6.

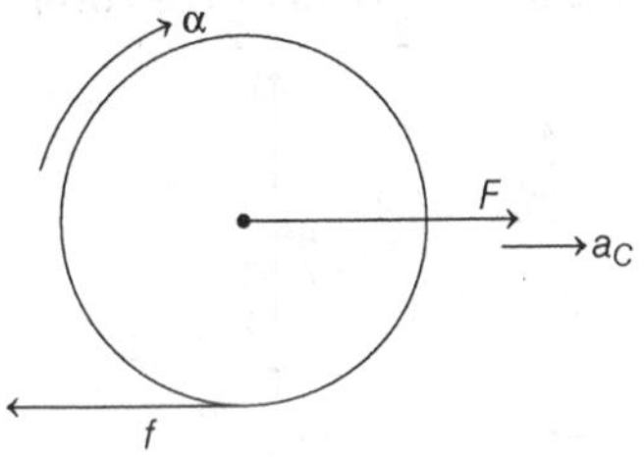

$F - f = ma_c \Rightarrow fR = I_C\alpha$

$a_C - \alpha R = 0 \Rightarrow F - I_C\dfrac{\alpha}{R} = ma_c$

$$a_C = \frac{F}{\dfrac{I_C}{R^2} + m}$$

$$f = \frac{I_C\alpha}{R} = \frac{I_C}{R^2}, a_C = \frac{I_C}{R^2}\frac{F}{\left[\dfrac{I_C}{R^2} + m\right]}$$

$$f = \frac{F}{\left(m + \dfrac{I_C}{R^2}\right)}$$

Thin walled hollow cylinder,

$I_C = mR^2 \Rightarrow a_C = \dfrac{F}{2m}$

$fR = I_C\alpha = \dfrac{I_C a_C}{R} \Rightarrow f = \dfrac{I_C a_C}{R^2} \le \mu mg$

$$a_C \le \frac{\mu mgR^2}{I_C}$$

For solid cylinder, $I_C = \dfrac{mR^2}{2}$

$$a_C \le 2\,\mu g \Rightarrow (a_C)_{max} = 2\,\mu g$$

7.

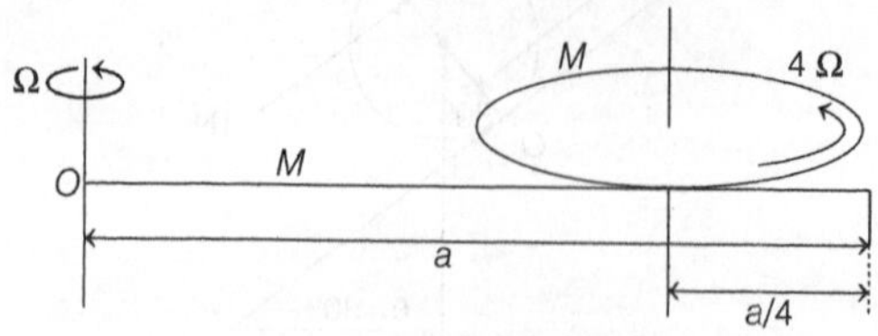

Angular momentum of disc about O is

$$L_{DO} = M\left(\frac{3a}{4}\right)\left(\frac{3a}{4}\right)\Omega + \frac{M}{2}\left(\frac{a}{4}\right)^2(4\Omega)$$

Angular momentum of rod about O is

$$L_{RO} = \frac{Ma^2}{3}\Omega$$

So, $\quad L_O = L_{DO} + L_{RO} = \dfrac{49}{48}(Ma^2\Omega)$

So, $\quad n = 49$

8. When the bar makes an angle θ, the height of its COM (mid-point) is $\dfrac{L}{2}\cos\theta$.

$\therefore$ Displacement $= L - \dfrac{L}{2}\cos\theta = \dfrac{L}{2}(1-\cos\theta)$

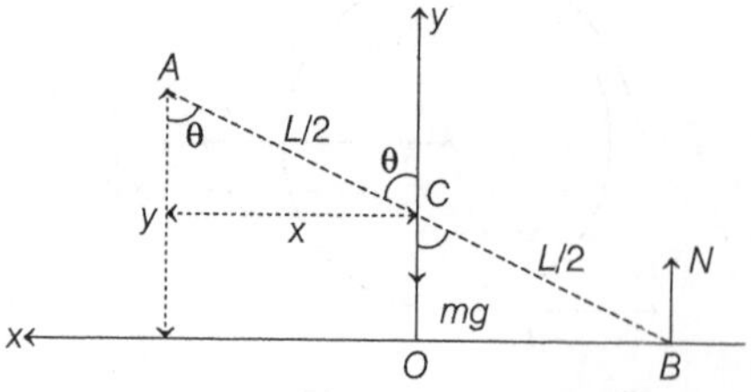

Since, forces on the rod are only along the vertical direction (mg at C and N at B), hence COM will fall vertically downwards. Instantaneous torque about point of contact is

$$\tau = mg \times \frac{L}{2}\sin\theta \quad \text{or} \quad \tau \propto \sin\theta$$

Now, $\quad x = \dfrac{L}{2}\sin\theta;\ y = L\cos\theta$

$$\frac{x^2}{(L/2)^2} + \frac{y^2}{L^2} = 1$$

Path of A is an ellipse.

9. Question is not very clear.

10. If height of the cone $h >> r$

Then, $\quad \mu N = mg \quad \Rightarrow \quad \mu m(R-r)\omega_0^2 = mg$

$$\omega_0 = \sqrt{\frac{g}{\mu(R-r)}}$$

11.

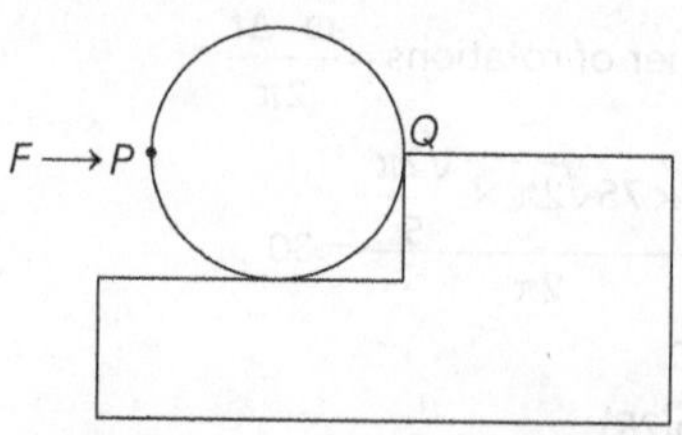

(a) If force is applied normal to surface at P, then line of action of force will pass from Q and thus, $\tau = 0$.

(b) Wheel can climb.

(c) $\tau = F(2R\cos\theta) - mgR\cos\theta,\ \tau \propto \cos\theta$

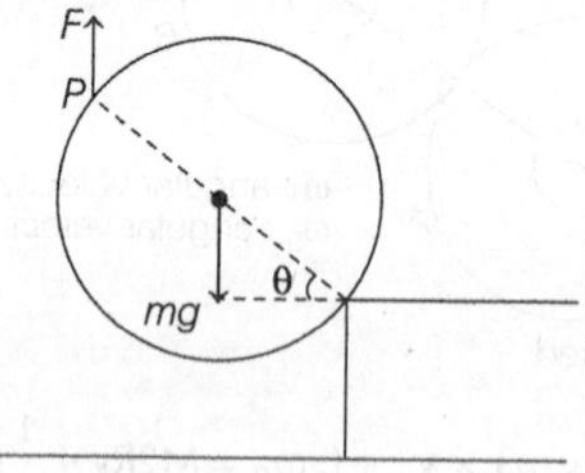

Hence, as θ increases

τ decreases. So it is correct.

(d)

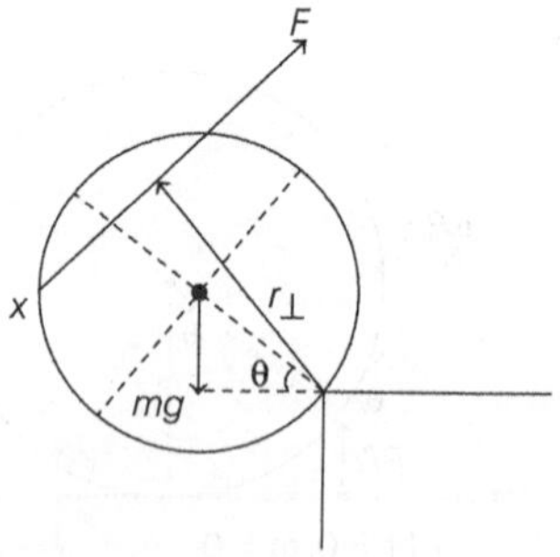

$\tau = Fr_\perp - mg\cos\theta$

τ increases with θ.

12.

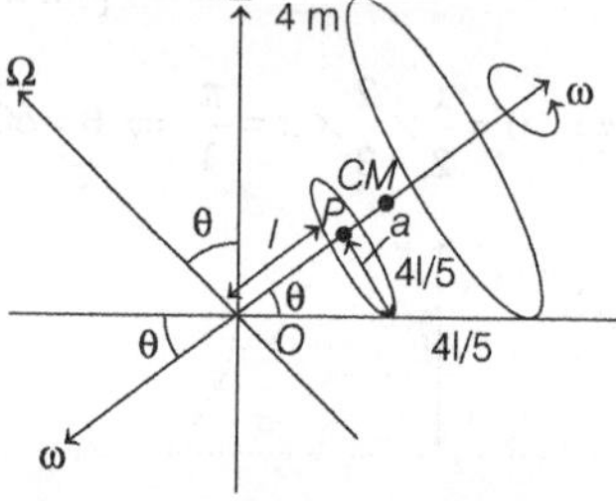

$$\cos\theta = \frac{l}{\sqrt{l^2+a^2}} = \frac{\sqrt{24}}{5}$$

(a) $\quad L_z = L_{CM-O}\cos\theta - L_{D-CM}\sin\theta$

$$= \frac{81\sqrt{24}}{5}a^2 m\omega \times \frac{\sqrt{24}}{5} - \frac{17\,ma^2\omega}{2} \times \frac{1}{\sqrt{24}}$$

$$= \frac{81 \times 24 ma^2\omega}{25} - \frac{17ma^2\omega}{2\sqrt{24}}$$

(b) $\quad L_{CM-O} = (5m)\left[\dfrac{9l}{5}\omega\right]\dfrac{9l}{5} = \dfrac{81\,ml^2\omega}{5} = \dfrac{81\,ml^2}{5} \times \dfrac{a\omega}{l}$

$$L_{CM-O} = \frac{81 mla\omega}{5} = \frac{81\sqrt{24}\,a^2 m\omega}{5}$$

(c) Velocity of point P : $a\omega = 1\,\omega$ then

$$\omega = \frac{a\omega}{1} = \text{Angular velocity of C.M. w.r.t. point } O.$$

Angular velocity of CM w.r.t. Z-axis $= \omega_0 \cos\theta$

$$\omega_{CM-z} = \frac{a\omega}{1}\frac{\sqrt{24}}{5} = \frac{a\omega}{\sqrt{24}\,a}\frac{\sqrt{24}}{5}$$

$$\omega_{CM-z} = \frac{\omega}{5}$$

(d) $L_{D-CM} = \dfrac{ma^2}{2}\omega + \dfrac{4m(2a)^2}{2}\omega = \dfrac{17\,ma^2\omega}{2}$

13. In case of pure rolling, mechanical energy remains constant (as work-done by friction is zero). Further in case of a disc,

$$\frac{\text{translational kinetic energy}}{\text{rotational kinetic energy}} = \frac{K_T}{K_R} = \frac{\frac{1}{2}mv^2}{\frac{1}{2}I\omega^2}$$

$$= \frac{mv^2}{\left(\frac{1}{2}mR^2\right)\left(\frac{v}{R}\right)^2} = \frac{2}{1}$$

or $\quad K_T = \dfrac{2}{3}$ (Total kinetic energy)

or Total kinetic energy

$$K = \frac{3}{2}K_T = \frac{3}{2}\left(\frac{1}{2}mv^2\right) = \frac{3}{4}mv^2$$

Decrease in potential energy = increase in kinetic energy

or $\quad mgh = \dfrac{3}{4}m\,(v_f^2 - v_i^2)$

or $\quad v_f = \sqrt{\dfrac{4}{3}gh + v_i^2}$

As final velocity in both cases is same.

So, value of $\sqrt{\dfrac{4}{3}gh + v_i^2}$ should be same in both cases.

$\therefore \quad \sqrt{\dfrac{4}{3}\times 10\times 30 + (3)^2} = \sqrt{\dfrac{4}{3}\times 10 \times 27 + (v_2)^2}$

Solving this equation, we get

$$v_2 = 7 \text{ m/s}$$

14. $I_P > I_Q$

In case of pure rolling, $\quad a = \dfrac{g\sin\theta}{1 + I/mR^2}$

$a_Q > a_P$ as its moment of inertia is less. Therefore, Q reaches first with more linear speed and more translational kinetic energy.

Further, $\omega = \dfrac{v}{R}$ or $\omega \propto v$

$\therefore \quad \omega_Q > \omega_P$ as $v_P > v_Q$

15. Velocity of point O is

$$v_O = (3R\omega)\,\hat{\mathbf{i}}$$

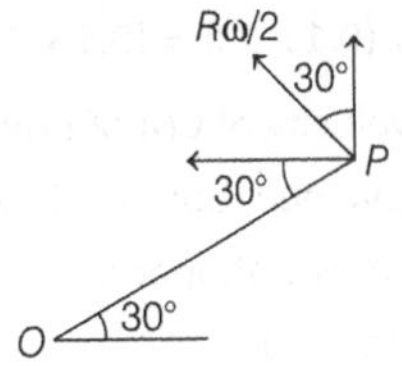

$\mathbf{v}_{PO}$ is $\dfrac{R\cdot\omega}{2}$ in the direction shown in figure.

In vector form

$$\mathbf{v}_{PO} = -\frac{R\omega}{2}\sin 30°\,\hat{\mathbf{i}} + \frac{R\omega}{2}\cos 30°\,\hat{\mathbf{k}}$$

$$= -\frac{R\omega}{4}\hat{\mathbf{i}} + \frac{\sqrt{3}R\omega}{4}\hat{\mathbf{k}}$$

But $\quad \mathbf{v}_{PO} = \mathbf{v}_P - \mathbf{v}_O$

$\therefore \quad \mathbf{v}_P = \mathbf{v}_{PO} + \mathbf{v}_O = \left(-\dfrac{R\omega}{4}\hat{\mathbf{i}} + \dfrac{\sqrt{3}R\omega}{4}\hat{\mathbf{k}}\right) + 3R\omega\,\hat{\mathbf{i}}$

$$= \frac{11}{4}R\omega\,\hat{\mathbf{i}} + \frac{\sqrt{3}}{4}R\omega\,\hat{\mathbf{k}}$$

16.

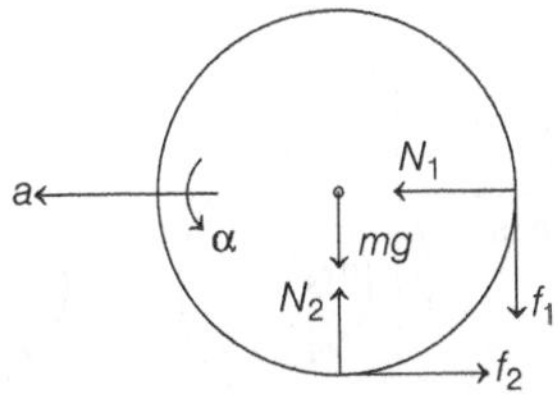

There is no slipping between ring and ground. Hence f_2 is not maximum. But there is slipping between ring and stick. Therefore, f_1 is maximum. Now let us write the equations.

$$I = mR^2 = (2)(0.5)^2 = \frac{1}{2}\text{kg - m}^2$$

$$N_1 - f_2 = ma$$

or $\quad N_1 - f_2 = (2)(0.3) = 0.6$ N $\quad$ ...(i)

$$a = R\alpha = \frac{R\tau}{I}$$

$$= \frac{R(f_2 - f_1)R}{I} = \frac{R^2(f_2 - f_1)}{I}$$

$\therefore \quad 0.3 = \dfrac{(0.5)^2(f_2 - f_1)}{(1/2)}$

or $\quad f_2 - f_1 = 0.6$ N $\quad$ ...(ii)

$N_1^2 + f_1^2 = (2)^2 = 4 \quad$ ...(iii)

Further $\quad f_1 = \mu N_1 = \left(\dfrac{P}{10}\right)N_1 \quad$ ...(iv)

Solving above four equations, we get

$$P \simeq 3.6$$

17. The data is incomplete. Let us assume that friction from ground on ring is not impulsive during impact.

From linear momentum conservation in horizontal direction, we have

$$(-2\times 1)+(0.1\times 20)=(0.1\times 0)+(2\times v) \quad \overset{-ve \quad +ve}{\longleftrightarrow}$$

Here, v is the velocity of CM of ring after impact.

Solving the above equation, we have $v=0$

Thus, CM becomes stationary.

∴ Correct option is (a).

Linear impulse during impact

(i) In horizontal direction

$$J_1=\Delta p=0.1\times 20=2\text{ N-s}$$

(ii) In vertical direction

$$J_2=\Delta p=0.1\times 10=1\text{ N-s}$$

$$PM=PN-MN=0.75-0.5=0.25\text{ m}$$

$$PC=0.5\text{ m}$$

$$\sin\theta=\frac{0.25}{0.5}=\frac{1}{2}$$

$$\therefore \quad \theta=30°$$

$$MC=PC\cos 30°=\frac{1}{2}\times\frac{\sqrt{3}}{2}$$

Writing the equation (about CM)

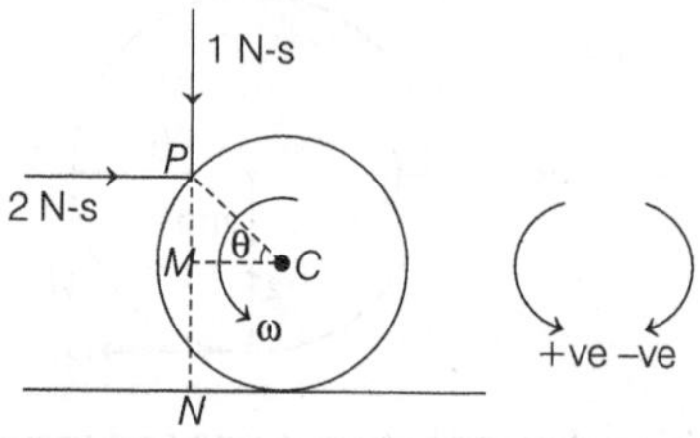

Angular impulse = Change in angular momentum

We have,

$$1\times\left(\frac{\sqrt{3}}{2}\times\frac{1}{2}\right)-2\times 0.5\times\frac{1}{2}=2\times(0.5)^2\left[\omega-\frac{1}{0.5}\right]$$

Solving this equation ω comes out to be positive or anti-clockwise. So just after collision rightwards slipping is taking place.

Hence, friction is leftwards.

Therefore, option (c) is also correct.

18. $a=R\alpha$

$$\therefore \quad \frac{2kx-f}{M}=R\left[\frac{fR}{\frac{1}{2}MR^2}\right]$$

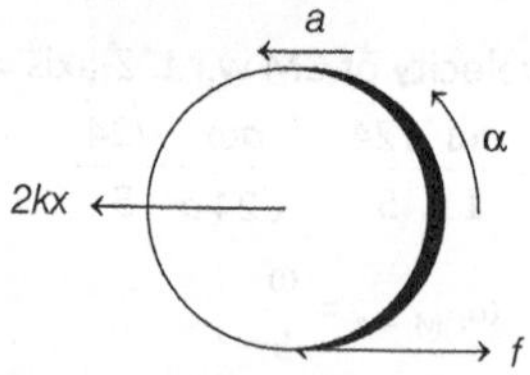

Solving this equation, we get

$$f=2kx/3$$

$$\therefore \quad |F_{net}|=2kx-f$$

$$=2kx-\frac{2kx}{3}=\frac{4kx}{3}$$

This is opposite to displacement.

$$\therefore \quad F_{net}=-\frac{4kx}{3}$$

19. $F_{net}=-\left(\frac{4kx}{3}\right)$

$$\therefore \quad a=\frac{F_{net}}{M}=-\left(\frac{4k}{3M}\right)x=-\omega^2 x$$

$$\therefore \quad \omega=\sqrt{\frac{4k}{3M}}$$

20. In case of pure rolling, mechanical energy will remain conserved.

$$\therefore \quad \frac{1}{2}Mv_0^2+\frac{1}{2}\left(\frac{1}{2}MR^2\right)\left(\frac{v_0}{R}\right)^2=2\left[\frac{1}{2}kx^2_{max}\right]$$

$$\therefore \quad x_{max}=\sqrt{\frac{3M}{4k}}\,v_0$$

As, $\quad f=2kx/3$

$$\therefore \quad F_{max}=\mu Mg=\frac{2kx_{max}}{3}=\frac{2k}{3}\sqrt{\frac{3M}{4k}}\,v_0$$

$$\therefore \quad v_0=\mu g\sqrt{3M/k}$$

CHAPTER~05

GRAVITATION

LEVEL 01 Starter Level

5.1 Universal Law of Gravitation

1 A mass (M) is split into two parts (m) and (M – m) which are then separated by a certain distance. What ratio m/M will maximise the gravitational force between the parts?

2 Two solid spheres of same size of a metal are placed in contact by touching each other.

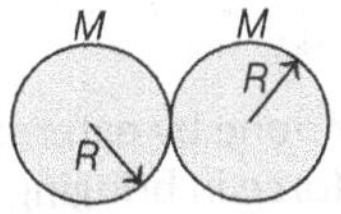

Prove that the gravitational force acting between them is directly proportional to the fourth power of their radius.

3 Two particles of masses m_1 and m_2, initially at rest at infinite distance from each other, move under the action of mutual gravitational pull. Show that at any instant their relative velocity of approach is $\sqrt{2G(m_1+m_2)/R}$, where R is their separation at that instant.

4 Two particles of equal mass (m) each move in a circle of radius (r) under the action of their mutual gravitational attraction. Find the speed of each particle.

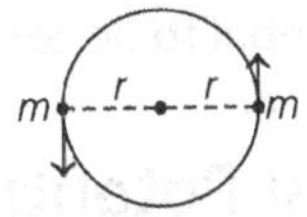

5 Three particles A, B and C each of mass m, are placed in a line with AB = BC = d. Find the gravitational force on a fourth particle P of same mass, placed at a distance d from the particle B on the perpendicular bisector of the line AC as shown in figure.

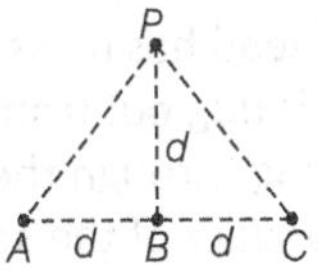

6 An infinite number of particles each of mass m are placed on the positive X-axis at 1m, 2m, 4m, 8m, ... from the origin. Find the magnitude of the resultant gravitational force on mass m kept at the origin.

7 Find gravitational force exerted by point mass m on uniform rod (mass M and length L)

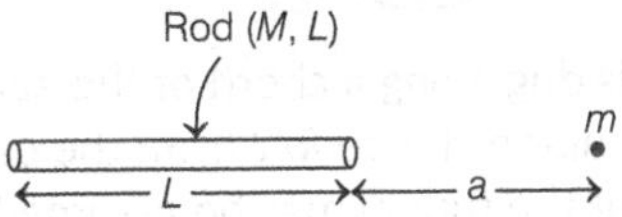

5.2 Gravitational Field Intensity

1. Find the distance of a point from the earth's centre where the resultant gravitational field due to the earth and the moon is zero. The mass of the earth is 6.0×10^{24} kg and that of the moon is 7.4×10^{22} kg. The distance between the earth and the moon is 4.0×10^{5} km.

2. A thin uniform rod has mass M and length L. Find gravitational field intensity at a point whose distance from each end of rod is L.

3. A thin rod of mass M and length L is bent in a semi-circle as shown in figure.

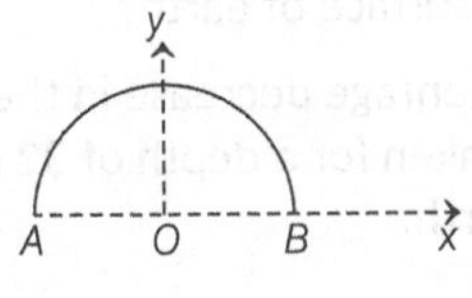

(a) What is its gravitational force (both magnitude and direction) on a particle with mass m at O, the centre of curvature?

(b) What would be the force on m if the rod is, in the form of a complete circle?

4. Calculate distance of the point on the axis of a uniform ring of mass M and radius R from its centre where gravitational field intensity is maximum.

5. A uniform solid sphere of mass M and radius a is surrounded symmetrically by a uniform thin spherical shell of equal mass and radius $2a$. Find the gravitational field at a distance (a) $3a/2$ from the centre, (b) $5a/2$ from the centre.

6. Inside a uniform sphere of density ρ there is a spherical cavity whose centre is at a distance l from the centre of the sphere. Find the strength of the gravitational field inside the cavity.

7. A solid sphere of lead has mass M and radius R. A spherical hollow is dug out from it (see figure). Its boundary is passing through the centre and also touching the boundary of the solid sphere. Deduce the gravitational force on a mass m placed at P, which is distant $2R$ from the centre.

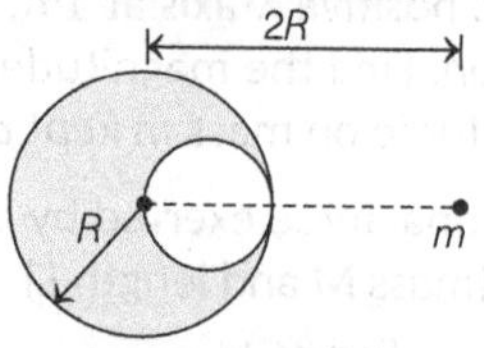

8. A tunnel is dug along a chord of the earth at a perpendicular distance $R/2$ from the earth's centre. The wall of the tunnel may be assumed to be frictionless. Find the force exerted by the wall on a particle of mass m when it is at a distance x from the centre of the tunnel. Mass of earth = M, Radius of earth = R

5.3 Acceleration Due to Gravity

1. Earth's mass is 80 times that of the moon and their diameters are 12800 and 3200 kms respectively. What is the value of g at the moon? (g on earth = 980 cm/s^2)

2. How much above the surface of earth does the acceleration due to gravity reduce by 36% of its value on the surface of earth?

3. Find the percentage decrease in the weight of the body when taken for a depth of 32 km below the surface of earth.

4. A man can jump 1.5 m on the Earth. Calculate the approximate height he might be able to jump on a planet whose density is one-quarter that of the Earth and whose radius is one-third that of the Earth.

5. The diameter of a planet is four times that of the earth. Find the time period of a pendulum on the planet, if it is a seconds pendulum on the earth. Take the mean density of the planet equal to that of the earth.

6. Find the height over the earth's surface at which the weight of a body becomes half of its value at the surface.

7. At what rate should the earth rotate so that the apparent g at the equator becomes zero? What will be the length of the day in this situation?

5.4 Gravitational Potential

1. (i) Find out potential at P and Q due to the two point mass system.

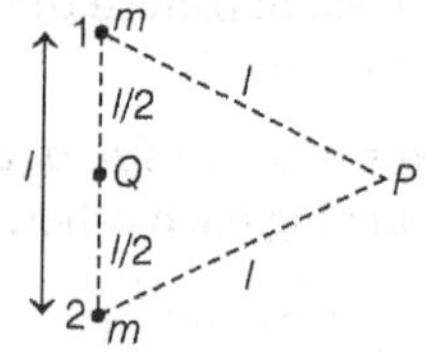

(ii) Find out work done by external agent and gravitational force in bringing a particle of mass m_0 from P to Q.

2. Find potential at a point P at a distance x on the axis away from centre of a ring of mass M and radius R.

3. A particle of mass m is placed at the centre of a uniform spherical shell of equal mass and radius a. Find the gravitational potential at a point P at a distance $a/2$ from the centre.

4. Calculate the gravitational potential at the centre of base of a solid hemisphere of mass M, radius R.

5. If $V = 2x^2 + 3y^2 + zx$, find gravitational field at a point (x, y, z).

6. The gravitational field due to a mass distribution is given by $E = -k/x^3$ in x-direction. Taking the gravitational potential to be zero at infinity, find its value at a distance x.

5.5 Gravitational Potential Energy

1. The gravitational field in a region is given by the equation $E = (5\hat{i} + 12\hat{j})$ N/kg. If a particle of mass 2 kg is moved from the origin to the point (12m, 5m) in this region, find the change in the gravitational potential energy.

2. The gravitational potential difference between the surface of a planet and a point 20m above it is 16 J/kg. Calculate the work done in moving a 2kg mass by 8m on a slope of 60° from the horizontal.

3. Three particles each of mass m are placed at the corners of an equilateral triangle of side a as shown in figure. Calculate

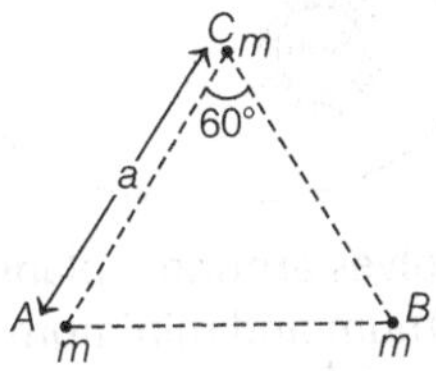

(a) potential energy of the system

(b) work done by the external agent to change the side of the triangle from a to $2a$.

4. Find the minimum energy required to disassemble a system of four particles, each of mass m placed at the vertices of a square of side l.

5. If g is acceleration due to gravity on the earth's surface, find the gain in the potential energy of an object of mass m raised from the surface of earth to a height equal to the radius R of the earth.

6. A small body is dropped from a height equal to the radius of the Earth . Find its speed just before reaching the surface of earth if g is acceleration due to gravity on the earth's surface.

7. A particle is projected with a velocity $\sqrt{\frac{3gR}{2}}$ vertically upward from the surface of the earth, R being the radius of the earth and g being the acceleration due to gravity on the surface of the earth. Find maximum height attained by it from the surface of earth.

8. A rocket is fired with a speed $v = 2\sqrt{gR}$ near the earth's surface and directed upwards. Find its speed in the interstellar space.

9. Two particles of masses m and M are initially at rest at an infinite distance apart. They move towards each other and gain speeds due to gravitational attraction. Find their speeds when the separation between the masses becomes equal to d.

5.6 Escape Velocity

1. A planet in a distant solar system is 10 times more massive than the earth and its radius is 10 times smaller. Given that escape velocity from the earth is 11km/s, find the escape velocity from the surface of the planet.

2. Find escape velocity from a space station which is at a height equal to radius of earth from the surface of earth.

3. Find radius of such planet on which the man escapes through jumping. The capacity of jumping of person on earth is 1.5 m. Density of planet is same as that of earth.

4. A very small groove is made in the earth, and a particle of mass m_0 is placed at $R/2$ distance from the centre. Find the escape speed of the particle from that place.

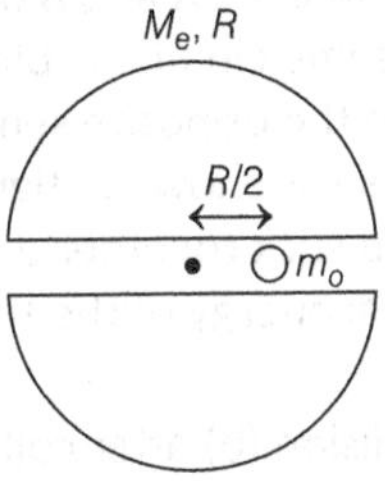

5. Distance between centres of two stars is $10a$. The masses of these stars are M and $16M$ and their radii are a and $2a$ respectively. A body is fired straight from the surface of the larger star towards the smaller star. What should be its minimum initial speed to reach the surface of the smaller star?

5.7 Satellite

1. An artificial satellite is describing an equatorial orbit at 1600 km above the surface of the earth.

(a) Calculate its orbital speed and the period of revolution.

(b) If the satellite is travelling in the same direction as the rotation of the earth (i.e, from west to east), calculate the interval between two successive times at which it will appear vertically overhead to an observer at a fixed point on the equator. (Radius of earth = 6400 km.)

2. (a) What is the height of a geo-stationary satellite from the surface of earth?

(b) What will be the time period of a spy satellite orbiting a few hundred km above the earth's surface? (Radius of earth = 6,400 km)

3. An artificial satellite of the earth is to be established in the equatorial plane of the earth and to an observer at the equator it is required that the satellite will move eastward, completing one round trip per day. Determine the distance of the satellite from the centre of the earth. The mass of the earth is $M = 6.00 \times 10^{24}$ kg and its angular velocity $\omega_0 = 7.30 \times 10^{-5}$ rad/s.

4. A satellite orbits the earth at a height of 3.6×10^{6} m from its surface. Compute its (a) kinetic energy, (b) potential energy, (c) total energy. Mass of the satellite = 500kg, mass of the earth $=6\times10^{24}$ kg, radius of the earth $=6.4\times10^{6}$ m, $G=6.67\times10^{-11}$ Nm^{2} kg^{-2}.

5. A 400kg satellite is in a circular orbit of radius $2R_E$ about the earth. How much energy is required to transfer it to a circular orbit of radius $4R_E$?

6. Consider two satellites *A* and *B* of equal masses, moving in the same circular orbit of radius *r* around the earth but in the opposite sense and therefore, on a collision course as shown in figure. They collide inelastically and stick together as wreckage. Find the total mechanical energy of the two satellites + earth system

(a) before collision (b) after collision. Describe the subsequent motion of the combined satellite.

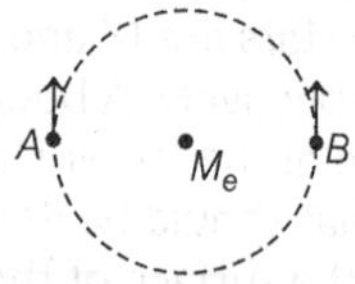

5.8 Kepler's Laws

1. The mean distance of a planet from the sun is approximately 4 times that of earth from the sun. Find the number of years required for planet to make one revolution about the sun.

2. Suppose a planet is revolving around the sun in an elliptical path given by $\frac{x^2}{a^2}+\frac{y^2}{b^2}=1$. Find time period of revolution. Angular momentum of the planet about the sun is *L*

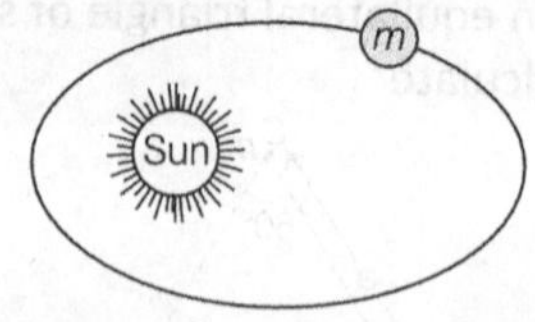

3. A satellite revolves around a planet in an elliptical orbit. Its maximum and minimum distances from the planet are 1.5×10^{7} m and 0.5×10^{7} m respectively. If the speed of the satellite at the farthest point be 5×10^{3} m/s, calculate the speed at the nearest point.

4. An artificial satellite is in an elliptical orbit around the earth with aphelion of 6*R* and perihelion of 2*R* where *R* is radius of the earth = 6400 km. Calculate the eccentricity of the elliptical orbit.

5. A planet of mass *m* moves along an ellipse around the Sun of mass *M* so that its maximum and minimum distances from Sun are *a* and *b* respectively. Prove that the angular momentum *L* of this planet relative to the centre of the Sun is $L=m\sqrt{\frac{2GMab}{(a+b)}}$.

6. A planet of mass *m* revolves around the sun (of mass *M*) in an elliptical orbit. The semi major axis of the orbit is *a*. Find the total mechanical energy of the system.

LEVEL 02 JEE Main Level

Single Choice Correct Questions

1. Three uniform sphere of mass *M* and radius *R* each are kept in such a way that each touches the other two. The magnitude of gravitational force on any of the spheres due to other two is

(a) $\frac{\sqrt{3}}{4}\frac{GM^2}{R^2}$ (b) $\frac{3}{2}\frac{GM^2}{R^2}$

(c) $\frac{\sqrt{3}GM^2}{R^2}$ (d) $\frac{\sqrt{3}GM}{R^2}$

2. *A*, *B*, *C* and *D* are four masses each of mass *M* lying on the vertices of a square of side *a*. They always move along a common circle with velocity *v*. Find *v* so that they always remain on the vertices of the square

(a) $\sqrt{\frac{GM(2\sqrt{2}+1)}{2\sqrt{2}a}}$ (b) $\sqrt{\frac{GM(\sqrt{2}+1)}{2a}}$

(c) $\sqrt{\frac{GM\sqrt{2}(2+1))}{a}}$ (d) None of these

3. Find the force of attraction on a particle of mass *m* placed at the centre of a quarter ring of mass *m* and radius *R* as shown in figure.

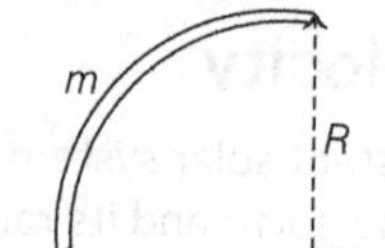

(a) $\frac{\sqrt{2}Gm^2}{R^2}$ (b) $\frac{2\sqrt{2}Gm^2}{R^2}$ (c) $\frac{\sqrt{2}Gm^2}{\pi R^2}$ (d) $\frac{2\sqrt{2}Gm^2}{\pi R^2}$

4. A spherical shell is cut into two pieces along a chord as shown in the figure. P is a point on the plane of the chord. The gravitational field at P due to the upper part is E_1, and that due to the lower part is E_2. What is the relation between them?

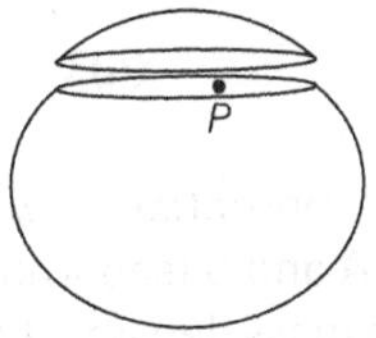

(a) $E_1 > E_2$ (b) $E_1 < E_2$
(c) $E_1 = E_2$ (d) Nothing can be said

5. Figure show a hemispherical shell having uniform mass density. The direction of gravitational field intensity at point P will be along

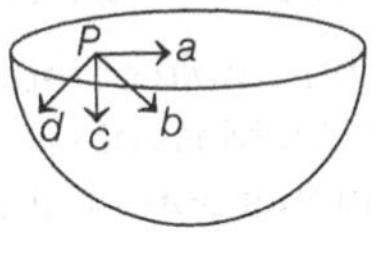

(a) a (b) b (c) c (d) d

6. A solid sphere of uniform density and radius R applies a gravitational force of attraction equal to F_1 on a particle placed at A at a distance $2R$ from the centre of the sphere. A spherical cavity of radius $R/2$ is now made in the body. The new mass now applies a gravitational force F_2 on the same particle placed at A. The ratio F_2/F_1 will be

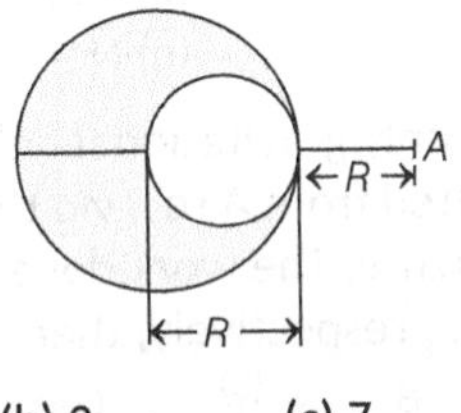

(a) 1/2 (b) 3 (c) 7 (d) 7/9

7. Two uniform solid spheres of equal radii R, but mass M and $4M$ have a center to center separation $6R$ as shown. The two spheres are held fixed. The position of neutral point(s) with respect to smaller mass is

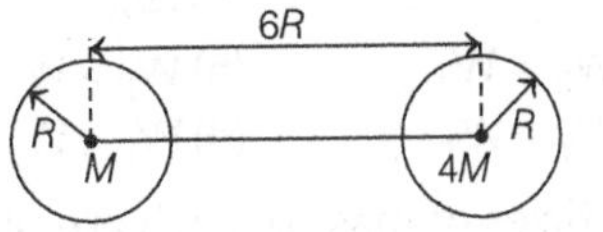

(a) $2R, -6R$ (b) $2R, 6R$ (c) $2R$ (d) $6R$

8. Two astronauts have deserted their spaceship in a region of space far from the gravitational attraction of any other body. Each has a mass of 100kg and they are 100m apart. They are initially at rest relative to one another. How long will it be before the gravitational attraction brings them 1cm closer together?

(a) 2.52 days (b) 1.41 days
(c) 0.70 days (d) 1.41 s

9. A tunnel is dug along a diameter of the earth. The force on a particle of mass m placed in the tunnel at a distance r from the surface of earth

(a) $\frac{GM_e mr}{R_e^2}$ (b) $\frac{GM_e m(R_e - r)}{R_e^3}$

(c) $\frac{GM_e mr^2}{R_e^2}$ (d) $\frac{GM_e mr}{R_e^3}$

10. Two lead spheres each of mass M are suspended by two long strings each of length L. The distance between the upper ends of the strings is also L. The angle which the strings make with the vertical due to mutual attraction of the spheres is

(a) $\tan^{-1}\left(\frac{GM}{gL}\right)$ (b) $\tan^{-1}\left(\frac{GM}{gL^2}\right)$

(c) $\tan^{-1}\left(\frac{GM}{2gL^2}\right)$ (d) $\tan^{-1}\left(\frac{Gm}{2gL^3}\right)$

11. Two spherical bodies of mass M and $8M$ and radii R and $2R$ respectively are released in free space with initial separation between their centres equal to $12R$. If they attract each other due to gravitational force only, then the distance covered by the smaller body just before collision is

(a) $4R$ (b) $6R$
(c) $8R$ (d) $32R/3$

12. Weight of a body of mass m decreases by 1% when it is raised to height h above the Earth's surface. If the body is taken to a depth h in a mine, then its weight will

(a) decrease by 0.5% (b) decrease by 2%
(c) increase by 0.5% (d) increase by 1%

13. At what altitude will the acceleration due to gravity be 25% of that at the earth's surface (given radius of earth is R)?

(a) $R/4$ (b) R
(c) $3R/8$ (d) $R/2$

14. The mass and diameter of a planet are twice those of earth. What will be the period of oscillation of a pendulum on this planet if it is a seconds pendulum on earth?

(a) $\sqrt{2}$ s (b) $2\sqrt{2}$ s (c) $\frac{1}{\sqrt{2}}$ s (d) $\frac{1}{2\sqrt{2}}$ s

15. Two planets of radii r_1 and r_2 are made from the same material. The ratio of the acceleration of gravity g_1/g_2 at the surfaces of the two planets is

(a) r_1/r_2 (b) r_2/r_1
(c) $(r_1/r_2)^2$ (d) $(r_2/r_1)^2$

16. A planet has mass 1/10 of that of earth, while radius is 1/3 that of earth. If a person can throw a stone on earth surface to a height of 90m, then he will be able to throw the stone on that planet to a height

(a) 90 m (b) 40 m
(c) 100 m (d) 45 m

17. A uniform solid sphere A is surrounded symmetrically by a uniform thin spherical shell B of equal mass but twice its radius (i.e. $r_B = 2r_A$). The gravitational field g is plotted as a function of the distance from the center of the solid sphere r. Which of the following shows the correct plot?

(a)
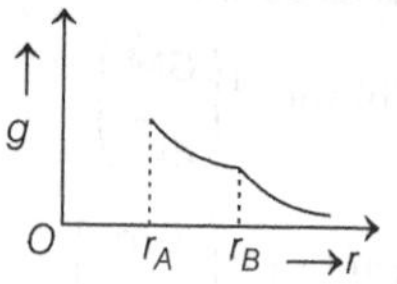

(b)
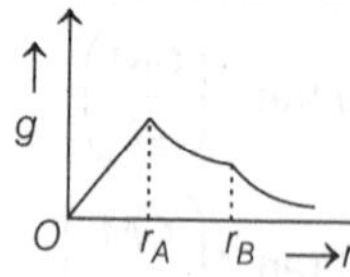

(c)
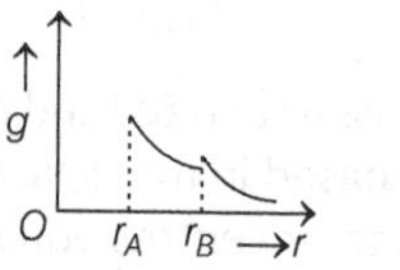

(d)
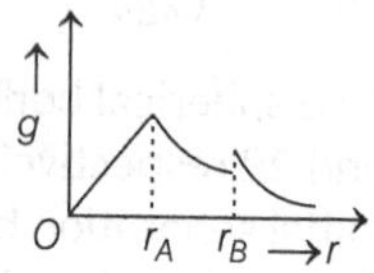

18. The rotation of the earth having radius R about its axis speeds upto a value such that a man at latitude angle 60° feels weightless. The duration of the day in such case will be

(a) $8\pi\sqrt{\frac{R}{g}}$ (b) $8\pi\sqrt{\frac{g}{R}}$
(c) $\pi\sqrt{\frac{R}{g}}$ (d) $4\pi\sqrt{\frac{g}{R}}$

19. A very large number of particles of same mass m are kept at horizontal distances of 1m, 2m, 4m, 8m and so on from (0,0) point. The total gravitational potential at this point (0, 0) is

(a) $-8Gm$ (b) $-3Gm$ (c) $-4Gm$ (d) $-2Gm$

20. Two bodies of masses m and M are placed at a distance d apart. The gravitational potential at the position where the gravitational field due to them is zero is V

(a) $V = -\frac{G}{d}(m+M)$ (b) $V = -\frac{Gm}{d}$
(c) $V = -\frac{GM}{d}$ (d) $V = -\frac{G}{d}(\sqrt{m}+\sqrt{M})^2$

21. Let gravitation field in a space be given as $E = -k/r$. If the reference point is at distance d_i where potential is V_i, then relation for potential is

(a) $V = k\ln\frac{r}{V_i} + 0$ (b) $V = k\ln\frac{r}{d_i} + V_i$
(c) $V = \ln\frac{r}{d_i} + KV_i$ (d) $V = \ln\frac{r}{d_i} + \frac{V_i}{K}$

22. The gravitational potential of two homogeneous spherical shells A and B (separated by large distance) of same surface mass density at their respective centres are in the ratio 3 : 4. If the two shells coalesce into single one such that surface mass density remains same, then the ratio of potential at an internal point of the new shell to shell A is equal to

(a) 3 : 2 (b) 4 : 3 (c) 5 : 3 (d) 3 : 5

23. There is a concentric hole of radius R in a solid sphere of radius $2R$. Mass of remaining portion is M, then the gravitational potential at centre is

(a) $\frac{-5GM}{7R}$ (b) $\frac{-7GM}{14R}$
(c) $\frac{-3GM}{7R}$ (d) $\frac{-9GM}{14R}$

24. A person brings a mass of 1kg from infinity to a point A. Initially the mass was at rest but it moves at a speed of 2m/s as it reaches A. The work done by the person on the mass is −3J. The potential at A is

(a) −3J / kg (b) −2J / kg
(c) −5J / kg (d) None of these

25. In a region of only gravitational field of mass M a particle is shifted from A to B *via* three different paths in the figure. The work done in different paths are W_1, W_2, W_3 respectively, then

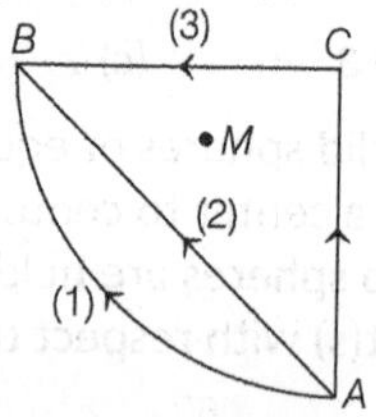

(a) $W_1 = W_2 = W_3$ (b) $W_1 > W_2 > W_3$
(c) $W_1 = W_2 > W_3$ (d) $W_1 < W_2 < W_3$

26. Three particles of mass m each are placed at three corners of an equilateral triangle of side a. The work which should be done on this system to increase the side of the triangle to $2a$ is

(a) $\frac{3GM^2}{a}$ (b) $\frac{3Gm^2}{2a}$ (c) $\frac{Gm^2}{2a}$ (d) $\frac{3Gm^2}{4a^2}$

27. A particle of mass m is placed on the centre of a fixed non-uniform semi-circular ring of radius R and mass M as shown. Then, work required to displace the particle slowly from centre of ring to infinity is

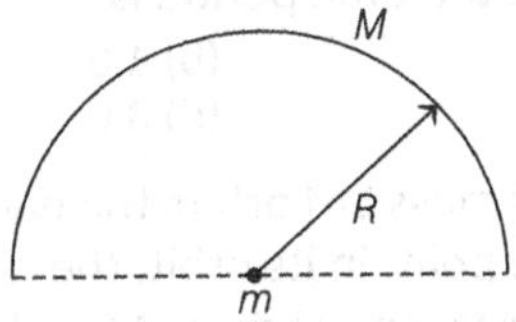

(Assume only gravitational interaction of ring and particle)

(a) $\frac{GMm}{R}$ (b) $-\frac{GMm}{R}$

(c) $\frac{GMm}{pR}$ (d) $-\frac{GMm}{pR}$

28. A body of mass m rises to height $h = R/5$ from the earth's surface, where R is earth's radius. If g is acceleration due to gravity at earth's surface, the increase in potential energy is

(a) $\frac{5}{6}mgR$ (b) $\frac{1}{6}mgR$

(c) $\frac{3}{5}mgR$ (d) $\frac{6}{7}mgR$

29. A body starts from rest at a point, distance R_0 from the centre of the earth of mass M, radius R. The velocity acquired by the body when it reaches the surface of the earth will be

(a) $GM\left(\frac{1}{R}-\frac{1}{R_0}\right)$ (b) $2\,GM\left(\frac{1}{R}-\frac{1}{R_0}\right)$

(c) $\sqrt{2\,GM\left(\frac{1}{R}-\frac{1}{R_0}\right)}$ (d) $2GM\sqrt{\left(\frac{1}{R}-\frac{1}{R_0}\right)}$

30. Two particles of mass m_1 and m_2 are initially at rest at infinite distance. Find their velocity of approach due to gravitational attraction, when separation is d

(a) $\sqrt{\frac{2G(m_1+m_2)}{d}}$ (b) $\sqrt{\frac{G(2m_1+m_2)}{3d}}$

(c) $\sqrt{\frac{3G(2m_1+m_2)}{d}}$ (d) $\sqrt{\frac{G(m_1+m_2)}{d}}$

31. A particle is projected with a velocity $\sqrt{\frac{4gR}{3}}$ vertically upward from the surface of the earth, R being the radius of the earth and g being the acceleration due to gravity on the surface of the earth. The velocity of the particle, when it is at half the maximum height reached by it is

(a) $\sqrt{\frac{gR}{2}}$ (b) $\sqrt{\frac{gR}{3}}$ (c) $\sqrt{gR}$ (d) $\sqrt{\frac{2gR}{3}}$

32. Suppose, if a tunnel is dug along the diameter of the earth and a body of mass m is released from a point A at a distance $2R$ above earth along the line of tunnel. If M is the mass of the earth and R is the radius of the earth. The velocity of the body during its fall when it crosses the point B at a distance $R/2$ below the earth centre as shown.

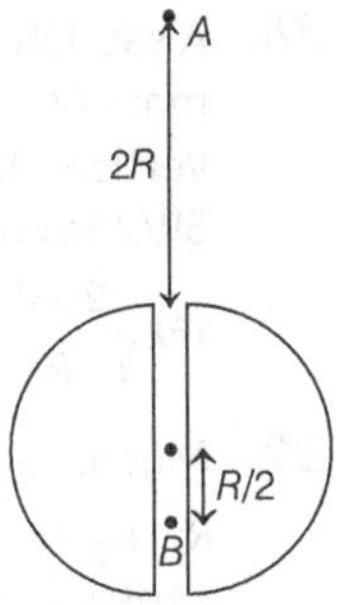

(a) $\frac{5}{2}\sqrt{\frac{GM}{3R}}$ (b) $\sqrt{\frac{GM}{3R}}$

(c) $2\sqrt{\frac{GM}{3R}}$ (d) $\frac{3}{2}\sqrt{\frac{GM}{3R}}$

33. The escape velocity for a body projected vertically upwards from the surface of earth is 11 km/s. If the body is projected at an angle of 45° with the vertical, the escape velocity will be

(a) $11\sqrt{2}$ km/s (b) 22 km/s

(c) 11 km/s (d) $11\sqrt{2}$ km/s

34. A projectile is fired from the surface of earth of radius R with a speed kv_e in radially outward direction (where, v_e is the escape velocity and $k < 1$). Neglecting air resistance, the maximum height from centre of earth is

(a) $\frac{R}{k^2+1}$ (b) k^2R

(c) $\frac{R}{1-k^2}$ (d) kR

35. The escape velocity from the earth is about 11 km/s. The escape velocity from a planet having twice the radius and the same mean density as the earth is

(a) 22 km/s (b) 11 km/s (c) 5.5 km/s (d) 15.5 km/s

36. The escape speed for a projectile in the case of earth is 11.2 km/sec. A body is projected from the surface of the earth with a velocity which is equal to twice the escape speed. The velocity of the body when at infinite distance from the centre of the earth is

(a) 11.2 km/s (b) 22.4 km/s

(c) $11.2\sqrt{3}$ km/s (d) $11.2\sqrt{2}$ km/s

37. A spherical uniform planet is rotating about its axis. The velocity of a point on its equator is v. Due to the rotation of planet about its axis the acceleration due to gravity g at equator is 1/2 of g at poles. The escape velocity of a particle on the pole of planet in terms of v.

(a) $v_e = 2v$ (b) $v_e = v$ (c) $v_e = v/2$ (d) $v_e = \sqrt{3}\,v$

38. A satellite is fired from the surface of the moon of mass M and radius R, with speed v_0 at 30° with the vertical. The satellite reaches a maximum distance of $5R/2$ from the centre of the moon. The value of v_0 is

(a) $\sqrt{\frac{2GM}{R}}$ (b) $\sqrt{\frac{5GM}{R}}$ (c) $\sqrt{\frac{5GM}{4R}}$ (d) $\sqrt{\frac{2GM}{37R}}$

39. Masses and radii of Earth and Moon are M_1, M_2 and R_1, R_2 respectively. The distance between their centre is d. The minimum velocity given to mass M from the mid point of line joining their centre so that it will escape is

(a) $\sqrt{\frac{4G(M_1+M_2)}{d}}$ (b) $\sqrt{\frac{4G\,(M_1 M_2)}{d(M_1+M_2)}}$

(c) $\sqrt{\frac{2G}{d}\left(\frac{M_1+M_2}{M_1 M_2}\right)}$ (d) $\sqrt{\frac{2G}{d}(M_1+M_2)}$

40. The orbital velocity of an artificial satellite in a circular orbit just above the surface of the earth is v_0. The value of the orbital velocity for another satellite orbiting at an altitude of half of earth's radius is :

(a) $\sqrt{\frac{3}{2}}v_0$ (b) $\sqrt{\frac{2}{3}}v_0$ (c) $\frac{2}{3}v_0$ (d) $\frac{1}{3}v_0$

41. If the gravitational force were to vary inversely as mth power of the distance, then the time period of a planet in circular orbit of radius r around the sun will be proportional to

(a) $r^{-3m/2}$ (b) $r^{3m/2}$ (c) $r^{(m+1)/2}$ (d) $r^{\frac{m+1}{2}}$

42. Two planets A and B have radius in the ratio 1 : 6. A satellite revolving near the surface of planets have same time period of revolution. The ratio of density of planets A and B is

(a) 1 : 6 (b) 6 : 1 (c) 1 : 1 (d) 36 : 1

43. A satellite can be in a geostationary orbit around earth at a distance r from the centre. If the angular velocity of earth about its axis doubles, a satellite can now be in a geostationary orbit around earth if its distance from the centre is

(a) $\frac{r}{2}$ (b) $\frac{r}{2\sqrt{2}}$ (c) $\frac{r}{(4)^{1/3}}$ (d) $\frac{r}{(2)^{1/3}}$

44. A satellite is seen after each 8h over the equator at a place on the earth when its sense of rotation is opposite to the earth. The time interval after which it can be seen at the same place when the sense of rotation of the earth and the satellite is the same will be

(a) 8 h (b) 12 h (c) 24 h (d) 6 h

45. A satellite is launched into a circular orbit of radius R around earth while a second satellite is launched into an orbit of radius $1.02R$. The percentage difference in the time period is

(a) 0.7 (b) 1.0
(c) 1.5 (d) 3.0

46. A satellite of mass $5M$ orbits the earth in a circular orbit. At one point in its orbit, the satellite explodes into two pieces, one of mass M and the other of mass $4M$. After the explosion, the mass M ends up travelling in the same circular orbit, but in opposite direction. After the explosion, motion of the mass $4M$

(a) will be in a bound orbit
(b) will be in an unbound orbit
(c) will be in a partially bound orbit
(d) will not be possible to decide due to insufficient information

47. The radius of a planet is R. A satellite revolves around it in a circle of radius r with angular velocity ω_0. The acceleration due to the gravity on planet's surface is

(a) $\frac{r^3\omega_0}{R}$ (b) $\frac{r^3\omega_0^3}{R^2}$ (c) $\frac{r^3\omega_0^2}{R}$ (d) $\frac{r^3\omega_0^2}{R^2}$

48. The correct graph representing the variation of total energy(E), kinetic energy(K) and potential energy (U) of a satellite with its distance from the centre of earth is

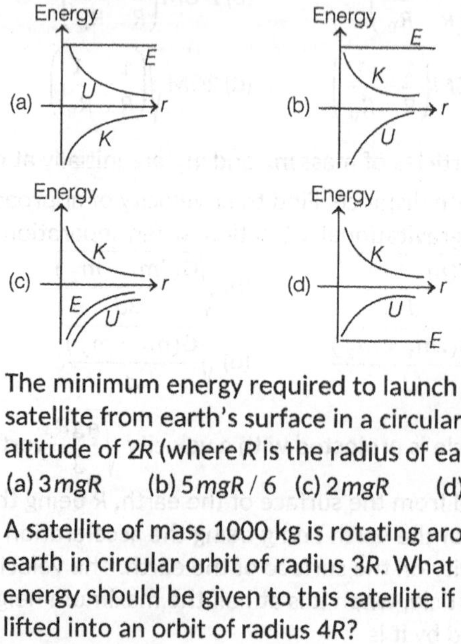

49. The minimum energy required to launch a m kg satellite from earth's surface in a circular orbit at an altitude of $2R$ (where R is the radius of earth) will be

(a) $3mgR$ (b) $5mgR/6$ (c) $2mgR$ (d) $mgR/3$

50. A satellite of mass 1000 kg is rotating around the earth in circular orbit of radius $3R$. What extra energy should be given to this satellite if it is to be lifted into an orbit of radius $4R$?

(a) 2.61×10^{24} J (b) 1.81×10^{19} J
(c) 1.81×10^{20} J (d) 2.61×10^{9} J

51. A space ship is launched into a circular orbit close to the earth's surface. What additional velocity should now be imparted to the space ship in the orbit to overcome the gravitational pull (radius of earth = 6400 km and g = 9.8 m/s^2).
(a) 4.2 km/s (b) 4.8 km/s
(c) 2.2 km/s (d) 3.3 km/s

52. A planet of mass m moves around the sun of mass M in an elliptical orbit. The maximum and minimum distance of the planet from the sun are r_1 and r_2 respectively. The time period of the planet is proportional to
(a) $r_1^{3/2}$ (b) $r_2^{3/2}$
(c) $(r_1+r_2)^{3/2}$ (d) $(r_1-r_2)^{3/2}$

53. The figure shows the motion of a planet around the sun in an elliptical orbit with sun at the focus. The shaded areas can be assumed to be equal. If t_1 and t_2 represent the time taken for the planet to move from A to B and C to D respectively, then

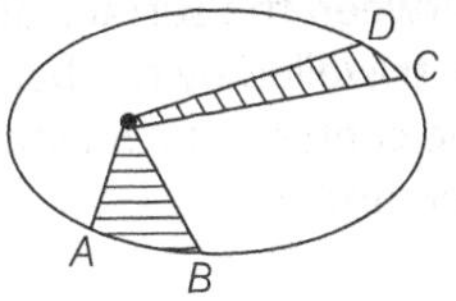

(a) $t_1 < t_2$ (b) $t_1 > t_2$
(c) $t_1 = t_2$ (d) None of these

54. A small satellite is in elliptical orbit around earth as shown. If L denotes the magnitude of its angular momentum and K denotes kinetic energy

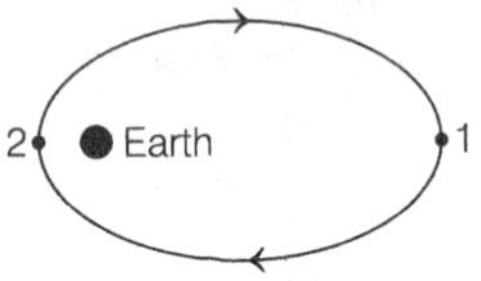

(a) $L_2 > L_1$ and $K_2 > K_1$ (b) $L_2 > L_1$ and $K_2 = K_1$
(c) $L_2 < L_1$ and $K_2 = K_1$ (d) $L_2 = L_1$ and $K_2 > K_1$

55. If the distance between the earth and the sun were half its present value, the number of days in a year would have been
(a) 64.5 (b) 129
(c) 182.5 (d) 730

56. A planet of mass m is in an elliptical orbit about the sun ($m << M_{sun}$) with an orbital period T. If A be the area of orbit, then its angular momentum would be
(a) $\frac{2mA}{T}$ (b) mAT
(c) $\frac{mA}{2T}$ (d) $2mAT$

57. A planet moves around Sun in an elliptical orbit of eccentricity e. The ratio of the velocity at perigee v_p and at apogee v_a is given by

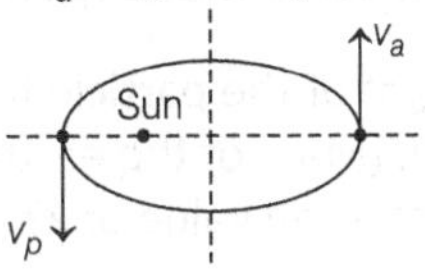

(a) $\frac{v_p}{v_a} = \frac{1+e}{1-e}$ (b) $\frac{v_p}{v_a} = \frac{1-e}{1+e}$
(c) $\frac{v_p}{v_a} = \sqrt{\frac{1+e}{1-e}}$ (d) $\frac{v_p}{v_a} = \sqrt{\frac{1-e}{1+e}}$

58. If a satellite is revolving around a planet of mass M in an elliptic orbit of semi major axis a, then the orbital speed of the satellite when it is at a distance r from the focus will be given by
(a) $\sqrt{GM\left(\frac{1}{r}-\frac{1}{a}\right)}$ (b) $\sqrt{2GM\left(\frac{1}{r}-\frac{1}{a}\right)}$
(c) $\sqrt{GM\left(\frac{2}{r}-\frac{1}{a}\right)}$ (d) $\sqrt{GM\left(\frac{1}{r}-\frac{2}{a}\right)}$

Numerical Value Questions

1. A satellite is launched in the equatorial plane in such a way that it can transmit signals upto 60° latitude on the earth. The orbital velocity of the satellite is found to be $\sqrt{\frac{GM}{\alpha R}}$ Find the value of α.

2. An artificial satellite is moving in a circular orbit around the earth with a speed equal to half the magnitude of the escape velocity from the earth. If the satellite is stopped suddenly in its orbit and allowed to fall freely on the earth, find the speed (in km/s) with which it hits the surface of earth. (g = 10 m/s^2 and R = 6400 km)

3. A planet revolves about the sun in elliptical orbit of semi-major axis 2 x 10^{12} m. The areal velocity of the planet when it is nearest to the sun is 4.4 x 10^{16} m/s. The least distance between planet and the sun is 1.8×10^{12} m. Find the minimum speed of the planet in km/s.

4. The difference between the time periods (in s) of a seconds pendulum at a depth of 64 km from Earth's surface and on earth surface is ΔT ? Fill the value of $100\Delta T$ in OMR sheet.

5. If the areal velocity of one planet is 2 times the areal velocity of other planet, then find the ratio of their radii of circular motion around the sun.

6. A particle of mass m_0 is projected vertically upward from surface of earth with a speed of $\sqrt{\frac{5GM_e}{4R}}$. The maximum height of the particle from the earth surface is $kR/3$. [Mass of the earth M_e and R is radius of earth]. What is the value of k?

7. A particle of mass m is moving in circular motion of radius r with constant speed v in influence of two fixed particles of mass M. Plane of circular motion is perpendicular to line joining fixed particles as shown. Speed of particle is given as $v = \sqrt{\frac{GM}{nr}}$ find value of n $(a = r\sqrt{3})$

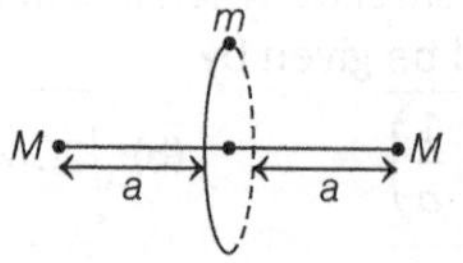

8. A student can throw a ball at a speed on earth which can just cross a river of width 10 m. He reaches on an imaginary planet whose mean density is twice of the earth. Find out the maximum possible radius of planet (in km) so that if he throws the ball at same speed it may escape from planet. Given radius of earth 6.4×10^6 m.

9. Two large spherical object of mass M each (uniformly distributed) are fixed as shown in figure. A small point mass m is projected from point A heading towards center C_2 of second sphere. The minimum velocity of point mass so that it can reach upto second object at point B is $\frac{n}{3}\sqrt{\frac{GM}{5R}}$, then calculate n. [Neglect other gravitational forces]

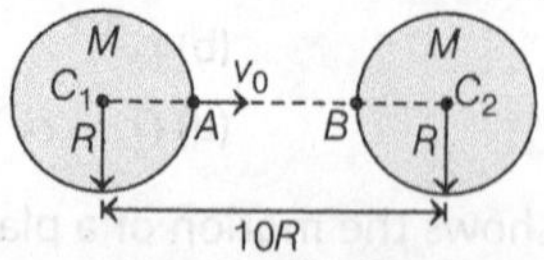

10. A smooth tunnel is dug along the radius of the earth that ends at the centre. A ball is released from the surface of earth along the tunnel. The coefficient of restitution between the surface and ball is 0.2. If the total distance travelled by the ball before second collision at the centre is $nR/5$ where R is the radius of the earth, then find n.

LEVEL 03 JEE Advanced Level

Single Choice Correct Questions

1. Find the distance between centre of gravity and centre of mass of a two particle system attached to the ends of a light rod. Each particle has same mass. Length of the rod is R, where R is the radius of Earth

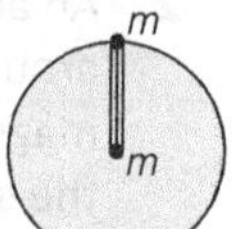

(a) R (b) $R/2$ (c) zero (d) $R/4$

2. Six stars of equal mass m moving about the centre of mass of the system such that they are always on the vertices of a regular hexagon of side length a. Their common time period of revolution around centre will be

(a) $4\pi\sqrt{\frac{a^3}{Gm}}$ (b) $2\pi\sqrt{\frac{4\sqrt{3}a^3}{Gm(5\sqrt{3}+4)}}$

(c) $2\pi\sqrt{\frac{3a^3}{Gm\,(5\sqrt{3}+4)}}$ (d) $2\pi\sqrt{\frac{3a^3}{Gm(5\sqrt{3}-4)}}$

3. A uniform ring of mass M is lying at a distance $\sqrt{3}\,R$ from the centre of a uniform sphere of mass m just below the sphere as shown in the figure where R is the radius of the ring as well as that of the sphere. Then, gravitational force exerted by the ring on the sphere is

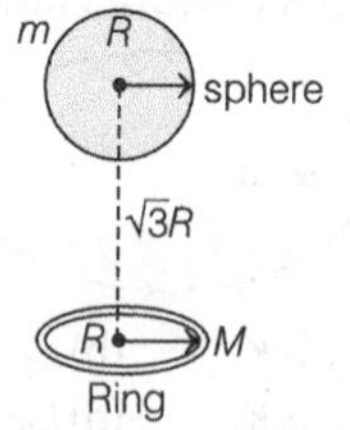

(a) $\frac{GMm}{8R^2}$ (b) $\frac{GMm}{3R^2}$ (c) $\sqrt{3}\frac{GMm}{R^2}$ (d) $\sqrt{3}\frac{GMm}{8R^2}$

4. A straight rod of length l extends from $x = \alpha$ to $x = l + \alpha$ as shown in the figure. If the mass per unit length is $(a + bx^2)$, the gravitational force it exerts on a point mass m placed at $x = 0$ is given by

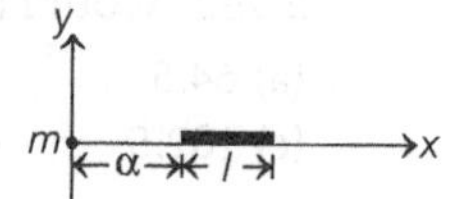

(a) $Gm\left(a\left(\frac{1}{\alpha} - \frac{1}{\alpha + l}\right) + bl\right)$ (b) $\frac{Gm(a + bx^2)}{l^2}$

(c) $Gm\left(\alpha\left(\frac{1}{a} - \frac{1}{a + l}\right) + bl\right)$ (d) $Gm\left(a\left(\frac{1}{\alpha + l} - \frac{1}{\alpha}\right) + bl\right)$

5. A hypothetical spherical planet of radius R and its density varies as $\rho = kr$, where k is constant and r is the distance from the center. The pressure caused by gravitational pull inside ($r < R$) the planet at a distance r measured from its center given by

(a) $\frac{k^2G\pi(R^4 - r^4)}{4}$ (b) $\frac{k^2G\pi(R^4 - r^4)}{2}$

(c) $2k^2G\pi(R^4 - r^4)$ (d) $4k^2G\pi(R^4 - r^4)$

6. In older times, people used to think that the earth was flat. Imagine that the earth is indeed not a sphere of radius R, but an infinite plate of thickness H. What value of H is needed to allow the same gravitational acceleration to be experienced as on the surface of the actual earth?

(Assume that the earth's density is uniform and equal in the two models.)

(a) 2R/3 (b) 4R/3

(c) 8R/3 (d) R/3

7. The density of the core of a planet is ρ_1 and that of the outer shell is ρ_2. The radii of the core and that the planet are R and 2R respectively. Gravitational acceleration at the surface of the planet is same as at a depth R. Find the ratio ρ_1/ρ_2

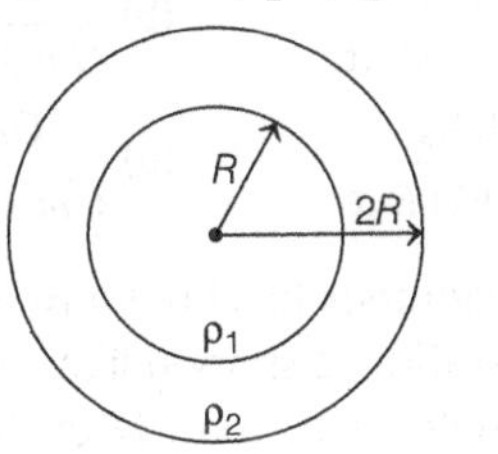

(a) 3/7 (b) 4/9

(c) 7/3 (d) 3/8

8. Two blocks of masses m each are hung from a balance as shown in the figure. The scale pan A is at height H_1 whereas scale pan B is at height H_2. Net torque of weights acting on the system about point C, will be (length of the rod is l and H_1 and H_2 are $<< R$) ($H_1 > H_2$)

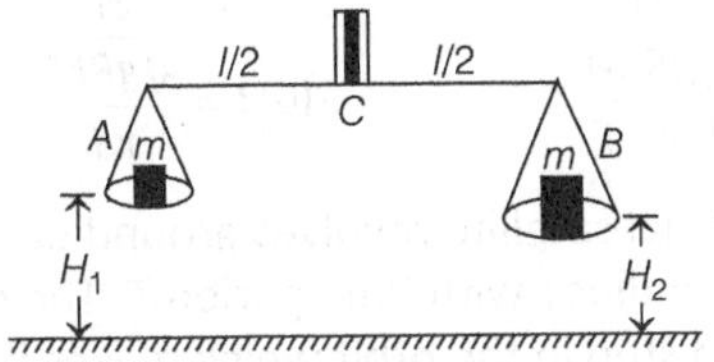

(a) $mg\left(\frac{1-2H_1}{R}\right)l$ (b) $\frac{mg}{R}(H_1 - H_2)l$

(c) $\frac{2mg}{R}(H_1 + H_2)l$ (d) $2mg\frac{H_2H_1}{H_1 + H_2}l$

9. The two planets with radii R_1, R_2 have densities ρ_1, ρ_2 and atmospheric pressures p_1 and p_2 respectively. Therefore, the ratio of masses of their atmospheres, neglecting variation of g and ρ within the limits of atmosphere, is

(a) $\frac{p_1R_2\rho_1}{p_2R_1\rho_2}$ (b) $\frac{p_1R_2\rho_2}{p_2R_1\rho_1}$ (c) $\frac{p_1R_1\rho_1}{p_2R_2\rho_2}$ (d) $\frac{p_1R_1\rho_2}{p_2R_2\rho_1}$

10. A small body of superdense material, whose mass is twice the mass of the earth but whose size is very small compared to the size of the earth, starts from rest at a height $H << R$ *above the* earth's surface, and reach the Earth's surface in time t. Then, t is equal to

(a) $\sqrt{2H/g}$ (b) $\sqrt{H/g}$

(c) $\sqrt{2H/3g}$ (d) $\sqrt{4H/3g}$

11. A thin uniform annular disc (see figure) of mass M has outer radius 4R and inner radius 3R. The work required to take a mass m from point P on its axis to infinity is

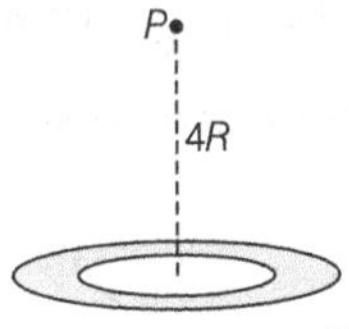

(a) $\frac{2GMm}{7R}(4\sqrt{2}-5)$ (b) $-\frac{2GMm}{7R}(4\sqrt{2}-5)$

(c) $\frac{GMm}{2R}$ (d) $\frac{2GMm}{5R}(\sqrt{2}-1)$

12. Consider two configurations in fig(i) and fig(ii). The work done by external agent in changing the configuration from fig(i) to fig(ii) is

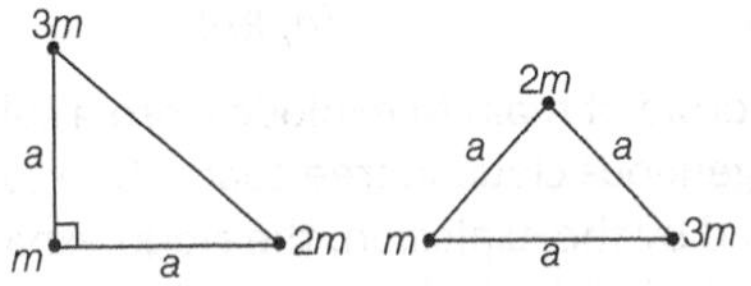

Fig (i) Fig (ii)

(a) zero (b) $-\frac{6Gm^2}{a}\left(1+\frac{1}{\sqrt{2}}\right)$

(c) $-\frac{6Gm^2}{a}\left(1-\frac{1}{\sqrt{2}}\right)$ (d) $-\frac{6Gm^2}{a}\left(2-\frac{1}{\sqrt{2}}\right)$

13. There is a crater of depth R/100 on the surface of the moon (radius R). A projectile is fired vertically upward from the crater with velocity, which is equal to the escape velocity v from the surface of the moon. Find the maximum height attained by the projectile.

(a) 90R (b) 95R

(c) 99.5R (d) 50R

14. The acceleration due to gravity on the surface of earth is g and radius R. A ball is projected horizontally from point P_1 on the surface of earth (as shown in the figure) If the maximum height attained by the ball above the earth surface is $3R$, then speed of projection v_0 is (neglect cosmic dust resistance and earth rotation about its axis)

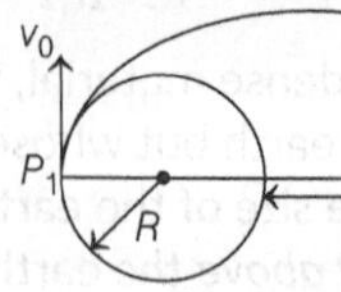

(a) $\sqrt{\frac{8}{5}gR}$ (b) $\sqrt{2gR}$
(c) $\sqrt{gR}$ (d) $\sqrt{\frac{6}{5}gR}$

15. A projectile of mass m is fired from the surface of the earth at an angle $\alpha = 60°$ from the vertical. The initial speed v_0 is equal to $\sqrt{\frac{GM}{R}}$. How high does the projectile rise? Neglect air resistance and the earth's rotation.

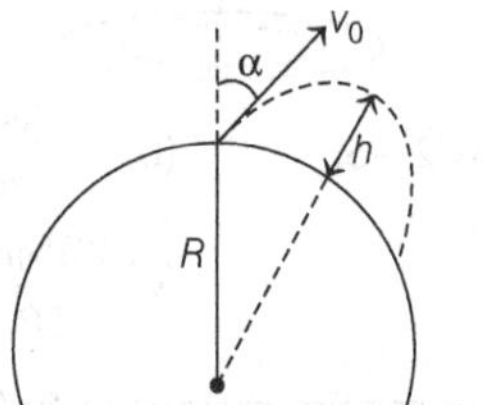

(a) R/2 (b) R/5
(c) R/4 (d) R/8

16. An asteroid of mass M explodes into a spherical homogeneous cloud in free space. Due to energy received by the explosion, the cloud expands and the expansion is spherically symmetric. At an instant, when radius of the cloud is R_0, all of its particles on the surface are observed receding radially away from the centre of the cloud with a velocity v_0. What will the radius of the cloud be, when its expansion ceases?

(a) $\frac{GMR_0}{2GM - R_0 v_0^2}$ (b) $\frac{2GMR_0}{2GM - R_0 v_0^2}$
(c) $\frac{GMR_0}{2GM + R_0 v_0^2}$ (d) $\frac{GMR_0}{2GM - R_0 v_0^2}$

17. A skylab of mass m is first launched from the surface of the earth in a circular orbit of radius $2R$ and then it is shifted from this circular orbit to another circular orbit of radius $3R$. The minimum energy required to place the lab in the first orbit and to shift the lab from first orbit to the second orbit are

(a) $3mgR/4$, $mgR/6$ (b) $3mgR/4$, $mgR/12$
(c) mgR, mgR (d) $2mgR$, mgR

18. A satellite is moving on a circular orbit around a planet. A sharp impulse is given to the satellite such that it escapes from the gravitational field of the planet. The impulse can be given in two different ways as shown. The ratio of the impulse given in the two different cases P_1/P_2 is

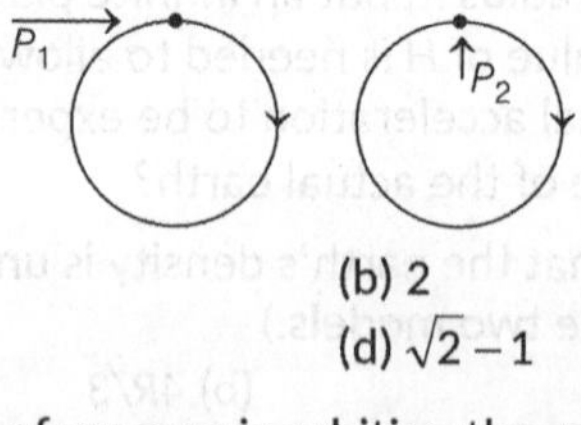

(a) $\sqrt{2}$ (b) 2
(c) $\sqrt{2}+1$ (d) $\sqrt{2}-1$

19. A satellite of mass m is orbiting the earth in a circular orbit of radius r. It starts losing energy slowly at a constant rate k due to friction. M_e and R_e denote the mass and radius of the earth respectively, the satellite takes a limit time t to fall on the earth. The radius r is

(a) $\frac{GmM_eR_e}{GmM_e - 4kR_et}$ (b) $\frac{GmM_eR_e}{Gm\,M_e + 2kR_et}$
(c) $\frac{GmM_eR_e}{Gm\,M_e + 2kR_et}$ (d) $\frac{GmM_eR_e}{Gm\,M_e - 2kR_et}$

20. A crew of scientists has built a new space station. The space station is shaped like a wheel of radius R, with essentially all its mass M at the rim. When the crew arrives, the station will be set rotating at a rate that causes an object at the rim to have radial acceleration g, thereby simulating earth's surface gravity. This is accomplished by two small rockets, each with thrust T newtons, mounted on the station's rim. How long a time t does one need to fire the rockets to achieve the desired condition?

(a) $t = \frac{\sqrt{gR^3}M}{2T}$ (b) $t = \frac{\sqrt{gRM}}{2T}$
(c) $t = \sqrt{\frac{gR}{\pi}\frac{M}{T}}$ (d) $t = \frac{\sqrt{gRM}}{\pi T}$

21. An artificial satellite revolves around earth in circular orbit of radius r with time period T. The satellite is made to stop in the orbit which makes it fall onto earth. Time of fall of the satellite on to earth is given by

(a) $\sqrt{3}\frac{T}{6}$ (b) $\frac{\sqrt{2}}{8}T$ (c) $\frac{T}{\sqrt{3}}$ (d) $\sqrt{\frac{2}{3\pi}}T$

22. An artificial satellite of mass m is moving in a circular orbit at a height equal to the radius R of the earth. Suddenly due to internal explosion the satellite breaks into two parts of equal masses. One part of the satellite stops just after the explosion and then falls to the surface of the earth. The increase in the mechanical energy of the system (satellite + earth) due to explosion will be (Given, acceleration due to gravity on the surface of earth is g)

(a) mgR (b) $mgR/2$ (c) $mgR/4$ (d) $3mgR/4$

23. A small ball of mass m is released at a height R above the Earth surface, as shown in the figure. If the maximum depth of the ball to which it goes is $R/2$ inside the earth through a narrow groove before coming to rest momentarily. The groove, contain an ideal spring of spring constant K and natural length R, the value of K is
(R is radius of earth and M mass of earth)

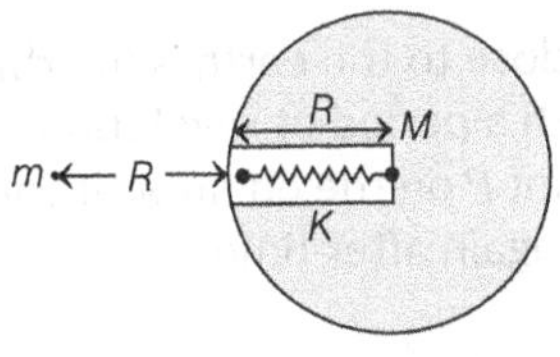

(a) $\frac{3GMm}{R^3}$ (b) $\frac{6GMm}{R^3}$ (c) $\frac{9GMm}{R^3}$ (d) $\frac{7GMm}{R^3}$

24. If gravitational forces alone prevent a spherical rotating neutron star from disintegrating, find minimum time period of star that has a mean density of magnitude $\left(\frac{9\pi}{20}\right)\times 10^{11}$ kg/m^3,

$$G = \frac{20}{3}\times 10^{-11}\ \text{N-m}^2/\text{kg}^2$$

(a) 1 s (b) 1.5 s
(c) 3 s (d) 5 s

25. An isolated triple star system consists of two identical stars, each of mass m and a fixed star of mass M. The identical masses revolve around the central star in the same circular orbit of radius r. The two orbiting stars are always at opposite ends of a diameter of the orbit. The time period of revolution of each star around the fixed star is equal to

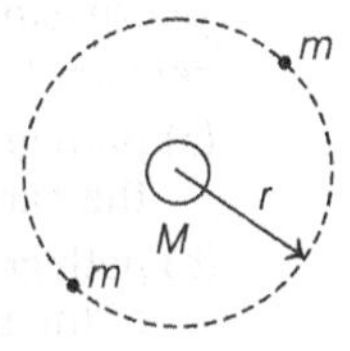

(a) $\frac{4\pi r^{3/2}}{\sqrt{G(4M+m)}}$ (b) $\frac{2\pi r^{3/2}}{\sqrt{GM}}$

(c) $\frac{2\pi r^{3/2}}{\sqrt{G(M+m)}}$ (d) $\frac{4\pi r^{3/2}}{\sqrt{G(M+m)}}$

26. A planet moves around the sun in an elliptical orbit as shown. Ecentricity of ellipse is 1/2. Time taken by planet to move from D to B ($D\rightarrow A\rightarrow B$) and B to D ($B\rightarrow C\rightarrow D$) are respectively T_{DAB} and T_{BCD}.

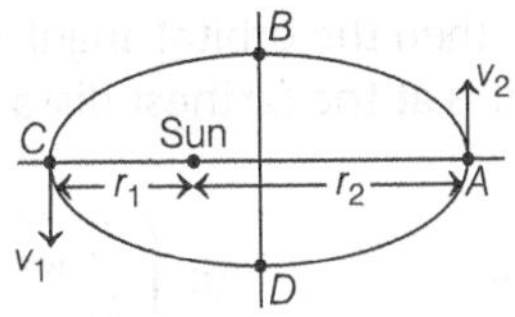

(a) $\frac{T_{DAB}}{T_{BCD}} = \frac{\pi+2}{\pi-2}$

(b) $\frac{T_{DAB}}{T_{BCD}} = \frac{2\pi+1}{2\pi-1}$

(c) velocity of planet at point B is $\sqrt{3}\,v_2$

(d) velocity of planet at point B is $\sqrt{2}\,v_2$

27. The velocity of a satellite travelling in an elliptical orbit, when it reaches point C on the end of the semiminor axis is

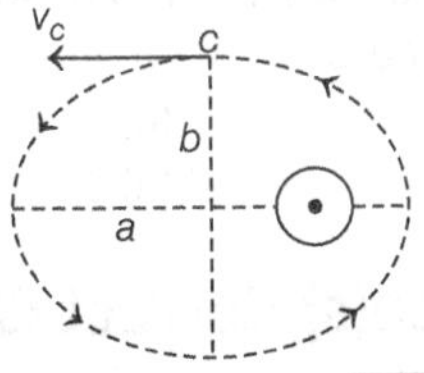

(a) $\sqrt{\frac{2GM}{a}}$ (b) $\sqrt{\frac{GM}{a}}$

(c) $\sqrt{\frac{GM}{2a}}$ (d) $\sqrt{\frac{2GM}{\sqrt{3}a}}$

28. Spaceman Fred's spaceship (which has negligible mass) is in an elliptical orbit about planet Bob. The minimum distance between the spaceship and the planet is R; the maximum distance between the spaceship and the planet is $2R$. At the point of maximum distance, spaceman Fred is traveling at speed v_0. He then fires his thrusters so that he enters a circular orbit of radius $2R$. What is his new speed ?

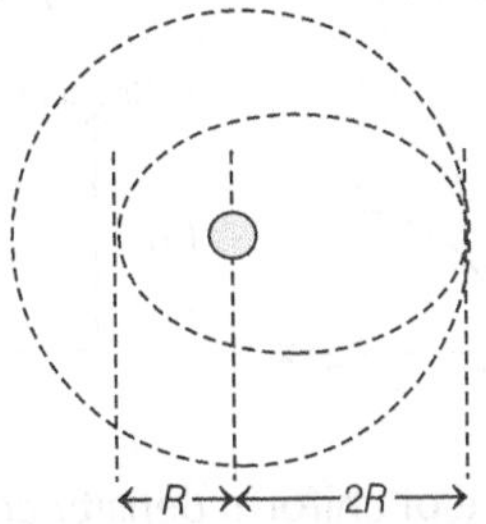

(a) $\sqrt{\frac{3}{2}}v_0$ (b) $\sqrt{5}\,v_0$ (c) $\sqrt{\frac{3}{5}}v_0$ (d) $\sqrt{2}\,v_0$

29. A planet is revolving around the sun in an elliptical orbit. Its closest distance from the Sun is r_{min}. The farthest distance from the Sun is r_{max}. If the orbital angular velocity of the planet when it is nearest to the sun is ω, then the orbital angular velocity at the point when it is at the farthest distance from the sun is

(a) $\left(\sqrt{\frac{r_{min}}{r_{max}}}\right)\omega$ (b) $\left(\sqrt{\frac{r_{max}}{r_{min}}}\right)\omega$

(c) $\left(\frac{r_{max}}{r_{min}}\right)^2 \omega$ (d) $\left(\frac{r_{min}}{r_{max}}\right)^2 \omega$

30. A small satellite of mass *m* is revolving around earth in a circular orbit of radius r_0 with speed v_0. At certain point of its orbit, the direction of motion of satellite is suddenly changed by angle $\cos^{-1}(3/5)$ by turning its velocity vector such that speed remains constant. The satellite consequently goes to elliptical orbit around earth. The ratio of speed at perigee to speed at apogee is

(a) 3 (b) 9
(c) 1/3 (d) 1/9

Multiple Choice(s) Correct Questions

1. A tunnel is dug along a chord of the earth at a perpendicular distance $R/2$ from the earth's centre. The wall of the tunnel may be assumed to be frictionless. A particle is released from one end of the tunnel. The pressing force by the particle on the wall and the acceleration of the particle varies with x (distance of the particle from the centre) according to

(a) 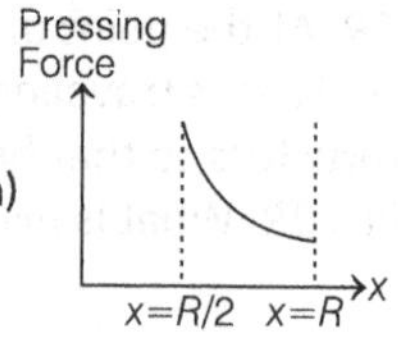

(b) 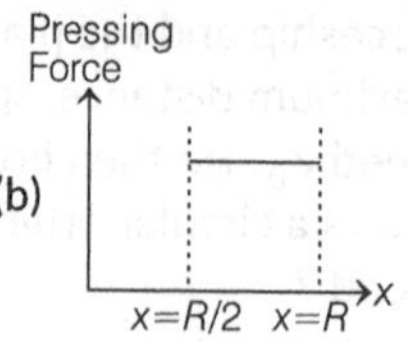

(c) 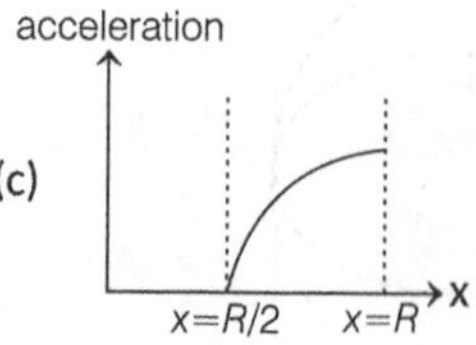

(d) 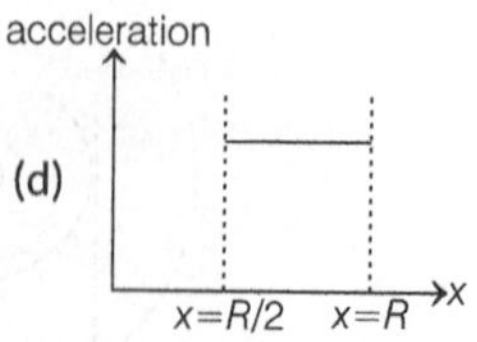

2. A solid sphere of uniform density and radius 4 units is located with its centre at the origin O of coordinates. Two spheres of equal radii 1 unit, with their centres at $A(-2, 0, 0)$ and $B(2, 0, 0)$ respectively, are taken out of the solid leaving behind spherical cavities as shown in figure. Then

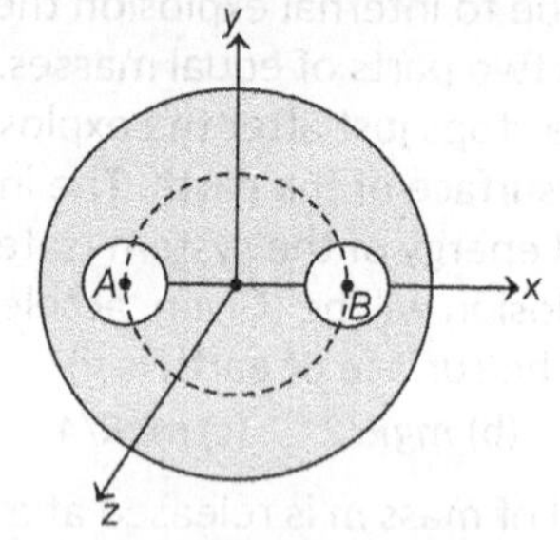

(a) the gravitational field due to this object at the origin is zero
(b) the gravitational field at the point $B(2, 0, 0)$ is zero
(c) the gravitational potential is the same at all points of circle $y^2 + z^2 = 36$
(d) the gravitational potential is the same at all points on the circle $y^2 + z^2 = 4$

3. A satellite close to the earth is in orbit above the equator with a period of revolution of 1.5 h. If it is above a point *P* on the equator at some time, it will be above *P* again after time

(a) 1.5 h
(b) 1.6 h, if it is rotating from west to east
(c) 24/17 h, if it is rotating from east to west
(d) 24/17 h, if it is rotating from west to east

4. An orbiting satellite will escape if

(a) its speed is increased by $(\sqrt{2}-1)100\%$
(b) its speed in the orbit is made $\sqrt{1.5}$ times of its initial value
(c) its kinetic energy is doubled
(d) it stops moving in the orbit

5. An artificial satellite is in a circular orbit around the earth. The universal gravitational constant starts decreasing at time $t = 0$ at a constant rate with respect to time *t*. Then, the satellite has its

(a) path gradually spiraling out away from the centre of the earth.
(b) path gradually spiraling in towards from the centre of the earth.
(c) angular momentum about the centre of the earth remains constant
(d) potential energy increases

6. Two satellites S_1 and S_2 of equal masses revolve in the same sense around a heavy planet in coplanar circular orbit of radii R and $4R$

(a) the ratio of period of revolution S_1 and S_2 is 1 : 8.
(b) their velocities are in the ratio 2 : 1

(c) their angular momentum about the planet are in the ratio 2 : 1

(d) the ratio of angular velocities of S_2 w.r.t. S_1 when all three are in the same line is 9 : 5.

7. A satellite is to be stationed in an orbit such that it can be used for relay purposes (such a satellite is called a geostationary satellite). The conditions such a should fulfill is/are

(a) its orbit must lie in equatorial plane

(b) its sense of rotation must be from west to east

(c) its orbital radius must be 42400 km

(d) its orbit must not be elliptical and should be circular

8. Three planets of same density and with radii R_1, R_2 and R_3 such that $R_1 = 2R_2 = 3R_3$ have gravitation fields on the surfaces g_1, g_2 and g_3 and escape velocities v_1, v_2 and v_3 respectively.

(a) $\frac{g_1}{g_2} = 2$ (b) $\frac{g_1}{g_3} = 3$ (c) $\frac{v_1}{v_2} = \frac{1}{2}$ (d) $\frac{v_1}{v_3} = 3$

9. A geostationary satellite is at a height h above the surface of earth. The earth radius is R

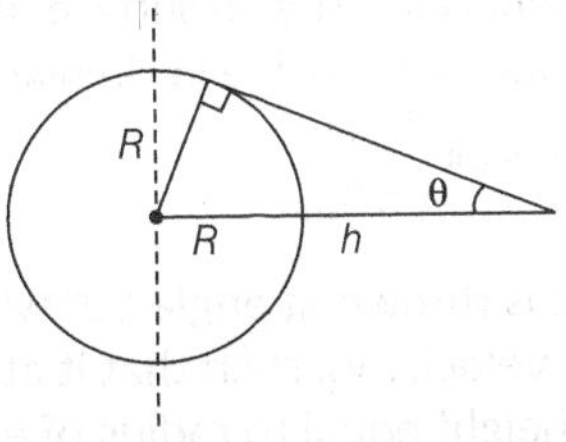

(a) The minimum colatitude on earth upto which the satellite can be used for communication is $\sin^{-1}\left(\frac{R}{R+h}\right)$.

(b) The maximum colatitudes on earth upto which the satellite can be used for communication is $\sin^{-1}\left(\frac{R}{R+h}\right)$.

(c) The area on earth escaped from this satellite is given as $2\pi R^2(1+\sin\theta)$

(d) The area on earth escaped from this satellite is given as $2\pi R^2(1+\cos\theta)$

10. Inside a uniform sphere of mass M (M is mass of complete sphere) and radius R, a cavity of radius R/3 is made in the sphere as shown

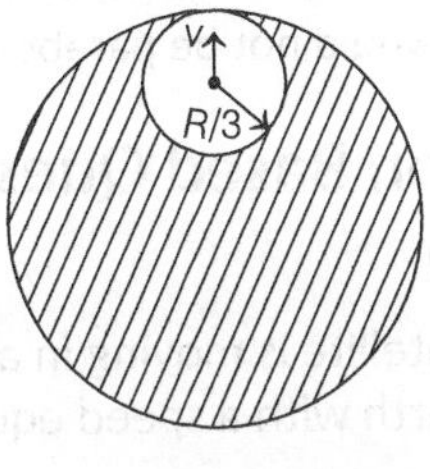

(a) gravitational field inside the cavity is uniform

(b) gravitational field intensity in the cavity is $\frac{8\pi G\rho R}{9}$ at the centre.

(c) the escape velocity of a particle projected from centre of cavity is $\sqrt{\frac{88GM}{45R}}$

(d) the escape velocity of a particle projected from centre of cavity is $\sqrt{\frac{20GM}{9R}}$.

11. A binary star system consists of two stars having masses M and $2M$. The distance between their centers is equal to R. They revolve about their common center of mass under their mutual gravitational force of interaction. Which of the following is/are correct ?

(a) Heavier star revolves in orbit of radius $R/3$

(b) Both the stars will revolve with the same time period which is equal to $\frac{2\pi}{\sqrt{3GM}}R^{3/2}$

(c) Kinetic energy of lighter star is twice that of the other.

(d) Kinetic energy of lighter star is 4 times that of the other.

12. A satellite of mass m is moving in a circular orbit of radius r around the earth. This satellite is shifted in circular orbit of radius $2r$. (Mass of the earth is M).

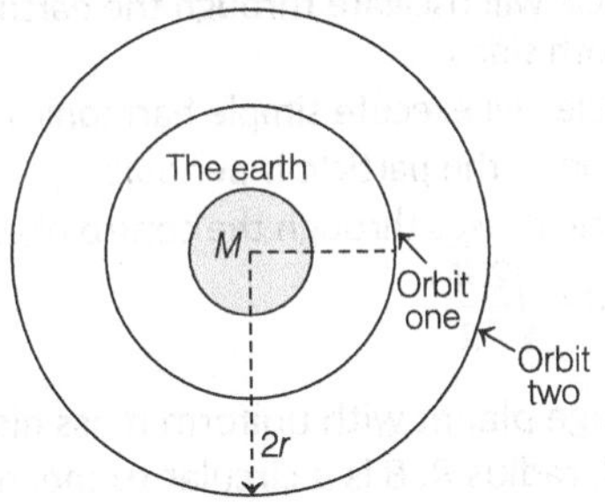

(a) The minimum energy required to shift the satellite in new orbit is $\frac{GMm}{2r}$

(b) Time period of satellite in new orbit will be double that time period of previous orbit

(c) The acceleration of satellite in new orbit becomes 1/4 of acceleration in previous orbit.

(d) The minimum energy required to shift the satellite in new orbit is $\frac{GMm}{4r}$.

13. At the equator on a spherical planet, a body weighs one third of that at the pole. Radius of planet is R. The time period of revolution of the planet around its axis is equal to $T = 60$ min.
(Take : $G = \frac{20}{3} \times 10^{-11}\ Nm^2/kg^2$)

(a) The average density ρ of the planet is $\frac{\pi}{192} \times 10^6\ kg/m^3$.
(b) The height of geostationary satellite from the surface of planet is $\left(3\sqrt{\frac{3}{2}} - 1\right)R$.
(c) At a latitude of 60°, the weight of the body is half the weight at pole
(d) The geostationary satellite can be in a plane passing through the poles.

14. A particle is dropped from a height equal to the radius of the earth above the tunnel dug through the earth as shown in the figure.

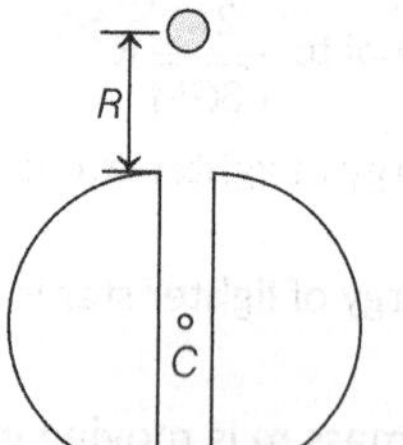

R : Radius of earth, M : Mass of earth

(a) Particle will oscillate through the earth to a height R on both sides
(b) Particle will execute simple harmonic motion
(c) Motion of the particle is periodic
(d) Particle passes through the centre of earth with a speed $= \sqrt{\frac{2GM}{R}}$.

15. A is a huge planet with uniform mass distribution, mass M, radius R. B is a circular tunnel made in it, concentric with planet. Radius of tunnel is r, $(r = R/2)$ cross-sectional diameter is $d (d << r)$. C is a small ball of mass $m (m << M)$ which is moving freely inside the tunnel without friction in a uniform circular motion, take acceleration due to gravity on surface of A as g

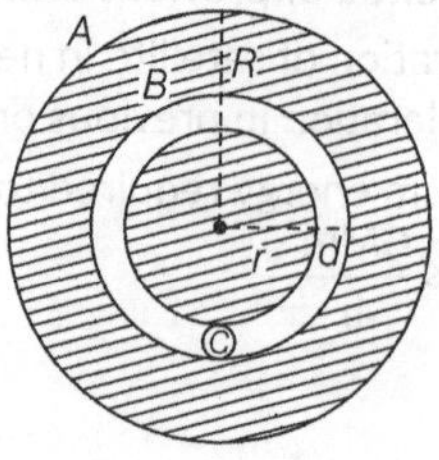

(a) If contact force on C is double the gravitational force, its time period $= 2\pi\sqrt{\frac{R}{3g}}$
(b) If contact force on C is double the gravitational force, its time period $= 2\pi\sqrt{\frac{R}{g}}$
(c) If contact force is zero, time period T, radius of tunnel r, then $T \propto r$
(d) If contact force is zero, time period T, radius of tunnel r, then T would be independent of r.

16. Mass density of a planet varies as $\rho(r) = \frac{\rho_0 r}{R}$ where R is radius of planet and r is distance from center of planet.

(a) A particle of mass m is to be projected from surface so as to escape the planet, its velocity of projection relative to surface is $\sqrt{2\pi G\rho_0 R^2}$.
(b) A particle of mass m is to be projected from surface so as to escape the planet, its velocity of projection relative to surface is $2\sqrt{2\pi G\rho_0 R^2}$
(c) Gravitational intensity on surface of planet is $\pi G\rho_0 R$.
(d) Time period of a satellite in circular orbit very close to planet is $2\pi\sqrt{\frac{R}{\pi G\rho_0}}$.

17. A projectile is thrown at angle 30° with surface of earth, with velocity v_0 such that it attains a maximum height equal to radius of earth, then

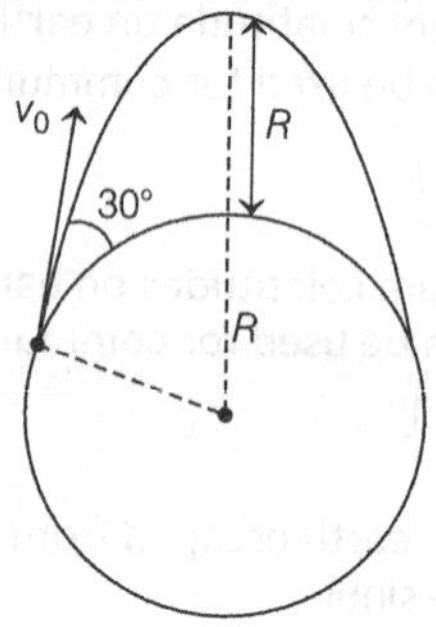

(a) minimum velocity would be $\frac{v_0}{4}$
(b) minimum velocity would be $\frac{\sqrt{3}v_0}{4}$
(c) at maximum height velocity will be zero.
(d) trajectory would not be parabolic

Comprehension Based Questions

Comprehension - 1

An artificial satellite is moving in a circular orbit around the earth with a speed equal to half the magnitude of escape velocity from the surface of earth. R is the radius of earth and g is acceleration due to gravity at the surface of earth. (R = 6400 km)

1. Then the distance of satellite from the surface of earth is

(a) 3200 km (b) 6400 km
(c) 12800 km (d) 4800 km

2. The time period of revolution of satellite in the given orbit is

(a) $2\pi\sqrt{\frac{2R}{g}}$ (b) $2\pi\sqrt{\frac{4R}{g}}$
(c) $2\pi\sqrt{\frac{8R}{g}}$ (d) $2\pi\sqrt{\frac{6R}{g}}$

3. If the satellite is stopped suddenly in its orbit and allowed to fall freely onto the earth, the speed with which it hits the surface of the earth.

(a) $\sqrt{gR}$ (b) $\sqrt{1.5gR}$
(c) $\sqrt{\frac{gR}{2}}$ (d) $\sqrt{\frac{gR}{\sqrt{2}}}$

Comprehension - 2

A pair of stars rotates about their center of mass. One of the stars has a mass M and the other has mass m such that $M = 2m$. The distance between the centres of the stars is d(d being large compared to the size of either star).

4. The period of rotation of the stars about their common centre of mass (in terms of d, m, G.) is

(a) $\sqrt{\frac{4\pi^2}{Gm}d^3}$ (b) $\sqrt{\frac{8\pi^2}{Gm}d^3}$
(c) $\sqrt{\frac{2\pi^2}{3Gm}d^3}$ (d) $\sqrt{\frac{4\pi^2}{3Gm}d^3}$

5. The ratio of the angular momentum of the two stars about their common centre of mass (L_m/L_M) is

(a) 1 (b) 2
(c) 4 (d) 9

6. The ratio of kinetic energies of the two stars (K_m/K_M) is

(a) 1 (b) 2
(c) 4 (d) 9

Comprehension - 3

Many planets are revolving around the fixed sun, in circular orbits of different radius (R) and different time period (T). To estimate the mass of the sun, the orbital radius (R) and time period (T) of planets were noted. Then $\log_{10} T$ v/s $\log_{10} R$ curve was plotted.

The curve was found to be approximately straight line (as shown in figure) having y intercept = 6.0 (Neglect the gravitational interaction among the planets [Take $G = (20/3)\times10^{-11}$ in MKS, $\pi^2 = 10$]

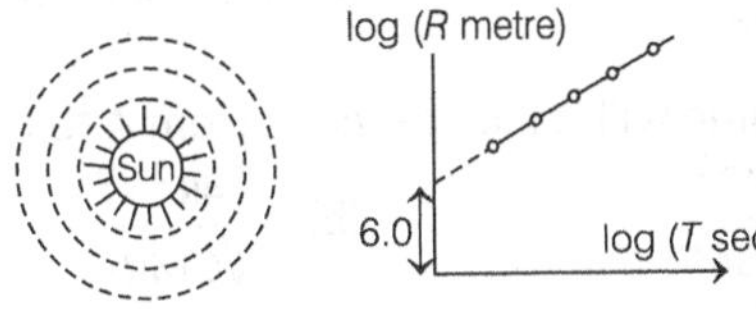

7. The slope of the line should be

(a) 1 (b) $\frac{3}{2}$ (c) $\frac{2}{3}$ (d) $\frac{19}{4}$

8. Estimate the mass of the sun

(a) 6×10^{29} kg (b) 5×10^{20} kg
(c) 8×10^{25} kg (d) 3×10^{35} kg

9. Two planets A and B, having orbital radius R and $4R$ are initially at the closest position and rotating in the same direction. If angular velocity of planet B is ω_0, then after how much time will both the planets be again in the closest position? (Neglect the interaction between planets).

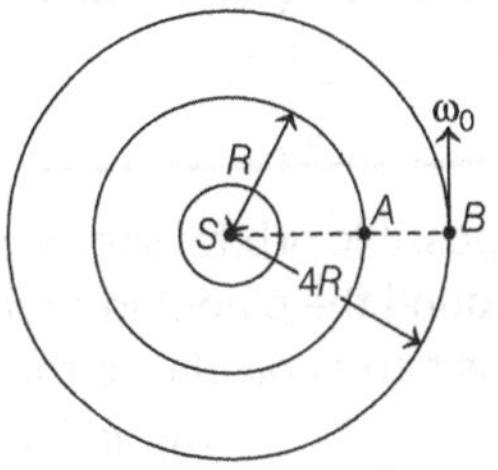

(a) $\frac{2\pi}{7\omega_0}$ (b) $\frac{2\pi}{9\omega_0}$
(c) $\frac{2\pi}{\omega_0}$ (d) $\frac{2\pi}{5\omega_0}$

Comprehension-4

A solid sphere of mass M and radius R is surrounded by a spherical shell of same mass M and radius 2R as shown. A small particle of mass m is released from rest from a height h(<<R) above the shell. There is a hole in the shell.

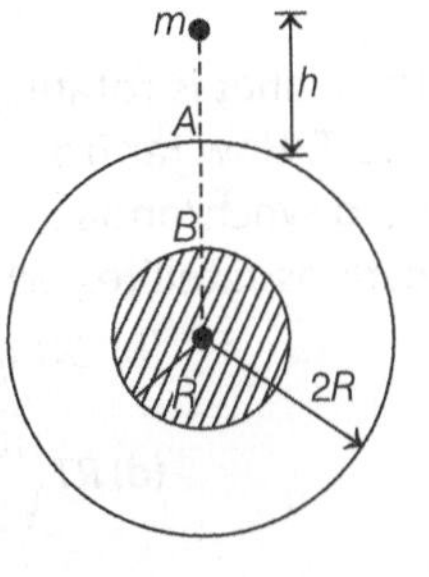

10. In what time will it enter the hole at A

(a) $2\sqrt{\frac{hR^2}{GM}}$ (b) $\sqrt{\frac{2hR^2}{GM}}$

(c) $\sqrt{\frac{hR^2}{GM}}$ (d) None of these

11. What time will it take to move from A to B?

(a) $= \frac{4R^2}{\sqrt{GMR}}$ (b) $> \frac{4R^2}{\sqrt{GMR}}$

(c) $< \frac{4R^2}{\sqrt{GMR}}$ (d) None of these

12. With what approximate speed will it collide at B ?

(a) $\sqrt{\frac{2GM}{R}}$ (b) $\sqrt{\frac{GM}{2R}}$

(c) $\sqrt{\frac{3GM}{2R}}$ (d) $\sqrt{\frac{GM}{R}}$

Comprehension-5

Consider a hypothetical planet which is very long and cylindrical. The density of the planet is ρ and its radius is R.

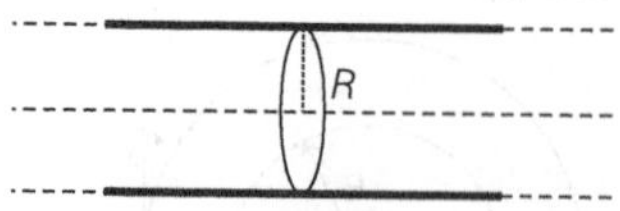

13. What is the possible orbital speed of the satellite in moving around the planet in circular orbit in a plane which is perpendicular to the axis of planet?

(a) $R\sqrt{\pi G\rho}$ (b) $2R\sqrt{\pi G\rho}$

(c) $R\sqrt{2\pi G\rho}$ (d) $R\sqrt{\frac{G\rho}{2\pi}}$

14. If an object is projected radially outwards from the surface such that it reaches upto a maximum distance of 3R from the axis, then what should be the speed of projection?

(a) $R\sqrt{\frac{2}{3}\pi\rho G}$ (b) $2R\sqrt{\pi\rho G \ln 3}$

(c) $R\sqrt{\frac{4}{3}\pi\rho G}$ (d) $R\sqrt{\frac{2}{3}\pi\rho G \ln 3}$

15. Assume that the planet is rotating about its axis with time period T. How far from the axis of the planet do the geo synchronous telecommunications satellites orbit?

(a) $RT\sqrt{\pi G\rho}$ (b) $2RT\sqrt{\pi G\rho}$

(c) $RT\sqrt{2\pi G\rho}$ (d) $RT\sqrt{\frac{G\rho}{2\pi}}$

Comprehension-6

In the picture below, the planet orbits around the sun with a period of 40 months and takes 12 months to translate from the point D to point E and 1 month from point B to C. The area of the ellipse is A. Mass of the satellite is m.

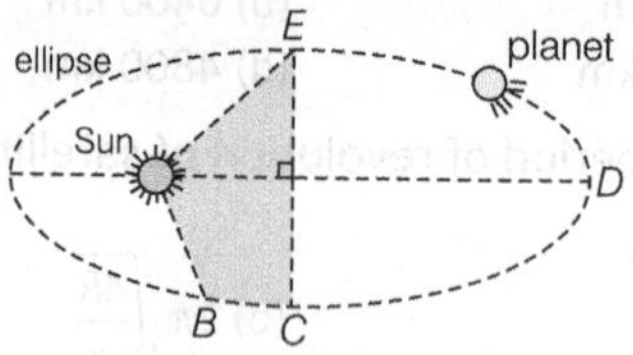

16. The area of the shaded region

(a) A/20 (b) A/8

(c) A/40 (d) A/4

17. The angular momentum of planet per unit mass per unit area is

(a) 5×10^{-8} /s (b) 16×10^{-8} /s

(c) 2×10^{-8} /s (d) 0

Comprehension-7

Let us identify the system as the spacecraft and the earth but not the portion of the fuel in the spacecraft that we use to change the orbit.

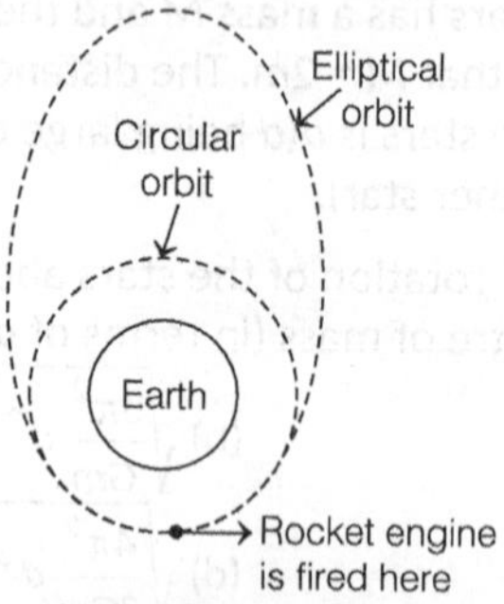

In a given orbit, the mechanical energy of the spacecraft-earth system is given by $E = -\frac{GMm}{2r}$. This energy includes the kinetic energy of the spacecraft and the potential energy associated with the gravitational force between the spacecraft and the earth. If the rocket engines are fired, the thrust force moves the spacecraft through a displacement. As a result, the mechanical energy of the spacecraft–earth system increases. The spacecraft has a new higher energy but is constrained to be in an orbit that includes the original starting point. It can not be in a higher energy circular orbit having a larger radius because this orbit would not contain the starting point. The only possibility is that the orbit is elliptical as shown in figure.

$$E = -\frac{GMm}{2a}$$

Above equation gives the energy of the spacecraft–earth system for an elliptical orbit where a is semi-major axis. Thus if we know the new energy of the orbit, we can find the semi-major axis of the elliptical orbit. Conversely, if we know the semi-major axis of an elliptical orbit we would like to achieve,we can calculate how much additional energy is required from the rocket engines. A spacecraft is moving in a circular orbit around the Earth (Radius 6400 km), at a height of 300 km from the surface. To place the spacecraft in an elliptical orbit, the magnitude of the mechanical energy of the spacecraft-earth system is decreased by 10.0%.

18. If the spacecraft -earth system had initial energy $(-E_0)$, then the total mechanical energy of the system after firing the rocket will be

(a) $-1.1E_0$ (b) $-0.9E_0$
(c) $-E_0$ (d) None of these

19. Semi-major axis of the new elliptical orbit is

(a) 7444.4 km (b) 7111.1 km
(c) 7888.9 km (d) 6777.77 km

20. Maximum height of the spacecraft above the surface of the earth will be

(a) 1177.8 km (b) 677.8 km
(c) 300 km (d) 1788.9 km

Comprehension-8

A meteorite of mass m collides with a satellite of mass 10 m which was orbiting around a planet in a circular path of radius R. Due to collision, the meteorite sticks to the satellite and the satellite is seen to have gone into an orbit whose minimum distance from the planet is $R/2$. Mass of the planet is M.

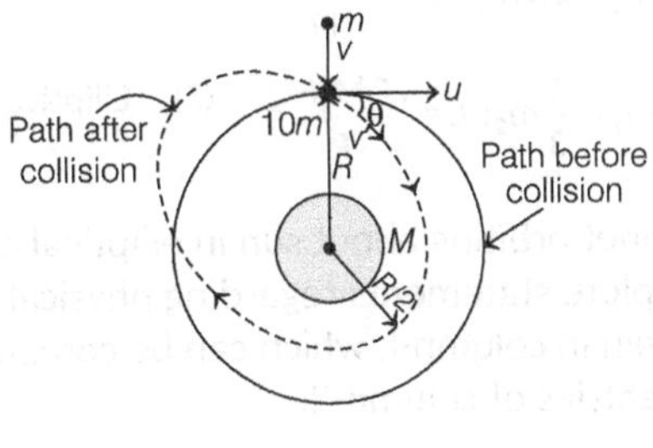

21. Velocity of meteorite before collision

(a) $\sqrt{\frac{11GM}{R}}$ (b) $\sqrt{\frac{58GM}{R}}$
(c) $\sqrt{\frac{10GM}{11R}}$ (d) $\sqrt{\frac{58GM}{11R}}$

22. Angular momentum of (satellite + meteorite) system about the center of planet is

(a) $10\sqrt{GMm^2R}$ (b) $\sqrt{110\ GMm^2R}$
(c) $\sqrt{\frac{58}{11}GMm^2R}$ (d) $11\sqrt{GMm^2R}$

Comprehension-9

The minimum and maximum distances of a satellite from the centre of the earth are $2R$ and $4R$ respectively, where R is the radius of earth and M is the mass of earth.

23. Its minimum and maximum speeds are

(a) $\sqrt{\frac{GM}{9R}}, \sqrt{\frac{2GM}{R}}$ (b) $\sqrt{\frac{GM}{5R}}, \sqrt{\frac{3GM}{2R}}$
(c) $\sqrt{\frac{GM}{6R}}, \sqrt{\frac{2GM}{3R}}$ (d) $\sqrt{\frac{GM}{3R}}, \sqrt{\frac{5GM}{2R}}$

24. The radius of curvature at the point of minimum distance is

(a) $8R/3$ (b) $5R/3$
(c) $4R/3$ (d) $7R/3$

Match The Columns Questions

1. If earth decreases its rotational speed, match the following

Table 1	Table 2
(A) Value of g at pole	(P) will remain same
(B) Value of g at equator	(Q) will increase
(C) Distance of geostationary satellite	(R) will decrease
(D) Energy of geostationary satellite	(S) cannot say

2. In elliptical orbit of a planet, as the planet moves from apogee position to perigee position, match the following table

Table - 1	Table - 2
(A) Speed of planet	(P) remains same
(B) Distance of planet from the centre of sun	(Q) decreases
(C) Potential energy	(R) increases
(D) Angular momentum about the centre of sun	(S) cannot say

3. A particle is projected vertically up from the surface of the earth with speed $\sqrt{gR}$.

Column -I	Column -II
(A) Maximum height attained by the particle is αR then α is	(P) 2
(B) Time taken by the particle to reach the maximum height is $\beta\sqrt{\frac{R^3}{GM}}$, then β is	(Q) $\frac{\pi}{4}+1$
(C) Value of acceleration due to gravity at maximum height is $\gamma\frac{GM}{4R^2}$, then γ is	(R) $\frac{\pi}{2}+1$
(D) Orbital velocity of a satellite revolving at maximum height is $\delta\sqrt{\frac{GM}{2R}}$, then δ is	(S) 1
	(T) None of these

4. A satellite is revolving round the earth in a circular orbit of radius a with velocity v_0. A particle is projected from the satellite in forward direction with relative velocity $v=\left[\sqrt{\frac{5}{4}}-1\right]v_0$. During subsequent motion of particle, match the following

Column -I	Column - II
(A) Total energy of particle	(P) $-\frac{3GM_e m}{8a}$
(B) Minimum distance of particle from the earth	(Q) $-\frac{5}{8}\frac{GM_e m}{a}$
(C) Maximum distance of particle from the earth	(R) $5a/3$
	(S) $2a/3$
	(T) a

5. A sphere of radius of uniform density and R has a spherical cavity of radius $R/2$ as shown in the figure. BD is a diameter of the sphere. A is a point on this diameter far away from B. No other masses are present in the surrounding. PQ is the diameter of the cavity perpendicular to BD. Match the List – I with List – II.

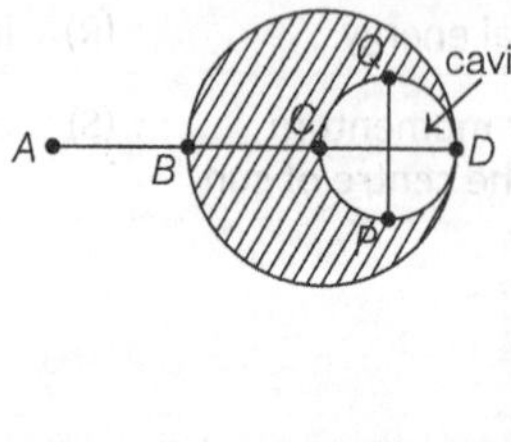

Column -I	Column - II
(A) From A to B along the straight line	(P) gravitational potential decreases
(B) From B to C along the straight line	(Q) gravitational potential remains constant
(C) From C to D along the straight line	(R) gravitational potential first decreases and then increases
(D) From P to Q along the straight line	(S) gravitational potential increases

6. A satellite is to be launched and established in its orbit around the earth. For this purpose it is raised to a certain height (equal to its orbit distance) with a rocket and held stationary by some mechanism and an explosion is carried out instantly to provide the required velocity to the satellite. Let the original mass of satellite is M_s, mass of the earth M_e, radius of the required orbit R and universal gravitational constant G. As a result of explosion the satellite breaks into two parts of masses m_1 and m_2 and energy released is given by E. List-I gives certain combination of m_1, m_2 and E while list-II gives the nature of orbit followed by m_2. Match them suitably (If $v>v_e$; orbit is hyperbolic,

$v=v_e$; orbit is parabolic and

$v<v_e$; orbit is eliptical where v_e is escape velocity and v is velocity of the part)

List -I	List - II
(A) $m_1=m_2$; $E=\frac{GM_eM_s}{R}$	(P) Parabolic orbit
(B) $m_1=2m_2$; $E=\frac{GM_eM_s}{4R}$	(Q) Hyperbolic orbit
(C) $m_1=3.5\,m_2$; $E=\frac{GM_eM_s}{4R}$	(R) Circular orbit
(D) $m_1=\frac{1}{3}m_2$; $E=\frac{2GM_eM_s}{R}$	(S) Elliptical orbit

7. For planet orbiting about sun in elliptical orbit, some incomplete statements regarding physical quantities are given in column-I, which can be completed by using entries of column-II.

Column -I	Column - II
(A) Maximum potential energy of sun planet system	(P) is independent of semi-major axis of orbit
(B) Maximum speed of planet	(Q) is at apogee

	Column -I		Column - II
(C)	Minimum potential energy of sun planet system	(R)	is dependent on mass of planet
(D)	Minimum KE of planet	(S)	is at perigee
		(T)	depends upon mass of sun

8. Density of a planet is two times the density of earth. Radius of this planet is half the radius of earth. Match the following. (As compared to earth)

	Column -I		Column - II
(A)	Acceleration due to gravity on this planet's surface	(P)	Half
(B)	Gravitational potential on the surface	(Q)	Same
(C)	Gravitational potential at centre	(R)	Two times
(D)	Gravitational field strength at centre	(S)	Four times

Numerical Value Questions

1. You are at a distance of $R = 1.5 \times 10^6$ m from the centre of an unknown planet. You notice that if you throw a ball horizontally it goes completely around the planet hitting you in the back 90,000 seconds later with exactly the same speed that you originally threw it. If the length of semi-major axis of ball is 2R, what is the mass of the planet. Express in scientific notation $(\alpha \times 10^{\beta})$ kg and fill $(\alpha + \beta)$ in OMR sheet.

[Take, $G = (20/3) \times 10^{-11} Nm^2/Kg^2, \pi^2 = 10$]

2. A solid sphere of mass M of radius R is moving with speed $\sqrt{\frac{GM}{R}} = 100\sqrt{10}\ ms^{-1}$ in free space. Due to application of external impulsive force, it breaks into eight spheres of same radius in such a way that the total mechanical energy before breaking and after breaking of sphere remains same. Find the speed (in m/s) of each sphere when separation between them is very large. Assume at that instant speed of each sphere is same.

3. A tunnel is dug along the chord of the earth at a perpendicular distance R/2 from the earth's centre. Walls of tunnel are frictionless. A particle of mass m is released into tunnel. Find the ratio of normal reactions at point P and Q between tunnel and particle as shown in the figure.

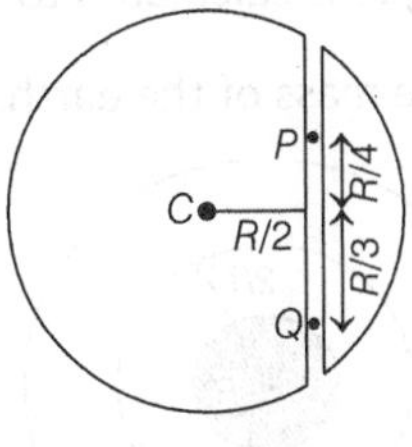

4. An astronaut in a circular orbit around earth observes a celestial body moving in a lower circular orbit around earth in same plane as his orbit and in the same sense. He observes that the body moves at a speed of 5 m/s relative to himself when it is closest to him. The minimum distance between him and the body if he is moving at a speed of 5000 m/s is *n* km. Fill the value of *n* in OMR sheet. (Mass of earth $= 6 \times 10^{24}$ kg and round off the value of *n* to the nearest integer).

5. Figure shows a binary star system revolving about their COM. The masses of star *A* and *B* are 15×10^{30} kg and 45×10^{30} kg respectively. Find the ratio of area swept by star *A* to area swept by star *B* in a common time interval.

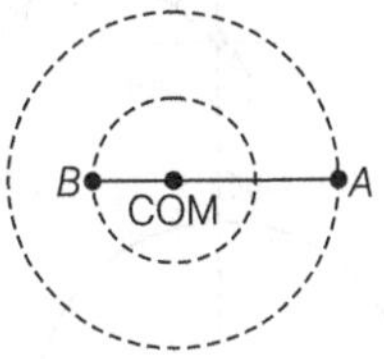

6. A composite solid sphere *S* of radius *R* has density 2ρ in spherical region *S'* of radius *R*/2 while remaining region has density ρ. Gravitational force exerted by this composite body on a point mass (*m*) placed as shown in the figure is $\pi R\rho GM\left(\frac{k}{25}\right)$. Find *k*.

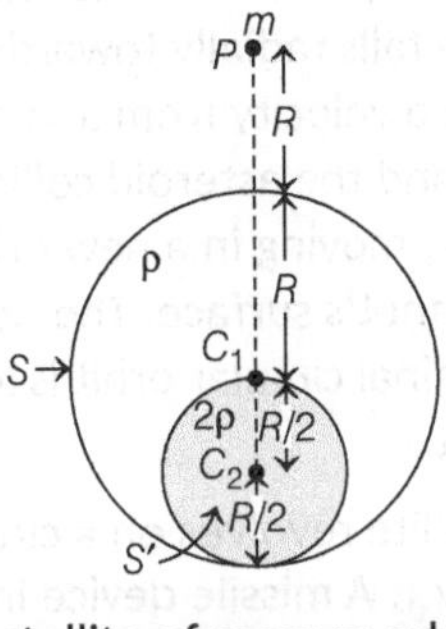

7. An artificial satellite of mass *m* orbiting the earth in a circular orbit of radius twice the earth's radius *R*. It is to be taken in another circular orbit of radius 4*R*.

The transfer is accomplished through an elliptical orbit as shown in the figure. The energy needed to complete the job is calculated to be equal to $\frac{1}{k}\frac{GMm}{R}$ where M is the mass of the earth. Find the value of k.

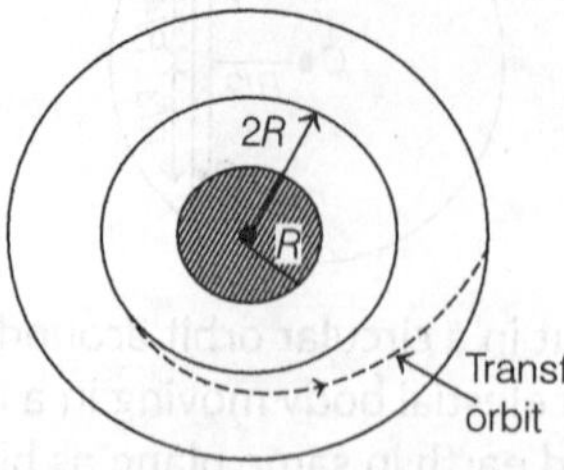

8. A particle is projected from point A, that is at a distance $4R$ from the centre of the earth, with speed v_1 in a direction making 30° with the line joining the centre of the earth and point A, as shown. Find the speed v_1 if particle passes grazing the surface of the earth. Consider gravitational interaction only between these two.

(use $\frac{Gm}{R} = 6.4 \times 10^7 \ m^2/s^2$) Express you answer in the form $(500\sqrt{2}X)$ m/s and write the value of X.

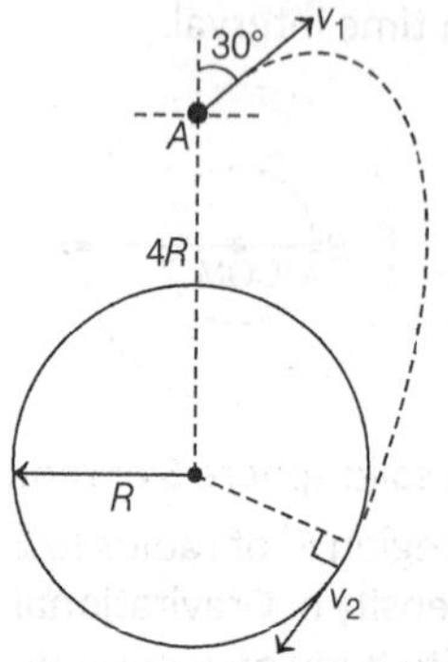

9. A satellite of mass m is in a circular orbit around an airless spherical planet of radius R. An asteroid of equal mass m falls radially towards the planet, starting at zero velocity from a very large distance. The satellite and the asteroid collide inelastically and stick together, moving in a new orbit such that it just misses the planet's surface. The radius of the satellite's original circular orbit is $(\alpha + \sqrt{11})R$. Find the value of α.

10. An Earth satellite revolves on a circular orbit at a linear speed v_0. A missile device increases the absolute value of this speed to $1.5v_0$, and the satellite goes into an unknown path as shown (Fig). With what speed will the satellite leave the gravitational field of earth? The resistance of the cosmic dust is not taken into account. Mass of earth is M. If your answer is $\frac{v_0}{\alpha}$, fill α in OMR sheet.

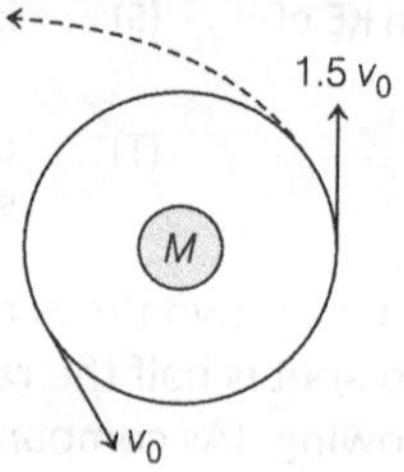

Previous Years Questions

JEE Main

1 The acceleration due to gravity on the surface of earth is g. If the diameter of earth reduces to half of its original value and mass remains constant, then acceleration due to gravity on the surface of earth would be **[2024, 27 Jan Shift-I]**

(a) $\frac{g}{2}$ (b) $4g$

(c) $\frac{g}{4}$ (d) $2g$

2 Given below are two statements : one is labelled as **Assertion (A)** and other is labelled as **Reason (R)**.

Assertion (A) The angular speed of the moon in its orbit about the earth is more than the angular speed of the earth in its orbit about the sun.

Reason (R) The moon takes less time to move around the earth than the time taken by the earth to move around the sun.

In the light of the above statements, choose the **most appropriate** answer from the options given below **[2024, 27 Jan Shift-II]**

(a) Both (A) and (R) are correct but (R) is not the correct explanation of (A).

(b) Both (A) and (R) are correct and (R) is the correct explanation of (A).

(c) (A) is correct but (R) is not correct.

(d) (A) is not correct but (R) is correct.

3. At what distance above and below the surface of the earth a body will have same weight. (take radius of earth as R) **[2024, 29 Jan Shift-I]**

(a) $\sqrt{5}R - R$ (b) $\frac{\sqrt{5}R - R}{2}$

(c) $\frac{R}{2}$ (d) $\frac{\sqrt{3}R - R}{2}$

4 A planet takes 200 days to complete one revolution around the Sun. If the distance of the planet from Sun is reduced to one fourth of the original distance, how many days will it take to complete one revolution **[2024, 29 Jan Shift-II]**

(a) 25 (b) 20
(c) 100 (d) 50

5 Escape velocity of a body from earth is 11.2 km/s. If the radius of a planet be one-third the radius of earth and mass be one-sixth that of earth, the escape velocity from the planet is **[2024, 30 Jan Shift-II]**

(a) 8.4 km/s (b) 11.2 km/s
(c) 4.2 km/s (d) 7.9 km/s

6 A simple pendulum is placed at a place where its distance from the earth's surface is equal to the radius of the earth. If the length of the string is 4 m, then the time period of small oscillations will be .... s. [Take, $g = \pi^2 \text{ms}^{-2}$] **[2024, 30 Jan Shift-II]**

7 Two identical particles each of mass m go round a circle of radius a under the action of their mutual gravitational attraction. The angular speed of each particle will be **[2023, 15 April Shift-I]**

(a) $\sqrt{\frac{Gm}{4a^3}}$ (b) $\sqrt{\frac{Gm}{2a^3}}$
(c) $\sqrt{\frac{Gm}{a^3}}$ (d) $\sqrt{\frac{Gm}{8a^3}}$

8 Two particles of equal mass m move in a circle of radius r under the action of their mutual gravitational attraction. The speed of each particle will be **[2023, 29 Jan Shift-I]**

(a) $\sqrt{\frac{Gm}{4r}}$ (b) $\sqrt{\frac{4Gm}{r}}$
(c) $\sqrt{\frac{Gm}{2r}}$ (d) $\sqrt{\frac{Gm}{r}}$

9 The time period of a satellite of earth is 24 hours. If the separation between the earth and the satellite is decreased to one-fourth of the previous value, then its new time period will become **[2023, 29 Jan Shift-II]**

(a) 1 hour (b) 6 hours
(c) 3 hours (d) 4 hours

10 If the distance of the Earth from the Sun is 1.5×10^6 km, then the distance of an imaginary planet from the Sun, if its period of revolution is 2.83 years is **[2023, 24 Jan Shift-II]**

(a) 3×10^7 km (b) 6×10^6 km
(c) 3×10^6 km (d) 6×10^7 km

11 The weight of a body on the Earth is 400 N. Then weight of the body when taken to a depth half of the radius of the earth will be **[2023, 8 April Shift-I]**

(a) 300 N (b) Zero (c) 100 N (d) 200 N

12 The acceleration due to gravity at height h above the earth if $h << R$ (Radius of earth) is given by **[2023, 8 April Shift-II]**

(a) $g' = g\left(1 - \frac{h^2}{2R^2}\right)$ (b) $g' = g\left(1 - \frac{2h^2}{R^2}\right)$
(c) $g' = g\left(1 - \frac{2h}{R}\right)$ (d) $g' = g\left(1 - \frac{h}{2R}\right)$

13 Given below are two statements:

Statement I Rotation of the Earth shows effect on the value of acceleration due to gravity (g)

Statement II The effect of rotation of the Earth on the value of 'g' at the equator is minimum and that at the pole is maximum.

In the light of the above statements, choose the correct answer from the options given below **[2023, 10 April Shift-II]**

(a) Both Statement I and Statement II are true
(b) Statement I is true but statement II is false
(c) Both Statement I and Statement II are false
(d) Statement I is false but statement II is true

14 Two planets A and B of radii R and $1.5R$ have densities ρ and $\rho/2$ respectively. The ratio of acceleration due to gravity at the surface of B to A is **[2023, 13 April Shift-II]**

(a) 3 : 4 (b) 4 : 3 (c) 2 : 3 (d) 2 : 1

15 The weight of a body at the surface of earth is 18 N. The weight of the body at an altitude of 3200 km above the earth's surface is (Given, radius of earth, $R_e = 6400$ km). **[2023, 24 Jan Shift-I]**

(a) 9.8 N (b) 19.6 N
(c) 8 N (d) 4.9 N

16 Given below are two statements.

Statement I Acceleration due to earth's gravity decreases as go 'up' or 'down' from earth's surface.

Statement II Acceleration due to earth's gravity is same at a height h and depth d from earth's surface, if $h = d$.

In the light of the above statements, choose the most appropriate answer from the options given below. **[2023, 24 Jan Shift-II]**

(a) Both Statement I and II are correct.
(b) Statement I is correct but Statement II is incorrect.
(c) Both Statement I and Statement II are incorrect.
(d) Statement I is incorrect but Statement II is correct.

17 If V is the gravitational potential due to sphere of uniform density on it's surface, then it's value at the centre of sphere will be **[2023, 11 April Shift-II]**

(a) $\frac{V}{2}$ (b) V (c) $\frac{3V}{2}$ (d) $\frac{4}{3}V$

18 If the gravitational field in the space is given as $\left(-\frac{K}{r^2}\right)$. Taking the reference point to be at $r = 2$ cm with gravitational potential $V = 10$ J/kg. Find the gravitational potential at $r = 3$ cm in SI unit

(Given, $K = 6$ J-cm/kg) **[2023, 30 Jan Shift I]**

(a) 12 (b) 9
(c) 10 (d) 11

19 Given below are two statements : One is labelled as **Assertion (A)** and the other is labelled as **Reason (R)**.

Assertion (A) Earth has atmosphere whereas moon doesn't have any atmosphere.

Reason (R) The escape velocity on moon is very small as compared to that on earth.

In the light of the above statements, choose the correct answer from the options given below **[2023, 6 April Shift-I]**

(a) Both A and R are correct but R is not the correct explanation of A
(b) A is true but R is false
(c) A is false but R is true
(d) Both A and R are correct and R is the correct explanation of A

20 The time period of a satellite, revolving above earths surface at a height equal to R will be (Given, $g = \pi^2$ m/s^2 and R = radius of earth) **[2023, 10 April Shift-II]**

(a) $\sqrt{2R}$ (b) $\sqrt{8R}$
(c) $\sqrt{4R}$ (d) $\sqrt{32R}$

21 A planet having mass $9M_e$ and radius $4R_e$, where M_e and R_e are mass and radius of Earth respectively, has escape velocity in km/s given by (Given, escape velocity on earth $v_e = 11.2 \times 10^3$ m/s) **[2023, 13 April Shift-I]**

(a) 11.2 (b) 33.6
(c) 67.2 (d) 16.8

22 Two satellites of masses m and $3m$ revolve around the earth in circular orbits of radii r & $3r$ respectively. The ratio of orbital speeds of the satellites respectively is **[2023, 10 April Shift-I]**

(a) 9 : 1 (b) $\sqrt{3} : 1$
(c) 1 : 1 (d) 3 : 1

23 A space ship of mass 2×10^4 kg is launched into a circular orbit close to the Earth's surface. The additional velocity to be imparted to the space ship in the orbit to overcome the gravitational pull will be (if $g = 10$ m/s^2 and radius of earth = 6400 km) **[2023, 11 April Shift-II]**

(a) $11.2(\sqrt{2}-1)$ km/s (b) $7.9(\sqrt{2}-1)$ km/s
(c) $8(\sqrt{2}-1)$ km/s (d) $7.4(\sqrt{2}-1)$ km/s

24 The ratio of escape velocity of a planet to the escape velocity of the Earth will be
Given : Mass of the planet is 16 times mass of earth and radius of the planet in 4 times the radius of the Earth. **[2023, 12 April Shift-I]**

(a) 1 : 4 (b) $1 : \sqrt{2}$
(c) 2 : 1 (d) 4 : 1

25 Two satellites A and B move round the Earth in the same orbit. The mass of A is twice the mass of B. The quantity which is same for the two satellites will be **[2023, 12 April Shift-I]**

(a) Total energy (b) Kinetic energy
(c) Speed (d) Potential energy

26 If earth has a mass nine times and radius twice to that of a planet P, then $\frac{v_e}{3}\sqrt{x}$ ms^{-1} will be the minimum velocity required by a rocket to pull out of gravitational force of P, where v_e is escape velocity on earth. The value of x is **[2023, 1 Feb Shift I]**

(a) 18 (b) 1
(c) 2 (d) 3

27 The escape velocities of two planets A and B are in the ratio 1 : 2. If the ratio of their radii respectively is 1 : 3, then the ratio of acceleration due to gravity of planet A to the acceleration of gravity of planet B will be **[2023, 1 Feb Shift II]**

(a) 4/3 (b) 3/4
(c) 3/2 (d) 2/3

28 The time period of a satellite revolving around earth in a given orbit is 7 h. If the radius of orbit is increased to three times its previous value, then approximate new time period of the satellite will be **[2022, 29 June Shift-II]**

(a) 40 h (b) 36 h (c) 30 h (d) 25 h

29 Two objects of equal masses placed at certain distance from each other attract each other with a force of F. If one-third mass of one object is transferred to the other object, then the new force will be **[2022, 28 June Shift-II]**

(a) $\frac{2}{9}F$ (b) $\frac{16}{9}F$ (c) $\frac{8}{9}F$ (d) F

30 Two planets A and B of equal mass are having their period of revolutions T_A and T_B, such that $T_A = 2T_B$. These planets are revolving in the circular orbits of radii r_A and r_B, respectively. Which of the following would be the correct relationship for their orbits? **[2022, 28 June Shift-I]**

(a) $2r_A^2 = r_B^3$ (b) $r_A^3 = 2r_B^3$

(c) $r_A^3 = 4r_B^3$ (d) $T_A^2 - T_B^2 = \frac{\pi^2}{GM}(r_B^3 - 4r_A^3)$

31 If the radius of earth shrinks by 2% while its mass remains same. The acceleration due to gravity on the earth's surface will approximately **[2022, 28 July Shift-I]**

(a) decrease by 2% (b) decrease by 4%
(c) increase by 2% (d) increase by 4%

32 The percentage decrease in the weight of a rocket, when taken to a height of 32 km above the surface of Earth will, be (Radius of Earth = 6400 km) **[2022, 26 July Shift-I]**

(a) 1% (b) 3%
(c) 4% (d) 0.5%

33 An object is taken to a height above the surface of earth at a distance $\frac{5}{4}R$ from the centre of the earth. Where radius of earth, $R = 6400$km. The percentage decrease in the weight of the object will be **[2022, 25 July Shift-II]**

(a) 36% (b) 50%
(c) 64% (d) 25%

34 Given below are two statements. One is labelled as Assertion A and the other is labelled as Reason R.

Assertion (A) If we move from poles to equator, the direction of acceleration due to gravity of earth always points towards the centre of earth without any variation in its magnitude.

Reason (R) At equator, the direction of acceleration due to the gravity is towards the centre of earth.
In the light of above statements, choose the correct answer from the options given below **[2022, 26 June Shift-II]**

(a) Both A and R are true and R is the correct explanation of A.
(b) Both A and R are true but R is not the correct explanation of A.
(c) A is true but R is false.
(d) A is false but R is true.

35 The variation of acceleration due to gravity (g) with distance (r) from the centre of the earth is correctly represented by (Given, R = radius of earth) **[2022, 26 June Shift-I]**

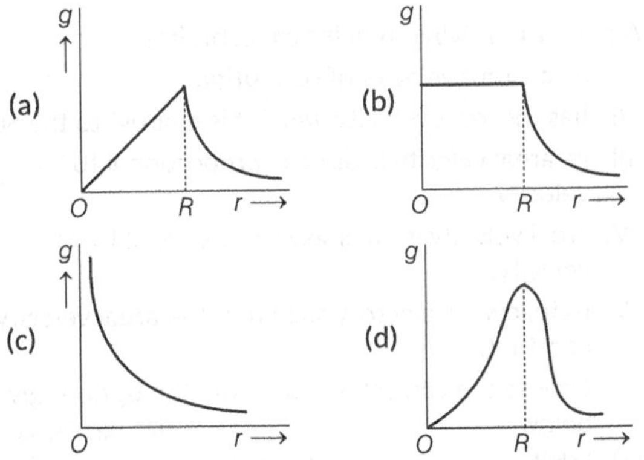

36 The height of any point P above the surface of earth is equal to diameter of earth. The value of acceleration due to gravity at point P will be (Given, g = acceleration due to gravity at the surface of earth) **[2022, 25 June Shift-I]**

(a) $\frac{g}{2}$ (b) $\frac{g}{4}$

(c) $\frac{g}{3}$ (d) $\frac{g}{9}$

37 The approximate height from the surface of earth at which the weight of the body becomes $\frac{1}{3}$ of its weight on the surface of earth is [Radius of earth, $R = 6400$ km and $\sqrt{3} = 1.732$] **[2022, 27 June Shift I]**

(a) 3840 km (b) 4685 km
(c) 2133 km (d) 4267 km

38 The escape velocity of a body on a planet A is 12 kms^{-1}. The escape velocity of the body on another planet B, whose density is four times and radius is half of the planet A is **[2022, 29 June Shift-I]**

(a) 12 kms^{-1} (b) 24 kms^{-1}
(c) 36 kms^{-1} (d) 6 kms^{-1}

39 A solid sphere of radius R gravitationally attracts a particle placed at 3R from its centre with a force F_1. Now, a spherical cavity of radius $(R/2)$ is made in the sphere (as shown in figure) and the force becomes F_2. The value of $F_1 : F_2$ is **[2021, 25 Feb Shift-I]**

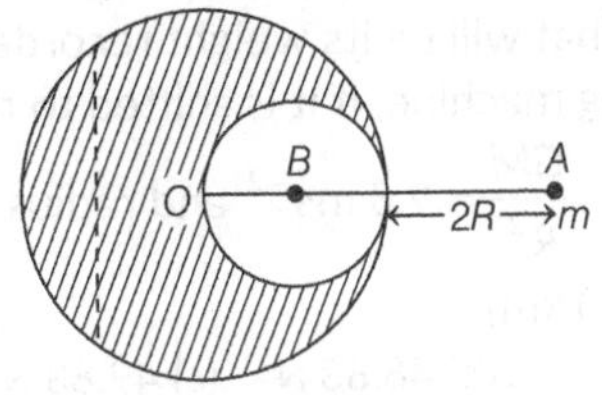

(a) 25 : 36 (b) 36 : 25
(c) 50 : 41 (d) 41 : 50

40 A planet revolving in elliptical orbit has

I. a constant velocity of revolution

II. has the least velocity when it is nearest to the Sun

III. its areal velocity is directly proportional to its velocity

IV. areal velocity is inversely proportional to its velocity.

V. to follow a trajectory such that the areal velocity is constant.

Choose the correct answer from the options given below. **[2021, 26 Feb Shift-I]**

(a) Only I (b) Only IV
(c) Only III (d) Only V

41 The maximum and minimum distance of a comet from the Sun are 1.6×10^{12} m and 8.0×10^{10} m, respectively. If the speed of the comet at the nearest point is 6×10^4 ms^{-1}, then the speed at the farthest point is **[2021, 16 March Shift-I]**

(a) 1.5×10^3 m/s (b) 6.0×10^3 m/s
(c) 3.0×10^3 m/s (d) 4.5×10^3 m/s

42 A geostationary satellite is orbiting around an arbitrary planet P at a height of $11R$ above the surface of P, R being the radius of P. The time period of another satellite in hours at a height of $2R$ from the surface of P is .... P has the time period of 24 h. **[2021 , 17 March Shift-II]**

(a) $6\sqrt{2}$ (b) $6/\sqrt{2}$ (c) 3 (d) 5

43 The time period of a satellite in a circular orbit of radius R is T. The period of another satellite in a circular orbit of radius $9R$ is **[2021, 18 March Shift-I]**

(a) $9T$ (b) $27T$ (c) $12T$ (d) $3T$

44 If the angular velocity of Earth's spin is increased such that the bodies at the equator start floating, the duration of the day would be approximately

(Take $2g = 10$ ms^{-2}, the radius of Earth, $R = 6400 \times 10^3$ m, take $\pi = 3.14$) **[2021, 18 March Shift-II]**

(a) 60 min (b) does not change
(c) 1200 min (d) 84 min

45 A body weights 49 N on a spring balance at the North pole. What will be its weight recorded on the same weighing machine, if it is shifted to the equator ?

(Use, $g = \frac{GM}{R^2} = 9.8$ ms^{-2} and radius of earth, $R = 6400$ km) **[2021, 24 Feb Shift-II]**

(a) 49 N (b) 48.83 N (c) 49.83 N (d) 49.17 N

46 Find the gravitational force of attraction between the ring and sphere as shown in the figure, where the plane of the ring is perpendicular to the line joining the centres. If $\sqrt{8}R$ is the distance between the centres of a ring (of mass m) and a sphere (of mass M), where both have equal radius R. **[2021, 26 Feb Shift-I]**

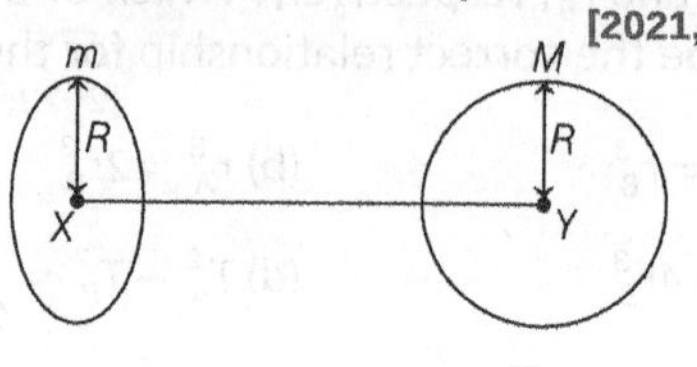

(a) $\frac{\sqrt{8}}{9} \cdot \frac{GmM}{R}$ (b) $\frac{2\sqrt{2}}{3} \cdot \frac{GMm}{R^2}$
(c) $\frac{1}{3\sqrt{8}} \cdot \frac{GMm}{R^2}$ (d) $\frac{\sqrt{8}}{27} \cdot \frac{GmM}{R^2}$

47 A person standing on a spring balance inside a stationary lift measures 60 kg. The weight of that person, if the lift descends with uniform downward acceleration of 1.8 m/s^2 will be .... N. [$g = 10$ m/s^2] **[2021, 26 Feb Shift-I]**

48 In the reported figure of Earth, the value of acceleration due to gravity is same at point A and C but it is smaller than that of its value at point B (surface of the Earth). The value of $OA : AB$ will be $x : y$. The value of x is .... **[2021, 26 Feb Shift-II]**

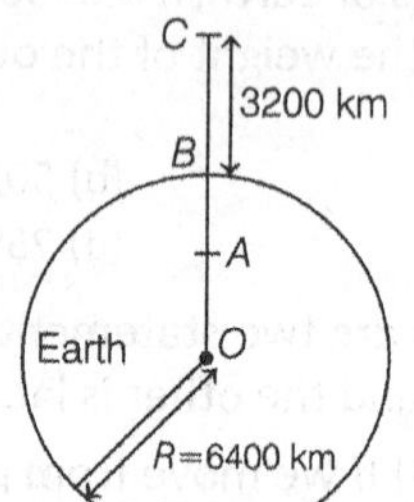

49 A person whose mass is 100 kg travels from Earth to Mars in a spaceship. Neglect all other objects in sky and take acceleration due to gravity on the surface of the Earth and Mars as 10 m/s^2 and 4 m/s^2, respectively. Identify from the below figures, the curve that fits best for the weight of the passenger as a function of time. **[2021, 20 July Shift-I]**

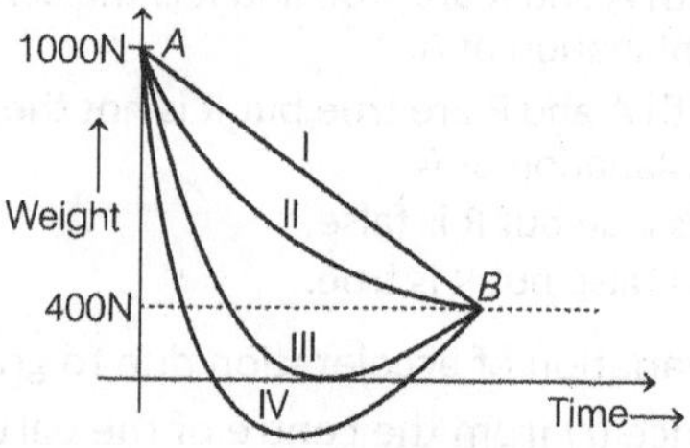

(a) III (b) I
(c) IV (d) II

JEE Advanced

1 Two satellites P and Q are moving in different circular orbits around the Earth (radius R). The heights of P and Q from the Earth surface are h_P and h_Q, respectively, where $h_P = R/3$. The accelerations of P and Q due to Earth's gravity are g_P and g_Q, respectively. If $g_P / g_Q = 36/25$, what is the value of h_Q? **(2023)**

(a) $\frac{3R}{5}$ (b) $\frac{R}{6}$ (c) $\frac{6R}{5}$ (d) $\frac{5R}{6}$

2 Two spherical stars A and B have densities ρ_A and ρ_B, respectively. A and B have the same radius, and their masses M_A and M_B are related by $M_B = 2M_A$. Due to an interaction process, star A loses some of its mass, so that its radius is halved, while its spherical shape is retained, and its density remains ρ_A. The entire mass lost by A is deposited as a thick spherical shell on B with the density of the shell being ρ_A. If v_A and v_B are the escape velocities from A and B after the interaction process, the ratio $\frac{v_B}{v_A} = \sqrt{\frac{10n}{15^{1/3}}}$. The value of n is .... **(2022)**

3 The distance between two stars of masses $3M_S$ and $6M_S$ is 9R. Here R is the mean distance between the centers of the Earth and the Sun, and M_S is the mass of the Sun. The two stars orbit around their common center of mass in circular orbits with period nT, where T is the period of Earth's revolution around the Sun. The value of n is ______ . **(2021)**

4 A rocket is launched normal to the surface of the Earth, away from the Sun, along the line joining the Sun and the Earth. The Sun is 3×10^5 times heavier than the Earth and is at a distance 2.5×10^4 times larger than the radius of Earth. The escape velocity from Earth's gravitational field is $v_e = 11.2 \text{ km s}^{-1}$. The minimum initial velocity (v_s) required for the rocket to be able to leave the Sun-Earth system is closest to (Ignore the rotation and revolution of the Earth and the presence of any other planet) **(2017)**

(a) $v_s = 72 \text{km s}^{-1}$ (b) $v_s = 22 \text{km s}^{-1}$
(c) $v_s = 42 \text{km s}^{-1}$ (d) $v_s = 62 \text{km s}^{-1}$

5 A bullet is fired vertically upwards with velocity v from the surface of a spherical planet. When it reaches its maximum height, its acceleration due to the planet's gravity is $\frac{1}{4}$th of its value at the surface of the planet. If the escape velocity from the planet is $v_{sec} = v\sqrt{N}$, then the value of N is (ignore energy loss due to atmosphere) **(2015)**

6 A large spherical mass M is fixed at one position and two identical masses m are kept on a line passing through the centre of M (see figure). The point masses are connected by a rigid massless rod of length l and this assembly is free to move along the line connecting them.

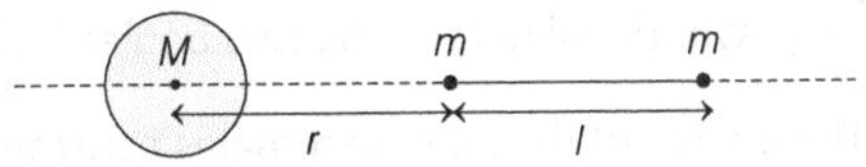

All three masses interact only through their mutual gravitational interaction. When the point mass nearer to M is at a distance $r = 3l$ from M the tension in the rod is zero for $m = k\left(\frac{M}{288}\right)$. The value of k is **(2015)**

7 A spherical body of radius R consists of a fluid of constant density and is in equilibrium under its own gravity. If P(r) is the pressure at $r(r < R)$, then the correct options is/are **(2015)**

(a) $P(r = 0) = 0$ (b) $\frac{P\left(r = \frac{3R}{4}\right)}{P\left(r = \frac{2R}{3}\right)} = \frac{63}{80}$

(c) $\frac{P\left(r = \frac{3R}{5}\right)}{P\left(r = \frac{2R}{5}\right)} = \frac{16}{21}$ (d) $\frac{P\left(r = \frac{R}{2}\right)}{P\left(r = \frac{R}{3}\right)} = \frac{20}{27}$

8 A planet of radius $R = \frac{1}{10} \times$ (radius of earth) has the same mass density as earth. Scientists dig a well of depth $\frac{R}{5}$ on it and lower a wire of the same length and of linear mass density 10^{-3} kg m^{-1} into it. If the wire is not touching anywhere, the force applied at the top of the wire by a person holding it in place is (take the radius of earth $= 6 \times 10^6$ m and the acceleration due to gravity of earth is 10 ms^{-2}) **(2014)**

(a) 96 N
(b) 108 N
(c) 120 N
(d) 150 N

9 Two bodies, each of mass M, are kept fixed with a separation 2L. A particle of mass m is projected from the mid-point of the line joining their centres, perpendicular to the line. The gravitational constant is G. The correct statement(s) is (are) **(2013)**

(a) The minimum initial velocity of the mass m to escape the gravitational field of the two bodies is $4\sqrt{\frac{GM}{L}}$

(b) The minimum initial velocity of the mass m to escape the gravitational field of the two bodies is $2\sqrt{\frac{GM}{L}}$

(c) The minimum initial velocity of the mass m to escape the gravitational field of the two bodies is $\sqrt{\frac{2GM}{L}}$

(d) The energy of the mass m remains constant

10 Two spherical planets P and Q have the same uniform density ρ, masses M_P and M_Q, and surface areas A and $4A$, respectively. A spherical planet R also has uniform density ρ and its mass is $(M_P + M_Q)$. The escape velocities from the planets P, Q and R, are v_P, v_Q and v_R, respectively. Then **(2012)**

(a) $v_Q > v_R > v_P$

(b) $v_R > v_Q > v_P$

(c) $v_R/v_P = 3$

(d) $v_P/v_Q = 1/2$

Answer Key

LEVEL 1

5.1 Universal Law Of Gravitation

1. 1:2 4. $v = \frac{1}{2}\sqrt{\frac{Gm}{r}}$ 5. $\frac{Gm^2}{d^2}\left(1 + \frac{1}{\sqrt{2}}\right)$ along PB 6. $\frac{4}{3}Gm^2$ 7. $\frac{GMm}{(L+a)a}$

5.2 Gravitational Field Intensity

1. $x = 3.6 \times 10^5$ km. 2. $\frac{2GM}{\sqrt{3}L^2}$ 3. (a) $\frac{2\pi GMm}{L^2}$ (b) zero 4. $\pm\frac{R}{\sqrt{2}}$ 5. (a) $\frac{4GM}{9a^2}$ (b) $\frac{8GM}{25a^2}$

6. $\frac{4\pi}{3}G\rho l$ 7. $\frac{7GMm}{36R^2}$ 8. $\frac{GMm}{2R^2}$

5.3 Acceleration Due to Gravity

1. 196 cm/s^2 2. 1600 km 3. 0.5% 4. 18 m 5. 1s 6. $(\sqrt{2}-1)R_e$ 7. $\omega = \sqrt{\frac{g_s}{R_e}}$, length of day = 84.57 min

5.4 Gravitational Potential

1. (i) $V_P = -\frac{2Gm}{l}, V_Q = \frac{4GM}{l}$ (ii) $W_{ext} = -\frac{2Gmm_0}{l}; W_{gr} = \frac{2Gmm_0}{l}$ 2. $-\frac{GM}{\sqrt{R^2+x^2}}$

3. $-\frac{3Gm}{a}$ 4. $\frac{-3GM}{2R}$ 5. $\mathbf{E} = -[(4x+z)\hat{\mathbf{i}} + 6y\hat{\mathbf{j}} + x\hat{\mathbf{k}}]$ 6. $\frac{-k}{2x^2}$

5.5 Gravitational Potential Energy

1. −240 J 2. 11 J 3. (a) $-\frac{3Gm^2}{a}$ (b) $\frac{3Gm^2}{2a}$ 4. $\frac{Gm^2}{l}(4+\sqrt{2})$ 5. $mgR/2$

6. $\sqrt{gR}$ 7. 3R 8. $\sqrt{2gR}$ 9. $v_1 = \sqrt{\frac{2GM^2}{d(M+m)}}, v_2 = \sqrt{\frac{2Gm^2}{d(M+m)}}$

5.6 Escape Velocity

1. 110 km/s 2. $\sqrt{gR}$ 3. $R_p = \sqrt{R_E h}$ 4. $v_e = \sqrt{\frac{11GM_e}{4R}}$ 5. $\frac{3}{2}\sqrt{\frac{5GM}{a}}$

5.7 Satellite

1. (a) 7.083 km/s, 1.97 hr, (b) 2.15 s 2. (a) 36000 km (b) 1.4 hr 3. 2.66×10^{7}m 4. (a) 10^{10} J (b) -2×10^{10} J (c) -10^{10} J

5. 3.13×10^9 J 6. (a) $-\frac{GM_e m}{r}$ (b) $-\frac{2GM_e m}{r}$

5.8 Kepler's Laws

1. 8 years 2. $\frac{2\pi mab}{L}$ 3. 1.5×10^4 m/s 4. 0.5 6. $-\frac{GMm}{2a}$

Level 2

Single Choice Correct Questions

1. (a)	2. (a)	3. (d)	4. (c)	5. (c)	6. (d)	7. (c)	8. (b)	9. (b)	10. (b)
11. (c)	12. (a)	13. (b)	14. (b)	15. (a)	16. (c)	17. (d)	18. (c)	19. (d)	20. (d)
21. (b)	22. (c)	23. (d)	24. (c)	25. (a)	26. (b)	27. (a)	28. (b)	29. (c)	30. (a)
31. (b)	32. (a)	33. (c)	34. (c)	35. (a)	36. (c)	37. (a)	38. (c)	39. (a)	40. (b)
41. (d)	42. (c)	43. (c)	44. (c)	45. (d)	46. (b)	47. (d)	48. (c)	49. (b)	50. (d)
51. (d)	52. (c)	53. (c)	54. (d)	55. (b)	56. (a)	57. (a)	58. (c)		

Numerical Value Questions

1. (2)	2. (8)	3. (40)	4. (1)	5. (4)	6. (5)	7. (4)	8. (4)	9. (8)	10. (7)

Level 3

Single Choice Correct Questions

1. (b)	2. (b)	3. (d)	4. (a)	5. (a)	6. (a)	7. (c)	8. (b)	9. (d)	10. (c)
11. (a)	12. (c)	13. (c)	14. (a)	15. (a)	16. (b)	17. (b)	18. (d)	19. (d)	20. (b)
21. (b)	22. (c)	23. (d)	24. (a)	25. (a)	26. (c)	27. (b)	28. (a)	29. (d)	30. (b)

Multiple Choice(s) Correct Questions

1. (b, c)	2. (a,c,d)	3. (b, c)	4. (a, c)	5. (a, c, d)	6. (a, b, d)	7. (a,b,c,d)	8. (a, b, d)	9. (a, c)	10. (a, b, d)
11. (a, b, c)	12. (c, d)	13. (a, b)	14. (a, c, d)	15. (a, d)	16. (a, c, d)	17. (b, d)			

Comprehension Based Questions

1. (b)	2. (c)	3. (a)	4. (d)	5. (b)	6. (b)	7. (c)	8. (a)	9. (a)	10. (a)
11. (c)	12. (d)	13. (c)	14. (b)	15. (d)	16. (b)	17. (c)	18. (b)	19. (a)	20. (d)
21. (b)	22. (a)	23. (c)	24. (a)						

Match the Columns Question

1. A→P; B→Q; C→Q; D→Q
2. A→R; B→Q; C→Q; D→P
3. A→S; B→R; C→S; D→S
4. A→P; B→T; C→R
5. A→P; B→R; C→S; D→Q
6. A→P; B→R; C→Q; D→S
7. A→QRT; B→ST; C→RST; D→QRT
8. A→Q; B→P; C→P; D→Q

Numerical Value Questions

1. (23)	2. (100)	3. (1)	4. (32)	5. (9)	6. (9)	7. (8)	8. (8)	9. (4)	10. (2)

Previous Years Questions

JEE Main

1. (b)	2. (b)	3. (b)	4. (a)	5. (d)	6. (8)	7. (a)	8. (a)	9. (c)	10. (c)
11. (d)	12. (c)	13. (b)	14. (a)	15. (c)	16. (b)	17. (c)	18. (d)	19. (a)	20. (d)
21. (d)	22. (b)	23. (c)	24. (c)	25. (c)	26. (c)	27. (b)	28. (b)	29. (c)	30. (c)
31. (d)	32. (a)	33. (*)	34. (d)	35. (a)	36. (d)	37. (b)	38. (a)	39. (c)	40. (d)
41. (c)	42. (c)	43. (b)	44. (d)	45. (b)	46. (d)	47. (492)	48. (4)	49. (a)	

JEE Advanced

1. (a)	2. (2.30)	3. (9)	4. (c)	5. (2)	6. (7)	7. (b,c)	8. (b)	9. (b,d)	10. (b,d)

SOLUTIONS

Level 1

5.1 Universal Law of Gravitation

1. $F = \dfrac{G(M-m)m}{r^2}$

$\dfrac{dF}{dm} = \dfrac{G}{r^2}(M-2m) = 0$

$\Rightarrow \quad \dfrac{m}{M} = \dfrac{1}{2}$

2. $F = \dfrac{GM_1M_2}{r^2} = \dfrac{G(\rho\frac{4}{3}\pi R^3)(\rho\frac{4}{3}\pi R^3)}{(2R)^2}$

$\Rightarrow \quad F \propto R^4$

3. $F = \dfrac{Gm_1m_2}{r^2}; a_1 = \dfrac{F}{m_1}$ and $a_2 = \dfrac{F}{m_2}$

$a_{rel} = a_1 - (-a_2) = \dfrac{G(m_1+m_2)}{r^2}$

$\Rightarrow \quad v_{rel}\dfrac{dv_{rel}}{dr} = \dfrac{G(m_1+m_2)}{r^2}$

$\Rightarrow \quad \displaystyle\int_0^{v_{rel}} v_{rel}dv_{rel} = G(m_1+m_2)\int_\infty^R \frac{dr}{r^2}$

$v_{rel} = \sqrt{\dfrac{2G(m_1+m_2)}{r}}$

4. $F = \dfrac{mv^2}{r} \Rightarrow \dfrac{Gm(m)}{2r^2} = \dfrac{mv^2}{r} \Rightarrow v = \sqrt{\dfrac{Gm}{4r}}$

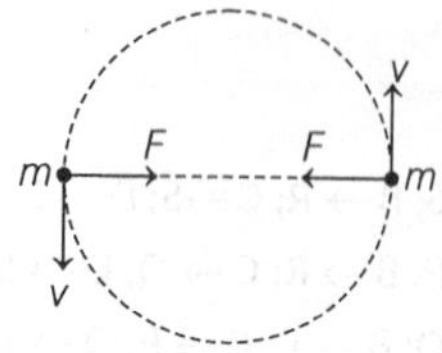

5. $F_1 = \dfrac{Gmm}{(\sqrt{2}d)^2}$ and $F_2 = \dfrac{Gmm}{d^2}$

$F_{net} = F_2 + 2F_1\cos 45°$

$= \dfrac{Gm^2}{d^2}\left(1 + \dfrac{1}{\sqrt{2}}\right)$

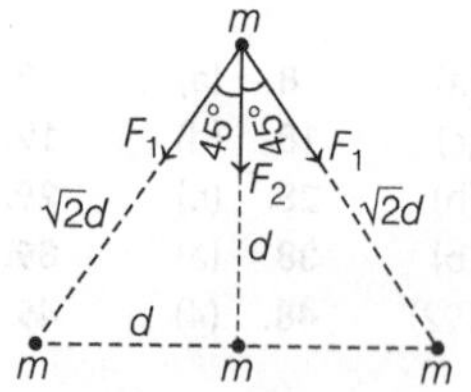

6. $F = Gm^2\left(\dfrac{1}{1^2} + \dfrac{1}{2^2} + \dfrac{1}{4^2} + \dfrac{1}{8^2} + \ldots\right)$

$F = \dfrac{4}{3}Gm^2$

7.

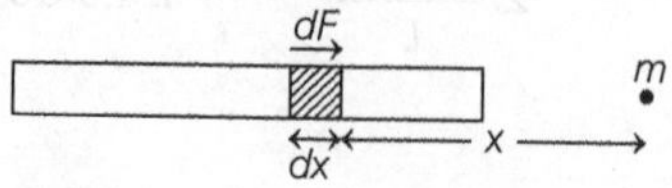

$\displaystyle\int dF = \int_a^{a+L} G\frac{\left(\frac{M}{L}\right)dxm}{x^2} \Rightarrow F = \frac{GMm}{(L+a)a}$

5.2 Gravitational Field Intensity

1. $E_{net} = \dfrac{Gm_1}{x_2} - \dfrac{Gm_2}{(r-x)^2} = 0$

$\Rightarrow \quad \dfrac{x}{r-x} = \sqrt{\dfrac{m_1}{m_2}} = 9$

$\Rightarrow \quad x = \dfrac{9r}{10} = 3.6 \times 10^5$ km

2. $E_x = \dfrac{G\lambda}{r}(\sin\alpha + \sin\beta)$

$= \dfrac{Gm/L}{L\cos 30°}(\sin 30° + \sin 30°) = \dfrac{2GM}{\sqrt{3}L^2}$

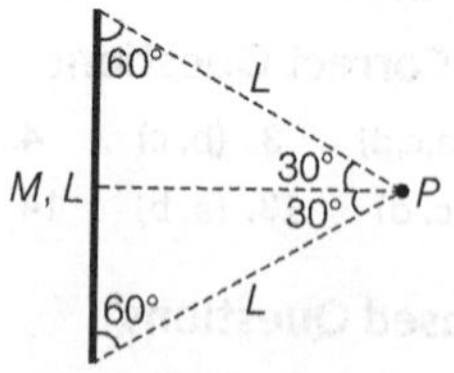

3. (a) $F = mE = m\left(\dfrac{2G(M/L)}{R}\right) = \dfrac{2\pi GMm}{L^2}$

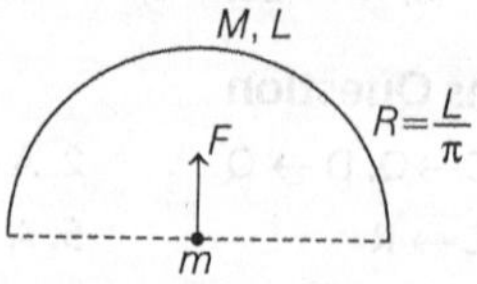

(b) For complete ring, gravitational field at the centre is zero. So $F = 0$

4. $E = \dfrac{GMx}{(R^2+x^2)^{3/2}}$

For E to be maximum, $\dfrac{dE}{dx} = 0$

$\Rightarrow \quad \dfrac{(R^2+x^2)^{3/2}(1) - x\frac{3}{2}(R^2+x^2)^{1/2}(2x)}{(R^2+x^2)^3} = 0$

$\Rightarrow \quad x = \pm\dfrac{R}{\sqrt{2}}$

5. (a) $E = E_1 + E_2 = \dfrac{GM}{(3a/2)^2} + 0 = \dfrac{4GM}{9a^2}$

(b) $E = E_1 + E_2 = \dfrac{GM}{(5a/2)^2} + \dfrac{GM}{(5a/2)^2} = \dfrac{8GM}{25a^2}$

6.

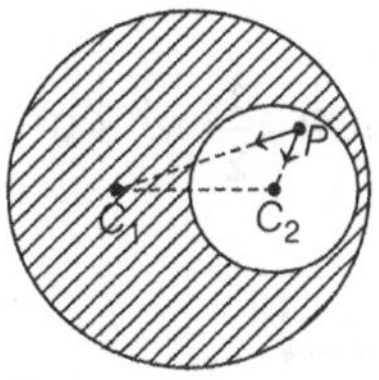

Gravitational field inside a solid sphere

$$= -\frac{4\pi G\rho}{3}\mathbf{r}$$

$$\mathbf{E} = \mathbf{E}_1 - \mathbf{E}_2$$

$$= \frac{4\pi G\rho}{3}(\mathbf{PC}_1) - \frac{4\pi G\rho}{3}\mathbf{PC}_2$$

$$= \frac{4\pi G\rho}{3}\mathbf{C}_2\mathbf{C}_1$$

$$|\mathbf{E}| = \frac{4\pi Gl\rho}{3}$$

7. $E = E_1 - E_2 = \dfrac{GM}{(2R)^2} - \dfrac{G(M/8)}{(3R/2)^2} = \dfrac{7}{36}\dfrac{GM}{R^2}$

$$F = mE = \frac{7GMm}{36R^2}$$

8. $F = \left(\dfrac{GM}{R^3}x\right)m$

$$N = F\cos\theta = \frac{GMxm}{R^3}\left(\frac{R/2}{x}\right) = \frac{GMm}{2R^2}$$

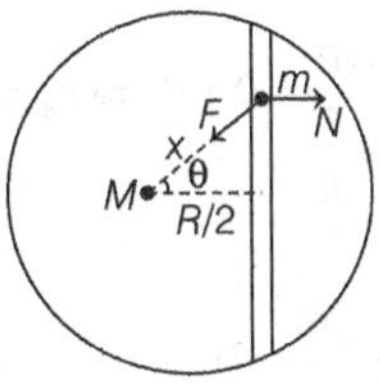

5.3 Acceleration due to gravity

1. $g = \dfrac{GM}{R^2} \Rightarrow \dfrac{g_1}{g_2} = \dfrac{M_1}{M_2}\left(\dfrac{R_2}{R_1}\right)^2$

$$\Rightarrow \quad \frac{g_1}{980} = \left(\frac{1}{80}\right)\left(\frac{12800}{3200}\right)^2$$

$$\Rightarrow \quad g_1 = 196 \text{ cm/s}^2$$

2. $g' = \dfrac{g}{\left(1+\dfrac{h}{R}\right)^2}$

$$\Rightarrow \quad 0.64g = \frac{g}{\left(1+\dfrac{h}{R}\right)^2}$$

$$\Rightarrow \quad h = \frac{R}{4} = 1600 \text{ km}$$

3. % decrease in $g = \dfrac{d}{R} \times 100$

$$= \frac{32\text{km}}{6400 \text{ km}} \times 100 = 0.5\%$$

4. $g = \dfrac{GM}{R^2} = \dfrac{G\rho}{R^2}\left(\dfrac{4}{3}\pi R^3\right) = \dfrac{4G\pi\rho R}{3}$

$$\frac{g_1}{g_2} = \frac{\rho_1 R_1}{\rho_2 R_2} \Rightarrow \frac{g_1}{g_2} = \left(\frac{1}{4}\right)\left(\frac{1}{3}\right) = \frac{1}{12}$$

$$H = \frac{u^2}{2g} \Rightarrow \frac{H_1}{H_2} = \frac{g_2}{g_1} \Rightarrow \frac{H_1}{1.5} = 12$$

$$\Rightarrow \quad H_1 = 18 \text{ m}$$

5. $g = \dfrac{4}{3}G\pi\rho R \Rightarrow g \propto R$

$$T = 2\pi\sqrt{\frac{l}{g}} \Rightarrow T \propto \frac{1}{\sqrt{g}} \Rightarrow T \propto \frac{1}{\sqrt{R}}$$

$$\frac{T_P}{T_E} = \sqrt{\frac{R_E}{R_P}} \Rightarrow \frac{T_P}{2} = \sqrt{\frac{R_E}{4R_E}}$$

$$\Rightarrow \quad T_P = 1 \text{ s}$$

6. $w = mg' = \dfrac{mg}{\left(1+\dfrac{h}{R}\right)^2} = \dfrac{mg}{2}$

$$\Rightarrow \quad h = (\sqrt{2} - 1)R$$

7. $g_{\text{app}} = g - \omega^2 R = 0 \Rightarrow \omega = \sqrt{\dfrac{g}{R}}$

$$T = \frac{2\pi}{\omega} = 2\pi\sqrt{\frac{R}{g}} = 84.57 \text{ min}$$

5.4 Gravitational Potential

1. (i) $V_P = -\dfrac{Gm}{l} - \dfrac{Gm}{l} = -\dfrac{2Gm}{l}$

$$V_Q = -\frac{Gm}{(l/2)} - \frac{Gm}{(l/2)} = -\frac{4Gm}{l}$$

(ii) $W_{\text{ext}} = m_0\Delta V = m_0(V_Q - V_p) = -\dfrac{2Gmm_0}{l}$

$$W_{\text{gr}} = -m_0\Delta V = \frac{2Gmm_0}{l}$$

2. $V = -\dfrac{G\int dm}{\sqrt{R^2+x^2}} = -\dfrac{GM}{\sqrt{R^2+x^2}}$

3. $V = V_1 + V_2 = -\dfrac{Gm}{(a/2)} - \dfrac{Gm}{a} = -\dfrac{3Gm}{a}$

4. Inside a solid sphere

$$V = -\frac{GM}{2R^3}(3R^2 - x^2)$$

At the centre, $V = \dfrac{-3GM}{2R}$

Expression for potential at the centre of a solid hemisphere will be same.

5. $\mathbf{E} = \dfrac{-\partial V}{\partial x}\hat{\mathbf{i}} - \dfrac{\partial V}{\partial y}\hat{\mathbf{j}} - \dfrac{\partial V}{\partial z}\hat{\mathbf{k}} = -[(4x+z)\hat{\mathbf{i}} + 6y\hat{\mathbf{j}} + x\hat{\mathbf{k}}]$

6. $dV = -\mathbf{E} \cdot dr$

$$\Rightarrow \int_0^V dV = \int_\infty^x \frac{k}{x^3} dx \Rightarrow V = -\frac{k}{2x^2}$$

5.5 Gravitational Potential Energy

1. $\Delta V = -\int \mathbf{E} \cdot d\mathbf{r} = -(5\hat{i} + 12\hat{j}) \cdot (12\hat{i} + 5\hat{j})$

$$= -120 \text{ J/kg}$$

$$\Delta U = m\Delta V = 2(-120) = -240 \text{ J}$$

2. $E = \frac{\Delta V}{\Delta r} = \frac{16}{20} = 0.8 \text{ N/kg}$

$$W = m(E\Delta r) = 2 \times 0.8 \times 8 \sin 60° = 11 \text{ J}$$

3. (a) $U = 3\left(-\frac{Gm(m)}{a}\right) = -\frac{3Gm^2}{a}$

(b) $W_{ext} = U_2 - U_1$

$$= -\frac{3Gm^2}{2a} - \left(\frac{-3Gm^2}{a}\right) = \frac{3Gm^2}{2a}$$

4. $U_1 = \left(\frac{-Gm^2}{l}\right) \times 4 + \left(-\frac{Gm^2}{\sqrt{2}l}\right) \times 2 = -(4 + \sqrt{2})\frac{Gm^2}{l}$

$$U_2 = 0$$

$$W_{ext} = \Delta U = U_2 - U_1 = (4 + \sqrt{2})\frac{Gm^2}{l}$$

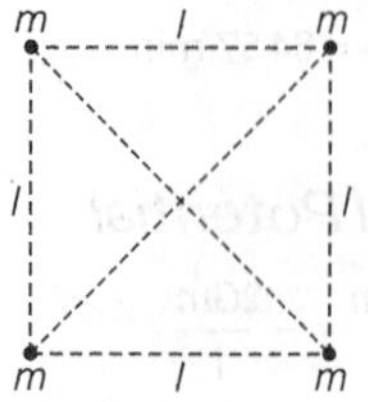

5. $U = -\frac{mgR}{1 + \frac{h}{R}}$

$$h = 0 \Rightarrow U_1 = -mgR$$

$$h = R \Rightarrow U_2 = -\frac{mgR}{2}$$

$$\Delta U = U_2 - U_1 = \frac{mgR}{2}$$

6. $K_1 + U_1 = K_2 + U_2$

$$\Rightarrow 0 - \frac{mgR}{2} = \frac{1}{2}mv^2 - mgR$$

$$\Rightarrow v = \sqrt{gR}$$

7. $K_1 + U_1 = K_2 + U_2$

$$\Rightarrow \frac{1}{2}m\left(\sqrt{\frac{3gR}{2}}\right)^2 - mgR = 0 - \left(\frac{mgR}{1 + \frac{h}{R}}\right)$$

$$\Rightarrow \quad h = 3R$$

8. $K_1 + U_1 = K_2 + U_2$

$$\Rightarrow \frac{1}{2}m(2\sqrt{gR})^2 - mgR = \frac{1}{2}mv^2 + 0$$

$$\Rightarrow v = \sqrt{2gR}$$

9.

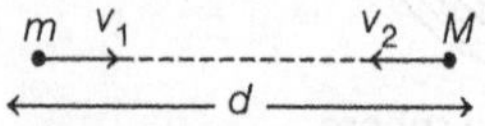

Applying linear momentum conservation for the system,

$$0 + 0 = mv_1 - Mv_2 \quad \text{...(i)}$$

Applying mechanical energy conservation,

$$K_1 + U_1 = K_2 + U_2$$

$$\Rightarrow (0 + 0) + 0 = \left(\frac{1}{2}mv_1^2 + \frac{1}{2}Mv_2^2\right) - \frac{GMm}{d} \quad \text{...(ii)}$$

Solving Eqs. (i) and (ii), we get

$$v_1 = \sqrt{\frac{2GM^2}{d(M + m)}} \text{ and } v_2 = \sqrt{\frac{2Gm^2}{d(M + m)}}$$

5.6 Escape Velocity

1. $v_e = \sqrt{\frac{2GM}{R}} \Rightarrow \frac{v_1}{v_2} = \sqrt{\frac{M_1R_2}{M_2R_1}}$

$$\Rightarrow \frac{v_1}{11} = \sqrt{10 \times 10} \Rightarrow 5v_1 = 110 \text{ km/s}$$

2. $K_1 + U_1 = K_2 + U_2$

$$\Rightarrow \quad \frac{1}{2}mv_e^2 - \frac{mgR}{1 + \frac{R}{R}} = 0 + 0 \Rightarrow v_e = \sqrt{gR}$$

3. For planet,

$$\frac{1}{2}mv^2 - \frac{GM_pm}{R_P} = 0 \quad \text{...(i)}$$

On earth,

$$\frac{1}{2}mv^2 = m\left(\frac{GM_E}{R_E^2}\right)h \quad \text{...(ii)}$$

From Eqs. (i) and (ii), we get

$$\frac{M_P}{M_E} = \frac{hR_P}{R_E^2}$$

$$\Rightarrow \quad \frac{\rho\left(\frac{4}{3}\pi R_P^3\right)}{\rho\left(\frac{4}{3}\pi R_E^3\right)} = \frac{hR_P}{R_E^2}$$

$$\Rightarrow \quad R_P = \sqrt{R_E h}$$

4. $K_1 + U_1 = K_2 + U_2$

$$\Rightarrow \quad \frac{1}{2}mv_e^2 - \frac{GMm}{2R^3}\left(3R^2 - \left(\frac{R}{2}\right)^2\right) = 0 + 0$$

$$\Rightarrow \quad v_e = \sqrt{\frac{11GM_e}{4R}}$$

5.

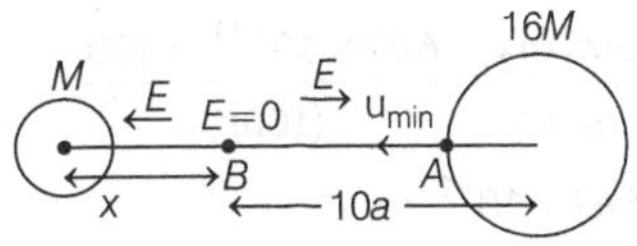

At B, $E = \frac{GM}{x^2} - \frac{G(16M)}{(10a - x)^2} = 0$

$\Rightarrow \quad x = 2a$

Applying conservation of energy between A and B,

$K_A + U_A = K_B + U_B$

$$\Rightarrow \frac{1}{2}mu_{min}^2 + \left(\frac{-G(16M)}{2a} - \frac{GM}{8a}\right) = 0 + \left(-\frac{GM}{2a} - \frac{G(16M)}{8a}\right)$$

$$\Rightarrow \quad u_{min} = \frac{3}{2}\sqrt{\frac{5GM}{a}}$$

5.7 Satellite

1. (a) $v = \sqrt{\frac{GM}{r}} = \sqrt{\frac{gR^2}{R+h}} = \sqrt{\frac{4gR}{5}} = 7.083$ km/s

$$T = 2\pi\sqrt{\frac{r^3}{GM}} = 1.97 \text{ hr}$$

(b) $\omega_{rel} = \omega_1 - \omega_2 = \frac{2\pi}{1.97} - \frac{2\pi}{24}$

$$T = \frac{2\pi}{\omega} = \frac{24(1.97)}{24 - 1.97} = 2.15 \text{ hr}$$

2. (a) $T = 2\pi\sqrt{\frac{r^3}{GM}} = 24 \times 3600$

$\Rightarrow \quad r \approx 36000$ km

(b) $T^2 \propto r^3 \Rightarrow \frac{T_1}{T_2} = \left(\frac{r_1}{r_2}\right)^{3/2}$

$$\Rightarrow \quad T_1 = \left(\frac{6400}{42400}\right)^{3/2}(24\text{hr}) = 1.4 \text{ hr}$$

3. $\omega_{rel} = \omega_1 - \omega_2 \Rightarrow \frac{2\pi}{\omega_0} = \frac{2\pi}{\omega} - \frac{2\pi}{\omega_0}$

$\Rightarrow \quad \omega = 2\omega_0 = 14.6 \times 10^{-5}$

$$\omega = \sqrt{\frac{GM}{r^3}} = 14.6 \times 10^{-5}$$

$\Rightarrow \quad r = 2.66 \times 10^7$ m

4. (a) $K = \frac{1}{2}mv^2 = \frac{1}{2}m\left(\sqrt{\frac{GM}{r}}\right)^2 = \frac{GMm}{2r} = 10^{10}$ J

(b) $U = -\frac{GMm}{r} = -2 \times 10^{10}$ J

(c) $E = K + U = -10^{10}$ J

5. $\Delta E = E_2 - E_1 = -\frac{GMm}{2(4R_E)} - \left(\frac{-GMm}{2(2R_E)}\right)$

$$= \frac{GMm}{8R_E} = \frac{mgR_E}{8} = 3.13 \times 10^9 \text{ J}$$

6. (a) $E_1 = \frac{-GMm}{2r} - \frac{GMm}{2r} = -\frac{GMm}{r}$

(b) Applying linear momentum conservation,

$$mv + m(-v) = 2mv'$$

$\Rightarrow \quad v' = 0$

So, the combined mass will come to rest and it will posses only potential energy.

$$E_2 = -\frac{-GMm}{r} - \frac{GMm}{r} = -\frac{2GMm}{r}$$

The combined mass will fall vertically down to earth.

5.8 Kepler's Laws

1. $T^2 \propto r^3 \Rightarrow \frac{T_1}{T_2} = \left(\frac{r_1}{r_2}\right)^{3/2}$

$$\Rightarrow \quad \frac{T_1}{1\text{ yr}} = \left(\frac{4r}{r}\right)^{3/2}$$

$\Rightarrow \quad T_1 = 8$ yr

2. Area $= \pi ab$, Areal velocity $= \frac{dA}{dt} = \frac{L}{2m}$

$$\Rightarrow \quad \pi ab = \left(\frac{L}{2m}\right)T$$

$$\Rightarrow \quad T = \frac{2\pi mab}{L}$$

3. $mv_1r_1 = mv_2r_2$

$\Rightarrow \quad 5 \times 10^3 \times 1.5 \times 10^7 = v_2(0.5 \times 10^7)$

$\Rightarrow \quad v_2 = 1.5 \times 10^4$ m/s

4. $a(1+e) = 6R$ ...(i)

$a(1-e) = 2R$ ...(ii)

From Eqs. (i) and (ii), we get $e = 0.5$

5. $mv_1a = mv_2b$ ...(i)

$$\frac{1}{2}mv_1^2 - \frac{GMm}{a} = \frac{1}{2}mv_2^2 - \frac{GMm}{b} \quad \text{...(ii)}$$

Solving Eqs., we get

$$v_1 = \sqrt{\frac{2GMb}{a(a+b)}}$$

So, $L = mv_1a = m\sqrt{\frac{2GMab}{a+b}}$

6. $mv_1r_1 = mv_2r_2$ ...(i)

$$\frac{1}{2}mv_1^2 - \frac{GMm}{r_1} = \frac{1}{2}mv_2^2 - \frac{GMm}{r_2} \quad \text{...(ii)}$$

Solving Eqs. (i) and (ii), we get

$$v_1 = \sqrt{\frac{2GMr_2}{r_1(r_1+r_2)}}$$

So, $E = K_1 + U_1 = \frac{1}{2}mv_1^2 - \frac{GMm}{r_1} = -\frac{GMm}{2a}$

LEVEL 2

Single Choice Correct Questions

1. $F = \dfrac{GM(M)}{(2R)^2} = \dfrac{GM^2}{4R^2}$

$F_{net} = 2F\cos 30° = \dfrac{\sqrt{3}GM^2}{4R^2}$

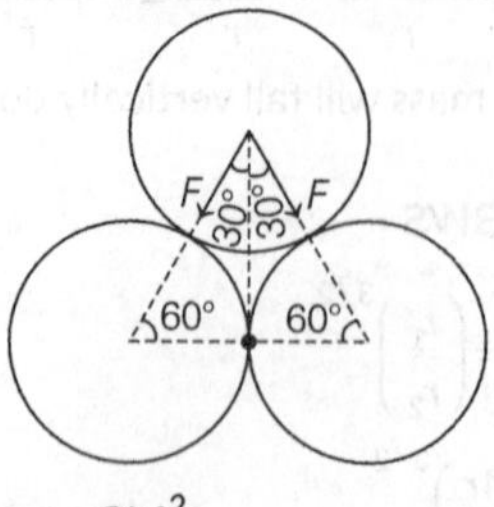

2. $F_1 = \dfrac{GM^2}{a^2}$ and $F_2 = \dfrac{GM^2}{(\sqrt{2}a)^2}$

Net force on $A = F_2 + 2F_1 \cos 45°$

$\Rightarrow \left(\dfrac{1}{2} + \sqrt{2}\right)\dfrac{GM^2}{a^2}$

$\Rightarrow \quad F_{net} = \dfrac{Mv^2}{r} = \left(\dfrac{2\sqrt{2}+1}{2}\right)\dfrac{GM^2}{a^2}$, where $r = \dfrac{a}{\sqrt{2}}$

$\Rightarrow v = \sqrt{\dfrac{GM(2\sqrt{2}+1)}{2\sqrt{2}a}}$

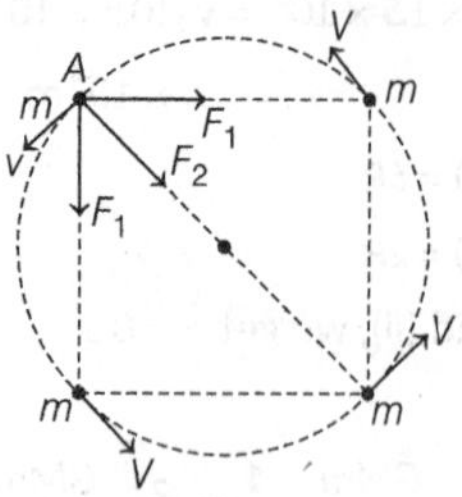

3. $F = mE = m\left(\dfrac{\sqrt{2}G\lambda}{R}\right)$,

where $\lambda = \dfrac{m}{(\pi R/2)} \Rightarrow F = \dfrac{2\sqrt{2}Gm^2}{\pi R^2}$

4. $E_1 = E_2$ because net gravitational field at P is zero.

5. If we keep another hemispherical shell over it to complete the sphere, then, net gravitational field at P due to both the hemispherical shells is zero. So, from symmetry, the gravitational field due to the hemispherical shell should be along c.

6. $F_1 = \dfrac{GMm}{(2R)^2}$, $F_2 = \dfrac{GMm}{(2R)^2} - \dfrac{G(M/8)m}{(3R/2)^2} = \dfrac{7GMm}{36R^2}$

So, $\dfrac{F_2}{F_1} = \dfrac{7}{9}$

7. Let distance of neutral point from smaller mass be x.

$$E = \frac{GM}{x^2} - \frac{G(4M)}{(6R-x)^2} = 0 \Rightarrow x = 2R$$

8. $a_1 = \dfrac{F}{m_1} = \dfrac{Gm_1m_2}{m_1r^2} = \dfrac{6.67 \times 10^{-11} \times 100}{(100)^2}$

$= 6.67 \times 10^{-13}\ \text{m/s}^2$

$a_2 = \dfrac{F}{m_2} = 6.67 \times 10^{-13}\ \text{m/s}^2$

$a_{rel} = a_1 - (-a_2) = 13.34 \times 10^{-13}\ \text{m/s}^2$

$s = ut + \dfrac{1}{2}at^2 \Rightarrow 0.01 = \dfrac{1}{2} \times 13.34 \times 10^{-13} t^2$

$\Rightarrow \quad t = 1.41$ days

9. $F = mE = m\left(\dfrac{GM_e(R_e - r)}{R_e^3}\right)$

10. $F = \dfrac{GM^2}{(L - 2L\sin\theta)^2} = \dfrac{GM^2}{L^2}$ $\quad [\because (\theta \to 0)]$

$T\sin\theta = F$ ...(i)

$T\cos\theta = Mg$ ...(ii)

Dividing Eqs. (i) by (ii)

$\theta = \tan^{-1}\left(\dfrac{GM}{gL^2}\right)$

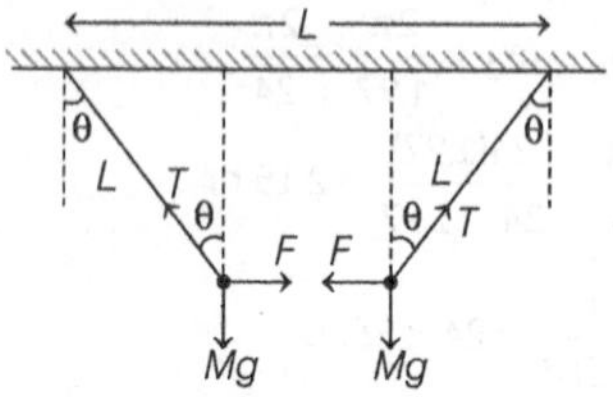

11. External force of the system is zero. So centre of mass of the system will not move.

$s_{CM} = \dfrac{Mx - 8M(9R - x)}{M + 8M} = 0$

$\Rightarrow \quad x = 8R$

12. When body is taken above the earth's surface,

$\dfrac{\Delta g}{g} \times 100 = -\dfrac{2h}{R} \times 100$

$\Rightarrow \quad -1\% = -\dfrac{2h}{R} \times 100$

$\Rightarrow \quad \dfrac{h}{R} \times 100 = 0.5\%$

When body is taken below the earth's surface,

$\dfrac{\Delta g}{g} \times 100 = -\dfrac{h}{R} \times 100 = -0.5\%$

So, weight decreases by 0.5%.

13. $g' = \dfrac{GM}{(R+h)^2} \Rightarrow \dfrac{g}{4} = \dfrac{GM}{R^2\left(1 + \dfrac{h}{R}\right)^2}$

$\Rightarrow \quad h = R$

14. On earth, $T = 2\pi\sqrt{\dfrac{l}{g}} = 2$

On planet, $g' = \frac{G(2M)}{(2R)^2} = \frac{g}{2}$

$$T' = 2\pi\sqrt{\frac{l}{(g/2)}} = \sqrt{2}T = 2\sqrt{2}\text{ s}$$

15. $g = \frac{GM}{R^2} = \frac{G\left(\rho\frac{4}{3}\pi R^3\right)}{R^2} = \frac{4}{3}G\rho\pi R$

$$\frac{g_1}{g_2} = \frac{\rho_1 r_1}{\rho_1 r_2} = \frac{r_1}{r_2} \qquad [\because (\rho_1 = \rho_2)]$$

16. $g' = \frac{G(M/10)}{(R/3)^2} = \frac{9g}{10}$

$$H' = \frac{u^2}{2\left(\frac{9g}{10}\right)} = \frac{10}{9} \Rightarrow H = \frac{10}{9} \times 90 = 100\text{ m}$$

17. $E = \frac{GMr}{r_A^3}$ (for $r < r_A$)

$= \frac{Gm}{r^2}$ (for $r_A \le r < r_B$)

$= \frac{2Gm}{r^2}$ for $r \ge r_B$

18. $g_{app} = g - \omega^2 R\cos^2\lambda = 0$

$$\Rightarrow \omega = 2\sqrt{\frac{g}{R}},\quad T = \frac{2\pi}{\omega} = \pi\sqrt{\frac{R}{g}}$$

19. $V = V_1 + V_2 + V_3 + \ldots\ldots$

$$= -\frac{Gm}{1} - \frac{Gm}{2} - \frac{Gm}{4} - \frac{Gm}{8}\ldots\ldots$$

$$= -Gm\left(1 + \frac{1}{2} + \frac{1}{4} + \frac{1}{8} + \ldots\ldots\right)$$

$$= -\frac{Gm(1)}{1 - \frac{1}{2}} = -2Gm$$

20.

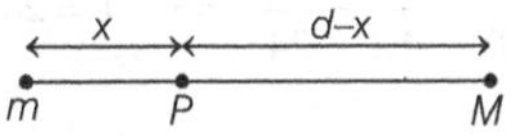

At P, $E = \frac{Gm}{x^2} - \frac{GM}{(d-x)^2} = 0$

$$\Rightarrow x = \frac{\sqrt{m}\,d}{\sqrt{M} + \sqrt{m}}$$

$$V = V_1 + V_2 = -\frac{Gm}{x} - \frac{GM}{d-x} = -\frac{G}{d}(\sqrt{M} + \sqrt{m})^2$$

21. $dV = -E\,dr$

$$\Rightarrow \int_{V_i}^{V} dV = +\int_{d_i}^{r} \frac{k}{r}\,dr$$

$$\Rightarrow V - V_i = +k\ln\left(\frac{r}{d_i}\right)$$

$$\Rightarrow V = V_i + k\ln\left(\frac{r}{d_i}\right)$$

22. $V = -\frac{Gm}{R} = -\frac{G\sigma(4\pi R^2)}{R} = -G\sigma 4\pi R$

$$\frac{V_A}{V_B} = \frac{R_A}{R_B} = \frac{3}{4}$$

When shells A and B coalesce into single shell,

$$\sigma 4\pi R_A^2 + \sigma 4\pi R_B^2 = \sigma 4\pi R_C^2$$

$$\Rightarrow R_C = \sqrt{R_A^2 + R_B^2}$$

$$V_c = -G\sigma 4\pi R_c = -G\sigma 4\pi\sqrt{R_A^2 + R_B^2}$$

$$\frac{V_C}{V_A} = \frac{\sqrt{R_A^2 + R_B^2}}{R_A} = \sqrt{1 + \left(\frac{R_B}{R_A}\right)^2} = \frac{5}{3}$$

23. $\rho = \frac{M}{\frac{4}{3}\pi((2R)^3 - R^3)} = \frac{3M}{28\pi R^3}$

$$V = V_1 - V_2 = -\frac{3}{2}\frac{G\rho\frac{4}{3}\pi(2R)^3}{2R} + \frac{3}{2}\frac{G\rho\frac{4}{3}\pi R^3}{R} = -\frac{9GM}{14R}$$

24. $W_{ext} + W_{gravitational} = \Delta K$

$$\Rightarrow -3 - 1(v_A - 0) = \frac{1}{2} \times 1 \times 2^2 - 0$$

$$\Rightarrow v_A = -5\text{ J/kg}$$

25. $W = m(V_B - V_A)$, work done is independent of the path taken.

So, $W_1 = W_2 = W_3$

26. $W = \Delta U = -\frac{Gm^2 \times 3}{2a} - \left(-\frac{Gm^2}{a} \times 3\right) = \frac{3Gm^2}{2a}$

27. $W = \Delta U = m\Delta V = m\left(0 - \left(-\frac{GM}{R}\right)\right) = \frac{GMm}{R}$

28. $U = -\frac{mgR}{1 + \frac{h}{R}}$, $U_1 = -mgR$, when $h = 0$,

$$U_2 = -\frac{5mgR}{6}, \text{ when } h = \frac{R}{5}$$

$$\Delta U = U_2 - U_1 = \frac{mgR}{6}$$

29. $K_1 + U_1 = K_2 + U_2$

$$\Rightarrow 0 - \frac{GMm}{R_0} = \frac{1}{2}mv^2 - \frac{GMm}{R} \Rightarrow v = \sqrt{2GM\left(\frac{1}{R} - \frac{1}{R_0}\right)}$$

30. Loss in gravitational PE = Gain in KE

$$\Rightarrow \frac{Gm_1m_2}{d} = \frac{1}{2}\mu v_{rel}^2 \text{ where } \mu = \frac{m_1m_2}{m_1 + m_2}$$

$$\Rightarrow v_{rel} = \sqrt{\frac{2G(m_1 + m_2)}{d}}$$

31. $K_1 + U_1 = K_2 + U_2$

$$\Rightarrow \frac{1}{2}m\left(\sqrt{\frac{4gR}{3}}\right)^2 - mgR = 0 - \frac{mgR}{1 + \frac{h_{max}}{R}}$$

$\Rightarrow h_{max} = 2R,$

$K_1 + U_1 = K_2 + U_2$

$$\Rightarrow \frac{1}{2}m\left(\sqrt{\frac{4gR}{3}}\right)^2 - mgR = \frac{1}{2}mv^2 - \frac{mgR}{1+\frac{R}{R}} \Rightarrow v = \sqrt{\frac{gR}{3}}$$

32. $V_A = -\frac{GM}{3R}; V_B = -\frac{GM}{2R^3}\left(3R^2 - \left(\frac{R}{2}\right)^2\right) = -\frac{11GM}{8R}$

$K_A + U_A = K_B + U_B$

$$\Rightarrow 0 + M\left(\frac{-GM}{3R}\right) = \frac{1}{2}Mv_B^2 + M\left(-\frac{11GM}{8R}\right)$$

$$\Rightarrow \quad v_B = \frac{5}{2}\sqrt{\frac{GM}{3R}}$$

33. Escape velocity is independent of the angle of projection.

34. $K_1 + U_1 = K_2 + U_2$

$$\Rightarrow \frac{1}{2}m(kv_e)^2 - \frac{GMm}{R} = 0 - \frac{GMm}{r}$$

$$\Rightarrow \quad \frac{1}{2}m\left(k\sqrt{\frac{2GM}{R}}\right)^2 - \frac{GMm}{R} = -\frac{GMm}{r}$$

$$\Rightarrow \quad r = \frac{R}{1-k^2}$$

35. $v_e = \sqrt{\frac{2GM}{R}} = \sqrt{\frac{2G\rho}{R}\left(\frac{4}{3}\pi R^3\right)} = \sqrt{\frac{8G\pi\rho R^2}{3}}$

$$\frac{v_1}{v_2} = \left(\sqrt{\frac{\rho_1}{\rho_2}}\right)\frac{R_1}{R_2} \Rightarrow \frac{v_1}{11} = 1(2)$$

$$\Rightarrow \quad v_1 = 22 \text{ km/s}$$

36. $K_1 + U_1 = K_2 + U_2$

$$\Rightarrow \frac{1}{2}m(2v_e)^2 - \frac{GMm}{R} = \frac{1}{2}mv^2 + 0$$

$$\Rightarrow v = \sqrt{4v_e^2 - v_e^2} = \sqrt{3}v_e = 11.2\sqrt{3} \text{ km/s}$$

37. $v = \omega R$

$$g_{app} = g - \omega^2 R = \frac{g}{2} \Rightarrow g = 2\omega^2 R$$

$$v_e = \sqrt{2gR} = \sqrt{2(2\omega^2 R)R}$$

$$= 2\omega R = 2v$$

38. Applying conservation of mechanical energy,

$$K_1 + U_1 = K_2 + U_2$$

$$\Rightarrow \frac{1}{2}mv_0^2 - \frac{GMm}{R} = \frac{1}{2}mv^2 - \frac{GMm}{(5R/2)} \quad \text{...(i)}$$

Applying angular momentum conservation about the centre of the moon,

$$m(v_0 \sin 30°)R = mv\left(\frac{5R}{2}\right) \quad \text{... (ii)}$$

Solving Eqs. (i) and (ii), we get

$$v_0 = \sqrt{\frac{5GM}{4R}}$$

39. $K_1 + U_1 = K_2 + U_2$

$$\Rightarrow \frac{1}{2}Mv_{min}^2 - M\left(\frac{-GM_1}{(d/2)} - \frac{GM_2}{(d/2)}\right) = 0 + 0$$

$$\Rightarrow \quad v_{min} = \sqrt{\frac{4G(M_1 + M_2)}{d}}$$

40. $v_0 = \sqrt{\frac{GM}{R}}, \; v = \sqrt{\frac{GM}{3R/2}} = \left(\sqrt{\frac{2}{3}}\right)v_0$

41. $F = \frac{GMm}{r^m} = m\omega^2 r \Rightarrow \omega = \frac{1}{r^{(m+1)/2}}$

$$T = \frac{2\pi}{\omega} \Rightarrow T \propto r^{(m+1)/2}$$

42. $T = 2\pi\sqrt{\frac{R^3}{GM}} = 2\pi\sqrt{\frac{R^3}{G\rho\left(\frac{4}{3}\pi R^3\right)}} = 2\pi\sqrt{\frac{3}{4G\rho\pi}}$

$$\frac{T_1}{T_2} = \sqrt{\frac{\rho_2}{\rho_1}} \Rightarrow 1 = \frac{\rho_2}{\rho_1} \Rightarrow \frac{\rho_1}{\rho_2} = 1$$

43. $T = 2\pi\sqrt{\frac{r^3}{GM}} = \frac{2\pi}{\omega_{earth}}$ ...(i)

$$2\pi\sqrt{\frac{r_1^3}{GM}} = \frac{2\pi}{(2\omega_{earth})} \quad \text{...(ii)}$$

On solving, we get

$$r_1 = \frac{r}{(4)^{1/3}}$$

44. When earth and satellite rotate in the opposite sense,

$$\omega_{rel} = \omega_1 + \omega_2$$

$$\Rightarrow \quad \frac{2\pi}{8} = \frac{2\pi}{T_1} + \frac{2\pi}{24}$$

$$\Rightarrow \quad T_1 = 12 \text{ h}$$

When earth and satellite rotate in the same sense,

$$\omega_{rel} = \omega_1 - \omega_2$$

$$\Rightarrow \quad \frac{2\pi}{T} = \frac{2\pi}{12} - \frac{2\pi}{24} \Rightarrow T = 24 \text{ h}$$

45. $T^2 \propto R^3$

$$\Rightarrow \quad 2\frac{\Delta T}{T} = 3\frac{\Delta R}{R}$$

$$\Rightarrow \quad \frac{\Delta T}{T} = \frac{3}{2}\frac{\Delta R}{R}$$

$$\Rightarrow \quad \frac{\Delta T}{T} \times 100 = \frac{3}{2}\left(\frac{1.02R - R}{R}\right) \times 100 = 3\%$$

46. Conserving linear momentum for explosion,

$$5M\sqrt{\frac{GM_e}{r}} = M\left(-\sqrt{\frac{GM_e}{r}}\right) + 4Mv_2$$

$$\Rightarrow \quad v_2 = \frac{3}{2}\sqrt{\frac{GM_e}{r}}$$

$$K_2 = \frac{1}{2}(4M)v_2^2 = \frac{9GM_eM}{2r}$$

$$U_2 = -\frac{G(4M)M_e}{r}$$

$$E_2 = K_2 + U_2 = \frac{GM_eM}{2r} > 0$$

So, 4M will be in an unbound orbit.

47. $\frac{GMm}{r^2} = m\omega_0^2 r \Rightarrow \omega_0 = \sqrt{\frac{GM}{r^3}}$

$\Rightarrow \quad GM = \omega_0^2 r^3$

$$g = \frac{GM}{R^2} = \frac{\omega_0^2 r^3}{R^2}$$

48. $E = \frac{U}{2} = -K = -\frac{GMm}{2r}$

49. $E_1 = U_1 + K_1 = -mgR + 0$

$E_2 = -\frac{GMm}{2(3R)} = -\frac{mgR}{6}$

$\Delta E = E_2 - E_1 = \frac{5\,mgR}{6}$

50. $E_1 = -\frac{GMm}{2(3R)} = \frac{-GMm}{6R}$

$E_2 = -\frac{GMm}{2(4R)} = -\frac{GMm}{8R}$

$\Delta E = E_2 - E_1 = \frac{GMm}{24R}$

$= \frac{mgR}{24} = \frac{1000 \times 9.8 \times 6.4 \times 10^6}{24} = 2.61 \times 10^9$ J

51. $v = \sqrt{\frac{GM}{R}} = \sqrt{gR}$

$v_e = \sqrt{2gR}$

Additional velocity to be imparted $= v_e - v$

$= (\sqrt{2} - 1)\sqrt{gR}$

$= 3.3$ km/s

52. $a = \frac{r_1 + r_2}{2}, T^2 \propto a^3$

$\Rightarrow \quad T^2 \propto (r_1 + r_2)^3$

$\Rightarrow \quad T \propto (r_1 + r_2)^{3/2}$

53. $\frac{dA}{dt} = \frac{A}{t_1} = \frac{A}{t_2} \Rightarrow t_1 = t_2$

54. Angular momentum is conserved.

So, $L_1 = L_2$

$mv_1r_1 = mv_2r_2 \Rightarrow v_2 > v_1 \quad (\because r_2 < r_1)$

$\Rightarrow \quad K_2 > K_1$

55. $T^2 \propto r^3 \Rightarrow \frac{T_1}{T_2} = \left(\frac{r_1}{r_2}\right)^{3/2}$

$\Rightarrow \quad \frac{T_1}{365} = \left(\frac{r/2}{r}\right)^{3/2}$

$\Rightarrow T_1 = \frac{365}{2\sqrt{2}} = 129$ days

56. $\frac{dA}{dt} = \frac{A}{T}$

$\Rightarrow \quad \frac{L}{2m} = \frac{A}{T} \Rightarrow L = \frac{2mA}{T}$

57. $r_p = a(1-e)\,;\, r_a = a(1+e)$

$mv_pr_p = mv_ar_a \Rightarrow \frac{v_p}{v_a} = \frac{1+e}{1-e}$

58. $mv_1r_1 = mv_2r_2$ ...(i)

$\frac{1}{2}mv_1^2 - \frac{GMm}{r_1} = \frac{1}{2}mv_2^2 - \frac{GMm}{r_2}$ ...(ii)

Solving Eqs. (i) and (ii), we get

$$v_1 = \sqrt{\frac{2GMr_2}{r_1(r_1 + r_2)}}$$

So, $E = K_1 + U_1 = \frac{1}{2}mv_1^2 - \frac{GMm}{r_1}$

$= -\frac{GMm}{2a} = \text{constant}$

Now, $\frac{1}{2}mv^2 - \frac{GMm}{r} = -\frac{GMm}{2a}$

$\Rightarrow \quad v = \sqrt{GM\left(\frac{2}{r} - \frac{1}{a}\right)}$

Numerical Value Questions

1. $CP = \frac{R}{\cos 60°} = 2R,$

$v = \sqrt{\frac{GM}{r}} = \sqrt{\frac{GM}{2R}}$

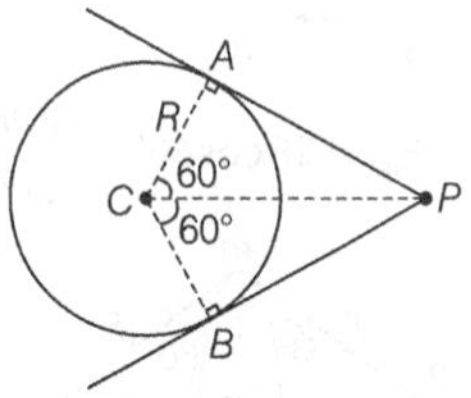

2. $v = \frac{v_e}{2} \Rightarrow \sqrt{\frac{GM}{r}} = \frac{1}{2}\sqrt{\frac{2GM}{R}}$

$\Rightarrow \quad r = 2R$

Applying mechanical energy conservation,

$K_1 + U_1 = K_2 + U_2$

$\Rightarrow \quad 0 - \frac{GMm}{2R} = \frac{1}{2}mv^2 - \frac{GMm}{R}$

$\Rightarrow \quad v = \sqrt{\frac{GM}{R}} = \sqrt{gR}$ = 8 km/s

3. $r_1 = 1.8 \times 10^{12}$ m

$a = 2 \times 10^{12}$ m

$r_2 = 2a - r_1 = 2.2 \times 10^{12}$ m

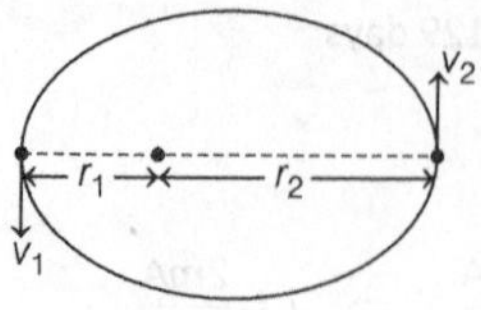

$$\frac{dA}{dt}=\frac{L}{2m}=\frac{v_2 r_2}{2}$$

$$\Rightarrow 4.4\times10^{16}=\frac{v_2(2.2\times10^{12})}{2} \quad \Rightarrow \quad v_2 = 40 \text{ km/s}$$

4. $g' = g\left(1-\frac{h}{R}\right) = g\left(1-\frac{64}{6400}\right) = 0.99g$

$$T = 2\pi\sqrt{\frac{l}{g}} \quad \Rightarrow \quad \frac{\Delta T}{T} = \frac{1}{2}\frac{\Delta g}{g}$$

$$\Rightarrow \quad \frac{\Delta T}{2} = \frac{1}{2}\left(\frac{g-0.99g}{g}\right)$$

$$\Rightarrow \quad \Delta T = 0.01 \text{ s}$$

5. Areal velocity, $= \frac{L}{2m} = \frac{vr}{2} = \left(\sqrt{\frac{Gm}{r}}\right)\frac{r}{2} \propto \sqrt{r}$

$$\frac{(\text{Areal velocity})_1}{(\text{Areal velocity})_2} = \frac{\sqrt{r_1}}{\sqrt{r_2}} = 2$$

$$\Rightarrow \quad \frac{r_1}{r_2} = 4$$

6. $K_1 + U_1 = K_2 + U_2$

$$\Rightarrow \frac{1}{2}m_0\left(\sqrt{\frac{5GM_e}{4R}}\right)^2 - \frac{GM_e m_o}{R} = 0 - \frac{GM_e m_o}{r}$$

$$\Rightarrow \quad r = \frac{8R}{3}$$

$$h = r - R = \frac{8R}{3} - R = \frac{5R}{3}$$

7. $F = \frac{GMm}{(2r)^2} \quad \Rightarrow \quad F_{net} = 2F\cos 60° = \frac{GMm}{4r^2}$

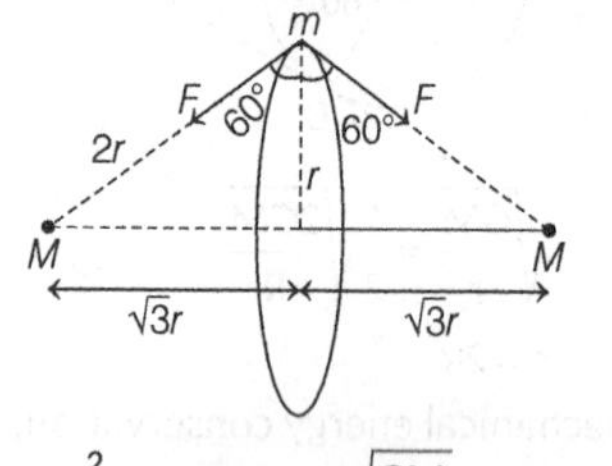

$$\frac{GMm}{4r^2} = \frac{mv^2}{r} \quad \Rightarrow \quad v = \sqrt{\frac{GM}{4r}}$$

8. Let speed of projection be v.

$$R_{max} = \frac{v^2 \sin 90°}{g} = 10 \quad \Rightarrow \quad v = \sqrt{10g}$$

$$v_e = \sqrt{\frac{2GM}{R}} = \sqrt{\frac{2G\left(\frac{\rho 4}{3}\pi R^3\right)}{R}} = R\sqrt{\frac{8\pi G\rho}{3}}$$

Let escape velocity for earth be v_e and for the planet be v_P,

$$\frac{v_e}{v_P} = \frac{R_e}{R_P}\sqrt{\frac{\rho_e}{\rho_P}}$$

$$\Rightarrow \quad \frac{\sqrt{2gR_e}}{\sqrt{10g}} = \frac{R_e}{R_P}\sqrt{\frac{\rho_e}{2\rho_e}}$$

$$\Rightarrow \quad R_P = \sqrt{2.5R_e} = 4 \text{ km}$$

9. Let C be the midpoint of the line joining C_1 and C_2. Gravitational field Intensity at C is zero. So, we just need to make the point mass reach C with negligible velocity. Once it crosses C, it will be pulled by the second sphere.

Applying energy conservation between A and C

$$K_1 + U_1 = K_2 + U_2$$

$$\Rightarrow \quad \frac{1}{2}mv_0^2 + m\left(\frac{-GM}{R} - \frac{GM}{9R}\right) = 0 + m\left(\frac{-GM}{5R} - \frac{GM}{5R}\right)$$

$$\Rightarrow \quad v_0 = \frac{8}{3}\sqrt{\frac{GM}{5R}}$$

10. Let speed of the ball just before first collision be v_1.

$$K_1 + U_1 = K_2 + U_2$$

$$\Rightarrow \quad 0 - \frac{GMm}{R} = \frac{1}{2}mv_1^2 - \frac{3GM}{2R}$$

$$\Rightarrow \quad v_1 = \sqrt{\frac{GM}{R}}$$

Speed of ball just after Ist collision,

$$v_2 = ev_1 = \frac{1}{5}\sqrt{\frac{GM}{R}}$$

Lets take maximum height reached to be h after first collision,

$$K_1 + U_1 = K_2 + U_2$$

$$\frac{1}{2}m\left(\frac{1}{5}\sqrt{\frac{GM}{R}}\right)^2 - \frac{3GMm}{2R} = 0 - \frac{GMm}{2R^3}(3R^2 - h^2)$$

$$\Rightarrow \quad h = \frac{R}{5}$$

Total distance travelled before second collision

$$= R + 2h = \frac{7R}{5}$$

LEVEL 3

Single Choice Correct Questions

1. $g_1 = g$ and $g_2 = 0$

$$y_{cg} = \frac{(m_1g_1)y_1 + (m_2g_2)y_2}{m_1g_1 + m_2g_2} = \frac{mgR + 0}{mg + 0} = R$$

$$y_{cm} = \frac{m_1y_1 + m_2y_2}{m_1 + m_2} = \frac{mR + 0}{m + m} = \frac{R}{2}$$

$$y_{cg} - y_{cm} = R - \frac{R}{2} = \frac{R}{2}$$

2.

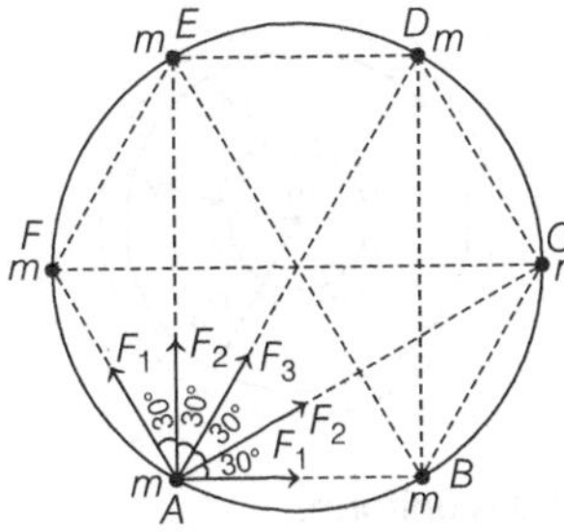

$$F_1 = \frac{Gm^2}{a^2}; F_2 = \frac{Gm^2}{(\sqrt{3}a)^2}; F_3 = \frac{Gm^2}{(2a)^2}$$

Net force on $A = F_3 + 2F_2 \cos 30° + 2F_1 \cos 60°$

$$= \frac{Gm^2}{a^2}\left(\frac{1}{4} + \frac{1}{\sqrt{3}} + 1\right) = \frac{Gm^2}{a^2}\left(\frac{5\sqrt{3}+4}{4\sqrt{3}}\right)$$

Centripetal force of $A = m\omega^2 a = \frac{Gm^2}{a^2}\left(\frac{5\sqrt{3}+4}{4\sqrt{3}}\right)$

$$\Rightarrow \qquad \omega = \sqrt{\frac{Gm}{a^3}\left(\frac{5\sqrt{3}+4}{4\sqrt{3}}\right)}$$

$$\Rightarrow \qquad T = \frac{2\pi}{\omega} = 2\pi\sqrt{\frac{4\sqrt{3}a^3}{Gm(5\sqrt{3}+4)}}$$

3. Lets take an element of mass dm on the ring.

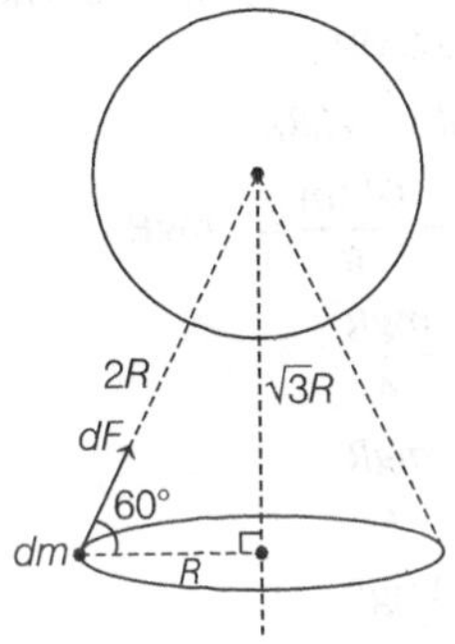

$$dF = dm\frac{GM}{(2R)^2}$$

$$F_{net} = \int dF \sin 60° = \int dm \frac{GM}{(2R)^2}\sin 60°$$

$$= \frac{\sqrt{3}Gm}{8R^2}\int dm = \frac{\sqrt{3}GMm}{8R^2}$$

4. Lets first calculate gravitation field intensity due to the rod at origin.

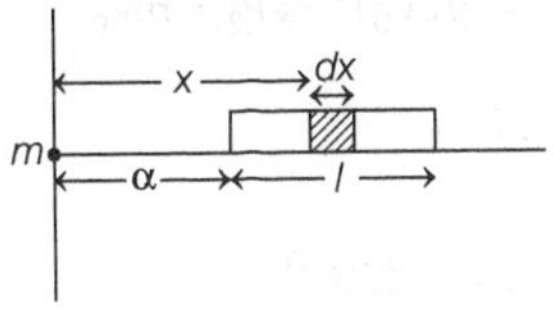

$$dm = (a + bx^2)dx$$

$$\int dE = \int_{\alpha}^{l+\alpha} \frac{G(a+bx^2)\,dx}{x^2}$$

$$E = G\left[-\frac{a}{x} + bx\right]_{\alpha}^{l+\alpha} = G\left(a\left(\frac{1}{\alpha} - \frac{1}{l+\alpha}\right) + bl\right)$$

$$F = mE = Gm\left(a\left(\frac{1}{\alpha} - \frac{1}{l+\alpha}\right) + bl\right)$$

5. Consider a small elemental spherical shell,
$dm = (kr)(4\pi r^2 dr)$

$\Rightarrow M = k\pi r^4$ = Total mass of sphere of radius r

Pressure × Area = weight = dmg

$$\Rightarrow \quad -dp \times 4\pi r^2 = \frac{Gm}{r^2}dm \Rightarrow -dp = \frac{Gk\pi r^4 \times (kr)4\pi r^2 dr}{4\pi r^4}$$

$$\Rightarrow \qquad -dp = Gk^2\pi r^3 dr$$

Pressure will increase from surface to centre.

$$-\int_0^p dp = Gk^2\pi\int_R^r r^3 dr \Rightarrow p = k^2G\pi\left(\frac{R^4 - r^4}{4}\right)$$

6. Gauss law for gravitation, $\int \mathbf{g}.ds = -m_{in}(4\pi G)$

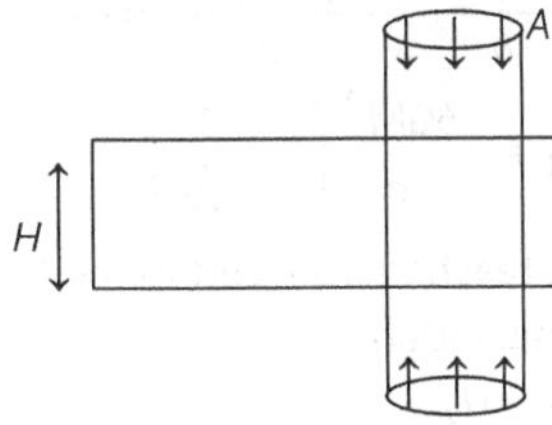

$$\Rightarrow \qquad 2\left(\frac{GM}{R^2}\right)A = \left(\frac{M}{\frac{4}{3}\pi R^3}\right)(AH)4\pi G \Rightarrow H = \frac{2R}{3}$$

7. $$g_1 = \int_0^R \frac{G(\rho_1 4\pi x^2 dx)}{(2R)^2} + \int_R^{2R} \frac{G\rho_2 4\pi x^2 dx}{(2R)^2} = \frac{G\pi R}{3}(\rho_1 + 7\rho_2)$$

$$g_2 = \int_0^R \frac{G(\rho_1 4\pi x^2 dx)}{R^2} = \frac{4G\pi R\rho_1}{3}$$

$$g_1 = g_2 \Rightarrow \frac{G\pi R}{3}(\rho_1 + 7\rho_2) = \frac{4G\pi R\rho_1}{3} \Rightarrow \frac{\rho_1}{\rho_2} = \frac{7}{3}$$

8. Net torque $= (mg_2)\frac{l}{2} - (mg_1)\left(\frac{l}{2}\right)$

$$= m\left(g\left(1 - \frac{2H_2}{R}\right)\right)\frac{l}{2} - m\left(g\left(1 - \frac{2H_1}{R}\right)\right)\frac{l}{2} = \frac{mg}{R}(H_1 - H_2)l$$

9. $$p = \rho_{atm}gh = \frac{m}{\frac{4}{3}\pi[(R+h)^3 - R^3]}\left(\frac{GM}{R^2}\right)h$$

$$\Rightarrow \qquad p = \frac{m}{\frac{4}{3}\pi R^3\left[\left(1 + \frac{h}{R}\right)^3 - 1\right]}\left(\frac{G\left(\rho\frac{4}{3}\pi R^3\right)}{R^2}\right)h$$

$$\Rightarrow \qquad p = \frac{mG\rho}{3R} \Rightarrow m \propto \frac{pR}{\rho}$$

10. $a_{body} = g \Rightarrow a_{earth} = \frac{2Mg}{M} = 2g$

$a_{rel} = g - (-2g) = 3g$

$s = ut + \frac{1}{2}at^2$

$\Rightarrow H = \frac{1}{2}(3g)t^2 \Rightarrow t = \sqrt{\frac{2H}{3g}}$

11. $\sigma = \frac{M}{\pi(4R)^2 - (3R)^2} = \frac{M}{7\pi R^2}$

$V_p = -\int_{3R}^{4R} \frac{G(\sigma 2\pi x\, dx)}{\sqrt{x^2 + (4R)^2}} = -\frac{2GM}{7R}(4\sqrt{2} - 5)$

$W_{ext} = m\Delta V = m(V_\infty - V_p) = \frac{2GMm}{7R}(4\sqrt{2} - 5)$

12. $U_1 = -\frac{G(2m)m}{a} - \frac{G(3m)m}{a} - \frac{G(3m)(2m)}{\sqrt{2}a} = -\frac{Gm^2}{a}(5 + 3\sqrt{2})$

$U_2 = -\frac{Gm(3m)}{a} - \frac{Gm(2m)}{a} - \frac{G(2m)(3m)}{a} = -\frac{11Gm^2}{a}$

$W_{ext} = \Delta U = U_2 - U_1 = -\frac{6GM^2}{a}\left(1 - \frac{1}{\sqrt{2}}\right)$

13. Let maximum height reached from surface be h.
Applying energy conservation,

$K_1 + U_1 = K_2 + U_2$

$\Rightarrow \frac{1}{2}m\left(\sqrt{\frac{2GM}{R}}\right)^2 - \frac{GMm}{2R^3}\left(3R^2 - \left(\frac{99R}{100}\right)^2\right) = 0 - \frac{GMm}{R+h}$

$\Rightarrow \frac{GMm}{R} - \frac{2.0199GMm}{2R} = -\frac{GMm}{R+h}$

$\Rightarrow h = 99.5\,R$

14. Conserving angular momentum about the centre of earth,

$mv_0R = mv(4R)$ ...(i)

Conserving mechanical energy of the system,

$K_1 + U_1 = K_2 + U_2$

$\Rightarrow \frac{1}{2}mv_0^2 - \frac{GMm}{R} = \frac{1}{2}mv^2 - \frac{GMm}{4R}$ ...(ii)

Solving Eqs. (i) and (ii), we get

$v_0 = \sqrt{\frac{8gR}{5}}$

15. Applying angular momentum conservation about the centre of earth,

$m(v_0 \sin 60°)R = mvr$ ...(i)

Applying mechanical energy conservation,

$K_1 + U_1 = K_2 + U_2$

$\Rightarrow \frac{1}{2}mv_0^2 - \frac{GMm}{R} = \frac{1}{2}mv^2 - \frac{GMm}{r}$ ...(ii)

Solving Eqs. (i) and (ii), we get

$r = \frac{3R}{2}$, So $h = r - R = \frac{R}{2}$

16.

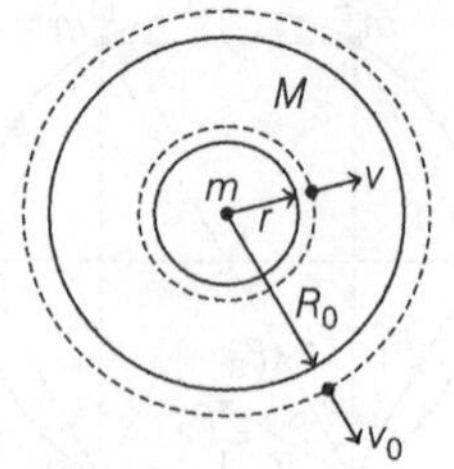

Density of cloud is uniform.

So, $\rho_1 = \rho_2 \Rightarrow \frac{m}{\frac{4}{3}\pi r^3} = \frac{M}{\frac{4}{3}\pi R^3} \Rightarrow r = \left(\frac{m}{M}\right)^{1/3} R$

$\Rightarrow \frac{dr}{dt} = \left(\frac{m}{M}\right)^{1/3}\frac{dR}{dt} \Rightarrow v = \left(\frac{r}{R_0}\right)v_0$

$K = \int dK = \int_0^{R_0} \frac{1}{2}\left(\frac{M}{\frac{4}{3}\pi R^3}\right)(4\pi r^2 dr)\left(\frac{r v_0}{R_0}\right)^2 = \frac{3}{10}Mv_0^2$

Applying energy conservation

$K_1 + U_1 = K_2 + U_2$

$\Rightarrow \frac{3}{10}Mv_0^2 - \frac{3}{5}\frac{GM^2}{R_0} = 0 - \frac{3}{5}\frac{GM^2}{R}$

[$\because K_2 = 0$ when expansion ceases]

$\Rightarrow R = \frac{2GMR_0}{2GM - v_0^2R_0}$

17. $E_1 = K_1 + U_1 = 0 - \frac{GMm}{R} = -mgR$

$E_2 = -\frac{GMm}{2(2R)} = -\frac{mgR}{4}$

$E_3 = -\frac{GMm}{2(3R)} = -\frac{mgR}{6}$

$\Delta E_1 = E_2 - E_1 = \frac{3mgR}{4}$

$\Delta E_2 = E_3 - E_2 = \frac{mgR}{12}$

18. $v_0 + \frac{P_1}{m} = v_e \Rightarrow v_0 + \frac{P_1}{m} = \sqrt{2}v_0 \Rightarrow P_1 = mv_0(\sqrt{2} - 1)$

$\sqrt{v_0^2 + \left(\frac{P_2}{m}\right)^2} = v_e$

$\Rightarrow v_0^2 + \left(\frac{P_2}{m}\right)^2 = (\sqrt{2}v_0)^2 \Rightarrow P_2 = mv_0$

So, $\frac{P_1}{P_2} = \sqrt{2} - 1$

19. $E_i = -\frac{GM_em}{2r}; E_f = -\frac{GM_em}{2R_e}$

$\Rightarrow E_i - E_f = kt$

$\Rightarrow \frac{-GM_em}{2r} + \frac{GM_em}{2R_e} = kt \Rightarrow r = \frac{GM_emR_e}{GM_em - 2kR_et}$

20. $g=\omega^2R \Rightarrow \omega=\sqrt{\frac{g}{R}}$

$$\Sigma\tau=I\alpha \Rightarrow 2TR=(MR^2)\alpha \Rightarrow \alpha=\frac{2T}{MR}$$

$$\omega=\omega_0+\alpha t \Rightarrow \sqrt{\frac{g}{R}}=\left(\frac{2T}{MR}\right)t \Rightarrow t=\frac{M\sqrt{gR}}{2T}$$

21. On stopping, the satellite will fall along the radius r of the orbit which can be regarded as a limiting case of an ellipse with semi-major axis $\frac{r}{2}$.

Using Kepler's third law,

$$T\propto r^{3/2} \text{ and } T_1\propto\left(\frac{r}{2}\right)^{3/2} \Rightarrow T_1=\frac{T}{\sqrt{8}}$$

$$\text{Time of fall}=\frac{T_1}{2}=\frac{\sqrt{2}T}{8}$$

22. Before collision, $v_0=\sqrt{\frac{GM}{2R}}$

Applying linear momentum conservation for explosion,

$$mv_0=\frac{m}{2}(0)+\left(\frac{m}{2}\right)v \Rightarrow v=2v_0$$

$$\Delta E=\Delta K=K_2-K_1$$

$$=\frac{1}{2}\left(\frac{m}{2}\right)(2v_0)^2-\frac{1}{2}mv_0^2=\frac{mv_0^2}{2}=\frac{GMm}{4R}=\frac{mgR}{4}$$

23. $K_1+U_1=K_2+U_2$

$$\Rightarrow 0+\left(\frac{-GMm}{2R}+0\right)$$

$$=0+\left(\frac{-GMm}{2R^3}\left(3R^2-\left(\frac{R}{2}\right)^2\right)+\frac{1}{2}K\left(\frac{R}{2}\right)^2\right) \Rightarrow K=\frac{7GMm}{R^3}$$

24. $g>\omega^2R \Rightarrow \frac{G\rho\left(\frac{4}{3}\pi R^3\right)}{R^2}>\left(\frac{2\pi}{T}\right)^2R$

$$T_{min}=\sqrt{\frac{3\pi}{G\rho}}=1s$$

25. The net gravitational force on a given star provides the necessary centripetal force.

$$\frac{GMm}{r^2}+\frac{G(m)(m)}{(2r)^2}=m\omega^2r \Rightarrow \omega=\sqrt{\frac{G(4M+m)}{4r^3}}$$

$$T=\frac{2\pi}{\omega}=\frac{4\pi r^{3/2}}{\sqrt{G(4M+m)}}$$

26. $b=a\sqrt{1-e^2}=\frac{\sqrt{3}a}{2}$

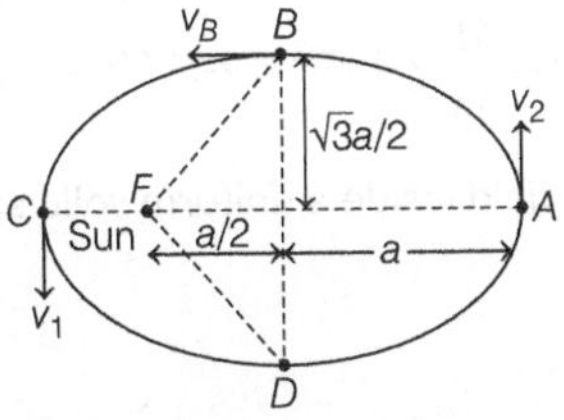

From conservation of angular momentum,

$$mv_2\left(a+\frac{a}{2}\right)=mv_B\left(\frac{\sqrt{3}a}{2}\right) \Rightarrow v_B=\sqrt{3}v_2$$

Since, areal velocity is constant, time required will be proportional to area swept.

$$\frac{T_{DAB}}{T_{BCD}}=\frac{\text{Area of FDAB}}{\text{Area of FBCD}}=\frac{\frac{\pi ab}{2}+\frac{1}{2}(\sqrt{3}a)\left(\frac{a}{2}\right)}{\frac{\pi ab}{2}-\frac{1}{2}(\sqrt{3}a)\left(\frac{a}{2}\right)}=\frac{\pi+1}{\pi-1}$$

27.

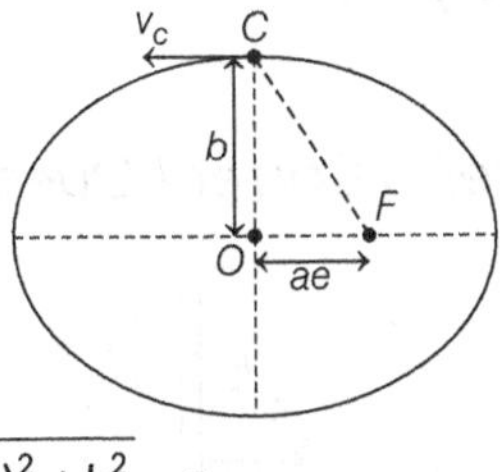

$$CF=\sqrt{(ae)^2+b^2}=a$$

At C, $E=-\frac{GMm}{2a}$

$$\Rightarrow \frac{1}{2}mv_c^2-\frac{GMm}{a}=-\frac{GMm}{2a} \Rightarrow v_c=\sqrt{\frac{GM}{a}}$$

28. For elliptical orbit, $a=\frac{2R+R}{2}=\frac{3R}{2}$

At the point of maximum distance,

$$\frac{1}{2}mv_0^2-\frac{GMm}{2R}=-\frac{GMm}{2(3R/2)}$$

$$\Rightarrow v_0=\sqrt{\frac{GM}{3R}}$$

For circular orbit, $v=\sqrt{\frac{GM}{(2R)}}=\left(\sqrt{\frac{3}{2}}\right)v_0$

29. $L=mv_1r_1=mv_2r_2$

$$\Rightarrow(\omega_1r_1)r_1=(\omega_2r_2)r_2 \Rightarrow \frac{\omega_1}{\omega_2}=\frac{r_2^2}{r_1^2} \Rightarrow \omega_1=\left(\frac{r_{min}}{r_{max}}\right)^2\omega$$

30.

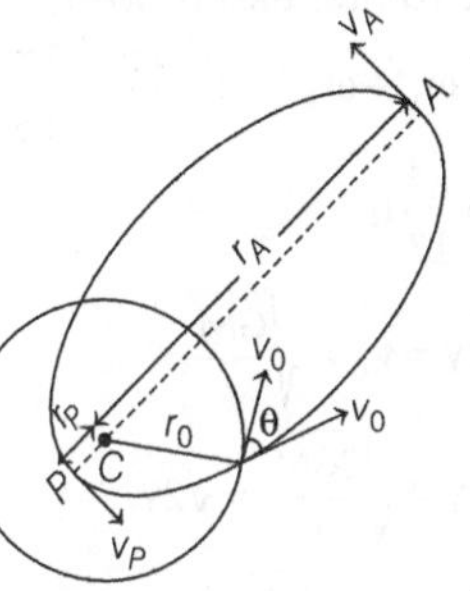

Applying conservation of angular momentum about C

$$mv_pr_p=mv_Ar_A=mv_0r_0\cos\theta$$

$$\Rightarrow v_Ar_A=v_pr_p=\frac{3v_0r_0}{5}$$

Applying conservation of energy

$$\frac{1}{2}mv_A^2 - \frac{GMm}{r_A} = \frac{1}{2}mv_0^2 - \frac{GMm}{r_0}$$

$$\Rightarrow \frac{9v_0^2r_0^2}{50r_A^2} - \frac{v_0^2r_0}{r_A} + \frac{v_0^2}{2} = 0$$

$$\Rightarrow 9\left(\frac{r_0}{r_A}\right)^2 - 50\left(\frac{r_0}{r_A}\right) + 25 = 0$$

$$\Rightarrow \frac{r_0}{r_A} = \frac{5}{9} \Rightarrow r_A = \frac{9r_0}{5} \text{ and } r_p = \frac{r_0}{5}$$

So, $\frac{v_p}{v_A} = \frac{r_A}{r_p} = 9$

Multiple Choice(s) Correct Questions

1.

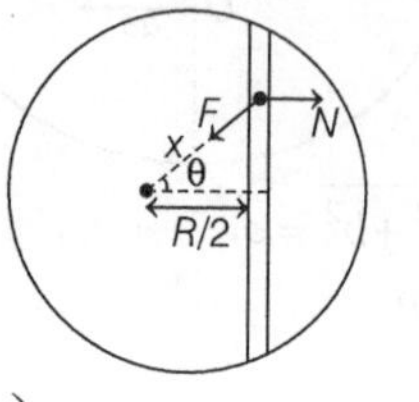

$$F = \left(\frac{GMx}{R^3}\right)m$$

$$N = F\cos\theta = \left(\frac{GMm}{R^3}\right) x \left(\frac{R/2}{x}\right) = \frac{GMm}{2R^2} = \text{constant}$$

$$a = \frac{F\sin\theta}{m} = \frac{GM}{R^3}\sqrt{x^2 - \frac{R^2}{4}}$$

2. Since, both the spheres are cutout symmetrically, gravitational field at the origin is zero. Gravitational field at (2, 0, 0) will be non-zero.

All the points on the given circle are symmetrically located w.r.t. the remaining sphere. So, potential will be same at all points on the given circles in *YZ*-plane.

3. When satellite rotates west to east, $\omega_{rel} = \omega_1 - \omega_2$

$$\Rightarrow \frac{2\pi}{T} = \frac{2\pi}{1.5} - \frac{2\pi}{24} \Rightarrow T = 1.6 \text{ h}$$

When satellite rotates east to west,

$$\omega_{rel} = \omega_1 + \omega_2 \Rightarrow \frac{2\pi}{T} = \frac{2\pi}{1.5} + \frac{2\pi}{24}$$

$$\Rightarrow T = \frac{24}{17} \text{ h}$$

4. Orbital velocity $= v_0 = \sqrt{\frac{GM}{r}}$

Escape velocity $= \sqrt{\frac{2GM}{r}} = \sqrt{2}v_0$

5. Gravitational force will decrease in magnitude but it is still directed towards the centre of the earth. So, torque of gravitational force is zero about the centre and angular momentum will be conserved.

$L = mvr$ = constant

$$F = \frac{GMm}{r^2} = \frac{mv^2}{r} \Rightarrow r \propto \frac{1}{G} \qquad [\because v^2r^2 = \text{constant}]$$

Hence, as *G* decreases, *r* increases.

$$U = -\frac{GMm}{r}$$

As *G* decreases and *r* increases $\frac{GMm}{r}$ will decrease and *U* will increase.

6. (a) $T^2 \propto R^3 \Rightarrow \frac{T_1}{T_2}\left(\frac{R_1}{R_2}\right)^{3/2} = \frac{1}{8}$

(b) $v \propto \frac{1}{\sqrt{r}} \Rightarrow \frac{v_1}{v_2} = \sqrt{\frac{r_2}{r_1}} = 2:1$

(c) $L = mvr \Rightarrow L \propto \sqrt{r} \Rightarrow \frac{L_1}{L_2} = \frac{1}{2}$

(d) When both have velocity in opposite direction

$$(\omega_{rel})_1 = \frac{2v + v}{5R} = \frac{3v}{5R}$$

When both have velocity in same direction

$$(\omega_{rel})_2 = \frac{2v - v}{3R} = \frac{v}{3R} \Rightarrow \frac{(\omega_{rel})_1}{(\omega_{rel})_2} = \frac{9}{5}$$

7. (A, B, C, D) Informative.

8. $g = \frac{GM}{R^2} = \frac{G\left(\rho\frac{4}{3}\pi R^3\right)}{R^2} \Rightarrow g \propto R$

$$v_e = \sqrt{\frac{2GM}{R}} = \sqrt{\frac{2G\rho\frac{4}{3}\pi R^3}{R}} \Rightarrow v_e \propto R$$

Hence, $\frac{g_1}{g_2} = \frac{R_1}{R_2} = 2, \frac{g_1}{g_3} = \frac{R_1}{R_3} = 3$

$$\frac{v_1}{v_2} = \frac{R_1}{R_2} = 2, \frac{v_1}{v_3} = \frac{R_1}{R_3} = 3$$

9.

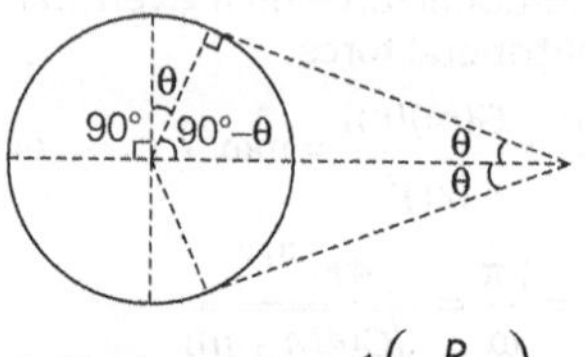

Minimum co-latitude $= \theta = \sin^{-1}\left(\frac{R}{R+h}\right)$

Ω = solid angle $= 2\pi(1 - \cos(90° + \theta)) = 2\pi(1 + \sin\theta)$

Area escaped $= \frac{\Omega}{4\pi} \times 4\pi R^2 = 2\pi R^2(1 + \sin\theta)$

10. Gravitational field inside a uniform solid sphere $= -\frac{4\pi G\rho r}{3}$

At point *P*,

$$E = E_1 - E_2 = \frac{4\pi G\rho}{3}PC_1 - \frac{4\pi G\rho}{3}PC_2 = \frac{4\pi G\rho}{3}(C_2C_1)$$

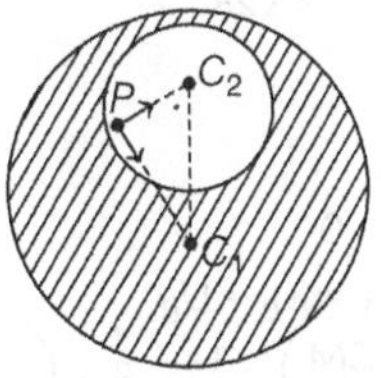

Hence, gravitational field inside cavity is uniform.

$$E = \frac{4\pi G\rho}{3}\left(\frac{2R}{3}\right) = \frac{8\pi G\rho R}{9}$$

At $C_2, V = V_1 - V_2$

$$= -\frac{GM}{2R^3}\left(3R^2 - \left(\frac{2R}{3}\right)^2\right) - \left(\frac{-3}{2}\frac{(GM/27)}{(R/3)}\right)$$

$$= -\frac{10GM}{9R}$$

$K_1 + U_1 = K_2 + U_2$

$$\Rightarrow \frac{1}{2}mv_e^2 - \frac{10GMm}{9R} = 0 + 0 \Rightarrow v_e = \sqrt{\frac{20GM}{9R}}$$

11.

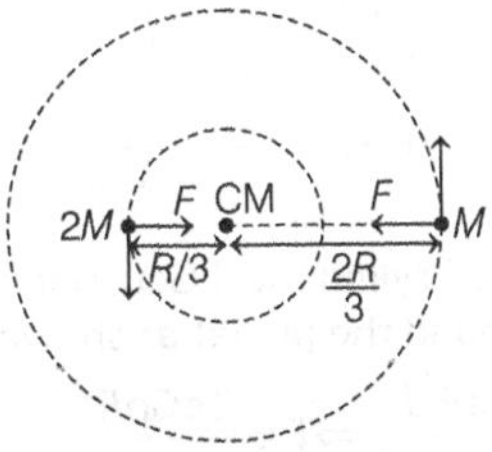

$$F = \frac{G(2M)(M)}{R^2} = M\omega^2\left(\frac{2R}{3}\right) \Rightarrow \omega = \sqrt{\frac{3GM}{R^3}}$$

Hence, $T = \frac{2\pi}{\omega} = \frac{2\pi}{\sqrt{3GM}}R^{3/2}$

$$v_1 = \omega\left(\frac{2R}{3}\right) \text{ and } v_2 = \omega\left(\frac{R}{3}\right)$$

$$K_1 = \frac{1}{2}mv_1^2 \text{ and } K_2 = \frac{1}{2}(2M)v_2^2$$

Hence, $\frac{K_1}{K_2} = 2$

12. (b) $\frac{T_1}{T_2} = \left(\frac{R_1}{R_2}\right)^{3/2} \Rightarrow \frac{T_2}{T} = \left(\frac{2r}{r}\right)^{3/2} \Rightarrow T_2 = 2\sqrt{2}T$

(c) $a = \frac{v^2}{r} = \frac{GM}{r^2} \Rightarrow a \propto \frac{1}{r^2} \Rightarrow \frac{a_1}{a_2} = \frac{r_2^2}{r_1^2} = 4$

(d) $\Delta E = E_2 - E_1 = -\frac{GMm}{2(2r)} - \left(\frac{-GMm}{2r}\right) = \frac{GMm}{4r}$

13. (a) At equator, $g_{app} = g - \omega^2 R \Rightarrow \frac{g}{3} = g - \omega^2 R$

$$\Rightarrow \quad \omega = \sqrt{\frac{2g}{3R}} = \sqrt{\frac{2GM}{3R^3}}$$

$$T = \frac{2\pi}{\omega} = 2\pi\sqrt{\frac{3R^3}{2G(\rho\frac{4}{3}\pi R^3)}} = 60 \times 60$$

$$\Rightarrow \quad \rho = \frac{\pi}{192} \times 10^6 \text{ kg/m}^3$$

(b) $T = 2\pi\sqrt{\frac{(R+h)^3}{GM}} = 2\pi\sqrt{\frac{3R^3}{2GM}} \Rightarrow h = \left(\sqrt[3]{\frac{3}{2}} - 1\right)R$

(c) $g_{app} = g - \omega^2 R\cos^2\lambda = g - \omega^2 R\cos^2 60°$

$$= g - \left(\frac{2g}{3}\right)\left(\frac{1}{4}\right) = \frac{5g}{6}$$

14. $K_1 + U_1 = K_2 + U_2$

$$\Rightarrow 0 - \frac{GMm}{2R} = \frac{1}{2}mv^2 - \frac{3}{2}\frac{GMm}{R} \Rightarrow v = \sqrt{\frac{2GM}{R}}$$

Motion of the particle is periodic. When particle is travelling inside earth, its motion is SHM.

15. (a) $F_G = \frac{GMm}{R^3}\left(\frac{R}{2}\right) = \frac{GMm}{2R^2}$

$$N - F_G = m\omega^2\left(\frac{R}{2}\right)$$

$$\Rightarrow \quad 2F_G + F_G = m\omega^2\left(\frac{R}{2}\right) \Rightarrow \omega = \sqrt{\frac{3GM}{R^3}}$$

$$T = \frac{2\pi}{\omega} = 2\pi\sqrt{\frac{R}{3g}}$$

$$F_G = m\omega^2 r \Rightarrow \frac{GMmr}{R^3} = m\omega^2 r$$

$\Rightarrow \omega = \text{constant}$

$\Rightarrow T = \text{constant}$

16. Mass of planet, $M = \int_0^R \left(\frac{\rho_0 r}{R}\right)4\pi r^2 dr \Rightarrow M = \pi\rho_0 R^3$

(a) $\frac{1}{2}mv_e^2 - \frac{GMm}{R} = 0 \Rightarrow v_e = \sqrt{2\pi G\rho_0 R^2}$

(c) $E = \frac{GM}{R^2} = \pi G\rho_0 R$

(d) $v_0 = \sqrt{\frac{GM}{R}} = \sqrt{\pi\rho_0 G R^2} \Rightarrow T = \frac{2\pi R}{v_0} = 2\pi\sqrt{\frac{R}{\pi G\rho_0}}$

17. Conserving angular momentum about the centre of earth,

$$m(v_0\cos 30°)R = mv_{min}(2R) \Rightarrow v_{min} = \frac{\sqrt{3}v_0}{4}$$

Trajectory is elliptical.

Comprehension Based Questions

1. $v = \frac{v_e}{2} \Rightarrow \sqrt{\frac{GM}{R+h}} = \frac{1}{2}\sqrt{\frac{2GM}{R}} \Rightarrow h = R = 6400$ km

2. $T = 2\pi\sqrt{\frac{(R+h)^3}{GM}} = 2\pi\sqrt{\frac{8R^3}{GM}} = 2\pi\sqrt{\frac{8R}{g}}$

3. $K_1 + U_1 = K_2 + U_2$

$$\Rightarrow \quad 0 - \frac{GMm}{2R} = \frac{1}{2}mv^2 - \frac{GMm}{R}$$

$$\Rightarrow \quad v = \sqrt{\frac{GM}{R}} = \sqrt{gR}$$

4.

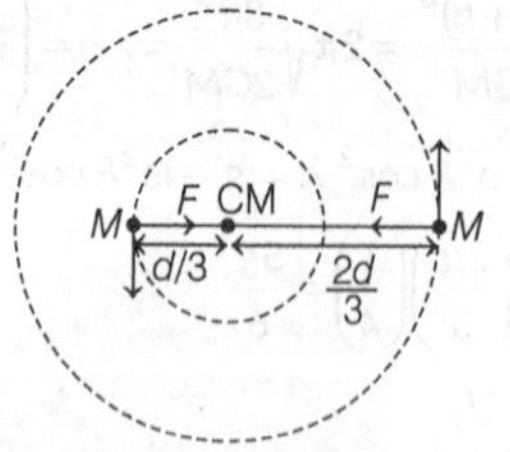

$$F = \frac{G(2m)(m)}{d^2} = m\omega^2\left(\frac{2d}{3}\right) \Rightarrow \omega = \sqrt{\frac{3Gm}{d^3}}$$

Hence, $T = \frac{2\pi}{\omega} = \sqrt{\frac{4\pi^2 d^3}{3Gm}}$

5. $\frac{L_m}{L_M} = \frac{m\left(\frac{2d}{3}\right)^2 \omega}{M\left(\frac{d}{3}\right)^2 \omega} = 2$

6. $K_m = \frac{1}{2}m\left(\omega\left(\frac{2d}{3}\right)\right)^2$ and $K_M = \frac{1}{2}M\left(\frac{\omega d}{3}\right)^2$

So, $\frac{K_m}{K_M} = 2$

7. $T^2 = \frac{4\pi^2 R^3}{GM}$

$$\Rightarrow 2\log_{10} T = 3\log_{10} R + \log_{10}\left(\frac{4\pi^2}{GM}\right)$$

$$\Rightarrow \log_{10} R = \frac{2}{3}\log_{10} T - \frac{1}{3}\log_{10}\left(\frac{4\pi^2}{GM}\right)$$

So, slope of line $= \frac{2}{3}$

8. y-intercept' $= -\frac{1}{3}\log_{10}\left(\frac{4\pi^2}{GM}\right) = 6$

$$\Rightarrow \frac{4(10)}{(20/3)\times 10^{-11} M} = 10^{-18} \Rightarrow M = 6\times 10^{29} \text{ kg}$$

9. $\omega = \sqrt{\frac{GM}{R^3}} \Rightarrow \frac{\omega_A}{\omega_B} = \left(\frac{4R}{R}\right)^{3/2} \Rightarrow \omega_A = 8\omega_0$

$$\omega_{rel} = \omega_A - \omega_B = 8\omega_0 - \omega_0 = 7\omega_0$$

$$T = \frac{2\pi}{\omega_{rel}} = \frac{2\pi}{7\omega_0}$$

10. $E_A = E_1 + E_2 = \frac{GM}{(2R)^2} + \frac{GM}{(2R)^2} = \frac{GM}{2R^2}$

$$s = ut + \frac{1}{2}at^2 \Rightarrow h = \frac{1}{2}\left(\frac{GM}{2R^2}\right)T^2$$

$$\Rightarrow \quad T = 2\sqrt{\frac{hR^2}{GM}}$$

11. Since, $h << R : v_A \approx 0$

$$K_A + U_A = K_B + U_B$$

$$\Rightarrow \quad 0 + \left(\frac{-GM}{2R} - \frac{GM}{2R}\right) = \frac{1}{2}mv_B^2 + \left(\frac{-GM}{R} - \frac{GM}{2R}\right)$$

$$\Rightarrow \quad v_B = \sqrt{\frac{GM}{R}}$$

As particle goes from A to B, its acceleration increases. So,

$$t < \frac{v_B}{a_A} = t < \frac{\sqrt{\frac{GM}{R}}}{\frac{GM}{4R^2}} \Rightarrow t < \frac{4R^2}{\sqrt{GMR}}$$

12. $v_B = \sqrt{\frac{GM}{R}}$

13.

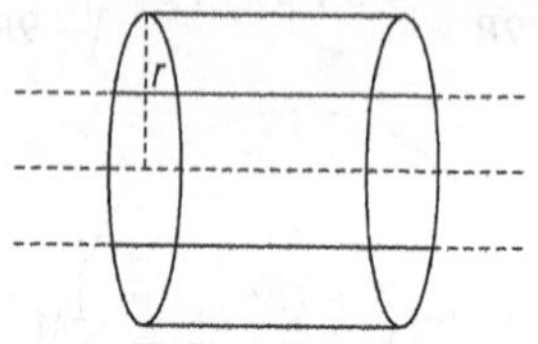

Consider a closed cylinderical Gaussian surface of radius r and length l around the planet as shown in figure,

$$E(2\pi rl) = \frac{\rho\pi R^2 l}{(1/4\pi G)} \Rightarrow E = \frac{2\pi G\rho R^2}{r}$$

To rotate a satellite around the planet in the orbit of radius r, centripetal force is provided by the gravitational force.

$$mE = \frac{mv^2}{r} = m\left(\frac{2\pi G\rho R^2}{r}\right) = \frac{mv^2}{r}$$

$$\Rightarrow \quad v = (\sqrt{2\pi G\rho})R$$

14. $W_g = \Delta K$

$$\Rightarrow \quad -\int_R^{3R} \frac{2\pi G\rho R^2 m}{r} dr = 0 - \frac{1}{2}mv_0^2$$

$$\Rightarrow v_0 = 2R\sqrt{\pi\rho G(\ln 3)}$$

15. $T = \frac{2\pi r}{v} = \frac{2\pi r}{R\sqrt{2\pi G\rho}} \Rightarrow r = RT\sqrt{\frac{G\rho}{2\pi}}$

16. Areal velocity is constant.

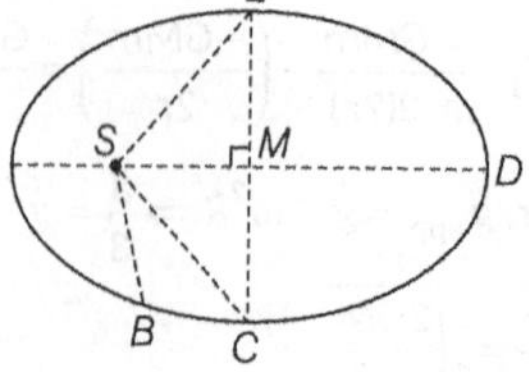

$$\frac{dA}{dt} = \frac{A}{40}$$

$$\Delta_{DES} = \frac{A}{40}(12) = \frac{3A}{10}$$

$$\Delta_{DEM} = \frac{A}{4}$$

So, $\Delta_{EMS} = \Delta_{DES} - \Delta_{DEM} = \frac{3A}{10} - \frac{A}{4} = \frac{A}{20}$

$$\Delta_{SBC} = \frac{A}{40}(1) = \frac{A}{40}$$

$$\Delta_{SBCE} = 2\Delta_{EMS} + \Delta_{SBC} = 2\left(\frac{A}{20}\right) + \frac{A}{40} = \frac{A}{8}$$

17. $\frac{dA}{dt} = \frac{A}{40 \times 30 \times 86400} = \frac{L}{2m} \Rightarrow \frac{L}{mA} = 2 \times 10^{-8}\ s^{-1}$

18. Magnitude of mechanical energy is decreased by 10%.

So, $E' = -(E_0 - 0.1E_0) = -0.9E_0$

19. $\frac{-GMm}{2a} = -0.9E_0 = -0.9\left(\frac{GMm}{2r}\right)$

$$\Rightarrow \quad a = \frac{r}{0.9} = \frac{6700}{0.9} = 7444.4 \text{ km}$$

20. $H_{max} = 2a - (2R + h) = 1788.9$ km

21. Orbital velocity of satellite $= u = \sqrt{\frac{GM}{R}}$

Applying linear momentum conservation for collision.

$10mu\hat{\mathbf{i}} + mv\hat{\mathbf{j}} = 11m\mathbf{v}$

$$\mathbf{v} = \frac{10u}{11}\hat{\mathbf{i}} + \frac{v}{11}\hat{\mathbf{j}}$$

Let v be velocity at the closest distance of approach.

From angular momentum conservation.

$$(11m)\left(\frac{10u}{11}\right)R = 11mv\left(\frac{R}{2}\right) \Rightarrow v = \frac{20u}{11}$$

From energy conservation,

$$\frac{1}{2}(11m)\left(\sqrt{\left(\frac{10u}{11}\right)^2 + \left(\frac{v}{11}\right)^2}\right)^2 - \frac{GM(11m)}{R}$$

$$= \frac{1}{2}(11m)v^2 - \frac{GM(11m)}{(R/2)}$$

$$\Rightarrow \quad v = \sqrt{\frac{58GM}{R}}$$

22. $L = (11m)\left(\frac{10u}{11}\right)R = 10muR$

$$= 10m\left(\sqrt{\frac{GM}{R}}\right)R = 10\sqrt{GMm^2R}$$

23. $a = \frac{r_{max} + r_{min}}{2} = \frac{4R + 2R}{2} = 3R$

$$E = \frac{1}{2}mv_{max}^2 - \frac{GMm}{2R} = -\frac{GMm}{2(3R)}$$

$$\Rightarrow v_{max} = \sqrt{\frac{2GM}{3R}}$$

$$E = \frac{1}{2}mv_{min}^2 - \frac{GMm}{4R} = -\frac{GMm}{2(3R)}$$

$$\Rightarrow v_{min} = \sqrt{\frac{GM}{6R}}$$

24. $a_c = \frac{v_\perp^2}{r} \Rightarrow \frac{GM}{(2R)^2} = \frac{v_{max}^2}{r} \Rightarrow r = \frac{8R}{3}$

Match the Columns Questions

1. (a) g at pole will remain same as there is no effect of rotation at poles.

(b) At equator, $g_{app} = g - \omega^2 R$

If ω decreases, g_{app} increases.

(c) $T = 2\pi\sqrt{\frac{(R+h)^3}{GM}} = \frac{2\pi}{\omega}$

If ω decreases, h increases.

(d) $E = -\frac{GMm}{2r}$

If ω decreases, r increases and hence E will increase.

2. $L = mv_1r_1 = mv_2r_2$ = constant

(a) Speed increases as $v \propto \frac{1}{r}$

(b) r decreases

(c) $U = -\frac{GMm}{r}$. Since r decreases, U decreases.

(d) L = constant

3. (a) $K_1 + U_1 = K_2 + U_2 \Rightarrow \frac{1}{2}m(\sqrt{gR})^2 - mgR = 0 - \frac{mgR}{1 + \frac{h}{R}}$

$$\Rightarrow \quad h = R$$

(b) $K_1 + U_1 = K_2 + U_2$

$$\Rightarrow \quad \frac{1}{2}m(\sqrt{gR})^2 - \frac{GMm}{R} = \frac{1}{2}mv^2 - \frac{GMm}{r}$$

$$\Rightarrow \quad v = \sqrt{\frac{GM}{Rr}(2R - r)}$$

$$\Rightarrow \quad \int_R^{2R} \frac{\sqrt{r}\,dr}{\sqrt{2R - r}} = \sqrt{\frac{GM}{R}}\int_0^T dt$$

Substitute $r = 2R\sin^2\theta$,

$$\Rightarrow \quad dr = 4R\sin\theta\cos\theta\, d\theta$$

$$\Rightarrow \quad \int_{\pi/4}^{\pi/2} \frac{\sqrt{2R}\sin\theta(4R\sin\theta\cos\theta\, d\theta)}{\sqrt{2R}\cos\theta} = \sqrt{\frac{GM}{R}}\int_0^T dt$$

$$\Rightarrow \quad T = \left(\frac{\pi}{2} + 1\right)\sqrt{\frac{R^3}{GM}}$$

(c) $g' = \frac{GM}{(2R^2)} = \frac{GM}{4R^2}$

(d) $v = \sqrt{\frac{GM}{2R}}$

4. $v_p = v_{\text{particle, satellite}} + v_{\text{satellite}}$

$$= \left(\sqrt{\frac{5}{4}} - 1\right)v_0 + v_0 = \sqrt{\frac{5}{4}}v_0$$

Applying conservation of angular momentum,

$mv_p a = mvr$

$$\Rightarrow \quad v = \frac{v_p a}{r} = \sqrt{\frac{5}{4}}\left(\frac{v_0 a}{r}\right)$$

Applying conservation of energy,

$$\frac{1}{2}m\left(\sqrt{\frac{5}{4}}v_0\right)^2 - \frac{GMm}{a}$$

$$= \frac{1}{2}m\left(\sqrt{\frac{5}{4}}\frac{v_0 a}{r}\right)^2 - \frac{GMm}{r}$$

$$\Rightarrow \quad \frac{1}{2}m\left(\frac{5}{4}v_0^2\right) - \frac{GMm}{a} = \frac{1}{2}m\left(\frac{a^2}{r^2}\frac{5v_0^2}{4}\right) - \frac{GMm}{r}$$

Substituting $v_0 = \sqrt{\frac{GM}{a}}$, we get

$$3r^2 - 8ar + 10a = 0 \Rightarrow r = a, \frac{5a}{3}$$

So, $r_{min} = a$ and $r_{max} = \frac{5a}{3}$

$$\text{Total Energy} = \frac{1}{2}m\left(\sqrt{\frac{5}{4}}\sqrt{\frac{GM}{a}}\right)^2 - \frac{GMm}{a} = -\frac{3GMm}{8a}$$

5. (a) As we are moving in the direction of gravitational field, gravitational potential decreases.

(b) As we are moving from *B* to *C*, gravitational field (radially inwards) decreases, becomes zero and then increases (radially outwards). So, the potential first decreases and then increases.

(c) Gravitational field inside cavity is uniform. Its direction is parallel to line joining centre of the sphere and the cavity and leftward. So, in moving from *C* to *D*. we are going against the direction of gravitational field and hence, potential increases.

(d) Line *PQ* is perpendicular to gravitational field, so potential remains constant along line *PQ*.

6. $K = \frac{p^2}{2m}; K \propto \frac{1}{m}$

(a) $\frac{m_1}{m_2} = 1 \Rightarrow \frac{K_1}{K_2} = 1 \Rightarrow K_2 = \frac{E}{2}$

$$\Rightarrow \quad \frac{1}{2}\left(\frac{M_s}{2}\right)v_2^2 = \frac{1}{2}\left(\frac{GM_eM_s}{R}\right)$$

$$\Rightarrow \quad v_2 = \sqrt{\frac{2GM_e}{R}} = v_e$$

So, m_2 will go in parabolic orbit.

(b) $\frac{m_1}{m_2} = 2 \Rightarrow \frac{K_1}{K_2} = \frac{1}{2} \Rightarrow K_2 = \frac{2E}{3}$

$$\Rightarrow \quad \frac{1}{2}\left(\frac{M_s}{3}\right)v_2^2 = \frac{2}{3}\left(\frac{GM_eM_s}{4R}\right) \Rightarrow v_2 = \sqrt{\frac{GM_e}{R}}$$

So, m_2 will go in circular orbit.

(c) $\frac{m_1}{m_2} = \frac{7}{2} \Rightarrow \frac{K_1}{K_2} = \frac{2}{7} \Rightarrow K_2 = \frac{7E}{9}$

$$\Rightarrow \quad \frac{1}{2}\left(\frac{2M_s}{9}\right)v_2^2 = \frac{7}{9}\left(\frac{GM_eM_s}{4R}\right) \Rightarrow v_2 = \sqrt{\frac{7GM_e}{2R}} > v_e$$

So, m_2 will go in hyperbolic orbit.

(d) $\frac{m_1}{m_2} = \frac{1}{3} \Rightarrow \frac{K_1}{K_2} = 3 \Rightarrow K_2 = \frac{E}{4}$

$$\Rightarrow \quad \frac{1}{2}\left(\frac{3M_s}{4}\right)v_2^2 = \frac{1}{4}\left(\frac{2GM_eM_s}{R}\right) \Rightarrow v_2 = \sqrt{\frac{4GM_e}{3R}} < v_e$$

So, m_2 will go in elliptical orbit.

7. Speed of planet is maximum at perigee and minimum at apogee. So, kinetic energy is maximum at perigee and minimum at apogee. Potential energy and kinetic energy are dependent on mass of planet, mass of sun and semi-major axis.

8. (a) $g = \frac{GM}{R^2} = \frac{G\rho\left(\frac{4}{3}\pi R^3\right)}{R^2} = \frac{4G\rho\pi R}{3}$

$$\frac{g_1}{g_2} = \frac{\rho_1 R_1}{\rho_2 R_2} \Rightarrow \frac{g_P}{g} = (2)\left(\frac{1}{2}\right) = 1$$

(b) $V = -\frac{GM}{R} = -\frac{G\rho\left(\frac{4}{3}\pi R^3\right)}{R} = -\frac{4G\rho\pi R^2}{3}$

$$\frac{V_1}{V_2} = \frac{\rho_1 R_1^2}{\rho_2 R_2^2} \Rightarrow \frac{V_P}{V} = (2)\left(\frac{1}{4}\right) = \frac{1}{2}$$

(c) $V = -\frac{3GM}{2R}; \frac{V_P}{V} = \frac{1}{2}$

(d) $E_{\text{centre}} = 0$

Numerical Value Questions

1. $T = 2\pi\sqrt{\frac{a^3}{GM}} \Rightarrow 9000 = 2\pi\sqrt{\frac{(2 \times 1.5 \times 10^6)^3}{(20/3) \times 10^{-11} M}}$

$$\Rightarrow \quad M = 2 \times 10^{21} \text{ kg}$$

So, $\alpha + \beta = 2 + 21 = 23$

2. Using conservation of energy,

$$\frac{-3GM^2}{5R} + \frac{1}{2}Mv_0^2 = -\frac{3G(M/8)^2}{5(R/2)} \times 8 + 8 \times \left(\frac{1}{2} \times \frac{M}{8} \times v^2\right)$$

Substituting, $v_0 = \sqrt{\frac{GM}{R}}$, we get

$$v = \sqrt{\frac{GM}{10R}} = 100 \text{ m/s}$$

3. $N = F\cos\theta = \left(\frac{GMm}{R^3}r\right)\left(\frac{x}{r}\right) = \frac{GMmx}{R^3}$ = constant

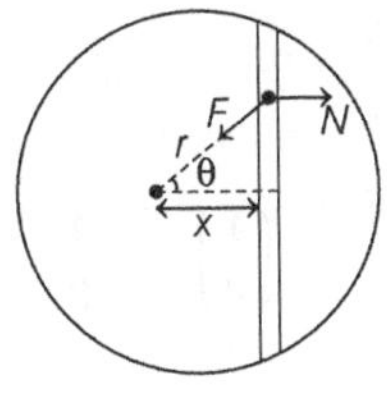

So, $\frac{N_P}{N_Q} = 1$

4. For astronaut, $v_{ast} = \sqrt{\frac{GM}{R_2}}$

For body, $v_{body} = \sqrt{\frac{GM}{R_1}}$

$$v_{ast} = 5000 \text{ m/s},$$

$$v_{body} = v_{body,\,ast} + v_{ast}$$

$$= 5 + 5000 = 5005 \text{ m/s}$$

$$R_2 - R_1 = \frac{GM}{(5000)^2} - \frac{GM}{(5005)^2} = 32 \text{ km}$$

5. $A = r^2\theta \Rightarrow \frac{dA}{dt} = r^2\frac{d\theta}{dt} = r^2\omega$

$$\frac{\left(\frac{dA}{dt}\right)_A}{\left(\frac{dA}{dt}\right)_B} = \left(\frac{r_A}{r_B}\right)^2 = \left(\frac{m_B}{m_A}\right)^2 = 9$$

6. Given body =

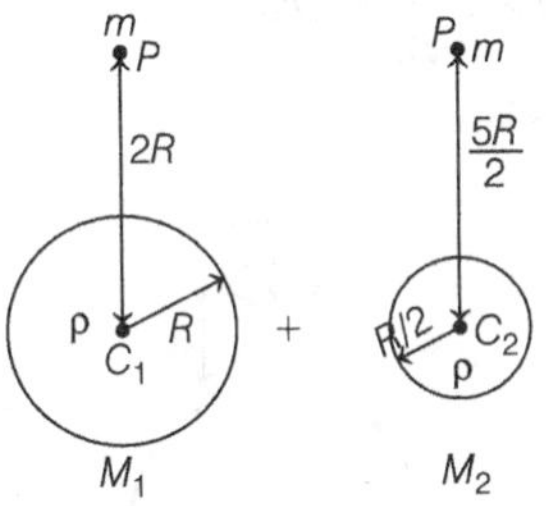

By superposition,

$$F = F_1 + F_2 = \frac{GM_1M}{(2R)^2} + \frac{GM_2M}{\left(\frac{5R}{2}\right)^2}$$

Substituting, $M_1 = \rho\left(\frac{4}{3}\pi R^3\right)$ and $M_2 = \rho\left(\frac{4}{3}\pi\left(\frac{R}{2}\right)^3\right)$

we get, $F = \frac{9\pi R\rho GM}{25}$

7. $\Delta E = E_2 - E_1 = -\frac{GMm}{2(4R)} - \left(\frac{-GMm}{2(2R)}\right) = \frac{GMm}{8R}$

8. Conserving angular momentum,

$$m(v_1\cos 60°)4R = mv_2R$$

$$\Rightarrow \quad v_2 = 2v_1$$

Conserving energy of the system,

$$\frac{-GMm}{4R} + \frac{1}{2}mv_1^2 = -\frac{GMm}{R} + \frac{1}{2}mv_2^2$$

$$\Rightarrow \quad v_1 = \sqrt{\frac{GM}{2R}} = \sqrt{\frac{6.4\times 10^7}{2}}$$

$$= \frac{8000}{\sqrt{2}} \text{ m/s}$$

9. Velocity of asteroid just before collision

$$= \sqrt{\frac{2GM}{r}} = \sqrt{2}v_0$$

Orbital velocity of satellite before collision

$$= \sqrt{\frac{GM}{r}} = v_0$$

By linear momentum conservation for collision,

$$mv_0\hat{i} + m(\sqrt{2}v_0)\hat{j} = 2m\mathbf{v}$$

$$\Rightarrow \quad \mathbf{v} = \frac{v_0}{2}\hat{i} + \frac{v_0}{\sqrt{2}}\hat{j}$$

Speed of combined mass $= \sqrt{\left(\frac{v_0}{2}\right)^2 + \left(\frac{v_0}{\sqrt{2}}\right)^2} = \frac{\sqrt{3}v_0}{2}$

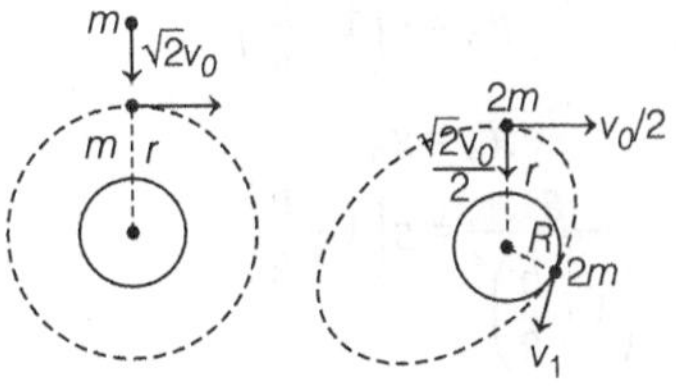

Just Before Collision After Collision

By angular momentum conservation,

$$2m\left(\frac{v_0}{2}\right)r = 2m\,v_1R$$

$$\Rightarrow \quad v_1 = \frac{v_0r}{2R}$$

By energy conservation,

$$\frac{1}{2}(2m)\left(\frac{\sqrt{3}v_0}{2}\right)^2 - \frac{GM(2m)}{r} = \frac{1}{2}(2m)v_1^2 - \frac{GM(2m)}{R}$$

$$\Rightarrow r^2 - 8Rr + 5R^2 = 0$$

$$\Rightarrow \quad r = (4+\sqrt{11})R$$

10. $K_1 + U_1 = K_2 + U_2$

$$\Rightarrow \frac{1}{2}m(1.5v_0)^2 - \frac{GMm}{r} = \frac{1}{2}mv^2 + 0$$

$$\Rightarrow \quad \frac{9}{8}mv_0^2 - mv_0^2 = \frac{1}{2}mv^2 \qquad \because \left[\frac{GM}{r} = v_0^2\right]$$

$$\Rightarrow \quad v = \frac{v_0}{2}$$

Previous Years Questions

JEE Main

1. Initially, $g = \dfrac{GM}{R^2}$

Under given condition

$$g' = \frac{GM}{(R/2)^2} = \frac{4GM}{R^2} = 4g$$

2. $T_{earth} = 365$ days

$T_{moon} = 27$ days

As, $T = \dfrac{2\pi}{\omega}$, then $\omega_{moon} > \omega_{earth}$

Both Assertion and Reason are correct and Reason is the correct explanation of Assertion.

3. Given,

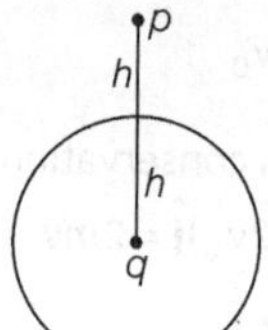

$$g_p = \frac{gR^2}{(R+h)^2}$$

$$g_q = g\left(1 - \frac{h}{R}\right)$$

$$g_p = g_q$$

$$\frac{g}{\left(1+\frac{h}{R}\right)^2} = g\left(1 - \frac{h}{R}\right)$$

$$\Rightarrow \left(1+\frac{h}{R}\right)\left(1+\frac{h}{R}\right)\left(1-\frac{h}{R}\right) = 1$$

$$\left(1 - \frac{h^2}{R^2}\right)\left(1 + \frac{h}{R}\right) = 1$$

Take, $\dfrac{h}{R} = x$

So, $x^3 - x + x^2 = 0$

$$x = \frac{\sqrt{5}-1}{2}$$

$$\Rightarrow \quad h = \frac{R}{2}(\sqrt{5}-1)$$

option, $h = \dfrac{\sqrt{5}R - R}{2}$

4. For the planet,

$T_1 = 200$ days

$R_1 = R$

$R_2 = \dfrac{R}{4}$

$\therefore \quad T_2 = ?$

According to Kepler's law

$T^2 \propto R^3$

$$\therefore \quad \frac{T_2}{T_1} = \left(\frac{R_2}{R_1}\right)^{3/2}$$

$$= \left(\frac{R/4}{R}\right)^{3/2} = \left(\frac{1}{4}\right)^{3/2} = \frac{1}{8}$$

$$\therefore \quad T_2 = \frac{T_1}{8}$$

$$= \frac{200}{8} = 25 \text{ days}$$

5. Escape speed from earth is

$$v_e = \sqrt{\frac{2GM}{R}} = 11.2 \text{ km/s}$$

Now for planet, $R_p = \dfrac{1}{3}R$

and $\quad M_P = \dfrac{1}{6}M$

So, escape speed for planet is

$$v_p = \sqrt{\frac{2GM_p}{R_p}}$$

$$= \sqrt{\frac{2G\left(\frac{M}{6}\right)}{\left(\frac{R}{3}\right)}}$$

$$= \sqrt{\frac{GM}{R}} = \frac{1}{\sqrt{2}} ve$$

$$= 11.2 \times \frac{1}{\sqrt{2}} = 7.92 \frac{\text{km}}{\text{s}}$$

$$\approx 7.9 \text{ km/s}$$

6.

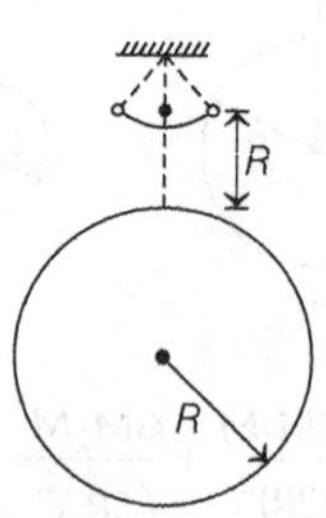

Acceleration due to gravity at height h above earth's surface is,

$$g_h = g \cdot \frac{R^2}{(R+h)^2}$$

Here, $\quad g = \pi^2 \dfrac{\text{m}}{\text{s}^2}$ and $h = R$

$$\therefore \quad g_h = g\frac{R^2}{4R^2} = \frac{g}{4} = \frac{\pi^2}{4} \text{ m/s}^2$$

Time period of pendulum at that height is,

$$T = 2\pi\sqrt{\frac{l}{g_h}} = 2\pi\sqrt{\frac{4}{\frac{\pi^2}{4}}} = 4 \times 2$$

$$= 8 \text{ s}$$

7. Due to mutual gravitational attraction, the particles will be at the position shown below.

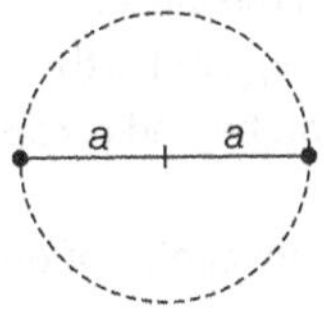

Here, centripetal force
= gravitational force

$$\Rightarrow \quad ma\omega^2 = \frac{Gm^2}{(2a)^2} \Rightarrow \omega = \sqrt{\frac{Gm}{4a^3}}$$

8. Particles moves along their COM,

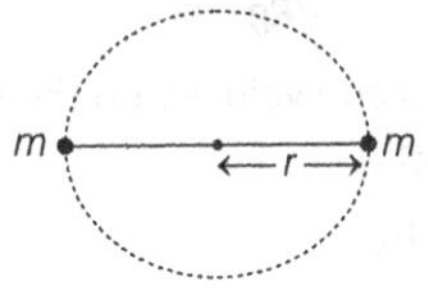

Force on each particle $= \frac{Gmm}{(2r)^2} = \frac{Gm^2}{4r^2}$

This force acts like centripetal pull so,

$$\frac{mv^2}{r} = \frac{Gm^2}{4r^2} \Rightarrow v = \sqrt{\frac{Gm}{4r}}$$

9. According to Kepler's third law,

$$T^2 \propto r^3$$

We get, $\frac{T_2^2}{T_1^2} = \frac{r_2^3}{r_1^3}$

or $T_2^2 = T_1^2\left(\frac{r_2}{r_1}\right)^3$

Here, $T_1 = 24 \text{ h}, \frac{r_2}{r_1} = \frac{1}{4}$

So, $T_2^2 = (24)^2 \times \frac{1}{4^3}$

or $T_2 = 3 \text{ h}$

10. Using $T^2 \propto r^3$ we get, $\frac{T_2^2}{T_1^2} = \frac{(r_2)^3}{(r_1)^3}$

Here, $T_1 = 1$ year, $r_1 = 1.5 \times 10^6$ km,

$T_2 = 2.83$ years, $r_2 = ?$

So, $r_2^3 = \frac{(2.83)^2}{1^2} \times (1.5 \times 10^6)^3$

$\Rightarrow \quad r_2^3 = 8.0089 \times (1.5 \times 10^6)^3$

or $\quad r_2 \approx [8 \times (1.5 \times 10^6)^3]^{1/3}$

$\Rightarrow \quad r_2 = 2 \times 1.5 \times 10^6 \approx 3 \times 10^6$ km

11. Acceleration due to gravity on the surface of the Earth is;

$$g = \frac{GM}{R^2} = \frac{4}{3}\pi G\rho R$$

And acceleration due to gravity at depth d is;

$$g' = \frac{4}{3}\pi G \cdot \rho(R - d)$$

Here $\quad d = \frac{R}{2}$

So, $\quad g' = \frac{4}{3}\pi G\rho \cdot \frac{R}{2} = \frac{g}{2}$

Hence, weight of a body at a depth $d = \frac{R}{2}$ is;

$$mg' = \frac{mg}{2} = \frac{400}{2} = 200 \text{ N}$$

12. Acceleration due to gravity at surface of earth, $g = \frac{GM}{R^2}$

At height h, acceleration due to gravity will be,

$$g_h = \frac{GM}{(R+h)^2}$$

$$\Rightarrow \quad \frac{g_h}{g} = \frac{R^2}{(R+h)^2} = \left(1 + \frac{h}{R}\right)^{-2}$$

$$= 1 - \frac{2h}{R} \text{ (when } h << R)$$

$$\Rightarrow \quad g_h = g\left(1 - \frac{2h}{R}\right)$$

13. Statement I is true as rotation causes variation is value of g.

i.e. $\quad g' = g - r\omega^2 \cos^2 \lambda$

At pole, $\quad g = g_s$ (no effect)

At equator, $g = g_s - r\omega^2 \cos^2 \lambda = g_s - r\omega^2$

($\because \cos^2 \lambda_{\max}$ at $\lambda = 0°$, is at equator)

Hence, the value of g is maximum at equator. Therefore, statement II is incorrect.

14.

	Planet-A	Planet-B
Radius	R	$1.5\,R$
Density	ρ	$\frac{\rho}{2}$

$$g = \frac{4}{3}\pi G\rho R$$

$$\Rightarrow \quad \frac{g_{BS}}{g_{AS}} = \frac{\frac{4}{3}\pi G\rho_B R_B}{\frac{4}{3}\pi G\rho_A \cdot R_A}$$

$$\frac{g_{BS}}{g_{AS}} = \frac{\rho_B R_B}{\rho_A \cdot R_A}$$

$$= \frac{\left(\frac{\rho}{2}\right) \times (1.5)R}{\rho R} = \frac{1.5}{2} = \frac{3}{2 \times 2} = \frac{3}{4}$$

15. Acceleration due to gravity on surface of earth,

$$g = \frac{GM}{R^2} \quad \text{...(i)}$$

At height h acceleration is,

$$g' = \frac{GM}{(R+h)^2} \quad \text{... (ii)}$$

Dividing Eq. (i) by Eq. (ii), we get

$$\frac{g}{g'} = \frac{(R+h)^2}{R^2} \Rightarrow g' = \frac{gR^2}{(R+h)^2}$$

If mass of body is m, then weight of body at height h is

$$mg' = \frac{(mg)\cdot R^2}{(R+h)^2}$$

Substituting given values, we get weight at height h, 1

$$w' = mg' = \frac{18 \times (6400)^2}{(6400+3200)^2}$$

$$= \frac{18 \times 6400 \times 6400}{9600 \times 9600} = 8 \text{ N}$$

16. As, we go up or down from earth's surface, acceleration due to gravity decreases. So statement I is correct.

Now,

$g_h = g_d$ gives,

Now, for small $h (h << R)$ we have,

$$g\left(1 - \frac{2h}{R}\right) = g\left(1 - \frac{d}{R}\right)$$

$$2h = d \text{ or } h = d/2$$

So, statement II is incorrect.

17. $V = \frac{GM}{2R^3}(3R^2 - r^2)$

at $r = R \Rightarrow V = \frac{GM}{R}$

at $r = 0$, $V_0 = \frac{3GM}{2R} \Rightarrow V = \frac{GM}{R}$

$$V_0 = \frac{3}{2} \cdot \frac{GM}{R}$$

Put the value of V, $V_0 = \frac{3}{2} V$

18. So, Gravitational potential V is given by

$$\frac{dV}{dr} = -E \text{ or } dV = -Edr$$

$$\int_{V_i}^{V_f} dV = -\int_{2 \text{ cm}}^{3 \text{ cm}} Edr = -\int_2^3 \frac{-K}{r^2} dr$$

$$= \left[\frac{-K}{r}\right]_2^3 = -K\left[\frac{1}{3} - \frac{1}{2}\right] = \frac{K}{6} = \frac{6}{6} = 1 \text{ Jkg}^{-1}$$

$\Rightarrow V_f - V_i = 1$

$\Rightarrow V_f - 10 = 1$

$\Rightarrow V_f = 11 \text{ J kg}^{-1}$

19. $v_{\text{escape}} = \sqrt{\frac{2GM}{R}} = \sqrt{2gR}$

Radius of moon is less than that of the Earth and acceleration due to gravity is also less on moon as compared to that on the Earth.

Thus, v_{esp} of moon < v_{esp} of Earth

This is also the reason behind escape of atmosphere from the moon.

20. Height of satellite from centre of earth $= 2R$

Therefore,

$$\frac{mv^2}{2R} = \frac{GMm}{(2R)^2} \Rightarrow v = \sqrt{\frac{GM}{2R}} = \sqrt{\frac{Rg}{2}}$$

If satellite takes time T to revolve around the Earth with velocity, v, then

$$T = \frac{2\pi(2R)}{v} = \frac{4\pi R\sqrt{2}}{\sqrt{Rg}} = \sqrt{32.2R} \approx \sqrt{32\,R}$$

21. We know that, escape velocity on the surface of the Earth.

$$v_e = \sqrt{\frac{2GM_e}{R_e}}$$

and on the surface of planet

$$v_p = \sqrt{\frac{2GM_p}{R_p}} = \sqrt{2G \cdot \frac{9M_e}{4R_e}} \quad (\because M_p = 9M_e, R_p = 4R_e)$$

$$= \frac{3}{2}\sqrt{\frac{2GM_e}{R_e}} = \frac{3}{2} v_e = \frac{3}{2} \times 11.2 = 16.8 \text{ km/s}$$

22. Orbital speed of a satellite orbiting in a radius r is

$$v = \sqrt{\frac{GM}{r}}$$

So, ratio of orbital speeds for 2-earth satellites is,

$$\frac{v_1}{v_2} = \sqrt{\frac{r_2}{r_1}} \Rightarrow \frac{v_1}{v_2} = \sqrt{\frac{3r}{r}} = \frac{\sqrt{3}}{1}$$

(Given $r_2 = 3r$ and $r_1 = r$)

23. $v_{\text{circular}} = \sqrt{\frac{GM}{R}} = \sqrt{gR}$

$$v_{\text{escape}} = \sqrt{\frac{2GM}{R}} = \sqrt{2gR}$$

$$\Delta v = v_{\text{esp}} - v_{\text{circular}} = \sqrt{2gR} - \sqrt{gR}$$

$$= (\sqrt{2} - 1)\sqrt{gR}$$

$$= (\sqrt{2} - 1)\sqrt{\frac{10}{1000} \times 6400} = (\sqrt{2} - 1)8 \text{ km/s}$$

24. Given, mass of planet $M_p = 16M_e$

radius of planet, $R_p = 4R_e$

Escape velocity, $v_e = \sqrt{\frac{2GM}{R}}$

$\therefore v_e$ for planet $= \sqrt{\dfrac{2G(16M_e)}{(4R_e)}} = 2\sqrt{\dfrac{2GM_e}{R_e}}$

$= 2\,(v_e$ for earth)

i.e., $\dfrac{v_p \text{ for planet}}{v_e \text{ for earth}} = \dfrac{2}{1}$

25. Given, mass of satellite A is twice the mass of B. i.e.,

$$M_A = 2M_e$$

For satellite, we know that,

$$PE = \frac{-GM_PM_A}{R} \text{ and } KE = \frac{+GM_PM_A}{2R}$$

$$TE = \frac{-GM_PM_A}{2R}$$

and Speed, $v = \sqrt{\dfrac{GM_p}{R}}$

Therefore, orbital speed of the satellite is independent of mass of the satellite.

26. The escape velocity from surface of any planet is given as

$$v = \sqrt{\frac{2GM}{R}} \quad \text{...(i)}$$

For given planet, $M = \dfrac{M_e}{9}, R = \dfrac{R_e}{2}$

From Eq. (i),

$$v = \sqrt{\frac{2G\left(\dfrac{M_e}{9}\right)}{\dfrac{R_e}{2}}} = \sqrt{\frac{2}{9}}\sqrt{\frac{2GM_e}{R_e}}$$

$$= \sqrt{\frac{2}{9}}\,v_e = \frac{\sqrt{2}}{3}v_e$$

$\Rightarrow \quad x = 2$

27. Escape velocity of any planet from surface is given as

$$v_e = \sqrt{2gR}$$

For two planets A and B,

$$\frac{(v_e)_A}{(v_e)_B} = \sqrt{\frac{g_A}{g_B}}\sqrt{\frac{R_A}{R_B}} \quad \text{...(i)}$$

Given that, $\dfrac{(v_e)_A}{(v_e)_B} = \dfrac{1}{2}, \dfrac{R_A}{R_B} = \dfrac{1}{3}$

From Eq. (i), $\dfrac{1}{2} = \sqrt{\dfrac{g_A}{g_B}}\sqrt{\dfrac{1}{3}}$

or $\sqrt{\dfrac{g_A}{g_B}} = \dfrac{\sqrt{3}}{2}$ or $\dfrac{g_A}{g_B} = \dfrac{3}{4}$

28. For a satellite, time period of revolution is dependent on its orbit as, $T^2 \propto R^3$

Therefore, $\dfrac{T_2}{T_1} = \left(\dfrac{R_2}{R_1}\right)^{3/2}$

Here, $T_1 = 7\text{ h}, \dfrac{R_2}{R_1} = 3$

So, $T_2 = 7 \times (3)^{3/2} = 7 \times 5.19$

$= 36.37\text{ h} \approx 36\text{ h}$

29. Initially, force between two masses is given by Newton's law as

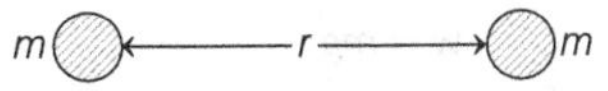

$$F = \frac{Gm \times m}{r^2} = \frac{Gm^2}{r^2}$$

When $\dfrac{1}{3}$rd of second mass is transferred to other, masses will be $\dfrac{4}{3}m$ and $\dfrac{2}{3}m$.

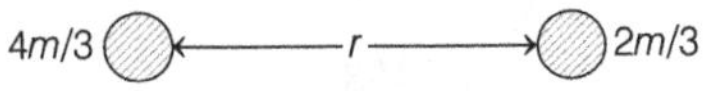

Now, force of attraction will be

$$F' = \frac{G\dfrac{4m}{3} \times \dfrac{2m}{3}}{r^2} \Rightarrow F' = \frac{8}{9}\frac{Gm^2}{r^2}$$

$\Rightarrow \quad F' = \dfrac{8}{9}F$

30. For a planet in a circular orbit,

$$T^2 \propto R^3 \text{ (Kepler's law)}$$

For planets A and B, we have,

$\Rightarrow \quad \dfrac{T_A^2}{T_B^2} = \dfrac{r_A^3}{r_B^3}$

Given, $\quad T_A = 2T_B$

so, $\quad \dfrac{(4T_B^2)}{T_B^2} = 4 = \dfrac{r_A^3}{r_B^3} \Rightarrow r_A^3 = 4r_B^3$

31. Given, radius of Earth shrinks by 2%

i.e. $\dfrac{\Delta R}{R} \times 100 = -2\%$

We know that, acceleration due to gravity, $g = \dfrac{GM}{R^2}$

$\Rightarrow \quad g \propto \dfrac{1}{R^2}$

$\Rightarrow \quad \dfrac{\Delta g}{g} = -2\dfrac{\Delta R}{R} = -2(-2\%) = 4\%$

Hence, acceleration due to gravity is increased by 4%.

32. Weight of rocket,

$$w = mg$$

$$w = m\left(\frac{Gm}{R^2}\right) \qquad \left(g = \frac{Gm}{R^2}\right)$$

$$w \propto \frac{1}{R^2}$$

$\Rightarrow \quad \dfrac{\Delta w}{w} = \dfrac{2\Delta R}{R} = 2 \times \dfrac{32}{6400}$

$(\because R = 6400\text{ km}, \Delta R = 32\text{ km})$

$= \dfrac{1}{100}$

$\therefore$ Percentage decrease in weight $= \dfrac{\Delta w}{w} \times 100 = \dfrac{1}{100} \times 100\%$

$= 1\%$

33. Weight of object on the surface of earth,

$$w = mg \quad \text{...(i)}$$

At height, $h = \dfrac{5}{4}R$, the value of acceleration due to gravity,

$$g' = \frac{g}{\left(1 + \frac{h}{R}\right)^2} = \frac{g}{\left(1 + \frac{\frac{5}{4}R}{R}\right)^2} = \frac{g}{\left(\frac{9}{4}\right)^2} = \frac{16g}{81}$$

$$\Rightarrow \quad g' = \frac{16g}{81}$$

Weight of object at this height,

$$w' = mg' = m \times \frac{16g}{81}$$

$$\Rightarrow \quad w' = \frac{16mg}{81}$$

$\therefore$ percentage decrease in weight

$$= \frac{w - w'}{w} \times 100$$

$$= \frac{mg - \frac{16mg}{81}}{mg} \times 100$$

$$= \frac{65}{81} \times 100 = 80.2\%$$

34. At every location, the direction of acceleration due to gravity is always towards the centre of earth, but its magnitude changes at different locations i.e. if we move from poles to equator, the direction of acceleration due to gravity of the earth always points towards centre of earth but its magnitude decreases and becomes minimum on reaching at equator.

Hence, A is false but R is true.

35. With the depth r the acceleration due to gravity changes as, $g' = g\left(1 - \dfrac{r}{R}\right)$, where R is radius of thew earth.

So, as depth increases, acceleration due to gravity decreases and reaches minimum at centre.

But with height, $g' = g\left(1 - \dfrac{2r}{R}\right)$

So, g' decreases as r increases.

Therefore, the graph of g *versus* r is plotted as

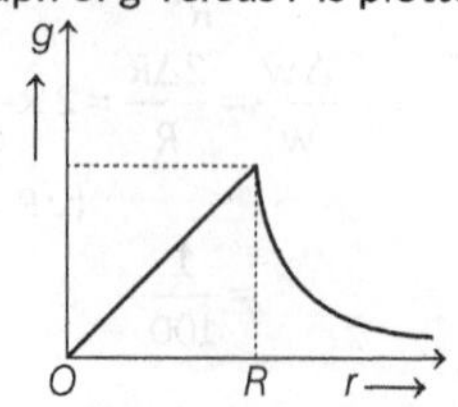

36. Given, height of any point P,

h = diameter of the earth $= 2R_e$

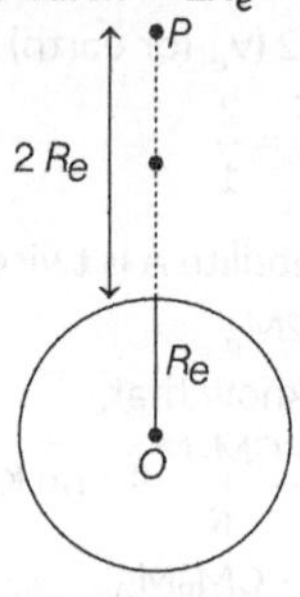

Acceleration due to gravity at height h from the surface of earth is given as

$$g_h = \frac{g}{\left(1 + \frac{h}{R_e}\right)^2} = \frac{g}{\left(1 + \frac{2R_e}{R_e}\right)^2} = \frac{g}{(3)^2} = \frac{g}{9}$$

37. Let h be required height,

i.e. weight of body at height h

$$= \frac{\text{weight of body on the surface of earth}}{3}$$

$$\Rightarrow \quad mg_h = \frac{mg}{3}$$

$$\Rightarrow \quad g_h = \frac{g}{3} \Rightarrow \frac{g}{\left(1 + \frac{h}{R_e}\right)^2} = \frac{g}{3}$$

$$\Rightarrow \quad \left(1 + \frac{h}{R_e}\right)^2 = 3 \Rightarrow 1 + \frac{h}{R_e} = \sqrt{3}$$

$$\Rightarrow \quad h = (\sqrt{3} - 1)R_e = (1.732 - 1)6400$$

$$= 0.732 \times 6400 = 4684.8 \text{ km}$$

$$\simeq 4685 \text{ km}$$

38. Escape velocity of a mass over a planet,

$$v_{esc} = \sqrt{\frac{2GM}{R}}, M = \frac{4}{3}\pi R^3 \cdot \rho$$

$$\Rightarrow \quad v_{esc} = \sqrt{\frac{8}{3}G\pi R^2 \cdot \rho} \text{ or } v_{esc} \propto R\sqrt{\rho}$$

$$\Rightarrow \quad \frac{v_B}{v_A} = \frac{R_B}{R_A} \cdot \sqrt{\frac{\rho_B}{\rho_A}}$$

Here, $v_A = 12 \text{ km/s}, \rho_B = 4\rho_A$

and $R_B = \dfrac{1}{2}R_A$

Hence $\dfrac{v_B}{v_A} = \dfrac{1}{2} \times \sqrt{4}$

$$\Rightarrow \quad v_B = v_A \text{ or } v_B = 12 \text{ km/s}$$

39. Given, radius of sphere $= R$

Distance of particle from centre of Earth $= 3R$

Force between sphere and particle $= F_1$

Radius of cavity $= R/2$

Let mass of sphere $= M$

Mass of sphere with cavity $= M'$
Mass of particle $= m$

Now, $M' = \rho \cdot \frac{4}{3}\pi\left(\frac{R}{2}\right)^3 = \frac{M}{8}$

By using concept of gravitational force,

$$F_1 = \frac{GMm}{(3R)^2} = \frac{GMm}{9R^2} \quad \text{... (i)}$$

and $$F_{cavity} = \frac{GM'm}{(AB)^2} = \frac{G(M/8)m}{(2R + R/2)^2} = \frac{4GMm}{25 \times 8R^2} \quad \text{... (ii)}$$

$$\therefore \quad F_2 = F_1 - F_{cavity} = \frac{GMm}{9R^2} - \frac{4}{25 \times 8}\frac{GMm}{R^2}$$

$$= \frac{GMm}{R^2}\left(\frac{1}{9} - \frac{1}{50}\right) = \frac{41}{50 \times 9}\frac{GMm}{R^2}$$

$$\because \quad \frac{F_1}{F_2} = \frac{50}{41}$$

40. According to Kepler's second law of planetary motion, areal velocity of every planet moving around the sun should remain constant in elliptical orbit.

41. Given, maximum distance of comet from the Sun,
$r_1 = 1.6 \times 10^{12}$ m

Minimum distance of comet from the Sun,
$$r_2 = 8.0 \times 10^{10} \text{m}$$

Speed of the comet at nearest point, $v_2 = 6 \times 10^4 \text{ms}^{-1}$

Applying law of conservation of angular momentum,
$$mv_1 r_1 = mv_2 r_2$$
($\because$ mass of comet will remain same)

$$\Rightarrow \quad v_1 = \frac{v_2 r_2}{r_1}$$

$$= \frac{6 \times 10^4 \times 8 \times 10^{10}}{1.6 \times 10^{12}} = \frac{48 \times 10^{14}}{1.6 \times 10^{12}}$$

$$= 3 \times 10^3 \text{ m/s}$$

42. Given,
Height of satellite from planet's surface, $h = 11R$
So, the total distance from the centre of planet
$$= 11R + R = 12R$$
Time period of planet $= 24$ h
Similarly, the total distance of second satellite from the centre of planet $= 2R + R = 3R$
Using the Kepler's law
$$T^2 \propto R^3$$

$$\Rightarrow \quad \left(\frac{T_1}{T_2}\right) = \left(\frac{R_1}{R_2}\right)^{3/2}$$

Substituting the values in the above equation, we get

$$\left(\frac{24}{T}\right) = \left(\frac{12R}{3R}\right)^{3/2}$$

$$T = 3 \text{ h}$$

$\therefore$ The time period of another satellite is 3 h.

43. According to Kepler's third law,
$$T^2 \propto R^3$$

$$\Rightarrow \quad \frac{T_2}{T_1} = \left(\frac{R_2}{R_1}\right)^{3/2}$$

$$\Rightarrow \quad \frac{T_2}{T} = \left(\frac{9R}{R}\right)^{3/2} \quad \left[\because R_1 = R, \; R_2 = 9R\right]$$

$$\Rightarrow \quad T_2 = 27T$$

44. Condition of weightlessness, $g_{equator} = 0$

$g_{equator} = g - \omega^2 R$

The radius of the Earth, $R = 6400$ km $= 6.4 \times 10^6$ m

$$\Rightarrow \quad \omega = \sqrt{\frac{g}{R}} \Rightarrow \omega = \sqrt{\frac{10}{6.4 \times 10^6 \text{ m}}}$$

$$\Rightarrow \quad \omega = \frac{1}{800} \text{ rad/s}$$

The duration of the day,

$$T = \frac{2\pi}{\omega} \Rightarrow T = \frac{2\pi}{\frac{1}{800}}$$

$$\Rightarrow \quad T = 5024 \text{ s}$$

$$\Rightarrow \quad T = \frac{5024}{60} \text{ min}$$

$$\Rightarrow \quad T = 84 \text{ min}$$

Hence, the duration of the day would be 84 min.

45. Given, weight of body at North pole,
$$w_p = mg = 49 \text{ N}$$
Radius of Earth, $R = 6400$ km
Let weight of body at equator be w_e.
At equator, $g_e = g - R\omega^2$

$$\therefore \quad w_e = mg_e = m(g - R\omega^2)$$

Since, $w_p > w_e \Rightarrow w_e < 49$ N
Hence, above condition is satisfied by only option (b).

46. Given, distance between centre of ring and sphere,
$d = \sqrt{8}R$

Since, gravitational field at the axis of ring, $E = \frac{Gmd}{(d^2 + R^2)^{3/2}}$

Here, G is the gravitational constant.

$$\Rightarrow \quad E = \frac{GmR\sqrt{8}}{(8R^2 + R^2)^{3/2}} = \frac{GmR\sqrt{8}}{(3R)^3}$$

$$\Rightarrow \quad E = \frac{GmR\sqrt{8}}{27R^3} = \frac{Gm\sqrt{8}}{27R^2}$$

Force between ring and sphere,
$$F = ME \quad \text{...(i)}$$
Substituting the value of E in Eq. (i), we get
$$F = \frac{\sqrt{8}}{27}\frac{GmM}{R^2}$$

47. Given, mass of man $(m) = 60$ kg

Downward acceleration of lift, $a = 1.8\,\text{ms}^{-2}$

Let T be the tension in the rope connected with lift, g be the acceleration due to gravity $(10\,\text{ms}^{-2})$.

As, lift is moving in downward direction

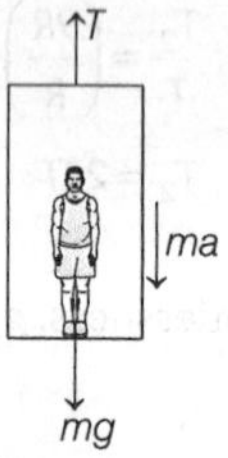

$\therefore\ mg - T = ma$

$\Rightarrow\quad T = mg - ma = m(g - a)$

$= 60(10 - 1.8) = 60 \times 8.2 = 492$ N

Hence, the weight of the man during downward acceleration is 492 N.

48. Given, $g_A = g_C$

Radius of Earth, $R = 6400$ km

Height, $\quad h = 3200 \text{ km} = \dfrac{R}{2}$

Since, $\quad g = \dfrac{GM}{R^2}$

where, G is gravitational constant.

$$\therefore\quad g_A = \frac{GM(OA)}{R^3} \quad \text{... (i)}$$

and $$g_C = \frac{GM}{(OC)^2} = \frac{GM}{R+h}$$

$$= \frac{GM}{(R + R/2)^2} = \frac{GM}{(3R/2)^2} \quad \text{... (ii)}$$

According to given information from Eqs. (i) and (ii), we get

$$\frac{GM(OA)}{R^3} = \frac{GM}{9R^2/4}$$

$$\Rightarrow\quad OA = \frac{4}{9}R = \frac{4}{9} \times 6400$$

and $\quad AB = OB - OA$

$$\Rightarrow\quad AB = 6400 - \frac{4}{9} \times 6400$$

$$= 6400\,(1 - 4/9) = 6400 \times 5/9$$

Now, $\quad OA : AB = \dfrac{6400 \times 4/9}{5/9 \times 6400} = \dfrac{4}{5}$

Hence, $\quad x = 4$

49. Given,

Acceleration due to gravity on Earth, $g_E = 10\,\text{m/s}^2$

and acceleration due to gravity on Mars, $g_M = 4\,\text{m/s}^2$

We know that, g_E (at height h)$= g_{\text{Earth}}\left(1 - \dfrac{2h}{R}\right)$

$\therefore$ Weight at Earth,

$$mg_E = 100 \times 10 = 1000 \text{ N}$$

As the spaceship moves far away from Earth, the value of g_E decreases to zero at a point where $g_E + g_M = 0$ and hence weight will also be zero.

This point is called neutral point and is shown by graph (III) in the given figure.

Then, g_E increases 4ms^{-2} at Mars surface and weight becomes 400N which is also exhibited by graph (III).

JEE Advanced

1. We know that,

$$g = \frac{GM}{r^2}$$

for satellite P, $r = R + h_P$

$$g_P = \frac{GM}{(R + h_P)^2} \quad \text{...(i)}$$

For satellite Q, $r = R + h_Q$

$$\therefore\quad g_Q = \frac{GM}{(R + h_Q)^2} \quad \text{...(ii)}$$

From Eqs. (i) and (ii), we get

$$\frac{g_P}{g_Q} = \frac{(R + h_Q)^2}{(R + h_P)^2}$$

$$\Rightarrow\quad \frac{36}{25} = \left[\frac{R + h_Q}{R + h_Q}\right]^2$$

$$\Rightarrow\quad \frac{6}{5} = \frac{R + h_Q}{R + h_P}$$

$$\Rightarrow\quad \frac{6}{5} + \frac{R + \frac{R}{3}}{R + h_P} \Rightarrow h_P = \frac{3R}{5}$$

2. v_A : Mass $\propto$ (Radius)^3

Radius of A is reduced to half. So, mass of A will become $\dfrac{M_A}{8}$.

$$v_A = \sqrt{\frac{\left(2G\dfrac{M_A}{8}\right)}{\left(\dfrac{R}{2}\right)}} = \sqrt{\frac{GM_A}{2R}} \quad \text{...(i)}$$

v_B : $\dfrac{7M_A}{8}$ mass is deposited over B.

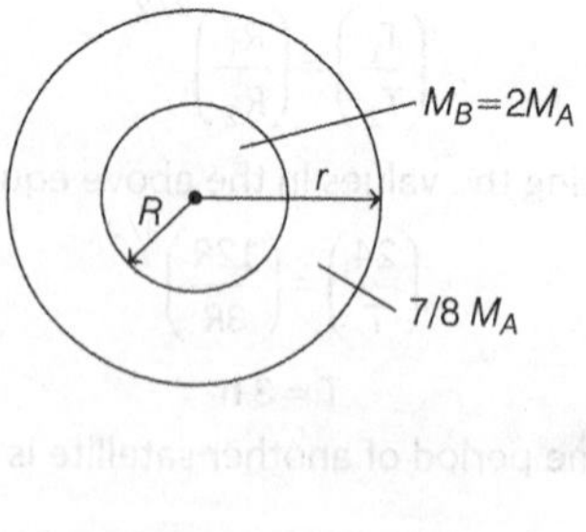

$$\rho_A = \frac{M_A}{\frac{4}{3}\pi R^3} \quad \text{...(ii)}$$

$$\frac{4}{3}\pi(r^3 - R^3)(\rho_A) = \frac{7}{8}M_A \quad \text{...(iii)}$$

Solving Eqs. (ii) and (iii), we get

$$r = \left(\frac{15}{8}\right)^{\frac{1}{3}} R$$

Now, $$v_B = \sqrt{\frac{2G\left(2M_A + \frac{7}{8}M_A\right)}{\left(\frac{15}{8}\right)^{\frac{1}{3}} R}} \quad \text{...(iv)}$$

From Eqs. (i) and (iv), we get

$$\frac{v_B}{v_A} = \sqrt{\frac{2.30 \times 10}{(15)^{\frac{1}{3}}}}$$

$\therefore \quad n = 2.30$

3. For earth-sun system,

$$T_0^2 = \frac{4\pi^2}{GM_S} \times R^3 \quad \text{...(i)}$$

For binary system

$$T^2 = \frac{4\pi^2}{G[3M_S + 6M_S]} \times (9R)^3 \quad \text{...(ii)}$$

Using Eqs. (i) and (ii), we get

$$T = 9T_0$$

So, $n = 9$

4. Given, $v_e = 11.2 \text{ km/ s} = \sqrt{\frac{2GM_e}{R_e}}$

From energy conservation,

$$K_i + U_i = K_f + U_f$$

$$\frac{1}{2}mv_s^2 - \frac{GM_s m}{r} - \frac{GM_e m}{R_e} = 0 + 0$$

Here, r = distane of rocket from sun

$$\Rightarrow \quad v_s = \sqrt{\frac{2GM_e}{R_e} + \frac{2GM_s}{r}}$$

Given, $M_s = 3 \times 10^5 M_e$ and $r = 2.5 \times 10^4 R_e$

$$\Rightarrow \quad v_s = \sqrt{\frac{2GM_e}{R_e} + \frac{(2G)3 \times 10^5 M_e}{2.5 \times 10^4 R_e}}$$

$$= \sqrt{\frac{2GM_e}{R_e}\left(1 + \frac{3 \times 10^5}{2.5 \times 10^4}\right)}$$

$$= \sqrt{\frac{2GM_e}{R_e} \times 13}$$

$$= \sqrt{13} \times 11.2 \text{ km/ s}$$

$$\Rightarrow \quad v_s \simeq 42 \text{ km/s}$$

5. At height h,

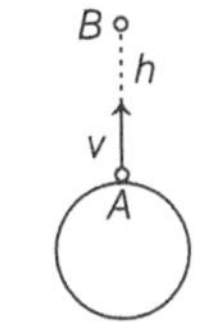

$$g' = \frac{g}{\left(1 + \frac{h}{R}\right)^2} \quad \text{...(i)}$$

Given, $g' = \frac{g}{4}$

Substituting in equation (i) we get,

$$h = R$$

Now, from A to B,

decrease in kinetic energy = increase in potential energy

$$\Rightarrow \quad \frac{1}{2}mv^2 = \frac{mgh}{1 + \frac{h}{R}}$$

$$\Rightarrow \quad \frac{v^2}{2} = \frac{gh}{1 + \frac{h}{R}} = \frac{1}{2}gR \quad (h = R)$$

$$\Rightarrow \quad v^2 = gR$$

or $\quad v = \sqrt{gR}$

Now, $\quad v_{esc} = \sqrt{2gR} = v\sqrt{2}$

$$\Rightarrow \quad N = 2$$

6. For point mass at distance $r = 3l$

$$\frac{GMm}{(3l)^2} - \frac{Gm^2}{l^2} = ma \quad \text{....(i)}$$

For point mass at distance $r = 4l$

$$\frac{GMm}{(4l)^2} + \frac{Gm^2}{l^2} = ma \quad \text{(ii)}$$

Equating the two equations, we have

$$\frac{GMm}{9l^2} - \frac{Gm^2}{l^2} = \frac{GMm}{16l^2} + \frac{Gm^2}{l^2}$$

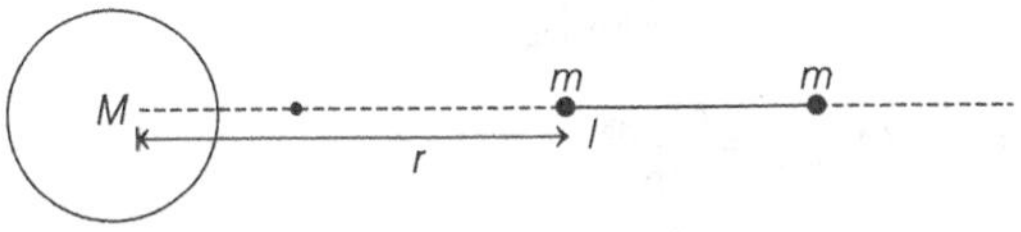

$$\frac{7GMm}{144} = \frac{2Gm^2}{l^2}$$

$$m = \frac{7M}{288}$$

7. Gravitational field at a distance r due to mass 'm'

$$E = \frac{Gm}{r^2} = \frac{4G\rho\pi r}{3}$$

Consider a small element of width dr and area ΔA at a distance r.

Pressure force on this element outwards = gravitational force on 'dm' from 'm' inwards

$$\Rightarrow (dp)\Delta A = E(dm) \quad \Rightarrow -dp \cdot \Delta A = \left(\frac{4}{3}G\pi\rho r\right)(\Delta A\, dr \cdot \rho)$$

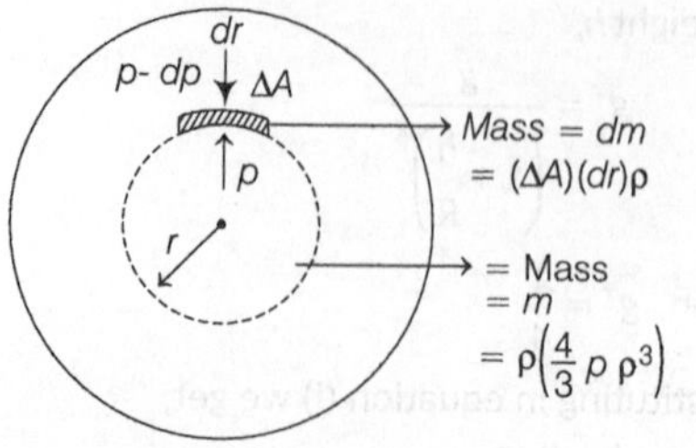

$$-\int_O^P dp = \int_R^r \left(\frac{4G\rho^2\pi}{3}\right) r\,dr$$

$$-p = \frac{4G\rho^2\pi}{3\times 2}[r^2 - R^2] \Rightarrow p = c(R^2 - r^2)$$

$$r = \frac{3R}{4},\ p_1 = c\left(R^2 - \frac{9R^2}{16}\right) = c\left(\frac{7R^2}{16}\right)$$

$$r = \frac{2R}{3},\ p_2 = c\left(R^2 - \frac{4R^2}{9}\right) = c\left(\frac{5R^2}{9}\right)$$

$$\frac{p_1}{p_2} = \frac{63}{80}$$

$$r = \frac{3R}{5},\ p_3 = c\left(R^2 - \frac{9}{25}R^2\right) = c\left(\frac{16R^2}{25}\right)$$

$$r = \frac{2R}{5},\ p_4 = c\left(R^2 - \frac{4R^2}{25}\right) = c\left(\frac{21R^2}{25}\right)$$

$$\frac{p_3}{p_4} = \frac{16}{21}$$

8. Given, $R_{\text{planet}} = \frac{R_{\text{earth}}}{10}$ and density, $\rho = \frac{M_{\text{earth}}}{\frac{4}{3}\pi R_{\text{earth}}^3}$

$$= \frac{M_{\text{planet}}}{\frac{4}{3}\pi R_{\text{planet}}^3}$$

$$\Rightarrow \quad M_{\text{planet}} = \frac{M_{\text{earth}}}{10^3}$$

$$g_{\text{surface of planet}} = \frac{GM_{\text{planet}}}{R_{\text{planet}}^2} = \frac{GM_e \cdot 10^2}{10^3 \cdot R_e^2} = \frac{GM_e}{10R_e^2}$$

$$= \frac{g_{\text{surface of earth}}}{10}$$

$$g_{\text{depth of planet}} = g_{\text{surface of planet}}\left(\frac{x}{R}\right)$$

where, x = distance from centre of planet.

∴ Total force on wire

$$F = \int_{4R/5}^{R} \lambda\, dx\, g\left(\frac{x}{R}\right) = \frac{\lambda g}{R}\left[\frac{x^2}{2}\right]_{4R/5}^{R}$$

Here, $g = g_{\text{surface of planet}},\ R = R_{\text{planet}}$

Substituting the given values, we get $F = 108$ N

9.

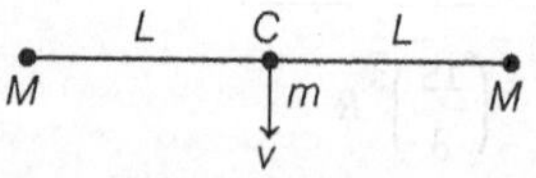

Let v is the minimum velocity. From energy conservation,

$$U_c + K_c = U_\infty + K_\infty$$

$$\therefore \quad mV_c + \frac{1}{2}mv^2 = 0 + 0$$

$$\therefore \quad v = \sqrt{-2V_c} = \sqrt{(-2)\left(\frac{-2GM}{L}\right)} = 2\sqrt{\frac{GM}{L}}$$

10. Surface area of Q is four times. Therefore, radius of Q is two times. Volume is eight times. Therefore, mass of Q is also eight times.

So, let $\quad M_P = M$ and $R_P = r$

Then, $\quad M_Q = 8\,M$ and $R_Q = 2r$

Now, mass of R is $(M_P + M_Q)$ or 9 M. Therefore, radius of R is $(9)^{1/3} r$. Now, escape velocity from the surface of a planet is given by

$$v = \sqrt{\frac{2GM}{r}} \quad (r = \text{radius of that planet})$$

$$\therefore \quad v_P = \sqrt{\frac{2GM}{r}}$$

$$\Rightarrow \quad v_Q = \sqrt{\frac{2G(8M)}{(2r)}}$$

$$\Rightarrow \quad v_R = \sqrt{\frac{2G(9M)}{(9)^{1/3} r}}$$

From here we can see that, $\frac{v_P}{v_Q} = \frac{1}{2}$ and $v_R > v_Q > v_P$

CHAPTER~06

ELASTICITY

LEVEL 01 Starter Level

6.1 Stress and Strain

1 One end of a uniform wire of length L and of weight w is attached rigidly to a point in the roof and a weight w_1 is suspended from its lower end. If S is the area of cross- section of the wire, find the stress in the wire at a height $3L/4$ from its lower end.

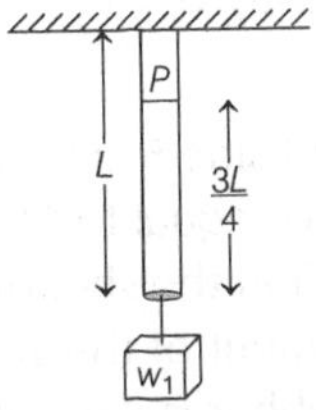

2 Two equal and opposite forces act on a rod of uniform cross-sectional area A, as shown in the figure. Find the (i) tensile (ii) shearing stress on the section $PQRS$.

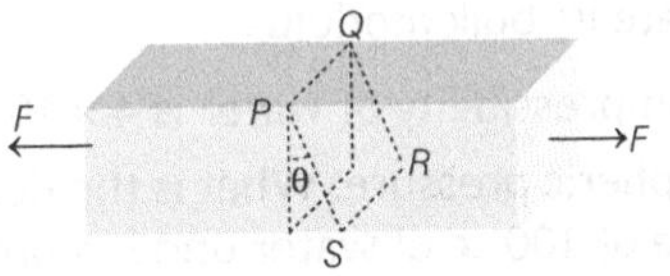

3 A wire is stretched to double its length. What is the strain in it?

4 A cube of aluminium of sides 0.1 m is subjected to a shearing force of 100 N. The top face of the cube is displaced through 0.02 cm with respect to the bottom face. Find the shearing strain.

5 A uniform cube is subjected to volume compression. If each side is decreased by 1%, then what is bulk strain?

6.2 Young's modulus

1 A vertical metal cylinder of radius 2 cm and length 2 m is fixed at the lower end and a load of 100 kg is put on it. Find (a) the stress (b) the strain and (c) the compression of the cylinder. Young's modulus of the metal $= 2 \times 10^{11}$ N/m^2.

2 Two persons pull a rope towards themselves. Each person exerts a force of 100 N on the rope. Find the Young's modulus of the material of the rope, if it extends in length by 1 cm. Original length of the rope = 2 m and the area of cross-section = 2 cm.

3 Two wires A and B are made of same material. The wire A has a length l and diameter d while the wire B has a length $2l$ and diameter $d/2$. If the two wires are stretched by the same force, find the ratio of elongation in A to the elongation in B.

4 A 5 m long aluminium wire ($Y_{Al} = 6 \times 10^{10}$ N/m²) of diameter 3 mm supports a 40 kg mass. In order to have the same elongation in a copper wire ($Y_{Cu} = 12 \times 10^{10}$ N/m) of the same length under the same weight, what should be the diameter of the copper wire?

5 Three blocks A, B and C each of mass 3 kg are attached as shown in figure. Both the wires have equal cross-sectional area 5×10^{-7} m². The surface is smooth. Find the longitudinal strain in each wire, if Young modulus of both the wires is 2×10^{11} N/m² ($g = 10$ m/s²)

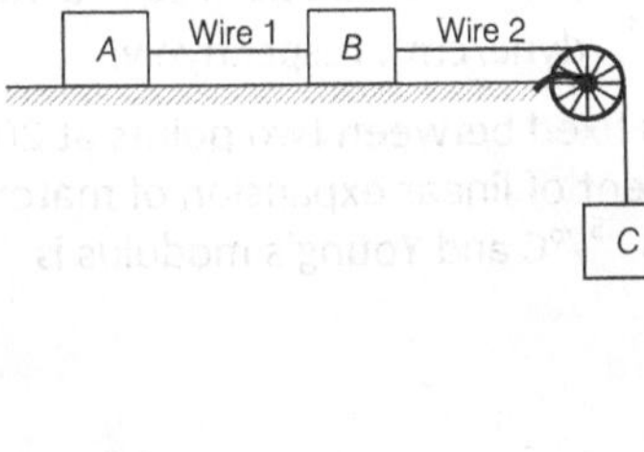

6 A steel wire and a copper wire of equal length and equal cross-sectional area are joined end to end and the combination is subjected to a tension. Find the ratio of (a) the stresses developed in the two wires and (b) the strains developed.
$Y_{\text{steel}} = 2 \times 10^{11}\ \text{N/m}^2, Y_{\text{Cu}} = 1.3 \times 10^{11}\ \text{N/m}^2$.

7 Two blocks of masses 1 kg and 2 kg are connected by a metal wire going over a smooth pulley as shown in figure. The breaking stress of the metal is 2×10^9 N/m. What should be the minimum radius of the wire used, if it is not to break ? Take, $g = 10\ \text{m/s}^2$.

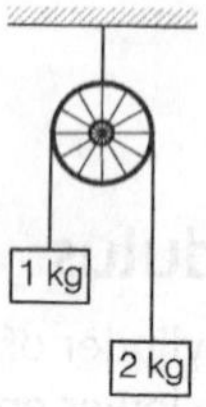

8 An aluminium rod has a breaking strain 0.2%. What will be the minimum cross-sectional area of the rod in order to support a load of 10^4 N ? (Young's modulus is $7 \times 10^9\ \text{Nm}^{-2}$)

9 A copper rod of length L and radius r is suspended from the ceiling by one of its ends. Find the elongation of the rod due to its own weight when ρ and Y are the density and Young's modulus of the copper respectively.

10 A uniform copper bar of density ρ, length L, cross-sectional area S and Young's modulus Y is moving horizontally on a frictionless surface with constant acceleration a_0. Find

(a) the stress at the centre of the bar,

(b) total elongation of the bar.

11 A light rod of length 200 cm is suspended from the ceiling horizontally by means of two vertical wires of equal length tied to its end. One of the wires is made of steel and is of cross-section 0.1 cm² and the other of brass of cross-section 0.2 cm². Along the rod at which distance a weight be hung to produce

(a) equal stresses in both the wires

(b) equal strains in both the wires?

Y for steel and brass are 20×10^{11} dyne/cm² and 10×10^{11} dyne/cm², respectively.

12 A rod is fixed between two points at 20° C. The coefficient of linear expansion of material of rod is 1.1×10^{-5}/°C and Young's modulus is 1.2×10^{11} N/m². Find the stress developed in the rod, if temperature of rod becomes 10° C.

6.3 Modulus of Rigidity

1 The drawing shows a 160 kg crate hanging from the end of a steel bar. The length of the bar is 0.10 m, and its cross-sectional area is 3.2×10^{-4} m². Neglect the weight of the bar itself and determine

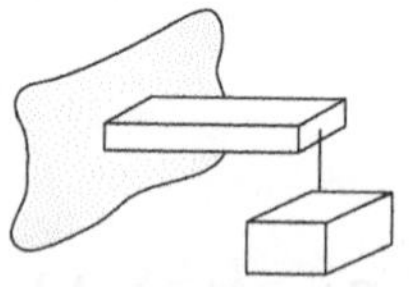

(a) the shear stress on the bar and

(b) the vertical deflection of the right end of the bar shear modulus of steel $= 8.1 \times 10^{10}\ \text{N/m}^2$.

2 A box shaped piece of gelatin dessert has a top area of 15 cm² and a height of 3 cm. When a shearing force of 0.50 N is applied to the upper surface, the upper surface displaces 4 mm relative to the bottom surface. What are the shearing stress, the shearing strain, and the shear modulus for the gelatin?

3 A rubber cube of side 5 cm has one side fixed while a tangential force equal to 1800 N is applied to opposite face. Find the shearing strain and the lateral displacement of the strained face. Modulus of rigidity for rubber is $2.4 \times 10^6\ \text{N/m}^2$.

6.4 Bulk Modulus

1 A spherical ball contracts in volume by 0.001% when it is subjected to a pressure of 100 atm. Calculate its bulk modulus.

2 The compressibility of water is 4×10^{-5} per unit atmospheric pressure. What is the decrease in volume of 100 cc of water under a pressure of 100 atm?

3 Find the depth of a lake at which the density of water is 1% greater than at the surface, if compressibility of water is 50×10^{-6} atm
[Take, $g = 10\ \text{m/s}^2$ and 1 atm $= 10^5\ \text{N/m}^2$]

4 What is the ratio of the adiabatic to isothermal elasticities of a triatomic gas?

5 A gas undergoes a process in which the pressure and volume are related by $Vp^n =$ constant. Find the bulk modulus of the gas.

6.5 Poisson's Ratio

1 A 3 cm long copper wire is stretched to increase its length by 0.3 cm. Find the lateral strain in the wire, if the Poisson's ratio for copper is 0.26.

2 A uniform bar of length L and cross-sectional area A is subjected to a tensile load F, Y be the Young's modulus and σ be the Poisson's ratio, then find the volumetric strain.

3 A rod has Poisson's ratio 0.2. If a rod suffers a longitudinal strain of 2×10^{-3}, then what is the % change in its volume?

6.6 Elastic Potential Energy

1 A wire suspended vertically from one of its ends is stretched by attaching a weight of 200 N to the lower end. The weight stretches the wire by 1 mm, then find the elastic energy stored in the wire.

2 Calculate the increase in energy of a brass bar of length 0.2 m and cross-sectional area 1 cm^2 when compressed with a load of 5 kg-weight along its length.
(Young's modulus of brass $= 1.0 \times 10^{11}$ N/m^2 and $g = 9.8$ m/s^2).

3 When the load on a wire increased slowly from 2 kg wt. to 4 kg wt, the elongation increases from 0.6 mm to 1.00 mm. How much work is done during the extension of the wire? [$g = 9.8$ m/s^2]

4 If work done in stretching a wire by 1 mm is 2 J. find the work necessary for stretching another wire of same material, but with double the radius and half the length by 1 mm.

5 A copper rod of length L and radius r is suspended from the ceiling by one of its ends. ρ and Y are the density and Young's modulus of the copper, respectively. Find the elastic potential energy stored in the rod due to its own weight.

6.7 Stress-Strain Curve

1 The stress *versus* strain graphs for wires of two materials A and B are as shown in the figure.

If Y_A and Y_B are the Young's moduli of the materials, then find Y_A/Y_B.

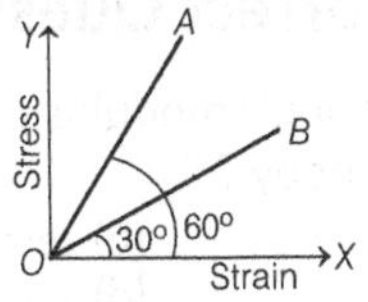

2 A graph is shown between stress and strain for a metal.

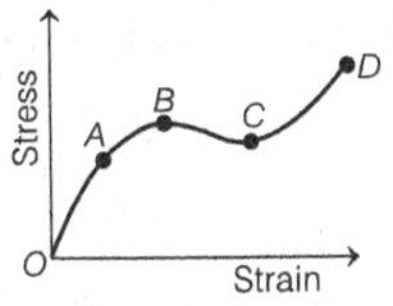

(i) Which point is the yield point?
(ii) Which point is the breaking point?
(iii) In which region Hooke's law holds good?
(iv) In which region internal forces are conservative?
(v) In which region the wire behaves like a viscous liquid?

3 The stress-strain graphs for materials A and B are shown in figure. The graphs are drawn to the same scale

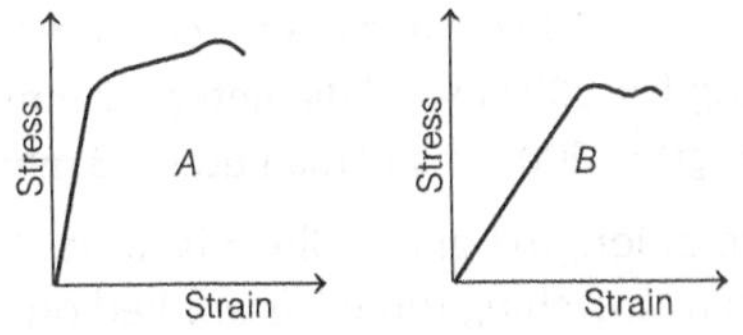

(a) Which of the material has greater Young's modulus. Explain?
(b) Which material is more ductile. Explain?
(c) Which is more brittle. Explain?

4 The strain-stress curves of three wires of different materials are shown in the figure. P, Q and R are the elastic limits of the wires. Which wire is the most elastic?

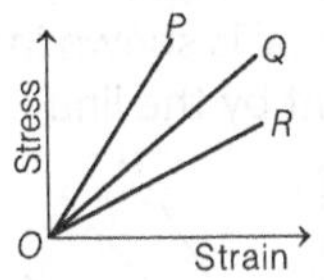

LEVEL 02 JEE Main Level

Single Choice Correct Questions

1 What is the Young's modulus of elasticity for a perfectly rigid body ?

(a) infinity (b) zero
(c) 1 (d) – 1

2 The Young's modulus of a wire of length L and radius r is Y. If the length and radius are reduced to $L/2$ and $r/2$, then its Young's modulus will be

(a) $\frac{Y}{2}$ (b) Y
(c) $2Y$ (d) $4Y$

3. The ratio of diameters of two wires of same material in $n:1$. The length of each wire is 4 m. On applying the same load, the increase in length of thin wire will be ($n > 1$)

(a) n^2 times (b) n times
(c) $2n$ times (d) $(2n+1)$ times

4 The following four wires are of the same material. Which of these will have the largest extension when the same tension is applied?

(a) Length = 50 cm and diameter = 0.5 mm
(b) Length = 100 cm and diameter = 1 mm
(c) Length = 200 cm and diameter = 2 mm
(d) Length = 300 cm and diameter = 3 mm

5 A wire of length L and radius r is fixed at one end. When a stretching force F is applied on the free end, the extension in the wire is l. Another wire of length $2L$ and radius $2r$ and of the same material is also fixed at one end. If a stretching force $2F$ is applied on the other end, then the elongation in the length of the wire will be

(a) $\frac{l}{2}$ (b) l
(c) $2l$ (d) $4l$

6 The load *versus* elongation graph for four wires of the same material is shown in figure. The thinnest wire is represent by the line

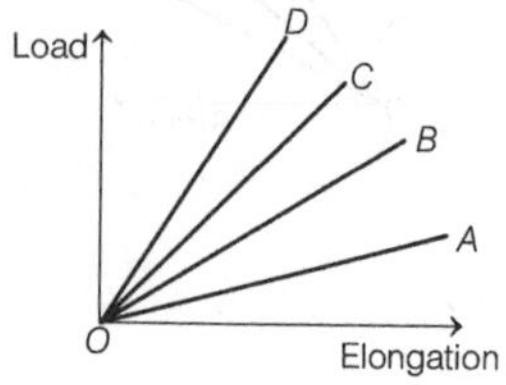

(a) OC (b) OD (c) OA (d) OB

7 On applying a stress of 7×10^8 N/m^2, the length of a wire of some elastic material is doubled. Then, the value of the Young's modulus (in N/m^2) for this material should be

(a) 3.5×10^8
(b) 14×10^8
(c) 7×10^8
(d) Insufficient data Y cannot be inferred

8 The adjacent graph shows the extension (Δl) of a wire of length 1 m suspended from the top of a roof at one end and with a load w connected to the other end. If the cross-sectional area of the wire is 10^{-6} m^2, calculate the Young's modulus of the material of the wire.

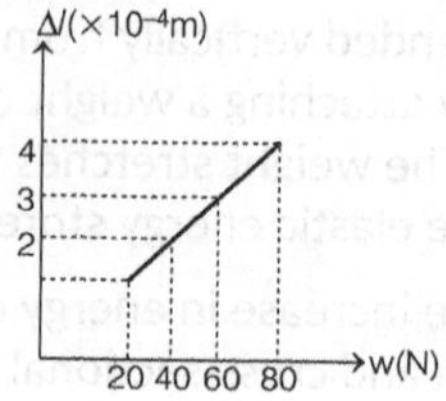

(a) 2×10^{11} N/m² (b) 2×10^{-11} N/m^2
(c) 3×10^{-12} N/m² (d) 3×10^{12} N/m^2

9 The elastic limit of an elevator cable is 2×10^9 N/m^2. The maximum upward acceleration that an elevator of mass 2×10^3 kg can have when supported by a cable whose cross-sectional area is 10^{-4} m^2, provided the stress in cable would not exceed half of the elastic limit would be

(a) 10 m/s^2 (b) 50 m/s^2
(c) 40 m/s²
(d) Not possible to move up

10 To break a wire, a stress of 10^6 N/m² is required. If the density of the material is 3×10^3 kg/m^3, then the minimum length of the wire which will break by its own weight will be

(a) 34 m (b) 30 m (c) 300 m (d) 3 m

11 If the ratio of lengths, radii and Young's modulii of steel and brass wires in the figure are a, b and c respectively. Then the corresponding ratio of increase in their lengths would be

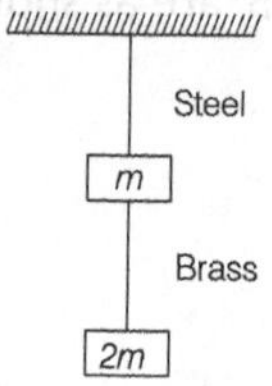

(a) $\frac{2ac}{b^2}$ (b) $\frac{3a}{2b^2c}$ (c) $\frac{3c}{2ab^2}$ (d) $\frac{2a^2c}{b}$

12 A uniform rod of length L, has a mass per unit length λ and area of cross-section A. The elongation in the rod is l due to its own weight, if it is suspended from the ceiling of a room. The Young's modulus of the rod is

(a) $\frac{3\lambda g L^2}{Al}$ (b) $\frac{\lambda g L^2}{2Al}$ (c) $\frac{2\lambda g L}{Al}$ (d) $\frac{\lambda g L^2}{Al}$

13 A steel ring of radius r and cross-section area A is fitted on to a wooden disc of radius $R(R > r)$. If Young's modulus be E, then the force with which the steel ring is expanded is

(a) $AE\frac{R}{r}$ (b) $AE\left(\frac{R-r}{r}\right)$

(c) $\frac{E}{A}\left(\frac{R-r}{A}\right)$ (d) $\frac{Er}{AR}$

14 A wire of radius r, Young's modulus Y and length l is hung from a fixed point and supports a heavy metal cylinder of volume V at its lower end. The change in length of the wire when cylinder is immersed in a liquid of density ρ, is in fact

(a) decreases by $\frac{Vl\rho g}{Y\pi r^2}$ (b) increases by $\frac{Vr\rho g}{Y\pi l^2}$

(c) decreases by $\frac{V\rho g}{Y\pi r}$ (d) increases by $\frac{V\rho g}{\pi l}$

15 The length of a metal wire is l_1 when the tension in it is T_1 and is l_2 when the tension is T_2. The natural length of the wire is

(a) $\frac{l_1 + l_2}{2}$ (b) $\sqrt{l_1 l_2}$

(c) $\frac{l_1 T_2 - l_2 T_1}{T_2 - T_1}$ (d) $\frac{l_1 T_2 + l_2 T_1}{T_2 + T_1}$

16 The breaking stress of a wire depends on

(a) material of the wire
(b) length of the wire
(c) radius of the wire
(d) shape of the cross-section

17 A rope 1 cm in diameter breaks, if the tension in it exceeds 500 N. The maximum tension that may be given to a similar rope of diameter 2 cm is

(a) 500 N (b) 250 N
(c) 1000 N (d) 2000 N

18 A body of mass 10 kg is attached to a wire 0.3 m long. Its breaking stress is 4.8×10^7 N/m^2. The area of cross-section of the wire is 10^{-6} m^2. The maximum angular velocity with which it can be rotated in a horizontal circle without breaking is

(a) 2 rad/s (b) 4 rad/s
(c) 6 rad/s (d) 8 rad/s

19 Two blocks of masses m and $2m$ are connected through a wire of breaking stress S passing over a frictionless pulley. The maximum radius of the wire to be used so that the wire may not break is

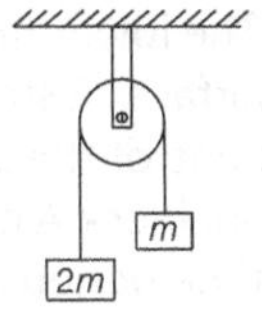

(a) $\sqrt{\frac{3}{4}\frac{mg}{\pi S}}$ (b) $\sqrt{\frac{4}{3}\frac{mg}{S}}$

(c) $\sqrt{\frac{4}{3}\frac{mg}{\pi S}}$ (d) $\sqrt{\frac{1}{2}\frac{mg}{\pi S}}$

20 A copper wire of a metre length, cross-sectional area 10^{-6} m^2 and of negligible mass, is kept on a smooth horizontal table with one end fixed. A 1 kg ball is attached to the other end. The wire and ball are rotating with an angular velocity of 20 rad/s. The wire elongated by 10^{-3} m. The Young's modulus of wire is

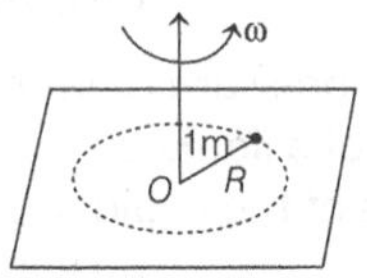

(a) 4×10^{10} N/m^2 (b) 3×10^{11} N/m^2
(c) 4×10^{11} N/m^2 (d) 3×10^{10} N/m^2

21 In the Q. No. 20, if angular velocity is raised to 100 rad/s, the wire breaks. Then, the breaking stress of the wire is

(a) 10^{11} N/m^2 (b) 10^4 N/m^2
(c) 10^6 N/m^2 (d) 10^{10} N/m^2

22 A wire of cross-sectional area A is stretched horizontal between two clamps located at a distance $2l$ from each other. A weight w is suspended from the mid-point of the wire. The strain produced in the wire, (if the vertical distance through which the mid-point of the wire moves down $x << l$) will be

(a) $\frac{x^2}{l^2}$ (b) $\frac{2x^2}{l^2}$

(c) $\frac{x^2}{2l^2}$ (d) $\frac{x}{2l}$

23 In above question, the stress in the string is

(a) $\frac{4xw}{lA}$ (b) $\frac{2xw}{lA}$

(c) $\frac{wl}{4xA}$ (d) $\frac{wl}{2xA}$

24 A highly rigid cubical block A of small mass M and side L is fixed rigidly onto another cubical block B of same dimensions and of low modulus of rigidity η such that lower face of A completely covers the upper face of B. The lower face of B is rigidly held on a horizontal surface. A small force F is applied perpendicular to one of the side face of A. After the force is withdrawn, block A executes small oscillations, the time period of which is given by

(a) $2\pi\sqrt{M\eta L}$ (b) $2\pi\sqrt{\frac{ML}{\eta}}$

(c) $2\pi\sqrt{\frac{M\eta}{L}}$ (d) $2\pi\sqrt{\frac{M}{\eta L}}$

25 A 50 kg motor rests on four cylindrical rubber blocks. Each block has a height of 4 cm and a cross-sectional area of 16 cm^2. The shear modulus of rubber is 2×10^6 N/m^2. A sideways force of 500 N is applied to the motor. The distance that the motor moves sideways is

(a) 0.156 cm (b) 1.56 cm

(c) 0.312 cm (d) 0.204 cm

26 An increase in pressure required to decrease the 200 L volume of a liquid by 0.004% in container is (bulk modulus of the liquid = 2100 MPa)

(a) 188 kPa (b) 8.4 kPa

(c) 18.8 kPa (d) 84 kPa

27 A cube is subjected to a uniform volume compression. If the side of the cube decreases by 2%, the bulk strain is

(a) 0.02 (b) 0.03 (c) 0.04 (d) 0.06

28 A metal block is experiencing an atmospheric pressure of 1×10^5 N/m^2. When the same block is placed in a vacuum chamber, find the fractional change in its volume. The bulk modulus of metal is 1.25×10^{11} N/m^2.

(a) 2×10^{-7} (b) 4×10^{-7}

(c) 6×10^{-7} (d) 8×10^{-7}

29 A ball falling in a lake of 200 m shows a decrease of 0.1% in its volume. The bulk modulus of elasticity of the material of the ball is ($g = 10$ m/s^2)

(a) 10^9 N/m^2 (b) 2×10^9 N/m^2

(c) 3×10^9 N/m^2 (d) 4×10^9 N/m^2

30 Compressibility of water is 5×10^{-5} atm. The change in pressure required to increase the density of water by 0.1% is

(a) 2×10^9 Nm^{-2} (b) 2×10^8 Nm^{-2}

(c) 2×10^6 Nm^{-2} (d) 2×10^4 Nm^{-2}

31 A gas undergoes a change according to the law, $p = p_0 e^{\alpha V}$. The bulk modulus of the gas is

(a) p (b) αpV (c) αp (d) $\frac{pV}{\alpha}$

32 The mean density of sea water is ρ, and bulk modulus is B. The change in density of sea water in going from the surface of water to a depth h is

(a) $\frac{\rho gh}{B}$ (b) $B\rho gh$ (c) $\frac{\rho^2 gh}{B}$ (d) $\frac{B\rho^2}{gh}$

33 A solid sphere of radius R made of material of bulk modulus k is surrounded by a liquid in a cylindrical container. A massless piston of area A floats on the surface of liquid. When a mass m is placed on the piston to compress the liquid, the fractional change in the radius of the sphere $\frac{\Delta R}{R}$ is

(a) $\frac{mg}{Ak}$ (b) $\frac{mg}{3Ak}$ (c) $\frac{mg}{A}$ (d) $\frac{3mg}{Ak}$

34 A uniform pressure p is exerted on all sides of a solid cube at temperature t°C. By what amount should the temperature of the cube be raised in order to bring back to its original volume, it had before pressure was applied? (The bulk modulus and coefficient of volume expansion of the material are B and γ, respectively)

(a) $\frac{p\gamma}{B}$ (b) $\frac{pB}{\gamma}$ (c) $\frac{\gamma}{pB}$ (d) $\frac{p}{\gamma B}$

35 Which of the following statements is correct?

(a) Hooke's law is applicable only within elastic limit.

(b) The adiabatic and isothermal elastic constants of a gas are equal.

(c) Young's modulus is dimensionless.

(d) Stress multiplied by strain is equal to the stored energy.

36 Which one of the following substance possesses the highest elasticity?

(a) Rubber (b) Glass (c) Steel (d) Copper

37 If there is no change in the volume of wire on stretching, then poisson's ratio for the material of wire is

(a) -1 (b) 0 (c) 0.5 (d) 0.25

38 When a wire of length 10 m is subjected to a force of 100 N along its length, the lateral strain produced is 0.01×10^{-3}. The Poisson's ratio was found to be 0.4. If the area of cross-section of wire is 0.025 m^2, then its Young's modulus is

(a) 1.6×10^8 N/m^2 (b) 2.5×10^{10} N/m^2

(c) 12.5×10^{11} N/m^2 (d) 16×10^9 N/m^2

39 Poisson's ratio of a certain material is 0.2. If a longitudinal strain of 4×10^{-3} is produced in a uniform rod of this material, the percentage change in its volume will be
(a) 0.24 % (b) 0.32 % (c) 0.48 % (d) 0.56 %

40 A tensile force F is applied on all six surfaces of a cube of side unity, then increase in length of each side will be (Y = Young's modulus, σ = Poisson's ratio)
(a) $\frac{F}{Y(1-\sigma)}$ (b) $\frac{F}{Y(1+\sigma)}$
(c) $\frac{F(1-2\sigma)}{Y}$ (d) $\frac{F}{Y(1+2\sigma)}$

41 A steel wire at 20°C and of 2 mm diameter is pulled between two points. When the temperature becomes 10°C, the tension in the wire will be (coefficient of linear expansion of steel $= 10^{-5}$/°C and $Y = 2 \times 10^{11}$ N/m^2)
(a) 6.28 N (b) 62.8 N (c) 20.7 N (d) 11 N

42 A metal rod of Young's modulus 2×10^{10} Nm^{-2} undergoes an elastic strain of 0.06%. The energy per unit volume stored in J m^{-3} is
(a) 3600 (b) 7200 (c) 10800 (d) 14400

43 A uniform metal rod of 2 mm^2 cross-section is heated from 0°C to 20°C. The coefficient of linear expansion of the rod is 12×10^{-6}/°C, its Young's modulus is 10^{11} N/m^2. The energy stored per unit volume of the rod is
(a) 2880 J/m^3 (b) 1500 J/m^3
(c) 5760 J/m^3 (d) 1440 J/m^3

44 Two wires of the same material and length but diameter in the ratio 1 : 2 are stretched by the same force. The ratio of potential energy per unit volume for the two wires when stretched will be
(a) 1 : 1 (b) 2 : 1 (c) 4 : 1 (d) 16 : 1

45 A metal wire 4 m long and 2×10^{-7} m^2 in cross-section is stretched by a force of 30 N. If the work done in stretching that wire is 4.5×10^{-2} J, the Young's modulus of the wire is
(a) 2×10^{11} Pa (b) 4×10^{11} Pa
(c) 2×10^{12} Pa (d) 4×10^{12} Pa

46 The rubber cord catapult has a cross-sectional area 1 mm² and total unstretched length 10.0 cm. It is stretched to 12.0 cm and then released to project a missile of mass 5.0 g. Taking Young's modulus for rubber as 5.0×10^8 Nm^{-2}, the tension in the cord is
(a) 1000 N (b) 100 N
(c) 10 N (d) 1 N

47 In above question, the velocity of projection of the missile is
(a) 0.2 ms^{-1} (b) 2 ms^{-1} (c) 20 ms^{-1} (d) 200 ms^{-1}

48 Each of three blocks shown in figure has a mass 3 kg. The wire connecting blocks A and B has area of cross-section 0.005 cm^2 and Young's modulus of elasticity $Y = 2 \times 10^{11}$ N/m^2. Neglect friction. Find the elastic potential energy stored per unit volume in wire connecting blocks A and B in steady state (in J/m^3) ($g = 10$ m/s^2)

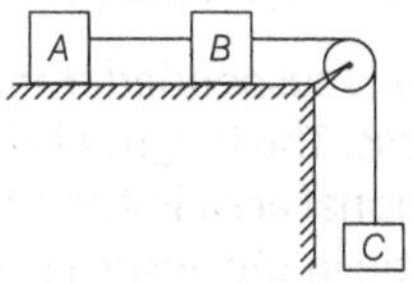

(a) 500 (b) 1000 (c) 2000 (d) 3000

49 A smooth uniform string of natural length l, cross-sectional area A and Young's modulus Y is pulled along its length by a force F on a horizontal surface. Find the elastic potential energy stored in the string.
(a) $U = \frac{F^2 l}{AY}$ (b) $U = \frac{F^2 l}{3AY}$ (c) $U = \frac{F^2 l}{6AY}$ (d) $U = \frac{F^2 l}{2AY}$

50 Two wires of equal length and cross-section area are suspended as shown in figure. Their Young's modulus are Y_1 and Y_2, respectively. The equivalent Young's modulus will be

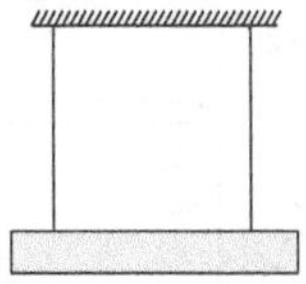

(a) $Y_1 + Y_2$ (b) $\frac{Y_1 + Y_2}{2}$ (c) $\frac{Y_1 Y_2}{Y_1 + Y_2}$ (d) $\sqrt{Y_1 Y_2}$

51 Two elastic rods are joined between fixed supports as shown in the figure. Condition for no change in the lengths of individual rods with the increase of temperature is (α_1, α_2 = linear expansion coefficient, A_1, A_2 = area of rods, Y_1, Y_2 = Young modulus

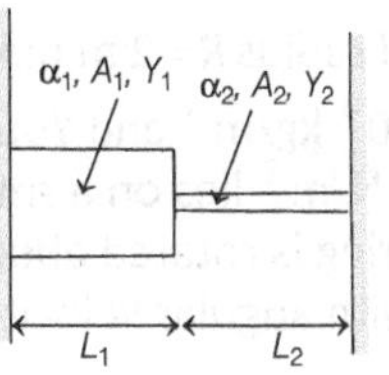

(a) $\frac{A_1}{A_2} = \frac{\alpha_1 Y_1}{\alpha_2 Y_2}$ (b) $\frac{A_1}{A_2} = \frac{L_1 \alpha_1 Y_1}{L_2 \alpha_2 Y_2}$
(c) $\frac{A_1}{A_2} = \frac{L_2 \alpha_2 Y_2}{L_1 \alpha_1 Y_1}$ (d) $\frac{A_1}{A_2} = \frac{\alpha_2 Y_2}{\alpha_1 Y_1}$

52 On loading, a metal wire of cross-section $10\ m^2$ and length 2 m by a mass of 210 kg, it extends by 16 mm and suddenly broke from the point of support. If density of that metal is $8000\ kgm^{-3}$ and its specific heat is $420\ J\ Kg^{-1}\ K^{-1}$, the rise in temperature of wire is

(a) 2.5 °C (b) 5 °C
(c) 6 °C (d) 10 °C

Numerical Value Questions

1 A 0.1 kg mass is suspended from a wire of negligible mass. The length of the wire is 1 m and its cross-sectional area is $4.9 \times 10^{-7}\ m^2$. If the mass is pulled a little in the vertically downward direction and released, it performs simple harmonic motion of angular frequency $140\ rad\ s^{-1}$. If the Young's modulus of the material of the wire is $n \times 10^9\ Nm^{-2}$, find the value of n.

2 A square brass plate of side 1.0 m and thickness 0.005 m is subjected to a force F on its smaller opposite edges, causing a displacement of 0.02 cm, If the shear modulus of brass is $0.4 \times 10^{11}\ N/m^2$, find the value of the force F (in kN).

3 Calculate the force F (in kN) needed to punch a 1.46 cm diameter hole in a steel plate 1.27 cm thick (Figure). The ultimate shear strength of steel is $3.45 \times 10^8\ Nm^{-2}$.

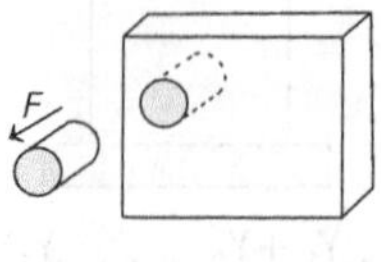

4 Two steel wires of same length but radii r and $2r$ are connected together end to end and tied to a wall as shown. The force stretches the combination by 10 mm. How far does the mid-point A move? (in mm)

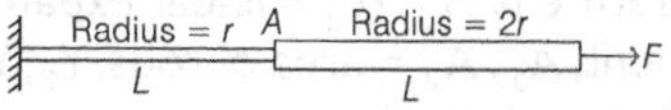

5 A thin ring of radius $R = 2$ m made of material of density $\rho = 10^4\ kg/m^3$ and Young modulus $Y = 2 \times 10^{11}\ N/m^2$ lies on a smooth horizontal table. If the ring is rotated about its centre in its own plane with angular velocity $\omega = 10$ rad/s, calculate the small change in radius. (In multiple of 10^{-5} m)

6 The Poisson's ratio of a material is 0.4. If a force is applied to a wire of this material, then there is a decrease of cross-sectional area by 2%. Find the percentage increase in its length.

7 Find the elastic potential energy per unit volume of water (in $\times 10^3\ Jm^{-3}$) at a depth of 1 km. Given, compressibility of water $= 5 \times 10^{-10}$ SI units and density of water $= 1000\ kg\ m^{-3}$)

8 What is the density of water (in kgm^{-3}) near the bottom of the ocean, where the pressure is about 501 atm? Given, density of water at the surface, where pressure is 1 atm is $1000\ kgm^{-3}$ and bulk modulus of water is $2.0 \times 10^9\ Nm^{-2}$.

9 One end of a steel wire is fixed to ceiling of an elevator moving up with an acceleration $2\ m/s^2$ and a load of 10 kg hangs from other end. Area of cross-section of the wire is $2\ cm^2$. If the longitudinal strain in the wire $n \times 10^{-6}$, then find n. (Take, $g = 10\ m/s^2$ and $Y = 2 \times 10^{11}\ N/m^2$)

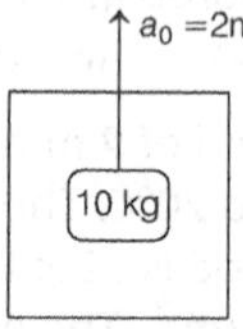

10 A block of weight 100 N is suspended by copper and steel wires of same cross-sectional area $0.5\ cm^2$ and length $\sqrt{3}$ m and 1 m, respectively. Their other ends are fixed on a ceiling as shown in figure. The angles subtended by copper and steel wires with ceiling are 30° and 60°, respectively. If elongation in copper wire is (Δl_c) and elongation in steel wire is (Δl_s), then find the ratio $\frac{\Delta l_c}{\Delta l_s}$. [Young's modulus for copper and steel are $1 \times 10^{11}\ N/m^2$ and $2 \times 10^{11}\ N/m^2$, respectively]

LEVEL 03 JEE Advanced Level

Single Choice Correct Questions

1 Forces of 10^5 N each are applied in opposite direction on the upper and lower faces of a cube of side 10 cm, shifting the upper face parallel to itself by 0.5 cm. If the side of the cube were 20 cm, the displacement would be

(a) 1 cm (b) 0.5 cm (c) 0.25 cm (d) 0.125 cm

2 Choose correct statement.

(a) The strain in a body is caused by stress.
(b) The stress in a body is caused by strain.
(c) Both stress and strain are caused by some external force.
(d) Stress and strain are unrelated.

3 A uniform slender rod of length L, cross-sectional area A and Young's modulus Y is acted upon by the forces shown in the figure. The elongation of the rod is

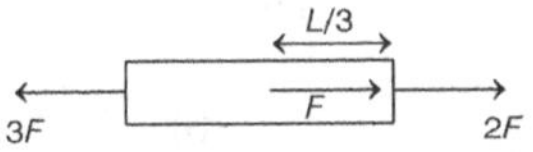

(a) $\frac{3FL}{5AY}$ (b) $\frac{2FL}{5AY}$ (c) $\frac{3FL}{8AY}$ (d) $\frac{8FL}{3AY}$

4 The bar shown in the figure is made of a single piece of material. It is fixed at one end. It consists of two segments of equal length $L/2$ but different cross-sectional area A and $2A$. What is the change in length of the entire system under the action of an axial force F? Consider the shape of joint to remain circular. (Given, Y = Young's modulus).

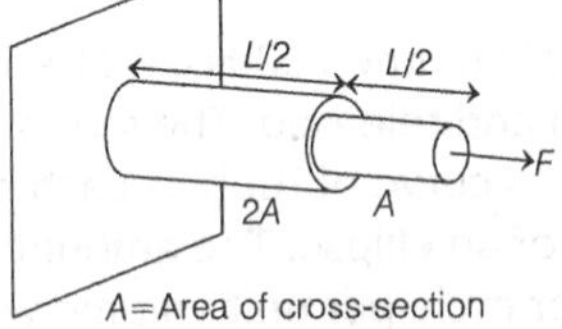

A=Area of cross-section

(a) $\frac{3FL}{4AY}$ (b) $\frac{3FL}{8AY}$

(c) $\frac{3FL}{2AY}$ (d) None of these

5 A conical wire is stretched by two forces F applied parallel to its length and in opposite direction, normal to end faces. The length of wire is L and its end radius are r_1 and r_2. Find out the extension produced.

(Y = Young's modulus of wire)

(a) $\frac{FL}{\pi r_1^2 Y}$ (b) $\frac{FL}{\pi r_1 Y}$ (c) $\frac{FL}{\pi r_1 r_2 Y}$ (d) $\frac{FLY}{\pi r_1 r_2}$

6 A steel rod of length L, density d and cross-sectional area A, is hinged at one end, so that it can rotate freely in a vertical plane. The rod is released from a horizontal position. When it becomes vertical, the stress at its mid-point is

(a) $\frac{13dLg}{8}$ (b) $\frac{12dLg}{8}$ (c) $\frac{2dLg}{5}$ (d) $\frac{dLg}{2}$

7 The diagram shows a horizontal steel girder AB of length 1 m, area of cross-section 10 cm^2 from the ends of which a load of 10^3 kg is suspended by two strings of length 1 m each. The compression in the girder is

($Y_{steel} = 2 \times 10^{11}$ N/m^2, $g = 10$ ms^{-2})

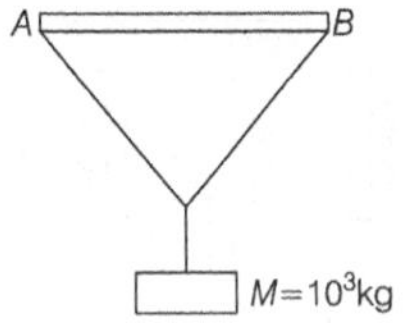

(a) $\frac{1}{\sqrt{3}} \times 10^{-5}$ m (b) $\frac{5}{\sqrt{3}} \times 10^{-5}$ m

(c) $\frac{5}{2\sqrt{3}} \times 10^{-5}$ m (d) $\frac{1}{\sqrt{3}} \times 10^{-4}$ m

8 A constant force F_0 is applied on a uniform elastic string placed over a smooth horizontal surface as shown in figure. Young's modulus of string is Y and area of cross-section is S. The elongation in the string is

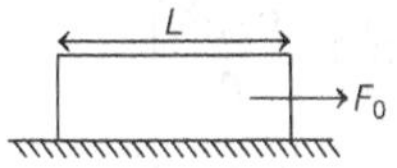

(a) $\frac{F_0 L}{SY}$ (b) $\frac{2F_0 L}{SY}$ (c) $\frac{F_0 L}{2SY}$ (d) $\frac{F_0 Y}{2SL}$

9 A wire of length 2 m is clamped horizontally between two fixed supports. A mass $m = 5$ kg is hanged from middle of wire. The vertical depression in wire in equilibrium is (Young's modulus of wire $= 2.4 \times 10^9$ N/m^2, cross-sectional area $= 1$ cm^2)

(a) 4.68 cm (b) 1.52 cm (c) 1.12 cm (d) 5.92 cm

10 A ring of radius R made of lead wire breaking strength σ and density ρ, rotated about a stationary vertical axis passing through its centre and perpendicular to the plane of the ring. Calculate the number of rotations per second at which the ring ruptures.

(a) $\frac{1}{2\pi R}\sqrt{\frac{\sigma}{\rho}}$ (b) $\frac{1}{\pi R}\sqrt{\frac{\sigma}{\rho}}$ (c) $\frac{1}{2R}\sqrt{\frac{\sigma}{\rho}}$ (d) $\frac{1}{R}\sqrt{\frac{\sigma}{\rho}}$

11 A thin uniform copper rod of length l and area cross-section A and mass m rotates uniformly with an angular velocity ω in a horizontal plane about a vertical axis passing through one of its end. The elongation of the rod is

(a) $\frac{m\omega^2 l^2}{AY}$ (b) $\frac{m\omega^2 l^2}{2AY}$

(c) $\frac{m\omega^2 l^2}{3AY}$ (d) $\frac{m\omega^2 l^2}{6AY}$

12 A steel rod of cross-sectional area 15 cm^2 and two brass rods each of cross-sectional area 10 cm^2 together support a load of 4000 kg as shown in figure. The stress in brass rod will be (Take, Y for steel $= 2.0 \times 10^6$ N/cm^2 and for brass $= 1.0 \times 10^6$ N/cm^2, $g = 10$ m/s^2)

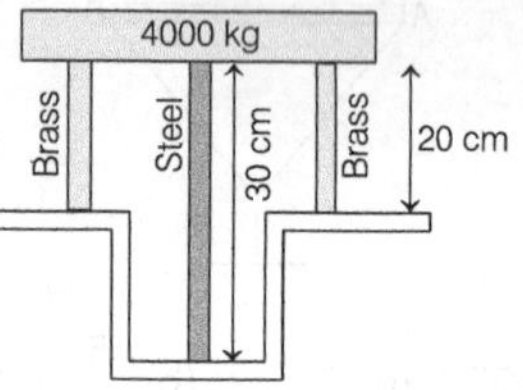

(a) 5 MPa (b) 10 MPa
(c) 15 MPa (d) 20 MPa

13 Estimate the pressure deep inside the sea at a depth h below the surface. Assume that the density of water is ρ_0 at sea level and its bulk modulus is B. p_0 is the atmosphere pressure at sea level. p is the pressure at depth h;

(a) $p = p_0 - B\ln\left(1 - \frac{\rho_0 gh}{B}\right)$

(b) $p = p_0 + B\ln\left(1 - \frac{\rho_0 gh}{B}\right)$

(c) $p = p_0 - B\ln\left(1 + \frac{\rho_0 gh}{B}\right)$

(d) $p = p_0 + \ln\left(1 + \frac{\rho_0 gh}{B}\right)$

14 A liquid of volumetric thermal expansion coefficient $= \gamma$ and bulk modulus B is filled in a spherical tank of negligible heat expansion coefficient. Its radius is R and wall thickness is t ($t << R$). When the temperature of the liquid is raised by θ, the tensile stress developed in the walls of the tank is

(a) $\frac{B\gamma\theta R}{2t}$ (b) $\frac{B\gamma\theta R}{t}$

(c) $\frac{2B\gamma\theta R}{t}$ (d) $\frac{B\gamma\theta R}{4t}$

15 A uniform steel wire hangs from the ceiling and elongates due to its own weight. The ratio of elongation of the upper half of the wire to the elongation of the lower half of wire is

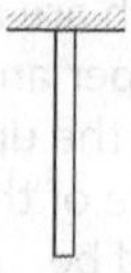

(a) 4 : 1 (b) 3 : 1 (c) 3 : 2 (d) None

16 Two wires of the same material (Young's modulus Y) and same length L but radii R and $2R$ respectively, are joined end to end and a weight w is suspended from the combination as shown in the figure. The elastic potential energy in the system is

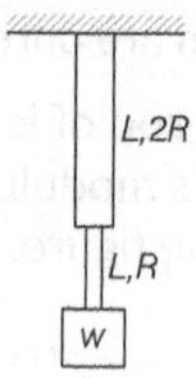

(a) $\frac{3w^2L}{4\pi R^2 Y}$ (b) $\frac{3w^2L}{8\pi R^2 Y}$

(c) $\frac{5w^2L}{8\pi R^2 Y}$ (d) $\frac{w^2L}{\pi R^2 Y}$

17 An iron bar (Young's modulus $= 10^{12}$ dyne/cm^2, $\alpha = 10^{-6}$/°C) 100 cm long and 10 cm² in cross-section is heated from 0°C to 100°C without being permitted to bend or expand. The compressive elastic energy developed inside the bar is

(a) 100 mJ (b) 200 mJ (c) 500 mJ (d) None

18 A rubber of volume 2000 cc is alternately subjected to tension and released. The stress figure shows the stress-strain curve of rubber. Each curve is a quadrant of an ellipse. The amount of energy lost as heat per cycle per unit volume will be

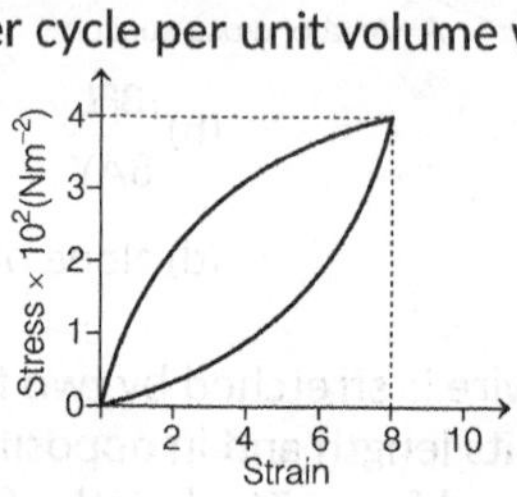

(a) $\left(\frac{\pi}{2} - 1\right) \times 16 \times 10^2$ J (b) $\left(\frac{\pi}{4} - 1\right) \times 8 \times 10^2$ J

(c) $\left(\frac{\pi}{4} - 1\right) \times 32 \times 10^2$ J (d) $\left(\frac{\pi}{2} - 1\right) \times 32 \times 10^2$ J

Multiple Choice(s) Correct Questions

1 The wires A and B shown in the figure, are made of the same material and have radii r_A and r_B. A block of mass m kg is tied between them. If the force F is $mg/3$, one of the wires breaks.

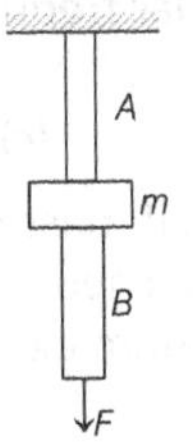

(a) A will break before B, if $r_A < 2r_B$
(b) A will break before B, if $r_A = r_B$
(c) Either A or B will break, if $r_A = 2r_B$
(d) The lengths of A and B must be known to decide which wire will break.

2 A uniform metallic ring of mass m, radius R, cross-sectional area a and Young's modulus Y is kept on a smooth cone of radius $2R$ and semi-vertical angle 45° as shown. [Assume that extension in the ring is small]

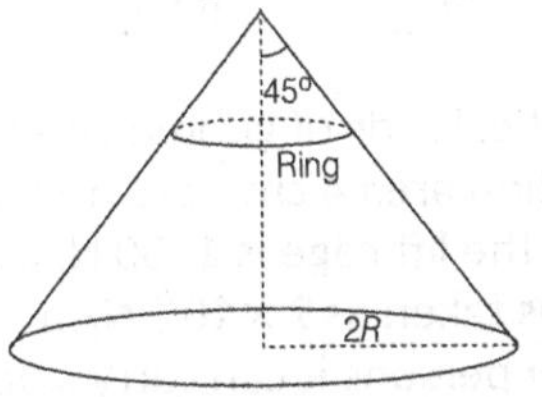

(a) The tension in the ring will be same throughout.
(b) The tension in the ring will be independent of radius of ring.
(c) The extension in the ring will be $\frac{mgR}{aY}$
(d) Elastic potential energy stored in the ring will be $\frac{m^2g^2R}{8\pi Ya}$

3 A small cube of liquid of surface area A is considered at a depth of h from the surface of liquid. If its density is ρ, bulk modulus is B, the elastic energy density inside the cube is proportional to

(a) h^2 (b) A
(c) $\frac{1}{B}$ (d) ρ

4 A uniform plank is resting over a smooth horizontal surface. It is subjected to a horizontal force at its one end. Which of the following statements are not correct?

(a) Stress developed in plank material is maximum at the end at which force is applied and decreases linearly to zero at the other end.
(b) A uniform tensile stress is developed in the plank material.
(c) Since plank is pulled at one end only, plank starts to accelerate along direction of the force. Hence, no stress is developed in the plank material.
(d) Stress at the ends is the same but it changes in between.

5 A rod is made of uniform material and has non-uniform cross-section. It is fixed at both the ends as shown and heated at mid-section. Which of the following statements are not correct?

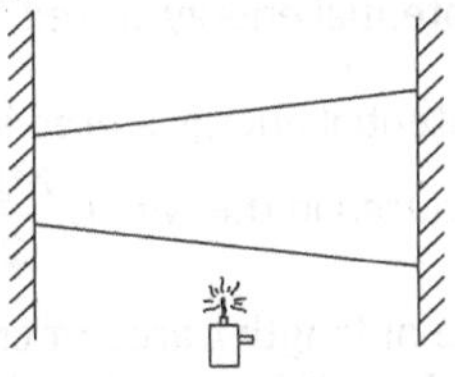

(a) Force of compression in the rod will be maximum at mid-section.
(b) Compressive stress in the rod will be maximum at left end.
(c) Since rod is fixed at both the ends, its length will remain unchanged. Hence, no strain will be induced in it.
(d) Force of compression is the same throughout the rod.

6 The figure shows the stress-strain graphs for materials A and B. From the graph it follows that

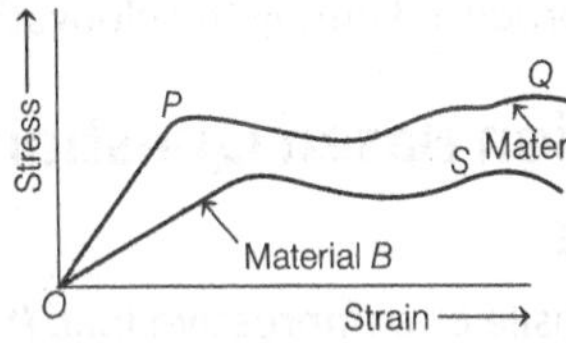

(a) material A has a higher Young's modulus
(b) material B is more ductile
(c) material A can withstand greater stress
(d) material B can withstand greater stress

7 Which of the following are correct?

(a) For a small deformation of a material, the ratio (stress/strain) constant.
(b) For a large deformation of a material, the ratio (stress/strain) decreases.
(c) Two wires made of different materials, having the same diameter and length are connected end to end. A force is applied. This stretches their combined length by 2 mm. Now, the strain is same in both the wires but stress is different.
(d) None of the above

8 Which of the following are correct ?
(a) The shear modulus of a liquid is infinite.
(b) Bulk modulus of a perfectly rigid body is infinite.
(c) When length of a bar is increased by stretching it, its volume must decrease.
(d) When length of a bar is increased by stetching it, its volume must remain same.

9 When a body of mass M is attached to lower end of a wire (of length L) whose upper end is fixed, then the elongation of the wire is l. In this situation, mark out the correct statement(s).
(a) Loss in gravitational potential energy of M is Mgl.
(b) Elastic potential energy stored in the wire is $\frac{Mgl}{2}$.
(c) Elastic potential energy stored in the wire is Mgl.
(d) Heat produced in the wire is $\frac{Mgl}{2}$.

10 A metal wire of length L area of cross-section A and Young's modulus Y is stretched by a variable force F such that F is always slightly greater than the elastic force of resistance in the wire. When the elongation of the wire is l,
(a) the work done by F is $\frac{YA^2}{L}$
(b) the work done by F is $\frac{YAl^2}{2L}$
(c) the elastic potential energy stored in the wire is $\frac{YAl^2}{2L}$
(d) heat is produced during the elongation

Comprehension Based Questions

Comprehension-1

When a tensile or compressive load P is applied to rod or cable, its length changes. The change in length x which, for an elastic material is proportional to the force (Hook's law).
$P \propto x$ or $P = kx$.
The above equation is similar to the equation of spring. For a rod of length L, area A and Young's modulus Y, the extension x can be expressed as
$x = \frac{PL}{AY}$ or $P = \frac{AY}{L}x$, hence $k = \frac{AY}{L}$
Thus, rods or cables attached to lift can be treated as springs. The energy stored in rod is called strain energy and equal to $\frac{1}{2}Px$. The loads placed or dropped on the floor of lift cause stresses in the cables and can be evaluated by spring analogy. If the cable of lift is previously stressed and load is placed or dropped, then maximum extension in cable can be calculated by energy conservation.

1 If rod of length 4 m, area 4 cm^2 and Young's modulus 2×10^{10} N/m is attached with mass 200 kg, then angular frequency of SHM (rad/s) of mass is equal to
(a) 1000 (b) 10 (c) 100 (d) 10 P

2 In above problem, if mass of 10 kg falls on the massless collar attached to rod from the height of 99 cm, then maximum extension in the rod is equal ($g = 10$ m/s^2)
(a) 9.9 cm (b) 10 cm (c) 0.99 cm (d) 1 cm

3 In the above problem, the maximum stress developed in the rod is equal to
(a) 5×10^7 N/m^2 (b) 5×10^8 N/m^2
(c) 4×10^7 N/m^2 (d) 4×10^8 N/m^2

4 If two rods of same length 4 m and cross-section areas 2 cm^2 and 4 cm^2 with same Young's modulus 2×10^{10} N/m^2 are attached one after the other with mass 600 kg, then angular frequency is
(a) $\frac{1000}{3}$ (b) $\frac{10}{3}$ (c) $\frac{100}{3}$ (d) $\frac{10\pi}{3}$

5 Four identical rods of geometry each of cross-section area 4 cm^2 are attached with lift. If weight of the lift cage is 1000 N, and elastic limit of each rod is taken as 9×10^6 N/m^2, then the number of persons it can carry safely is equal to ($g = 10$ m/s^2, assume average mass of a person as 50 kg and lift moves with constant speed)
(a) 7 (b) 26 (c) 24 (d) 25

Comprehension-2

Figure shows a bar of uniform cross-section of area s. Equal and opposite tensile forces are applied at the ends of the bar. Each force has a magnitude F. $ABCD$ is a plane through the bar and inclined at angle θ with the perpendicular to the length of the bar.

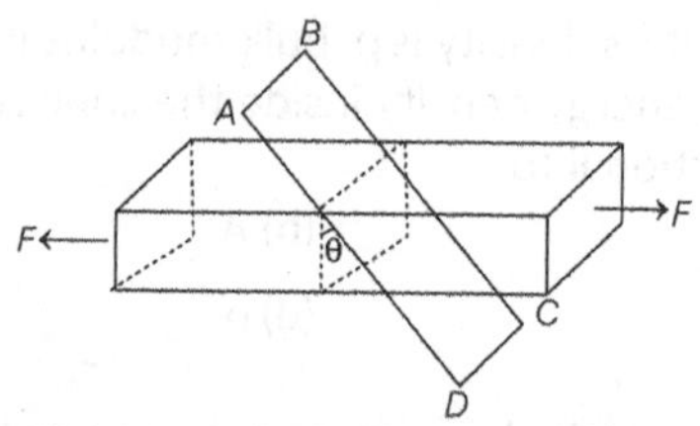

6 Normal stress at the plane which is inclined with the plane perpendicular to the length of the bar is
(a) $\frac{F}{s}$ (b) $\frac{F\cos\theta}{s}$ (c) $\frac{F\cos^2\theta}{s}$ (d) $\frac{F}{s\cos\theta}$

7 Shear stress on the plane which is inclined with the plane perpendicular to the length of the bar is

(a) $\frac{F\sin\theta}{s}$ (b) $\frac{F}{s\cos\theta}$ (c) $\frac{F\tan\theta}{s}$ (d) $\frac{F\sin 2\theta}{2s}$

8 Shear stress on the said plane will be maximum for $\theta =$

(a) 90° (b) 45° (c) 30° (d) 0°

Comprehension-3

A sphere of mass *m* attached with the free end of a steel wire of a length *l* swings in the vertical plane from the horizontal position.

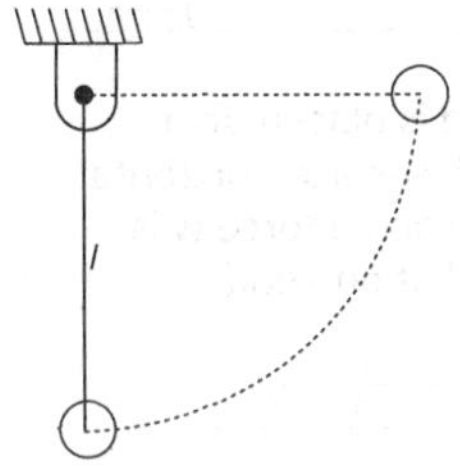

9 Elongation of the wire in the vertical position is

(a) $\frac{mgl}{Y(\pi r^2)}$ (b) $\frac{2mgl}{Y(\pi r^2)}$ (c) $\frac{mgl}{3Y(\pi r^2)}$ (d) $\frac{3mgl}{Y(\pi r^2)}$

10 Elastic energy stored in the wire in the vertical position is

(a) $\frac{9m^2g^2l}{2Y\pi r^2}$ (b) $\frac{7m^2g^2l}{2Y\pi r^2}$

(c) $\frac{9m^2g^2l}{Y\pi r^2}$ (d) $\frac{9m^2g^2l}{4Y\pi r^2}$

Comprehension-4

A body hangs from the mid-point of a light wire of length $2l$ and cross-sectional area *A* such that the wire sags through a vertical distance $y (y << l)$. The Young's modulus of the wire is *Y*.

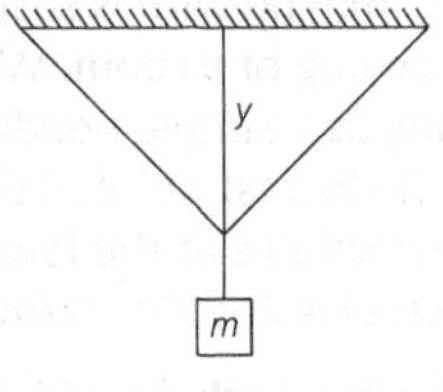

11 The strain in the wire is

(a) $\frac{y^2}{2l^2}$ (b) $\frac{y^2}{3l^2}$ (c) $\frac{y^2}{4l^2}$ (d) $\frac{2y^2}{l^2}$

12 What is the elastic energy stored?

(a) $\frac{YAy^4}{2l^3}$ (b) $\frac{YAy^4}{6l^3}$ (c) $\frac{YAy^4}{4l^3}$ (d) $\frac{YAy^4}{3l^3}$

Comprehension-5

A thin wire of cross-section *a* is made to form a flexible circular loop of radius *R*. If the loop spins with angular speed ω, (Assume $\rho =$ density and $Y =$ Young's modulus of wire)

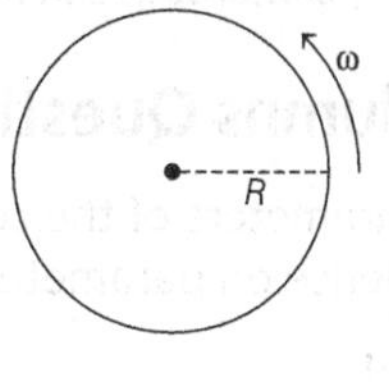

13 Stress in the wire will be

(a) $\rho R^2\omega^2$ (b) $\rho R\omega$

(c) $\frac{R^2\omega^2}{\rho}$ (d) $\frac{R^2\omega^2}{2\rho}$

14 Small increase in radius (ΔR) of loop will be

(a) $\frac{\rho\omega^2R^3}{Y}$ (b) $\frac{\rho\omega^2R^3}{2Y}$

(c) $\frac{2\rho\omega^2R^3}{Y}$ (d) $\frac{\rho\omega^2R^3}{4Y}$

Comprehension-6

In the figure shown, *A* and *B* are two short steel rods each of cross-sectional area 5 cm^2. The lower ends of *A* and *B* are welded to a fixed plate *CD*. The upper end of *A* is welded to the L-shaped piece *EFG* which can slide without friction on upper end of *B*. A horizontal pull of 1200 N is exerted at *G* as shown. Neglect the weight of *EFG* wire

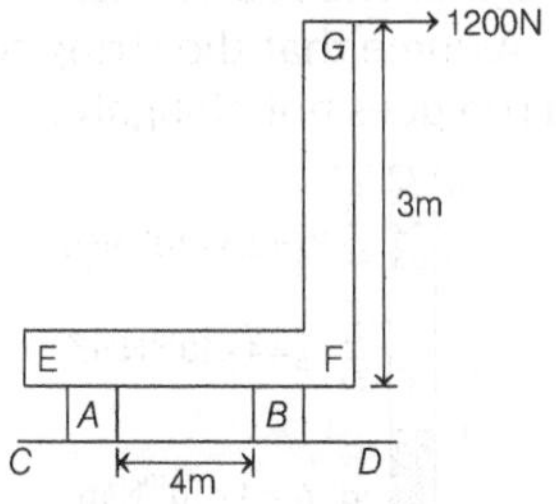

15 Mark out the correct statements(s).

(a) Shearing stress in *A* is zero.

(b) Shearing stress in *B* is zero.

(c) Shearing stress in both *A* and *B* is zero.

(d) Shearing stress in both *A* and *B* is non-zero.

16 Longitudinal stress in *A* is

(a) 180 N/cm^2, tensile in nature

(b) 240 N/cm^2, tensile in nature

(c) 180 N/cm^2, compressive in nature

(d) 240 N/cm^2, compressive in nature

17 Longitudinal stress in *B* is
(a) 180 N/cm^2, tensile in nature
(b) 240 N/cm^2, tensile in nature
(c) 180 N/cm^2, compressive in nature
(d) 240 N/cm^2, compressive in nature

Match The Columns Questions

1 Match the parameters of the column-I according to their dependence on parameters of column-II.

Column-I	Column-II
A. Young's modulus of the wire	P. Material of the wire
B. Breaking stress of the wire	Q. Length of the wire
C. Strain due to applied force in the wire	R. Radius of the wire
D. Potential energy stored in the wire	S. Applied force

2 Match the following

Column-I	Column-II
A. Longitudinal stress	P. Volume changes
B. Shear stress	Q. Shape changes
C. Volume changes	R. Volume does not change
D. Tensile stress	S. Shape does not change

3 A light rod of uniform cross-section of 10^{-4} m^2 is shown in figure. The rod consists of three different materials. Assume that the string connecting the block and rod does not elongate.

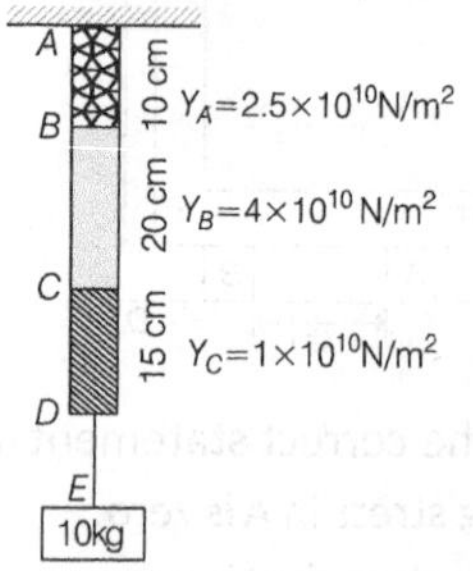

Column-I (Points)	Column-II (Displacement in μm)
A. B	P. 4
B. C	Q. 9
C. D	R. 12
D. E	S. 15
	T. 24

4 In column -I a uniform rod of length *L* is shown with the applied force(s). The cross sectional area of the rod is *A* and the weight of the rod is *w*. In column-II the elastic potential energy of the rod in different cases are given. Match the columns (Young's modulus is *Y*)

Column-I	Column-II
A. 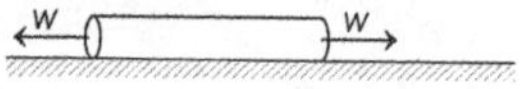 Both ends are pulled by force W on smooth surface	P. $\frac{w^2L}{2AY}$
B. 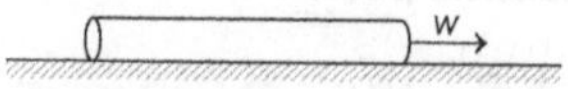 The rod is placed on a smooth surface horizontal surface and a force *w* is applied at one end.	Q. $\frac{w^2L}{6AY}$
C. 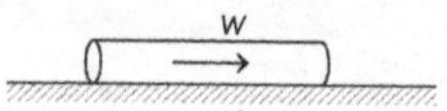 The rod is placed on a smooth surface horizontal surface and a force equal to *w* is applied at the centre of the rod.	R. $\frac{w^2L}{24AY}$
	S. Zero

Numerical Value Questions

1 The cross-section of a bar is given by $\left[1+\frac{x^2}{100}\right]$ cm^2, where *x* is the distance from one end. The extension under a load of 20 kN on a length of 10 cm is $\lambda \times 10^{-3}$ cm. Find λ. $Y = 2 \times 10^7$ N/cm^2

2 A sphere of radius 0.1 m and mass 8π kg is attached to the lower end of a steel wire of length 5.0 m and diameter 10^{-3} m. The wire is suspended from 5.22 m high ceiling of a room. When the sphere is made to swing as a simple pendulum, it just grazes the floor at the lowest point. Calculate the velocity (in m/s) of the sphere at the lowest position. Young modulus of steel is 2×10^{11} N/m^2.

3 Two vertical wires each, $l = 150$ cm long one of steel having cross-sectional area $A_s = 2 \times 10^{-6}$ m^2 and second of bronze of cross-sectional area $A_b = 1 \times 10^{-6}$ m^2 are suspended from a ceiling with horizontal distance $r = 55$ cm as shown in figure. A light but rigid horizontal rod connect lower ends of wires. A vertical downward force *F* is applied on the rod at a distance *x* cm from steel wire as shown in figure such that the rod remains horizontal even after application of force. Find x. Given, $Y_s = 2\times10^{11}$ N/m^2, $Y_b = 1.5\times10^{11}$ N/m^2.

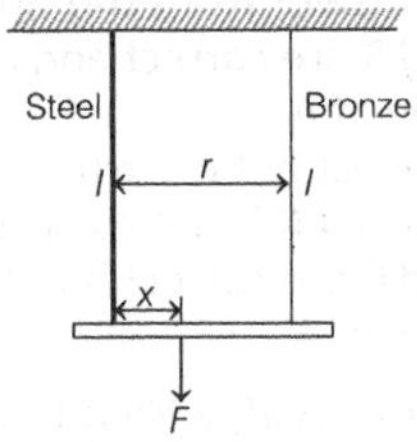

4 A stone of 0.5 kg mass is attached to one of a 0.8 m long aluminium wire of 0.7 mm diameter and suspended vertically. The stone is now rotated in a horizontal plane at a rate such that the wire makes an angle of 85° with the vertical. Find the increase in the length (in mm) of the wire. [Young's modulus of aluminium $= 7\times10^{10}$ N/m^2, $\sin 85° = 0.9962$ and $\cos 85° = 0.0872$]

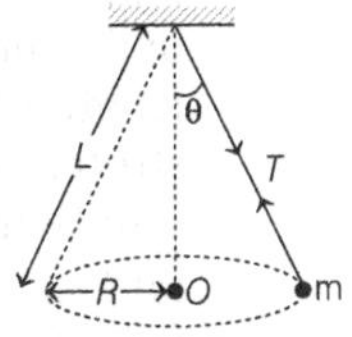

5 A block is hanged by means of two identical wires having cross section area A (1 mm^2) as shown in the diagram. If temperature is lowered by ΔT (10°C), find the mass (in kg) to be added to hanging mass such that junction remains at initial position. Given, that co-efficient of linear expansion $\alpha = 2\times10^{-5}$/°C and Young's modulus $Y = 5\times10^{11}$ N/m^2 for the wire.

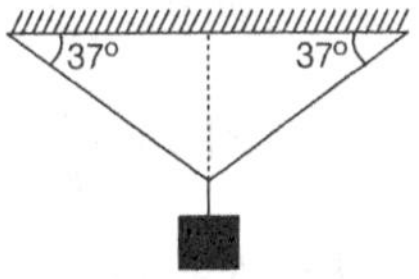

6 A ring of radius R made of wire of density ρ is rotated about a stationary vertical axis passing through its centre and perpendicular to the plane of the ring. Determine the angular velocity (in rad/s) of ring at which the ring breaks. The wire breaks at tensile stress σ. Ignore gravity. Take, $\frac{\sigma}{\rho} = 4$ and $R = 1$ m.

7 A steel rod of cross-sectional area 0.1 m² is acted upon by forces shown in figure. Determine the elongation of the length BD of the bar (in μm). Take, $Y = 2.0\times10^{11}$ N/m^2.

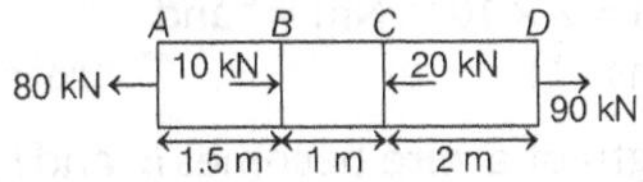

8 A balloon is filled with helium at the atmospheric pressure p_0 The volume of the balloon is V_0. The balloon is made of the material of mass m and density ρ_0. After being released, the balloon bursts at an altitude, where the atmospheric pressure is (p_0/2). Immediately before bursting, the balloon has a volume of 1.25 V_0. Assume that the temperature of helium remains constant, the balloon remains spherical, and the density of the material remains virtually constant. If the maximum stress that the balloon material can withstand is $\frac{\alpha p_0 V_0 \rho_0}{\beta m}$, then find at $\alpha + \beta$.

9 The average depth of Indian ocean is about 3 km. Find the percentage compression $\left(\frac{\Delta V}{V}\times 100\right)$ of water at the bottom of the ocean. Given, bulk modulus of water is 2.2×10^9 Nm^{-2}, density of water = 1000 kgm^{-3} and $g = 9.8$ m/s^2.

Previous Years Questions

JEE Main

1 If average depth of an ocean is 4000 m and the bulk modulus of water is 2×10^9 Nm^{-2}, then fractional compression $\frac{\Delta V}{V}$ of water at the bottom of ocean is $\alpha\times10^{-2}$. The value of α is ....
(Given, $g = 10$ ms^{-2}, $\rho = 1000$ kg m^{-3})
[2024, 27 Jan Shift-I]

2 Given below are two statements : one is labelled as **Assertion (A)** and other is labelled as **Reason (R)**.

Assertion (A) The property of body, by virtue of which it tends to regain its original shape when the external force is removed, is elasticity.

Reason (R) The restoring force depends upon the bonded interatomic and intermolecular force of solids.

In the light of the above statements, choose the **correct** answer from the options given below
[2024, 27 Jan Shift-II]

(a) Both (A) and (R) are true but (R) is not the correct explanation of (A).
(b) (A) is false but (R) is true.
(c) Both (A) and (R) are true and (R) is the correct explanation of (A).
(d) (A) is true but (R) is false.

3 A wire of length L and radius r is clamped at one end. If its other end is pulled by a force F, its length increases by l. If the radius of the wire and the applied force both are reduced to half of their original values keeping original length constant, the increase in length will become **[2024, 29 Jan Shift-II]**

(a) 3/2 times
(b) 4 times
(c) 2 times
(d) 3 times

4 Young's modulus of material of a wire of length L and cross-sectional area A is Y. If the length of the wire is doubled and cross-sectional area is halved, then Young's modulus will be **[2024, 30 Jan Shift-I]**
(a) $4Y$ (b) Y
(c) $2Y$ (d) $\frac{Y}{4}$

5 The depth below the surface of sea to which a rubber ball be taken, so as to decrease its volume by 0.02% is .... m.
(Take density of sea water $= 10^3$ kg m^{-3}.
Bulk modulus of rubber $= 9 \times 10^8$ Nm^{-2}, and $g = 10$ ms^{-2}) **[2024, 31 Jan Shift-I]**

6 A wire of length L and radius r is clamped rigidly at one end. When the other end of the wire is pulled by a force f, its length increases by l. Another wire of same material of length $2L$ and radius $2r$ is pulled by a force $2f$. Then the increase in its length will be **[2023, 15 April Shift-I]**
(a) $2l$ (b) l
(c) $4l$ (d) $l/2$

7 Young's moduli of the material of wires A and B are in the ratio of 1 : 4, while its area of cross-sections are in the ratio of 1 : 3. If the same amount of load is applied to both the wires, the amount of elongation produced in the wires A and B will be in the ratio of
(Assume length of wires A and B are same) **[2023, 10 April Shift-II]**
(a) 1 : 12 (b) 36 : 1
(c) 12 : 1 (d) 1 : 36

8 An aluminium rod with Young's modulus $Y = 7.0 \times 10^{10}$ N/m^2 undergoes elastic strain of 0.04%. The energy per unit volume stored in the rod in SI unit is **[2023, 8 April Shift-I]**
(a) 2800 (b) 11200
(c) 8400 (d) 5600

9 A 100 m long wire having cross-sectional area 6.25×10^{-4} m^2 and Young's modulus is 10^{10} Nm^{-2} is subjected to a load of 250 N, then the elongation in the wire will be **[2023, 24 Jan Shift - I]**
(a) 4×10^{-4} m (b) 4×10^{-3} m
(c) 6.25×10^{-3} m (d) 6.25×10^{-6} m

10 Given below are two statements: one is labelled as Assertion (A) and the other is labelled as Reason (R). **[2023, 24 Jan Shift - II]**
Assertion (A) Steel is used in the construction of buildings and bridges.
Reason (R) Steel is more elastic and its elastic limit is high.
In the light of above statements, choose the most appropriate answer from the options given below.
(a) Both A and R are correct and R is the correct explanation of A.
(b) A is not correct but R is true.
(c) A is correct but R is not correct.
(d) Both A and R are correct but R is not the correct explanation of A.

11 Under the same load, wire A having length 5.0 m and cross-section 2.5×10^{-5} m^2 stretches uniformly by the same amount as another wire B of length 6.0 m and a cross-section of 3.0×10^{-5} m^2 stretches. The ratio of the Young's modulus of wire A to that of wire B will be **[2023, 31 Jan Shift - I]**
(a) 1 : 2 (b) 1 : 4
(c) 1 : 1 (d) 1 : 10

12 Choose the correct relationship between Poisson ratio (σ), bulk modulus (K) and modulus of rigidity (η) of a given solid object. **[2023, 30 Jan Shift - I]**
(a) $\sigma = \frac{3K + 2\eta}{6K + 2\eta}$ (b) $\sigma = \frac{6K - 2\eta}{3K - 2\eta}$
(c) $\sigma = \frac{3K - 2\eta}{6K + 2\eta}$ (d) $\sigma = \frac{6K + 2\eta}{3K - 2\eta}$

13 A steel rod has a radius of 20 mm and a length of 2.0 m. A force of 6.28 kN stretches it along its length. Young's modulus of steel is 2.0×10^{11} N/m^2. The longitudinal strain produced in the wire is .... $\times 10^{-5}$. **[2023, 6 April Shift-I]**

14 A metal block of mass m is suspended from a rigid support through a metal wire of diameter 14 mm. The tensile stress developed in the wire under equilibrium state is 7×10^5 Nm^{-3}. The value of mass m in kg.
(Take, $g = 9.8$ ms^{-2} and $\pi = \frac{22}{7}$) **[2023, 6 April Shift-II]**

15 Two wires each of radius 0.2 cm and negligible mass, one made of steel and the other made of brass are loaded as shown in the figure. The elongation of the steel wire is .... $\times 10^{-6}$ m. (Young's modulus for steel $= 2 \times 10^{11}$ Nm^{-2} and $g = 10$ ms^{-2}) **[2023, 10 April Shift-I]**

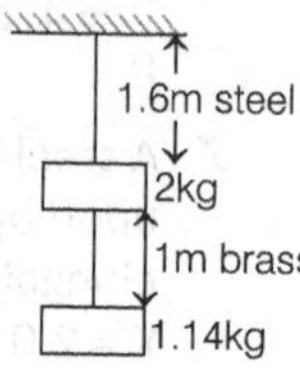

16 The length of a wire becomes l_1 and l_2 when 100 N and 120 N tensions are applied, respectively. If $10l_2 = 11l_1$, the natural length of wire will be $\frac{1}{x}l_1$. Here the value of x is .... **[2023, 11 April Shift-I]**

17 The elastic potential energy stored in a steel wire of length 20 m stretched through 2 cm is 80 J. The cross-sectional area of the wire is .... mm^2.

(Given, $y = 2.0 \times 10^{11}\ Nm^{-2}$). **[2023, 13 April Shift-I]**

18 The area of cross-section of the rope used to lift a load by a crane is $2.5 \times 10^{-4}\ m^2$. The maximum lifting capacity of the crane is 10 metric tons. To increase the lifting capacity of the crane to 25 metric tons. The required area of cross-section of the rope should be (Take, $g = 10\ ms^{-2}$) **[2022, 26 July Shift-II]**

(a) $6.25 \times 10^{-4}\ m^2$ (b) $10 \times 10^{-4}\ m^2$
(c) $1 \times 10^{-4}\ m^2$ (d) $1.67 \times 10^{-4}\ m^2$

19 A uniform heavy rod of weight $10\ kg\ ms^{-2}$, cross-sectional area $100\ cm^2$ and length 20 cm is hanging from a fixed support. Young's modulus of the material of the rod is $2 \times 10^{11}\ Nm^{-2}$. Neglecting the lateral contraction, find the elongation of rod due to its own weight. **[2021, 31 Aug Shift-I]**

(a) 2×10^{-9} m (b) 5×10^{-8} m
(c) 4×10^{-8} m (d) 5×10^{-10} m

20 When a rubber ball is taken to a depth of ...... m in deep sea, its volume decreases by 0.5%.
(The bulk modulus of rubber $= 9.8 \times 10^8\ Nm^{-2}$. Density of sea water $= 10^3\ kg\ m^{-3}$, $g = 9.8\ m/s^2$) **[2021, 31 Aug Shift-I]**

21 Four identical hollow cylindrical columns of mild steel support a big structure of mass 50×10^3 kg. The inner and outer radii of each column are 50 cm and 100 cm, respectively. Assuming, uniform local distribution, calculate the compression strain of each column. [Use, $Y = 2.0 \times 10^{11}$ Pa, $g = 9.8\ m/s^2$]. **[2021, 31 Aug Shift-II]**

(a) 3.60×10^{-8} (b) 2.60×10^{-7}
(c) 1.87×10^{-3} (d) 7.07×10^{-4}

22 If Y, K and η are the values of Young's modulus, bulk modulus and modulus of rigidity of any material, respectively. Choose the correct relation for these parameters. **[2021, 24 Feb Shift-I]**

(a) $Y = \dfrac{9K\eta}{2\eta + 3K}\ N/m^2$

(b) $Y = \dfrac{9K\eta}{3K - \eta}\ N/m^2$

(c) $K = \dfrac{Y\eta}{9\eta - 3Y}\ N/m^2$

(d) $\eta = \dfrac{3YK}{9K + Y}\ N/m^2$

23 An object is located at 2 km beneath the surface of the water. If the fractional compression $\Delta V/V$ is 1.36%, the ratio of hydraulic stress to the corresponding hydraulic strain will be ....
(Take, density of water is $1000\ kg\ m^{-3}$ and $g = 9.81\ ms^{-2}$) **[2021, 17 March Shift-II]**

(a) $1.96 \times 10^7\ Nm^{-2}$
(b) $1.44 \times 10^7\ Nm^{-2}$
(c) $2.26 \times 10^9\ Nm^{-2}$
(d) $1.44 \times 10^9\ Nm^{-2}$

24 The area of cross-section of a railway track is $0.01\ m^2$. The temperature variation is 10°C. Coefficient of linear expansion of material of track is 10^{-5}/°C. The energy stored per metre in the track is ...... J/m. (Take, Young's modulus of material of track is $10^{11}\ Nm^{-2}$) **[2021, 22 July Shift-II]**

25 Given below are two statements: one is labelled as Assertion A and the other is labelled as Reason R.

Assertion (A) When a rod lying freely is heated, no thermal stress is developed in it.

Reason (R) On heating, the length of the rod increases.

In the light of the above statements, choose the correct answer from the options given below **[2021, 25 Feb Shift-I]**

(a) Both A and R are true but R is not the correct explanation of A.
(b) A is false but R is true.
(c) A is true but R is false.
(d) Both A and R are true and R is the correct explanation of A.

JEE Advanced

1 A cubical solid aluminium (bulk modulus $= -V\dfrac{dP}{dV} = 70$ GPa) block has an edge length of 1 m on the surface of the earth. It is kept on the floor of a 5 km deep ocean. Taking the average density of water and the acceleration due to gravity to be $10^3\ kg\ m^{-3}$ and $10\ ms^{-2}$, respectively, the change in the edge length of the block in mm is ______. **(2020)**

2 One end of a horizontal thick copper wire of length $2L$ and radius $2R$ is welded to an end of another horizontal thin copper wire of length L and radius R. When the arrangement is stretched by applying forces at two ends, the ratio of the elongation in the thin wire to that in the thick wire is **(2013)**

(a) 0.25 (b) 0.50
(c) 2.00 (d) 4.00

Answer Key

Level 1

6.1 Stress and Strain

1. $\frac{w_1 + (3w/4)}{S}$ 2. (a) $\frac{F}{A}\cos^2\theta$ (b) $\frac{F}{A}\sin\theta\cos\theta$ 3. 1 4. 0.002 5. 0.03

6.2 Young's Modulus

1. (a) 7.80×10^5 N/m^2 (b) 3.9×10^{-6} (c) 7.8×10^{-6}m 2. 1×10^8 N/m^2 3. 1/8

4. 2.12 mm 5. $10^{-4}, 2 \times 10^{-4}$ 6. (a) 1 (b) 13/20 7. 4.6×10^{-5} cm 8. 7.1×10^{-4} m^2

9. $\frac{\rho g L^2}{2y}$ 10. (a) $L\rho a_0/2$ (b) $\rho a_0 L^2/2Y$ 11. (a) $x = (4/3)$m (b) $x = 1$ m 12. 1.32×10^7 N/m^2

6.3 Modulus of Rigidity

1. (a) 4.9×10^6 N/m^2 (b) 6.0×10^{-6}m 2. 333 Pa, 0.133, 2.5 kPa 3. 0.3, 1.5 cm

6.4 Bulk Modules

1. 10^7 atm 2. 0.4 cc 3. 2 km 4. 4/3 5. p/n

6.5 Poisson's Ratio

1. 0.026 2. $\frac{F}{AY}(1 - 2\sigma)$ 3. +0.12%

6.6 Elastic Potential Energy

1. 0.1 J 2. 2.4×10^{-5} J 3. 13.72×10^{-3} J 4. 16 J 5. $\frac{1}{6}\frac{\pi r^2 \rho^2 g^2 L^3}{Y}$

6.7 Stress-Strain Curve

1. 3

2. (i) (*B*) (ii) (*D*) (iii) (*OA*) (iv) (*OB*) (v)(*BC*)

3. (a) Material *A* has greater Young's modulus. *Y* = Stress/Strain; Slope *A* > Slope *B*.

(b) Material *A* is more ductile as the length of plastic region is more for material *A*.

(c) Material *B* is more brittle, as length of plastic region is shorter for material *B*.

4. Wire *P*

Level 2

Single Choice Correct Questions

1. (a)	2. (b)	3. (a)	4. (a)	5. (b)	6. (c)	7. (c)	8. (a)	9. (c)	10. (a)
11. (b)	12. (b)	13. (b)	14. (a)	15. (c)	16. (a)	17. (d)	18. (b)	19. (c)	20. (c)
21. (d)	22. (c)	23. (d)	24. (d)	25. (a)	26. (d)	27. (d)	28. (d)	29. (b)	30. (c)
31. (b)	32. (c)	33. (b)	34. (d)	35. (a)	36. (c)	37. (c)	38. (a)	39. (a)	40. (c)
41. (b)	42. (a)	43. (a)	44. (d)	45. (a)	46. (b)	47. (c)	48. (b)	49. (c)	50. (b)
51. (d)	52. (a)								

Numerical Value Questions

1. 4	2. 40	3. 200	4. 8	5. 4	6. 2.5	7. 24
8. 1025	9. 3	10. 2				

Level 3

Single Choice Correct Questions

1. (c)	2. (c)	3. (d)	4. (a)	5. (c)	6. (a)	7. (c)	8. (c)	9. (d)	10. (a)
11. (c)	12. (b)	13. (a)	14. (a)	15. (b)	16. (c)	17. (c)	18. (d)		

Multiple Choice(s) Correct Questions

1. (a, b, c)	2. (a, b, c)	3. (a, c)	4. (b, c, d)	5. (a, c)	6. (a, c)	7. (a, b)
8. (a, b)	9. (a, b, d)	10. (b, c)				

Comprehension Based Questions

1. (c)	2. (d)	3. (a)	4. (c)	5. (b)	6. (c)	7. (d)	8. (b)	9. (d)	10. (a)
11. (a)	12. (c)	13. (a)	14. (a)	15. (b)	16. (a)	17. (c)			

Match the Columns Questions

1. $A \rightarrow P, B \rightarrow P, C \rightarrow PRS, D \rightarrow PQRS$
2. $A \rightarrow PS, B \rightarrow QR, C \rightarrow PS, D \rightarrow PS$
3. $A \rightarrow P, B \rightarrow Q, C \rightarrow T, D \rightarrow T$
4. $A \rightarrow P, B \rightarrow P, C \rightarrow R$

Numerical Value Questions

1. 8	2. 8.76	3. 15	4. 1.67	5. 12	6. 2	7. 12.5
8. 25	9. 1.36					

Previous Years Questions

JEE Main

1. (2)	2. (c)	3. (c)	4. (b)	5. (18)	6. (b)	7. (c)	8. (d)	9. (b)	10. (a)
11. (c)	12. (c)	13. (25)	14. (11)	15. (20)	16. (2)	17. (40)	18. (a)	19. (d)	20. (500)
21. (b)	22. (c)	23. (d)	24. (5)	25. (a)					

JEE Advanced

1. (0.24)	2. (c)

SOLUTIONS

Level 1

6.1 Stress and Strain

1. Tension at $P = w_1 + \frac{3w}{4}$

   Stress $= \frac{F_1}{A} = \frac{1}{S}\left(w_1 + \frac{3w}{4}\right)$

2. Area of section $PQRS = \frac{A}{\cos\theta} = A\sec\theta$

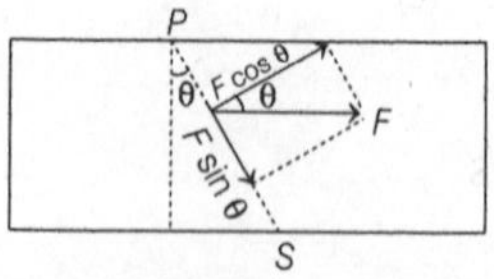

   Tensile stress $= \frac{F_\perp}{A} = \frac{F\cos\theta}{A\sec\theta} = \frac{F}{A}\cos^2\theta$

   Shearing stress $= \frac{F_\parallel}{A} = \frac{F\sin\theta}{A\sec\theta} = \frac{F}{A}\sin\theta\cos\theta$

3. Strain $= \frac{\Delta L}{L} = \frac{2L - L}{L} = 1$

4. Shearing strain $= \frac{\Delta L}{L} = \frac{0.02\times10^{-2}}{0.1} = 0.002$

5. $V = a^3 \Rightarrow \frac{\Delta V}{V} = 3\left(\frac{\Delta a}{a}\right)$

   Bulk strain $= \frac{\Delta V}{V} = 3\left(\frac{\Delta a}{a}\right) = 3(0.01) = 0.03$

6.2 Young's Modulus

1. (a) Stress $= \frac{F}{A} = \frac{100\times9.8}{3.14\times(0.02)^2} = 7.80\times10^5\ \text{N/m}^2$

   (b) Strain $= \frac{\text{Stress}}{Y} = \frac{7.80\times10^5}{2\times10^{11}} = 3.9\times10^{-6}$

   (c) Strain $= \frac{\Delta L}{L} \Rightarrow 3.9\times10^{-6} = \frac{\Delta L}{2} \Rightarrow \Delta L = 7.8\times10^{-6}$ m

2. Stress $= \frac{100}{2\times10^{-4}} = 5\times10^5\ \text{N/m}^2$

   Strain $= \frac{1\times10^{-2}}{2} = 5\times10^{-3}$

   $Y = \frac{\text{Stress}}{\text{Strain}} = \frac{5\times10^5}{5\times10^{-3}} = 10^8\ \text{N/m}^2$

3. $\Delta L = \frac{FL}{AY} = \frac{4FL}{\pi d^2 Y} \Rightarrow \Delta L \propto \frac{L}{d^2}$

   $\Rightarrow \frac{\Delta L_A}{\Delta L_B} = \left(\frac{L_A}{L_B}\right)\left(\frac{d_B}{d_A}\right)^2 = \left(\frac{l}{2l}\right)\left(\frac{\frac{d}{2}}{d}\right)^2 = \frac{1}{8}$

4. $\Delta L = \frac{FL}{AY} = \frac{4FL}{\pi d^2 Y} \Rightarrow d \propto \frac{1}{\sqrt{Y}}$

   $\Rightarrow \frac{d_{Al}}{d_{Cu}} = \sqrt{\frac{Y_{Cu}}{Y_{Al}}} \Rightarrow \frac{3\text{mm}}{d_{Cu}} = \sqrt{\frac{12\times10^{10}}{6\times10^{10}}}$

   $\Rightarrow d_{Cu} = \frac{3}{\sqrt{2}}$ mm $= 2.12$ mm

5. $\Sigma F = ma \Rightarrow 30 - T_2 = 3a$ ...(i)

   $T_2 - T_1 = 3a$ ..(ii)

   $T_1 = 3a$ ...(iii)

   Solving we get, $a = \frac{10}{3}$ m/s^2, $T_1 = 10$ N, $T_2 = 20$ N

   In wire 1, Stress $= \frac{10}{5\times10^{-7}} = 2\times10^7\ \text{N/m}^2$

   Strain $= \frac{2\times10^7}{2\times10^{11}} = 10^{-4}$

   In wire 2, Stress $= \frac{20}{5\times10^{-7}} = 4\times10^7\ \text{N/m}^2$

   Strain $= \frac{4\times10^7}{2\times10^{11}} = 2\times10^{-4}$

6. F ← | Steel | Copper | → F

   (a) σ = stress $= \frac{F}{A} \Rightarrow \frac{\sigma_1}{\sigma_2} = 1$

   (b) Strain $= \frac{\text{Stress}}{Y}$

   $\Rightarrow \frac{\text{Strain in steel wire}}{\text{Strain in copper wire}} = \frac{Y_{Cu}}{Y_{steel}} = \frac{13}{20}$

7. $T = \frac{2m_1m_2g}{m_1+m_2} = \frac{40}{3}$ N

   Breaking stress $= \frac{T}{A} \Rightarrow 2\times10^9 = \frac{\frac{40}{3}}{\pi r^2}$

   $\Rightarrow \quad r = 4.6\times10^{-5}$ m

8. Strain $= \frac{\text{Stress}}{Y} \Rightarrow \frac{0.2}{100} = \frac{10^4}{A(7\times10^9)}$

   $\Rightarrow A = 7.1\times10^{-4}\ \text{m}^2$

9. $T = (\rho\pi r^2 x)\,g$

   Stress $= \frac{\rho\pi r^2 xg}{\pi r^2} = \rho xg$

   Strain $= \frac{\rho xg}{Y}$

   $\Rightarrow \frac{dl}{dx} = \frac{\rho xg}{Y} \Rightarrow \int dl = \int_0^L \frac{\rho gx\,dx}{Y}$

   $\Rightarrow \Delta l = \frac{\rho g L^2}{2Y}$

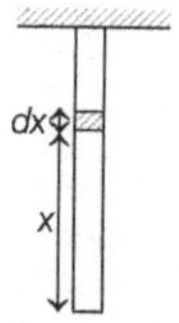

10. 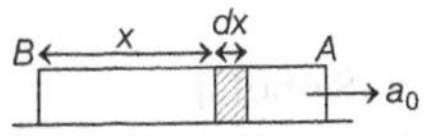

(a) At centre, $T = \left(\frac{m}{2}\right)a_0 = \left(\frac{L}{2}S\rho\right)a_0$

$\text{Stress} = \frac{T}{S} = \frac{L}{2}\rho a_0$

(b) At a distance x from end B, $T_x = (xS\rho)a_0$

$\text{Strain} = \frac{\text{Stress}}{Y} \Rightarrow \frac{dl}{dx} = \frac{(xS\rho)a_0}{SY}$

$\Rightarrow \int dl = \frac{\rho a_0}{Y}\int_0^L x\,dx \Rightarrow \Delta l = \frac{\rho a_0 L^2}{2Y}$

11. 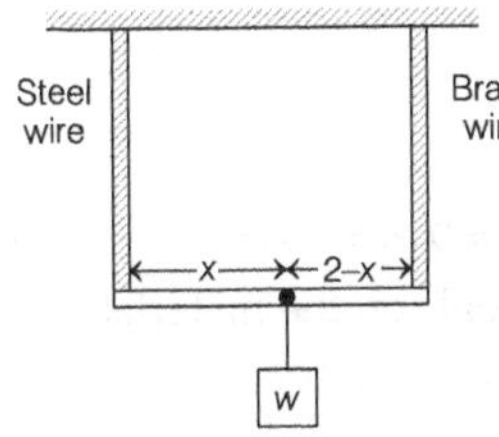

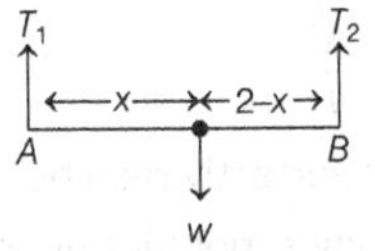

For equilibrium of system about C, $\Sigma\tau = 0$

$\Rightarrow \quad T_1 x - T_2(2 - x) = 0$

$\Rightarrow \quad \frac{T_1}{T_2} = \frac{2 - x}{x}$

(a) For equal stresses,

$\frac{T_1}{A_1} = \frac{T_2}{A_2} \Rightarrow \frac{T_1}{T_2} = \frac{A_1}{A_2} \Rightarrow \frac{2 - x}{x} = \frac{0.1}{0.2}$

$\Rightarrow \quad x = \frac{4}{3}\text{ m}$

(b) For equal strains,

$\frac{T_1}{A_1Y_1} = \frac{T_2}{A_2Y_2} \Rightarrow \frac{T_1}{T_2} = \left(\frac{A_1}{A_2}\right)\left(\frac{Y_1}{Y_2}\right)$

$\Rightarrow \quad \frac{2 - x}{x} = \left(\frac{0.1}{0.2}\right)\left(\frac{20 \times 10^{11}}{10 \times 10^{11}}\right)$

$\Rightarrow \quad x = 1\text{ m}$

12. Thermal stress $= Y\alpha\Delta T = 1.2 \times 10^{11} \times 1.1 \times 10^{-5} \times (20 - 10)$

$= 1.32 \times 10^7\text{ N/m}^2$

6.3 Modulus of Rigidity

1. (a) Shear stress $= \frac{F}{A} = \frac{160 \times 9.8}{3.2 \times 10^{-4}} = 4.9 \times 10^6\text{ N/m}^2$

(b) $\Delta L = \frac{FL}{A\eta} = \frac{160 \times 9.8 \times 0.1}{3.2 \times 10^{-4} \times 8.1 \times 10^{10}} = 6.0 \times 10^{-6}\text{ m}$

2. Shearing stress $= \frac{F}{A} = \frac{0.50}{15 \times 10^{-4}} = 333\text{ Pa}$

Shearing strain $= \frac{\Delta L}{L} = \frac{0.4}{3} = 0.133$

Shear modulus $= \frac{\text{Shearing stress}}{\text{Shearing strain}} = \frac{333}{0.133} = 2.5\text{ kPa}$

3. Shearing stress $= \frac{F}{A} = \frac{1800}{(0.05)^2} = 7.2 \times 10^5\text{ N/m}^2$

Shearing strain $= \frac{F}{A\eta} = \frac{7.2 \times 10^5}{2.4 \times 10^6} = 0.3$

$\frac{\Delta L}{L} = 0.3 \Rightarrow \frac{\Delta L}{5} = 0.3 \Rightarrow \Delta L = 1.5\text{ cm}$

6.4 Bulk Modulus

1. $B = -\frac{\Delta p}{\left(\frac{\Delta V}{V}\right)} = -\frac{100}{\left(-\frac{0.001}{100}\right)} = 10^7\text{ atm}$

2. $B = \frac{\Delta p}{\left(\frac{\Delta V}{V}\right)} \Rightarrow \frac{\Delta V}{V} = \frac{\Delta p}{B}$

$\Rightarrow \quad \frac{\Delta V}{(100\text{ cc})} = (100\text{ atm})(4 \times 10^{-5}\text{ atm}^{-1})$

$\Rightarrow \quad \Delta V = 0.4\text{ cc}$

3. $\rho = \frac{m}{V} \Rightarrow \frac{\Delta V}{V} = -\frac{\Delta\rho}{\rho}$

$B = -\frac{\Delta p}{\left(\frac{\Delta V}{V}\right)} \Rightarrow B = -\frac{\Delta p}{\left(-\frac{\Delta\rho}{\rho}\right)} = \frac{\rho g h}{\left(\frac{\Delta\rho}{\rho}\right)}$

$\Rightarrow \frac{1}{50 \times 10^{-6} \times 10^{-5}} = \frac{10^3 \times 10 \times h}{\left(\frac{1}{100}\right)}$

$\Rightarrow \quad h = 2\text{ km}$

4. B_{adi} = Adiabatic elasticity $= \gamma p$

B_{iso} = isothermal elasticity $= p$

$\frac{B_{adi}}{B_{iso}} = \gamma = \frac{4}{3}$

5. Vp^n = constant

$\Rightarrow \quad Vnp^{n-1}\frac{dp}{dV} + p^n = 0 \Rightarrow \frac{dp}{dV} = -\frac{p}{nV}$

Bulk modulus $= \frac{dp}{\left(\frac{dV}{V}\right)} = \frac{p}{n}$

6.5 Poisson's Ratio

1. Longitudinal strain $= \frac{\Delta L}{L} = \frac{0.3}{3} = 0.1$

$\sigma = \frac{\text{Lateral strain}}{\text{Longitudinal strain}}$

$\Rightarrow \quad 0.26 = \frac{\text{Lateral strain}}{0.1}$

$\Rightarrow$ Lateral strain $= 0.026$

2. $V = \pi r^2 l \Rightarrow \frac{\Delta V}{V} = \frac{2\Delta r}{r} + \frac{\Delta l}{l}$

$$= 2\left(-\sigma\frac{\Delta l}{l}\right) + \frac{\Delta l}{l} \qquad \left\{\because \sigma = \frac{-\frac{\Delta r}{r}}{\frac{\Delta l}{l}}\right\}$$

$$= (1-2\sigma)\frac{\Delta l}{l} = \frac{F}{AY}(1-2\sigma)$$

3. $\frac{\Delta V}{V} = (1-2\sigma)\frac{\Delta l}{l}$

$\Rightarrow \frac{\Delta V}{V} \times 100 = (1 - 2(0.2))(2\times 10^{-3}) \times 100 = 0.12\%$

6.6 Elastic Potential Energy

1. Elastic energy stored $= \frac{mgl}{2} = \frac{200\times 1\times 10^{-3}}{2} = 0.1$ J

2. Stress $= \frac{F}{A} = \frac{5\times 9.8}{1\times 10^{-4}} = 4.9\times 10^{5}$ N/m^2

Energy stored $= \frac{(\text{Stress})^2}{2Y}\times$ Volume

$= \frac{(4.9\times 10^5)^2}{2\times 1\times 10^{11}}\times(1\times 10^{-4}\times 0.2)$

$= 2.4\times 10^{-5}$ J

3. $W = \frac{F\Delta l}{2}$

$W_1 = \frac{(2\times 9.8)(0.6\times 10^{-3})}{2}$, $W_2 = \frac{(4\times 9.8)(1\times 10^{-3})}{2}$

Work done $= W_2 - W_1 = 13.72\times 10^{-3}$ J

4. $F = \frac{AY\Delta l}{l} \Rightarrow F = \frac{\pi r^2 Y\Delta l}{l} \Rightarrow F \propto \frac{r^2}{l}$

$\Rightarrow \quad \frac{F_1}{F_2} = \left(\frac{r_1}{r_2}\right)^2\left(\frac{l_2}{l_1}\right) = \left(\frac{r_1}{2r_1}\right)^2\left(\frac{l_1/2}{l_1}\right) = \frac{1}{8}$

$W = \frac{F\Delta l}{2} \Rightarrow \frac{W_1}{W_2} = \frac{F_1}{F_2} = \frac{1}{8} \Rightarrow \frac{2}{W_2} = \frac{1}{8}$

$\Rightarrow \quad W_2 = 16$ J

5. $T = (\rho\pi r^2 x)g$

$\sigma = \frac{T}{A} = \rho g x$

$\int dU = \int \frac{\sigma^2}{2Y}dV$

$\Rightarrow \quad U = \int_0^L \frac{(\rho g x)^2}{2Y}\pi r^2 dx = \frac{1}{6}\frac{\pi r^2\rho^2 g^2 L^3}{Y}$

6.7 Stress-Strain Curve

1. $Y = \frac{\text{Stress}}{\text{Strain}} = \text{Slope} = \tan\theta$

$\frac{Y_A}{Y_B} = \frac{\tan 60^\circ}{\tan 30^\circ} = 3$

2. (i) *B* (ii) *D* (iii) *OA* (iv) *OB* (v) *BC*

3. (a) $Y = \text{Slope} \Rightarrow Y_A > Y_B$ $\{\because (\text{Slope})_A > (\text{Slope})_B\}$
   (b) Material *A* is more ductile as the length of plastic region is more for material *A*.
   (c) Material *B* is more brittle as the length of plastic region is shorter for material *B*.

4. Young's modulus is maximum for wire *P*. So, elasticity is maximum for wire *P*.

Level 2

Single Choice Correct Questions

1. $Y = \frac{\frac{F}{A}}{\frac{\Delta l}{l}}$

For perfectly rigid body, $\Delta l = 0 \Rightarrow Y \to \infty$

2. Young's modulus depends only on the material.

3. $\Delta l = \frac{Fl}{AY} = \frac{4Fl}{\pi d^2 Y} \Rightarrow \Delta l \propto \frac{1}{d^2}$

4. $\Delta l = \frac{Fl}{AY} = \frac{4Fl}{\pi d^2 Y} \Rightarrow \Delta l \propto \frac{l}{d^2}$

5. $\Delta l = \frac{Fl}{\pi r^2 Y} \Rightarrow \frac{\Delta l_1}{\Delta l_2} = \left(\frac{F_1}{F_2}\right)\left(\frac{l_1}{l_2}\right)\left(\frac{r_2}{r_1}\right)^2$

$\Rightarrow \quad \frac{l}{\Delta l_2} = \left(\frac{F}{2F}\right)\left(\frac{L}{2L}\right)\left(\frac{2r}{r}\right)^2$

$\Rightarrow \quad \Delta l_2 = l$

6. Slope $= \frac{F}{\Delta l} = \frac{AY}{l} \Rightarrow$ Slope $\propto A$

Slope is least for wire *A*. So, wire *A* will be thinnest.

7. $Y = \frac{\text{Stress}}{\text{Strain}} = \frac{7\times 10^8}{\left(\frac{2L-L}{L}\right)} = 7\times 10^8$ N/m^2

8. $\Delta l = \frac{Fl}{AY}$,

Slope $= \frac{\Delta l}{F} = \frac{(4-1)\times 10^{-4}}{80-20}$

$\Rightarrow \quad \frac{l}{AY} = \frac{1}{20}\times 10^{-4}$

$\Rightarrow \quad \frac{1}{10^{-6}Y} = \frac{1}{20}\times 10^{-4}$

$\Rightarrow \quad Y = 2\times 10^{11}$ N/m^2

9. $T - mg = ma$

$\Rightarrow \quad T = m(g+a)$

Stress $= \frac{T}{A} = \frac{m(g+a)}{A} = \frac{2\times 10^3(10+a)}{10^{-4}}$

Stress $= \frac{1}{2}$(elastic limit)

$\Rightarrow \quad 2\times10^7(10+a)=\frac{1}{2}\times2\times10^9$

$\Rightarrow \quad a=40\text{ m/s}^2$

10. Stress $=\frac{mg}{A}$

$\Rightarrow 10^6=\frac{(3\times10^3\times Al)(9.8)}{A} \Rightarrow l=34\text{ m}$

11. $\Delta l=\frac{Fl}{AY}$

$\Rightarrow \quad \frac{\Delta l_1}{\Delta l_2}=\left(\frac{F_1}{F_2}\right)\left(\frac{l_1}{l_2}\right)\left(\frac{r_2}{r_1}\right)^2\left(\frac{Y_2}{Y_1}\right)$

$=\left(\frac{3mg}{2mg}\right)(a)\left(\frac{1}{b}\right)^2\left(\frac{1}{c}\right)=\frac{3a}{2b^2c}$

12. $\Delta l=\frac{Fl}{AY} \Rightarrow l=\frac{(\lambda Lg)\left(\frac{L}{2}\right)}{AY}$

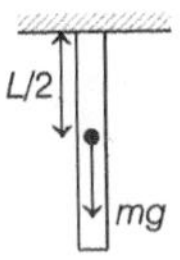

$\Rightarrow \quad Y=\frac{\lambda gL^2}{2Al}$

13. $E=\frac{\text{Stress}}{\text{Strain}} \quad \Rightarrow \quad E=\frac{\frac{F}{A}}{\left(\frac{2\pi R-2\pi r}{2\pi r}\right)}$

$\Rightarrow \quad F=AE\left(\frac{R-r}{r}\right)$

14. Loss in weight = Buoyant force $=\rho Vg$

$\Delta l=\frac{Fl}{AY}=\frac{\rho Vgl}{\pi r^2 Y}$

15. Let natural length be l.

$F=kx$

$\Rightarrow \quad T_1=k(l_1-l)$ ...(i)

and $\quad T_2=k(l_2-l)$ ...(ii)

Dividing Eq. (i) by Eq. (ii), we get

$l=\frac{l_1T_2-l_2T_1}{T_2-T_1}$

16. Breaking stress depends only on the material of wire.

17. Breaking stress $=\frac{F_1}{A_1}=\frac{F_2}{A_2}$

$\Rightarrow \quad \frac{500}{\pi(0.5)^2}=\frac{F_2}{\pi(1)^2} \Rightarrow F_2=2000\text{ N}$

18. $T=m\omega^2 l$

Breaking stress $=\frac{T}{A}=\frac{m\omega_{max}^2 l}{A}=4.8\times10^7$

$\Rightarrow \quad \frac{10\times\omega_{max}^2\times0.3}{10^{-6}}=4.8\times10^7$

$\Rightarrow \quad \omega_{max}=4\text{ rad/s}$

19. $T=\frac{2m_1m_2g}{m_1+m_2}=\frac{4mg}{3}$

Breaking stress $=\frac{T}{A} \Rightarrow S=\frac{\frac{4mg}{3}}{\pi r^2} \Rightarrow r=\sqrt{\frac{4mg}{3\pi S}}$

20. $Y=\frac{\text{Stress}}{\text{Strain}}=\frac{\frac{m\omega^2 l}{A}}{\frac{\Delta l}{l}}=\frac{m\omega^2 l^2}{A\Delta l}$

$=\frac{1\times(20)^2\times(1)^2}{10^{-6}\times10^{-3}}$

$=4\times10^{11}\text{ N/m}^2$

21. Breaking stress $=\frac{m\omega^2 l}{A}$

$=\frac{1(100)^2(1)}{10^{-6}}=10^{10}\text{ N/m}^2$

22.

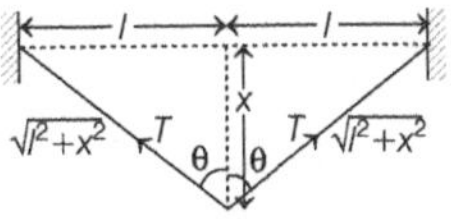

Strain $=\frac{\Delta l}{l}=\frac{2\sqrt{l^2+x^2}-2l}{2l}=\left(1+\frac{x^2}{l^2}\right)^{\frac{1}{2}}-1$

$=1+\frac{x^2}{2l^2}-1 \quad \because \{x<<l\}$

$=\frac{x^2}{2l^2}$

23. $2T\cos\theta=w$

$\Rightarrow \quad T=\frac{w}{2\cos\theta}=\frac{w\sqrt{l^2+x^2}}{2x}$

Stress $=\frac{T}{A}=\frac{w\sqrt{l^2+x^2}}{2xA}=\frac{wl}{2xA} \quad \because \{x<<l\}$

24. $\eta=\frac{\text{Stress}}{\text{Strain}} \Rightarrow \eta=\frac{\frac{F}{L^2}}{\frac{\Delta L}{L}}$

$\Rightarrow \quad F=\eta L\Delta L$

Restoring force $=-(\eta L)\Delta L$

So, force constant $=\eta L$

$T=2\pi\sqrt{\frac{M}{k}}=2\pi\sqrt{\frac{M}{\eta L}}$

25. $\Delta L=\frac{FL}{A\eta}=\frac{500\times0.04}{(4\times16\times10^{-4})(2\times10^6)}=0.156\times10^{-2}\text{ m}$

$=0.156\text{ cm}$

26. $B=\frac{\Delta p}{\left(\frac{\Delta V}{V}\right)} \quad \Rightarrow \quad 2100\times10^6=\frac{\Delta p}{\left(\frac{0.004}{100}\right)} \quad \Rightarrow \quad \Delta p=84\text{ kPa}$

27. Bulk strain $=\frac{\Delta V}{V}=3\left(\frac{\Delta l}{l}\right)=3\left(\frac{2}{100}\right)=0.06$

28. $B = \frac{\Delta p}{\left(\frac{\Delta V}{V}\right)} \Rightarrow \frac{\Delta V}{V} = \frac{\Delta p}{B} = \frac{1\times10^5}{1.25\times10^{11}} = 8\times10^{-7}$

29. $B = \frac{\Delta p}{\left(\frac{\Delta V}{V}\right)} \Rightarrow B = \frac{\rho g h}{\left(\frac{\Delta V}{V}\right)} = \frac{10^3\times10\times200}{\left(\frac{0.1}{100}\right)}$

$= 2\times10^9\ \text{N/m}^2$

30. $\rho = \frac{m}{V} \Rightarrow \frac{\Delta V}{V} = -\frac{\Delta\rho}{\rho} \Rightarrow \frac{\Delta V}{V} = -\left(\frac{0.1}{100}\right)$

$\Delta p = -B\left(\frac{\Delta V}{V}\right) = -\frac{1}{C}\left(\frac{\Delta V}{V}\right) = -\frac{1}{(5\times10^{-5}\times10^{-5})}\left(-\frac{0.1}{100}\right)$

$= 2\times10^6\ \text{Nm}^{-2}$

31. $p = p_0\rho^{\alpha V} \Rightarrow \frac{dp}{dV} = p_0 e^{\alpha V}(\alpha)$

$B = \frac{dp}{\left(\frac{dV}{V}\right)} = V(p_0 e^{\alpha V}\alpha) = \alpha p V$

32. $\rho = \frac{m}{V} \Rightarrow \frac{\Delta\rho}{\rho} = -\frac{\Delta V}{V}$

$B = -\frac{\Delta p}{\left(\frac{\Delta V}{V}\right)} \Rightarrow B = -\frac{\Delta p}{\left(-\frac{\Delta\rho}{\rho}\right)} = \frac{\rho^2 g h}{\Delta\rho}$

$\Rightarrow \Delta\rho = \frac{\rho^2 g h}{B}$

33. $V = \frac{4}{3}\pi R^3 \Rightarrow \frac{\Delta V}{V} = \frac{3\Delta R}{R}$

$B = \frac{\Delta p}{\left(\frac{\Delta V}{V}\right)} \Rightarrow k = \frac{\frac{mg}{A}}{3\left(\frac{\Delta R}{R}\right)} \Rightarrow \frac{\Delta R}{R} = \frac{mg}{3Ak}$

34. $B = \frac{\Delta p}{\left(\frac{\Delta V}{V}\right)} \Rightarrow \frac{\Delta V}{V} = \frac{\Delta p}{B}$

$\Rightarrow \gamma\Delta T = \frac{p}{B} \Rightarrow \Delta T = \frac{p}{B\gamma}$

35. Hooke's law is applicable only with elastic limit.

36. Steel has the highest value of modulus of elasticity among the given materials.

37. $\frac{dV}{V} = (1-2\sigma)\frac{\Delta l}{l} = 0 \Rightarrow \sigma = 0.5$

38. Longitudinal strain $= \frac{\text{Lateral strain}}{\sigma} = \frac{0.01\times10^{-3}}{0.4}$

$= 2.5\times10^{-5}$

Longitudinal stress $= \frac{F}{A} = \frac{100}{0.025} = 4\times10^3\ \text{N/m}^2$

$Y = \frac{4\times10^3}{2.5\times10^{-5}} = 1.6\times10^8\ \text{Nm}^{-2}$

39. $\frac{\Delta V}{V} = (1-2\sigma)\frac{\Delta l}{l} = (1-2(0.2))(4\times10^{-3}) = 0.24\times10^{-2}$

$\frac{\Delta V}{V}\times100 = (0.24\times10^{-2})\times100 = 0.24\%$

40. $\sigma_x = \sigma_y = \sigma_z = \frac{F}{A}$

In x-direction, Strain $= \frac{\sigma_x}{Y} - \sigma\left(\frac{\sigma_y}{Y}\right) - \sigma\left(\frac{\sigma_z}{Y}\right)$

$\Rightarrow \frac{\Delta l}{1} = \frac{F}{AY}(1-2\sigma)$

$\Rightarrow \Delta l = \frac{F}{AY}(1-2\sigma)$

41. $T = AY\alpha\,\Delta T = \pi(1\times10^{-3})^2\times2\times10^{11}\times1\times10^{-5}\times10$

$= 62.8$ N

42. Energy per unit volume

$= \frac{1}{2}Y(\text{Strain})^2 = \frac{1}{2}\times2\times10^{10}\times\left(\frac{0.06}{100}\right)^2$

$= 3600\ \text{Jm}^{-3}$

43. Strain $= \frac{\Delta L}{L} = \alpha\Delta T = 12\times10^{-6}\times20$

$= 2.4\times10^{-4}$

Energy stored per unit volume $= \frac{1}{2}Y(\text{Strain})^2$

$= \frac{1}{2}\times10^{11}\,(2.4\times10^{-4})^2 = 2880\ \text{Jm}^{-3}$

44. $\sigma = \frac{F}{A} = \frac{F}{\pi r^2} \Rightarrow \sigma \propto \frac{1}{r^2} \Rightarrow \frac{\sigma_1}{\sigma_2} = \left(\frac{r_2}{r_1}\right)^2$

$U = \frac{(\text{Stress})^2}{2Y} \Rightarrow U \propto \sigma^2$

$\Rightarrow \frac{U_1}{U_2} = \left(\frac{\sigma_1}{\sigma_2}\right)^2 = \left(\frac{r_2}{r_1}\right)^4$

$= \left(\frac{2r}{r}\right)^4 = 16:1$

45. $W = \frac{F\Delta l}{2} \Rightarrow 4.5\times10^{-2} = \frac{30\times\Delta l}{2}$

$\Rightarrow \Delta l = 3\times10^{-3}$ m

$Y = \frac{\text{Stress}}{\text{Strain}} = \frac{Fl}{A\Delta l} = \frac{30\times4}{2\times10^{-7}\times3\times10^{-3}} = 2\times10^{11}$ Pa

46. Strain $= \frac{\Delta l}{l} = \frac{12-10}{10} = 0.2$

$Y = \frac{\text{Stress}}{\text{Strain}} \Rightarrow 5\times10^8 = \frac{T}{(1\times10^{-6})(0.2)} \Rightarrow T = 100$ N

47. $U = \frac{1}{2}Y\,(\text{Strain})^2\,(\text{Volume}) = \frac{1}{2}mv^2$

$\Rightarrow \frac{1}{2}\times5\times10^8\,(0.2)^2\,(1\times10^{-6}\times10\times10^{-2})$

$$= \frac{1}{2} \times 5 \times 10^{-3} v^2$$

$\Rightarrow \quad v = 20 \text{ m/s}$

48. $\Sigma F = ma \Rightarrow 30 - T_1 = 3a$ ...(i)

$T_2 - T_1 = 3a$ ...(ii)

$T_2 = 3a$ ...(iii)

Solving we get, $T_2 = 10$ N

$$U_{AB} = \frac{(\text{Stress})^2}{2Y}$$

$$= \frac{1}{2}\left(\frac{10}{0.005 \times 10^{-4}}\right)^2 \left(\frac{1}{2 \times 10^{11}}\right) = 1000 \text{ J/m}^3$$

49. $T_x = \left(\frac{m}{l}x\right)\left(\frac{F}{m}\right) = \frac{Fx}{l}$

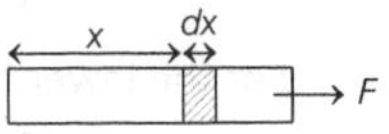

$$\text{Stress} = \frac{T_x}{A} = \frac{Fx}{Al}$$

$$\int dU = \int_0^l \frac{(\text{Stress})^2}{2Y}(Adx) \Rightarrow U = \frac{F^2 l}{6AY}$$

50. $k_{eq} = k_1 + k_2 \Rightarrow \frac{(2A)Y_{eq}}{L} = \frac{AY_1}{L} + \frac{AY_2}{L}$

$$\Rightarrow \quad Y_{eq} = \frac{Y_1 + Y_2}{2}$$

51. For no change in the lengths of individual rods, the compressive forces in both rods due to thermal expansion should be equal. So,

$$A_1 Y_1 \alpha_1 \Delta T = A_2 Y_2 \alpha_2 \Delta T$$

$$\Rightarrow \quad \frac{A_1}{A_2} = \frac{\alpha_2 Y_2}{\alpha_1 Y_1}$$

52. Energy stored = Heat produced

$$\Rightarrow \frac{1}{2}(\text{Stress})\ (\text{Strain})\ (\text{Volume}) = ms\Delta T$$

$$\Rightarrow \frac{1}{2}\left(\frac{210 \times 9.8}{10^{-6}}\right)\left(\frac{16 \times 10^{-3}}{2}\right)(10^{-6} \times 2)$$

$$= (8000 \times 10^{-6} \times 2)(420)\,\Delta T$$

$$\Rightarrow \quad \Delta T = 2.45° \text{ C}$$

Numerical Value Questions

1. $F = \left(\frac{AY}{l}\right)\Delta l \Rightarrow$ Force constant $= \frac{AY}{l}$

$$\omega = \sqrt{\frac{k}{m}} = \sqrt{\frac{AY}{ml}} = \sqrt{\frac{4.9 \times 10^{-7} Y}{0.1 \times 1}} = 140$$

$$\Rightarrow \quad Y = 4 \times 10^9 \text{ Nm}^{-2}$$

2. $F = \eta A \frac{\Delta l}{l}$

$$= 0.4 \times 10^{11} \times (1 \times 0.005) \times \left(\frac{0.02 \times 10^{-2}}{1.0}\right) = 40 \text{ kN}$$

3. $F = \sigma A = \sigma(2\pi rt)$

$$= 3.45 \times 10^8 (2 \times 3.14 \times 0.73 \times 10^{-2} \times 1.27 \times 10^{-2}) = 200 \text{ kN}$$

4. $k = \frac{(\pi r^2)Y}{L} \Rightarrow \frac{k_1}{k_2} = \left(\frac{r_1}{r_2}\right)^2 = \frac{1}{4}$

$\Delta l_1 + \Delta l_2 = 10$ mm ...(i)

$k_1 \Delta l_1 = k_2 \Delta l_2 \Rightarrow \frac{\Delta l_1}{\Delta l_2} = \frac{k_2}{k_1} = 4$ ...(ii)

Solving Eqs. (i) and (ii), we get

$\Delta l_1 = 8$ mm

5. $2T \sin\left(\frac{d\theta}{2}\right) = dm\omega^2 R$

$$\Rightarrow \quad Td\theta = (\rho A R d\theta)\omega^2 R$$

$$\Rightarrow \quad T = \rho A \omega^2 R^2$$

$$\text{Stress} = \frac{T}{A} = \rho\omega^2 R^2$$

$$\text{Strain} = \frac{\Delta l}{l} = \frac{2\pi(R + \Delta R) - 2\pi R}{2\pi R} = \frac{\Delta R}{R}$$

$$Y = \frac{\text{Stress}}{\text{Strain}} \Rightarrow 2 \times 10^{11} = \frac{(10^4)(10)^2(2)^2}{\left(\frac{\Delta R}{2}\right)}$$

$$\Rightarrow \Delta R = 4 \times 10^{-5} \text{ m}$$

6. $A = \pi r^2 \Rightarrow \frac{\Delta A}{A} \times 100 = 2\left(\frac{\Delta r}{r} \times 100\right)$

$$\Rightarrow \quad 2\% = 2\left(\frac{\Delta r}{r} \times 100\right)$$

$$\Rightarrow \quad \frac{\Delta r}{r} \times 100 = 1\%$$

$$\sigma = \frac{\frac{\Delta r}{r}}{\frac{\Delta l}{l}} \Rightarrow \frac{\Delta l}{l} \times 100 = \frac{1}{\sigma}\left(\frac{\Delta r}{r} \times 100\right) = \frac{1}{0.4}(1\%) = 2.5\%$$

7. Elastic potential energy per unit volume

$$= \frac{1}{2}(\text{Stress})\ (\text{Strain}) = \frac{1}{2}(\text{Stress})\left(\frac{\text{Stress}}{B}\right)$$

$$= \frac{1}{2}(\text{Stress})^2\ (\text{Compressibility})$$

$$= \frac{1}{2}(\rho g h)^2\ (C) = \frac{1}{2} \times (10^3 \times 9.8 \times 10^3)^2 (5 \times 10^{-10})$$

$$= 24 \times 10^3 \text{ Jm}^{-3}$$

8. Consider 1 m^3 of water at the surface. Let us calculate change in volume ΔV of this water when it is at a pressure of 501 atm.

$$\Delta V = \frac{(\Delta p)V}{B} = \frac{(501 - 1) \times 10^5 \times 1}{2 \times 10^9} = 0.025 \text{ m}^3$$

$$\text{New density} = \frac{m}{V - \Delta V} = \frac{1000}{1 - 0.025} = 1025 \text{ kg m}^{-3}$$

9. $\sigma = \frac{T}{A} = \frac{m(g + a)}{A}$

$$\text{Strain} = \frac{\sigma}{Y} = \frac{m(g+a)}{AY}$$

$$= \frac{10(10+2)}{2\times10^{-4}\times2\times10^{11}} = 3\times10^{-6}$$

10. $\Sigma F_x = 0 \Rightarrow T_1 \cos 60° = T_2 \cos 30°$

$$\Rightarrow \quad \frac{T_1}{T_2} = \sqrt{3}$$

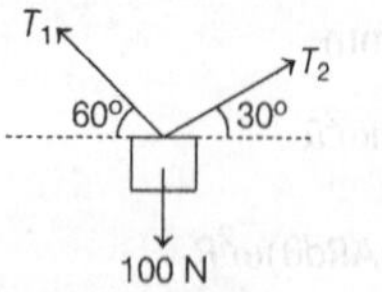

$$\Delta l = \frac{Fl}{AY} \Rightarrow \frac{\Delta l_C}{\Delta L_S} = \left(\frac{T_C}{T_S}\right)\left(\frac{l_C}{l_S}\right)\left(\frac{Y_S}{Y_C}\right)$$

$$= \left(\frac{1}{\sqrt{3}}\right)\left(\frac{\sqrt{3}}{1}\right)\left(\frac{2\times10^{11}}{1\times10^{11}}\right) = 2$$

Level 3

Single Choice Correct Questions

1. $\Delta L = \frac{FL}{A\eta} = \frac{FL}{L^2\eta} \Rightarrow \Delta L \propto \frac{1}{L}$

$$\Rightarrow \frac{\Delta L_1}{\Delta L_2} = \frac{L_2}{L_1} \Rightarrow \frac{0.5}{\Delta L_2} = \frac{20}{10}$$

$$\Rightarrow \Delta L_2 = 0.25 \text{ cm}$$

2. Both stress and strain are caused by some external force.

3.

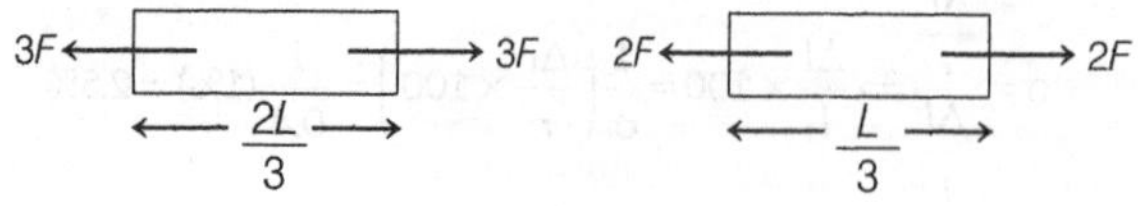

$$\Delta L = \Delta L_1 + \Delta L_2 = \frac{(3F)\left(\frac{2L}{3}\right)}{AY} + \frac{(2F)\left(\frac{L}{3}\right)}{AY} = \frac{8FL}{3AY}$$

4. $\Delta L = \Delta L_1 + \Delta L_2 = \frac{F\left(\frac{L}{2}\right)}{AY} + \frac{F\left(\frac{L}{2}\right)}{(2A)Y} = \frac{3FL}{4AY}$

5.

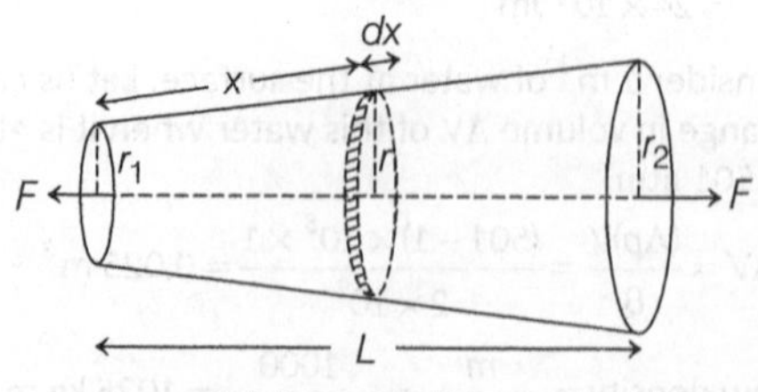

Consider an elemental ring of radius r and width dx at a distance x as shown in figure.

$$r = r_1 + \left(\frac{r_2 - r_1}{L}\right)x$$

Elongation of element, $dl = \frac{Fdx}{AY} = \frac{Fdx}{\pi r^2 Y}$

$$\int dl = \int_0^L \frac{Fdx}{\pi\left(r_1 + \left(\frac{r_2 - r_1}{L}\right)x\right)^2 Y}$$

$$\Rightarrow \quad \Delta l = \frac{FL}{\pi r_1 r_2 Y}$$

6. Using energy conservation,
Loss in gravitational, PE = Gain in KE

$$\Rightarrow \quad mg\left(\frac{L}{2}\right) = \frac{1}{2}\left(\frac{mL^2}{3}\right)\omega^2 \Rightarrow \omega = \sqrt{\frac{3g}{L}}$$

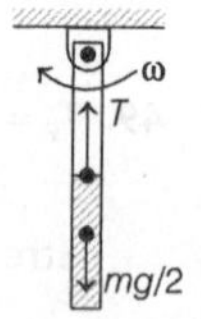

For the lower half rod,

$$T - \frac{mg}{2} = \left(\frac{m}{2}\right)\omega^2\left(\frac{3L}{4}\right)$$

$$\Rightarrow \quad T - \frac{mg}{2} = \left(\frac{m}{2}\right)\left(\frac{3g}{L}\right)\left(\frac{3L}{4}\right)$$

$$\Rightarrow \quad T = \frac{13}{8}mg$$

$$\text{Stress at mid-point} = \frac{13mg}{8A} = \frac{13dALg}{8A} = \frac{13\,dLg}{8}$$

7.

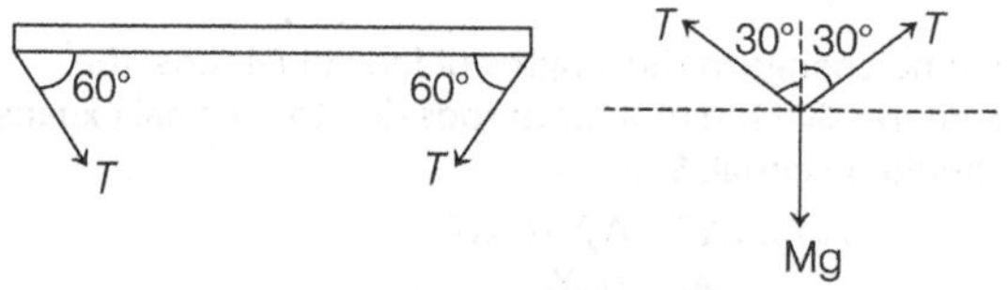

$$2T\cos 30° = Mg \Rightarrow T = \frac{Mg}{\sqrt{3}} = \frac{10000}{\sqrt{3}}$$

$$\Delta l = \frac{Fl}{AY} = \frac{(T\cos 60°)l}{AY}$$

$$= \frac{5000\times1}{\sqrt{3}\times10\times10^{-4}\times2\times10^{11}}$$

$$= \frac{5}{2\sqrt{3}}\times10^{-5}\text{ m}$$

8. $\Sigma F = ma \Rightarrow F_0 = ma \Rightarrow a = \frac{F_0}{m}$

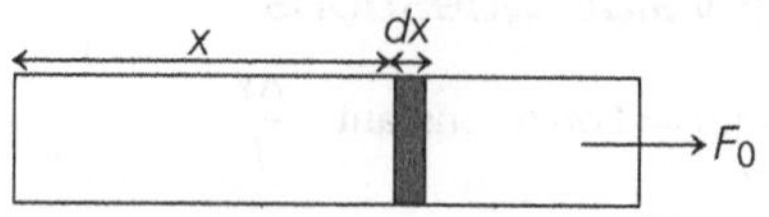

$$T_x = \left(\frac{m}{L}x\right)a = \frac{F_0 x}{L}$$

$$\text{Stress} = \frac{T_x}{S} = \frac{F_0 x}{SL}$$

$$\text{Strain in } dx \text{ element} = \frac{dl}{dx} = \frac{F_0 x}{SLY}$$

$$\Rightarrow \int dl = \frac{F_0}{SLY}\int_0^L x\,dx \quad \Rightarrow \quad \Delta l = \frac{F_0 L}{2SY}$$

9. Strain in the wire $= \dfrac{2\sqrt{1+y^2}-2}{2} = (1+y^2)^{\frac{1}{2}} - 1$

$$= 1 + \frac{y^2}{2} - 1 = \frac{y^2}{2}$$

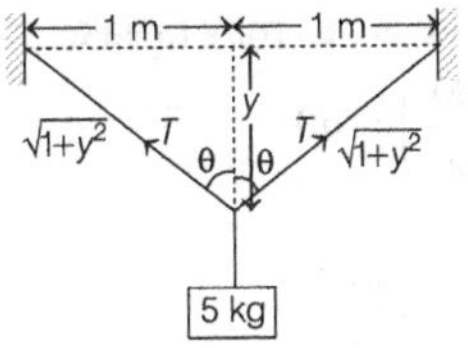

$$2T\cos\theta = 50 \Rightarrow 2T\left(\frac{y}{\sqrt{1+y^2}}\right) = 50$$

$$\Rightarrow \quad T = \frac{25}{y} \qquad \because \{y << 1\}$$

Stress in the wire $= \dfrac{T}{A} = \dfrac{25}{y \times 1 \times 10^{-4}} = \dfrac{25 \times 10^4}{y}$

$$Y = \frac{\text{Stress}}{\text{Strain}} \Rightarrow 2.4 \times 10^9 = \frac{25 \times 10^4}{y \times \left(\frac{y^2}{2}\right)}$$

$$\Rightarrow \quad y = 5.92 \text{ cm}$$

10. $2T\sin\left(\dfrac{d\theta}{2}\right) = dm\omega^2 R$

$$\Rightarrow \quad T d\theta = (\rho A R d\theta)\omega^2 R$$

$$\Rightarrow \quad T = \rho A \omega^2 R^2$$

Breaking stress $= \dfrac{T}{A} = \rho\omega^2 R^2 = \sigma$

$$\Rightarrow \quad \rho(2\pi f)^2 R^2 = \sigma$$

$$\Rightarrow \quad f = \frac{1}{2\pi R}\sqrt{\frac{\sigma}{\rho}}$$

11. $T_x = \left(\dfrac{m}{l}(l-x)\right)\omega^2\left(\dfrac{l+x}{2}\right)$

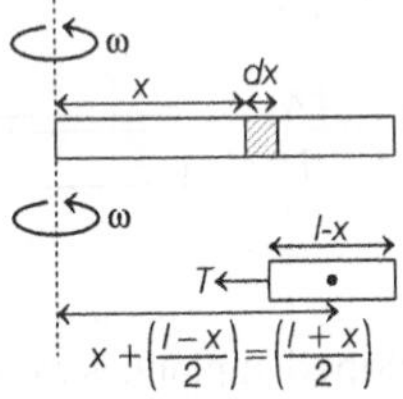

Stress $= \dfrac{T_x}{A} = \dfrac{m\omega^2(l^2 - x^2)}{2Al}$

Strain in dx element $= \dfrac{dl}{dx}$

$$\frac{dl}{dx} = \frac{m\omega^2(l^2 - x^2)}{2AYl}$$

$$\Delta l = \int dl = \int_0^l \frac{m\omega^2(l^2 - x^2)}{2AYl}dx = \frac{m\omega^2 l^2}{3AY}$$

12. Let compressive forces in steel and brass rods be T_1 and T_2, respectively.

$$T_1 + 2T_2 = 4000g \qquad \text{...(i)}$$

Compressions in both steel and brass rods will be equal.

$$\Rightarrow \quad \Delta l_1 = \Delta l_2$$

$$\Rightarrow \quad \frac{T_1 l_1}{A_1 Y_1} = \frac{T_2 l_2}{A_2 Y_2} \Rightarrow \frac{T_1(30)}{15 \times 2 \times 10^6} = \frac{T_2(20)}{10 \times 1 \times 10^6}$$

$$\Rightarrow \quad T_1 = 2T_2 \qquad \text{...(ii)}$$

From Eqs. (i) and (ii), we get

$$T_1 = 2 \times 10^4 \text{ N}$$

$$T_2 = 10^4 \text{ N}$$

Stress in brass rod $= \dfrac{T_2}{A_2} = \dfrac{10^4}{10 \times 10^{-4}} = 10$ MPa

13. $\dfrac{dp}{dh} = -\rho g \qquad \text{...(i)}$

$$B = -\frac{dp}{\left(\frac{dV}{V}\right)} \qquad \text{...(ii)}$$

$$\rho = \frac{M}{V} \Rightarrow \frac{d\rho}{\rho} = -\frac{dV}{V} \qquad \text{...(iii)}$$

From Eqs. (i), (ii) and (iii), we get

$$B\frac{d\rho}{\rho} = \rho g dh$$

$$\Rightarrow \quad \int_{\rho_0}^{\rho}\frac{d\rho}{\rho^2} = \frac{g}{B}\int_0^h dh \Rightarrow \frac{1}{\rho_0} - \frac{1}{\rho} = \frac{gh}{B}$$

$$\Rightarrow \quad \rho = \frac{\rho_0 B}{B - \rho_0 gh}$$

Substituting value of ρ in Eqs. (i), we get

$$\int_{p_0}^{p} dp = -\int_0^h \frac{\rho_0 Bg dh}{B - \rho_0 gh}$$

$$\Rightarrow \quad p = p_0 - B\ln\left(1 - \frac{\rho_0 gh}{B}\right)$$

14. For thermal expansion, $\dfrac{\Delta V}{V} = \gamma\theta$

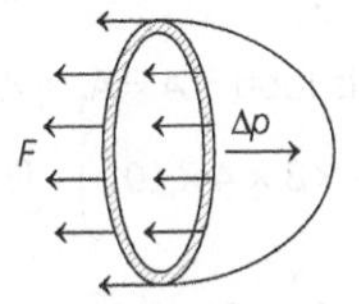

Bulk modulus, $B = \dfrac{\Delta p}{\left(\frac{\Delta V}{V}\right)} \Rightarrow B = \dfrac{\Delta p}{\gamma\theta} \Rightarrow \Delta p = \gamma\theta B$

$$\Delta p = \frac{F}{\pi R^2} = \gamma\theta B$$

$$\Rightarrow \quad F = \gamma\theta B\pi R^2$$

Tensile stress $= \dfrac{F}{2\pi Rt} = \dfrac{\gamma\theta B\pi R^2}{2\pi Rt} = \dfrac{\gamma\theta BR}{2t}$

15. $T = \left(\dfrac{m}{L}x\right)g$

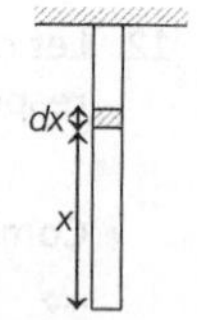

$$\text{Stress} = \frac{T}{A} = \frac{mgx}{AL}$$

$$\text{Strain} = \frac{dl}{dx} = \frac{mgx}{AYL}$$

$$\int dl = \int \frac{mgx}{AYL}\,dx$$

Elongation in upper half,

$$\int dl = \int_{L/2}^{L} \frac{mgx}{AYL}\,dx \Rightarrow \Delta l_1 = \frac{3mgL}{8AY}$$

Elongation in lower half,

$$\int dl = \int_{0}^{L/2} \frac{mgx}{AYL}\,dx \Rightarrow \Delta l_2 = \frac{mgL}{8AY} \Rightarrow \frac{\Delta l_1}{\Delta l_2} = 3$$

16. $U = \dfrac{1}{2}\dfrac{(\text{Stress})^2}{Y} \times \text{Volume}$

$$U = U_1 + U_2 = \frac{1}{2}\frac{\left(\frac{w}{\pi R^2}\right)^2}{Y}(\pi R^2 L) + \frac{1}{2}\frac{\left(\frac{w}{\pi (2R)^2}\right)^2}{Y}(\pi (2R)^2 L)$$

$$= \frac{5w^2L}{8\pi R^2 Y}$$

17. Thermal stress $= Y\alpha\Delta T = 10^{11} \times 10^{-6} \times 100 = 10^7\ \text{N/m}^2$

$$\text{Elastic energy stored} = \frac{1}{2}\frac{(\text{Stress})^2}{Y} \times \text{Volume}$$

$$= \frac{1}{2}\frac{(10^7)^2}{10^{11}} \times (10 \times 10^{-4} \times 1) = 500\ \text{mJ}$$

18. Hystersis loss corresponding to elasticity per unit volume of a substance is given by the area of hystersis loop.

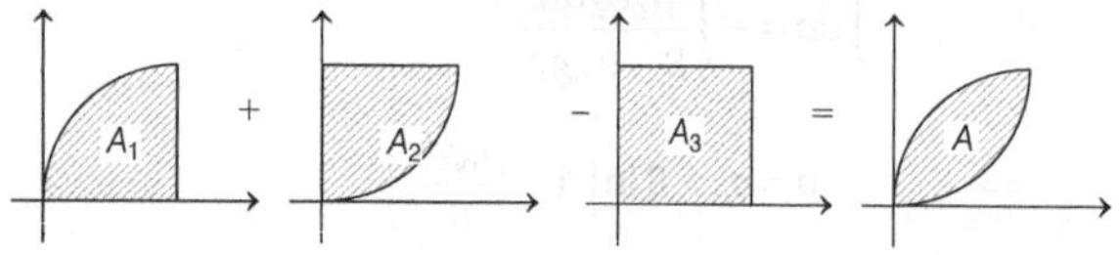

Area of ellipse $= \pi \times$ (Semi-major axis) $\times$ (Semi-minor axis)

$$A_1 = A_2 = \frac{1}{4}(\pi \times 8 \times 4 \times 10^2) \text{ and } A_3 = 8 \times 4 \times 10^2$$

Area of hysteresis loop $= A = A_1 + A_2 - A_3$

$$= 2\left(\frac{\pi}{4} \times 8 \times 4 \times 10^2\right) - (8 \times 4 \times 10^2)$$

$$= \left(\frac{\pi}{2} - 1\right) \times 32 \times 10^2\ \text{J}$$

Multiple Choice(s) Correct Questions

1. Tension in $B = T_B = \dfrac{mg}{3}$

Tension in $A = T_A = T_B + mg = \dfrac{4mg}{3}$

$\therefore \quad T_A = 4T_B$

Stress, $S = \dfrac{T}{\pi r^2}$

Wire breaks when S is equal to breaking stress.

For $r_A = r_B$, $S_A = 4S_B \Rightarrow A$ breaks before B.

For $r_A = 2r_B$, $S_A = S_B$

$\Rightarrow$ Either of the wires may break.

2. $T_0 = 2T \sin\left(\dfrac{d\theta}{2}\right) = Td\theta$

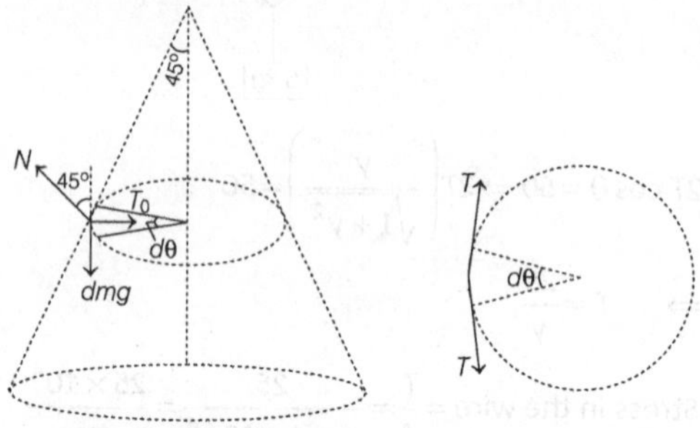

$$N \cos 45° = dmg \quad \text{...(i)}$$

$$N \sin 45° = T_0 = Td\theta \quad \text{...(ii)}$$

From Eqs. (i) and (ii), we get

$$Td\theta = (dm)g$$

$$\Rightarrow Td\theta = \left(\frac{m}{2\pi R} Rd\theta\right)g \Rightarrow T = \frac{mg}{2\pi}$$

$$\text{Extension in the ring} = \frac{FL}{AY} = \left(\frac{mg}{2\pi}\right)\frac{2\pi R}{aY} = \frac{mgR}{aY}$$

$$\text{Energy stored in the ring} = \frac{1}{2}\frac{(\text{Stress})^2}{Y} \times (\text{Volume})$$

$$= \frac{1}{2}\left(\frac{mg}{2\pi a}\right)^2 \frac{1}{Y}(2\pi R a)$$

$$= \frac{m^2 g^2 R}{4\pi Y a}$$

3. $E = \dfrac{(\text{Stress})^2}{2B} = \dfrac{p^2}{2B} = \dfrac{(\rho g h)^2}{2B} = \dfrac{1}{2}\dfrac{\rho^2 g^2 h^2}{B}$

So, $E \propto h^2$ and $E \propto \dfrac{1}{B}$

4. $T_x = \left(\dfrac{m}{l}x\right)\left(\dfrac{F}{m}\right) = \dfrac{Fx}{l}$

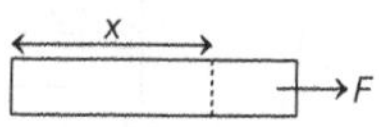

$$\sigma = \frac{T_x}{A} = \frac{Fx}{Al}$$

So, stress developed in plank is maximum at the end at which force is applied and decreases linearly to zero at the other end.

5. Force of compression is the same throughout the rod. Compressive stress will be maximum at the left end because cross-section area is minimum.

6. $Y = \dfrac{\text{Stress}}{\text{Strain}}$ = Slope of stress-strain curve

$Y_A > Y_B \because (\text{Slope})_A > (\text{Slope})_B$

Material A has higher breaking stress.

7. (A) Within elastic limit, $\frac{\text{Stress}}{\text{Strain}} = \text{Constant}$

(B) Beyond elastic limit, a small increase in stress produces large deformation i.e. large strain. So, $\frac{\text{Stress}}{\text{Strain}}$ decreases.

(C) Both the wires will have same stress. Since, Y is different, strain will be different.

8. (A) As liquid has no fixed shape, it can't bear any tangential stress. Hence, shear modulus of liquid is infinite.

(B) For perfectly rigid body, deformation is zero. So, bulk modulus will be infinite.

(C) $\frac{\Delta V}{V} = (1-2\sigma)\frac{\Delta L}{L}$. When a bar is stretched, its volume may increase, decrease or remain same depending on the poisson's ratio value.

9. (A) Loss in gravitational potential energy of M is Mgl as M falls down by l.

(B) Elastic potential energy stored $= \frac{1}{2} \times \text{stress} \times \text{strain} \times \text{volume}$

$$= \frac{1}{2}\left(\frac{Mg}{A}\right)\left(\frac{l}{L}\right)(AL) = \frac{Mgl}{2}$$

(D) Heat produced $= Mgl - \frac{Mgl}{2} = \frac{Mgl}{2}$

10. $F = kx = \left(\frac{AY}{L}\right)l$

$$W_F = \int F dl = \int_0^l \left(\frac{AY}{L}\right) l\, dl = \frac{AYl^2}{2L}$$

Since the wire is elongated slowly, elastic potential energy stored in the wire will be equal to work done by F and heat produced will be zero.

Comprehension Based Questions

Comprehension-1

1. $k = \frac{AY}{L} = \frac{4\times10^{-4}\times2\times10^{10}}{4} = 2\times10^6$ N/m

Angular frequency $= \omega = \sqrt{\frac{k}{m}} = \sqrt{\frac{2\times10^6}{200}} = 100$ rad/s

2. Let maximum extension in the rod be x.

Using energy conservation,

Loss in gravitational PE = Gain in strain energy

$$\Rightarrow \quad 10\times10\times(0.99+x) = \frac{1}{2}\times(2\times10^6)x^2$$

$$\Rightarrow \quad x = 0.01 \text{ m} = 1 \text{ cm}$$

3. Strain $= \frac{\Delta l}{l} = \frac{0.01}{4}$

Stress $= Y$ (Strain) $= 2\times10^{10}\times\left(\frac{0.01}{4}\right) = 5\times10^7$ N/m^2

4. For series combination, $\frac{1}{k_{eq}} = \frac{1}{k_1} + \frac{1}{k_2}$

$$\Rightarrow \quad \frac{1}{k_{eq}} = \frac{4}{2\times10^{-4}\times2\times10^{10}} + \frac{4}{4\times10^{-4}\times2\times10^{10}}$$

$$\Rightarrow \quad k_{eq} = \frac{2}{3}\times10^6 \text{ N/m}$$

$$\omega = \sqrt{\frac{k_{eq}}{m}} = \sqrt{\frac{2\times10^6}{3\times600}} = \frac{100}{3} \text{ rad/s}$$

5. Let the number of persons be n and tension in each rod be T.

Total weight $= 1000 + (50n)g = 500(2+n)$

$$4T = 500(2+n) \Rightarrow T = 125(2+n)$$

Stress in each rod $= \frac{T}{A} = \frac{125(2+n)}{4\times10^{-4}} = 9\times10^6 \Rightarrow n = 26.8$

So, the maximum number of person, it can carry safely will be 26.

6. New area of cross-section $= \frac{s}{\cos\theta}$

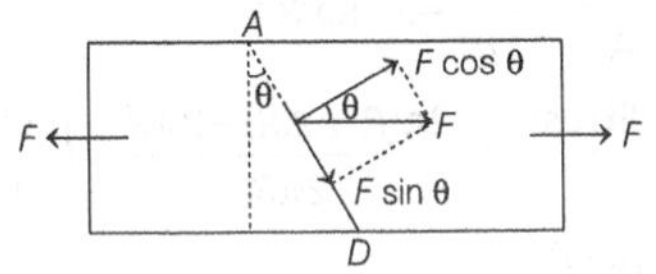

Normal stress $= \frac{F_\perp}{A} = \frac{F\cos\theta}{\left(\frac{s}{\cos\theta}\right)} = \frac{F\cos^2\theta}{s}$

7. Shear stress $= \frac{F_T}{A} = \frac{F\sin\theta}{\left(\frac{s}{\cos\theta}\right)} = \frac{F\sin2\theta}{2s}$

8. Shear stress will be maximum when $\sin2\theta = 1$

$$\Rightarrow \quad 2\theta = 90° \Rightarrow \theta = 45°$$

9. Using energy conservation for sphere,

Loss in gravitational PE = Gain in KE

$$mgl = \frac{1}{2}mv^2 \Rightarrow v = \sqrt{2gl}$$

In vertical position,

$$T - mg = \frac{mv^2}{l}$$

$$\Rightarrow \quad T - mg = \frac{m}{l}(\sqrt{2gl})^2$$

$$\Rightarrow \quad T = 3mg$$

Elongation $= \frac{FL}{AY} = \frac{3mgl}{\pi r^2 Y}$

10. Elastic energy stored $= \frac{1}{2}k(\Delta l)^2$

$$= \frac{1}{2}\left(\frac{\pi r^2 Y}{l}\right)\left(\frac{3mgl}{\pi r^2 Y}\right)^2 = \frac{9m^2g^2l}{2Y\pi r^2}$$

11. $\Delta l = 2\sqrt{l^2+y^2} - 2l = 2l\left(\left(1+\frac{y^2}{l^2}\right)^{\frac{1}{2}} - 1\right)$

$$= 2l\left(1+\frac{y^2}{2l^2}-1\right)=\frac{y^2}{l}$$

$$\text{Strain} = \frac{\Delta l}{l} = \frac{\frac{y^2}{l}}{2l} = \frac{y^2}{2l^2}$$

12. Elastic energy stored $= \frac{1}{2}Y\,(\text{Strain})^2 \times (\text{Volume})$

$$= \frac{1}{2}Y\left(\frac{y^2}{2l^2}\right)^2 (A(2l)) = \frac{AYy^4}{4l^3}$$

13. $2T\sin\left(\frac{d\theta}{2}\right) = dm\omega^2 R$

$\Rightarrow \quad Td\theta = (\rho a R d\theta)\omega^2 R$

$\Rightarrow \quad T = \rho a\omega^2 R^2$

$$\text{Stress} = \frac{T}{A} = \frac{\rho a\omega^2 R^2}{a} = \rho\omega^2 R^2$$

14. $\text{Strain} = \frac{\text{Stress}}{Y} \Rightarrow \frac{2\pi(R+\Delta R)-2\pi R}{2\pi R} = \frac{\rho\omega^2R^2}{Y}$

$$\Rightarrow \Delta R = \frac{\rho\omega^2 R^2}{Y}$$

15. Lets draw the free body diagram of the steel rod and the L-shaped structure as shown in the figure.

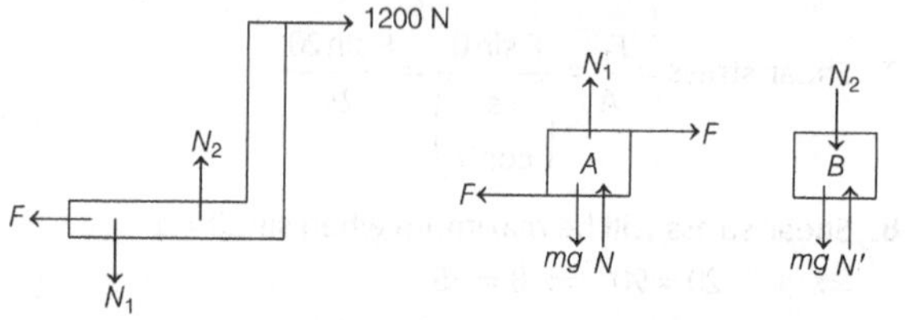

The direction of N_1 and N_2 can be found by using the equilibrium condition.

For L-shaped structure,

Vertical equilibrium, $N_1 = N_2$

Horizontal equilibrium, $F = 1200$ N

For rotational equilibrium, torque about $E = 0$

$\Rightarrow \quad N_2 \times 4 - 1200 \times 3 = 0$

$\Rightarrow \quad N_2 = 900$ N

Shearing stress in $A = \frac{F}{A} = \frac{1200}{5} = 240\ \text{N/cm}^2$

Shearing stress in $B = 0$

16. Longitudinal stress in $A = \frac{N_1}{A} = \frac{900}{5} = 180\ \text{N/cm}^2$, Tensile

17. Longitudinal stress in $B = \frac{N_2}{A} = \frac{900}{5}$

$= 180\ \text{N/cm}^2$, Compressive

Match The Columns Questions

1. (A) Young's modulus depends only on the material of the wire.

(B) Breaking stress is property of the material of the wire.

(C) $\text{Strain} = \frac{F}{AY} = \frac{F}{\pi r^2 Y}$

So, strain depends on applied force F, radius of wire r and material of wire Y.

(D) $U = \frac{1}{2}F\Delta l = \frac{1}{2}F\left(\frac{FL}{AY}\right) = \frac{F^2 l}{2\pi r^2 Y}$

So, potential energy stored in the wire depends on applied force F, length l, radius r and material of the wire Y.

2. (A) Longitudinal stress causes the volume to change and doesn't affect the shape.

(B) Shear stress causes the shape of an object to change but the volume remains same.

(C) Volume changes generally doesn't cause the shape to change.

(D) Same as A.

3. Elongation in a rod $= \Delta l = \frac{FL}{AY}$

Elongation in rod $AB = \Delta l_{AB} = \frac{100 \times (10 \times 10^{-2})}{10^{-4} \times (2.5 \times 10^{10})} = 4\ \mu\text{m}$

Elongation in rod $BC = \Delta l_{BC} = \frac{100 \times (20 \times 10^{-2})}{10^{-4} \times (4 \times 10^{10})} = 5\ \mu\text{m}$

Elongation in rod $CD = \Delta l_{CD} = \frac{100 \times (15 \times 10^{-2})}{10^{-4} \times (1 \times 10^{10})} = 15\ \mu\text{m}$

Displacement of point $B = \Delta l_{AB} = 4\ \mu\text{m}$

Displacement of point $C = \Delta l_{AB} + \Delta l_{BC} = 9\ \mu\text{m}$

Displacement of point $D = \Delta l_{AB} + \Delta l_{BC} + \Delta l_{CD} = 24\ \mu\text{m}$

Displacement of point $E = \Delta l_{AB} + \Delta l_{BC} + \Delta l_{CD} + \Delta l_{DE}$

$= 24\ \mu\text{m} \qquad \because \{\Delta l_{DE} = 0\}$

4. (A) The rod will be uniformly stressed,

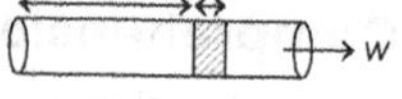

$\text{Stress} = \frac{w}{A}$

$$\text{Elastic potential energy} = \frac{(\text{Stress})^2}{2Y} \times \text{Volume}$$

$$= \frac{\left(\frac{w}{A}\right)^2}{2Y}(AL) = \frac{w^2 L}{2AY}$$

(B) $T_x = \frac{wx}{L}$

$$\text{Stress} = \frac{T_x}{A} = \frac{wx}{AL}$$

$$\int dU = \int_0^L \frac{1}{2Y}\left(\frac{wx}{AL}\right)^2 A\,dx \Rightarrow U = \frac{w^2 L}{6AY}$$

(C)

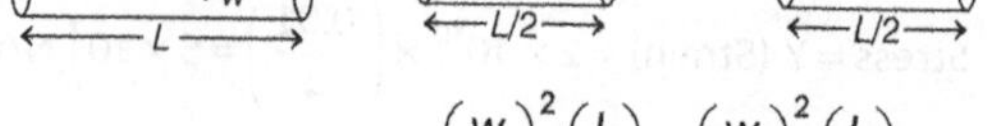

$$U = U_1 + U_2 = \frac{\left(\frac{w}{2}\right)^2\left(\frac{L}{2}\right)}{6AY} + \frac{\left(\frac{w}{2}\right)^2\left(\frac{L}{2}\right)}{6AY} = \frac{w^2 L}{24AY}$$

Numerical Value Questions

1. $\Delta l = \int \frac{Fdx}{AY} = \frac{20\times10^3}{2\times10^7}\int_0^{10}\frac{dx}{1+\frac{x^2}{100}}$

$= 10^{-3}\times\frac{1}{\left(\frac{1}{10}\right)}\left[\tan^{-1}\left(\frac{x}{10}\right)\right]_0^{10}$

$= \frac{10\pi}{4}\times10^{-3}\text{ cm} = 8\times10^{-3}\text{ cm}$

2. Let ΔL be the extension of wire when the sphere is at mean position. Then, $L + \Delta L + 2r = 5.22$

$\Rightarrow \quad 5 + \Delta L + 0.2 = 5.22$

$\Rightarrow \quad \Delta L = 0.02$ m

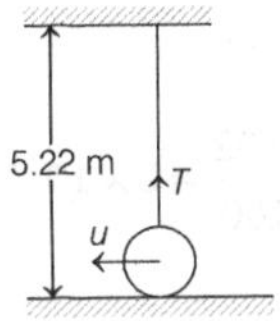

Let T be tension in the wire at mean position.

$T = \left(\frac{AY}{L}\right)\Delta L = \left(\frac{\pi(0.5\times10^{-3})^2(2\times10^{11})}{5}\right)(0.02)$

$= 200\pi$ N

Also, at mean position $T - mg = \frac{mv^2}{R}$

$\Rightarrow \quad 200\pi - (8\pi)(10) = \frac{(8\pi)v^2}{5.12} \quad \Rightarrow \quad v = 8.76$ m/s

3. Let tension in steel and bronze wires be T_1 and T_2, respectively.

For equilibrium of rod, net torque = 0

$\Rightarrow \quad T_1x - T_2(55 - x) = 0$

$\Rightarrow \quad \frac{T_1}{T_2} = \frac{55 - x}{x}$

For rod to remain horizontal, elongation in both the wires will have to be equal.

$\Delta l_1 = \Delta l_2 \quad \Rightarrow \quad \frac{T_1 l}{A_1Y_1} = \frac{T_2 l}{A_2Y_2}$

$= \frac{T_1(150)}{2\times10^{-6}\times2\times10^{11}} = \frac{T_2(150)}{1\times10^{-6}\times1.5\times10^{11}}$

$\Rightarrow \quad \frac{T_1}{T_2} = \frac{8}{3}$

So, $\frac{55 - x}{x} = \frac{8}{3} \Rightarrow x = 15$ cm

4. $T\cos 85° = mg \Rightarrow T = \frac{mg}{\cos 85°} = \frac{0.5\times9.8}{0.0872}$

$\Delta l = \frac{Fl}{AY} = \left(\frac{0.5\times9.8}{0.0872}\right)\frac{(0.8)}{3.14(0.35\times10^{-3})^2(7\times10^{10})}$

$= 1.668\times10^{-3}$ m $= 1.67$ mm

5. Compressive stress due to decrease in temperature,

$\sigma_1 = Y\alpha\Delta T = 5\times10^{11}\times2\times10^{-5}\times10 = 10^8$ N/m^2

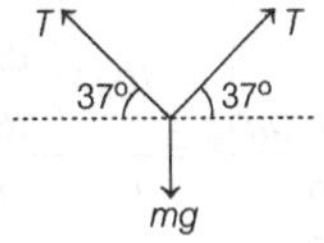

$\Sigma F_y = 0 \Rightarrow 2T\sin 37° = mg \Rightarrow T = \frac{25m}{3}$

σ_2 = Tensile stress due to hanging mass $= \frac{T}{A} = \frac{25m}{3\times10^{-6}}$

For junction to remain at initial position,

$\sigma_1 = \sigma_2 \Rightarrow 10^8 = \frac{25m}{3\times10^{-6}} \Rightarrow m = 12$ kg

6. $2T\sin\left(\frac{d\theta}{2}\right) = dm\omega^2R$

$\Rightarrow \quad Td\theta = (\rho ARd\theta)\omega^2R$

$\Rightarrow \quad T = \rho A\omega^2R^2$

Stress in the ring $= \frac{T}{A} = \rho\omega^2R^2$

For ring to break, $\sigma = \rho\omega^2R^2$

$\Rightarrow \quad \omega = \frac{1}{R}\sqrt{\frac{\sigma}{\rho}} = 2$ rad/s

7. Elongation in a rod $= \frac{Fl}{AY}$

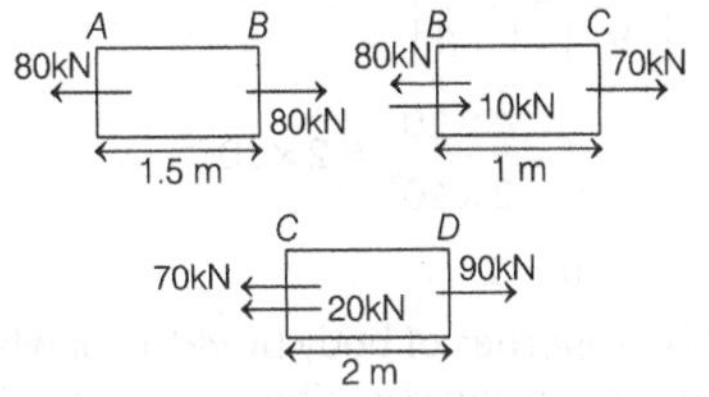

Elongation in $BC = \Delta l_{BC} = \frac{70\times10^3\times1}{0.1\times2\times10^{11}} = 3.5\times10^{-6}$ m

Elongation in $CD = \Delta l_{CD} = \frac{90\times10^3\times2}{0.1\times2\times10^{11}} = 9\times10^{-6}$ m

Elongation in $BD = \Delta l_{BC} + \Delta l_{CD} = 3.5 + 9 = 12.5\,\mu$m

8. For isothermal process, $p_1V_1 = p_2V_2$

$\Rightarrow p_0V_0 = p\left(\frac{5}{4}V_0\right) \Rightarrow p = 0.8p_0$

Net outward pressure on the surface of balloon

$= 0.8p_0 - 0.5p_0 = 0.3p_0$

Net pressure force $= (0.3p_0)\pi R^2$ and also $\frac{5}{4}V_0 = \frac{4}{3}\pi R^3$

But this force must just balance the elastic force $\sigma\Delta A$ where, $\Delta A = 2\pi Rt$ (t is the thickness of balloon material)

$\rho_0 = \frac{m}{(4\pi R^2)t} \Rightarrow t = \frac{m}{(4\pi R^2)\rho_0}$

So, $\sigma(2\pi R)\left(\frac{m}{(4\pi R^2)\rho_0}\right)=(0.3p_0)\pi R^2$

$$\Rightarrow \quad \sigma=\frac{(0.6)\pi R^3 p_0\rho_0}{m}=\frac{(0.6)\left(\frac{15}{16}V_0\right)p_0\rho_0}{m}$$

$$=\frac{9p_0V_0\rho_0}{16m}$$

So, $\alpha+\beta=9+16=25$

9. $\frac{\Delta V}{V}=\frac{\Delta p}{B}=\frac{\rho g h}{B}=\frac{10^3\times 10\times 3\times 10^3}{2.2\times 10^9}=1.36\times 10^{-2}$

$$\frac{\Delta V}{V}\times 100=1.36\times 10^{-2}\times 100=1.36\%$$

Previous Years Questions

JEE Main

1. Bulk modulus, $B=-\frac{P}{\frac{\Delta V}{V}}$

$P=$ hydraulic stress

$\frac{\Delta V}{V}=$ volume strain

$$P=\rho g h=1000\times 10\times 4000$$
$$=4\times 10^7\ \text{N/m}$$

$$\left|\frac{\Delta V}{V}\right|=\left|-\frac{P}{B}\right|$$
$$=\frac{4\times 10^7}{2\times 10^9}=2\times 10^{-2}$$

$\alpha=2$

2. Elasticity is properties of body by virtue of which it tends to regain their shape and size after removing external force and restoring force depends upon the bonded interatomic and intermolecular force of solid.

Both Assertion and Reason are true and Reason is correct explanation of Assertion.

3. We know that,

$$Y=\frac{F/A}{\Delta l/l}$$
$$=\frac{Fl}{A\Delta l}$$
$$Y=\frac{Fl}{\pi r^2\Delta l}$$
$$\Rightarrow \quad \Delta l=\frac{Fl}{\pi r^2 Y}$$
$$\Rightarrow \quad \Delta l\propto\frac{F}{r^2}$$
$$\therefore \quad \frac{\Delta l_2}{\Delta l_1}=\frac{F_2}{F_1}\times\left(\frac{r_1}{r_2}\right)^2$$
$$=\frac{F_1/2}{F_1}\times\left(\frac{r_1}{r_1/2}\right)^2$$
$$=\frac{1}{2}\times 4$$
$$=2$$
$$\therefore \quad \Delta l_2=2\Delta l_1$$

4. Young's modulus describe the relation between stress and strain.

$$Y=\frac{\text{Stress}}{\text{Strain}}$$

It is independent of geometrical factor.

Hence, it will remain same as Y.

5. Decrease in volume of rubber ball

$$\frac{\Delta V}{V}\times 100=0.02$$
$$\Rightarrow \quad \frac{\Delta V}{V}=\frac{0.02}{100}=2\times 10^{-4}$$

Bulk modulus,

$$B=\frac{F/A}{\Delta V/V}=\frac{p}{\Delta V/V}$$

$\Rightarrow$ Pressure, $p=B\times\frac{\Delta V}{V}$

or $\quad \rho g h=B\times\frac{\Delta V}{V}$

$\Rightarrow$ Height of water column,

$$h=\frac{B\times\Delta V/V}{\rho\times g}$$
$$\Rightarrow \quad h=\frac{9\times 10^8\times 2\times 10^{-4}}{1000\times 10}$$
$$=18\ \text{m}$$

6. We know that,

$$Y=\frac{fL}{\pi r^2 l}\Rightarrow l=\frac{fL}{\pi r^2 Y}$$
$$\Rightarrow \quad l\propto\frac{fL}{r^2}$$
$$\Rightarrow \quad \frac{l_2}{l_1}=\frac{f_2}{f_1}\times\frac{L_2}{L_1}\times\left(\frac{r_1}{r_2}\right)^2$$

Here, $f_2=2f, f_1=f$

$L_2=2L, L_1=L$

$r_2=2r, r_1=r$

$$\therefore \quad \frac{l_2}{l_1}=\frac{2f}{f}\times\frac{2L}{L}\times\left(\frac{r}{2r}\right)^2=1$$
$$\Rightarrow \quad l_2=l_1=l$$

7. Young's modulus of elasticity is given by

$$Y=\frac{FL}{A\Delta L}$$

According to question,

$$\frac{Y_A}{Y_B}=\frac{1}{4}=\frac{\frac{FL}{A\Delta L_A}}{\frac{FL}{3A\Delta L_B}} \Rightarrow \frac{\Delta L_A}{\Delta L_B}=\frac{3A}{A}\times 4=12$$

$$\therefore \quad \frac{\Delta L_A}{\Delta L_B}=\frac{12}{1}$$

8. Strain Energy per unit volume in a rod is given by

$$u=\frac{U}{V}=\frac{1}{2}\times \text{Stress}\times\text{Strain}=\frac{1}{2}\varepsilon^2 Y$$

$\varepsilon=$ strain

Given $\varepsilon = 0.04\% = \frac{0.04}{100} = 4\times 10^{-4}$

and $Y=7\times 10^{10}\ \frac{\text{N}}{\text{m}^2}$

Hence, strain energy per unit volume is,

$$u_E=\frac{1}{2}\varepsilon^2 Y=\frac{1}{2}\times(4\times 10^{-4})^2\times 7\times 10^{10}$$

$$=\frac{1}{2}\times 16\times 10^{-8}\times 7\times 10^{10}$$

$$=5600\ \text{J/m}^3$$

9. Given, $A=6.25\times 10^{-4}\text{m}^2$

$Y=10^{10}\text{Nm}^{-2}$

$l=100$ m, $F=250$ N

$$\because \quad \Delta l=\frac{Fl}{AY}=\frac{250\times 100}{6.25\times 10^{-4}\times 10^{10}}=4\times 10^{-3}\ \text{m}$$

10. Steel is elastic and can withstand high loads. This property enables steel to use as structure in reinforced cement and concrete works.

Hence, Both (A) and (R) are correct and (R) is correct explanation of (A).

11. Given that $L_A=5$ m, $A_A=2.5\times 10^{-5}\ \text{m}^2$

$L_B=6$ m, $A_B=3\times 10^{-5}\ \text{m}^2$

From Hooke's law,

$$Y=\frac{FL}{A\Delta L}$$

If F and ΔL are same, then

$$Y\propto\frac{L}{A}$$

For two wires A and B,

$$\frac{Y_A}{Y_B}=\frac{L_A}{L_B}\cdot\frac{A_B}{A_A}=\frac{5}{6}\cdot\frac{3\times 10^{-5}}{2.5\times 10^{-5}}$$

$$\Rightarrow \quad \frac{Y_A}{Y_B}=\frac{1}{1}$$

12. We have following emperical relations,

$$Y=2\eta(1+\sigma) \quad \text{... (i)}$$

$$Y=3K(1-2\sigma) \quad \text{... (ii)}$$

Where, symbols have their usual meaning.

From Eq. (i) and Eq. (ii), we get

$$\Rightarrow \quad 2\eta(1+\sigma)=3K(1-2\sigma)$$

$$\Rightarrow \quad 2\eta+2\eta\sigma=3K-6K\sigma$$

$$\Rightarrow \quad \sigma(2\eta+6K)=3K-2\eta$$

$$\Rightarrow \quad \sigma=\frac{3K-2\eta}{2\eta+6K}$$

13. We know, $Y=\frac{\text{Stress}}{\text{Strain}}$

$$\therefore \quad \text{Strain}=\frac{\text{Stress}}{Y},\ \text{Stress}=\frac{F}{A}$$

$$\text{Strain}=\frac{F}{A\cdot Y}$$

Putting the given value, we get

$$\text{Longitudinal strain}=\frac{62.8\times 1000}{\pi r^2\times 2\times 10^{11}}$$

$$=\frac{62.8\times 1000}{3.14\times 400\times 10^{-6}\times 2\times 10^{11}}$$

$$=\frac{200}{8}\times 10^{-5}=25\times 10^{-5}=x\times 10^{-5} \quad \text{(Given)}$$

So, $x=25$

14. We know, Stress $=\frac{\text{Force}}{\text{Area}}=\frac{mg}{A}$

$$\therefore \quad m=\frac{S\times A}{g}=\frac{7\times 10^5\times\pi R^2}{g}$$

$$=\frac{7\times 10^5\times\frac{22}{7}\times(7\times 10^{-3})^2}{9.8}=11\ \text{kg}$$

15. Steel wire is elongated due to a load of mass

$m=2+1.14$

$=3.14\ \text{kg}=\pi\ \text{kg}$

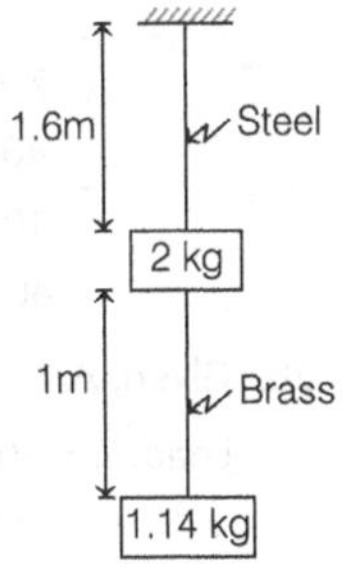

Now using,

$$Y=\frac{Fl}{A\Delta l}$$

$$\therefore \quad \Delta l=\frac{F\cdot l}{Y\cdot A}$$

$$=\frac{\pi(1.6)g}{2\times 10^{11}\times\pi\times(0.2\times 10^{-2})^2}$$

$$=\frac{\pi\times 1.6g}{2\times 10^{11}\times\pi\times(0.2)^2\times 10^{-4}}$$

$$=\frac{\pi\times 16\times 10^{-1}g}{2\times 10^{11}\times\pi\times 2^2\times 10^{-2}\times 10^{-4}}$$

$$=20\times 10^{-6}\ \text{m}$$

16. We know that,

$$F=kx$$

$$\therefore \quad F=\frac{YA}{l_0}\cdot x$$

When $F=100$ N

$$100=K(l_1-l_0) \quad \text{...(i)}$$

When $F=120$ N

$$120=K(l_2-l_0) \quad \text{...(ii)}$$

So, $\frac{120}{100} = \frac{k(l_2 - l_0)}{k(l_1 - l_0)}$

Given,

$$10l_2 = 11l_1, l_2 = 1 \cdot 1l_1$$

$$\frac{120}{100} = \frac{(1 \cdot 1l_1 - l_0)}{l_1 - l_0}$$

$$1 \cdot 2l_1 - 1 \cdot 2l_0 = 1 \cdot 1l_1 - l_0$$

$$0 \cdot 1l_1 = 0 \cdot 2l_0$$

$$l_0 = \frac{l_1}{2}$$

So, $x = 2$

17. Length of steel wire,

$$L = 20 \text{ m}$$

Change in length,

$$\Delta L = 2 \text{ cm} = 2 \times 10^{-2} \text{ m}$$

$$Y = 2 \times 10^{11} \text{ Nm}^{-2}$$

We know that,
elastic potential energy.

$$U = \frac{1}{2} \times \text{stress} \times \text{strain} \times \text{volume}$$

$$v = \frac{1}{2} \times Y \times (\text{strain})^2 \times (A \times L)$$

$$\Rightarrow \quad A = \frac{2U}{Y \times (\text{strain})^2 \times L}$$

$$= \frac{2U}{Y \times \left(\frac{\Delta L}{L}\right)^2 \times L} = \frac{2UL}{Y \times (\Delta L)^2}$$

$$= \frac{2 \times 80 \times 20}{2 \times 10^{11} \times (2 \times 10^{-2})^2}$$

$$= \frac{400}{10^7} = 4 \times 10^{-5} \text{ m}^2$$

$$= 40 \times 10^{-6} \text{ m}^2 = 40 \text{ mm}^2$$

18. Given, $A_1 = 2.5 \times 10^{-4} \text{m}^2$

Load, $F_1 = 10$ metric tonne $\times g$

$$= 10 \times 1000 \text{ kg} \times g = 10^4 g\text{N}$$

For second condition,

$$F_2 = 25 \text{ metric tonne} \times g$$

$$= 25 \times 1000 \times g = 2.5 \times 10^4 g \text{ N}$$

For the condition of elastic limit,

$$\frac{F_1}{A_1} = \frac{F_2}{A_2}$$

$$\Rightarrow \quad A_2 = \frac{F_2}{F_1} A_1$$

$$= \frac{2.5 \times 10^4 g}{10^4 g} \times 2.5 \times 10^{-4}$$

$$= 6.25 \times 10^{-4} \text{m}^2$$

19. Given, weight of rod, $w = 10 \text{kg ms}^{-2}$

Area of cross- section, $A = 100 \text{ cm}^2 = 100 \times 10^{-4} \text{m}^2$

Length of rod, $l = 20 \text{ cm} = 20 \times 10^{-2} \text{m}$

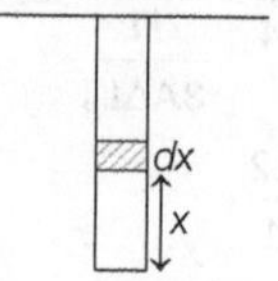

Young's modulus $(Y) = 2 \times 10^{11} \text{ Nm}^{-2}$

Let, elongation $= \Delta l$

Since, Young's modulus, $Y = \frac{dmg\ x}{A \Delta l}$

Mass of element dx at distance x,

$$dm = \frac{m}{l} dx$$

$$\Rightarrow \quad \Delta l = \frac{\left(\frac{mg}{l}\right) x\ dx}{AY} \Rightarrow \Delta l = \frac{mg}{AlY} \left.\frac{x^2}{2}\right|_0^l$$

$$\Rightarrow \quad \Delta l = \frac{mg}{AlY} \frac{l^2}{2} = \frac{mgl}{2AY} = \frac{wl}{2AY}$$

$$= \frac{10 \times 20 \times 10^{-2}}{2 \times 100 \times 10^{-4} \times 2 \times 10^{11}}$$

$$= 5 \times 10^{-10} \text{ m}$$

20. Given, decrease in volume

$$(\Delta V / V) = -\frac{0.5}{100}$$

Bulk modulus of rubber,

$$B = 9.8 \times 10^8 \text{ Nm}^{-2}$$

Density of sea water, $\rho = 10^3 \text{kgm}^{-3}$

Acceleration due to gravity, $g = 9.8 \text{ ms}^{-2}$

Let h be the depth at which ball is dipped.

Since, $\quad B = \frac{\Delta p}{-\Delta V / V}$

where, Δp is change in pressure $= \rho g h$

$$\therefore \quad \rho g h = -B \frac{\Delta V}{V}$$

$$\Rightarrow \quad h = -\frac{1}{\rho g} B \frac{\Delta V}{V}$$

$$\Rightarrow \quad h = -\frac{1}{10^3 \times 9.8} \times 9.8 \times 10^8 \times \left(-\frac{0.5}{100}\right)$$

$$= 0.5 \times 10^{8-3-2} = 0.5 \times 10^3 = 500 \text{ m}$$

21. Let inner and outer radii of hollow cylindrical column are r and R, respectively.

Given that, $r = 50$ cm, $R = 100$ cm

Mass supported on four columns,

$$M = 50 \times 10^3 \text{ kg}$$

Mass supported on each column, $m = \frac{M}{4}$

$$\Rightarrow \quad m = \frac{50 \times 10^3}{4} = 12.5 \times 10^3 \text{ kg}$$

Now, weight, $w = mg = 12.5 \times 9.8 \times 10^3 \text{ N} = 1.225 \times 10^5 \text{ N}$

Area of cross-section of each column

$$A = \pi(R^2 - r^2)$$

$$= 3.14\{(100)^2 - (50)^2\} \times 10^{-4} \text{ m}^2 = 2.35 \text{ m}^2$$

Young's modulus, $Y = 2.0 \times 10^{11}$ Pa

By using Hooke's law,

$$\text{Stress} = Y \times \text{Strain}$$

$$\therefore \text{Compressive strain} = \frac{\text{Stress}}{Y} = \frac{w}{AY}$$

Substituting the values, we get

$$\text{Compressive strain} = \frac{1.225 \times 10^5}{2.35 \times 2.0 \times 10^{11}}$$

$$= 2.60 \times 10^{-7}$$

22. We know that,

$$Y = 3K(1 - 2\sigma)$$

$$\Rightarrow \quad \sigma = \frac{1}{2}\left(1 - \frac{Y}{3K}\right) \quad \text{... (i)}$$

Also, $\quad Y = 2\eta(1 + \sigma)$

$$\Rightarrow \quad \sigma = \frac{Y}{2\eta} - 1 \quad \text{... (ii)}$$

On comparing Eqs. (i) and (ii), we get

$$\left(1 - \frac{Y}{3K}\right)\frac{1}{2} = \frac{Y}{2\eta} - 1$$

On solving, we get

$$K = \frac{\eta Y}{9\eta - 3Y} \text{ N/m}^2$$

23. Given, The volumetric strain is $\frac{\Delta V}{V} = 1.36\%$

The depth beneath the water surface, $h = 2$ km

The pressure inside the water surface up to 2 km, $p = \rho g h$

Substituting the values in the above equation, we get

$$p = 1000 \times 9.81 \times 2000$$

$$p = 19.62 \times 10^6 \text{Pa}$$

The bulk modulus of the object, $\beta = \dfrac{p}{\frac{\Delta V}{V}}$

Substituting the values in the above equation, we get

$$\beta = \frac{19.62 \times 10^6}{\frac{1.36}{100}} = 1.44 \times 10^9 \text{N/m}^2$$

Hence, the ratio of the hydraulic stress to the corresponding hydraulic strain will be $1.44 \times 10^9 \text{N/m}^2$.

24. Given, area of cross-section, $A = 0.01 \text{ m}^2$

Change of temperature, $\Delta T = 10°\text{C}$

Coefficient of linear expansion, $\alpha = 10^{-5}$ /°C

Young's modulus, $Y = 10^{11} \text{Nm}^{-2}$

Energy stored per unit length

$$U = \text{Energy stored per unit volume} \times \text{Area}$$

$$= \frac{1}{2} Y(\text{strain})^2 \times A$$

$$U = \frac{1}{2} Y(\alpha \Delta T)^2 \times A \quad \left[\therefore \frac{\Delta l}{l} = \alpha \Delta T\right]$$

$$= \frac{1}{2} \times 10^{11}(10^{-5} \times 10)^2 \times 0.01$$

$$= \frac{1}{2} \times 10^{11} \times 10^{-8} \times 0.01$$

$$= 5 \text{ J/m}$$

25. Thermal stress is defined as the stress, experienced by any rod on heating between two fixed rigid supports. On heating, the size of the rod increases but, if the two ends are free, rod will not experience any stress. i.e, there is no thermal stress will be produced in it.

Hence, option (a) is the correct.

JEE Advanced

1. $\frac{dV}{V} = -\frac{dp}{B}$ (where, B = bulk modulus)

$$V = l^3$$

$$\frac{\Delta V}{V} = 3\frac{\Delta l}{l}$$

$$3\frac{\Delta l}{l} = \left|-\frac{\Delta p}{B}\right| = \frac{\rho g h}{B}$$

$$\therefore \quad \Delta T = \frac{\rho g h l}{3B}$$

Substituting the given values, we get $\Delta l = 0.24$ mm

2. $\Delta l = \frac{FL}{AY} = \frac{FL}{(\pi r^2)Y}$

$$\Rightarrow \quad \Delta l \propto \frac{L}{r^2}$$

$$\therefore \quad \frac{\Delta l_1}{\Delta l_2} = \frac{L/R^2}{2L/(2R)^2} = 2$$

CHAPTER~07

FLUIDSTATICS

LEVEL 01 Starter Level

7.1 Pressure Variation in a Fluid

1 Find the absolute pressure at points *A*, *B* and *C* as shown in the figure (10^5 Pa = 1atm)

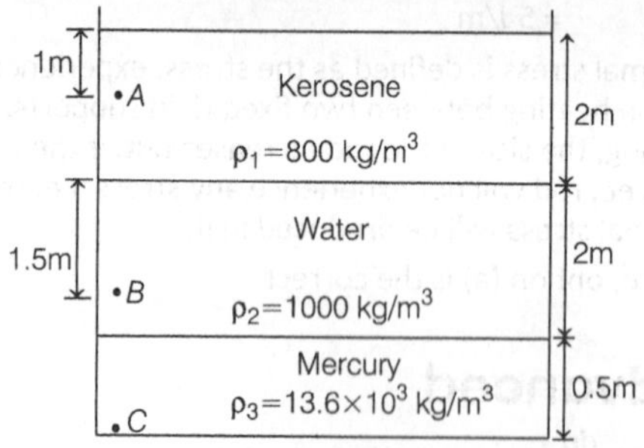

2 If pressure at half the depth of a lake is equal to (2/3)rd of pressure at the bottom of the lake, then what is the depth of the lake?

3 When a large bubble rises from the bottom of a lake to the surface, its radius doubles. If atmospheric pressure is equal to that of column of water height *H*, then what is the depth of lake?

4 For the system shown in figure, the cylinder on the left at *L*, has a mass of 800 kg and a cross-sectional area of 400 cm^2. The piston on the right at *S*, has cross-sectional area 25 cm^2 and negligible weight. If the apparatus is filled with oil of density 0.9 g/cm^3, find the force *F* required to hold the system in equilibrium as shown in figure.

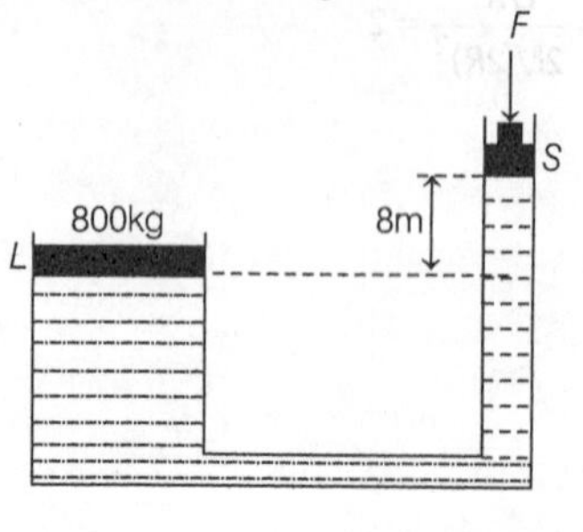

5 A vertical U-tube of uniform inner cross-section contains mercury in both sides of its arms. A glycerin (density = 1.3 g/cm^3) column of length 10 cm is introduced into one of its arms. Oil of density 0.8 gm/cm^3 is poured into the other arm until the upper surfaces of the oil and glycerin are in the same horizontal level. Find the length of the oil column. Density of mercury = 13.6 g/cm^3.

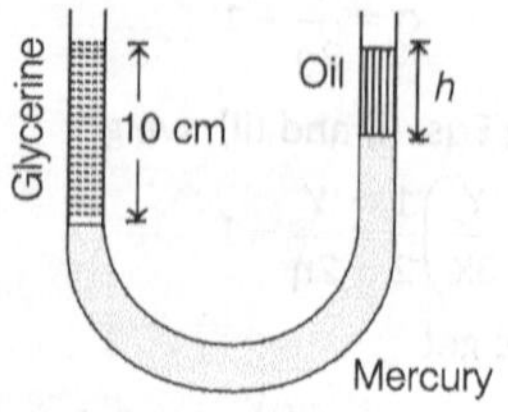

6 Find out pressure at points *A* and *B*. Also, find angle θ.

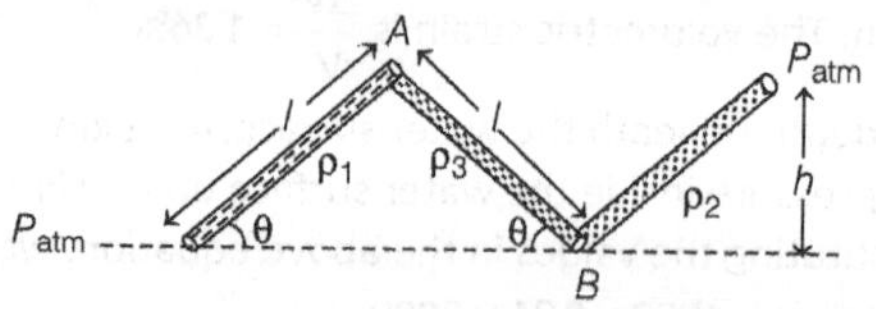

7.2 Fluid In Accelerated Vessels

1 A liquid stands at the same level in the U-tube when at rest. If area of cross-section of both the limbs are equal, what is the difference in height *h* of the liquid in the two limbs of U-tube, when the system is given an acceleration a in horizontal direction as shown?

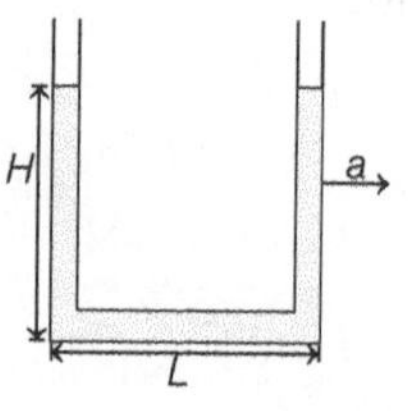

2 A rectangular box is completely filled with a liquid of density ρ, as shown in figure. The box is accelerated horizontally with a constant acceleration a. Determine the gauge pressures at the four points A, B, C and D,

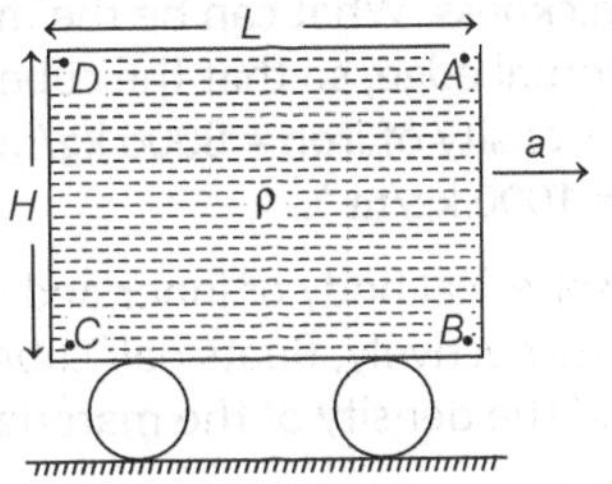

3 An open rectangular tank with dimensions 5m × 4m × 3m contains water upto a height of 2m. It is accelerated horizontally along the longer side.

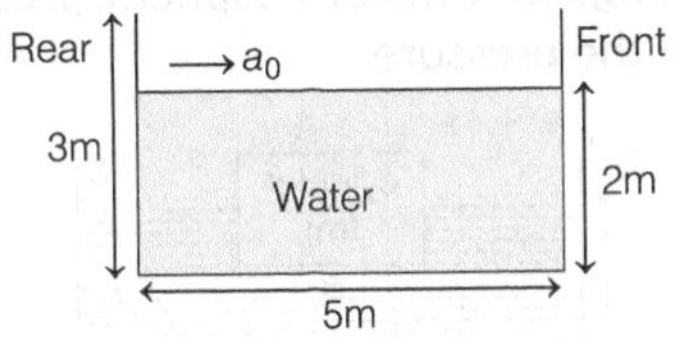

(a) Determine the maximum acceleration that can be given without spilling the water.

(b) If this acceleration is increased by 20%, calculate the percentage of water spilt over.

(c) If initially, the tank is closed at the top and is accelerated horizontally by 9 m/s^2, find the gauge pressure at the bottom of the front and rear walls of the tank. (g = 10 m/s^2)

4 In the given figure, the container slides down with acceleration a on an incline of angle θ. Liquid is stationary with respect to container. Find the

(i) angle made by surface of liquid with horizontal plane.

(ii) angle if $a = g\sin\theta$.

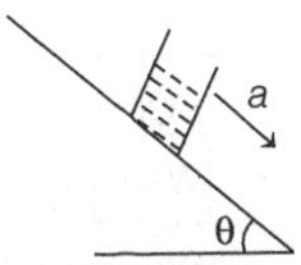

5 A U-shaped tube contains a liquid of density ρ and it is rotated about the line as shown in the figure. Find the difference in the levels of liquid column.

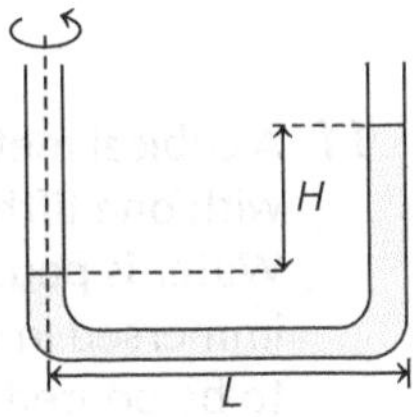

6 A cylinder of radius $R = 1$m and height $H = 3$m, two thirds filled with water, is rotated about its vertical axis, as shown in figure. Determine the speed of rotation when,

(a) the water starts spilling over the rim

(b) the centre of the base is just exposed

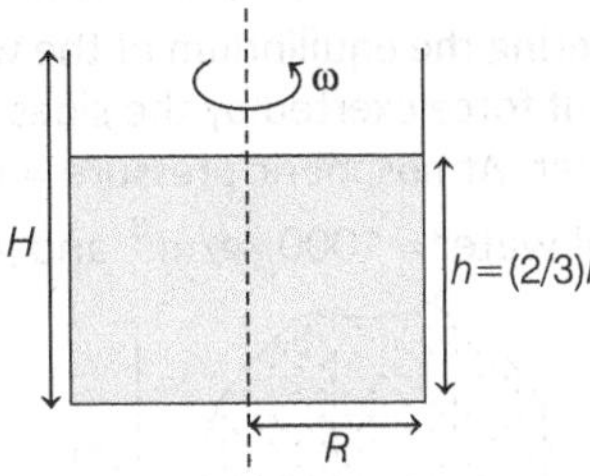

7.3 HYDROSTATIC FORCE

1 Water stands at a depth h behind the vertical face of a dam. It exerts a resultant horizontal force on the dam tending to slide it along its foundation and a torque tending to overturn the dam about the point O. Find

(a) horizontal force (b) torque about O,

l = cross-sectional length. Neglect atmospheric pressure.

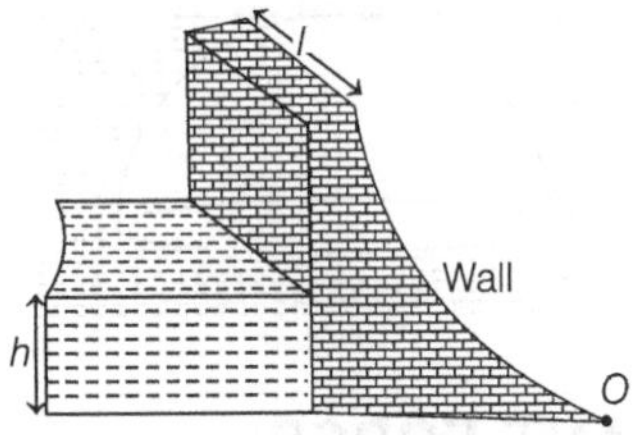

2 Water and liquid is filled up behind a square wall of side l = 10 m. Find out forces on part AB and BC of wall, (Density of water = 1000 kg/m^3, Density of liquid = 2000 kg/m^3, Atmospheric pressure = 10^5Pa)

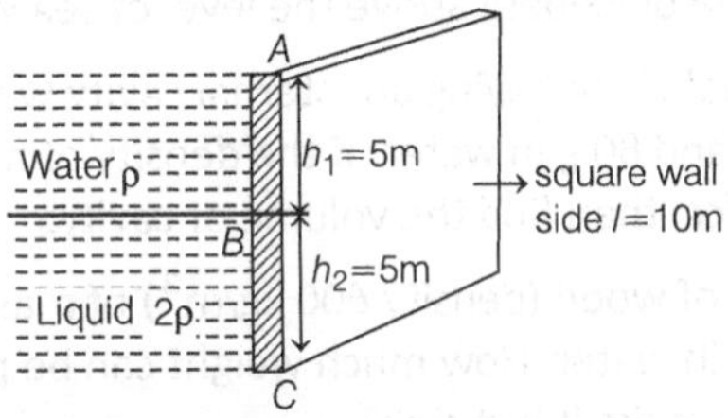

3 Find the hydrostatic force acting on the circular patch of radius R on the vertical wall of dam as shown in figure. Density of water is ρ and atmospheric pressure $= p_0$

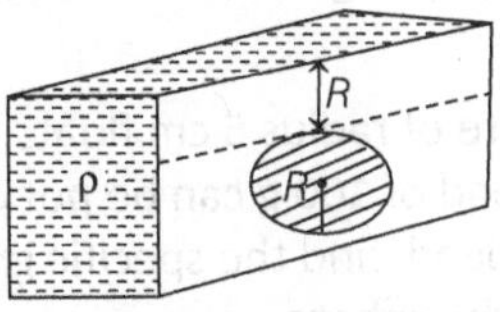

4 A glass full of water has a bottom of area 20 cm^2, top of area 20 cm^2, height 20 cm and volume half a litre.

(a) Find the force exerted by the water on the bottom.

(b) Considering the equilibrium of the water, find the resultant force exerted by the sides of the glass on the water. Atmospheric pressure $= 1.0 \times 10^5 \text{ N/m}^2$

Density of water = 1000 kg/m^3 and g = 10 m/s^2.

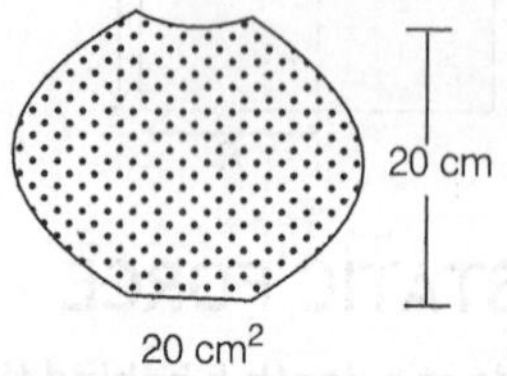

5 A solid hemisphere of radius R is made to just sink in a liquid of density ρ. Find

(a) the vertical thrust on the curved surface

(b) the vertical thrust on the flat surface

(c) the side thrust on the hemisphere

(d) the total hydrostatic force acting on the hemisphere

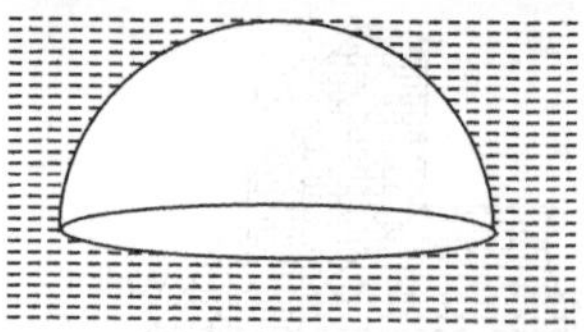

7.4 BUOYANT FORCE

1 An iceberg is floating partially immersed in sea water. If the density of sea water is 1.03 gm/cc and that of ice is 0.92 gm/cc, find the fraction of the total volume of iceberg above the level of sea water.

2 A metal block having an internal cavity weighs 110 g in air and 80 g in water. If the density of metal is 5.5 g/cc, then find the volume of cavity.

3 A raft of wood (density 600 kg/m^3) of mass 120 kg floats in water. How much weight can be put on the raft to make it just sink?

4 A necklace weighing 50 g in air, but it weight 46 g in water. Assume copper is mixed with gold to prepare the necklace. How much copper is present in it? (Specific gravity of gold is 20 and that of copper is 10)

5 A solid sphere of radius 5 cm floats in water. If a maximum load of 100 g can be put on it without wetting the load, find the specific gravity of the material of the sphere.

6 A block of wood weighs 12 kg and has a relative density 0.6. It is to be in water with 0.9 of its volume immersed. What weight of a metal is needed (a), if the metal is on the top of wood, (b) if the metal is attached below the wood? (Relative density of metal = 7)

7 A cubical box is to be constructed with iron sheets 1mm in thickness. What can be the minimum value of the external edge, so that the cube does not sink in water? Density of iron = 8000 kg/m^3 and density of water = 1000 kg/m^3.

8 A hollow spherical body of inner and outer radii 6 cm and 8 cm respectively, floats half submerged in water. Find the density of the material of the sphere.

9 A liquid of density ρ is filled in a beaker of cross-section S to a height H and then a cylinder of mass m and cross-section s is made to float in it as shown in figure. If the atmospheric pressure is p_0, then find the pressure

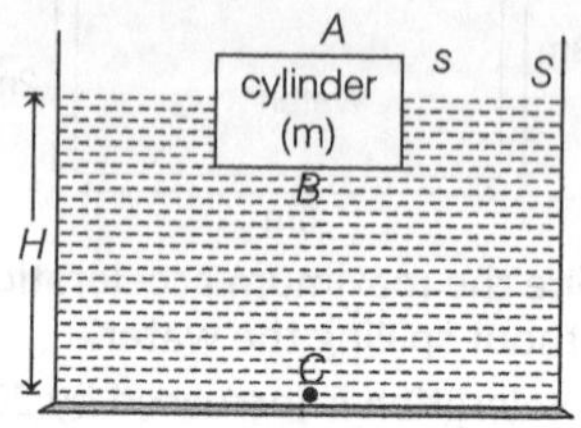

(a) at the top face A of the cylinder

(b) at the bottom face B of the cylinder and

(c) at the base C of the beaker. Can ever these three pressure be equal?

10 A cubical block of wood of side of 10 cm, floats at the interface between oil and water as shown in figure. Find the height of the cube submerged inside water. The density of oil is 0.6 g/cm^3. The mass of the block is 680 gm.

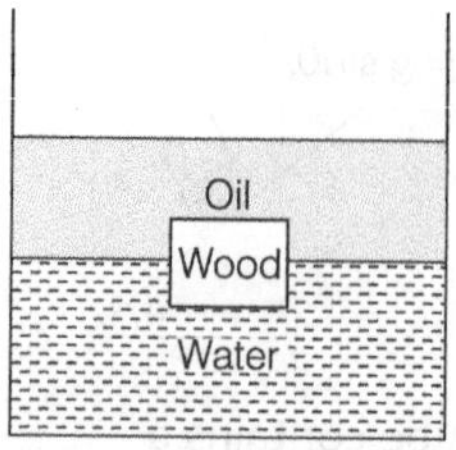

11 A cubical metal block of edge 12 cm floats in mercury with one fifth of the height inside the mercury. Water is poured till the surface of the block is just immersed in it. Find the height of the water column to be poured. Specific gravity of mercury =13.6.

12 A spring balance reads 10 kg when a bucket of water is suspended from it. What is the reading of the spring balance when

(a) an ice cube of mass 1.5 kg is put into the bucket?

(b) an iron piece of mass 7.8 kg suspended by another string is immersed with half its volume inside the water in the bucket? (Relative density of iron = 7.8).

13 A piece of ice is floating in water. What will happen to the level of water when all ice melts? What will happen, if the beaker is filled not with water but with liquid (a) denser than water (b) lighter than water?

14 A solid sphere of mass $m = 2$ kg and specific gravity $\sigma = 0.5$ is held stationary relative to a tank filled with water as shown in figure. The tank is accelerating vertically upward with acceleration $a = 2$ m/s^2.

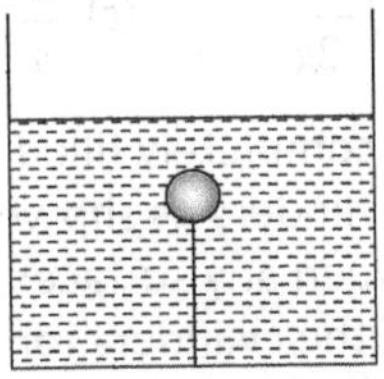

(a) Calculate tension in the thread connected between the sphere and the bottom of the tank.

(b) If the thread snaps, calculate acceleration of sphere with respect to the tank.

(Density of water is $\rho = 1000$ kg/m^3, $g = 10$ m/s^2)

15 A wooden plank of length 1m and uniform cross-section is hinged at one end to the bottom of a tank as shown. The tank is filled with water upto a height of 0.5m. The specific gravity of the plank is 0.5. Find the angle θ made by the plank in equilibrium position.

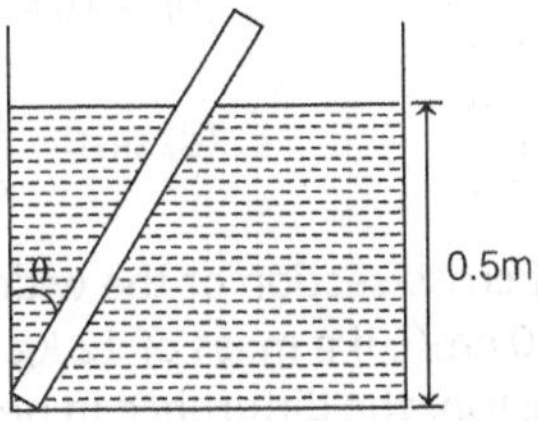

LEVEL 02 JEE Main Level

Single Choice Correct Questions

1 The pressure at the bottom of a tank of water is $3p$, where p is the atmospheric pressure. If the water is drawn out till the level of water is lowered by one fifth, the pressure at the bottom of the tank will now be

(a) $2p$ (b) $(13/5)\,p$ (c) $(8/5)\,p$ (d) $(4/5)\,p$

2 The volume of an air bubble become three times as it rises from the bottom of a lake to its surface. Assuming atmospheric pressure to be 75 cm of Hg and density of water to be 1/10 of the density of mercury, the depth of the lake is

(a) 5 m (b) 10 m (c) 15 m (d) 20 m

3 An open-ended U-tube of uniform cross-sectional area contains water (density 1.0 gm/cm^3) standing initially 20 cm from the bottom in each arm. An immiscible liquid of density 4.0 gm/cm^3 is added to one arm until a layer 5 cm high forms, as shown in the figure above. What is the ratio h_2/h_1 of the heights of the liquid in the two arms?

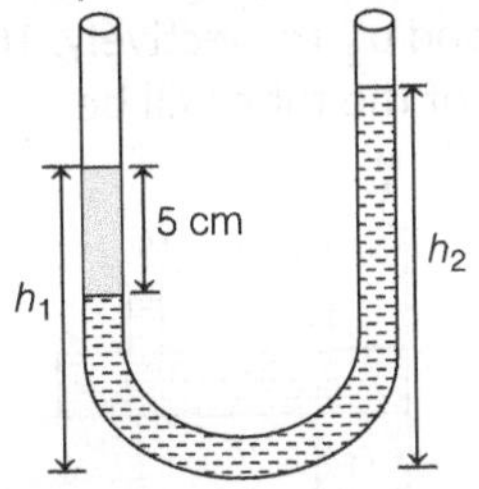

(a) 3/1 (b) 5/2 (c) 2/1 (d) 3/2

4 A U-tube having horizontal arm of length 20 cm, has uniform cross-sectional area = 1 cm^2. It is filled with water of volume 60 cc. What volume of a liquid of density 4 g/cc should be poured from one side into the U-tube, so that no water is left in the horizontal arm of the tube?

(a) 60 cc (b) 45 cc
(c) 50cc (d) 35cc

5 Two communicating vessels contain mercury. The diameter of one vessel is n times larger than the diameter of the other. A column of water of height h is poured into the left vessel. The mercury level in the right vessel will rise by (σ = relative density of mercury)

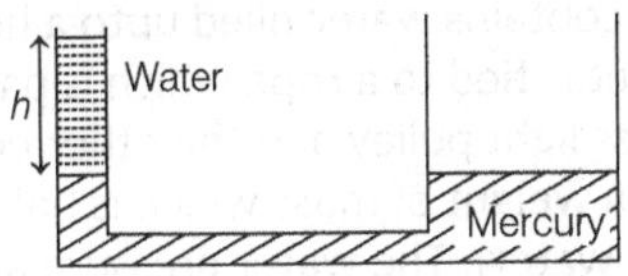

(a) $\dfrac{n^2h}{(n+1)^2\sigma}$

(b) $\dfrac{h}{(n^2+1)\sigma}$

(c) $\dfrac{h}{(n+1)^2\sigma}$

(d) $\dfrac{h}{n^2\sigma}$

6 A small uniform tube is bent into a circle of radius r whose plane is vertical. The equal volumes of two fluids whose densities are ρ and σ ($\rho > \sigma$), fill half the circle. Find the angle that the radius passing through the interface makes with the vertical.

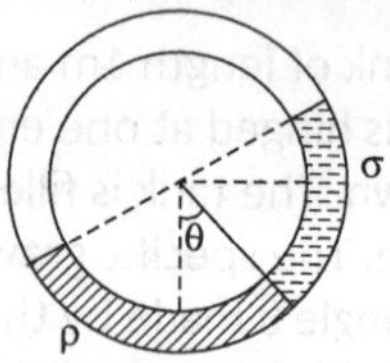

(a) $\cos\theta = \dfrac{\rho-\sigma}{\rho+\sigma}$ (b) $\tan\theta = \dfrac{\rho-\sigma}{\rho+\sigma}$

(c) $\sin\theta = \dfrac{\rho+\sigma}{\rho-\sigma}$ (d) $\sin\theta = \dfrac{\rho}{\sigma}$

7 The area of cross-section of the wider tube shown in figure is 800 cm^2. If a mass of 12 kg is placed on the massless piston, the difference in heights h in the level of water in the two tubes is

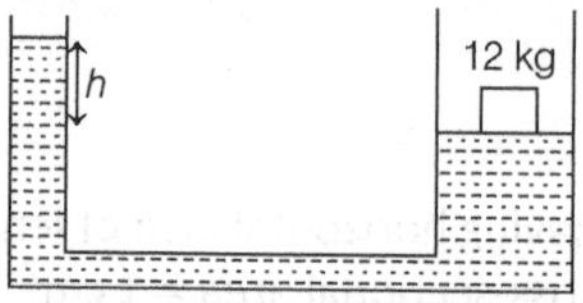

(a) 10 cm (b) 6 cm (c) 15 cm (d) 2 cm

8 The hydraulic press shown in the figure is used to raise the mass M through a height of 5.0 mm by performing 500 J of work at the small piston. The diameter of the large piston is 10 cm while that of the smaller one is 2cm. The mass M is of

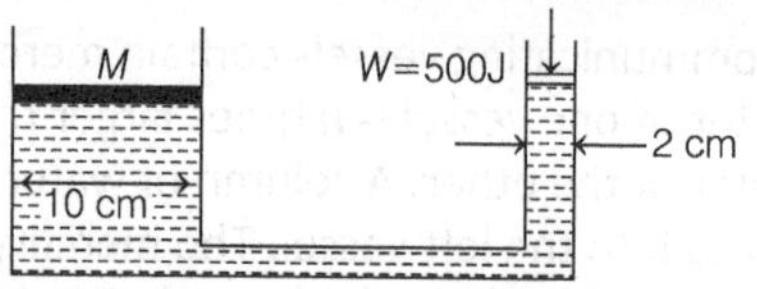

(a) 10^4 kg (b) 10^3 kg (c) 100 kg (d) 10^5 kg

9 A bucket contains water filled upto a height = 15 cm. The bucket is tied to a rope which is passed over a frictionless light pulley and the other end of the rope is tied to a weight of mass which is half of that of the (bucket + water). The water pressure above atmosphere pressure at the bottom is

(a) 0.5 kPa (b) 1 kPa
(c) 5 kPa (d) None of these

10 An open cubical tank was initially fully filled with water. When the tank was accelerated on a horizontal plane along one of its side it was found that one third of volume of water spilled out. The acceleration was

(a) $g/3$ (b) $2g/3$
(c) $3g/2$ (d) None of these

11 A U-tube of base length L filled with same volume of two liquids of densities ρ and 2ρ is moving with an acceleration a on the horizontal plane as shown in the figure. If the height difference between the two surfaces (open to atmosphere) becomes zero, then the height H is given by

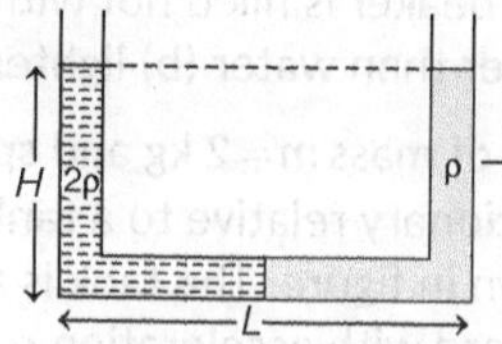

(a) $\dfrac{aL}{2g}$ (b) $\dfrac{3aL}{2g}$ (c) $\dfrac{aL}{g}$ (d) $\dfrac{2aL}{3g}$

12 A narrow tube completely filled with a liquid is lying on a series of cylinders as shown in figure. Assuming no sliding between any surfaces, the value of acceleration of the cylinders for which liquid will not come out of the tube from anywhere is given by

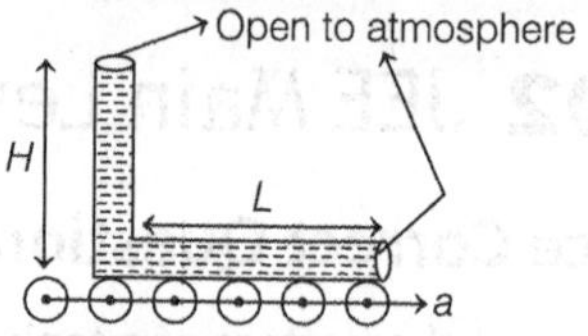

(a) $\dfrac{gH}{2L}$ (b) $\dfrac{gH}{L}$ (c) $\dfrac{2gH}{L}$ (d) $\dfrac{gH}{\sqrt{2L}}$

13 A rectangular box containing water is accelerated upwards at 3 m/s^2 on an inclined plane making 30° to the horizontal. The slope of the free liquid surface is

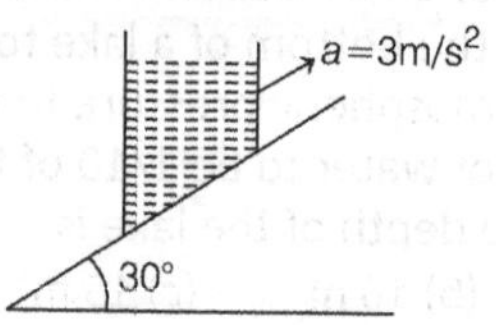

(a) 0.23 (b) $\dfrac{1}{\sqrt{3}}$ (c) $\sqrt{3}$ (d) 0.32

14 A tube filled with water of density ρ and closed at both ends uniformly rotates in a horizontal plane about a vertical axis. The manometers fixed in the tube at distances r_1 and r_2 from the axis indicate pressure p_1 and p_2 respectively. The angular velocity ω of rotation of the tube will be

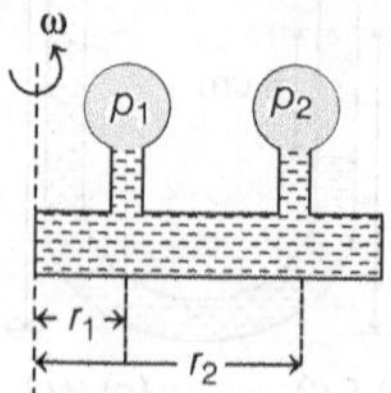

(a) $\sqrt{\dfrac{2(p_2 - p_1)}{\rho(r_2^2 - r_1^2)}}$ (b) $\sqrt{\dfrac{2(p_2 + p_1)}{\rho(r_2^2 + r_1^2)}}$

(c) $\sqrt{\dfrac{2}{\rho}\left(\dfrac{p_2}{r_2^2} - \dfrac{p_1}{r_1^2}\right)}$ (d) $\sqrt{\dfrac{2}{\rho}\left(\dfrac{p_2}{r_2} - \dfrac{p_1}{r_1}\right)}$

15 A liquid is kept in a cylindrical vessel which is being rotated about a vertical axis through the centre of the circular base. If the radius of the vessel is r and angular velocity of rotation is ω, then the difference in the heights of the liquid at the centre of the vessel and the edge is

(a) $\dfrac{r\omega}{2g}$ (b) $\dfrac{r^2\omega^2}{2g}$

(c) $\sqrt{2gr\omega}$ (d) $\dfrac{\omega^2}{2gr^2}$

16 A square gate of size 1 m × 1 m is hinged at its mid-point. A fluid of density ρ fills the space to the left of the gate. The force F required to hold the gate stationary is

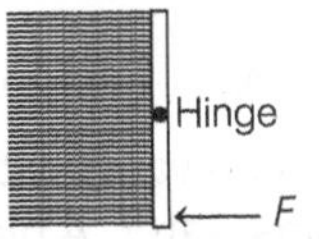

(a) $\dfrac{\rho g}{3}$ (b) $\dfrac{\rho g}{2}$

(c) $\dfrac{\rho g}{6}$ (d) None of these

17 Figure here shows the vertical cross-section of a vessel filled with a liquid of density ρ. The normal thrust per unit area on the walls of the vessel at point P, as shown, will be

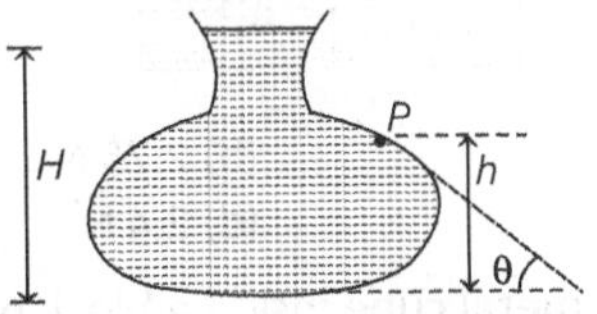

(a) $h\rho g$ (b) $H\rho g$

(c) $(H-h)\,\rho g$ (d) $(H-h)\,\rho g\cos\theta$

18 The force F needed to support the liquid of density ρ and the vessel on top in figure is

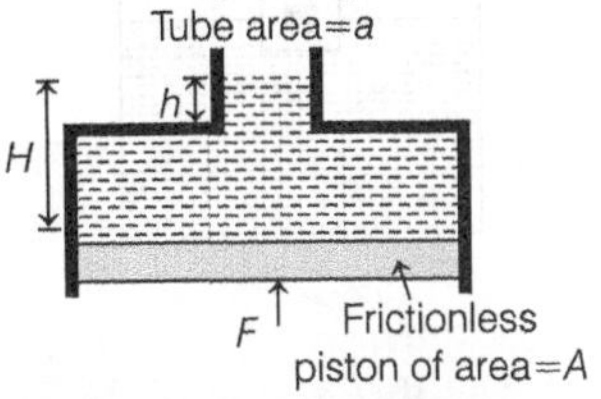

(a) $\rho g\,\{ha - (H-h)A\}$ (b) ρgHA

(c) ρgHa (d) $\rho g\,(H-h)A$

19 A liquid of mass 1 kg is filled in a flask as shown in figure. The force exerted by the flask on the liquid is ($g = 10\ m/s^2$) (Neglect atmospheric pressure)

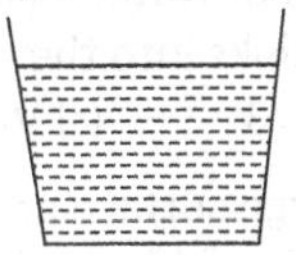

(a) 10 N (b) greater than 10 N

(c) less than 10 N (d) Zero

20 The three vessels shown in figure have same base area. Equal masses of a liquid are poured in each vessel. The force exerted by the liquid at the base area will be

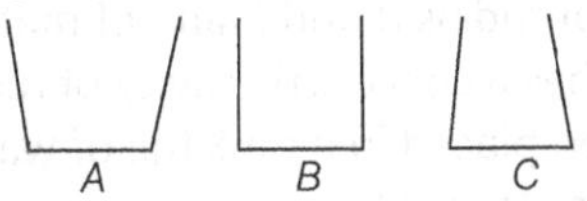

(a) equal in all vessels
(b) maximum in vessel *A*
(c) maximum in vessel *B*
(d) maximum in vessel *C*

21 A hemispherical portion of radius R is removed from the bottom of a cylinder of radius R. The volume of the remaining cylinder is V and mass M. It is suspended by a string in a liquid of density ρ, where it stays vertical. The upper surface of the cylinder is at a depth h below the liquid surface. The force on the bottom of the cylinder by the liquid is

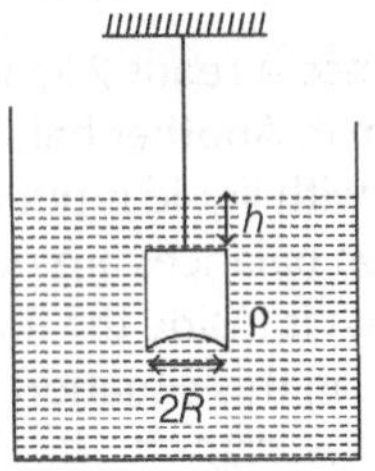

(a) Mg (b) $Mg - V\rho g$

(c) $Mg + \pi R^2 h\rho g$ (d) $\rho g(V + \pi R^2 h)$

22 A sample of metal weighs 210 g in air, 180 g in water and 120 g in an unknown liquid. Then

(a) the density of metal is 3 g/cm^3
(b) the density of the metal is 7 g/cm^3
(c) the density of liquid is 4 gm/cm^3
(d) the metal will float on liquid

23 A wooden cube just floats inside water, when a 200 g mass is placed on it. When the mass is removed, the cube is 2 cm above the water level. The size of the cube is

(a) 5 cm (b) 10 cm

(c) 15 cm (d) 20 cm

24 A hollow sphere of volume V is floating on water surface half immersed in it. What should be the minimum volume of water inside the sphere so that the sphere now sinks into the water?

(a) $V/2$ (b) $V/3$ (c) $V/4$ (d) V

25 A container of large surface area is filled with liquid of density ρ. A cubical block of side edge a and mass M is floating in it with four-fifth of its volume submerged. If a coin of mass m placed gently on the top surface of the block is just submerged, M is

(a) $4m/5$ (b) $m/5$
(c) $4m$ (d) $5m$

26 A sphere of radius R and made of material of relative density σ has a concentric cavity of radius r. It just floats when placed in a tank full of water. The value of the ratio R/r will be

(a) $\left(\dfrac{\sigma}{\sigma-1}\right)^{1/3}$ (b) $\left(\dfrac{\sigma-1}{\sigma}\right)^{1/3}$

(c) $\left(\dfrac{\sigma+1}{\sigma}\right)^{1/3}$ (d) $\left(\dfrac{\sigma-1}{\sigma+1}\right)^{1/3}$

27 A crown made of gold and copper weighs 210 g in air and 198 g in water. The weight of gold in crown is (density of gold = 19.3 g/cm^3 and density of copper = 8.5 g/cm^3).

(a) 93 g (b) 100 g
(c) 150 g (d) 193 g

28 The spring balance A reads 2 kg with a block m suspended from it. Another balance B reads 5 kg, when a beaker with liquid is put on the pan of the balance. The two balances are now, so arranged that the hanging mass is inside the liquid in the beaker as shown in figure. In this situation

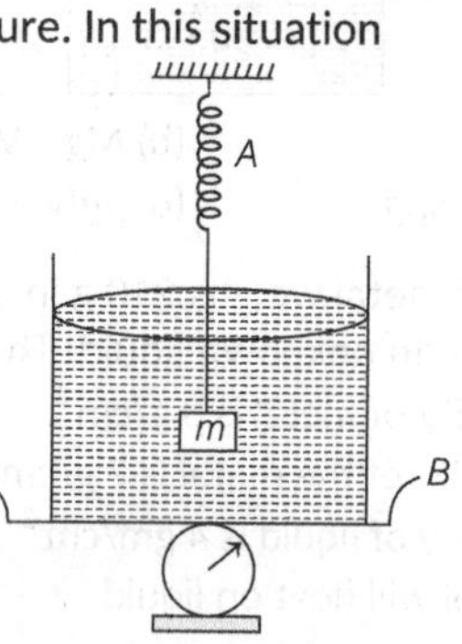

(a) the balance A will read more than 2 kg
(b) the balance B will read less than 5 kg
(c) the balance A will read less than 2 kg and B will read more than 5 kg
(d) the balances A and B will read 2 kg and 5 kg respectively.

29 A beaker containing water is placed on the platform of a spring balance. The balance reads 1.5 kg. A stone of mass 0.5 kg and density 500 kg/m^3 is completely immersed in water without touching the walls of beaker. What will be the balance reading now?

(a) 2 kg (b) 2.5 kg
(c) 1 kg (d) 3 kg

30 A cylindrical block of area of cross-section A and of material of density ρ is placed in a liquid of density one-third of density of block. The block compresses a spring and compression in the spring is one-third of the length of the block. If acceleration due to gravity is g, the spring constant of the spring is

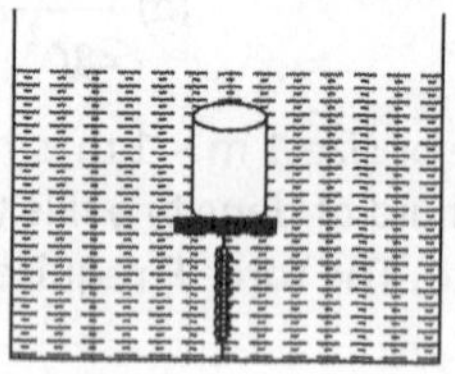

(a) ρAg (b) $2\rho Ag$ (c) $2\rho Ag/3$ (d) $\rho Ag/3$

31 A tank accelerates upwards with acceleration, $a = 1$ m/s^2 contains water. A block of mass 1 kg and density 0.8 g/cm^3 is held stationary inside the tank with the help of the string as shown in figure. The tension in the string is (Given, density of water = 1000 kg/m^3)

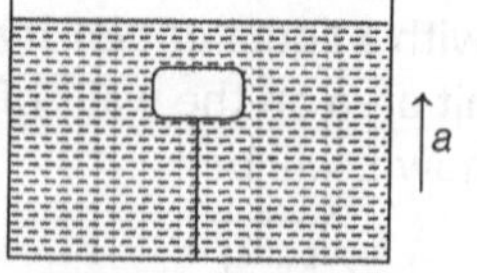

(a) 2.2 N (b) 2.75 N
(c) 3 N (d) 2.4 N

32 There is a metal cube inside a block of ice which is floating on the surface of water. The ice melts completely and metal falls in the water. Water level in the container

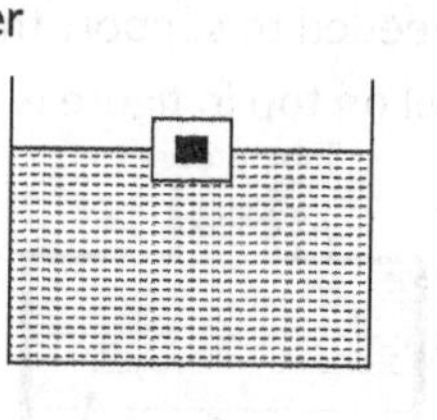

(a) rises
(b) falls
(c) remains same
(d) Nothing can be concluded

33 A small wooden ball of density ρ is immersed in water of density σ to depth h and then released. The height H above the surface of water up to which the ball will jump out of water is

(a) $\frac{\sigma h}{\rho}$ (b) $\left(\frac{\sigma}{\rho}-1\right)h$

(c) h (d) zero

34 A cubical block is floating in a liquid with half of its volume immersed in the liquid. When the whole system accelerates upward with a net acceleration $g/3$, the fraction of volume immersed in the liquid will be

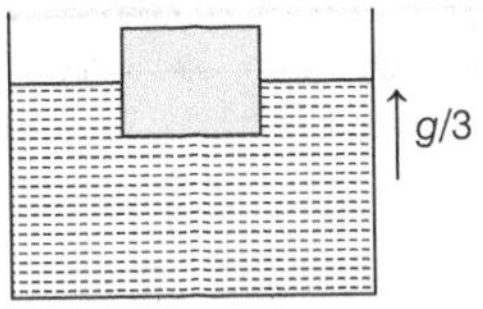

(a) 1/2 (b) 3/8

(c) 2/3 (d) 3/4

35 A homogeneous solid cylinder of length L is immersed such that it floats with its axis vertical at the liquid-liquid interface with length $L/4$ in the denser liquid as shown in the figure. The lower density liquid is open to atmosphere having pressure p_0. Then, density D of solid is given by

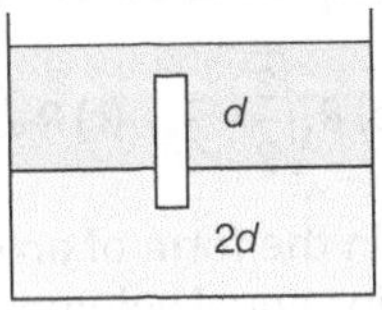

(a) $5d/4$ (b) $4d/5$

(c) $4d$ (d) $d/5$

Numerical Value Questions

1 An open tank 10 m long and 2 m deep is filled upto height 1.5 m of oil of specific gravity 0.80. The tank is accelerated uniformly from rest to a speed of 10 m/s. What is the shortest time (in seconds) in which this speed may be attained without spilling any oil. $(g = 10\,\text{m/s}^2)$

2 A hollow cone floats with its axis vertical upto one-third of its height in a liquid of relative density 0.8 and with its vertex submerged. When another liquid of relative density ρ is filled in it upto one-third of its height, the cone floats upto half its vertical height. The height of the cone is 0.10 m and the radius of the circular base is 0.05 m. Find the specific gravity ρ.

3 Figure shows a cubical block of side 10 cm and relative density 1.5 suspended by a wire of cross-sectional area $10^{-6}\ \text{m}^2$. The breaking stress of the wire is $7\times10^6\ \text{N/m}^2$. The block is placed in a beaker of base area 200 cm^2 and initially i.e. at $t =$ 0, the top surface of water and the block coincide. There is a pump at the bottom corner which ejects 2 cm^3 of water per sec constantly. Find the time (in seconds) at which the wire will break.

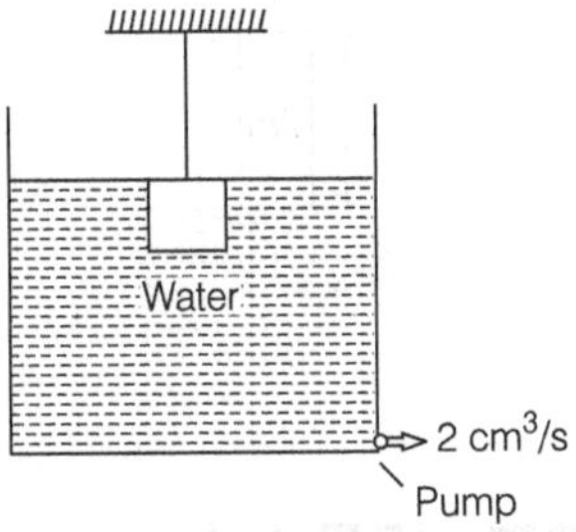

4 A cube (density 0.5 gm/cc) of side 10 cm is floating in water kept in a cylindrical beaker of base area 1500 cm^2. When a mass m is kept on wooden block the level of water rises in the beaker by 2 mm. Find the mass m (in g).

5 A uniform plastic sphere of radius R floating almost fully immersed in a fluid of density ρ as shown. The force of the fluid pressure on the lower half of the sphere (excluding the contribution of the atmospheric pressure) is $\frac{5}{n}\pi R^3\rho g$. Find n.

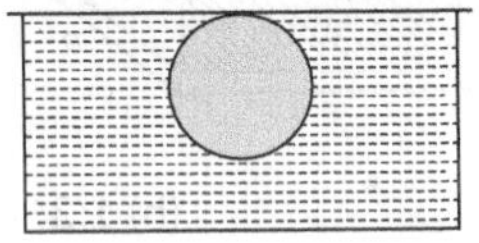

6 A rod of length 12 m has specific gravity ρ (= 25/36). One end of the rod is tied to 5 m long rope, which in turn is tied to the floor of a pool 10 m deep as shown. Find the length (in m) of the part of rod, which is out of water.

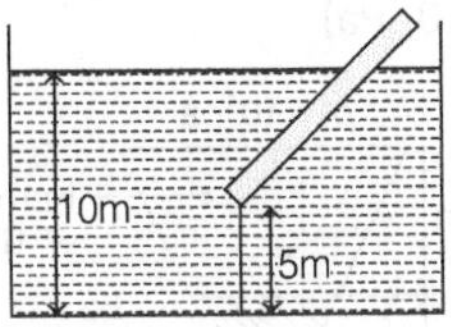

7 A uniform cylinder of mass 2 m is connected to a block of mass m though a string passing over a smooth pulley. The system is released from position, where the lower end of the cylinder just touches a liquid surface in a tank. Length and cross-section area of cylinder are L and A, respectively. The cylinder just stops at instant when its upper edge reaches liquid surface. If density of liquid is $\frac{nm}{AL}$, then find value of n.

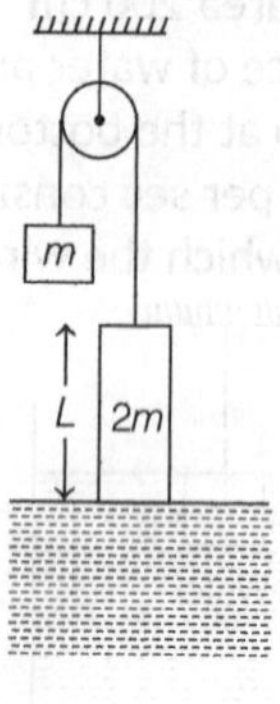

LEVEL 03 JEE Advanced Level

Single Choice Correct Questions

1 A cuboid ($a \times a \times 2a$) is filled with two immiscible liquids of density 2ρ and ρ as shown in the figure. Neglecting atmospheric pressure, ratio of force on base and side wall of the cuboid is

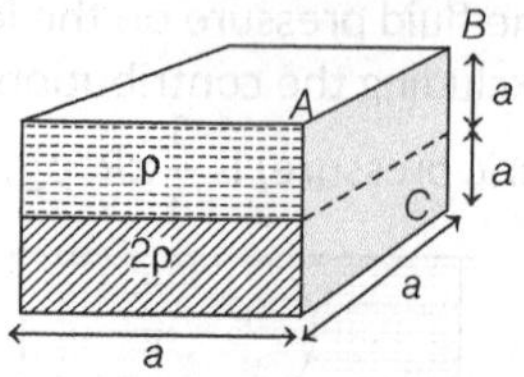

(a) 2:3 (b) 1:3
(c) 5:6 (d) 6:5

2 The figure shows a conical container of half-apex angle 37° filled with certain quantities of kerosene and water. The force exerted by the water on the kerosene is approximately. (Take atmospheric pressure $= 10^5$ Pa)

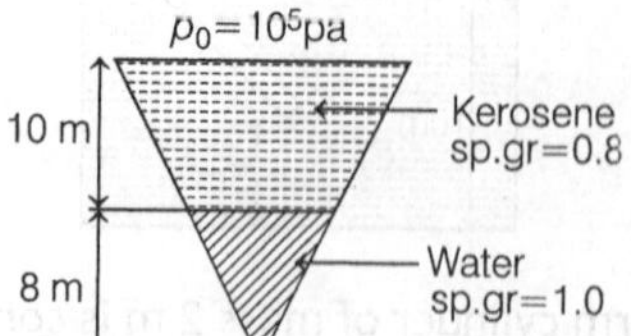

(a) 2×10^7 N
(b) 3×10^7 N
(c) 4×10^7 N
(d) 5×10^7 N

8 A vertical U-tube is spinned about the vertical axis passing through the left hand limb, with an angular speed ω, such that the liquid columns in the limbs have heights h and $3h$, as shown in the figure. If the value of ω is $\sqrt{\frac{5g}{nh}}$ then find n.

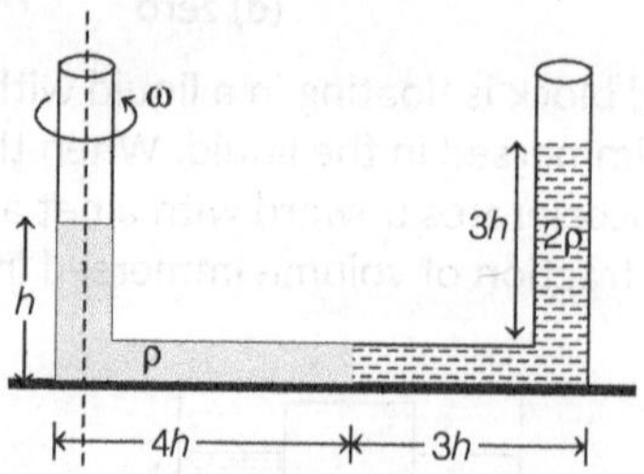

3 In the figure shown, the heavy cylinder (radius R) resting on smooth surface separates two liquids of denisities 2ρ and 3ρ. The height h for the equilibrium of cylinder must be

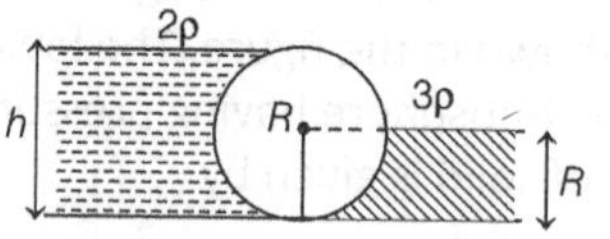

(a) $\frac{3R}{2}$ (b) $R\sqrt{\frac{3}{2}}$ (c) $R\sqrt{2}$ (d) $R\sqrt{\frac{3}{4}}$

4 A closed tube in the form of an equilateral triangle of side 6m contains equal volumes of three liquids which do not mix and is placed vertically with its lowest side horizontal. Find x in the figure, if the densities of the liquids are in A.P.

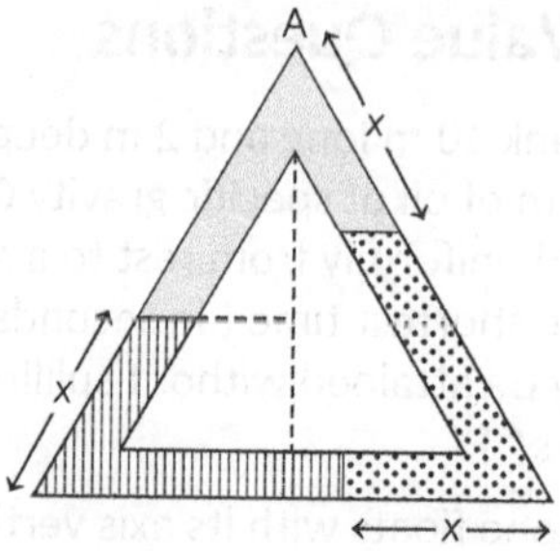

(a) 1 m (b) 1.5 m (c) 2 m (d) 3 m

5 The vertical limbs of a U shaped tube are filled with a liquid of density ρ upto a height h on each side. The horizontal portion of the U-tube having length $2h$ contains a liquid of density 2ρ. The U-tube is moved horizontally with an acceleration $g/2$ parallel to the horizontal arm. Find the difference in heights in liquid levels in the two vertical limbs, at steady state.

(a) $4h/7$ (b) $5h/7$ (c) $6h/7$ (d) $8h/7$

6 A light semi-cylindrical gate of radius R is piovted at its mid point O, of the diameter as shown in the figure holding liquid of density ρ. The force F required to prevent the rotation of the gate is equal to

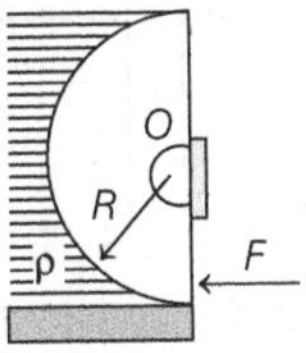

(a) $2\pi R^3 \rho g$ (b) $2\rho g R^3 l$

(c) $\frac{2R^2 l \rho g}{3}$ (d) None of these

7 A fluid container is containing a liquid of density ρ is accelerating upward with acceleration a along the inclined place of inclination α as shown. Then, the angle of inclination θ of free surface is

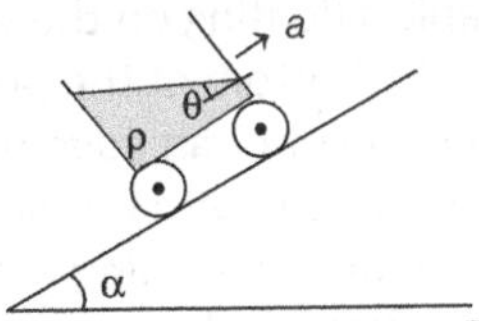

(a) $\theta = \alpha$ (b) $\tan^{-1}\left[\frac{a+g \sin \alpha}{g \cos \alpha}\right]$

(c) $\tan^{-1}\left[\frac{a-g \sin \alpha}{g(1+\cos \alpha)}\right]$ (d) $\tan^{-1}\left[\frac{a-g \sin \alpha}{g(1-\cos \alpha)}\right]$

8 Length of the horizontal arm of a uniform cross-section U - tube is 5 cm and both ends of the vertical arms are open to the surrounding pressure of 7700 N/m^2. A liquid of density $\rho = 10^3$ kgm^{-3} is poured into the tube such that the liquid just fills the horizontal part of the tube. Now, one of the open ends is sealed and the tube is then rotated about a vertical axis passing through the other vertical arm with angular velocity ω due to which the liquid rises up to half the length of the vertical arm. If length of each vertical arm is 6 cm, what is the value of ω?

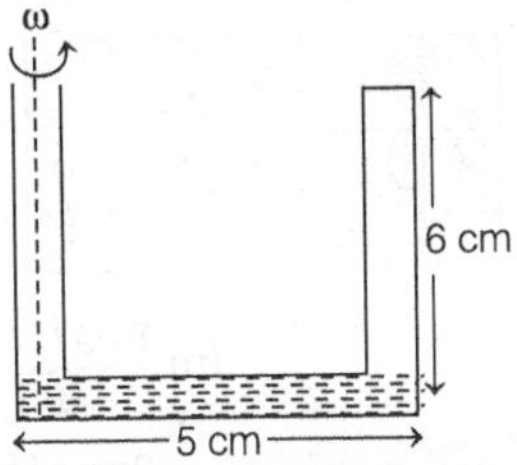

(a) 25 rad/s (b) 50 rad/s
(c) 75 rad/s (d) 100 rad/s

9 A conical block, floats in water with 90% height immersed in it. Height h of the block is equal to the diameter of the block i.e., 20 cm. The mass to be kept on the block, so that the block just floats at the surface of water is

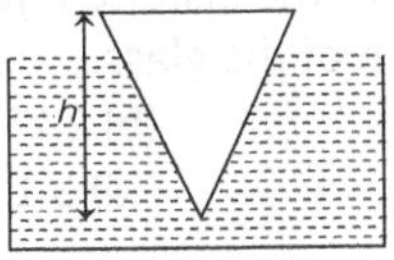

(a) 568 g (b) 980 g
(c) 112 g (d) 196 g

10 A block of mass 10 kg, connected to another hollow block of same size and negligible mass, by a spring of spring constant 500 N/m, floats in water as shown in the figure. The compression in the spring is ($\rho_{\text{water}} = 1\times10^3 \text{ kg/m}^3, g = 10 \text{ m/s}^2$)

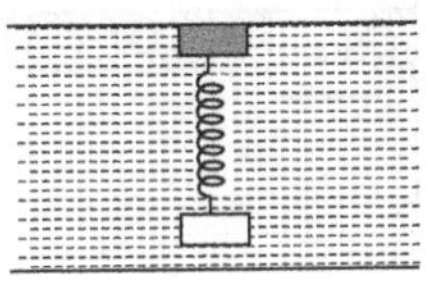

(a) 10 cm (b) 20 cm
(c) 50 cm (d) 100 cm

11 Two cubes of size 1.0 m sides, one of relative density 0.60 and another of relative density = 1.15 are connected by weightless wire and placed in a large tank of water. Under equilibrium the lighter cube will project above the water surface to a height of

(a) 50 cm
(b) 25 cm
(c) 10 cm
(d) zero

12 A dumbbell is placed in water of density ρ. It is observed that by attaching a mass m to the rod, the dumbbell floats with the rod horizontal on the surface of water and each sphere exactly half submerged as shown in the figure. The volume of the mass m is negligible. The value of length l is

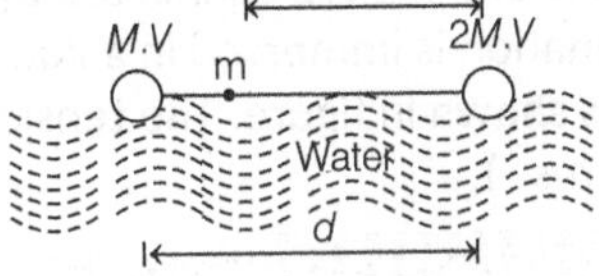

(a) $\frac{d(V\rho-3M)}{2(V\rho-2M)}$ (b) $\frac{d(V\rho-2M)}{2(V\rho-3M)}$

(c) $\frac{d(V\rho+2M)}{2(V\rho-3M)}$ (d) $\frac{d(V\rho-2M)}{2(V\rho+3M)}$

13 A cube of ice of edge 4 cm is placed in an empty cylindrical glass of inner diameter 6 cm. Assume that the ice melts uniformly from each side, so that it always retains its cubical shape. Remembering that ice is lighter than water, find the length of the edge of the ice cube at the instant, it just leaves contact with the bottom of the glass.

(a) 1.85 cm (b) 2.26 cm
(c) 2.77 cm (d) 3.13 cm

14 A rectangular bar of soap has density 800 kg/m^3 floats in water of density 1000 kg/ m^3. Oil of density 300 kg/m^3 is slowly added, forming a layer that does not mix with the water. When the top surface of the oil is at the same level as the top surface of the soap, what is the ratio of the oil layer thickness to the soap's thickness, x/L ?

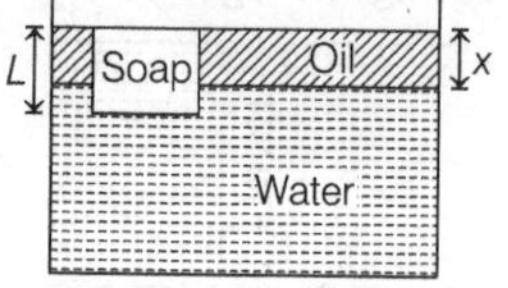

(a) 1/5 (b) 2/7
(c) 3/10 (d) 3/8

15 In the arrangement shown, m_B = 3m, density of liquid is ρ and density of block B is 2ρ. The system is released from rest so that block B moves up when in liquid and moves down when out of liquid with the same acceleration. Find the mass of block A.

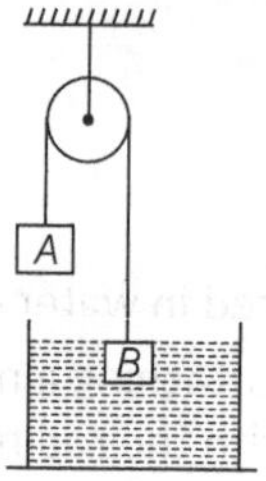

(a) 7m/4 (b) 2m (c) 9m/2 (d) 9m/4

16 Two spheres of volume 250 cc each but of relative densities 0.8 and 1.2 are connected by a string and the combination is immersed in a liquid in vertical position as shown in figure. The tension in the string is (g = 10 m/s^2)

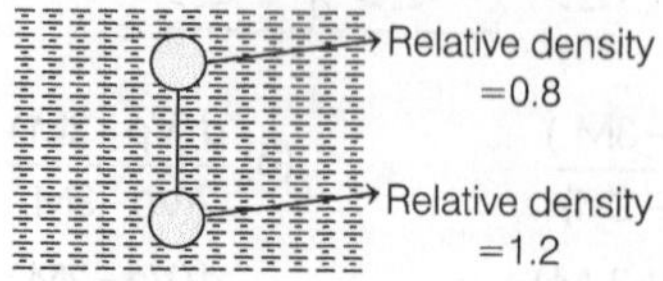

(a) 5.0 N (b) 0.5 N (c) 1.0 N (d) 2.0 N

17 A solid cylinder of height h and mass m is floating in a liquid of density ρ as shown in the figure. Find the acceleration of the vessel containing liquid for which the relative downward acceleration of the completely immersed cylinder with respect to vessel becomes equal to one-third of that of the vessel.

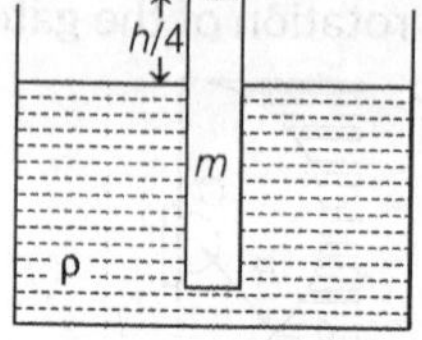

(a) 2g/3 (b) 4g/3 (c) 3g/4 (d) g/2

18 A concrete sphere of radius R has a cavity of radius r which is packed with sawdust. The relative densities of concrete and sawdust are 2.4 and 0.3 respectively. For this sphere to float with its entire volume submerged under water, the ratio of the mass of concrete to the mass of sawdust will be

(a) 8 (b) 4 (c) 3 (d) zero

19 A wooden plank is floating on the water in a pool. It is tethered to the bottom of the pool by a string attached at mid-point of an edge of bottom face, which causes it to float with the diagonal of its vertical cross-section coinciding with the level surface of the water, as shown in the figure. What is the specific gravity of the wood?

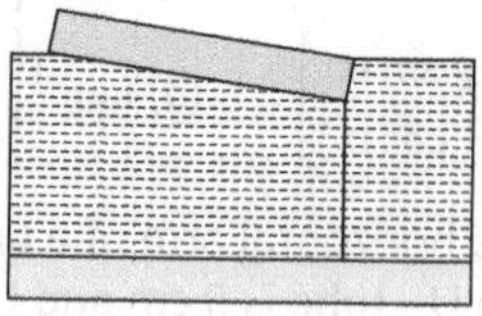

(a) 1/5 (b) 1/4 (c) 1/3 (d) 1/2

20 A non-uniform cylinder of mass m, length l and radius r is having its centre of mass at a distance l/4 from the centre and lying on the axis of the cylinder. The cylinder is kept in a liquid of uniform density ρ. The moment of inertia of the rod about the centre of mass is I. The angular acceleration of point A relative to point B just after the rod is released from the position shown in figure is

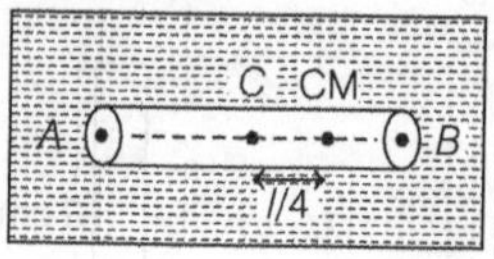

(a) $\frac{\pi\rho g l^2 r^2}{I}$ (b) $\frac{\pi\rho g l^2 r^2}{4I}$

(c) $\frac{\pi\rho g l^2 r^2}{2I}$ (d) $\frac{3\pi\rho g l^2 r^2}{4I}$

21 A slender homogeneous rod of length 2L floats partly immersed in water, being supported by a string fastened to one of its ends, as shown. The specific gravity of the rod is 0.75. The length of rod that extends out of water is

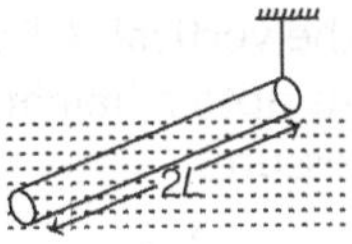

(a) L (b) L/2
(c) L/4 (d) 2L/3

22 A wax candle floats vertically in a liquid of density twice that of wax. The candle burns at the rate of 4 cm/h. Then, with respect to the surface of the liquid the upper end of the candle will

(a) fall at the rate of 4 cm/h
(b) fall at the rate of 2 cm/h
(c) rise at the rate of 2 cm/h
(d) remain at the same height

23 A wooden stick of length L, radius R and density ρ has a small metal piece of mass m (of negligible volume) attached to its one end. Find the minimum value for the mass m that would make the stick float vertically in stable equilibrium in a liquid of density σ.

(a) $2\pi R^2 L\rho\left(\sqrt{\frac{\sigma}{\rho}}-1\right)$ (b) $\pi R^2 L\rho\left(\sqrt{\frac{2\sigma}{\rho}}-1\right)$
(c) $\pi R^2 L\rho\left(\sqrt{\frac{\sigma}{\rho}}-1\right)$ (d) $\pi R^2 L\rho\left(\sqrt{\frac{\sigma}{2\rho}}-1\right)$

24 A cubical block of volume V and density 3ρ is placed inside a liquid of density ρ and attached to a spring of spring constant k as shown in the figure. Assuming ideal spring and pulley and spring is attached at A which is at R/2 from centre. The compression in the spring at equilibrium is

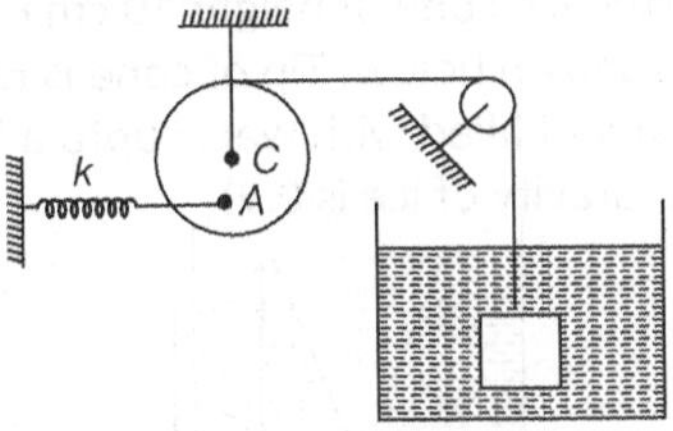

(a) $\frac{4\rho Vg}{k}$ (b) $\frac{2\rho Vg}{k}$
(c) $\frac{3\rho Vg}{k}$ (d) $\frac{\rho Vg}{k}$

25 A conical flask of mass 10 kg and base area $10^3\ cm^2$ is floating in liquid of specific gravity 1.2 as shown in the figure. The force that liquid exerts on curved surface of conical flask is ($g = 10\ m/s^2$)

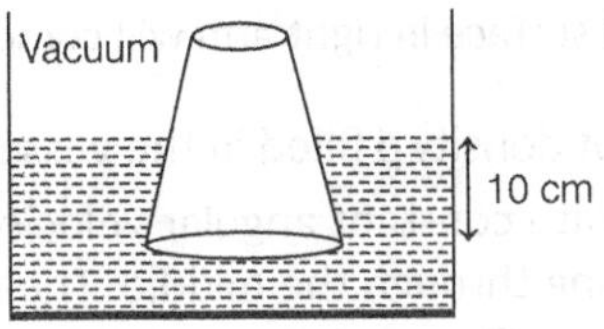

(a) 20 N in downward direction
(b) 40 N in downward direction
(c) 20 N in upward direction
(d) 40 N in upward direction

Multiple Choice(s) Correct Questions

1 A piston of mass $M = 3$ kg and radius $R = 4$ cm has a hole into which a thin pipe of radius $r = 1$ cm is inserted. The piston can enter a cylinder tightly and without friction, and initially it is at the bottom of the cylinder. 750 gm of water is now poured into the pipe, so that the piston and pipe are lifted up as shown. If the height of water in the cylinder is H and height of water in the pipe is h, then

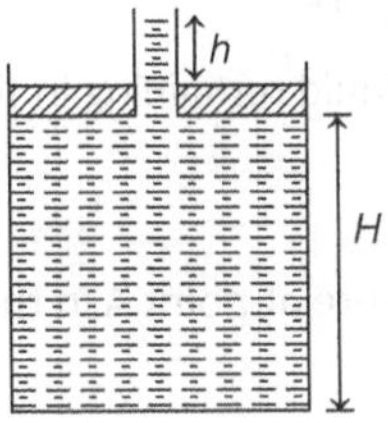

(a) $h = \frac{1}{\pi} m$ (b) $H = \frac{11}{32\pi} m$
(c) $h = \frac{2}{\pi} m$ (d) $H = \frac{11}{16\pi} m$

2 A long U-tube is filled with a liquid of density ρ such that length of tube above liquid is a in both arm. One side of tube (right arm) is sealed and the tube is inverted. (p_0 = atmospheric pressure)

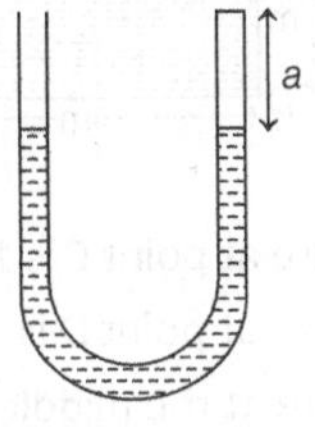

(a) Liquid will spill out the left tube if $a < \frac{p_0}{4\rho g}$

(b) Liquid will not spill out the left tube for any value of a

(c) Liquid surface in left arm will not move if $a = \frac{p_0}{2\rho g}$

(d) Liquid surface in right arm will come down

3 A liquid of density ρ filled in the vessel as shown is rotated with constant angular velocity ω about the axis passing through the middle. The radius of cylinder is R. Then

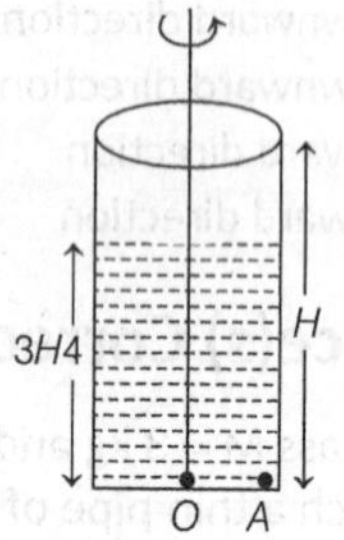

(a) the minimum value of ω for which the liquid comes out, is $\sqrt{\frac{gH}{R^2}}$

(b) the value of ω for which the base of container is just exposed is $\sqrt{\frac{2gH}{R^2}}$

(c) volume of liquid remaining in the container in case (B) is $\frac{\pi R^2 H}{2}$

(d) gauge pressure at point A in the container in case (B) is $\rho g H$

4 A container having dimensions $5\text{m} \times 4\text{m} \times 3\text{m}$ is accelerated along its breadth in horizontal. Container is filled with water up to the height of 1.5 m. Container is accelerated with 7.5 m/s^2. (Take $g = 10$ m/s^2, density of water is 10^3 kg/m^3)

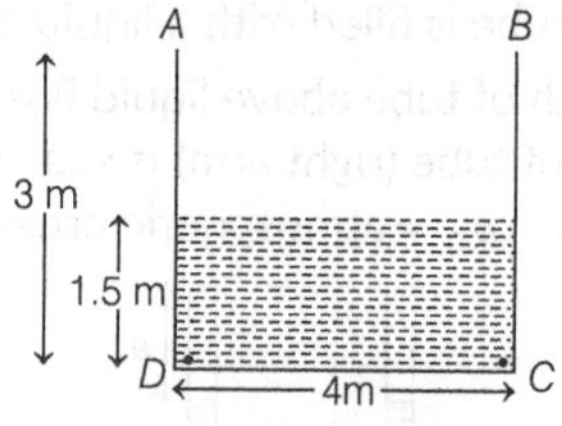

(a) Gauge pressure at point C is 10^4 Pa

(b) Gauge pressure at point D is 3×10^4 Pa

(c) Gauge pressure at the middle of the base is 1.5×10^4 Pa

(d) Remaining volume of liquid inside the container is 20 m^3

5 The vessel shown in the figure has two sections. The lower part is a rectangular vessel with area of cross-section A and height h. The upper part is a conical vessel of height h with base area A and top area a and the walls of the vessel are inclined at an angle 30° with the vertical. A liquid of density ρ fills both the sections upto a height $2h$. Neglecting atmospheric pressure.

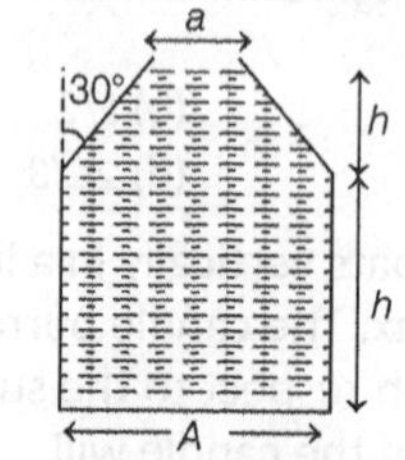

(a) The force F exerted by the liquid on the base of the vessel is $2h\rho g \frac{(A+a)}{2}$

(b) The pressure p at the base of the vessel is $2h\rho g \frac{A}{a}$

(c) The weight of the liquid W is greater than the force exerted by the liquid on the base.

(d) The walls of the vassel exert a downward force $(F - W)$ on the liquid.

6 A stick is tied to the floor of the water tank with a string as shown in the figure. The length of stick is 2 m. Area of cross-section of stick is 10^{-3} m^2. Specific gravity of stick is 0.25. Take, $g = 10$ m/s^2. Then

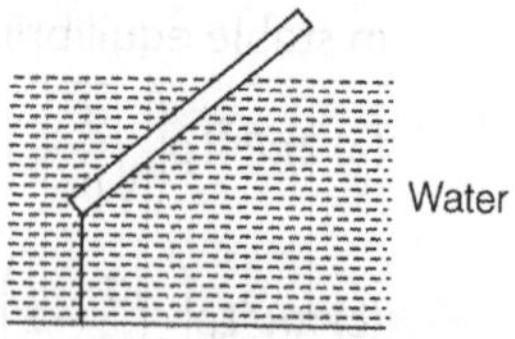

(a) tension in the string is 5 N.

(b) buoyancy force acting on stick is 10 N

(c) length of stick immersed in water is 1m.

(d) when string is cut, initial acceleration of stick is 1 m/s^2.

7 An inverted ice cone of height 10 cm is immersed in water as shown below. Tip of cone is touching the base of vessel filled with water upto a height of 9 cm. (Specific Gravity of ice is 0.9)

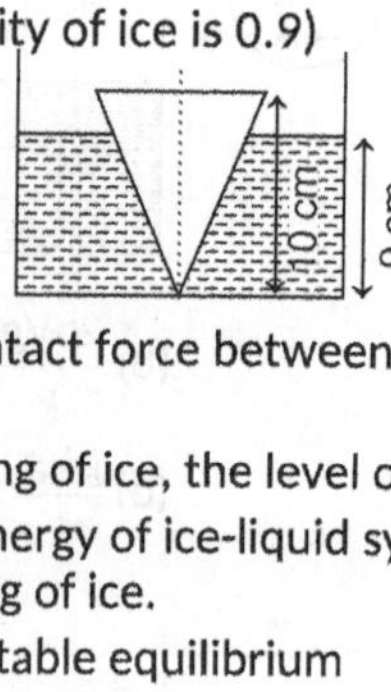

(a) Normal contact force between cone and vessel is zero.

(b) After melting of ice, the level of water will increase

(c) Potential energy of ice-liquid system will decrease after melting of ice.

(d) Cone is in stable equilibrium

8 A solid hemisphere of radius R is made to just sink in a liquid of density ρ. Consider hydrostatic force only i.e., do not take atmospheric pressure into consideration. Mark the correct statements

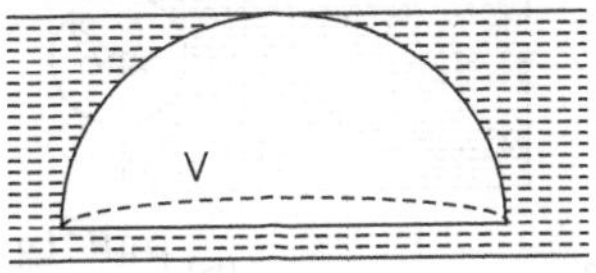

(a) Vertical hydrostatic force on the curved surface is given by $\frac{\pi\rho g R^3}{3}$

(b) Vertical hydrostatic force on the curved surface is given by $\frac{2\pi\rho g R^3}{3}$

(c) Horizontal hydrostatic force on right half of curved surface $\frac{4}{3}\rho g R^3$

(d) Horizontal hydrostatic force on right half of curved surface $\frac{(3\pi - 4)\rho g R^3}{6}$

9 A light cylindrical tube T of length l and radius r containing air is inverted in water (density d). One end of the tube is open and the other is closed. A block B of density $2d$ is kept on the tube as shown in the figure. The tube stays in equilibrium in the position shown. (Assume the atmospheric pressure is to be p_0) Pick up the correct statement(s). (Neglect mass of tube and mass of air enclosed)

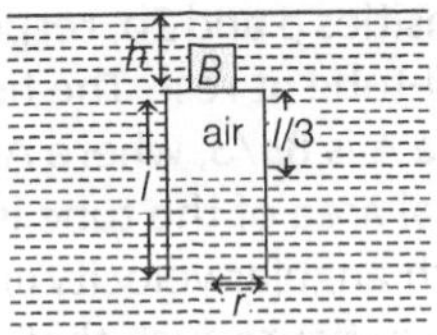

(a) The volume of block B is $\frac{\pi r^2 l}{3}$

(b) The volume of block B is $\frac{2\pi r^2 l}{3}$

(c) The pressure of air trapped in the tube is $p_0 + dg\left(h + \frac{l}{3}\right)$

(d) The pressure of air trapped in the tube is $p_0 + dg\left(h + \frac{2l}{3}\right)$

10 A cylinder container has an irregular shaped dent on the side wall of container due to which its volume decreases by V. Container is filled completely with a liquid of density ρ (here in the options below, side wall refers to all the curved and dent part of the cylinder). Then,

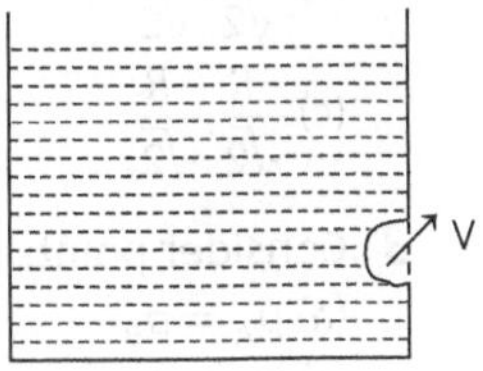

(a) force on liquid due to side wall may be greater or equal to $V\rho g$ depending on location of dent.

(b) force on liquid due to side wall is always equal to $V\rho g$.

(c) force on liquid due to side wall is independent of shape of dent provided volume reduction due to dent remains same.

(d) force on liquid due to side wall is dependent on shape of dent, even if volume reduction due to dent remains constant.

11 A small solid ball of density ρ is held inside at point A of a cubical container of side L, filled with an ideal liquid of density 4ρ as shown. The container is closed at the top. Now, if the container starts moving with constant acceleration 'a' horizontally and the ball is released from point A, simultaneously. Then,

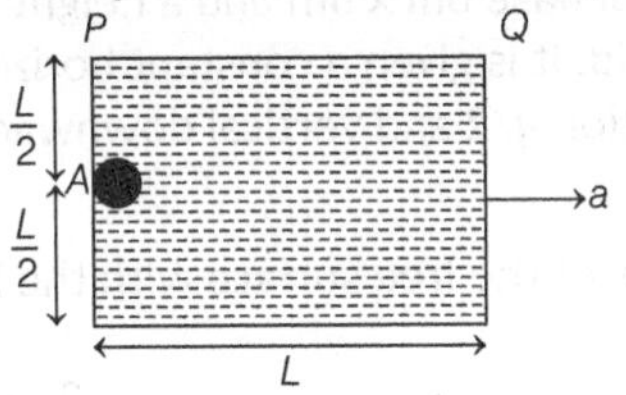

(a) for the ball to hit top of container at end Q, $a = 3g$

(b) for the ball to hit top of container at end Q, $a = 2g$

(c) ball hits the top of container at end Q after a time $t = \sqrt{\frac{L}{3g}}$

(d) ball hits the top of container at end Q after a time $t = \sqrt{\frac{L}{2g}}$

Comprehension Based Questions

Comprehension-1

A hollow sphere is completely filled with a liquid having a density ρ. The radius of sphere is R. Now, sphere is pulled with a constant horizontal acceleration of g on a horizontal surface. Take, centre of sphere as origin of co-ordinate system as shown in the figure.

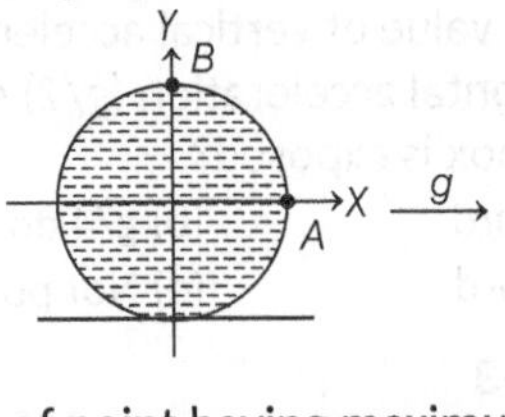

1 Co-ordinate of point having maximum pressure is

(a) $\frac{R}{\sqrt{2}}, \frac{R}{\sqrt{2}}$ (b) $\frac{R}{2}, \frac{R}{2}$ (c) $\frac{-R}{\sqrt{2}}, \frac{-R}{\sqrt{2}}$ (d) $\frac{-R}{2}, \frac{-R}{2}$

2 Co-ordinate of point having minimum pressure is

(a) $\frac{R}{\sqrt{2}}, \frac{R}{\sqrt{2}}$ (b) $\frac{R}{2}, \frac{R}{2}$

(c) $\frac{-R}{\sqrt{2}}, \frac{-R}{\sqrt{2}}$ (d) $\frac{-R}{2}, \frac{-R}{2}$

3 Consider points A and B as shown in figure

(a) $p_A = p_B$ (b) $p_A > p_B$

(c) $p_B > p_A$ (d) $p_A = p_B = 0$

Comprehension - 2

If the container filled with liquid gets accelerated horizontally or vertically, pressure in liquid gets changed. In case of horizontally accelerated liquid (a_x), the free surface has the slope a_x/g. In case of vertically accelerated liquid (a_y) for calculation of pressure, effective g is used. A closed box with horizontal base 6m × 6m and a height 2 m is half filled with liquid. It is given a constant horizontal acceleration $g/2$ and vertical downward acceleration $g/2$.

4 The angle of the free surface with the horizontal is equal to

(a) 30° (b) $\tan^{-1}\frac{2}{3}$

(c) $\tan^{-1}\frac{1}{3}$ (d) 45°

5 Length of exposed portion of top of box is equal to

(a) 2 m (b) 3 m (c) 4 m (d) 2.5 m

6 Water pressure at the bottom of centre of box is equal to

(atmospheric pressure $= 10^5 \text{N/m}^2$ density of water $= 1000 \text{kg/m}^3, g = 10 \text{m/s}^2$)

(a) 1.1 MPa (b) 0.11 MPa

(c) 0.104 MPa (d) 0.014 MPa

7 Maximum value of water pressure in the box is equal to

(a) 1.4 MPa (b) 0.14 MPa

(c) 0.104 MPa (d) 0.014 MPa

8 What is the value of vertical acceleration of box for given horizontal acceleration ($g/2$) so that no part of bottom of box is exposed?

(a) g/2 upward (b) g/4 downward

(c) g/4 upward (d) Not possible

Comprehension-3

A cylinder of radius R is kept embedded along the wall of a dam as shown. Take density of water as ρ. Take length as L.

9 The vertical force exerted by water on the cylinder is

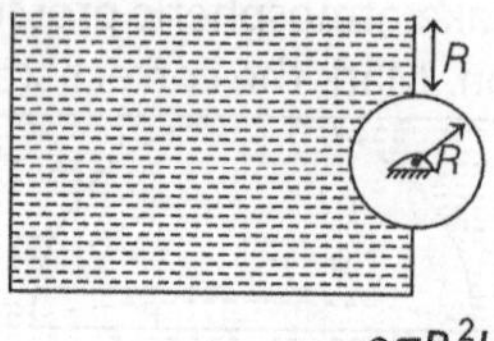

(a) $\rho\pi R^2 Lg$ (b) $\frac{\rho\pi R^2 Lg}{2}$

(c) zero (d) None of these

10 The net torque exerted by liquid on the cylinder is

(a) $\frac{2\rho R^2 Lg}{3}$ (b) $\frac{\rho R^2 Lg}{3}$

(c) $\frac{\rho R^2 Lg}{2}$ (d) 0

11 The force exerted by liquid on the cylinder in horizontal direction is (neglecting atmospheric pressure).

(a) $2R^2\rho Lg$ (b) $R^2\rho Lg$

(c) $4R^2\rho Lg$ (d) $1.61\, R^2\rho Lg$

Comprehension - 4

A U-tube containing two different liquids of density ρ and 2ρ is fixed vertically on a rotating table as shown in the figure. Initially, table is at rest and table can rotate about a vertical axis passing through the centre of the table. The interface of two liquids of densities ρ and 2ρ, respectively lies at the point A in a U-tube at rest. The height of liquid column above A is $8a/3$, where $AB = 2a$. The cross-sectional area of the tube is S. Now, the table is whirled with angular velocity ω about a vertical axis as shown in figure such that the interface of the liquids shifts towards B by $2a/3$, then at this instant,

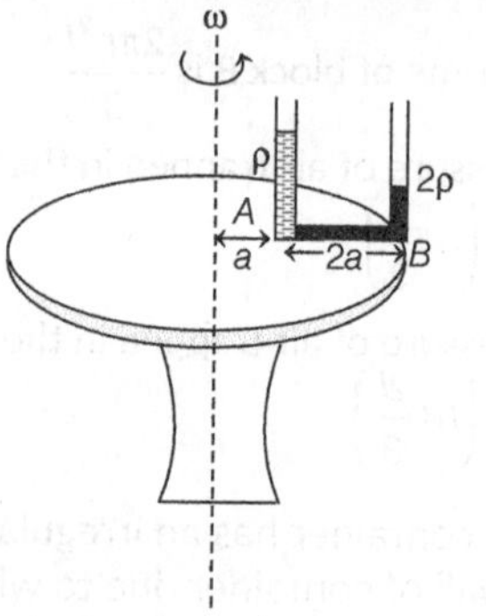

12 find $p_B - p_A$.

(a) ρga (b) $2\rho ga$

(c) $3\rho ga$ (d) $4\rho ga$

13 find the value of ω.

(a) $\sqrt{\frac{9g}{4a}}$ (b) $\sqrt{\frac{9g}{32a}}$

(c) $\sqrt{\frac{9g}{8a}}$ (d) $\sqrt{\frac{9g}{16a}}$

14 find the force exerted by liquid of ρ on liquid of 2ρ at the interface.

(a) $\rho Sag\left(\frac{9}{4}\right)$ (b) $\rho Sag\left(\frac{29}{3}\right)$

(c) $\rho Sag\left(\frac{9}{10}\right)$ (d) $\rho Sag\left(\frac{29}{10}\right)$

Comprehension - 5

A cone made of a material of relative density 27/64 and height 4 m floats with its apex downwards in water.

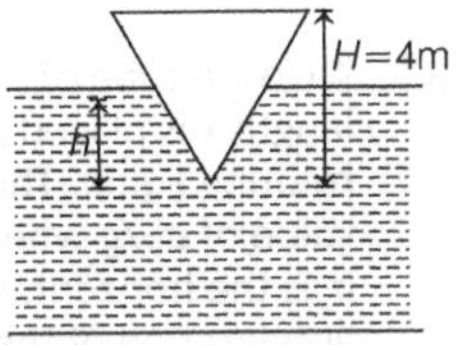

15 The submerged height h is

(a) 3 m (b) 4 m

(c) 2 m (d) None of these

16 The time period of vertical SHM, if it is slightly displaced from equilibrium position ($g = 10\ \text{m/s}^2$)

(a) 1 s (b) 1.98 s

(c) 2 s (d) 2.98 s

17 If the above whole arrangement starts falling with an acceleration equal to g, then

(a) time period of SHM remain same

(b) time period of SHM increases

(c) time period of SHM decreases

(d) None of the above

Comprehension - 6

A cylindrical container of height 7 m and radius 2 m is given some angular velocity ω such that the liquid rises 1 m above the original level. The liquid is filled upto height 5 m. Then,

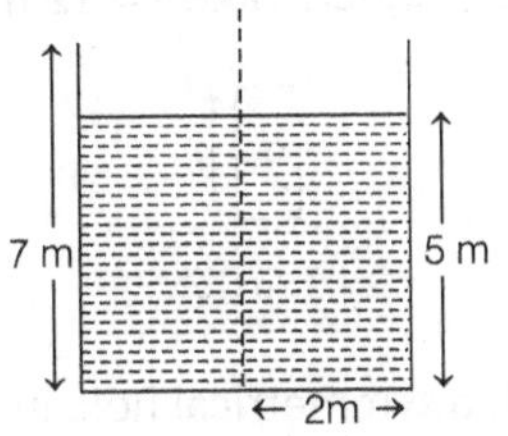

18 The minimum height of the liquid from the base of the container

(a) 3 m (b) 4 m

(c) 5 m (d) 6 m

19 The angular velocity ω is

(a) $\sqrt{5}$ rad/s (b) $\sqrt{10}$ rad/s

(c) $\sqrt{20}$ rad/s (d) $\sqrt{40}$ rad/s

20 The rise in height of the liquid at the ends with respect to the vertex of the liquid

(a) 2 m (b) 3 m

(c) 4 m (d) None of these

Match The Columns Questions

1 A rectangular tank 1.5 m wide, 3 m long and 1.8 m deep contains water to a depth of 1.2 m. Find the horizontal acceleration which may be imparted to the tank in the direction of its length, so that ($g = 10\ \text{m/s}^2$)

	Column-I		Column-II
(A)	There is just no spilling of water from the tank (m/s^2)	(P)	1.35
(B)	The front bottom corner of the tank is just exposed (m/s^2)	(Q)	12
(C)	The bottom of the tank is exposed upto its mid-point (m/s^2)	(R)	4
(D)	Calculate the volume of water (in m^3) that would spill out from the tank in the case (B).	(S)	6

2 A cubical box is completely filled with mass m of a liquid and is given horizontal acceleration a as shown in the figure. Match the force due to fluid pressure on the faces of the cube with their appropriate values (assume zero pressure as minimum pressure)

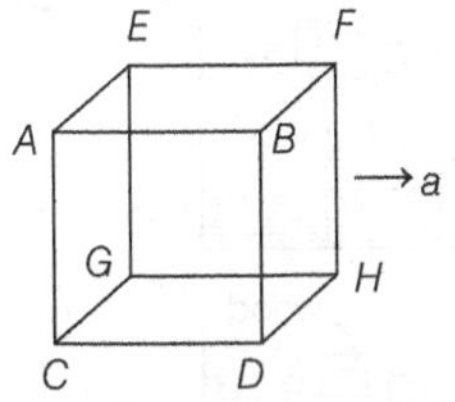

	Column I		Column II
(A)	Force on face ABFE	(P)	$ma/2$
(B)	Force on face BFHD	(Q)	$mg/2$
(C)	Force on face ACGE	(R)	$\frac{ma}{2}+\frac{mg}{2}$
(D)	Force on face CGHD	(S)	$\frac{ma}{2}+mg$
		(T)	$ma+\frac{mg}{2}$

3 Shown below is a cylinder of radius R floating in vessel containing liquids A and B. Neglecting atmospheric pressure match the quantities mentioned in column I with corresponding expression in column II.

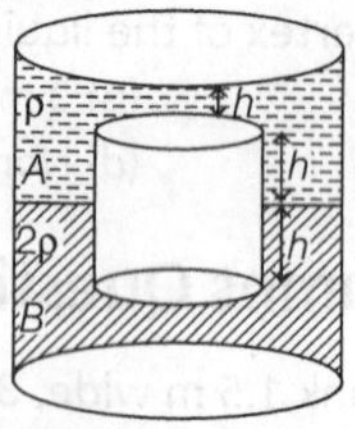

	Column I		Column II
(A)	Net force exerted by liquid A of density ρ on the cylinder	(P)	$9\rho gRh^2$
(B)	Net force exerted by liquid B of density 2ρ on the cylinder	(Q)	$\pi\rho gR^2h$
(C)	Net force exerted by liquids A and B on the left half of the curved part of cylinder	(R)	$4\pi\rho gR^2h$
(D)	Net force exerted by liquid A and B on the cylinder.	(S)	$3\pi\rho gR^2h$

4 When ice melts completely, level of liquid in which ice is submerged.

	Column I		Column II
(A)	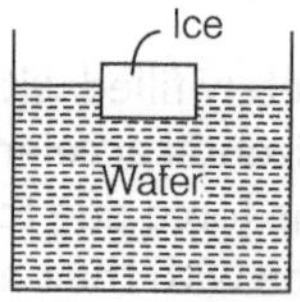	(P)	Increases
(B)	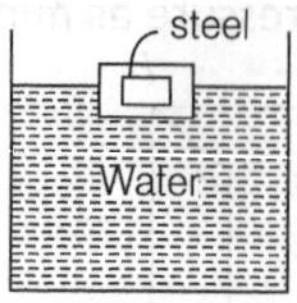	(Q)	Decreases
(C)	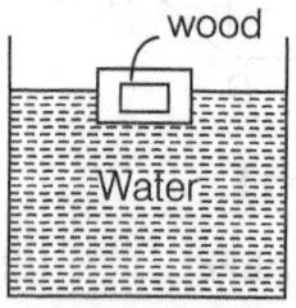	(R)	Remains same
(D)	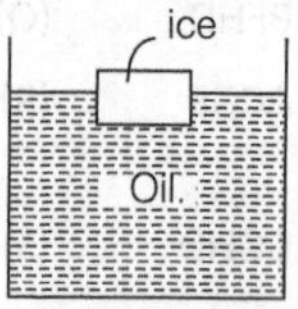 Density of oil is greater than density of ice	(S)	May increase or decrease

5 Match the following column.

	Column-I		Column-II
(A)	A cube of mass m and density σ is pulled by a force $\mathbf{F} = mg\hat{\mathbf{i}}$ in an accelerating liquid of density ρ. The value of a_x/a_y is 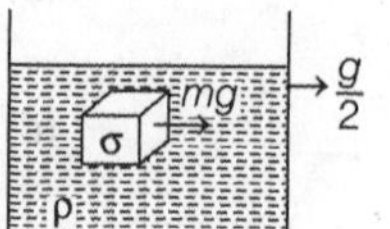	(P)	$\dfrac{\rho}{\sigma}$
(B)	The sphere of mass m is pulled horizontally by a force $F_x = mg$ in a non-accelerating liquid. The value of a_x/a_y is 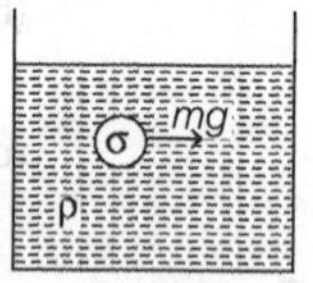	(Q)	1:1
(C)	A closed tube of length x is placed in a rotating liquid. The value of a_x/g where a_x is the horizontal acceleration of the cube, is 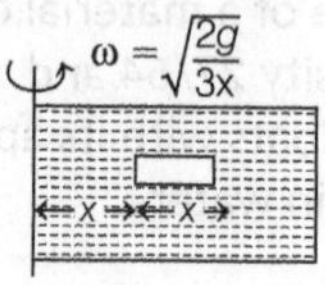	(R)	$\dfrac{\sigma}{\rho-\sigma}$
(D)	The string of a pendulum makes an angle θ with vertical, when the cart moves with an acceleration a. If the cart is filled with liquid of density $\rho<\sigma$ (density of the bob), the value of the angle of inclination with the vertical becomes θ'. Then $\tan\theta'/\tan\theta$ is  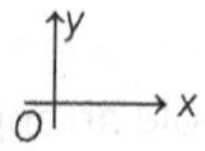	(S)	$\dfrac{2\sigma+\rho}{2(\sigma-\rho)}$

Numerical Value Questions

1 A uniform vertical cylinder is released from rest with its lower end just touching the liquid surface of a deep lake. Calculate the maximum displacement (in m) of the cylinder. Take, $l = 12$ m, $\dfrac{\sigma}{\rho} = \dfrac{1}{3}$

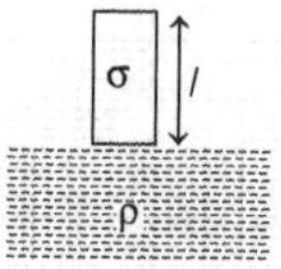

2 A vessel with a symmetrical hole in its bottom is fastened on a cart. The mass of the vessel and the cart is 1.5 kg. With what force F(in N) should the cart be pulled so that the maximum amount of water remains in the vessel? The dimensions of the vessel are as shown in figure. Given, that $b = 50$ cm, $c = 10$ cm, area of base $A = 40\text{ cm}^2$, $L = 20$ cm, $g = \text{m/s}^2$.

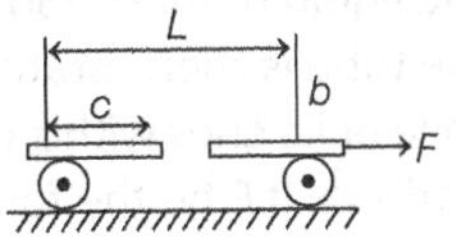

3 The horizontal part of the U-shaped tube shown in the figure is 10 cm, and its vertical branches are long enough. The cross-section of the tube is 1 cm^2. First, 20 cm^3 water is poured into the tube, then 20 cm^3 oil is poured into the left branch. (density of water = 1000 kg/m^3, density of oil = 800 kg/m^3), The whole system is accelerated towards the left, at an acceleration of $a = 10\text{ m/s}^2$. Determine the difference between the level of water and the level of oil (in cm).

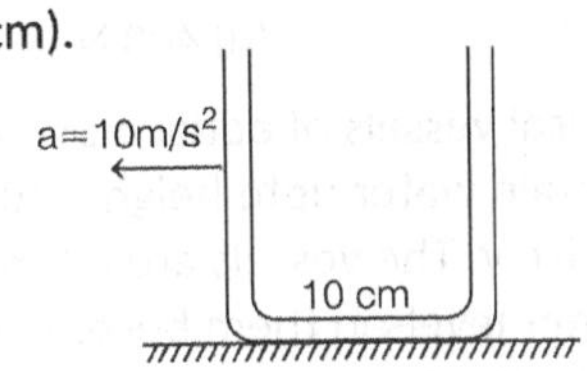

4 As the drawing illustrates, a pond full of water has the shape of an inverted cone with the tip sliced off and has a depth of 30 m. The atmospheric pressure above the pond is 1.0×10^5 Pa. The circular top surface (radius $= R_2$) and circular bottom surface (radius $= R_1$) of the pond are both parallel to the ground. The magnitude of the force acting on the top surface is the same as the magnitude of the force acting on the bottom surface. Obtain R_2/R_1.

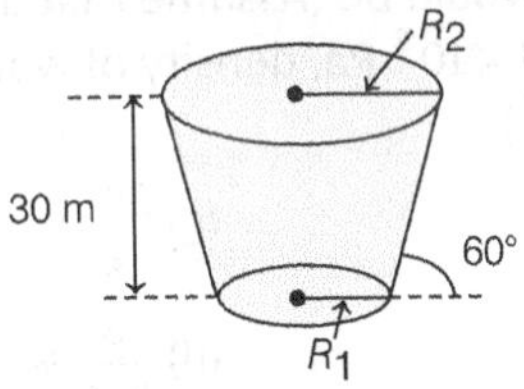

5 A vertical glass tube of length $l = 2$ m is open both the ends. It is immersed in water in vertical position. After lifting it out while we close the upper end with a finger, we find that half the length of the tube is filled with water. What was the length of air column (in cm) before lifting out? (Take, $p_{atm} = 10^5\text{ N/m}^2$ and neglect surface tension).

6 A cylindrical wooden float whose base area is 4 m^2 and height 1 m drifts on the water surface in vertical position. Density of wood is 500 kg/m^3 and that of water is 1000 kg/m^3, What minimum work (in kJ) must be performed to take the float out of the water?

7 We have a vessel in shape of a cuboid partially filled with water. Its base is square with an area of 5 dm^2 and vessel contains water upto 20 cm height. Then, we place a wooden cube inside water. The wood has mass of 4 kg and specific gravity 0.5. The base of wooden cube is horizontal. Find the height (in cm) of water level above the base.

8 A conical cup of height b, semi-vertical angle α rests open end down on a flat surface as shown. The cup is filled to height H with liquid of density ρ and a small hole is punched at the apex of the cone. The upward lifting force on the cup is

$$F = \pi\rho g\left[bH^2 - \frac{H^3}{n}\right]\tan^2\alpha, \text{ then } n \text{ is.}$$

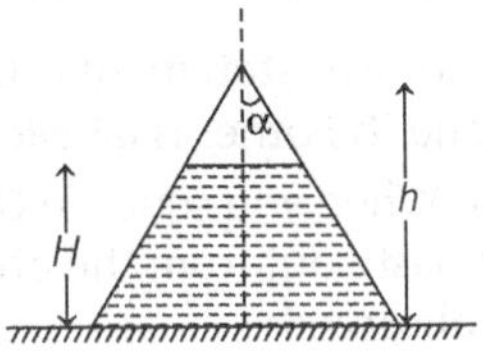

9 Schematic cross-sectional view of dam gate is shown in the figure. Find value of $\left(\frac{h}{l}\right)^2$, such that water is not allowed to flow?

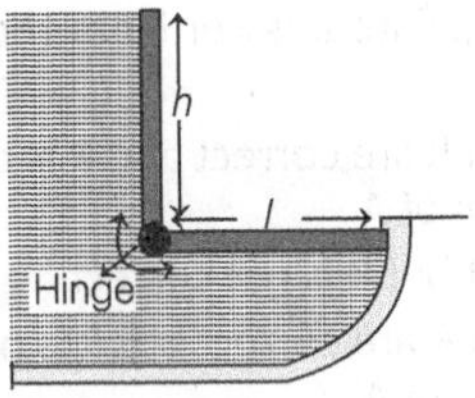

10 Figure shows a metal ball suspended by thread of negligible mass from an upright cylinder that floats partially submerged in water. The cylinder has height 6 cm, face area 11 cm^2 on the top and bottom and density 0.5g/cm^3. 4 cm of cylinder's height is inside the water surface. If density of the metal ball is 8 gm/cm^3, then its radius is equal to $\left(\frac{3}{x}\right)^{1/3}$ cm.

Calculate x. ($\rho_w = 1\text{g/cm}^3$)

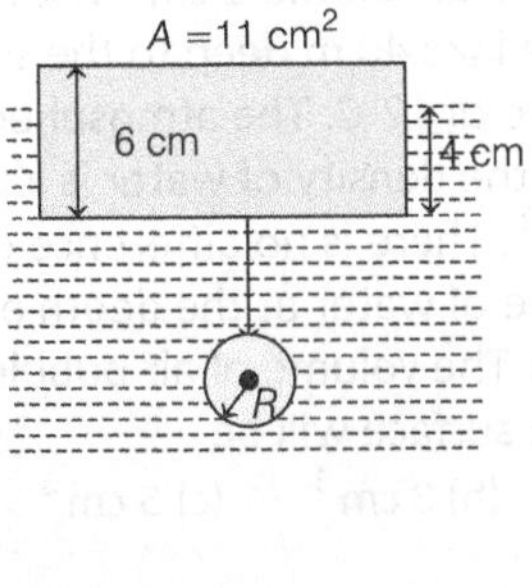

Previous Years Questions

JEE Main

1 Given below are two statements :

Statement I Pressure in a reservoir of water is same at all points at the same level of water.

Statement II The pressure applied to enclosed water is transmitted in all directions equally.

In the light of the above statements, choose the correct answer from the options given below : **[2023, 10 April Shift-I]**

(a) Both Statement I and Statement II are false
(b) Statement I is false but Statement II is true
(c) Both Statement I and Statement II are true
(d) Statement I is true but Statement II is false

2 Given below are two statements : One is labelled as **Assertion A** and the other is labelled as **Reason R**

Assertion A When you squeeze One end of a tube to get toothpaste out from the other end, Pascal's principle is observed.

Reason R A change in the pressure applied to enclosed incompressible fluid is transmitted undiminished to every portion of the fluid and to the walls of its container.

In the light of the above statements, choose the most appropriate answer from the options given below **[2023, 6 April Shift-II]**

(a) Both A and R are correct and R is the correct explanation of A
(b) A is correct but R is not correct
(c) Both A and R are correct but R is not the correct explanation of A
(d) A is not correct but R is correct

3 A hydraulic automobile lift is designed to lift vehicles of mass 5000 kg. The area of cross-section of the cylinder carrying the load is 250 cm^2. The maximum pressure the smaller piston would have to bear is (Assume $g = 10\ m/s^2$) **[2023, 8 April Shift-II]**

(a) $2 \times 10^{+5}$ Pa (b) $200 \times 10^{+6}$ Pa
(c) $20 \times 10^{+6}$ Pa (d) $2 \times 10^{+6}$ Pa

4 An air bubble of volume 1 cm^3 rises from the bottom of a lake 40 m deep to the surface at a temperature of 12°C. The atmospheric pressure is 1×10^5 Pa, the density of water is 1000 kg/m^3 and $g = 10\ m/s^2$. There is no difference of the temperature of water at the depth of 40 m and on the surface. The volume of air bubble when it reaches the surface will be **[2023, 8 April Shift-I]**

(a) 4 cm^3 (b) 3 cm^3 (c) 5 cm^3 (d) 2 cm^3

5 A tube of length 50 cm is filled completely with an incompressible liquid of mass 250 g and closed at both ends. The tube is then rotated in horizontal plane about one of its ends with a uniform angular velocity $x\sqrt{F}$ rad s^{-1}. If F be the force exerted by the liquid at the other end, then the value of x will be .... **[2022, 29 July Shift-II]**

6 A pressure-pump has a horizontal tube of cross-sectional area 10 cm^2 for the outflow of water at a speed of 20 m/s. The force exerted on the vertical wall just infront of the tube which stops water horizontally flowing out of the tube, is (given, density of water = 1000 kg/m^3) **[2022, 28 July Shift-II]**

(a) 300 N (b) 500 N
(c) 250 N (d) 400 N

7 Two cylindrical vessels of equal cross-sectional area 16 cm^2 contain water upto heights 100 cm and 150 cm, respectively. The vessels are interconnected so that the water levels in them become equal. The work done by the force of gravity during the process, is (Take, density of water = 10^3 kg/m^3 and $g = 10\ ms^{-2}$) **[2022, 27 July Shift-I]**

(a) 0.25 J (b) 1 J
(c) 8 J (d) 12 J

8 The pressure acting on a submarine is 3×10^5 Pa at a certain depth. If the depth is doubled, the percentage increase in the pressure acting on the submarine would be (Assume that atmospheric pressure is 1×10^5 Pa, density of water is 10^3 kg m^{-3}, $g = 10\ ms^{-2}$) **[2021, 16 March Shift-I]**

(a) $\frac{200}{3}\%$ (b) $\frac{200}{5}\%$
(c) $\frac{5}{200}\%$ (d) $\frac{3}{200}\%$

9 A hydraulic press can lift 100 kg when a mass m is placed on the smaller piston. It can lift ...... kg when the diameter of the larger piston is increased by 4 times and that of the smaller piston is decreased by 4 times keeping the same mass m on the smaller piston. **[2021, 24 Feb Shift-I]**

10 An air bubble of radius 1 cm in water has an upward acceleration 9.8 cm s^{-2}. The density of water is 1 g/cm^3 and water offers negligible drag force on the bubble. The mass of the bubble is (Take, $g = 980\ cm/s^2$) **[2020, 4 Sep Shift-I]**

(a) 1.52 g (b) 4.51 g
(c) 4.15 g (d) 3.15 g

11 A hollow spherical shell at outer radius R floats just submerged under the water surface. The inner radius of the shell is r. If the specific gravity of the shell material is $\frac{27}{8}$ with respect to water, value of r is

[2020, 5 Sep Shift-I]

(a) $\frac{8}{9}R$ (b) $\frac{1}{3}R$ (c) $\frac{2}{3}R$ (d) $\frac{4}{9}R$

JEE Advanced

1 A cylindrical tube, with its base as shown in the figure, is filled with water. It is moving down with a constant acceleration a along a fixed inclined plane with angle $\theta = 45°$. p_1 and p_2 are pressures at points 1 and 2, respectively, located at the base of the tube. Let $\beta = (p_1 - p_2)/(\rho g d)$, where ρ is density of water, d is the inner diameter of the tube and g is the acceleration due to gravity. Which of the following statement(s) is(are) correct? **(2021)**

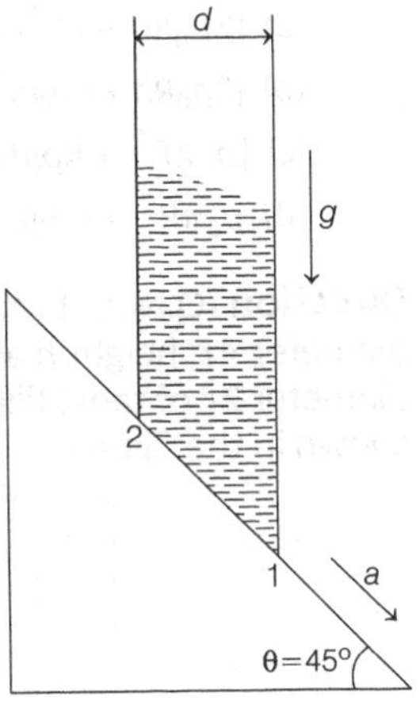

(a) $\beta = 0$, when $a = g/\sqrt{2}$

(b) $\beta > 0$, when $a = g/\sqrt{2}$

(c) $\beta = \frac{\sqrt{2}-1}{\sqrt{2}}$, when $a = g/2$

(d) $\beta = \frac{1}{\sqrt{2}}$, when $a = g/2$

2 An open-ended U-tube of uniform cross-sectional area contains water (density 10^3 kg m^{-3}). Initially the water level stands at 0.29 m from the bottom in each arm. Kerosene oil (a water-immiscible liquid) of density 800 kg m^{-3} is added to the left arm until its length is 0.1 m, as shown in the schematic figure below. The ratio (h_1/h_2) of the heights of the liquid in the two arms is **(2020)**

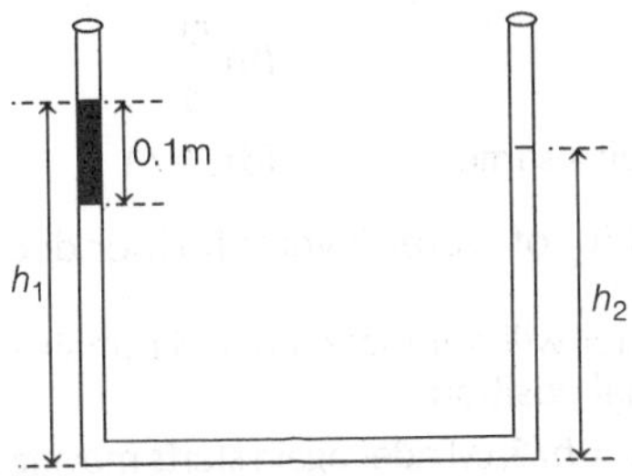

(a) $\frac{15}{14}$ (b) $\frac{35}{33}$ (c) $\frac{7}{6}$ (d) $\frac{5}{4}$

3 A hot air balloon is carrying some passengers, and a few sandbags of mass 1 kg each so that its total mass is 480 kg. Its effective volume giving the balloon its buoyancy is V. The balloon is floating at an equilibrium height of 100 m. When N number of sandbags are thrown out, the balloon rises to a new equilibrium height close to 150 m with its volume V remaining unchanged. If the variation of the density of air with height h from the ground is

$pho(h) = \rho_0 e^{-\frac{h}{h_0}}$, where $\rho_0 = 1.25$ kg m^{-3} and $h_0 = 6000$ m, the value of N is ________. **(2020)**

4 A uniform cylinder of length L and mass M having cross-sectional area A is suspended, with its length vertical from a fixed point by a massless spring of force constant k such that it is half submerged in a liquid of density σ at equilibrium position. The extension x_0 of the spring when it is in equilibrium is **(2013)**

(a) $\frac{Mg}{k}$ (b) $\frac{Mg}{k}\left(1 - \frac{LA\sigma}{M}\right)$

(c) $\frac{Mg}{k}\left(1 - \frac{LA\sigma}{2M}\right)$ (d) $\frac{Mg}{k}\left(1 + \frac{LA\sigma}{M}\right)$

5 A solid sphere of radius R and density ρ is attached to one end of a massless spring of force constant k. The other end of the spring is connected to another solid sphere of radius R and density 3ρ. The complete arrangement is placed in a liquid of density 2ρ and is allowed to reach equilibrium. The correct statement(s) is (are) **(2013)**

(a) the net elongation of the spring is $\frac{4\pi R^3 \rho g}{3k}$

(b) the net elongation of the spring is $\frac{8\pi R^3 \rho g}{3k}$

(c) the light sphere is partially submerged

(d) the light sphere is completely submerged

6 A thin uniform cylindrical shell, closed at both ends, is partially filled with water. It is floating vertically in water in half-submerged state. If ρ_c is the relative density of the material of the shell with respect to water, then the correct statement is that the shell is **(2012)**

(a) more than half-filled if ρ_c is less than 0.5

(b) more than half-filled if ρ_c is more than 1.0

(c) half-filled if ρ_c is more than 0.5

(d) less than half-filled if ρ_c is less than 0.5

Direction (Q.Nos 7 to 9) A small spherical monoatomic ideal gas bubble $(\gamma = 5/3)$ is trapped inside a liquid of density ρ_l (see figure). Assume that the bubble does not exchange any heat with the liquid. The bubble contains n moles of gas. The temperature of the gas when the bubble is at the bottom is T_0, the height of the liquid is H and the atmospheric pressure is p_0 (Neglect surface tension)

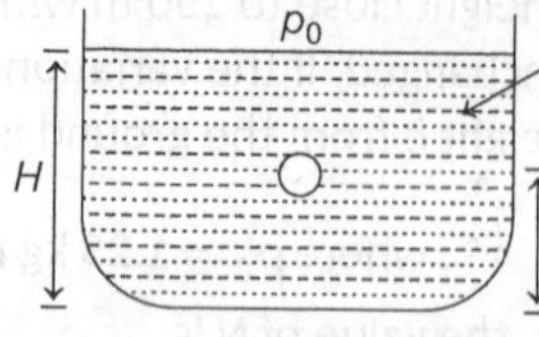

7 As the bubble moves upwards, besides the buoyancy force the following forces are acting on it. **(2008)**

(a) Only the force of gravity
(b) The force due to gravity and the force due to the pressure of the liquid
(c) The force due to gravity, the force due to the pressure of the liquid and the force due to viscosity of the liquid
(d) The force due to gravity and the force due to viscosity of the liquid

8 When the gas bubble is at a height y from the bottom, its temperature is **(2008)**

(a) $T_0\left(\dfrac{p_0+\rho_l gH}{p_0+\rho_l gy}\right)^{2/5}$ (b) $T_0\left(\dfrac{p_0+\rho_l g(H-y)}{p_0+\rho_l gH}\right)^{2/5}$

(c) $T_0\left(\dfrac{p_0+\rho_l gH}{p_0+\rho_l gy}\right)^{3/5}$ (d) $T_0\left(\dfrac{p_0+\rho_l g(H-y)}{p_0+\rho_l gH}\right)^{3/5}$

9 The buoyancy force acting on the gas bubble is (Assume R is the universal gas constant) **(2008)**

(a) $\rho_l nRgT_0\dfrac{(p_0+\rho_l gH)^{2/5}}{(p_0+\rho_l gy)^{2/5}}$

(b) $\dfrac{\rho_l nRgT_0}{(p_0+\rho_l gH)^{2/5}[p_0+\rho_l g(H-y)]^{3/5}}$

(c) $\rho_l nRgT_0\dfrac{(p_0+\rho_l gH)^{3/5}}{(p_0+\rho_l gy)^{8/5}}$

(d) $\dfrac{\rho_l nRgT_0}{(p_0+\rho_l gH)^{3/5}[p_0+\rho_l g(H-y)]^{2/5}}$

10 Water is filled up to a height h in a beaker of radius R as shown in the figure. The density of water is ρ, the surface tension of water is T and the atmospheric pressure is p_0. Consider a vertical section $ABCD$ of the water column through a diameter of the beaker. The force on water on one side of this section by water on the other side of this section has magnitude **(2007)**

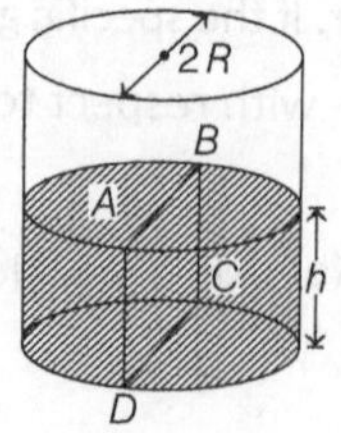

(a) $|2p_0Rh+\pi R^2\rho gh-2RT|$
(b) $|2p_0Rh+R\rho gh^2-2RT|$
(c) $|p_0\pi R^2+R\rho gh^2-2RT|$
(d) $|p_0\pi R^2+R\rho gh^2+2RT|$

Direction (Q.Nos. 11 to 13) A wooden cylinder of diameter $4r$, height h and density $\rho/3$ is kept on a hole of diameter $2r$ of tank, filled with liquid of density ρ as shown in the figure.

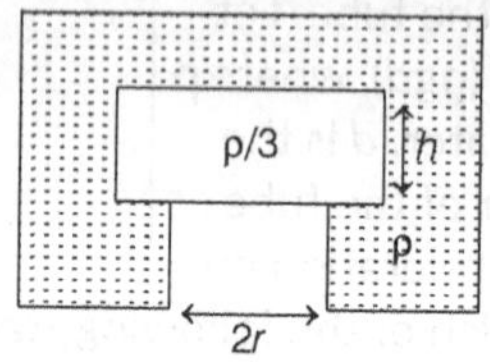

11 Now level of the liquid starts decreasing slowly. When the level of liquid is at a height h_1 above the cylinder the block starts moving up. At what value of h_1, will the block rise? **(2006)**

(a) $4h/9$ (b) $5h/9$
(c) $5h/3$ (d) Remains same

12 The block in the above question is maintained at the position by external means and the level of liquid is lowered. The height h_2 when this external force reduces to zero is **(2006)**

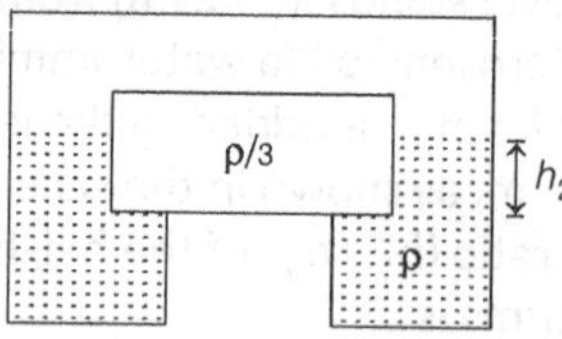

(a) $\dfrac{4h}{9}$ (b) $\dfrac{5h}{9}$
(c) Remains same (d) $2h/3$

13 If height h_2 of water level is further decreased, then **(2006)**

(a) cylinder will not move up and remains at its original position
(b) for $h_2=h/3$, cylinder again starts moving up
(c) for $h_2=h/4$, cylinder again starts moving up
(d) for $h_2=h/5$, cylinder again starts moving up

Answer Key

Level 1

7.1 Pressure Variation in a Static Liquid

1. $p_A = 1.08$ atm, $p_B = 1.31$ atm, $p_C = 2.04$ atm
2. 20 m
3. $7H$
4. 320 N
5. 9.6 cm
6. $p_A = p_{atm} - \rho_1 gl \sin\theta$; $p_B = p_{atm} + \rho_2 gh$; $\theta = \sin^{-1}\left(\frac{\rho_2 h}{(\rho_3 - \rho_1)l}\right)$

7.2 Fluid in Accelerated Vessels

1. La/g
2. $p_A = 0, p_B = \rho gH$, $p_C = \rho gH + \rho aL$, $p_D = \rho aL$
3. (a) 4 m/s^2 (b) 10% (c) zero, 4.5×10^4 Pa
4. (i) $\phi = \tan^{-1}\frac{a\cos\theta}{(g - a\sin\theta)}$ (ii) $\phi = \theta$
5. $H = \omega^2 L^2 / 2g$
6. (a) $\sqrt{40}$ rad/s (b) $\sqrt{60}$ rad/s

7.3 Hydrostatic Force

1. (a) $\frac{\rho gl h^2}{2}$ (b) $\frac{\rho glh^3}{6}$
2. (a) 6.25×10^6N, 10^7N (b) Total force $= 6.25 \times 10^6$N
3. $(p_0 + 2\rho gR)\pi R^2$
4. (a) 204 N (b) 1 N
5. (a) $\rho g\pi R^3/3$ (down) (b) $\rho g\pi R^3$ (upward) (c) 0 (d) $2\rho g\pi R^3/3$ (upward)

7.4 Buoyant Force

1. 10.7%
2. 10 cc
3. 80kg
4. 30g
5. 0.8
6. (a) 6kg (b) 7 kg
7. 4.8 cm
8. 865 kg/m^3
9. (a) 1/20 (b) 19/20
10. 2 cm
11. 10.4 cm
12. (a) 11.5 kg (b) 10.5 kg
13. remains unchanged (a) level rises (b) level falls
14. (a) 24 N, (b) 12 m/s^2
15. 45°

Level 2

Single Choice Correct Questions

1. (b)	2. (c)	3. (c)	4. (d)	5. (b)	6. (b)	7. (c)	8. (a)	9. (b)	10. (b)
11. (b)	12. (a)	13. (a)	14. (a)	15. (b)	16. (c)	17. (c)	18. (b)	19. (a)	20. (d)
21. (d)	22. (b)	23. (b)	24. (a)	25. (c)	26. (a)	27. (d)	28. (c)	29. (b)	30. (b)
31. (b)	32. (b)	33. (b)	34. (a)	35. (a)					

Numerical Value Questions

1. 10	2. 1.9	3. 100	4. 300	5. 3	6. 2	7. 2	8. 41

Level 3

Single Choice Correct Questions

1. (d)	2. (a)	3. (b)	4. (c)	5. (d)	6. (d)	7. (b)	8. (d)	9. (a)	10. (a)
11. (b)	12. (b)	13. (b)	14. (b)	15. (d)	16. (b)	17. (d)	18. (b)	19. (c)	20. (b)
21. (a)	22. (b)	23. (c)	24. (a)	25. (a)					

Multiple Choice(s) Correct Questions

1. (b,c)	2. (a,c)	3. (abcd)	4. (b,c)	5. (d)	6. (abc)	7. (bc)
8. (ad)	9. (ac)	10. (bc)	11. (bc)			

Comprehension Based Questions

1. (c)	2. (a)	3. (a)	4. (d)	5. (c)	6. (b)	7. (b)	8. (a)	9. (b)	10. (d)
11. (c)	12. (b)	13. (b)	14. (a)	15. (a)	16. (b)	17. (d)	18. (b)	19. (b)	20. (a)

Match the Columns Questions

1. A→ r; B→ s; C→ q; D→ p
2. A→ p; B→ q; C→ t; D→ s
3. A→ q; B→ r; C→ p; D→ s
4. A→ r; B→ q; C→ r; D→ q
5. A→ s; B→ r; C→ p; D→ q

Numerical Value Question

1. 8	2. 100	3. 6	4. 2	5. 90	6. 5	7. 28
8. 3	9. 3	10. 8				

Previous Years Questions

JEE Main

1. (c)	2. (a)	3. (d)	4. (c)	5. (4)	6. (d)	7. (b)
8. (a)	9. (25600)	10. (c)	11. (a)			

JEE Advanced

1. (a,c)	2. (b)	3. 4	4. (c)	5. (a, d)	6. (a)	7. (d)
8. (b)	9. (b)	10. (b)	11. (c)	12. (a)	13. (a)	

SOLUTIONS

Level 1

7.1 Pressure Variation in a Fluid

1. $p_A = p_0 + \rho_1 g h_A = 10^5 + 800 \times 10 \times 1 = 1.08$ atm

$p_B = p_0 + \rho_1 g h_1 + r_2 g h_B = 10^5 + 800 \times 10 \times 2$

$+1000 \times 10 \times 1.5 = 1.31$ atm

$p_C = p_0 + \rho_1 g h_1 + \rho_2 g h_2 + \rho_3 g h_3$

$= 10^5 + 8000 \times 10 \times 2 + 1000 \times 10 \times 2 + 13.6 \times 10^3 \times 10 \times 0.5$

$= 2.04$ atm

2. $p_0 + \rho g\left(\frac{h}{2}\right) = \frac{2}{3}(p_0 + \rho g h)$

$h = \frac{2p_0}{\rho g} = \frac{2 \times 10^5}{10^3 \times 10} = 20\text{m}$

3. $p_1 V_1 = p_2 V_2 \Rightarrow (p_0 + \rho g h)\frac{4}{3}\pi R^3 = p_0\left(\frac{4}{3}\pi (2R)^3\right)$

$h = \frac{7p_0}{\rho g} = \frac{7\rho g H}{\rho g} = 7\,H$

4. $p_1 = p_2$

$\Rightarrow p_0 + \frac{800 \times 10}{400 \times 10^{-4}} = p_0 + \frac{F}{25 \times 10^{-4}} + 900 \times 10 \times 8$

$\Rightarrow \quad F = 320$ N

5. $p_1 = p_2 \Rightarrow p_0 + 1.3g(10)$

$= p_0 + 0.8gh + 13.6g(10 - h)$

$\Rightarrow \; h = 9.6$ cm

6. $p_A = p_{atm} - \rho_1 g(l \sin\theta)$

$p_B = p_{atm} + \rho_2 g h$

$p_B = p_A + \rho_3 g(l \sin\theta)$

$\Rightarrow \quad (p_{atm} + \rho_2 g h) = (p_{atm} - \rho_1 g l \sin\theta) + \rho_3 g l \sin\theta$

$\Rightarrow \quad \theta = \sin^{-1}\left(\frac{\rho_2 h}{(l_3 - \rho_1)l}\right)$

7.2 Fluid in Accelerated Vessels

1.

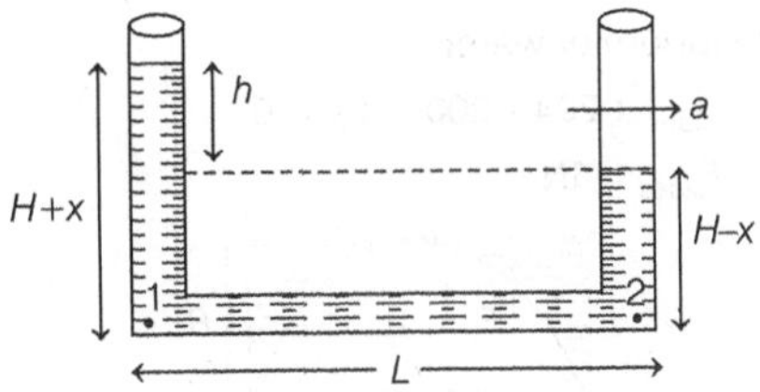

$p_1 = p_0 + \rho g(H + x), p_2 = p_0 + \rho g(h - x)$

$p_1 = p_2 + \rho a L$

$\Rightarrow \quad (p_0 + \rho g(H + x) = (p_0 + \rho g(H - x)) + \rho a L$

$\Rightarrow \quad x = \frac{aL}{2g}$

So, $h = (H + x) - (H - x) = 2x = \frac{aL}{g}$

2. Gauge pressure

at A, $p_A = 0$

at B, $p_B = p_A + \rho g H = \rho g H$

at C, $p_C = p_B + \rho a L = \rho(gH + aL)$

at D, $p_D = p_A + \rho a L = \rho a L$

3. (a) Initial volume of water $= 5 \times 2 \times 4 = 40\,\text{m}^3$

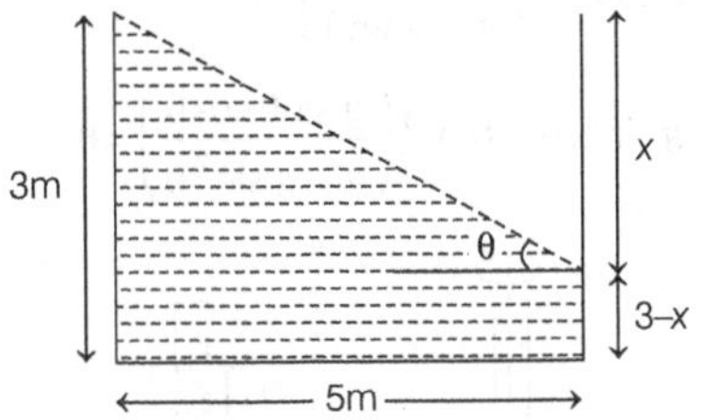

Volume of water $= \frac{1}{2}(3 + (3 - x))5 \times 4 = 40\,\text{m}^3$

$\Rightarrow \quad x = 2\,\text{m}$

$\tan\theta = \frac{x}{5} = \frac{a}{g} \Rightarrow a = \frac{2g}{5} = 4\,\text{m/s}^2$

(b) New acceleration $= 4 + 4 \times \frac{20}{100} = 4.8\,\text{m/s}^2$

$\tan\theta = \frac{x}{5} = \frac{4.8}{10} \Rightarrow x = 2.4\text{m}$

Volume of water retained $= \frac{1}{2}(3 + (3 - 2.4))(5) \times 4 = 36\text{m}^3$

Volume of water spilt out $= 40 - 36 = 4\,\text{m}^3$

% of water spilt out $= \frac{4}{40} \times 100 = 10\%$

(c) $\quad \tan\theta = \frac{a}{g} = \frac{9}{10} = \frac{y}{x} \Rightarrow y = \frac{9x}{10}$

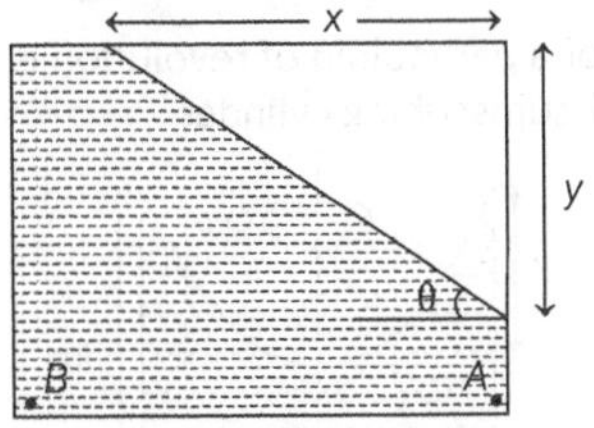

Empty volume $= \frac{1}{2}(x \times y)4 = 60 - 40$

$\Rightarrow \quad xy = 10$

$\Rightarrow \quad x\left(\frac{9x}{10}\right) = 10 \Rightarrow x = \frac{10}{3}\,\text{m and } y = 3\,\text{m}$

So, $\quad p_A = 0$

$p_B = p_A + \rho a(5) = 4.5 \times 10^4\,\text{Pa}$

4. (a)

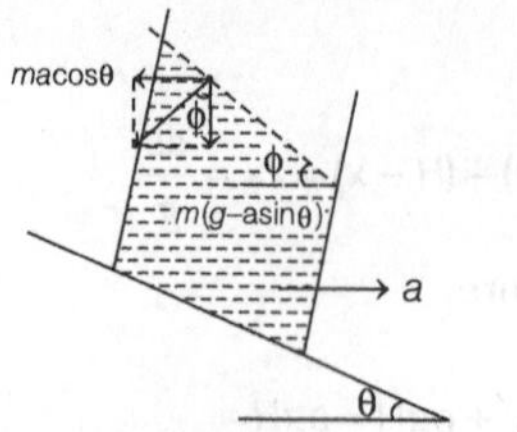

$$\tan\phi = \frac{ma\cos\theta}{mg - ma\sin\theta}$$

$$\phi = \tan^{-1}\left(\frac{a\cos\theta}{g - a\sin\theta}\right)$$

(b) If $a = g\sin\theta$, $\phi = \tan^{-1}\left(\frac{g\sin\theta\cos\theta}{g - g\sin^2\theta}\right) = \theta$

5.

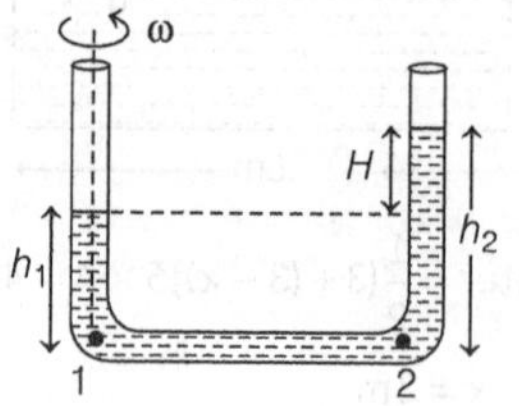

Along vertical,

$$p_1 = p_0 + \rho g h_1$$

and $\quad p_2 = p_0 + \rho g h_2$

Along horizontal,

$$\Delta p = \int_0^L \rho(\omega^2 x)dx$$

$$\Rightarrow \quad p_2 - p_1 = \frac{\rho\omega^2 L^2}{2}$$

$$\Rightarrow \quad (p_0 + \rho g h_2) - (p_0 + \rho g h_1) = \frac{\rho\omega^2 L^2}{2}$$

$$\Rightarrow \quad H = \frac{\omega^2 L^2}{2g}$$

6. (a) Volume of a paraboloid of revolution is half of the volume of circumscribing cylinder

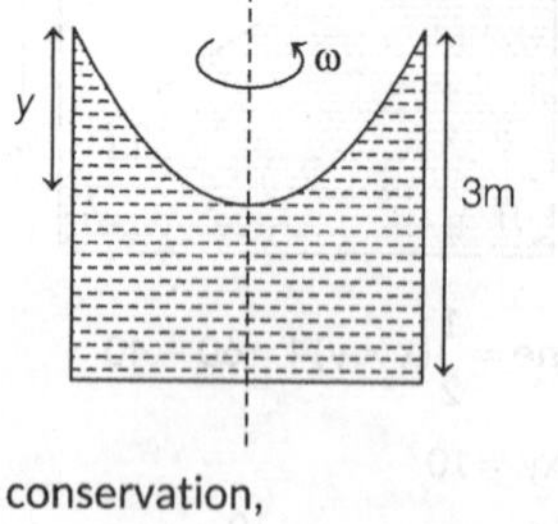

From volume conservation,

$$\pi R^2(2) = \pi R^2(3 - y) + \frac{1}{2}(\pi R^2 y) \Rightarrow y = 2\,\text{m}$$

The equator of parabolic surface

$$y = \frac{\omega^2 x^2}{2g} \Rightarrow 2 = \frac{\omega^2(1)^2}{2 \times 10} \Rightarrow \omega = \sqrt{40}\ \text{rad/s}$$

(b) $y = \frac{\omega^2 x^2}{2g} \Rightarrow 3 = \frac{\omega^2(1)^2}{2 \times 10} \Rightarrow \omega = \sqrt{60}\ \text{rad / s}$

7.3 Hydrostatic Force

1. (a) $dF = pdA = (\rho g y)(l dy)$

$$F = \int_0^h \rho g y l dy = \frac{\rho g l h^2}{2}$$

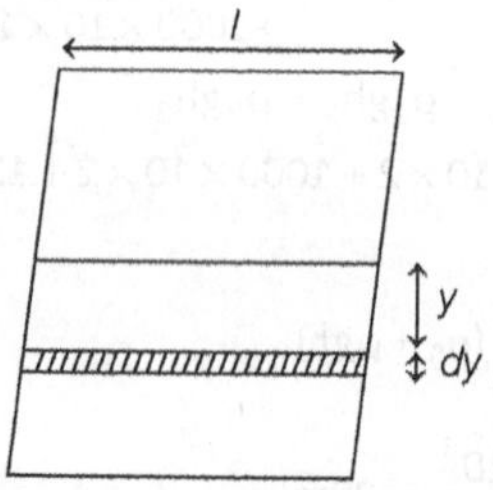

(b) $d\tau = dF(h - y)$

$$\Rightarrow \int d\tau = \int_0^h \rho g y l dy(h - y) = \frac{\rho g l h^3}{6}$$

2. $F_{AB} = p_C A = \left(p_0 + \frac{\rho g h_1}{2}\right) l h_1 = 6.25 \times 10^6\,\text{N}$

$$F_{BC} = p_C A = \left(p_0 + \rho g h_1 + (2\rho) g \frac{h_2}{2}\right) l h_2 = 10^7\,\text{N}$$

3. $F = p_C A = (p_0 + \rho g(2R))\pi R^2$

$$= (p_0 + 2\rho g R)\pi R^2$$

4. (a) $F = pA = (p_0 + \rho g h)A$

$$= (10^5 + 10^3(10)(0.2))(20 \times 10^{-4}) = 204\text{N}$$

(b) Resultant force due to sides of the glass on water will be upward.

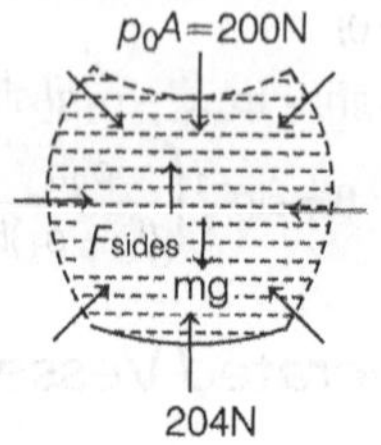

For equilibrium of water

$$F_{sides} + 204 - 200 - mg = 0$$

$$\Rightarrow \quad F_{sides} = 1\text{N}$$

5. (a)

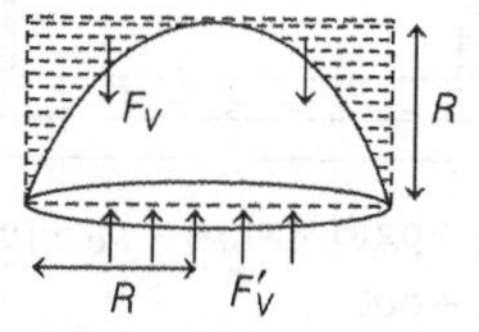

Vertical thrust of the liquid is equal to weight of the liquid column above the curved spherical surface.

$$F_V = \rho V g$$

where, V = Volume of cylinder - Volume of the hemisphere

$$= (\pi R^2)R - \frac{2}{3}\pi R^3 = \frac{\pi R^3}{3}$$

$$\text{So, } F_v = \frac{\rho\pi R^3 g}{3} \text{ (down)}$$

(b) $F_V' = PA = (\rho g R)\pi R^2 = \rho g \pi R^3$ (upward)

(c) Side thrust = 0

(d) Total hydrostatic force $= F_V' - F_1$

$$= \rho g \pi R^3 - \frac{\rho g \pi R^3}{3}$$

$$= \frac{2\rho g \pi R^3}{3} \text{ (upward)}$$

7.4 Buoyant Force

1. Fraction submerged $= \frac{\rho_{ice}}{\rho_w}$

Fraction outside $= 1 - \frac{\rho_{ice}}{\rho_w} = 1 - \frac{0.92}{1.03} = 10.7\%$

2. Apparent weight $= mg - B$

$\Rightarrow \quad 80\,g = 110g - 1(V)g \Rightarrow V = 30\text{cc}$

Volume of metal $= \frac{110}{5.5} = 20$ cc

Volume of cavity $= 30 - 20 = 10$ cc

3. $B = (M+m)g \Rightarrow 1000 \times \frac{120}{600} \times g = (120+m)g$

$\Rightarrow \quad m = 80\,\text{kg}$

4. Let volume of copper $= V_1$ and

Volume of gold $= V_2$

$10\,V_1 + 20\,V_2 = 50$

$V_1 + 2V_2 = 5$ ...(i)

$\Rightarrow$ Buoyant force = Loss in weight

$\Rightarrow \quad 1(V_1 + V_2)\,g = 50\,g - 46\,g$

$\Rightarrow \quad V_1 + V_2 = 4$ ...(ii)

Solving Eqs. (i) and (ii), we get

$V_1 = 3$ and $V_2 = 1$

Mass of copper $= 10\,V_1 = 10\,(3) = 30$ g

5. $B = (M+m)g$

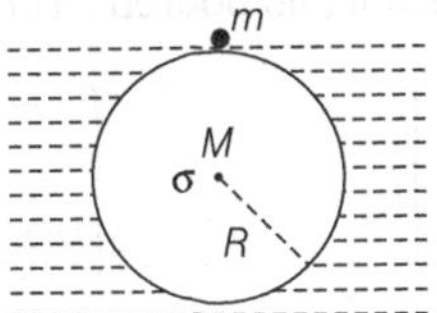

$$\Rightarrow \quad 1\left(\frac{4}{3}\pi(5)^3\right)g = \left[\left(\sigma\frac{4}{3}\pi(5)^3\right) + 100\right]g$$

$\Rightarrow \quad \sigma = 0.8$

6. (a) $B_1 = (m_1 + m_2)g$

$$\Rightarrow 1000\left(0.9 \times \frac{12}{600}\right)g = (12+m)g \Rightarrow m = 6\,\text{kg}$$

(b) $B_1 + B_2 = (m_1 + m_2)\,g$

$$\Rightarrow \quad 1000\left(0.9 \times \frac{12}{600}\right)g + 1000\left(\frac{m}{7000}\right)g = (12+m)g$$

$\Rightarrow \quad m = 7\,\text{kg}$

7. Let external edge of the box $= L$

mass of box $= \rho V = 8000 \times (6L^2) \times 1 \times 10^{-3}$

$B = mg \Rightarrow 1000 \times L^3 \times g$

$= 8000 \times (6L^2) \times 1 \times 10^{-3} \times g$

$\Rightarrow \quad L = 4.8$ cm

8.

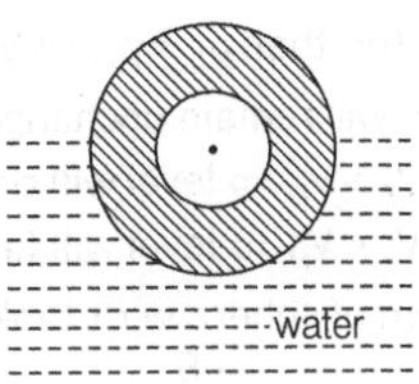

$B = mg$

$$\Rightarrow \quad \rho_w \frac{2}{3}\pi R^3 g = \sigma\left(\frac{4}{3}\pi R^3 - \frac{4}{3}\pi r^3\right)g$$

$$\Rightarrow \quad \sigma = \frac{\rho_w R^3}{2(R^3 - r^3)} = 865\,\text{kg/m}^3$$

9. (a) $p_A = p_0$ as top is exposed to atmosphere.

(b) $p_B = p_o$ + (Pressure due to weight of cylinder)

$$= p_o + \frac{mg}{s}$$

(c) $p_c = p_o + \rho g h$

If the system is in a state of free fall, then $g_{eff} = 0$ and $p_A = p_B = p_c = p_0$

10. Let height of the cube submerged inside water is h.

$B_1 + B_2 = mg$

$\Rightarrow \quad 1 \times (10^2 h) \times g + 0.6(10^2(10-h)g = 680g$

$\Rightarrow \quad h = 2$ cm

11. Initially block floats with one fifth volume submerged in side mercury.

$$B = mg \Rightarrow \rho_{Hg}\left(\frac{V}{5}\right)g = \rho_s V g$$

$$\Rightarrow \quad \rho_s = \frac{13.6}{5}\,\text{gm/cc}$$

Let height of water column $= h$

$B_1 + B_2 = mg$

$$\Rightarrow \quad 13.6(12 \times 12 \times (12-h))g + 1(12 \times 12 \times h) = \left(\frac{13.6}{5}\right)(12)^3 g$$

$\Rightarrow \quad h = 10.4$ cm

12. (a) Reading of spring balance = Total weight of system

$$= 10g + 1.5g = 11.5\text{ kg}$$

(b) Reading of spring balance = Weight of bucket of water + Buoyant force on water due to iron piece

$$= 10g + 1000\left(\frac{1}{2} \times \frac{7.8}{7800}\right)g$$

$$= 10.5\text{ kgf}$$

13. Let mass of ice block = M

V_D = Volume of the liquid displaced by block $= \frac{M}{\rho_L}$

V_F = Volume of water formed on melting $= \frac{M}{\rho_w}$

If the liquid is water, then $\rho_L = \rho_w \Rightarrow V_F = V_D$

So, level of water will remain unchanged.

(a) If $\rho_L > \rho_w \Rightarrow V_F > V_D \Rightarrow$ level will rise.

(b) If $\rho_L < \rho_w \Rightarrow V_F < V_D \Rightarrow$ level will fall.

14. (a) For equilibrium of sphere w.r.t tank,

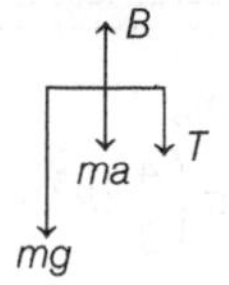

$$B = mg + ma + T$$

$$\Rightarrow \quad \rho V(g + a) = 2(g + a) + T$$

$$\Rightarrow \quad 1000 \times \frac{2}{500} \times 12 = 2 \times 12 + T$$

$$\Rightarrow \quad T = 24\text{N}$$

(b) $\Sigma F = ma \Rightarrow B - m(g + a) = ma'$

$$\Rightarrow \quad 48 - 24 = 2a'$$

$$\Rightarrow \quad a' = 12\text{ m/s}^2$$

15. Buoyancy force will act at the centre of the submerged part of the rod.

Let Cross-section area of plank = S

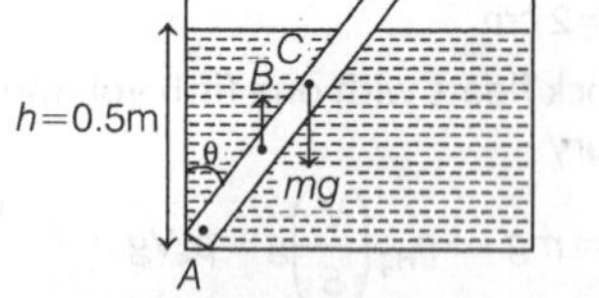

Taking torque about hinge A,

$$mg\left(\frac{L}{2}\sin\theta\right) - B\left[\left(\frac{h}{2\cos\theta}\right)\sin\theta\right] = 0$$

$$500[S(1)]g\left(\frac{1}{2}\sin\theta\right) - 1000\left[S\left(\frac{0.5}{\cos\theta}\right)\left(\frac{0.5}{2\cos\theta}\right)\right]\sin\theta = 0$$

$$\Rightarrow \quad \cos\theta = \frac{1}{\sqrt{2}}$$

$$\Rightarrow \quad \theta = 45°$$

LEVEL 2

Single Choice Correct Questions

1. $3p = p + \rho gh \Rightarrow h = \frac{2p}{\rho g}$

$$p_{\text{bottom}} = p + \rho g\left(\frac{4h}{5}\right) = p + \rho g\left(\frac{4}{5}\left(\frac{2p}{\rho g}\right)\right) = \frac{13p}{5}$$

2. $p_0 = \rho_{Hg} g\ (75\text{ cm})$

For air inside bubble,

$$p_1V_1 = p_2V_2$$

$$\Rightarrow \quad (p_0 + \rho_w gh)V = p_0(3V)$$

$$\Rightarrow \quad \rho_w gh = 2p_0$$

$$\Rightarrow \quad \frac{1}{10}\rho_{Hg} gh = 2\rho_{Hg} g(75\text{ cm}) \Rightarrow h = 15\text{ m}$$

3.

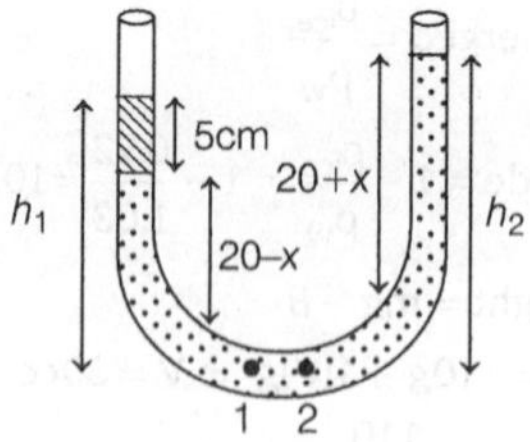

$$p_1 = p_2$$

$$\Rightarrow \quad p_0 + 4g(5) + 1g(20 - x) = p_0 + 1g(20 + x)$$

$$\Rightarrow \quad x = 10\text{ cm}$$

$$\frac{h_2}{h_1} = \frac{20 + x}{(20 - x) + 5} = \frac{30}{15} = 2$$

4.

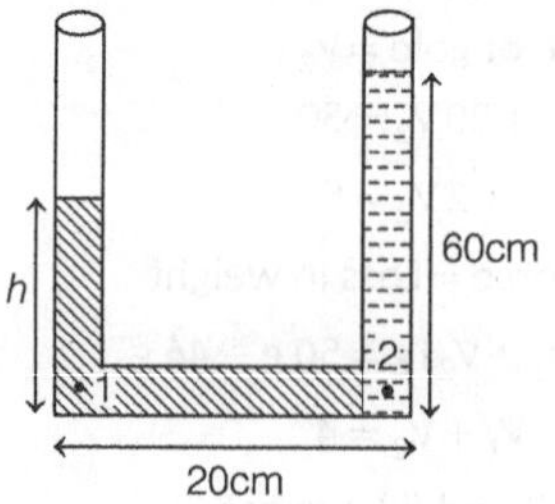

$p_1 = p_2 \Rightarrow p_0 + 4gh = p_0 + 1g(60)$

$\Rightarrow \quad h = 15\text{ cm}$

Length of liquid column = 20 + 15 = 35 cm

Volume of liquid poured = $(1\text{ cm}^2)(35\text{ cm}) = 35\text{ cc}$

5.

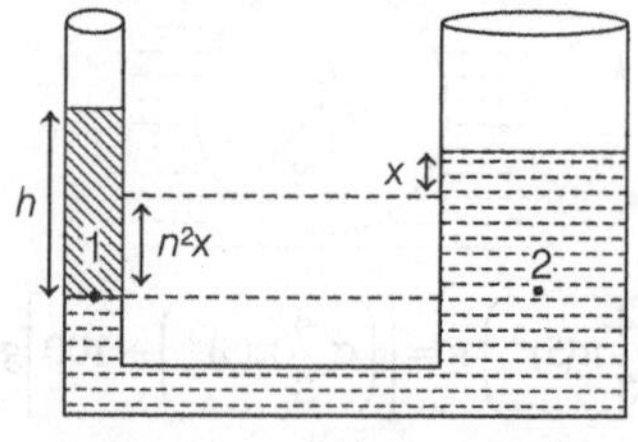

$p_1 = p_2 \Rightarrow p_0 + \rho_w gh = p_0 + \sigma\rho_w(n^2x + x)$

$$\Rightarrow \quad x = \frac{h}{(n^2+1)\sigma}$$

6.

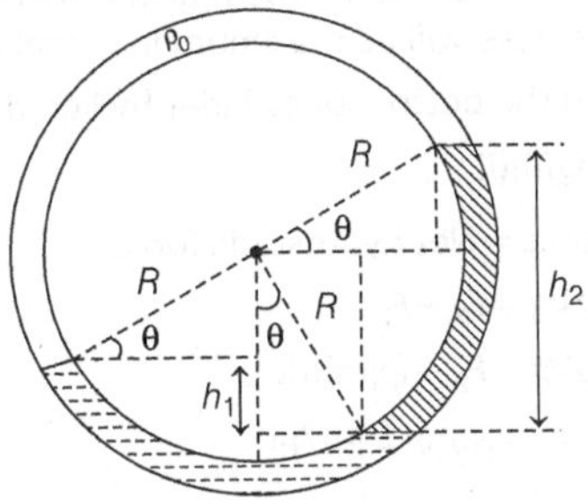

Pressure at interface $= p_0 + \rho g h_1 = p_0 + \sigma g h_2$

$$\Rightarrow \quad \rho g(R\cos\theta - R\sin\theta) = \sigma g(R\cos\theta + R\sin\theta)$$

$$\Rightarrow \quad \rho\cos\theta - \rho\sin\theta = \sigma\cos\theta + \sigma\sin\theta$$

$$\Rightarrow \quad \tan\theta = \frac{\rho-\sigma}{\rho+\sigma}$$

7. $p_1 = p_2 \Rightarrow p_0 + 1000gh = p_0 + \dfrac{12g}{800\times 10^{-4}}$

$$\Rightarrow \quad h = 15 \text{ cm}$$

8. $W = mgh \Rightarrow 500 = M(10)(5\times 10^{-3})$

$$\Rightarrow \quad M = 10^4 \text{kg}$$

9. $2mg - T = 2ma$ ...(i)

$T - mg = ma$ ...(ii)

Solving Eqs. (i) and (ii), we get $a = \dfrac{g}{3}$

So, bucket is going down with acceleration g/3.

$$p_{\text{bottom}} = p_0 + \rho g_{\text{eff}} h = p_0 + \rho\left(g - \frac{g}{3}\right)h$$

Gauge pressure at bottom

$$= \frac{2\rho g h}{3} = \frac{2}{3}\times 1000\times 10\times 15\times 10^{-2}$$

$$= 1\text{kPa}$$

10.

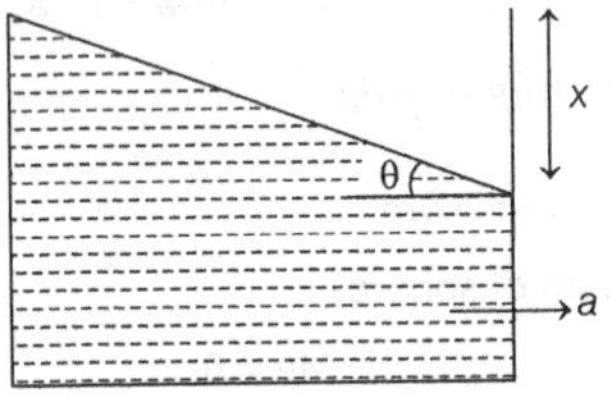

Let side of cubical tank $= l$

Empty volume = Volume of water spilled out

$$\Rightarrow \quad \left(\frac{1}{2}xl\right)l = \frac{1}{3}l^3$$

$$\Rightarrow \quad x = \frac{2l}{3}$$

$$\tan\theta = \frac{x}{l} = \frac{a}{g} \Rightarrow a = \frac{2g}{3}$$

11.

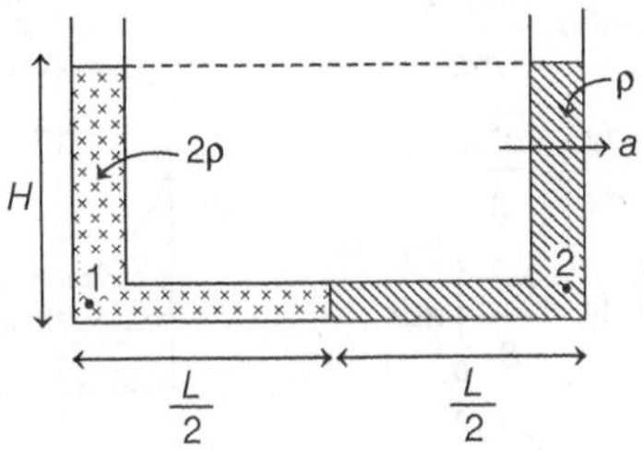

Along vertical,

$$p_1 = p_0 + (2\rho)gh$$
$$p_2 = p_0 + \rho gh$$

Along horizontal,

$$p_1 = p_2 + \rho a\left(\frac{L}{2}\right) + 2\rho a\left(\frac{L}{2}\right)$$

$$\Rightarrow \quad (p_0 + 2\rho gH) = (p_0 + \rho gH) + \frac{3\rho aL}{2}$$

$$\Rightarrow \quad H = \frac{3aL}{2g}$$

12.

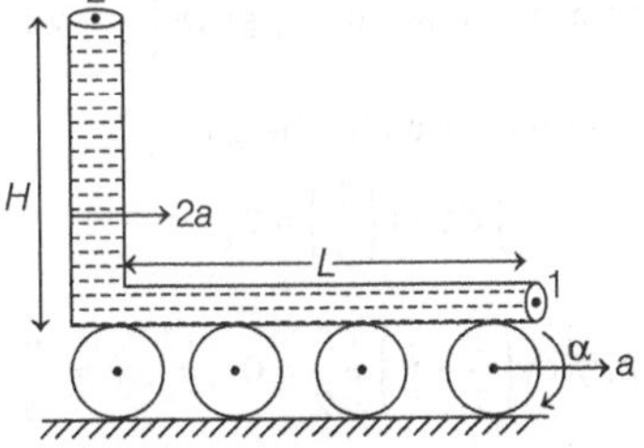

$$p_1 = p_2 + \rho gH - \rho(2a)L$$

$$\Rightarrow \quad p_0 = p_0 + \rho gH - 2\rho aL$$

$$\Rightarrow \quad a = \frac{gH}{2L}$$

13.

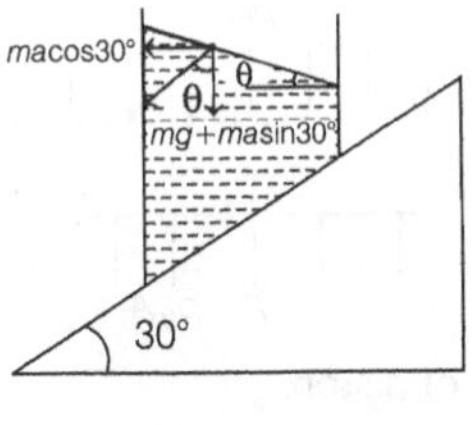

$$\tan\theta = \frac{ma\cos 30^\circ}{mg + ma\sin 30^\circ} = \frac{3\sqrt{3}}{23} = 0.23$$

14. $\displaystyle\int_{p_1}^{p_2} dp = \int_{r_1}^{r_2} \rho(\omega^2 r)\,dr$

$$\Rightarrow \quad p_2 - p_1 = \rho\omega^2\left(\frac{r_2^{\,2} - r_1^{\,2}}{2}\right)$$

$$\Rightarrow \quad \omega = \sqrt{\frac{2(p_2 - p_1)}{\rho(r_2^{\,2} - r_1^{\,2})}}$$

15. $\tan\theta = \dfrac{m\omega^2 x}{mg}$

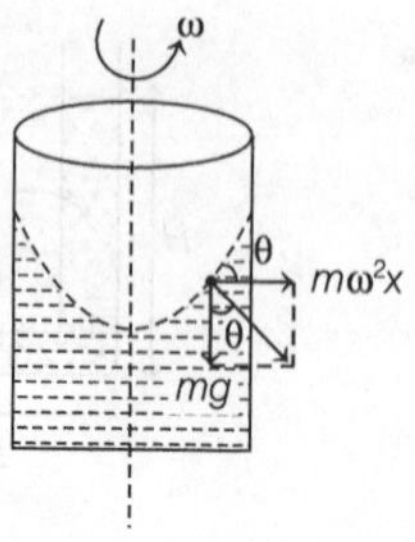

$\Rightarrow \quad \dfrac{dy}{dx} = \dfrac{\omega^2 x}{g}$

$\Rightarrow \quad \displaystyle\int_0^y dy = \dfrac{\omega^2}{g}\int_0^r x\,dx$

$\Rightarrow \quad y = \dfrac{\omega^2 r^2}{2g}$

16. The net force acting on the gate element of width dy at a depth y from the surface of the fluid.

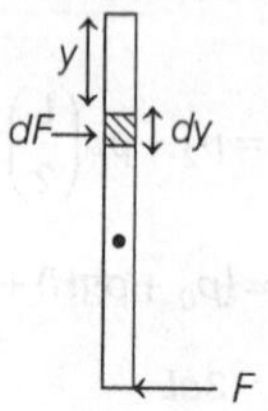

$$dF = (p_0 + \rho g y - P_0)(1dy)$$

Torque about the hinge $d\tau = \rho g y\, dy\left(\dfrac{1}{2} - y\right)$

Net torque experienced by the gate.

$$\int d\tau + F\left(\frac{1}{2}\right) = 0$$

$\Rightarrow \quad \displaystyle\int_0^1 \rho g y\, dy\left(\frac{1}{2} - y\right) + \frac{F}{2} = 0 \Rightarrow F = \frac{\rho g}{6}$

17. Normal thrust at point p,

$$dF = (p_0 + \rho g\,(H - h) - p_0)\,dA$$

Normal thrust per unit area $= \dfrac{dF}{dA} = \rho g\,(H - h)$

18.

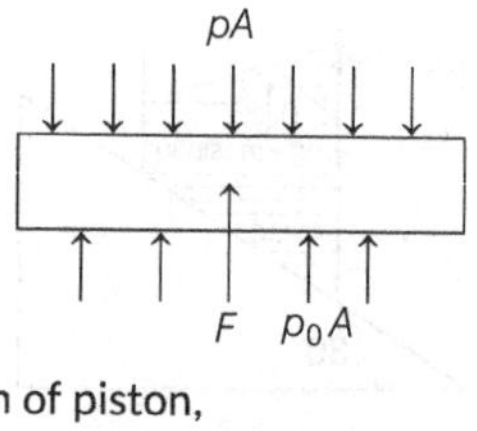

For equilibrium of piston,

$$pA = p_0 A + F$$

$\Rightarrow \quad (p_0 + \rho g H)A = p_0 A + F$

$\Rightarrow \quad F = \rho g H A$

19. For equilibrium of liquid column, resultant force exerted by the flask on the liquid will be equal to weight of liquid.

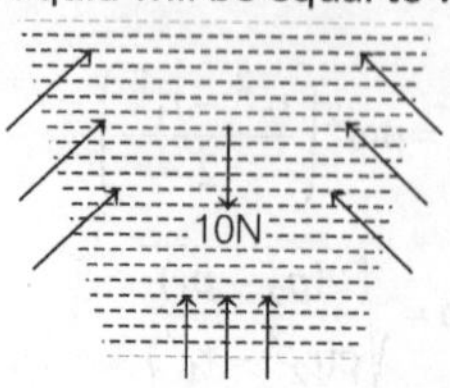

20. Force exerted by the liquid at the base $= pA$

$$= (p_0 + \rho g H)A$$

Height of liquid column will be maximum in vessel C. So, force at the base will be maximum in vessel C.

21. Let force on the bottom of cylinder by liquid be F_2.

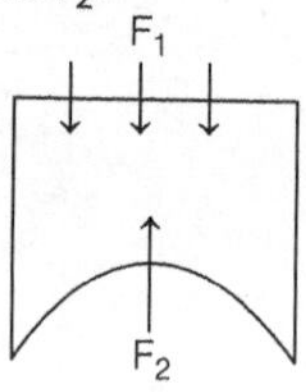

$F_1 = pA = (\rho g h)\pi R^2$

Buoyant Force = Net hydrostatic force

$\Rightarrow \quad \rho V g = F_2 - F_1$

$\Rightarrow \quad \rho V g = F_2 - (\rho g h)\pi R^2$

$\Rightarrow \quad F_2 = \rho g(V + \pi R^2 h)$

22. Buoyant force, $w_{app} = w - B$

$\Rightarrow \quad 180\,g = 210\,g - 1\,Vg$

$\Rightarrow \quad V = 30$ cc

Density of metal $= \dfrac{210}{30} = 7\,\text{gm/cc}$

When metal is put in unknown liquid,

$$w_{app} = w - B$$

$\Rightarrow \quad 120\,g = 210\,g - \rho_L(30)\,g$

$\Rightarrow \quad \rho_L = 3\,g/\text{cc}$

23. Weight removed = Decrease in buoyant force

$\Rightarrow \quad 200\,g = 1(l^2 \times 2)g$

$\Rightarrow \quad l = 10$ cm

24. Weight of water added = Additional buoyant force

$\Rightarrow \quad \rho_w V' g = \rho_w\left(\dfrac{V}{2}\right)g$

$\Rightarrow \quad V' = \dfrac{V}{2}$

25. For equilibrium of block,

$$Mg = B \Rightarrow Mg = \rho\left(\frac{4V}{5}\right)g \Rightarrow \rho V g = \frac{5}{4}Mg$$

When the coin is placed on the block.

$$(M + m)g = B' \Rightarrow (M + m)g = \rho V g$$

$\Rightarrow \quad (M + m)g = \dfrac{5}{4}Mg$

$\Rightarrow \quad M = 4m$

26. For equilibrium of sphere,

$$Mg = B$$

$\Rightarrow \quad (\sigma\,\rho_w)\dfrac{4}{3}\pi(R^3 - r^3)g = \rho_w\left(\dfrac{4}{3}\pi R^3\right)g$

$\Rightarrow \quad \dfrac{R}{r} = \left(\dfrac{\sigma}{\sigma - 1}\right)^{1/3}$

27. Let volume of gold $= V_1$

and volume of copper $= V_2$

Mass of crown $= 19.3V_1 + 8.5V_2 = 210$ ...(i)

$\Rightarrow$ Buoyant force = Loss in weight in water

$$\Rightarrow \quad 1(V_1 + V_2)g = 210 - 198$$

$$\Rightarrow \quad V_1 + V_2 = 12 \quad \text{... (ii)}$$

Solving Eqs. (i) and (ii), we get

$$V_1 = 10\text{cc} \text{ and } V_2 = 2\text{cc}$$

Mass of gold $= 19.3 \times 10 = 193$ gm

28. Block experiences a buoyant force due to liquid in upward direction. So, reading of spring balance will be less than 2 kg.

Liquid will experience buoyant force due to block in downward direction. So, reading of balance *B* will be more than 5kg.

29. Buoyant force an stone

$$= \rho_L V_S g = 1000 \times \left(\frac{0.5}{500}\right) \times 10 = 10\text{N}$$

So, the stone will exert a buoyant force of 10 N (1 kgf)

Hence, the balance reading $= 1.5 + 1 = 2.5$ kg

30. For equilibrium of block,

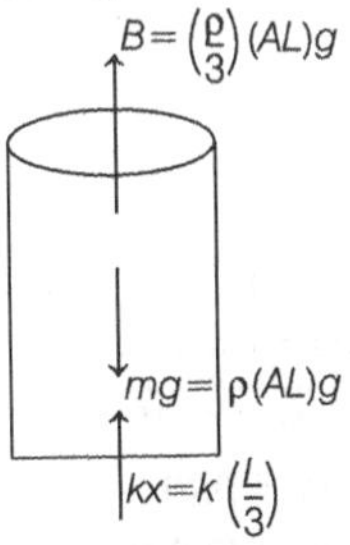

$$\Sigma F = 0$$

$$\Rightarrow \quad B + kx = mg$$

$$\Rightarrow \quad \frac{\rho}{3} ALg + k\left(\frac{L}{3}\right) = \rho ALg$$

$$\Rightarrow \quad K = 2\rho Ag$$

31.

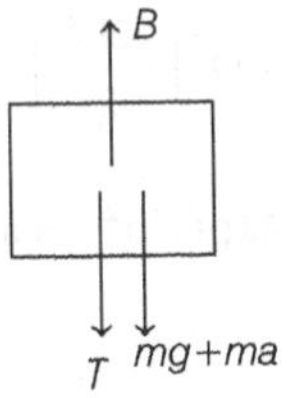

$$\Sigma F = 0$$

$$\Rightarrow \quad B = T + mg + ma$$

$$\Rightarrow \quad \rho_L V(g + a) = T + m(g + a)$$

$$\Rightarrow \quad 1000\left(\frac{1}{800}\right)(10 + 1) = T + 1(10 + 1)$$

$$\Rightarrow \quad T = 2.75\text{N}$$

32. Since, metal is denser than ice, water displaced will be more than the water formed on melting, so the level of water falls.

33. Applying work-energy theorem for the fall,

$$W_{mg} + W_B = \Delta K$$

$$\Rightarrow \quad -(\rho V)g(H + h) + (\sigma V g)h = 0 - 0$$

$$\Rightarrow \quad H = \left(\frac{\sigma}{\rho} - 1\right)h$$

34. Fraction of volume immersed $\dfrac{V_d}{V} = \dfrac{\rho_s}{\rho_L}$

It depends upon the densities of solid and liquid only. It is independent of acceleration of system. So, no change in fraction of volume immersed.

35. For equilibrium of cylinder,

$$B_1 + B_2 = mg$$

$$\Rightarrow \quad (2d)\left(A\frac{L}{4}\right)g + dA\left(\frac{3L}{4}\right)g = D(AL)g$$

$$\Rightarrow \quad D = \frac{5d}{4}$$

Numerical Value Questions

1.

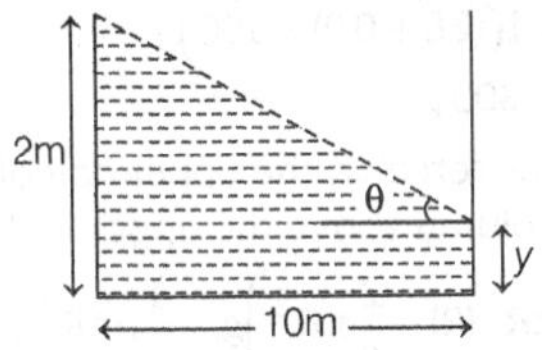

From volume conservation,

$$\frac{1}{2}(2 + y)(10)l = 10 \times 1.5 \times l \Rightarrow \quad y = 1\text{m}$$

$$\tan\theta = \frac{2 - y}{10} = \frac{a}{g} \Rightarrow a = 1\,\text{m/s}^2$$

$$v = u + at \Rightarrow 10 = 0 + 1(t) \Rightarrow t = 10\text{ s}$$

2. Weight of liquid added = Increase in buoyant force

$$\Rightarrow \quad (\rho\rho_w)\left(\frac{1}{3}\pi\left(\frac{r}{3}\right)^2\left(\frac{h}{3}\right)\right)g = (0.8\rho_w)\left(\frac{1}{3}\pi\left(\frac{r}{2}\right)^2\left(\frac{h}{2}\right) - \frac{1}{3}\pi\left(\frac{r}{3}\right)^2\left(\frac{h}{3}\right)\right)g$$

$$\Rightarrow \quad \rho = 1.9$$

3. As water level decreases, buoyant force on the block decreases and tension in the wire increases. Let water level comes down by y, then wire breaks.

$$T = mg - B$$

$$\Rightarrow \quad 7 \times 10^6 \times 10^{-6} = 1500 \times (0.1)^3 g - 1000 \times (0.1)^2 \frac{(10 - y)}{100} g$$

$$y = 2\text{ cm}$$

Let the level descends by 2 cm in time it.

$$2t = (200 - 100)2 \Rightarrow t = 100\text{ s}$$

4. 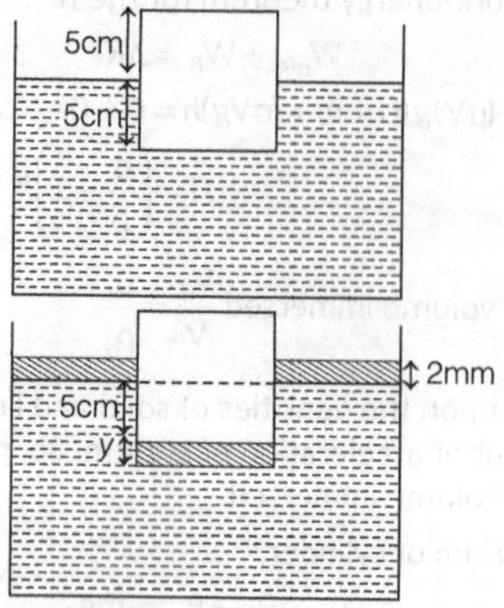

Let the cube dips further by y cm and water level rises by 2 mm.

Volume of water raised = Volume of extra depth of wood

$\Rightarrow \quad 100\,y = (1500 - 100)\left(\frac{2}{10}\right) \Rightarrow y = 2.8$ cm

Additional weight = Extra upthrust

$\Rightarrow \quad mg = 1((2.8 + 0.2) \times 100)g$

$\Rightarrow \quad m = 300$ g

5. F_1 = Hydrostatic force on the upper half of sphere = weight of the liquid column above the upper half of sphere

$$= \rho\left(\pi R^2 (R) - \frac{2}{3}\pi R^3\right)g = \frac{1}{3}\rho\pi R^3 g \text{ (downward)}$$

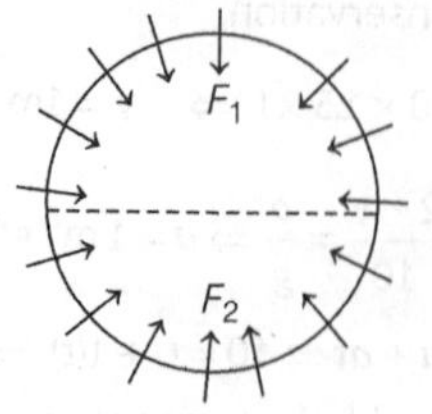

$$F_2 - F_1 = B \Rightarrow F_2 - \frac{1}{3}\rho\pi R^3 g = \rho\left(\frac{4}{3}\pi R^3\right)g$$

$\Rightarrow \quad F_2 = \frac{5}{3}\rho\pi R^3\, g$

6. 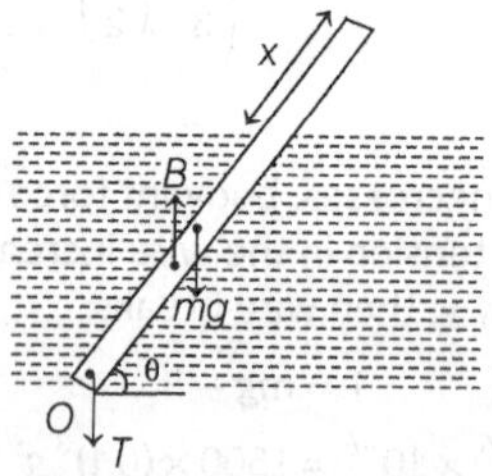

Balancing torque about O,

$$\left(\frac{25}{36}\rho_w\right)(12A)g(6\cos\theta) - \rho_w$$

$$[(12 - x)A]g\left(\frac{12 - x}{2}\right)\cos\theta = 0$$

$\Rightarrow \quad (12 - x)^2 = 100$

$\Rightarrow \quad x = 2$ m

7. 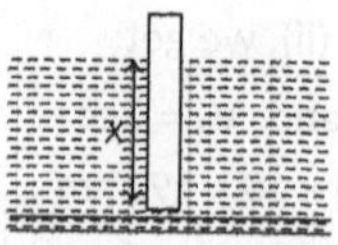

$$W_{\text{gravity}} + W_B = \Delta K$$

$\Rightarrow \quad (2mgL - mgL) - \int_0^L (\rho Axg)dx = 0 - 0$

$(2mg\,L - mgL) - \int_0^L (\rho Axg)dx = 0 - 0$

$\Rightarrow \quad mgL - \frac{\rho AgL^2}{2} = 0 \Rightarrow \rho = \frac{2m}{AL}$

So, $\quad n = 2$

8. 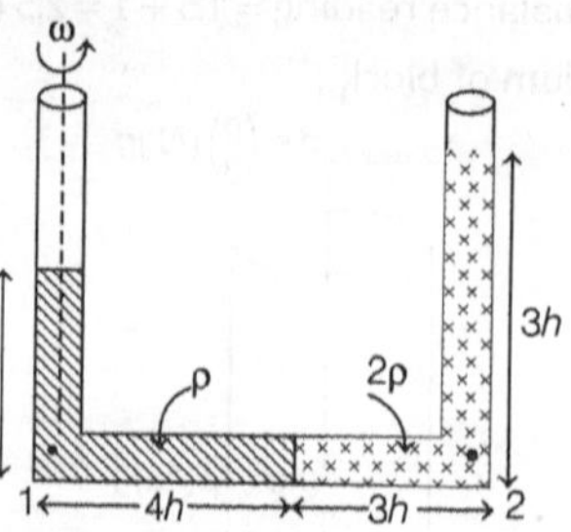

Along vertical, $p_1 = p_0 + \rho gh$

$p_2 = p_0 + (2\rho)g(3h) = p_0 + 6\rho gh$

Along horizontal,

$$\int dp = \int \rho\omega^2 x\, dx$$

$$\int_{p_1}^{p_2} dP = \int_0^{4h} \rho\omega^2 x\, dx + \int_{4h}^{7h} (2\rho)\omega^2 x\, dx$$

$\Rightarrow \quad p_2 - p_1 = \rho\omega^2\left(\frac{16h^2}{2}\right) + 2\rho\omega^2\left(\frac{33h^2}{2}\right)$

$\Rightarrow \quad 5\rho gh = 41\rho\omega^2 h^2 \Rightarrow \omega = \sqrt{\frac{5g}{41h}}$

Level 3

Single Choice Correct Questions

1. F_1 = Force on base = Pressure at base × Area

$= (\rho ga + 2R ga)(a \times a) = 3\rho g a^3$

F_2 = Force on side wall $= p_1 A_1 + p_2 A_2$

$$= \rho g\left(\frac{a}{2}\right)(a \times a) + \left(\rho g a + 2\rho g\left(\frac{a}{2}\right)\right) \times (a \times a) = \frac{5}{2}\rho g a^3$$

$F_1 : F_2 = 6 : 5$

2. $\tan 37° = \dfrac{r}{8} \Rightarrow r = 6\text{ m}$

$$F = pA = (p_0 + \rho g h)\pi r^2$$

$$= (10^5 + 800 \times 10 \times 10)(3.14)(6)^2 = 2 \times 10^7\text{ N}$$

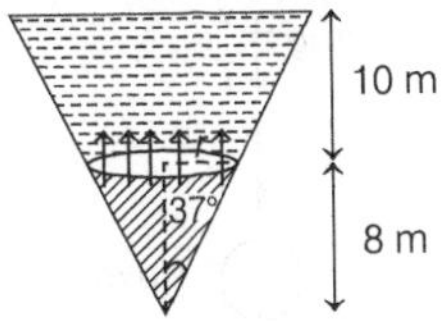

3. For equilibrium of cylinder in horizontal,

$$F_{LHS} = F_{RHS}$$

$$\Rightarrow \quad p_1 A_1 = p_2 A_2$$

$$\Rightarrow \quad \left(2\rho g\left(\frac{h}{2}\right)\right)(hl) = \left(3\rho g\left(\frac{R}{2}\right)\right)(Rl) \Rightarrow h = R\sqrt{\frac{3}{2}}$$

4. Let the densities be ρ-d, ρ and $\rho + d$

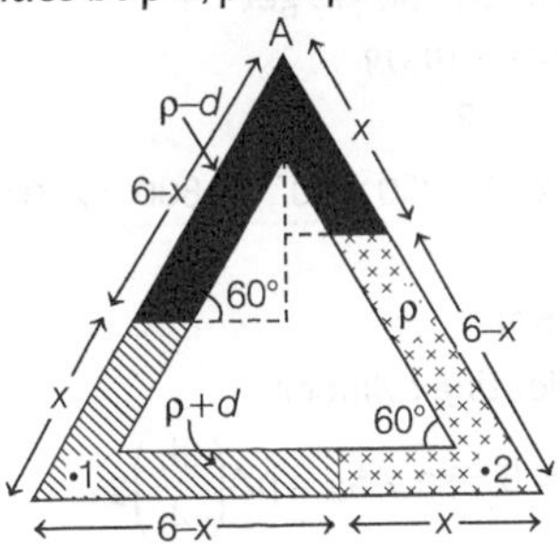

$$p_1 = p_2$$

$$\Rightarrow (\rho - d)g(6-x)\sin 60° + (\rho + d)gx\sin 60°$$

$$= (\rho - d)gx\sin 60° + \rho g(6-x)\sin 60°$$

$$\Rightarrow \quad (\rho - d)(6-x) + (\rho + d)x = (\rho - d)x + \rho(6-x)$$

$$\Rightarrow \quad x = 2\text{ m}$$

5.

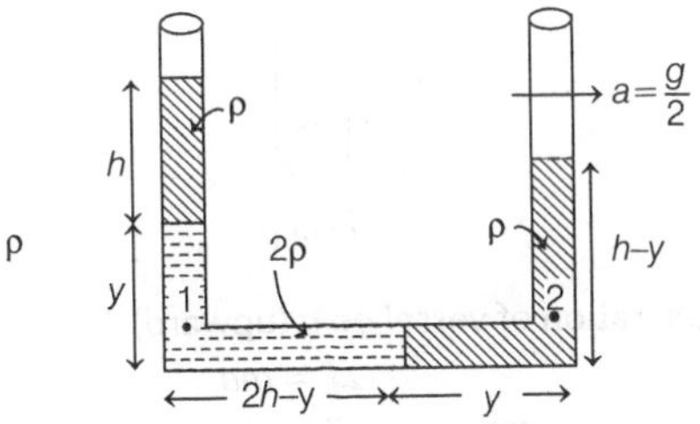

Along vertical, $p_1 = p_0 + \rho g h + (2\rho)g y$ ...(i)

$p_2 = p_0 + \rho g(h - y)$ ...(ii)

Along horizontal,

$$p_1 - p_2 = 2\rho\left(\frac{g}{2}\right)(2h - y) + \rho\left(\frac{g}{2}\right)y \quad \text{...(iii)}$$

Solving Eqs. (i), (ii) and (iii), we get

$$y = \frac{4h}{7}$$

So, $\Delta h = (h + y) - (h - y) = 2y = 8h/7$

6. Torque due to hydrostatic force on any point on the cylinder about hinge is zero. Since net torque is zero, $F = 0$.

7.

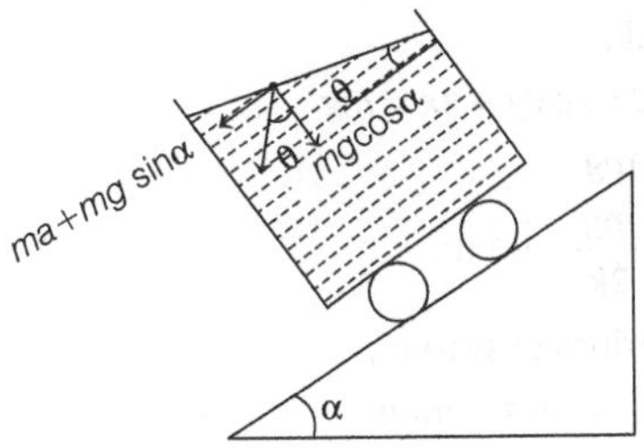

$$\tan\theta = \frac{ma + mg\sin\alpha}{mg\cos\alpha}$$

$$\theta = \tan^{-1}\left(\frac{a + g\sin\alpha}{g\cos\alpha}\right)$$

8.

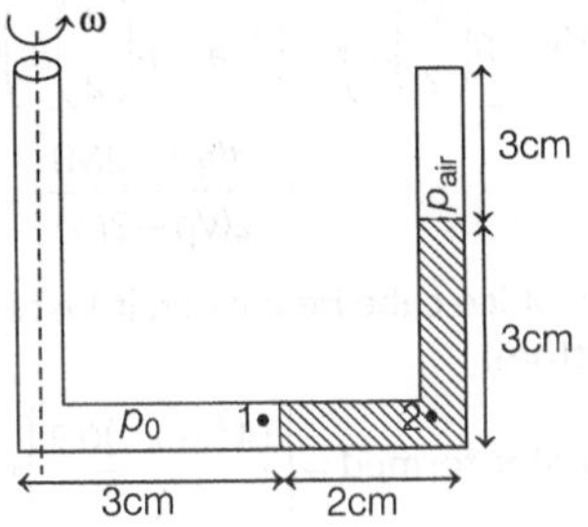

For air column in the right vertical arm

$$p_1 V_1 = p_2 V_2 \Rightarrow 7700 \times 6 = p_{air} \times 3$$

$$\Rightarrow \quad p_{air} = 15400\text{ N/m}^2$$

Along vertical, $p_2 = p_{air} + \rho g h$

$$= 15400 + 10^3 \times 10 \times (3 \times 10^{-2}) = 15700\text{ N/m}^2$$

Along horizontal, $p_2 - p_1 = \displaystyle\int_{0.03}^{0.05} \rho\omega^2 x\, dx$

$$\Rightarrow \quad 15700 - 7700 = 1000\omega^2\left(\frac{(0.05)^2 - (0.03)^2}{2}\right)$$

$$\Rightarrow \quad \omega = 100\text{ rad/s}$$

9. Additional weight = Extra buoyant force

$$mg = 1\left(\frac{1}{3}\pi(10)^2(20) - \frac{1}{3}\pi(9)^2(18)\right)g$$

$$\Rightarrow \quad m = \frac{542\pi}{3} = 568\text{ gm}$$

10.

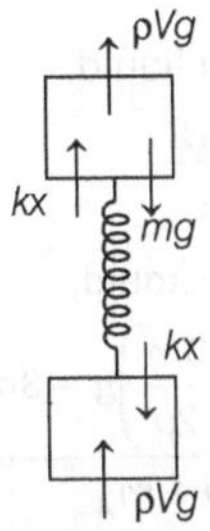

For lower block,

$$\Sigma F = 0 \Rightarrow \rho V g = kx$$

For upper block,

$$\Sigma F = 0 \Rightarrow \rho V g + kx = mg$$

$$\Rightarrow \quad 2kx = mg$$

$$\Rightarrow \quad x = \frac{mg}{2k} = 0.1 \text{ m}$$

11. For the equilibrium of system,

$$B_1 + B_2 = m_1 g + m_2 g$$

$$\Rightarrow \quad 1(100)^2(100 - h)g + 1(100)^3 g = 0.6(100)^3 g + 1.15(100)^3 g$$

$$\Rightarrow \quad h = 25 \text{ cm}$$

12. Taking torque about m,

$$\left(2Mg - \rho\left(\frac{V}{2}\right)g\right)l - \left(Mg - \rho\left(\frac{V}{2}\right)g\right)(d - l) = 0$$

$$\Rightarrow \quad l = \frac{d(V\rho - 2M)}{2(V\rho - 3M)}$$

13. Let the edge of ice cube be x when it just leaves contact with the bottom.

$$\text{Volume of water formed} = \left[\frac{(4^3 - x^3)0.9}{1}\right] \text{cm}^3$$

Let water rises to height h is the cylinder,

$$[\pi(3)^2 - x^2]h = (4^3 - x^3)(0.9)$$

$$h = \frac{(4^3 - x^3)(0.9)}{\pi(3)^2 - x^2}$$

When ice block loses contact with the bottom,

$$B = mg$$

$$\Rightarrow \quad 1\left(x^2\left(\frac{(4^3 - x^3)(0.9)}{\pi(3)^2 - x^2}\right)\right)g = (0.9x^3)g$$

$$\Rightarrow \quad x = \frac{64}{9\pi} = 2.26 \text{ cm}$$

14. $B_1 + B_2 = mg$

$$\Rightarrow \quad 300(Ax)g + 1000A(L - x)g = 800(AL)g$$

$$\Rightarrow \quad \frac{x}{L} = \frac{2}{7}$$

15. $a = \dfrac{\text{Net pulling force}}{\text{Total mass}}$

When block B is out of liquid,

$$a = \frac{3mg - m_A g}{3m + m_A} \quad \text{...(i)}$$

When block B is inside liquid,

$$a = \frac{m_A g + \rho\left(\frac{3m}{2\rho}\right)g - 3mg}{3m + m_A} \quad \text{...(ii)}$$

From Eqs. (i) and (ii), we get

$$m_A = \frac{9m}{4}$$

16.

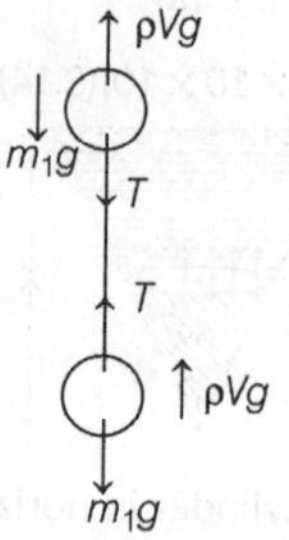

For lower sphere,

$$m_1 g - \rho V g = T \quad \text{...(i)}$$

For upper sphere,

$$\rho V g - m_2 g = T \quad \text{...(ii)}$$

Adding Eqs. (i) and (ii) we get

$$T = \frac{(m_1 - m_2)g}{2}$$

$$= \frac{(1200 \times 250 \times 10^{-6} - 800 \times 250 \times 10^{-6})(10)}{2}$$

$$= 0.5 \text{ N}$$

17. Initially for floating cylinder,

$$mg = B \Rightarrow \rho_s A h g = \rho A\left(\frac{3h}{4}\right)g$$

$$\Rightarrow \quad \rho_s = \frac{3\rho}{4}$$

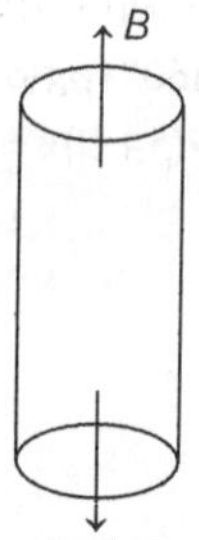

Let acceleration of vessel be a (upward)

$$\Sigma F = ma$$

$$\Rightarrow \quad mg + ma - B = m\,a_{rel}$$

$$\Rightarrow \quad \left(\frac{3\rho}{4}Ah\right)(g + a) - \rho(Ah)(g + a) = \left(\frac{3\rho Ah}{4}\right)\frac{a}{3}$$

$$\Rightarrow \quad a = -g/2$$

$$\Rightarrow \quad a = g/2 \text{ (downward)}$$

18. For equilibrium of sphere,

$$B = m_1 g + m_2 g$$

$$\Rightarrow 1\left(\frac{4}{3}\pi R^3\right)g = 0.3\left(\frac{4}{3}\pi R^3\right)g + 2.4\left(\frac{4}{3}\pi(R^3 - r^3)\right)g$$

$$\Rightarrow \quad \frac{R^3}{r^3} = \frac{3}{2}$$

$$\frac{M_{\text{concrete}}}{M_{\text{sawdust}}}=\frac{2.4\left(\frac{4}{3}\pi(R^3-r^3)\right)}{0.3\left(\frac{4}{3}\pi r^3\right)}=8\left(\frac{R^3}{r^3}-1\right)=4$$

19. Weight acts at centre of gravity C and buoyancy force acts at centre of buoyancy B

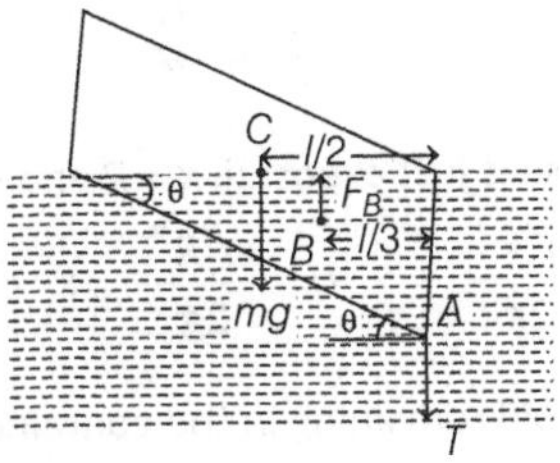

Taking torque about A,

$$mg\left(\frac{l}{2}\right)=F_B\left(\frac{l}{3}\right)$$

$$\Rightarrow\quad (\rho_s V)g\left(\frac{l}{2}\right)=\left(\rho_w\frac{V}{2}\right)g\left(\frac{l}{3}\right)$$

$$\Rightarrow\quad \frac{\rho_s}{\rho_w}=\frac{1}{3}$$

20.

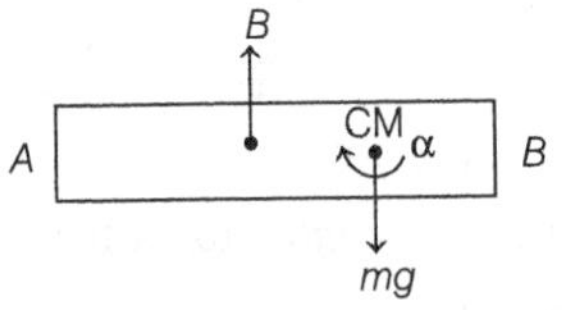

About the CM,

$$\Sigma\tau=I\alpha$$

$$\Rightarrow\quad B\left(\frac{l}{4}\right)=I\alpha\ \Rightarrow\ \rho(\pi r^2 l)g\frac{l}{4}=I\alpha$$

$$\Rightarrow\quad \alpha=\frac{\pi\rho g l^2 r^2}{4I}$$

21.

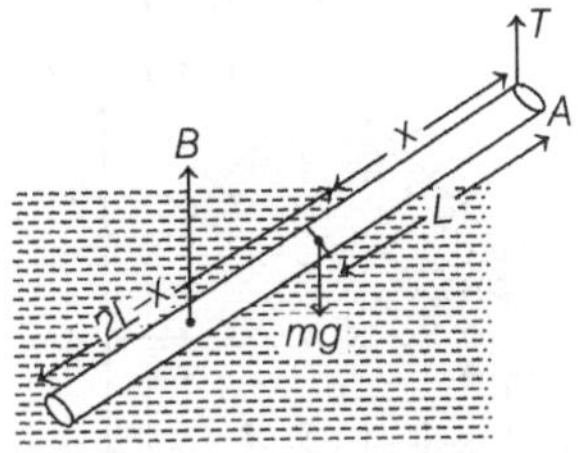

Taking torque about A,

$$\Rightarrow\quad mg(L\cos\theta)-B\left(x+\frac{2L-x}{2}\right)\cos\theta=0$$

$$\Rightarrow\quad (0.75\rho_w)(A(2L))g(L\cos\theta)$$
$$-(\rho_w A(2L-x)g)\left(\frac{2L+x}{2}\right)\cos\theta=0$$

$$\Rightarrow\quad x=L$$

22.

$$\rho_s=\frac{\rho_L}{2}$$

$\Rightarrow$ The candle is floating with 50% of its length submerged. The candle burns at a rate of 4cm/hr, so after 1h length of candle will decrease by 4cm and half of it would remain in liquid and half outside. So, the upper end will fall at a rate 2 cm/h wrt the surface of liquid.

23. Centre of buoyancy must be above the centre of mass,

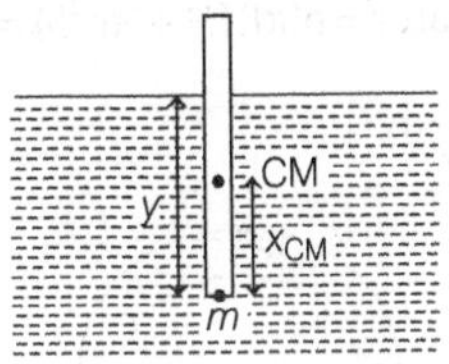

$$x_{cm}=\frac{m_1x_1+m_2x_2}{m_1+m_2}=\frac{(\pi R^2L\rho)(L/2)+m(0)}{\pi R^2L\rho+m}$$

$$=\frac{\pi R^2L^2\rho}{2(\pi R^2L\rho+m)}$$

$$\Sigma F_y=0\Rightarrow W=B\ \Rightarrow\ (M+m)g=\sigma(\pi R^2y)g$$

$$\Rightarrow\quad \rho\pi R^2L+m=\sigma\pi R^2y\ \Rightarrow\ y=\frac{\rho\pi R^2L+m}{\sigma\pi R^2}$$

For equilibrium, $\frac{y}{2}\geq x_{cm}$

$$\Rightarrow\quad \frac{1}{2}\left(\frac{\rho\pi R^2L+m}{\sigma\pi R^2}\right)\geq\frac{\pi R^2L^2\rho}{2(\pi R^2L\rho+m)}$$

$$\Rightarrow\quad m+\pi R^2L\rho\geq\pi R^2L\sqrt{\rho\sigma}$$

$$\Rightarrow\quad m_{min}=\pi R^2L(\sqrt{\sigma\rho}-\rho)$$

24. $T=mg-B\Rightarrow T=3\rho Vg-\rho Vg=2\rho Vg$

$$\Sigma\tau=0\Rightarrow TR-kx\left(\frac{R}{2}\right)=0$$

$$\Rightarrow\quad (2\rho Vg)R-kx\left(\frac{R}{2}\right)=0\Rightarrow x=\frac{4\rho Vg}{k}$$

25.

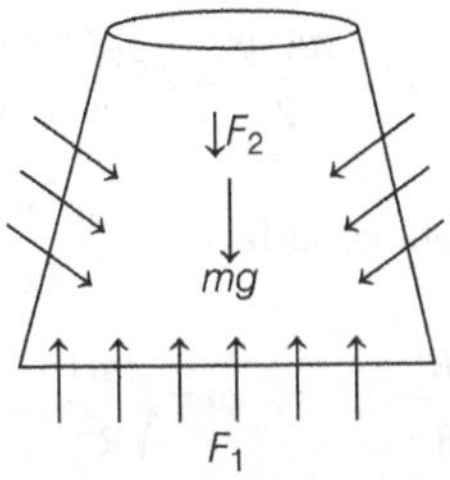

$$F_1 = pA = \rho g h A$$
$$= 1200 \times 10 \times 0.1 \times (10^3 \times 10^{-4}) = 120 \text{ N}$$

F_2 = Resultant force that liquid exerts on the curved surface in downward direction.

For equilibrium of cone, $\Sigma F_y = 0$

$\Rightarrow \quad F_1 = mg + F_2$

$\Rightarrow \quad 120 = 100 + F_2$

$\Rightarrow \quad F_2 = 20 \text{ N (downward)}$

Multiple Choice(s) Correct Questions

1. $p_1 = p_2 \Rightarrow p_0 + \dfrac{Mg}{\pi(R^2 - r^2)} = p_0 + \rho g h$

$\Rightarrow \quad h = \dfrac{M}{\rho\pi(R^2 - r^2)} = \dfrac{2}{\pi} \text{ m}$

Total mass of water $= \rho(\pi R^2 H + \pi r^2 h) = 0.75$

$\Rightarrow \quad H = \dfrac{11}{32\pi} \text{ m}$

2.

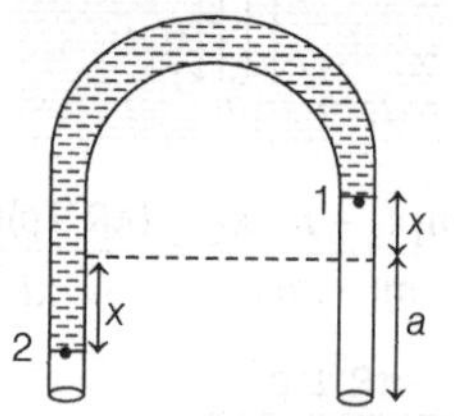

Let pressure of air in the right arm in inverted position be p.

So, $\quad p_1 V_1 = p_2 V_2$

$\Rightarrow \quad p(a + x) = p_0\, a \quad$ ...(i)

$\quad p_2 = p_1 + \rho g\,(2x)$

$\Rightarrow \quad p_0 = p + 2\rho g\, x \quad$ ...(ii)

Solving, we get $\quad x = \dfrac{p_0}{2\rho g} - a$

3. From volume conservation,

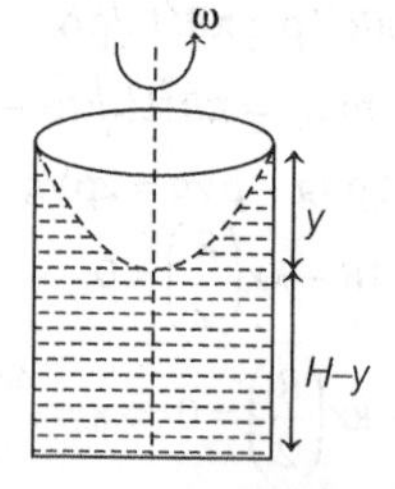

$$\pi R^2 (H - y) + \frac{\pi R^2 y}{2} = \pi R^2 \left(\frac{3H}{4}\right) \Rightarrow y = \frac{H}{2}$$

Equation of parabolic surface, $y = \dfrac{\omega^2 x^2}{2g}$

$\Rightarrow \quad \dfrac{H}{2} = \dfrac{\omega^2 R^2}{2g} \quad \Rightarrow \omega = \sqrt{\dfrac{gH}{R^2}}$

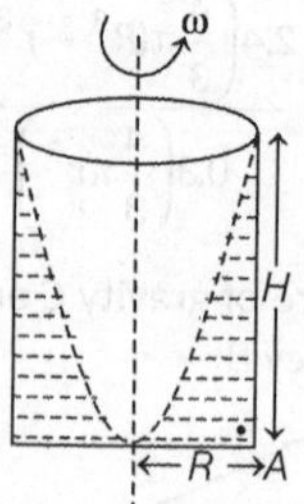

When the base is just exposed, $x = R$ and $y = H$

$$y = \frac{\omega^2 x^2}{2g} \Rightarrow H = \frac{\omega^2 R^2}{2g} \Rightarrow \omega = \sqrt{\frac{2gH}{R^2}}$$

Volume of liquid remaining in the container $= \dfrac{1}{2}\pi R^2 H$

Gauge pressure at $A = \rho g H$

4. $\tan\theta = \dfrac{a}{g} = \dfrac{7.5}{10} = \dfrac{3}{4}$

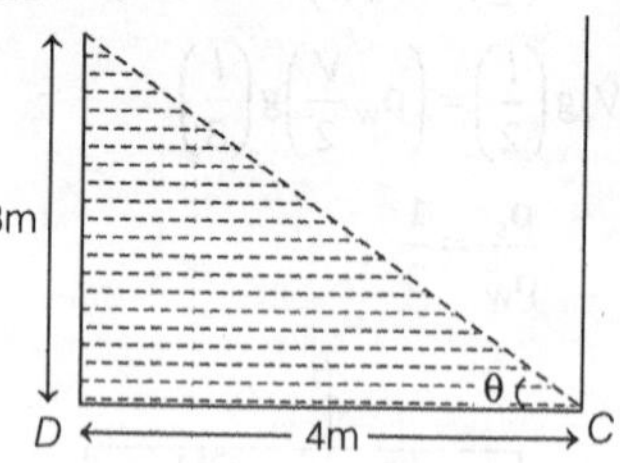

Gange pressure at $C = 0$

Gange pressure at $D = \rho g h = 10^3 \times 10 \times 3 = 3 \times 10^4$ Pa

No liquid spills out

5. Pressure at the base of the vessel $= \rho g(2h)$

F = Force exerted by the liquid on the base of the vessel $= (2\rho g h)A$

Let the resultant force exerted by the walls on the liquid be F_1 (down)

For equilibrium of liquid,

$$F_1 + w = F$$

$\Rightarrow \quad F_1 = F - w$

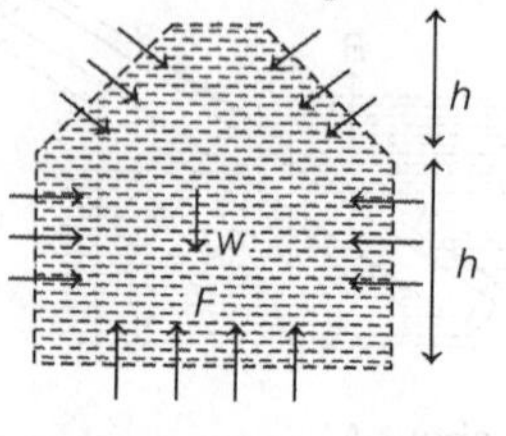

6. Let length of stick immersed in water be x.

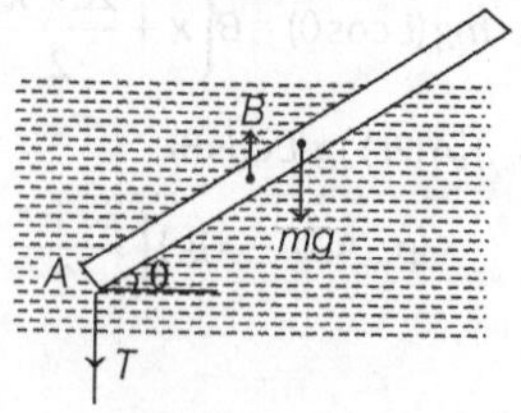

Taking torque about A, $\Sigma\tau = 0$

$\Rightarrow \quad mg(1\cos\theta) - B\left(\frac{x}{2}\right)\cos\theta = 0$

$\Rightarrow \quad (250\times10^{-3}\times2)g(1\cos\theta)$

$$-(1000\times10^{-3}\times xg)\left(\frac{x}{2}\right)\cos\theta = 0$$

$\Rightarrow \quad x = 1\text{ m}$

So, $B = 1000\times10^{-3}\times1\times10 = 10\text{ N}$

$$T = B - mg = 10 - 250\times10^{-3}\times2\times10 = 5\text{ N}$$

When string is cut, $\Sigma F = ma$

$\Rightarrow \quad B - mg = ma$

$\Rightarrow \quad 10 - 5 = 0.5a \Rightarrow a = 10\text{ m/s}^2$

7. Weight of ice cone $= 0.9\left(\frac{1}{3}\pi R^2(10)\right)g$

Buoyant force $= 1\left(\frac{1}{3}\pi\left(\frac{9R}{10}\right)^2 9\right)g$

$$N = mg - B > 0$$

Volume of water formed on melting of ice

$$= \frac{\text{Mass of ice melted}}{\text{Density of water}}$$

$$= \frac{0.9}{1}\left(\frac{1}{3}\pi R^2(10)\right)$$

Since, volume of water formed is greater than water displaced by the cone, level of water will increase.

Potential energy of ice-water system will decrease because work done by gravity on the system is positive and centre of mass of the system descends.

8. Vertical hydrostatic force on the curved surface
= Weight of the liquid column just above the hemisphere

$$= \rho\left(\pi R^2(R) - \frac{2}{3}\pi R^2\right)g = \frac{\pi\rho g R^3}{3}$$

Horizontal hydrostatic force on the right half of curved surface

$$= P_c A_{\text{projected}} = \left(\rho g\left(R - \frac{4R}{3\pi}\right)\right)\left(\frac{\pi R^2}{2}\right)$$

$$= \frac{(3\pi - 4)\rho g R^3}{6}$$

9.

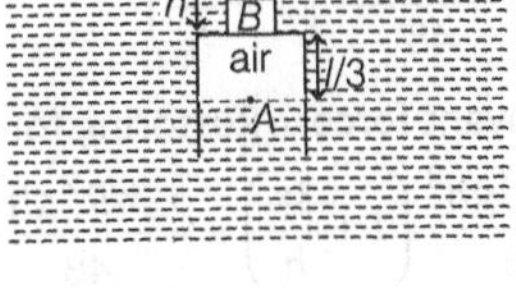

For equilibrium of system,

Weight = Buoyant force

$\Rightarrow \quad 2dVg = d\left(V + \pi r^2\frac{l}{3}\right)g$

$\Rightarrow \quad V = \frac{\pi r^2 l}{3}$

p_A = pressure of air trapped in the tube

$$= p_0 + dg\left(h + \frac{l}{3}\right)$$

10. Force on liquid due to side wall = Force on the side wall due to liquid = Weight of displaced liquid $= \rho Vg$

This force is independent of the shape of dent provided that V = constant.

11. Pseudo force $= \rho va$

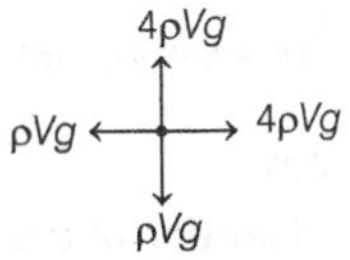

Horizontal buoyant force $= 4\rho Va$

Vertical buoyant force $= 4\rho Vg$

$$\tan\theta = \frac{4\rho Vg - \rho Vg}{4\rho Va - \rho Va} = \frac{L/2}{L}$$

$\Rightarrow \quad a = 2g$

$$s_x = u_x t + \frac{1}{2}a_x t^2$$

$\Rightarrow \quad L = \frac{1}{2}\left(\frac{3\rho Va}{\rho V}\right)t^2$

$\Rightarrow \quad t = \sqrt{\frac{L}{3g}}$

Comprehension Based Questions

1.

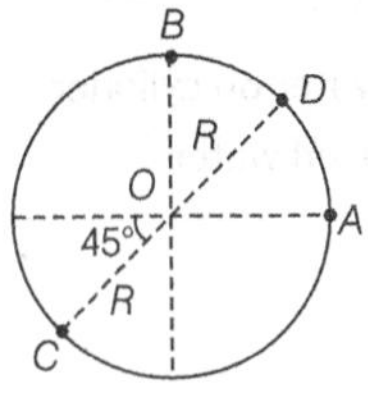

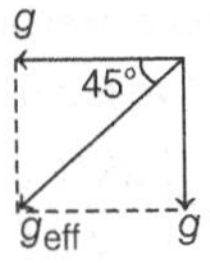

g_{eff} is along OC. So, maximum pressure will be at point C.
coordinates of $C \equiv (-R\cos45°, -R\sin45°)$

2. Minimum pressure is at point D.

Coordinate of $D \equiv (R\cos45°, R\sin45°)$

3. Line joining A and B is perpendicular to direction of g_{eff}. So, A and B lie on an isobaric line. Hence, $p_A = p_B$

4. $\tan\theta = \frac{g/2}{g - g/2} = 1$

$\Rightarrow \quad \theta = 45°$

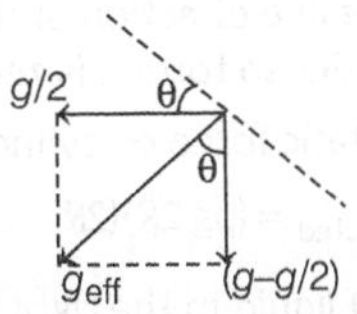

5.

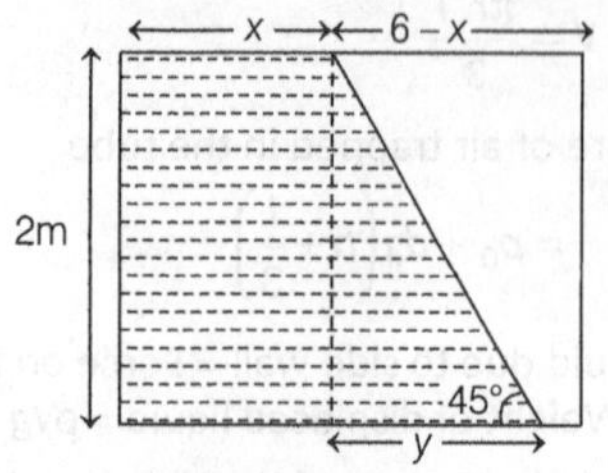

$$\tan 45° = \frac{2}{y} \Rightarrow y = 2\text{ m}$$

$$\text{Volume of liquid} = \frac{1}{2}(x + x + y)(2)(6) = 6 \times 16$$

$$\Rightarrow \quad x = 2\text{ m}$$

So, length of exposed portion of top $= 6 - 2 = 4$ m

6. Free surface passes through the centre of the box.

So, $p = p_0 + \rho g h = 10^5 + 1000 \times 10 \times 1 = 0.11$ MPa

7. $p_{max} = p_0 + \rho g h = 10^5 + 1000 \times 10 \times 4 = 0.14$ MPa

8. $$\tan\theta = \frac{a_x}{a_y + g} = \frac{1}{3}$$

$$\Rightarrow \quad a_y = \frac{g}{2}, \text{ upwards}$$

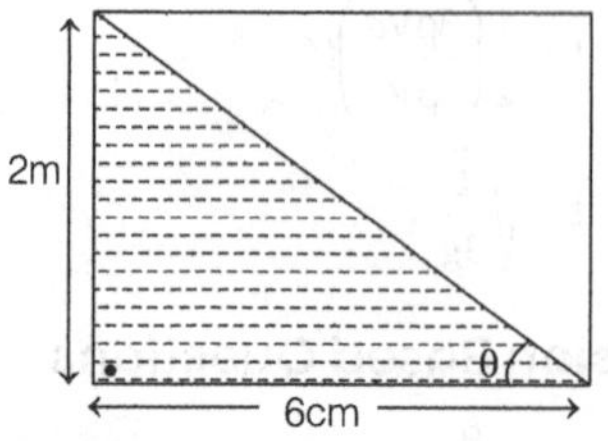

9. Vertical force exerted by water on cylinder

= Weight of displaced water

$$= \rho\left(\frac{\pi R^2 L}{2}\right) g$$

10.

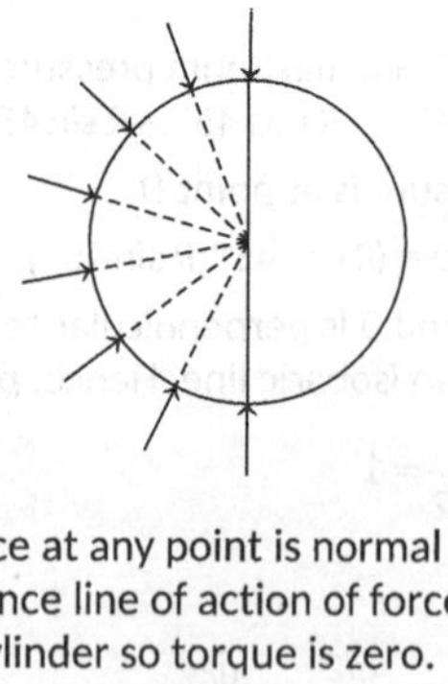

Hydrostatic force at any point is normal to the surface of cylinder and hence line of action of force passes through the centre of cylinder so torque is zero.

11. Horizontal hydrostatic force on cylinder.

$$= p_C A_{projected} = (\rho g 2R)(2R \times L) = 4\rho g L R^2$$

12. Let initial height of liquid in the right limb = h

$$p_A = p_B \Rightarrow \rho g\left(\frac{8a}{3}\right) = 2\rho g h$$

$$\Rightarrow \quad h = \frac{4a}{3}$$

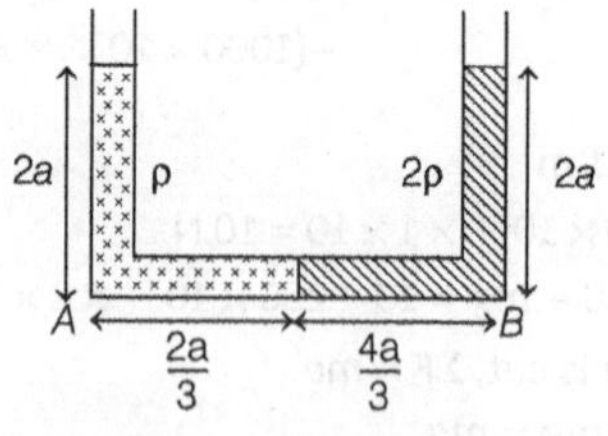

$$p_B = 2\rho g(2a); \; p_A = \rho g(2a)$$

$$\Rightarrow \quad p_B - p_A = 2\rho g a$$

13. $$\int_{p_A}^{p_B} dp = \int_a^{5a/3} \rho(\omega^2 x)dx + \int_{5a/3}^{3a} 2\rho(\omega^2 x)dx$$

$$\Rightarrow \quad p_B - p_A = \frac{64}{9}\omega^2 a^2 \rho$$

$$\Rightarrow \quad 2\rho g a = \frac{64}{9}\omega^2 a^2 e \Rightarrow \omega = \sqrt{\frac{9g}{32a}}$$

14. Let pressure at the interface $= p_C$

$$\int_{p_A}^{p_C} dp = \int_a^{5a/3} \rho\omega^2 x\, dx$$

$$\Rightarrow \quad p_C - \rho g(2a) = \rho\left(\frac{9g}{32}\right)\frac{1}{2}\left(\frac{25}{9} - 1\right)a^2$$

$$\Rightarrow \quad p_C = \frac{9}{4}\rho g a \quad \Rightarrow \quad F = p_C A = \rho S a g\left(\frac{9}{4}\right)$$

15. For equilibrium of cone, $w = B$

$$\Rightarrow \quad \left(\frac{27}{16}\rho_w\right)\left(\frac{1}{3}\pi R^2 (4)\right)g = \rho_w\left(\frac{1}{3}\pi\left(\frac{hR}{4}\right)^2 h\right)g$$

$$\Rightarrow \quad h = 3\text{ m}$$

16. $$B = \left(\frac{\rho_w \pi R^2 g}{48}\right)h^3$$

Let's displace the cone downward by a distance x,

$$B' = \frac{\rho_w \pi R^2 g}{48}(h + x)^3 = \frac{\rho_w \pi R^2 g h^3}{48}\left(1 + \frac{x}{h}\right)^3$$

$$= \frac{\rho_w \pi R^2 g h^3}{48}\left(1 + \frac{3x}{h}\right)$$

Additional buoyant force = Restoring force

$$\Rightarrow \quad \frac{\rho_w \pi R^2 g h^3}{48}\left(1 + \frac{3x}{h}\right) - \frac{\rho_w \pi R^2 g h^3}{48} = -ma$$

$$\Rightarrow \quad \frac{\rho_w \pi R^2 g h^2 x}{16} = -\left(\frac{27}{16}\rho_w\right)\left(\frac{1}{3}\pi R^2 (4)\right)a$$

$$\Rightarrow \quad a = -gx$$

$$T = \frac{2\pi}{\omega}$$

$$\Rightarrow \quad T = \frac{2\pi}{\sqrt{g}} = \frac{2\pi}{\sqrt{10}} \approx 1.98 \text{ s}$$

17. $B = \rho V g_{eff}$

In free fall, $g_{eff} = 0 \Rightarrow B = 0$

So, the cone will be in free fall too.

18.

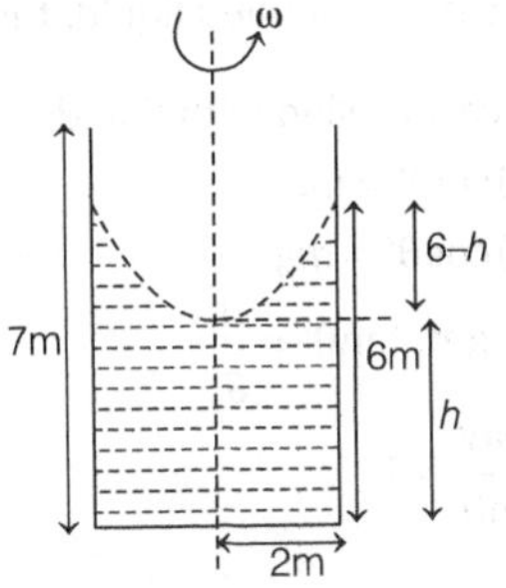

From volume conservation,

$$\pi R^2(5) = \pi R^2 h + \frac{1}{2}(\pi R^2(6-h))$$

$$\Rightarrow \quad h = 4 \text{ m}$$

19. $y = \dfrac{\omega^2 x^2}{2g} \Rightarrow 6 - 4 = \dfrac{\omega^2 (2)^2}{2(10)} \Rightarrow \omega = \sqrt{10}$ rad/s

20. Rise in height of the liquid at the ends with respect to the vertex of the liquid $= 6 - h = 2\text{m}$

Match the Columns Questions

1. (A)

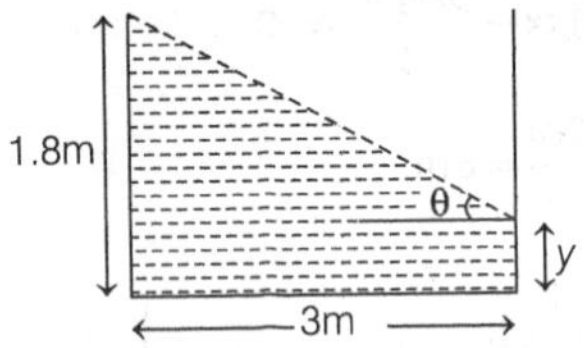

From volume conservation,

$$\frac{1}{2}(1.8 + y)(3)(1.5) = 3 \times 1.2 \times 1.5$$

$$\Rightarrow \quad y = 0.6 \text{ m}$$

$$\tan\theta = \frac{1.8 - y}{3} = \frac{a}{g} \Rightarrow a = 4 \text{ m/s}^2$$

(B) $\tan\theta = \dfrac{1.8}{3} = \dfrac{a}{g} \Rightarrow a = 6 \text{ m/s}^2$

(C) $\tan\theta = \dfrac{1.8}{1.5} = \dfrac{a}{g} \Rightarrow a = 12 \text{ m/s}^2$

(D) Volume remaining $= \dfrac{1}{2}(3 \times 1.8)(1.5) = 4.05 \text{m}^3$

Original volume $= 3 \times 1.2 \times 1.5 = 5.40 \text{m}^3$

Volume of water spilled $= 5.40 - 4.05 = 1.35 \text{ m}^3$

2. Pressure variation with height, $p = \rho g h$

Pressure variation in horizontal, $p = \rho l a$

Force, $F = p_C A$

$$F_{ABFE} = \left(\rho \frac{l}{2} a\right) l^2 = \frac{\rho l^3 a}{2} = \frac{ma}{2}$$

$$F_{BFHD} = \left(\rho \left(\frac{l}{2}\right) g\right) l^2 = \frac{mg}{2}$$

$$F_{ACGE} = \left(\rho l a + \rho \frac{l}{2} g\right) l^2 = ma + \frac{mg}{2}$$

$$F_{CGHD} = \left(\rho l g + \rho\left(\frac{l}{2}\right) a\right) l^2 = mg + \frac{ma}{2}$$

3. (A) $F_A = pA = (\rho g h)\pi R^2$

(B) $F_B = pA = [\rho g(2h) + 2\rho g h]\pi R^2 = 4\rho g h \pi R^2$

(C) $p_C = \rho g \left(\dfrac{3h}{2}\right)$

$$p_D = \rho g(2h) + 2\rho g\left(\frac{h}{2}\right) = 3\rho g h$$

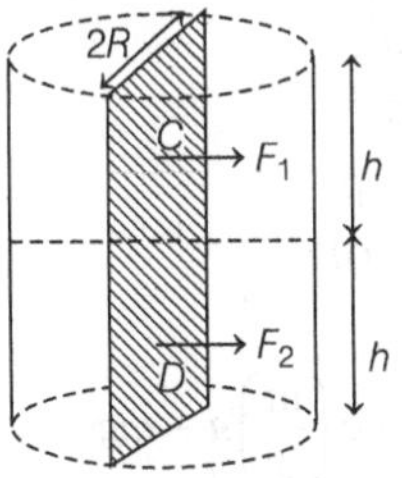

$$F = F_1 + F_2$$

$$= \rho g\left(\frac{3h}{2}\right)(2Rh) + (3\rho g h)(2Rh)$$

$$= 9\rho g R h^2$$

(D) $F_{net} = F_B - F_A = 3\rho g h \pi R^2$

4. (A) When ice melts completely, volume of water formed will be equal to volume of water displaced, so level of water remains same.

(B) Since, steel is denser than ice, volume of water formed will be less than volume of water displaced. So, level of water decreases.

(C) Wood will float on water. So, water level remains same.

(D) $\rho_{ice} < \rho_{oil} < \rho_{water}$

Let mass of ice $= m$ and volume of oil displaced by ice $= V_i$

$$B = mg \Rightarrow \rho_{oil} V_i g = mg \Rightarrow V_i = \frac{m}{\rho_{oil}}$$

On melting of ice, volume of water formed $= V_f = \dfrac{m}{\rho_w}$

$$V_f < V_i$$

$$\because \quad \rho_w > \rho_{oil}$$

Hence, level of liquid decreases.

5. (A) FBD of the cube w.r.t. the container,

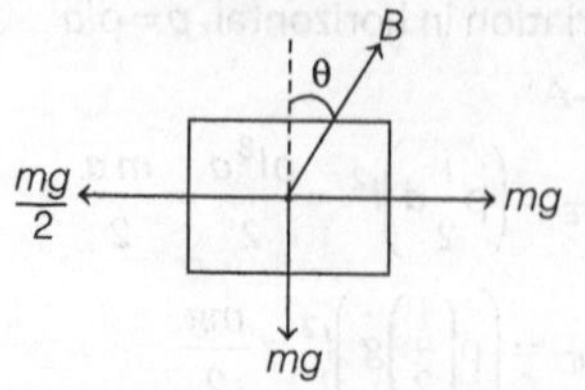

$$B=\rho\left(\frac{m}{\sigma}\right)g_{\text{eff}}=\frac{m\rho}{\sigma}\sqrt{g^2+\left(\frac{g}{2}\right)^2}=\frac{\sqrt{5}m\rho g}{2\sigma}$$

$$\tan\theta=\frac{g/2}{g}=\frac{1}{2}$$

$$\Rightarrow \quad \sin\theta=\frac{1}{\sqrt{5}} \text{ and } \cos\theta=\frac{2}{\sqrt{5}}$$

$$\Sigma F_x=ma_x \Rightarrow mg-\frac{mg}{2}+B\sin\theta=ma_x$$

$$\Rightarrow \quad a_x=g\left(1+\frac{\rho}{2\sigma}\right)$$

$$\Sigma F_y=ma_y \Rightarrow B\cos\theta-mg=ma_y$$

$$\Rightarrow \quad a_y=g\left(\frac{\rho}{\sigma}\right)-1$$

Hence, $\frac{a_x}{a_y}=\frac{2\sigma+\rho}{2(\rho-\sigma)}$

(B) $a_x=g$

$$a_y=\frac{B-mg}{m}=\frac{\rho\left(\frac{m}{\sigma}\right)g-mg}{m}$$

$$=\left(\frac{\rho}{\sigma}-1\right)g$$

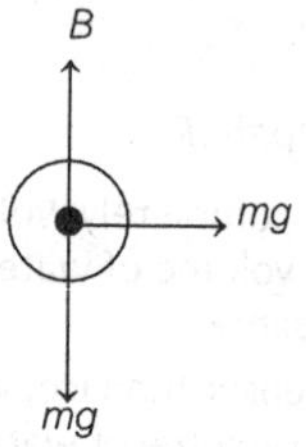

Hence, $\frac{a_x}{a_y}=\frac{\sigma}{\rho-\sigma}$

(C)

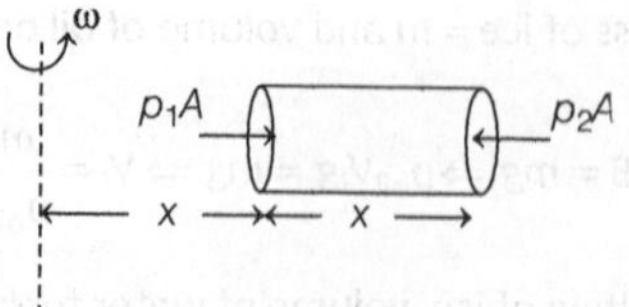

$$\Sigma F_x=ma_x \Rightarrow (p_2-p_1)A=ma_x$$

$$\Rightarrow \quad \int_x^{2x}\rho(\omega^2x)dx\,A=ma_x$$

$$\Rightarrow \quad \frac{\rho}{2}\omega^2(3x^2)A=(\sigma Ax)a_x$$

$$\Rightarrow \quad \frac{\rho}{2}\left(\frac{2g}{3x}\right)(3x^2)A=(\sigma Ax)a_x$$

$$\Rightarrow \quad \frac{a_x}{g}=\frac{\rho}{\sigma}$$

(D) When the cart is not filled liquid, $\tan\theta=\frac{a}{g}$

When the cart is filled with liquid,

$(T+B)\sin\theta'=ma$ ...(i)

$(T+B)\cos\theta'=mg$ ...(ii)

Solving we get, $\tan\theta'=\frac{a}{g}$

Hence, $\frac{\tan\theta'}{\tan\theta}=1$

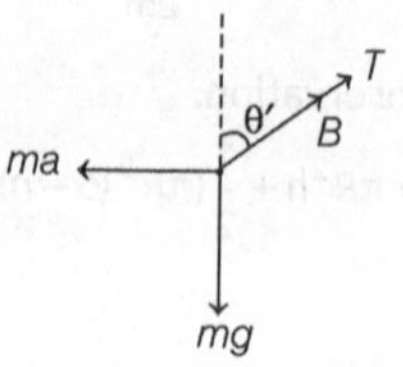

Numerical Value Questions

1. $W_{mg}+W_B=\Delta K$

$$\Rightarrow \quad +mg\,x-\int_0^x\rho(Ax)g\,dx=0-0$$

$$\Rightarrow \quad (\sigma Al)gx-\frac{\rho Agx^2}{2}=0$$

$$\Rightarrow \quad x=\frac{2\sigma l}{\rho}=8\text{m}$$

2.

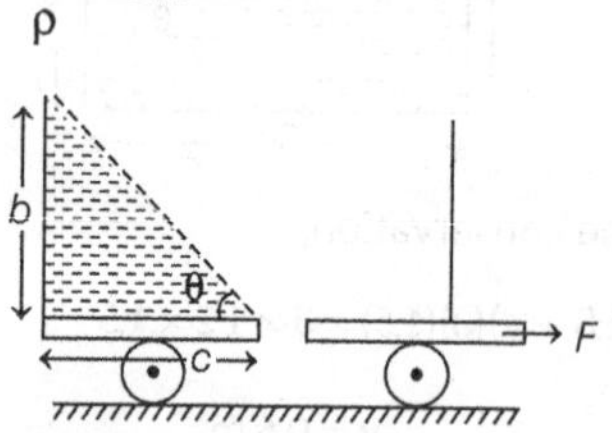

$$\tan\theta=\frac{b}{c}=\frac{a}{g}$$

$$\Rightarrow \quad a=\frac{gb}{c}=50\,\text{m/s}^2$$

Volume of water retained $=\left(\frac{1}{2}bc\right)\left(\frac{A}{L}\right)$

$m=$ Mass of water retained $=\rho\left(\frac{1}{2}\frac{bcA}{L}\right)=0.5$ kg

$F=(M+m)a=(1.5+0.5)(50)=100$ N

3. $a = 10\,\text{m/s}^2$

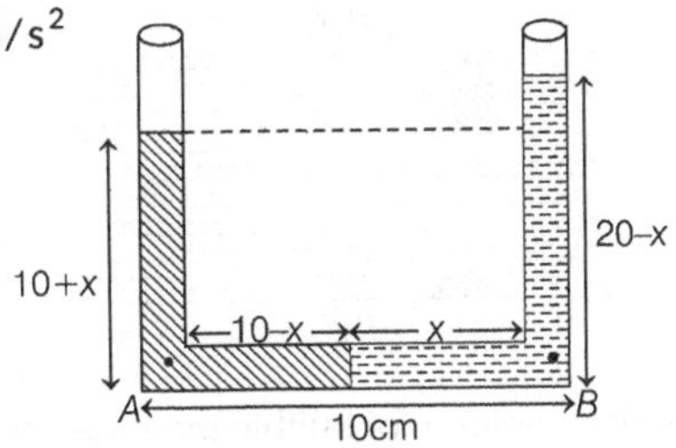

Along vertical,

$$p_A = p_0 + \rho_{oil} g(10 + x) \qquad \text{...(i)}$$

$$p_B = p_0 + \rho_w g(20 - x) \qquad \text{...(ii)}$$

Along horizontal,

$$p_B - p_A = \rho_{oil} a(10 - x) + \rho_w a x \qquad \text{...(iii)}$$

Solving, we get $x = 2$ cm

Difference between level in two limbs

$$= (20 - x) - (10 + x) = 6 \text{ cm}$$

4. $F_1 = F_2 \Rightarrow p_0(\pi R_2^2) = (p_0 + \rho g h)\pi R_1^2$

$$\Rightarrow \quad \frac{R_2}{R_1} = \sqrt{\frac{p_0 + \rho g h}{p_0}} = 2$$

5. Let length of air column before lifting out $= x$

After the tube has been lifted out of water,

$$p_{air} + 1000 \times 10 \times 1 = 10^5$$

$$\Rightarrow \quad p_{air} = 9 \times 10^4 \text{ Pa}$$

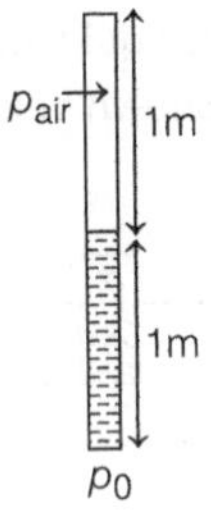

For the air column under isothermal conditions,

$$p_1 V_1 = p_2 V_2$$

$$\Rightarrow \quad 10^5 (Ax) = 9 \times 10^4 A(1) \quad \Rightarrow \quad x = 0.9 \text{ m} = 90 \text{ cm}$$

6. For floatation, $B = mg$

$$\Rightarrow \quad 1000 \times Ah \times g = 500 A(1) g$$

$$\Rightarrow \quad h = 0.5 \text{ m}$$

Applying work-energy theorem,

$$W_{ext} + W_{gravity} + W_{buoyant\ force} = \Delta K$$

$$\Rightarrow \quad W_{ext} - mgh + \int_0^h 100\,Axg\,dx = 0 - 0$$

$$\Rightarrow W_{ext} - (500 \times 4 \times 1)(10)(0.5) + \frac{1000 \times 4 \times 10 \times (0.5)^2}{2} = 0$$

$$\Rightarrow \quad W_{ext} = 5000 \text{ J} = 5 \text{ kJ}$$

7. Let side of cube be x.

$$x^3 = \frac{m}{\sigma} = \frac{4}{500} \Rightarrow x = 0.2 \text{ m}$$

Volume of water $= (5 \times 10^{-2})(0.2) = 10^{-2}\ \text{m}^3$

For equlibrium of floating cube, $B = mg$

$$\Rightarrow \quad 1000 V_d g = 4g \quad \Rightarrow \quad V_d = 4 \times 10^{-3} \text{m}^3$$

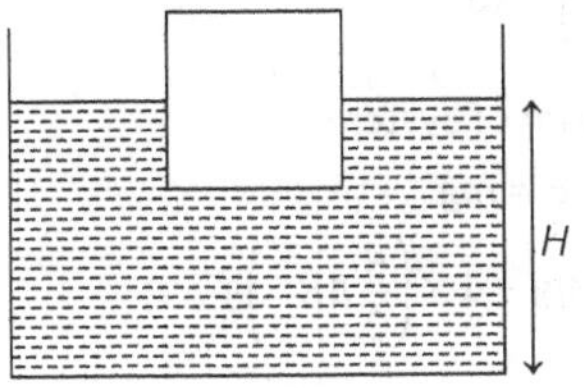

$$A = 5 \times 10^{-2} \text{m}^2$$

Volume of water $= AH - V_d$

$$\Rightarrow \quad 10^{-2} = 5 \times 10^{-2} H - 4 \times 10^{-3} \Rightarrow H = 0.28 \text{ m} = 28 \text{ cm}$$

8. $r = (b - y)\tan\alpha$

$dF = (p_0 + \rho g(H - y) - p_0)(2\pi r dr)$

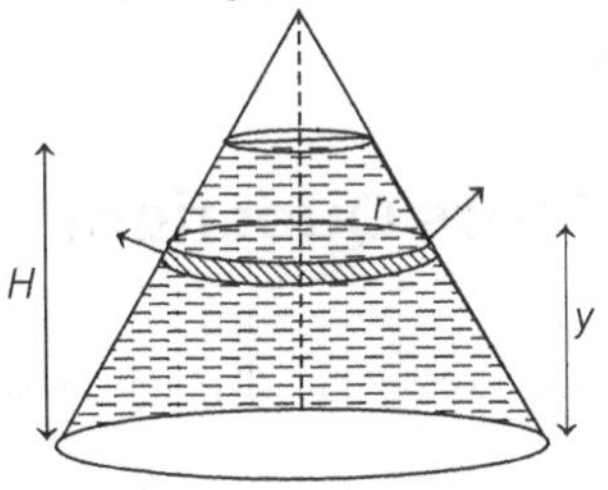

$$dr = -dy \tan\alpha$$

$$\Rightarrow \quad dF = \rho g(H - y) 2\pi r dr$$

$$\Rightarrow \quad dF = \rho g(H - y) 2\pi (b - y)\tan\alpha(-dy\tan\alpha)$$

$$\Rightarrow \quad \int dF = -2\rho g \pi \tan^2\alpha \int_H^0 (H - y)(b - y)\,dy$$

$$\Rightarrow \quad F = \pi \rho g \left[bH^2 - \frac{H^3}{3} \right]$$

Hence, $n = 3$

9.

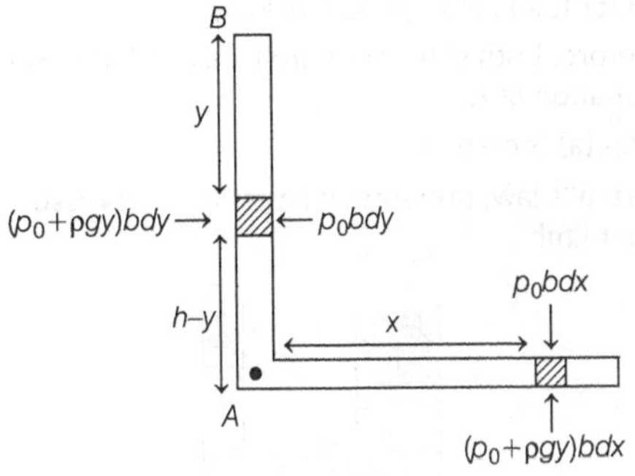

$$\text{Torque on } AB = \int_0^h (p_0 + \rho g y - p_0) b\,dy (h - y) = \frac{\rho g b h^3}{6}$$

Torque on $AC = \int_0^l (p_0 + \rho gh - p_0)(b\,dx)x = \frac{\rho gbl^2h}{2}$

For equilibrium of gate, $\tau_{AB} = \tau_{AC}$

$\Rightarrow \quad \frac{\rho gbh^3}{6} = \frac{\rho gbl^2h}{2}$

$\Rightarrow \quad \left(\frac{h}{l}\right)^2 = 3$

10. For equilibrium of system,

$B = mg$

$\Rightarrow 1\times(11\times 4)g + 1\times\left(\frac{4}{3}\pi R^3\right)g$

$= 0.5(11\times 6)g + 8\left(\frac{4}{3}\pi R^3\right)g$

$\Rightarrow \frac{4}{3}\times\frac{22}{7}R^3 = \frac{11}{7}$

$\Rightarrow R = \left(\frac{3}{8}\right)^{1/3}$

Hence, $x = 8$

Previous Years Questions

JEE Main

1. For a fluid mass, pressure at all points on same level is equal.

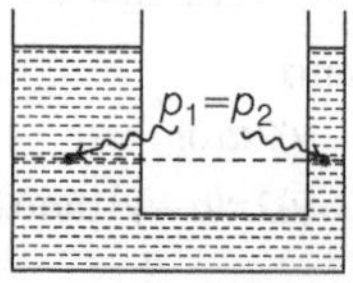

Also by pascal's law, pressure applied anywhere in a fluid is equally transmitted in all directions.

2. As per pascal's law, when we apply pressure to an ideal liquid it is equally distributed in the entire liquid and to the walls as well since due to applied pressure, every morning, the tooth paste does not get compressed and we can safely consider it an incompressible liquid.

Therefore, both statement are true and R is correct explanation of A.

Option (a) is correct.

3. By Pascal's law, pressure at larger limb = pressure at smaller limb.

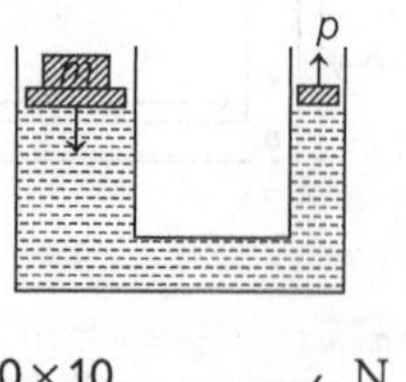

So, $p = \frac{Mg}{A} = \frac{5000\times 10}{250\times 10^{-4}} = 2\times 10^{-6}\ \frac{\text{N}}{\text{m}^2} = 2\times 10^{6}$ Pa

4.

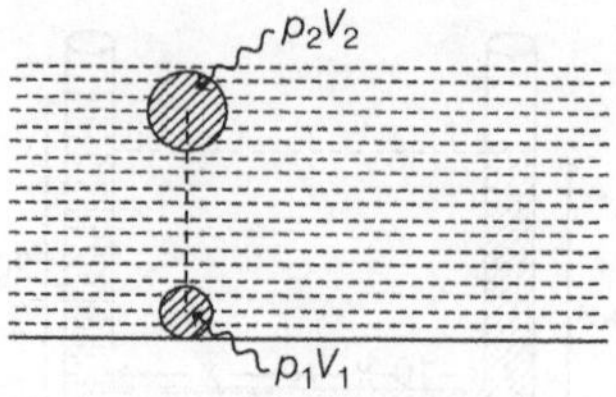

As bubble rises, volume of bubble increases due to decrease of pressure.

It is also given temperature remains constant so;

$$p_1V_1 = p_2V_2 \qquad \text{...(i)}$$

Here, $\quad p_1 = p_{\text{atm}} + p_{\text{water}} = p_{\text{atm}} + h\rho g$

Now, $p_{\text{atm}} = 1\times 10^5$Pa

And $h\rho g = 40\times 1000\times 10 = 4\times 10^5$ Pa

So; $\quad p_1 = 1\times 10^5 + 4\times 10^5 = 5\times 10^5$Pa

and $\quad V_1 = 1\text{ cm}^3$

Also $\quad p_2$ = pressure at surface
= atmospheric pressure
$= 1\times 10^5$ Pa

So substituting value in Eq. (i) we get;

$p_1V_1 = p_2V_2$

$\Rightarrow (5\times 10^5\text{Pa})(1\text{ cm}^3) = (1\times 10^5\text{Pa})(V_2)$

$\Rightarrow \quad V_2 = 5\text{ cm}^3$

5. Given, length of tube, $l = 50$ cm $= 0.5$ m

Mass of incompressible liquid, $m = 250g = 0.25$ kg

The given situation is shown below.

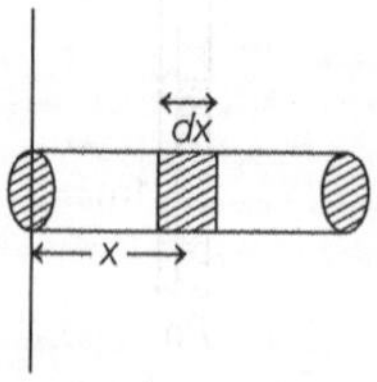

Force exerted by the liquid at the other end due to rotation,

$$F = \int (dm)\omega^2 x$$

where, $dm = \frac{m}{L}\cdot dx$

$\therefore \quad F = \int_0^L \frac{m}{L}dx\cdot\omega^2 x = \frac{m}{L}\cdot\omega^2\left[\frac{x^2}{2}\right]_0^L$

$F = \frac{m\omega^2 L}{2}$

$\Rightarrow \quad \omega = \sqrt{\frac{2F}{mL}} = \sqrt{\frac{2F}{0.25\times 0.5}}$

$= \sqrt{16F} = 4\sqrt{F} = x\sqrt{F}$ (given)

$\therefore \quad x = 4$

6. Given, cross-section area of tube, $A = 10\ cm^2$
$= 10 \times 10^{-4} m^2$

Speed of outflow of water, $v = 20\ ms^{-1}$

Density of water, $\rho_w = 1000\ kgm^{-3}$

As we know, force exerted by water flow on the wall,
F_w = momentum loss of water per second = mass of hitting the wall per second × speed of water

$$\Rightarrow \quad F_w = (\rho_w A v_w) \times v_w = \rho_w A v_w^2$$
$$= 1000 \times 10 \times 10^{-4} \times (20)^2 = 400\ N$$

7. The given situation is shown below,

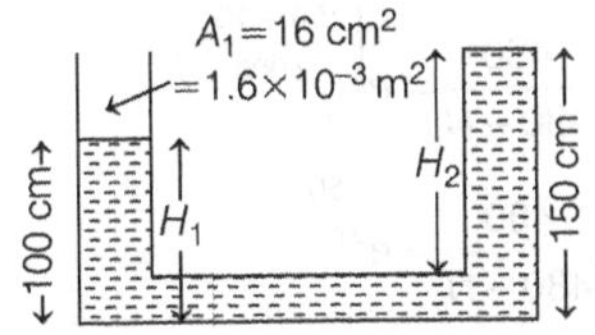

Here, $H_1 = 100\ cm = 1\ m$, $H_2 = 150\ cm = 1.5\ m$
Density of water, $\rho = 10^3 kg/m^3$, $g = 10\ m/s^2$

Total initial energy of two vessels before interconnection,
$$E_i = m_1 g \frac{H_1}{2} + m_2 g \frac{H_2}{2}$$

Since, $m_1 = \rho A.H_1$ and $m_2 = \rho A H_2$

$$\therefore \quad E_i = \rho A H_1\, g \frac{H_1}{2} + \rho A H_2 g \frac{H_2}{2}$$
$$= \frac{\rho A g}{2}(H_1^2 + H_2^2) = \frac{\rho A g}{2}(1^2 + 1.5^2)$$
$$\Rightarrow \quad E_i = \frac{3.25}{2}\rho A g \quad \text{...(i)}$$

Similarly, total final energy of the two vessels after interconnecting them,
$$E_f = \frac{\rho A g}{2}(H_1^2 + H_2^2)$$
$$= \frac{\rho A g}{2}(H^2 + H^2) \quad (\because H_1 = H_2 = H)$$
$$= \frac{\rho A g}{2}(2H^2) \quad \left(H = \frac{H_1 + H_2}{2} = \frac{1 + 1.5}{2} = 1.25 m\right)$$
$$= \rho A g (1.25)^2 = \frac{3.125\,\rho A g}{2}$$

Work done by the force of gravity, $W = E_i - E_f$
$$= \frac{\rho A g}{2}(3.25 - 3.125)$$
$$= \frac{10^3 \times 1.6 \times 10^{-3} \times 10 \times 0.125}{2} = 1\ J$$

8. Given, pressure on submarine at a certain depth,
$$p_i = 3 \times 10^5 Pa$$

Since, we know that at a certain depth or below the surface of a liquid of density ρ, pressure is given as
$$p_i = p_0 + \rho g h$$
$$\Rightarrow \quad 3 \times 10^5 = p_0 + \rho g h$$
$$\Rightarrow \quad 3 \times 10^5 = 1 \times 10^5 + \rho g h \quad (\because p_0 = 1 \times 10^5 Pa)$$
$$\Rightarrow \quad 3 \times 10^5 - 1 \times 10^5 = \rho g h$$
$$\Rightarrow \quad 2 \times 10^5 = \rho g h \quad \text{...(i)}$$

When the depth is doubled, then final pressure will be
$$p_f = p_0 + \rho g 2h = 1 \times 10^5 + 2(\rho g h)$$
$$= 1 \times 10^5 + 2(2 \times 10^5) \quad \text{[using Eq. (i)]}$$
$$= 1 \times 10^5 + 4 \times 10^5$$
$$\Rightarrow \quad p_f = 5 \times 10^5 Pa$$

∴ Percentage increase in pressure
$$= \frac{p_f - p_i}{p_i} \times 100 = \frac{(5-3) \times 10^5}{3 \times 10^5} \times 100 = \frac{200}{3}\%$$

9. According to Pascal's law,
$$\frac{F_1}{A_1} = \frac{F_2}{A_2}$$

Initially, $$\frac{100g}{A_1} = \frac{mg}{A_2} \quad \text{...(i)}$$

Finally, $$\frac{Mg}{16A_1} = \frac{mg}{\left(\frac{A_2}{16}\right)} \quad \text{...(ii)}$$

On dividing Eqs. (i) by (ii), we get
$$\frac{100 \times 16}{M} = \frac{1}{16}$$
$$\therefore \quad M = 25600\ kg$$

10. From free body diagram,
$B - mg = ma$(here, B = buoyant force)
$\rho_w V g - mg = ma$ (here, V = volume)
$$\rho_w V g = mg + ma$$
$$\rho_w V g = m(g + a)$$
$$\Rightarrow \quad m = \frac{\rho_w V g}{g + a} \quad \text{...(i)}$$

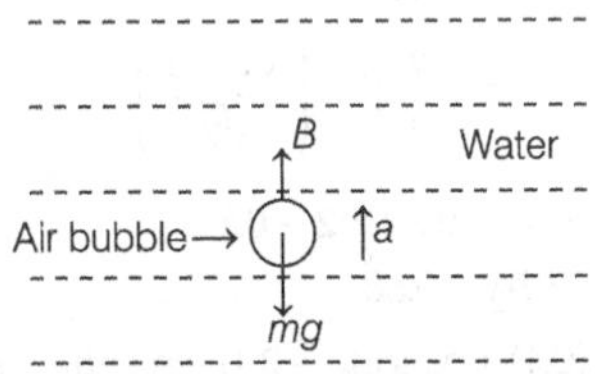

Given, $\rho_w = 1\ g/cm^3$ $g = 980\ cm/s^2$,
$a = 9.8\ cm/s^2$ and $r = 1\ cm$

Substituting all values in eq. (i), we get
$$m = \frac{(1) \times \frac{4}{3}\pi r^3 \times 980}{980 + 9.8} = \frac{\frac{4}{3} \times \frac{22}{7} \times (1)^3 \times 980}{989.8}$$
$$= \frac{4 \times 22 \times 980}{3 \times 7 \times 989.8} = 4.148\ g \simeq 4.15\ g$$

Hence, correct option is (c).

11. Relative density or specific gravity,

$$\rho_r = \frac{\text{Density of object}}{\text{Density of water}} = \frac{\rho_o}{\rho_w} = \frac{27}{8}$$

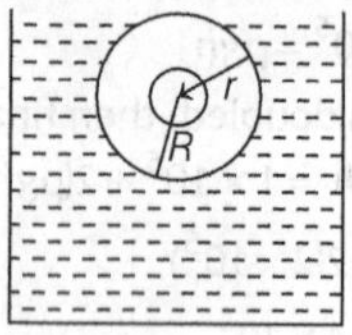

In equilibrium,

$$\frac{4}{3}\pi R^3 \rho_w g = \frac{4}{3}\pi(R^3 - r^3)\rho_o \cdot g$$

$$\Rightarrow \quad R^3 = (R^3 - r^3)\left(\frac{27}{8}\right)$$

$$\Rightarrow \quad 8R^3 = 27R^3 - 27r^3$$

$$\Rightarrow \quad 27r^3 = 27R^3 - 8R^3$$

$$\Rightarrow \quad 27r^3 = 19R^3$$

$$\Rightarrow \quad \frac{r^3}{R^3} = \frac{19}{27}$$

$$\Rightarrow \quad r = \left(\frac{19}{27}\right)^{1/3} R = \frac{2.66}{3} R = 0.88R$$

$$\Rightarrow \quad r \approx \frac{8}{9}R$$

Hence, correct option is (a).

JEE Advanced

1. $(p_1 - p_2)ds = \rho d s d\sqrt{2}(g \sin 45° - a)$

$$(p_1 - p_2)ds = \rho d(g - a\sqrt{2})$$

$$\beta = \frac{(p_1 - p_2)}{\rho g d} = \left(1 - \frac{a\sqrt{2}}{g}\right)$$

When $\quad a = \frac{g}{\sqrt{2}}, \beta = 0$

When $\quad a = \frac{g}{2}, \beta = \left(\frac{\sqrt{2} - 1}{\sqrt{2}}\right)$

2. We have, $h_1 + h_2 = 0.29 \times 2 + 0.1$

$$h_1 + h_2 = 0.68 \qquad \text{... (i)}$$

$\Rightarrow p_0 + \rho_k g(0.1) + \rho_w g(h_1 - 0.1) - \rho_w g h_2 = p_0$

where, ρ_k = density of kerosene and ρ_w = density of water.

$$\Rightarrow \quad \rho_k g(0.1) + \rho_w g h_1 - \rho_w g \times (0.1) = \rho_w g h_2$$

$$\Rightarrow \quad 800 \times 10 \times 0.1 + 1000 \times 10 \times h_1 - 1000 \times 10 \times 0.1 = 1000 \times 10 \times h_2$$

$$\Rightarrow \quad 10000(h_1 - h_2) = 200$$

$$\Rightarrow \quad h_1 - h_2 = 0.02 \qquad \text{... (ii)}$$

Solving Eqs. (i) and (ii), we get

$$h_1 = 0.35 \text{ and } h_2 = 0.33$$

So, $\quad \frac{h_1}{h_2} = \frac{35}{33}$

3. Weight = Upthrust

$$mg = F_u$$

$$480 \times 10 = \rho V g$$

$$480 \times 10 = \rho_0 e^{-\frac{h}{h_0}}$$

$$480 \times 10 = \rho_0 e^{-\frac{100}{6000}} Vg \qquad \text{... (i)}$$

$$(480 - N \times 1)\,10 = \rho' Vg$$

$$(480 - N)\,10 = \rho_0 e^{-\frac{150}{6000}} Vg \qquad \text{... (ii)}$$

Dividing Eq. (i) by Eq. (ii), we get

$$\frac{480}{480 - N} = e^{\left(\frac{150 - 100}{6000}\right)}$$

$$\frac{480}{480 - N} = e^{\frac{50}{6000}}$$

$$\frac{480}{480 - N} = e^{\frac{1}{120}}$$

$$N = 4$$

4. In equilibrium, Upward force = Downward force

$$kx_0 + F_B = mg$$

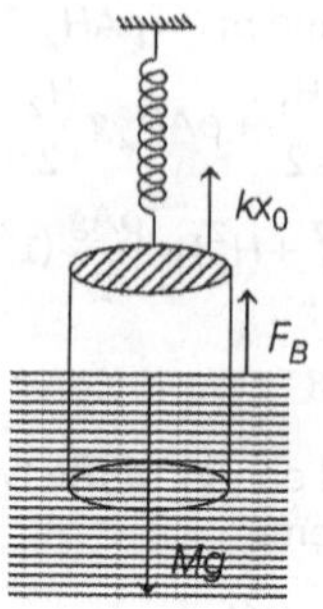

Here, kx_0 is restoring force of spring and F_B is buoyancy force.

$$kx_0 + \sigma \frac{L}{2} Ag = Mg$$

$$x_0 = \frac{Mg - \frac{\sigma L A g}{2}}{k} = \frac{Mg}{k}\left(1 - \frac{\sigma LA}{2M}\right)$$

5.

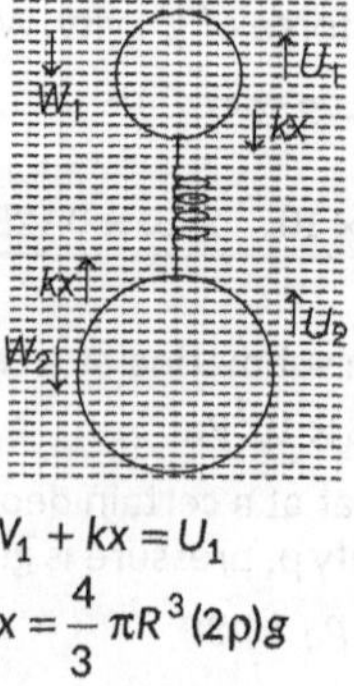

On small sphere, $W_1 + kx = U_1$

$$\therefore \quad \frac{4}{3}\pi R^3(\rho)g + kx = \frac{4}{3}\pi R^3(2\rho)g \qquad \text{...(i)}$$

On second sphere (large)

$$W_2 = U_2 + kx$$

$$\therefore \quad \frac{4}{3}\pi R^3(3\rho)g = \frac{4}{3}\pi R^3(2\rho)g + kx \qquad \text{...(ii)}$$

By Eqs. (i) and (ii), we get

$$x = \frac{4\pi R^3 \rho g}{3k}$$

Here, U represents upthrust.

6. Let V_1 = total material volume of shell
   V_2 = total inside volume of shell and
   x = fraction of V_2 volume filled with water.

   In floating condition,
   Total weight = Upthrust

$$\therefore \quad V_1\rho_c g + (xV_2)(1)\,g = \left(\frac{V_1 + V_2}{2}\right)(1)\,g$$

$$\text{or} \quad x = 0.5 + (0.5 - \rho_c)\frac{V_1}{V_2}$$

   From here we can see that, $x > 0.5$ if $\rho_c < 0.5$

7. As the bubble moves upwards, besides the buoyancy force (cause of which is pressure difference) only force of gravity and force of viscosity will act.
   $\therefore$ Correct option is (d).

8. As there is no exchange of heat. Therefore, process is adiabatic. Applying,

$$T^{\gamma}p^{1-\gamma} = \text{constant}$$

$$\text{or} \quad Tp^{\frac{1-\gamma}{\gamma}} = \text{constant}$$

$$\Rightarrow \quad T_2 p_2^{\frac{1-\gamma}{\gamma}} = T_1 p_1^{\frac{1-\gamma}{\gamma}}$$

$$\text{or} \quad T_2 = T_1\left(\frac{p_1}{p_2}\right)^{\frac{1-\gamma}{\gamma}} = T_1\left(\frac{p_2}{p_1}\right)^{\frac{\gamma-1}{\gamma}}$$

   Substituting the values, we have

$$T_2 = T_0\left[\frac{p_0 + \rho_l g(H - y)}{p_0 + \rho_l gH}\right]^{\frac{5/3-1}{5/3}}$$

$$= T_0\left[\frac{p_0 + \rho_l g(H - y)}{p_0 + \rho_l gH}\right]^{\frac{2}{5}}$$

   $\therefore$ Correct option is (b).

9. Buoyancy force

$$F = \text{(volume of bubble)}\,(\rho_l)g = \left(\frac{nRT_2}{p_2}\right)\rho_l g$$

$$\text{Here,} \quad T_2 = T_0\left[\frac{p_0 + \rho_e g(H - y)}{p_0 + \rho_l gh}\right]^{\frac{2}{5}}$$

$$\text{and} \quad p_2 = p_0 + \rho_l g(H - y)$$

   Substituting the values, we get

$$F = \frac{\rho_l nRgT_0}{(p_0 + \rho_l gH)^{2/5}[p_0 + \rho_l g(H - y)]^{3/5}}$$

   $\therefore$ Correct option is (b)

10. Force from right hand side liquid on left hand side liquid.
    (i) Due to surface tension force $= 2RT$ (towards right)
    (ii) Due to liquid pressure force

$$= \int_{x=0}^{x=h} (p_0 + \rho gh)(2R\cdot x)\,dx$$

$$= (2p_0Rh + R\rho gh^2) \text{ (towards left)}$$

$$\therefore \text{ Net force is } |2p_0Rh + R\rho gh^2 - 2RT|$$

11. Let A_1 = Area of cross-section of cylinder $= 4\pi r^2$
    A_2 = Area of base of cylinder in air $= \pi r^2$
    and A_3 = Area of base of cylinder in water
    $= A_1 - A_2 = 3\pi r^2$

    Drawing free body diagram of cylinder

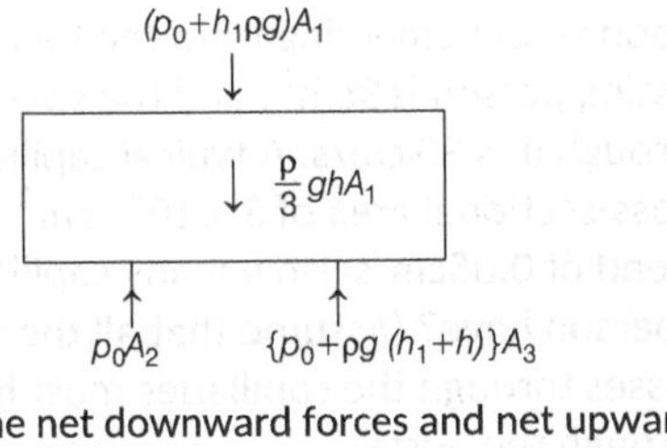

    Equating the net downward forces and net upward forces, we get, $h_1 = \frac{5}{3}h$.

12. Again equating the forces, we get

$$h_2 = \frac{4h}{9}$$

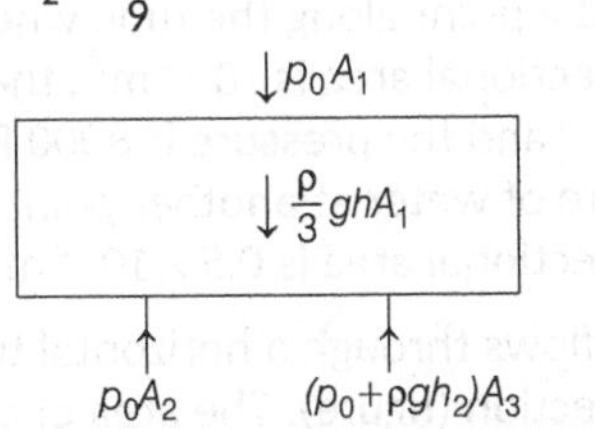

13. For $h_2 < 4h/9$, buoyant force will further decrease. Hence, the cylinder remains at its original position.

CHAPTER~08

FLUID DYNAMICS

LEVEL 01 Starter Level

8.1 Equation of Continuity

1. Two water pipes of diameters 4 cm and 8 cm are connected with main supply line. The velocity of flow of water in the pipe of 8 cm diameter is 10 cm/s, then what is velocity of flow in 4 cm diameter pipe?

2. The cross-sectional area of the aorta (the major blood vessel emerging from the heart) of a normal resting person is $3 cm^2$, and the speed of blood through it is 30 cm/s. A typical capillary has cross-sectional area of $3 \times 10^{-7} cm^2$ and a flow speed of 0.05cm/s. How many capillaries does such a person have? (Assume that all the blood that passes through the capillaries must have passed through the aorta).

8.2 Bernoulli's Equation

1. A horizontal pipe line carries water in a streamline flow. At a point along the tube where the cross-sectional area is $10^{-2} m^2$, the water velocity is $2 ms^{-1}$ and the pressure is 8000 Pa. Find the pressure of water at another point where the cross-sectional area is $0.5 \times 10^{-2} m^2$.

2. Water flows through a horizontal tube of variable cross-section (figure). The area of cross-section at A and B are $4 mm^2$ and $2 mm^2$ respectively. If 1 cc of water enters per second through A, find (a) the speed of water at A, (b) the speed of water at B and (c) the pressure difference $p_A - p_B$.

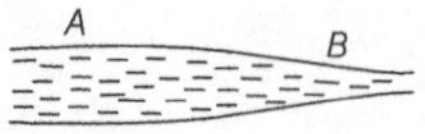

3. Suppose the tube in the previous problem is kept vertical with A upward but the other conditions remain the same. The separation between the cross-sections at A and B is 15/16 cm. Repeat parts (a), (b) and (c) of the previous problem. Take $g = 10 m/s^2$.

4. Water flows through a tube shown in figure. The areas of cross-section at A and B are $1 cm^2$ and $0.5 cm^2$ respectively. The height difference between A and B is 5 cm. If the speed of water at A is 10 cm/s find (a) the speed at B and (b) the difference in pressures at A and B.

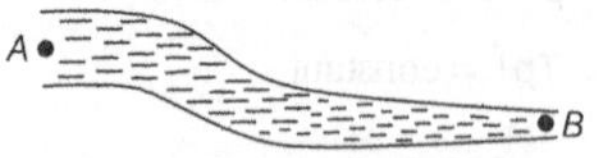

5. Air is streaming past a horizontal aeroplane wing such that the speed of air is 120 m/s over the upper surface and 90 m/s at the lower surface, with respect to the plane. If the density of air is $1.3 kg/m^3$, find the difference in pressure between the top and bottom of the wing. If the wing is 10 m long and has an average width of 2 m, calculate the gross lift of the wing.

6. Water is flowing continuously from a tap having an internal diameter 8×10^{-3} m. The water velocity as it leaves the tap is $0.4 ms^{-1}$. Find the diameter of the water stream at a distance 20 cm below the tap.

7. Water flows through a horizontal tube as shown in figure. If the difference of heights of water column in the vertical tubes are 2 cm, and the areas of cross-section at A and B are $4 cm^2$ and $2 cm^2$ respectively, find the rate of flow of water across any section.

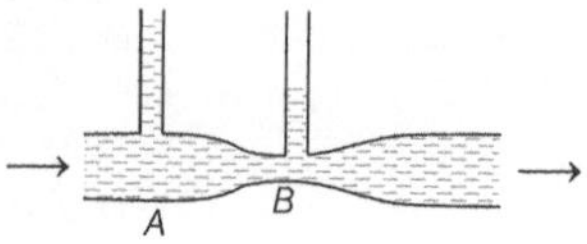

8. Water flows through the tube shown in figure. The areas of cross-section of the wide and the narrow portions of the tube are 5 cm^2 and 2 cm^2 respectively. The rate of flow of water through the tube is 500 cm^3/s. Find the difference of mercury levels in the U-tube.

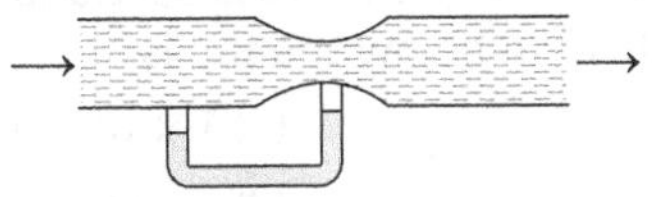

8.3 Velocity of Efflux

1. A tank is filled with water upto height H. Water is allowed to come out of a hole P in one of the walls at a depth D below the surface of water as shown in the figure.

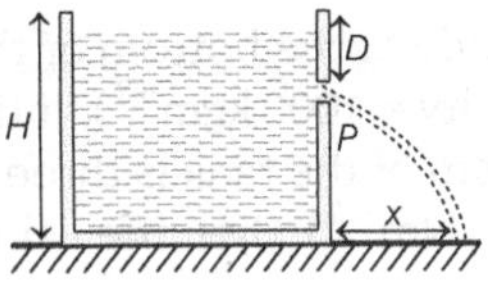

(a) Express the horizontal distance x in terms of H and D.

(b) What will be value of D for which horizontal distance x will be maximum?

2. A large cylindrical tank of cross-sectional area $1 m^2$ is filled with water. It has a small hole at a height of 1 m from the bottom. A movable piston of mass 5 kg is fitted on the top of the tank such that it can slide in the tank freely. A load of 45 kg is applied on the top of water by piston, as shown in figure. Find the value of v when piston is 7m above the bottom. ($g = 10 m/s^2$).

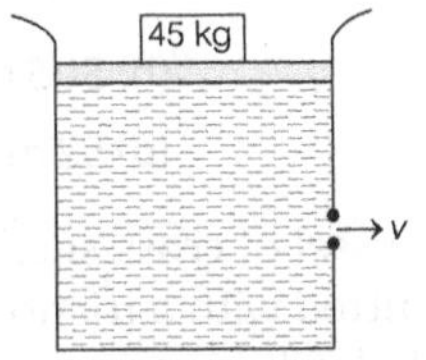

3. A tank is filled with two immiscible liquids of densities ρ and 2ρ each of height h as shown in figure. A small hole is punched at depth $3h/2$ from the surface of lighter liquid. Find the velocity (v) of efflux from the hole.

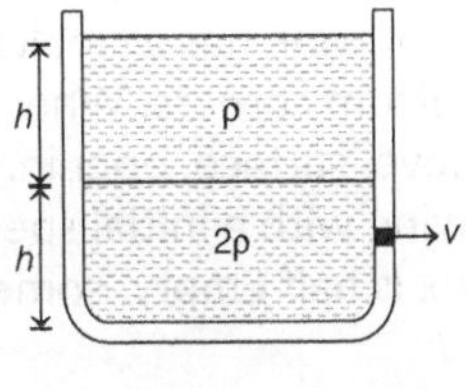

4. A cylindrical container of cross-section area, A is filled up with water upto height h. Water may exit through a tap of cross-section area a in the bottom of container. Find

(a) velocity of water just after opening of tap.

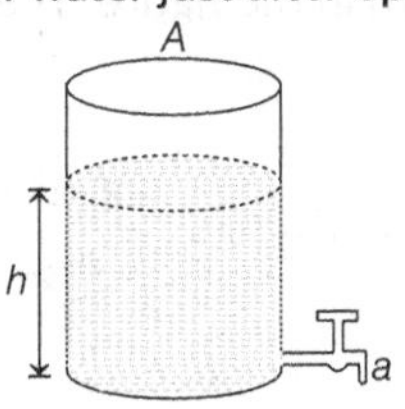

(b) time in which container becomes empty.

(Given, $\left(\frac{a}{A}\right)^{1/2} = 0.02$, $h = 20$ cm)

5. A siphon tube is discharging a liquid of specific gravity 0.9 from a reservoir as shown in the figure. (use $g = 10 m/s^2$ and $p_{atm} = 10^5 Pa$)

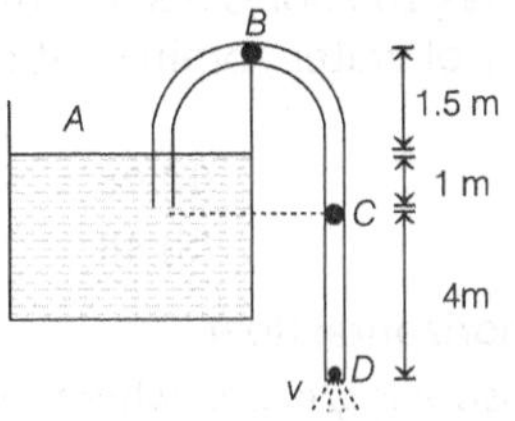

(a) Find the velocity of the liquid through the siphon.

(b) Find the pressure at the highest point B.

(c) Find the pressure at point C.

6. A non-viscous liquid of constant density 1000 kg/m^3 flows in streamline motion along a tube of variable cross-section. The tube is kept inclined in the vertical plane as shown in the figure. The area of cross-section of the tube at two points P and Q at heights of 2m and 5m are respectively $4 \times 10^{-3} m^2$ and $8 \times 10^{-3} m^2$. The velocity of the liquid at point P is 1 m/s. Find the work done per unit volume by the pressure and the gravity forces as the fluid flows from point P to Q.

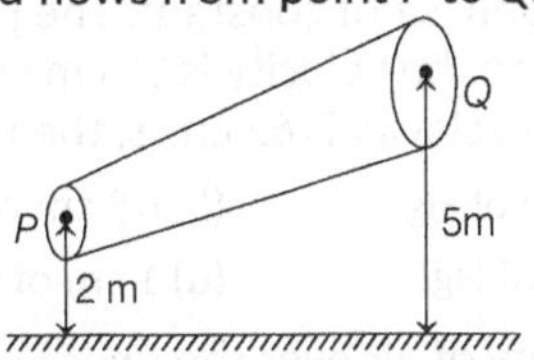

7. A vertical tank, open at the top, is filled with a liquid and rests on a smooth horizontal surface. A small hole is opened at the centre of one side of the tank. The area of cross-section of the tank is N times the area of the hole, where N is a large number. Neglect mass of the tank itself. Find the initial acceleration of the tank.

LEVEL 02 JEE Main Level

Single Choice Correct Questions

1. An incompressible liquid flows through a horizontal tube as shown in the figure. Then, the velocity v of the fluid is

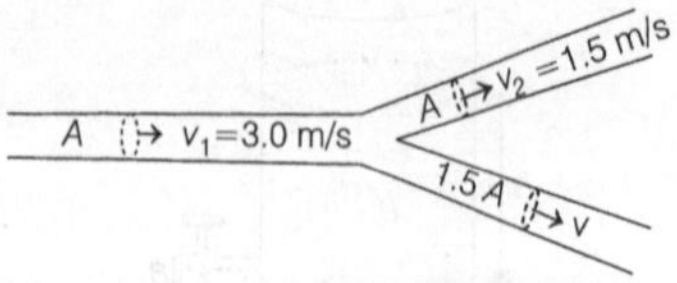

(a) 3.0 m/s (b) 1.5 m/s
(c) 1.0 m/s (d) 2.25 m/s

2. Fountains usually seen in gardens are generated by a wide pipe with an enclosure at one end having many small holes. Consider one such fountain which is produced by a pipe of internal diameter 2 cm in which water flows at a rate $3\ ms^{-1}$. The enclosure has 100 holes each of diameter 0.05 cm. The velocity of water coming out of the holes is (in ms^{-1})

(a) 0.48 (b) 96
(c) 24 (d) 48

3. In steady horizontal flow

(a) the pressure is greatest where the speed is least
(b) the pressure is independent of speed
(c) the pressure is least where the speed is least
(d) a and c are correct.

4. Water is flowing through two horizontal pipes of different radii which are connected together. In the first pipe speed of water is $4\ ms^{-1}$ and the pressure is $1.25 \times 10^4\ Nm^{-2}$. Then pressure of water in the second pipe is (radii of those pipes are in the ratio 1 : 2)

(a) $0.5 \times 10^4 Nm^{-2}$ (b) $0.75 \times 10^4\ Nm^{-2}$
(c) $1 \times 10^4\ Nm^{-2}$ (d) $2 \times 10^4\ Nm^{-2}$

5. Water flows along a horizontal pipe whose cross-section is not constant. The pressure is 1 cm of Hg where the velocity is 35 cm/ s. At a point where the velocity is 65 cm/s, the pressure will be

(a) 0.89 cm of Hg (b) 8.9 cm of Hg
(c) 0.5 cm of Hg (d) 1 cm of Hg

6. The velocity of air over the upper surface of airplane wing is $40\ ms^{-1}$ and that on the lower surface is $30\ ms^{-1}$. The area of the wing is $4\ m^2$. If the mass of the wing is 200 kg, the net force acting on it is (density of air $= 1.3\ kgm^{-3}$ $(g = 9.8\ m/s^2)$)

(a) 140 N up (b) 140 N down
(c) 280 N up (d) 280 N down

7. Water from a tap emerges vertically downwards with an initial speed of 1 m/s. The cross-sectional area of tap is $10^{-4}\ m^2$. Assume that the pressure is constant throughout the stream of water and that the flow is steady, the cross-sectional area of stream 0.15 m below the tap is

(a) $5 \times 10^{-4}\ m^2$ (b) $1 \times 10^{-4}\ m^2$
(c) $5 \times 10^{-5}\ m^2$ (d) $2 \times 10^{-5}\ m^2$

8. To get the maximum flight, a ball must be thrown as

(a) 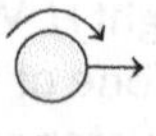 (b) 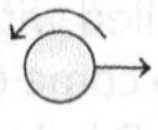
(c) 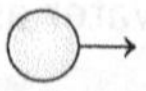 (d) any of (A), (B), and (C)

9. A hole is made at the bottom of the tank filled with water (density $= 1000\ kgm^{-3}$). If the total pressure at the bottom of the tank is three atmospheres ($1\ atm = 10^5\ Nm^{-2}$), then the velocity of efflux is

(a) $\sqrt{400}\ ms^{-1}$ (b) $\sqrt{200}\ ms^{-1}$
(c) $\sqrt{600}\ ms^{-1}$ (d) $\sqrt{500}\ ms^{-1}$

10. Where is filled in a cylindrical container to a height of 3 m. The ratio of the cross-sectional area of the orifice and the beaker is 0.1. The square of the speed of the liquid coming out from the orifice is $(g = 10\ m/s^2)$

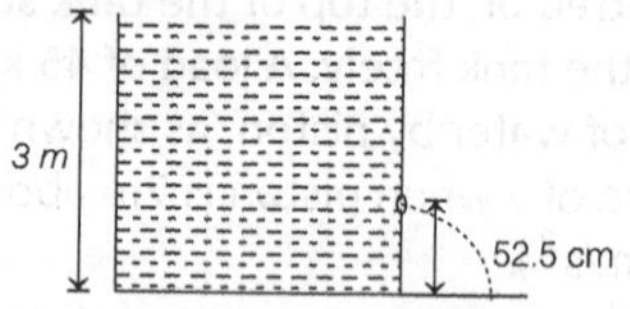

(a) $50\ m^2/s^2$ (b) $50.5\ m^2/s^2$
(c) $51\ m^2/s^2$ (d) $52\ m^2/s^2$

11. A cylindrical vessel of cross-sectional area $1000\ cm^2$, is fitted with a frictionless piston of mass 10 kg, and filled with water completely. A small hole of cross-sectional area $10\ mm^2$ is opened at a point 50 cm deep from the lower surface of the piston. The velocity of efflux from the hole will be

(a) 10.5 m/s (b) 3.4 m/s
(c) 0.8 m/s (d) 0.2 m/s

12. A cubical box of wine has a small spout located in one of the bottom corners. When box is full and placed on a level surface, opening the spout result in a flow of wine with a initial speed of v_o (see fig). When the box is half empty, someone tilts it at 45°

so that the spout is at the lowest point. When the spout is opened the wine will flow out with a speed of

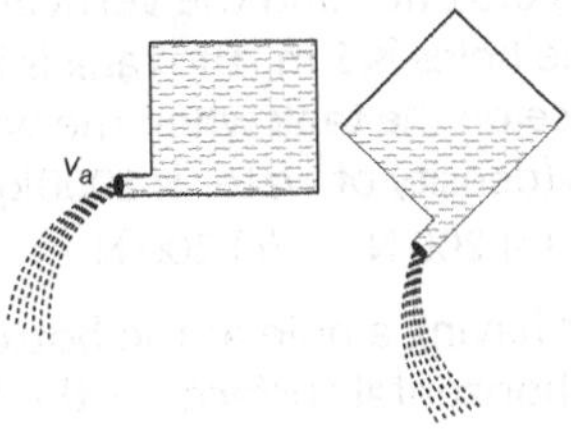

(a) v_0 (b) $v_0/2$ (c) $v_0/\sqrt{2}$ (d) $v_0/\sqrt[4]{2}$

13. A large open tank has two holes in the wall. One is a square hole of side L at a depth y from the top and the other is a circular hole of radius R at a depth $4y$ from the top. When the tank is completely filled with water, the quantities of water flowing out per second from both holes are the same. Then radius R, is equal to

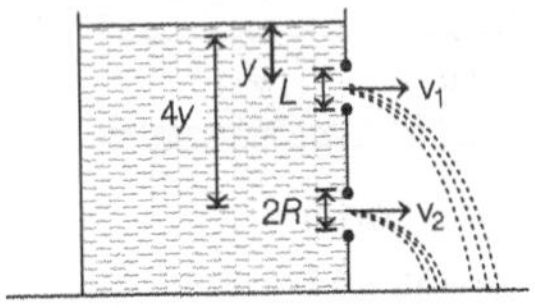

(a) $\frac{L}{\sqrt{2\pi}}$ (b) $2\pi L$ (c) L (d) $\frac{L}{2\pi}$

14. A tube is attached as shown in the closed vessel containing water. The velocity of water coming out from a small hole is

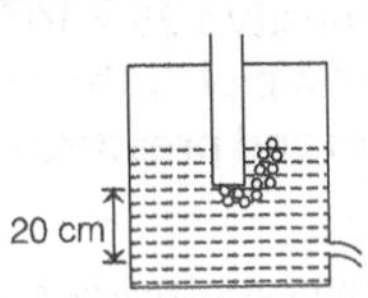

(a) $\sqrt{2}$ m/s (b) 2 m/s
(c) depends on pressure of air inside vessel
(d) None of these

15. The velocity of the liquid coming out of a small hole of a large vessel containing two different liquids of densities 2ρ and ρ as shown in figure is

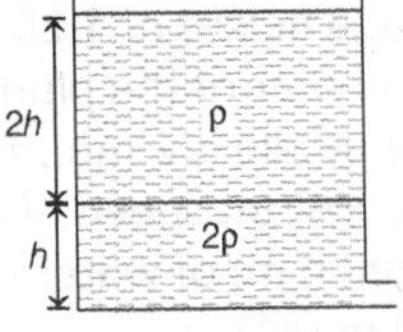

(a) $\sqrt{6gh}$ (b) $2\sqrt{gh}$
(c) $2\sqrt{2gh}$ (d) $\sqrt{gh}$

16. A large tank is filled with water (density $= 10^3$ kg/m^3). A small hole is made at a depth 10 m below water surface. The range of water issuing out of the hole is R on ground. What extra pressure must be applied on the water surface so that the range becomes $2R$ (take 1 atm $= 10^5$ Pa and $g = 10$ m/s^2)

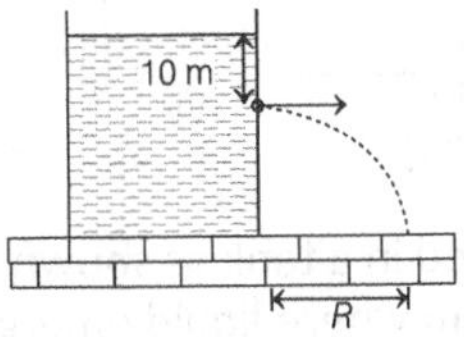

(a) 9 atm
(b) 4 atm
(c) 5 atm
(d) 3 atm

17. A tank with vertical wall is mounted so that its base is at a height H above the horizontal ground. The tank is filled with water to a depth h. A hole is punched in the side wall of the tank at a depth X below the water surface. To have maximum range of the emerging steam, the value of X is

(a) $\frac{H+h}{4}$ (b) $\frac{H+h}{2}$
(c) $\frac{H+h}{3}$ (d) $\frac{3(H+h)}{4}$

18. As shown in the figure water squirts horizontally out of two small holes in the side of the cylinder and the two streams strike the ground at the same point. It hole Q is at a height h above ground and level of water stands to a height H, then the height of P above ground level is

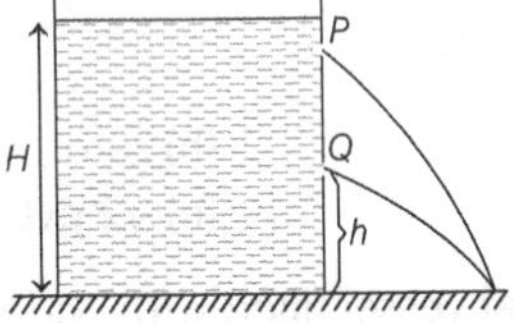

(a) $2h$ (b) $H - 2h$
(c) $(H - h)$ (d) None

19. A large tank filled with water a height h is to be emptied through a small hole at the bottom. The ratio of times taken for the level for water to fall from h to $h/2$ and from $h/2$ to zero is

(a) $\sqrt{2}$ (b) $\frac{1}{\sqrt{2}}$
(c) $\sqrt{2} - 1$ (d) $\frac{1}{\sqrt{2} - 1}$

20. For a fluid which is flowing steadily in a horizontal tube as shown in the figure, the level in the vertical tubes is best represented by

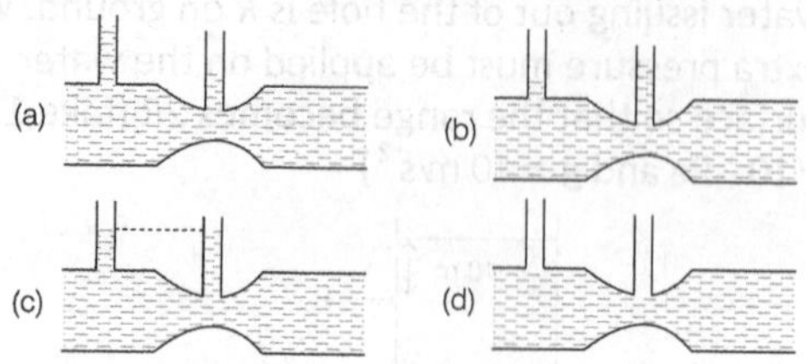

21. Water is filled in a tank as shown in figure. There is a hole from where liquid emerges with speed v. If air is blown over the tank, the speed v

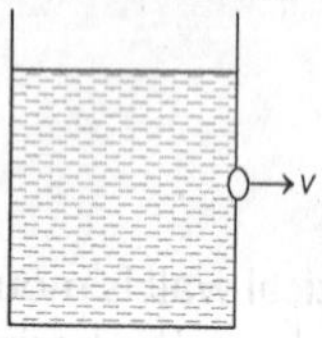

(a) will decrease
(b) will increase
(c) will remain same
(d) may increase or decrease. It will depend on density of liquid

22. A fire hydrant (as shown in the figure) delivers water of density ρ at a volume rate L. The water travels vertically upward through the hydrant and then does 90° turn to emerge horizontally at speed v. The pipe and nozzle have uniform cross-section throughout. The force exerted by the water on the corner of the hydrant is

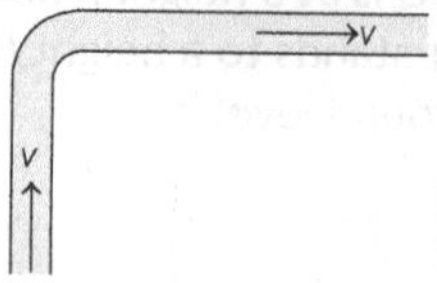

(a) ρvL (b) zero
(c) $2\rho vL$ (d) $\sqrt{2}\,\rho vL$

23. A cylindrical vessel filled with water of density ρ upto height of H stands on a horizontal plane. The side wall of the vessel has a plugged circular hole touching the bottom. The coefficient of friction between the bottom of vessel and plane is μ and total mass of water plus vessel is M. What should be minimum diameter of hole so that the vessel begins to move on the floor if plug is removed?

(a) $\sqrt{\dfrac{2\mu M}{\pi \rho H}}$ (b) $\sqrt{\dfrac{\mu M}{2\pi\rho H}}$

(c) $\sqrt{\dfrac{\mu M}{\rho H}}$ (d) none

24. There are two holes one each along the opposite sides of a wide rectangular tank. The cross-section of each hole is $0.01\ \text{m}^2$ and the vertical distance between the holes is 1 m. The tank is filled with water. The net force on the tank when the water flows out of the holes is (density of water is $1000\text{kg}/\text{m}^3$)
(a) 100 N (b) 200 N (c) 300 N (d) 400 N

25. A container having a hole at the bottom is free to move on a horizontal surface. As the liquid comes out, the container moves in backward direction with an acceleration α and finally acquires a velocity v (when all the liquid has drained out). Neglect the mass of container. The correct option out of the following is

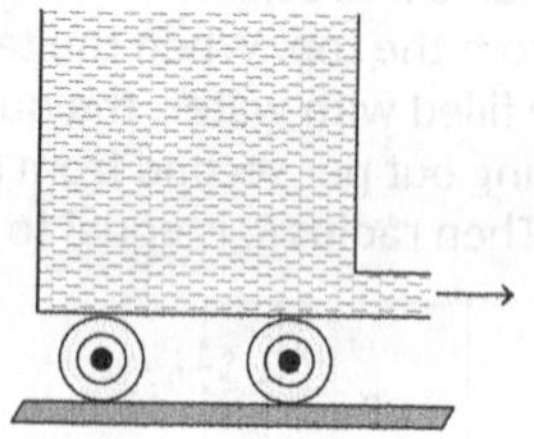

(a) Only v depends on h
(b) Only α depends on h
(c) Both v and α depend on h
(d) Neither v nor α depends on h.

Numerical Value Questions

1. Calculate the rate of flow (in multiple of $10^{-1}\text{m}^3/\text{s}$) of glycerine of density $1.25\times10^3\,\text{kg}/\text{m}^3$ through the conical section of a pipe if the radii of its ends are 0.1 m and 0.05 m and pressure drop across its length is $1.5\times10^5\text{N/m}^2$.

2. The diagram shows venturimeter through which water is flowing. The speed of water at X is 2 cm/s. Find the speed (in cm/s) of water at Y ($g = 1000\ \text{cm/s}^2$).

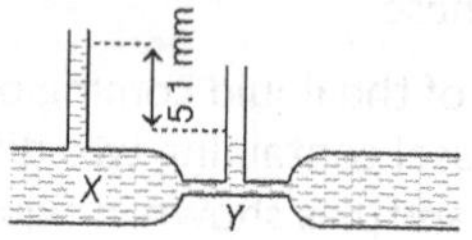

3. Consider a horizontally oriented syringe containing water located at a height of 1.25 m above the ground. The diameter of the plunger is 8 mm and the diameter of the nozzle is 2 mm. The plunger is pushed with a constant speed of 0.25 m/s. Find the horizontal range (in m) of water stream on the ground. ($g = 10\ \text{m}/\text{s}^2$)

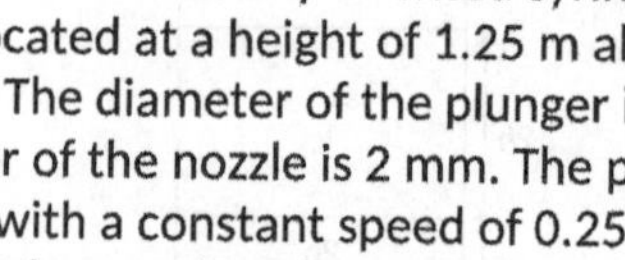

4. Water shoots out of a pipe and nozzle as shown in the figure. The cross-sectional area for the tube at point A is four times that of the nozzle. The pressure of water at point A is 41×10^3 Nm^{-2} (guage). Find the height h (in m) above the nozzle to which water jet will shoot. Neglect all the losses occurred in the above process. [$g = 10 \text{ m/s}^2$]

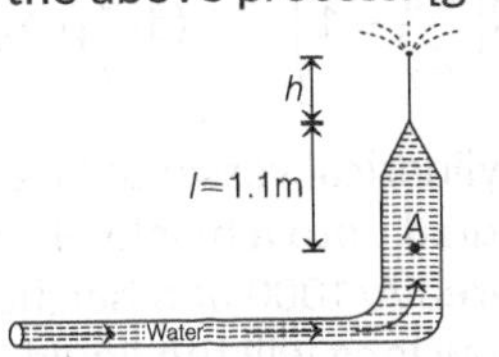

5. A long cylindrical tank of radius 1m is being filled by a pipe of radius 2 cm. The incoming water has a velocity of 1m/s. The tank has a hole of radius 1 cm at the bottom. What is the height of water (in cm) in the tank in steady state?

6. For the arrangement shown in the figure, find the time interval in seconds after which the water jet ceases to cross the wall. Area of the cross-section of the tank $A = \sqrt{5}$ m^2 and area of the orifice $a = 32$ cm^2. [Assume that the container remaining fixed]. (Take $g = 10 \text{ m/s}^2$).

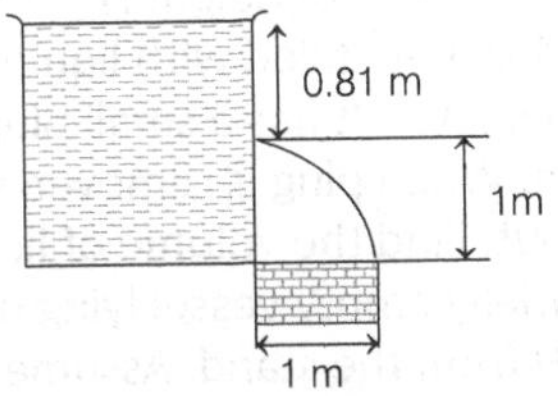

7. A fluid tank is full of water. The tank has area A and there is a hole at the side near bottom with area A/100. Water is filled upto height H. What is the total momentum (in kNs) imparted to the water till the tank becomes empty? $H = 5\text{m}$, $A = 3\text{m}^2$.

8. A fixed cylindrical tank having large cross-section area is filled with two liquids of densities ρ and 2ρ and in equal volumes as shown in the figure. A small hole of area of cross-section $a = \sqrt{6}$ cm^2 is made at height $h/2$ from the bottom. Find the area of cross-section (in cm^2) of stream of liquid just before it hits the ground.

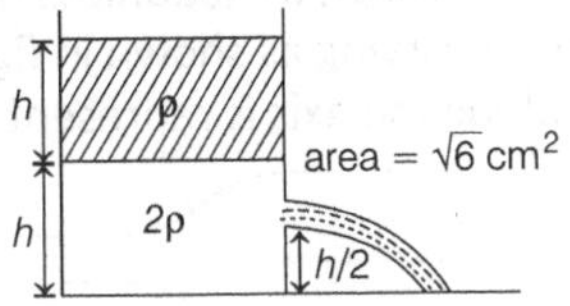

9. Water filled in an empty tank of area 60A through a tap of cross-sectional area A. The speed of water flowing out of tap is given by $v\ (\text{m/s}) = 10\left[4 - \pi \sin \frac{\pi}{30}(\text{s}^{-1})t\right]$. Find the level of water (in m) in tank at $t = 15$ s.

10. A tank containing gasoline is sealed and the gasoline is under pressure p_0 as shown in the figure. The store gasoline has a density of 660 kg m^{-3}. A sniper fires a rifle bullet into the gasoline tank, making a small hole 53 m below the surface of gasoline. The total height of gasoline is 73 m from the base. The jet of gasoline shooting out of the hole strikes the ground at a distance of 80 m from the tank initially. The local atmospheric pressure is 10^5Nm^{-2}. If the pressure p above the gasoline surface is $n \times 10^5 \text{Nm}^{-2}$ then find n.

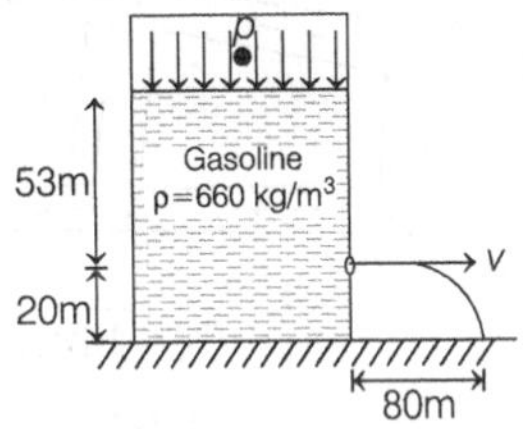

LEVEL 03 JEE Advanced Level

Single Choice Correct Questions

1. A portion of a tube is shown in the figure. Fluid is flowing from cross-section area A_1 to A_2. The two cross-sections are at distance ℓ from each other. The velocity of the fluid at section A_2 is $\sqrt{\frac{gl}{2}}$. If the pressures at A_1 and A_2 are same, then the angle made by the tube with the horizontal will be

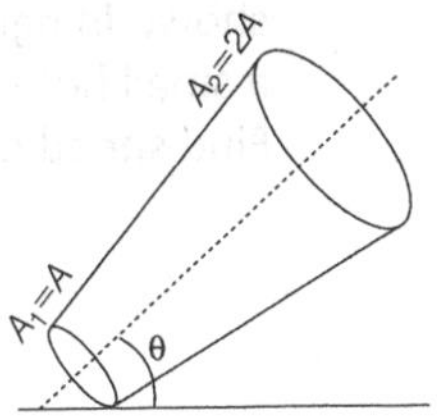

(a) 37°
(b) $\sin^{-1} 3/4$
(c) 53°
(d) None of these

2. A mercury manometer is connected as shown in the figure. The difference in height Δh is (symbols have usual meaning).

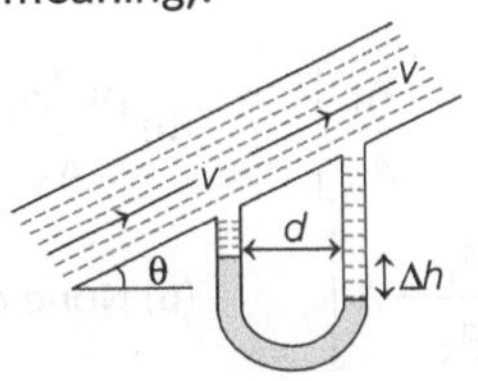

(a) $\frac{\rho d \cot\theta}{\rho_{Hg}}$ (b) $\frac{\rho d \tan\theta}{\rho_{Hg}}$

(c) $\frac{\rho d \sin\theta}{\rho_{Hg}}$ (d) None of these

3. Water flows through a frictionless duct with a cross-section varying as shown in figure. Pressure p at points along the axis is represented by :

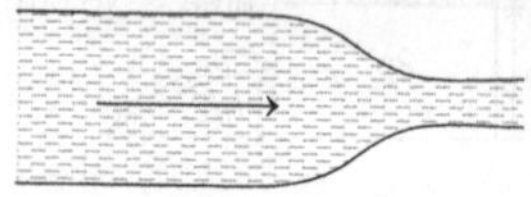

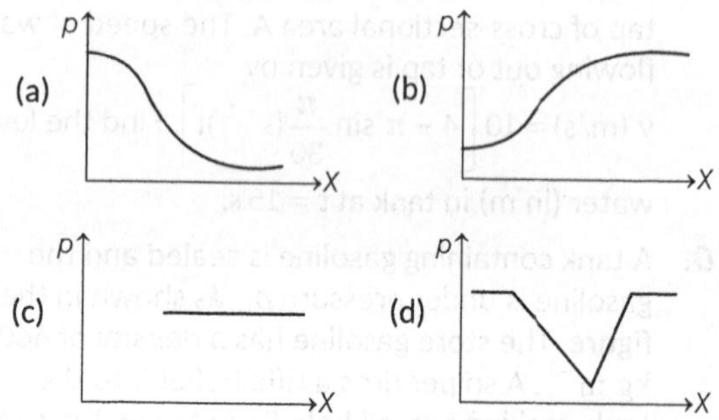

4. An ideal liquid is flowing in two pipes, AC is inclined and BD is horizontal. Both the pipes are connected by the Fig. The flow is streamlined in both the pipes. If velocity of liquid at A, B and C are 2 m/s, 4 m/s and 4 m/s respectively, the velocity at D will be

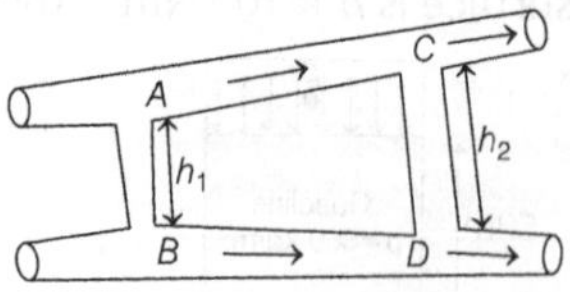

(a) 4 m/s (b) $\sqrt{14}\text{m}/\text{s}$

(c) $\sqrt{28}\ \text{m}/\text{s}$ (d) None

5. In a tube as shown in figure water coming in per second is equal to water going out per second. Find out the magnitude of the force exerted by water on the tube if inlet velocity is v_0

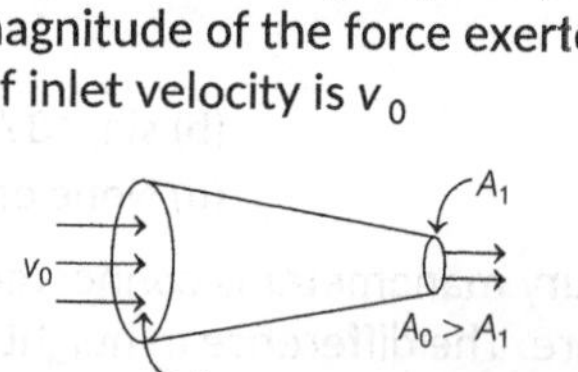

(a) $\rho A_0 v_0^2\left[1-\frac{A_1}{A_0}\right]$ (b) $\frac{\rho v_0^2 A_1^2}{A_0}$

(c) $\rho A_0 v_0^2\left[\frac{A_0}{A_1}-1\right]$ (d) None of these

6. In last question find out change in kinetic energy of liquid per unit time by the tube.

(a) $\frac{1}{4}\rho A_0 v_0^3\left(\frac{A_0^2}{A_1^2}-1\right)$ (b) $\frac{1}{4}\rho A_0 v_0^3\left(\frac{A_0}{A_1}-1\right)$

(c) $\frac{1}{2}\rho A_0 v_0^3\left(\frac{A_0}{A_1}-1\right)$ (d) $\frac{1}{2}\rho A_0 v_0^3\left(\frac{A_0^2}{A_1^2}-1\right)$

7. An open cylindrical vessel of large cross-section A contains liquid upto a height H= 120 cm. After an orifice of area $A/1000$ at a height of h = 20cm is opened, how long will the liquid be falling on the plate? Given that plate AB is of length 60 cm. (g = 10 m/s^2)

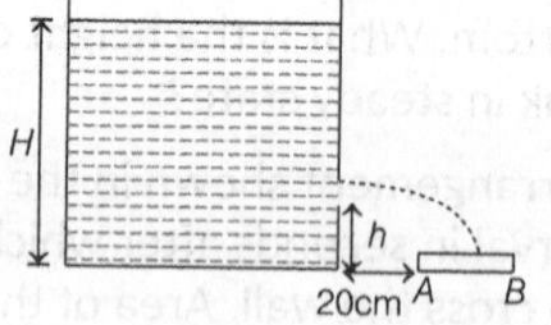

(a) 100 s (b) 200s

(c) 300 s (d) 400 s

8. A cylindrical vessel of height H = 4 m and area of cross section 1 m^2 filled with liquid rests on a stand of same height H. It has a small plugged hole near its bottom. When plug is removed the liquid starts to come out. Find the volume of liquid collected in a large initially empty vessel lying on floor at a distance H from the stand. Assume that liquid falling on to the floor does not flow into the vessel.

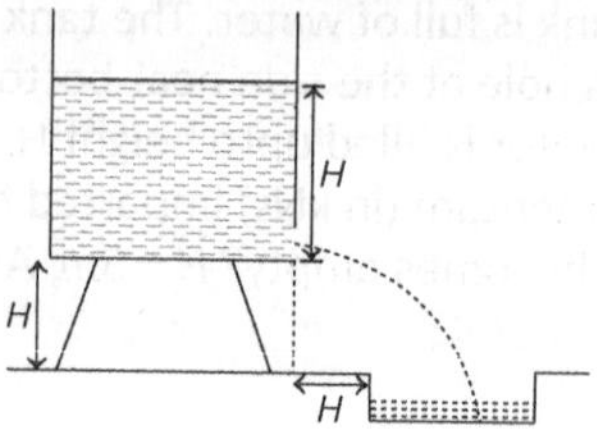

(a) 1m^3 (b) 2m^3

(c) 3m^3 (d) 4 m^3

9. Two immiscible liquids are filled in conical flask as shown in figure. The area of cross-section is shown, a small hole of area a is made in lower end of cone. Find speed of liquid flow from hole.

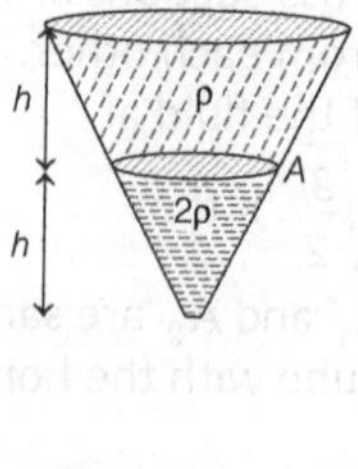

(a) $\sqrt{\dfrac{2gh}{1-\dfrac{17a^2}{A^2}}}$ (b) $\sqrt{\dfrac{gh}{1-\dfrac{17a^2}{A^2}}}$

(c) $\sqrt{\dfrac{2gh}{1-\dfrac{17a^2}{32A^2}}}$ (d) $\sqrt{\dfrac{3gh}{1-\dfrac{17a^2}{32A^2}}}$

10. A small hole is made at the bottom of a symmetrical jar as shown in figure. A liquid is filled into the jar upto a certain height. The rate of descension of liquid is independent of the level of the liquid in the jar. Then the surface of the jar is a surface of revolution of the curve–

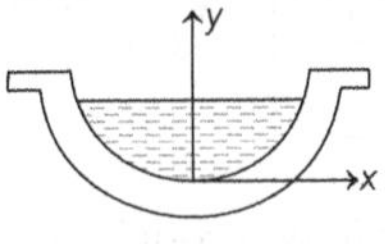

(a) $y = kx^4$
(b) $y = kx^2$
(c) $y = kx^3$
(d) $y = kx^5$

11. A container of height 'H' is filled completely by 2 immiscible liquid of same mass and density ratio 1 : 2. Cross-sectional area of container is A. A hole of area S is punched in the bottom of the container. ($S << A$). Find the time of flow out denser liquid.

(a) $\dfrac{A}{S}(4-\sqrt{2})\sqrt{\dfrac{H}{g}}$ (b) $\dfrac{4A}{S}\sqrt{\dfrac{H}{g}}$

(c) $\dfrac{A}{S}(3-\sqrt{2})\sqrt{\dfrac{H}{3g}}$ (d) $\dfrac{A}{S}(2-\sqrt{2})\sqrt{\dfrac{H}{3g}}$

12. An L-shaped glass tube is just immersed in flowing water such that its opening is pointing against flowing water. If the speed of water current is v, then

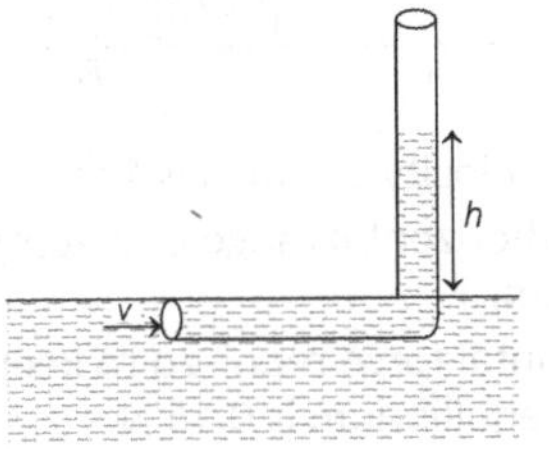

(a) the water in the tube rises to height $\dfrac{v^2}{2g}$
(b) the water in the tube rises to height $\dfrac{v^2}{4g}$
(c) the water in the tube does not rise at all
(d) None of these

13. A cylindrical container of radius R and height h is completely filled with a liquid. Two horizontal L-shaped pipes of small cross-section area a are connected to the cylinder as shown in the figure. Now the two pipes are opened and fluid starts coming out of the pipes horizontally in opposite directions. Then the torque due to ejected liquid on the system is

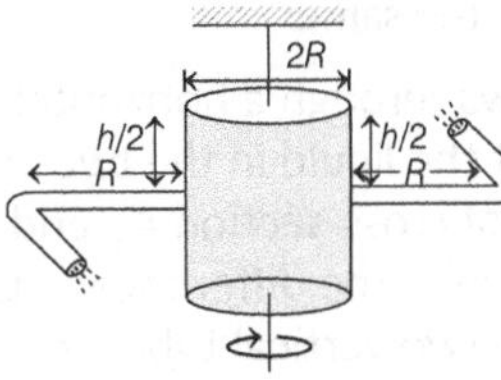

(a) $4agh\rho R$
(b) $8agh\rho R$
(c) $2agh\rho R$
(d) None of the above

14. There is a small hole in the bottom of a fixed container containing a liquid upto height h. The top of the liquid as well as the hole at the bottom are exposed to atmosphere. Area of the hole is a and that of the top surface is A. As the liquid comes out of the hole, the top surface of the liquid
(a) accelerates with acceleration $= g$
(b) accelerates with acceleration $= g\dfrac{a^2}{A^2}$
(c) retards with retardation $= g\dfrac{a}{A}$
(d) retards with retardation $= \dfrac{ga^2}{A^2}$

15. A large tank of (height $h_1 = 4\text{m}$) water has a hose connected to it, as shown in figure. The tank is sealed at the top and has compressed air between the water surface and the top. When the water height h_2 is 3 m, the gauge pressure of air is $p_1 = 1\times 10^5 \text{N/m}^2$. Assume that the air above the water surface expands isothermally. The velocity of flow out of the hose when h_2 has decreased to 2 m is (Assume ideal fluid flow and $p_{atm} = 10^5 \text{N/m}^2$)

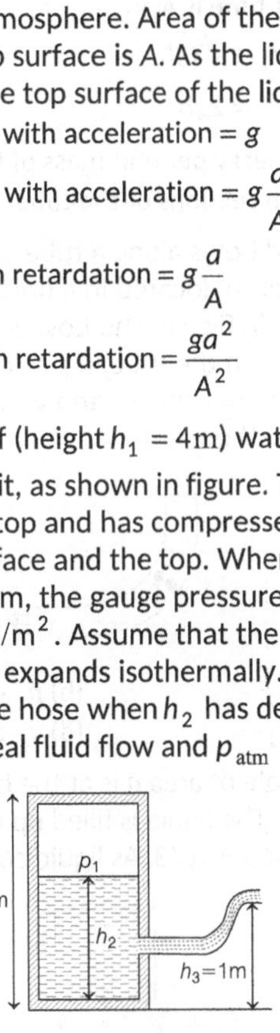

(a) 4 m/s (b) $\sqrt{20}$ m/s
(c) 5 m/s (d) $\sqrt{30}$ m/s

Multiple Choice(s) Correct Questions

1. In a streamline flow,
(a) the speed of a particle always remains same
(b) the velocity of a particle always remains same
(c) the kinetic energies of all the particles arriving at a given point are the same
(d) the momenta of all the particles arriving at a given point are the same

2. A liquid flows through a horizontal tube. The velocities of the liquid in the two sections, which have areas of cross-section A_1 and A_2, are v_1 and v_2 respectively. The difference in the levels of the liquid in the two vertical tubes is h

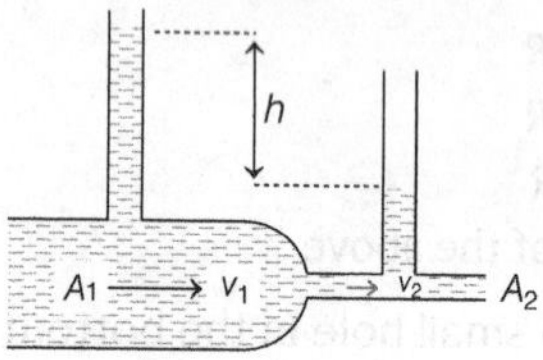

(a) The volume of the liquid flowing through the tube in unit time is $A_1 v_1$
(b) $v_2 - v_1 = \sqrt{2gh}$
(c) $v_2^2 - v_1^2 = 2gh$
(d) The energy per unit mass of the liquid is the same in both sections of the tube.

3. Ideal fluid flows along a tube of uniform cross-section, located in a horizontal plane and bent as shown in figure. The flow is steady, 1 and 2 are two points in the tube. If p_1 and p_2 are pressure at the two points and v_1 and v_2 are the respective velocities, then

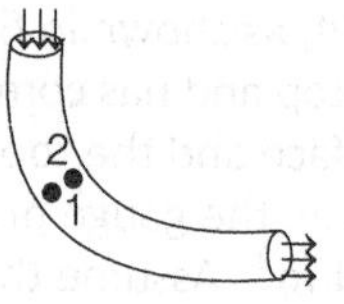

(a) $p_1 > p_2$ (b) $p_1 < p_2$
(c) $v_1 < v_2$ (d) $v_1 > v_2$

4. A small hole of area a is at the bottom of a container of area A. The liquid is filled up to height h from base. Given that $a = A/3$. As liquid comes out then

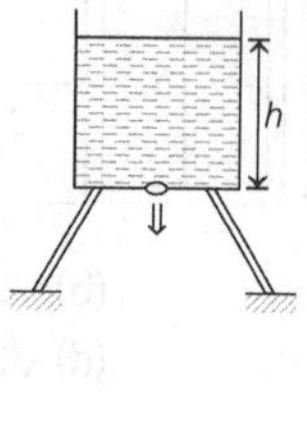

(a) level of liquid in container falls at rate of $\sqrt{\frac{gh}{4}}$
(b) magnitude of acceleration of top surface of liquid is $g/8$
(c) velocity of liquid coming out of hole is $\sqrt{2gh}$.
(d) None of these

5. A siphon has a uniform circular base of diameter $8/\sqrt{\pi}$ cm with its crest A, 1.8m above the water level. Vessel is of large cross-section $g = 10\text{ms}^{-2}$ and atmospheric pressure $p_0 = 10^5 \text{ N/m}^2$)

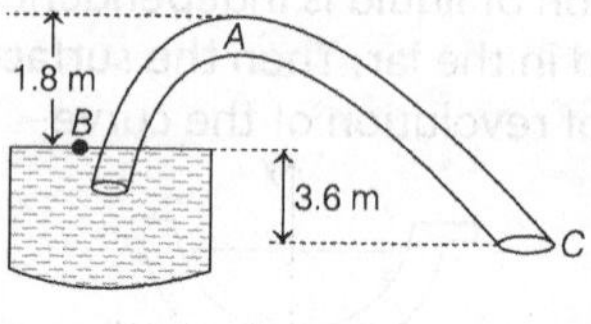

(a) Velocity of flow through pipe is $6\sqrt{2}$ m/s
(b) Discharge rate of flow through pipe is $96\sqrt{2} \times 10^{-4} \text{m}^3/\text{s}$
(c) Velocity of flow through pipe is 6 m/s.
(d) Pressure at A is $0.46 \times 10^{-5} \text{N/m}^2$

6. Curved surface of a vessel has shape of a truncated cone having semivertex angle 37°. Vessel is full of water (density = 1000 kg/m^3) upto a height of 13 cm and is placed on a smooth horizontal plane. Upper surface is opened to atmosphere. A hole of 1.5 cm^2 is made on curved wall at a height of 8 cm from bottom as shown in figure. Area of water surface in the vessel is large as compared to the area of hole.

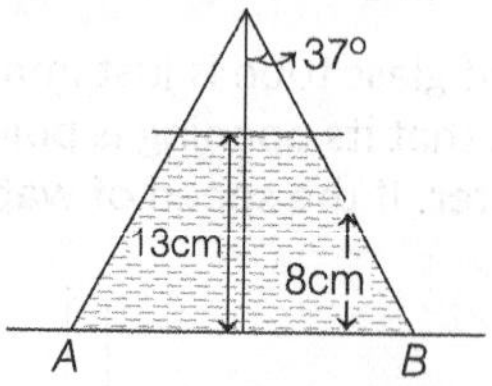

(a) Initial velocity of efflux is 1 m/s.
(b) Initial horizontal range of water jet from point B is 6.65 cm.
(c) Horizontal force required to keep the vessel in static equilibrium is 0.15 N.
(d) Horizontal force required to keep the vessel in static equilibrium is 0.12 N.

7. The figures shows a cart of mass 10 kg initially kept at rest on a frictionless surface. A jet of liquid of density 1000 kg/m^3 is directed on the cart. Velocity of the jet is 10 m/s and its cross-section area is 2×10^{-4} m^2. If at $t = 0$, cart is released and allowed to move freely in horizontal direction then choose the CORRECT statement(s).

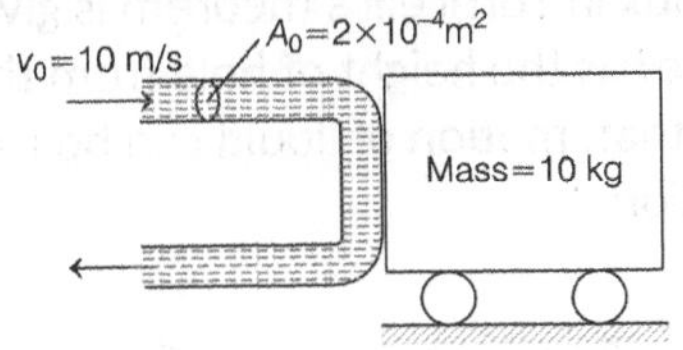

(a) Force on the cart at $t = 0$ s is 40 N
(b) Velocity of cart at $t = 10$ s is 8 m/s
(c) Acceleration of cart at $t = 10$ s is 1 m/s^2.
(d) Power supplied to the cart when cart is moving with velocity 5 m/s is 50 W.

8. Oil enters the bend of a pipe in the horizontal plane with velocity $4ms^{-1}$ and pressure $280 \times 10^3 Nm^{-2}$ as shown in figure. (Take specific gravity of oil as 0.9 and $\sin 37° = 0.6$)

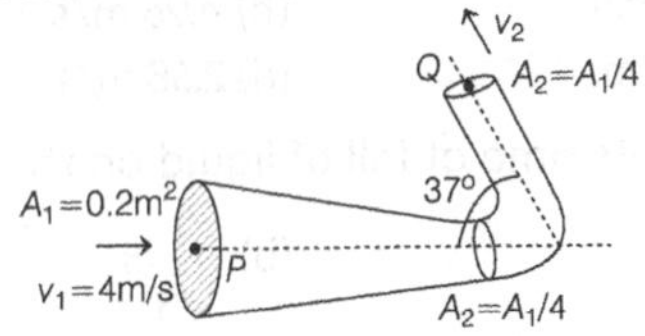

(a) the pressure of oil at the point Q, $(p_2) = 172 \times 10^3 N/m^2$
(b) the pressure of oil at the point Q, $(p_2) = 388 \times 10^3 N/m^2$
(c) the force required to hold the bend in the place is 63×10^3N
(d) the force required to hold the bend in the place is 76×10^3N

9. Figure shows inverted T shaped fixed pipe. Liquid is released from rest from the position shown. Liquid is non-viscous.

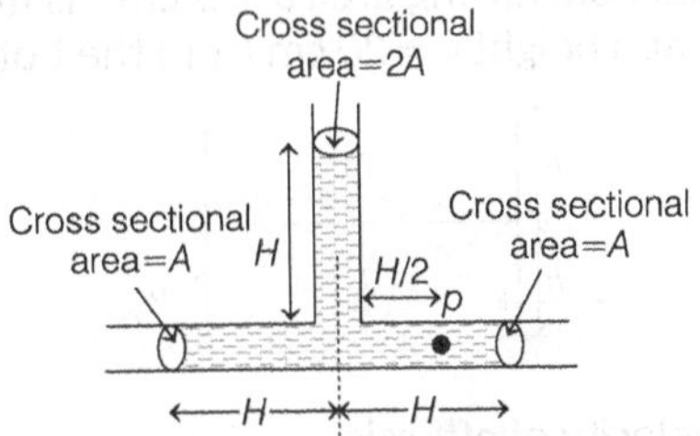

(a) Velocity of fluid particle in vertical part of tube when level of liquid in it remains $H/2$ will be $\sqrt{\frac{3gH}{8}}$
(b) The initial acceleration of the fluid particle in vertical tube will be $g/2$
(c) Initial gauge pressure at point P will be $\rho gH/4$.
(d) None of the above

Comprehension Based Questions

Comprehension-1

The figure shows the commonly observed decrease in diameter of a water stream as it falls from a tap. The tap has internal diameter D_0 and is connected to a large tank of water. The surface of the water is at a height b above the end of the tap. By considering the dynamics of a thin "cylinder" of water in the stream, answer the following : (Ignore any resistance to the flow and any effects of surface tension, given ρ_w = density of water).

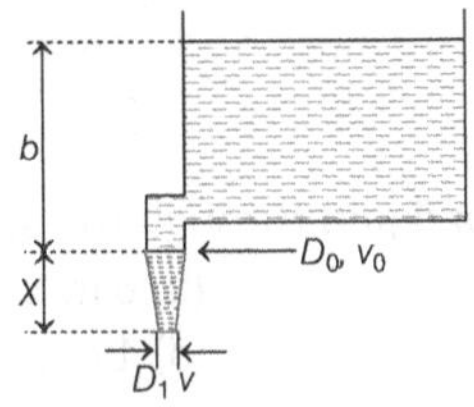

1. Equation for the flow rate, i.e. the mass of water flowing through a given point in the stream per unit time, as function of the water speed v will be
(a) $v\rho_w \pi D^2/4$
(b) $v\rho_w (\pi D^2/4 - \pi D_0^2/4)$
(c) $v\rho_w \pi D^2/2$
(d) $v\rho_w \pi D_0^2/4$

2. Which of the following equation expresses the fact that the flow rate at the tap is the same as at the stream point with diameter D and velocity v (i.e. D in terms of D_0, v_0 and v will be)
(a) $D = \frac{D_0 v_0}{v}$
(b) $D = \frac{D_0 v_0^2}{v^2}$
(c) $D = \frac{D_0 v}{v_0}$
(d) $D = D_0\sqrt{\frac{v_0}{v}}$

3. The equation for the water speed v as a function of the distance x below the tap will be
(a) $v = \sqrt{2gb}$
(b) $v = [2g(b+x)]^{1/2}$
(c) $v = \sqrt{2gx}$
(d) $v = [2g(b-x)]^{1/2}$

4. Equation for the stream diameter D in terms of x and D_0 will be :
(a) $D = D_0\left(\frac{b}{b+x}\right)^{1/4}$
(b) $D = D_0\left(\frac{b}{b+x}\right)^{1/2}$
(c) $D = D_0\left(\frac{b}{b+x}\right)$
(d) $D = D_0\left(\frac{b}{b+x}\right)^2$

5. A student observes after setting up this experiment that for a tap with $D_0 = 1$ cm at $x = 0.3$ m the stream diameter $D = 0.9$ cm. The height b of the water above the tap in this case will be :
(a) 5.7 cm
(b) 57 cm
(c) 27 cm
(d) 2.7 cm

Comprehension-02

A siphon tube is discharging a liquid of density 900 kg m^{-3} as shown in figure.
$(p_0 = 1.01 \times 10^5 \text{N/m}^2)$

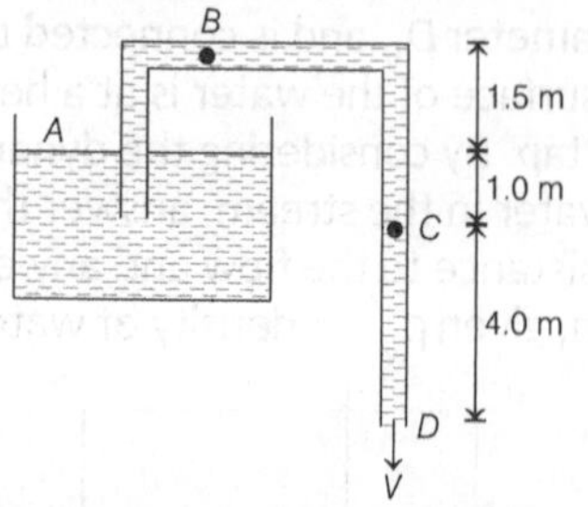

6. The speed of liquid through the siphon is
(a) 6 m/s (b) 8 m/s
(c) 10 m/s (d) 12 m/s

7. Pressure at point B is
(a) $4.25 \times 10^4 \text{ N/m}^2$ (b) $6.25 \times 10^4 \text{N/m}^2$
(c) $2.50 \times 10^4 \text{N/m}^2$ (d) $2.0 \times 10^5 \text{N/m}^2$

8. Pressure at point C is
(a) $5.5 \times 10^4 \text{N/m}^2$
(b) $6.5 \times 10^4 \text{N/m}^2$
(c) $8.0 \times 10^4 \text{N/m}^2$
(d) $10.5 \times 10^4 \text{N/m}^2$

Comprehension-03

A tank of height H and base area A is half filled with water and there is a small orifice at the bottom and there is a heavy solid cylinder having base area $A/3$ and height of the cylinder is same as that of the tank. The water is flowing out of the orifice. Here cylinder is put into the tank to increase the speed of water flowing out.

9. The speed of water flowing out of the orifice after the cylinder is kept inside it is
(a) $\sqrt{\frac{gH}{2}}$ (b) $\sqrt{\frac{3gH}{2}}$
(c) $\sqrt{2gH}$ (d) $\sqrt{3gH}$

10. After long time, when the height of water inside the tank again becomes equal to $H/2$, the solid cylinder is taken out. Then the velocity of liquid flowing out of the orifice (just after removing the cylinder) will be
(a) $\sqrt{\frac{gH}{3}}$ (b) $\sqrt{\frac{3gH}{2}}$
(c) $\sqrt{2g\left(\frac{H}{3}\right)}$ (d) $\sqrt{2g\left(\frac{H}{2}\right)}$

Comprehension -04

Velocity of efflux in Torricelli's theorem is given by $v = \sqrt{2gh}$, here h is the height of hole from the top surface, after that, motion of liquid can be treated as projectile motion.

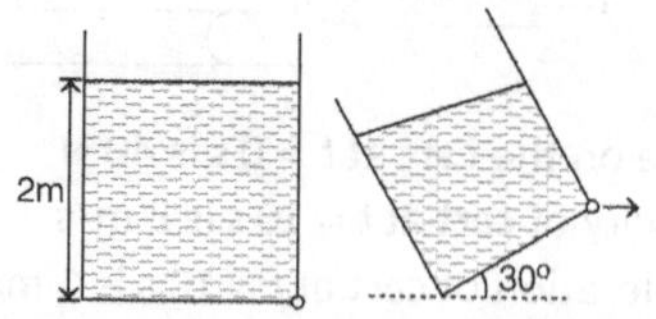

11. Liquid is filled in a vessel of square base (2m × 2m) upto a height of 2 m as shown in figure (i). In figure (ii) the vessel is tilted from horizontal at 30°. What is the velocity of efflux in this case? Liquid does not spill out.
(a) 3.29 m/s (b) 4.96 m/s
(c) 5.67 cm (d) 2.68 m/s

12. What is its time of fall of liquid on the ground?
(a) $\frac{1}{\sqrt{2}}$ s (b) $\frac{1}{\sqrt{3}}$ s
(c) $\frac{1}{\sqrt{5}}$ s (d) O2s

13. At what distance from point O, will be liquid strike on the ground?
(a) 5.24 m (b) 6.27 m
(c) 4.93 m (d) 3.95 m

Comprehension-05

A cylindrical tank having cross-sectional area $A = 0.5 \text{ m}^2$ is filled with two liquids of density $\rho_1 = 900 \text{kg/m}^3$ and $\rho_2 = 600 \text{kg/m}^3$ to a height $h = 60$ cm each as shown in figure. A small hole having area $a = 5 \text{ cm}^2$ is made in right vertical wall at a height $y = 20$ cm from the bottom.

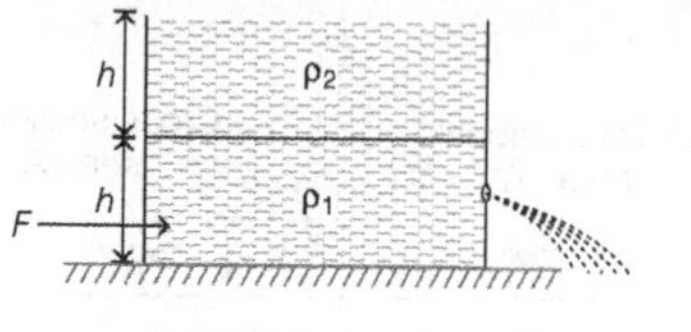

14. The velocity of efflux is
(a) 10 m/s (b) 20 m/s
(c) 4 m/s (d) 35 m/s

15. Horizontal force F required to keep the cylinder in static equilibrium, if it is placed on a smooth horizontal plane, is
(a) 7.2 N (b) 10 N
(c) 15.5 N (d) 20.4 N

16. Minimum and maximum values of F to keep the cylinder in static equilibrium, if coefficient of friction between the cylinder and the plane is $\mu = 0.01$. $(g = 10\ m/s^2)$

(a) 0, 40 N (b) 5.4 N, 52.2 N
(c) 0, 70 N (d) 0, 52.2 N

Comprehension-06

A liquid having density 6000 kg/m^3 stands to a height of 4m in a sealed tank as shown in the figure. The tank contains compressed air at a gauge pressure of 3 atm. The horizontal outlet pipe has a cross-sectional area of 6 cm^2 and 3cm^2 at larger and smaller sections.

Atmospheric pressure

$$= 1\text{ atm}, g = 10\ m/s^2, 1\text{ atm} = 10^5 N/m^2$$

Assume that depth of liquid in the tank remains constant due to its very large base and air pressure above it remains constant. Based on the above information, answer the following questions.

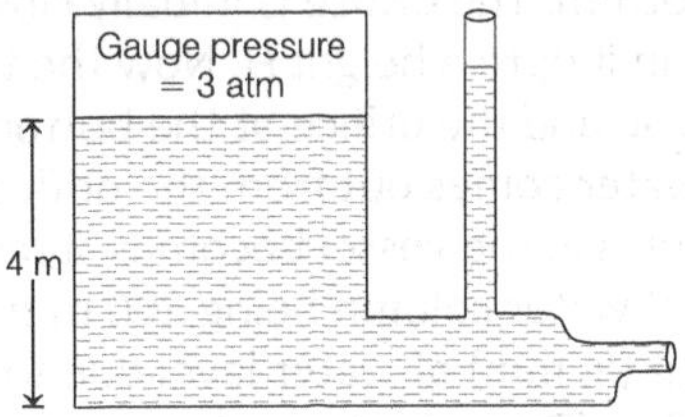

17. The height at which liquid will stand in the open end of the pipe is

(a) 4 m (b) 3.5 m (c) 4.5 m (d) 6.75 m

18. The discharge rate from the outlet is

(a) $4.02 \times 10^{-3} m^3/s$ (b) $6 \times 10^{-5} m^3/s$
(c) $7.56 \times 10^{-3} m^3/s$ (d) $4.02 \times 10^{-5} m^3/s$

19. If a hole is created in the tank at its top end, then the height of liquid level in the open end of the pipe is

(a) 4 m (b) 3 m (c) 3.5 m (d) 3.8 m

Match the Column Questions

1.

	Column I		Column II
(A)	Bernoulli's theorem	(P)	Narrower pipes have less pressure
(B)	Ball moving with spin	(Q)	Paint gun
(C)	Artificial high pressure	(R)	Non-viscous fluids
(D)	Streamlined flow	(S)	Conservation of energy
		(T)	Uplift due to pressure difference

2. A bottle is filled with water, above which a little air at atmospheric pressure is present. Plugs are blocking the three small holes (A, B and C).

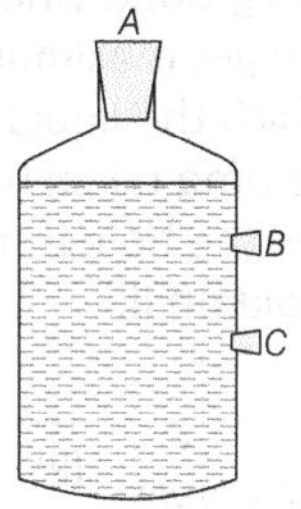

	Column I		Column II
(A)	A and C are opened	(P)	Air comes into the bottle from upper most open hole
(B)	B and C are opened	(Q)	Water flows out of holes B and C
(C)	Only C is opened	(R)	Very little water comes out and the flow stops
(D)	All the holes are opened	(S)	Pressure of air inside bottle above the water remains unchanged.

3. A long cylindrical tank of cross-sectional area A is filled with two immiscible liquids of densities ρ and 2ρ. It has two holes of cross-section $A/10$; One is just above liquid interface (hole B) other one at the bottom (hole A) as shown in figure. A movable piston of cross-sectional area almost equal to A is fitted on the top of the tank. A load kept on smooth horizontal surface.

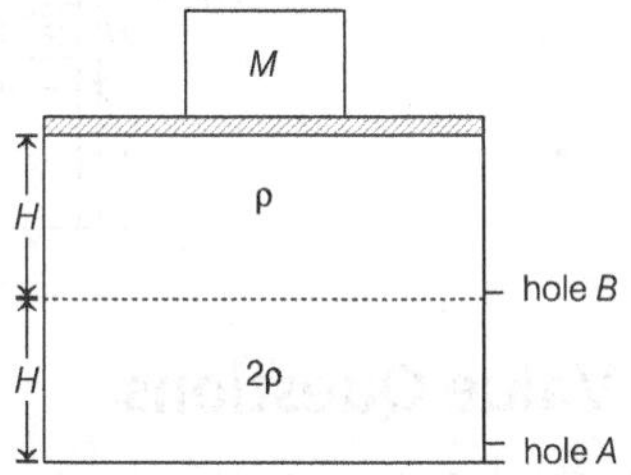

	Column I		Column II
(A)	Initial speed of water jet at hole A	(P)	$\sqrt{\frac{Mg}{\rho A} + 3gH}$
(B)	Initial speed of water jet at hole B	(Q)	$\sqrt{\frac{2Mg}{\rho A} + 2gH}$
(C)	Maximum force exerted by water jet of hole A on the tank	(R)	$\frac{Mg + 3\rho AgH}{5}$
(D)	Maximum force exerted by water jet of hole B on the tank	(S)	$\frac{Mg + \rho AgH}{5}$

4. In column-II, liquid (s) are filled in a container of large base area as shown in the figures. If h is the height above the ground where a small hole to be made in order to get maximum range, R. v is the velocity with which the liquid comes out from the hole and t is the time taken by the liquid to reach ground just after the hole is made. Then match the column I with column II.

	Column I		Column II
(A)	$\sqrt{\frac{gH}{2}} \le v \le 2\sqrt{2gH}$	(P)	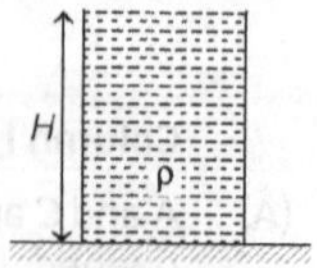
(B)	$H \le R \le 2\sqrt{2}H$	(Q)	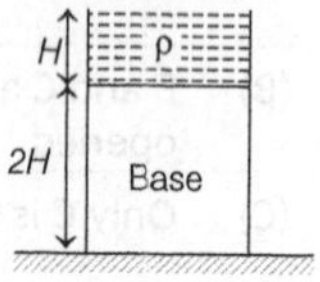
(C)	$H \le h \le 3h$	(R)	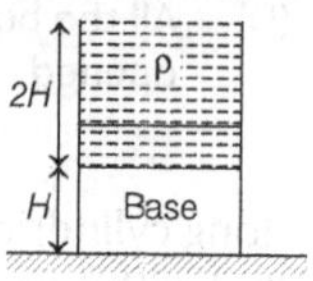
(D)	$\sqrt{\frac{H}{g}} \le t \le 2\sqrt{\frac{H}{g}}$	(S)	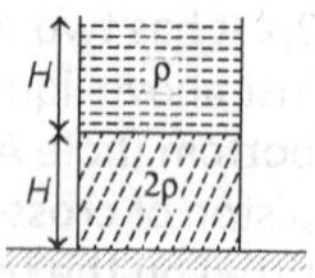
		(T)	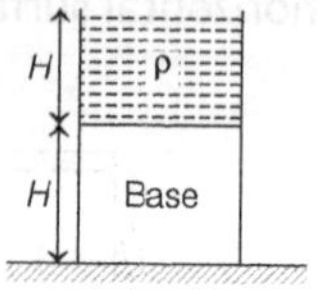

Numerical Value Questions

1. A liquid of density $\rho = \rho_0 (1 + \alpha y)$ is stored in a container where y is the distance from the liquid surface and $\alpha = \frac{2}{3} m^{-1}$. A small hole is made at the bottom of the container. Find velocity of efflux (in m/s) when the liquid height is 1m. Assume flow is laminar ($g = 10 ms^{-2}$).

2. Figure shows a siphon, the vessel area is very large as compared to cross-section of tube. Tube has a uniform cross-section, its lower end is 6m below the surface of water. What is maximum height H (in m) of the upper end for siphon to work? Take density of water $= 10^3 kg/m^3$, atmospheric pressure $= 10^5 N/m^2$.

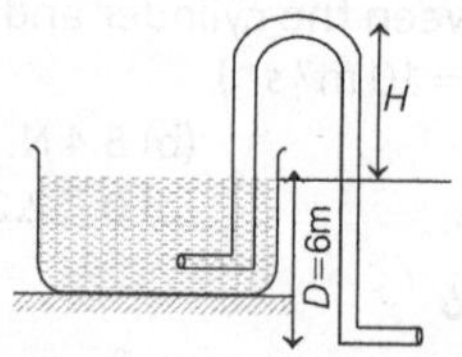

3. A conical container of radius $R = 1$ m and height $H = 5$ m is filled completely with liquid. There is a hole at the bottom of container of area $\pi \times 10^{-3} m^2$ (see figure). Find the time taken (in sec) to empty the conical container. Take $g = 10 ms^{-2}$.

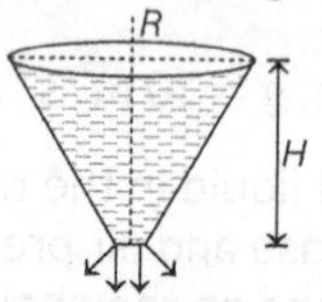

4. A cylindrical vessel of height 500 mm has an orifice at its bottom. The orifice is initially closed and water is filled in it upto a height H. Now the top is sealed with a cap and the orifice at the bottom is opened. Some water comes out from the orifice and the water level in the vessel becomes steady with height of water column being 200 mm. Find the fall in height (in mm) of water level due to opening of the orifice. (Take atmospheric pressure $= 1.0 \times 10^5 N/m^2$, density of water $1000 kg/m^3$ and $g = 10 ms^{-2}$, Neglect any effect of surface tension.)

5. Water is filled in a uniform container of area of cross-section A. A hole of cross-section area a ($<< A$) is made in the container at a height of 20 m above the base. Water streams out and hits a small block on surface at some distance from container. Block is moved on surface in such a way that stream always hits the block. The initial velocity of the block (in m/s) is (Given $\frac{a}{A} = \frac{1}{20}$).
[Take $g = 10 ms^{-2}$]

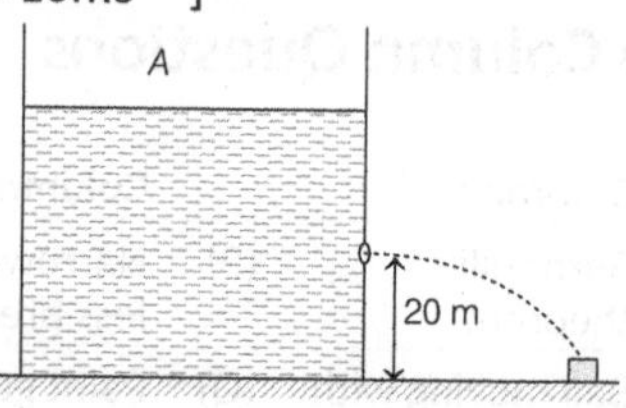

6. A horizontal oriented tube AB of length 5 m rotates with a constant angular velocity 0.5 rad/s about a stationary vertical axis OO' passing through the end A. The tube is filled with ideal fluid. The end A of the tube is open, the closed end B has a very small

orifice. Find the velocity with which the liquid comes out from the hole in m/s.

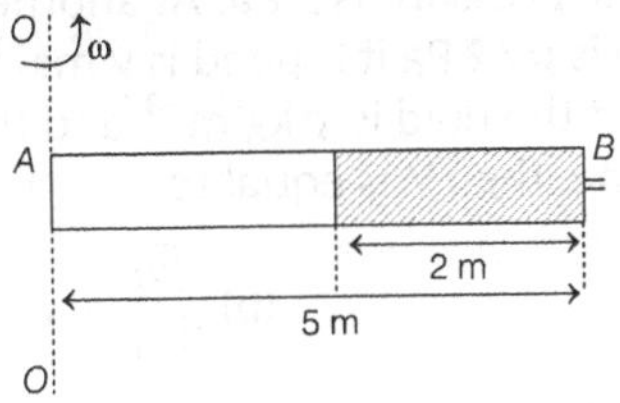

7. The tap in the garden was closed inappropriately resulting in the water flowing freely out of it which forms a downward narrowing beam. The beam of water has a circular cross-section, the diameter of the circle is 6 mm at one point and 3 cm below it is only 3 mm as shown in figure. If the rate of water wasted is $(n \times \pi)$ mL/minute then find the value of n. (Neglect the effect of viscosity and surface tension of the flowing water)

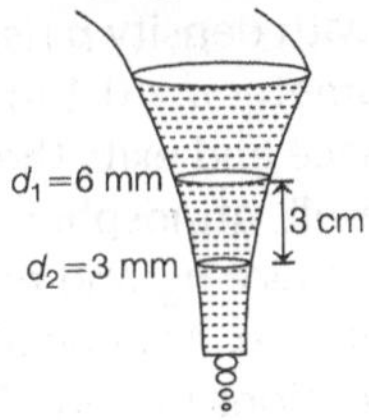

8. A rectangular opening on the side of a tank has a width l. The top of the opening is at a depth h_1 below the surface of the water and the bottom is at a depth h_2 (Figure). The volume of water that emerges from the opening in a unit time is given by $\alpha\sqrt{2g}\ m^3/s$.

Find α. (Given $h_1 = 1m$, $h_2 = 4m$ and $l = 1.5$ m)

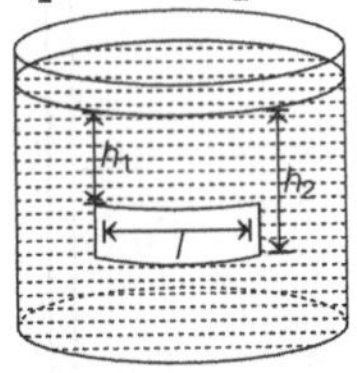

9. A pipe of circular cross-section of inner radius r and outer radius $2r$ is bent into a semi-circle as shown in the diagram. A fluid of density $\rho = 10^3 kg/m^3$ is flowing through it. The breaking stress of the material of the pipe is $3 \times 10^7 N/m^2$. Find the maximum velocity (in m/s) with which the fluid can flow in the pipe.

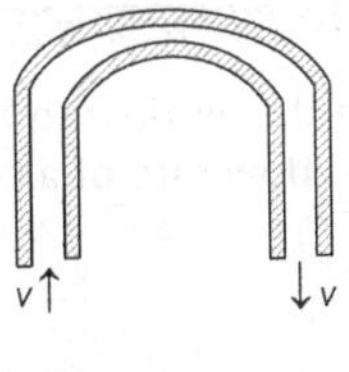

10. A tank of cross-sectional area A is filled with water to a height H. It stands on a smooth horizontal surface. A small orifice is made at the bottom of the vertical wall. The water flows out of the orifice and the tank recoils. Find the speed (in m/s) of the tank when it gets emptied. Assume mass of empty tank to be negligible.

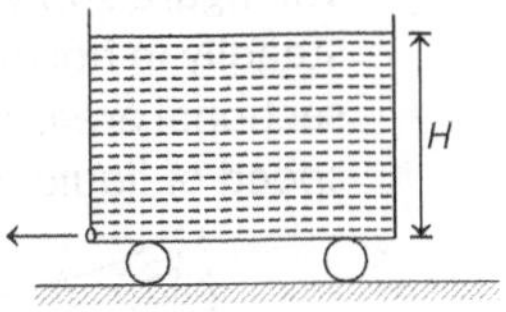

Given, $H = 5$ m, $g = 10$ ms^{-2}

Previous Years Questions

JEE Main

1 The reading of pressure metre attached with a closed pipe is $4.5 \times 10^4 N/m^2$. On opening the valve, water starts flowing and the reading of pressure metre falls to $2.0 \times 10^4 N/m^2$. The velocity of water is found to be $\sqrt{v}$ m/s. The value of v is .... **[2024, 27 Jan Shift-II]**

2 In a test experiment on a model aeroplane in wind tunnel, the flow speeds on the upper and lower surfaces of the wings are 70 ms^{-1} and 65 ms^{-1} respectively. If the wing area is 2 m^2, the lift of the wing is .... N. (Given density of air = 1.2 kg m^{-3}) **[2024, 29 Jan Shift-I]**

3 A fully loaded boeing aircraft has a mass of 5.4×10^5 kg. Its total wing area is 500 m^2. It is in level flight with a speed of 1080 km/h. If the density of air ρ is 1.2 kg m^{-3}, the fractional increase in the speed of the air on the upper surface of the wing relative to the lower surface in percentage will be.
($g = 10$ m/s^2) **[2023 29 Jan Shift-II]**
(a) 10 (b) 8 (c) 16 (d) 6

4 Figure below shows a liquid being pushed out of the tube by a piston having area of cross-section 2.0 cm^2. The area of cross-section at the outlet is 10 mm. If the piston is pushed at a speed of 4 cm s^{-1}, the speed of outgoing fluid is cm s^{-1}. **[2023, 10 April Shift-II]**

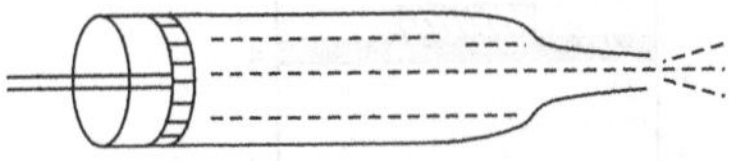

5 The surface of water in a water tank of cross-section area 750 cm^2 on the top of a house is h m above the top level. The speed of water coming out through the top of cross-section area 500 mm^2 is 30 cm/s. At that instant, dh/dt is $x \times 10^{-3}$ m/s. The value of x will be .... **[2023, 1 Feb Shift-II]**

6 The figure shows a liquid of given density flowing steadily in horizontal tube of the section. Cross-sectional areas at A is 1.5 cm^2, and B is 25 mm^2, if speed of liquid at B is 60 cm/s then $(p_A - p_B)$ is

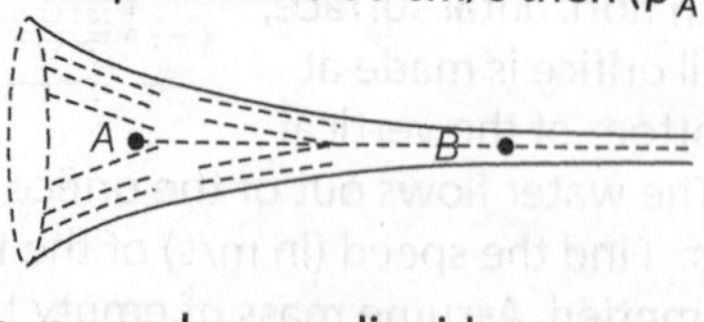

(Given, p_A and p_B are liquid pressure at A and B points.
density, $\rho = 1000 \text{ kg m}^{-3}$
A and B are on the axis of tube **[2023, 13 April Shift-I]**

(a) 36 Pa (b) 135 Pa (c) 175 Pa (d) 27 Pa

7 The area of cross-section of a large tank is 0.5 m^2. It has a narrow opening near the bottom having area of cross-section 1 cm^2. A load of 25 kg is applied on the water at the top in the tank. Neglecting the speed of water in the tank, the velocity of the water, coming out of the opening at the time when the height of water level in the tank is 40 cm above the bottom, will be ...... cms^{-1}.
(Take, $g = 10 \text{ ms}^{-2}$) **[2022, 27 June Shift-I]**

8 A light cylindrical vessel is kept on a horizontal surface. Area of base is A. A hole of cross-sectional area a is made just at its bottom side. The minimum coefficient of friction necessary to prevent sliding the vessel due to the impact force of the emerging liquid is $(a << A)$. **[2021, 27 July Shift-I]**

(a) $\frac{A}{2a}$ (b) None (c) $\frac{2a}{A}$ (d) $\frac{a}{A}$

9 Consider a water tank as shown in the figure. It's cross-sectional area is 0.4 m^2. The tank has an opening B near the bottom whose cross-section area is 1 cm^2. A load of 24 kg is applied on the water at the top when the height of the water level is 40 cm above the bottom, the velocity of water coming out the opening B is $v \text{ ms}^{-1}$. The value of v, to the nearest integer, is ....
(Take value of g to be 10 ms^{-2}) **[2021, 18 March Shift-II]**

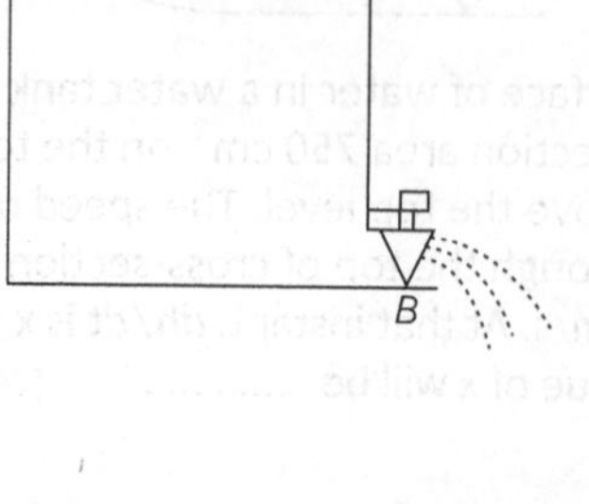

10 A fluid is flowing through a horizontal pipe of varying cross-section with speed $v \text{ ms}^{-1}$ at a point where the pressure is p Pa. At another point, where pressure is $p/2$ Pa its speed is $V \text{ ms}^{-1}$. If the density of the fluid is $\rho \text{ kg m}^{-3}$ and the flow is streamline, then V is equal to **[2020, 6 Sep Shift-II]**

(a) $\sqrt{\frac{p}{\rho}} + v$ (b) $\sqrt{\frac{2p}{\rho} + v^2}$

(c) $\sqrt{\frac{p}{2\rho} + v^2}$ (d) $\sqrt{\frac{p}{\rho} + v^2}$

JEE Advanced

1. A cylindrical furnace has height (H) and diameter (D) both 1 m. It is maintained at temperature 360 K. The air gets heated inside the furnace at constant pressure p_a and its temperature becomes $T = 360$ K. The hot air with density p rises up a vertical chimney of diameter $d = 0.1$ m and height $h = 9$ m above the funace and exits the chimney (see the figure). As a result, atmospheric air of density $p_a = 1.2 \text{ kg m}^{-3}$, pressure p_a and temperature $T_a = 300$ K enters the furnace. Assume air as an ideal gas, neglect the variations in ρ and T inside the chimeny and the furnace. Also ignore the viscous effects.
(Given : The acceleration due to gravity $g = 10 \text{ ms}^{-2}$ and $\pi = 3.14$) **(2023)**

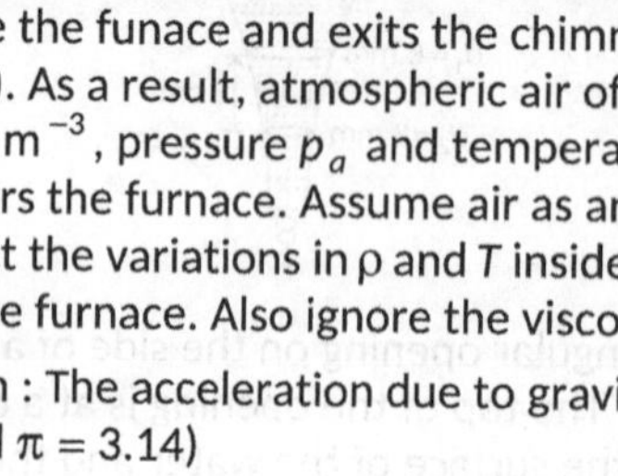

I. Considering the air flow to be streamline, the steady mass flow rate of air exiting the chimney is ...... gm s^{-1}.

II. When the chimney is closed using a cap at the top, a pressure difference Δp develops between the top and the bottom surfaces of the cap. If the changes in the temperature and density of the hot air, due to the stoppage of air flow, are negligible, then the value of Δp is ...... Nm^{-2}.

2. A train with cross-sectional area S_t is moving with speed v_0 inside a long tunnel of cross-sectional area $S_0 (S_0 = 4S_t)$. Assume that almost all the air (density ρ) in front of the train flows back between its sides and the walls of the tunnel. Also, the air flow with respect to the train is steady and laminar. Take the ambient pressure and that inside the train to be p_0. If the pressure in the region between the sides of the train and the tunnel walls is p then $p_0 - p = \frac{7}{2N}\rho v_t^2$. The value of N is ______. **(2020)**

Direction (Q. Nos. 3 and 4) A spray gun is shown in the figure where a piston pushes air out of nozzle. A thin tube of uniform cross-section is connected to the nozzle. The other end of the tube is in a small liquid container. As the piston pushes air through the nozzle, the liquid from the container rises into the nozzle and is sprayed out. For the spray gun shown, the radii of the piston and the nozzle are 20 mm and 1 mm respectively. The upper end of the container is open to the atmosphere. **(2014)**

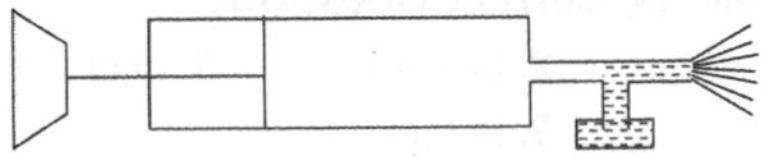

3. If the piston is pushed at a speed of $5\ mms^{-1}$, the air comes out of the nozzle with a speed of

(a) $0.1\ ms^{-1}$ (b) $1\ ms^{-1}$
(c) $2\ ms^{-1}$ (d) $8\ ms^{-1}$

4. If the density of air is ρ_a and that of the liquid ρ_l, then for a given piston speed the rate (volume per unit time) at which the liquid is sprayed will be proportional to

(a) $\sqrt{\frac{\rho_a}{\rho_l}}$ (b) $\sqrt{\rho_a \rho_l}$

(c) $\sqrt{\frac{\rho_l}{\rho_a}}$ (d) ρ_l

Answer Key

Level 1

8.1 Equation of Continuity

1. 40 cm/s 2. 6×10^9

8.2 Bernoulli's Equation

1. 2000 Pa 2. (a) 25 cm/s (b) 50 cm/s (c) 93.75 Pa 3. (a) 25 cm (b) 50 cm/s (c) 0
4. (a) 20 cm/s (b) 485 Pa 5. $4.1 \times 10^3\ N/m^2, 8.2 \times 10^4\ N$
6. 3.6×10^{-3} m 7. 146 cm^3/s 8. 1.97 cm

8.3 Velocity of Efflux

1. (a) $2\sqrt{D(H-D)}$ (b) $D = \frac{H}{2}$ 2. 11 m/s 3. $\sqrt{2gh}$ 4. (a) 2 m/s (b) 500 s
5. (a) 10 m/s (b) 4.15×10^4 Pa (c) 6.4×10^4 Pa 6. 29025 J/m^3, 29400 J/m^3 7. $\frac{g}{N}$

Level 2

Single Choice Correct Questions

1. (c)	2. (d)	3. (a)	4. (d)	5. (a)	6. (b)	7. (c)	8. (b)	9. (a)	10. (a)
11. (b)	12. (d)	13. (a)	14. (b)	15. (b)	16. (d)	17. (b)	18. (c)	19. (c)	20. (a)
21. (a)	22. (d)	23. (a)	24. (b)	25. (a)					

Numerical Value Questions

1. 1.26	2. 32	3. 2	4. 3.2	5. 80	6. 125	7. 100
8. 2	9. 5	10. 2.78				

Level 3

Single Choice Correct Questions

1. (b)	2. (b)	3. (a)	4. (c)	5. (c)	6. (d)	7. (c)	8. (c)	9. (d)	10. (a)
11. (d)	12. (a)	13. (a)	14. (d)	15. (b)					

Multiple Choice(s) Correct Questions

1. (c, d)	2. (a, c, d)	3. (a,c)	4. (a,b)	5. (a,b,d)	6. (a,d)	7. (a,b,d)
8. (a, d)	9. (a,b,c)					

Comprehension Based Questions

1. (a)	2. (d)	3. (b)	4. (a)	5. (b)	6. (c)	7. (a)
8. (b)	9. (b)	10. (c)	11. (b)	12. (c)	13. (d)	14. (c)
15. (a)	16. (d)	17. (d)	18. (a)	19. (b)		

Match the Columns Questions

1. A → RS; B → T; C → Q; D → PR
2. A → PS; B → PQ; C → R; D → PQS
3. A → P; B → Q; C → R; D → S
4. A → PQRST; B → PQST; C → PQRST; D → QRT

Numerical Value Questions

1. 4	2. 4	3. 200	4. 6	5. 1	6. 2	7. 108
8. 7	9. 300	10. 20				

Previous Years Questions

JEE Main

1. (50)	2. (810)	3. (a)	4. (80)	5. (2)	6. (c)
7. (300)	8. (c)	9. (3)	10. (d)		

JEE Advanced

1. I. (7850) II. (20)	2. 9	3. (c)	4. (a)

SOLUTIONS

Level 1

8.1 Equation of continuity

1. $A_1v_1 = A_2v_2$

$\Rightarrow \quad \dfrac{\pi(4)^2}{4}v_1 = \dfrac{\pi(8)^2}{4}\times 10$

$\Rightarrow \quad v_1 = 40\text{ cm/s}$

2. $A_1v_1 = A_2v_2$

$\Rightarrow \quad 3\times 30 = (n\times 3\times 10^{-7})(0.05)$

$\Rightarrow \quad n = 6\times 10^9$

8. 2. Bernoulli's equation

1. Equation of continuity, $A_1v_1 = A_2v_2$

$\Rightarrow \quad 10^{-2}\times 2 = 0.5\times 10^{-2}\times v$

$\Rightarrow \quad v = 4\text{ m/s}$

Bernoulli's equation in a horizontal pipe,

$$p_1 + \frac{1}{2}\rho v_1^2 = p_2 + \frac{1}{2}\rho v_2^2$$

$\Rightarrow 8000 + \dfrac{1}{2}\times 10^3\times 2^2 = p_2 + \dfrac{1}{2}\times 10^3\times 4^2$

$\Rightarrow \quad p_2 = 2000\text{ Pa}$

2. (a) $\dfrac{dV}{dt} = Av$

$\Rightarrow \quad 1\text{ cm}^3/\text{s} = (4\times 10^{-2}\text{ cm}^2)v_A$

$\Rightarrow \quad v_A = 25\text{ cm/s}$

(b) $\dfrac{dV}{dt} = Av$

$\Rightarrow \quad 1\text{ cm}^3/\text{s} = (2\times 10^{-2}\text{cm}^2)v_B$

$v_B = 50\text{ cm/s}$

(c) Applying Bernoulli's equation,

$$p_A + \frac{1}{2}\rho v_A^2 = p_B + \frac{1}{2}\rho v_B^2$$

$\Rightarrow p_A - p_B = \dfrac{1}{2}\rho(v_B^2 - v_A^2)$

$= \dfrac{1}{2}\times 1000\times[(50)^2 - (25)^2]\times 10^{-4}$

$= 93.75\text{ Pa}$

3. (a) $\dfrac{dV}{dt} = Av$

$\Rightarrow 1\text{ cm}^3/\text{s} = (4\times 10^{-2}\text{cm}^2)v_A \Rightarrow v_A = 25\text{ cm/s}$

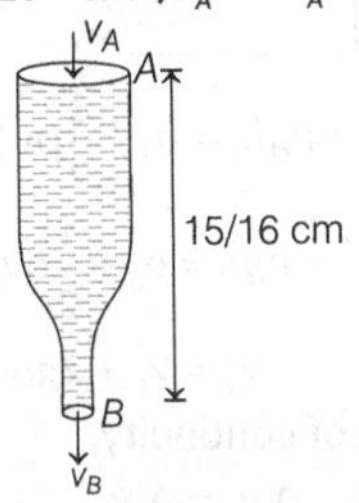

(b) $\dfrac{dV}{dt} = Av$

$\Rightarrow \quad 1\text{ cm}^3/\text{s} = (2\times 10^{-2}\text{cm}^2)v_B$

$\Rightarrow \quad v_B = 50\text{ cm/s}$

(c) Applying Bernoulli's equation,

$$p_A + \frac{1}{2}\rho v_A^2 + \rho g h_A = p_B + \frac{1}{2}\rho v_B^2 + \rho g h_B$$

$p_A - p_B = \dfrac{1}{2}\rho(v_B^2 - v_A^2) - \rho g(h_A - h_B)$

$= \dfrac{1}{2}\times 1000[(50)^2 - (25)^2]\times 10^{-4}$

$- 1000\times 10\left(\dfrac{15}{16} - 0\right)\times 10^{-2}$

$= 0$

4. Equation of continuity,

$A_1v_1 = A_2v_2$

$\Rightarrow \quad 1\times 10 = 0.5\,v_2$

$\Rightarrow \quad v_2 = 20\text{ cm/s}$

Bernoulli's equation, $p_1 + \dfrac{1}{2}\rho v_1^2 + \rho g h_1$

$= p_2 + \dfrac{1}{2}\rho v_2^2 + \rho g h_2$

$\Rightarrow \quad p_1 - p_2 = \dfrac{1}{2}\rho(v_2^2 - v_1^2) - \rho g(h_1 - h_2)$

$= \dfrac{1}{2}\times 1000[(20)^2 - (10)^2]\times 10^{-4}$

$- 1000\times 10\times(5\times 10^{-2} - 0)$

$= -485\text{ Pa}$

5. Applying Bernoulli's equation,

$$p_1 + \frac{1}{2}\rho v_1^2 = p_2 + \frac{1}{2}\rho v_2^2$$

1 ⟶ 120 m/s
2 ⟶ 90 m/s

$\Rightarrow \quad p_2 - p_1 = \dfrac{1}{2}\rho(v_1^2 - v_2^2)$

$= \dfrac{1}{2}\times 1.3\times[(120)^2 - (90)^2]$

$= 4095\text{ Pa} = 4.1\times 10^3\text{Pa}$

Gross lift $= (p_2 - p_1)A$

$= 4095\times 10\times 2 = 81900\text{ N} = 8.2\times 10^4\text{ N}$

6. Applying Bernoulli's equation,

$$p_1 + \frac{1}{2}\rho v_1^2 + \rho g h_1 = p_2 + \frac{1}{2}\rho v_2^2 + \rho g h_2$$

$\Rightarrow \quad v_2^2 = v_1^2 + 2g(h_1 - h_2) \qquad \{\because p_1 = p_2\}$

$\Rightarrow \quad v_2^2 = (0.4)^2 + 2\times 9.8(0.2 - 0)$

$\Rightarrow \quad V_2 \simeq 2\text{ m/s}$

Applying equation of continuity,

$A_1v_1 = A_2v_2$

$$\Rightarrow \pi(4\times10^{-3})^2\times0.4=\frac{\pi d^2}{4}\times2$$

$$\Rightarrow \qquad d \simeq 3.6\times10^{-3}\text{ m}$$

7. $p_A = p_0 + \rho g h_1$ and $p_B = p_0 + \rho g h_2$

$$p_A - p_B = \rho g(h_1 - h_2)$$

$$= 1000\times10\times2\times10^{-2} = 200\text{ Pa}$$

Applying equation of continuity,

$$A_1v_1 = A_2v_2 \Rightarrow 4v_1 = 2v_2$$

$$\Rightarrow \qquad v_2 = 2v_1$$

Applying Bernoulli's equation,

$$p_1+\frac{1}{2}\rho v_1^2 = p_2+\frac{1}{2}\rho v_2^2$$

$$\Rightarrow \qquad p_1 - p_2 = \frac{1}{2}\rho(v_2^2 - v_1^2)$$

$$\Rightarrow \qquad 200 = \frac{1}{2}\times1000((2v_1)^2 - v_1^2)$$

$$\Rightarrow \qquad v_1 = \sqrt{\frac{2}{15}}\text{ m/s}$$

Rate of flow of water

$$= A_1v_1 = 4\times\left(\sqrt{\frac{2}{15}}\times10^2\right) = 146\text{ cm}^3/\text{s}$$

8. $\frac{dV}{dt} = A_1v_1 \Rightarrow 500 = 5v_1 \Rightarrow v_1 = 100\text{ cm/s}$

$$\Rightarrow \qquad \frac{dV}{dt} = A_2v_2 \Rightarrow 500 = 2v_2 \Rightarrow v_2 = 250\text{ cm/s}$$

Applying Bernoulli's equation,

$$p_1+\frac{1}{2}\rho_w v_1^2 = p_2+\frac{1}{2}\rho_w v_2^2$$

$$\Rightarrow \qquad p_1 - p_2 = \frac{1}{2}\rho_w(v_2^2 - v_1^2)$$

$$\Rightarrow \qquad \rho_{Hg} g h = \frac{1}{2}\rho_w(v_2^2 - v_1^2)$$

$$\Rightarrow 13.6\times980\times h = \frac{1}{2}\times[(250)^2 - (100)^2]$$

$$\Rightarrow \qquad h = 1.97\text{ cm}$$

8.3 Velocity of efflux

1. (a) Applying Bernoulli's equation between points 1 and 2,

$$(p_0+\rho g D) + 0 = p_0 + \frac{1}{2}\rho v^2 \Rightarrow v = \sqrt{2gD}$$

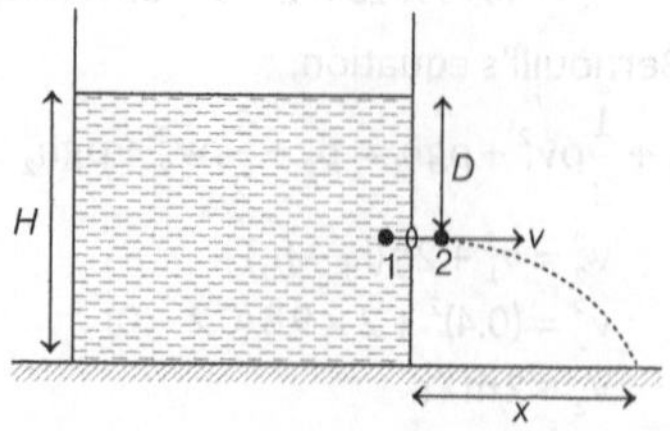

Time of flight, $T = \sqrt{\frac{2h}{g}} = \sqrt{\frac{2(H-D)}{g}}$

Horizontal range

$$= x = vT = \sqrt{2gD}\sqrt{\frac{2(H-D)}{g}} = 2\sqrt{D(H-D)}$$

(b) $x = 2\sqrt{DH - D^2}$

For x to be maximum, $\frac{dx}{dD} = 0$

$$\Rightarrow \quad 2\frac{1}{2\sqrt{DH-D^2}}(H-2D) = 0$$

$$\Rightarrow \qquad D = \frac{H}{2}$$

2. Applying Bernoulli's equation,

$$p_1+\frac{1}{2}\rho v_1^2 = p_2+\frac{1}{2}\rho v_2^2$$

$$\Rightarrow \left(p_0+\rho g h+\frac{mg}{A}\right)+0 = p_0+\frac{1}{2}\rho v_2^2$$

$$\Rightarrow \qquad v_2 = \sqrt{2gh+\frac{2mg}{\rho A}}$$

$$= \sqrt{2\times10\times6+\frac{2(45+5)(10)}{1000\times1}}$$

$$= 11\text{ m/s}$$

3. Applying Bernoulli's equation between points 1 and 2

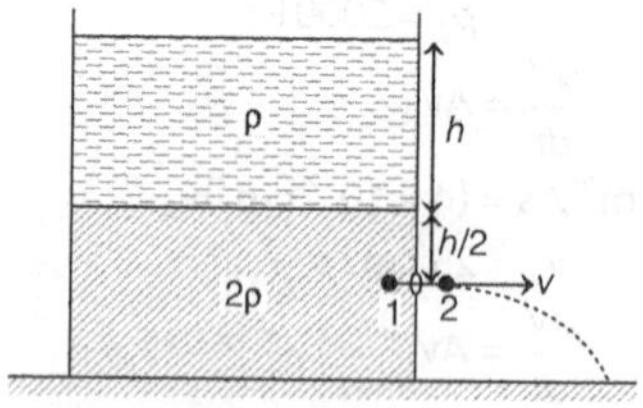

$$p_1+\frac{1}{2}\rho v_1^2 = p_2+\frac{1}{2}\rho v_2^2$$

$$\Rightarrow \qquad \left(p_0+\rho g h+2\rho g\left(\frac{h}{2}\right)\right)+0 = p_0+\frac{1}{2}(2\rho)v^2$$

$$\Rightarrow \qquad v = \sqrt{2gh}$$

4. Applying Bernoulli's equation between points 1 and 2,

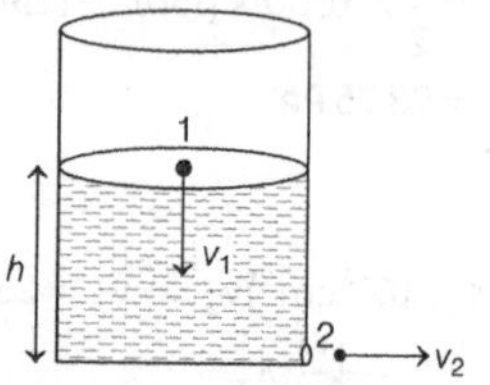

$$p_1+\frac{1}{2}\rho v_1^2+\rho g h_1 = p_2+\frac{1}{2}\rho v_2^2+\rho g h_2$$

$$\Rightarrow \qquad p_0+\frac{1}{2}\rho v_1^2+\rho g h = p_0+\frac{1}{2}\rho v_2^2+0$$

$$\Rightarrow \qquad v_2^2 = v_1^2+2gh \qquad \text{... (i)}$$

Applying equation of continuity,

$$A_1v_1 = A_2v_2$$

$\Rightarrow \quad Av_1 = av_2 \quad$ ... (ii)

Solving Eqs. (i) and (ii), we get

$$v_2 = \sqrt{\frac{2gh}{1-\left(\frac{a}{A}\right)^2}} = 2\text{m/s}$$

(b) At any height h, $v_2 = \sqrt{2gh}$

$$A_1v_1 = A_2v_2 \Rightarrow Av_1 = a\sqrt{2gh} \Rightarrow v_1 = \frac{a}{A}\sqrt{2gh}$$

$$v_1 = \frac{-dh}{dt} = \frac{a}{A}\sqrt{2gh}$$

$$\Rightarrow \frac{1}{\sqrt{2g}}\int_h^0 \frac{dh}{\sqrt{h}} = -\frac{a}{A}\int_0^T dt$$

$$\Rightarrow T = \frac{A}{a}\sqrt{\frac{2h}{g}} = \frac{1}{(0.02)^2}\sqrt{\frac{2(0.2)}{10}} = 500 \text{ s}$$

5. (a) Applying Bernoulli's equation between points A and D.

$$p_1 + \rho g h_1 + \frac{1}{2}\rho v_1^2 = p_2 + \rho g h_2 + \frac{1}{2}\rho v_2^2$$

$$\Rightarrow p_0 + \rho g(4+1) + 0 = p_0 + 0 + \frac{1}{2}\rho v_D^2$$

$$\Rightarrow v_D = 10 \text{ m/s}$$

(b) Applying Bernoulli's equation between points A and B.

$$p_1 + \rho g h_1 + \frac{1}{2}\rho v_1^2 = p_2 + \rho g h_2 + \frac{1}{2}\rho v_2^2$$

$$\Rightarrow p_0 + 0 + 0 = p_B + 900 \times 10 \times 1.5 + \frac{1}{2} \times 900 \times (10)^2$$

$$\Rightarrow p_B = 4.15 \times 10^4 \text{ Pa}$$

(c) Applying Bernoulli's equation between between points C and D.

$$p_1 + \rho g h_1 + \frac{1}{2}\rho v_1^2 = p_2 + \rho g h_2 + \frac{1}{2}\rho v_2^2$$

$$\Rightarrow p_C + 900 \times 10 \times 4 + \frac{1}{2} \times 900 \times (10)^2$$

$$= 10^5 + 0 + \frac{1}{2} \times 900 \times (10)^2$$

$$\Rightarrow p_C = 6.4 \times 10^4 \text{ Pa}$$

6. Using equation of continuity,

$$A_1v_1 = A_2v_2$$

$$\Rightarrow 4 \times 10^{-3} \times 1 = 8 \times 10^{-3} v_Q$$

$$\Rightarrow v_Q = 0.5 \text{ m/s}$$

Work done per unit volume by the pressure

$$= p_1 - p_2$$

$$= \rho g(h_2 - h_1) + \frac{1}{2}\rho(v_2^2 - v_1^2)$$

$$= 10^3 \times 9.8\,(5-2) + \frac{1}{2} \times 10^3 \times [(0.5)^2 - (1)^2]$$

$$= 29025 \text{ J/m}^3$$

Work done per unit volume by gravity

$$= \rho g(h_2 - h_1) = 10^3 \times 9.8\,(5-2)$$

$$= 29400 \text{ J/m}^3$$

7. Velocity of efflux, $v = \sqrt{2g\left(\frac{h}{2}\right)} = \sqrt{gh}$

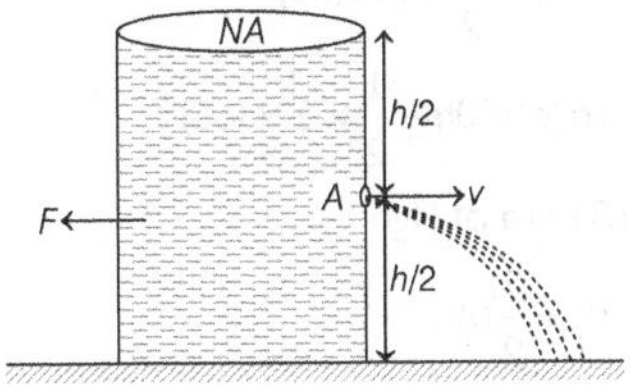

$$F = \frac{dp}{dt} = \frac{d(mv)}{dt}$$

$$= \frac{d}{dt}(\rho V v) = \rho v \frac{dV}{dt}$$

$$= \rho A v^2$$

Initial acceleration of tank

$$= \frac{F}{m} = \frac{\rho A(\sqrt{gh})^2}{\rho(NA)h} = \frac{g}{N}$$

Level 2

Single Choice Correct Questions

1. Applying equation of continuity,

$$A_1v_1 = A_2v_2 + A_3v_3$$

$$\Rightarrow A(3) = A(1.5) + (1.5A)v$$

$$\Rightarrow v = 1.0 \text{ m/s}$$

2. Applying equation of continuity,

$$A_1v_1 = A_2v_2$$

$$\Rightarrow \frac{\pi(2)^2 \times 3}{4} = 100 \times \frac{\pi(0.05)^2}{4} v_2$$

$$\Rightarrow v_2 = 48 \text{ m/s}$$

3. In steady horizontal flow,

$$p + \frac{1}{2}\rho v^2 = \text{constant}$$

So, pressure is greatest where the speed is least.

4. Applying equation of continuity,

$$A_1v_1 = A_2v_2$$

$$\Rightarrow \pi r^2 \times 4 = \pi(2r)^2 v_2$$

$$\Rightarrow v_2 = 1 \text{ m/s}$$

Applying Bernoulli's equation in the horizontal pipes,

$$p_1 + \frac{1}{2}\rho v_1^2 = p_2 + \frac{1}{2}\rho v_2^2$$

$$\Rightarrow 1.25 \times 10^4 + \frac{1}{2} \times 1000 \times 4^2 = p_2 + \frac{1}{2} \times 1000 \times 1^2$$

$$\Rightarrow p_2 = 2 \times 10^4 \text{ N/m}^2$$

5. Applying Bernoulli's equation for the horizontal pipe,

$$p_1 + \frac{1}{2}\rho v_1^2 = p_2 + \frac{1}{2}\rho v_2^2$$

$$\Rightarrow \rho_{Hg} g(1 \text{ cm}) + \frac{1}{2}\rho_\omega (35 \text{ cm/s})^2$$

$$= \rho_{Hg} gh + \frac{1}{2}\rho_{\omega}(65 \text{ cm/s})^2$$

$$\Rightarrow 13.6 \times 980 \times 1 + \frac{1}{2} \times 1 \times (35)^2$$

$$= 13.6 \times 980h + \frac{1}{2} \times 1 \times (65)^2$$

$\Rightarrow \quad h = 0.89$ cm of Hg

6. $p_1 + \frac{1}{2}\rho v_1^2 = p_2 + \frac{1}{2}\rho v_2^2$

$$\Rightarrow p_1 - p_2 = \frac{1}{2}\rho(v_2^2 - v_1^2)$$

$$= \frac{1}{2} \times 1.3[(40)^2 - (30)^2] = 455 \text{ N/m}$$

Uplift $= (p_1 - p_2)A = 455 \times 4 = 1820$ N

Net force $= 200 \times 9.8 - 1820 = 140$ N, down

7. Applying Bernoulli's equation,

$$p_1 + \frac{1}{2}\rho v_1^2 + \rho g h_1 = p_2 + \frac{1}{2}\rho v_2^2 + \rho g h_2$$

$\Rightarrow \quad v_2^2 = v_1^2 + 2g(h_1 - h_2) \qquad \because \{p_1 = p_2\}$

$\Rightarrow \quad v_2^2 = (1)^2 + 2 \times 10 \times (0.15)$

$\Rightarrow \quad v_2 = 2$ m/s

Applying equation of continuity,

$$A_1 v_1 = A_2 v_2$$

$\Rightarrow \quad 10^{-4} \times 1 = A_2(2)$

$\Rightarrow \quad A_2 = 5 \times 10^{-5} \text{m}^2$

8. If a ball is moving from left to right and also spinning about a horizontal axis in anti-clockwise direction of motion, then relative to the ball air will be moving from right to left. The resultant velocity of air above and below the ball will be $(v + \omega r)$ and $(v - \omega r)$, respectively.

So, according to Bernoulli's principle, due to this differences of pressure, an upward force will act on the ball and hence the ball will get maximum flight.

9. Applying Bernoulli's equation,

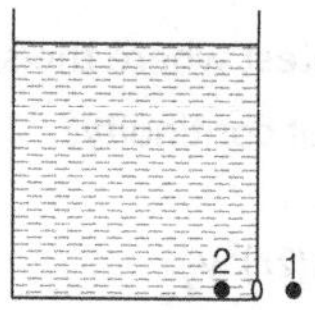

$$p_1 + \frac{1}{2}\rho v_1^2 = p_2 + \frac{1}{2}\rho v_2^2$$

$\Rightarrow \quad 10^5 + \frac{1}{2} \times 10^3 v^2 = 3 \times 10^5 + 0$

$\Rightarrow \quad v = \sqrt{400}$ m/s

10. $v^2 = \dfrac{2gh}{1 - \left(\dfrac{a}{A}\right)^2}$

$$= \frac{2 \times 10 \times (3 - 0.525)}{1 - (0.1)^2} = 50 \text{ m}^2/\text{s}^2$$

11. Applying Bernoulli's equation,

$$p_1 + \frac{1}{2}\rho v_1^2 = p_2 + \frac{1}{2}\rho v_2^2$$

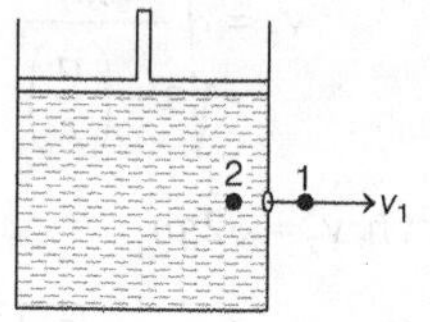

$\Rightarrow \quad 10^5 + \frac{1}{2} \times 10^3 v_1^2$

$$= \left(10^5 + 10^3 \times 9.8 \times 0.5 + \frac{10 \times 9.8}{1000 \times 10^{-4}}\right) + 0$$

$\Rightarrow \quad v_1 = 3.4$ m/s

12. Let side of the cubical box be L.

Velocity of efflux, $v = \sqrt{2gh}$

When the box is full, $h = l$

$\Rightarrow \quad v_0 = \sqrt{2gL}$

When the box is half empty and tilted, $h = \frac{l}{\sqrt{2}}$

$\Rightarrow \quad v = \sqrt{2g\left(\frac{L}{\sqrt{2}}\right)} \Rightarrow v = \frac{v_0}{\sqrt[4]{2}}$

13. Volume flow rate $= \frac{dV}{dt} = Av$

Volume flow rate is same for both holes.

$\Rightarrow \quad A_1 v_1 = A_2 v_2$

$\Rightarrow \quad (L^2)\sqrt{2gy} = (\pi R^2)(\sqrt{2g(4y)})$

$\Rightarrow \quad R = \frac{L}{\sqrt{2\pi}}$

14. $v = \sqrt{2gh} = \sqrt{2 \times 10 \times 0.2} = 2$m/s

15. Applying Bernoulli's equation,

$$p_1 + \frac{1}{2}\rho v_1^2 = p_2 + \frac{1}{2}\rho v_2^2$$

$$\Rightarrow (p_0 + \rho g(2h) + (2\rho)gh) + 0 = p_0 + \frac{1}{2}(2\rho)v^2$$

$\Rightarrow \quad v = 2\sqrt{gh}$

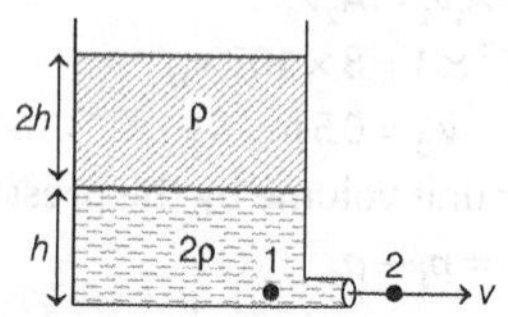

16. Applying Bernoulli's equation,

$$p_1 + \frac{1}{2}\rho v_1^2 = p_2 + \frac{1}{2}\rho v_2^2$$

$$\Rightarrow (p_0 + 10^3 \times 10 \times 10) + 0 = p_0 + \frac{1}{2} \times 10^3 v_2^2$$

$\Rightarrow \quad v_2 = \sqrt{200}$ m/s

So horizontal range, $R = v_2 T$

$$2R = v'T$$

$$\Rightarrow \quad v_2' = 2v_2 = 2\sqrt{200} \text{ m/s}$$

Applying Bernoulli's equation,

$$p_1 + \frac{1}{2}\rho v_1^2 = p_2 + \frac{1}{2}\rho v_2^2$$

$$\Rightarrow (p_0 + 10^3 \times 10 \times 10 + p_{extra}) + 0 = p_0 + \frac{1}{2} \times 10^3 \times (2\sqrt{200})^2$$

$$\Rightarrow \quad p_{extra} = 3 \times 10^5 \text{Pa} = 3 \text{ atm}$$

17. $v = \sqrt{2gX}$, $T = \sqrt{\frac{2(H+h-X)}{g}}$

$$R = vT = 2\sqrt{X(H+h-X)}$$

To maximize R, $\frac{dR}{dX} = 0$

$$\Rightarrow \quad \frac{2}{2\sqrt{X(H+h-X)}}(H+h-2X) = 0$$

$$\Rightarrow \quad X = \frac{H+h}{2}$$

18. Let height of p above ground be y.

$v_p = \sqrt{2g(H-y)}$ and $v_Q = \sqrt{2g(H-h)}$

$R_1 = R_2$

$$\Rightarrow \sqrt{2g(H-y)}\sqrt{\frac{2y}{g}} = \sqrt{2g(H-h)}\sqrt{\frac{2h}{g}}$$

$$\Rightarrow \quad y = H - h$$

19. $T = \frac{A_1}{A_2}\left(\sqrt{\frac{2H}{g}} - \sqrt{\frac{2h}{g}}\right)$

When water level falls from h to $\frac{h}{2}$.

$$T_1 = \frac{A_1}{A_2}\left(\sqrt{\frac{2h}{g}} - \sqrt{\frac{2(h/2)}{g}}\right)$$

When water level falls from h/2 to 0.

$$T_2 = \frac{A_1}{A_2}\left(\sqrt{\frac{2(h/2)}{g}} - 0\right)$$

So, $\frac{T_1}{T_2} = \sqrt{2} - 1$

20. Where tube is narrower, liquid is faster and hence according to Bernoulli's principle pressure will be lesser. So, height of liquid in the vertical tubes will be lesser where the tube is narrower.

21. When air is blown over the tank, atmospheric pressure over the tank decreases. Due to lesser pressure difference at the hole, velocity of efflux decreases.

22. Initial momentum of liquid = $d\,mv\hat{j}$

Final momentum of liquid = $d\,mv\hat{i}$

Change in momentum, **dp** = $dmv(\hat{i} - \hat{j})$

$$\Rightarrow \quad dp = \sqrt{2}dmv$$

$$\Rightarrow \quad \frac{dp}{dt} = \sqrt{2}\frac{dm}{dt}v = \sqrt{2}\frac{d(\rho V)}{dt}v$$

$$\Rightarrow \quad F = \sqrt{2}\rho L V$$

23. For the vessel to just begin moving,

$$F = F_L$$

$$\Rightarrow \quad \rho A v^2 = \mu M g$$

$$\Rightarrow \rho\left(\frac{\pi d^2}{4}\right)(\sqrt{2gH})^2 = \mu M g$$

$$\Rightarrow \quad d = \sqrt{\frac{2\mu M}{\pi \rho H}}$$

24. $F_1 = \rho A v_1^2$, $F_2 = \rho A v_2^2$

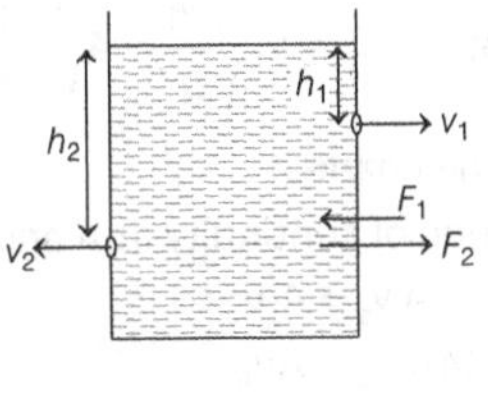

Net force $= F_2 - F_1 = \rho A(v_2^2 - v_1^2)$

$$= \rho A(2gh_2 - 2gh_1) = 2\rho A g h$$

$$= 2 \times 10^3 \times 0.01 \times 10 \times 1 = 200 \text{ N}$$

25. $F = \rho a v^2$

$$\Rightarrow \quad m\alpha = \rho a(\sqrt{2gh})^2$$

$$(\rho A h)\alpha = \rho a(2gh)$$

$$\Rightarrow \quad \alpha = \frac{2ga}{A}$$

So, acceleration at any instant is independent of h.

Velocity acquired by container,

$$v = u + at \Rightarrow v = \frac{2gat}{A}$$

Hence, v depends on h as t depends on h.

Numerical Value Questions

1.

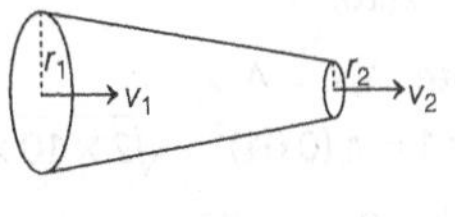

Equation of continuity, $A_1 v_1 = A_2 v_2$

$$\Rightarrow \quad \pi(0.1)^2 v_1 = \pi(0.05)^2 v_2$$

$$\Rightarrow \quad v_2 = 4v_1$$

Bernoulli's equation, $p_1 + \frac{1}{2}\rho v_1^2 = p_2 + \frac{1}{2}\rho v_2^2$

$$\Rightarrow \quad p_1 - p_2 = \frac{1}{2}\rho(v_2^2 - v_1^2)$$

$$\Rightarrow \quad 1.5 \times 10^5 = \frac{1}{2} \times 1.25 \times 10^3 \times [(4v_1)^2 - v_1^2]$$

$$\Rightarrow \quad v_1 = 4 \text{ m/s}$$

Rate of flow $= A_1 v_1 = 3.14(0.1)^2 \times (4) = 1.26 \times 10^{-1} \text{m}^3/\text{s}$

2. $p_1+\frac{1}{2}\rho v_1^2=p_2+\frac{1}{2}\rho v_2^2$

$\Rightarrow \quad p_1-p_2=\frac{1}{2}\rho(v_2^2-v_1^2)$

$\Rightarrow \quad \rho gh=\frac{1}{2}\rho(v_2^2-v_1^2)$

$\Rightarrow 1000\times 5.1\times 10^{-1}=\frac{1}{2}[(v_2^2-(2)^2)]$

$\Rightarrow \quad v_2=32$ cm/s

3. Equation of continuity, $A_1v_1=A_2v_2$

$\Rightarrow \quad \frac{\pi(8)^2}{4}\times 0.25=\frac{\pi(2)^2}{4}v_2$

$\Rightarrow \quad v_2=4$ m/s

Horizontal range $=v_2T=v_2\sqrt{\frac{2h}{g}}=4\sqrt{\frac{2(1.25)}{10}}=2\text{m}$

4. Let point B at the nozzle.

Applying equation of continuity at A and B,

$A_1v_1=A_2v_2$

$\Rightarrow \quad (4A)v_A=Av_B$

$\Rightarrow \quad v_A=\frac{v_B}{4}$

Applying Bernoulli's equation between A and B,

$p_1+\frac{1}{2}\rho v_1^2+\rho gh_1=p_2+\frac{1}{2}\rho v_2^2+\rho gh_2$

$\Rightarrow p_A+\frac{1}{2}\rho v_A^2+0=p_B+\frac{1}{2}\rho v_B^2+\rho gl$

$\Rightarrow (p_0+41\times 10^3)+\frac{1}{2}\times 10^3\times\left(\frac{v_B}{4}\right)^2$

$=p_0+\frac{1}{2}\times 10^3\times v_B^2+10^3\times 10\times 1.1$

$\Rightarrow \quad v_B=8\text{ m/s}$

$\Rightarrow \quad h=\frac{v_B^2}{2g}$

$\Rightarrow \quad h=\frac{(8)^2}{2(10)}=3.2\text{ m}$

5. In steady state, $A_1v_1=A_2v_2$

$\Rightarrow \pi(0.02)^2\times 1=\pi(0.01)^2\times\sqrt{2\times 10\times h}$

$h=0.8\text{ m}=80\text{ cm}$

6. $R=v\sqrt{\frac{2h}{g}} \quad \Rightarrow 1=v\sqrt{\frac{2(1)}{10}} \quad \Rightarrow v=\sqrt{5}$ m/s

$v=\sqrt{2gh} \quad \Rightarrow \quad \sqrt{5}=\sqrt{2gh}$

$\Rightarrow \quad h=0.25$ m

$t=\frac{A}{a}\sqrt{\frac{2}{g}}(\sqrt{H}-\sqrt{h})$

$\Rightarrow \quad t=\frac{\sqrt{5}}{32\times 10^{-4}}\sqrt{\frac{2}{10}}(\sqrt{0.81}-\sqrt{0.25})$

$\Rightarrow \quad t=125$ s

7. Equation of continuity, $A_1v_1=A_2v_2$

$\Rightarrow \quad A\left(-\frac{dh}{dt}\right)=\left(\frac{A}{100}\right)\sqrt{2gh}$

$\Rightarrow \quad dt=-\frac{100dh}{\sqrt{2gh}}$

Total momentum imparted $=\int Fdt=\int\rho av^2dt$

$=\int_5^0 10^3\left(\frac{A}{100}\right)2gh\left(\frac{-100\,dh}{\sqrt{2gh}}\right)$

$=10^5\text{Ns}=100\text{ kNs}$

8. Applying Bernoulli's equation,

$p_1+\frac{1}{2}\rho v_1^2=p_2+\frac{1}{2}\rho v_2^2$

$\Rightarrow\left(p_0+\rho gh+2\rho g\left(\frac{h}{2}\right)\right)+0=p_0+\frac{1}{2}(2\rho)v_2^2$

$\Rightarrow \quad v_2=\sqrt{2gh}$

Speed just before hitting the ground,

$v=\sqrt{v_2^2+\left(2g\left(\frac{h}{2}\right)\right)}=\sqrt{3gh}$

Applying equation of continuity,

$A_1v_1=A_2v_2$

$\Rightarrow \quad \sqrt{6}\times\sqrt{2gh}=A\sqrt{3gh}$

$\Rightarrow \quad A=2\text{cm}^2$

9. Equation of continuity,

$A_1v_1=A_2v_2$

$\Rightarrow (60\,A)\frac{dh}{dt}=A\left(10\left(4-\pi\sin\left(\frac{\pi t}{30}\right)\right)\right)$

$\Rightarrow \quad \int dh=\int\frac{1}{6}\left(4-\pi\sin\left(\frac{\pi t}{30}\right)\right)dt$

$\Rightarrow \quad h=\frac{1}{6}\left[4t+30\cos\left(\frac{\pi t}{30}\right)\right]_0^{15}=5\text{ m}$

10. $R=v\sqrt{\frac{2h}{g}}$

$\Rightarrow \quad 80=v\sqrt{\frac{2(20)}{10}}$

$\Rightarrow \quad v=40\text{ m/s}$

Applying Bernoulli's equation,

$p_1+\frac{1}{2}\rho v_1^2=p_2+\frac{1}{2}\rho v_2^2$

$\Rightarrow(p+660\times 10\times 53)+0=10^5+\frac{1}{2}\times 660\times(40)^2$

$p=2.78\times 10^5\text{Pa}$

Level 3

Single Choice Correct Questions

1. Applying equation of continuity,

$$A_1v_1 = A_2v_2$$

$$\Rightarrow \quad Av_1 = 2A\left(\sqrt{\frac{gl}{2}}\right) \Rightarrow v = \sqrt{2gl}$$

Applying Bernoulli's equation,

$$p_1 + \rho g h_1 + \frac{1}{2}\rho v_1^2 = p_2 + \rho g h_2 + \frac{1}{2}\rho v_2^2$$

$$\Rightarrow p + 0 + \frac{1}{2}\rho(\sqrt{2gl})^2 = p + \rho g(l\sin\theta) + \frac{1}{2}\rho\left(\sqrt{\frac{gl}{2}}\right)^2$$

$$\Rightarrow \quad \sin\theta = \frac{3}{4} \Rightarrow \theta = \sin^{-1}\left(\frac{3}{4}\right)$$

2.

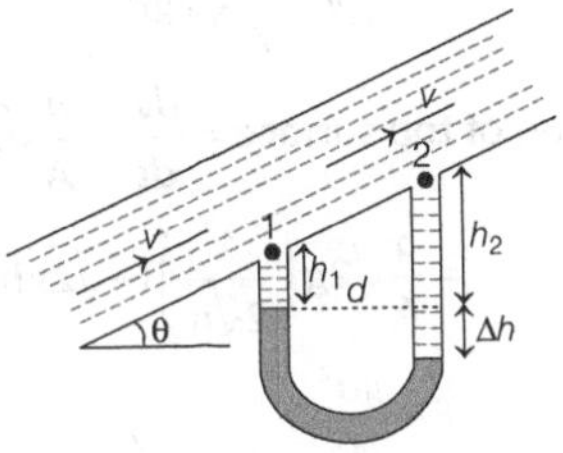

Applying Bernoulli's equation for points 1 and 2,

$$p_1 + \rho g h_1 + \frac{1}{2}\rho v_1^2 = p_2 + \rho g h_2 + \frac{1}{2}\rho v_2^2$$

$$\Rightarrow \quad p_1 + \rho g h_1 + \frac{1}{2}\rho v^2 = p_2 + \rho g h_2 + \frac{1}{2}\rho v^2$$

$$\Rightarrow \quad p_1 - p_2 = \rho g(h_2 - h_1)$$

$$\Rightarrow \quad \rho_{Hg} g\Delta h = \rho g(d\tan\theta)$$

$$\Rightarrow \quad \Delta h = \frac{\rho d\tan\theta}{\rho_{Hg}}$$

3. As we move along the axis of the pipe, cross-section area decreases. So, speed of water flow will increase and hence pressure will decrease as in a horizontal pipe, $p + \frac{1}{2}\rho v^2 =$ constant.

4. Applying Bernoulli's equation for the points *B* and *D*,

$$p_B + \frac{1}{2}\rho v_B^2 = p_D + \frac{1}{2}\rho v_D^2 \quad ...(i)$$

Applying Bernoulli's equation for the points *A* and *C*,

$$p_A + \rho g h_1 + \frac{1}{2}\rho v_A^2 = p_C + \rho g h_2 + \frac{1}{2}\rho v_C^2 \quad ...(ii)$$

Along vertical, $\quad p_B = p_A + \rho g h_1 \quad ...(iii)$

$$p_D = p_C + \rho g h_2 \quad ...(iv)$$

Solving Eqs. (i), (ii), (iii) and (iv), we get

$$\Rightarrow \quad v_B^2 - v_A^2 = v_D^2 - v_C^2$$

$$\Rightarrow \quad v_D = \sqrt{v_C^2 + v_B^2 - v_A^2} = \sqrt{28} \text{ m/s}$$

5. Applying equation of continuity, $A_0v_0 = A_1v_1$

$$\Rightarrow \quad v_1 = \frac{A_0v_0}{A_1}$$

dp = Change in momentum of dm mass of liquid $= dm(v_1 - v_0)$

$$F = \frac{dp}{dt} = \frac{dm}{dt}(v_1 - v_0) = \rho A_0 v_0\left(\frac{A_0v_0}{A_1} - v_0\right)$$

$$= \rho A_0 v_0^2\left(\frac{A_0}{A_1} - 1\right)$$

6. $$\frac{dk}{dt} = \frac{1}{2}\frac{dm}{dt}(v_1^2 - v_0^2)$$

$$= \frac{1}{2}(\rho A_0 v_0)\left(\left(\frac{A_0v_0}{A_1}\right)^2 - v_0^2\right) = \frac{1}{2}\rho A_0 v_0^3\left(\frac{A_0^2}{A_1^2} - 1\right)$$

7. Let height of the liquid above orifice be h_1.

$$v = \sqrt{\frac{2gh_1}{1 - \frac{\left(\frac{A}{1000}\right)^2}{A^2}}} = \sqrt{2gh_1}$$

Horizontal range,

$$R = v\sqrt{\frac{2h}{g}} = \sqrt{2gh_1}\sqrt{\frac{2h}{g}} = 2\sqrt{hh_1}$$

For liquid to fall on the plate *AB*, $20 < R < 80$

$$\Rightarrow \quad 20 < 2\sqrt{20h_1} < 80$$

$$\Rightarrow \quad 5 < h_1 < 80$$

Time for which liquid falls on plate

$$= \frac{A_2}{A_1}\left(\sqrt{\frac{2H}{g}} - \sqrt{\frac{2h}{g}}\right)$$

$$= \frac{A}{\left(\frac{A}{1000}\right)}\left(\sqrt{\frac{2(0.8)}{10}} - \sqrt{\frac{2(0.05)}{10}}\right)$$

$$= 300 \text{ s}$$

8. Let height of liquid in the vessel be *h*.

Velocity of efflux $= \sqrt{2gh}$

Horizontal range, $R = vT = \sqrt{2gh}\sqrt{\frac{2H}{g}} = 2\sqrt{Hh}$

Collection of liquid will stop, when $R \le H$

$$\Rightarrow \quad 2\sqrt{Hh} \le H$$

$$\Rightarrow \quad h \le \frac{H}{4} \Rightarrow h \le 1 \text{ m}$$

Volume of liquid collected

$$= A(H - h) = 1(4 - 1) = 3\text{m}^3$$

9. Applying Bernoulli's equations for points 1 and 2,

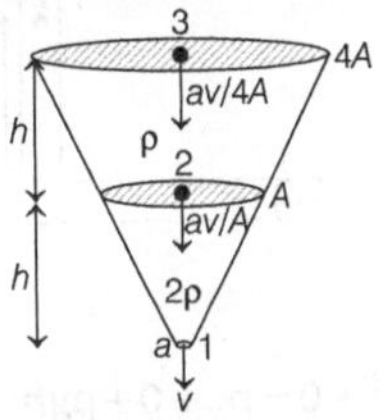

$$p_0 + \frac{1}{2}(2\rho)v^2 = p_2 + 2\rho gh + \frac{1}{2}(2\rho)\left(\frac{av}{A}\right)^2$$

Applying Bernoulli's equation for points 2 and 3,

$$p_2 + 0 + \frac{1}{2}\rho\left(\frac{av}{A}\right)^2 = p_0 + \frac{1}{2}\rho\left(\frac{av}{4A}\right)^2 + \rho gh$$

Solving we get, $v = \sqrt{\dfrac{3gh}{1 - \dfrac{17a^2}{32A^2}}}$

10. Let height of liquid be y at any instant.
Applying equation of continuity,

$$A_1v_1 = A_2v_2$$

$$\Rightarrow \quad a\sqrt{2gy} = (\pi x^2)\left(-\frac{dy}{dt}\right)$$

π, g and $\dfrac{dy}{dt}$ are constants.

Squaring the equation, we get $y = kx^4$

11.

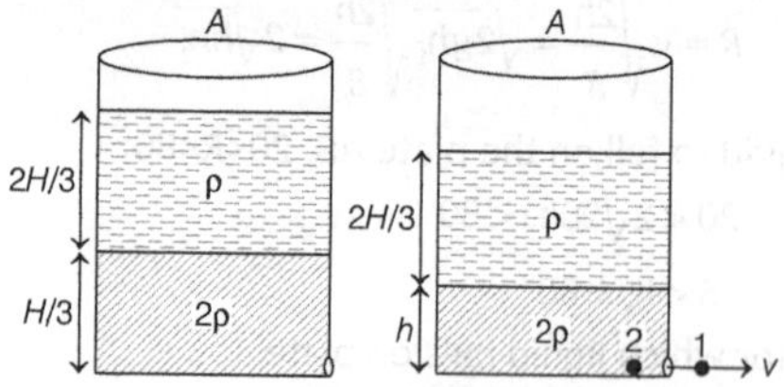

Applying Bernoulli's equation for points 1 and 2,

$$p_0 + \frac{1}{2}(2\rho)v^2 = \left(p_0 + \rho g\left(\frac{2H}{3}\right) + 2\rho gh\right) + 0$$

$$\Rightarrow \quad v = \sqrt{2g\left(\frac{H}{3} + h\right)}$$

Applying equation of continuity,

$$A_1v_1 = A_2v_2$$

$$\Rightarrow \quad S\sqrt{2g\left(\frac{H}{3} + h\right)} = A\left(-\frac{dh}{dt}\right)$$

$$\Rightarrow \quad \frac{A}{S\sqrt{2g}}\int_{H/3}^{0}\frac{dh}{\sqrt{\frac{H}{3} + h}} = -\int_0^t dt$$

$$\Rightarrow \quad t = \frac{A}{S}(2 - \sqrt{2})\sqrt{\frac{H}{3g}}$$

12. Applying Bernoulli's equation for points 1 and 2,

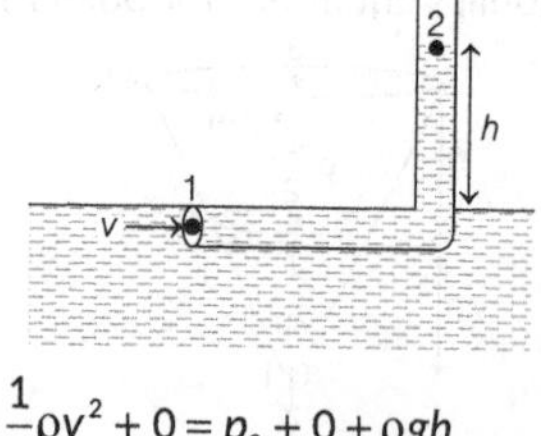

$$p_0 + \frac{1}{2}\rho v^2 + 0 = p_0 + 0 + \rho gh$$

$$\Rightarrow \quad h = \frac{v^2}{2g}$$

13. Velocity of efflux of liquid, $v = \sqrt{2g\left(\frac{h}{2}\right)} = \sqrt{gh}$

Force on ejected liquid $= \rho av^2 = \rho agh$

Torque of these forces about the axis

$$= (\rho agh)2R + (\rho agh)2R$$

$$= 4agh\rho R$$

14. Velocity of liquid coming out of hole $= \sqrt{2gh}$

Let velocity of top surface be v.

Using equation of continuity, $A_1v_1 = A_2v_2$

$$\Rightarrow \quad Av = a\sqrt{2gh}$$

$$\Rightarrow \quad v = \frac{a}{A}\sqrt{2gh}$$

Acceleration of top surface $= \dfrac{dv}{dt} = \dfrac{a}{A}\sqrt{2g}\left(\dfrac{1}{2\sqrt{h}}\right)\dfrac{dh}{dt}$

$$= \frac{a}{A}\sqrt{2g}\left(\frac{1}{2\sqrt{h}}\right)(-\sqrt{2gh})$$

$$= -\frac{ga^2}{A^2}$$

15. For isothermal process, $p_1V_1 = p_2V_2$

$$\Rightarrow \quad (10^5 + 10^5)A(1) = p_2A(2)$$

$$\Rightarrow \quad p_2 = 10^5 \text{ Pa}$$

Applying Bernoulli's equation,

$$p_1 + \rho gh_1 + \frac{1}{2}\rho v_1^2 = p_2 + \rho gh_2 + \frac{1}{2}\rho v_2^2$$

$$\Rightarrow \quad 10^5 + 10^3 \times 10 \times 1 + \frac{1}{2} \times 10^3 v^2$$

$$= 10^5 + 10^3 \times 10 \times 2 + 0$$

$$\Rightarrow \quad v = \sqrt{20} \text{ m/s}$$

Multiple Choice(s) Correct Questions

1. (c, d)
2. (a) $\dfrac{dV}{dt} = A_1v_1 = A_2v_2$

(c) Applying Bernoulli's equation for the horizontal tube,

$$p_1 + \frac{1}{2}\rho v_1^2 = p_2 + \frac{1}{2}\rho v_2^2$$

$$\Rightarrow \quad p_1 - p_2 = \frac{1}{2}\rho(v_2^2 - v_1^2)$$

$$\Rightarrow \quad \rho gh = \frac{1}{2}\rho(v_2^2 - v_1^2)$$

$$\Rightarrow \quad v_2^2 - v_1^2 = 2gh$$

(d) Total energy per unit mass is conserved.

3. Fluid particles passing through the bend are in circular motion. The centripetal acceleration is provided by the variation in pressure.

$$(p_1 - p_2)A = ma_c$$

$\Rightarrow \quad p_1 > p_2$

Applying Bernoulli's equation at 1 and 2,

$$p_1 + \frac{1}{2}\rho v_1^2 + \rho g h_1 = p_2 + \frac{1}{2}\rho v_2^2 + \rho g h_2$$

$\Rightarrow \quad v_1 < v_2 \quad \because (p_1 > p_2 \text{ and } h_1 = h_2)$

4. $$v = \sqrt{\frac{2gh}{1 - \frac{a^2}{A^2}}} = \sqrt{\frac{2gh}{1 - \frac{\left(\frac{A}{3}\right)^2}{A^2}}} = 3\sqrt{\frac{gh}{4}}$$

Applying equation of continuity, $A_1 v_1 = A_2 v_2$

$$\Rightarrow \quad \left(\frac{A}{3}\right) 3\sqrt{\frac{gh}{4}} = A v_2$$

$$\Rightarrow \quad v_2 = \sqrt{\frac{gh}{4}}$$

Acceleration of top surface of liquid

$$= \frac{dv_2}{dt} = \sqrt{\frac{g}{4}}\left(\frac{1}{2\sqrt{h}}\right)\frac{dh}{dt}$$

$$= \left(\sqrt{\frac{g}{4}}\right)\left(\frac{1}{2\sqrt{h}}\right)\left(-\sqrt{\frac{gh}{4}}\right)$$

$$= \frac{-g}{8}$$

5. Applying Bernoulli's equation at B and C,

$$p_0 + 0 + 10^3 \times 10(3.6) = p_0 + \frac{1}{2} \times 10^3 v_C^2 + 0$$

Discharge rate of flow

$$= Av = \pi\left(\frac{4}{\sqrt{\pi}} \times 10^{-2}\right)^2 (6\sqrt{2})$$

$$= 96\sqrt{2} \times 10^{-4}\ \text{m}^3/\text{s}$$

Applying Bernoulli's equation at A and C,

$$p_A + \frac{1}{2} \times 10^3 \times (6\sqrt{2})^2 + 10^3 \times 10 \times (1.8 + 3.6)$$

$$= 10^5 + \frac{1}{2} \times 10^3 \times (6\sqrt{2})^2 + 0$$

$$\Rightarrow \quad p_A = 0.46 \times 10^5\ \text{Pa}$$

6. (A) $v = \sqrt{2gh} = \sqrt{2 \times 10 \times 0.05} = 1\ \text{m/s}$

(B) $s_y = u_y t + \frac{1}{2}a_y t^2$

$$\Rightarrow -0.08 = (1\sin 37^\circ)t + \frac{1}{2}(-10)t^2$$

$$\Rightarrow \quad t = 0.2\ \text{s}$$

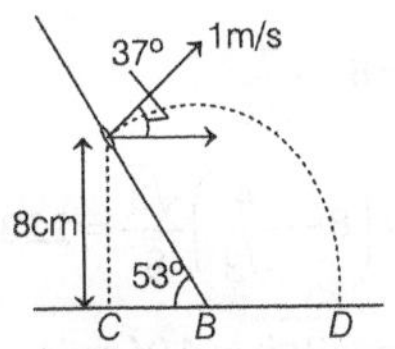

$$CD = (1\cos 37^\circ)(0.2) = 0.16\text{m} = 16\ \text{cm}$$

$$BD = CD - BC = 16 - 8\tan 37^\circ = 10\ \text{cm}$$

(D) $F_H = \rho A v^2 \cos 37^\circ$

$$= 10^3 \times 1.5 \times 10^{-4} \times (1)^2 \times (0.8) = 0.12\ \text{N}$$

7. (A) $F = 2\rho A v^2 = 2 \times 1000 \times 2 \times 10^{-4} \times (10)^2 = 40\text{N}$

(B) $F = 2\rho A(v - v_c)^2$

$$\Rightarrow \quad m\frac{dv_c}{dt} = 2\rho A(v - v_c)^2$$

$$\Rightarrow \quad \int_0^{v_c} \frac{dv_c}{(v - v_c)^2} = \frac{2\rho A}{m}\int_0^t dt$$

$$\Rightarrow \quad v_c = \frac{2\rho A v^2 t}{m + 2\rho A v t}$$

At $\quad t = 10\ \text{s}, v_c = 8\ \text{m/s}$

(C) $\quad a_c = \frac{F}{m} = \frac{2\rho A(v - v_c)^2}{m}$

At $t = 10$ s, $\quad a_c = 0.16\ \text{m/s}^2$

(D) When $v = 5\ \text{m/s}$, $F = 2\rho A(v - v_c^2) = 10\text{N}$

$$P = Fv = 10 \times 5 = 50\text{W}$$

8. (A) Applying equation of continuity,

$$A_1 v_1 = A_2 v_2$$

$$\Rightarrow \quad A_1(4) = \left(\frac{A_1}{4}\right)v_2$$

$$\Rightarrow \quad v_2 = 16\ \text{m/s}$$

Applying Bernoulli's equation at P and Q,

$$p_1 + \frac{1}{2}\rho v_1^2 = p_2 + \frac{1}{2}\rho v_2^2$$

$$\Rightarrow 280 \times 10^3 + \frac{1}{2} \times 900 \times (4)^2$$

$$= p_2 + \frac{1}{2} \times 900 \times (16)^2$$

$$\Rightarrow \quad p_2 = 172 \times 10^3\text{N/m}^2$$

(D) $F_x = p_1 A_1 + p_2 A_2 \cos 37^\circ + \rho(A_1 v_1)(v_1 + v_2\cos 37^\circ)$

$$= 74.98\ \text{N}$$

$$F_y = p_2 A_2 \sin 37^\circ + \rho(A_1 v_1)(v_2 \sin 37^\circ)$$

$$= 12.07\ \text{N}$$

$$F_{net} = \sqrt{F_x^2 + F_y^2} = 76 \times 10^3\text{N}$$

9. (A) Loss in gravitational PE = Gain in KE

$$\Rightarrow (\rho(2AH))g\left(\frac{H}{2}\right) - \left(\rho\left(2A\left(\frac{H}{2}\right)\right)\right)g\left(\frac{H}{4}\right)$$

$$= \frac{1}{2}\rho(4AH)v^2$$

$$\Rightarrow \quad v = \sqrt{\frac{3gh}{8}}$$

(B) $\quad \Sigma F = ma$

$$\Rightarrow \rho(2AH)g = \rho(4AH)a$$

$$a = \frac{g}{2}$$

(C) For the shaded liquid column, $\Sigma F = ma$

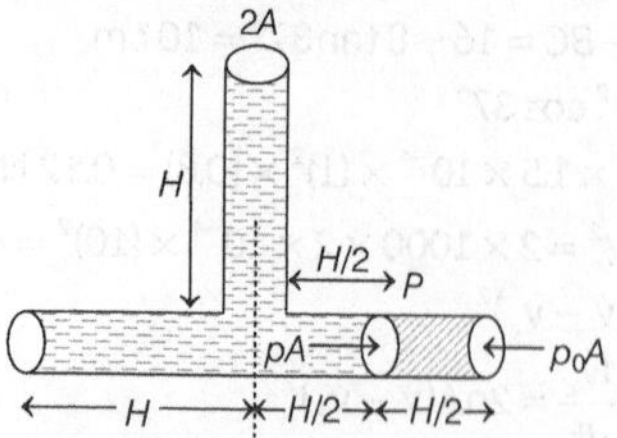

$$\Rightarrow pA - p_0A = \left(\rho A\left(\frac{H}{2}\right)\right)\left(\frac{g}{2}\right)$$

$$\Rightarrow \quad p - p_0 = \frac{\rho g H}{4}$$

$$\Rightarrow \text{Gauge pressure at } p = \frac{\rho g H}{4}$$

Comprehension Based Questions

1. $\frac{dm}{dt} = \rho\frac{dV}{dt} = \rho A v = \rho_w\left(\frac{\pi D^2}{4}\right)v$

2. $A_1 v_1 = A_2 v_2$

$$\Rightarrow \quad \left(\frac{\pi D_0^2}{4}\right)v_0 = \left(\frac{\pi D^2}{4}\right)v$$

$$\Rightarrow \quad D = D_0\sqrt{\frac{v_0}{v}}$$

3. Applying Bernoulli's equation,

$$p_1 + \frac{1}{2}\rho v_1^2 + \rho g h_1 = p_2 + \frac{1}{2}\rho v_2^2 + \rho g h_2$$

$$\Rightarrow p_0 + \frac{1}{2}\rho v^2 + 0 = p_0 + 0 + \rho g(b + x)$$

$$\Rightarrow \quad v = \sqrt{2g(b + x)}$$

4. $D = D_0\sqrt{\frac{v_0}{v}} = D_0\sqrt{\frac{\sqrt{2gb}}{\sqrt{2g(b+x)}}} = D_0\left(\frac{b}{b+x}\right)^{1/4}$

5. $D = D_0\left(\frac{b}{b+x}\right)^{1/4}$

$$0.9 = 1\left(\frac{b}{b+0.3}\right)^{1/4}$$

$$\Rightarrow \quad b = 57 \text{ cm}$$

6. Applying Bernoulli's equation at A and D,

$$p_1 + \frac{1}{2}\rho v_1^2 + \rho g h_1 = p_2 + \frac{1}{2}\rho v_2^2 + \rho g h_2$$

$$\Rightarrow p_0 + 0 + 900 \times 10 \times 5 = p_0 + \frac{1}{2} \times 900 \times v_D^2 + 0$$

$$\Rightarrow \quad v_D = 10 \text{ m/s}$$

7. Applying Bernoulli's equation at B and D,

$$p_1 + \frac{1}{2}\rho v_1^2 + \rho g h_1 = p_2 + \frac{1}{2}\rho v_2^2 + \rho g h_2$$

$$\Rightarrow p_B + \frac{1}{2} \times 900 \times (10)^2 + 900 \times 10 \times 6.5$$

$$= 1.01 \times 10^5 + \frac{1}{2} \times 900 \times (10)^2 + 0$$

$$\Rightarrow \quad p_B = 4.25 \times 10^4 \text{ N/m}^2$$

8. Applying Bernoulli's equation at C and D,

$$p_1 + \frac{1}{2}\rho v_1^2 + \rho g h_1 = p_2 + \frac{1}{2}\rho v_2^2 + \rho g h_2$$

$$\Rightarrow p_C + \frac{1}{2} \times 900 \times (10)^2 + 900 \times 10 \times 4$$

$$= 1.01 \times 10^5 + \frac{1}{2} \times 900 \times (10)^2 + 0$$

$$\Rightarrow \quad p_C = 6.5 \times 10^4 \text{ N/m}^2$$

9. Let new height of water in the tank be h.

Volume of water $= \frac{AH}{2} = \left(A - \frac{A}{3}\right)h \quad \Rightarrow \quad h = \frac{3H}{4}$

Speed of water flowing out of the orifice

$$= \sqrt{2gh} = \sqrt{2g\left(\frac{3H}{4}\right)} = \sqrt{\frac{3gH}{2}}$$

10. When the solid cylinder has been taken out,

$$\left(A - \frac{A}{3}\right)\left(\frac{H}{2}\right) = Ah$$

$$\Rightarrow \quad h = \frac{H}{3}$$

Speed of water $= \sqrt{2gh} = \sqrt{\frac{2gH}{3}}$

11. Volume of liquid $= 2 \times 2 \times 2 = 8 \text{m}^2$

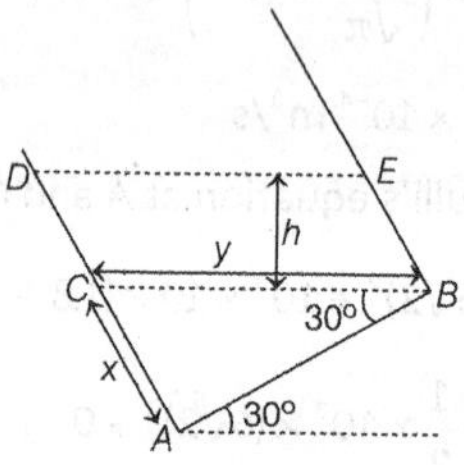

$\tan 30° = \frac{x}{2} \Rightarrow x = \frac{2}{\sqrt{3}} \text{m}$

Volume of $ABC = \frac{1}{2} \times 2 \times x \times 2 = \frac{4}{\sqrt{3}} \text{m}^3$

$$\sin 30° = \frac{x}{y} \Rightarrow y = 2x = \frac{4}{\sqrt{3}} \text{m}$$

Volume of $BCDE = 8 - \frac{4}{\sqrt{3}}$

$$\Rightarrow \quad y \times h \times 2 = 8 - \frac{4}{\sqrt{3}}$$

$$\Rightarrow \quad h = \left(8 - \frac{4}{\sqrt{3}}\right)\frac{\sqrt{3}}{8} = 1.232 \text{m}$$

Velocity of efflux $= \sqrt{2gh} = 4.96 \text{ m/s}$

12. $T = \sqrt{\frac{2H}{g}} = \sqrt{\frac{2(2\sin 30^\circ)}{10}} = \frac{1}{\sqrt{5}}$ s

13. Range $= 2\cos 30^\circ + vT = 3.95$m

14. Applying Bernoulli's equation,

$$p_1 + \frac{1}{2}\rho v_1^2 = p_2 + \frac{1}{2}\rho v_2^2$$

$$\Rightarrow p_0 + \frac{1}{2} \times 900 \times v^2$$

$$= (p_0 + 600 \times 10 \times 0.6 + 900 \times 10 \times 0.4) + 0$$

$$\Rightarrow \quad v = 4 \text{ m/s}$$

15. $F = \rho a v^2 = 900 \times (5 \times 10^{-4}) \times 4^2 = 7.2$N

16. $f_L = \mu mg = 0.01\,(900 \times 0.5 \times 0.6 + 600 \times 0.5 \times 0.6)\,10$

$= 45$N

$$F_{max} = f_L + F = 45 + 7.2 = 52.2\text{N}$$

Since $F < f_L, F_{min} = 0$

17.

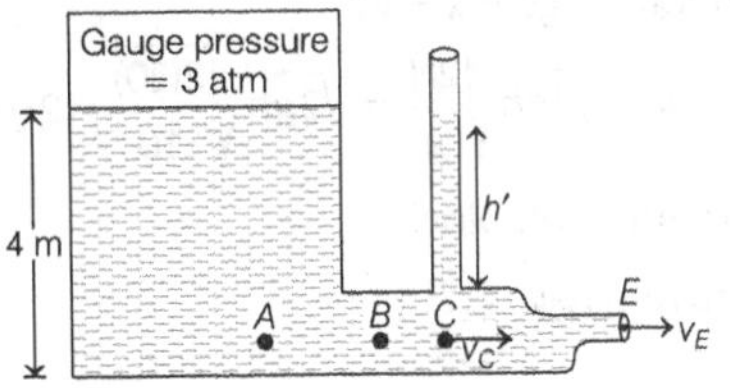

$$p_A = p_0 + p + \rho g h$$

$$\Rightarrow \quad p_A = 10^5 + 3 \times 10^5 + 6 \times 10^3 \times 10 \times 4$$

$$= 6.4 \times 10^5 \text{ Pa}$$

Applying Bernoulli's theorem at A and E,

$$6.4 \times 10^5 + 0 = 10^5 + \frac{1}{2} \times (6 \times 10^3) v_E^2$$

$$\Rightarrow \quad v_E = \sqrt{180} = 13.4 \text{m/s}$$

Applying equation of continuity at C and E,

$$\Rightarrow \quad A_1 v_1 = A_2 v_2$$

$$\Rightarrow (6 \times 10^{-4}) v_C = (3 \times 10^{-4})(13.4)$$

$$\Rightarrow \quad v_C = 6.7 \text{m/s}$$

Applying Bernoulli's theorem at A and C,

$$6.4 \times 10^5 + 0 = p_C + \frac{1}{2} \times 6000 \times (6.7)^2$$

$$\Rightarrow \quad p_C = 5.05 \times 10^5 \text{ Pa}$$

From hydrostatics, $p_C = p_0 + \rho g h'$

$$\Rightarrow 5.05 \times 10^5 = 10^5 + 6 \times 10^3 \times 10 \times h'$$

$$\Rightarrow \quad h' = 6.75 \text{ m}$$

18. Discharge rate from outlet $= A_E v_E$

$$= 3 \times 10^{-4} \times 13.4$$

$$= 4.02 \times 10^{-3} \text{m}^3/\text{s}$$

19. When hole is created, pressure at the top will be

$$p_0 = 10^5 \text{ Pa}$$

Applying Bernoulli's equation at A and E,

$$p_A + \frac{1}{2}\rho v_A^2 = p_E + \frac{1}{2}\rho v_E^2$$

$$\Rightarrow (10^5 + 6 \times 10^3 \times 10 \times 4) + 0$$

$$= 10^5 + \frac{1}{2} \times (6 \times 10^3) v_E^2$$

$$\Rightarrow \quad v_E = \sqrt{80} \text{ m/s}$$

Applying continuity equation at C and E,

$$A_1 v_1 = A_2 v_2$$

$$\Rightarrow 6 \times 10^{-4} v_C = 3 \times 10^{-4} (\sqrt{80}) \Rightarrow v_C = \sqrt{20} \text{ m/s}$$

Applying Bernoulli's equation at A and C,

$$p_A + \frac{1}{2}\rho v_A^2 = p_C + \frac{1}{2}\rho v_C^2$$

$$\Rightarrow (10^5 + 6 \times 10^3 \times 10 \times 4) + 0$$

$$= (10^5 + 6 \times 10^3 \times 10 \times h') + \frac{1}{2} \times 6 \times 10^3 \times (\sqrt{20})^2$$

$$\Rightarrow \quad h' = 3\text{m}$$

Match the Column Questions

1. (A) Bernoulli's theorem is applicable for incompressible, non-viscous liquids with streamlined flow. It is based on the principle of conservation of energy.

(B) A ball moving with a spin will have higher velocity of air above the ball than below. So, the pressure below will be more than that above causing a lift.

(C) Based on the principle of Bernoulli's theorem., artificial high pressure created pushes the paint through the gun.

(D) Streamlined flow is possible in only non-viscous medium. As the streamline passes through narrower pipes, the velocity increases causing the pressure to fall.

2. A- PS; B - PQ; C-R ; D - PQS

3. (A) Applying Bernoulli's theorem,

$$p_1 + \frac{1}{2}\rho v_1^2 = p_2 + \frac{1}{2}\rho v_2^2$$

$$\Rightarrow \left(p_0 + \frac{Mg}{A} + \rho g H + 2\rho g H\right) + 0 = p_0 + \frac{1}{2}(2\rho) v_A^2$$

$$\Rightarrow \quad v_A = \sqrt{\frac{Mg}{\rho A} + 3gH}$$

(B) Applying Bernoulli's theorem,

$$p_1 + \frac{1}{2}\rho v_1^2 = p_2 + \frac{1}{2}\rho v_2^2$$

$$\Rightarrow \left(p_0 + \frac{Mg}{A} + \rho g H\right) + 0 = p_0 + \frac{1}{2}\rho v_B^2$$

$$\Rightarrow \quad v_B = \sqrt{\frac{2Mg}{\rho A} + 2gH}$$

(C) $F_A = (2\rho) a v_A^2 = (2\rho)\left(\frac{A}{10}\right)\left(\frac{Mg}{\rho A} + 3gH\right) = \frac{Mg + 3\rho A g H}{5}$

(D) $F_B = \rho\left(\frac{A}{10}\right) v_B^2 = \rho\left(\frac{A}{10}\right)\left(\frac{2Mg}{\rho A} + 2gH\right) = \frac{Mg + \rho A g H}{5}$

4. A-PQRST; B - PQST; C - PQRST; D- QRT

Numerical Value Questions

1. Density of liquid at the bottom $= \rho_0\left(1+\frac{2}{3}(1)\right) = \frac{5\rho_0}{3}$

Pressure at the bottom

$$= p_0 + \int_0^1 \rho_0(1+\alpha y)gdy = p_0 + \frac{40\rho_0}{3}$$

Applying Bernoulli's theorem,

$$p_1 + \frac{1}{2}\rho v_1^2 = p_2 + \frac{1}{2}\rho v_2^2$$

$$\Rightarrow \left(p_0 + \frac{40\rho}{3}\right) + 0 = p_0 + \frac{1}{2}\left(\frac{5\rho}{3}\right)v_2^2$$

$$\Rightarrow \quad v_2 = 4 \text{ m/s}$$

2.

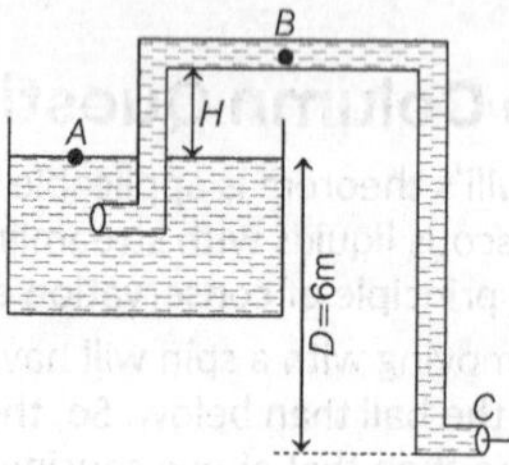

Applying Bernoulli's theorem at A and C,

$$p_A + \rho g h_B + \frac{1}{2}\rho v_A^2 = p_C + \rho g h_C + \frac{1}{2}\rho v_C^2$$

$$\Rightarrow 10^5 + 10^3 \times 10 \times 6 + 0 = 10^5 + 0 + \frac{1}{2} \times 10^3 \times v_C^2$$

$$\Rightarrow \quad v_C = \sqrt{120} \text{ m/s}$$

For equation of continuity, $v_B = v_C = \sqrt{120}$ m/s

Applying Bernoulli's equation at B and C,

$$p_B + \rho g h_B + \frac{1}{2}\rho v_B^2 = p_C + \rho g h_C + \frac{1}{2}\rho v_C^2$$

$$\Rightarrow p_B + 10^3 \times 10\,(6+H) + \frac{1}{2}\rho v_B^2 = 10^5 + 0 + \frac{1}{2}\rho v_B^2$$

$$\Rightarrow \quad p_B = 10^5 - 10^4(6+H)$$

For siphon to work, $p_B > 0$

$$\Rightarrow \quad 10^5 - 10^4(6+H) > 0$$

$$\Rightarrow \quad H < 4\text{m}$$

$$\Rightarrow \quad H_{max} = 4\text{m}$$

3. Let height of liquid be h at any instant.

$$A_1v_1 = A_2v_2$$

$$\Rightarrow (\pi \times 10^{-3})\sqrt{2gh} = \pi(h\tan\theta)^2\left(-\frac{dh}{dt}\right)$$

$$\Rightarrow \quad \int_0^T dt = -\frac{1000\tan^2\theta}{\sqrt{2g}}\int_5^0 h^{3/2}dh$$

$$\Rightarrow \quad T = \frac{1000\left(\frac{1}{5}\right)^2}{\sqrt{20}} \times \left(\frac{2}{5} \times (5)^{5/2}\right) = 200 \text{ s}$$

4. Water will stop coming out of orifice when pressure at the bottom becomes equal to atmospheric pressure.

$$p_{bottom} = p_{top} + \rho gh$$

$$\Rightarrow \quad 10^5 = p_{top} + 10^3 \times 10 \times 0.2$$

$$\Rightarrow \quad p_{top} = 9.8 \times 10^4 \text{Pa}$$

For the air above water,

$$p_1V_1 = p_2V_2$$

$$\Rightarrow 10^5 \times A\,(0.5 - H) = 9.8 \times 10^4 A\,(0.5 - 0.2)$$

$$\Rightarrow \quad H = 0.206\text{m} = 206 \text{ mm}$$

Fall in height $= 206 - 200 = 6$ mm

5. From equation of continuity, $A_1v_1 = A_2v_2$

$$\Rightarrow \quad a\sqrt{2gh} = A\left(\frac{dh}{dt}\right)$$

$$\Rightarrow \quad \frac{dh}{dt} = \frac{a}{A}\sqrt{2gh}$$

Horizontal range $= x = vT$

$$\Rightarrow \quad x = \sqrt{2gh}\sqrt{\frac{2H}{g}} = \sqrt{2gh}\sqrt{\frac{2(20)}{10}} = 2\sqrt{2gh}$$

For stream to hit block,

velocity of block $= \frac{dx}{dt}$

$$= 2\sqrt{2g}\left(\frac{1}{2\sqrt{h}}\right)\left(\frac{dh}{dt}\right)$$

$$= 2\sqrt{2g}\left(\frac{1}{2\sqrt{h}}\right)\left(\frac{a}{A}\sqrt{2gh}\right) = 1 \text{ m/s}$$

6. $\int_{p_0}^{p_B} dp = \int_3^5 \rho(\omega^2 x)dx$

$$\Rightarrow \quad p_B - p_0 = \rho(0.5)^2\left[\frac{x^2}{2}\right]_3^5$$

$$\Rightarrow \quad p_B = p_0 + 2\rho$$

Applying Bernoulli's theorem,

$$p_1 + \frac{1}{2}\rho v_1^2 = p_2 + \frac{1}{2}\rho v_2^2$$

$$\Rightarrow \quad p_0 + 2\rho + 0 = p_0 + \frac{1}{2}\rho v_2^2$$

$$\Rightarrow \quad v_2 = 2 \text{ m/s}$$

7. Let velocities be v_1 and v_2 at the two cross-sections using equation of continuity,

$$A_1v_1 = A_2v_2$$

$$\Rightarrow \quad \pi(3)^2 v_1 = \pi(1.5)^2 v_2$$

$$\Rightarrow \quad v_2 = 4v_1$$

Using Bernoulli's theorem,

$$p_1 + \frac{1}{2}\rho v_1^2 + \rho g h_1 = p_2 + \frac{1}{2}\rho v_2^2 + \rho g h_2$$

$$\Rightarrow \quad v_2^2 = v_1^2 + 2g(h_1 - h_2) \qquad \because \{p_1 = p_2\}$$

$$\Rightarrow \quad (4v_1)^2 = v_1^2 + 2 \times 10 \times 3 \times 10^{-2}$$

$$\Rightarrow \quad v_1 = 0.2 \text{ m/s}$$

Rate of water flow $= A_1 v_1$

$$= \pi (3 \times 10^{-3})^2 (0.2)\, m^3/s$$
$$= \pi \times 9 \times 10^{-6} \times 0.2 \times 10^6 \times 60\, mL/min$$
$$= 108\, \pi\, mL/min$$

8. Lets take a strip of thickness dh at depth h. Velocity of liquid flowing out of the strip

$$= v = \sqrt{2gh}$$

Volume flow rate

$$= \frac{dV}{dt} = \int_{h_1}^{h_2} (\sqrt{2gh})(l dh) = (\sqrt{2g})\, l \left[\frac{h^{3/2}}{3/2}\right]_{h_1}^{h_2}$$
$$= 7\sqrt{2g}\ m^3/s$$

9. $T = F \cos 45° = \rho A v^2 = \rho(\pi r^2) v^2$

Breaking stress $= \dfrac{T}{\pi(2r)^2 - \pi r^2} = \dfrac{\rho \pi r^2 v^2}{3\pi r^2}$

$$\Rightarrow \quad 3 \times 10^7 = \frac{10^3 v^2}{3}$$
$$\Rightarrow \quad v = 300\ m/s$$

10. T = Time taken to empty the tank

$$= \frac{A}{a}\sqrt{\frac{2H}{g}} = \frac{A}{a}$$

Force on the tank $= \rho a v^2$

$$\Rightarrow \quad m\frac{dv}{dt} = \rho a (2gh)$$
$$\Rightarrow \quad (\rho A h)\frac{dv}{dt} = \rho a (2gh)$$
$$\Rightarrow \quad \int_0^v dv = \frac{2ga}{A}\int_0^T dt$$
$$\Rightarrow \quad v = \frac{2ga}{A}\left(\frac{A}{a}\right) = 20\, m/s$$

Previous Years Questions

JEE Main

1. In given question,

$$p_1 = 4.5 \times 10^4 N/m^2$$
$$p_2 = 2.0 \times 10^4 N/m^2$$

Applying Bernoulli's principle,

$$p_1 = p_2 + \frac{1}{2}\rho v^2$$
$$4.5 \times 10^4 = 2.0 \times 10^4 + \frac{1}{2}\rho v^2$$
$$4.5 \times 10^{-4} - 2.0 \times 10^4 = \frac{1}{2}\rho v^2$$
$$2.5 \times 10^4 = \frac{1}{2}\rho v^2$$
$$5.0 \times 10^4 = \rho v^2$$
$$\frac{5.0 \times 10^4}{\rho} = v^2$$
$$\frac{5.0 \times 10^4}{10^3} = v^2$$
$$5.0 \times 10^4 \times 10^{-3} = v^2$$
$$v = \sqrt{50}\ m/s$$

2.

$$F = \frac{1}{2}\rho\,(v_1^2 - v_2^2)\, A,$$
$$\rho = 1.2\ kg/m^3$$
$$F = \frac{1}{2} \times 1.2 \times (70^2 - 65^2) \times 2$$
$$= 1.2 \times (4900 - 4225) = 810\ N$$

3. For balancing the weight of aircrafts $Mg = (p_1 - p_2)A$

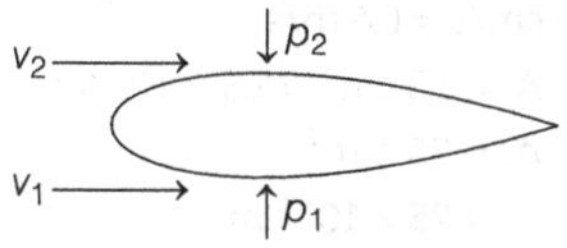

$$\Rightarrow \quad p_1 - p_2 = \frac{Mg}{A} = \frac{5 \cdot 4 \times 10^5 \times 10}{500}$$
$$= 10 \cdot 8 \times 10^3 \text{ units.}$$

Now, by Bernoulli's theorem,

$$p_1 + \frac{1}{2}\rho v_1^2 = p_2 + \frac{1}{2}\rho v_2^2$$

(Assuming height of plane small)

$$\Rightarrow \quad p_1 - p_2 = \frac{1}{2}\rho(v_2^2 - v_1^2)$$
$$\Rightarrow \quad (v_2 - v_1)\left(\frac{v_2 + v_1}{2}\right) = \frac{p_1 - p_2}{\rho}$$

Here, $\dfrac{v_2 + v_1}{2} = 1080\dfrac{km}{h} = 300\dfrac{m}{s}$ and $\rho = 1 \cdot 2\ kg/m^3$

So, $v_2 - v_1 = \dfrac{p_1 - p_2}{\rho\left(\dfrac{v_1 + v_2}{2}\right)} = \dfrac{10.8 \times 10^3}{1.2 \times 300} = 30$

Also, $\quad v_1 + v_2 = 600$

So, $v_2 = 315$ m/s and $v_1 = 285$ m/s

% change in velocity $= \dfrac{v_2 - v_1}{v_1} \times 100$

$$= \frac{315 - 285}{285} \times 100$$
$$= 10.52\% \simeq 10\%$$

4. From equation of continuity,

$$A_1 v_1 = A_2 v_2$$

Here, $A_1 = 2\ cm^2$, $A_2 = 10\ mm^2$

$$= 10 \times 10^{-2}\ cm^2$$
$$v_1 = 4\ cm\ s^{-1}$$

Thus, $v_2 = \dfrac{A_1 v_1}{A_2} = \dfrac{2 \times 4}{10 \times 10^{-2}} = 80$ cm/s

5. By using equation of continuity,

$$A_1v_1 = A_2v_2$$

Given that,

$$A_1 = 750\ \text{cm}^2,\ A_2 = 500\ \text{mm}^2$$
$$= 500\times 10^{-2}\ \text{cm}^2$$
$$v_2 = 30\ \text{cm/s}$$
$$v_1 = \frac{A_2v_2}{A_1} = \frac{500\times 10^{-2}\times 30}{750}$$
$$v_1 = 2\times 10^{-1}\ \text{cm/s}$$
$$v_1 = 2\times 10^{-3}\ \text{m/s}$$

Given that $\frac{dx}{dt} = v = x\times 10^{-3}$ m/s

Therefore, $x = 2$

6. Given, $v_2 = 60$ cm/s $= 0.6$ m/s

$$A_1 = 1.5\ \text{cm}^2 = 1.5\times 10^{-4}\text{m}^{-2}$$
$$A_2 = 25\ \text{mm}^2$$
$$= 25\times 10^{-6}\ \text{m}^2$$

According to equation of continuity,

$$A_1v_1 = A_2v_2$$
$$\Rightarrow \quad v_1 = \frac{A_2v_2}{A} = \frac{25\times 10^{-6}\times 0.6}{1.5\times 10^{-4}} = 0.1\ \text{m/s}$$

∴ According to Bernoulli's principle,

$$p_A - p_B = \frac{1}{2}\rho(v_2^2 - v_1^2)$$
$$= \frac{1}{2}\times 1000[(0.6)^2 - (0.1)^2]$$
$$= 500[0.35] = 175.00 = 175\ \text{Pa}$$

7. The pressure at the surface of the water in the tank is that due to the atmosphere and due to load.

$$\therefore\ p_A = p_0 + \frac{25\times 10}{0.5} = p_0 + 500\ \text{N/m}^2$$

At the opening, the pressure is due to the atmosphere. Using Bernoulli's equation,

$$\Rightarrow \quad p_A + \rho gh + \frac{1}{2}\rho v_A^2 = p_B + \frac{1}{2}\rho v_B^2$$
$$\Rightarrow \quad p_0 + 500 + (1000\times 10\times 0.4) + 0$$
$$= p_0 + \left(\frac{1}{2}\times 1000\right)v_B^2$$
$$500 + 4000 = 500\ v_B^2$$
$$\frac{4500}{500} = v_B^2$$
$$\Rightarrow \quad v_B^2 = 9$$
$$\Rightarrow \quad v_B = 3\ \text{ms}^{-1} = 300\ \text{c ms}^{-1}$$

8. ∵ Force exerted by leaving water on the container,

$$F = \left(\frac{dm}{dt}\right)v = (\rho av)v$$
$$F = \rho av^2$$

Also, by conservation of energy,

$$v = \sqrt{2gh} \Rightarrow F = \rho a(\sqrt{2gh})^2$$
$$\Rightarrow \quad F = \rho a(2gh)$$

∵ For no sliding of vessel,

$$\mu mg \geq F$$
$$\Rightarrow \quad \mu mg \geq \rho a\,(2gh)$$
$$\Rightarrow \quad \mu\rho(Ah)g \geq \rho a\,2gh$$
$$\Rightarrow \quad \mu_{\min} = \frac{2a}{A}$$

9. Given, cross-sectional area of the tank, $A = 0.4\text{m}^2$

Cross-sectional area of the opening at B,

$$A = 4\ \text{cm}^2$$
$$= 1\times 10^{-4}\text{m}^2$$

Load applied on the top of the tank,

$$m = 24\ \text{kg}$$

Height of the water level, $h = 40$ cm

From the figure,

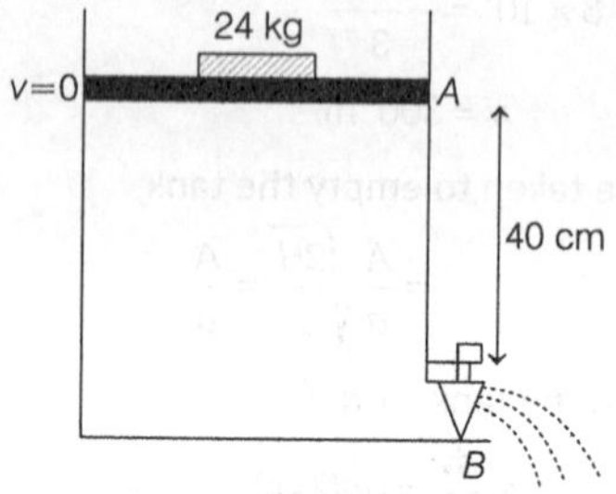

Using the Bernoulli's principle equation,

$$p_0 + \frac{mg}{A} + \rho gh + \frac{\rho v_A^2}{2} = p_0 + \frac{\rho v_B^2}{2}$$
$$\Rightarrow \quad 0 + \frac{(24)10}{0.4} + 1000\times 10\times 0.4 + \frac{\rho(0)^2}{2}$$
$$= 0 + \frac{1000\times v_B^2}{2}$$
$$v_B = 3\ \text{m/s}$$

Hence, the value of v to the nearest integer is 3.

10. Since, pipe is horizontal. Applying Bernoulli's equation at two different cross-section,

$$p_1 + \rho gh_1 + \frac{1}{2}\rho v_1^2 = p_2 + \rho gh_2 + \frac{1}{2}\rho v_2^2$$

For same level, $p + \frac{1}{2}\rho v_1^2 = \frac{p}{2} + \frac{1}{2}\rho v_2^2$

Given, $v_1 = v$ m/s and $v_2 = V$ m/s

$$\frac{p}{2} = \frac{1}{2}\rho(V^2 - v^2)$$
$$\Rightarrow \quad V^2 - v^2 = \frac{p}{\rho}$$
$$\Rightarrow \quad V = \sqrt{\frac{p}{\rho} + v^2}$$

Hence, correct option is (d).

JEE Advanced

1. I. The situation is shown below.

Using Bernoulli's principle between top and bottom points of furnace,

$$p_a = \frac{1}{2}\rho_2 v^2 = p_a + \rho g H + \frac{1}{2}\rho v^2 \quad \text{...(i)}$$

Since, $p_a \times 300 = \rho \times 360°$

$\Rightarrow \quad 1.2 \times 300 = \rho \times 360° \Rightarrow \rho = 1\ \text{kgm}^{-3}$

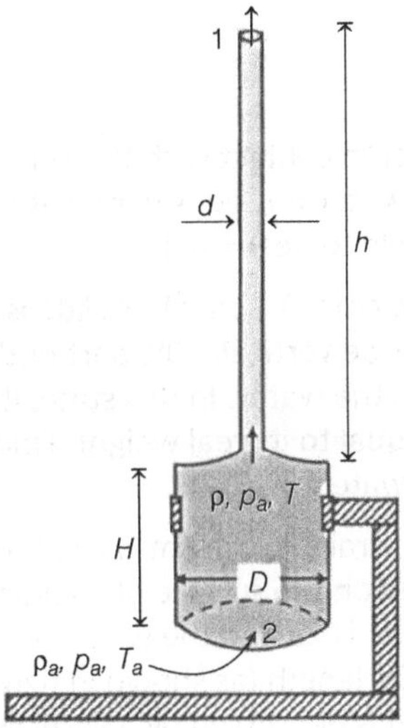

from Eq. (i),

$$\frac{1}{2}\rho_a v^2 = \rho g H + \frac{1}{2}\rho v^2$$

$$\Rightarrow \frac{1}{2}(\rho_a - \rho)v^2 = \rho g H$$

$$\Rightarrow \frac{1}{2}(1.2 - 1)v^2 = 1 \times 10 \times 1$$

$$\Rightarrow \quad 0.1 \times v^2 = 10$$

$$\Rightarrow \quad v = 10\ \text{m/s}$$

$$\therefore \text{Mass flow rate} = v \times \frac{\pi D^2}{4} \times \rho = 10 \times \frac{3.14}{4} \times 1 \times 1 \times 1$$

$$= 7.85\ \text{kg/s}$$

$$= 7850\ \text{g/s}$$

II. For the given condition,

$$p_1 = p_{\text{inside}} + \rho g H$$

$$\Rightarrow \quad p_{\text{inside}} = p_a - \rho g H$$

$$= \rho_a g H - \rho g H$$

$$= (\rho_0 - \rho) g H$$

$$= (1.2 - 1) \times 10 \times 10$$

$$= 0.2 \times 10 \times 10 = 20\ \text{N/m}^2$$

2.

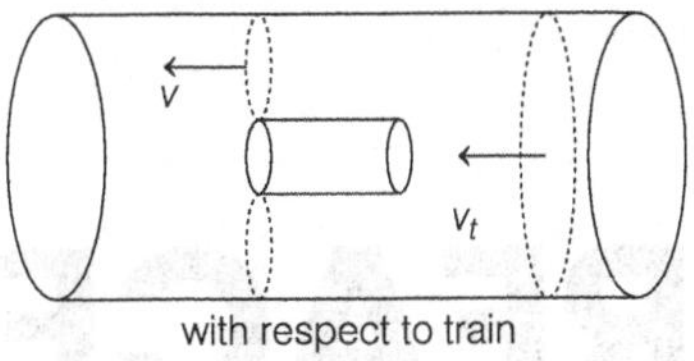

Applying Bernoulli's equation,

$$p_0 + \frac{1}{2}\rho v_1^2 = p + \frac{1}{2}\rho v^2$$

$$p_0 - p = \frac{1}{2}\rho(v^2 - v_1^2) \quad \text{... (i)}$$

From equation of continuity,

$$4S_t v_t = v \times 3S_t$$

$$\Rightarrow \quad v = \frac{4}{3}v_t \quad \text{... (ii)}$$

From Eqs. (i) and (ii), we get

$$p_0 - p = \frac{1}{2}\rho\left(\frac{16}{9}v_t^2 - v_t^2\right) = \frac{1}{2}\rho\frac{7v_t^2}{9}$$

$$\therefore \quad N = 9$$

3. From continuity equation,

$$A_1 v_1 = A_2 v_2$$

Here, $A_1 = 400A_2$

because $r_1 = 20r_2$ and $A = \pi r^2$

$$\therefore \quad v_2 = \frac{A_1}{A_2}(v_1) = 400\,v_1$$

$$= 400(5)\ \text{mm/s}$$

$$= 2000\ \text{mm/s}$$

$$= 2\ \text{m/s}$$

4.

$$p_1 - p_2 = \frac{1}{2}\rho_a v_a^2$$

$$\Rightarrow \quad p_3 - p_2 = \frac{1}{2}\rho_l v_l^2$$

$$p_3 = p_1$$

$$\therefore \quad \frac{1}{2}\rho_l v_l^2 = \frac{1}{2}\rho_a v_a^2$$

$$\Rightarrow \quad v_l = \sqrt{\frac{\rho_a}{\rho_l}}\,v_a$$

$$\therefore \text{ Volume flow rate} \propto \sqrt{\frac{\rho_a}{\rho_l}}$$

CHAPTER~09

SURFACE TENSION

LEVEL 01 Starter Level

9.1 Force due to Surface Tension

1 A body of mass m is placed on the liquid surface, whose surface tension is T. If F is the minimum force required to pull it away from the liquid, then find value of F for different bodies in the following cases.

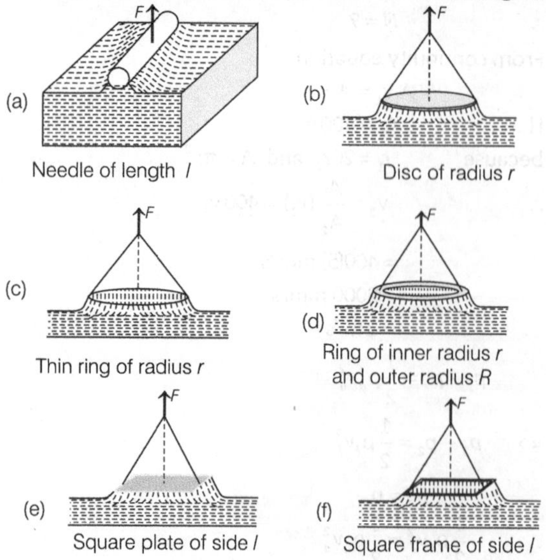

2 A liquid film is formed over a frame $ABCD$ as shown in figure. Wire CD can slide without friction. Find the mass to be hung from CD to keep it in equilibrium.

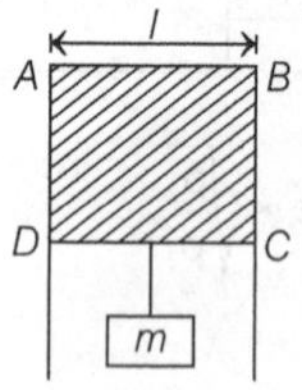

3 A cube of edge a with mass m wettable by water floats on the surface of water. What is the distance between the lower face of the cube and the surface of the water in contact with the cube? [Surface tension of water $= T$, density of water $= d$; assume contact angle to be $\theta = 0°$]

4 A 15 cm × 6 cm × 0.1 cm glass slide is suspended with its longest side vertical. 10% part of this slide is dipped into the water. In this state, its apparent weight is equal to its real weight. Find the surface tension of water.

5 A long thin straight uniform wire of negligible radius is supported on the surface of a liquid. The width of the container is $2d$ and the wire is kept at its centre, parallel to its length (as shown in figure). The surface of the liquid is depressed by a vertical distance $y(y << d)$ at the centre as shown in figure. If the wire has mass per unit length λ, what is the surface tension of the liquid? Ignore end effects.

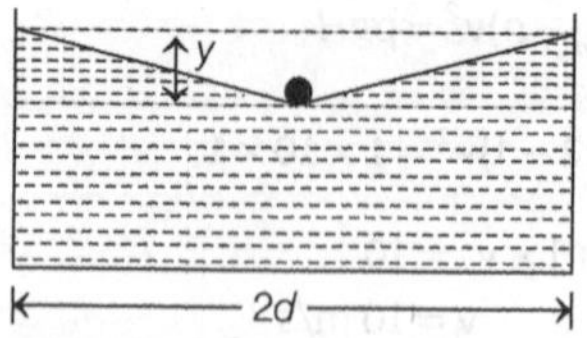

9.2 Surface Energy

1 What is the work done in blowing a soap bubble of radius r under isothermal conditions? The surface tension of soap film is T. What is the additional work required to double its radius to $2r$?

2 A water drop of radius 1 mm is broken into 10^6 identical drops. Surface tension of water is 72 dyne /cm. Find the energy spent in this process.

3 If a number of little droplets of water, all of the same radius r coalesce to form a single drop of radius R, show that the rise in temperature of the water is given by $\frac{3T}{J}\left(\frac{1}{r}-\frac{1}{R}\right)$, where J is the mechanical equivalent of heat and T is the surface tension of water.

4 What is the amount of work done in increasing the size of a soap film from 10×6 cm to 10×10 cm? (Surface tension $= 30 \times 10^{-3}$ N/m)

5 If two bubbles of radii r_1 and r_2 coalesce isothermally in vacuum, then find the radius of new bubble.

9.3 Excess Pressure

1 Find the excess pressure inside
(a) a drop of mercury of radius 2 mm
(b) a soap bubble of radius 4 mm and
(c) an air bubble of radius 4 mm formed inside a tank of water.
Surface tension of mercury, soap solution and water are 0.465N/m, 0.03 N/m and 0.076 N/m, respectively.

2 The ratio of excess pressures in two soap bubbles is 3:1, find the ratio of their volumes.

3 A soap bubble of radius r_1, and another soap bubble of radius $r_2 (> r_1)$ are brought together, so that they have a common interface. Find the radius of the interface.

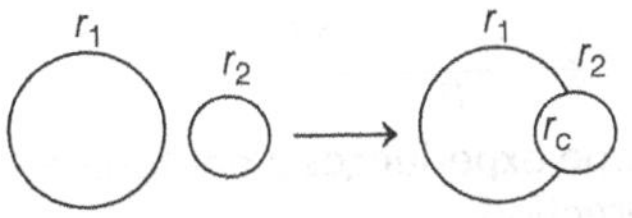

4 Under isothermal condition two soap bubbles of radii a and b coalesce to form a single bubble of radius c. If the external pressure is p_0, show that the surface tension $T = \dfrac{p_0(c^3 - a^3 - b^3)}{4(a^2 + b^2 - c^2)}$.

5 An empty container has a circular hole of radius r at its bottom. The container is pushed into water very slowly as shown. To what depth the lower surface of container (from surface of water) can be pushed into water such that water does not flow into the container? (Surface tension of water $= T$, density of water $= \rho$)

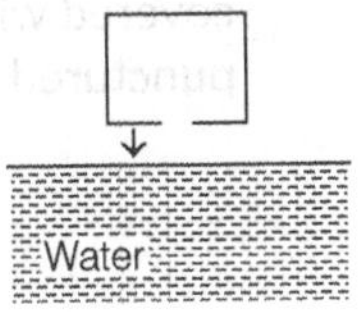

6 A U-tube has 2 tubes of radius 1.5 mm and 1 mm. What will be the difference in water level in two limbs? Given, Contact angle $\theta = 0°$, surface tension $= 7.5 \times 10^{-2}$ N/m.

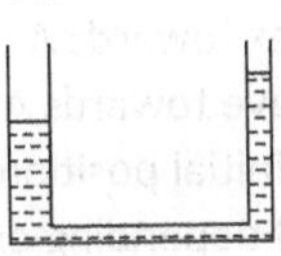

9.4 Capillary

1 A tube of 1 mm bore is dipped into a vessel containing a liquid of density 0.8 g/cm^3, surface tension 30 dyne/cm and angle of contact zero. Calculate the length which the liquid will occupy in the tube when the tube is held (a) vertical (b) inclined to the vertical at an angle of 60°.

2 Water rises to a height of 10 cm in a capillary tube and mercury falls to a depth of 3.5 cm in the same capillary tube. If the density of mercury is 13.6 g/cc and its angle of contact is 135° and density of water is 1 g/cc and its angle of contact is 0°, then find the ratio of surface tensions of the water and mercury. $\left(\dfrac{1}{\sqrt{2}} = 0.7\right)$

3 Water rises to a height of 20 mm in a capillary. If the radius of the capillary is made one-third of its previous value, then what is the new value of the capillary rise?

4 A long vertical capillary of radius R is dipped in a liquid having surface tension T. Find the gauge pressure at the mid-point of the liquid column in the capillary. Take angle of contact $= \theta$.

5 A long capillary of radius R is immersed in liquid of surface tension T. The tube is slowly pulled out of the liquid vertically. Find the length of liquid column left in the capillary tube when it is out of liquid. ($\rho =$ density of liquid, $g =$ acceleration due to gravity). Assume liquid wets the capillary completely.

6 A glass rod of diameter $d_1 = 1.5$ mm is inserted symmetrically into a glass capillary with inside diameter $d_2 = 2$ mm. Then, the whole arrangement is vertically oriented and brought in contact with the surface of water. To what height will the water rise in the capillary?
Surface tension of water $= 73 \times 10^{-3}$ N/m, Angle of contact $= 0°$. (use $g = 10 \text{ m/s}^2$)

7 When a capillary tube is dipped in liquid it rises up to 8 cm in the tube. Now the tube is pushed down such that its end is only 5 cm above the outside liquid level. Will the liquid overflow? What will happen to the radius of the meniscus?

8 A vertical capillary with inside diameter 0.50 mm is submerged into water, so that the length of its part emerging outside the water surface is equal to 25mm. Find the radius of curvature of the meniscus. Surface tension of water is 73×10^{-3} N/m.

LEVEL 02 JEE Main Level

Single Choice Correct Questions

1 A wooden stick 2 m long is floating on the surface of water. The surface tension of water 0.07 N/m. By putting soap solution on one side of the sticks the surface tension is reduced to 0.06 N/m. The net force on the stick will be

(a) 0.07 N (b) 0.06 N
(c) 0.01 N (d) 0.02 N

2 A thin metal disc of radius r floats on water surface and bends the surface downwards along the perimeter making an angle θ with vertical edge of disc. If the disc displaces a weight of water w and surface tension of water is T, then the weight of metal disc is

(a) $2\pi rT + w$
(b) $2\pi rT\cos\theta - w$
(c) $2\pi rT\cos\theta + w$
(d) $w - 2\pi rT\cos\theta$

3 A metallic wire of density ρ floats horizontal in water. The maximum radius of the wire, so that the wire may not sink will be : (surface tension of water $= T$ and angle of contact $\theta = 0°$)

(a) $\sqrt{\dfrac{2T}{\pi\rho g}}$ (b) $\sqrt{\dfrac{4T}{\rho g}}$
(c) $\sqrt{\dfrac{T}{\pi\rho g}}$ (d) $\sqrt{\dfrac{T\rho}{\pi g}}$

4 A film of soap solution is trapped between a vertical frame and a light wire ab of length 0.1 m. If $g = 10\,\text{m/s}^2$, surface tension of soap solution is 25×10^{-3} N/m, then the load w that should be suspended from the wire to keep it in equilibrium is

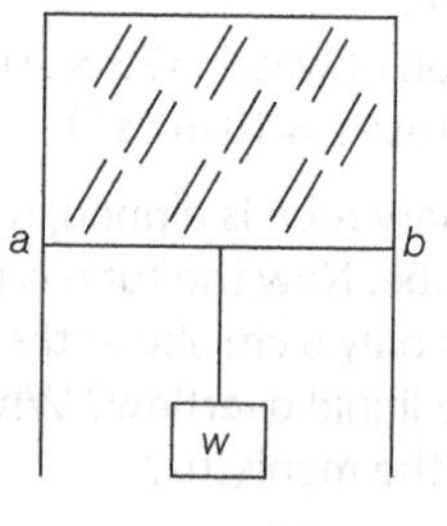

(a) 0.2 g (b) 0.3 g
(c) 0.4 g (d) 0.5 g

5 The surface tension of water is 75 dyne/cm. Find the minimum vertical force required to pull a thin wire ring up (refer figure) if it is initially resting on a horizontal water surface. The circumference of the ring is 20 cm and its weight is 0.1 N.

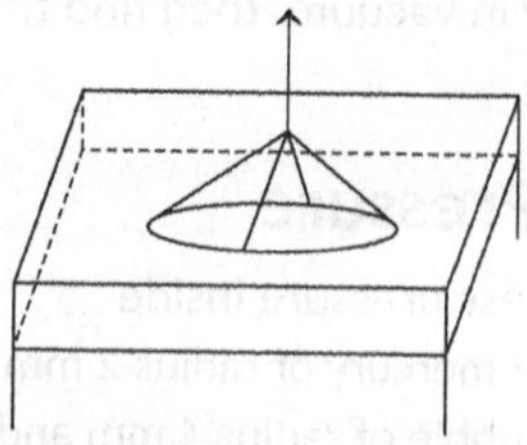

(a) 0.125 N (b) 0.225 N (c) 0.115 N (d) 0.130 N

6 A light, rigid sheet of triangular shape has a curved portion cut from it as shown in figure. It floats on the surface of water. Some soap solution is dropped over dotted region. Surface tension of water and soap film are T_1 and T_2, respectively. $T_1 = 1.5\,T_2$. Mark correct option.

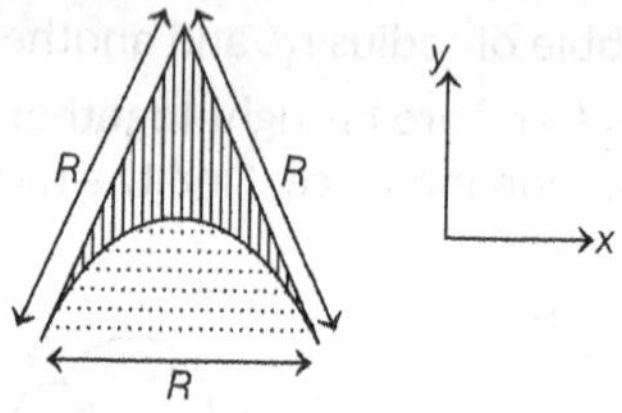

(a) The frame experiences a net force $F = (T_1 - T_2)R$ in $y < 0$ direction
(b) The frame experiences force $F = (T_1 - T_2)R$ in $y > 0$ direction
(c) The frame experiences force $(T_1 - T_2)(2 - \pi)R$ in $y > 0$ direction
(d) Resultant force on wire frame is zero

7 A thread is tied slightly loose to a wire frame as shown in the figure. And the frame is dipped into a soap solution and taken out. The frame is completely covered with the film. When the portion A is punctured with a pin, the thread :

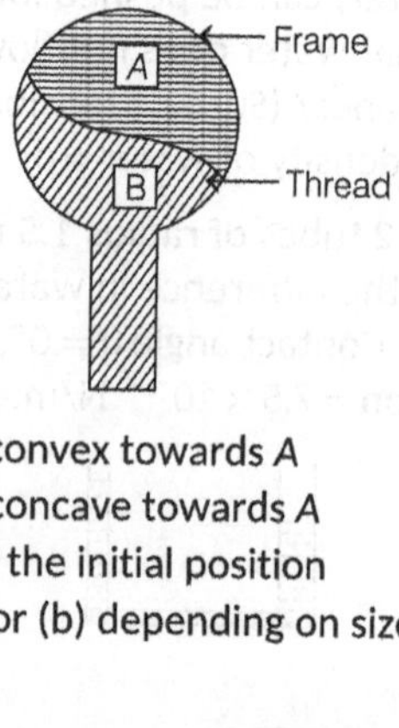

(a) becomes convex towards A
(b) becomes concave towards A
(c) remains in the initial position
(d) either (a) or (b) depending on size of A w.r.t. B

8 There is a horizontal film of soap solution. On it a thread is placed in the form of a loop. The film is pierced inside the loop and the thread becomes a circular loop of radius R. If the surface tension of the loop be S, then what will be the tension in the thread?

(a) $\pi R^2 / S$ (b) $\pi R^2 S$ (c) $2\pi RS$ (d) $2RS$

9 Two small drops of mercury, each of radius r, coalesce to form a single large drop. The ratio of the total surface energies before and after the change is

(a) $1 : 2^{1/3}$ (b) $2^{1/3} : 1$

(c) $2 : 1$ (d) $1 : 2$

10 The work done in blowing a soap bubble of 10 cm radius is (surface tension of the soap solution is 0.03 N/m)

(a) 75.36×10^{-4} J (b) 37.68×10^{-4} J

(c) 150.72×10^{-4} J (d) 75.36 J

11 Air is pushed into a soap bubble of diameter d to double its diameter. If the surface tension of the soap solution is S, the work done in the process is :

(a) $3\pi d^2 S$ (b) $6\pi d^2 S$

(c) $12\pi d^2 S$ (d) $24\pi d^2 S$

12 If the work done in blowing a bubble of volume V is W, then the work done in blowing the bubble of volume 2V from the same soap solution will be

(a) $W/2$ (b) $\sqrt{2}W$

(c) $\sqrt[3]{2}W$ (d) $\sqrt[3]{4}\,W$

13 A film of water is formed between two straight parallel wires of length 10cm each separated by 0.5cm. If their separation is increased by 1 mm, while still maintaining their parallelism, how much work will have to be done? (Surface tension of water $= 7.2 \times 10^{-2}$ N/m)

(a) 7.22×10^{-6} J (b) 1.44×10^{-5} J

(c) 2.88×10^{-5} J (d) 5.76×10^{-5} J

14 A water drop of radius R is split into n identical drops. If the surface tension of water is T, the energy required to split the drop is given by

(a) $T(n-1)4\pi R^2$ (b) $T(n^{1/3}-1)4\pi R^2$

(c) $T(n^{2/3}-1)4\pi R^2$ (d) None

15 A large number of liquid drops each of radius a coalesce to form a single spherical drop of radius b. The energy released in the process is converted into kinetic energy of the big drop formed. The speed of big drop will be

(a) $\sqrt{\frac{6T}{\rho}\left[\frac{1}{a}-\frac{1}{b}\right]}$ (b) $\sqrt{\frac{4T}{\rho}\left[\frac{1}{a}-\frac{1}{b}\right]}$

(c) $\sqrt{\frac{8T}{\rho}\left[\frac{1}{a}-\frac{1}{b}\right]}$ (d) $\sqrt{\frac{5T}{\rho}\left[\frac{1}{a}-\frac{1}{b}\right]}$

16 A spherical soap bubble is blown such that its radius increases at a constant rate. Which of following curves represents power required to increase surface energy of the bubble *versus* radius of drop?

(a) 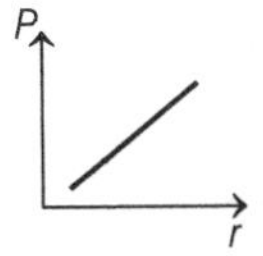

(b) 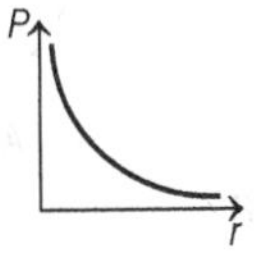

(c) 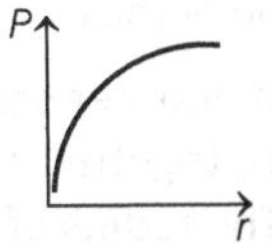

(d) 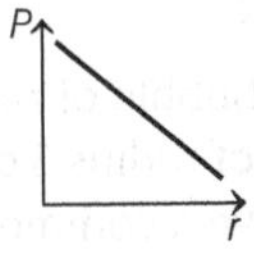

17 A water drop is divided into 8 equal droplets. The pressure difference between the inner and outer side of the big drop will be:

(a) same as for smaller droplet

(b) 1/2 of that for smaller droplet

(c) 1/4 of that for smaller droplet

(d) twice that for smaller droplet

18 If two soap bubbles of different radii are connected by a thin tube with each other then

(a) Air flows from the larger bubble into the smaller one until the two bubbles are of equal size

(b) Air flows from the smaller bubble into the larger one and the larger bubble grows at the expense of smaller one

(c) The size of bubbles remain the same

(d) Air may flow from any one bubble into the other depending on the temperature

19 Pressure inside two soap bubbles are 1.01 and 1.02 atmospheres. Ratio between their volumes is

(a) 102 : 101 (b) $(102)^3 : (101)^3$

(c) 8 : 1 (d) 2 : 1

20 A tiny air bubble of radius r in water is at a depth h below the water surface at some instant. If p_0 is atmospheric pressure and d and T are the density and surface tension of water respectively, the pressure inside the bubble will be:

(a) $p_0 + hdg - \frac{4T}{r}$ (b) $p_0 + hdg + \frac{2T}{r}$

(c) $p_0 + hdg - \frac{2T}{r}$ (d) $p_0 + hdg + \frac{4T}{r}$

21 A soap bubble of radius R is surrounded by another soap bubble of radius $2R$, as shown. Take, surface tension $= S$. Then, the pressure inside the smaller soap bubble, in excess of the atmospheric pressure, will be

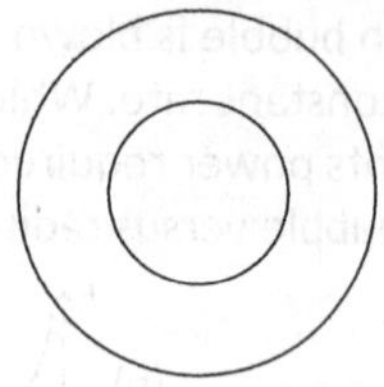

(a) $4S/R$ (b) $3S/R$
(c) $6S/R$ (d) None of these

22 A soap bubble of radius 4 cm and another soap bubble of radius 3 cm are brought together so that they have a common interface. The radius of the interface is
(a) 1 cm (b) 5 cm (c) 7 cm (d) 12 cm

23 Two spherical soap bubbles of radii 3 cm and 4 cm in vacuum coalesce under isothermal conditions. The resulting bubble has a radius equal to :
(a) 1 cm (b) 5 cm (c) 7 cm (d) 12 cm

24 Figs (A) and (B) show water drop and mercury drop in two identical conical glass pipes, then

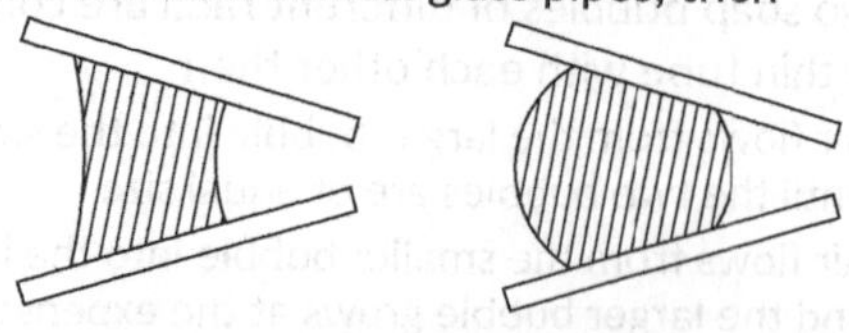

(A) (B)

(a) the water drop tends to move towards narrow end and mercury drop towards wide end.
(b) the water drop tends to move towards wide end and mercury drop towards narrow end.
(c) both tend to move towards wide end.
(d) both tend to move towards narrow end.

25 A soap bubble is being blown on a tube of radius 1 cm. The surface tension of the soap solution is 0.05 N/m and the bubble makes an angle of 60° with the tube as shown. The excess of pressure over the atmospheric pressure in the tube is :

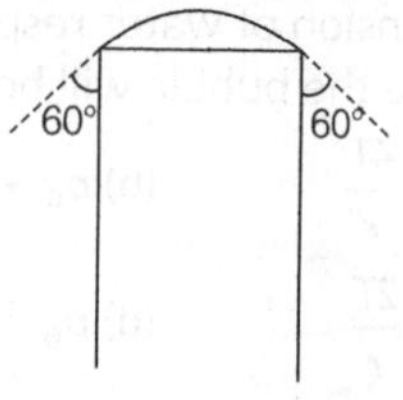

(a) 1 Pa (b) 5 Pa (c) 10 Pa (d) 20 Pa

26 A vessel whose bottom has round holes with a diameter of $d = 0.1$ mm is filled with water. The maximum height of the water level h at which the water does not flow out, will be : (The water does not wet the bottom of the vessel)
[S.T of water = 70 dyne/cm]
(a) 24.0 cm (b) 25.0 cm (c) 26.0 cm (d) 28.0 cm

27 The angle of contact between glass and water is 0° and water (surface tension 70 dyne/cm) rises in a glass capillary up to 6 cm. Another liquid of surface tension 140 dyne/cm, angle of contact 60° and relative density 2 will rise in the same capillary up to
(a) 12 cm (b) 24 cm (c) 3 cm (d) 6 cm

28 Water rises in a vertical capillary tube upto a height of 2.0 cm. If the tube is inclined at an angle of 60° with the vertical, then upto what length the water will rise in the tube?
(a) 2.0 cm (b) 4.0 cm (c) $\frac{4}{\sqrt{3}}$ cm (d) $2\sqrt{2}$ cm

29 A 20 cm long capillary tube is dipped in water. The water rises upto 8 cm. If the entire arrangement is put in a freely falling elevator, the length of water column in the capillary tube will be
(a) 8 cm (b) 10 cm
(c) 4 cm (d) 20 cm

30 A capillary tube of radius R is immersed in water and water rises in it to a height H. Mass of water in the capillary tube is M. If the radius of the tube is doubled, mass of water that will rise in the capillary tube will now be
(a) M (b) $2M$
(c) $M/2$ (d) $4M$

31 One end of a glass capillary tube with radius $r = 0.05$ cm is immersed into water to a depth of $h = 2$ cm. What pressure is required to blow an air bubble out of the lower end of the tube?
($T = 7 \times 10^{-2}$ N/m and $\rho = 10^3$ kg/m^3)
(a) 480 N/m^2 (b) 680 N/m^2
(c) 120 N/m^2 (d) 820 N/m^2

32 Water rises in a capillary tube to a certain height such that the upward force due to surface tension is balanced by 75×10^{-4} N force due to the weight of the liquid. If the surface tension of water is 6×10^{-2} N/m, the inner circumference of the capillary must be
(a) 1.25×10^{-2} m (b) 0.50×10^{-2} m
(c) 6.5×10^{-2} m (d) 12.5×10^{-2} m

33 One end of a uniform capillary tube of inner radius 1.0 mm is held vertically such that one end is just dipped in water (surface tension = 0.07 N/m) and a length of 1 cm is outside water. Which of the following options is true?

(a) The liquid will keep on overflowing from the open end as the tube length is insufficient

(b) The liquid will rise upto the top and will assume flat surface

(c) The liquid will rise the full exposed length and the radius of its meniscus will be equal to the radius of the capillary (= 1.0 mm)

(d) The liquid will rise the full length of the tube and will assume a meniscus of radius= 1.4 mm

34 A vertical glass capillary tube of radius r open at both ends contains some water (surface tension T and density ρ). If L be the length of the water column, then

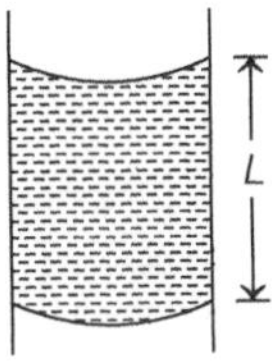

(a) $L = \dfrac{4T}{r\rho g}$ (b) $L = \dfrac{2T}{r\rho g}$

(c) $L = \dfrac{T}{4r\rho g}$ (d) $L = \dfrac{T}{2r\rho g}$

35 The radii of the two columns in a U tube are r_1 and r_2 . When a liquid of density ρ [angle of contact is 0°] is filled in it, the level difference of the liquid in the two arms in h. The surface tension of the liquid is [g = acceleration due to gravity]

(a) $\dfrac{\rho g h r_1 r_2}{2(r_2 - r_1)}$ (b) $\dfrac{\rho g h(r_2 r_1)}{2(r_2 + r_1)}$

(c) $\dfrac{2(r_1 - r_2)}{\rho g h r_1 r_2}$ (d) $\dfrac{\rho g h}{2(r_2 - r_1)}$

36 Two large parallel glass plates placed at small separation d are dipped in a liquid having density ρ and surface tension T. Find the height of the liquid level between the plates w.r.t. the outside liquid level. The angle of contact for liquid glass interface is θ.

(a) $\dfrac{2T\cos\theta}{d\rho g}$ (b) $\dfrac{T\cos\theta}{d\rho g}$

(c) $\dfrac{4T\cos\theta}{d\rho g}$ (d) $\dfrac{2T}{d\rho g\cos\theta}$

Numerical Value Questions

1 A microscope slide measures 6.0 cm × 1.5 cm × 0.20 cm. It is suspended with its face vertical and with its longest side horizontal and is lowered into a liquid until it is half immersed. Its apparent weight is then found to be the same as its weight in air. Calculate the surface tension of liquid in dyne/cm, assuming the angle of contact to be zero. Density of liquid is $1\ g/cm^3$. Round off to nearest integer

2 An air bubble of radius 3.5 μm is at a depth of 6 m below the water surface. Taking atmospheric pressure as 10^5 Pa, surface tension of water as 0.07 N/m, and density of atmospheric air as $1.2\ kg/m^3$. Find the density (in kg/m^3) of air inside the air bubble.

3 There is an air bubble of radius R inside a drop of water of radius 3R. Find the ratio of gauge pressure at point A to the gauge pressure at point B.

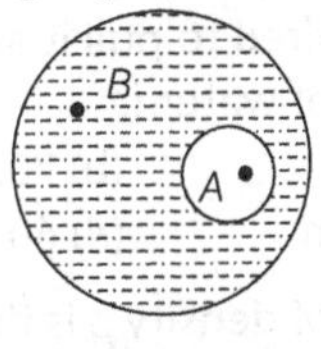

4 Due to the excess pressure of surface tension, find the change in the radius (in Å) of a liquid drop of surface tension 0.075 N/m and bulk modulus $1.25\times 10^8\ N/m^2$.

5 A liquid of specific gravity 1.5 is observed to rise 3.0 cm in a capillary tube of diameter 0.50 mm and the liquid wets the surface of the tube. Calculate the excess pressure (in $dyne/cm^2$) inside a spherical bubble of 1.0 cm diameter blown from the same liquid. Angle of contact = 0°, $g = 1000\ cm/s^2$.

6 Two spherical soap bubbles coalesece. If V is the consequent change in volume of the contained air and S is the change in the total surface area and T is the surface tension of the soap solution, then if relation between p_0, V.S and T is $\lambda p_0 V + 4ST = 0$, then find λ.
(p_0 is atmospheric pressure and assume temperature of the air remains same in all the bubbles).

7 A capillary of 1 mm diameter, is dipped vertically in a pot of water. Find the gauge pressure (in N/m^2) of the water in the tube 5.0 cm below the surface. Surface tension of water = 0.075 N/m.
(Take, $g = 10\ m/s^2$ and $\rho_w = 1000\ kg/m^3$)

8 There is a soap bubble of radius 1.92×10^{-5}m in air cylinder which is originally at the pressure $10^5\ N/m^2$. The air in the cylinder is now compressed isothermally until the radius of the bubble is halved. If now the pressure of air in the cylinder is $n \times 10^5\ N/m^2$, then find n. The surface tension of the soap solution is 0.08 N/m.

LEVEL 03 JEE Advanced Level

Single Choice Correct Questions

1 A mosquito with 8 legs stands on water surface. Each leg makes depression of radius a. If the surface tension and angle of contact are T and zero respectively, then the weight of mosquito is:

(a) $8Ta$ (b) $16\pi Ta$ (c) $16Ta$ (d) $32\pi Ta$

2 A ring is cut from a platinum tube 8.5 cm internal and 8.7 cm external diameter. It is supported horizontally from a pan of a balance, so that it comes in contact with the water in a glass vessel. If an extra 3.97 g-wt is required to pull it away from water, the surface tension of water is

(a) 72 dyne/cm (b) 70.80 dyne/cm
(c) 63.35 dyne/cm (d) 60 dyne/cm

3 A drop of liquid of density ρ is floating half-immersed in a liquid of density d. If σ is the surface tension, the diameter of the drop of the liquid is:

(a) $\sqrt{\dfrac{\sigma}{g(2\rho-d)}}$ (b) $\sqrt{\dfrac{2\sigma}{g(2\rho-d)}}$

(c) $\sqrt{\dfrac{6\sigma}{g(2\rho-d)}}$ (d) $\sqrt{\dfrac{12\sigma}{g(2\rho-d)}}$

4 A cube of mass 20 g wettable by water floats on the surface of water. Each face of the cube is 3 cm long, The distance between lower face of cube and surface of water is (surface tension of water = 70 dyne/cm, $g = 1000\ \text{cm/s}^2$, assume contact angle is 0°) :

(a) 1.012 cm (b) 1.631 cm
(c) 2.315 cm (d) 2.52 cm

5 A soap bubble has radius R and thickness d (<< R) as shown. It collapses into a spherical drop. The ratio of excess pressure in the drop to the excess pressure inside the bubble is

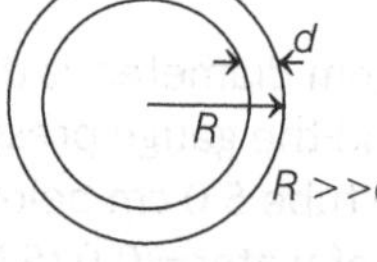

(a) $\left(\dfrac{R}{3d}\right)^{\frac{1}{3}}$ (b) $\left(\dfrac{R}{6d}\right)^{\frac{1}{3}}$ (c) $\left(\dfrac{R}{24d}\right)^{\frac{1}{3}}$ (d) None

6 A cylinder with a movable piston contains air under a pressure p_1, and a soap bubble of radius r. The pressure p_2 to which the air should be compressed by slowly pushing the piston into the cylinder for the soap bubble to reduce its size by half will be : (The surface tension is σ and the temperature T is maintained constant)

(a) $\left[8p_1 + \dfrac{24\sigma}{r}\right]$ (b) $\left[4p_1 + \dfrac{24\sigma}{r}\right]$

(c) $\left[2p_1 + \dfrac{24\sigma}{r}\right]$ (d) $\left[2p_1 + \dfrac{12\sigma}{r}\right]$

7 A soap bubble with a radius r is placed on another bubble with a radius R (figure). Angles between the films at the points of contact will be

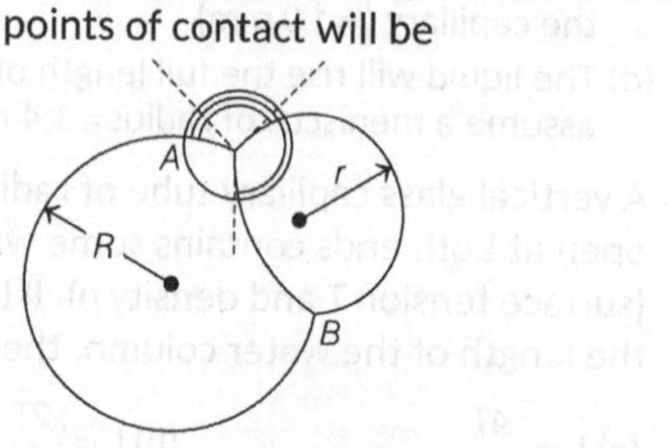

(a) 120° (b) 30°
(c) 45° (d) 90°

8 The high domes of ancient buildings have structural value (besides beauty). It arises from pressure difference on the two faces due to curvature (as in soap bubbles). There is a dome of radius 5 m and uniform (but small) thickness. The surface tension of its masonary structure is about 500 N/m. Treated as hemispherical, the maximum load the dome can support is nearest to

(a) 1500 kg wt (b) 3000 kg wt
(c) 6000 kg wt (d) 12000 kg w

9 A liquid is filled in a spherical container of radius R till a height h. At this position the liquid surface at the edges is also horizontal. The contact angle is

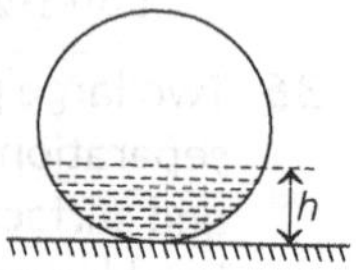

(a) 0 (b) $\cos^{-1}\left(\dfrac{R-h}{R}\right)$

(c) $\cos^{-1}\left(\dfrac{h-R}{R}\right)$ (d) $\sin^{-1}\left(\dfrac{R-h}{R}\right)$

10 Water of density ρ in a clean aquarium forms a meniscus, as illustrated in the figure. Calculate the difference in height h between the centre and the edge of the meniscus. The surface tension of water is γ.

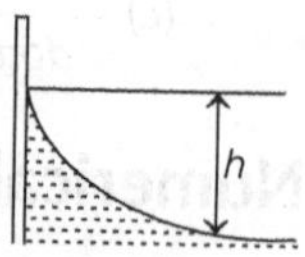

(a) $\sqrt{\dfrac{2\gamma}{\rho g}}$ (b) $\sqrt{\dfrac{\gamma}{\rho g}}$ (c) $\dfrac{1}{2}\sqrt{\dfrac{\gamma}{\rho g}}$ (d) $2\sqrt{\dfrac{\gamma}{\rho g}}$

11 On heating water, bubbles beings formed at the bottom of the vessel detatch and rise. Take the bubbles to be spheres of radius R and making a circular contact of radius r with the bottom of the vessel. If $r << R$ and the surface tension of water is T, value of r just before bubbles detatch is : (density of water is ρ_w)

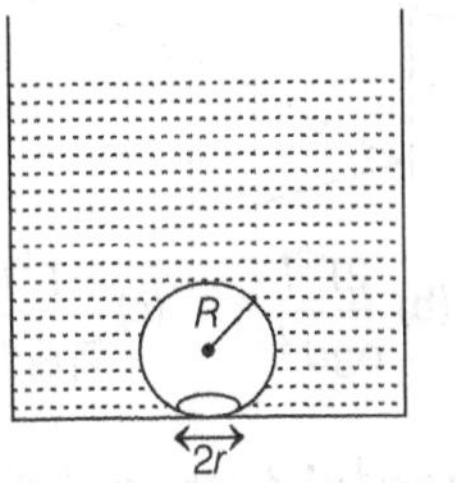

(a) $R^2\sqrt{\dfrac{2\rho_w g}{3T}}$ (b) $R^2\sqrt{\dfrac{\rho_w g}{6T}}$

(c) $R^2\sqrt{\dfrac{\rho_w g}{T}}$ (d) $R^2\sqrt{\dfrac{3\rho_w g}{T}}$

12 An open capillary tube is lowered in a vessel with mercury. The difference between the levels of the mercury in the vessel and in the capillary tube $\Delta h =$ 4.6mm. What is the radius of curvature of the mercury meniscus in the capillary tube? Surface tension of mercury is 0.46 N/m, density of mercury is 13.6 g/cc.

(a) $\dfrac{1}{340}$ m (b) $\dfrac{1}{680}$ m

(c) $\dfrac{1}{1020}$ m (d) Information insufficient

13 A long capillary tube of mass π gm, radius 2mm and negligible thickness is partially immersed in a liquid of surface tension 0.1 N/m. Take contact angle to be 60° and neglect buoyant force. The force required to hold the tube vertically will be. ($g = 10\,m/s^2$)

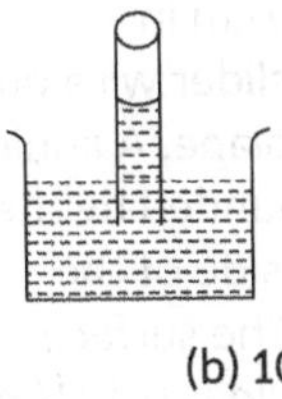

(a) $10.4\,\pi$ mN (b) $10.8\,\pi$ mN

(c) $0.8\,\pi$ mN (d) $4.8\,\pi$ mN

14 Water rises to a height h in a capillary tube lowered vertically into water to a depth l as shown in the figure. The lower end of the tube is now closed, the tube is then taken out of the water and opened again. The length of the water column remaining in the tube will be

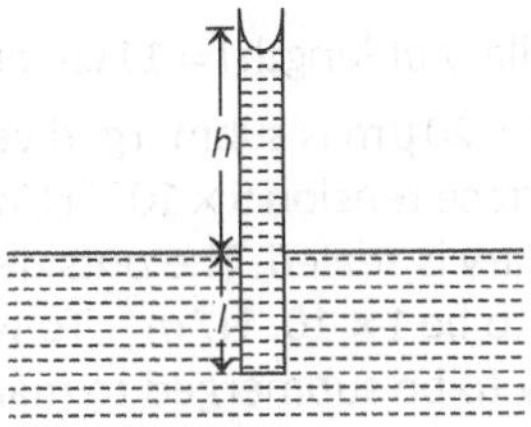

(a) $2h$ if $l \geq h$ and $l + h$ if $l \leq h$

(b) h if $l \geq h$ and $l + h$ if $l \leq h$

(c) $4h$ if $l \geq h$ and $l - h$ if $l \leq h$

(d) $h/2$ if $l \geq h$ and $l + h$ if $l \leq h$

15 A glass capillary tube is of the shape of a truncated cone with an apex angle, α so that its two ends have cross-sections of different radii. When dipped in water vertically, water rises in it to a height h, where the radius of its cross-section is b. If the surface tension of water is S, its density is ρ and its contact angle with glass is θ, the value of h will be (g is the acceleration due to gravity)

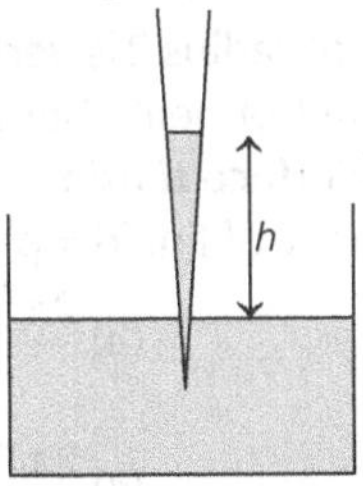

(a) $\dfrac{2S}{b\rho g}\cos(\theta - \alpha)$ (b) $\dfrac{2S}{b\rho g}\cos(\theta + \alpha)$

(c) $\dfrac{2S}{b\rho g}\cos\left(\theta - \dfrac{\alpha}{2}\right)$ (d) $\dfrac{2S}{b\rho g}\cos\left(\theta + \dfrac{\alpha}{2}\right)$

16 A container has two immiscible liquids of densities ρ_1 and ρ_2. A capillary tube of radius r is inserted in the liquid so that its bottom reaches upto the denser liquid. The denser liquid rises in the capillary and attains a height h from the interface of the liquids, which is equal to the column length of the lighter liquid. Assuming angle of contact to be zero, the surface tension of heavier liquid is

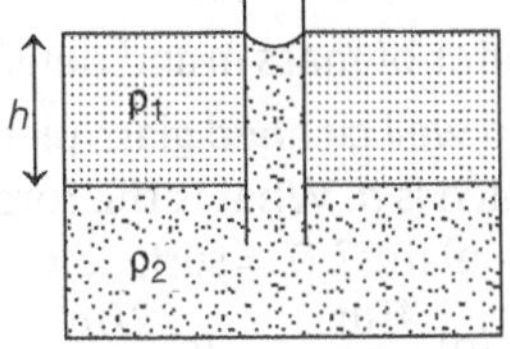

(a) $2\pi r\rho_2 gh$ (b) $\dfrac{\rho_2 rgh}{2}$

(c) $\dfrac{r}{2}(\rho_2 - \rho_1)gh$ (d) $2\pi r(\rho_2 - \rho_1)gh$

17 A glass capillary of length $l = 11$ cm and inside diameter, $d = 20\ \mu$m is submerged vertically into a liquid of surface tension 5×10^{-2} N/m. The upper end of the capillary is sealed. The outside pressure is considered to be $1 \times 10^5 \text{N/m}^2$. To what length, has the capillary to be submerged to make the water levels inside and outside the capillary coincide?

(a) 1 cm (b) 2 cm
(c) 4 cm (d) 5.5 cm

18 A coaxial cylinder made of glass is immersed in liquid of surface tension S. Radius of inner and outer surface of cylinder are R_1 and R_2, respectively. Height till which liquid will rise is (Density of liquid is ρ)

(a) $\dfrac{2S}{R_2 \rho g}$ (b) $\dfrac{2S}{R_1 \rho g}$
(c) $\dfrac{S}{(R_2 - R_1)\rho g}$ (d) $\dfrac{2S}{(R_2 - R_1)\rho g}$

19 A capillary tube of radius R is vertically immersed in a liquid. The amount of heat liberated when liquid rises in tube is (Surface tension of liquid $= T$, Angle of contact $= \theta$, density of liquid $= \rho$)

(a) $\dfrac{2\pi T \cos^2 \theta}{\rho g}$ (b) $\dfrac{2\pi^2 T \cos^2 \theta}{\rho g}$
(c) $\dfrac{2\pi T^2 \sin^2 \theta}{\rho g}$ (d) $\dfrac{2\pi T^2 \cos^2 \theta}{\rho g}$

20 An air bubble of radius R is formed in a narrow tube having a radius b, where $R >> b$. Air of density ρ is blown inside the tube with velocity v. The air molecules collide perpendicularly with the wall of the bubble and stop. Find the radius at which the bubble separates from the tube. Take surface tension of the bubble as T.

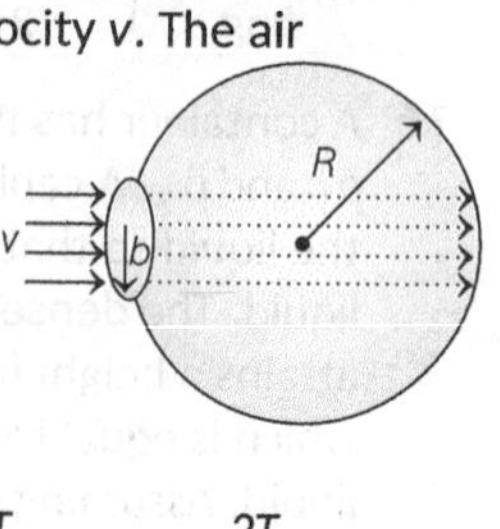

(a) $\dfrac{4T}{\rho v^2}$ (b) $\dfrac{2T}{\rho v^2}$ (c) $\dfrac{T}{\rho v^2}$ (d) $\dfrac{2T}{\rho v}$

21 A drop of water of mass m and density ρ is placed between two well cleaned glass plates, the distance between which is d. What is the force of attraction between the plates? ($T =$ surface tension)

(a) $\dfrac{Tm}{2\rho d^2}$ (b) $\dfrac{4Tm}{\rho d^2}$ (c) $\dfrac{2Tm}{\rho d^2}$ (d) $\dfrac{Tm}{\rho d^2}$

22 Two vertical parallel plates are partially submerged in water. The distance between plate is equal to d. Water rises due to surface tension T, the width of plate is l and contact angle of water with glass is 0°. Find the force of attraction between the plates.

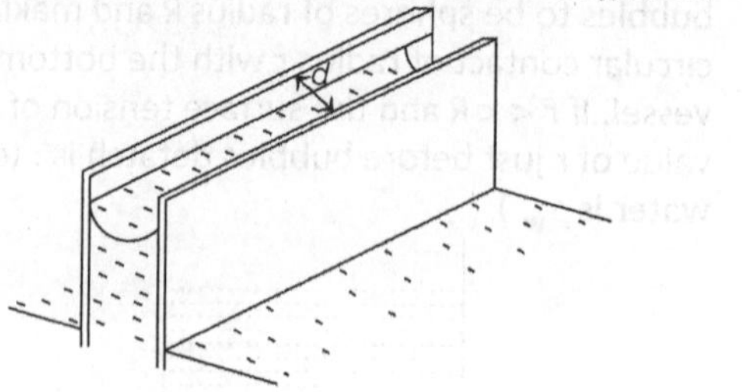

(a) $\dfrac{T^2 l}{\rho g d^2}$ (b) $\dfrac{2T^2 l}{\rho g d^2}$ (c) $\dfrac{T^2 l}{2\rho g d^2}$ (d) $\dfrac{T^2 l}{4\rho g d^2}$

Multiple Choice(s) Correct Questions

1 A soap film (surface tension $= S$) is formed on a rectangular wire frame as shown in figure. A small, light, inextensible loop of thread of length l is gently placed over the soap film. The loop stays on the film in the irregular fashion in which it was placed. Now, a hole is pricked in the film inside the loop with a needle and the thread finally comes to equilibrium position. Choose the correct option(s)

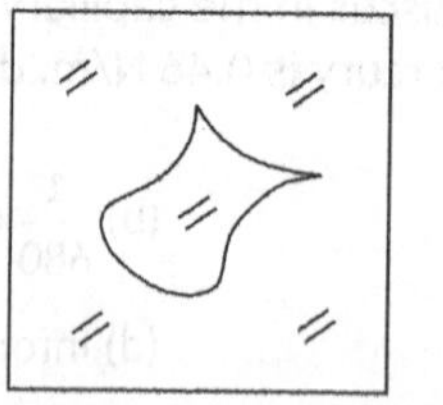

(a) The thread will take a square shape
(b) The thread will take a circular shape
(c) Tension in the thread will be $2Sl$
(d) Tension in the thread will be $\dfrac{Sl}{\pi}$

2 A circular wire, 10 cm in diameter, with a slider wire on it, is in a horizontal plane. A liquid film is formed, bounded by the wires, on the left side of the slider, as shown. The surface tension of the liquid is 0.1 N/m. An applied force 16mN, perpendicular to the slider, maintains the film in equilibrium. Ignore the sag in the film. What can be the distance between point P and slider?

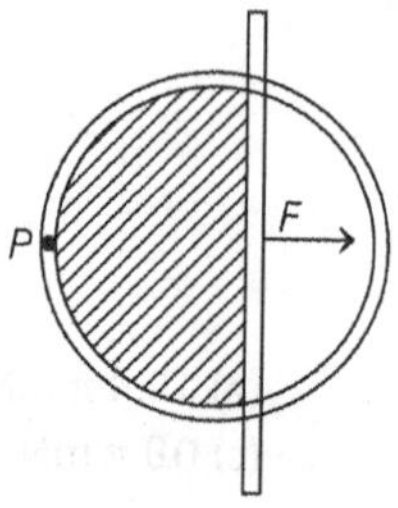

(a) 8 cm
(b) 2 cm
(c) 5 cm
(d) slider cannot be in equilibrium.

3 A soap film is formed on a vertical equilateral triangular frame *ABC*. Side *BC* can move vertically always remaining horizontal. If *m* is the mass of rod *BC* and *T* is surface tension of soap film. Mark the correct statement(s) :

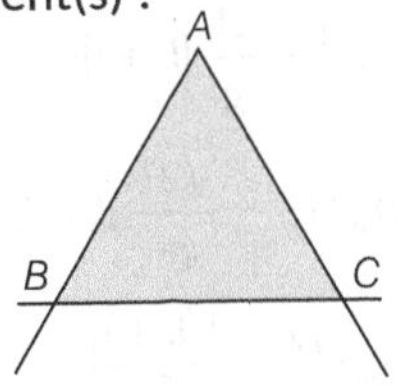

(a) The length of *BC* in equilibrium is $mg/2T$.
(b) The length of *BC* in equilibrium is mg/T.
(c) The time period of small oscillations about the equilibrium position is $\pi\sqrt{\frac{\sqrt{3}m}{T}}$
(d) The time period of small oscillations about the equilibrium position is $\pi\sqrt{\frac{m}{\sqrt{3}T}}$

4 *n* drops of a liquid, each with surface energy *E* join to form a single drop, then
(a) some energy will be released in the process
(b) some energy will be absorbed in the process.
(c) the energy released or absorbed will be $E(n - n^{2/3})$
(d) the energy released or absorbed will be $nE(2^{2/3} - 1)$

5 Excess pressure can be $(2T/R)$ for
(a) spherical drop
(b) spherical meniscus
(c) cylindrical bubble in air
(d) spherical bubble in water

6 When a capillary tube is dipped in a liquid, the liquid rises to a height *h* in the tube. The free liquid surface inside the tube is hemispherical in shape. The tube is now pushed down so that the height of the tube outside the liquid is less than *h*. Then,
(a) the liquid will come out of the tube like in a small fountain
(b) the liquid will ooze out of the tube slowly
(c) the liquid will fill the tube but not come out of its upper end
(d) the free liquid surface inside the tube will not be hemispherical

7 Which of the following statements are correct?
(a) If angle of contact is obtuse, the liquid rises in capillary
(b) If angle of contact is acute, then liquid wets solid
(c) If angle of contact is obtuse, the shape of liquid meniscus is convex upwards
(d) Surface tension of liquids decreases with rise in temperature

8 A glass capillary tube is dipped vertically in water as shown in the figure. Due to capillary action water rises upto height *h*. Now a small pin hole is made in capillary at point *P* shown in the figure. Choose the correct statement(s) :

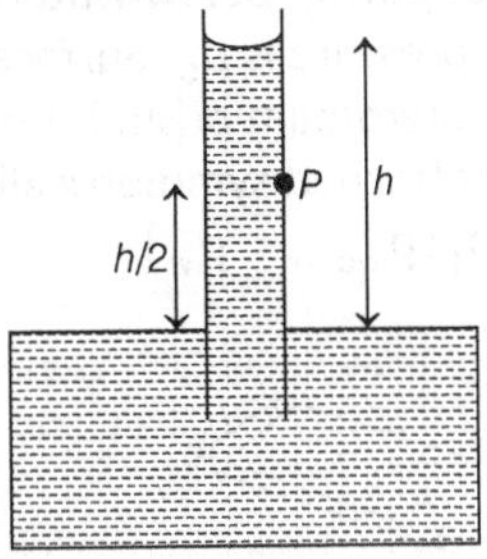

(a) Water will not come out of the tube from pinhole of the capillary
(b) Surface of the meniscus on pinhole will be convex outward.
(c) Pressure at point *P* inside the liquid is equal to atmospheric pressure.
(d) Pressure inside the liquid at point *P* is less than the atmospheric pressure.

9 A capillary tube of radius *r* is lowered into water whose surface tension is α and density *d*. The liquid rises to a height *h*. Assume that the contact angle is zero. Choose the correct statement(s):
(a) Magnitude of work done by force of surface tension is $\frac{4\pi\alpha^2}{dg}$
(b) Magnitude of work done by force of surface tension is $\frac{2\pi\alpha^2}{dg}$
(c) Potential energy acquired by the water is $\frac{2\pi\alpha^2}{dg}$
(d) The amount of heat developed is $\frac{2\pi\alpha^2}{dg}$

10 A vertical glass capillary tube, open at both ends, contains some water. Which of the following shapes may not be taken by the water in the tube ?

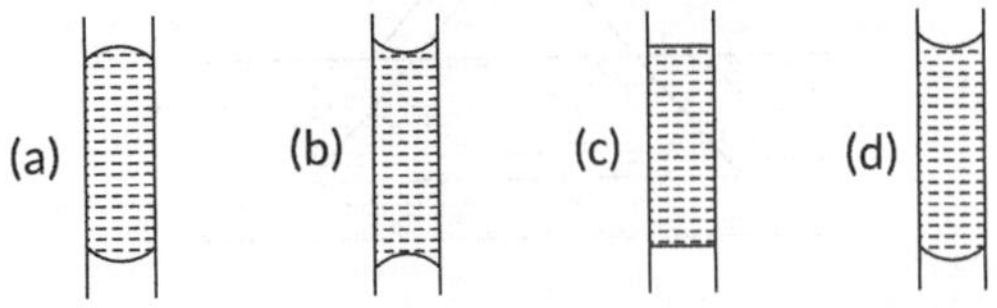

Comprehension Based Questions

Comprehension-1

A prism shaped styrofoam of density $\rho_{styrofoam} < \rho_{water}$ is held completely submerged in water. It lies with its base horizontal. The base of foam is at a depth h_0, below water surface and atmospheric pressure is p_0. Surface is open to atmosphere. Styrofoam prism is held in equilibrium by the string attached symmetrically. (Take : $\rho_{styrofoam} = \rho_f ; \rho_{water} = \rho_w$)

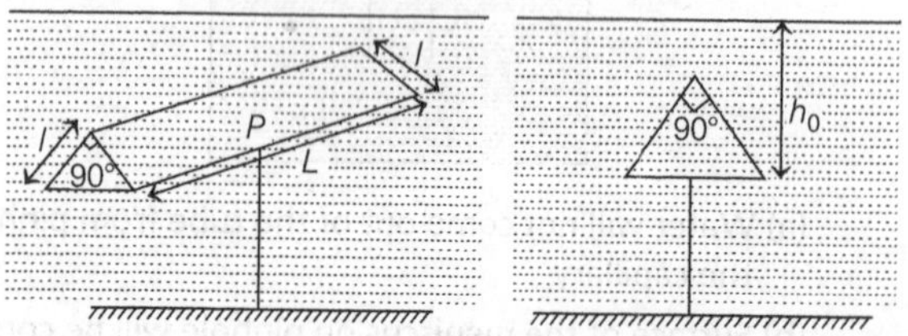

1 Net force exerted by liquid on the styro foam is

(a) $\sqrt{2}\rho_w g l^2 L$ (b) $2\rho_w g l^2 L$

(c) $\rho_w g \dfrac{l^2 L}{2}$ (d) $\rho_w g l^2 L$

2 Magnitude of force on any one of the slant face of styrofoam is

(a) $(p_0 + \rho_w g(h_0 - \sqrt{2}l))Ll$

(b) $\left(p_0 + \rho_w g\left(h_0 - \dfrac{l}{\sqrt{2}}\right)\right)Ll$

(c) $\left(p_0 - \rho_w g\left(h_0 - \dfrac{l}{\sqrt{2}}\right)\right)Ll$

(d) $\left(p_0 + \rho_w g\left(h_0 - \dfrac{l}{2\sqrt{2}}\right)\right)Ll$

3 Now string is cut and styrofoam is allowed to come to surface. A point mass is to be placed symmetrically on the upper surface of styrofoam such that it is in equilibrium with its base in horizontal plane.

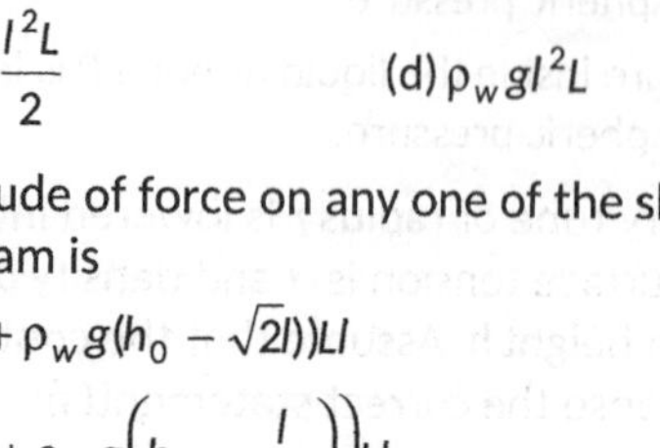

In equilibrium position styrofoam has half of its slant length submerged. Surface tension of water is T, contact angle is 0°. Determine mass m to achieve equilibrium.

(a) $\dfrac{\rho_f L l^2}{2} + \dfrac{3}{4}\rho_w L l^2 - \dfrac{2T}{g}[L + l]$

(b) $\dfrac{-\rho_f L l^2}{2} + \dfrac{3}{8}\rho_w L l^2 - \dfrac{\sqrt{2}T}{g}[L + l]$

(c) $\dfrac{-\rho_f L l^2}{2} + \dfrac{3}{8}\rho_w L l^2 - \dfrac{T[L + l]}{\sqrt{2}g}$

(d) None of the above

Comprehension-2

A long glass capillary (radius R) is taken out of liquid (surface tension S and density ρ) in vertical position. Angle of contact everywhere is zero. Atmospheric pressure is p_0. It is observed that the capillary retains some liquid.

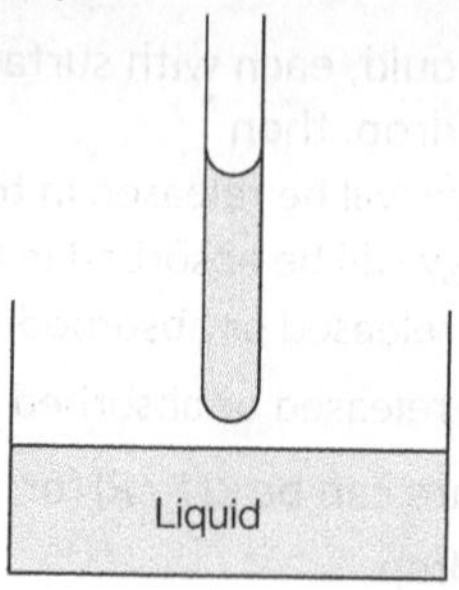

4 The radius of curvature of meniscus at the bottom of tube is

(a) R (b) ∞

(c) $R/2$ (d) $R/3$

5 The length of liquid column retained in the capillary is

(a) $\dfrac{3S}{\rho R g}$ (b) $\dfrac{2S}{\rho R g}$

(c) $\dfrac{4S}{\rho R g}$ (d) Zero

6 Assume equal angle of contact everywhere, the angle of contact, if the length of capillary would have been $\dfrac{S}{\rho R g}$ is

(a) $\cos^{-1}\left(\dfrac{1}{3}\right)$ (b) $\cos^{-1}\left(\dfrac{1}{2}\right)$

(c) $\cos^{-1}\left(\dfrac{1}{4}\right)$ (d) zero

Match the Columns Questions

1 Capillary rise and shape of droplets on a plate due to surface tension are shown in column II.

	Column I		Column I
(A)	Adhesive forces are greater than cohesive forces	(P)	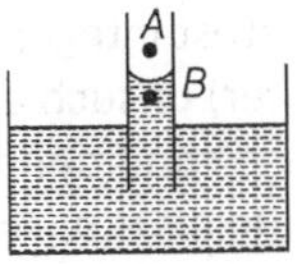
(B)	Cohesive forces are greater than adhesive forces	(Q)	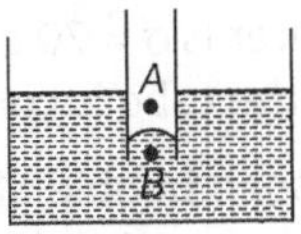
(C)	Pressure at A > pressure at B	(R)	A mercury drop is pressed between two parallel plates of glass 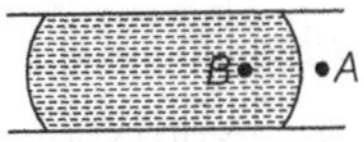
(D)	Pressure at B > pressure at A	(S)	Mercury drop on glass plate 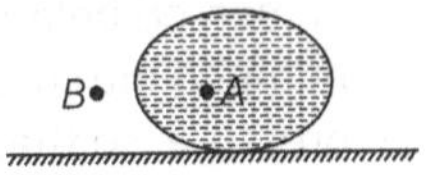

2

	Column I		Column I
(A)	Excess pressure inside a drop	(P)	decreases with increase in radius
(B)	Excess pressure inside a soap bubble	(Q)	$\frac{2T}{R}$
(C)	Excess pressure inside an air cavity	(R)	$\frac{4T}{R}$
(D)	Surface tension	(S)	decreases with increase in temperature

3 Column-I contains different arrangements and column-II contains capillary rise of water in those arrangements. Surface tension of water is S and density is ρ. Match the following

	Column I		Column I
(A)	Silver tube of radius R immersed in water	(P)	$\frac{2S}{R\rho g}$
(B)	Glass tube of radius R immersed in water	(Q)	$\frac{4S}{R\rho g}$
(C)	Hollow co-axial cylinder made of glass, having inner and outer radius R and $2R$ respectively immersed in water	(R)	$\frac{3S}{2R\rho g}$
(D)	Two parallel glass plates separated by distance R immersed in water	(S)	Zero

4

	Column I		Column I
(A)	Spliting of bigger drop into small drops	(P)	Temperature changes
(B)	Formation of bigger drop from small drops.	(Q)	Temperature remains constant
(C)	Spraying of liquid	(R)	Surface energy changes
(D)	Spliting of bigger soap bubble into small soap bubble of same thickness	(S)	Surface energy remain unchanged

Numerical Value Questions

1 A capillary of radius $r = 0.2$ mm is dipped vertically in a liquid of density ($\rho = 1$ g/cc). A small piston (x) is inserted inside the capillary which maintains the constant pressure of air ($p_1 = 200$ dyne/cm^2) above the hemispherical meniscus. If ambient pressure is $p_0 = 1000$ dyne/cm^2 and surface tension of liquid is $T = 72$ dyne/cm, then find the height h of liquid in cm. (weight of curved part of liquid is ignored)

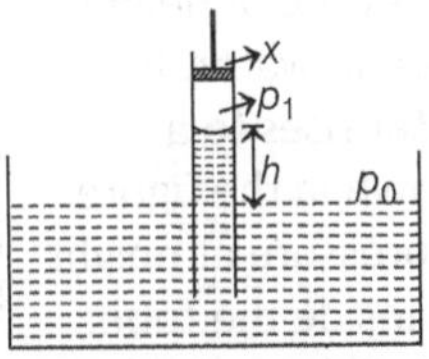

2 A container of width 2 m is filled with a liquid. A thin wire of mass per unit length 10 g/m is gently placed over the liquid surface in the middle of the surface as shown in the figure. As a result, the liquid surface is depressed by a distance 1 cm. Determine the surface tension (in SI unit) of the liquid. Assume suitable approximation.

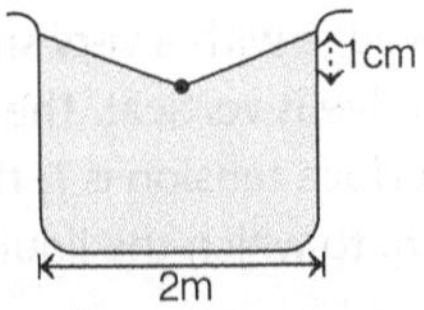

3 A capillary tube with very thin walls is attached to the beam of a balance which is then equalized. The lower end of the capillary is brought in contact with the surface of water after which an additional load of $p = 0.135$ gm force is needed to regain equilibrium. If the radius of the capillary is $\frac{\lambda}{10}$ mm, then find λ. The surface tension of water is 70 dyne/cm. ($g = 9.8\text{ m/s}^2$)

4 In a soap film experiment an originally semicircle shaped thread of radius 10 cm can be deformed to two semicircles with a force of 0.01 N exerted at the middle of the thread. Calculate the surface tension (in 10^{-2} N/m)

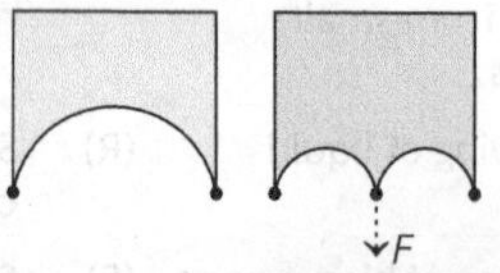

5 Suppose there is an air bubble of radius $R/2$ inside the air cavity of radius R inside a water drop of radius $3R$ as shown in figure. Find the ratio of gauge pressure at point C to gauge pressure at point B.

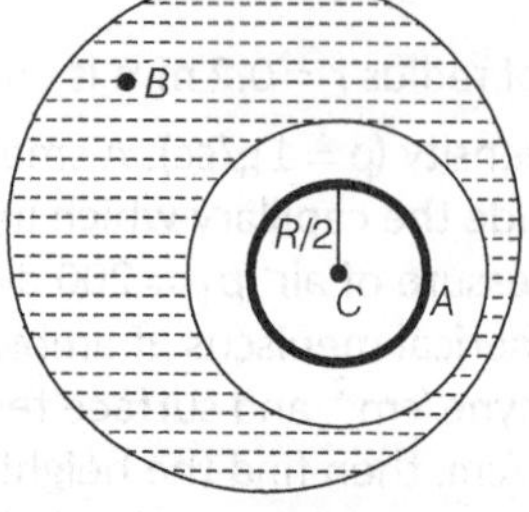

6 A capillary glass tube of height $2h$ is just dipped in water. In effect, the water rises to a height h as shown in the figure. Let p_1 be the pressure at height $h/3$ as shown inside the tube. The entire system is put in an elevator moving up with a constant acceleration of g. Let the new pressure at the same point be p_2. If $\Delta p = p_1 - p_2$ be change in pressure at a height $h/3$ inside the tube, find $\frac{\rho g h}{\Delta p}$.

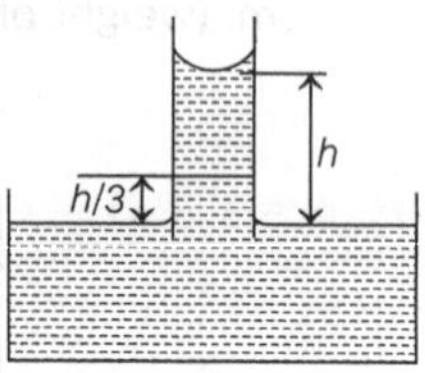

7 Two vertical plates submerged partially in a wetting liquid form a wedge with a very small angle $\delta\theta$. The edge of this wedge is vertical. The density of the liquid is ρ its surface tension is T, the contact angle is 0°. The height h, to which the liquid rises, as a function of the distance x from the edge is $\frac{nT}{\rho g x(\delta\theta)}$.

Find the value of n.

8 A capillary tube sealed at the top has an internal radius of $r = 0.05$ cm. The tube is placed vertically in water with its open end dipped in water. Find greatest integer corresponding to the length (in meter) of such a tube be for the water in it to rise in these conditions to a height $h = 1$ cm ? The pressure of the air is $p_0 = 1\text{ atm} = 76$ cm of Hg, density of Hg $= 13.6\text{ g/cm}^3$, $g = 9.8\text{ m/s}^2$. The surface tension of water is $\sigma = 70$ dyne/cm. (Assume temperature of air in the tube is constant)

9 A soap bubble of radius r and surface tension T is given a potential of V volt. If the new radius R of the bubble is related to its initial radius by equation,

$$p_0[R^3 - r^3] + \lambda T[R^2 - r^2] - \frac{1}{2}\varepsilon_0 V^2 R = 0,$$

where p_0 is the atmospheric pressure. Then, find λ.

10 The figure shows an inverted U like tube with straight limbs of unequal radii $r_1 = 0.25$ mm and $r_2 = 0.50$mm. Both the open ends of the tube are immersed below the free surface of water. The air is pumped into the upper part of the tube at such pressure, so that the water in the wider tube is at level with the water outside. Find the height h (in mm) of water in the other limb. Take, angle of contact as zero and surface tension of water $= 7 \times 10^{-2}$ N/m.

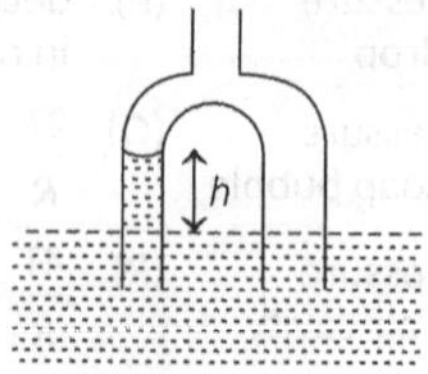

Previous Years Questions

JEE Main

1 Given below are two statements.

Statement I If a capillary tube is immersed first in cold water and then in hot water, the height of capillary rise will be smaller in hot water.

Statement II If a capillary tube is immersed first in cold water and then in hot water, the height of capillary rise will be smaller in cold water.

In the light of the above statements, choose the **most appropriate** from the options given below

[2024, 29 Jan Shift-I]

(a) Both Statement I and Statement II are true
(b) Both Statement I and Statement II are false
(c) Statement I is false but Statement II is true
(d) Statement I is true but Statement II is false

2 A small liquid drop of radius R is divided into 27 identical liquid drops. If the surface tension is T, then the work done in the process will be **[2024, 29 Jan Shift-II]**

(a) $3\pi R^2 T$ (b) $4\pi R^2 T$ (c) $\frac{1}{8}\pi R^2 T$ (d) $8\pi R^2 T$

3 A big drop is formed by coalescing 1000 small identical drops of water. If E_1 be the total surface energy of 1000 small drops of water and E_2 be the surface energy of single big drop of water, then $E_1 : E_2$ is $x : 1$ where $x =$ .... **[2024, 30 Jan Shift-II]**

4 The height of liquid column raised in a capillary tube of certain radius when dipped in liquid A vertically is 5 cm. If the tube is dipped in a similar manner in another liquid B of surface tension and density double the values of liquid A, the height of liquid column raised in liquid B would be .... m. **[2023, 30 Jan Shift-I]**

(a) 0.10 (b) 0.05
(c) 0.20 (d) 0.5

5 If 1000 droplets of water of surface tension 0.07 N/m, having same radius 1 mm each, combine to form a single drop. In the process, the released surface energy is $\left(\text{Take, } \pi = \frac{22}{7}\right)$ **[2023, 31 Jan Shift-I]**

(a) 7.92×10^{-6} J (b) 8.8×10^{-5} J
(c) 9.68×10^{-4} J (d) 7.92×10^{-4} J

6 A mercury drop of radius 10^{-3} m is broken into 125 equal size droplets. Surface tension of mercury is 0.45 Nm^{-1}. The gain in surface energy is **[2023, 1 Feb Shift-I]**

(a) 5×10^{-5} J (b) 2.26×10^{-5} J
(c) 17.5×10^{-5} J (d) 28×10^{-5} J

7 There is an air bubble of radius 1.0 mm in a liquid of surface tension 0.075 Nm^{-1} and density 1000 kg m^{-3} at a depth of 10 cm below the free surface. The amount by which the pressure inside the bubble is greater than the atmospheric pressure is .... Pa $(g = 10 \text{ m}^{-2})$ **[2023, 15 April Shift-I]**

8 The surface tension of soap solution is $3.5 \times 10^{-2} \text{ Nm}^{-1}$. The amount of work done required to increase the radius of soap bubble from 10 cm to 20 cm is .... $\times 10^{-4}$ J.
(Take, $\pi = 27/7$) **[2023, 11 April Shift-II]**

9 A spherical drop of liquid splits into 1000 identical spherical drops. If U_i is the surface energy of the original drop and U_f is the total surface energy of the resulting drops, the (ignoring evaporation), $\frac{U_f}{U_i} = \left(\frac{10}{x}\right)$. Then value of x is .... **[2023, 25 Jan Shift-II]**

10 Given below are two statements One is labelled as Assertion (A) and the other is labelled as Reason (R).

Assertion (A) Clothes containing oil or grease stains cannot be cleaned by water wash.

Reason (R) Because the angle of contact between the oil/ grease and water is obtuse.

In the light of the above statements, choose the correct answer from the option given below. **[2022, 29 July Shift-I]**

(a) Both (A) and (R) are true and (R) is the correct explanation of (A).
(b) Both (A) and (R) are true but (R) is not the correct explanation of (A).
(c) (A) is true but (R) is false.
(d) (A) is false but (R) is true.

11 A spherical soap bubble of radius 3 cm is formed inside another spherical soap bubble of radius 6 cm. If the internal pressure of the smaller bubble of radius 3 cm in the above system is equal to the internal pressure of the another single soap bubble of radius r cm. The value of r is .... **[2022, 27 July Shift-II]**

12 A water drop of radius 1 cm is broken into 729 equal droplets. If surface tension of water is 75 dyne/cm, then the gain in surface energy upto first decimal place will be (Given, $\pi = 3.14$) **[2022, 26 July Shift-I]**

(a) 8.5×10^{-4} J
(b) 8.2×10^{-4} J
(c) 7.5×10^{-4} J
(d) 5.3×10^{-4} J

13 A water drop of diameter 2 cm is broken into 64 equal droplets. The surface tension of water is 0.075 N/m. In this process, the gain in surface energy will be : **[2022, 28 June Shift-I]**

(a) 2.8×10^{-4} J (b) 1.5×10^{-3} J
(c) 1.9×10^{-4} J (d) 9.4×10^{-5} J

14 A soap bubble of radius 3 cm is formed inside the another soap bubble of radius 6 cm. The radius of an equivalent soap bubble which has the same excess pressure as inside the smaller bubble with respect to the atmospheric pressure is .... cm. **[2021, 26 Aug Shift-I]**

15 Two spherical soap bubbles of radii r_1 and r_2 in vacuum combine under isothermal conditions. The resulting bubble has a radius equal to **[2021, 25 July Shift-II]**

(a) $\frac{r_1 r_2}{r_1 + r_2}$ (b) $\sqrt{r_1 r_2}$ (c) $\sqrt{r_1^2 + r_2^2}$ (d) $\frac{r_1 + r_2}{2}$

16 Two small drops of mercury each of radius R coalesce to form a single large drop. The ratio of total surface energy before and after the change is **[2021, 20 July Shift-II]**

(a) $2^{1/3} : 1$ (b) $1 : 2^{1/3}$
(c) $2 : 1$ (d) $1 : 2$

17 When two soap bubbles of radii a and $b (b > a)$ coalesce, the radius of curvature of common surface is **[2021, 17 March Shift-I]**

(a) $\frac{ab}{b-a}$ (b) $\frac{a+b}{ab}$ (c) $\frac{b-a}{ab}$ (d) $\frac{ab}{a+b}$

18 A large number of water drops, each of radius r, combine to have a drop of radius R. If the surface tension is T and mechanical equivalent of heat is J, the rise in heat energy per unit volume will be **[2021, 26 Feb Shift-I]**

(a) $\frac{2T}{J}\left(\frac{1}{r} - \frac{1}{R}\right)$ (b) $\frac{2T}{rJ}$
(c) $\frac{3T}{rJ}$ (d) $\frac{3T}{J}\left(\frac{1}{r} - \frac{1}{R}\right)$

JEE Advanced

1. An incompressible liquid is kept in a container having a weightless piston with a hole. A capillary tube of inner radius 0.1 mm is dipped vertically into the liquid through the airtight piston hole, as shown in the figure. The air in the container is isothermally compressed from its original volume V_0 to $100/101\, V_0$ with the movable piston. Considering air as an ideal gas, the height (h) of the liquid column in the capillary above the liquid level in cm is ......
[Given : Surface tension of the liquid is 0.075 Nm^{-1}, atmospheric presure is 10^5 Nm^{-2}, acceleration due to gravity (g) is 10 ms^{-2}, density of the liquid is 10^3 kg m^{-3} and contact angle of capillary surface with the liquid is zero] **(2023)**

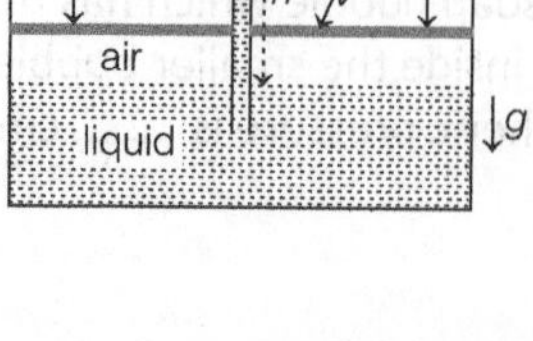

2. When water is filled carefully in a glass, one can fill it to a height h above the rim of the glass due to the surface tension of water. To calculate h just before water starts flowing, model the shape of the water above the rim as a disc of thickness h having semicircular edges, as shown schematically in the figure. When the pressure of water at the bottom of this disc exceeds what can be withstood due to the surface tension, the water surface breaks near the rim and water starts flowing from there. If the density of water, its surface tension and the acceleration due to gravity are 10^3 kg m^{-3}, 0.07 Nm^{-1} and 10 ms^{-2}, respectively, the value of h (in mm) is ______. **(2020)**

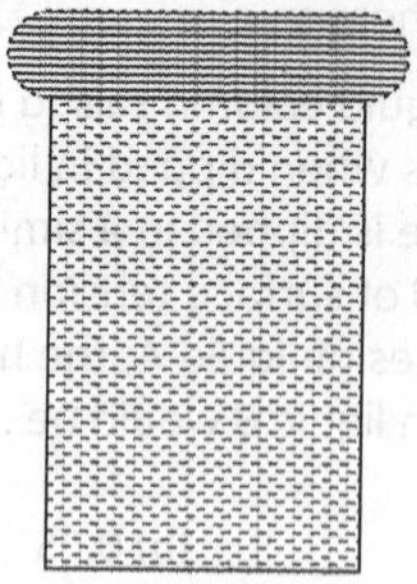

3. A uniform capillary tube of inner radius r is dipped vertically into a beaker filled with water. The water rises to a height h in the capillary tube above the water surface in the beaker. The surface tension of water is σ. The angle of contact between water and the wall of the capillary tube is θ. Ignore the mass of water in the meniscus. Which of the following statements is (are) true ? **(2018)**
(a) For a given material of the capillary tube, h decreases with increase in r
(b) For a given material of the capillary tube, h is independent of σ
(c) If this experiment is performed in a lift going up with a constant acceleration, then h decreases
(d) h is proportional to contact angle θ

4. A drop of liquid of radius $R = 10^{-2}$ m having surface tension $S = \frac{0.1}{4\pi}$ Nm^{-1} divides itself into K identical drops. In this process the total change in the surface energy $\Delta U = 10^{-3}$ J. If $K = 10^{\alpha}$, then the value of α is **(2017)**

5. A glass capillary tube is of the shape of truncated cone with an apex angle α so that its two ends have cross-sections of different radii. When dipped in water vertically, water rises in it to a height h, where the radius of its cross-section is b. If the surface tension of water is S, its density is ρ, and its contact

angle with glass is θ, the value of h will be (g is the acceleration due to gravity) **(2014)**

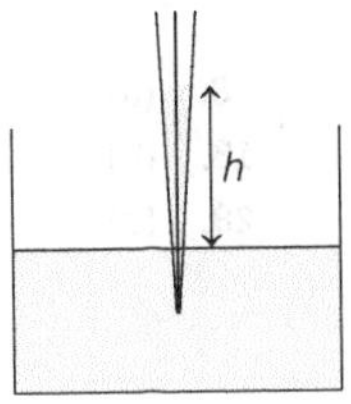

(a) $\frac{2S}{b\rho g}\cos(\theta-\alpha)$ (b) $\frac{2S}{b\rho g}\cos(\theta+\alpha)$

(c) $\frac{2S}{b\rho g}\cos(\theta-\alpha/2)$ (d) $\frac{2S}{b\rho g}\cos(\theta+\alpha/2)$

Direction (Q. Nos. 6-8) When liquid medicine of density ρ is to be put in the eye, it is done with the help of a dropper. As the bulb on the top of the dropper is pressed, a drop forms at the opening of the dropper. We wish to estimate the size of the drop.We first assume that the drop formed at the opening is spherical because that requires a minimum increase in its surface energy. To determine the size, we calculate the net vertical force due to the surface tension T when the radius of the drop is R. When this force becomes smaller than the weight of the drop, the drop gets detached from the dropper. **(2010)**

6. If the radius of the opening of the dropper is r, the vertical force due to the surface tension on the drop of radius R (assuming $r << R$) is

(a) $2\pi rT$ (b) $2\pi RT$

(c) $\frac{2\pi r^2 T}{R}$ (d) $\frac{2\pi R^2 T}{r}$

7. If $r = 5\times10^{-4}$ m, $\rho = 10^3$ kg m^{-3}, $g = 10$ ms^{-2}, $T = 0.11$ Nm^{-1}, the radius of the drop when it detaches from the dropper is approximately

(a) 1.4×10^{-3} m (b) 3.3×10^{-3} m

(c) 2.0×10^{-3} m (d) 4.1×10^{-3} m

8. After the drop detaches, its surface energy is

(a) 1.4×10^{-6} J (b) 2.7×10^{-6} J

(c) 5.4×10^{-6} J (d) 8.1×10^{-9} J

9. Two soap bubbles A and B are kept in a closed chamber where the air is maintained at pressure 8 Nm^{-2}. The radii of bubbles A and B are 2 cm and 4 cm, respectively. Surface tension of the soap-water used to make bubbles is 0.04 Nm^{-1}. Find the ratio $\frac{n_B}{n_A}$, where n_A and n_B are the number of moles of air in bubbles A and B, respectively. [Neglect the effect of gravity] **(2009)**

Answer Key

Level 1

9.1 Force due to Surface Tension

1. (a) $mg+2Tl$ (b) $mg+2\pi Tr$ (c) $mg+T(4\pi r)$ (d) $mg+T[2\pi(R+r)]$ (e) $mg+4Tl$ (f) $mg+8Tl$
2. $\frac{2Tl}{g}$
3. $\frac{mg+4Ta}{a^2 dg}$
4. 72.3dyne/cm
5. $\frac{\lambda dg}{2y}$

9.2 Surface Energy

1. $8\pi r^2T, 24\pi r^2T$
2. 89.5×10^{-6}J
4. 2.4×10^{-4}J
5. $r=\sqrt{r_1^2+r_2^2}$

9.3 Excess Pressure

1. (a) $465 N/m^2$ (b) $30 N/m^2$ (c) $38 N/m^2$
2. $\frac{1}{27}$
3. $r=\frac{r_1r_2}{r_1-r_2}$
5. $\frac{2T}{\rho gr}$
6. 5mm

9.4 Capillary

1. (a) 1.53 cm (b) 3.06 cm
2. 5/34
3. 60 mm
4. $\frac{-T\cos\theta}{R}$
5. $\frac{4T}{\rho gR}$
6. 5.84 cm
7. Liquid won't overflow and radius of meniscus will increase.
8. $\simeq 0.6$ mm

Level 2

Single Choice Correct Questions

1. (d) 2. (c) 3. (a) 4. (d) 5. (d) 6. (b) 7. (b) 8. (d) 9. (b) 10. (a)
11. (b) 12. (d) 13. (b) 14. (b) 15. (a) 16. (a) 17. (b) 18. (b) 19. (c) 20. (b)
21. (c) 22. (d) 23. (b) 24. (a) 25. (c) 26. (d) 27. (c) 28. (b) 29. (d) 30. (b)
31. (a) 32. (d) 33. (d) 34. (a) 35. (a) 36. (a)

Numerical Value Questions

1. 73 2. 2.4 3. 4 4. 4 5. 450 6. 3 7. 200 8. 9

Level 3

Single Choice Correct Questions

1. (b) 2. (a) 3. (d) 4. (c) 5. (c) 6. (a) 7. (a) 8. (b) 9. (b) 10. (a)
11. (a) 12. (b) 13. (a) 14. (a) 15. (d) 16. (c) 17. (a) 18. (d) 19. (d) 20. (a)
21 (c) 22 (b)

Multiple Choice(s) Correct Questions

1. (b, d) 2. (a, b) 3. (a, c) 4. (a, c) 5. (a,b, c, d) 6. (c, d) 7. (b, c, d)
8. (a, d) 9. (a, c, d) 10. (a. b. c)

Comprehension Based Questions

1. (c) 2. (d) 3. (b) 4. (a) 5. (c) 6. (c)

Match the Columns Questions

1. A→ P; B→ QRS; C→ PS; D→ QR
2. A→ PQS; B→ PQS; C→ PRS; D→ S
3. A→ S; B→ P; C→ P; D→ P
4. A→ PR; B→ PR; C→ PR; D→ QS

Numerical Value Questions

1. 8 2. 5 3. 15 4. 5 5. 16 6. 3 7. 2
8. 5 9. 4 10. 28

Previous Years Questions

JEE Main

1. (d) 2. (d) 3. (10) 4. (b) 5. (d) 6. (b) 7. (1130) 8. (264) 9. (1) 10. (a)
11. (2) 12. (c) 13. (a) 14. (2) 15. (c) 16. (a) 17. (a) 18. (d)

JEE Advanced

1.(25.00) 2.(3.741) 3. (a,c) 4. (6) 5. (d) 6. (c) 7. (a) 8. (b) 9. (6 : 1)

SOLUTIONS

Level 1

9.1 Force due to Surface Tension

1. (a) $F = mg + T(2l) = mg + 2Tl$
   (b) $F = mg + T(2\pi r) = mg + 2\pi Tr$
   (c) $F = mg + T(2\pi r + 2\pi r) = mg + T(4\pi r)$
   (d) $F = mg + T(2\pi R + 2\pi r) = mg + T[2\pi(R + r)]$
   (e) $F = mg + T(4l) = mg + 4Tl$
   (f) $F = mg + T(4l + 4l) = mg + 8Tl$

2. For wire CD, $F_{\text{due to surface tension}} = mg$

$$\Rightarrow \quad T(2l) = mg$$

$$\Rightarrow \quad m = \frac{2Tl}{g}$$

3. F = Force due to surface tension on the cube $= T(4a)$

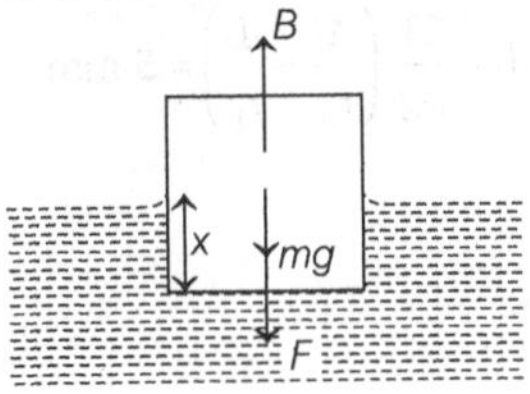

For equilibrium of cube,

$$B = mg + F$$

$$\Rightarrow \quad d(a^2x)g = mg + T(4a)$$

$$\Rightarrow \quad x = \frac{mg + 4Ta}{a^2dg}$$

4.

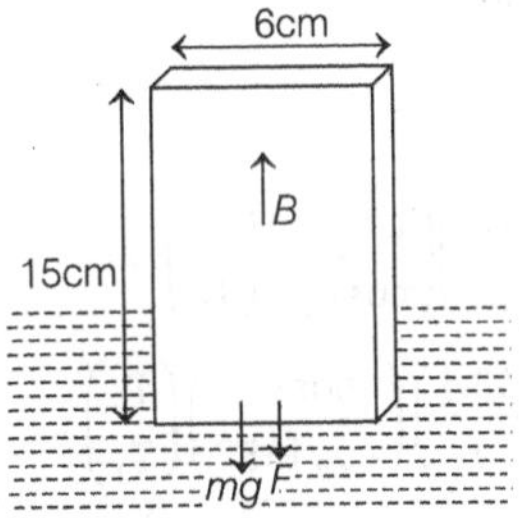

Apparent weight $= mg - B + F$

$$\Rightarrow \quad mg = mg - B + F$$

$$\Rightarrow \quad F = B$$

$$\Rightarrow T[2(6 + 0.1)] = 1 \times \left(\frac{10}{100} \times 15 \times 6 \times 0.1\right) \times 980$$

$$\Rightarrow \quad T = 72.3 \text{ dyne/cm}$$

5.

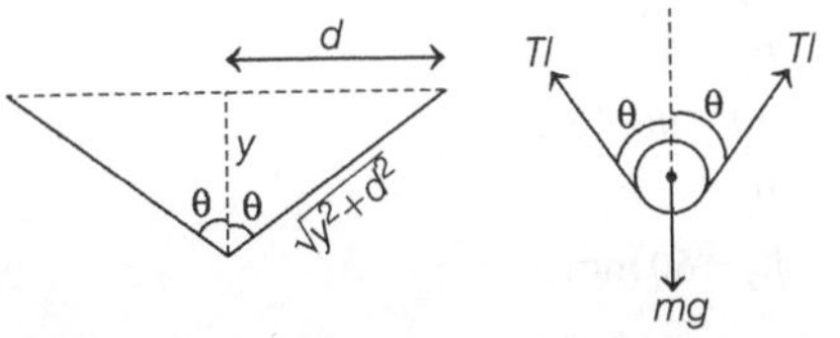

$$\cos\theta = \frac{y}{\sqrt{y^2 + d^2}} = \frac{y}{d} \qquad [\because y << d]$$

For equilibrium of wire, $\Sigma F_y = 0$

$$\Rightarrow \quad 2Tl\cos\theta = mg$$

$$\Rightarrow \quad 2Tl\left(\frac{y}{d}\right) = (\lambda l)g$$

$$\Rightarrow \quad T = \frac{\lambda dg}{2y}$$

9.2 Surface Energy

1. $W = \Delta U = U_2 - U_1 = T(2 \times 4\pi r^2) - 0 = 8T\pi r^2$

   Additional work to double the radius,

$$W = \Delta U = U_2 - U_1$$
$$= T[2 \times 4\pi(2r)^2] - T(2 \times 4\pi r^2)$$
$$= 24T\pi r^2$$

2. Let radius of each drop formed is r.

   For volume conservation, $\frac{4}{3}\pi R^3 = n\left(\frac{4}{3}\pi r^3\right)$

$$\Rightarrow \quad r = \frac{R}{n^{1/3}}$$

Energy spent $= \Delta U = U_2 - U_1$

$$= T[n(4\pi r^2)] - T(4\pi R^2)$$
$$= 4\pi TR^2(n^{1/3} - 1)$$
$$= 4 \times 3.14 \times (72 \times 10^{-3})(1 \times 10^{-3})^2 [(10^6)^{1/3} - 1]$$
$$= 89.5 \times 10^{-6} \text{ J}$$

3. From volume conservation, $n\left(\frac{4}{3}\pi r^3\right) = \frac{4}{3}\pi R^3$

$$\Rightarrow \quad n = \left(\frac{R}{r}\right)^3$$

Heat produced $= U_1 - U_2 = n[T(4\pi r^2)] - T(4\pi R^2)$

$$= \left[\left(\frac{R^3}{r^3}\right)r^2 - R^2\right]4\pi T$$
$$= 4\pi R^2T\left(\frac{R}{r} - 1\right)$$

Heat produced $= ms\Delta\theta$

$$\Rightarrow \quad 4\pi R^2T\left(\frac{R}{r} - 1\right) = \left(1 \times \frac{4}{3}\pi R^3\right)(1 \times J)\Delta\theta$$

$$\Rightarrow \quad \Delta\theta = \frac{3T}{J}\left(\frac{1}{r} - \frac{1}{R}\right)$$

4. $W = \Delta U = T\Delta A$

$$= 30 \times 10^{-3}(2 \times 10 \times 10 \times 10^{-4} - 2 \times 10 \times 6 \times 10^{-4})$$
$$= 2.4 \times 10^{-4} \text{ J}$$

5. For isothermal condition,

$$U_1 = U_2$$

$$\Rightarrow T(8\pi r_1^2) + T(8\pi r_2^2) = T(8\pi r^2)$$

$$\Rightarrow \quad r = \sqrt{r_1^2 + r_2^2}$$

9.3 Excess Pressure

1. (a) $\Delta p = \dfrac{2T}{R} = \dfrac{2 \times 0.465}{2 \times 10^{-3}} = 465\ \text{N/m}^2$

(b) $\Delta p = \dfrac{4T}{R} = \dfrac{4 \times 0.03}{4 \times 10^{-3}} = 30\ \text{N/m}^2$

(c) $\Delta p = \dfrac{2T}{R} = \dfrac{2 \times 0.076}{4 \times 10^{-3}} = 38\ \text{N/m}^2$

2. $\Delta p = \dfrac{4T}{R} \Rightarrow \dfrac{R_1}{R_2} = \dfrac{\Delta p_2}{\Delta p_1} = \dfrac{1}{3}$

$$V = \frac{4}{3}\pi R^3 \Rightarrow \frac{V_1}{V_2} = \left(\frac{R_1}{R_2}\right)^3 = \frac{1}{27}$$

3.

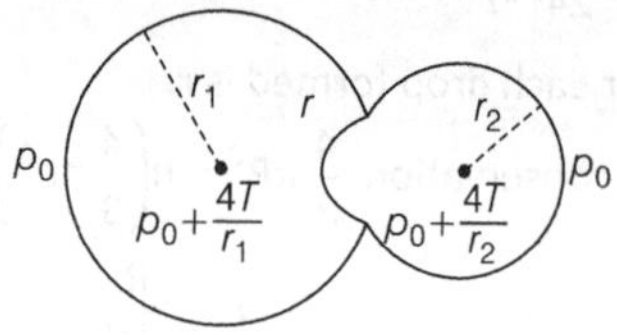

Pressure inside bubble of radius, $r_1 = p_0 + \dfrac{4T}{r_1}$

Pressure inside bubble of radius, $r_2 = p_0 + \dfrac{4T}{r_2}$

For the interface,

$$\text{Excess pressure} = \left(p_0 + \frac{4T}{r_2}\right) - \left(p_0 + \frac{4T}{r_1}\right)$$

$$\Rightarrow \quad \frac{4T}{r} = \left(p_0 + \frac{4T}{r_2}\right) - \left(p_0 + \frac{4T}{r_1}\right)$$

$$\Rightarrow \quad r = \frac{r_1 r_2}{r_1 - r_2}$$

4. Under isothermal condition for the air inside bubbles,

$$p_1V_1 + p_2V_2 = p_3V_3$$

$$\Rightarrow \left(p_0 + \frac{4T}{a}\right)\left(\frac{4}{3}\pi a^3\right) + \left(p_0 + \frac{4T}{b}\right)\left(\frac{4}{3}\pi b^3\right) = \left(p_0 + \frac{4T}{c}\right)\left(\frac{4}{3}\pi c^3\right)$$

$$\Rightarrow \quad T = \frac{p_0(c^3 - a^3 - b^3)}{a^2 + b^2 - c^2}$$

5.

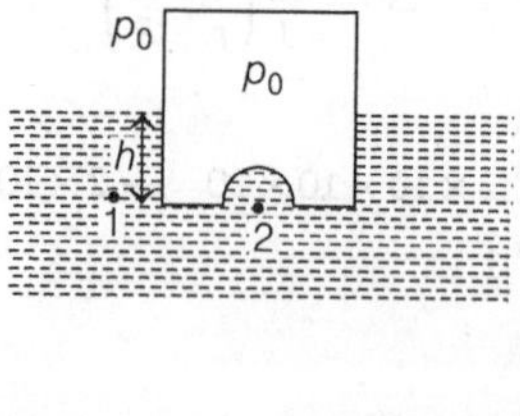

$$p_1 = p_2$$

$$\Rightarrow \quad p_0 + \rho gh = p_0 + \frac{2T}{r}$$

$$\Rightarrow \quad h = \frac{2T}{\rho gr}$$

6.

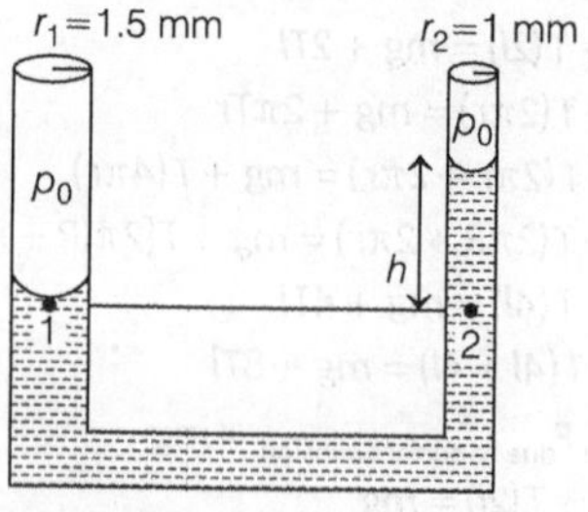

$$p_1 = p_2$$

$$\Rightarrow \quad p_0 - \frac{2T}{r_1} = p_0 - \frac{2T}{r_2} + \rho gh$$

$$\Rightarrow \quad h = \frac{2T}{\rho g}\left(\frac{1}{r_2} - \frac{1}{r_1}\right) = 5\ \text{mm}$$

9.4 Capillary

1. (a) $h = \dfrac{2T\cos\theta}{\rho gR}$

$$= \frac{2 \times 30 \times \cos 0^\circ}{0.8 \times 980 \times \left(\frac{0.1}{2}\right)} = 1.53\ \text{cm}$$

(b) $h = l\cos\theta$

$$\Rightarrow 1.53 = l\cos 60^\circ$$

$$\Rightarrow \quad l = 3.06\ \text{cm}$$

2. $h = \dfrac{2T\cos\theta}{\rho gR}$

$$\Rightarrow \quad \frac{h_1}{h_2} = \left(\frac{\rho_2}{\rho_1}\right)\left(\frac{\cos\theta_1}{\cos\theta_2}\right)\left(\frac{T_1}{T_2}\right)$$

$$\Rightarrow \quad \frac{10}{-3.5} = \left(\frac{13.6}{1}\right)\left(\frac{\cos 0^\circ}{\cos 135^\circ}\right)\left(\frac{T_1}{T_2}\right)$$

$$\Rightarrow \quad \frac{T_1}{T_2} = \frac{5}{34}$$

3. $h = \dfrac{2T\cos\theta}{\rho gR}$

$$\Rightarrow \quad h \propto \frac{1}{R}$$

$$\Rightarrow \quad \frac{h_1}{h_2} = \frac{R_2}{R_1}$$

$$\Rightarrow \quad \frac{20}{h_2} = \frac{(R_1/3)}{R_1}$$

$$\Rightarrow \quad h_2 = 60\ \text{mm}$$

4.

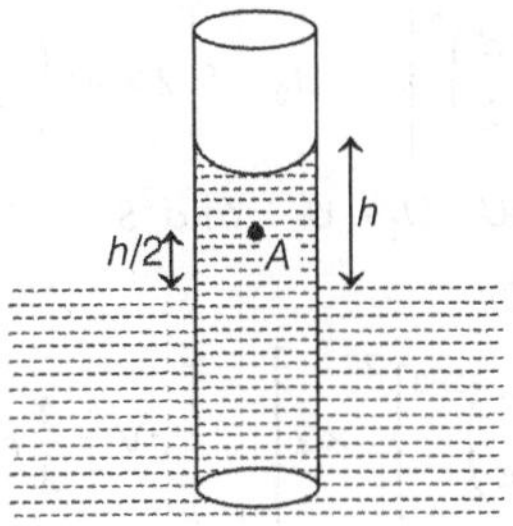

$p_A = p_0 - \rho g\left(\frac{h}{2}\right)$, where $h = \frac{2T\cos\theta}{\rho g R}$

$$= p_0 - \rho g\left(\frac{2T\cos\theta}{2(\rho g R)}\right) = p_0 - \frac{T\cos\theta}{R}$$

Gauge pressure at $A = -\frac{T\cos\theta}{R}$

5.

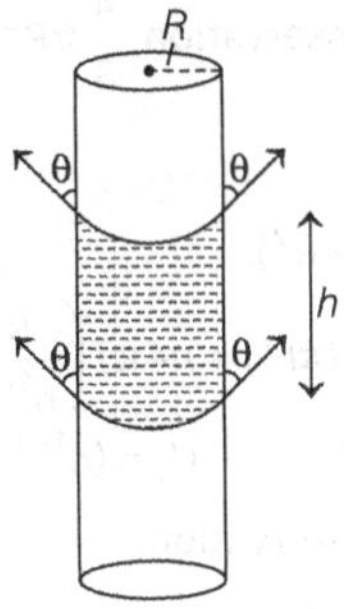

For equilibrium of liquid column,

$$T(2\pi R)\cos\theta + T(2\pi R)\cos\theta = mg$$

$$\Rightarrow \quad 2T(2\pi R)\cos\theta = \rho(\pi R^2 h)g$$

$$\Rightarrow \quad h = \frac{4T\cos\theta}{\rho g R} \Rightarrow h = \frac{4T}{\rho g R} \quad \because \{\theta = 0°\}$$

6.

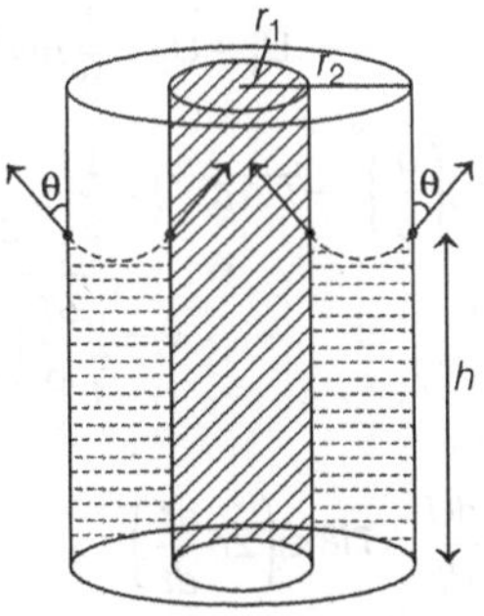

For equilibrium of liquid column inside capillary,

$$F_1 + F_2 = mg$$

$$\Rightarrow \quad T(2\pi r_1)\cos\theta + T(2\pi r_2)\cos\theta = [\rho\pi(r_2^2 - r_1^2)h]g$$

$$\Rightarrow \quad h = \frac{2T\cos\theta}{\rho g(r_2 - r_1)}$$

$$= \frac{2\times 73\times 10^{-3}\cos 0°}{1000\times 10\times 0.25\times 10^{-3}}$$

$$= 5.84 \text{ cm}$$

7. For capillary of insufficient length, liquid does not overflow and radius of meniscus increases.

$$h = \frac{2T}{\rho g r} \Rightarrow r \propto \frac{1}{h} \Rightarrow hr = \text{constant}$$

As h decreases, r increases.

8. $h = \frac{2T\cos\theta}{\rho g R} = \frac{2\times 73\times 10^{-3}\times\cos 0°}{1000\times 10\times 0.25\times 10^{-3}}$

$$= 0.059 \text{ m} = 59 \text{ mm}$$

h_1 = Length of capillary outside water = 25 mm

Since, $h_1 < h$, this is capillary of insufficient length.

So, $hr = h_1 r_1$

$$\Rightarrow \quad 59\left(\frac{0.25}{\cos 0°}\right) = 25 r_1$$

$$\Rightarrow \quad r_1 = 0.59 \text{ mm} \simeq 0.6 \text{ mm}$$

Level 2

Single Choice Correct Questions

1. Net force on the stick $= T_1 l - T_2 l = (T_1 - T_2)l$

$$= (0.07 - 0.06)2 = 0.02 \text{ N}$$

2. $\Sigma F_y = 0 \Rightarrow B + T(2\pi r)\cos\theta = w_{disc}$

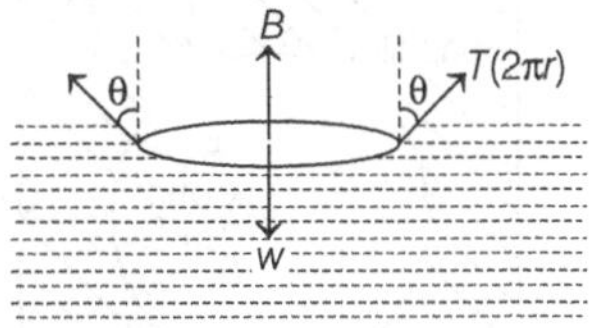

$$\Rightarrow \quad w_{disc} = w + 2\pi r T\cos\theta$$

3. For equilibrium of wire,

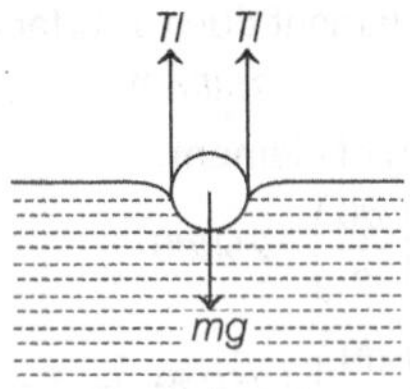

$$2Tl = mg$$

$$\Rightarrow \quad 2Tl = (\rho\pi r^2 l)g$$

$$\Rightarrow \quad r = \sqrt{\frac{2T}{\pi\rho g}}$$

4. For equilibrium of wire ab,

$$2Tl = mg$$

$$\Rightarrow \quad m = \frac{2Tl}{g} = \frac{2\times 25\times 10^{-3}\times 0.1}{10} = 0.5 \text{ g}$$

5. $F = mg + T(2\times 2\pi r)$

$$= 0.1 + 75\times 10^{-3}(2\times 0.2)$$

$$= 0.130 \text{ N}$$

6. $F_y = T \times$ Projected length

Net force $= T_1 R - T_2 R$

$= (T_1 - T_2)R$ in + y-direction

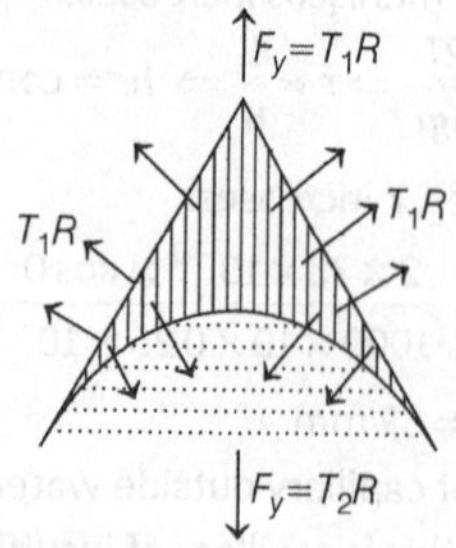

7. When film A is punctured, film B will try to minimise its area. So, thread will become concave towards A.

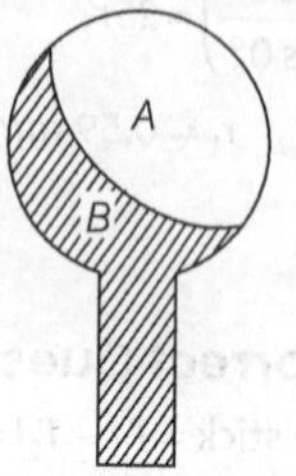

8. Lets take an element of angular width $d\theta$ on the thread.

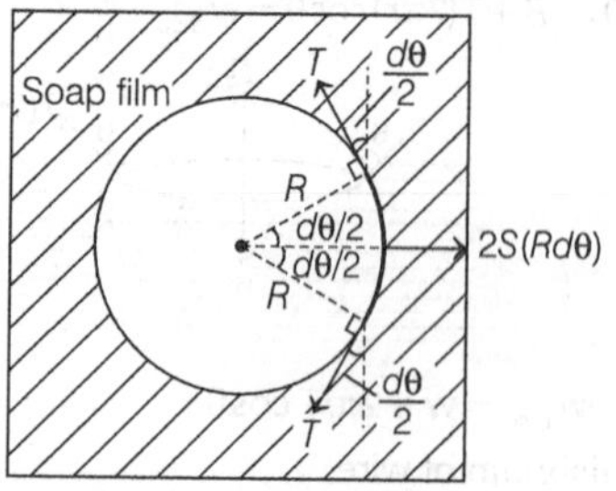

Force on the element due to surface tension

$$= 2S(Rd\theta)$$

For equilibrium of element,

$$2T \sin\left(\frac{d\theta}{2}\right) = 2SRd\theta$$

$$\Rightarrow \quad 2T\left(\frac{d\theta}{2}\right) = 2SRd\theta \Rightarrow T = 2SR$$

9. Let radius of single large drop be R.

For volume conservation, $2\left(\frac{4}{3}\pi r^3\right) = \frac{4}{3}\pi R^3$

$$\Rightarrow \quad R = 2^{1/3} r$$

$$U_1 = T(4\pi r^2) \times 2,$$

$$U_2 = T(4\pi R^2)$$

$$\frac{U_1}{U_2} = \frac{T(8\pi r^2)}{T(4\pi R^2)} = \frac{2r^2}{(2^{1/3} r)^2} = 2^{1/3} : 1$$

10. $W = \Delta U = U_2 - U_1$

$$= T(4\pi r^2 \times 2) - 0$$

$$= 0.03 \times 4 \times 3.14 \times (0.1)^2 \times 2$$

$$= 75.36 \times 10^{-4}\ \text{J}$$

11. $U_1 = S\left[2 \times 4\pi\left(\frac{d}{2}\right)^2\right], \quad U_2 = S\left[2 \times 4\pi\left(\frac{2d}{2}\right)^2\right]$

$$W = \Delta U = U_2 - U_1 = 6\pi d^2 S$$

12. $W = T(4\pi r^2 \times 2)$

$$= T\left[4\pi\left\{\left(\frac{3V}{4\pi}\right)^{1/3}\right\}^2 \times 2\right] \quad \left\{\because V = \frac{4}{3}\pi r^3 \Rightarrow r = \left(\frac{3V}{4\pi}\right)^{1/3}\right\}$$

$$\Rightarrow \quad W \propto V^{2/3}$$

$$\Rightarrow \quad \frac{W_1}{W_2} = \left(\frac{V_1}{V_2}\right)^{2/3} \Rightarrow \frac{W}{W_2} = \left(\frac{V}{2V}\right)^{2/3}$$

$$\Rightarrow \quad W_2 = 2^{2/3} W = \sqrt[3]{4}\, W$$

13. $W = T\Delta A = 7.2 \times 10^{-2} \times (0.1 \times 10^{-3} \times 2) = 1.44 \times 10^{-5}\ \text{J}$

14. From volume conservation, $\frac{4}{3}\pi R^3 = n\left(\frac{4}{3}\pi r^3\right)$

$$\Rightarrow \quad r = \frac{R}{n^{1/3}}$$

$$U_1 = T(4\pi R^2),$$

$$U_2 = nT(4\pi r^2) = n4\pi T\left(\frac{R}{n^{1/3}}\right)^2 = n^{1/3} T(4\pi R^2)$$

$$W = \Delta U = U_2 - U_1 = (n^{1/3} - 1)T(4\pi R^2)$$

15. From volume conservation,

$$n\frac{4}{3}\pi a^3 = \frac{4}{3}\pi b^3$$

$$\Rightarrow \quad n = \left(\frac{b}{a}\right)^3$$

$$U_1 = T(4\pi a^2)n, \quad U_2 = T(4\pi b^2)$$

Energy released $= \Delta K$

$$\Rightarrow \quad U_1 - U_2 = \frac{1}{2} mv^2$$

$$\Rightarrow \quad T(4\pi a^2)\left(\frac{b}{a}\right)^3 - T(4\pi b^2) = \frac{1}{2}\left(\rho \frac{4}{3}\pi b^3\right) v^2$$

$$\Rightarrow \quad v = \sqrt{\frac{6T}{\rho}\left(\frac{1}{a} - \frac{1}{b}\right)}$$

16. $U = T(8\pi r^2)$

$$P = \frac{dU}{dt} = T(8\pi)\left(2r\frac{dr}{dt}\right)$$

$$\Rightarrow \quad P \propto r \quad \because \left\{\frac{dr}{dt} \text{ is constant}\right\}$$

So, P versus r graph will be straight line passing through origin.

17. $\frac{4}{3}\pi R^3 = 8\left(\frac{4}{3}\pi r^3\right) \Rightarrow r = \frac{R}{2}$

$$\Delta p = \frac{2T}{r} \Rightarrow \Delta p \propto \frac{1}{r}$$

$$\Rightarrow \frac{\Delta p_{\text{big drop}}}{\Delta p_{\text{small drop}}} = \frac{r}{R} = \frac{1}{2} \Rightarrow \Delta p_{\text{big drop}} = \frac{1}{2}\Delta p_{\text{small drop}}$$

18. p_1 = Pressure inside larger bubble $= p_0 + \frac{4T}{R}$

p_2 = Pressure inside smaller bubble $= p_0 + \frac{4T}{r}$

$$p_2 > p_1 \qquad [\because (r < R)]$$

So, air blows from smaller bubble into the larger bubble.

19. $\Delta p_1 = 1.01 - 1 = 0.01$ atm

$\Delta p_2 = 1.02 - 1 = 0.02$ atm

$$\Delta p = \frac{4T}{r} \Rightarrow \frac{r_1}{r_2} = \frac{\Delta p_2}{\Delta p_1} = 2$$

$$V_1 : V_2 = r_1^3 : r_2^3 = 8 : 1$$

20. Air bubble inside water has only one free surface. So, excess pressure will be $\frac{2T}{r}$.

$$p = (p_0 + hdg) + \frac{2T}{r}$$

21. $p_2 = p_0 + \frac{4S}{(2R)} = p_0 + \frac{2S}{R}$

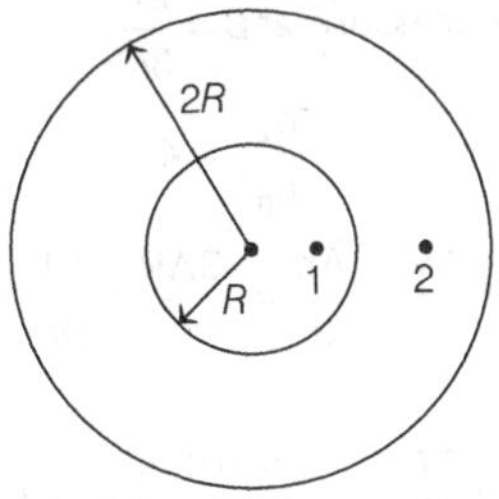

$$p_1 = p_2 + \frac{4S}{R} = \left(p_0 + \frac{2S}{R}\right) + \frac{4S}{R} = p_0 + \frac{6S}{R}$$

Excess pressure inside the smaller bubble $= \frac{6S}{R}$

22. p_1 = Pressure inside bigger bubble $= p_0 + \frac{4T}{r_1}$

p_2 = Pressure inside smaller bubble $= p_0 + \frac{4T}{r_2}$

Excess pressure for interface $= p_2 - p_1$

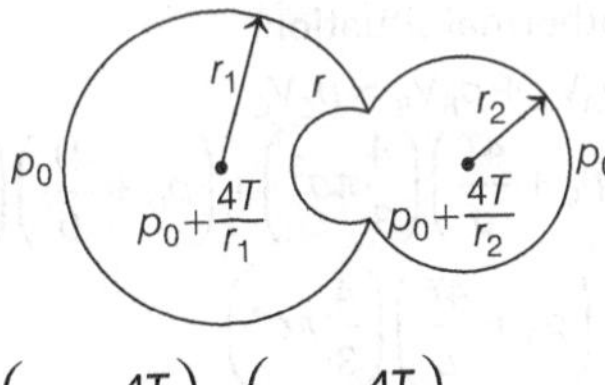

$$\Rightarrow \quad \frac{4T}{r} = \left(p_0 + \frac{4T}{r_2}\right) - \left(p_0 + \frac{4T}{r_1}\right)$$

$$\Rightarrow \quad r = \frac{r_1 r_2}{r_1 - r_2} = 12 \text{ cm}$$

23. Under isothermal condition, $U_1 = U_2$

$$\Rightarrow \quad T(8\pi r_1^2) + T(8\pi r_2^2) = T(8\pi r^2)$$

$$\Rightarrow \quad r = \sqrt{r_1^2 + r_2^2} = 5 \text{ cm}$$

24. Pressure difference on two sides of a curved surface is inversely proportional to the radius of curvature.

25. $\cos 60° = \frac{r}{R} \Rightarrow \frac{1}{2} = \frac{1}{R} \Rightarrow R = 2$ cm

$$\Delta p = \frac{4T}{R} = \frac{4 \times 0.05}{2 \times 10^{-2}} = 10 \text{ Pa}$$

26.

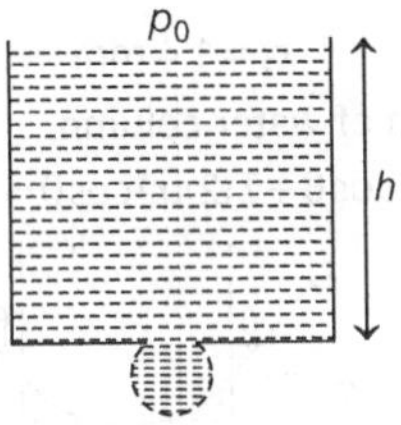

$$p_0 + \rho g h - \frac{2T}{r} = p_0$$

$$\Rightarrow \quad h = \frac{2T}{\rho g r} = \frac{2 \times 70}{1 \times 1000 \times 0.005} = 28.0 \text{ cm}$$

27. $\frac{h_1}{h_2} = \left(\frac{T_1}{T_2}\right)\left(\frac{\cos\theta_1}{\cos\theta_2}\right)\left(\frac{\rho_2}{\rho_1}\right)$

$$= \left(\frac{70}{140}\right)\left(\frac{\cos 0°}{\cos 60°}\right)\left(\frac{2}{1}\right) \Rightarrow h_2 = 3\text{cm}$$

28. $h = l\cos\theta$

$$\Rightarrow \quad 2 = l\cos 60° \Rightarrow l = 4 \text{ cm}$$

29. $h = \frac{2T\cos\theta}{\rho g_{\text{eff}} R}$

For freely falling elevator, $g_{\text{eff}} = 0 \Rightarrow h \to \infty$

So, capillary will be completely filled with water.

30. $H = \frac{2T\cos\theta}{\rho g R} \Rightarrow H \propto \frac{1}{R}$

So, when radius is double, H will be halved.

$$M' = \rho\left[\pi(2R)^2\left(\frac{H}{2}\right)\right] \text{ and } M = \rho(\pi R^2 H)$$

$$\frac{M'}{M} = 2 \Rightarrow M' = 2M$$

31. $h = \frac{2T\cos\theta}{\rho g R} = \frac{2 \times 7 \times 10^{-2} \times \cos 0°}{10^3 \times 10 \times 0.05 \times 10^{-2}} = 2.8$ cm

Pressure required to flow an air bubble at the lower end

$$= \rho g h = 10^3 \times 10 \times (2.8 + 2) \times 10^{-2}$$

$$= 480 \text{ N/m}^2$$

32. $T(2\pi r)\cos\theta = w$

$$\Rightarrow \text{Circumference} = 2\pi r = \frac{w}{T\cos\theta}$$

$$= \frac{75 \times 10^{-4}}{6 \times 10^{-2}\cos 0°} = 12.5 \times 10^{-2} \text{ m}$$

33. $h = \frac{2T\cos\theta}{\rho g R} \Rightarrow h = \frac{2 \times 0.07 \times \cos 0°}{10^3 \times 10 \times 1 \times 10^{-3}}$

$$= 0.014 \text{ m} = 1.4 \text{ cm}$$

So, this is capillary of insufficient length $h = \frac{2T}{\rho g r}$

$$\Rightarrow \quad h \propto \frac{1}{r} \Rightarrow h_1 r_1 = h_2 r_2$$

$$\Rightarrow \quad (1.4 \text{ cm})\left(\frac{1 \text{ mm}}{\cos 0°}\right) = (1 \text{ cm})\, r_2$$

$$\Rightarrow \quad r_2 = 1.4 \text{ mm}$$

34. For equilibrium of water column,

$$T(2\pi r)\cos\theta + T(2\pi r)\cos\theta = mg$$

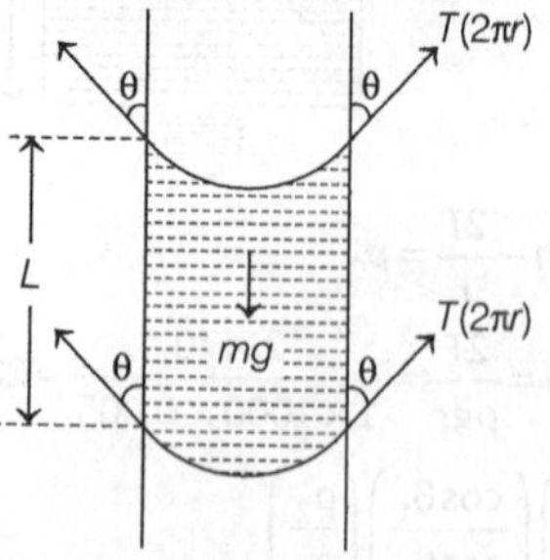

$$\Rightarrow \quad T(4\pi r)\cos 0° = (\rho \pi r^2 L)g \Rightarrow L = \frac{4T}{\rho g r}$$

35. $p_1 = p_2$

$$\Rightarrow p_0 - \frac{2T}{r_2} = p_0 - \frac{2T}{r_1} + \rho g h \quad \Rightarrow \quad T = \frac{\rho g h r_1 r_2}{2(r_2 - r_1)}$$

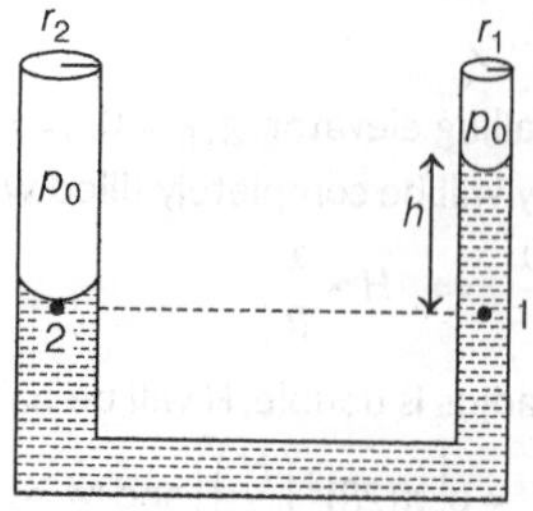

36. For equilibrium of liquid column,

$$2Tl\cos\theta = mg$$

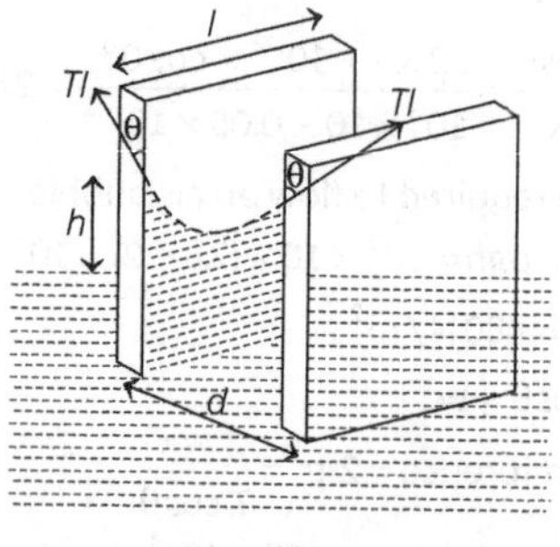

$$\Rightarrow \quad 2Tl\cos\theta = \rho(lhd)g \Rightarrow h = \frac{2T\cos\theta}{\rho g d}$$

Numerical Value Questions

1. F = Force due to surface tension $= T \times [2(6 + 0.2)] = 12.4\, T$

Apparent weight $= mg - B + F$

$$\Rightarrow \quad mg = mg - B + F$$

$$\Rightarrow \quad F = B$$

$$\Rightarrow \quad 12.4T = 1 \times \left(\frac{50}{100} \times 6 \times 1.5 \times 0.2\right) \times 1000$$

$$\Rightarrow \quad T = 72.58 \text{ dyne/cm} \simeq 73 \text{ dyne/cm}$$

2. $p = p_0 + \rho g h + \frac{2T}{R}$

$$= 10^5 + 10^3 \times 10 \times 6 + \frac{2 \times 0.07}{3.5 \times 10^{-6}} = 2 \times 10^5 \text{ Pa}$$

$$\rho = \frac{pM}{RT} \Rightarrow \frac{\rho_1}{\rho_2} = \frac{p_1}{p_2}$$

$$\Rightarrow \quad \frac{1.2}{\rho_2} = \frac{10^5}{2 \times 10^5}$$

$$\Rightarrow \quad \rho_2 = 2.4 \text{ kg/m}^3$$

3. $p_B = p_0 + \frac{2T}{3R},\ p_A = p_B + \frac{2T}{R} = p_0 + \frac{8T}{3R}$

$$p_A{}' = \text{Gauge pressure at } A = \frac{8T}{3R}$$

$$p_B{}' = \text{Gauge pressure at } B = \frac{2T}{3R}$$

$$\Rightarrow \quad \frac{p_A{}'}{p_B{}'} = 4$$

4. $B = \frac{\Delta p}{\left(\frac{\Delta V}{V}\right)} \Rightarrow \frac{\Delta V}{V} = \frac{\Delta p}{B} \Rightarrow \frac{3\Delta R}{R} = \frac{2T}{BR}$

$$\Rightarrow \quad \Delta R = \frac{2T}{3B} = \frac{2 \times 0.075}{3 \times 1.25 \times 10^8} = 4 \times 10^{-10} \text{ m} = 4 \text{ Å}$$

5. $h = \frac{2T\cos\theta}{\rho g R}$

$$\Rightarrow \quad 3 = \frac{2T\cos 0°}{1.5 \times 1000 \times 0.25 \times 10^{-1}}$$

$$\Rightarrow \quad T = 56.25 \text{ dyne/cm}$$

$$\Delta p = \frac{4T}{r} = \frac{4 \times 56.25}{0.5} = 450 \text{ dyne/cm}^2$$

6. For an isothermal situation,

$$p_A V_A + p_B V_B = p_C V_C$$

$$\Rightarrow \quad \left(p_0 + \frac{4T}{a}\right)\left(\frac{4}{3}\pi a^3\right) + \left(p_0 + \frac{4T}{b}\right)\left(\frac{4}{3}\pi b^3\right)$$

$$= \left(p_0 + \frac{4T}{c}\right)\left(\frac{4}{3}\pi c^3\right)$$

$$\Rightarrow \quad p_0\left(\frac{4}{3}\pi a^3 + \frac{4}{3}\pi b^3 - \frac{4}{3}\pi c^3\right) + \frac{4T}{3}(4\pi a^2 + 4\pi b^2 - 4\pi c^2) = 0$$

$$\Rightarrow \quad p_0 V + \left(\frac{4T}{3}\right) S = 0 \Rightarrow 3p_0 V + 4TS = 0$$

So, $\lambda = 3$

7. $h = \frac{2T\cos\theta}{\rho g R} = \frac{2 \times 0.075 \times \cos 0°}{10^3 \times 10 \times 0.5 \times 10^{-3}} = 3 \text{ cm}$

Depth of the point from the water level in the pot

$$= 5 - 3 = 2 \text{ cm}$$

Gauge pressure $= \rho g h = 10^3 \times 10 \times 2 \times 10^{-2} = 200 \text{ N/m}^2$

8. Initial pressure inside bubble $= p_0 + \dfrac{4T}{r}$

Final pressure inside bubble $= p_{\text{new}} + \dfrac{4T}{(r/2)}$

For isothermal condition,

$p_1V_1 = p_2V_2$

$$\Rightarrow \quad \left(p_0 + \frac{4T}{r}\right)\left(\frac{4}{3}\pi r^3\right) = \left(p_{\text{new}} + \frac{8T}{r}\right)\frac{4}{3}\pi\left(\frac{r}{2}\right)^3$$

$$\Rightarrow \quad p_{\text{new}} = 8p_0 + \frac{24T}{r} = 8 \times 10^5 + \frac{24 \times 0.08}{1.92 \times 10^{-5}}$$

$$= 9 \times 10^5 \text{ N/m}^2$$

Level 3

Single Choice Correct Questions

1. F = Force on each leg due to surface tension $= T(2\pi a)$
   So, $W = 8F = 8[T(2\pi a)] = 16\pi Ta$
2. $F = T[2\pi(R + r)]$
   $\Rightarrow \quad 3.97 \times 980 = T(2 \times 3.14(4.35 + 4.25))$
   $\Rightarrow \quad T = 72$ dyne/cm
3. For equilibrium of drop, $mg = B + F$
   $$\Rightarrow \quad \rho\left(\frac{4}{3}\pi r^3\right)g = d\left(\frac{2}{3}\pi r^3\right)g + \sigma(2\pi r)$$
   $$\Rightarrow \quad r = \sqrt{\frac{3\sigma}{g(2\rho - d)}}$$
   Diameter of drop $= 2r = \sqrt{\dfrac{12\sigma}{g(2\rho - d)}}$
4. For equilibrium of cube, $B = mg + F$

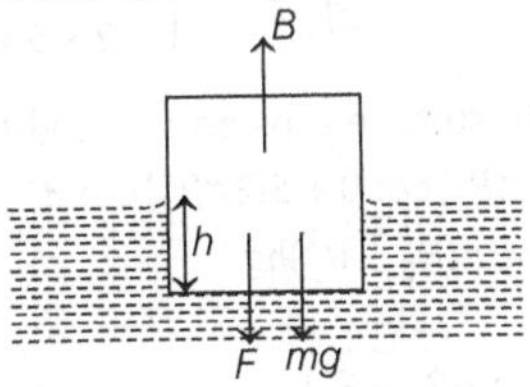

$\Rightarrow 1 \times (3^2 \times h) \times 1000 = 20 \times 1000 + 70(4 \times 3)$

$\Rightarrow \quad h = 2.315$ cm

5. From volume conservation, $(4\pi R^2)d = \dfrac{4}{3}\pi r^3$
   $$\Rightarrow \quad r = (3R^2 d)^{1/3}$$
   Δp_1 = Excess pressure in the drop $= \dfrac{2T}{r}$

   Δp_2 = Excess pressure in the bubble $= \dfrac{4T}{R}$

   $$\frac{\Delta p_1}{\Delta p_2} = \frac{R}{2r} = \frac{R}{2(3R^2d)^{1/3}} = \left(\frac{R}{24d}\right)^{1/3}$$
6. For isothermal situation,
   $$p_1V_1 = p_2V_2$$
   $$\Rightarrow \quad \left(p_1 + \frac{4\sigma}{r}\right)\left(\frac{4}{3}\pi r^3\right) = \left(p_2 + \frac{4\sigma}{(r/2)}\right)\frac{4}{3}\pi\left(\frac{r}{2}\right)^3$$
   $$\Rightarrow \quad p_2 = 8p_1 + \frac{24\sigma}{r}$$
7. From Lami's theorem, $\dfrac{F}{\sin\alpha} = \dfrac{F}{\sin\beta} = \dfrac{F}{\sin\gamma}$

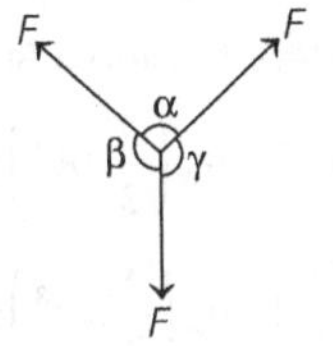

$\Rightarrow \quad \alpha = \beta = \gamma$

$\because \quad \alpha + \beta + \gamma = 360°$

$\Rightarrow \quad \alpha = \beta = \gamma = 120°$

8. Maximum load $= \Delta p(\pi R^2) = \left(\dfrac{4T}{R}\right)\pi R^2$
   $= 4T\pi R = 4 \times 500 \times 3.14 \times 5$
   $= 31400$ N
   $\simeq 3000$ kg-wt
9. $\cos\theta = \dfrac{R - h}{R}$

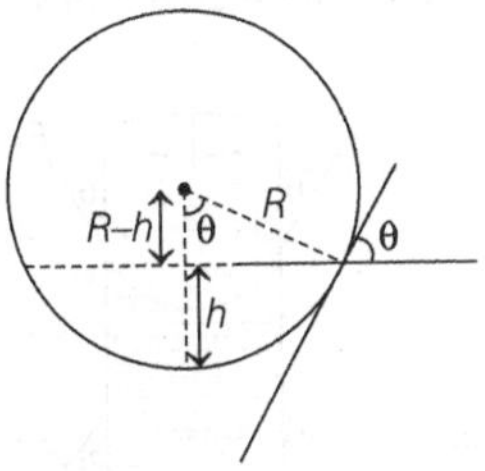

$$\Rightarrow \quad \theta = \cos^{-1}\left(\frac{R - h}{R}\right)$$

10. $F_1 = p_{\text{avg}}(lh) = \left(p_0 - \rho g\dfrac{h}{2}\right)lh$

$F_2 = p_0(lh)$

$F_3 = \gamma l$

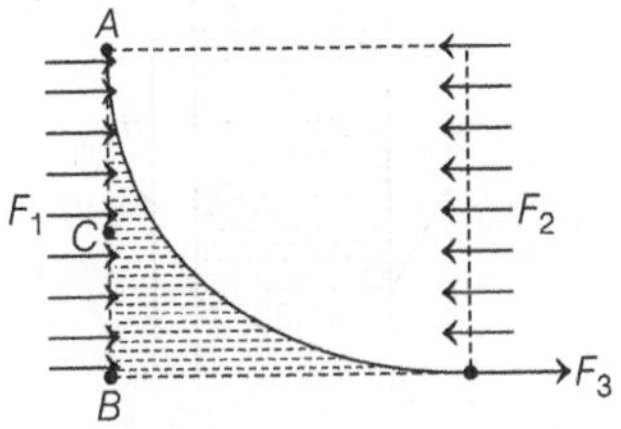

For equilibrium of liquid column,

$F_1 + F_3 = F_2$

$$\Rightarrow \quad \left[p_0 - \rho g\left(\frac{h}{2}\right)\right]lh + \gamma l = p_0(lh) \Rightarrow h = \sqrt{\frac{2\gamma}{\rho g}}$$

11. For bubble to detach,

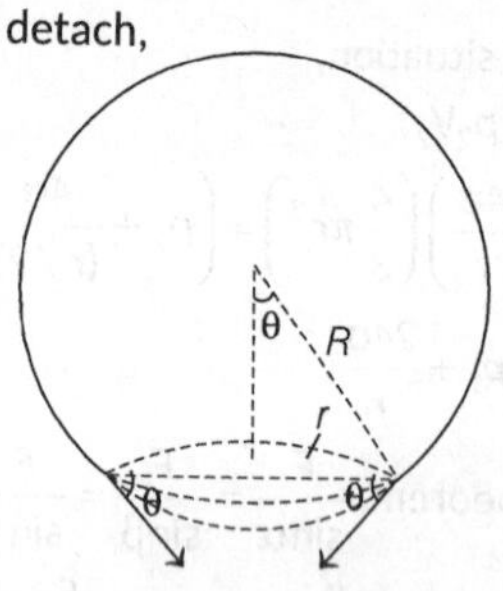

Force due to surface tension = Buoyant force

$$\Rightarrow \quad T(2\pi r)\sin\theta = \rho_w\left(\frac{4}{3}\pi R^3\right)g$$

$$\Rightarrow \quad T(2\pi r)\left(\frac{r}{R}\right) = \rho_w\left(\frac{4}{3}\pi R^3\right)g$$

$$\Rightarrow \quad r = R^2\sqrt{\frac{2\rho_w g}{3T}}$$

12. $\Delta h = \dfrac{2T}{\rho g r}$

$$\Rightarrow r = \frac{2T}{\rho g \Delta h} = \frac{2\times 0.46}{13600\times 10\times 4.6\times 10^{-3}} = \frac{1}{680}\text{ m}$$

13.
$$\begin{aligned} F &= mg + F_1\cos\theta + F_2\cos\theta \\ &= mg + T(2\pi R)\cos\theta + T(2\pi R)\cos\theta \\ &= mg + 2T\pi R = 10.4\,\pi\text{ mN} \end{aligned}$$

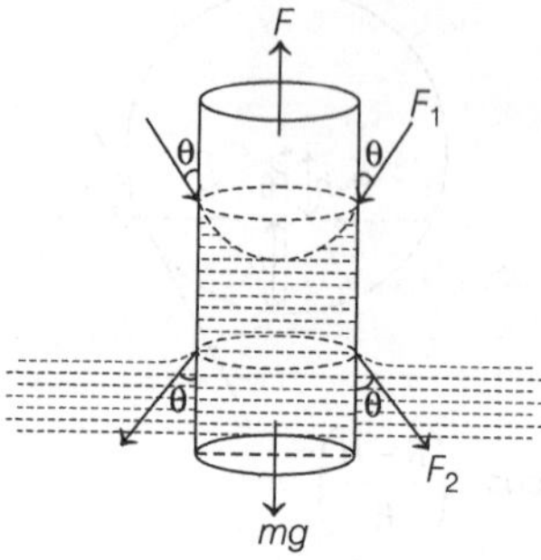

14. $2(T(2\pi R)\cos\theta) = (\rho\pi R^2 h_{max})g$

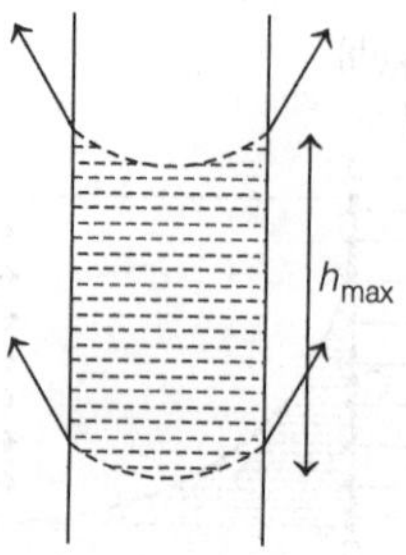

$$\Rightarrow \quad 2(\rho\pi R^2 hg) = \rho\pi R^2 h_{max} g$$

$$\Rightarrow \quad h_{max} = 2h$$

The length of water column remaining will be $2h$, if $l > h$ and $l + h$ if $l < h$

15. $R\cos\left(\theta + \dfrac{\alpha}{2}\right) = b$

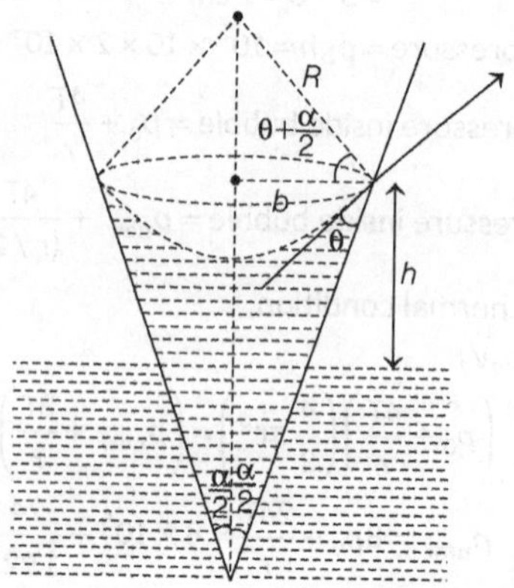

Excess pressure on concave side of meniscus $= \dfrac{2S}{R}$

$$\Rightarrow \quad \rho g h = \frac{2S}{R} \quad \Rightarrow \quad h = \frac{2S}{\rho g R} = \frac{2S}{\rho g b}\cos\left(\theta + \frac{\alpha}{2}\right)$$

16. $p_0 + \rho_1 g h = p_0 - \dfrac{2T}{r} + \rho_2 g h \Rightarrow T = \dfrac{r}{2}(\rho_2 - \rho_1)gh$

17. For air inside capillary under isothermal condition,

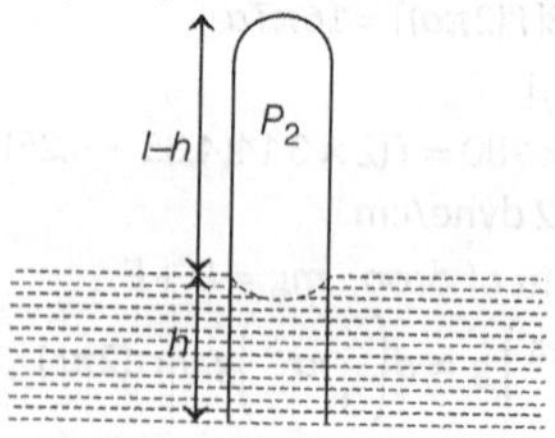

$$p_1V_1 = p_2V_2$$

$$\Rightarrow \quad p_0Al = \left(p_0 + \frac{2T}{r}\right)A(l-h)$$

$$\Rightarrow \quad h = \frac{l}{1 + \dfrac{p_0 r}{2T}} = \frac{11}{1 + \left(\dfrac{10^5\times 10\times 10^{-6}}{2\times 5\times 10^{-2}}\right)} = 1\text{ cm}$$

18. Force due to surface tension = Weight of liquid risen

$$\Rightarrow \quad S(2\pi R_1)\cos\theta + S(2\pi R_2)\cos\theta = \rho\pi(R_2^2 - R_1^2)hg$$

$$\Rightarrow \quad h = \frac{2S}{\rho g(R_2 - R_1)} \qquad [\because \theta = 0°]$$

19. In equilibrium, $T(2\pi R)\cos\theta = (\rho\pi R^2 h)g$

W = Work done by surface tension $= [T(2\pi R)\cos\theta]h = \rho\pi R^2 h^2 g$

ΔU = Increase in gravitational potential energy of liquid

$$= (\rho\pi R^2 h)\,g\left(\frac{h}{2}\right) = \frac{\rho\pi R^2 g h^2}{2}$$

Heat produced $= W - \Delta U$

$$= \rho\pi R^2 h^2 g - \frac{\rho\pi R^2 g h^2}{2}$$

$$= \frac{\rho\pi R^2 gh^2}{2} = \frac{\rho\pi R^2 g}{2}\left(\frac{2T\cos\theta}{\rho g R}\right)^2$$

$$= \frac{2\pi T^2\cos^2\theta}{\rho g}$$

20. Force due to colliding air molecules

$$= \frac{dp}{dt} = \frac{d(\rho V v)}{dt} = \rho\frac{dV}{dt}v = \rho A v^2 = \rho\pi b^2 v^2$$

Force due to surface tension $= T(2\pi b)\cos\theta \times 2$

When bubble separates, $2T(2\pi b)\left(\frac{b}{R}\right) = \rho\pi b^2 v^2$

$$\Rightarrow \qquad R = \frac{4T}{\rho v^2}$$

21. Δp = Pressure difference for a cylindrical surface.

$$= \frac{T}{R} = \frac{T}{(d/2)} = \frac{2T}{d}$$

$$\text{Force} = \Delta p A = \left(\frac{2T}{d}\right)\left(\frac{V}{d}\right) = \frac{2T}{d^2}\left(\frac{m}{\rho}\right) = \frac{2Tm}{\rho d^2}$$

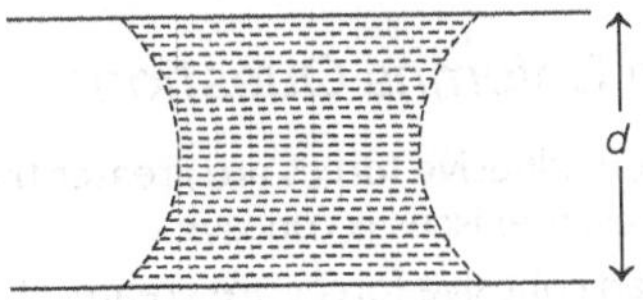

22. For equilibrium of liquid risen,

$$T(2l) = \rho(lhd)g \Rightarrow h = \frac{2T}{\rho g d}$$

Work done in separating the plates should be equal to rise in potential energy to raise the water to height h.

Work done $= \rho(lhd)g\left(\frac{h}{2}\right)$

If F is the force of attraction,

$$Fd = \rho g\left(\frac{h}{2}\right)(lhd)$$

$$\Rightarrow \qquad F = \frac{\rho g l h^2}{2} = \frac{\rho g l}{2}\left(\frac{2T}{\rho g d}\right)^2 = \frac{2T^2 l}{\rho g d^2}$$

Multiple Choice(s) Correct Questions

1. The thread will take a circular shape as the remaining film will try to minimise its area. Lets take an element of width $Rd\theta$ on the thread.

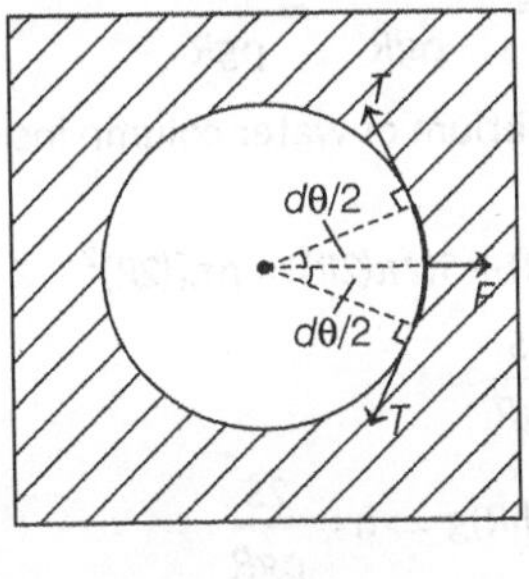

For equilibrium of element,

$$2T\sin\left(\frac{d\theta}{2}\right) = F$$

$$\Rightarrow \qquad Td\theta = 2S(Rd\theta)$$

$$\Rightarrow \qquad T = 2SR = 2S\left(\frac{l}{2\pi}\right) = \frac{Sl}{\pi}$$

2.

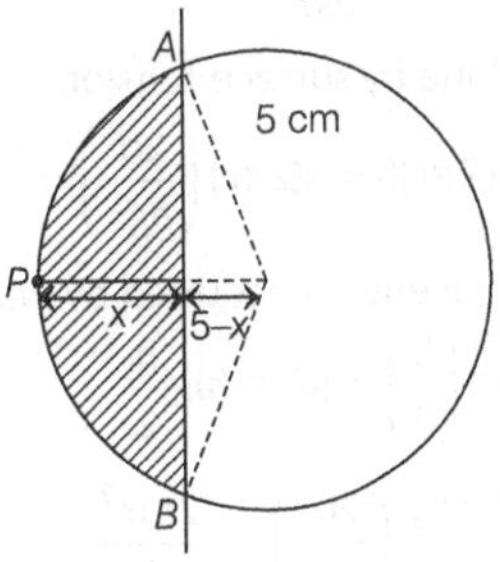

$$F_{AB} = 2Tl_{AB}$$

$$\Rightarrow \qquad 16\times 10^{-3} = 2(0.1)l_{AB}$$

$$\Rightarrow \qquad l_{AB} = 8 \text{ cm}$$

$$l_{AB} = 2\sqrt{5^2 - (5-x)^2} = 8$$

$\Rightarrow x = 2$ cm and $x = 8$ cm

3. In equilibrium, $2Tl = mg \Rightarrow l = \frac{mg}{2T}$

Lets displace wire BC by a distance x from equilibrium position.

$$\Sigma F = ma \Rightarrow mg - 2T(l + 2x\tan 30°) = ma$$

$$\Rightarrow \qquad a = -\left(\frac{4T}{\sqrt{3}m}\right)x$$

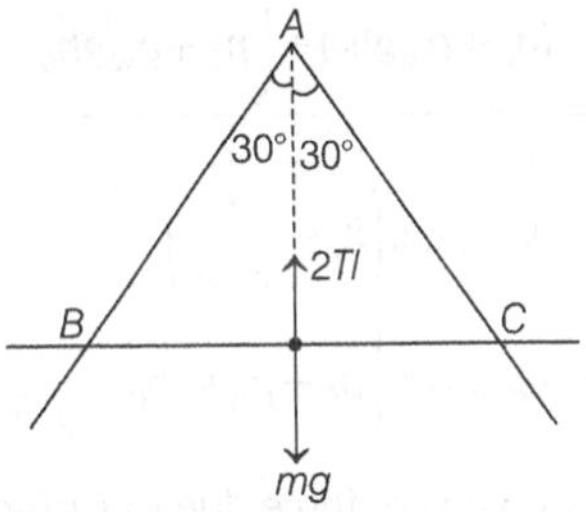

$$T = 2\pi\sqrt{\frac{\sqrt{3}m}{4T}} = \pi\sqrt{\frac{\sqrt{3}m}{T}}$$

4. From volume conservation, $n\frac{4}{3}\pi r^3 = \frac{4}{3}\pi R^3$

$$\Rightarrow \qquad R = n^{1/3}r$$

Energy released $= E_2 - E_1 = nT(4\pi r^2) - T(4\pi R^2)$

$$= T(4\pi r^2)\left(n - \left(\frac{R}{r}\right)^2\right) = E(n - n^{2/3})$$

5. A, B, C, D

6. For capillary of insufficient length, liquid will not come out of capillary and radius of meniscus increases.

7. (B, C, D)

8. Pressure at $p = p_0 - \rho g \frac{h}{2}$

Since, pressure at p is less than p_0, water will not come out of the tube from pinhole.

9. Capillary rise $= h = \frac{2\alpha}{dgr}$

W = Work done by surface tension

$$= \alpha(2\pi r)h = \alpha(2\pi r)\left(\frac{2\alpha}{dgr}\right) = \frac{4\pi\alpha^2}{dg}$$

ΔU = Potential energy acquired by water

$$= mg\left(\frac{h}{2}\right) = (d\pi r^2 h)g\frac{h}{2}$$

$$= \frac{d\pi r^2 g}{2}\left(\frac{2\alpha}{dgr}\right)^2 = \frac{2\pi\alpha^2}{dg}$$

Heat developed $= W - \Delta U$

$$= \frac{4\pi\alpha^2}{dg} - \frac{2\pi\alpha^2}{dg} = \frac{2\pi\alpha^2}{dg}$$

10. The two tree liquid surfaces must provide a net upward force due to surface tension to balance the weight of the liquid column.

Comprehension Based Questions

1. Net force exerted by liquid on styrofoam is buoyant force

$$= \rho_w g \frac{l^2 L}{2}$$

2. F = Force on any one of the slant face

$$p_{avg} = \frac{(p_0 + \rho_w g h_0) + \left(p_0 + \rho_w g h_0 - \frac{l}{\sqrt{2}}\right)}{2}$$

$$= p_0 + \rho_w g\left(h_0 - \frac{l}{2\sqrt{2}}\right)$$

$$F = p_{avg}A = \left[p_0 + \rho_w g\left(h_0 - \frac{l}{2\sqrt{2}}\right)\right]Ll$$

3. Resultant downward force due to surface tension

$$= \sqrt{2}T(L + l)$$

$$B = \text{Buoyant force} = \frac{3}{8}\rho_w g L l^2$$

$$\text{Weight} = \frac{\rho_f g L l^2}{2}$$

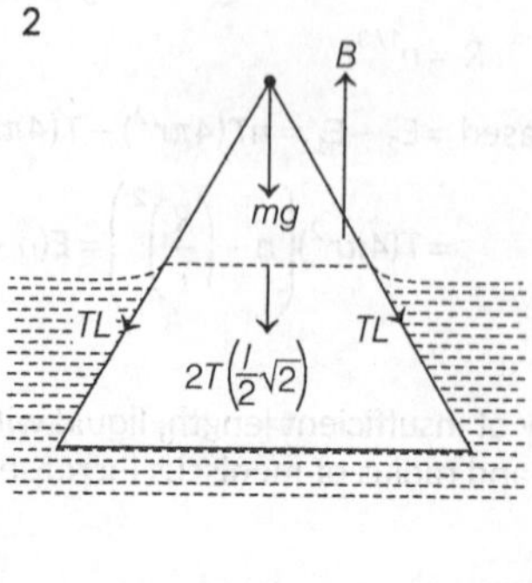

For equilibrium,

$$\Rightarrow \quad mg + \frac{\rho_f g L l^2}{2} + \sqrt{2}T(L + l) = \frac{3}{8}\rho_w g L l^2$$

$$\Rightarrow \quad m = -\frac{\rho_f L l^2}{2} + \frac{3}{8}\rho_w L l^2 - \frac{\sqrt{2}T(L + l)}{g}$$

4. $r = \frac{R}{\cos\theta} \Rightarrow r = \frac{R}{\cos 0^\circ} = R$

5. $S(2\pi R) + S(2\pi R) = (\rho\pi R^2 h)g$

$$h = \frac{4S}{\rho R g}$$

6. For capillary of insufficient length,

$$h_1 r_1 = h_2 r_2 \Rightarrow \left(\frac{4s}{\rho R g}\right)R = \left(\frac{S}{\rho R g}\right)\left(\frac{R}{\cos\theta}\right)$$

$$\Rightarrow \quad \cos\theta = \frac{1}{4}$$

$$\Rightarrow \quad \theta = \cos^{-1}\left(\frac{1}{4}\right)$$

Match the Columns Questions

1. (a) When adhesive forces are greater than cohesive forces, meniscus is concave.

(b) When cohesive forces are greater than adhesive forces, meniscus is convex.

(c) and (d) Pressure on concave side is more than pressure on convex side.

2. (a) $\Delta p_{drop} = \frac{2T}{R} \Rightarrow \Delta p_{drop} \propto \frac{1}{R}$

As temperature increases, surface tension decreases. Hence, Δp also decreases.

(b) $\Delta p_{\text{soap bubble}} = \frac{4T}{R} \Rightarrow \Delta p_{\text{soap bubble}} \propto \frac{1}{R}$

(c) $\Delta p_{\text{air cavity}} = \frac{4T}{R} \Rightarrow \Delta p_{\text{air cavity}} \propto \frac{1}{R}$

(d) Surface tension decreases with increase in temperature.

3. (a) For silver tube in water, angle of contact is 90°. So,

$$h = \frac{2S\cos\theta}{\rho g R} = 0$$

(b) For glass tube in water, angle of contact is 0°.

$$\text{So, } h = \frac{2S\cos 0^\circ}{\rho g R} = \frac{2S}{\rho g R}$$

(c) For equilibrium of water column inside hollow glass cylinder,

$$S(2\pi R) + S(2\pi(2R)) = \rho\pi[(2R)^2 - R^2]hg$$

$$\Rightarrow \quad h = \frac{2S}{\rho g R}$$

(d) $Sl + Sl = \rho(lhR)g \Rightarrow h = \frac{2S}{\rho g R}$

4. (a) When bigger drop splits into small drops, surface area increases and hence surface energy increases and temperature changes.
(b) Surface energy decreases and temperature changes.
(c) In spraying of liquid, surface area increases. Hence, surface energy increases and temperature changes.
(d) $(4\pi R^2)t = n(4\pi r^2)t \Rightarrow 4\pi R^2 = n(4\pi r^2)$

Surface area remains unchanged. So, surface energy and temperature will remain unchanged.

Numerical Value Questions

1. $p_1 - \frac{2T}{R} + \rho gh = p_0$

$\Rightarrow \quad 200 - \frac{2\times 72}{0.02} + 1\times 1000 \times h = 1000$

$\Rightarrow \quad h = 8$ cm

2. For equilibrium of wire, $2Tl\sin\theta = mg$

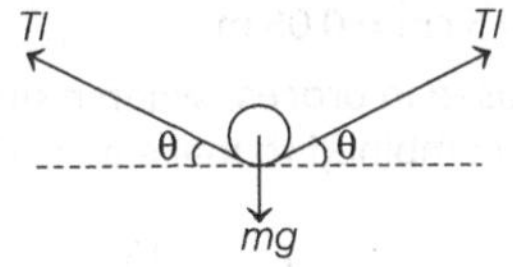

$\Rightarrow \quad 2Tl\left(\frac{a}{\sqrt{1^2+(0.01)^2}}\right) = \lambda lg$

$\Rightarrow \quad T = \frac{\lambda g}{2a} = \frac{10\times 10^{-3}\times 10}{2\times 0.01} = 5$ N/m

3. Force due to water on the capillary

$= T(2\pi R) + T(2\pi R) = T(4\pi R)$

$T(4\pi R) = 0.135\times 980$

$\Rightarrow \quad 70\times 4\times 3.14R = 0.135\times 980$

$\Rightarrow \quad R = 0.15$ cm $= 1.5$ mm

So, $\lambda = 15$

4. For figure (a)

$2T = 2\sigma(2R)$

$\Rightarrow \quad 2T = 4\sigma R$

$\Rightarrow \quad T = 2\sigma R$

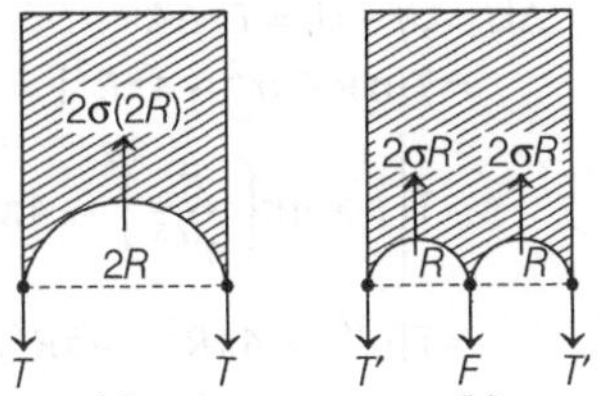

(a) (b)

For figure (b)

$F + 2T' = 2\sigma R + 2\sigma R$

$\Rightarrow \quad F + 2T' = 4\sigma R$

$\Rightarrow \quad F + 2\left(\frac{T}{2}\right) = 4\sigma R$

$\Rightarrow \quad F + 2\sigma R = 4\sigma R$

$\Rightarrow \quad F = 2\sigma R$

$\Rightarrow \quad \sigma = \frac{F}{2R} = \frac{0.01}{2\times 0.1} = 5\times 10^{-2}$ N/m

5. $p_B = p_0 + \frac{2T}{3R}$,

$p_C = p_0 + \frac{2T}{3R} + \frac{2T}{R} + \frac{4T}{(R/2)} = p_0 + \frac{32T}{3R}$

$p_A' =$ Gauge pressure at $A = \frac{2T}{3R}$

$p_C' =$ Gauge pressure at $C = \frac{32T}{3R}$

$\frac{p_C'}{p_A'} = 16$

6. $p_1 = p_0 - \rho g\left(\frac{h}{3}\right)$

$p_2 = p_0 - \rho g_{\text{eff}}\left(\frac{h}{3}\right) = p_0 - \rho(g+g)\left(\frac{h}{3}\right)$

$\Delta p = p_1 - p_2 = \frac{\rho gh}{3} \Rightarrow \frac{\rho gh}{\Delta p} = 3$

7. Lets consider a liquid column of height h and width dx at a distance x from the edge as shown in the figure.

Length of this strip $= x\,\delta\theta$

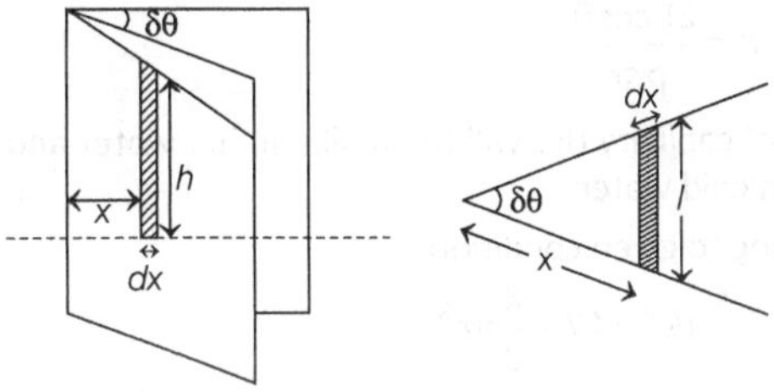

For equilibrium of strip,

$W = F_{\text{due to surface tension}}$

$\Rightarrow \rho(hdx)(x\,\delta\theta)g = 2Tdx$

$\Rightarrow \quad h = \frac{2T}{\rho gx\,\delta\theta}$

8. Let length of the tube be L.

For the air column inside capillary under isothermal condition,

$p_1V_1 = p_2V_2$

$\Rightarrow \quad p_0AL = \left(p_0 - \rho gh + \frac{2T}{r}\right)A(L-h)$

$\Rightarrow \quad L = \frac{p_0hr}{2T - \rho ghr} + h$

$\Rightarrow \quad L = \frac{(1.01\times 10^5)(0.01)(0.05\times 10^{-2})}{2\times 70\times 10^{-3} - (10^3)(9.8)(0.01)(0.05\times 10^{-2})} + 0.01$

$\Rightarrow \quad L = 5.56$ m

9. $V = \frac{\sigma R}{\varepsilon_0} \Rightarrow \sigma = \frac{V\varepsilon_0}{R}$

$$p_1V_1 = p_2V_2$$

$$\Rightarrow \left(p_0 + \frac{4T}{r}\right)\frac{4}{3}\pi r^3 = \left(p_0 + \frac{4T}{R} - \frac{\sigma^2}{2\varepsilon_0}\right)\frac{4}{3}\pi R^3$$

$$\Rightarrow p_0(R^3 - r^3) + 4T(R^2 - r^2) - \frac{1}{2}\varepsilon_0 V^2 R = 0$$

So, $\lambda = 4$

10. For the wider limb $p - \frac{2T}{r_2} = p_0$

$$\Rightarrow \qquad p = p_0 + \frac{2T}{r_2}$$

For the narrower limb, $p - \frac{2T}{r_1} + \rho gh = p_0$

$$\Rightarrow \qquad \left(p_0 + \frac{2T}{r_2}\right) - \frac{2T}{r_1} + \rho gh = p_0$$

$$\Rightarrow \qquad h = \frac{2T}{\rho g}\left(\frac{1}{r_1} - \frac{1}{r_2}\right)$$

$$\Rightarrow \qquad h = \frac{2 \times 7 \times 10^{-2}}{10^3 \times 10}\left(\frac{1}{0.25 \times 10^{-3}} - \frac{1}{0.5 \times 10^{-3}}\right)$$

$$= 0.028 \text{ m} = 28 \text{ mm}$$

Previous Years Questions

JEE Main

1. Surface tension will be less as temperature increases,

$$h = \frac{2T\cos\theta}{\rho gr}$$

Height of capillary rise will be smallar in hot water and larger in cold water.

2. According to given condition,

$$\frac{4}{3}\pi R^3 = 27 \times \frac{4}{3}\pi r^3$$

Where, r is radius of small liquid drop

$$\therefore \qquad R = 3r$$

$$\Rightarrow \qquad r = \frac{R}{3} \qquad \text{...(i)}$$

$\therefore$ Work done $= T \times \Delta A$

$$= T[27 \times 4\pi r^2 - 4\pi R^2]$$

$$= 4T\left[27\pi \times \left(\frac{R}{3}\right)^2 - \pi R^2\right] \qquad \text{[From Eq. (i)]}$$

$$= T[8\pi R^2]$$

$$= 8\pi TR^2$$

3. Surface energy = Surface tension × Area

$$\Rightarrow \qquad E_1 = S \times 4\pi r^2 \times 1000$$

and $\qquad E_2 = S \times 4\pi R^2$

where, $1000 \times \frac{4}{3}\pi r^3 = \frac{4}{3}\pi R^3$

So, $\frac{r}{R} = \frac{1}{10}$

Hence, $\frac{E_1}{E_2} = 1000 \times \left(\frac{r}{R}\right)^2 = \frac{1000}{100} = 10$

4. Height of a liquid column in a capillary is given by;

$$H = \frac{2S\cos\theta}{\rho Rg}$$

In liquid A, $H = 5$ cm,

$$5 = \frac{2S_A\cos\theta}{\rho_A Rg} \qquad \text{... (i)}$$

In liquid B, $h = \frac{2S_B\cos\theta}{\rho_B Rg} \qquad \text{... (ii)}$

Form Eqs. (i) and (ii), we get

$$\frac{h}{5} = \frac{S_B}{S_A}\cdot\frac{\rho_A}{\rho_B} = \frac{2S_A}{S_A}\cdot\frac{\rho_A}{2\rho_A} \qquad (\because S_B = 2S_A \text{ and } \rho_B = 2\rho_A)$$

$$= 1$$

$$\Rightarrow \qquad h = 5 \text{ cm} = 0.05 \text{ m}$$

5. Energy released in process when n small identical drops of radius r are combined to make a big drop of radius R is given as

$$\Delta U = 4\pi r^2 \times T\left(n - n^{\frac{2}{3}}\right)$$

where, T = Surface tension

Here, $\quad T = 0.07$ N/m or 7×10^{-2}N/m

$$r = 1 \text{ mm} = 10^{-3} \text{ m}$$

$$\Delta U = 4 \times \frac{22}{7} \times (10^{-3})^2 \times 7 \times 10^{-2}(1000 - 100)$$

$$\Rightarrow \Delta U = 7.92 \times 10^{-4} \text{ J}$$

6. Let the radius of bigger drop and smaller drops of mercury be R and r respectively.

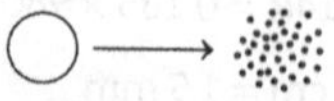

$$V = \text{constant}$$

$$\frac{4}{3}\pi R^3 = n \times \frac{4}{3}\pi r^3$$

$$\Rightarrow \qquad R = n^{\frac{1}{3}} r$$

Gain in surface energy,

$$\Delta U = U_f - U_i = T \cdot \Delta A$$

$$= T[n \times 4\pi r^2 - 4\pi R^2]$$

$$= T\left[n \times 4\pi\left(\frac{R}{n^{1/3}}\right)^2 - 4\pi R^2\right]$$

$$= T[n^{1/3} \times 4\pi R^2 - 4\pi R^2]$$

$$\Delta U = T \times 4\pi R^2[n^{\frac{1}{3}} - 1]$$

Given that, $T = 0.45 \text{ Nm}^{-1}$

$$R = 10^{-3} \text{ m}$$

$\Rightarrow \quad n = 125$

$\therefore \quad \Delta U = 0.45 \times 4\pi \times (10^{-3})^2 \quad [(125)^{1/3} - 1]$

$\Delta U = 2.26 \times 10^{-5}$ J

7. Given, depth,

$h = 10$ cm $= 0.1$ m

Radius of bubble, $r = 1$ mm $= 10^{-3}$ m

Surface, tension, $T = 0.075$ N/m

$\therefore$ Excess pressure in side the air bubble

$$\Delta p = \rho gh + \frac{2T}{r}$$
$$= 10^3 \times 9.8 \times 0.1 + \frac{2 \times 0.075}{10^{-3}}$$
$$= 1130 \text{ N/m}^2$$

8. Given,

$$S.T = 3.5 \times 10^{-2} \text{ N/m}$$
$$r_2 = 20 \text{ cm} = 20 \times 10^{-2} \text{ m} = 0.2 \text{ m}$$
$$r_1 = 0.1 \text{ m}$$

Workdone $=$ ST $\times$ (Change in Area) $\times 2$

$$= 3.5 \times 10^{-2} \times 2 \times (4\pi r_2^2 - 4\pi r_1^2)$$
$$= 3.5 \times 10^{-2} \times 2 \times 4\pi \times (r_2^2 - r_1^2)$$
$$= 3.5 \times 10^{-2} \times 8\pi(4-1) \times 10^{-4}$$
$$= 3.5 \times 10^{-2} \times 8\pi \times 3 \times 10^{-4}$$
$$= 3.5 \times 10^{-2} \times 8 \times \frac{22}{7} \times 3 \times 10^{-4}$$
$$= 264 \times 10^{-4} \text{ J}$$

9. If R be the radius of big (original) spherical drop and r be the radius of small drops, then

$$\frac{4}{3}\pi R^3 = 1000 \times \frac{4}{3}\pi r^3$$

$\Rightarrow \quad R = 10r \Rightarrow r = \frac{R}{10} \quad$ ...(i)

Initial surface area of spherical drop,

$$A = 4\pi R^2$$

$\therefore$ Initial surface energy of original drop,

$$U_i = T \cdot A = T \cdot 4\pi R^2$$

$U_i = 4\pi R^2 T \quad$ ...(ii)

When original drop splits into 1000 drops, then final energy,

$$U_f = 1000 \times 4\pi r^2 \cdot T$$

$= 1000 \times 4\pi \times \left(\frac{R}{10}\right)^2 T \quad$ [From Eq. (i)]

$$= 40\pi R^2 T$$

$\therefore \quad \frac{U_f}{U_i} = \frac{40\pi R^2 T}{4\pi R^2 T} = \frac{10}{1} = \left(\frac{10}{x}\right) \quad$ [given]

$\therefore \quad x = 1$

10. The water-oil contact angle is as shown below where; $\theta_c =$ Contact angle

Clearly $\theta_c > 90°$ (obtuse contact angle)

$\therefore$ Cohesive force > adhesive force

Hence, clothes containing oil or grease cannot be cleaned by water.

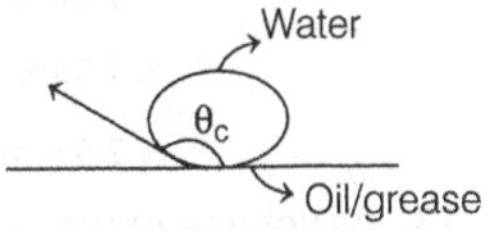

11. According to the given situation,

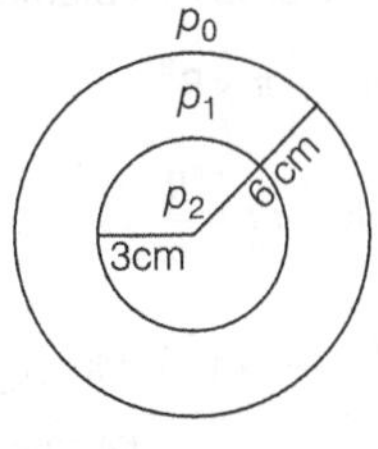

We know, excess pressure inside a soap bubble $= \frac{4T}{r}$

where, $T =$ surface tension of liquid soap solution

$\therefore \quad p_1 - p_0 = \frac{4T}{6}$ and $p_2 - p_1 = \frac{4T}{3}$

Adding both we get,

$$p_2 - p_0 = \frac{4T}{6} + \frac{4T}{3} = \frac{4T + 8T}{6} = \frac{12T}{6}$$

$\therefore \quad p_2 - p_0 = 2T \quad$ ...(i)

Also, according to the given situation,

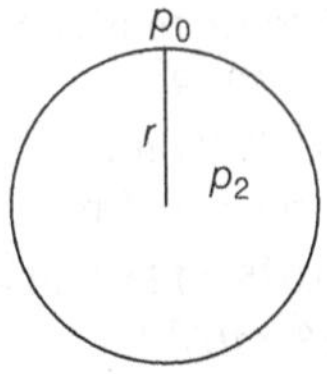

$p_2 - p_0 = \frac{4T}{r} \quad$ ...(ii)

$\therefore \quad$ From Eqs. (i) and (ii),

$$2T = \frac{4T}{r} \Rightarrow r = 2 \text{ cm}$$

12. Let R and r be the radius of big water drop and small water droplet, then

Volume of 1 big water drop $= 729 \times$ Volume of one small droplet

$\Rightarrow \quad \frac{4}{3}\pi R^3 = 729 \times \frac{4}{3}\pi r^3$

$\Rightarrow \quad R^3 = (9r)^3 \Rightarrow R = 9r$

$\Rightarrow \quad r = \frac{R}{9} = \frac{1}{9}$ cm $\quad (\because R = 1$ cm$)$

Gain in surface energy, $\Delta E = T.\Delta A$

$\Rightarrow \quad \Delta E = T \times (729 \times 4\pi r^2 - 4\pi R^2)$

$$= 75\left(729 \times 4\pi \times \frac{1}{9^2} - 4\pi(1)^2\right)$$
$$= 75(36\pi - 4\pi) = 32\pi \times 75$$
$$= 7.54 \times 10^3 \text{ dyne-cm}$$
$$= 7.54 \times 10^3 \times 10^{-7} \text{ N-m}$$

$[\because 1$ dyne-cm $= 10^{-7}$ N-m$]$

$= 7.54 \times 10^{-4}$ N-m

$= 7.54 \times 10^{-4}$ J

$\approx 7.5 \times 10^{-4}$ J

13. As volume of water remains same when water drop is broken into 64 water droplets.

$\therefore$ Volume of 64 small drops = Volume of 1 large drop

$$\Rightarrow \quad \frac{4}{3}\pi r^3 \times 64 = \frac{4}{3}\pi \times R^3$$

$$\Rightarrow \quad (4r)^3 = R^3 \text{ or } r = \frac{R}{4}$$

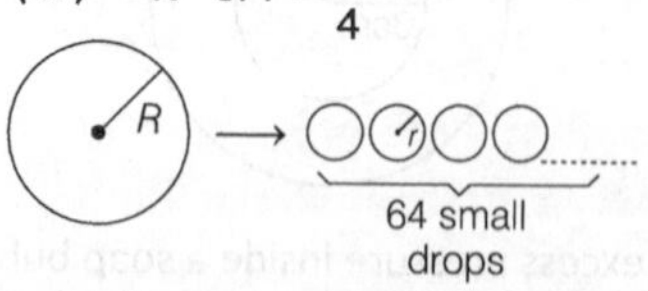

Now, increase in surface area of liquid drops

= surface area of 64 drops − surface area of initial large drop

$= 64 \times 4\pi r^2 - 4\pi R^2$

$= 64 \times 4\pi\left(\frac{R}{4}\right)^2 - 4\pi R^2$

$= 16\pi R^2 - 4\pi R^2$

$= 4\pi R^2(4-1) = 12\pi R^2$

Now, increase in surface energy,

ΔE = Surface tension × increase in surface area

$= T \times 12\pi R^2$

Here, $T = 0.075$ N / m,

$R = 1$ cm $= 10^{-2}$ m

$\Rightarrow \quad \Delta E = 0.075 \times 12 \times 3.14 \times (10^{-2})^2$

$= 2.8 \times 10^{-4}$ J

14. The given situation is shown below

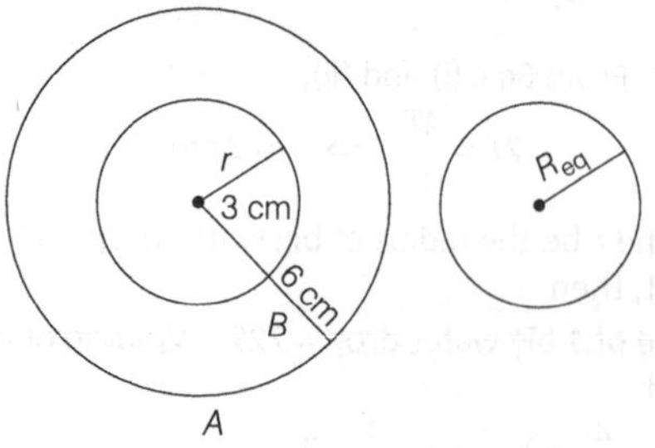

$r_A = 6$ cm

$r_B = 3$ cm

Excess pressure inside the soap bubble is given by

$$(\Delta p)_{\text{excess}} = \frac{4S}{r_A} + \frac{4S}{r_B}$$

According to the given question,

$$\frac{4S}{r_A} + \frac{4S}{r_B} = \frac{4S}{R_{eq}}$$

$$\Rightarrow \quad \frac{1}{r_A} + \frac{1}{r_B} = \frac{1}{R_{eq}} \Rightarrow \frac{1}{6} + \frac{1}{3} = \frac{1}{R_{eq}}$$

$$\Rightarrow \quad \frac{1+2}{6} = \frac{1}{R_{eq}} \Rightarrow \frac{1}{R_{eq}} = \frac{1}{2}$$

$$\Rightarrow \quad R_{eq} = 2\text{cm}$$

15. Given, radius of bubbles is r_1 and r_2, respectively.

Let, the radius of combined new bubble be r.

Excess pressure inside a soap bubble is

$$p = \frac{4T}{r}$$

where, T is surface tension.

and volume of a soap bubble is

$$V = \frac{4}{3}\pi r^3$$

By using law of conservation of energy

$$pV = p_1V_1 + p_2V_2$$

$$\frac{4T}{r} \times \frac{4}{3}\pi r^3 = \frac{4T}{r_1} \times \frac{4}{3}\pi r_1^3 + \frac{4T}{r_2} \times \frac{4}{3}\pi r_2^3$$

$$\Rightarrow \quad r^2 = r_1^2 + r_2^2$$

$$\Rightarrow \quad r = \sqrt{r_1^2 + r_2^2}$$

16. According to question, two small drops of mercury each of radius R coalesce to form a single large drop of radius R'.

According to question,

Volume of 1st small drop + Volume of 2nd small drop = Volume of a big drop

$$\frac{4}{3}\pi R^3 + \frac{4}{3}\pi R^3 = \frac{4}{3}\pi R'^3$$

$$\Rightarrow \quad R^3 + R^3 = R'^3$$

$$\Rightarrow \quad 2R^3 = R'^3$$

$$\text{or} \quad R'^3 = 2R^3$$

$$\Rightarrow \quad R' = (2)^{\frac{1}{3}}(R^3)^{\frac{1}{3}}$$

$$\Rightarrow \quad R' = 2^{\frac{1}{3}}(R) \quad \text{...(i)}$$

$\because$ So, considering the given scenario, we can write

$\text{Area}_{\text{initially}} = 4\pi R^2 + 4\pi R^2 = 2(4\pi R^2)$

and $\text{Area}_{\text{finally}} = 4\pi R'^2$

$$\therefore \quad \frac{\text{Surface energy initially}}{\text{Surface energy finally}}, \frac{U_i}{U_f} = \frac{A_i}{A_f}$$

$$\Rightarrow \quad \frac{U_i}{U_f} = \frac{2(4\pi R^2)}{4\pi R'^2}$$

$$\Rightarrow \quad \frac{U_i}{U_f} = \frac{2R^2}{R'^2} \quad \text{...(ii)}$$

$\therefore$ From Eqs. (i) and (ii), we get

$$\frac{U_i}{U_f} = \frac{2R^2}{(2^{1/3})^2 \cdot (R)^2}$$

$$\Rightarrow \quad \frac{U_i}{U_f} = \frac{2R^2}{2^{2/3} \cdot R^2}$$

$$\Rightarrow \quad \frac{U_i}{U_f} = 2^{1-\frac{2}{3}} \Rightarrow \frac{U_i}{U_f} = 2^{1/3}$$

$$\Rightarrow \quad U_i : U_f = 2^{1/3} : 1$$

17. When two soap bubbles of radii a and b ($b > a$) coalesce, it can be shown as follows

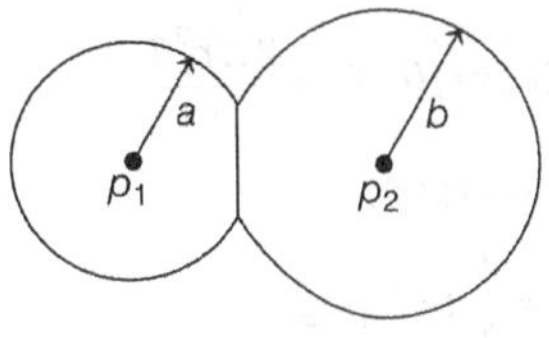

Pressure inside the bubble 1, $p_1 = p_0 + \frac{4T}{a}$

where, p_0 is the initial pressure,
T is the surface tension
and a is the radius of the bubble 1.

Similarly, pressure inside the bubble 2, $p_2 = p_0 + \frac{4T}{b}$

where, b is the radius of the bubble 2.

Excess pressure at common surface is given by

$$p_{ex} = p_1 - p_2$$

Let, r be the radius of common surface, then

$$\Rightarrow \quad \frac{4T}{r} = \left(p_0 + \frac{4T}{a}\right) - \left(p_0 + \frac{4T}{b}\right)$$

$$\Rightarrow \quad \frac{4T}{r} = p_0 + \frac{4T}{a} - p_0 - \frac{4T}{b}$$

$$\Rightarrow \quad \frac{4T}{r} = \frac{4T}{a} - \frac{4T}{b} \Rightarrow \frac{1}{r} = \frac{1}{a} - \frac{1}{b}$$

$$\Rightarrow \quad \frac{1}{r} = \frac{b-a}{ab} \Rightarrow r = \frac{ab}{b-a}$$

Which is the required expression for radius of curvature at common surface.

18. Given, radius of small drop $= r$

Radius of big drop $= R$

Surface tension $= T$

and mechanical equivalent of heat $= J$

As, small drops combine to form big drop.

$\therefore$ Volume of big drop $(V_B) = n \times$ Volume of small drop (V_S)

$$\Rightarrow \quad \frac{4}{3}\pi R^3 = n.\frac{4}{3}\pi r^3$$

$$\Rightarrow \quad nr^3 = R^3$$

$$\Rightarrow \quad r = \frac{R}{n^{1/3}} \quad \text{...(i)}$$

Surface energy of small drop

$(E_S) =$ Surface tension $(T) \times$ Area (A)

$$\Rightarrow \quad E_S = n \times 4\pi r^2 T \quad \text{and} \quad E_B = 4\pi R^2 T$$

Now, change in energy will be

$$\Delta E = E_B - E_S = 4\pi T(nr^2 - R^2)$$

$\therefore$ Heat energy per unit volume

$$= \frac{\Delta E}{V} = \frac{4\pi T(nr^2 - R^2)}{J \times \frac{4}{3}\pi R^3} = \frac{3T}{J}\left(\frac{nr^2}{R^3} - \frac{1}{R}\right)$$

$$= \frac{3T}{J}\left(n\frac{R^2}{n^{2/3}R^3} - \frac{1}{R}\right)$$

$$= \frac{3T}{J}\left[\frac{n^{1/3}}{R} - \frac{1}{R}\right] \quad \text{[from Eq. (i)]}$$

$$= \frac{3T}{J}\left[\frac{1}{r} - \frac{1}{R}\right]$$

JEE Advanced

1. $T =$ constant

$\Rightarrow \quad pV =$ constant

$p \propto \frac{1}{V}$, Volume $= \frac{100}{101}$ times,

so, pressure $= \frac{101}{100}$ times $= 1.01$ times

$\Rightarrow \quad p_r = 1.01\, p_0$

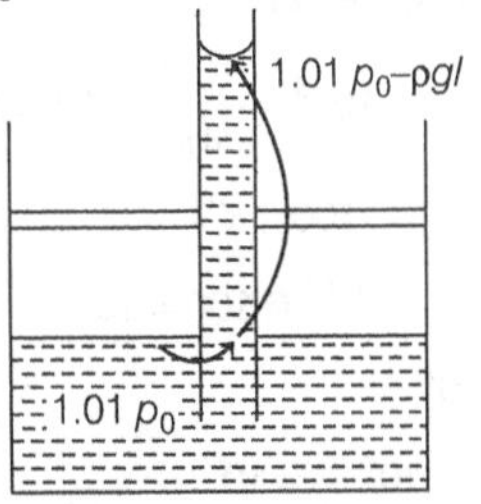

$$p_0 - \frac{2T}{R} = 1.01\, p_0 = \rho g h$$

$$\Rightarrow \quad \rho g h = 0.01\, p_0 + \frac{2T}{R}$$

$$\Rightarrow \quad (10^3)(10)h = (0.01)(10^5) + \frac{2 \times 0.075}{0.1 \times 10^{-3}}$$

$$\Rightarrow \quad h = \frac{2500}{10^4}\text{ m} = 25\text{ cm}$$

2. Pressure at the bottom of disc = Pressure due to surface tension

$$\rho g h = T\left(\frac{1}{R_1} + \frac{1}{R_2}\right)$$

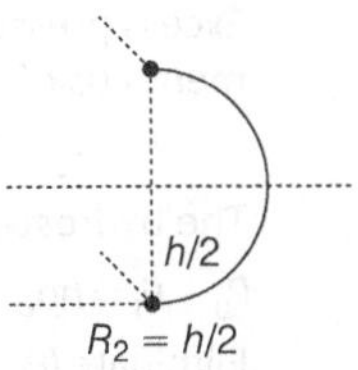

$$R_1 >>> R_2$$

So, $\frac{1}{R_1} <<< \frac{1}{R_2}$ and $R_2 = h/2$

$$\therefore \quad \rho g h = T\left(\frac{1}{R_1} + \frac{1}{R_2}\right) = T\left(0 + \frac{1}{h/2}\right)$$

$$h^2 = \frac{2T}{\rho g}$$

$$\Rightarrow \quad h = \sqrt{\frac{2T}{\rho g}} = \sqrt{\frac{2 \times 0.07}{10^3 \times 10}} = \sqrt{\frac{14 \times 100}{10^4 \times 100}}$$

$$h = \sqrt{14}\text{ mm} = 3.741$$

3. $h = \dfrac{2\sigma\cos\theta}{r\rho g}$

(a) $\rightarrow h \propto \dfrac{1}{r}$

(b) h depends upon σ.

(c) If lift is going up with constant acceleration.

$$g_{\text{eff}} = (g+a) \quad \Rightarrow h = \frac{2\sigma\cos\theta}{r\rho(g+a)}$$

It means h decreases.

(d) h is proportional to $\cos\theta$.

4. Equating the volumes, we have

$$\frac{4}{3}\pi R^3 = K \cdot \frac{4}{3}\pi r^3$$

$$\Rightarrow \qquad R = K^{1/3} r$$

$$\therefore \qquad \Delta U = T\Delta A = T(K \cdot 4\pi r^2 - 4\pi R^2)$$

$$= T(K \cdot 4\pi R^2 K^{-2/3} - 4\pi R^2)$$

$$\Delta U = 4\pi R^2 T[K^{1/3} - 1]$$

Putting the values, we get

$$10^{-3} = \frac{10^{-1}}{4\pi} \times 4\pi \times 10^{-4}[K^{1/3} - 1]$$

$$100 = K^{1/3} - 1$$

$$\Rightarrow \qquad K^{1/3} \cong 100 = 10^2$$

Given that $K = 10^{\alpha}$

$$\therefore \qquad 10^{\alpha/3} = 10^2$$

$$\Rightarrow \qquad \frac{\alpha}{3} = 2 \Rightarrow \alpha = 6$$

5. Let R be the radius of the meniscus formed with a contact angle θ. By geometry, this radius makes an angle $\theta + \dfrac{\alpha}{2}$ with the horizontal and,

$$\cos\left(\theta + \frac{\alpha}{2}\right) = b/R \qquad \text{...(i)}$$

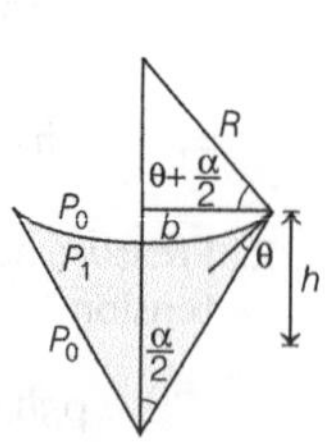

Let P_0 be the atmospheric pressure and P_1 be the pressure just below the meniscus. Excess pressure on the concave side of meniscus of radius R is,

$$P_0 - P_1 = 2S/R \qquad \text{...(ii)}$$

The hydrostatic pressure gives,

$$P_0 - P_1 = h\rho g \qquad \text{...(iii)}$$

Eliminate $(P_0 - P_1)$ from second and third equations and substitute R from first equation to get,

$$h = \frac{2S}{\rho g R} = \frac{2S}{b\rho g}\cos\left(\theta + \frac{\alpha}{2}\right)$$

6. Vertical force due to surface tension,

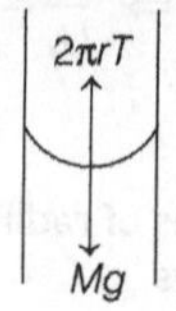

$$F_v = F\sin\theta = (T 2\pi r)(r/R) = \frac{2\pi r^2 T}{R}$$

$\therefore$ Correct option is (c).

7. $\dfrac{2\pi r^2 T}{R} = mg = \dfrac{4}{3}\pi R^3 \cdot \rho \cdot g$

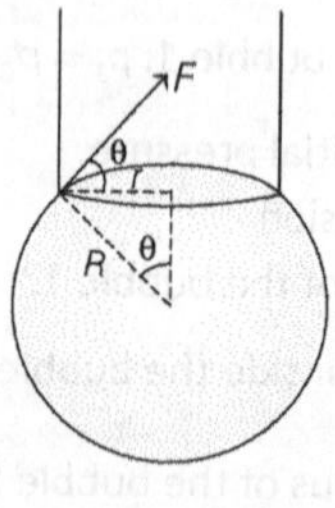

$$\therefore \qquad R^4 = \frac{3r^2 T}{2\rho g}$$

$$= \frac{3 \times (5 \times 10^{-4})^2 (0.11)}{2 \times 10^3 \times 10}$$

$$= 4.125 \times 10^{-12}\ \text{m}^4$$

$$\therefore \qquad R = 1.425 \times 10^{-3}\text{m}$$

$$\approx 1.4 \times 10^{-3}\ \text{m}$$

$\therefore$ Correct option is (a).

8. Surface energy, $E = (4\pi R^2)T$

$$= (4\pi)(1.4 \times 10^{-3})^2 (0.11)$$

$$= 2.7 \times 10^{-6}\ \text{J}$$

$\therefore$ Correct option is (b).

9. Although not given in the question, but we will have to assume that temperatures of A and B are same.

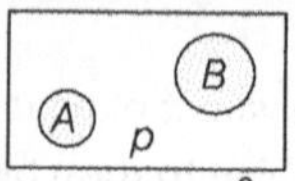

$p = 8\ \text{Nm}^{-2}$

$$\frac{n_B}{n_A} = \frac{p_B V_B / RT}{p_A V_A / RT} = \frac{p_B V_B}{p_A V_A}$$

$$= \frac{(p + 4S/r_A) \times (4/3)\pi (r_A)^3}{(p + 4S/r_B) \times (4/3)\pi (r_B)^3} \quad (S = \text{surface tension})$$

Substituting the values, we get

$$\frac{n_B}{n_A} = 6$$

CHAPTER~10

VISCOSITY

LEVEL 01 Starter Level

10.1 Newton's Law of Viscosity

1 A plate of area 2 m^2 is made to move horizontally with a speed of 2 m/s by applying a horizontal tangential force over the free surface of a liquid. If the depth of the liquid is 0.5 m and the liquid in contact with the plate is stationary. Coefficient of viscosity of liquid is 0.01 poise. Find the tangential force needed to move the plate.

2 A man is rowing a boat with a constant velocity v_0 in a river, the contact area of boat is A and coefficient of viscosity is η. The depth of river is *D*. Find the force required to row the boat.

3 A cubical block (of side 2 m) of mass 20 kg slides on inclined plane lubricated with the oil of viscosity $\eta = 10^{-1}$ poise with constant velocity of 10 m/s. Find out the thickness of layer of liquid. ($g = 10$ m/s^2)

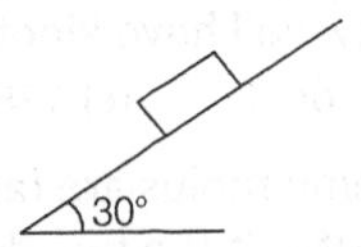

4 The velocity distribution in a viscous flow over a plate is given by $v = 4y - y^2$ for $y \leq 2$ m, where v = velocity in m/s at a point distant y from the plate. If the coefficient of dynamic viscosity is 1.5 Pa-s, determine the shear stress at $y = 0$ and at $y = 2.0$ m.

5 The space between two co-axial disks each of 20 cm diameter is filled with oil of 0.01 cm thickness. If the coefficient of viscosity of the oil is 0.08 N-s/m^2, calculate the torque required to rotate one disk relative to the other at 10 rev/s.

6 As per the shown figure, the central solid cylinder starts with initial angular velocity ω_0. Find out the time after which the angular velocity becomes half.

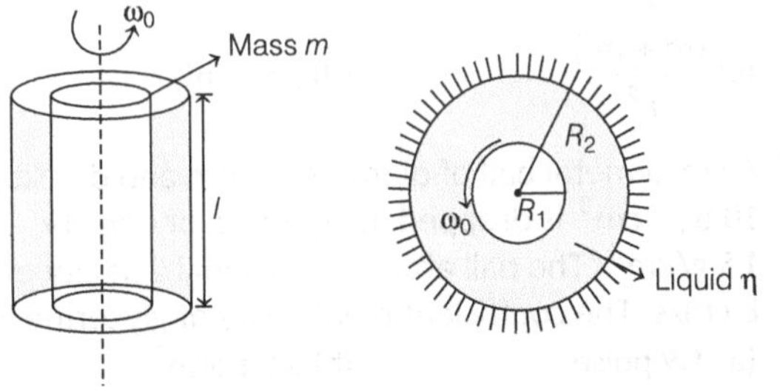

10.2 Stokes' Law

1 An air bubble of radius $r = 3$ mm moves up in a viscous liquid with a constant velocity $v = 0.7$ cm/s. If the density of the liquid is 1.75 gm/cc, find the viscosity of liquid (in poise). Neglect the density of air in comparison to that of the liquid.

2 If the terminal speed of a sphere of gold (density = 19.5 kg/m^3) is 0.2 m/s in a viscous liquid (density 1.5 kg/m^3), find the terminal speed of a sphere of silver (density = 10.5 kg/m^3) of the same size in the same liquid.

3 Eight equal drops of water each of radius $r = 2$ mm are falling through air with a terminal velocity of 16 cm/s. The eight drops combine to form a big drop. Calculate the terminal velocity of big drop.

4 A powder comprising particles of various sizes is stirred up in a vessel filled to a height of 10 cm with water. Assuming the particles to be spherical, find the size of the largest particle that will remain in suspension after 1 h (density of powder = 4 g/cm^3, viscosity of water = 0.01 poise).

5 A sphere having radius r and density 2ρ is projected vertically upwards in a liquid of density ρ and viscosity η with a velocity v_0. Find the time when the sphere is at its highest position in terms of v_0 and g.
(Given, $v_0 = \dfrac{2\rho r^2 g}{9\eta}$)

10.3 Reynold's Number

1 Calculate the Renyolds number for blood flowing at 30 cm/s through an aorta of radius 1.0 cm. Assume that the blood has a viscosity of 4 mPa-s and density of 1060 kg / m^3 . What is the nature of flow?

2 The diameter of the tap is 1.25 cm and the flow rate through it is 5×10^{-6} m^3 s^{-1} Is the flow turbulent? Given, coefficient of viscosity of water is 10^{-3} poise.

LEVEL 02 JEE Main Level

Single Choice Correct Questions

1 A ball of mass m and radius r is gently released in a viscous liquid. The mass of the liquid displaced by it is m', such that $m > m'$. The terminal velocity is proportional to

(a) $\dfrac{m - m'}{r}$ (b) $\dfrac{m + m'}{r}$

(c) $\dfrac{(m + m')}{r^2}$ (d) $(m - m') r^2$

2 A small metal ball of diameter 4 mm and density 10.5 g/ cm^3 is dropped in glycerine of density 1.5 g/cm^3. The ball attains a terminal velocity of 8 cm/s. The coefficient of viscosity of glycerine is

(a) 4.9 poise (b) 9.8 poise
(c) 98 poise (d) 980 poise

3 Neglecting the density of air, the terminal velocity obtained by a raindrop of radius 0.3mm falling through the air of viscosity 1.8×10^{-5} N / m^2 will be

(a) 10.9 m/s (b) 8.3 m/s
(c) 9.2 m/s (d) 7.6 m/s

4 A sphere of brass released in a long liquid column attains a terminal speed v_0. If the terminal speed is attained by a sphere of marble of the same radius and released in the same liquid is nv_0, then the value of n will be (Given, the specific gravities of brass, marble and liquid are 8.5, 2.5 and 0.8, respectively)

(a) 5/17 (b) 17/77 (c) 11/31 (d) 17/5

5 A spherical ball falls through viscous medium with terminal velocity v. If this ball is replaced by another ball of the same mass but half the radius, then the terminal velocity will be (neglect the effect of buoyancy).

(a) v (b) $2v$ (c) $4v$ (d) $8v$

6 When a ball is released from rest in a very long column of viscous liquid, its downward acceleration is a (just after release). Then its acceleration when it has acquired two-third of the maximum velocity is

(a) $a/3$ (b) $2a/3$
(c) $a/6$ (d) None of these

7 Which of the following is the incorrect graph for a sphere falling in a viscous liquid? (Given at $t = 0$, velocity $v = 0$ and displacement $x = 0$)

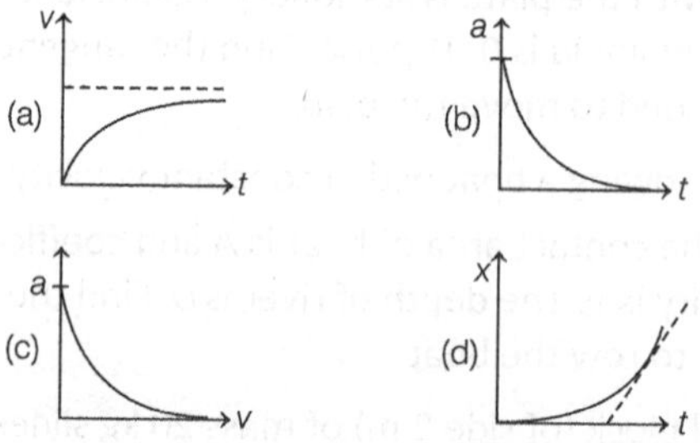

8 A spherical raindrop reaching the ground with terminal velocity has kinetic energy K. Another drop of twice the radius, also reaching the ground with terminal velocity, will have kinetic energy

(a) 16 K (b) 64 K (c) 128 K (d) 256 K

9 Two drops of same radius are falling through air with steady velocity of v. If the two drops coalesce, what would be the terminal velocity?

(a) 4 v (b) $(4)^{1/3} v$ (c) 2 v (d) 64 v

10 Between a plate of area 100 cm^2 and another plate of area 100 m^2, there is a 1 mm, thick layer of water. If the coefficient of viscosity of water is 0.01 poise, then the force required to move the smaller plate with a velocity 10 cm/s with reference to large plate is

(a) 100 dyne (b) 10^4 dyne
(c) 10^6 dyne (d) 10^9 dyne

11 Two large vertical parallel plates separated by a gap of d have a highly viscous liquid of density ρ and viscosity coefficient η, flowing steadily under gravity in the gap. The velocity gradient of flow near plates surface is

(a) $\frac{2\rho dg}{\eta}$

(b) $\frac{3\rho dg}{\eta}$

(c) $\frac{\rho dg}{3\eta}$

(d) $\frac{\rho dg}{2\eta}$

12 A rectangular metal plate has dimensions of $10 \text{ cm} \times 20 \text{ cm}$. A thin film of oil separates the plate from a fixed horizontal surface. The separation between the rectangular plate and the horizontal surface is 0.2 mm. An ideal string is attached to the plate and passes over an ideal pulley to a mass m. When $m = 125$ g, the metal plate moves at constant speed of 5 cm/s across the horizontal surface, then the coefficient of viscosity of oil in dyne-s/cm^2 is (Use, $g = 1000 \text{ cm/s}^2$)

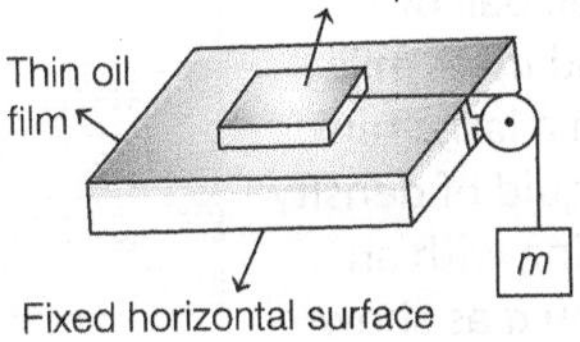

(a) 5 (b) 25
(c) 2.5 (d) 50

13 A plastic circular disc of radius R is placed on a thin oil film, spread over a flat horizontal surface. The torque required to spin the disc about its central vertical axis with a constant angular velocity is proportional to

(a) R^2 (b) R^3
(c) R^4 (d) R^6

14 Water flows at a speed of 6 cm s^{-1} through a tube of radius 1 cm. Coefficient of viscosity of water at room temperature is 0.01 poise. The Reynolds number is

(a) 1000 (b) 1100
(c) 1200 (d) 1400

Numerical Value Questions

1 A sphere of radius 10 cm and density 500 kg/m^3 is under water of density 1000kg/m^3. The acceleration of the sphere is 9.80 m/s^2 upward. Viscosity of water is 1.0 centipoise. If $g = 9.81 \text{m/s}^2$, what is the velocity (in m/s) of the sphere ?

2 A spherical ball of radius 1×10^{-4} m and density 10^4 kg/m^3 falls freely under gravity through a distance h before entering a tank of water. If after entering the water, the velocity of the ball does not change, find h. The viscosity of water is $9.8 \times 10^{-6} \text{ N-s/m}^2$.

3 A thin square plate of side $l = 10$ cm is dragged with constant velocity $v = 3$ cm/s in caster oil of thickness $d = 2$ mm. Find the horizontal force (in N) required to move it, if $\eta = 150$ poise.

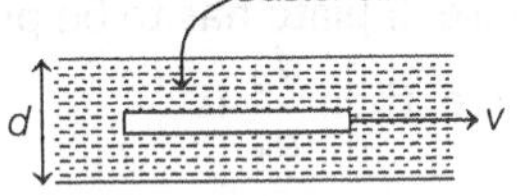

4 A liquid of density $\rho = 1000 \text{ kg/m}^3$ and coefficient of viscosity $\eta = 0.1 \text{ Ns/m}^2$ is flowing down in vertical pipe of large cross-section. A small ball of density $\rho_0 = 100 \text{ kg/m}^3$ and radius $r = 5$ cm is at rest in flowing liquid. Find velocity (in m/s) of flowing liquid.

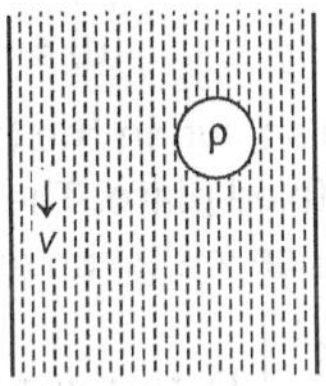

5 An air bubble of radius $r = 3$ mm moves up in a viscous liquid with a constant velocity $v = 0.7$ cm/s. If the density of the liquid is 1.75 gm/cc, find the viscosity of liquid (in poiseuille). Neglect the density of air in comparison to that of the liquid.

6 A small spherical ball falling under gravity in a viscous medium heats the medium due to viscous drag force. The rate of heating is proportional to r^n, where r is the radius of the sphere. Find n.

LEVEL 03 JEE Advanced Level

Single Choice Correct Questions

1 A space 2.5 cm wide between two large plane surfaces is filled with oil. Force required to drag a very thin plate of area $0.5\ m^2$ just mid-way the surfaces at a speed of 0.5 m/s is 1 N. The coefficient of viscosity in $N\text{-}s/m^2$ is

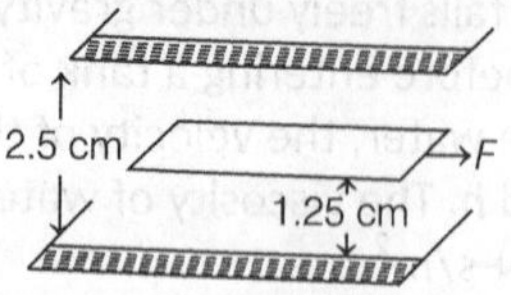

(a) 5×10^{-2} (b) 2.5×10^{-2}
(c) 1×10^{-2} (d) 7.5×10^{-2}

2 A thin plate separates two liquids of coefficients of viscosity η and 4η kept between two fixed plates as shown in figure. If plate has to be pulled by applying minimum force, then $\frac{d_2}{d_1}$ is

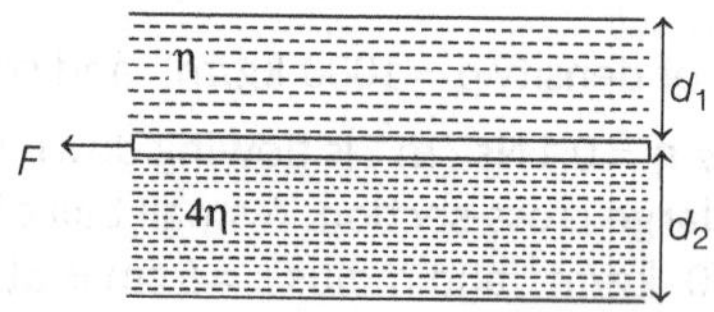

(a) 1 (b) 2
(c) 3 (d) 4

3 For the situation shown in the figure, water flows on the surface of a fixed plate. The velocity of water as a function of distance y is given as

$u = \alpha\left[\frac{y}{h} - 2\left(\frac{y}{h}\right)^2\right]$. Determine the magnitude of the shear stress that the water applies at the base of the plate. Coefficient of viscosity is η.

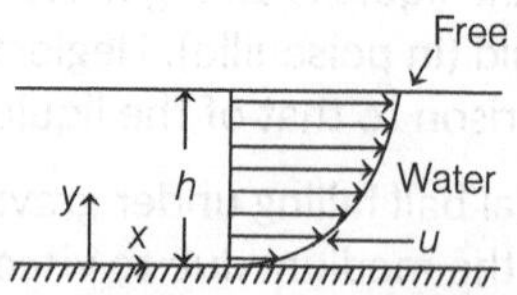

(a) $\frac{3\alpha\eta}{h}$ (b) $\frac{2\alpha\eta}{h}$ (c) $\frac{4\alpha\eta}{h}$ (d) $\frac{\alpha\eta}{h}$

4 A cylindrical piston of length l and radius R is moved with constant velocity v in a cylindrical tube filled with oil. If the clearance between the piston and tube is h (<< R), assuming η as the coefficient of viscosity of the oil, find the external force required to drive the piston with constant velocity.

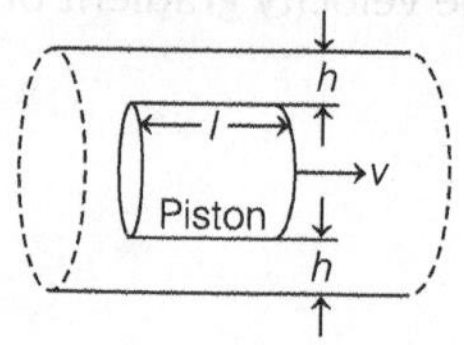

(a) $F = \pi R \eta \frac{vl}{h}$ (b) $F = 2\pi R \eta \frac{vl}{h}$
(c) $F = \pi R^2 \eta \frac{vl}{h}$ (d) $F = 2\pi R^2 \eta \frac{vl}{h}$

5 A spherical solid ball of volume V is made of a material of density ρ_0. It is falling through a liquid of density $\rho (\rho < \rho_0)$. Assume that, the liquid applies a viscous force on the ball that is proportional to the square of its speed v i.e. $F_{viscous} = -kv^2, k > 0$. The terminal speed of the ball is

(a) $\sqrt{\frac{Vg(\rho_0 - \rho)}{k}}$ (b) $\frac{Vg\rho_0}{k}$
(c) $\sqrt{\frac{Vg\rho_0}{k}}$ (d) $\frac{V(\rho_0 - \rho)}{k}$

6 A very small ball of radius r and mass m is released in a large tank having a liquid of density ρ and moving with an acceleration a as shown in figure. If coefficient of viscosity of the liquid is η, then terminal speed of the ball will be (neglect buoyant force)

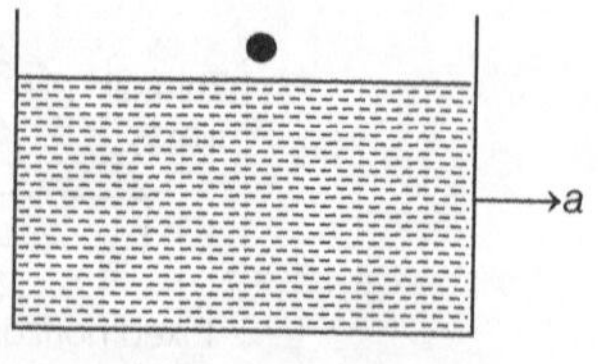

(a) $\frac{mg}{6\pi\eta r}$ (b) $\frac{ma}{6\pi\eta r}$
(c) $\frac{m}{6\pi\eta r}\sqrt{g^2 + a^2}$ (d) $\frac{m}{6\pi\eta r}\sqrt{g + a}$

7 A hollow cylinder of radius R and height h (<< R) is completely filled with a liquid having coefficient of viscosity η. Now, a cylinder of radius R is placed over it and is rotated with constant angular velocity ω by an external agent as shown.

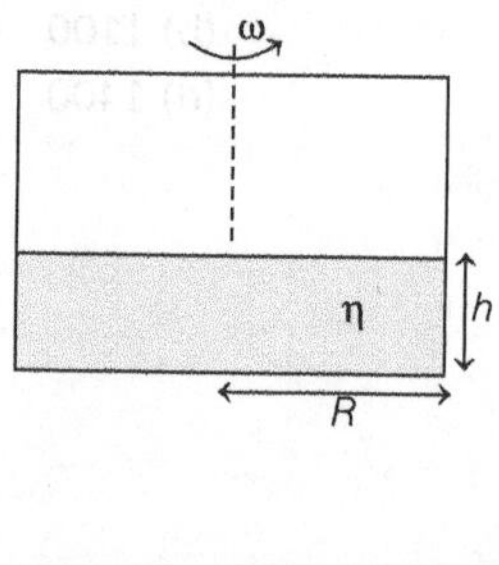

(a) External power required to rotate the cylinder with constant angular velocity ω is zero.

(b) External torque required to rotate the cylinder with constant angular velocity ω is $\frac{\pi \omega R^4 \eta}{h}$.

(c) External torque required to rotate the cylinder with constant angular velocity ω is $\frac{\pi \omega R^4 \eta}{2h}$.

(d) External power required to rotate the cylinder with constant angular velocity ω is $\frac{\pi \omega^2 R^4 \eta}{h}$.

Multiple Choice(s) Correct Questions

1 An oil drop falls through air with a terminal velocity of 5×10^{-4} m/s. Viscosity of air is 1.8×10^{-5} N-s / m^2 and density of oil is 900 kg/m^3 (neglect density of air as compared to that of oil).

(a) The radius of drop is 4.18×10^{-6} m

(b) The radius of drop is 2.14×10^{-6} m

(c) The terminal velocity of a drop of half of this radius is 1.25×10^{-4} m/s.

(d) The terminal velocity of a drop of half of this radius is 2.5×10^{-4} m/s.

2 A solid sphere moves at a terminal velocity of 20 m/s in air at a place, where $g = 10$ m/s^2 downwards. The sphere is taken in a hall, where $g = 5$ m/s^2 downwards having air of same viscosity and sphere is pushed down at a speed of 40 m/s. [Neglect buoyancy of air]

(a) Its initial acceleration will be 15 m/s^2 downward.

(b) Its initial acceleration will be 15 m/s^2 upward

(c) The magnitude of acceleration will decrease as time passes and becomes zero after sometime

(d) New terminal velocity of the solid sphere will be 10 m/s downwards.

3 A tube of length l and radius R carries a steady flow of fluid, whose density is ρ and viscosity η. The velocity of flow is given by $v = v_0\left(1 - \frac{r^2}{R^2}\right)$, where r is the distance of flowing fluid from the axis.

(a) The volume of fluid, flowing across the section of the tube, in unit time is $2\pi v_0 (R^2/4)$.

(b) The kinetic energy of the fluid within the volume of the tube is $KE = \pi \rho l v_0^2 (R^2/6)$

(c) The frictional force exerted on the tube by the fluid is $F = 4\pi \eta l v_0$.

(d) The pressure difference at the ends of tube is $p = \frac{4 \eta l v_0}{R^2}$.

Comprehension Based Questions

Comprehension-1

A spherical soap bubble with internal air density ρ_i, temperature T_i and radius R_0 is surrounded by air with density ρ_a, atmospheric pressure p_a and temperature T_a. The soap film has surface tension γ. The mass and the surface tension of the soap solution do not change with the temperature. Assume that air both inside and outside behaves like same ideal gas.

1 When the bubble is first formed, the air within is warmer ($T_i > T_a$). The buoyant force acting on the soap bubble must be equal to the weight for it to float in air. For finding the mass of the soap film, you can assume that the density of the soap solution is ρ_s and that the thickness of the film is t ($t << R_0$). The minimum value of T_i, so that the bubble can float in still air is

(a) $\frac{R_0 \rho_a T_a}{R_0 \rho_a - 3\rho_s t}\left[1 + \frac{3\gamma}{R_0 p_a}\right]$

(b) $\frac{R_0 \rho_a T_a}{R_0 \rho_a - 3\rho_s t}\left[1 + \frac{\gamma}{R_0 p_a}\right]$

(c) $\frac{R_0 \rho_a T_a}{R_0 \rho_a - 3\rho_s t}\left[1 + \frac{\gamma}{2R_0 p_a}\right]$

(d) $\frac{R_0 \rho_a T_a}{R_0 \rho_a - 3\rho_s t}\left[1 + \frac{4\gamma}{R_0 p_a}\right]$

2 After due time, the temperature of air within the bubble becomes equal to that of the surrounding air. Now, the soap bubble floats in air due to an air current flowing upwards. Find the minimum velocity v of the air, so that viscous drag and buoyancy will balance the weight of the soap bubble. The coefficient of viscosity of air is η. The soap bubble finally acquires radius R, when it is in thermal equilibrium with surroundings

(a) $\frac{2Rg}{3\eta}\left(\rho_s t + \frac{2\gamma \rho_a}{3p_a}\right)$

(b) $\frac{Rg}{3\eta}\left(\rho_s t + \frac{4\gamma \rho_a}{3p_a}\right)$

(c) $\frac{2Rg}{3\eta}\left(\rho_s t + \frac{4\gamma \rho_a}{3p_a}\right)$

(d) $\frac{2Rg}{\eta}\left(\rho_s t + \frac{4\gamma \rho_a}{3p_a}\right)$

Comprehension-2

Consider a disk of mass m, radius R lying on a liquid layer of thickness t and coefficient of viscosity η as shown in the figure.

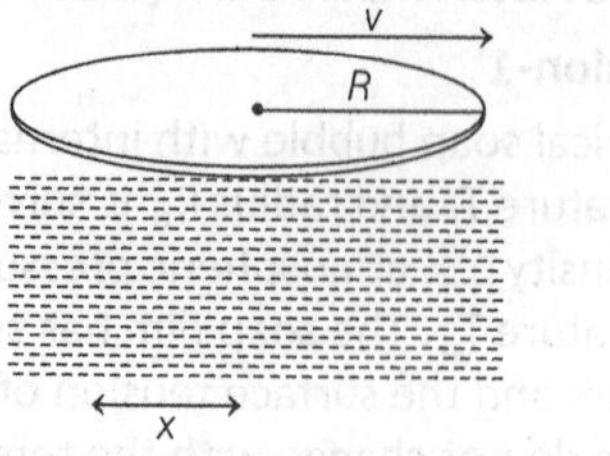

3 The coefficient of viscosity varies as $\eta = \eta_0 x$ (x measured from as shown in the figure). At the given instant, the disk is floating towards right with a velocity v as shown. Find the force required to move the disk slowly at the given instant.

(a) $\frac{2\pi \eta_0 R^3 v}{3t}$ (b) $\frac{\pi \eta_0 R^2 v}{t}$

(c) $\frac{\pi \eta_0 R^3 v}{3t}$ (d) $\frac{4\pi \eta_0 R^3 v}{3t}$

4 The torque required to rotate the disk at a constant angular velocity ω is (given the viscosity is uniformly η)

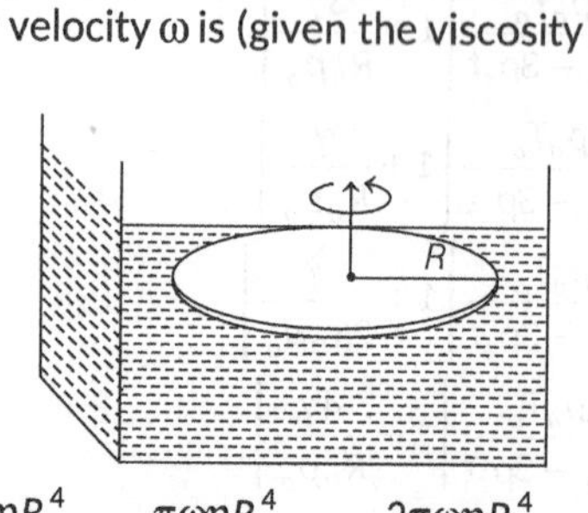

(a) $\frac{4\pi\omega\eta R^4}{t}$ (b) $\frac{\pi\omega\eta R^4}{2t}$ (c) $\frac{2\pi\omega\eta R^4}{t}$ (d) $16\pi\omega\eta R^4$

5 A disc rotating with angular velocity ω_0 is placed on a viscous liquid of thickness t. Find the angle rotated by the disc before it comes to rest (Viscosity $= \eta$, mass of disc $= m$, radius of disc $= R$)

(a) $\frac{4\omega_0 tm}{\eta\pi R^2}$ (b) $\frac{2\omega_0 tm}{\eta\pi R^2}$ (c) $\frac{\omega_0 tm}{\eta\pi R^2}$ (d) $\frac{\omega_0 tm}{2\eta\pi R^2}$

Comprehension-3

When a viscous liquid flows, adjacent layers oppose their relative motion by applying a viscous force given by

$F = -\eta A \frac{dv}{dz}$, where $\eta =$ coefficient of viscosity,

$A =$ *surface area of adjacent layers in contact and* $\frac{dv}{dz} =$ *velocity gradient.*

Now, a viscous liquid having coefficient of viscosity η is flowing through a fixed tube of length l and radius R under a pressure difference p between the two ends of the tube.

Now, consider a cylindrical volume of liquid of radius r. Due to steady flow, net force on the liquid in cylindrical volume should be zero.

$$-\eta 2\pi r l \frac{dv}{dr} = p\pi r^2 \Rightarrow -\int_v^0 dv = \frac{p}{2\eta l}\int_r^R r\,dr$$

($\because$ layer in contact with the tube is stationary)

Now, the volume of the liquid flowing per second through the tube is

$$Q = \int_0^R v 2\pi r dr = \int_0^R v_0\left(1 - \frac{r^2}{R_2}\right) 2\pi r dr$$

$$\therefore Q = \frac{\pi P R^4}{8\eta l}$$

This is called Poiseuille's equation.

6 The viscous force on the cylindrical volume of the liquid varies as

(a) $F \propto r^2$ (b) $F \propto r$

(c) $F \propto 1/r$ (d) $F \propto 1/r^2$

7 Force acting on the tube due to the liquid is

(a) $\pi \eta \ell v_0$ (b) $2\pi\eta\ell v_0$

(c) $4\pi\eta\ell v_0$ (d) $6\pi\eta\ell v_0$

Numerical Value Questions

1 A spherical ball of density ρ and radius 0.003m is dropped into a tube containing a viscous fluid filled up to the 0 cm mark as shown in the figure. Viscosity of the fluid $= 1.260\ \text{Nm}^{-2}$ and its density $\rho_L = \rho/2 = 1260\ \text{kgm}^{-3}$. Assume the ball reaches a terminal speed by the 10 cm mark. The time taken (in s) by the ball to traverse the distance between the 10 cm and 20 cm mark is (g = acceleration due to gravity $= 10\ \text{ms}^{-2}$)

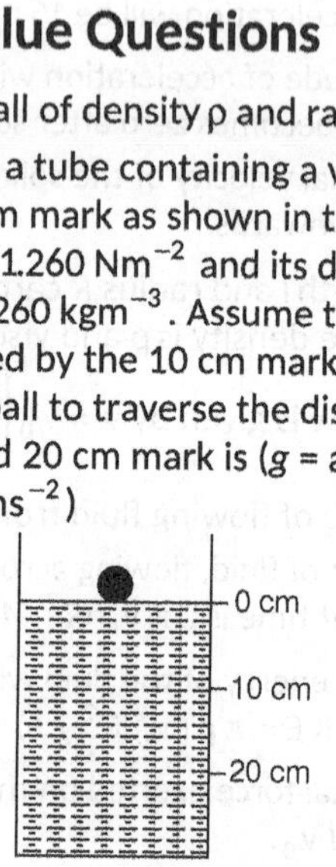

2 Two identical balls are connected by weightless inextensible cord thrown over ideal pulley. One of the balls is immersed into a vessel with a liquid. With what steady velocity v (in m/s) will the ball move, if it is known that the established rate of fall of a single ball in the same liquid is equal to 8 m/s? Resistance force is proportional to fluid velocity. The density of the liquid is ρ and density of the material of balls is 2ρ.

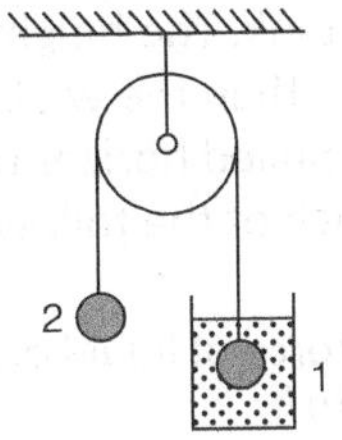

Previous Years Questions

JEE Main

1 Given below are two statements

Statement I Viscosity of gases is greater than that of liquids.

Statement II Surface tension of a liquid decreases due to the presence of insoluble impurities.

In the light of the above statements, choose the **most appropriate** answer from the options given below. **[2024, 27 Jan Shift-I]**

(a) Both Statement I and Statement II are correct.
(b) Statement I is incorrect but Statement II is correct.
(c) Both Statement I and Statement II are incorrect.
(d) Statement I is correct but Statement II is incorrect.

2 A small steel ball is dropped into a long cylinder containing glycerine. Which one of the following is the correct representation of the velocity time graph for the transit of the ball? **[2024, 31 Jan Shift-I]**

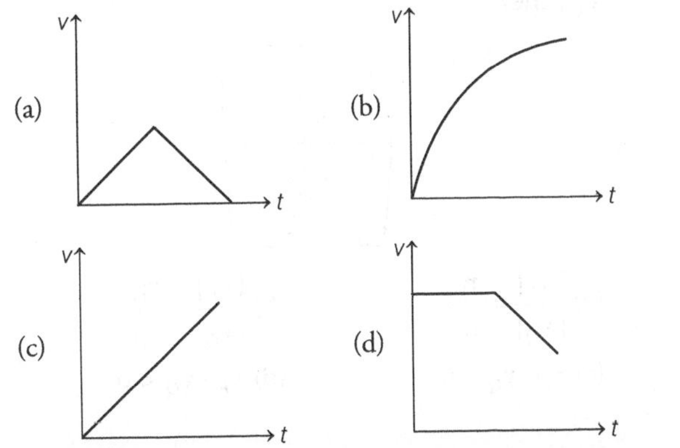

3 A small spherical ball of radius r, falling through a viscous medium of negligible density has terminal velocity v. Another ball of the same mass but of radius $2r$, falling through the same viscous medium will have terminal velocity **[2024, 31 Jan Shift-II]**

(a) $\frac{v}{4}$ (b) $\frac{v}{2}$ (c) $4v$ (d) $2v$

4 A small ball of mass M and density ρ is dropped in a viscous liquid of density ρ_0. After some time, the ball falls with a constant velocity. What is the viscous force on the ball ? **[2023, 6 April Shift-I]**

(a) $F = Mg\left(1 + \frac{\rho}{\rho_0}\right)$ (b) $F = Mg\left(1 + \frac{\rho_0}{\rho}\right)$

(c) $F = Mg\left(1 - \frac{\rho_0}{\rho}\right)$ (d) $F = Mg\,(1 \pm \rho\rho_0)$

5 A spherical ball of radius 1 mm and density 10.5 g/cc is dropped in glycerine of coefficient of viscosity 9.8 poise and density 1.5 g/cc. Viscous force on the ball by which it attains constant velocity is 3696×10^{-x} N. The value of x is .... (Given, $g = 9.8$ m/s^2 and $\pi = 22/7$) **[2023, 24 Jan Shift-II]**

6 Eight equal drops of water are falling through air with a steady speed of 10 cm/s. If the drops coalesce, the new velocity is **[2023, 11 April Shift-II]**

(a) 16 cm/s (b) 40 cm/s
(c) 10 cm/s (d) 5 cm/s

7 An air bubble of diameter 6 mm rises steadily through a solution of density 1750 kg/m^2 at the rate of 0.35 cm/s. The coefficient of viscosity of the solution (neglect density of air) is P as (given, $g = 10$ ms^{-2}). **[2023, 8 April Shift-I]**

8 The velocity of a small ball of mass m and density d_1, when dropped in a container filled with glycerine, becomes constant after sometime. If the density of glycerine is d_2, then the viscous force acting on the ball, will be **[2022, 27 June Shift-I]**

(a) $mg\left(1 - \frac{d_1}{d_2}\right)$ (b) $mg\left(1 - \frac{d_2}{d_1}\right)$

(c) $mg\left(\frac{d_1}{d_2} - 1\right)$ (d) $mg\left(\frac{d_2}{d_1} - 1\right)$

9 The diameter of an air bubble which was initially 2 mm, rises steadily through a solution of density 1750 kg m^{-3} at the rate of 0.35 cms^{-1}. The coefficient of viscosity of the solution is .... poise (in nearest integer). (The density of air is negligible). **[2022, 28 July Shift-I]**

10 A small spherical ball of radius 0.1 mm and density 10^4 kg m^{-3} falls freely under gravity through a distance h before entering a tank of water. If after entering the water, the velocity of ball does not change and it continue to fall with same constant velocity inside water, then the value of h will be......m.

(Given $g = 10$ ms^{-2}, viscosity of water $= 1.0 \times 10^{-5}$ N-sm^{-2}). **[2022, 29 June Shift-II]**

11 A water drop of radius 1 μm falls in a situation where the effect of buoyant force is negligible. Coefficient of viscosity of air is 1.8×10^{-5}N-s-m^{-2} and its density is negligible as compared to that of water (10^6 gm^{-3}). Terminal velocity of the water drop is (Take, acceleration due to gravity = 10 ms^{-2}) **[2022, 28 June Shift-II]**

(a) 145.4×10^{-6} ms^{-1}
(b) 118.0×10^{-6} ms^{-1}
(c) 132.6×10^{-6} ms^{-1}
(d) 123.4×10^{-6} ms^{-1}

12 If ρ is the density and η is coefficient of viscosity of fluid which flows with a speed v in the pipe of diameter d, the correct formula for Reynolds number R_e is **[2022, 26 June Shift-II]**

(a) $R_e = \dfrac{\eta d}{\rho v}$

(b) $R_e = \dfrac{\rho v}{\eta d}$

(c) $R_e = \dfrac{\rho v d}{\eta}$

(d) $R_e = \dfrac{\eta}{\rho v d}$

13 The terminal velocity v_t of the spherical rain drop depends on the radius (r) of the spherical rain drop as **[2022, 25 June Shift-I]**

(a) $r^{1/2}$ (b) r
(c) r^2 (d) r^3

14 In Millikan's oil drop experiment, what is viscous force acting on an uncharged drop of radius 2.0×10^{-5} m and density 1.2×10^3 kgm^{-3}? Take viscosity of liquid $= 1.8 \times 10^{-5}$Nsm^{-2}. (Neglect buoyancy due to air). **[2021, 27 Aug Shift-I]**

(a) 3.8×10^{-11}N (b) 3.9×10^{-10}N
(c) 1.8×10^{-10}N (d) 5.8×10^{-10}N

JEE Advanced

1 Water from a pipe is coming at a rate of 100 liters per minute. If the radius of the pipe is 5 cm, the Reynolds number for the flow is of the order of (density of water = 1000 kg/m^3, coefficient of viscosity of water = 1 mPa s) **(2019)**

(a) 10^3 (b) 10^4 (c) 10^2 (d) 10^6

2 Consider a thin square plate floating on a viscous liquid in a large tank. The height h of the liquid in the tank is much less than the width of the tank. The floating plate is pulled horizontally with a constant velocity u_0. Which of the following statements is (are) true? **(2018)**

(a) The resistive force of liquid on the plate is inversely proportional to h
(b) The resistive force of liquid on the plate is independent of the area of the plate
(c) The tangential (shear) stress on the floor of the tank increases with u_0
(d) The tangential (shear) stress on the plate varies linearly with the viscosity η of the liquid

3 Consider two solid spheres P and Q each of density 8 gm cm^{-3} and diameters 1 cm and 0.5 cm, respectively. Sphere P is dropped into a liquid of density 0.8 gm cm^{-3} and viscosity η=3 poiseulles. Sphere Q is dropped into a liquid of density 1.6 gm cm^{-3} and viscosity η = 2 poiseulles. The ratio of the terminal velocities of P and Q is .... **(2016)**

4 Two spheres P and Q of equal radii have densities ρ_1 and ρ_2, respectively. The spheres are connected by a massless string and placed in liquids L_1 and L_2 of densities σ_1 and σ_2 and viscosities η_1 and η_2, respectively. They float in equilibrium with the sphere P in L_1 and sphere Q in L_2 and the string being taut (see figure). If sphere P alone in L_2 has terminal velocity $\mathbf{v}_P$ and Q alone in L_1 has terminal velocity $\mathbf{v}_Q$, then **(2015)**

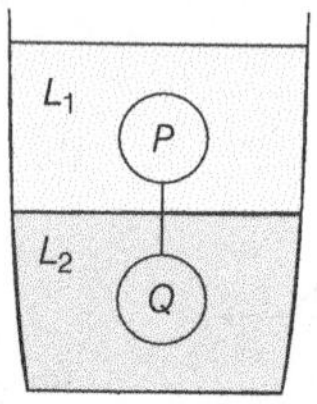

(a) $\dfrac{|\mathbf{v}_P|}{|\mathbf{v}_Q|} = \dfrac{\eta_1}{\eta_2}$ (b) $\dfrac{|\mathbf{v}_P|}{|\mathbf{v}_Q|} = \dfrac{\eta_2}{\eta_1}$

(c) $\mathbf{v}_P \cdot \mathbf{v}_Q > 0$ (d) $\mathbf{v}_P \cdot \mathbf{v}_Q < 0$

Answer Key

Level 1

10.1 Newton's Law of Viscosity

1. 8×10^{-3}N 2. $\frac{\eta A v_0}{D}$ 3. 4mm 4. 6 Pa–s, 0 5. 7.89 N-m 6. $\frac{m(R_2-R_1)\ln 2}{4\pi\eta l R_1}$

10.2 Stokes Law

1. 50 poise 2. 0.1 m/s 3. 64 cm/s 4. 2×10^{-6}m 5. $t=\frac{2v_0\ln 2}{g}$

10.3 Reynolds Number

1. 1590, laminar 2. $R_e=5100$, turbulent

Level 2

Single Choice Correct Questions

1. (a) 2. (b) 3. (a) 4. (b) 5. (b) 6. (a) 7. (c) 8. (c) 9. (b) 10. (a)
11. (d) 12. (c) 13. (c) 14. (c)

Numerical Value Questions

1. 11 2. 20.4 3. 9 4. 50 5. 5 6. 5

Level 3

Single Choice Correct Questions

1. (b) 2. (b) 3. (d) 4. (b) 5. (a) 6. (c) 7. (c)

Multiple Choice(s) Correct Questions

1. (b, c) 2. (b, c, d) 3. (a, b, c, d)

Comprehension Based Questions

1. (d) 2. (c) 3. (a) 4. (b) 5. (c) 6. (a) 7. (c)

Numerical Value Questions

1. 5 2. 8

Previous Years Questions

JEE Main

1. (b) 2. (b) 3. (b) 4. (c) 5. (7) 6. (b) 7. (10) 8. (b) 9. (11) 10. (20)
11. (d) 12. (c) 13. (c) 14. (b)

JEE Advanced

1. (b) 2. (a,c,d) 3. (3) 4. (a,d)

SOLUTIONS

Level 1

10.1 Newton's Law of Viscosity

1. $\eta = 0.01$ poise $= 0.001$ deca-poise

$$F = \eta A \frac{dv}{dx} = (0.001)(2)\left(\frac{2}{0.5}\right) = 8 \times 10^{-3}\,\text{N}$$

2. $F = \eta A \dfrac{dv}{dx} = \eta A \left(\dfrac{v_0 - 0}{D - 0}\right) = \dfrac{\eta A v_0}{D}$

3. For block, $\Sigma F = 0$

$$\Rightarrow \quad mg\sin 30^\circ = F$$

$$\Rightarrow \quad mg\sin 30^\circ = \eta A \frac{dv}{dx}$$

$$\Rightarrow 20 \times 10 \times \frac{1}{2} = 10^{-2} \times 2^2 \times \left(\frac{10-0}{t}\right)$$

$$\Rightarrow \quad t = 4 \times 10^{-3}\,\text{m} = 4\,\text{mm}$$

4. $F = \eta A \dfrac{dv}{dy}$

$$\Rightarrow \text{Shear stress} = \frac{F}{A} = \eta\frac{dv}{dy} = 1.5\,(4 - 2y)$$

At $y = 0$, shear stress $= 1.5\,(4 - 2y) = 6\,\text{N/m}^2$

and at $y = 2$, shear stress $= 1.5\,(4 - 2 \times 2) = 0$

5. Lets take an elemental ring of radius r and thickness dr on the disc.

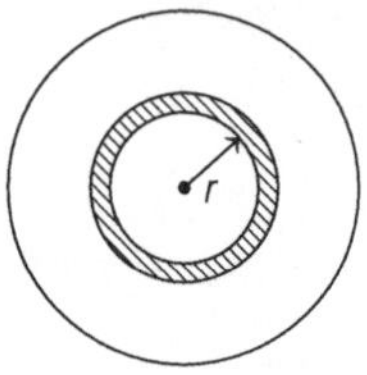

Tangential force on the ring $= \eta(2\pi r dr)\left(\dfrac{\omega r - 0}{t}\right)$

$d\tau =$ Retarding torque on the ring $= \eta(2\pi r dr)\left(\dfrac{\omega r}{t}\right)r$

$$\Rightarrow \int d\tau = \int_0^R \eta(2\pi r dr)\left(\frac{\omega r}{t}\right)r$$

$$\tau = \frac{\pi\eta\omega R^4}{2t} = \frac{\pi\,(0.08)\,(2\pi\,10)(0.1)^4}{2 \times 0.01 \times 10^{-2}} = 7.89\,\text{N-m}$$

6. Let angular velocity of solid cylinder be ω at any instant.

$$F = \eta A \frac{dv}{dx} = \eta(2\pi R_1 l)\left(\frac{\omega R_1 - 0}{R_2 - R_1}\right)$$

$$\tau = I\alpha$$

$$\Rightarrow \quad -\eta(2\pi R_1 l)\frac{(\omega R_1)R_1}{R_2 - R_1} = \left(\frac{mR_1^2}{2}\right)\frac{d\omega}{dt}$$

$$\Rightarrow \quad \int_0^t dt = -\frac{m(R_2 - R_1)}{4\pi\eta R_1 l}\int_{\omega_0}^{\frac{\omega_0}{2}} \frac{d\omega}{\omega}$$

$$\Rightarrow \quad t = \frac{m(R_2 - R_1)}{4\pi\eta R_1 l}\ln 2$$

10.2 Stokes' Law

1. $v_T = \dfrac{2}{9}\dfrac{r^2(\rho - \sigma)g}{\eta}$

$$\Rightarrow \quad 0.7 \times 10^{-2} = \frac{2}{9}\frac{(3 \times 10^{-3})^2(1750 - 0)10}{\eta}$$

$$\Rightarrow \quad \eta = 5 \text{ deca-poise} = 50 \text{ poise}$$

2. $v_T = \dfrac{2r^2(\sigma - \rho)g}{9\eta}$

$$\Rightarrow \quad \frac{v_1}{v_2} = \frac{\sigma_1 - \rho}{\sigma_2 - \rho} \Rightarrow \frac{0.2}{v_2} = \frac{19.5 - 1.5}{10.5 - 1.5}$$

$$\Rightarrow \quad v_2 = 0.1\,\text{m/s}$$

3. From volume conservation,

$$8\left(\frac{4}{3}\pi r^3\right) = \frac{4}{3}\pi R^3$$

$$\Rightarrow \quad R = 2r,$$

$$v_T \propto r^2$$

$$\Rightarrow \quad \frac{v_1}{v_2} = \frac{r^2}{R^2} \Rightarrow \frac{16\,\text{cm/s}}{v_2} = \frac{r^2}{(2r)^2}$$

$$\Rightarrow \quad v_2 = 64\,\text{cm/s}$$

4. Terminal velocity of the largest particle which is just about to settle at the bottom of the vessel,

$$v_T = \frac{10 \times 10^{-2}}{3600}\,\text{m/s}$$

Let r be the radius of that particle, then

$$v_T = \frac{2}{9}r^2\frac{(\sigma - \rho)}{\eta}g$$

$$\Rightarrow \quad \frac{10 \times 10^{-2}}{3600} = \frac{2}{9}r^2\frac{(4 \times 10^3 - 0)}{(0.01 \times 10^{-1})} \times 10$$

$$\Rightarrow \quad r = 2 \times 10^{-6}\,\text{m}$$

5. $\Sigma F = ma \Rightarrow B - mg - 6\pi r\eta v = ma$

$$\Rightarrow \rho\left(\frac{4}{3}\pi r^3\right)g - 2\rho\left(\frac{4}{3}\pi r^3\right)g - 6\pi\eta r v = 2\rho\left(\frac{4}{3}\pi r^3\right)\frac{dv}{dt}$$

$$\Rightarrow \quad \int_0^t dt = -\int_{v_0}^0 \frac{2dv}{1 + \dfrac{9\eta v}{2\rho r^2 g}}$$

$$\Rightarrow \quad t = \frac{2v_0 \ln 2}{g}$$

10.3 Reynolds Number

1. $R_e = \frac{\rho v d}{\eta} = \frac{1060 \times 0.3 \times (2 \times 10^{-2})}{4 \times 10^{-3}} = 1590$

Since $R_e < 2000$, flow will be laminar.

2. Flow rate $= Av = 5 \times 10^{-6}$

$$\Rightarrow \quad \pi\left(\frac{1.25}{2} \times 10^{-2}\right)^2 v = 5 \times 10^{-6}$$

$$\Rightarrow \quad v = 4.07 \times 10^{-2} \text{ m/ s}$$

$$R_e = \frac{\rho v d}{\eta} = \frac{10^3 \times 4.07 \times 10^{-2} \times 1.25 \times 10^{-2}}{10^{-3} \times 10^{-1}} = 5087$$

Since $R_e > 3000$, flow will be turbulent.

Level 2

Single Choice Correct Questions

1. $v_T = \frac{2}{9}\frac{(\sigma - \rho)r^2 g}{\eta} = \frac{2}{9}\frac{\left(\sigma\left(\frac{4}{3}\pi r^3\right) - \rho\left(\frac{4}{3}\pi r^3\right)\right) r^2 g}{\frac{4}{3}\pi r^3}$

$$\Rightarrow \quad v_T = \frac{2}{9}\frac{(m - m')g}{\left(\frac{4}{3}\pi r\right)}$$

$$\Rightarrow \quad v_T \propto \left(\frac{m - m'}{r}\right)$$

2. $v_T = \frac{2}{9}\frac{(\sigma - \rho)r^2 g}{\eta}$

$$\Rightarrow \quad 8 = \frac{2}{9}\frac{(10.5 - 1.5)(0.2)^2 \times 980}{\eta}$$

$$\Rightarrow \quad \eta = 9.8 \text{ poise}$$

3. $v_T = \frac{2}{9}\frac{(\sigma)r^2 g}{\eta}$

$$\Rightarrow v_T = \frac{2}{9} \times \frac{10^3 \times (0.3 \times 10^{-3})^2 \times (9.8)}{1.8 \times 10^{-5}}$$

$$= 10.9 \text{ m / s}$$

4. $v_T = \frac{2}{9}\frac{(\sigma - \rho)r^2 g}{\eta}$

$$\Rightarrow \quad \frac{v_1}{v_2} = \frac{\sigma_1 - \rho}{\sigma_2 - \rho} \Rightarrow \frac{v_0}{\eta v_0} = \frac{8.5 - 0.8}{2.5 - 0.8}$$

$$\Rightarrow \quad \eta = \frac{17}{77}$$

5. $m = \sigma\left(\frac{4}{3}\pi r^3\right)$

$$\Rightarrow \quad \sigma \propto \frac{1}{r^3} \Rightarrow \frac{\sigma_1}{\sigma_2} = \frac{r_2^3}{r_1^3}$$

$$\Rightarrow \quad \sigma_2 = 8\sigma_1$$

$$v_T = \frac{2}{9}\frac{\sigma r^2 g}{\eta}$$

$$\Rightarrow \quad \frac{v_1}{v_2} = \left(\frac{\sigma_1}{\sigma_2}\right)\left(\frac{r_1}{r_2}\right)^2$$

$$\Rightarrow \quad \frac{v}{v_2} = \left(\frac{\sigma_1}{8\sigma_1}\right)\left(\frac{r_1}{r_1/2}\right)^2$$

$$\Rightarrow \quad v_2 = 2v$$

6. When the ball is released from rest,

$$mg - B - 6\pi\eta r(0) = ma$$

$$\Rightarrow \quad mg - B = ma \quad \text{... (i)}$$

When the ball acquires terminal velocity,

$$mg - B - 6\pi\eta r v_T = 0 \quad \text{... (ii)}$$

When $v = \frac{2v_T}{3}$,

$$mg - B - 6\pi\eta r\left(\frac{2v_T}{3}\right) = ma_1 \quad \text{...(iii)}$$

Solving Eqs. (i), (ii) and (iii), we get

$$a_1 = \frac{a}{3}$$

7. $mg - B - 6\pi\eta r v = ma$

So, *a versus v* graph will straight line with negative slope. Hence, option (c) is incorrect.

8. $m = \rho\left(\frac{4}{3}\pi r^3\right) \Rightarrow m \propto r^3$

$$v_T = \frac{2}{9}\frac{(\sigma - \rho)r^2 g}{\eta} \Rightarrow v_T \propto r^2$$

$$K = \frac{1}{2}mv_T^2 \Rightarrow K \propto r^7$$

$$\Rightarrow \quad \frac{K_1}{K_2} = \left(\frac{r_1}{r_2}\right)^7 \Rightarrow \frac{K}{K_2} = \left(\frac{r_1}{2r_1}\right)^7$$

$$\Rightarrow \quad K_2 = 128K$$

9. From volume conservation,

$$2\left(\frac{4}{3}\pi r^3\right) = \frac{4}{3}\pi R^3$$

$$\Rightarrow \quad R = (2)^{1/3} r$$

$$v_T \propto r^2 \Rightarrow \frac{v_1}{v_2} = \left(\frac{r_1}{r_2}\right)^2 \Rightarrow \frac{v}{v_2} = \left(\frac{r}{2^{1/3} r}\right)^2$$

$$\Rightarrow \quad v_2 = (4^{1/3})v$$

10. $F = \eta A \frac{dv}{dx} = (0.01)(100)\left(\frac{10 - 0}{0.1}\right) = 100 \text{ dyne}$

11. $2\eta A \frac{dv}{dx} = mg \Rightarrow 2\eta A \frac{dv}{dx} = (\rho A d)g$

$$\Rightarrow \quad \frac{dv}{dx} = \frac{\rho d g}{2\eta}$$

12. $\eta A\dfrac{dv}{dx} = mg$

$\Rightarrow \quad \eta(10\times 20)\left(\dfrac{5-0}{0.02}\right) = 125\times 1000$

$\Rightarrow \quad \eta = 2.5 \text{ dyne -s / cm}^2$

13. Lets take an elemental ring of radius r and thickness dr on the disc.

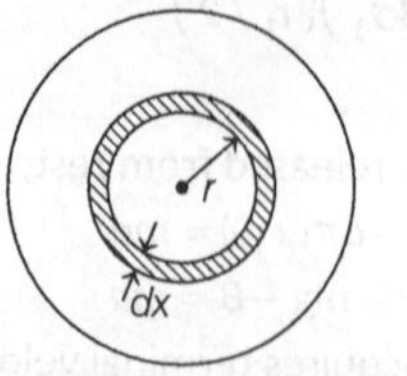

$$F = \eta A\frac{dv}{dx} \Rightarrow dF = \eta(2\pi r dr)\left(\frac{\omega r - 0}{t}\right)$$

$$\int d\tau = \int_0^R \eta(2\pi r dr)\left(\frac{\omega r}{t}\right) r$$

$$\tau = \frac{2\pi\eta\omega}{t}\int r^3 dr = \frac{\pi\eta\omega R^4}{2t}$$

$\Rightarrow \quad \tau \propto R^4$

14. $R_e = \dfrac{\rho v d}{\eta} = \dfrac{1\times 6\times 2}{0.01} = 1200$

Numerical Value Questions

1. $B - mg - 6\pi\eta r v = ma$

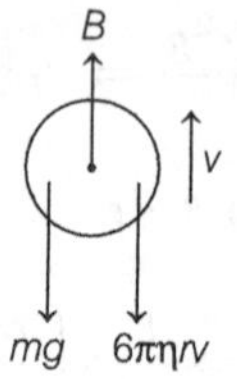

$$v = \frac{B - m(g+a)}{6\pi\eta r}$$

$$= \frac{1000\times\frac{4}{3}\pi r^3 g - 500\times\frac{4}{3}\pi r^3(g+a)}{6\pi\eta r}$$

$$= \frac{1000}{9}\left(\frac{r^2(g-a)}{\eta}\right) = \frac{1000}{9}\left(\frac{(0.1)^2(9.81-9.80)}{1\times 10^{-3}}\right)$$

$$= 11.11 \text{ m / s}$$

2. $v_T = \dfrac{2}{9}\dfrac{(\sigma-\rho)r^2 g}{\eta} = \sqrt{2gh}$

$\Rightarrow \quad \dfrac{2}{9}\dfrac{(10^4 - 10^3)(1\times 10^{-4})^2(9.8)}{9.8\times 10^{-6}} = \sqrt{2\times 9.8 h}$

$\Rightarrow \quad h = 20.4\text{m}$

3. F_1 = Viscous force on upper surface

$$= \eta A\frac{dv}{dx} = \eta A\left(\frac{v-0}{d/2}\right) = 2\eta\frac{Av}{d}$$

F_2 = viscous force on lower surface $= \dfrac{2\eta A v}{d}$

$$F_{ext} = F_1 + F_2 = \frac{4\eta A v}{d}$$

$$= \frac{4(150\times 10^{-1})(0.1)^2(3\times 10^{-2})}{2\times 10^{-3}} = 9\text{N}$$

4. In fluid frame, ball is moving with constant velocity and resultant of all forces acting on it is zero.

$$v_T = \frac{2}{9}\frac{(\rho-\sigma)r^2 g}{\eta}$$

$$= \frac{2}{9}\frac{(1000-100)(0.05)^2(10)}{0.1}$$

$$= 50 \text{ m / s}$$

5. $v_T = \dfrac{2}{9}\dfrac{(\rho-\sigma)r^2 g}{\eta}$

$\Rightarrow \quad 0.7 = \dfrac{2}{9}\dfrac{(1.75-0)(0.3)^3\times 1000}{\eta}$

$\Rightarrow \eta = 50 \text{ poise} = 5 \text{ poisuelle}$

6. Rate of production of heat $= P = Fv_T = (6\pi\eta r v_T)v_T$

$P \propto r v_T^2$

$P \propto r^5 \because \{v_T \propto r^2\}$

Level 3

Single Choice Correct Questions

1. $F = F_1 + F_2$

$$1 = \eta(0.5)\left(\frac{0.5}{1.25\times 10^{-2}}\right) + \eta(0.5)\left(\frac{0.5}{1.25\times 10^{-2}}\right)$$

$\Rightarrow \quad \eta = 2.5\times 10^{-2} \text{ N-s/m}^2$

2. $F = F_1 + F_2 = \eta A\dfrac{v}{d_1} + 4\eta A\dfrac{v}{d_2}$

$\Rightarrow \quad F = \eta A v\left(\dfrac{1}{d_1} + \dfrac{4}{d_2}\right) = \eta A v\left(\dfrac{1}{d_1} + \dfrac{4}{d - d_1}\right)$

For force to be minimum, $\dfrac{dF}{dd_1} = 0$

$\Rightarrow \eta A v\left(-\dfrac{1}{d_1^2} - \dfrac{4}{(d-d_1)^2}(-1)\right) = 0$

$\Rightarrow \quad d_1 = \dfrac{d}{3}$

So, $\quad \dfrac{d_2}{d_1} = \dfrac{2d/3}{d/3} = 2$

3. $F = \eta A\dfrac{du}{dy}$

$\Rightarrow$ Shear stress $= \dfrac{F}{A} = \eta\dfrac{du}{dy} = \eta\alpha\left(\dfrac{1}{h} - \dfrac{2(2y)}{h^2}\right)$

At the base of plate, $y = 0$

$\Rightarrow$ Shear stress $= \dfrac{\eta\alpha}{h}$

4. $F = \eta A \dfrac{dv}{dx}$

$$\Rightarrow \quad F = \eta(2\pi Rl)\left(\frac{v-0}{h}\right) = 2\pi R\eta\frac{vl}{h}$$

5. $\Sigma F = ma \Rightarrow mg - B - F_{viscous} = ma$

$$\Rightarrow \quad \rho_o Vg - \rho Vg - kv^2 = ma$$

For terminal velocity, $a = 0$

$$\Rightarrow \quad \rho_o Vg - \rho Vg - kv_T^2 = 0$$

$$\Rightarrow \quad v_T = \sqrt{\frac{Vg(\rho_0 - \rho)}{k}}$$

6. For terminal velocity, $F_{net} = 0$

$$\Rightarrow \quad m\sqrt{g^2 + a^2} - 6\pi\eta r v_T = 0$$

$$\Rightarrow \quad v_T = \frac{m\sqrt{g^2 + a^2}}{6\pi\eta r}$$

7. Lets take an elemental ring of radius r and thickness dr.

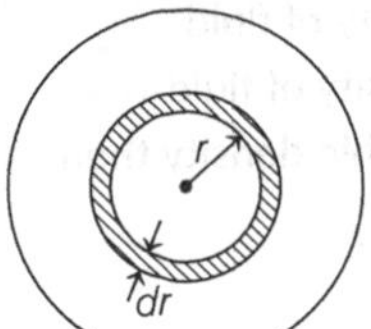

$$dF = \eta(2\pi r dr)\left(\frac{\omega r}{h}\right)$$

$$\int d\tau = \int_0^R \eta(2\pi r dr)\left(\frac{\omega r}{h}\right) r$$

$$\Rightarrow \quad \tau_{ext} = \frac{\pi\omega\eta R^4}{2h}$$

$$P_{ext} = \tau_{ext}\,\omega = \frac{\pi\omega^2\eta R^4}{2h}$$

Multiple Choice(s) Correct Questions

1. $v_T = \dfrac{2}{9}\dfrac{(\sigma - \rho)r^2 g}{\eta}$

$$\Rightarrow \quad 5 \times 10^{-4} = \frac{2}{9}\frac{(900-0)r^2(9.8)}{1.8 \times 10^{-5}}$$

$$\Rightarrow \quad r = 2.14 \times 10^{-6}\,\text{m}$$

$$v_T \propto r^2 \Rightarrow \frac{v_1}{v_2} = \frac{r_1^2}{r_2^2} \Rightarrow \frac{5 \times 10^{-4}}{v_2} = \frac{r_1^2}{(r_1/2)^2}$$

$$\Rightarrow \quad v_2 = 1.25 \times 10^{-4}\,\text{m/s}$$

2. Initially, $mg = 6\pi\eta r v_T$

$$\Rightarrow \quad m(10) = 6\pi\,\eta r(20)$$

$$\Rightarrow \quad 6\,\pi\eta r = \frac{m}{2}$$

In the hall, $mg' - 6\pi\eta r v = ma$

$$\Rightarrow \quad m(5) - \left(\frac{m}{2}\right)40 = ma$$

$\Rightarrow a = -15\,\text{m/s}^2 = 15\,\text{m/s}^2$, upward

For new terminal velocity,

$$m(5) - 6\pi\eta r v_T = 0$$

$$\Rightarrow \quad m(5) - \left(\frac{m}{2}\right)v_T = 0$$

$$\Rightarrow \quad v_T = 10\,\text{m/s}$$

3. (A) Let us consider a cylindrical section at a distance r and having thickness dr.

Volume flow rate

$$= \int_0^R (2\pi r dr)\left(v_0\left(1 - \frac{r^2}{R^2}\right)\right) = \frac{2\pi v_0 R^2}{4}$$

(B) $$K = \int \frac{1}{2} dm v^2 = \frac{1}{2}\int_0^R (\rho(2\pi r dr)l)\left(v_0\left(1 - \frac{r^2}{R^2}\right)\right)^2 = \frac{\pi r l v_0^2 R^2}{6}$$

(C) $$F = \eta A\left(\frac{dv}{dr}\right)_{r=R} = \eta(2\pi Rl)\left(-\frac{2v_0}{R}\right) = 4\pi\eta l v_0$$

(D) $$\Delta p = \frac{F}{A} = \frac{4\pi\eta l v_0}{\pi R^2} = \frac{4\eta l v_0}{R^2}$$

Comprehension Based Questions

1. Weight of inside air + Weight of film = Buoyant force

$$\Rightarrow \quad \rho_i\left(\frac{4}{3}\pi R_0^3\right)g + \rho_s(4\pi R_0^2 t)g = \rho_a\left(\frac{4}{3}\pi R_0^3\right)g$$

$$\Rightarrow \quad \rho_i R_0 + 3\rho_s t = \rho_a R_0 \qquad \text{... (i)}$$

Also, $$\frac{p_i}{\rho_i T_i} = \frac{p_a}{\rho_a T_a} \Rightarrow \frac{p_i}{p_a} = \frac{\rho_i T_i}{\rho_a T_a} \qquad \text{... (ii)}$$

Also, $p_i = p_a + \dfrac{4\gamma}{R_0}$

$$\Rightarrow \quad \frac{p_i}{p_a} = \left(1 + 4\frac{\gamma}{R_0 p_a}\right) \qquad \text{... (iii)}$$

Solving Eqs. (i), (ii) and (iii), we get

$$T_i = \frac{R_0\rho_a T_a}{(\rho_a R_0 - 3\rho_s t)}\left(1 + \frac{4\gamma}{p_a R_0}\right)$$

2. $F_{Buoyant} + F_{viscous} = F_{gravity}$

$$\Rightarrow \quad \rho_a\left(\frac{4}{3}\pi R^3\right)g + 6\pi\eta R v$$

$$= \rho_i\left(\frac{4}{3}\pi R^3\right)g + \rho_s 4\pi R^2 t g \qquad \text{... (i)}$$

Also, $$\frac{\rho_i}{\rho_a} = \frac{p_i}{p_a} = \left(1 + \frac{4\gamma}{Rp_a}\right) \qquad \text{... (ii)}$$

Solving Eqs. (i) and (ii), we get

$$v = \frac{2Rg}{3\eta}\left[\rho_s t + \frac{4\gamma\rho_a}{3p_a}\right]$$

3. Consider a ring of radius x and thickness dx.

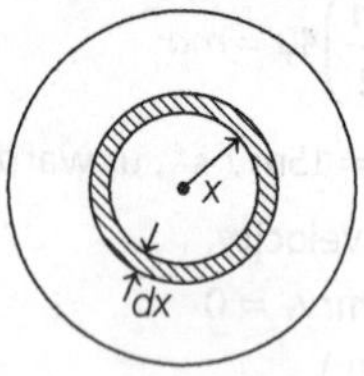

$$\int dF = \int_0^R (\eta_0 x)(2\pi x dx)\left(\frac{v}{t}\right)$$

$$F = \frac{2}{3}\frac{\pi\eta_0 R^3 v}{t}$$

4. $dF = \eta(2\pi x dx)\left(\frac{\omega x}{t}\right)$

$$\int d\tau = \int_0^R \eta(2\pi x dx)\left(\frac{\omega x}{t}\right)x$$

$$\Rightarrow \quad \tau = \frac{\pi\omega\eta R^4}{2t}$$

5. $\tau = I\alpha$

$$\Rightarrow \quad \frac{\pi\omega\eta R^4}{2t} = -\left(\frac{mR^2}{2}\right)\left(\omega\frac{d\omega}{d\theta}\right)$$

$$\Rightarrow \quad \int_0^\theta d\theta = -\frac{tm}{\eta\pi R^2}\int_{\omega_0}^0 d\omega$$

$$\Rightarrow \quad \theta = \frac{\omega_0 tm}{\eta\pi R^2}$$

Numerical Value Questions

1. $v_T = \frac{2}{9}\frac{(\sigma-\rho)r^2 g}{\eta}$

$$= \frac{2}{9}(2520-1260)\frac{(0.003)^2(10)}{1.260}$$

$$= 2 \text{ cm/s}$$

$$\text{Time taken} = \frac{\text{Distance}}{\text{Speed}} = \frac{10}{2} = 5 \text{ s}$$

2. For single ball in fluid,

$$v_T = \frac{2}{9}\frac{(\sigma-\rho)r^2 g}{\eta}$$

$$\Rightarrow \quad 8 = \frac{2}{9}\frac{(2\rho-\rho)r^2 g}{\eta} \Rightarrow \frac{\rho r^2 g}{\eta} = 36$$

For two balls system, ball 2 will descend.

For ball 2, $2\rho Vg - T = 0$

For ball 1, $T + \rho Vg - 2\rho Vg - 6\pi\eta r v_T' = 0$

$$\Rightarrow \quad v_T' = \frac{\rho Vg}{6\pi\eta r} = \frac{\rho\left(\frac{4}{3}\pi r^3\right)g}{6\pi\eta r}$$

$$= \frac{2}{9}\frac{\rho r^2 g}{\eta} = \frac{2}{9}(36) = 8 \text{ m/s}$$

Previous Years Questions

JEE Main

1. Of all the fluids, gases have the lowest viscosities. Highly soluble impurities increases the value of surface tension of liquid whereas insoluble impurities decreases the surface tension of liquid.

2. Initially velocity of ball increases and that results in increase of opposing viscous force.

$$F_{\text{viscous}} = 6\pi\eta r v$$

When viscous force and buoyant force are equals to gravitational force, net force on ball is zero.

After that ball falls with constant terminal speed.

So, correct graph is

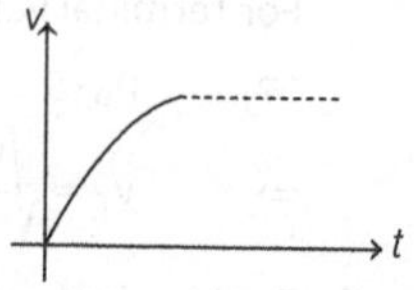

3. Terminal speed of a ball of radius r is given by,

$$v = \frac{2}{9}\frac{r^2(\rho-\sigma)g}{\eta}$$

ρ = density of ball

σ = density of fluid

η = viscosity of fluid

If fluid has negligible density then,

$$v = \frac{2}{9}\frac{r^2\rho g}{\eta}$$

Another ball has same mass as that of first and has radius $2r$.

$$\therefore \frac{4}{3}\pi r^3 \cdot \rho = \frac{4}{3}\pi(2r)^3 \cdot \rho'$$

$\Rightarrow$ For second ball, density is,

$$\rho' = \frac{\rho}{8}$$

Terminal speed of second ball is,

$$v' = \frac{2}{9}\frac{(r')^2 \cdot \rho' g}{\eta} = \frac{2}{9}\frac{(2r)^2\left(\frac{\rho}{8}\right)g}{\eta}$$

$$= \frac{1}{2}\cdot\frac{2}{9}\left(\frac{r^2\rho g}{\eta}\right) = \frac{1}{2}\cdot v$$

4. At terminal velocity, net force on the ball is zero.

$$Mg = f + B$$

$$Mg = f + V_{\text{ball}}\rho_0 g \quad \text{...(i)}$$

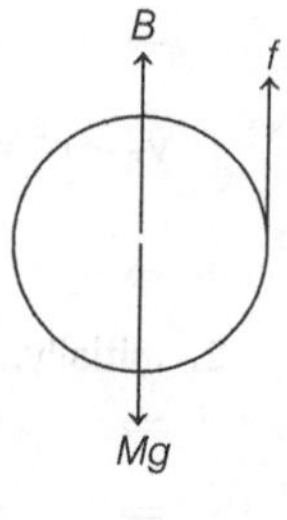

$$\text{Volume of ball} = \frac{M}{\rho}$$

From Eq. (i)

$$Mg = f + \frac{M}{\rho}\cdot\rho_0 g$$

$$\Rightarrow \quad f = Mg - \frac{M}{\rho}\rho_0 g$$

$$\Rightarrow \quad f = Mg\left(1 - \frac{\rho_0}{\rho}\right)$$

5. Ball attains constant velocity when net force on it is zero.

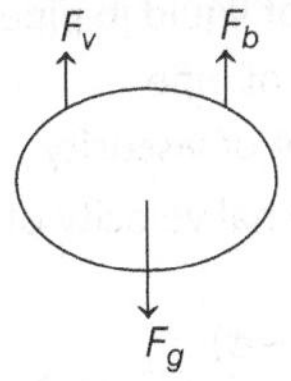

or $F_v + F_b = F_g$

(F_v = viscous force,

F_b = force of buoyancy, F_g = weight)

$\Rightarrow \quad F_v = F_g - F_b = (mg) - (m_f \cdot g)$

$= V \cdot \rho_b \cdot g - V \cdot \rho_f \cdot g = Vg(\rho_b - \rho_f)$

Here, ρ_b = density of ball

ρ_f = density of glycerine

V = volume of ball

= volume of glycerine displaced.

$= \frac{4}{3}\pi r^3 = \frac{4}{3}\pi \times (1 \times 10^{-3})^3 = 4.2 \times 10^{-9} m^3$

So, Viscous force is

$$F_v = 4.2 \times 10^{-9} \times 9.8\,(10.5 - 1.5) \times \frac{10^{-3}}{10^{-6}}$$

$= 4.2 \times 9.8 \times 9 \times 10^3 \times 10^{-9}$

$= 370.44 \times 10^{-6}$ N

$\approx 3700 \times 10^{-7}$ N

But $F_v = 3696 \times 10^{-x}$ N (Given)

So, $x = 7$

6. Given,

$v_s = 10$ cm/s, $R = n^{1/3} r$

$v_T \propto (\text{Radius})^2$

$\frac{v_f}{v_s} = \frac{R^2}{r^2}$ $[\because R = 8^{1/3} r]$

$\Rightarrow \quad \frac{v_f}{v_s} = \frac{(8^{1/3} r)^2}{r^2}$

$\Rightarrow \quad \frac{v_b}{v_s} = \frac{8^{2/3} r^2}{r^2}$

$\Rightarrow \quad \frac{v_f}{v_s} = [(8)^{1/3}]^2$

$\Rightarrow \quad \frac{v_b}{v_s} = (2)^2$

$\Rightarrow \quad v_f = 4v_s$

$\Rightarrow \quad v_f = 4 \times 10 = 40$ cm/s

7.

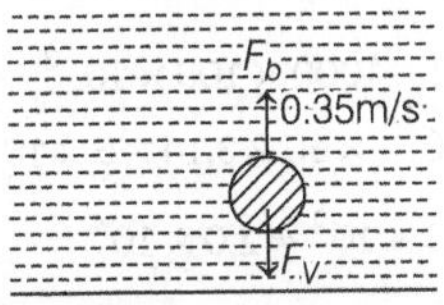

As bubble is rising steadily to upward, net force on it is zero.

Neglecting air density;

$F_{net} = 0$

$\Rightarrow \quad F_b = F_v$

where, F_b = Buoyant Force

F_v = Viscous Force

$\Rightarrow \quad \frac{4}{3}\pi r^2 (\rho_f) g = 6\pi\eta r v$

$$\eta = \frac{\frac{4}{3}\pi r^3 \cdot \rho_f \cdot g}{6\pi r v} = \frac{2}{9}\left(\frac{r^2 \rho_f g}{v}\right)$$

Substituting given values, we get

$$\eta = \frac{2 \times (3 \times 10^{-3})^2 \times 1750 \times 10}{9 \times 0.35 \times 10^{-2}}$$

$$= \frac{2 \times 6 \times 1750 \times 10^{-6} \times 10}{9 \times 35 \times 10^{-4}}$$

$= 10$ Pa.s

8. Let F_B be buoyant force and F_V be viscous force.

When terminal velocity is achieved, equation of motion is written as

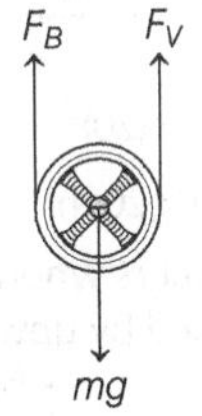

$F_{net} = 0$

$\Rightarrow \quad \Sigma F_{down} = \Sigma F_{up}$

$mg = F_B + F_V$

$\Rightarrow \quad mg = \left(\frac{m}{d_1}\right) d_2 g + F_V$

$\Rightarrow \quad F_V = mg\left(1 - \frac{d_2}{d_1}\right)$

9. Diameter of air bubble

$d = 2$ mm $= 2 \times 10^{-3}$ m

$\therefore$ Radius, $r = \frac{2}{2} \times 10^{-3}$ m $= 10^{-3}$ m

Density of solution, $\rho = 1750$ kgm^{-3}

Speed of bubble, $v = 0.35$ cms^{-1}

$= 3.5 \times 10^{-3}$ms^{-1}

According to given situation, bubble moves with terminal velocity v which is given as,

$$v = \frac{2r^2 g(\rho - \sigma)}{9\eta}$$

Here, σ = density of air ≈ 0

$$v = \frac{2r^2 g\rho}{9\eta}$$

$$\Rightarrow \quad \eta = \frac{2r^2 g\rho}{9v}$$

$$= \frac{2\times(10^{-3})^2 \times 10 \times 1750}{9 \times 3.5 \times 10^{-3}} = 1.1 \text{ N-s/m}^2$$

$$= 11 \text{ Poise} \qquad [\because 1 \text{ N-sm}^{-2} = 10 \text{ Poise}]$$

10. Given, radius of ball = 0.1 mm = 10^{-4} m

viscosity of water, $\eta = 10^{-5}$ N - sm^{-2}

density of ball, $l = 10^4$ kg m^{-3}

Velocity of ball does not change as it falls through water with terminal velocity.

So, $\quad v = v_T$

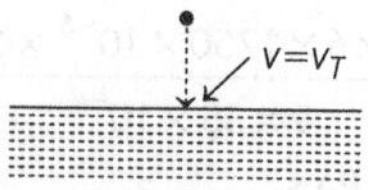

$$\Rightarrow \quad \sqrt{2gh} = \frac{2r^2(\rho - \rho_0)g}{9\eta}$$

$$\Rightarrow \quad \sqrt{2\times 10 \times h} = \frac{2\times(10^{-4})^2(10^4 - 10^3)\times 10}{9\times 1\times 10^{-5}}$$

$$\Rightarrow \quad 20h = (20)^2$$

$$\Rightarrow \quad h = 20 \text{ m}$$

11. Terminal velocity occurs when downward force of gravitation is balanced by upward stokes force,

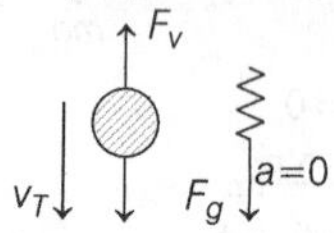

If v = terminal velocity

Then, neglecting buoyant force, we have

$$6\pi\eta r v = mg$$

$$\Rightarrow \quad 6\pi\eta r v = \frac{4}{3}\pi r^3 \cdot \rho \cdot g$$

or terminal velocity, $v = \dfrac{2}{9}\dfrac{\rho r^2 g}{\eta}$

Substituting, $r = 1\times 10^{-6}$ m,

$\rho = 10^3$ kg m^{-3}

$g = 10$ ms^{-2}, $\eta = 1.8\times 10^{-5}$ Ns m^{-2}

$$\Rightarrow \quad v = \frac{2}{9}\times\frac{10^3\times(10^{-6})^2\times 10}{1.8\times 10^{-5}}$$

$$= 123.4\times 10^{-6} \text{ m/s}$$

12. Reynold's number is a dimensionless parameter whose value is used to decide the nature of flow of a liquid through a pipe. It is given as

$$R_e = \frac{\rho v d}{\eta}$$

where, ρ = density of liquid,

v = velocity of liquid in pipe,

d = diameter of pipe

and $\quad x$ = coefficient of viscosity.

13. We know that, terminal velocity of spherical rain drop is given as

$$v_t = \frac{2gr^2(\rho - \sigma)}{9\eta} \Rightarrow v_t \propto r^2$$

where, ρ = density of rain drop, σ = density of air

and $\quad \eta$ = coefficient of viscosity of air.

14. Given, radius of oil drop, $r = 2.0\times 10^{-5}$ m

Density of oil drop, $\rho = 1.2\times 10^3$ kgm^{-3}

Viscosity of liquid, $\eta = 1.8\times 10^{-5}$ Nsm^{-2}

To neglect buoyancy, consider the density of air, $\rho_a = 0$

Viscous force acting on drop can be given as

$$F = 6\pi\eta r v \qquad \text{...(i)}$$

Here, v is terminal velocity.

The terminal velocity of drop can be given as

$$v = \frac{2r^2(\rho - \rho_a)g}{9\eta}$$

$$\Rightarrow v = \frac{2\times(2.0\times 10^{-5})^2(1.2\times 10^3 - 0)\times 9.8}{9\times 1.8\times 10^{-5}}$$

$$= 5.807\times 10^{-2} \text{ ms}^{-1}$$

Substituting all values in Eq. (i), we get

$$F = 6\pi\times 1.8\times 10^{-5}\times 2.0\times 10^{-5}\times 5.807\times 10^{-2}$$

$$= 3.94\times 10^{-10} \text{ N} \approx 3.9\times 10^{-10} \text{ N}$$

JEE Advanced

1. Reynolds' number for flow of a liquid is given by

$$R_e = \frac{\rho v D}{\eta}$$

where, velocity of flow,

$$v = \frac{\text{volume flow rate}}{\text{area of flow}} = \frac{V/t}{A}$$

So, $\quad R_e = \dfrac{\rho VD}{\eta At} = \dfrac{\rho V 2r}{\eta\times\pi r^2\times t} = \dfrac{2\rho V}{\eta\pi r t}$

Here, ρ = density of water = 1000 kgm^{-3}

$$\frac{V}{t} = \frac{100\times 10^{-3}}{60} \text{m}^3\text{s}^{-1}$$

where, η = viscosity of water = 1×10^{-3} Pa-s

and $\quad r$ = radius of pipe = 5×10^{-2} m

$$R_e = \frac{2\times 1000\times 100\times 10^{-3}}{1\times 10^{-3}\times 60\times 3.14\times 5\times 10^{-2}}$$

$$= 212.3\times 10^2 \approx 2.0\times 10^4$$

So, order of Reynolds' number is of 10^4.

2.

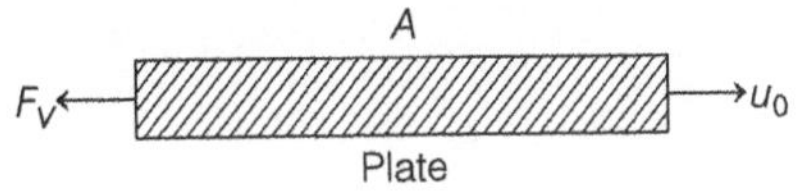

$$F_v = -\eta A\left(\frac{dv}{dy}\right)$$

Since, height h of the liquid in tank is very small.

$$\Rightarrow \quad \frac{dv}{dy} = \frac{\Delta v}{\Delta y} = \left(\frac{u_0}{h}\right)$$

$$\Rightarrow \quad F_v = -(\eta)A\left(\frac{u_0}{h}\right)$$

$$F_v \propto \left(\frac{1}{h}\right), F_v \propto u_0, F \propto A, F_v \propto \eta$$

Statement a, c and d are correct.

3. Terminal velocity is given by

$$v_T = \frac{2}{9}\frac{r^2}{\eta}(d-\rho)g$$

$$\frac{v_P}{v_Q} = \frac{r_P^2}{r_Q^2} \times \frac{\eta_Q}{\eta_P} \times \frac{(d-\rho_P)}{(d-\rho_Q)}$$

$$= \left(\frac{1}{0.5}\right) \times \left(\frac{2}{3}\right) \times \frac{(8-0.8)}{(8-1.6)}$$

$$= 4 \times \frac{2}{3} \times \frac{7.2}{6.4} = 3$$

4. For floating, net weight of system = net upthrust

$\Rightarrow (\rho_1 + \rho_2)Vg = (\sigma_1 + \sigma_2)Vg$

Since string is taut, $\rho_1 < \sigma_1$ and $\rho_2 > \sigma_2$

$$\mathbf{v}_P = \frac{2r^2g}{2\eta_2}(\sigma_2 - \rho_1) \quad \text{(upward terminal velocity)}$$

$$\mathbf{v}_Q = \frac{2r^2g}{9\eta_1}(\rho_2 - \sigma_1) \quad \text{(downward terminal velocity)}$$

$$\left|\frac{\mathbf{v}_P}{\mathbf{v}_Q}\right| = \frac{\eta_1}{\eta_2}$$

Further, $\mathbf{v}_P \cdot \mathbf{v}_Q$ will be negative as they are opposite to each other.